MILESTONES OF HISTORY

100 DECISIVE
THE HISTORY

 W·W·NORTON

MILESTONES OF HISTORY

EVENTS IN OF MANKIND

& COMPANY INC·NEW YORK

Library of Congress Catalog Card No: 76-139852

Manufactured in Italy

First published by W. W. Norton & Company, Inc. 1971
in association with the *Newsweek* Book Division

SBN 393-05432-2

Contents

Part Three The Expanding World of Man

Part Four   Twilight of Princes

Part Five Age of Optimism

Part Six Our Twentieth-Century World

Charts and Maps

General Introduction

This volume represents an entirely new approach to a unified history of the world. In the past attempts have been made to compress five thousand years of history into a book by condensing. That method is impossible to produce and unsatisfactory to read. The editors of Milestones of History have started afresh to produce a volume which is both scholarly and highly readable.

One hundred events have been selected as being Milestones along the path of history. Each of these Milestones has left the world a very different place from what it had been before. These events are described in depth by men whose lives have been devoted to studying the period, some of the most eminent names in the study of history. The event is described just as it happened. The stories are exciting and urgent. But in addition to the descriptive side, the events are fitted into the perspective of time so that the reader can see where and when they happened in relation to other events.

Each essay is illustrated with pictures and artefacts which are exactly contemporary with the event being described. Unlike many books of this kind, no artists' impressions or replicas have been used. Maps and diagrams have been especially commissioned to explain the more complex points and to give added impact.

In the pages of this magnificent book the reader will meet the men who have made the world what it is today, such as Alexander, who created an empire stretching from Greece to the Himalayas; Mohammed, founder of a great new religion; Cortes, conqueror of Mexico in the name of a newly expansive and assertive Europe; Isaac Newton, discoverer of the law of gravity; Napoleon Bonaparte, attempted conqueror of Europe; Mohandas Gandhi, champion of non-violence in a violent world.

Each event, whether a natural catastrophe, such as the eruption of Santorin, which destroyed the Mycenaean civilization; religious events such as the crucifixion of Jesus; battles such as Constantine's victory at the Milvian Bridge; political landmarks, such as the signing of the Magna Carta in 1215; cultural events, such as the writing of Shakespeare's *Hamlet* or the composition of Beethoven's *Eroica* Symphony: or social upheavals, such as the Russian Revolution of 1917, is a milestone in its impact on the past and the present. Significant moments in man's history are examined with fresh viewpoints and penetrating interpretations.

To supplement the text are 1500 superb illustrations—nearly one third of them in full color—that help capture the spirit of the time. Numerous maps and diagrams are included to highlight the narrative. Modern photographs are juxtaposed with illustrations of contemporary paintings, manuscripts, architecture, pottery and statuary.

The book is divided into six sections, each edited by a scholar of international reputation: S. G. F. Brandon, Professor of Comparative Religion at the University of Manchester (England); Friedrich Heer, Professor of the History of Ideas at the University of Vienna (Austria); Neville Williams, curator of England's Public Record Office; Christopher Hibbert, author of *Charles I* and many other books; Alan Palmer, author of *The Lands Between*; Hugh Thomas, Professor of History at the University of Reading (England). Each section includes chronological charts which help to relate the "milestones" with more every-day events of the period.

Through a comprehensive study of one hundred "milestones" of man's past, the volume encompasses the entire sweep of history. This meticulously researched, authoritatively written and beautifully illustrated work forms a virtual encyclopedia of world history.

Ancient Empires

Editor S. G. F. Brandon

3000 B.C. – A.D. **70**

Introduction

What is History? Many answers have been given to this question. To most people it is undoubtedly the record of past events. But a moment's reflection will show that it is not a record of everything that has happened, whether the subject be the history of mankind as a whole, or of a nation, a city, a religion or institution. History, as it is recorded by chroniclers or presented by historians, inevitably involves the selection of certain events as being especially significant among all that happened within a specific area of the past. And selection also implies criteria of interpretation by which events are considered significant. In other words, out of the complex of past happenings certain events are chosen as being "historical." This process of selection and interpretation is a very complicated one, and it has been going on ever since man first began to record his past—about the beginning of the third millennium B.C.

Selecting an "historical" event also involves a process of abstraction and concretion that is fundamentally artificial, yet instinctive to man and a basic factor of his rationality. It presupposes that the passage of time is made up of a series of "events," each distinct and identifiable. But, on analysis, this presupposition is very difficult to justify. What we call "Time" is essentially mysterious; it is one of the main categories of our consciousness, and we cannot get outside it and assess it objectively. Time presents itself to us primarily in the ever-changing pattern of our experience; if we were not conscious of such change, it is difficult to see how we should be aware of Time. But, although our apprehension of temporal change is continuous when we are conscious, some phenomena affect us more than others and we naturally endow them with especial significance; we abstract from a continuous sequence some specific section, and isolate it as a decisive "event." The section which we thus choose may extend over a period of some years as, for example, the French Revolution is designated a decisive event in French history; but generally our instinct is to select some more sharply defined happening that we can invest with definite significance as, for example, the storming of the Bastille on July 14, 1789 is said to constitute the beginning of the French Revolution—in other words, as being a "milestone" in French history.

The great German historian Leopold von Ranke (1795–1886) defined the historian's task as being that of describing the past "as it really happened" (*wie es eigentlich gewesen*). His definition will doubtless always stand as the ideal of scientifically objective history, and as a warning against the writing of history as propaganda or apologia for some nationalist, political or religious end. But it has come to be realized that this represents an ideal that can never be wholly achieved. As already noted, History inevitably implies selection and interpretation of the facts considered to be relevant. Both activities ultimately depend upon human minds, which are conditioned by many factors such as education, religion and nationality, quite apart from personal interests and consciously conceived aims. Throughout all ancient Hebrew historiography, for instance, runs the basic conviction that Time is a linear process in which the providence of Yahweh, the god of Israel, was being progressively revealed as History on behalf of his chosen people, the "children of Israel". By contrast, according to both the Hindu and Buddhist views, the empirical world is not reality but an illusory process of phenomena that moves unceasingly in repetitive cycles, so History can have no ultimate significance.

Nevertheless, even though von Ranke's ideal of History is beyond practical attainment, and all our records of the past contain an irreducible factor of personal evaluation, the conviction remains deep-rooted that History is important and worthy of study.

Introduction

It is so regarded partly because it attests that man is an effective agent in the working-out of his destiny. For, even though the Marxist view of History as the inevitable fulfillment of fundamental economic laws is now widely recognized as logical, a realistic assessment of the evidence warns us against accepting our past and present as merely the result of economic predestination. We have all seen enough during the six decades of this century to be convinced that imponderable factors, as well as economic ones, operate to prevent the future pattern of History being forecast, as astronomers can forecast the future position of the planets. Thus, although it might have been predicted that a second world war would have resulted from the European situation after World War I, no one could have foreseen the part that Adolf Hitler was to play in the 1920s, or even in the first years of the 1930s. Several events of World War II, where History turned on the personal equation, might well have produced vastly different consequences for all concerned: what would have resulted if the Battle of Britain in 1940 had been won by Nazi Germany, or the Battle of Stalingrad had gone the other way in 1942–43, or the first atomic bomb had been completed in Germany instead of America? All these events, seen in retrospect, can rightly be called milestones of History.

Any philosophical definition of historical fact or of History itself must surely admit that some happenings in the story of man have been more critical or decisive for his destiny than others. Hence, a sequential study of such milestones of History will provide, as it were, a synoptic chart of the past of our race, rather as anatomical charts show the synapses or nerve centers of the human body. By linking each milestone with essays to show the connection of each historical synapse with those before and after, an account of human culture and civilization should emerge that is both dramatic and instructive, recording some of the factors that have shaped our situation today.

This part of the volume deals with a sequence of sixteen milestones, ranging in time from *c.* 3000 B.C. to A.D. 70. Limitation of space has inevitably precluded many that would have merited inclusion in a larger volume; but reference will be made to these in the linking essays. The selection of the first milestone constituted a problem, because recorded History started about the same time in Egypt and Sumer—indeed, a famous Sumerologist, Professor S. N. Kramer, has written a book entitled *History Begins at Sumer*, thus advocating the priority of the civilization in which he specializes. A good case can, indeed, be made out for the chronological primacy of Sumer; but, whereas the Sumerians had established small city-states in Lower Mesopotamia by the end of the fourth millennium B.C., it was in Egypt that the first national state, with a centralized government, was set up about 3000 B.C. From then on, the cultural achievement of Egypt equaled, if it did not excel, that of Sumer. However, the establishment of these first civilized states in the Valley of the Nile and the plain between the Tigris and Euphrates was preceded by millennia of gradual cultural development of the human race. And, although no written records exist to inform us of decisive milestones, some of the basic discoveries made during that long, remote period laid the foundations for the later achievements of civilization.

The earliest skeletal remains of *homo sapiens* revealed by archeology, together with relics of his culture, date from about thirty thousand years ago. From this evidence it is clear that certain fundamental discoveries had already been made. The use of fire can, indeed, be traced back to 300,000 B.C.; indications of its use were found in the rock shelters at Chou K'ou Tien, which had been inhabited by the so-called "Peking Man", a remote hominian precursor of *homo sapiens*. How this ability, never achieved by the other animals, was first acquired by the sub-men who preceded the first ancestors of our race is unknown; but it was basic to man's conquest of his natural environment. The ability to make tools and weapons has, similarly, a long unknown ancestry. Although some animals are accustomed to employ materials for purposes beyond the range of their own physical endowment (e.g., the dam-building of beavers), man alone has had the talent continuously to improve his tools and weapons, giving him an increasing mastery over animals stronger and swifter than himself. During the Old Stone Age, man also became an artist, as the painted caves in France, Spain and elsewhere impressively show. This art seems to have been inspired not by esthetic ideas but by magical beliefs. Indeed, many other Palaeolithic practices show that already man was aware of problems, both natural and supernatural, which he sought to solve by religio-magical means. Thus he felt that the dead needed special tending: he carefully buried them with food, tools and ornaments, suggesting belief in some kind of *post-mortem* existence. He carved figurines representing women, with the maternal attributes grossly exaggerated and the faces left blank; and at Laussel, in the Dordogne area of France, he has left behind one such figure that, from its position, suggests a cult-object, deifying the Mother as the source of fertility and life.

Man in the Old Stone Age was a food-gatherer, who obtained his food chiefly by hunting. During the New Stone Age (*c.* 8000 B.C.), he became a food-producer. Agriculture began, although how and where remains unknown to us. But what has aptly been called the "Neolithic Revolution" laid the foundations of civilization. With the development of agriculture went the domestication of animals, and the in-

vention of pottery and weaving. Soon the first agrarian settlements were founded, with stone-built houses and defenses: at Jericho and Çatal Hüyük in Anatolia, they date back to the seventh millennium B.C. A fertility religion also developed, centered on a mother goddess and the virility of the bull. The complexity of this Neolithic culture presupposes the elaboration of language as a means of communication. How and when language first began is beyond our knowing, but such complex undertakings as cave-art suggest that it must surely have existed in some form in the Palaeolithic era.

Through these long and dim corridors of Time, before human thought and action began to be recorded in writing, there were doubtless many occasions which were truly milestones in the evolution of man. Who sowed the first seedcorn, made the first earthen pot, worked the first metal, sailed the first boat, wrought the first wheel, must remain forever unknown. Yet these acts, involving new concepts and the technical skill to translate them into practical realities, initiated the long technological development which made possible all later achievements of civilized living. Hence we must recognize that, though their exact date is unknown, there were many great milestones in the story of man long before History, as such, began.

S. G. F. BRANDON

Gift of the Nile

On the long road to civilization, the emergence of the national state—particularly in the context of the world in which we live—is of paramount importance. Although other countries, and in particular Mesopotamia, the modern Iraq, developed some of the arts of civilization earlier, Egypt was the first country to draw itself together with a national identity. The documents that survive from the period are few, and therefore it is all the more remarkable that we know as much as we do about the unification of Upper and Lower Egypt. The invention of writing occurred in Egypt shortly before the event, but there is no written history on which to rely. However, the significance of the event is plain for all to see. Under successive dynasties of pharaohs the country prospered and its civilization flourished. The brilliance of the Egyptian achievement and its continuity have inspired and influenced mankind profoundly.

If you travel south from Cairo, along the west bank of the Nile, you will see on your left a narrow strip of bright green vegetation, sometimes shadowed by palm groves and ending suddenly in the broad, slow-moving, mud-brown river. On your right the vegetation ends abruptly, and beyond it the Western Desert begins, a ridge of golden, wind-blown sand, with here and there eroded rocks that look as if they had been baked and split by the fierce sun.

The road swings to the right and climbs the desert ridge, and suddenly you see before you a mighty pyramid built in steps, surrounded by a high wall enclosing a large courtyard; and not only this, but many other pyramids rising out of a plateau of billowing sand that stretches endlessly to the west, as sterile and hostile as it was in the days of the pharaohs. You have arrived at the five-thousand-year-old cemetery of Saqqara, burial place of generations of kings, noblemen and high officials for more than a thousand years.

The Step Pyramid, built for the Pharaoh Djoser (*c.* 2800 B.C.) is the oldest large stone monument in the world, but it is far from being the oldest tomb at Saqqara. A little to the north of it are the ruins of a series of large mud-brick structures called *mastabas*—the Arabic word for bench. One of these, prosaically known to archaeologists as Tomb 3357, once contained the funerary equipment, and probably the body, of the first pharaoh of the First Dynasty, a ruler who preceded Djoser by at least four hundred years. His tomb or cenotaph—it is not certain which—has been variously dated as somewhere between 3200 and 3000 B.C. One of his names (for the pharaohs bore several) was Hor-Aha, and he was the first pharaoh to rule over a united Egypt.

Hor-Aha's reign, and that of his predecessor, Narmer, mark a momentous turning point in history, the point at which Egypt, until then an agglomeration of petty states loosely federated into two kingdoms, became one truly united state under one divine ruler, the pharaoh. The conquest was probably achieved mainly by Narmer, who came from southern or Upper Egypt, but the unification was advanced by Hor-Aha, one of whose names was Min or Men. It is significant that the historians of Greek classical times, who had access to Egyptian temple records long since destroyed, state that the founder of Egypt was *Menes*, which seems to be the classical Greek form of Men or Min. There is still some controversy among Egyptologists as to whether Menes was Hor-Aha or Narmer. Perhaps the two kings had become fused in folk memory as one man. What *is* certain is that Hor-Aha was the first pharaoh of the First Dynasty and that he ruled at some time between 3200 and 3000 B.C., after the conquests of his predecessor, Narmer, had laid the foundations of unification. It is important to remember that we are dealing with a period before the beginnings of written history, and the invention of writing seems to have occurred in Egypt only shortly before Narmer's conquest. The documents that have survived are thus few and rudimentary, and a great deal of speculation is involved.

Narmer's original capital was probably Hierakonpolis in the south. Unlike Lower (i.e. northern) Egypt, which consisted mainly of the flat, highly fertile Nile Delta, Upper (i.e. southern) Egypt covered more rugged land and probably bred a hardier race of people. Already by about 3200 B.C. the inhabitants of both Upper and Lower Egypt were at a fairly advanced state of civilization. They could make copper as well as stone weapons. They could write. They were capable of producing works of art such as the Slate Palette of Narmer and the famous ivory Mace-head of Hierakonpolis, both of which are carved with scenes apparently depicting Narmer's conquest of Lower Egypt.

The Slate Palette of Narmer found at Hierakonpolis is one of the most important historical

Seated statue of Pharaoh Djoser, from a chapel adjoining the Step Pyramid, his tomb.

Opposite The Step Pyramid of Saqqara is the oldest stone monument in the world. It dates from *c.* 2800 B.C. and was built to house the dead Pharaoh Djoser.

The unification of Egypt

Above Pre-dynastic stone vase in the form of a fish.

Right Pre-dynastic pottery group of mother and child.

Below One of the stone mace-heads from Hierakonpolis, now in the Ashmolean Museum in Oxford. It depicts King Narmer during the celebration of his jubilee festival.

documents discovered in Egypt. On one side there is a scene showing Narmer walking in procession, preceded by his attendants; on the same panel are rows of decapitated corpses of his enemies. Another section on the same side of the palette shows the pharaoh, in the form of a bull, demolishing an enemy fortress. On the reverse side, Narmer is shown in an attitude typical of that adopted by later pharaohs, with one hand grasping the hair of a kneeling captive, the other holding a club. Beneath this the king's enemies are shown in flight. The date of the palette is between 3200 and 3000 B.C. and the primitive hieroglyphs on the stone spell out the name Nar-Mer.

The Mace-head of Narmer is equally important. It shows Narmer seated on a throne and wearing the "Red Crown" of Lower Egypt. Above him hovers the vulture-goddess Nekhbet of Hierakonpolis; before him march the standard-bearers of his conquering army. There is also a little figure of a woman seated beneath a palanquin. This figure is believed to represent a princess of the conquered kingdom of Lower Egypt whom Narmer subsequently married—probably Queen Nit-hotep, whose lavish tomb was discovered at Nagadeh. The primitive hieroglyphic signs clearly depict the name Nar-Mer (within a rectangular structure called the *serekh*, probably representing the panelled façade of his palace) and various numerals that indicate 120,000 men, 400,000 oxen and 1,422,000 goats captured in war.

That Narmer was a mighty conqueror is without doubt; yet no large monuments of his period have yet been found north of Tarkhan, and his queen was buried at Nagadeh. A somewhat insignificant tomb, No. B10, at Abydos, also in the south, has been identified as his. But since the kings of this and later periods had two tombs, one in the south and another in the north (symbolizing their dominion over the two kingdoms of Upper and Lower Egypt), it is possible that the real tomb of Narmer still awaits discovery.

Hor-Aha, Narmer's successor and the first ruler of a united Egypt, bore a name that means "fighting hawk." This was his *Horus* name, as ruler of Upper Egypt, but to symbolize his rule over Lower Egypt, he used the *Nebti* name of Men (or Min) signifying "Established." The corelation of these two names was proved when an ivory plaque bearing them both was discovered in the tomb of Queen Nit-hotep. This ivory label also depicts a most important scene commemorating the unification of the two lands.

Hor-Aha fought successful campaigns against the Nubians beyond the First Cataract, and no doubt had to engage in other frontier wars, but, by right of both conquest and inheritance, he was the first ruler of a united Egypt. His greatest achievement was the foundation of a new capital, called by the Greeks Memphis, near the point at which the two main branches of the Nile divide, a little south of modern Cairo. This site was carefully chosen as the natural frontier between north and south. In order to create it Hor-Aha had to divert the course of the Nile (as Herodotus tells us) and drain the land in order to construct a huge dike.

Hor-Aha made a wise choice of site for his capital. The first Neolithic invaders of Egypt, attracted by the beneficent Nile with its annual gift of rich fertilizing mud and the abundance of wild game near its banks, had arrived some 2,000 years before Hor-Aha's time. Unlike their wandering hunter ancestors, these Neolithic people could settle permanently in one place. But they and their descendants lived in a conglomeration of petty tribal states scattered over both Lower and Upper Egypt, and it was chiefly by siting Memphis at a point that gave him control over an area from the Delta to the First Cataract, six hundred miles up the Nile, that Hor-Aha and his successors were able to create and maintain a unified Egypt.

Saqqara was the cemetery of Memphis, and if one stands on the edge of the plateau, one can see beyond the river and amid the palm groves on the east bank a cluster of mud-brick dwellings which is all that remains of what was once the richest and most powerful city on earth. It stretched some ten miles along the east bank of the Nile as far as modern Cairo and beyond. There lay the royal palace and the villas of the nobles and high officials of Pharaoh; there rose the temples of their gods, many-columned and magnificent. All were built of mud-brick, because at this time (*c.* 3200 B.C.) the Egyptians had not yet learned the art of building monumentally in stone. We know what these

Left The Slate Palette of Narmer, showing the Pharaoh (who wears the White Crown of Upper Egypt) seizing a kneeling captive.

Below Detail from the reverse side of the Palette of Narmer. The pharaoh is walking in procession, wearing the Red Crown of Lower Egypt, preceded by his standard-bearers. Before them are rows of decapitated enemies.

Egyptian civilization forges ahead

Above Detail of the Hunter's Palette, now in the British Museum; it shows Egyptians hunting lion, gazelle, ostrich, and other desert creatures.

Below left Gray-white marble bowl, probably Pre-dynastic.

Below right Bedjmes the shipbuilder, Third Dynasty; red granite statue now in the British Museum.

buildings looked like because they are crudely represented on the ivory tablets and slate palettes found in the tombs of the First and Second Dynasties. Further, when in the Third Dynasty (*c.* 2800 B.C.) the Egyptians raised their first great stone building, the Step Pyramid of Djoser and its surrounding walls, courtyards and temples, they reproduced in stone the type of architecture they had previously used for mud-brick and timber.

It is a curious fact that this type of architecture, with its characteristic "panelled façades" also occurs in ancient Sumer, in Lower Mesopotamia, at a somewhat earlier date. Moreover, some of the Egyptian hieroglyphics of this period seem to have been derived from Sumer. These similarities have led certain Egyptologists, notably Professor Walter Emery, Professor of Egyptology at University College, London, to put forward the theory that the founders of Egyptian civilization and the unifiers of Egypt were a foreign race, originating perhaps in Lower Mesopotamia, whose cultural influences spread both eastward to Sumer and westward to Egypt. Only further archaeological investigation can prove or disprove this theory. The majority of scholars continue to assume that the earliest rulers of ancient Egypt sprang from a native stock, though they were almost certainly influenced by the civilization that had arisen in Lower Mesopotamia.

It is unlikely that in Narmer's own time and that of his immediate successors the effect of the unification was widely felt. Sumer, the only comparable civilization, was very remote from Egypt and there appears to have been only a slight contact, though an important one—that is, unless one accepts Professor Emery's theory. Nevertheless, objects found in tombs and made during and after Hor-Aha's time prove that between approximately 3200 and 2800 B.C. Egyptian civilization was developing at a rapid rate. Magnificent stone vases show the skill of the Egyptians in stone carving, a skill that was eventually to reveal itself

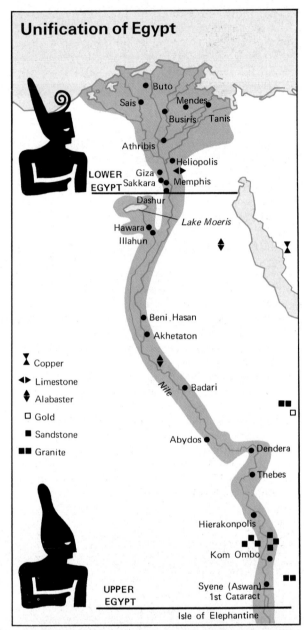

Unification of Egypt

Buto
Sais
Mendes
Busiris
Tanis
Athribis
Heliopolis
LOWER EGYPT
Giza
Sakkara
Memphis
Dashur
Hawara
Illahun
Lake Moeris
Beni Hasan
Akhetaton
Nile
Badari
Abydos
Dendera
Thebes
Hierakonpolis
Kom Ombo
UPPER EGYPT
Syene (Aswan)
1st Cataract
Isle of Elephantine

Copper
Limestone
Alabaster
Gold
Sandstone
Granite

Left Seated figure of a scribe, showing how a roll of papyrus was held in the left hand and gradually unrolled in use.

Below Egyptian hieroglyphs. The signs are colored, and outlined in black ink.

in the building of the pyramids, tombs, and temples of hewn stone. Carpentry, gold work and copper work make it clear that even at this remote period, before the first pyramid was built, Egypt was on the threshold of a long period of cultural expansion.

For the first few centuries after Hor-Aha (or Menes) the emphasis was on internal unification and the creation of an immense monolithic state. The tribal divisions became *nomes* (provinces), each with its own chief city. Agriculture flourished as the Egyptians learned how to control the flooding of their great river to produce an increasing abundance of food and provide for an increasing population. A large standing army was created. An elaborate hierarchy of officials controlled the kingdom. Expeditions were sent south into Nubia, partly for expansion and partly for trade, and also into Libya, in the Western Desert.

Writing, one of man's greatest inventions, developed swiftly and soon became very sophisti-cated. Scribal schools were set up, adjacent to the temples, and a new class of literate priests and their followers provided a body of tax collectors, civil servants and other officials who ran the economy of the newly united kingdom. In about 2700 B.C. the Pharaoh Khufu (or Cheops, to give him his Greek cognomen) built a monument of stone—the Great Pyramid—so enormous that it has been said to contain enough stone to reach two-thirds of the way round the world at the Equator. Similar pyramids were erected by Khufu's successors, notably at Saqqara, Abusir, and Dahshur, all intended to preserve for eternity the bodies of their royal builders.

After a period of civil war and internal disruption, the causes of which are unknown, the country revived under a new dynasty of pharaohs, those of the so-called Middle Kingdom (2100–1700 B.C.). The rising power of the *nomarchs*—governors of the *nomes* or provinces—was held in check, but dis-

Wooden panel carved in relief with the figure of Hesy-ra, one of Pharaoh Djoser's officials (c. 2000 B.C.). This is one of the earliest, and one of the finest, Egyptian sculptures in wood.

Narmer and Hor-Aha, however, was so strong that in the end a new dynasty of pharaohs, the Eighteenth, succeeded in driving out the invaders and creating the New Kingdom (1570–1085 B.C.), the first three centuries of which marked the most illustrious period of Egyptian power and influence. This was the period of imperial expansion that eventually led to Egyptian armies penetrating not only into Lebanon, Palestine and Syria but even as far as what is now northern Iraq. Egyptian colonies were set up along the Mediterranean coast and at strategic points in the hinterland, each under its governor.

In later years the innate conservatism of the Egyptians hindered their development in comparison with other peoples. For example, they learned to use the horse and chariot in warfare only after the Hyksos had beaten them with this weapon in about 1720 B.C. They continued to depend on bronze weapons when iron was rapidly coming into use in other lands, and even in Ptolemaic times (from the fourth century B.C.) they continued to follow their ancient customs—although the hieroglyphic inscriptions on temple walls reveal many errors, indications that the engravers had little or no knowledge of the early writings and had become mere copyists. This may be taken as symbolic of Egyptian culture as a whole. Great and splendid though it was in its prime, every generation tended to follow an accepted pattern laid down by their remote ancestors. Even when, in the first century B.C., Egypt became a province of the Roman Empire, the Caesars were represented on temple walls in the traditional dress, and performing the traditional ceremonies, of pharaohs just like Narmer and Hor-Aha. And to the very end of their civilization, which survived down to Greek and Roman times, they preserved the fiction of the Two Kingdoms of the South and North that had existed before the conquests of Narmer and Hor-Aha. The pharaoh was always known as "The King of Upper and Lower Egypt."

Yet the debt owed to Egypt by western Asia and eastern Europe is immense. The ancient Greeks, probably the most intelligent race that has ever lived, acknowledged this debt freely. From the time when their merchants began setting up trading posts in Egypt in the seventh and sixth centuries B.C. they were fascinated by Egypt, as one can tell from the pages of Herodotus and Diodorus. Archaic Greek art was clearly influenced by Egyptian sculpture, which at its best has few equals anywhere in the world. The Greeks copied Egyptian medicine and surgery and in many other fields of knowledge looked upon the Egyptian priests as their mentors. As one Egyptian said to an inquiring Greek, "You Greeks are like children, everlastingly asking questions." One may be sure that they would not have asked questions had they not expected useful and illuminating replies.

Narmer and his successors, by bringing the resources of the whole country under the control

ruptive forces threatened the central authority and weakened the power of the pharaohs. A group of tribes from western Asia, known to later historians as the Hyksos or "Shepherd Kings," seized the opportunity to occupy parts of Lower Egypt. Their leaders set themselves up as pharaohs, so that at one period there were two pharaohs, a Hyksos interloper ruling from Avaris, in the Delta, and a native Egyptian pharaoh ruling from Thebes in Upper Egypt.

The tradition of national unity established by

The development of arts and crafts

of one ruler, had achieved something of immense importance. For Egypt was one of the most fertile lands in the world and potentially one of the richest. From these beginnings great cities were to spring up, armies would be levied and trained, trade would expand, the arts and crafts would develop, and more and more power would be centered on the divine figure of the pharaoh, who claimed to be the "Son of Re," god of the sun and creator and maintainer of all living things. The unification laid the foundations of a civilized and powerful Egypt with a military and cultural influence extending far beyond its borders.

LEONARD COTTRELL

Above Wooden model of bakers and brewers.

Below Wooden model of men and oxen ploughing. Models such as these were frequently placed in Egyptian tombs, as part of the provisions made for the needs of the dead person in the after-life, which was thought to be very similar to life in this world.

The ancient Egyptians can be said to have been the first ancient people to create a national state. Another ancient people, however, can claim priority over the Egyptians in the invention of some of the arts of civilization and in the development of urban life. These were the inhabitants of ancient Mesopotamia, now called Iraq, the land through which the Tigris and Euphrates, the Twin Rivers, flow. The southern part of this land the inhabitants called Sumer. Excavations have shown that at a time when the Egyptians were still simple fishermen living in wattle and daub huts, using flint tools and storing their grain in baskets, there were people living in the valley of the Euphrates who already lived a life of some sophistication, in walled towns which (since this is a relative term only) we may call cities. They had built imposing towers and temples of mudbrick, ornamented with mosaic and fresco, and had achieved considerable technological mastery in stone-cutting, metallurgy and the potter's craft. The most remarkable evidence of this urban culture comes from Warka, about two hundred miles from the present

Urnanshe of Lagash with his family

head of the Persian Gulf, which was the site of ancient Uruk—the Biblical Erech. But similar remains, dating to the middle of the fourth millennium B.C., have been found at Ur, Nippur, Eridu and Lagash, and many other sites in Sumer, and also farther north at Mari, on the Euphrates near its junction with the Khabur, and at Tell Brak on its headwaters.

Life in Sumer

Agriculture and dairy farming were the bases of life in Sumer. The alluvium brought down by the rivers is very fertile and the productivity of the land remarkable; barley and wheat were the staple

crops, and the date palm and vine were cultivated. Fish abounded, and was an important source of food; so also were sheep and goats, of which there were many varieties. But the rivers, whose annual flood brought life to the fields of the Sumerians, were also a constant threat to their safety. Tradition preserved the memory of a disastrous flood which had once all but wiped out mankind; the hero Ziusudra, who escaped in a boat of bitumen and reeds built at the behest of the god Enki, the water-god, was the prototype of Noah.

Bronze model of mule-drawn chariot

The invention of writing

One of the greatest advances in the history of man was the invention, about 3500 B.C., of a system of writing. The earliest clay tablets are simple accounts—lists of objects, persons or animals, each depicted by a line drawing, or "pictogram," followed by a series of numerical signs or numbers. They are little more, in fact, than tallies, inscribed on small square cushions of clay. Gradually, however, the picture writing was stylized and the lines, jabbed for

Predynastic pictographic tablet

speed with the slanting edge of a reed stylus, became wedge-shaped, or cuneiform. This writing system evolved to such an extent that abstract ideas could be expressed.

Sumerian origins

The Sumerian language is quite different in structure and vocabulary from any other known language of the ancient world, and attempts to derive the Sumerians from an original home in the Caucasus mountains, or from the Iranian plateau, on linguistic grounds have so far failed. Nor does

Ziggurat ; Babylonian seal

archeology give us much help. It has been suggested that the curious temple-tower characteristic of Sumerian cities—the *ziggurat*, as it was called—is evidence that the Sumerians once worshiped their gods on the tops of mountains. Perhaps many strands were interwoven to make the fabric of their civilization. There may have been a Semitic element in the population of Mesopotamia from early times—certainly in the north at Mari, for the princes of Mari bore Semitic names, though they wore the sheepskin skirts and leather cloaks of the Sumerians and shared the same material civilization. And it was a Semite, a man called Sharrukin, or Sargon, who became cupbearer to the King of Kish (near Hillah) and finally seized power in that city. In a series of brilliant campaigns, Sargon wrested the hegemony of Sumer from the leading city of the time, Umma, establishing his new capital at Agade in Akkad, not far from Kish, in about 2370 B.C. Henceforward he was to rule as King of Sumer and Akkad. His successors claimed the title "King of the Four Quarters (of the World)." Both he and his grandson, Naram-Sin, led armies into North Syria and Anatolia, sources of copper, lead, silver and gold; they hewed conifers in the Amanus mountains and floated the logs down the Euphrates to build their palaces. For the first time Mesopotamia was united under a single, strong administration and the Akkadian kings dominated the whole of western Asia. The ships of the merchants of Agade sailed southwards from the port of Ur, down the Persian Gulf to Tilmun,

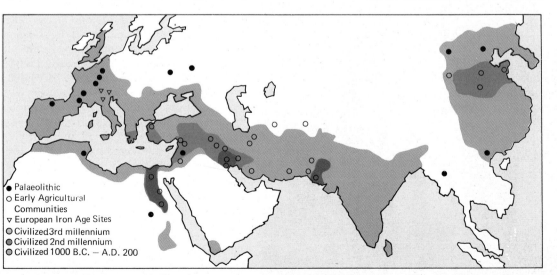

- ● Palaeolithic
- ○ Early Agricultural Communities
- ▽ European Iron Age Sites
- ◍ Civilized 3rd millennium
- ◍ Civilized 2nd millennium
- ◍ Civilized 1000 B.C. – A.D. 200

Early centers of culture

Sargon of Akkad

which is thought to be the island of Bahrein, and further south to the lands of Magan and Melukhkha. Magan, which may be the Makran coast of Persia, perhaps included also the coast of Oman on the other side of the Straits, a land rich in copper and stone. For

Akkadian ship

Magan furnished the Sumerians with the hard black stone for their statues, copper ore, and lumps of lapis lazuli, the valuable blue stone used in inlay and jewelry, which came many hundreds of miles from the mines in Afghanistan. Melukhkha lay even farther away: many scholars believe this is the Sumerian name for India.

Indus Valley Civilization

In the northwest corner of the continent of India at this time a great civilization had grown up in the basin of the Indus River. Its two chief cities, called today Mohenjo-Daro and Harappa, lay some five hundred miles apart. Each was a masterpiece of town-planning, with rectangular blocks of houses divided one from the other by a crisscross of streets broad enough to take the solid-wheeled ox-carts. Houses and public buildings were of burnt brick—a necessity in a

land of monsoon rain, whereas unbaked brick sufficed in Sumer—and there was an elaborate and skillfully planned drainage system to carry away both sewage and rainwater. More will be said of this Indus Valley Civilization, or Harappan Culture, as it is sometimes called, in a later chapter; suffice it here to say that ample evidence has recently been discovered of the existence at this time of Indian ports and trading stations in the Gulf of Cambay and on the Pakistan coast north of Karachi, and even on the south coast of Makran itself. Seals and other objects of Indus Valley workmanship found by excavators on Mesopotamian sites of the Akkadian period are evidence of contact between Sumer and the Indus

Bullock cart from Mohenjo-Daro

Valley, and some scholars are inclined to think that the civilization of Mohenjo-Daro and Harappa was either directly based on, or else inspired by, that of Sumer at an earlier period. There are, however, many essential differences between the two and the pictographic script of the Indus Valley owes nothing, so far as we can see (the language is unknown, for it is as yet undeciphered), to the cuneiform of Mesopotamia or its pictographic prototype. Moreover, the animals on the beautifully cut steatite seals are entirely those of the Indian fauna—the buffalo, the elephant and the rhinocerus, none of which was known in Sumer. While it cannot be denied that there was contact, either direct or indirect, between the two areas—perhaps over a long period, till the time of the First Dynasty of Babylon—the inspiration behind the civilization of the Indus Valley has yet to be traced.

Defeat of Naram-Sin

In Mesopotamia, Sumerian was gradually replaced in official documents by Semitic Akkadian, though Sumerian was retained in the temples. The administration of the

Figures from the Standard of Ur

kingdom was centralized and the old citizen army of the Sumerian states was replaced by a professional body trained in mountain warfare. The need for such an army was a real one, for enemies now began to press in upon the kingdom of Agade. Naram-Sin himself met with defeat from a coalition of mountain chieftains in the north of his realm, and though his successors managed for a time to stave off disaster, in about 2200 B.C. the Gutians, invaders from the Zagros mountains to the northeast of Iraq, captured Agade and took over the country.

In the south of the country, however, the old Sumerian cities seem to have been little affected by Gutian rule, and it was in these ancient centers of civilization, Uruk and Ur, that the people finally combined forces to drive out the invaders. Under the able rule of the Third Dynasty of Ur, the country was reunited and prosperity returned. Elam was made subject, and a profitable trade with the interior of Iran was thereby secured. Ships sailed again down the Persian Gulf, and among

Festival scene from Khafajan

the treasures they brought back were carved ivory figures and pearls. This was the golden age of Sumerian civilization. Temples were rebuilt on a grander scale than ever before, among them the great ziggurat at Ur, which became a landmark for miles around. Literature flourished under royal patronage, and a system of law was codified.

The significance of Sumerian culture lies not only in its antiquity and intrinsic achievement, but in that it was adopted, and adapted, by the Akkadians and their successors, the Babylonians and Assyrians. They adopted the pantheon of Sumerian gods and adjusted it to accommodate their own gods of desert and sky. They took over Sumerian script, adapting it to their own language, and kept Sumerian as the language of liturgy.

Thus after the collapse of the Ur dynasty, the ancient traditions continued. After a period of confusion, the city-states regrouped under new leaders: these were the Amorites, a Semitic people from the west who moved into the cities of Mesopotamia and gradually took control of many of them. Babylon was the seat of one of these Amorite dynasties, and Hammurabi its king.

An able warrior as well as a capable administrator, Hammurabi inherited from his Amorite predecessors a modest kingdom centered around the small town called Babil, or Babylon. Early in his reign he achieved some success, but he had to wait thirty years for his great victories. If one considers the significance of his reign in terms of human achievement, Hammurabi's name is connected with one remarkable document. This document, and its far-reaching significance, is to be the subject of the next chapter.

The First Law Code

As the political state evolved, the problem of its administration evolved too. The territory ruled over by Hammurabi of Babylon was composed not simply of two adjacent areas with similar characteristics—as in Narmer's Egypt—but of former independent states with very different traditions. Hammurabi had extended his territory by conquest, but as overlord he proved a conscientious ruler, dedicated to reform, and possibly the greatest tribute paid to him by his subjects was the comment, preserved in the chronicles of the country: "He established justice in the land." Inscribed on a stone, the memorial of his justice was providentially preserved for all time, despite its being carried off to Susa by an Elamite king early in the twelfth century B.C. Regardless of the fact that Hammurabi's immediate successors were unable to hold on to the territory he had won, his legacy to mankind constitutes a momentous milestone in the progress of human achievement.

Above The black basalt stele on which the Code of Hammurabi is inscribed. The lower part was erased by an Elamite king who captured the stele about 1200 B.C.

Opposite Relief on the stele of Hammurabi. The king is standing before a divinity, who is probably Shamash, the sun god, regarded as the law-giver.

Sometime toward the end of his reign, the great Babylonian king Hammurabi (*c.* 1792–1750 B.C.) inscribed a code of "laws" on a tall stele of hard stone. It was neither the first nor the last document of its type in Mesopotamia: at least half a dozen similar codes are known, of which the oldest dates from the end of the third millennium. But none of them so deserves to be considered the classic of its kind: no other is so broad in its scope and of such intellectual and literary perfection.

The Code of Hammurabi, in fact, provides both a brief history of, and a triumphant monument to, his reign. It is only toward the end of his life that a monarch feels the need to draw up an honors list of his successes and to give a summary of his experience and wisdom in order to inspire emulation as well as admiration. We know that the Babylonian empire as it appears in this code existed only during the great king's final years: in the prologue to the code, Hammurabi mentions victories that he did not win until the thirty-fifth or even the thirty-eighth year of his forty-year reign. It is because that reign marks one of the culminating points in the history of ancient Mesopotamia, a civilization that lasted for at least three or four thousand years, that the code is so important as documentary evidence.

In the 1,500 years before Hammurabi's reign, the "Land Between the Two Rivers" and above all the southern part of that territory, between present-day Baghdad and the Persian Gulf, had become the location of what one can call, compared with other minor prehistoric cultures, the oldest civilization in the world. Mesopotamian society was based on the systematic exploitation of land: the soil was cultivated intensively, and its natural productivity, already considerable, was increased by the establishment of a great system of canals that ensured effective irrigation. In those areas that had not been taken for agriculture or the cultivation of palm trees, stock raising flourished,

chiefly sheep and goats but also donkeys, cattle, pigs and other livestock. This work was carried out by the greater part of the population, both urban and rural. Its administration led to the establishment of a body of highly specialized civil servants, who preferred to live in the city near the palace and the temples; for it was there that the real rulers, the gods and their representative the king, had their headquarters.

The earth and all its produce belonged to the gods, as did the workers, who were their servants. Hence the harvest and the crops and the produce from herds (notably wool and skins) were brought for sale to the temples and stored in their warehouses. Once enough had been redistributed to meet the requirements of all citizens, according to their social standing, the rest was used as capital and as credit for huge commercial enterprises.

Since earliest times trade had been conducted with all the surrounding countries, and even farther afield—from the Lebanon and Asia Minor to Persia, both along the coast and in the mountainous interior, and as far as the western borders of India. Trade was vital to Mesopotamia because although it had a surplus of grain and animal products, it completely lacked certain raw materials that were necessary for civilized life. The soil provided only clay, bitumen and reeds; there was no timber whatever, no stone and no metal, although technicians had developed since at least the fourth millennium a technique of bronze work. Imported materials were worked by a host of skilled, often highly artistic craftsmen, who provided not only tools for farmers and stock breeders but also furnishings and works of art for the temples and palaces. These finished goods often found their way abroad as exports. One can see from this how well organized, how active and expanding the Mesopotamian economy was, and how systematized and orderly was its society.

The vast amount of accountancy that such

Hammurabi brings order to his kingdom

Above A letter from King Hammurabi to an official, instructing him to procure the ransom of a soldier with money from the treasury of the temple in the soldier's home town. The Code of Hammurabi includes detailed instructions as to who shall provide ransom money, according to the circumstances.

Right The Code of Hammurabi did not cover all the subjects that would now be dealt with in a code of law; its principal features are summarized in this diagram.

Code of Hammurabi

Gentleman   Freeman   Slave

The three types of citizen to whom the laws apply

Judge, bench of several in each city

Mayor and Council

Minor officials held office and land on feudal tenure from King available for military and other services

Offences

Death penalty
Killing of a child punishable in kind
Trial by ordeal in divine rivers — Tigris or Euphrates

Areas covered by the laws

Perjury
Theft
Feudal tenure
Land tenure and agriculture
Commercial dealing
Licensed drinking
Loans, trusts and debts
Marriage and divorce
Inheritance
Adoption
Medical treatment
Building
Hire of livestock
Hire of laborers
Hire of slaves

operations entailed had been considerably simplified about 2800 B.C. by what was virtually a stroke of genius: the invention of a system of writing. The system was still very complicated and was to remain so for a long period. Only specialists could understand and operate it, but they were to create the environment for the development of a truly intellectual culture. This writing was first used exclusively for keeping the accountancy records of the temples, but it was soon simplified and made more flexible and was then used for the compilation of dictionaries of signs and words, comprising all the symbols. Next it was used to record the deeds and exploits of kings, religious rites, and myths that the philosophers and theologians of the time had constructed to explain the great eternal problems of human existence and destiny. Finally it was used to express a certain number of scientific ideas and theories, the result of persistent observation and a profound desire to see the universe as orderly according to a particular perspective: divination, mathematics, medicine and jurisprudence.

This high degree of civilization, already established by the third millennium, was the product of a mixed population, of which the major elements and the most easy for us to identify were Semites and Sumerians. The former belonged to an ineradicable race of semi-nomadic shepherds who since the dawn of history have lived on the fringes of the great Syrian and Arabian deserts, and of whom a certain number have always been attracted by town life and have settled there. The Sumerians, whose provenance is unknown but who probably arrived from the east or the southeast by the fourth millennium at the latest, seem to have severed all ties with their former home and their kinsmen: in Mesopotamia they never received that infusion of new blood that has perpetually nourished and strengthened the Semitic part of the population. Consequently, while in the first half of Mesopotamian history, up to the end of the third millennium, the Sumerians appear to be the active, inventive and creative force in the development of civilization and at first more important in the political field, they were to find themselves gradually supplanted by the Semites.

Politically, the country was divided into a certain number of small states, each grouped around a city, with a majority of Semites in the north. These city-states sometimes allied with each other, sometimes fought against each other and were sometimes combined into larger kingdoms by the predominance of one or other among them. By the third millennium it was the Semites who seemed to have the advantage of the biggest alliances: first, at an early stage, around the city of Kish; and second, toward 2350 B.C. and for the following century and a half, around the city of Agade. At the beginning of the second millennium another Semitic dynasty, which seems to have been dominated by immigrants from the west, made Babylon their seat of power for three centuries

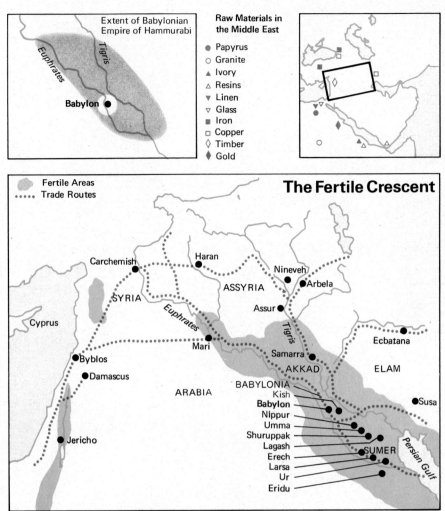

The Fertile Crescent

(about 1900–1600 B.C.). This gave the greatest of their kings the opportunity to create a third Semitic empire, displacing the Sumerians—who were this time completely absorbed and wiped forever off the map—and giving a special brilliance to the ancient civilization that had continued to expand and thrive for almost 2,000 years. This king was Hammurabi, whose "code" thus marked an achievement and a peak of civilization never before attained.

Hammurabi's impressive work—some 3,500 lines of cuneiform characters—is divided into three parts. There is a central section written in straight-forward, clear, unadorned prose. This section is framed by a prologue of three hundred lines and an epilogue of five hundred, which are sublime and lyrical in tone, with a choice of words and turns of phrase more like poetry.

It is from the central part that the monument derives its name of "code," which was bestowed upon it by its first decipherers. This section consists of a series of regulations—282 in all—that cover many secular activities. Some of these regulations concern crimes and their punishment:

If a man has brought an accusation of murder against another without being able to produce proof—the accuser shall be put to death.

Others are related to administrative problems, such as the proper conduct of business affairs:

If a man of business has entrusted to a shopkeeper either grain or wool or oil or any other merchandise to sell retail—once the sale has taken place and the purchase money has been accounted for, then the shopkeeper shall transmit it to the businessman, but shall receive from him a sealed document in evidence of the sum which has been remitted.

A listing of the subjects covered shows the range of these regulations. They concern false witness, theft, royal fiefs (lands allotted by the sovereign to members of his entourage, on condition that they share with him the produce), husbandry, town planning, commerce, deposits and pledges, marriage, divorce, second wives, the joint responsibility of husbands and wives for debts, preparations for marriage, the disposal of assets after the death of a spouse or parent, certain particular cases like the marriage of widows or priestesses, adoption, wet-nursing, assault and injuries, regulations for certain occupations, both professional and menial, and slavery.

Not all aspects of communal life appear in this list: for instance there is no reference to taxation.

Furthermore, when one looks at the code more

Left The stele of Naram Sin, King of Agade, who is shown standing before a mountain, his feet resting on slain enemies, while soldiers ascend a wooded path.

Right Map of Mesopotamia, showing the principal towns of the kingdom of Hammurabi and its natural resources.

1/25

Above The remains of the prisons of Hammurabi, excavated at Babylon.

Above right Gudea, the Ensi or ruler of Lagash, under whom the city of Lagash became the leading cultural center of Sumer.
The Sumerians were the earliest rulers of the civilization of Mesopotamia, and were displaced finally by the Semitic dynasty of Babylon under King Hammurabi.

closely the various paragraphs are all so concerned with specific and individual cases that it is impossible to describe them as "laws" in the proper sense of the word—that is to say, truly abstract and universal propositions. For example in the first paragraph quoted earlier, the question of false accusation on a capital charge relates only to murder, whereas there are numerous other possible examples like treason and sacrilege which should have been included for consideration. And in the second paragraph quoted, the need for scrupulous and documented accounts should surely extend to many business dealings other than the specific one between the man of business and his agent.

It is therefore a mistake to refer to a "code," at any rate if we mean to use the word in its true sense of a compilation of the entire legislation of a country and of a period. We are dealing rather with a collection of judgments originally pronounced to resolve actual cases, and subsequently classified into a sort of treatise on jurisprudence, illustrated by examples. We must realize that the ancient Mesopotamians were as yet incapable of formulating abstract and truly universal principles, i.e. laws. They chose to instruct in methods of ordering society by formulating examples from a

sufficiently large and typical selection of actual cases—in the way that we still teach our children grammar and arithmetic. The Code of Hammurabi is, then, both a manual on the art of judgment and a treatise on jurisprudence.

The prologue and epilogue enable us to understand better the significance that its author intended this imposing work to have. In the prologue Hammurabi confides to us his concept of himself and his role: he portrays himself as appointed by the gods to exercise royal power over his people, and he flatters himself that he has accomplished this great duty to perfection:

When Anu the Sublime, King of the gods together with Enlil, Lord of the sky and of the earth, the master of destiny of peoples, had bestowed upon Marduk, the eldest son of Enki, supreme power over all peoples and had enabled him to prevail over all the other gods, when they had pronounced the majestic name of Babylon and decreed the extension of its power over the whole universe and the establishment of an eternal kingdom based on foundations as immovable as those of the sky and the earth, then Anu and Enlil also pronounced my own name, Hammurabi, devout prince and worshiper of the gods, so that I might bring order to my people and so that I might free them from evil and wicked men, that

Farming and commerce thrive under Hammurabi

I should defend the weak from the oppression of the mighty, and that I might rise like the sun over men and cast my light over the whole country.

In order to prove his success, the sovereign then enumerates his great achievements, in both foreign affairs and internal politics. The list of the former is shorter and less detailed: it recalls how one after the other he had subdued and united in a vast empire centered on Babylon all the formerly autonomous cities that had made up Mesopotamia.

However, in Hammurabi's own eyes his most important achievement, the one most noble and the most welcome to the gods, was as an administrator who had kept his country in order and hence in a state of well-being and prosperity. This is why he lists the 282 articles, which were not only to immortalize his decisions and wise maxims, but also to demonstrate his real knowledge of law and his genuine gift of judgment.

Then, after this lengthy catalogue, the sovereign insists in the epilogue on the high ideals he has of kingship, and the zeal he has devoted to his divine mission. He presents himself as a model king and hands down his conduct, his experience and his knowledge as a source of instruction and inspiration for every sovereign worthy of the name who might come after him:

If any of my successors possesses the necessary understanding to keep the country in order, then let him pay attention to what I have engraved on my stele, for this will explain to him the course and the conduct to pursue by reminding him of the judgments which I have made for my people and the decisions which I have given them. In this way he will succeed in keeping his subjects in order, give them judgments and decisions, eradicate evil and wicked men from their midst and so achieve the well-being of the people! Yes, it is me, Hammurabi, the just king, upon whom the god Shamash has bestowed the understanding of justice!

After the end of the Hammurabi dynasty the political balance was profoundly altered: henceforth the struggle for supremacy was between the Semites of the south of the country, around Babylon, and those of the north, first around Assur and then around Nineveh. They were to contend for power for at least a thousand years to come, until Mesopotamia passed under the domination first of Persia (539 B.C.) and then of Greece (330 B.C.). About 1200 B.C. the Elamite king Shutruknahhunte, who had come to conquer and destroy Babylon, carried off the stele on which the code was inscribed to his capital, Susa, as a trophy of war. Here archaeologists found it 3,000 years later, broken in three pieces and partly damaged. As a work of literature and learning, however, this same code was to last right up to the end of the history of ancient Mesopotamia, continually studied, reread and recopied as one of the immortal classics of literary and intellectual achievement produced by this ancient civilization.

The Code of Hammurabi not only translates into clear language, with a precision of detail and

Two seals of the third millennium B.C. showing shepherds and their flocks (*above*) and river transport (*left*).

Two seals of the third millennium B.C. showing agricultural workers (*above*) and a hunting scene (*left*).

Laws for a thriving civilization

Above Six plaques showing figures from Mesopotamian life: a carpenter, a man with a goat, a woman suckling a child, a harpist, an itinerant showman with monkeys, and a married couple.

Opposite The golden head of a bull, decorating the front of a lyre from Ur.

an often remarkable exactitude, the principal institutions, the structure of the hierarchy and society, the administrative machinery and the economic mechanism of the great civilization of ancient Mesopotamia. It also conveys Mesopotamia's quintessential spirit: the supreme importance of the gods and their decisions to everything that happens here below; the nobility and importance of the monarchy; the ideals of order and justice that must govern society and inspire the ruling class; and a preoccupation with scientific analysis, order and clarity.

For all these reasons, the code is a significant milestone in that ancient heritage built up over thousands of years by our far-off ancestors on the

banks of the Euphrates and the Tigris, a heritage that fed two sources of our own civilization, Israel and Greece.

JEAN BOTTÉRO

The Babylonian kings who followed Hammurabi were unable to hold the wide territories that he had won. New enemies challenged the supremacy of Babylon in

Boundary stone from Khafajan

Mesopotamia; the south broke away and a new kingdom came into being, the dynasty of the Sea Land, with its center in the marshy region around the head of the Persian Gulf. The Babylonian army was more than once defeated by the Cassites, a mountain people from the region now known as Kurdistan, of whom we shall say more later. In the northwest, the Mari region regained independence. From the encircling highlands, barbarian newcomers were

Map of Babylon, c. 600 B.C.

pouring into the semicircle of river valleys and urban settlements known as the Fertile Crescent. The ethnic map of the Near East was undergoing the first of a series of violent changes, perhaps the most far-reaching of all in its effects on the history of man.

Cosmic order

A motif that recurs in the mythology of many ancient peoples is that of the emergence of order from disorder, of cosmos out of chaos. This is the theme of the creation legends of Mesopotamia and of Egypt. The concept of cosmic order, which the gods bring about and which mankind is concerned to maintain, is present in many ancient literatures. It implied the taming of the forces of nature, storm and fire and flood, and the defense of civilization against dangers from without. These dangers were ever-present, for throughout the whole of the ancient period and for many centuries afterwards, the areas of civilization were islands in a vast ocean of barbarism. To appreciate society and to understand its history, we must know something of this great hinterland of barbarian peoples, for their periodic incursions often constituted milestones of deep historical importance.

The civilized world of the ancient Near East was surrounded on all sides by barbarian lands that seemed to stretch to infinity. Of their peoples, only a fraction on the borderlands was known. South and west of Egypt extended the whole continent of Africa. But Egypt, owing to her geographical isolation, was not greatly troubled by the invasion of other African peoples. The situation was very different for the peoples of Western Asia. Northwards and eastwards lay the vast steppeland of Central Asia. The population of this huge expanse, though relatively sparse to the land over which they ranged, constituted an ever-present threat to the agricultural peoples of the more favored territories around the Fertile Crescent.

As a result of archeological research, particularly in the U.S.S.R., a certain amount is now becoming known about the inhabitants of this vast and hitherto little-known territory. It would appear that in Siberia and Mongolia a Palaeolithic economy, based on hunting, continued long after the rise of civilization in Western Asia. With the development of agriculture in areas that bordered on the steppeland, a mixed economy evolved, embracing both the growing of crops and the herding of animals; since they did not practice irrigation, and water was scarce, they

Copper bison from Lake Van

grew and harvested cereal crops after the season of rain and then moved on with their herds, seeking pasture over a wide range. This pattern of existence may be described as nomadic. At Tripolye, near Kiev, however, and at other sites in the Ukraine and eastern Rumania, remains of the settlements of stone-using agriculturalists have been found, dating to the third millennium B.C. They were not nomads, for they lived in large houses built of timber and clay, and had domesticated goats, cattle and dogs. The bones of horses also have been found in their settlements, and this is possibly the earliest evidence of the domestication of this friend of man.

A new weapon

Now in the Mari letters, and other documents of about the same date, there occur some names which are neither Sumerian nor Semitic. These names betray the presence of a new element in the population. The horse, too, makes its first appearance in the Near East, as a rare and precious gift sent by ruler to ruler. Usually two horses are mentioned, and it is evident that they were used in pairs as draft animals, to draw a new and revolutionary form of vehicle: the light war chariot. The Sumerians had used chariots to

Woman taming animals; Sumerian bowl

Near East and Babylon is eclipsed

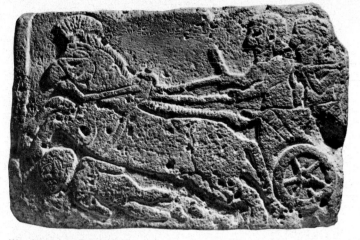

War chariot from Tell Halaf

Hittite civilization

Few Hurrian texts have yet been discovered, and it is probable that the Hurrians, like the Cassites, adopted the civilization of the country in which they found themselves and gradually lost their individuality. At any rate, it is difficult to pick out elements in their culture which are specifically Hurrian or specifically Cassite. With the Hittites we have more evidence. From the material remains of their civilization and from the many thousands of tablets on which their royal records, their prayers and liturgies, their treaties, contracts and laws are written, we can form a fairly complete picture of their national character and a good deal about their way of life. The basis of the economy was agriculture; corn, wine and oil were staple products. Barley and

Hittite king protected by a god

wheat grew in the valleys, and fruit on the hill slopes. The mountains were rich in minerals; copper, silver and lead were mined and also a little iron, probably the first to be smelted (in early Egypt the only iron known was in meteoric lumps hammered into shape). The

Babylonian model divining liver

medium of exchange was silver and a fixed tariff of prices, in terms of weight of silver, was laid down from time to time by the government.

The king's authority was absolute. He was the leader in war, high priest and lawgiver. Though he was not regarded as a god in his lifetime, as the Egyptian Pharaoh was, he was deified at death and offerings were made to the divine spirits of dead kings. Members of the royal family enjoyed special privileges: the queen in particular was often prominent in affairs of state. An elaborate and strict protocol governed court life. The nobles held land in fief from the king and were bound to him by the obligation of military and other service. In the old kingdom, an assembly of nobles advised the king and had some say in the appointment of his successor, but later these functions were no longer exercised and the king himself administered justice through his officers. Such laws as survive show that the Hittites had a well-developed legal system and a strong sense of justice. Great care was taken to sift all the evidence in a case, and penalties for crime were devised to compensate the injured party as well as to punish the wrongdoer.

great effect in battle, but they were heavy, clumsy affairs with solid wooden wheels, pulled by teams of the wild sort of asses, known as onagers, which are now extinct but once roamed the Syrian desert. From pictures of these Sumerian chariots in action, it can be seen that they must have thundered forward in a straight line, like a kind of tank, carrying two or three warriors with spears leveled, mowing down the enemy and spreading panic. The new chariots were quite different: very light, with spoked wheels, and built for speed. The military effectiveness of horse-drawn chariotry was quickly appreciated by those who suffered its onslaught, and it soon became an essential weapon of offense in every western Asiatic army. Its introduction is to be attributed to the newcomers, whom we know as the Hurrians, the Cassites and the Hittites.

The Hittites

The Hittites were the first to settle. Originally nomads with no knowledge of writing, they arrived in Anatolia at the end of the third millennium or the beginning of the second, and by about 1900 B.C. had begun to overrun eastern Turkey and to impose their rule on the native Hattians. During the following century they spread northwards, and about 1650 B.C. made the hilltop fortress of Hattusas (modern Boghazköi), in the bend of the river Halys, their capital. By this time they had adopted the cuneiform script of Mesopotamia and the first historical texts date from this period (known as the Hittite Old Kingdom).

The language of the Hittites of Hattusas is one of the Indo-European group of languages; that is to say, that though very different from Greek and Latin, the Germanic languages, and Sanskrit, it is basically akin to all these. Compare for instance the Hittite word *kuis* ("who") with Latin *quis; watar*, which in Hittite means water; and *mekkis* ("great"), which is like the Greek *megas*. The case endings of nouns and the inflection of verbs are also similar to those in various Indo-European languages. The Hittites, too, were great horse-breeders: it is interesting to find among the tablets from Boghazköi a treatise on the training of horses which is ascribed to a Hurrian expert in such matters, and which uses technical terms most nearly paralleled by Sanskrit.

Neither the Hurrians nor the Cassites were Indo-Europeans, judging by the remnant of their languages that is left to us; but by the sixteenth century, if not earlier, they were led by an aristocracy who spoke Indo-European languages, worshiped Aryan gods and were experts in the arts of warfare and the chase. In Babylonia the Cassites moved in to occupy the capital, Babylon, after an unexpected raid launched by the Hittite king Murshil, in 1530 B.C., in which the last of Hammurabi's successors perished. At about the same time, confederate Hurrian kingdoms were set up in North Syria and in the region now called the Jezira, between the Tigris and Euphrates. The greatest of these kingdoms was Mitanni, whose capital on the river Khabur has not yet been excavated. For a time, the kings of Mitanni were overlords of wide territories from Asia Minor to the foothills of Persia, and reckoned themselves the equals of any of the great powers of western Asia.

Hittite figures on rock relief

The Eruption of Santorin 1450 B.C.

By 2000 B.C. Crete, and its outpost the island of Santorin, was the home of a remarkable, flourishing civilization. Known as Minoan, after the legendary King Minos, this civilization ranks with Mesopotamia and Egypt as one of the great centers of human development and progress. The Cretans were great seafarers and traders, and they soon carried their civilization to other islands of the Aegean and to the Greek mainland. Archeology has shown us that round about 1700 palaces in Knossos and Phaistos, the two chief towns of Crete, were destroyed by fire. They were rebuilt, however, and a bright new chapter seemed to open up for Crete. Then suddenly an even greater disaster overtook Cretan civilization, on a scale unknown since. The whole of Santorin exploded, with devastating effects for the surrounding area. From that day Crete never recovered.

The legend of Atlantis—a tale, first told by Plato, of a great center of civilization suddenly and violently destroyed by the sea—has inspired generations of scholars to speculate on the possible historical reality of a lost continent. Some have subscribed to the theory that Atlantis may have been the Aegean island of Santorin, a flourishing outpost of Europe's earliest civilization, the one that took root in Crete during the third millennium B.C. For early in the fifteenth century B.C., Santorin and Crete were hit by a series of natural disasters on a scale that has never been repeated in the civilized world. Archaeological exploration will no doubt continue to reveal more about this cataclysmic series of events; meanwhile, we know enough to show how remarkable was the civilization these islanders had created.

The first inhabitants of Crete are believed to have reached its shores some eight thousand years ago. These earliest settlers were peasant farmers, who arrived in ships, bringing with them some of their animals and their seed-corn. Their tools were of stone, and they had not yet learned to work metal. Most likely they came to Crete from the east, either from the neighboring coasts of Anatolia or from farther afield in Cilicia or Syria.

The settlers continued to have some contact with the outside world. For making sharp-edged knife blades they used obsidian, a volcanic glass that they could have obtained from Melos in the Cyclades Islands, some ninety miles north of Crete. Some of their obsidian, however, seems to have been brought from the distant region of Kayseri in central Anatolia. In the course of time stone vases from Egypt and copper tools from other areas also began to reach Crete.

At the beginning of the third millennium B.C. new groups of immigrants from the east appear to have settled on the island. These may have been refugees escaping from the great political disturbances of the time. For it was about then that

the Nile valley was united by conquest under the rule of one king, Hor-Aha, to inaugurate the First Dynasty of Egypt. One of the earliest kings of Egypt's new dynasty extended his conquests into southern Palestine, and styles of pottery appearing in Crete suggest that refugees may have come to the island from that area.

Along with new styles of pottery, the art of metallurgy—making tools and weapons of copper and eventually of tin-bronze—seems to have been introduced to Crete at this time. In the centuries that followed, while the great pyramids were being erected in Egypt, other groups of immigrants found their way to Crete from the east. Some may have been fleeing the barbarous invaders who overran Syria and Palestine about the middle of the third millennium.

Brought to Crete by refugees, or by traders, ideas and arts such as those of stone vase-making, seal-engraving and writing, soon became established on the island. By the end of the third millennium the island had become the seat of a high civilization, the first on European soil, with cities and large palaces apparently belonging to rulers who were able to concentrate power and wealth in their hands.

This new civilization, while deriving much from Egypt, and even more perhaps from Syria and Mesopotamia, was something very different; and in turn it influenced the older cultures. The spiral designs that became fashionable in Egypt from about two thousand B.C. onwards, during the Middle Kingdom, may have been inspired by the spiral decoration on imported Cretan textiles. No such textiles have survived; but fine painted pottery from Crete, some of it with spiral decoration, has been found in Egypt, and many Egyptian objects—beads, scarabs, stone vases, and ivories—reached Crete.

The Cretans were evidently seafarers and traders. Many of their most important towns were

Patterns of spirals are found on many Cretan artifacts of the Bronze Age, and may have been the origin of the spiral patterns that became popular in Egypt *c.* 2000 B.C. This limestone amphora, from Knossos, dates from *c.* 1400 B.C., and is thus probably a little later than the Santorin eruption.

Opposite Part of the crater on the island of Nea Kameni, in the Santorin lagoon. The first of the Kameni islands (Palaea Kameni) was formed by volcanic activity in the second century B.C., and subsequent activity has created Nea Kameni. These islands, on which the volcano is still active today, represent the aftermath of the great eruption of the fifteenth century B.C.

A brilliant civilization in the Aegean

The art of metalwork was highly developed in Minoan Crete, as is evident from this finely worked decorative pinhead, which also reflects female fashion of the time, in the many-tiered skirt. This pinhead was found in one of the shaft graves at Mycenae.

Among the civilized arts of Crete was the making of faience figurines, and this statuette of a snake goddess, found in the palace at Knossos, is a notable example. The tiered skirt, wide belt and bared breasts are typical of the court fashion of the period.

on the coast where sandy beaches allowed the small ships of those days to be hauled ashore. Pictures of these ships on seal stones show them with single mast and square sail supplemented by oars or paddles.

In about 1700 B.C. the two largest palaces in Crete, at Knossos in the north and at Phaistos near the south coast, were destroyed by fire—whether by accident or as a result of earthquake or war is uncertain. Crete at this time appears to have been divided into several independent states, which probably indulged in intermittent warfare among themselves. The destruction of the palaces may also have been caused by foreign enemies, but if so, there is no evidence that they remained on the island.

After this destruction, the palaces at Knossos and Phaistos were rebuilt with even greater magnificence and splendor to inaugurate what was to be the most flourishing period of the Bronze Age civilization of Crete. Noble paintings in fresco now adorned the walls of the palaces and great houses. The arts of metal-working, gem-engraving, ivory-carving and faience-molding reached their highest perfection, although the art of pottery declined, probably because vases of metal—copper, gold and silver—were now in general use in the palaces and houses of the great.

This vigorous and attractive civilization soon began to spread beyond the shores of Crete, to the northern islands of the Aegean, and to large areas of the Greek mainland. Evidence of Cretan culture can be seen in the unplundered royal shaft graves at Mycenae, the chief city of the mainland. The earlier graves, which may date back to the seventeenth century B.C., contain some vases and other objects imported from Crete, while in the later graves, of the sixteenth and fifteenth centuries B.C., nearly all the vases, weapons and jewelry are of Cretan manufacture. Of course, it is hard to tell whether these were imports, or whether they are the work of Cretan artists employed at Mycenae or native artists trained in a Cretan style.

The spread of Cretan civilization to the mainland of Greece was perhaps largely the result of peaceful intercourse and admiring imitation. But there may have been a harsher side. In that imperialistic age it is only too likely that the rulers of Crete attempted to extort tribute from the princes of the mainland just as the contemporary pharaohs of Egypt did from the petty chieftains of Syria and Palestine.

Later Greek legends hint that there was a time when parts of mainland Greece were tributary to the kings of Knossos in Crete. Some of the most intriguing of these legends concern Minos, king and legislator of Crete, and the labyrinth at Knossos built to house his wife's monstrous offspring, the Minotaur. It seems possible that the legends concerning Minos' maritime conquests, even as far as Sicily, are based on considerable Cretan expansion in the Mediterranean and on

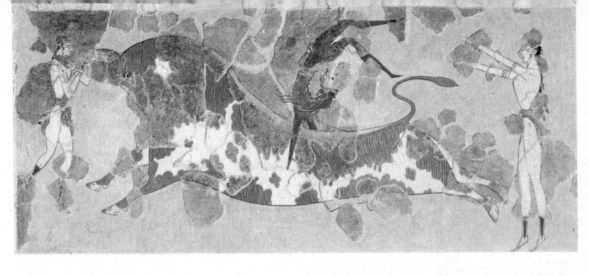

The famous bull games or dances of Minoan Crete are depicted in this fresco from the palace of Knossos. The religious significance of these games, if they had any, is unknown. Some have doubted whether the acrobatic feats shown were, in fact, ever accomplished.

kings who checked the piratical expeditions of their Aegean contemporaries.

Crete seems to have become heavily populated during this period from the seventeenth to the fifteenth centuries B.C. Everywhere throughout the island today there are traces of towns, villages and hamlets, even of isolated villas and farms, dating to those centuries. There may even have been a danger of overpopulation, the classic remedy for which, in later Greek times at least, was overseas colonization. Later Greek tradition recalls colonies of Cretans in the islands of the Cyclades, and archaeologists have identified a number of these, probably founded in the course of the sixteenth century B.C.

One of the islands settled by Cretan colonists was Santorin, the ancient Thera, seventy miles north of Crete and the nearest of the Cyclades to

the "homeland." Santorin is a volcano island; but at the time the Cretans settled there its volcano seems to have been long quiescent.

Crete and the Cyclades are much subject to earthquakes and tectonic disturbances of every kind—several times in each century some part of the main island suffers in this way. About 1550 B.C. or a bit later, an earthquake of unusual severity struck Knossos and many of the towns and settlements in the east of Crete. But the damage was soon repaired and the palace at Knossos and the houses there and elsewhere were restored.

Not long afterwards, however, early in the fifteenth century B.C., Crete was ravaged by another major earthquake. The destruction caused by this can also be traced at Knossos and the settlements of eastern Crete. This second earthquake may have been connected with a catastrophe

This scene, painted on the side of a stone sarcophagus from Hagia Triada in Crete, is thought to represent a funeral of the Minoan period. It dates from the fourteenth century B.C., but the styles of clothing are also typical of the period before the Santorin eruption.

Disaster strikes Crete

Above In the palace of Knossos foodstuffs—in particular oil and wine—were stored in giant jars called *pithoi* and in large storage pits in the floor. Many of these jars have been unearthed intact.

Right The alabaster throne of the rulers of Crete, in the throne room of the palace of Knossos. The frescoes on the wall behind are modern reconstructions carried out by Sir Arthur Evans.

on Santorin. For the volcano there, so long inactive, erupted about this time and buried the island's Cretan colonies. Most of the colonists, however, seem to have had time to escape, taking with them their most precious belongings. Excavations have revealed the houses of the colonists wonderfully preserved—as at Pompeii—below the debris of the volcano. Yet only one or two skeletons of human victims have been found, and there is little in the destroyed houses other than clay vases that were expendable.

Some time after this catastrophe—it may have been several years later—a few of the colonists appear to have come back to Santorin. Traces of new houses have been found above the debris of the eruption.

The third and final act in this drama of natural disasters was yet to come. The eruption on Santorin was merely the prelude to a cataclysm of a magnitude that has never been exceeded. A generation or so later, about the middle of the fifteenth century B.C., the whole island of Santorin exploded.

The only comparable natural disaster in history is the explosion in 1883 of the volcano island of Krakatoa in the Sunda Strait between Java and Sumatra, Indonesia. The sound of Krakatoa's eruption was heard as far away as Australia, the Philippines and Japan. The debris of stones and ash shot to a height estimated as seventeen miles or more; on islands in the neighborhood of Krakatoa the deposit of debris was thick enough to cover entire tropical forests, while finer dust, suspended in the atmosphere, eventually spread over the greater part of the surface of the globe. At Jakarta, a hundred miles away, day was turned into night, as debris darkened the sky for days. But the aftermath of the explosion was even more destructive. The great hollow crater left by the escape of debris collapsed and most of Krakatoa disappeared into this void. Where a cone 1,400 feet above sea level had once risen was now a gulf more than one thousand feet deep. Into this gulf the sea poured, causing immense tidal waves, between fifty and one hundred feet high. The waves swept over towns and settlements along the adjacent coasts, killing more than thirty-six thousand people.

The explosion of Santorin about 1450 B.C. is judged to have been on a very much greater scale than that of Krakatoa. The north coast of Crete, only seventy miles away across the open sea, was thickly studded with populous towns and settlements; these coastal settlements and many of those in the more protected interior of the island, must have been wrecked by the blast of the explosion. Some time afterwards the vast empty crater left by the escape of the debris collapsed. The island of Santorin, which had been more or less circular in shape, rising to a high cone in the center, became the jagged group of two islands that it is today. As in the case of Krakatoa, the sea swept into the deep void, causing huge tidal waves, probably as

Above The landscape of eastern Crete, showing in the distance the palace of Kato Zakro where traces of the Santorin disaster have been found.

much as a hundred and fifty feet high. When they bore down upon the north coast of Crete, such waves would have flattened all that the explosion had left standing. Meanwhile the debris from the eruption, hanging in the air, must have enveloped Crete in darkness for days on end, and poisonous fumes and vapors would have added to the suffering and terror of the survivors.

Many of the Cretan settlements destroyed at this time have been excavated. But at only one of them, Amnisos on the coast north of Knossos, has evidence of the tidal waves been noted, in the form of a layer of pumice stones over the ruins. Debris from the explosion has been identified in the wreckage of a palace at Zakro on the east coast. But the Zakro palace, and many of the buildings destroyed at this time elsewhere in Crete, had also been ravaged by fire. Moreover, although many fine vases of clay, stone and faience, bronze tools and inscribed clay tablets were recovered at Zakro, there was virtually no trace there of precious metals and none whatsoever of victims of the disaster. Here and elsewhere in Crete it looks as if people had some warning of catastrophe, and time enough to escape into the open with their most valued

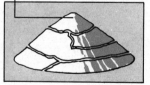

Cone of volcano blown off

Eruption causes tidal wave which hits Greece and Crete

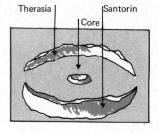

Therasia   Santorin
        Core

Above The lagoon of Santorin, where the sea has filled the crater of the volcano.
Right Diagram showing the stages of the Santorin eruption.

The end of an empire

possessions and household effects.

It has been suggested that the explosion of Santorin was triggered by an earthquake with its center in the seabed off the north coast of Crete. Earthquakes often begin with warning shocks, and result in fires spreading from hearths or lamps in houses. The initial destruction of the palace at Zakro, and of the other towns and settlements in Crete, may have been due to an earthquake and the fires it caused—followed by the explosion of Santorin and by the resulting tidal waves.

The material damage produced by this series of disasters was clearly immense. Most of the chief centers in the populous north and east of Crete had been totally destroyed, and those elsewhere had been wrecked. The eastern end of Crete seems to have been altogether uninhabited for a considerable period after the cataclysm. Because of the direction of prevailing winds, the deposit of debris must have been thicker there than elsewhere in Crete, and, laden as it was with poisonous chloride, would have killed vegetation and made life impossible for man and beast.

The towns in the east of Crete were eventually resettled, but the palaces there were never rebuilt. After the cataclysm, Knossos seems to have become the capital of a centralized bureaucratic state controlling most if not all of Crete. This may

have coincided with a change of dynasty at Knossos, perhaps with rulers who were strangers, either from another part of Crete or from abroad. It is possible that conquerors from the Greek mainland took advantage of the chaos and confusion that overwhelmed Crete after the cataclysm to gain control of Knossos. But the mainland too must have been seriously affected by the disaster, and the archaeological evidence for a subsequent conquest of Crete from abroad is ambiguous.

The palace of Knossos was destroyed yet again by fire, probably early in the fourteenth century B.C. But at this time it was not rebuilt. The inscribed clay tablets found in its ruins have been deciphered and tentatively identified as an early form of Greek. If the language of the tablets really is Greek, then it is highly probable that Greeks from the mainland won control of Knossos and ruled there after the Santorin catastrophe, but this decipherment is contested.

The explosion of Santorin may therefore have led to great political changes, but there is no certainty as to their character. The cataclysm happened to coincide with a marked decline in the quality of Cretan civilization. There is evidence of much wealth and splendor in Crete during the century or so between the cataclysm and the final

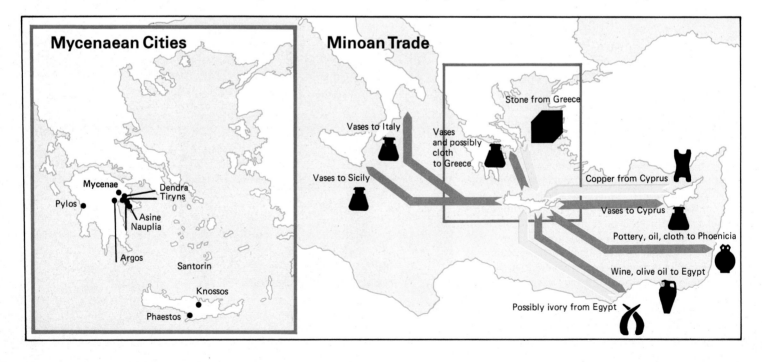

Mycenaean Cities

Mycenae
Pylos
Dendra
Tiryns
Asine
Nauplia
Argos
Santorin
Knossos
Phaestos

Minoan Trade

Stone from Greece
Vases to Italy
Vases and possibly cloth to Greece
Vases to Sicily
Copper from Cyprus
Vases to Cyprus
Pottery, oil, cloth to Phoenicia
Wine, olive oil to Egypt
Possibly ivory from Egypt

destruction of the palace at Knossos, but a deterioration is noticeable in taste and workmanship—except that employed in making tools and weapons.

The explosion of Santorin did not cause this decline, which seems to have begun much earlier. And the decline was accelerated after the final destruction of the palace at Knossos, a destruction that seems to have been the work of enemies. Afterwards, Crete, plundered and impoverished, may have become part of an empire ruled from Mycenae on the Greek mainland.

Towards the end of the thirteenth century B.C. Mycenae and the other chief centers of the Greek mainland were in turn destroyed by people moving into Greece from the north. Refugees from the devastated areas made their way overseas, and some of them came to Crete. After an interval, they were followed by other invaders, who occupied the fertile central parts of the island including the region around Knossos. Many of the previous inhabitants escaped abroad or took refuge in the mountains. Finally, at the very end of the Bronze Age, in the eleventh century B.C. the Dorian Greeks arrived to settle in Crete. With the coming of the Dorians the old Bronze Age civilization of Crete at last came to an end.

And for three thousand years—or until archeologists began probing Crete's ruins late in the nineteenth century—only such vague legends as that of the lost continent of Atlantis survived to remind man of Europe's earliest civilization.

M. S. F. HOOD

When Heinrich Schliemann discovered this gold mask at Mycenae he thought he had discovered the mask of Agamemnon, leader of the Greeks in the Trojan Wars, but it is now known to be at least three hundred years earlier.

Egypt becomes an imperial power and

We have seen that after the fall of Babylon in 1530 B.C. and the collapse of the Amorite kingdoms of the Euphrates area and North Syria, new peoples of different races entered the area and a new pattern of settlement developed. In the sixteenth and fifteenth centuries, the focus of our interest leaves the valley of the Two Rivers and is concentrated rather on Syria and Palestine, and in particular on the new kingdoms which, with a population now partly Semitic (or "Canaanite," the Biblical writers' term) and partly Hurrian, and often with an Indo-European aristocracy, were emerging as political entities. Their history is bound up with that of the rulers of Egypt, which now for the first time becomes an imperial power with widespread influence and far-reaching commerce.

Egypt in the Lebanon

The coastal plain of the Levant, later known as Phoenicia, and the Syrian hinterland as far as the Beqa', that is to say, the valley dividing the mountain ranges of Lebanon and Anti-Lebanon, had for some centuries past been in contact with the civilization of the Nile Valley. Originally, Egyptian influence had been confined to Byblos, a well-favored port north of the modern city of Beirut, and the forested slopes behind; from here, since the earliest historic period and perhaps even earlier, the Egyptians had brought the long timbers of pine and cedar they needed for shipbuilding, which were conspicuously lacking in the valley of the Nile. Their interest

Egyptian soldiers marching

had spread during the Middle Kingdom to include other parts of the Lebanon with which they established a trading relationship; in Palestine they may even have achieved some kind of military domination during the Twelfth Dynasty.

Egyptian influence had declined, however, as soon as the strong hand of the Twelfth Dynasty Pharaohs was withdrawn. Egyptian armies no longer marched north and, when the centralized control of the Pharaoh at last broke down and the country was split into principalities, even the sea link with Byblos was broken. The forts that had guarded the eastern frontier ceased to be effective. Bedouin bands infiltrated across the border, the trickle became a stream, and the small kingdom set up in the eastern Delta by these desert sheikhs (or Hyksos, the "shepherd kings" of

Greek tradition) grew in size till the Hyksos bid fair to take over the whole country. For something over a century, between approximately 1720 and 1600 B.C., the valley of the Nile was parceled out between Asiatic Hyksos in the north, native Egyptians in Upper Egypt and Nubian princes to the south, beyond the first cataract of the Nile. It took an almost superhuman effort for a family of local grandees in the Theban area, rallying patriotic support, to drive out the foreigners and restore unified control over the whole country. On the crest of a wave of military success, these first Phar-

Shipbuilding in Egypt

Defeat of Nubians

aohs of the Eighteenth Dynasty went on to win back Nubia (which in the Twelfth Dynasty they had controlled as far as the second cataract), and to carry their arms farther into Africa. At the same

time, they started northwards on the military road that was to lead them to the conquest of Syria and Palestine and to bring them face to face with the armies of both the Hurrians and, at length, the Hittites.

The confrontation was not, it seems, immediate. Tuthmosis I appears to have marched unimpeded to the Euphrates but after he withdrew, most of North Syria and even eastern Cilicia came under the overlordship of the Mitannian kings. The greatest of these, Shaushatar, controlled Assyria too and his authority reached as far as Kirkuk, east of the Tigris. But fifty years after Tuthmosis' surprising foray, the challenge was renewed and this time the Egyptian army found its way barred. The Mitannians had rallied to their aid the rulers of many of the small city-states of Syria, many of them now ruled by

Tuthmosis III smiting Asiatics

Hurrians, and Tuthmosis III, the greatest of Egypt's warrior kings, had to fight every inch of the way. In a series of seventeen campaigns from 1480 to 1454 B.C., he again and again fought in Retenu (the Egyptian name for Syria/Palestine), capturing cities, devastating the countryside, punishing rebel towns that threw out their garrisons and at least once putting to flight the main force of the Mitannian army. By the end of his reign he had driven Shaushatar from North Syria and set his frontier at the Euphrates.

Colonial administration

Tuthmosis III must be credited, too, with the organization of a rudimentary colonial administration. Native rulers were left in charge of their own city-states, but as vassals bound by solemn oaths of fealty to their overlord the Pharaoh. They were bound to pay a heavy war indemnity and to furnish annual tribute assessed in kind: large quantities of copper, gold and other metals, cattle and flocks and agricultural produce, honey, wine and oil. Their sons were taken to Egypt to serve as hostages for their good behavior and also to be given an Egyptian education to fit them for rule when their turn came. The daughters of vassals entered the Pharaoh's harem. Egyptian garrisons were left at strategic points, fortresses were built and Syrian harbors, supplied by local labor, served as supply bases.

Heyday of empire

This was a time of great prosperity for Egypt. In the heyday of the Egyptian empire, during the reigns of Amenophis II, his son Tuthmosis IV and his grandson Amenophis III, sometimes called the Magnificent, wealth poured into the coffers of Egypt. The gold mines of Nubia were exploited to the full and caravans brought to Pharaoh's treasury the exotic products of the Sudan—ivory and ebony, panther skins, frankincense and myrrh. Tribute poured in from Retenu, and valuable presents were sent by the rulers of the Near East, the Cassite kings of Babylonia, the Assyrians, the Mitannians (now bound in friendship to Egypt by a treaty of alliance), the rulers of Cyprus and of Crete and the Aegean islands. In the tombs at Thebes of great officials—the grand viziers, the treasurers and viceroys whose duty and privilege it was to receive foreign envoys and accept their gifts—many paintings are preserved, some-

Asiatics bring tribute to Pharaoh

times still in their original bright colors, depicting these ceremonial occasions. Here the ruler of Tunip can be seen, carrying on his arm his little son who is to be brought up in Egypt; with him are Syrians,

Goddess pregnant with Akhenaton

their brightly patterned tunics contrasting with the flowing white garments of the Egyptians. Here too are Mitannians—portly, bearded figures with voluminous robes wound round their bodies; and men in Mycenaean dress, identified as from "the isles in the midst of the Great Green (sea)," with bull's head drinking cups and other Aegean vessels familiar from the excavations of Heinrich Schliemann, Sir Arthur Evans and others in Crete and on the mainland of Greece. In some tombs, of the age of Tuthmosis III, the *Keftiu* or Cretans depicted with hair curling over their foreheads, bare chests and short loincloths, are certainly to be identified with the Minoans whose story was told in the previous chapter; they too we must imagine, came to marvel at the magnificence of Pharaoh and to gaze in awe at his huge temples and vast palaces, glittering with gold and precious stones, so different in concept and style from their own cool, frescoed halls.

The apostate Pharaoh

At the height of the empire's prosperity, a sudden internal crisis developed, which was to distract Egypt's attention for a time and to rule out all possibility of further conquest abroad. It was a strange crisis, one of the most curious episodes in the history of the ancient world, and we do not yet completely understand its cause or its effects. It arose from the personality of one individual—the son and heir of Amenophis III, who bore the same name, and who succeeded his father in about 1380 B.C. Around the figure of this king controversy has raged. Was he genius or madman? Was his religious reform prompted by mono-

theistic zeal, poetic inspiration or political astuteness? In opposition to the powerful and wealthy priesthood of the state cult of the god Amun, Amenophis IV restored the ancient cult of the sun-god, but gave it new expression in the form of the solar disc whose rays, ending in little hands, shed blessing and light upon the king and queen. He insisted that the worship of this sun-god, the Aton, should be exclusive and other cults were either proscribe or neglected. He changed his name to Akhenaton, "pleasing to Aton," and moved to a new capital at Tell el Amarna, which he named "The Horizon of Aton." Here he and his wife Nefertiti, whose beauty is familiar even to those who know nothing of

Akhenaton with Aton, the Sun Disk

her history, were able to worship their new god and live a life of domestic bliss (or so the relief sculptures in the tombs at Amarna would have us believe) with their

six daughters. In the hymns which were written in praise of the Aton, and which many people think he himself composed, there is great emphasis on truth and beauty, and on the universal nature of the sun's domain:

Thou appearest in beauty on
the horizon of heaven,
O living Aton, the beginning
of life!
When thou risest on the
eastern horizon
Thou fillest the earth with thy
beauty.
Thou art gracious, great,
glistening, high over every
land,
Thy rays encompass the earth
to the bounds of all that
thou hast made . . .

The phraseology of this hymn has been compared with one of the Biblical psalms (104), and Akhenaton's reforms have been regarded by some as foreshadowing and perhaps indirectly influencing the monotheism of the people of Israel. However this may be, he did not succeed in winning over the people of Egypt and after his death, the priests of Amun were again able to assert their influence. The young king Tutankhamen, who had been born into the Aton faith as Tutankhaton, changed his name and, while still a child, returned to Thebes, restored the neglected temples and reinstated Amun as the state god. Within a few years of Akhenaton's death, his memory was execrated and his capital razed. We shall see later how the authority of Egypt abroad suffered during this unhappy interlude, and how the Ramesside kings restored the prestige of Egypt in Syria.

Tutankhamen hunting

The Aryan Invasion of India *c.* **1400** B.C.

*Some four thousand years ago in India, around the Indus Valley at Mohenjo-daro and farther
north at Harappa, a civilization flourished rivaling those of Egypt and Mesopotamia.
Streets were laid out at right angles, brick houses existed, and an elaborate drainage system
was installed. Writing had also been invented. Pottery was produced, and there were certainly
trading contacts with Mesopotamia. However, round about 1750—and
continuing down to 1400—there is evidence that groups of Aryans from the North descended
into India, radically affecting the native civilization. They were not simply invaders, though
archeology has produced evidence of fighting at Mohenjo-daro—but settlers.
The Aryan invasions were in fact migrations of peoples. Among other things they introduced the
horse—hitherto unknown—to India, but much more significantly they brought a new language
and a new religion whose effects are still profoundly important in India today.*

The Indian subcontinent, bounded on the north
by the mountain ranges of the Himalayas and
elsewhere by the ocean, has always been relatively
immune from invasion. The would-be invader
must show an extraordinary degree of resourcefulness and tenacity if such natural obstacles as these
are to be overcome. On only two occasions in
historical times has India been invaded: by the
armies of Islam in the Middle Ages and by the
British (a process of gradual infiltration rather
than direct invasion) in the eighteenth and nineteenth centuries. Of the "prehistoric" invasions,
that of the Aryans in the second half of the second
millennium B.C. has left the profoundest marks on
Indian culture, and may fairly be called a milestone
in Indian history.

The precise dates and conditions of the Aryan
invasion, for reasons we shall discuss later, may
still elude scholarship, but this much is clear:
between 1750 and 1400 B.C. India was forced to
meet the onslaughts of waves of nomadic "barbarians" from the northwest. Materially, the
nomads were far inferior to the peoples they were
in the process of conquering; spiritually, they
were perhaps not inferior, but they were certainly
different.

The process of conquest, which appears to have
been gradual rather than sudden, as successive
tribes or groups of tribes crossed the mountains
into the Indus Valley and the Punjab, was greatly
facilitated by the Aryans' greater mobility, in
which the domestication of the horse played a
great part. But it cannot be stressed too strongly
that this did not mean that the original inhabitants
of the occupied area were simply exterminated.
They were displaced or subdued; patterns of
thought and conduct were imposed on them; and
by the time of the Aryans' further migration into
the Gangetic basin and western Central India,
Aryan ideals were certainly dominant in those
areas. But farther south and east, Aryanization was

both gradual and incomplete: and it remains so to
this day.

If history can be said to begin with the emergence
of chronicles and other written sources, then the
Aryan invasion belongs to prehistory. This is not
to say that there is no accessible material from
which knowledge of the invasion may be derived.
Such material is of two kinds: oral-literary, the
hymns of the *Rig Veda*, not reduced to writing until
many centuries after the events they reflect but
preserved with minute accuracy down through
the ages; and archaeological, a constantly growing
body of information that may yet require us
seriously to modify many accepted opinions and
many more tacit assumptions.

Neither source is absolutely precise or completely
exhaustive. Literary material such as the *Rig Veda*,
apart from not being susceptible to precise dating
or location, is thoroughly partisan. Take, for
instance, this quotation from a hymn dedicated to
the warrior god Indra:

> With all-outstripping chariot-wheel, O
> Indra, thou
> Far-famed, hast overthrown
> the twice ten kings of men
> With sixty thousand nine and ninety
> followers . . .
> Thou goest on from fight to fight
> intrepidly
> Destroying castle after
> castle here with strength. (*Rig Veda* 1:53)

The impression given by these and similar verses
is of a campaign of conquest and destruction; not
unnaturally, the hymns speak of the conquered
peoples only in terms of contempt. In contrast to
the light-skinned "nobles," they were dark, snub-
nosed barbarians (in the sense of speaking an
unintelligible language); contemptible phallus
worshippers who were nevertheless wealthy, with

Priest-king, or deity, from
Mohenjo-daro, in the Indus
Valley (*opposite and above*).
The people of this pre-Aryan
city were not the primitive
barbarians of Aryan legend.

A flourishing native culture

Impressions of cattle and an elephant, from superbly carved steatite seals from Mohenjo-daro.

cattle and fields and fortified cities. If they were destroyed by the "nobles," it was no more than they deserved: such is the impression given by the Aryans' own literary sources.

Until fairly recently, although it might have been suspected that this was not the whole truth, historians took the evidence of the *Rig Veda* literally. Indian culture, it was assumed, was a product of the Aryan mind, modified in the direction of inactivity and contemplation (the two unjustly equated) by long residence on the Indian plains. The pre-Aryan strain in the Indian population could not, it was thought, have contributed anything of value. True, this left historians, and not least historians of religion, with many uncomfortable facts to explain away; but the validity of what the *Rig Veda* had to say about the people the Aryans found in India was not questioned. In his book *Indian Philosophy* (1923), Radhakrishnan was thus able to write: "When the Aryans came to India they found the natives of India whom they called Dasyus (a word of uncertain meaning) opposing their free advance. These Dasyus were of a dark complexion, eating beef and indulging in Goblin worship. When the Aryans met them they desired to keep themselves aloof from them." When these words were written, it really seemed

as though the natives of northwest India were no more than a rabble of aboriginal savages.

Over the last half century, thanks to archeology, our picture of the Aryan invasions has to be completely revised. The reassessment ("revolution" might not be too strong a word) came early in the 1920s with the beginning of excavations at two sites: Harappa, in the Punjab, some 100 miles southwest of Lahore, and Mohenjo-daro ("the mound of the dead"), on the River Indus in Sind, two hundred miles north of Karachi. Since then further excavation over a very wide area has confirmed the fact that during the third and second millennia B.C. northwest India was the home not of barbarism but of a flourishing and in some ways extremely sophisticated urban culture, not unlike that of Mesopotamia. This is now known variously as the Indus Culture, the Harappa Culture and the Indus Valley Civilization. Some seventy sites are now known, covering an area of about half a million square miles. One of the most striking features of the Indus Culture is its elaborate and consistent practical development. This extends to such details as weights and measures, town planning and architecture, drainage, pottery, trade and commerce, art and (apparently) religion. As far as we know, Harappa and Mohenjo-daro

Front and side views of a terracotta female figurine from Mohenjo-daro, probably a representation of the mother goddess still worshiped in various forms all over India.

were the main centers, but we have no way of telling whether they were provincial or local capitals.

Despite such gaps in our knowledge, it is clear that the Indus Culture was far more advanced in practical ways than that of the invading nomadic Aryans. Spiritually, too, there is every reason to believe that the Indus Culture contributed much more to Hinduism than scholars were once prepared to allow.

One of the most celebrated finds from Mohenjo-daro is a seal bearing the image of a horned, three-faced male deity, seated in a yogic position and surrounded by animals—elephant, tiger, bull, rhinoceros and goat. This is evidently a prototype of the great god Shiva, lord of the beasts and prince of Yogins. Also connected with the worship of Shiva is the phallic symbol, or *lingam*, many representations of which have been found on Indus Culture sites. Many figures of nude or seminude females have also been found, explicable only as examples of the great mother-goddess still worshiped by various names all over India. The most spectacular building excavated at Mohenjo-daro—the "great bath"—probably points to the early practice of ritual washing, such as is still observed today in sacred rivers and temple baths in all parts of India. But the overriding impression of the spiritual basis of the Indus Culture provided by archeology is of a fertility religion: man's attempt to come to terms with the realities of his agrarian existence. Insofar as agriculture has remained the main basis of the Indian economy and way of life, Indian spiritual culture, still rooted to the soil, has taken over the heritage of the Indus Culture.

We must not, however, be too categorical when speaking of the intellectual aspects of the Indus Culture. There was a written language, but as yet no attempt to decipher the Indus script has met with undisputed success. It is thought that the language was probably Dravidian, perhaps therefore an ancestor of modern Tamil, but until a bilingual inscription is found—perhaps in Sumer?—the thought of pre-Aryan bronze age India must remain obstinately inaccessible.

Even the dates of the Indus Culture are a matter of dispute. It would probably not be too inaccurate to think in terms of an overall span of about a thousand years, from about 2500 to about 1500 B.C., since it is known that important trade contacts with Mesopotamia took place between 2300 and 2000 B.C., and radiocarbon dates have been obtained varying between 2300 and 1750 B.C. It seems relatively certain, however, that a decline began in about 1750 B.C., and that this decline and fall was in some way connected with the coming of the Aryans from the northwest.

But did the Aryans merely administer the final blows to a civilization already in decline? The evidence on this point is inconclusive. While in some areas the end of the Indus Culture seems to have been accompanied by extreme violence, elsewhere the transition may have been fairly

Formalized design showing three interlinked tigers, from a seal from Mohenjo-daro.

Three-headed animal seal from Mohenjo-daro, showing ibex, bull, and so-called "unicorn," which in fact is probably a bull in profile.

Horned deity with three faces, seated in a yogic posture and surrounded by animals; from Mohenjo-daro. This is evidently a prototype of the god Shiva, lord of the beasts and prince of Yogins.

A new people from the North

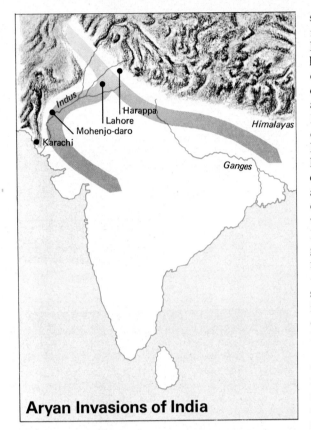

Aryan Invasions of India

peaceful. At Mohenjo-daro, the finding of un-buried skeletons in the streets points unmistakably to unexpected attack from some quarter; at Harappa, on the other hand, the evidence seems to suggest that peaceful settlement took place. Much has been made of changing climatic conditions as a factor contributing to the weakened state of the Indus Culture at that time, but we do not know how far it had declined when the first Aryan incursions began. What we do know is that, in two closely related areas of its culture, India was decisively affected by the invaders. The first of these is language; the second, religion.

The Aryan language belonged to the type classified later as Indo-European. The hieratic language of their religion was Sanskrit; the

Left The Great Bath of Mohenjo-daro, probably the scene of ritual bathing.

Right Drain at Mohenjo-daro, showing the high standard of building and engineering achieved by the pre-Aryan people of India.

spoken language was probably one of the dialects related to Sanskrit, of the type since called Prakrits. The Indus language, on the other hand, was probably Dravidian, belonging to an entirely different linguistic family. Within a few centuries, Sanskrit was established as the sacred and official language of northern India: the language of hymns, prayers and commentaries, epics and lyrics, codes of religious and secular law. Belonging to the Prakrits group is Pali, the sacred language of Buddhism; among direct descendants of Sanskrit are modern Hindi, Bengali, Marathi and Gujerati. Hence, in a real sense, the linguistic consequences of the Aryan invasion are still with us. Attempts currently being made in north India to establish Hindi as the official language of the whole of India—attempts partly motivated by its direct descent from Sanskrit—have been objected to by Dravidian-speaking southern Indians in particular as "north Indian imperialism." It is an incontestable fact that classical Indian culture expressed itself very largely in the tongue of the Aryans.

The religion of the Aryans was essentially different from that of the Indus peoples. The latter followed a fertility religion, based largely on the earth as giver of life. Aryan religion was centered on the great deities of the sky and atmosphere, sun and moon, storm and fire. The earliest Indian religious writings, the hymns of the *Rig Veda*, were probably in part brought into India by later waves of Aryan invaders, and in part composed after the invasions. They reflect a priestly religion, concerned above all with the maintenance of the natural order, *rta*, by regular sacrifice. Many hymns are dedicated to the god of storm and war, Indra, to the god of the sacrificial fire, Agni, and to the deified sacrificial drink, Soma, as well as to the more remote celestial gods, Varuna and Vishnu. The *Brahmanas*, prolix commentaries on the hymns showing sacrificial theory and practice, probably date from the beginning of the iron age and the second stage of the invasions. The *Upanishads*, mystical treatises concerning man and the universe, reflect some of the earliest stirrings of the Indian

speculative mind, possibly as a result of contact with Indus beliefs. On these foundations, though with many later elaborations, rests the complex edifice of Hinduism in its priestly aspect. To this day, one test of Hindu orthodoxy is the acceptance of the divine authority of these Vedic scriptures—largely, if not entirely, Aryan products.

But Hinduism is a social as well as a religious phenomenon. And there is probably no more tenacious social institution in the world than that of caste—still very much alive in India. It has been very extensively modified over the centuries, but that its roots date back to the Aryan invasion cannot be doubted. In the past, it has been too readily assumed that caste originated as a simple color bar between light-skinned Aryans and dark-skinned Dravidians. But this overlooks the fact that three of the four main caste groupings, those of priests, warriors and artisans, were classified as "twice-born," i.e. Aryan; only the fourth, the serfs, appear to have been non-Aryan. In fact, basic caste structure can be shown to correspond closely to the traditional structure of Aryan society: corroborative evidence can be found among other Indo-European peoples, such as the Celts and Romans. The conclusion must be that the invaders brought a rudimentary form of the caste system with them, and that after the invasions the conquered peoples were relegated in most cases to a subordinate role in society as serfs. In time, the emergent Indian society became more and more rigidly stratified under the growing influence of the Brahmanical priesthood—an influence that has persisted to modern times.

Down the centuries, the social and religious structure of Indian society became Aryanized in accordance with *varnàśrama dharma*, i.e. the caste law. To be a good Hindu, and by implication a good Indian, it was necessary to observe the laws of one's caste, as laid down in the priestly codes, such as the *Laws of Manu*. Language, trade and commerce, secular jurisprudence and education similarly followed Aryan patterns.

But this is not to say that India has ever become completely Aryanized. The contrast between the

Aryan north and the Dravidian south is still marked, and India's conflicts are still to some extent unresolved. Hinduism, although its superstructure and many of its philosophies are derived directly from the Vedic Aryans, is noticeably non-Aryan at the popular, grass-roots level. For the culture of India is a complex and composite entity, reducible to no simple categories and intolerant of simple explanations. India proved hospitable to the Aryan invaders of three thousand years ago; their coming altered the entire pattern of her future history. But the fact that it is still impossible to read India's history solely in Aryan terms demonstrates clearly that she did not entirely submit to the invasion.

ERIC J. SHARPE

Terracotta female figurine with "pannier" headdress, from Mohenjo-daro.

Terracotta model of bullock cart from Mohenjo-daro. The people of the Indus Valley Civilization were still predominantly agricultural; the elaborate cities that have been excavated were probably centers of trade and government.

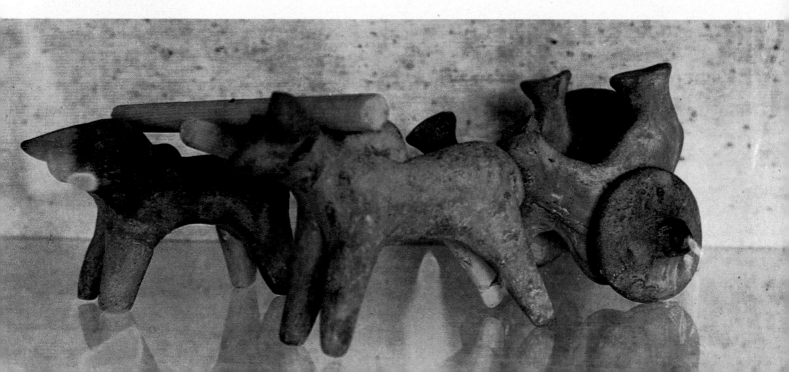

In the year 1887 an Egyptian peasant, digging in the ruins of an ancient city on the banks of the Nile, came across some baked clay tablets impressed with cuneiform writing. In due course these tablets came into the hands of dealers and eventually their importance realized. The city had once been the capital of Egypt,

Avenue of rams at temple of Karnak

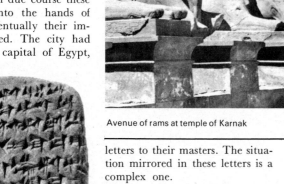

Cuneiform tablet from Tell el Amarna

for a brief time in the early fourteenth century B.C., and the tablets had come from the record office of the palace; they were letters, part of the files of the Foreign Office, the correspondence of the potentates and princes of the Near East with their ally, or in some cases their overlord, the Pharaoh of Egypt. They are written in Akkadian, the language of diplomacy in this age, as it had been in the time of the Mari letters, and we must imagine that in every prince's palace, even in countries remote from Babylonia, there were scribes who could read and write the language and would translate the

letters to their masters. The situation mirrored in these letters is a complex one.

The kings of Babylonia and Assyria, the kings of the Hurrian kingdom of Mitanni, and of the kingdom of Alashiya, which may be Cyprus, wrote to the Pharaohs as equals. They were bound to them by treaties of alliance cemented by marriage, and some of the letters discuss the amount of dowry which they propose to give to a daughter who is to be sent to Egypt to swell the Egyptian king's numerous harem. Rich presents were exchanged, and the vassal was to send a gift of gold equal value. This was, in fact, trade: an exchange of goods, value for value, on an official basis, and merchants were traveling as official agents of the kings and with their protection. Keftiu is not among those who sent these royal gifts: the Minoan envoys who once brought precious cargo from Crete to the court at Thebes came no longer. Knossos had been overwhelmed and was now in Mycenaean hands. But trade between Egypt and the Aegean continued, and Mycen-

aean pottery is found in some quantity at Tell el Amarna. It has recently been suggested that the memory of the Minoan civilization of Crete, after the disaster which overwhelmed Crete and the islands, was preserved in Egypt and was responsible for the legend of Atlantis, the fabulous island in the west where life was lived in fine palaces with elaborate drainage systems and which was overwhelmed by the sea. This story, according to Plato, was brought back from Egypt by his ancestor Solon. However this may be, it is true that in many details the description of Atlantis fits well

Daughters of Akhenaton and Nefertiti

with that which archeology tells us of Minoan Crete, and it is certainly tempting to see in the one a dim memory of the other.

Letters from the regents of vassal kingdoms, which form the bulk of the correspondence, protest their loyalty to the Pharaoh and frequently complain of the hostile activities of their neighbors and the treachery of fellow vassals. They paint a picture of turmoil and intrigue. It is clear that Egypt's control over her possessions in Syria and Palestine was far from complete, and that the Pharaohs Amenophis III and Amenophis IV (known by his own wish by the name of Akhenaton) were occu-

pied with problems of their own and failed to set forth on those constant demonstrations of strength and tours of inspection that were necessary, if a ruler was to maintain a firm hold on his possessions. Moreover, the Hittites were again casting envious eyes on North Syria. Some of the Amarna letters, from the vassals of Egypt in this region, show clearly how they were being forced or cajoled by Hittite agents into deserting their

Deity from Assur

alliance with Egypt. Historical narrative texts from Hattusas (modern Boghazköi), the Hittite capital, carry on the story of the Hittite capture of the kingdoms of North Syria and of the eclipse of Mitanni, from the Hittite point of view.

Weather god from Ras Shamra

Tribute-bearers from Carchemish

Tribute offered to El, god of Ugarit

The Kingdom of Ugarit

One of the vassals of Egypt, whose king at this time was forced to change his allegiance and become a tributary of the Hittite king, was the ruler of the wealthy kingdom of Ugarit, on the Syrian coast north of the modern town of Lattakia. Excavations on the site of this city, the modern Ras Shamra, have revealed the size

Idrimi, King of Alalakli

and importance of the town and its palace and here, too, valuable hoards of tablets have been found. Some of them are letters, couched in the same language of international diplomacy as the Amarna letters; they include the actual terms under which King Niqmaddu of Ugarit was to surrender to the Hittite king and the amount of tribute he was to pay. Other

tablets refer to domestic matters and it is these, and in particular the large number which are written in a simplified, alphabetic script of only thirty cuneiform characters, which give us insight into the daily life and beliefs of the people of this region in the fourteenth and thirteenth centuries B.C. At Ugarit, which must be reckoned a Canaanite city, we find myths of the high god El, of the bloodthirsty virgin goddess Anath, of Baal the storm god, who

Goddess from Ras Shamra

was to be the adversary of Yahweh, the national god of Israel, and of Yam the god of the sea, with whom Baal did battle. Many of the rites of sacrifice, the festivals and even the poetic phraseology find close parallels in the Old Testament. And this reminds us that the Hebrews came as nomadic wanderers into a civilization already old, and absorbed and adopted from the Canaanites much that they found in the Promised Land.

The mysterious Khapiru

Yahweh himself, as might be expected, has no part in the pantheon of Ugarit, but Ugaritic texts more than once mention a people called the Khapiru, a name which many historians equate with the Hebrews. The Khapiru are found over a wide area of the Near East. There is considerable doubt whether the word denotes some sort of ethnic group, a nation or a tribe, or whether it denotes a social class—a turbulent semi-nomadic element in the population of the kingdoms of Syria and Mesopotamia, who drove their flocks about the countryside and frequently succumbed to the temptation to plunder the fields and herds of their wealthier, settled

neighbors. In the Amarna letters they are greatly feared marauders, a constant threat to the safety of the kingdoms of Syria and Palestine. They had evidently formed a not inconsiderable part of the population of "Retenu" (as the Pharaohs called Syria and Palestine together) in the time of Amenophis II, since he lists 3,600 of them among his prisoners. Later, about 1310 B.C., they were encountered by the army of Seti I during his campaign in the Galilee area of Palestine.

The Khapiru are first mentioned as an element of the population of Mesopotamia, much earlier. So too are other Semitic groups. One of these groups, which received scant mention in the early texts but later grew into a formidable nation, were the Aramaeans. Hebrew tradition later affirmed that Abraham, their ancestor, had Aramaean kindred; the story of his wanderings from Ur to Harran fits well into a context of the years after 2000 B.C., when the lower Euphrates valley and the northern steppe-country (called today the Jezireh) between the Tigris and Euphrates were alike the scene of bedouin movements and migrations. We will now see how they settled in Egypt and then at last went to a "Promised Land."

Hittite hieroglyphs

Hittite, Mitannian, Elamite, Armorite, Assyrian, Akkadian cuneiform scripts

Ugaritic script

Cypro-Minoan script

Cretan linear script

Byblos script

Egyptian hieroglyphs

Egyptian hieratic

Sinai script

Early Forms of Writing

Syrian deity

Let My People Go!

The Hebrews were a nomadic people, some of whom settled in Egypt. They had their own God—Yahweh or Jehovah—and in this respect they differed little from the people around them. Yet the Israelites, led by Moses, were convinced that their God had promised them a land of their own, and that they must leave Egypt and go to Palestine. Their God was essentially a god of battle and, as such, invaluable as long as they were on the march. But what would happen once they settled down? Inevitably there were attempts to worship local gods also, but the basic conviction that there was only one god—and a moral god at that—the God of Israel, and that the Hebrews were his people, was never forgotten. For this reason the Hebrews are one of the most important peoples of antiquity. The Exodus or departure from Egypt was essential to the fulfillment of that role.

The blazing heat of early summer beat down upon the rocks and sand of the vast and mountainous wilderness of Sinai. In a parched valley, far from any human habitation, a band of some hundreds—perhaps even some thousands—of fugitives from the Nile Delta waited for the orders of their leader, Moses.

These "children of Israel" formed part of a group of tribes who had migrated into the Land of Canaan from the north several hundred years earlier. All claimed a common ancestor in Abraham and all shared a common religious belief. Then famine had struck the land, probably in about 1650 B.C. Some of the tribes had found food nearby; others—the ancestors of Moses' group—had wandered as far as Egypt in the search for sustenance, and they had remained there as serfs of the pharaohs, engaged in building public works. Though the life had been hard, there was at least food and water.

The tribes had stayed some four hundred years in Egypt, then had left everything at the behest of Moses. There had been long and stormy arguments between Moses and Pharaoh (probably Merneptah of the next chapter), before the children of Israel had managed to leave; and the departure itself had been unforgettably dramatic and unexpected. It has come down to us in the legends of ten plagues, each one more destructive than the last. The plagues had driven Pharaoh and the Egyptians to surrender to Moses' demand that this group of despised serfs be allowed to go and celebrate some strange rite beyond the boundaries of Egypt. Pharaoh had then regretted giving his permission, and there had been a dramatic escape. The children of Israel had successfully crossed the "Sea of Reeds" or the Red Sea, and the Egyptian chariots and horsemen pursuing them had met disaster. What precise incidents lie behind these legends we do not know, but no scholar today would deny that the experience was real, taking

place probably about 1280 B.C. Jewry has been celebrating that flight for more than 3,000 years in the festival of Passover, and we understand enough about primitive peoples to know that such a record arises only from experience.

The demand to "let my people go" had been made in the name of the God of Israel. For the tribe had retained belief in a single God who had called their ancestors to his especial service. It was to renew this service that, in spite of many misgivings and frequent complaints, they had followed Moses into the vast and deserted region of Sinai. And the culmination of their pilgrimage was the day of meeting with their God.

Moses was a man who had the irresistible power to gain complete acceptance and obedience from a whole people. While his life has attracted so many strange trappings that it is difficult to disentangle truth from legend, we could deny his existence only by creating someone with similar powers living at the same time and performing the same dynamic role in the spiritual evolution of a little band of former serfs. For the sojourn in Egypt of some of the people of Israel is history, and the survival of the Jewish people today as a result of the Exodus from Egypt and the events in the Sinai Desert is also history.

Though an Israelite, Moses had not been brought up to the drudgery of making and laying bricks. The Old Testament says that he grew up in the household of Pharaoh himself. If so, it had not made him forget the traditions of his ancestors, the worship of a God of whom there was no image, and the discipline of an ethical and moral, as well as a ritual, service to the Deity. Legend speaks of long years in the dry, steppe country east of Sinai, where he married and tended the sheep of his father-in-law, until a vision called him to his law-giving mission to his people.

If legend has surrounded the flight from Egypt and the life of Moses, still more has it surrounded

A view of Mount Sinai, at the summit of which Moses received from God the tables of the Law. Scholars do not doubt that the ethical discipline taught by Moses is the basis of the Biblical Ten Commandments.

Opposite The parched desert lands of the Middle East recall the grim terrain crossed by the Israelites under Moses in the Exodus from Egypt. (The picture shows the cracked soil and sparse vegetation of the Negev, near the Dead Sea.)

An Egyptian war-chariot of the type used in the pursuit of the Israelites. According to Hebrew tradition, the Egyptian army was drowned in the Red Sea, through which the Israelites had miraculously passed dry-shod. The feast of the Passover annually commemorates the Israelite Exodus from Egypt. The picture shows the Pharaoh Seti I; it is carved on the wall of the Temple of Amun at Karnak (ancient Thebes).

the "giving of the Law" at the foot of the mountain to which the Bible gives the names of Sinai and Horeb. The Bible recounts how Moses climbed to its summit and there spoke face to face with Yahweh, God and Redeemer of the children of Israel. The people waited below, awed by the lightning and thunderclouds hiding the summit of the mountain. We have no reason to doubt that the Ten Commandments—which prohibit murder, adultery, theft, lying and envy and which establish the Sabbath as a holy day—embody the core of the ethical discipline taught by Moses and accepted by the people as a whole. Nor would most scholars today hesitate to ascribe to the same period much of the communal law embodied in the Old Testament. Of particular interest are those laws embodied in the "Code of Holiness", in which the sanction is not a penalty, but a reminder of the covenant between God and Israel and the obligations that result therefrom. Typical of the laws are these two, concerning the poor and the weak:

When you reap the harvest of your land, you shall not reap your field to its very border, neither shall you gather the gleanings after your harvest . . . you shall leave them for the poor and the sojourner: I am the Lord your God. (*Leviticus* 19: 9–10)

You shall not curse the deaf or put a stumbling block before the blind, but you shall fear your God: I am the Lord. (*Leviticus* 14)

The central discipline is not any particular set of regulations, but the conviction of the whole people that they had accepted an obligation to live according to the Law, not as an act of obedience to an earthly ruler, but as a covenant between themselves and their God.

These words ascribed to Moses may have been written centuries later, but they contain the essence of the covenant:

See, I have set before you this day life and good, death and evil. If you obey the commandments of the Lord your God, by loving the Lord your God, by walking in his ways, and by keeping his commandments . . . then you shall live and multiply, and the Lord your God will bless you . . . But if your heart turns away and you will not hear . . . I declare to you this day that you shall perish. (*Deuteronomy* 30: 15–20)

The subsequent history of the children of Israel is the record of continual recall to the true meaning of the covenant, of continual struggle both with idolatry and with social injustice which defiled that covenant.

Some forty years after the giving of the Law, the children of Israel abandoned their nomadic life in and around the deserts of Sinai for a settled habitation in Palestine. According to their tradition, this had been promised them by their God. Palestine at that time contained an agglomeration of city-states, small kingdoms and semi-nomadic tribes of mixed ethnic origin. Still scattered among these people of Palestine were relatives of the children of Israel, who like them claimed descent from Abraham and to some extent retained the worship of his God. But they had not completely resisted

Pursued by Pharaoh's host, the Israelites go to Canaan

the local gods and goddesses and the fertility rites by which they were worshiped.

There was little to distinguish the newcomers from the rest of their neighbors. They interpreted the divine will in terms of very human ambitions. They were prepared to massacre and enslave other tribes, and they regarded the covenant with their God as an exclusive privilege. But the experience of the desert had given them particular status. One of the most remarkable developments during the next few centuries is that their settled relatives, who in fact had not undergone the long humiliation of Egyptian servitude, came to adopt the Egyptian experience as that of their own ancestors. The nature festivals that they shared with the peoples around were transformed into historical commemorations and remodeled as anniversaries of the Exodus from Egypt, the experience of Sinai and the acceptance of their God, Yahweh. Even that name was brought to them by those who had experienced the hardships of Egypt and the rigors of the desert.

In the earliest days of the settlement in Palestine the religion of Yahweh was preserved by groups of ecstatic devotees. Gradually they became dominated by the prophets, who proclaimed righteousness, denounced social injustice as fervently as religious idolatry and spoke with deepening insight about the nature and demands of a righteous God. It needed all their eloquence to instill into the people the true meaning of the covenant, and the fact that it involved responsibilities rather than privileges. "You only have I known of all the peoples of the earth," cries Amos in the name of Yahweh. "Therefore I will punish you for all your iniquities." (*Amos* 3:2) But the prophets also had to teach their people that the statement "you only have I known of all the peoples" did not mean that God had no concern for the rest of his creation. It is again Amos who says:

"Are you not like the Ethiopians unto me, O people of Israel?" says the Lord. "Did I not bring up Israel from the land of Egypt, and the Philistines from Caphtor and the Syrians from Kir?" (*Amos* 9:7)

The children of Israel were soon to meet disaster. They had established two small kingdoms which were constantly engaged in foolish quarrels with each other. The northern kingdom, with its capital at Samaria, was swallowed up by the Assyrian empire in about 721 B.C., and the ruling classes were deported to northern Mesopotamia. As an identifiable and creative society it disappeared from history. Less than two hundred years later, in 587 B.C., the southern kingdom, with its capital at Jerusalem, was likewise overthrown and its ruling classes deported by the Babylonians, who had succeeded the Assyrians. When Babylon was in turn destroyed by the Persians, Cyrus, the Persian king, issued an edict in 538 B.C. allowing the descendants of these exiles from the southern kingdom to return, and many did so. At the center of the southern kingdom had been the tribe of Judah, hence its inhabitants were known as "Judahites"—Hebrew, *Yehudim*; Latin, *Judaei*; English, *Jews*.

Though the story deals henceforth with "Jews," it is probable that descendants of the northern kingdom who wished to remain loyal to Yahweh migrated from northern Mesopotamia to the great centers of Jewish cultural life established by the Babylonians in the southern part of the land between the Tigris and the Euphrates. This was to be a center of the Jewish world for many centuries, indeed surviving until modern times.

During the century before Cyrus allowed them to return, the exiles had made two vital contributions to the future of their people. First, deprived of their Temple in Jerusalem, they had evolved a nonsacrificial form of worship, Sabbath by Sabbath, wherever Jews lived. This was the worship of the synagogue, and its present form is familiar to millions today wherever there are Christian churches or Muslim mosques. For it was without priestly sacrifices or rituals and consisted of prayer, praise and instruction, centered on Holy Scripture. The second achievement of the exiles lay in the collecting and editing of national records, history, prophetic utterances, psalms and sacred songs, from which the Scriptures were compiled. What is most striking about this compilation is that the whole of Jewish history is written in terms of obedience to the covenant. Kings whose victories added wide dominions and the revenue of subject peoples are dismissed in a few verses, with the words that they "did evil in the sight of the Lord." Kings like David, who were the object of deep affection and veneration, were represented without any attempt at whitewash. And the words of the

Above An Asiatic prisoner, Pharaoh Ramses II at Tell el a tile in the palace of the Pharaoh Ramses II at Tell el Yahudijah, in the Nile delta.

Below Three Canaanite idols: the weather god (*left*), holding a thunderbolt; deity holding a spear and a sword (*center*)—possibly Resheph, god of thunder and lightning: female figure from Beirut (*right*), possibly the goddess Astare.

To freedom in the Promised Land

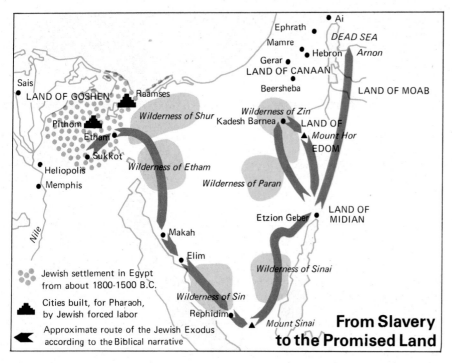

Jewish settlement in Egypt from about 1800-1500 B.C.

Cities built, for Pharaoh, by Jewish forced labor

Approximate route of the Jewish Exodus according to the Biblical narrative

From Slavery to the Promised Land

Ivory plaque from Megiddo, showing prisoners being led before a Canaanite ruler. The artist has imitated an Egyptian style.

prophets, who spared no one in their denunciations, are preserved with the utmost care.

The books of the Old Testament cover the traditions and chronicles of more than a thousand years. We can trace through them the slow growth of a national conviction that obedience to the covenant was the true goal of national life. But it was not until after these books were completed that those who had for many generations been pioneers and fighters for righteousness had their reward. In the supplementary books, called *The Apocrypha*, it is recorded how in 166 B.C. Antiochus, King of Syria, tried to make Israel desert its God. They were commanded to eat forbidden meats, "but many in Israel stood firm and were resolved

in their hearts not to eat unclean food. They chose to die, rather than to be defiled by food or to profane the holy covenant; and they did die" (*Maccabees*: 62–63). In consequence ordinary men and women became the first recorded martyrs in the long history of religious persecution.

The return to Judaea was a remarkable event, for in Babylon Jews had been prosperous and self-governing. They had a rich territory, which, compared with the infertile hills and ruined towns and villages around Jerusalem, should have argued in favor of staying in exile. But Jerusalem (often called Zion) and "the land of Israel" arouses an affection in the Jewish mind that may be illogical, may be irritating to others, but is a quite certain fact of history. The land of Babylon, for all its wealth, was *exile*, as the psalmist so well expressed:

By the waters of Babylon we sat down and wept,
> when we remembered thee, O Zion.
As for our harps we hanged them up upon the trees
> that are therein.
For they that led us away captive required of us
> then a song and melody in our heaviness: "Sing us
> one of the songs of Zion."
How shall we sing the Lord's song in a strange land?
If I forget thee, O Jerusalem, let my right hand
> forget her cunning.
> (*Psalms* 137: 1–5)

The return did not take place all at once, but in a series of caravans, and the future leader of the Jews came in one of the later groups. His name was Ezra, and he, together with his companions and disciples, ensured by their wise leadership the future of Judaism and the Jewish people. They brought with them from Babylon the institution of the synagogue and the main elements of a sacred Scripture. Ezra, however, added provision for a system of adult education by which the Law was regularly taught to the whole people.

When Jerusalem had been rebuilt from its ruins,

Left An Egyptian fresco showing a carpenter at work. *Below* Wooden model of Egyptian brickmakers. The Israelites were doubtless engaged in such activities when building "treasure cities" for Pharaoh in Egypt.

and the Temple was once more the center of national worship, Ezra arranged a solemn reading of the whole Law "before the Water Gate." The reading covered several days and was followed by a renewal, by the whole people, of the covenant with Yahweh. But Ezra did not merely read. He "gave the sense and caused the people to understand the meaning" (*Nehemiah* 8:8). Systematic teaching of the Law continued not merely on special occasions, but in every town, week by week, and by a trained body of teachers, recruited at first from local priestly families. They came to be known as scribes, because it was their duty not only to teach the Law, but to write copies of it, so that gradually every synagogue came to possess its own copy as well as its own teacher of the Law.

The inevitable consequence of this permeation of the whole life of the people by the revelation of Sinai soon followed. The local teachers became the local magistrates, for much of the Law dealt with matters, criminal and civil, that required adjudication; and the local magistrates in turn found themselves involved in the responsibility of reinterpretation necessary when a written code must be constantly adjusted to changes and developments in society. Judaism and Jewry were thus equipped to survive when Temple and State were destroyed in the disastrous wars with Rome.

JAMES PARKES

Although the Exodus of the "children of Israel" from Egypt is rightly to be regarded as one of the greatest milestones in human history, in the context of the age in which they lived it must have seemed a very small, even trivial event. The Egyptians themselves would have regarded it as just one more tiresome episode in a constantly recurring situation. For centuries the bedouin tribesmen of Sinai and south Palestine had been permitted from time to time to bring their flocks to the fringes of the fertile Delta in search of pasture; whenever there was famine on the steppelands, the cry would go around, "There is corn in Egypt!" And from time to time, when the nomads, grown numerous, sought to move farther in and settle, the army of Pharaoh would be sent to expel them from the borders once more. They had outstayed their welcome.

Archeology has not yet provided any material remains that

Egyptians harvesting corn

The reign of Ramses II

Ramses II is one of the most impressive figures in the whole history of the ancient Near East. His long reign of sixty-seven years (he lived to the age of ninety) was a time of great prosperity for Egypt. The resources of the country were developed, trade and industry flourished and a vast program of temple building was carried through. In every city in Egypt and Nubia his monuments proliferated. Quarries and mines were opened and wells dug in desert places to ease the lot of the miners. In front of the astonishing temple of Abu Simbel, carved in the living rock, there are four colossal figures representing, not the great gods of Egypt, but the king himself seated in fourfold

majesty, his face towards the rising sun. In the lofty hall of this temple and on the walls of others throughout the land, Ramses caused to be depicted, in flamboyant detail and in huge size, scenes from the great battle which he fought against the combined forces of the Hittites and their allies in the year 1300 B.C., the fourth year of his reign. The battle took place near the city of Kadesh in Syria. Almost singlehanded, if we are to believe his account, he

Hittite king and queen

had charged the enemy in his chariot and driven them sprawling backwards into the river Orontes. It was a theme of which the court poets and sculptors did not tire. In spite of his claim to have won a great victory, however, this trial of strength seems to have ended in stalemate. His greater achievement was the treaty of "brotherhood" which, after years of negotiation, he subsequently made with the Hittite king, Hattushil III, and which proved to be lasting. By a fortunate chance of survival, the text of this treaty survives in both the Hittite and the Egyptian versions, the one carved in hieroglyphics on a stone stele in the temple of Karnak, the other in

cuneiform on tablets found in the Hittite capital, Hattusas, the modern Boghazköi.

The treaty was cemented by the marriage of Ramses to the daughter of the Hittite king. She was sent to Egypt with an escort befitting so important a traveler and

Hittite war chariot

her way was made easy, we are told, by the storm god who caused the winter snows of Lebanon to melt and the sun to shine as she passed by. The *entente cordiale* was not thereafter broken by either side. The Hittites became increasingly preoccupied with struggles to maintain their empire in Anatolia and were content to maintain their position in North Syria, while Egypt was left in possession of the Phoenician coast and all of Palestine, and probably also of the land beyond the Jordan. If the armies of Joshua and Gideon were at this time moving into "the land of milk and honey," they must have found themselves in territory still at least nominally Egyptian, and in part garrisoned by Egyptian troops.

Canaanite strongholds

Unfortunately, archeological evidence for the destruction of the Bronze Age cities of Palestine mentioned in the Biblical narrative is curiously inconclusive. The

Statues at Abu Simbel

could throw light on the story of the sojourn in Egypt and of the Exodus. Circumstantial details contained in the narrative, however, and our knowledge of the wider history of the age, suggest that Joseph and Moses fit best into the context of the Nineteenth Dynasty, when the residence city of the Pharaohs was not Thebes or Memphis, but Pi-Ramesses in the eastern Delta, probably that same city called "Raamses" which the Hebrews are said to have helped to build. The Pharaoh of the Exodus in that case is likely to have been Ramses II, who founded this new city and embellished it with fine buildings and gardens.

Ramses II

Hittite warriors

The Hittite storm god

Achaean warriors

Warrior from Boghazköi

in Egyptian writings and suggests that by 1230 B.C., the approximate date of the events described in the long text of the stele, some Israelites were already established in the Promised Land.

Threats to the Hittites

The Hittite kingdom, meanwhile, was already running into difficulties. Assyrian armies were marching west and threatening Syria from across the Euphrates, and the turbulent Gasgas, barbarians from the northeastern mountains, constantly menaced the homeland. Hattushil had kept both at bay by military action and adroit diplomacy, but after his death in about 1250 B.C. his son, Tudkhaliya IV, met with opposition from a different quarter: from a hitherto friendly neighbor on the Aegean coast. This was the king of Ahhiyawa, who now began unwelcome interference in the affairs of the western dependencies of the Hittite empire.

The land of Ahhiyawa is still not certainly located. Many scholars, however, believe that the Ahhiyawans were the people who play the chief role in the Homeric epics—the Achaiwoi or Achaeans, warlike Greeks from the mainland and the islands who mustered their ships and under their leader, Agamemnon, sailed to attack

The Fall of Troy; Hellenistic bas-relief

Troy. The story of the ten years' siege of Troy by the Achaeans is the story of the *Iliad*. Now, judging by the geographical distribution of the confederate cities, and the description of the warriors' dress and accouterments as transmitted in

the tradition that survived till Homer's day, it is clear that these Achaeans were the same people whom archeologists have named the Mycenaeans, the Greek-speaking warrior race who occupied Crete and the islands of the Dodecanese after the fall of Knossos (see third chapter). Their seafaring merchants established colonies or trading posts over the whole of the eastern Mediterranean and even penetrated west of Sicily to the coasts of Italy, France and Spain. Mycenaean pottery is found in Cyprus, in the cities of the Levant and in Egypt, and some has been found, too, on the west coast of Turkey.

The kings of Ahhiyawa who sheltered fugitives from the Hittite court may well have been Achaean Greeks whose kingdom—somewhere on the fringe of the Hittite empire, perhaps in Caria or on the island of Rhodes—now constituted a threat to peace. In a treaty between Tudkhaliya IV and one of his vassals, the king of Amurru, the Hittite king refers to "the kings who are of equal rank with me: the king of Egypt, the king of Babylon, the king of Assyria and the king of Ahhiyawa." But the words "and the king of Ahhiyawa" were subsequently deliberately erased from the tablet. Fortunately the signs are still legible, and we are left wondering what crisis in Hittite affairs had led to the hasty removal of the offending phrase, perhaps by some scribe who had been lacking in discretion.

End of the Hittite Empire

In the reign of Tudkhaliya's successor, Arnuwanda III, the situation became more critical: a rebel made common cause with Ahhiyawa and occupied wide territories in the southwest of Asia Minor. In the east, a hostile attack by one Mita, or Midas, suggests that the Phrygians, who were destined later to occupy the Hittite

homeland, were already in league with other mountain peoples against their former overlords. In these texts we can dimly perceive the first stirrings of great movements of populations, the origin and direction of which we do not yet understand, but which were to topple the great empire of the Hittites and change the map of the Near East.

The end came in the reign of Arnuwanda's brother, Shuppiluliuma II, ill-fated bearer of a great name. At his accession, a little

before 1200 B.C., he must already have found himself at the head of an army fighting for its life. The records from Boghazköi tell of naval battles. Tablets from Ugarit, still a Hittite dependency, reflect a state of emergency in North Syria at the approach of an enemy who is not named. These tablets, some of them letters, were found in the oven in which they had been packed for baking; there had been no time to take them from the kiln when the city met its final destruction. Ugarit was sacked and burned, never to be rebuilt. Other cities of Anatolia and Syria met the same fate. Hattusas itself suffered a great conflagration, and wherever excavation has been undertaken on Hittite sites, the destruction is only too apparent. So complete was the disaster that no written record of it has survived, save in the annals of the one kingdom that was able to withstand the invaders. That kingdom was Egypt.

dramatic story of the fall of Jericho cannot nowadays be substantiated by the remains of fallen walls. On the sites of Lachish and Hazor—both mighty Canaanite strongholds—the evidence of pottery suggests a date late in the thirteenth century for the conquest, and Tell Beit Mersim, which is thought to have been the ancient city of Kiriath-Sepher, fell at about the same time. But in each case, no break in civilization is apparent between the levels below the layer of rubble and ash that marks destruction, and the levels of rebuilding above. It may rather be that one of the campaigns of Merneptah, the son and successor of Ramses II, was responsible for the calamity; in one of his inscriptions he claims to have crushed rebellion: "Canaan is plundered, Askalon is taken and Gezer seized; the people of Israel are desolate and have no seed. Palestine is widowed for Egypt."

This mention of Israel is unique

1191 B.C. Ramses III Defeats the Sea Peoples

For several years the Sea Peoples from the north had been drawing closer and closer to Egypt. Syria and Libya fell to them, and under the leadership of Mernera of Libya they began to prepare for an assault on Egypt itself. Merneptah, son of Ramses II, decided to take the initiative and attack first. His strategy was justified by his resounding victory, but the Sea Peoples learned a lesson and devised a new tactic. They began to infiltrate the country in families and groups. Unknown to the Egyptian administration, a new onslaught of Sea Peoples was about to occur. Happily for Egypt there was a man equal to the situation in the person of Ramses III.

Captive Sea People held by the hair; from Cairo Museum

Opposite Battle between the Egyptians and the Libyans; detail from the relief in the temple of Medinet-Habou commemorating Ramses III's second Libyan campaign.

In the eighth year of his reign, in 1191 B.C., Ramses III mobilized the Egyptian armies, together with their mercenaries, auxiliaries and allies, to halt an invasion of the Sea Peoples. Egypt was facing some of the toughest enemies in its history. Who were these mysterious Sea Peoples, as they are referred to in the official documents that chronicled the numerous campaigns fought against them during the reigns of Ramses II and Merneptah?

The Sea Peoples were nations of very diverse origins, engaged in joint expeditions of conquest and plunder. They included the Aqaivasha, who were probably Achaeans; the Tursha or Tyrrhenians; the Shakalsha or Zekel, who came from Sicily; the Shirdana or Sherden, who originated in Sardis or possibly Sardinia; the Denyen or Danaeans, originating from Greece; the Peleset, referred to in the Bible as Philistines; and the Louka or Lycians. These men, although from different stock, had one thing in common: Indo-European racial characteristics, with features astonishing to the Egyptians. They were "all northern peoples," declare the victory inscriptions of Merneptah in his temple at Karnak, "coming from all sorts of countries and remarkable for their blond hair and blue eyes."

These people were nomads, or perhaps they had been forced into a nomadic way of life by the great migrations of about 2000 B.C., which had completely changed the Near East and the Middle East. The descent of the Indo-Europeans into Greece, Asia and to some extent India had been irresistible and devastating. The Peleset, for example, who originated in Crete, established themselves first in the region of Syria and then in Palestine, warring against the Hebrews; while other tribes invaded the banks of the Orontes and the kingdom of the Amorites.

The conquest of Kheta, which had tried to oppose the insidious infiltration and brutal aggression of the Sea Peoples, and the defeat of the

Hittites put Egypt in great danger; for the great Delta, networked by numerous tributaries from the Nile, offered easy entry to the warships of the Indo-Europeans who aimed to command the seas. Some of these people already had entered the service of the pharaohs, who admired their military valor and gladly employed them as mercenaries. Among these were the Shakalsha, the Shirdana and the Louka. Others, like the Aqaivasha (the Achaeans who are found in Greece at virtually the same period) were newcomers.

Seti I had already been alarmed by the establishment of these Sea Peoples in Syria, and their obvious appetite for attacking neighboring countries and their large-scale irruption into Libya, where the native tribes had been overwhelmed. One of the principal aims of Seti's campaigns in Libya had been to neutralize their power. In this he succeeded, and he gave Egypt a long period of peace from these particular enemies. It was not until the end of the reign of Ramses II, Seti I's successor, that the threat from the Sea Peoples caused the pharaohs any great concern. Then came a considerable upheaval in Eastern Europe, principally in the Balkans and around the shores of the Black Sea, and nomads moved in the direction of Asia Minor, Greece and the Aegean islands, and finally Libya—that is to say, they moved in closer to Egypt. Once again it became necessary to take the offensive and fortify the frontiers, or better still, to attack the nomads before they became invincible.

Ramses II was eighty, too old, too tired and too disheartened to take the initiative. He handed the responsibility and the honor to his son Merneptah, who, in the fifth year of his reign (*c.* 1227 B.C.) attacked Libya. Merneptah justified this action in view of the preparations made by the Libyan king Merai, who was gathering the Sea Peoples together under his command. Tempted by the fertility of the Nile Valley, they were preparing to

A reforming Pharaoh

Below Captive Philistines, in feathered headdresses, being led away by the Egyptians. *Right* Detail showing three of the prisoners. From Medinet-Habou.

invade either by chariot along the land routes, or by sea.

The inscription called the "Stele of Israel," discovered in Merneptah's temple tomb in Thebes, records the events of the war and Merneptah's success; the inscriptions on the walls of the temple tell us more. The engagement took place at Per-Ir in the Delta, to the north of Memphis. After a battle lasting six hours, the Sea Peoples retreated; 9,000 prisoners were taken. In order to make his victory yet more effective, the Egyptian ruler pursued Merai's troops as far as Palestine and ravaged their settlements in the lands of Canaan and Ashkelon. This punitive expedition did not spare the Hebrews: "Israel is laid waste and its people no longer exist," the inscriptions record.

After this triumph, Merneptah had no more trouble with the Sea Peoples, nor did the five pharaohs who succeeded him. But Egypt was possibly enjoying a false sense of security. The Sea Peoples had learned prudence from their failure and never again risked a full-scale attack on their neighbor. But neither did they abandon the idea of infiltrating the Delta and taking possession of it.

It has been rightly said of Ramses III that he was "the last great king of the ancient empire." From the moment he succeeded to power in 1198 B.C., he was conscious of the vital need for reforms in his kingdom, above all in the administration and the army. Under his predecessors, foreign policy in regard to Asia had been feeble and neglected. Libya had re-established its power, and the Sea Peoples, in spite of their defeat at Per-Ir, were once again planning an attack on Egypt.

Their tactics, however, had changed. Un-observed by the frontier garrisons, they infiltrated the Delta in small groups of a few families each, then gradually moved south. Without the knowledge of the administration, they set up small collectives, apparently peaceful settlements but capable of becoming formidable instruments of war if their inhabitants banded together. The Egyptians over a long period had employed aliens, sometimes as soldiers and sometimes as workmen, and this facilitated the integration of these foreign races, who little by little mixed with the native population despite racial differences.

In the melting pot of this Afro-Asian immigration were Bedouins, Syrians, Cretans, Lydians and Canaanites. They were a motley crowd, lacking in discipline and hostile to the edicts of the administration and to the laws of a country to which they owed neither physical nor moral allegiance. Such internal disorder and lack of civic sense among people who lived in Egypt as though they had conquered it, yet who refused all the obligations that conquest entails, endangered the security and prosperity of Egypt. And this was at a time when Palestine, Syria, Naharin, Cilicia, Cyprus and the lands of the Amorites were in the hands of the Sea Peoples, before whose onslaughts even the powerful Hittite bastion had collapsed.

It was providential that at this time of great danger, a king who was wise, intelligent, energetic and bold succeeded to the throne. The bas-reliefs of the temple that Ramses built at Medinet-Habou record, in epic style and imposing pictures, the triumphs of the sovereign, the wheels of his war chariot grinding his enemies into dust. Along the north wall of the temple, a gateway almost 230 feet wide, scenes of the tremendous battles that brought about the undoing of the Sea Peoples unfold. But how could enemies so strongly entrenched around Egypt and so well established even in the Nile Valley itself have been defeated so completely? For after the victories of Ramses III they never again represented a serious danger to Egypt.

To understand the brilliance of Ramses III's tactics, one must recognize the patience, care and

Ramses spearing one of the enemy. In Egyptian battle scenes it was customary to show Pharaoh in the thick of the fight, personally responsible for the Egyptian triumph through his semi-divine power.

Invaders repelled

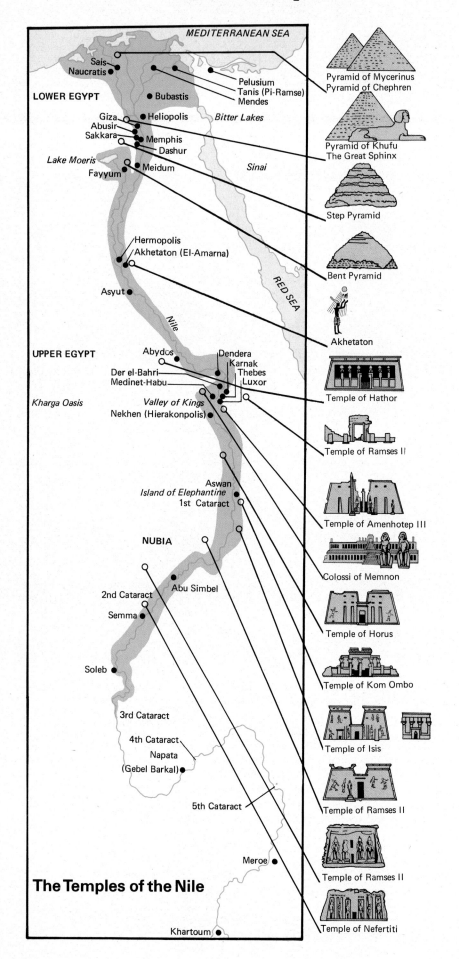

MEDITERRANEAN SEA

Sais
Naucratis

LOWER EGYPT

Bubastis

Pelusium
Tanis (Pi-Ramse)
Mendes

Bitter Lakes

Giza
Abusir
Sakkara

Heliopolis

Memphis
Dashur

Sinai

Lake Moeris

Meidum

Fayyum

Pyramid of Mycerinus
Pyramid of Chephren

Pyramid of Khufu
The Great Sphinx

Step Pyramid

Bent Pyramid

Hermopolis
Akhetaton (El-Amarna)

RED SEA

Asyut

Nile

Akhetaton

UPPER EGYPT

Abydos

Dendera
Karnak
Thebes
Luxor

Der el-Bahri
Medinet-Habu

Temple of Hathor

Kharga Oasis

Valley of Kings

Nekhen (Hierakonpolis)

Temple of Ramses II

Temple of Amenhotep III

Aswan
Island of Elephantine
1st Cataract

Colossi of Memnon

NUBIA

Temple of Horus

Abu Simbel

2nd Cataract

Semma

Temple of Kom Ombo

Soleb

3rd Cataract

4th Cataract
Napata
(Gebel Barkal)

Temple of Isis

5th Cataract

Temple of Ramses II

Meroe

The Temples of the Nile

Temple of Ramses II

Khartoum

Temple of Nefertiti

tenacity with which he pursued his policy of re-conquering Asia. The triumphant bas-reliefs of Medinet-Habou indicate a first expedition dating from the third or fourth year of his reign, or perhaps even earlier. This was against the Amorites, and the inscription reads: "The capital is reduced to ashes, the people taken into captivity, their race obliterated." Ramses III may well have used this opportunity to march against the Libyans and the Asians who, he said, had been the ruin of Egypt on former occasions. Perhaps he also stopped the Delta invasion of two new Indo-European bands of troops, who had come from Libya in swift warships and were disembarking along the coast.

This counter-blow, however effective temporarily, could not deter the aggressors, who were themselves being pressed by their own enemies. In the fifth year of Ramses' reign Libya was the scene of a concentration of hostile tribes, among whom were the Mashouash—who were beginning to acquire an alarming hegemony—and the less numerous Seped and Rebou. The Libyans had been restive ever since Ramses II, in order to assert his authority over this area, had installed as king a Libyan prince brought up in Egypt and loyal to the Pharaoh. The adherents of the legitimate Libyan dynasty overthrew this foreign intruder. Then, after summoning to their assistance all the scattered tribes of the Sea Peoples, they attacked the Egyptian garrisons at a place believed to be Canopus, where the Nile debouches. Their intention was to push on from there as far as Memphis.

Ramses III quickly surrounded the invaders, trapped them in swampy ground and slaughtered them so effectively that it would seem the whole race of the Sea Peoples must have been destroyed. However, the satisfaction gained from this victory was short-lived. Scarcely three years later, in 1191 B.C., the Denyen, the Tjeker, the Peleset, the Shakalsha and the Washash, more insolent and bolder than ever, and supported as always by the native population of Libya, the Tehenou, again attacked Egypt.

This war of 1191 B.C. finally broke the spirit of the Sea Peoples and disorganized their coalition. The tribes from Asia arriving by sea found the Delta protected by an Egyptian squadron much larger than any gathered there before. If one is to believe the accounts of the battle, each mouth of the Nile was blocked by ships close enough together to touch sides. Along the land frontier toward Palestine the Egyptians had built forts and had assembled a number of infantry regiments as well as squadrons of chariots. All the doors into Egypt had been securely locked.

Ramses' strategy was skillful: the enemy's assault would be broken by these impenetrable walls, and Ramses then would have only to drive back the discouraged and weakened aggressors to their point of departure. The bas-reliefs of Medinet-Habou show the fury of the naval battle. The Egyptian galleys rammed and sank the ships of the

Sea Peoples, whose prows, like the Viking long-
ships, terminated in birds' heads; Egyptian sailors
pierced with their lances the invaders, some of whom
wore the horned helmets so characteristic of the
Germanic nations during the later great migrations.

The invaders, annihilated at sea by a better-
armed fleet and blocked by land, retreated. They
left more than 12,500 dead and about a thousand
prisoners. The enemy dead were counted by a
curious system: each soldier cut off one hand (or
the genitals, if uncircumcized) of his victim and
took them to the scribes responsible for the census
and rewards.

Ramses III wished his glory to be recorded for
all time on the walls of his funerary temple, and it
is to this that we owe the magnificent and realistic
battle scenes. The Pharaoh—larger than life,

Above The gateway of the
temple of Medinet-Habou,
built in the style of an Asiatic
fortress.

Left Nubians bringing tribute
to the Pharaoh; wall painting
from the tomb of Sebekhotep
at Thebes.

Below The Pharaoh Ramses III,
depicted on each of this row of
colossal statues at Karnak.

1/63

Power and prosperity in Egypt

according to the convention for a figure already semi-divine in his own lifetime and after his death destined to be revered as a god—is piercing his enemies with his lance and crushing them with his mace. The sculptors have carved with great precision the racial peculiarities of the different peoples who allied together against Egypt: the projecting jaws of African Negroes, the Semitic noses, the feathered headdresses of the Philistines, the beards (presumably blond) and horned helmets of the northern tribes, huddled together in a single group, pitiful and suppliant. Elsewhere Ramses III, standing upright in front of a sort of rostrum, receives homage and reports from his generals, while lower down his secretaries count the corpses.

The victorious king was not exaggerating the glory of his successes. It is clear from the records of the Harris Papyrus and the inscriptions at Medinet-Habou that Egypt had escaped a catastrophe comparable to that which had wiped out the Hittites. Yet decisive as this victory was, it did not assure the impregnability of Egypt. Three years later, in the eleventh year of his reign, Ramses III had to take to the field yet again.

The Mashouash, who had occupied Libya and imposed their rule on the native Tehenou, had chosen as king a fearless and cunning tribal chief called Kaper. He first united all the small Indo-European tribes established in Libya and coerced the more or less reluctant Tehenou to join his federation. He then marched against the Egyptian frontier fortresses, and pushed forward to within fifty miles of the Nile before being halted by the royal chariots. Once again Ramses III was able to put on his victory memorials the triumphant inscription: "The race of men who menaced my country no longer exist, they have been ground into the dust, their hearts and souls have disappeared for all time."

We know from the inscriptions at Medinet-Habou that more than 2,000 Mashouash were killed, and that survivors were pursued for more than twelve miles. Prince Meshsher, who commanded the invading army, was taken prisoner, along with a considerable number of his men; when Kaper, the vanquished king, came to entreat Ramses to spare his son's life, they executed the prince in front of his eyes. Kaper himself was put in chains and condemned to slavery. The prisoners taken in the three campaigns (in the fifth, eighth and eleventh years of Ramses' reign) provided the king with 62,226 slaves, whom he employed to build and maintain his funerary temple.

The unruly neighbors of the Two Kingdoms were henceforth politically impotent. Dispersed, denied the cohesion that had made them so dangerous, driven out of all Egyptian territories, the Sea Peoples were once again reduced to piracy by sea and a nomadic life on land. The prestige of Ramses III was immense and his authority

A section of the Harris Papyrus, which records the exploits of Ramses III. It is the longest papyrus in the world. In this section the scribes have recorded instances of the justice meted out to his subjects by the Pharaoh. The papyrus is written in the hieratic script, which was developed by the scribes from the earlier hieroglyphic writing.

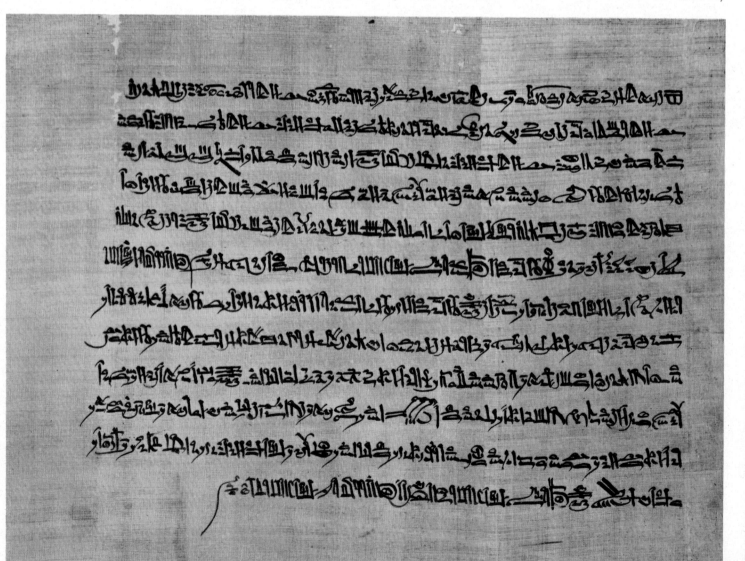

indisputable. The subject nations once again began to pay him tribute, and the sea routes once more were open to commerce. Ramses consolidated his empire by taking five cities of the Amorites and reducing the remnant of the Hittites in Syria to complete subordination. As for the Bedouins in Nubia, a few policing operations proved sufficient to reduce them to servility. Until Ramses III's death in 1166 B.C. nothing disturbed the prosperity and power of Egypt.

Ramses' personal life, however, was not so tranquil. In spite of the debt that his people owed him, showered as they were with glory and blessings, his life was endangered by several plots, one of which was engineered by his own vizier. At last, one of his wives, Queen Tiye, to further the covetousness and ambition of her son, resorted to a sorcerer who used magic charms and probably concocted poisonous drugs.

The plot was denounced and about sixty people, including six women, were condemned to death. Some of these were granted the favor of committing suicide; others were strangled or buried alive. The status and offices of the conspirators are known: a general by the name of Peyes, the commander of the Nubian archers, five senior officials, three royal scribes, five sculptors, the sorcerer Panhouibaounou, and certain concubines. Ramses never knew the outcome of the trial: he died some days before the verdict, after a reign of thirty-one years and forty days.

MARCEL BRION

Above Ramses III depicted with the "Theban Triad," the three principal deities of Thebes—Amon, Mut, and Khons. From the Harris Papyrus.

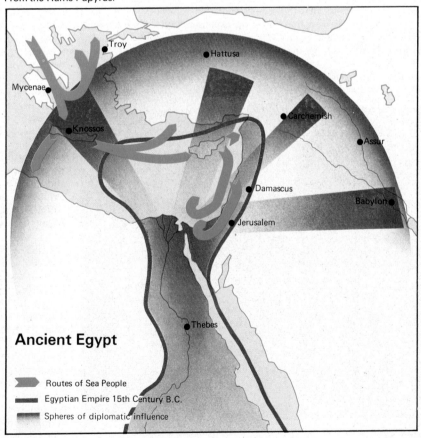

Ancient Egypt

➤ Routes of Sea People

▬ Egyptian Empire 15th Century B.C.

▮ Spheres of diplomatic influence

1/65

Hittite inscription

Ashurbanipal hunting

The vacuum left in Western Asia by the passage of the Sea Peoples was soon filled. New peoples infiltrated into the devastated areas and settled there. Some cities like Alalakh and Ugarit were never rebuilt; others rose again from their ashes. Tribes of Phrygians from Europe and their kin, the Mushki or Moschoi, divided the Anatolian plateau between them, but remnants of the Hittite peoples still continued to survive under their rule. Others, remaining outside the Phrygian orbit, retained their old traditions in the cities of southeastern Anatolia, the Taurus mountains and the plains of North Syria. Here they built temples to the old gods of the Hittite empire, and the inscriptions in their palaces are written in hieroglyphic script, the ancient writing that had coexisted with cuneiform since its beginning in Anatolia. In many of these "Neo-Hittite" states, however, the ruling element was soon Semitic, for camel-riding tribes-

men from the North Arabian desert moved into settled areas and took control of cities, setting up a series of political states. Once established, they flourished on commerce, acting as middlemen between the Mediterranean coast and the cities of Babylonia and Assyria. Competition, however, was to be their downfall: they proved incapable of combining. Their historical inscriptions celebrate victories over rivals, whereas a much greater danger threatened them from across the Euphrates.

Assyrian expansion

The Assyrians, now welded into a mighty military machine of formidable efficiency, were bent on expansion. One after another, as the Assyrian armies swept westwards, the Aramaean states crumpled and were swallowed up; one after another the cities of North Syria, Carchemish and

Arpad, Hamath and Damascus fell, and Israel and Judah paid tribute. The wealthy coastal cities of Phoenicia bought their freedom for a time, but they too were occupied, and by the seventh century Egypt herself was prostrate under the heel of Assyria. It was an empire such as the world had not seen before. The only kingdom to resist occupation, in spite of repeated campaigns, was the mountainous realm of Urartu, to the north of Assyria. Urartu's capital on the shores of Lake Van was impregnable to the attacks of the Assyrian siege engines. The Urartians, distant relatives of the Hurrians, had developed in their hilly fastness a remarkable civilization of their own, about which more is now beginning to be known, as excavation on sites in south Russia and northeastern Turkey uncovers their temples and palaces. Long at loggerheads with the Assyrians, who coveted their mineral resources, they eventually made a treaty with them. To the Assyrians, friendship with the Urartians had become desirable, for they were the last bulwark against a threat that now once more loomed terrifyingly large.

We have shown earlier how certain groups of nomads, some of them Indo-European in speech and custom, had poured over the mountains from the north and established themselves in Anatolia, Mesopotamia, Iran and northern India. But the steppelands of Central Asia continued to be a reservoir of nomadic peoples who periodically, in response to various pressures—famine maybe, or the impact of other, more distant migrations—invaded the civilized lands on their borders, from China in the east to Europe on the west. In about 1000 B.C. Indo-European groups began once more to overrun Persia from the direction of the Caucasus. Their bronze horse trappings and weapons are found in stone-built graves in the Luristan hills. Some were Iranian tribes,

forerunners of the Medes and Persians whose fortunes we shall briefly relate. Other invaders from the Russian steppes traveled more slowly and later, from about 800 B.C., nomadic groups known to classical writers as the Cimmerians, Thracians and Illyrians invaded the plains north of the Black Sea and the Danubian basin. Not long afterwards, a white-skinned horde of horse-riders known as the Yueh-Chi were troubling China.

Babylonian demon

The Scythian onslaught

The Cimmerians who invaded Asia Minor in the eighth century B.C. were escaping, so Herodotus tells us, from the Scythians who were hard on their heels. About the Scythians we are well informed, for a number of Greek writers describe their appearance and their customs and way of life. They were a short, bearded people who wore tunics and baggy thick trousers. Their covered wagons were drawn by oxen, and these were their only habitations. They were brilliant horsemen, skillful archers, scalp-hunters, and they practiced witchcraft and shaman-

Capture of Lachish

Coin of King Kanishka

ism, and drank from cups made from the skulls of their enemies. They succeeded, as the Cimmerians had not, in bringing to an end the Phrygian kingdom in Asia Minor. For fifty or perhaps a hundred years, their advance was stemmed on the west by the armies of Lydia, and to the south by those of Urartu and Assyria. Waves of Scythian onslaught beat in vain against the rocky strongholds of the armies of Van. But at last the kingdom of Urartu fell. At Karmir Blur, a rocky stronghold near the Russian border with Turkey, signs of a desperate last stand have been found: meals abandoned half-eaten, wine jars overturned, arrowheads of Scythian type embedded in the skeletons of those who had fallen in the streets or on the battlements.

Medes and Persians

The Assyrians, too, were to succumb. In 612 B.C. the Scythians joined an alliance with two other of Assyria's enemies, the Medes and the Babylonians; Nineveh fell and the empire was partitioned between the victors. It was, however, the more highly developed military power, the Medes, rather than the wild Scythians, into whose hands the northern part of the empire fell, while Babylonia took over Arabia, Phoenicia and Palestine.

We first hear of the Medes and Persians in the eighth century B.C., when both "Madai" and "Parsua" paid tribute to the Assyrian king Shalmaneser III. At this time the Medes were concentrated around the south of Lake Urmiah, in the north of Iran; later they moved south and made Ecbatana, the modern city now called Hamadan, their capital. Farther south, in Fars, the modern Shiraz district, a king of Parsua named Cyrus, a descendant of one Hakhamanish, or Achae-

menes, became a client of the last great king of Assyria, Ashurbanipal. After the fall of Nineveh, the Persians became vassals of the Median empire, but it was they, and not the Medes, who were destined to create the first Iranian empire, far wider than that of Assyria. It is often called the Achaemenid empire, after the founder of the line. In 539 B.C. a second and greater Cyrus, who had already captured Ecbatana and united Medes and Persians under his rule, conquered Babylon.

North Assyrian tribesman on camel

This date was truly a milestone in history, for it marked the end of the long political dominance of the Mesopotamian powers and the shift of leadership to Iran. Under its successive Achaemenid kings, Persian domination spread over the known world and into regions hitherto outside the ken of civilized peoples; not only the Fertile Crescent and Egypt, but the whole of the peninsula of Asia Minor as far as the Ionian coast was made subject, and to the east huge territories including Bactria and the region of the Hindu Kush, and even the Indus Valley, were made tributary. This empire, the greatest the world had yet known, continued until its overthrow, two centuries later, by the young and remarkable Macedonian adventurer, Alexander.

The rise of Persia

The success of the Achaemenids was perhaps due in part to their freshness of outlook, their youthful energy and their freedom from the shackles of tradition. In part it may

be ascribed to the bankruptcy and exhaustion of the ancient civilizations of the Near East, torn by internal discord and harassed by enemies from without. But largely it was due to the wise and liberal policy of the Achaemenid kings, a policy of adaptation and reconciliation whereby the old could be welded together with the new. The Persians respected local traditions, honored the gods of their subject peoples and interfered as little as possible in the affairs of their subjects. Their liberal attitude is in keeping with the tone of moral enlightenment and ethical balance which characterizes their religious outlook.

For great though their political achievement was, it is in the realm of religion that the Achaemenids left their mark indelibly on the world. For this, one man is responsible, Zarathustra—or Zoroaster as the Greeks called him. To him also is owed the earliest compositions of Persian literature, the *Gathas*, religious poems that were later incorporated into the sacred book known as the Avesta. We know very little of Zoroaster's life. The Gathas, which record his utterances, are difficult to interpret. Even the very date of his birth is widely disputed. Many authorities consider that the prince at whose court he found protection and encouragement was the father of Darius the Great; others consider that he lived some centuries earlier, or else that, although he may have lived in the sixth century, the effect of his teachings was not felt until much later. The question of whether or not the Achaemenid kings of Persia were themselves followers of Zoroaster is a matter of debate, though it is certain that they upheld one of the essential tenets of Zoroaster's faith: the belief in Ahura Mazda, the embodiment of goodness and wisdom and

Bronze buckle from the Caucasus

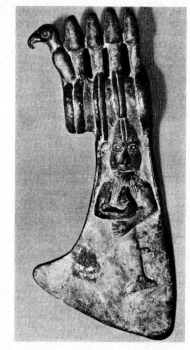

Axehead from Luristan

truth. Zoroastrian influence extended far beyond the frontiers of Iran; it had a profound effect on Judaism, especially in the realm of eschatology—the concepts of the afterlife, of purgatory, judgment and resurrection—and these ideas passed over into Christianity and became an integral part of orthodox Christian belief. In India today, Zoroastrianism continues as the faith of the relatively small but influential community of Parsees, and in Iran there are still areas where the ancient faith is still followed and the ancient rites performed.

Symbol of Ahura Mazda

It has been said that most scholars believe the most likely date for Zoroaster's birth is the early sixth century B.C., perhaps around 570, in the lifetime of the father of Darius. By a strange coincidence, within a few years, another great teacher was born whose religious doctrines, different though they were in many respects, were to have an equally profound effect on the lives of many millions. This was Gautama, the Buddha.

The Prophet of the East

As a young man, Gautama, or the Buddha as he came to be known, followed the usual pursuits of someone of his class. He hunted, played games, feasted and had many friends. He also inspired great personal devotion, which was to stand him in good stead later. Growing discontented with his life and determined to find enlightenment, he renounced his wealth and left Kapilavastu in order to lead an ascetic life. But Gautama found that this kind of existence, practiced in isolation, did not satisfy him. He believed that compassion for his fellow men should find practical expression. He returned to Gaya where he became the "fully-awakened", or Buddha, and began to teach. Although Buddhism—the faith he founded—did not become supreme in India, it won many followers in Ceylon, Burma, Thailand and Tibet and played a crucial role in the development of China and Japan.

In the forested foothills of the Himalayas, in the region that is now central Nepal, there was born around the year 563 B.C. a man whose life and teachings were to have a profound influence throughout Asia and beyond. His personal name was Siddhartha, but he was known also as Gautama, the name of the family group to which he belonged. The Gautama family were Sakyas, one of a number of clans who inhabited the area between the river Ganges and the Himalayas, roughly to the northeast and northwest of the modern city of Patna.

The young Gautama, who was later also to be called Sakyamuni, or "Sage of the Sakyas," grew up in the hill town of Kapilavastu. As the son of the leading clansman, Suddhodana, his lot must have been fairly pleasant, and Buddhist tradition tells us that he was protected from contact with the harsher of life's problems. Tradition also ascribes to his father the deliberate policy of shielding his son from knowledge of the evils of life, because at birth it had been predicted that the child was destined to become either a great ruler or a great ascetic, and his father was determined that it should be the former.

The nature of the human condition could not be hidden indefinitely, however, and Gautama's disillusionment with the artificially soft life he was enjoying came about in early manhood. Tradition represents this as happening through four chance encounters. First he met a very old man, "bent, decrepit, leaning on a staff, tottering as he walked, afflicted . . . ," a sight that caused the young Gautama to reflect that the same fate awaits all humanity. Next he encountered a sick man, suffering great disease, unable to raise himself, in acute pain, needing to be tended and washed by others; again the young man became aware that debilitating illness was a possibility that lay in store for all. Then he saw a corpse being carried out to the funeral pyre, attended by sorrowing

parents, relatives and friends. The same fate, he realized, awaits us all. Finally he encountered a *samana*, an ascetic holy man, with yellow robe and shaven head. Questioning him about his way of life, Gautama, concerned with the uncertainty and suffering that attends mortal existence, became attracted to the idea of the holy life.

As Gautama thought about these four encounters, he became convinced of the need to find a solution to the intolerable problem of suffering that he saw life entailed. He then resolved to leave the temporary and illusory pleasures of his privileged life in Kapilavastu and set out in pursuit of salvation.

Up to this point there is nothing to distinguish the young Gautama from other samanas who were seeking some kind of salvation from mortal ills. In his case, however, the ascetic life did not prove the answer. He engaged in the most rigorous of ascetic practices, in the course of which his body was reduced almost to a skeleton, yet he found no satisfying answer to his quest. Turning aside from the extreme rigors of asceticism, he took some food and came to a place on the bank of the river Neranjara, a tributary of the Ganges. There he saw a large tree, known subsequently to Buddhists as the bodhi or "enlightenment" tree. Here he sat down and remained for a long time, at length passing through certain well-defined, progressive stages of meditation. In the course of his meditation he was assailed by Mara the Evil One (literally, "the destroyer," or "lord of death"). Mara tried by various stratagems to deflect the Buddha-to-be from his progress toward enlightenment. Having failed to intimidate him, Mara then tried to divert Gautama by sending his three daughters to seduce him. But all Mara's efforts were futile. The earlier, Pali Buddhist scriptures present the temptation by Mara as a mental and spiritual attack by the elemental forces of mortal existence, the forces of *Kamadhatu*, the sensual

Above Shakravartin—"he who turns the wheel"—the ruler of the world, is shown in this marble relief of the school of Amaravati, dating from the first century B.C. or A.D.

Opposite The attack of Mara, a marble relief of the second century from Amaravati. In this relief the Buddha himself is not shown but is represented by the royal throne below the tree of enlightenment.

A prince abandons his luxurious life

sphere, which ultimately lead to death rather than life. In later versions the story of the temptation is embellished with highly sensational descriptions of Mara and his army in grand array, and of the seductive wiles of Mara's daughters. The temptations later became a favorite subject for pictorial decorations in Buddhist temples and monasteries in India and southeast Asia. The form of the *Buddha-rupa* or "Buddha image," in which the Buddha is shown seated in meditation with one hand pointing toward the ground, is sometimes known as the "Mara-renouncing" position.

At length, after being immersed in profound meditation throughout the night, there came to Gautama the clear insight by which he saw the true nature of all things; as day dawned he became "fully-awakened," or "Buddha." Buddha is in no sense a personal name, since in the view of Buddhists there had been other Buddhas before Gautama, and there will be others after him. The title Buddha, namely the "Awakened One" or "Enlightened One," indicates a spiritual or ontological status, a certain order of being. When he reached this state, the Buddha understood the transience that characterizes all mortal life and saw the ultimate transcendental end of existence, in Sanskrit called *nirvana*.

After this momentous insight, the Buddha remained for a week under the bodhi tree in continual meditation. Then, for a few weeks, he walked in the neighborhood of the tree. Once again Mara is said to have approached him and to have urged him to abandon mortal existence and enter fully and finally into nirvana. The Buddha rejected this subtle attempt of Mara's to get him out of the way, as he did all subsequent attempts. He replied that he must first instruct others in the truth he had experienced, set up an order of monks and see the order well established before he left this life. Mara, it is said, once again retired in defeat. It was to the

The Spread of Buddhism

mission he had described to Mara, and which Mara henceforth did everything he could to hinder, that the Buddha devoted the remaining forty years of his life.

To understand the significance of the Buddha's doctrine and the new religious community that he gathered round him, it is helpful to look first at what we know of the India he was born in. Our evidence comes mainly from the ancient Pali literature of the Buddhists, which shows a generally keener historical sense than either the Hindu Vedic texts or the Prakrit texts of the Jains, another contemporary religious group. Various critical studies have revealed that the republican groups of northeast India, such as the Sakyas, were suffering attacks from newly arisen neighboring monarchies, particularly those of Magadha and Kosala. These monarchies were absorbing the territories and people of the repub-

Scenes from the early life of the Buddha, depicted in carvings of the school of Amaravati.
Left The mother of the Buddha has a dream (*top right*), which is interpreted by a sage (*top left*). The birth of the Buddha ensues (*bottom right*), and he is presented to the tutelary spirits of the sakyas (*bottom left*).
Right The Buddha with his father, surrounded by women of the harem. Shielded by his father in a life of luxury, the Buddha grew to early manhood before realizing the sorrow of life.

lics, although the Sakyas themselves were probably not invaded during the Buddha's lifetime.

It was thus a time of social disturbance and political change and, consequently, a time also of psychological malaise. Men were asking with a new urgency questions about the meaning of existence and ultimate human destiny. The destruction of the old republican clans meant that people were being swept into the larger, more impersonal autocratic organization of the monarchy. They could no longer rely on the close-knit structure of the clan to give their lives ready-made significance. The individual became more acutely aware of his isolation and faced problems of personal conduct in which the old rules no longer applied. What, men were asking, are the causes of the indignities and injustices suffered by the individual? How should a man conduct himself? What other possible goal was there but to make the most of such opportunities as life provided to eat, drink and be merry? Such questions were not new in India, nor was the Buddha the first to suggest an answer. The need for answers was, however, being felt more acutely, and the Buddha offered a doctrine significantly different from others already available.

The religious philosophies and systems that existed in India at that time were broadly of two kinds; the distinction is epitomized by two characteristic classes of religious functionary, brahmans and samanas. The brahmans were priests brought by the Aryan invaders a thousand or so years earlier. They regarded themselves as a sacred elite, in whose keeping was the hereditary practice of the sacrificial system by which they believed the cosmos was maintained. It was a stupendous claim. To the ordinary householder, farmer or merchant, however, it was a claim that had little relevance to personal problems.

It was to the needs of such men that the samanas addressed themselves. The metaphysical views and ascetic disciplines that they recommended were various and often conflicting, but common to most of them was a belief in the liberation of the soul, or ego, by personal discipline, asceticism or esoteric meditational practices. These often involved renouncing the life of the householder and undertaking a rigorous training in self-mortification to enhance the soul's psychic powers, so that it might break out of the mortal realm into the sphere of supernatural bliss. The term "samana" indicates "one who labors," in this case spiritually.

Such was the background against which the Buddha set forth his doctrine, or *dharma*— according to tradition, in a deer park near the city of Benares. Unlike the teachings of most of the other great religions of the world, the Buddha-Dharma did not require belief in a supreme and omnipotent deity or creator, or make any reference to such a being. It consisted of an analysis of the human condition, as something given, rather than as a situation to be explained by speculation about cosmic origins. The latter kind of speculation was the basis of the brahmans' position; their theory of the importance of sacrifice the Buddha rejected. He also rejected their élitism: the doctrine he taught was true of all and true for all.

There are various ways of summarizing the Buddha-Dharma. One is in terms of the "four holy truths." The first truth to be apprehended is that all living beings have to suffer the disorder and imperfection of ordinary earthly existence; this may be variously described as "illness," "unsatisfactoriness," "imperfection," or "suffering." At times one may be temporarily unaware of this imperfection, but eventually it will always assert itself.

The second truth is that this suffering is caused by an attitude of craving, an insatiable thirst for that which one has not.

The third truth is that the experience of suffering

Buddhist pillar, decorated with scenes symbolizing the four main events of the Buddha's life—his birth, enlightenment, first sermon, death. The pillar with the Wheel of the Law, shown in the photograph, symbolizes the first sermon, given in the deer park at Benares.

The great departure. The Buddha leaves home, escorted as a prince for the last time, to abandon his luxurious life and become an ascetic.

A new religion is founded

Above Buddhists worshipping the Bodhi tree, beneath which the Buddha received enlightenment.

Below The miracle of Saraswati.

"soul," to which such importance had been attached and which was the cause of division between men through ideas of "I" and "mine," that real awakening was to be found. Destroy this egocentric view of the world, said the Buddha, and enter a freer, wider realm of being, which is nirvana. Moreover, it was a process that needed the experience of living in a community dedicated to the negation of the egoistic principle. Such a community was the Buddha-Sangha or Buddhist religious order.

The sangha, or order of *bhikkhus* (almsmen), provided the optimum conditions for living the Buddhist life. This community, which came into being when the first disciples attached themselves to the Buddha, was unique. Other groups of samanas sometimes formed groups for the period of the monsoon rains, when traveling was impossible and it became necessary to take shelter in one place. But these groups had only a temporary existence. Out of this practice, however, the Buddha and his disciples established a permanent community that existed to facilitate the practice of the Buddhist way. A recognized rule of life and conduct and a high standard of moral discipline were outstanding features of the order from the beginning.

In the course of the Buddha's lifetime, as the number of disciples grew, the code of conduct for members of the order was worked out and formally established. This code subsequently became embodied in the basic tradition as the *Vinaya*, that is, the Discipline. The other main feature of the tradition was the dharma, which had come to mean, besides the doctrine, the actual collection of discourses uttered by the Buddha. This took the form of parables, allegories, discussions, stories and verses, in order to render the doctrine as clear as possible to as many as possible, since the Buddha's teaching was intended for all men, whatever their station. Within the sangha there was no hierarchy apart from seniority in spiritual attainment; all social distinctions were (and still are) abandoned by those who entered.

The sangha thus offered some replacement for the communal life that India had lost with the destruction of the old republican societies. Later it was to acquire far wider significance, over a far greater area. For more reasons than one, a man went for refuge to the sangha. The common formula used by Buddhists from the earliest times as a simple affirmation of faith, and still universally adopted, runs as follows: "To the Buddha I go for refuge; to the dharma I go for refuge; to the sangha I go for refuge."

Among the early members of the sangha who accompanied the Buddha on his many journeys throughout northeast India and Nepal, and who devoted themselves to his mission and his needs (as Buddhist monks still minister to one another), are certain well remembered names, especially those of Ananda, often referred to as the "beloved disciple," Sariputta and Maha Kassapa. It was

ceases with the end of desire in all its aspects—greed, anger and false views of life. The cessation of craving is nirvana, the Buddhist goal.

The fourth truth is that there is a way by which such cessation can be achieved here and now, namely the way of the Buddha, the way opened up by him, to be followed by all men who have faith in the Buddha's knowledge. Such faith, however, is not blind faith, but "faith-with-a-view-to-verification." According to the Buddha, the following of the way itself provides the verification. The invitation that the Buddha offered was summed up in the phrase *"ehi passako"*—"Come and see," that is, verify the transcendent truth for yourself.

In addition to characterizing all human existence as suffering imperfection, the Buddha also emphasized its transitoriness. In ordinary earthly existence no state of being persists; all is continually in flux, and nothing endures. The third characteristic of existence, according to the Buddha, is the absence of any permanent individual ego. It was this that most clearly distinguished the Buddha's teaching from that of all the other samanas of India, and also from that of the brahmans. These others asserted the existence of a real permanent self or *atman* in each individual, and bade each man find within the depths of his *atman* the ultimate reality. The Buddha's doctrine was stigmatized by these "orthodox" teachers, as being *nairatmya*, that is, a "nonsoul" doctrine. But the Buddha asserted that it was in relinquishing this notion of a permanent

Ananda who approached the Buddha with a request from some of the women disciples that a parallel order for women should be established. After some hesitation the Buddha is said to have consented to this. From the earliest days an order of nuns, with its own parallel code of discipline and regulations, has been a feature of Buddhism.

At the age of eighty, his mortal body having come to the end of its span of existence, Gautama passed from the intermediate stage of the Buddha who still retains a mortal body to that of final and complete nirvana, or parinirvana. His bodily remains were cremated with great reverence, and his ashes were distributed among various groups who claimed a share in these sacred relics. The ceremony is described in one of the longest of the Pali texts, the *Parinirvana Sutta*. Over each share of the ashes, it is said, a memorial mound, or stupa, was raised. The stupa was a hemispherical structure of stone or brick with the sacred relic enshrined at its center. For Buddhists such structures became symbols and reminders of the Awakened One who had first taught them the dharma. In their later, developed form, known in Ceylon as *dagobas*, or pagodas, these stupas became a familiar feature of the Asian countries to which the Buddha-Dharma was carried by its missionary-monks.

In India the Buddhist sangha gradually grew in size and spread from the Ganges Valley around Patna northwestward toward the Punjab and Kashmir, where its monks came into contact with elements of Greco-Roman culture in the kingdom of Bactria (on the northwest borders of modern West Pakistan). There, some five centuries after the Buddha's death, a new form of Buddhism, known as the Mahayana, developed. It perhaps owed something to Greco-Roman influences, and something to the increasing numbers of brahmans who had by then, especially since the reign of the Buddhist emperor Asoka (third century B.C.), begun increasingly to enter the order.

These brahmans did not easily discard their old attitudes and ideas when they donned the yellow robe of the Buddhist monk. The result was the development within the Buddhist community of a high degree of speculative philosophizing, and an increasing use of non-Buddhist cults and practices among its lay supporters. By about A.D. 1200, partly for this reason, the practice of the way of the Buddha had disappeared almost entirely from India. From then on, however, Buddhism was expanding in influence in the neighboring lands of Tibet, Burma, Thailand, Laos, Cambodia and Vietnam, as well as in China and Japan, where it was already well established. Even in India the effects of the Buddha and his community influenced the philosophy, ethics and religious institutions of what had by then become Hinduism. In modern times India has begun to rediscover the way that was taught and practiced by one of her greatest sons, and the Buddhist community has once again begun a remarkable revival. TREVOR LING

One of the gates of the stupa at Sanchi. A stupa is a Buddhist temple designed to house sacred relics or to commemorate the sacred character of a place or of an important event. In shape it is based on the funerary mound of the Vedas, and symbolizes the cosmic mountain, the pivot of the world.

The dagoba, or stupa of Thuparama, in Ceylon. The oldest parts of this stupa date from the third century A.D.

The destruction of Knossos in 1450 B.C. precipitated the end of a brilliant period in Cretan civilization. The focus of power subsequently lay on the Greek mainland, in the great fortress-cities of Mycenae and Tiryns. These cities were remembered in Homeric legend, in the poems of the *Iliad* and the *Odyssey*. Confirmation as fact of what scholars had credited merely as legend was provided by the excavation of the site of Homer's "Mycenae rich in gold" by the German merchant-turned-archeologist, Heinrich Schliemann, in 1876. His discoveries there brought to light the "Mycenaean" civilization, which we now know to have been widespread in Greece from *c.* 1400–1200 B.C. It was the product of Indo-European settlers, and these Mycenaean Greeks took control of Crete, from where much of their culture originated, as the presence of Linear B tablets on both Crete and the mainland indicates.

The society which Homeric legend describes is not a society at its peak, as many scholars have noted, and the epics of "Homer" (whoever or whatever Homer might represent) foreshadow the downfall of the Mycenaean civilization. The decline of the Achaean Greeks was speeded by an abrupt end to their political supremacy, when the Dorian tribes swept southwards in about 1100 B.C. This may well have been part of a larger pattern of migrations that affected the western Mediterranean at about this time. The empire of the Hittites was overthrown, and Egypt was attacked by the "Peoples of the Sea." The Dorian invasion precipitated emigration of earlier Greek inhabitants from the mainland—Ionians from Attica fled to the coastal lands of Asia Minor, as did Aeolians from Thessaly; Achaeans moved into Arcadia and Cyprus.

The Trojan Horse of Homeric legend; from an early Greek vase

The Dorian invaders themselves settled in the Peloponnese and Crete, and in part of Asia Minor. The regional differences established during this period of movement and settlement were remembered by the Greeks—Sparta was always thought of as Dorian. After the Dorian invasion, Greece gradually assumed the political configuration that was to last until Alexander of Macedon reorganised the civilized world.

The city-state

The key to Greek political development, and indeed to Greek civilization, is the Greek city, or more accurately, city-state, the *polis*. The physical geography of Greece—small plains separated from each other by steep hills and mountain chains—must have influenced the development of small, closely-knit communities, though the choice of organization was the

Greeks'. They saw the *polis* as the only and the ultimate form of political and social life. Unlike elsewhere in the eastern Mediterranean, the Greek city was not part of a larger unit, such as a kingdom, but was an independent state in itself.

The cities of Greece must have provided their inhabitants with a stable and secure existence, for population in the cities had increased until it became a problem by the eighth century B.C. The geographic confinement which had partly determined the development of the cities also determined the limits of their growth—land was scarce. So still another migratory movement got under way. Yet this time it was not the helter-skelter movement of whole tribes, but the planned sending-out of real colonists. The knowledge that the Greeks possessed of the Mediterranean was somewhat hazy, but enough for many thousands to set out optimistically to find a new

life. They headed in the direction of southern Italy and Sicily, Asia Minor and the Black Sea, each pioneering group with its *oikistes*, the official "founder" of the new city. This colonization was not like the colonization of, for example, the British Empire, where the parent-country retained political control over its colonies. Once the settlers had made a landfall and established themselves in their new environment, they were on their own, virtually independent of their mother-city. Regular trading contacts were in many cases set up, the parent-cities tending to trade with their individual offspring. The wealth of a city like Corinth was undoubtedly augmented by trade with her many colonies, but the offspring prospered too—the Corinthian colony of Syracuse became one of the greatest of the Greek cities. The colonizing movement lasted for about two hundred years, from the eighth to the sixth century, and towards its end trade and commercial motivations had taken supremacy over the original "land-hunger" motive.

The political and economic

Mycenaean warrior; ivory

consequence of colonization for the Mediterranean world was that Greek influence and interests had spread far afield, ranging into the territories of diverse peoples. Southern Italy became predominately Greek (with Sicily, it was known as *Megale Hellas, Magna Graecia*), all along the coasts of Asia Minor there were Greek settlements, and Greeks even penetrated Egypt, establishing trading stations at Naucratis and Syria, and a colony at Al Mina.

The Phaistos Disk

Part of Linear B tablet from Knossos

Aramaean script

"Mistress of the Beasts"; Etruscan

Cultural interchange

Colonization was not the sole prerogative of the Greeks. Greek expansion in Sicily was limited by the colonizing efforts of the Phoenicians, the skillful sea-farers who inhabited the area of present-day Lebanon. They founded several important cities on the Mediterranean coast of Spain also, though perhaps their most important foundation was the city of Carthage in North Africa, whose famous son Hannibal will be the subject of a subsequent article.

Greek settlement in southern Italy was also limited by the expansion of the Etruscans in central Italy in the seventh and sixth centuries B.C. Etruscan kings ruled the small city of Rome during the sixth century, and the fate of the Greeks, the Carthaginians, the Etruscans and the Romans are all interlinked, as future articles will show. Political confrontation was to occur between various groupings of these powers, but an example of the importance of cultural interchange during this formative period is provided by the spread of the alphabet. The Linear B script was difficult and clumsy to write—only the Greeks

of Cyprus retained it for long—and in the eighth century the Greeks took over the Phoenician alphabet, and developed it in various forms. From the Greeks of Chalcis, the Etruscans adopted a version; from them the Romans borrowed and modified it. You are reading it now.

Cultural interchange on a large scale followed the Greek colonization of the East. The Greeks were eager to assimilate and learn from the eastern cultures. The "orientalizing" trend is evident in Greek pottery from the eighth century, with the use of motifs from Syria and Phoenicia (and the Phoenicians borrowed from the Egyptians). From the Greeks in Italy the Etruscans learned the arts of civilization; they were eager for all the trappings of Hellenization, as the material remains of their culture indicate. From them Rome absorbed Greek culture.

Our next article takes us to the point in Mediterranean history at which the expansion of the colonizing period has become with only minor exceptions a thing of the past, and expansion now means large-scale political confrontation. The cities of Greece were forced to unite to save themselves from domination by the mighty empire of Persia.

Political organization

However, the Greece that confronted Xerxes had evolved politically. Within the city-states of Greece, internal government went through a variety of forms. Sparta had two kings, whose power could vary according to the strength of their individual personalities *vis à vis* the council of elders—the ephors—who also made up the governing body of the state. Below the kings and ephors was an elite of citizens; and below them, various grades of semi-slaves and slaves. But, during the Archaic period, most Greek cities were

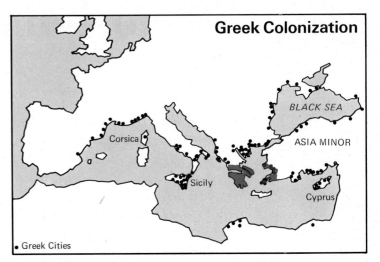

Greek Colonization

BLACK SEA

ASIA MINOR

Corsica

Sicily

Cyprus

• Greek Cities

ruled by aristocracies. As individual cities grew, and new economic interests and commercial expansion emerged, the hold of the landed aristocrats was challenged and gradually superceded by people of new wealth. The form of government thus tended to shift from aristocracy (rule or power of the best) to oligarchy (rule of the few). This shift in political power was often accompanied by improvements in justice—subjecting the administration of city life to the relative impartiality of written laws rather than the arbitrary and biased decisions of powerful landowners, the "princes who devour bribes and give crooked decisions" mentioned by Hesiod. The process of changing political organization to represent new interests was often hastened, from the seventh century on, by the appearance of "tyrants," individual leaders, frequently of noble ancestry, who were hostile to the aristocracy as a whole. Tyrants (only later did the word become symbolic of oppression) arose mainly in the coastal cities of Greece that had trading interests: the first tyrants were at Sicyon and Corinth. Athens, too, had her tyrant, a noble called Cylon, in 630 B.C., but her internal problems remained, and a reformer was given power to clear up some of the inconsistencies in Athens' political and social organization. The work of this senior citizen and law-giver, Solon, gave political recognition to new forces within Athenian society, but still many problems were unresolved, and thirty years later another tyrant emerged. He established himself firmly enough to found a dynasty. Although short-lived, the dynasty of the Peisistratids gave Athens a period of stability during which she

prospered. As it happened, the fall of the Peisistratids paved the way for democracy in Athens. In Greek politics, the tendency was for tyrants (individual rulers) to be succeeded by a coalition of important men, oligarchs. Two factions of nobles competed for control when the last tyrant had been deposed, and one faction, headed by a noble called Cleisthenes, had enlisted popular support. When Cleisthenes gained control, he carried out a thorough reform of the Athenian constitution, and considerably reduced the remaining power of the nobles that was vested in the council of the Areopagus. The assembly of the people of Athens became paramount: democracy (the power of the people) was achieved, and given perhaps its fullest expression ever.

At Salamis, the democratically elected leaders of the Athenian people confronted the power of an oriental autocrat, the fleet of Xerxes, Great King of the Persians. The empire that he ruled had emerged from the ruins of Assyrian and Median power. The Persians were given a new-found unity by Cyrus (559–529), and under his rule the Achaemenid empire expanded at a phenomenal rate. Lydia was conquered, then the Persians advanced to the edge of the Mediterranean, conquering the Greek cities there. Caria, Lycia and Cilicia came under Persian domination, Babylon fell, and Syria and Palestine were subdued. Egypt was conquered after Cyrus' death by his son Cambyses (525 B.C.). Thus the whole of the eastern Mediterranean was in Persian hands. The next chapter shows how the European expansion of Persian power was stemmed by a great naval battle in the Aegean.

Italian terracotta head; ivory head from Nimrod; head from Carthage

Victorious Athens

Greece was threatened by the advance of the Persians. But even in the face of such a threat, the Greeks were unable to unite as a nation. The basis of Greek life was the "polis" or city-state, and the concept of nationhood was completely foreign to this system. Eventually, however, a Hellenic league of Greek cities was formed, led by Athens and Sparta, and in 480 the Persians were defeated at sea at Salamis and in 479 on land at Plataea. Had the Persians been the victors, it is hard to tell how our civilization would have developed. Possibly democracy, as we know it, would never have survived. Paradoxically it was precisely because of Greece's weakness—the independence of the city-state—that democracy, particularly in Athens, reached its highest peak of development. Thanks to Salamis it was handed on to future generations, enshrined in the legacy of Greece.

Themistocles, whose far-sighted proposal that the Athenians should fight the Persians at sea rather than on land paved the way for the defeat of King Xerxes.

Opposite top The Pnyx at Athens, where Themistocles addressed the assembled citizens. In the distance is the Acropolis, the temple of Athena Parthenos, the most sacred spot in Athens.

Opposite bottom Greek warriors bid farewell to their womenfolk before setting out to battle; from a vase.

The Assembly on the Pnyx, Athens' "parliament hill," was packed; this would be a crucial debate. The mighty Xerxes of Persia, with the greatest invasion force that Greece had ever seen, had crossed the Dardenelles and was now advancing inexorably across Thrace towards Macedonia. His engineers had even cut a canal through the peninsula of Mt. Athos for the safe passage of the force's navy. The ruling dynasty of Thessaly had decided to collaborate with the invader, and the Macedonians had given him earth and water in token of submission. The district of Boeotia was rife with Persian sympathizers. The Spartans were ready to make a stand against Xerxes; the crucial question was, where would they make it? Their traditional line of defense was the Isthmus of Corinth. If they chose to hold that line now, Athens—to the north—would be left in isolation, exposed to the advance of the Persian war machine.

In two months or less, if nothing was done to halt him, Xerxes' fleet and army would reach Attica. The chance of the northern Greek states holding out—or indeed not actively collaborating with Xerxes—was plainly slim. Worse still, Xerxes had publicly declared that the prime purpose of his expedition was to punish Athens for the part that she had played, nearly twenty years earlier, in the revolt of Greek cities in Ionia against Persia. Any other state, then, might expect reasonable treatment from the Persian king; the Athenians could expect no mercy. Their alternatives were flight or resistance. The Delphic Oracle—while merely counseling other states to remain neutral—had already advised flight for the Athenians.

The big, thick-set man who stood on the speaker's platform of the Pnyx on that fine day in 480 B.C. was already a familiar figure. The crier's voice called out: "Pray silence for Themistocles, son of Neocles, of the Phrearri parish." Themistocles must have stood for some time, perhaps waiting till the buzz of voices died away, trying to

sense the Assembly's mood as he gazed out towards the plain of Marathon. There, he would have recalled, once before, only ten years earlier, Athenians had beaten off a Persian invasion. Themistocles had fought—and fought well—in that battle; so had many of those waiting this day for him to speak. But this crisis was different. At Marathon a citizen-army—men of property and breeding, who could afford their own armor—had marched out to defend their city and their country estates. Some of the men in his audience today, Themistocles knew, were anxious to do so again. Yet no infantry force Greece could put in the field would hold up this new invasion for long. To fight the Persians at sea was the only chance.

Three years before, against strong conservative opposition, Themistocles had put through a motion for Athens to build two hundred new warships, financed by the proceeds of a rich new lode in the Laurium silvermines. By June, 480, that fleet was ready, and Themistocles was determined to use it. We have no record of his actual speech to the Assembly on that historic occasion, but the arguments he employed are not in dispute.

Ever since the accession of King Darius, forty-two years earlier, in 522, Persian expansion had threatened Europe. Meanwhile, Egypt and Libya had fallen; so had several key islands in the eastern Aegean Sea. Darius had then boldly crossed the Bosporus, annexed Thrace and secured Macedonia's submission. The collapse of the Ionian Revolt (499–94) had made an invasion of the Greek mainland inevitable. In 490 the invasion came, to be repulsed by the Athenians at Marathon. Rebellion in the Persian empire, and the death of Darius in 486, had merely postponed the next, inevitable attack. Now Darius' son Xerxes was on the march.

Hysterical rumors estimated Xerxes' fleet at over 1,200 ships, and his army at well over a million (the actual figures are probably 650 and

The Persian menace

180,000 respectively). Themistocles' attempt to sell a naval-defense policy to the Greeks had already once fallen on deaf ears. The Hellenic League—a group of those Greek states determined to resist—had voted instead to send a land force of 10,000 men to hold the pass of Tempe in northern Greece, and Themistocles had agreed to serve as its commander. The expedition ended in a complete fiasco. The Greeks found that Xerxes could easily outflank them through central Greece; and the Thessalians, on whose help they had relied, went over *en bloc* to the enemy. It was immediately after this setback that Themistocles made his great speech to the Athenian assembly.

In a few days, there was to be an emergency meeting of the Hellenic League at the Isthmus of Corinth; but how the states would vote no one, at the moment, could foresee. Themistocles hoped for the acceptance of his own plan—a land-and-sea holding action at the pass of Thermopylae and in the waters off Artemisium. Yet he was a realist. No one had forgotten that the Spartans had arrived too late for Marathon. Worse still, they might vote to hold the Isthmus line and let everything to the north go. Cynics at Sparta might sacrifice their rival Athens to Xerxes and allow Persia to run northern Greece in the same *laissez-faire* way that she did Ionia. Sparta, south of the Isthmus, would retreat still further into isolation. In either case, Themistocles realized, adequate plans must now be made for the protection of Attica.

Thanks to archeology, we now know what those provisions were. In 1959 Professor Jameson of the University of Pennsylvania discovered a third-century B.C. inscription which preserves, in edited form, the motion passed by Themistocles in June, 480 B.C. Here are the key clauses from it, in Jameson's translation:

Gods. Resolved by the Council and People. Themistocles, son of Neocles, of Phrearri, made the motion. To entrust the city to Athena, the Mistress of Athens, and to all the other gods to guard and defend from the Barbarian for the sake of the land. The Athenians themselves and the foreigners who live in Athens are to send their children and women to safety in Troezen, their protector being Pittheus, the founding hero of the land. They are to send the old men and their movable possessions to safety on Salamis. The treasures and priestesses are to remain on the Acropolis, guarding the property of the gods.

All the other Athenians and foreigners of military age are to embark on the two hundred ships that are ready and defend against the Barbarian for the sake of their own freedom and that of the rest of the Greeks along with the Lacedaemonians, the Corinthians, the Aeginetans, and all others who wish to share the danger . . . When the ships have been manned, with a hundred of them they are to meet the enemy at Artemisium in Euboea, and with the other hundred they are to lie off Salamis and the coast of Attica and keep guard over the land. In order that all Athenians may be united in their defense against the Barbarian, those who have been sent into exile for ten years are to go to Salamis and stay there until the people come to some decision about them . . .

To get this motion passed was a real triumph for Themistocles: its measures were bound to be unpopular with those who had an old-fashioned attitude towards defending hearth, home and the shrines of one's ancestors. What landed gentleman would support a motion proposed by a man whose backing came from the "sailor rabble" of Piraeus—not least when its direct consequence might be the destruction of all farms and estates in Attica? When he called on Athens to evacuate Attica and trust to the fleet, Themistocles had the whole weight of prejudice and tradition against him.

Yet, somehow, he won. He argued that the "wooden wall" which—according to the Delphic prophecy—would not fail Athens in her hour of need—must refer to the fleet. He spoke of freedom and the glories of sacrifice. He changed his mood, becoming brisk and practical as he outlined the evacuation plan in detail. And he ended with a call to unite against the Barbarian. When he stopped speaking, the Assembly rose and cheered.

The Hellenic League, too, was swayed by Themistocles' arguments. Naval and land forces moved north to hold the Thermopylae-Artemisium line. The army, commanded by Sparta's King Leonidas, included some 4,000 Lacedaemonians, of whom only 300 were full Spartan citizens. Athens provided by far the largest contingent in the fleet: 147 triremes out of an initial 271. The priests at Delphi advised the Greeks to "pray to the winds." Meanwhile the Great King's host trudged southwards.

By the end of July the Greek fleet and army were in position. On August 12 the Persian fleet was anchored in minor harbors and anchorages around Cape Sepias and along the Pallene peninsula. Fire-signals from Skiathos brought the news to Artemisium. To prevent dissension, Themistocles had surrendered his command to the Spartan Eurybiades, but one can see his hand in what followed. The Greek fleet retreated to Chalcis, in

King Darius of Persia, whose attack on Greece had been repulsed ten years before Salamis, hunting lions; from an engraved cylinder seal.

the Straits of Euboea: Themistocles hoped to tempt the Persians into fighting in a confined space. Xerxes had dried out his fleet at Doriscus; the Greeks had not dared risk a similar operation. Thus the Persian vessels were now faster and more maneuverable than those of their opponents. Somehow this disadvantage had to be neutralized.

At dawn on August 13 the *meltemi*, the seasonal northeast winds, began to blow and for the next three days the Persian fleet was storm-bound, with heavy damage. As early as the fourteenth, the Greek naval commanders learned of this disaster—and heard also that the Persian land forces were approaching Thermopylae. The fleet now returned to Artemisium: it was strategically vital that King Leonidas should not have his right flank exposed. It was essential to maintain close liaison between land and sea forces.

For a day or two, nothing happened. The storm blew out by August 16, and the battered Persian fleet limped into Pagasae harbor. But on the following day Xerxes prepared for action. A squadron of two hundred ships was sent round Euboea to take the Greek fleet in the rear; perhaps news of this action drove the Greeks to fight their first naval engagement, on August 18. This clash coincided with the first land assault on Thermopylae, and it was equally inconclusive.

Praying to the winds seemed highly efficacious. Xerxes' outflanking squadron was now caught in a driving rain off the Hollows of Euboea and largely destroyed. Since the danger of an outflanking movement was now largely removed, the Greeks reinforced their Artemisium fleet with fifty-three ships relieved from the duty of guarding Attica. They hoped to snatch a decisive naval victory from the Persians. They were disappointed. On August 20 a bitter battle was fought with Xerxes' remaining squadrons, but its outcome was indecisive. Yet the Greeks still held the straits.

"They learned from their own behavior in the face of danger," Plutarch wrote, "that men who know how to come to close quarters and are determined to give battle have nothing to fear from

mere numbers of ships . . . they have simply to . . . engage the enemy hand-to-hand and fight it out to the bitter end." The engagement at Artemisium paved the way for Salamis. But while this encounter was taking place, another more famous and more desperate battle had been fought in the pass of Thermopylae.

For two days King Leonidas and his inadequate force held the pass against endless assaults by Xerxes' infantry. Then a traitor showed the Persians a concealed path over the mountains, a natural "corridor" by which Leonidas could be taken in the rear. The Phoenicians guarding it fled, possibly by design; the sources are not clear. At this news the bulk of the Peloponnesian units withdrew south. Once Xerxes' cavalry was through

Two Persians, from a frieze at Persepolis showing subjects paying homage to the Great King.

The Persian court, as seen by the Greek artist of the "Persian Vase," which was found in a burial chamber at Canossa.

Themistocles' strategy

the pass, those retreating Greek troops would be cut to ribbons. So Leonidas, without fuss or bother, made his last stand. The Spartans fought to the last man; when their spears were broken, they fought with their swords; and after that, with their hands and teeth. But they went down at last, and the pass to the south lay open.

Thermopylae and Artemisium were far from useless sacrifices. Their effect on Greek morale was incalculable, and they delayed the Persian advance just long enough. More important, and in conjunction with those two lucky storms, they had destroyed so many Persian ships and men that Xerxes hesitated to make the one move almost guaranteed to win him the campaign: a division of his forces. Demaratus, the renegade Spartan king who was acting as the Great King's adviser, urged

Xerxes to detach a task force of three hundred ships to the Peloponnese, while at the same time pressing home his attack on Athens. But Xerxes' brother Achaemenes vetoed such a project—too many ships had been lost already.

Battered and bloody, the Greek fleet withdrew south from Artemisium under the cover of darkness. The Athenians alone had had about half their vessels put out of commission. The allies made directly for Salamis, where the reserve fleet was to join them. The Athenians meanwhile sailed to Phaleron, to complete the evacuation of Attica before Xerxes' advance land forces crossed the frontier. The news that Themistocles and his exhausted crews received at Athens was not encouraging. The Peloponnesians—predictably— were reported to be "fortifying the Isthmus and

Above King Xerxes of Persia; from the palace at Persepolis.

Right A Greek warship, from a seal. Such ships as this defeated the Persian navy at Salamis.

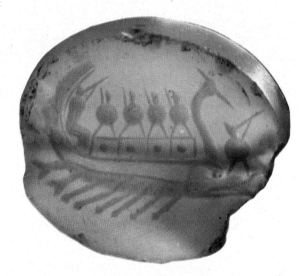

Aerial view of Salamis. Part of the island can be seen to the left (beyond the island of Psyttaleia), opposite Piraeus, the port of Athens.

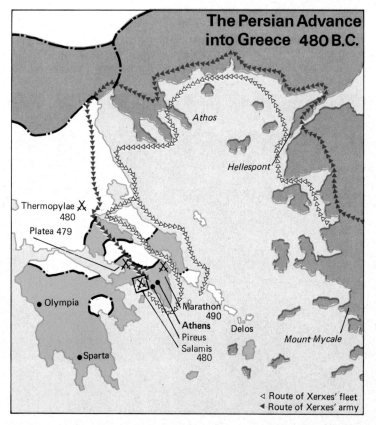

The Persian Advance into Greece 480 B.C.

Athos
Hellespont
Thermopylae 480
Platea 479
Olympia
Marathon 490
Athens
Pireus
Salamis 480
Delos
Mount Mycale
Sparta

◁ Route of Xerxes' fleet
◀ Route of Xerxes' army

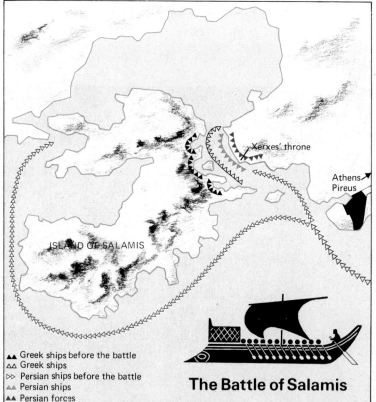

Xerxes' throne
Athens Pireus
ISLAND OF SALAMIS

▲▲ Greek ships before the battle
△△ Greek ships
▷▷ Persian ships before the battle
▲▲ Persian ships
▲▲ Persian forces

The Battle of Salamis

Greek hoplites (infantrymen) fighting in formation, protected by their round shields. Such soldiers defeated the army of Xerxes at Plataea, in the year following the battle of Salamis; relief from the Siphnian Treasury, at Delphi.

letting all else go." Some men still hoped to hold the Cithaeron-Parnes line with Spartan support. Again Themistocles acted swiftly and decisively. A token garrison was left on the Acropolis; within forty-eight hours the evacuation of Attica was complete, and the allies were firmly established on Salamis. Even then, Peloponnesian representatives at the council of war that followed were still in favor of pulling out and holding the Isthmus line.

Meanwhile the Persian army, virtually unopposed, was pressing on southwards. Delphi, mysteriously, was spared—perhaps as a reward for so many pro-Persian oracles. Boeotia surrendered, and collaborated. News came that the Persians were already in Attica, burning the countryside as they came. About August 27, Xerxes' advance column clattered through Athens' deserted streets to the foot of the Acropolis; his fleet reached Phaleron two days later, leaving behind a trail of smoke-blackened coastal villages. Soon after the beginning of September, the Persian army arrived in force, and on the fourth or fifth, watchers from Salamis saw a pall of smoke rise over the burning Acropolis.

Defeatism was in the air: several commanders were so alarmed that they walked out of a council meeting and "hoisted sail for immediate flight." Again there was talk of a retreat to the Isthmus. Themistocles told Eurybiades, in private, that once this happened, the whole allied fleet would break up. The Greeks, notorious individualists, possessed singularly little team spirit. In public, however, Themistocles argued that sea and land strategy were indissoluble. To fight in the Salamis channel would give the Greeks every advantage. In a confined space, tactics were more important than numbers or speed. Finally, Themistocles resorted to threats: if they refused to fight at Salamis, he said, he would pull out the entire Athenian contingent. At this, Eurybiades gave in, and the other commanders followed suit.

Xerxes had problems of his own. He could not attack the Peloponnese by sea until he had dealt with the fleet at Salamis. Whatever he did, he must act fast: it was already mid-September. Themistocles, who was a first-class judge of human nature, guessed that the Great King would grasp at anything that seemed to offer a quick solution. The Athenian therefore summoned his children's tutor, an Asiatic Greek named Sicinnus, and secretly sent him to Xerxes with a letter. In this letter Themistocles made three claims: that the allies were quarreling among themselves, that many would desert or change sides in a showdown battle, and that some already planned to slip away to the Isthmus during the night. If Xerxes blocked both exits from the straits, Themistocles advised, and struck at once, the Great King would capture or destroy the entire Greek fleet.

What Themistocles wrote was not only plausible, but in many respects was all too true. It was also just what Xerxes wanted to hear and he was therefore completely taken in by the deception. The duped Great King acted at once. The Egyptian squadron was sent to block the channel between Salamis and Megara. A large body of Persian infantry landed on the island of Psyttaleia at the entrance to the narrows. Other Persian and Phoenician squadrons moved up along the Attic coastline. Thus Xerxes' crews were up and active most of the night—and exhausted by morning. Xerxes had taken the bait, the blockade was complete. It only remained to be seen whether he would press home his attack into the sound. On that everything hung. As was said afterwards, all Greece that day stood on the razor's edge.

At first light of day on September 29, the Greek crews assembled by their ships, ready for action. Themistocles was chosen to address them and his speech, on the theme "All is at stake" became legendary. It fired his men's hearts, and, fiercely elated, the crews rowed out into the channel. But something more than mere patriotic fervor was needed to win the day and accounts of the battle suggest that meticulous planning had been under-

Two Greek soldiers, from a marble tombstone found at Salamis.

A golden age for Athens

The theater of Dionysus, at Athens, where Aeschylus' play *The Persians* was produced in 472 B.C. Aeschylus wrote the play for performance here, after having taken part in the Salamis campaign.

Horsemen in procession, taking part in a festival in honor of Athena; from a frieze in the Parthenon.

taken well before the battle actually took place.

The allied contingents were distributed among three harbors—Salamis itself, and the two shelving inlets north of the town, where the main force was concentrated. In Salamis harbor, detached from the fleet's battle formation were stationed the crack squadrons of Aegina and Megara. The northernmost position of the main force was held by the Corinthians, who had orders to guard the Bay of Eleusis against a surprise attack by the Egyptians in the Megara channel. The central allied line—Spartans on the right wing, Athenians on the left—moved out from shore to form beyond St. George's Island. At first the ships peeled off northwards—a critical moment, for this move was a carefully calculated feint to lure on the enemy.

Seeing the main part of the fleet heading north, the Persians must have believed that it was what they had been told to expect—a demoralized Greek retreat. A decision was taken at once. The Persian rowers bent to their oars, and the line moved forward through the narrows into the sound. From his golden throne, set on an eminence above the Attica shore, Xerxes watched their advance—at first with pride, then with mounting anxiety, and finally in anguish and despair. As more and more of his warships crowded into the narrows, they began to foul each other. Some had to be pulled out of line, causing considerable disorder. Xerxes was not the only commander to discover that it is much easier to start an advance than it is to stop it.

The leading Persian squadrons naturally slackened their speed when the Greeks—in battle formation now, and far from demoralized—came sweeping towards them in a wide crescent. To create yet greater chaos, the Persian admiral was killed almost at once, and his subordinate officers began shouting contradictory orders from every side. With such a press behind them, they could hardly have backed water now even if they had so wished. In a few minutes the whole channel was a logjam. The only alternative left to the Persians was to attack. But the Greeks, with more room to maneuver, encircled them in a tightening noose, pressing them still closer, brazen rams smashing through their timbers or shearing off their oar-banks. As the jammed Persian vessels struggled to withdraw, the Aeginetan squadron moved out from its reserve position and took them in the flank.

As the battle turned into a rout, Xerxes sprang up from his throne in agonized and impotent fury. Aeschylus, who fought at Salamis, afterwards memorialized the scene in his play *The Persians*:

Crushed hulls lay upturned on the sea, so thick
You could not see the water, choked with wrecks

And slaughtered men: while all the shores and reefs
Were strewn with corpses. Soon in wild disorder
All that was left of our fleet turned tail and fled.
But the Greeks pursued us, and with oars or broken
Fragments of wreckage split the survivors' heads
As if they were tunneys or a haul of fish:
And shrieks and wailing rang across the water
Till nightfall hid us from them.

Against all odds—and at the eleventh hour—
Greece had been saved; and not even his many
bitter enemies could deny that Themistocles had
saved her. Persian strategy had depended on close
cooperation between fleet and army; the fleet was
now virtually out of action, and the vast land force
had no option but to retreat. Xerxes' son-in-law
Mardonius remained in Greece, with perhaps
60,000 men; but a year later, in 479, an allied
army led by the Spartan Regent Pausanias
destroyed him also. Hostilities with Persia continued, sporadically, for years, but the specter of
invasion and occupation vanished after Salamis,
never to return.

Writing of Leonidas at Thermopylae—but it
might equally well have been of Themistocles at
Salamis—William Golding says, in a memorable
and moving essay: "If you were a Persian . . .
neither you nor Leonidas nor anyone else could
foresee that here thirty years' time was won for
shining Athens and all Greece and all humanity . . .
A little of Leonidas lies in the fact that I can go
where I like and write what I like. He contributed
to set us free." Salamis was the triumph of free men
over autocrats, of men who won, against odds,
precisely because they were fighting for an ideal.
Only free men, proud of their freedom, could
have produced the imperishable achievements in

architecture, sculpture, and drama that have
made Athens immortal: the vision of a Phidias,
the thundering choruses of Aeschylus, the proud,
gay, confident humor of Aristophanes. Under
Persian overlordship, Athens might have achieved
much; but not this, and not in the same spirit.

This story does not have a happy ending; not, at
least, in the short run. Less than ten years after his
great victory, Themistocles was hounded into
exile. He eventually died by his own hand,
a reluctant hanger-on at the court of the country
he had defeated, Persia. Pausanias was executed
by his own countrymen, probably on a trumped-up
charge. Under her new leaders, Athens, having
fought in the name of freedom, proceeded to build
an imperial system of her own, of "subject-allies"
who were not barbarians, but Greeks.

The fifth century, which had dawned so brightly,
ended in defeat and despair, with the long, drawn-
out struggle between Athens and Sparta. Yet
there is a moral here. Freedom means, in the last
resort, the freedom to go to hell in your own way;
better Athenian irresponsibility on an Assembly
vote than benevolent autocratic paternalism.
That is the lesson which Salamis bequeathed to
Greece, to Europe, and, ultimately to the whole
Western world. We forget it at our peril.

PETER GREEN

Pericles, the Athenian
statesman who was chiefly
responsible for the disastrous
war with Sparta. The drain on
the resources of Athens
caused by this lengthy and
bitter struggle led to her
defeat and to the temporary
collapse of the democracy that
had defeated the Persians.

83

The "classical" period of Greece, during which the finest products of Greek civilization were achieved, has been defined as beginning after the victory over the Persians. Its end is marked by the appearance of Macedonian soldiers in Greece, and the capitulation of the Greek cities to their semi-Greek conquerors from the north. This was the first stage in the vast program of military expansion under the Macedonian king, Alexander, which ended with his death, the subject of the next chapter. Macedonian expansion changed the whole face of the East: in the West events were less momentous, though in the same year as the battle of Salamis the Greeks of Syracuse held back a major attack on Sicily by the Carthaginians.

Achilles and Patroclus

The sea victory at Salamis had been engineered by the brilliant Athenian commander, Themistocles. The land victory at Plataea, which so decisively put an end to the Persian campaign in Greece, was the work of the Peloponnesians, especially of the Spartan commander, Pausanias, and his men. Pausanias was then given the task of liberating the Ionian coastal cities from Persia, but they seem to have feared his potential as a new tyrant, as did the Spartan *ephors* or elders, and he was relieved of his mission. Athens then took up the coastal war for which she was obviously so much better suited than Sparta, organizing the islands and cities into a confederacy under Athenian leadership, the Delian League. This league was put on a formal basis, with the allies contributing ships and money for defense. But, dominated as it was by Athens, it was only a question of time before it became a *de facto* Athenian empire. The Ionian kinship shared by its members might have been expected to form some basis for a closer tie, but the tradition and outlook of the

polis or city-state was not compatible with the idea of "nation" as we understand it today. The formation of a league was the nearest the Greeks came to national unity until the conquests of Alexander imposed a temporary unity on the Greek world. This meant that mainland Greece achieved an identity, if only through its geographical insignificance within a wider community, that of the *oikoumene* (the whole inhabited world).

But meanwhile, the formation of the Delian League consolidated the division of Greece into two main power blocs: the Peloponnesian League with Sparta at its head, and Athens and her "empire." These groups developed mutually hostile ideologies, based on the very different political system of Sparta and Athens.

Athens

Athens at this period had achieved the ultimate in Greek democracy. It was not total democracy, as we would understand it, for a large percentage of her population were

Relief of Demeter and Persephone

slaves, with very limited political rights. But Athens had developed a greater measure of popular representation than perhaps any other city or state has ever done.

Sparta

In contrast, Sparta was still theoretically ruled by her two kings and council of elders or ephors, below which were the citizen-élite, the *perioeci* and *helots*. Thus, oligarchy (rule of the few) was the basis of Spartan government, and democracy (the power of the *demos* or people) in Athens.

Athena

While the Delian League was successful in holding the allies together under Athens' leadership, and while Persia remained an obvious threat and a symbolic enemy to hold the Greeks together, no confrontation with the Peloponnesian bloc occurred. Persia was decisively beaten off Salamis (Cyprus) in 451, and obliged to conclude a peace with the Greeks. The Delian League clearly had less raison d'être now that the Persian menace had been contained, but Athens did not want to relinquish her position of dominance. The chains of empire were tightened by the establishment of colonies of Athenian citizens (*cleruchies*) at vital points in allied territory, guarding all-important supply routes to Athens. The champion of democracy might after all be a tyrant in disguise.

Leonidas, King of Sparta

Pericles

This extension of temporary military leadership into control of an empire took place under the rule of the great Pericles (470–429). The stability that lasted while Athens and her navy remained unchallenged in the Aegean enabled the arts of civilization to flourish in an unprecedented way. Athens itself was the glittering hub of intellectual and artistic activity. In the fifth century it became the center for philosophy, drawing together philosophers from all over the Greek world who previously had had no one meeting place. While the Greeks took much of their knowledge from the East—mathematics and astronomy in particular—they developed their own methods of scientific inquiry and philosophy. The power of pure reason led to the questioning of treasured concepts about life and society; and the Sophists, who advocated such a critical use of knowledge and education, provoked a strong reaction from the more conservative elements in Athens.

Socrates

The great teacher and philosopher became notorious for his ability to criticize anything and everything, though he was in fact challenging the extreme and wayward scepticism of the Sophists. He nevertheless became a scapegoat for the excesses of the Sophists' philosophical contortions, and preferred to die rather than recant. Such was the seriousness with which philosophy was treated by both its practitioners and the people of Athens.

Religion and temples

Philosophy did not entirely dispense with the gods, who were still an integral part of Greek culture everywhere. Since religion centered on the performance of the cult of a particular god or goddess, ceremonies mattered much more than doctrine, so philosophy was not a radical alternative. Religion was essentially bound up with the life of the *polis*, and large sums were spent on erecting temples to tutelary deities. These magnificent temples offered perfect opportunities for the expression of the

Socrates, Plato and Herodotus

Greek artistic genius, and the architecture and sculpture of this period has haunted European civilization from that time to the present day.

Greek drama

The Greeks of this period also produced remarkable new developments in literary form. The creation of the theatre, or more specifically, the creation of a permanent repertory of written plays, dates from the birth of Attic tragedy in the incomparable works of Aeschylus (525–456), written at the time of the struggle with Persia. Sophocles (497–406) and Euripides (480–406) continued the tradition of Attic drama,

Comic actors

and Aristophanes' (444–380) delightful plays, full of wit and sharp digs at the politicians, developed the new art of comedy.

Plato

Socrates' unwritten teachings were put into elegant and powerful words by the philosopher and writer Plato. His works, models of lucidity and style, include two stimulating and fundamental treatments of political theory, *The Republic* and *The Laws*.

The Athenian search for truth was passionate and pragmatic. Plato's works examined the real world of the Greek *polis*, and formulated more or less ideal solutions to the problems of city life, but he even tried out his theories in a practical experiment. The tyrant Dionysus II of Syracuse was at his own request carefully educated by Plato to be the "ideal ruler," the embodiment of Plato's wise philosopher-king. The experiment failed, as Dionysus proved too easily distracted by human pleasures, but it shows the extraordinary status of philosophy in Greek society.

Herodotus and Thucydides

The politics of the Periclean age profoundly influenced historical as well as other literary forms. Herodotus of Halicarnassus, proverbially "the father of history," produced a study of the Persian Wars that initiated true historical analysis where before only the uncritical tabulation of chronicles had existed. Athens' tight hold on the Aegean and the exacerbation of her relations with Sparta came to a head in 431, and war broke out. The ensuing conflict brought down the Athenian empire. Such a momentous event caused the historian Thucydides to ponder on the reasons for such a calamity. His work on the Peloponnesian War and the destruction of Athens' greatness, analyzing one of the most exciting and disturbing periods of history, is one of the most penetrating and skillful pieces of historical writing ever produced.

Victorious Sparta

The Peloponnesian War left Sparta victorious, and the Athenian navy and defenses were destroyed. Sparta was to enjoy only a brief period of hegemony in Greece. The war was concluded in 404: by 401 Sparta was embroiled with the Persians and, in Greece, was faced with an attack from her allies who were dissatisfied with her treatment of them. War followed.

Thebes

The city of Thebes, which had developed a highly efficient army under the brilliant general Epaminondas, emerged as victor from the struggle, destroying the Spartan army at Leuctra in 371. Victory brought with it leadership of the other Greek cities, but Thebes' domination was resented just as Sparta's (and Athens') had been. The pattern of intermittent wars, the shattering of one city's armed power to permit the emergence of another to dominate a federation of cities, was ominous in its repeti-

Head of charioteer

tion. Clearly the economic and political decline of Greece was a reality. The situation of the Greek cities could conceivably be exploited by a number of external powers—the Carthaginians' sphere of influence dangerously overlapped the Greek settlements in the western Mediterranean, and Persian ambitions might flourish again in the East. As it happened, the resolution of Greece's discord and decline came firmly from a direction that few people could have expected at the time.

Philip of Macedonia

To the north of Greece proper lay the kingdom of Macedonia, peopled by "barbarians" in Greek terms, though the ruling family was recognized as Greek. Feudal wars and local quarrels with the Illyrians were the Macedonians' traditional occupations, but a strong state emerged under King Philip II. He had spent some time as a hostage in Thebes and had absorbed knowledge of the Greek way of life, and, more important, knowledge of military procedure

from the famous Theban troops. Under his rule the military potential of Macedonia was developed and organized.

The new power of Macedonia grew visibly as Philip intervened in Thessaly and had himself elected as military commander. The presence of a strong state to the north produced various reactions among the Greeks. One line of thought, voiced by the orator Demosthenes, warned against Philip as a threat to the "liberty of Greece." The orator Isocrates championed the idea of Philip as the strong leader who was needed to unite the Greeks and lead them out of the morass of their political and military conflicts. The choice of the Greeks hardly mattered anyway. Philip was obviously aiming at the leadership of Greece, and there was no effective way to limit his designs. Military conflict with the Macedonians followed, and the last remaining Greek army of consequence, that of Thebes, was defeated together with Athenian soldiers at Chaeronea in 338. Philip became *hegemon*, or ruler, of

Philip II of Macedonia

yet another Greek league, comprising all the major Greek cities except Sparta, whose absence hardly mattered since she was no longer powerful.

Alexander

At the battle of Chaeronea, Philip's son Alexander played a decisive role in the victory, and proved himself a great military commander. His father dreamed of taking final revenge against the Persians on their own ground. Alexander inherited this ambition, and how he achieved this and much more is the subject of our next chapter.

The Death of Alexander the Great

In 336 Philip of Macedonia, in northern Greece, was assassinated. His successor, both as king and as leader of the League of Corinth, was his twenty-year-old son Alexander. In addition to the throne the young Alexander inherited his father's mission—to take revenge on the Persians on their own ground. The fulfilling of that mission and its consequences constitute one of the most glittering pages in the history of the ancient world. Alexander may not have wanted to fuse the traditions of East and West in the empire he created, but he gave Hellenism to posterity, thus bequeathing a truly international culture for the civilized world.

Twelve years had passed since Alexander, the young king of Macedonia and captain-general of the League of Corinth, had stood at the helm of his ship, guiding it over the Hellespont to the shores of Asia—twelve years and twenty thousand miles of Asian roads. Now, in 323 B.C., in a world that he himself had shaken and transformed, he lay dying in his Babylonian palace, and at the doors the soldiers clamored to see their leader. The rumor had spread that Alexander was dead already, and that his death had been concealed by the guards. At last the doors were thrown open to the rough horsemen and pikemen of Macedonia; with bewilderment on their faces, they crowded silently past the king's bed. Alexander was in his last fever, beyond speech and almost beyond life, but he made the effort to raise his yellowed face and nod some kind of greeting.

That night his generals—Seleucus and Peucestas, Peithon and Cleomenes—went to the temple of Serapis and asked if they should bring their leader to the god, but the oracle answered that it would be better for him to remain in his palace. There, soon afterwards, Alexander died. His illness had been malaria, the last of many bouts he had suffered on his campaigns; but it was malaria assisted by hard drinking and by the fury of a man fighting against unaccustomed ill-fortune.

Alexander died only seven years after the king he had displaced on the throne of Persia—Darius III, last of the Achaemenid line founded by the great Cyrus in the sixth century B.C. For almost two hundred years, since the fall of the Ionian cities to Cyrus in 545, Persia and Greece had been intimately linked. Darius I had been defeated at Marathon in 490, Xerxes at Salamis in 480 and Plataea in 479. But Persians still ruled over Greeks in Ionia, and by playing upon the rivalry between Sparta and Athens, they contrived to interfere in the affairs of the Greek states in Europe. Greeks sold their services to Persia, as mercenaries and craftsmen; they helped to build the great palaces at Susa and Persepolis; and as the Persians themselves grew soft from easy living, the paid Hellenes gradually became the most reliable corps in the vast and unwieldy army of the Persian King of Kings.

Accepting Persian pay, the Greeks observed Persian weaknesses. The epic story of the Ten Thousand—the Greek mercenaries who alone in the army of Cyrus the Younger stood firm at the battle of Cunaxa in 401, then fought their way to the Black Sea—became not only a literary classic in the hands of Xenophon, but also an inspiration to more ambitious men. King Agesilaus of Sparta was certainly not without hopes of considerably reducing the Persian domain in Asia Minor, and periodically the Athenians thought of revenge when they remembered how Xerxes had desecrated and destroyed their temples.

The great Attic orator Isocrates preached not only the union of the Hellenic world, but also a crusade against Persia, the natural enemy of the Hellenes. When he saw no one among the Greeks likely to fulfill his wishes, he looked to Philip II of Macedonia, a Hellenized barbarian who claimed descent from Achilles, Hercules and, for good measure, Perseus. Philip aspired to become the protector of neighboring Greece, and in 338 the League of Corinth entered into an arrangement for mutual defense with him and appointed him captain-general of the joint Greek and Macedonian armies. Philip persuaded the League to approve a war against Persia; before he could lead it, however, he was killed by an assassin. In 336 his son Alexander, twenty years old, succeeded to the throne of Macedonia and the captaincy of the League.

Never has any man been more fitted for his hour—an hour that offered a whole world to conquer and remake. Alexander's phenomenal beauty may be a legend fostered by flattering

Bust of Alexander as a young man; probably an idealized representation.

Opposite Alexander, on horseback, at the battle of Issus. This mosaic, found at Pompeii, is thought to be a copy of an original painting of *c.* 330 B.C.

Greek soldiers fighting Asiatics; a relief panel from the "Alexander Sarcophagus," which was found in the royal cemetery at Sidon, Phoenicia, and dates from the late fourth century B.C.

artists and chroniclers; but of his genius there can be no doubt. His strategic vision, his tactical originality and his grasp of military engineering are too well known to need discussion here. From the beginning the savage courage of Alexander the warrior was balanced by other, more humane forms of audacity. The influence of Aristotle, his childhood tutor, had not been in vain. Alexander's ruthlessness was Macedonian, but his intellectual curiosity and tolerance were Hellenic. More than any other great man of action, with the exception of Pericles, he represented the questing Greek mind. He became a great explorer and the inspirer of generations of geographers. In planning his expeditions he included philosophers, naturalists and topographers as well as military engineers. "If I were not Alexander, I would like to be Diogenes," he is supposed to have said. It is this combination of conqueror and philosopher that makes Alexander so fascinating and so historically significant.

The story of his conquests is familiar. He set out in 334 from his Macedonian capital of Pella, which he was never to see again. Crossing to Asia Minor, he defeated the Persians at the Battle of Granicus and liberated the Ionian cities. Late the next year, campaigning down the coast of Phoenicia, he defeated the main Persian army at Issus, and put Darius to ignominious flight. Taking his time to besiege and destroy Tyre and Gaza, he proceeded to Egypt, acquired a legendary parent in the god Amon, and showed a new, constructive side to his leadership by founding the first and greatest of all the Alexandrias, the queen city of the Hellenistic world.

Having consumed in such methodical fashion the western perimeter of the Persian empire, Alexander next aimed a blow at the heart. In the autumn of 331 he marched into Mesopotamia and met Darius on the field of Gaugamela. The elephants and the scythe-armed chariots of the Persian king, the multitudes of warriors he had drawn from every distant corner of the Achaemenid dominions, were of no avail against Alexander's cavalry and the Macedonian phalanx.

Totally defeated, Darius fled into the depths of Bactria; Alexander proceeded as conqueror to Babylon and Susa, then eventually to Persia proper, the center and birthplace of Darius' power. At last Alexander sat on the throne in the palace of Persepolis, built by Ionian craftsmen. The champion of Greece was transformed into the Great King of Asia, yet without entirely ceasing to be the champion of Greece. From then on the effort to reconcile his Hellenism with his Oriental power became the overriding element in Alexander's life.

The campaigns continued. Darius, pursued into Central Asia in a series of extraordinary marches, was killed by his own general, Bessus. Bessus and other Persian captains were slaughtered or incorporated into the Alexandrian pattern of government. Then, in 327, Alexander launched an expedition to India.

It was at this point that Alexander's incredible run of luck was reversed. Ironically, the first defeat of his life came at the hands of his own men. In 326, on the bank of the Jhelum River in India, his troops refused to pass beyond the Punjab into the lands of the great kings who ruled in middle India. "A commander like you, with an army like ours," his general Coenus said to him then, "has nothing to fear from any human enemy; but remember, fortune cannot be foretold, and no man may protect himself from what it will bring." Fortune had taken Alexander to the throne of the Achaemenid King of Kings in Persepolis, to the heartlands of Central Asia where Samarkand and Bukhara would later rise, and over the Hindu Kush in search of the great River of Ocean which he imagined washed the foothills of the Himalayas. But after the events on the Jhelum, he turned reluctantly back from the Punjab to fight his way down the Indus Valley, nearly dying from an arrow that pierced his lung when he assaulted the fortress of a fierce tribe in Sind.

There followed a terrible march over the deserts of Gedrosia, with men and beasts dying of thirst and Alexander sharing the privations his infantry endured. On his return to Babylon he found that

The savage courage of a warrior

many of the men he had left in charge had taken advantage of his absence in India to plunder the people and desecrate monuments. It was bad enough that Persians, who were indebted to him for his clemency, should do this; it was more bitter news to hear that Harpalus, his companion since childhood, had plundered the Persian treasure and then had fled to evade Alexander's wrath, dying at the hands of a fellow robber on the way back to Greece. Then, at Opis, there had been a mutiny by the Macedonian veterans, whom Alexander proposed to send home and replace by Persian levies; thirteen of his men were executed for that revolt. Finally his beloved friend Hephaestion had died in Ecbatana—perhaps also of malaria—and Alexander had abandoned himself to a prolonged and immoderate grief.

From all these misfortunes, Alexander emerged in the spring of 323 to plan an expedition that would revive his military glory and satisfy his perennial longing to know the unknown. To explore and subdue Arabia, a region little known even to the Persians, would make up for his failure to conquer India. A great harbor to hold a thousand ships had been dredged beside the Euphrates, and fleets had been assembled and manned by Phoenician and Ionian sailors. Troops had been recruited in Persia and Lydia and Caria; it would no longer be a Macedonian army that Alexander led, but an army of all the peoples under his rule. June 7, 323, was fixed for the start of the expedition. Five days before the scheduled departure, Alexander performed sacrifices to assure his success, gave wine to his men and drank heavily with his friends. Medius, his favorite since the death of

Above The pass of Issus, site of the battle in which Alexander defeated the main Persian army and put King Darius to flight.

Below Asiatics in Persian dress fighting a lioness; a relief panel from the "Alexander Sarcophagus."

Revenge on Persia

Hephaestion, induced him to continue drinking late into the night, and, before he went to sleep, the fever had already seized him. During the next few days Alexander insisted on continuing his sacrifices and giving orders to his army officers and to Nearchus, his admiral. But his condition became grave, and he was carried to a summer house beside the river, and finally to his palace. By this time he had lost the power of speech. Eleven days after the outset of his fever he died, at the age of thirty-three. The expedition to Arabia was never undertaken.

During his lifetime Alexander and his empire remained a disturbing enigma to his Greek and Macedonian followers. Remembering the leader who stood at Issus and exhorted his men with the cry, "We are free men, they are slaves," the Greeks were puzzled when Alexander tried to introduce into his court the Persian custom of prostration before the throne. When the sophist Callisthenes openly voiced his disapproval, he died—no one knows how—as a martyr to his own philosophic candor. Alexander's companions murmured angrily when the conquered Persians were welcomed as equals at the court. Finally, one night, after drinking heavily, the king quarreled with Cleitus, who had saved his life at the battle of Granicus, and killed him. The division between the ambitions of Alexander and the reservations of his followers put an end to the Indian expedition and sparked off the mutiny of Opis. After Alexander's death, there would be many Hellenes to claim that he turned away from Greece and became an Oriental ruler.

In a way, this was true. One can even mark a turning point at Ecbatana, in the spring of 330, when Alexander dismissed as allies the Greek soldiers of the League and rehired as mercenaries

Above Temple relief from Persepolis, showing a lion attacking a bull. The vigorous carving is typical of the art of the Persian empire at the time of Darius.

Below The ruins of the palace of Persepolis, the heart of Darius' great empire. It was built largely by Ionian Greeks, and was destroyed by Alexander.

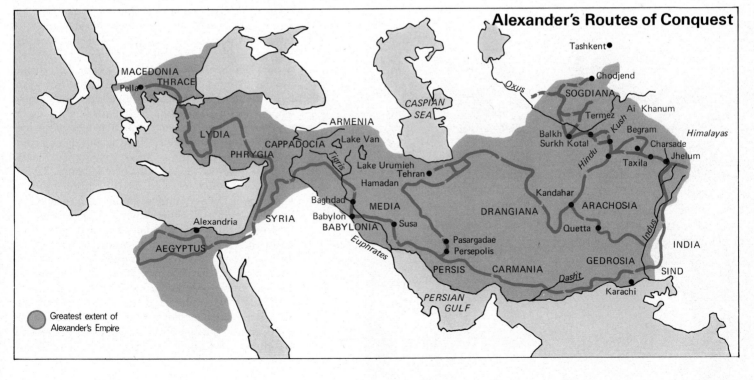

The excavated remains of the Persian palace at Susa, in eastern Mesopotamia.

those who chose to stay. His role as captain-general of Greece was discarded; now he claimed the Persian empire as his by right of conquest. Already, that winter, he had begun to fill his army with Persian recruits, trained in the Macedonian manner. In 325 he arranged an interracial mass marriage festival at Susa. Alexander had already in 327 married a Persian princess, Roxana, daughter of the Bactrian chieftain Oxyartes. Now he chose as a second wife the daughter of Darius, persuading eighty of his closest companions to pick Asiatic wives and ordering ten thousand soldiers to do likewise. Later, after the mutiny of Opis, there was a festival of reconciliation attended by nine thousand people; led by Greek priests and Persian Magi, the assembled guests prayed that the Macedonians and Persians might rule the empire together in true harmony.

For the claims that have been made that Alexander was the first ruler with a truly international vision, there is little further evidence. Diodorus Siculus, writing as a contemporary of Julius Caesar, certainly saw Alexander as believing in a real union of the people of Asia and Europe, but his view of history was necessarily influenced by the Stoic and Epicurean egalitarian ideas. It is difficult to argue against historians who claim that Alexander conceived not a true internationalism, but merely a renovated Persian empire, streamlined by Greek logic and efficiency and ruled by a dual master race.

What did Alexander plan for the physical extension of his empire? He had already won the greater part of the antique world. After Arabia he hoped to conquer the lands around the Caspian Sea. He had left garrisons in the Punjab and at the mouth of the Indus, and there is little doubt that one day he meant to complete the conquest of India. We can only speculate about his plans for the Mediterranean, but the fact that the Carthaginians, the Etruscans and even the far Iberians sent ambassadors to congratulate him on his conquests suggests an unseemly rush to make terms before his deep-eyed look turned westward. Writing his history of Alexander's expeditions, in the second century A.D., Arrian speaks of his

The legacy to the world

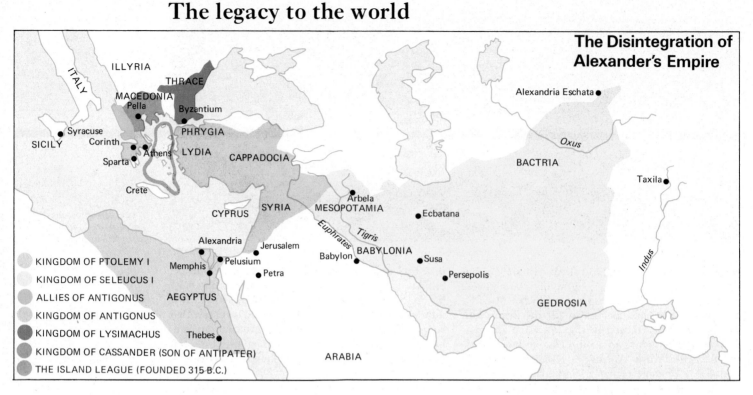

The Disintegration of Alexander's Empire

KINGDOM OF PTOLEMY I
KINGDOM OF SELEUCUS I
ALLIES OF ANTIGONUS
KINGDOM OF ANTIGONUS
KINGDOM OF LYSIMACHUS
KINGDOM OF CASSANDER (SON OF ANTIPATER)
THE ISLAND LEAGUE (FOUNDED 315 B.C.)

"insatiable desire to extend his possessions," and it is unlikely that, if he had lived, he would have left unattempted the conquest of Italy, France and Spain, where the Greeks had already long-established colonies. His eventual aim was almost certainly to unite under his own rule the whole of the known world.

Alexander profoundly affected the world through which he passed. At his death his empire was frozen within the boundaries he had created, and the only later extension of Hellenistic rule was in the eastern marches where he had merely conquered and passed on. Two centuries after his death the Greek kings of Bactria sent their cavalry probing toward the boundaries of the Chinese empire, and in the middle of the second century B.C. Menander, the Greek king of the Punjab and a philosophic warrior of the same temper as Alexander himself, fulfilled his predecessor's ambition by leading an army of Greeks and Persians down the valley of the Ganges to capture Pataliputra, the capital of Hindustan.

After Alexander's death, his empire fell immediately into disunity. His heir was Roxana's yet unborn child, the unfortunate Alexander IV, who was eventually murdered in 311 by Cassander, the son of Alexander's general Antipater. Antipater was nominal regent; in fact Alexander's generals, known as the Successors—Seleucus, Ptolemy, Antigonus, Lysimachus, Eumenes—divided the empire. Ptolemy departed first to his satrapy of Egypt, taking with him the body of Alexander to bury it in Alexandria. In 306, when all the heirs had been eliminated, the Successors, or *Diadochi*, named themselves kings. Only one of them, Ptolemy, died peacefully in his bed; the rest were killed in the bitter struggles dividing them. For a while it seemed as though Antigonus might reunite the empire, but Ptolemy and Seleucus were too strong for him, and the Hellenistic world remained divided between three great kingdoms—Macedonia, under the descendants of Antigonus, Egypt under the Ptolemies, and Syria, embracing also Persia and Mesopotamia, under the Seleucids. Smaller realms like Pergamum arose under the shadow of these great kingdoms, and new city-states like Rhodes and Byzantium became commercial powers in their own rights.

Despite all this fragmentation, the Hellenistic age was a time of vigorous civilization. It has been given too little credit for its achievements because historians have concentrated on its divisions and on the dramatic decline of its kingdoms in the face of the threat of Rome. The Successors, in spite of

Gold armlet from the Oxus Treasure.

their conflicts, ruled over a surprisingly homogeneous world. Asian kingdoms in Pontus and Bithynia and Cappadocia adopted the Hellenistic culture and political systems, and even the Parthian and Scythian rulers, finding their way into Greek Bactria, became Hellenized.

It was not entirely the kind of empire Alexander may have envisaged. The Successors had no use for his visions of copartnership between Greeks and Asians. Only Seleucus retained the Persian wife he had been given at the great marriage feast of Susa, and the ruling castes of all the Hellenistic kingdoms consisted either of Greeks—with a dwindling proportion of Macedonians—or of Hellenized members of the native aristocracy. This elite inhabited its own enclaves, typically Greek cities with democratic constitutions, and its settlements included people of all classes who migrated from the overpopulated Greece of the third and second centuries. The native people remained in the villages and retained their own cultures, so a marked horizontal rift, which Alexander had probably not foreseen, developed between Greeks and Asians. Yet, unlike the Romans, the Greeks of the diaspora never conceived a universal citizenship. They were citizens of their individual communities, subjects of the Greek kings, but the bonds that united a man in Alexandria of Egypt with a man in Alexandria Bucephala of the Punjab were cultural and not political.

The most durable of the Hellenistic states were those that eventually made some compromise with the native cultures. By the beginning of the second century the main states were decaying fast; by the middle of the century Macedonia and the Seleucid kingdom had been overwhelmed by the Romans, and the Greek kingdom of Bactria by the Sakas. But the Ptolemaic kings, who had accepted a place in the Egyptian religious hierarchy and had turned Alexandria into a great intellectual meeting place of East and West, survived; so did the Greek kings in India with their Buddhist affiliations. In fact, Cleopatra, last of the Ptolemies, and Hermaeus, last of the Indo-Greek monarchs, died at about the same time; the battle of Actium in 31 B.C. finally ended the political legacy of Alexander's conquests.

Yet even at Actium only one aspect of Alexander's heritage was destroyed. As Rostovtseff has pointed out, "the 'romanization' of the Hellenistic world was slight, the 'Hellenization' of the steadily expanding Latin world much more conspicuous." Later, from the eastern Rome of Constantinople, the Hellenistic world helped to give Eastern Christianity its special forms. To India, Alexander and his successors gave much of its art—the techniques of building and carving in stone and the Gandhara style—and the concept of a united rule that Chandragupta adopted when he founded the Mauryan empire. Even the Arabs, who finally destroyed the Greek cities of the East, retained Hellenistic science. Through Rome, Constantinople and the Arab world, Alexander contributed something to the new West of the Renaissance, even to

Greek influence on the art of western Asia was considerable. *Above* Sculptured scene in the Gandhara style of northwest India, an area once ruled by Hellenistic kings. *Below* Funerary busts from Palmyra, probably early-third century A.D. They illustrate the surviving influence of Hellenistic art.

lands he never conquered. If he failed to unify the world politically, he helped to turn it into an intellectual community, particularly when one remembers how much the great religions of Christianity, Mahayanist Buddhism and Islam owed to the exchange of ideas between Europe and Asia that he so materially assisted.

GEORGE WOODCOCK

The empire of Cyrus and Xerxes was vast. The empire left by Alexander on his death was even larger, and it did not outlast its founder. The most obvious reasons for its immediate breakup were the lack of overall homogeneity, the variety of individual characteristics and political traditions in the area it covered, and the virtual impossibility of establishing a strong central authority to hold it together. The theme of empire is a recurrent one throughout this volume: Xerxes, Alexander, Hannibal, Shih-huang-ti and lastly Augustus—all these men commanded empires. If we seek a key to the relative endurance of such empires, we should look for a durable and comprehensive administration. The great emperor Shih-huang-ti thoroughly organized the administration of his empire, and even though his dynasty was overthrown, the essential framework of the Chinese state remained. And we shall see that after the milestone of the battle of Actium, Augustus was to devote the greater part of his energy and ability to developing and improving an administration that would provide a lasting basis for the Roman Empire. Alexander's successors were more concerned with dividing the Near East among themselves than with pushing the territorial limits of their empire, as he had done, farther toward the mysterious East, as yet largely unknown to them. Contacts did

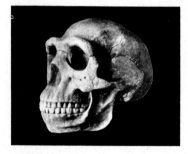

Skull of Peking Man

undoubtedly exist between the ancient Near East and China. Some scholars have sought to trace Mesopotamian influences in early Chinese culture, but they were extremely tenuous. However, a great civilization had been developing there from the second millennium B.C., and our next chapter will deal with a significant epoch in it. In preparation for it, we must now consider some of the fundamental aspects of Chinese civilization.

The Chinese thunder god

Prehistoric China

China has provided evidence of one of the earliest precursors of the human race (*homo sapiens*). In 1929 at the village of Chou K'ou Tien, about 26 miles southwest of Peking, skeletal remains were found of the so-called "Peking Man" (*Pithecanthropus pekinensis*). With a cranial capacity of about two-thirds of *homo sapiens*, this hominid, who lived about 300,000 B.C., made crude tools of stone and used fire. However, despite this early start, the subsequent development of culture in China during the Palaeolithic and Neolithic period remains obscure, chiefly because there has been relatively little archeological excavation.

The history of civilization in China is only adequately documented by archeological data from the Shang Dynasty (*c.* 1500–1027 B.C.). Later Chinese literature includes a rich mythology which tells of many emperors, beginning from 2356 B.C. As in similar records of other early peoples (e.g. the Sumerian King List and the genealogies in the *Book of Genesis*), incredibly long reigns are attributed to these emperors, who generally appear to have been of the culture-hero type. There are also a number of flood-myths, probably because the earliest centers of civilized life were in the area of the lower course of the Yellow River.

"Great Shang"

The most illuminating information about the culture of the Shang Dynasty has come from the excavation of its capital city, known as "Great Shang," near Anyang in north Honan, which dates from the twelfth and eleventh

centuries B.C. The most spectacular finds have been the "royal graves," which parallel, in the richness of the deposits and the number of skeletons, the "royal graves" found at the Sumerian city of Ur, in Mesopotamia. The remains of chariots, horses and their drivers show how important it was considered for the dead lord to take his transport with him into the tomb. The fine ritual bronzes which were found, some decorated with the celebrated *t'ao t'ieh* pattern, show the high quality of contemporary craftsmanship and the existence already of the distinctive characteristics of Chinese art.

"Oracle Bones"

Another kind of evidence, less impressive in appearance but of great historical significance, has been the so-called "Oracle Bones." It was apparently the practice at Anyang for augurs to apply a heated bronze implement to selected animal bones, and the resultant cracks were interpreted as answers to questions previously put. These questions and answers were often inscribed on the bones, and constitute the earliest extant evidence of Chinese writing.

A Confucian fable

Ancestor Worship

In primitive Chinese thought ancestor worship also involved a deep attachment to the soil, particularly to that bit of it where each family lived. It was the ancient custom to place both the newborn and the dying on the earth, thus symbolizing the need for contact with it at these two crises of man's life. In the primitive rural communities of China it was the custom also for marital intercourse to take place in the southwestern corner of the house, near to where the seed-corn was stored, and the dead, too, were buried close to this spot. Such customs sprang from the belief that the "family stock" lasted as long as the earth upon which the family lived. Thus, at any given moment, the greater part of the "family stock" lay buried in the family soil, with the living members, as it were, forming the individualized portion active above ground.

Within the ordinary family this sense of integration was expressed in a devoutly practiced cult of its ancestors. Their memories were preserved on tablets in the ancestral shrine, poor and meager though it may have been. On the son devolved the duties of being the chief mourner of his deceased father and minister of his mortuary ritual, while the grandson represented his deceased grandfather at the family cult. With the development of the ancestor cult in the feudal states of ancient China (*c.* 722–481 B.C.), the family of the ruler came to epitomize the various families of the state. The primitive connection between mankind and the soil was carefully preserved by siting the ancestral temple of the ruler in the seignorial town, close to the altar of the gods of soil and harvest.

Yin and Yang

It was probably during the feudal period of the later Chou Dynasty that another idea, which reflects a basic intuition of the Chinese mind, developed and found expression— the idea of *yin* and *yang*. This concept saw all cosmic existence as the product of an alternating rhythm of two complementary creative forces. The *yin* force or principle was regarded as feminine; it was associated with darkness, softness and inactivity. *Yang* was the male principle, characterized by light, hardness and activity; it was also associated with heaven, whereas *yin* was of the earth.

Human Nature

The *yin-yang* dualism was also used to explain human nature. Man was conceived with two souls which together with the body constituted him a living person. The *yin*-soul was identified with the primitive *kuei*, because it was of earthly origin and associated with the body from the moment of conception. During the individual's lifetime this *yin*-soul was called the *p'o*, and after death the *kuei*; it lingered on near the tomb but gradually faded to nothing. The *yang*-soul was regarded as the animating principle, which came from heaven as air or breath. It announced its presence in the first cry of the new-born infant, and it left the body as the last breath at death—there was a special ritual used by relatives for recalling this soul before it departed too far from the body. The *yang*-soul was known as the *hun* during life, and *shen* after death.

Ritual bronze vessel ; Shang dynasty

Confucius

The greatest figure in Chinese culture has been K'ung Fu-tsu or Confucius, as he is known in the West. He is reputed to have lived from 551 to 479 B.C., mainly in the small but cultured state of Lu (now in modern Shantung). Although his name has become associated with Confucianism, which is often regarded as the traditional religion of pre-Communist China, Confucius was not a religious prophet or teacher as, for example, were Moses, Zarathustra or the Buddha. Indeed, according to tradition, he definitely refused to discuss religious or

Confucius

metaphysical questions concerning divinity or human destiny. Confucius was essentially an ethical teacher. He taught that there was a *Tao*, or Way of Life, prescribed for men to follow, in order to maintain the proper balance or harmony that is fundamental to social happiness and the well-being of mankind.

Love of ancient rites

Confucius lived at a time when the old feudal society was breaking up, with resultant confusion of ideas and standards, strife and injustice. He seems to have belonged to, or became identified with, the *Ju*. These formed a scholar-class who were experts in the performance and interpretation of religious rites and exponents of a traditional learning. Looking back to what seemed the Golden Age of the Chou Dynasty, Confucius concluded that the proper observance of the ancient rites was necessary to integrate and preserve an ordered society. This Confucian view of the past profoundly affected the earliest extant records of Chinese history, particularly of the early Chou Dynasty. For these are largely idealized accounts of the establishment of the institutions and customs which Confucius and his followers approved.

Ti'en

Confucius certainly believed that the *Tao* or Way, which he presented, had divine authority. But his view of deity seems to have been essentially impersonal. Instead of using the ancient term *Shang Ti*, the Supreme Ancestor-Spirit or High God of the Shang Dynasty, he preferred *T'ien* (Heaven). He did, however, associate *T'ien* with a number of moral qualities, so that it does not appear only as a cold cosmic entity. Ritual in its various social forms, from the official sacrifices offered by the ruler to the mortuary service, owed by the individual to his ancestors, was essential to virtue.

Confucianism

Confucius achieved meager success during his lifetime, but his Way of Life appealed to the Chinese temperament, for his reputation steadily grew until he was recognized as China's greatest sage. He was honored by other high-sounding titles, and temples were dedicated to him; by some he was virtually regarded as a deity. There has been much discussion as to whether Confucianism, as the movement that stemmed from his teaching, should be described as a religion, for it lacks many distinctive religious attributes. Some scholars have preferred to call it an ethico-political philosophy.

Taoism

The idea of the *Tao* or Way, which Confucius invoked, was ancient and fundamental in Chinese culture. Confucius was primarily concerned with its social significance, although he was careful to emphasize its divine derivation. His idea, interpreted rather as an all-embracing cosmic process, was developed by other sages as a rival faith and practice; it appealed to

Han tomb interior

many who sought a more metaphysical creed than offered by Confucius and his disciples. Known as Taoism, with Lao-tzu as its legendary founder, this movement was based on the Chinese belief that man is a part of nature.

In time this Taoist belief produced a kind of nature-mysticism, and these ideas also inspired some beautiful painting, in which the Taoist sage merges into a landscape of mystical loveliness. Taoism, at its best, demanded of its devotees a high standard of intellectual ability as well as a capacity for mysticism; but because these qualities were not always to be found, the movement easily declined into forms of popular superstition. In this way, Taoism helped prepare the gradual establishment of Buddhism in China.

Sixth-century climacteric

Our milestones of history show the development of civilization throughout the world, and it is therefore worth noting here a curious but inexplicable phenomenon. The sixth century B.C. witnessed the beginnings of some of the great religions of mankind: Gautama, the Buddha, lived *c.* 563–483; Zarathustra was born about 570; Confucius about 551, and the foundations of Judaism were laid after the return of the exiled Jews from Babylonia. In the sixth century also came the dawn of a different movement which in the distant future was destined both to undermine and aid religion—in the cities of Ionia, Greek philosophy was born.

Building the Great Wall of China

Finding his country a patchwork of disparate states, Shih-huang-ti, the first Emperor of China, imposed upon it unity and coherence. Centralized administration demanded swift communications, so a vast network of roads and canals was thrown across the country. Weights and measures were standardized and the same writing script introduced throughout the land. But unity was of little avail without security, and to protect his new empire from the repeated invasions of Turco-Mongolian hordes, Shih-huang-ti built an immense wall that survives to this day. Across hill and valley, mile after mile, the mighty bastion is a vivid testimony to the willpower of an absolute monarch and the imagination of a creative genius.

The Great Wall (*opposite*) extends across some 1,400 miles of northern China. The section illustrated remains as it was when rebuilt by the Ming emperors (A.D. 1368–1644). The Wall had some 25,000 watchtowers, and models of it were a popular subject of Chinese art. The one above is of pottery, 33 inches high, and dates from the Han dynasty.

The Great Wall of China is probably the world's most stupendous monument to human ingenuity and industry, and purportedly is the only one of man's work that could be seen from the moon. The *Wan-li ch'ang ch'eng* or Wall of Ten Thousand *Li* (a *li* is approximately one-third of a mile) forms the country's northern boundary, extending some 1,400 miles from the Gulf of Chihli in the east to the sources of the Wei River in the far west of Kansu province.

Even today, centuries after its construction, the Wall remains an awe-inspiring sight. It climbs the sides of ravines and crests the watersheds of mountain ranges, doubling back on itself so frequently that its actual length is more than double 1,400 miles. In some stretches, particularly in the desolate desert regions of the far west, the Wall has been reduced to mere mounds of earth a few feet in height; other portions hundreds of miles in length are still in excellent repair—their stone, brick and mortar facings intact. The average height of these sections is twenty feet, and at top they are wide enough to permit six horsemen to pass abreast.

Although the Great Wall has been repaired and enlarged many times, the existing structure is mainly the result of restoration work undertaken during the Ming dynasty (A.D. 1368–1644). All reliable Chinese sources attribute the original building to the Ch'in dynasty ruler Shih-huang-ti, the self-styled First Emperor of all China. His imperial reign lasted only eleven years (221–210 B.C.), but for the preceding twenty-one years Shih-huang-ti had ruled the semi-barbaric border state of Ch'in in northwest China. With the assistance of able ministers, he had turned the full energies and resources of the Ch'in state to production and defense, and his kingdom rapidly became an irresistible military power.

In the year 211 B.C. the Ch'in ruler defeated the last of the feudal states into which China had been divided for centuries and proclaimed himself the First Emperor of China. Shih-huang-ti set himself the task of unifying his vast territories under the control of a strong centralized government and thus ending centuries of all but incessant internecine strife. Shih-huang-ti soon realized that the unification and pacification of his empire would be thwarted unless he could ensure the defense of his northern frontier, vulnerable to the constant incursions of China's traditional enemies, the warlike, nomadic Turco-Mongolian tribes who inhabited the northwestern steppes. Those barbarians, who "moved from place to place according to the water and grass, and had no walled cities or towns, settled habitation or agricultural occupation," had united under the Hsiung-nu, or Hun tribesman, by the time of the First Emperor.

From the beginning of his reign, the Emperor had been forced to send one expedition after another to drive back the swiftly moving Huns, who retreated over the wide Mongolian plains after each successful raid. Conquering the Mongols proved impossible; containing them within their own territories was all Shih-huang-ti could hope to achieve. To do so he embarked upon a construction project unparalleled in world history: the building of the Great Wall.

Shih-huang-ti was determined to construct a chain of strong fortifications and watchtowers along the entire length of his northern frontier and then to join them together by a massive wall. In 215 B.C. he dispatched General Meng-T'ien to the northern frontier with an army of 300,000 laborers and an uncounted number of political prisoners, convicted felons and other elements of the population that were considered dangerous or unproductive. There were already hundreds of miles of fortifications in existence along China's northern borders, built in earlier times by the states of Ch'in, Chao, Wei, and Yen to protect themselves from the Huns and the eastern Hu tribes. Those barriers were well

A new era is inaugurated

maintained, and wherever possible Meng-T'ien's engineers simply rebuilt and strengthened earlier fortifications.

Though there is little reliable information, numerous legends testify to the immensity of the builder's task, its appalling toll in human life and suffering and the remorseless speed of the Wall's construction. It has been estimated, for example, that if the materials used in building the Wall were to be transported to the equator, they would provide a wall eight feet high and three feet thick, encircling the entire globe. The Wall reportedly had 25,000 watchtowers within signaling distance of one another, each capable of accommodating one hundred men. Between the watchtowers, two parallel furrows, about twenty-five feet apart, were chiselled out of the solid rock. On this foundation, solid, squared granite blocks were then laid, and these were topped by two parallel courses of large bricks. The inner core was then filled with tamped earth. According to legend, the unwieldy granite blocks were often tied to teams of goats, who dragged them up the almost inaccessible ridges. It has been estimated that at one time roughly one-third of the able-bodied men of the empire were engaged either in building or defending the Wall, or in conveying the necessary supplies to the inhospitable regions that the Wall traversed.

So long as it could be effectively garrisoned, the Wall undoubtedly provided the rich agricultural plains of north China with some protection from Hun incursions, but it served another purpose as well. The Wall proved an effective barrier to those dissident indigenous groups within the empire who had been dispossessed of their lands and desired to defect to the enemy. Chinese scholars and peasants alike had much to offer the less sophisticated northern barbarians in the way of political, agricultural and economic expertise, and Shih-huang-ti was resolved that all defection attempts by sizeable groups should be frustrated.

The Wall solved another of Shih-huang-ti's domestic problems as well. Decades of almost ceaseless warfare had led to the creation of a huge standing army. Those soldiers, spread over the empire and inured to fighting, might easily prove a threat to the centralized government. Thus, the garrisoning of the Great Wall served a dual purpose, for besides protecting the frontier, it also kept a large part of the army permanently occupied some distance from the capital. In addition, it solved the problem of providing useful employment for China's vast numbers of landless vagabonds, prisoners and disillusioned scholars.

The sheer logistical problem of supplying those garrisons with food and equipment was an enormous drain on the economic resources of the empire, however. Apart from the Yellow River, few of north China's rivers were navigable for any appreciable distance, and the loaded supply barges

Above Head of a singer, from the period of the Warring States (fifth to third century B.C.), which ended with the establishment of the Ch'in dynasty under Shih-huang-ti, who proclaimed himself the first Emperor of China.

Below Bronze buckle with motif of struggling beasts, typifying the nomadic themes and vigorous execution of much early Chinese art.

had to be manhandled upstream against swiftly flowing currents. Carts traveling the barren regions often used up many of their supplies before reaching their intended destinations. Shih-huang-ti's attempts to supply provisions to the troops stationed along the Great Wall were a contributory cause in the speedy collapse of his empire.

Nevertheless, the Great Wall was a mighty material symbol of empire, an indication that for the first time in East Asian history a great power structure had arisen under the unified control of an absolute monarch. By almost every act, Shih-huang-ti repudiated China's centuries-old feudal-istic system. He saw himself as the inaugurator of a new era, and he ruthlessly destroyed the feudal states and their territorial magnates. The Emperor divided his lands into thirty-six (later forty-one) military districts, in which both military and civil authorities were responsible to the Emperor him-self. In those districts, the influence of the Confu-cian scholars was severely curtailed, and in 213 B.C. the Emperor moved to diminish further the power of the Confucians by ordering the destruction of those Confucian classics that the scholars invoked as "mirrors of the ancient golden age of universal peace and prosperity, under Sage-kings who ruled, not by force, but by virtue." State histories, except for those of Ch'in, and the writings of ancient philosophical schools were also destroyed.

The Confucian ideal of rule by etiquette and propriety and appeal to ancient precedents was replaced by standardized laws, which, though extremely harsh, were applicable to all. Peasants were given the right to own, buy and sell land. Agriculture was encouraged; commerce, which Shih-huang-ti regarded as non-productive, was repressed. Currency, weights and measures were all standardized—and by fixing the length of cart axles, communications along the roads through the loess-land of north China were measurably improved. Equally important was the unification of the written language through the introduction of a simplified script—a measure that, perhaps more than any other, advanced the cultural continuity of Chinese civilization.

To make organized revolt difficult, the weapons that had belonged to the feudal lords were melted down and their local fortifications were destroyed. Barbarian tribes that had inhabited north China for generations were expelled, while the southern barbarian tribes, who lived in what are now Kuangsi and Kuangtung provinces, were brought under Chinese jurisdiction by a brilliant campaign that included the digging of a twenty-mile-long canal to connect the great river systems of central and southern China.

The building of the Great Wall was not the First Emperor's only grandiose scheme. He put 700,000 convicts to work building a capital city, Hsien-yang in Shensi province, of a size and magnificence never before attempted. According to Chinese historians, 120,000 of the richest and most powerful families in the empire were transported

to the new capital. The Emperor sought to win them over by building exact replicas of the palaces those families had left behind and by loading them with titles and empty honors. For himself, Shih-huang-ti built an enormous palace near the capital, and a sepulcher under the shadow of Mount Li. Tree-lined radial roads fifty paces broad spread from Hsien-yang to all parts of the empire.

The First Emperor made frequent tours to different parts of his empire, and he often ascended the sacred mountains in outlying areas to make sacrifices. Extremely superstitious and morbidly fearful of death, Shih-huang-ti became the dupe of Taoist magicians, as he eagerly sought after the elixir of immortality. Impetuous, violent, cruel and despotic, Shih-huang-ti came to believe that

Kneeling girl, and convict without hands; two clay tomb figures from the early Han period. The amputation of the hands of convicts was a common punishment in China, but whether this is depicted here is uncertain, because of the state of preservation of the figure.

The vision of an empire-builder

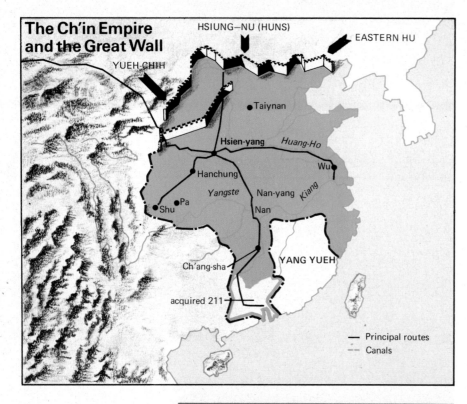

The Ch'in Empire and the Great Wall

HSIUNG—NU (HUNS)

EASTERN HU

YUEH-CHIH

Taiynan

Hsien-yang Huang-Ho

Wu

Hanchung

Yangste Nan-yang Kiang

Shu Pa Nan

YANG YUEH

Ch'ang-sha

acquired 211

— Principal routes
--- Canals

Bronze dagger and scabbard (Chou dynasty, seventh to sixth century B.C.), which owes much to nomadic influence both in its shape and in its decoration. The interlacing motif is probably derived from plaited ropes and leather thongs used by the nomads for their harness gear.

he was semidivine, and erected self-laudatory tablets throughout the empire. Gradually he became so mistrustful of even his closest associates that he segregated himself from his ministers and each night changed his sleeping quarters. Thus, towards the end of his life, the ruler of all China often could not be found when important matters needed decision.

Soon after the death of the First Emperor rebellion broke out, and within four years, in 206 B.C., the Ch'in dynasty came to an ignominious end. The concept of empire and the idea of the unity of all who lived south of the Great Wall were not lost, however, and even in times of imperial breakdown the vision of a united China remained. A centralized government had been established to promote large public works, exercise a monopoly over certain basic products, promote a common coinage and a common written language and maintain a large standing army.

The first ruler of the succeeding Han dynasty was astute enough to enforce most of the First Emperor's measures. There was a partial return to the old feudal system, however, as the new monarch granted fiefs to relatives and favorites. Furthermore, in his search for capable men to staff his huge administration he found it necessary to employ those who had been trained in Confucian ideas—and during the Han dynasty Confucianism came into its own.

The Huns, powerless against the First Emperor, once more renewed their pressure. Breaking through the Great Wall at its weakest point, they swept down on to the Yellow River plain and were only bought off by a huge present of silk, wine and grain. It was not until the reign of the Han dynasty emperor Wu-ti (140–87 B.C.) that the Chinese re-established their supremacy over the northern barbarians and even expanded their empire far beyond the Great Wall into Korea, and westwards towards central Asia.

The utility of the Great Wall as a means of defense has often been seriously questioned. Again and again throughout Chinese history the equestrian hordes of the Mongolian plains succeeded in detecting unguarded or weakly defended places, and poured through them on to the north China plain to wreak untold havoc. These comparatively primitive tribes of the inhospitable northern steppes found in the rich cities and well-cultivated homesteads south of the Wall an irresistible inducement to plunder. Their descent into China could sometimes be checked, but never permanently stopped. Only by keeping the Wall in constant repair and by garrisoning its whole length with well-seasoned and loyal troops could the government hope to keep out the intruders. In the days of the greatest of the Han, T'ang and Ming emperors the Wall provided a sure bastion against the invaders, but through long periods of internal weakness it proved entirely ineffective.

For some four centuries after the fall of the Han dynasty the whole of north China was governed by

barbarians. Throughout the fifth and the first half of the sixth centuries A.D. the Avars, a Mongol people variously called the Jou-jan or Juan-juan, maintained an empire north of the Great Wall extending from the borders of Korea to Lake Balkash, and they continually threatened north China. In 607 the Great Wall was again fortified, but at a prodigal cost: it is estimated that a million men worked for ten days during the summer of that year—and that half of them died. Later, in the Sung dynasty, the great Genghis Khan and his Mongol hordes were halted for two years by fanatical Chinese resistance; they did not break through the Wall until A.D. 1209.

The Great Wall not only helped to weld the Chinese people into a great nation, but it also helped to unify the peoples of the steppes into a political and military power. The building of the Wall marks a milestone, not only in the political history of China, but in that of Asia as a whole. It may have had a considerable effect in turning the Huns westwards to overrun Europe and thus change the course of European history. From the time that the Huns established a political hegemony over the region north of the Great Wall from Korea to central Asia, one power-structure after another rose to control that vast area. Yet none of them remained untouched by the cultural and civilizing influence of China. So strong was the cultural stability which developed in China that even when (for nearly four hundred years) north China was at the mercy of northern tribesmen, those non-Chinese conquerors gradually accepted Chinese culture and customs, and merged into the

civilization of those whom they had conquered. The same thing happened when the Mongols conquered China and founded their own dynasty. Chinese culture was immeasurably enriched by this admixture with peoples from beyond the Great Wall, but the basic structure of Chinese administration and life-style remained intact. In fact, neither the Mongols nor the Manchus could hope to be able to rule the vast Chinese empire without relying heavily on the Confucian scholar class.

After the Manchus took over the empire in A.D. 1644 the Great Wall ceased to be of military significance. Had the Chinese general Wu San-kuei defended the mighty fortress of Shan-hai-kuan at the eastern end of the Great Wall, a purely Chinese dynasty might have established itself in place of the effete Ming. Instead, he surrendered the fortress to the Manchu armies, who rapidly occupied the whole of north China and established their capital at Peking.

The empire of the Manchus was no longer bounded on the north by the Great Wall; Manchuria, Mongolia, Sinkiang and Tibet all remained outside it. New and entirely different enemies from over the seas began to engage the attention of the Chinese government, and the Wall, ungarrisoned and neglected, gradually fell into disrepair. Materials were even scavenged from it to construct the imperial tombs of the new dynasty. Today what remains of the Great Wall stands as an eternal witness to the dream of the First Emperor and great empire-builder, Shih-huang-ti.

D. HOWARD SMITH

Typical north China scenery in the neighborhood of Sian, with agricultural terraces on the slopes of the hills. It is through landscape such as this that the Great Wall runs for much of its length.

A window in a watchtower of the Great Wall.

The Great Wall of China did not always keep the invader out, but it did help to establish the geographical identity of the Chinese empire. The exact delineation of the boundaries of the empire gave its administration a positive geographical basis. The main subject of our next four chapters is Rome, and we shall be tracing some of the vicissitudes of her rise from small city-state to mistress of the Mediterranean world and Europe. The ultimate extension of Rome's power gave her a vast empire and, as with the empire of Shih-huang-ti, her territory was given a positive limit by permanent frontiers. The Great Wall of China has a smaller but still monumentally impressive parallel in Hadrian's Wall, built in the first years of the second century A.D. across the northern part of England, to keep out unconquered tribes from the north. The whole of the Roman Empire was ringed with systems of fortifications when natural barriers were not present, as the great forts of Germany and the *limes* (frontier system) of North Africa indicate. Our next chapter describes a remarkable episode. It is the story of an enemy of Rome who invaded Italy and conquered what one would have supposed was an insuperable natural barrier—the Alps.

Hannibal

The enemy was the Carthaginian leader Hannibal. His epic journey across from North Africa up through Spain, across southern France, *over* the Alps and into Italy is in the tradition of Alexander's vast journeys across deserts and mountains to conquer half the world. Hannibal himself was a

According to tradition Romulus and his brother were reared by a wolf

true product of the Hellenistic age that Alexander's conquests had ushered in. It was an age of the professional war-leader. The outcome of military struggles largely determined the political development of the Mediterranean world at this time, and the leader of a powerful army could carve out a kingdom for himself. Military power had assumed greater importance since Salamis—the size of the confrontation, the empire of Persia against the Greeks, was significant. In the East, Hellenistic princes made and unmade states. In the West, meanwhile, relatively modest campaigns in Italy were gradually bringing to power a small city-state. By 270 B.C. Rome had consolidated her position as the dominant power in central Italy. Before we look at the course of events that led to conflict with the North African empire of the Carthaginians, it is worth seeing how the city of Rome, now on the brink of a Mediterranean expansion that would lead to world domination, had grown up.

Origins of Rome

The Greeks, as we have seen, possessed very little information about their origins, though the Homeric epics had preserved for them some indications of a historic past. The Romans knew even less about their beginnings as a state, and for them legend provided the traditional account of Rome's early history. According to legend, Rome was founded in 735 B.C. by Romulus, son of Mars, on the hill known as the Palatine above the Tiber River. Rome's original constitution was monarchic; seven kings ruled over Rome until the last, Tarquinius Superbus, was

driven out and a republic set up. The last three kings were Etruscan. According to archeology and modern historical analysis, Rome was founded sometime in the eighth century B.C.; the oldest settlement, which was on the Palatine, merged with other settlements on the group of seven hills above the Tiber, and the hill called the Capitol was subsequently fortified. Rome's local power grew, and she gained the leadership of neighboring Latin towns, forming a league.

Jupiter, supreme Roman god

The Etruscans

The rise of the Etruscans to power in central and northern Italy

Fratricidal strife; Etruscan fresco

precipitated a clash with Rome. Rome lost the struggle and an Etruscan ruling house took over. Under this leadership Rome grew and prospered, learning the skills of civilization from the Etruscans as they had learned them from the Greeks. But at the beginning of the sixth century, the Etruscan domination was ended by a rebellion engineered by the more powerful families in Rome, and a republic was set up.

Etruscan couple; from a sarcophagus

Roman society

Rome's population was made up of various families or clans (*gentes*). Certain families were more important than others, and their heads functioned as a council of elders, called the Senate. In the days of the monarchy this council was the source of advice for the king, who was also chosen from among the ranks of the senators, or *patres* (fathers), as they were then called. The more important and richer families, the patricians, were distinguished from the lesser families, the plebeians. After the expulsion of the Etruscan Tarquin, two magistrates were henceforth elected instead of a king—they were later to be known as consuls. The word for king, *rex*, became a hated symbol of excessive power and it was never again used officially. When, centuries later, the Roman republic was transformed into the Empire under Octavius, as we shall see in a later chapter, the emperors, even though they were sole rulers at first, never used the term, but called themselves *imperator* (general, or one who exercises supreme power, *imperium*).

Patricians and plebeians

The decision-making body of early Rome was theoretically the *comitia*, or popular assembly, but in practice the Senate exercised power over it. In contrast, at Athens the popular assembly eventually curbed the power of the great nobles, as we have seen; Rome was thus never a democracy in the way that Athens was, but basically an oligarchy, increasingly dominated by powerful individuals. But unlike many Greek cities, Rome did achieve internal stability, and developed her constitution (and, perhaps almost as important, respect for it), without civil wars and the forcible imposition of rule by one group or another. The patricians and plebeians engaged in a long-drawn-out struggle for power, which was not simply rich against poor, for the ranks of the plebeians eventually contained influential families. The plebeians managed to obtain recognition of their own officials, the tribunes, who were then incorporated into the constitution of the Roman state. The calm conduct of what was a very real struggle is evident in the so-called

Roman patrician

"secession of the plebs," when the plebs withdrew their labor until their demands were met, thus showing by passive means their relevance to the Roman state.

Roman citizenship

In contrast to the Greek city-states, Rome's expansion did not stop at temporary domination over neighboring states. The Greeks, always respecting the idea of the autonomy of the city-state, did not conceive of a larger unity except in the form of a hegemony, or league, as we have seen. The Romans conquered peoples and cities in Italy, but their hegemony brought with it the chance of assimilation. Rome's "allies" achieved certain of the rights of Roman citizenship, and eventually all of Italy gained full Roman citizenship. The people of Rome, as in other city-states, had political expression through citizenship, but what distinguished Rome from city-states like Athens for example, was the emergence of the idea that citizenship could be extended wholesale to other peoples. This larger concept of citizenship paved the way for the absorption of foreign peoples and the resulting political unity that was to be the mainstay of the Empire of Rome. Alexander's conquests had set loose the idea of a community of Greek culture that embraced the

whole inhabited world, the *oikoumene;* the *oikoumene* was to be given a political framework within the conquests of Rome which provided for the continuity of Greek, or rather Greco-Roman, civilization around the Mediterranean.

Pyrrhus of Epirus

We now take up the story of Rome when she was as yet only a force inside Italy. In 270 B.C. Rome became involved in the quarrels of the Greek cities in the south of Italy. Her strong position in Italy gave her the potential role of arbiter, if not protector. In a dispute between Thurii and Tarentum, Thurii appealed to Rome for help, and it was given. Rome had

Elephants of King Pyrrhus

entered the sphere of Greek politics. The Tarentines, who saw Rome as a threat to their supremacy in southern Italy, enlisted the help of Pyrrhus, King of Epirus. Pyrrhus was a *condottiere* in the Hellenistic style, looking for a profitable cause to fight for, since his attempts to grab territory in Greece while the successors of Alexander were squabbling for power had been unsuccessful. Rome's first confrontation with the professional skill of Hellenistic mercenaries did not go well at first, and after a defeat at Heraclea, the Romans were forced back deep into Latium. The possible threat to Rome itself galvanized the Romans into uncompromising action: Pyrrhus was seen as a real

King Pyrrhus of Epirus

danger to Rome herself. He might play the war game for profit as did most of the Hellenistic war leaders, but Rome was in deadly earnest. Their stubborn efforts inflicted so many casualties on Pyrrhus that, although technically victor, he decided to withdraw from Italy (hence the proverbial Pyrrhic victory). He sailed off to Sicily to try his luck fighting for the Greek cities there against the Carthaginians. After a second try against the Romans in Italy, again without any real success, he returned to Greece where he was killed in a brawl at Argos.

Conflict with Carthage

Behind such campaigning, the realities of politics brought Rome and Carthage to a head-on collision. Carthaginian power had only just been kept at bay by the Greeks in Sicily for centuries. Rome's interests, and her involvement with the Greek cities of Magna Graecia, meant that two spheres of influence were beginning to overlap. Conflict came when Rome embarked on armed intervention in Sicily. The struggle with Carthage that followed was to last intermittently for more than half a century (264–202 B.C.), with the three Punic Wars—"Punic" from the Latin *poeni, poenicus* meaning Phoenician. For Carthage was the greatest offspring of Phoenician colonization in the western Mediterranean. Her great strength was her navy, and Rome was forced to become a sea-power almost overnight in order to have even a chance against the might of Carthage. Carthage was,

Phoenician ship

unlike most Phoenician colonies, also a great land power, whose vast territories in North Africa, stretching as far west as the Straits of Gibraltar, added to her possessions in Sicily and Sardinia, made her one of the foremost powers in the Mediterranean.

Carthaginian sarcophagus

The First and Second Punic Wars

The first war with Carthage ended with the ceding of Sicily to Rome, the first of Rome's overseas acquisitions and the beginning of her Empire. The Second Punic War brought to lasting fame the Carthaginian whose remarkable journey across the Alps is our next milestone. Hannibal was a great war leader, but he is distinguished from other Hellenistic captains of war by his sense of mission. It may not be acceptable to talk of destiny today, but to Hannibal and to the Romans it must have been a more valid concept. The destinies of Rome and Carthage were seen as intertwined in the Homeric past by the poet Virgil, who composed his epic poem *The Aeneid* in the reign of the Emperor Augustus. In this backward projection of history, the hero of the poem, Aeneas, a Trojan prince, leaves the ruins of defeated Troy and journeys to Italy to establish a new Troy—Rome—on the seven hills. On the way he stops off on the coast of North Africa, where he loves and leaves Dido, Queen of Carthage, who is building her great new capital. The deserted Queen swears perpetual vengeance against Aeneas' descendants and commits suicide. Hannibal is said to have sworn revenge on Rome on the altar of Melgart, and in the chapter that follows we shall see how his mission of revenge fared against the armies of Rome.

Aeneas sacrificing

Hannibal Challenges Rome 217 B.C.

*Two powers confronted each other to dispute mastery of the Mediterranean—Rome and Carthage.
The Carthaginians were interested in colonial expansion as an extension of their trading interests,
but were prepared to protect those interests if necessary. Rome's view was essentially different.
In fact some Romans believed that the fates of the two nations were inextricably linked, and that
they were doomed to a duel to the death. Because Carthage's sphere of influence extended over a
great deal of the western Mediterranean, Rome had to become a naval power virtually overnight.
But Carthage too was arming for the confrontation, and under the leadership of the general
Hamilcar moved the theatre of war to Spain. It remained for his son Hannibal—one of the greatest
military geniuses of all time—to challenge the Romans on their homeground by crossing both the
Pyrenees and the Alps. In the ancient world such a feat seemed impossible. Only Hannibal would
have dared embark on such a venture.*

In the spring of 218 B.C., an army of 100,000 men gathered in a town in eastern Spain, now Cartagena, under the command of a young general, Hannibal Barca. These soldiers had been recruited from all the warlike tribes of Spain and North Africa. The officers were Carthaginians, descended from the ancient Phoenician people who had left the Lebanon six or eight centuries earlier and had colonized first the coasts, then the interiors of present-day Tunisia and Andalusia. In the next two years these men were to accomplish one of the most astonishing feats of history. They were to travel more than 1,200 miles through hostile or savage countries, crossing one of the biggest rivers in Europe and two of the highest mountain chains. At the end of this formidable journey they were virtually to annihilate the finest armies of the time and to threaten the very survival of Rome's power in the heart of her own territory.

Hannibal's aim was to avenge the defeat that Rome had inflicted on Carthage twenty-three years earlier, at the end of the First Punic War, a struggle that had lasted for nearly a quarter of a century. (The Punic Wars were so called after the Roman name for Carthaginians: Poeni, i.e., Phoenicians.) His fantastic venture so astounded both his contemporaries and posterity that its romantic aspect has overshadowed the rational, one might almost say scientific, manner in which the undertaking was planned and executed. The facts, however, emerge from the account given by the Greek historian Polybius, one of the soundest intellects of antiquity despite his Roman bias. Thanks to him, we realize that Hannibal's campaign was not the whim of a rash young leader; it was prepared and led by one of the greatest political figures of all time. In spite of ultimate failure, it influenced decisively the evolution of Mediterranean civilization.

By the end of the fourth century B.C. Carthage had accumulated great wealth from its vast trading empire. Its kings had brought terror to the Greeks in Sicily, conquered Sardinia and sent exploratory expeditions along the river banks of tropical Africa and the boundaries of Europe. Carthaginian dominance over the western Mediterranean was well established. Then the great landowners rose to destroy the monarchy and for a time Carthage had sought to live at peace. Concentrating on trade, she had allowed the militant Roman republic to establish power over the whole of Italy without making any move, and had even refused to help her old allies the Etruscans, in spite of centuries-old treaties of mutual aid. The peasant soldiers of Latium had no apparent reason to interfere with Carthaginian merchants, and Rome's still-primitive economy could not rival the highly developed scientific agricultural system of the vast African estates.

But some of the Roman senators had formed fruitful associations with the merchants of Campania, who had pointed out to them the enormous profits that would accrue from the conquest of Sicily, the granary of the western Mediterranean, a great cultural center—and an island partially under Carthage's control. In 263 B.C. a Roman force had occupied Messina, thereby securing control of the straits between Sicily and Italy. Carthage could not tolerate this encroachment in an area that she considered as belonging to her "governorship" of Sicily, and the First Punic War broke out.

During the first years of the conflict the military superiority of the Romans on land was evident, and the Roman fleets held their own against the celebrated Carthaginian navy. The Carthaginians were able to retain only a few bases in Sicily, and that much was salvaged only because of their superiority in siege warfare. But in 256 B.C. the Romans, led by Regulus, were halted on one of their forays into Africa. The conflict had reached a stalemate. This prolonged warfare, however, was disastrous for a

This head, from a Carthaginian coin, is possibly a likeness of the great Carthaginian leader, Hannibal.

Opposite The elephants Hannibal took on his campaign across the Alps are probably its best-remembered feature; from a Carthaginian coin.

Confrontation between Rome and Carthage

country with a mercantile economy, such as Carthage. Exhausted and discouraged, in 241 B.C. the Carthaginian government finally renounced all claims over Sicily.

Following the end of the war, a grave social crisis was precipitated in Carthage by the mutiny of the mercenaries who had formed almost the entire part of the Punic army. The government fell and was replaced by a popular party, which handed power to Hamilcar Barca, Hannibal's father. This young general, already famous as head of commando units against the Romans, succeeded in controlling the mercenaries. Hamilcar recognized the basic weaknesses of the Punic government—weaknesses that had contributed to the loss of the war as well as to the revolt of the mercenaries. The problem was that government was in the hands of a self-centered plutocracy, with the ruling families vying with one another for power. While Hamilcar had little interest in internal politics, he modified the constitution to the extent necessary for him to carry out his plan of revenge against Rome.

Hamilcar did not in fact accept any possibility of compromise with the belligerent Italian republic. The Roman Senate had not attempted to subjugate Carthage even during the mutiny of the mercenaries, perhaps for fear of widespread revolution. But toward the end of Carthage's internal crisis Rome had annexed Sardinia, cynically and without regard for justice.

Hamilcar had three main aims: to have a free hand politically, without being obliged to account all the time to the rulers of Carthage; to be solely responsible for the country's economy and free to use its resources to influence both internal and foreign opinion; and to recruit an army that was efficient, well trained and completely loyal to him personally. He achieved all three aims in less than ten years, thanks to his conquest of southern Spain,

which he organized into a virtually independent kingdom on the model of those that Alexander's successors had created in Asia. The mountain chains of Andalusia concealed the richest mines in the Mediterranean world. These provided enough revenue to pay Rome the war reparations fixed by treaty, to afford resources for Hamilcar's electoral campaigns in Carthage and to hire Greek technicians and propagandists necessary for his great plan. The warlike Celtiberian tribes provided courageous soldiers whose fervent loyalty to their leaders offset the disadvantages of their rapacious behavior. All this took place on the fringe of the civilized world, beyond the regions regularly inspected by the Roman intelligence service.

Hamilcar was killed in a campaign in 229 B.C. The system of succession that he had devised required that one of his close relatives should succeed him. His eldest son Hannibal was still too young, and power passed into the hands of his son-in-law, Hasdrubal. He continued to organize the Spanish kingdom, but he seems to have sought to delay any further conflict with Rome.

The Greeks of Massilia (now Marseille) and of Emporiae in Catalonia, old enemies of the Phoenicians, had finally persuaded the Romans of the danger that the Barca empire represented. Hasdrubal signed a treaty that set the boundary of his domain at the river Ebro, or possibly the Júcar. But Hasdrubal was assassinated, and in 220 B.C. Hannibal succeeded to power.

Hannibal at once adopted a more uncompromising, aggressive policy. To make it quite clear that he ruled Spain and that his enemies could expect no help from Rome, he attacked and destroyed the Spanish town of Saguntum, which had a treaty of alliance with the Roman republic. The Senate, which had done nothing to save the people of Saguntum, demanded the punishment of the

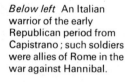

Below left An Italian warrior of the early Republican period from Capistrano; such soldiers were allies of Rome in the war against Hannibal.

Right Two Etruscans carrying a wounded comrade, from the lid of an urn. The Etruscans, too, were among the armies of Rome ranged against Hannibal.

Carthaginian "butcher." The Carthaginian government replied that the Barca state in Spain was autonomous and that Rome had recognized this when negotiating with Hasdrubal. The Roman ambassador could only point out the inevitability of war.

The Second Punic War was welcomed by Hannibal; and his moral responsibility for it was largely justified by the brutality and cynicism of Roman policy toward Carthage. The only question was whether the young Carthaginian leader had a reasonable chance of winning. Hannibal was convinced he had. Educated by Greeks, he had broadened his outlook to embrace the whole Mediterranean world and even the uncivilized countries beyond. No other statesmen except perhaps Alexander and Pyrrhus of Epirus had attained so international an outlook; and the quality of the information at the disposal of the Carthaginians made Hannibal well qualified to assess the geographical and political situation.

Hannibal had carefully considered the structure of the political organization that we call, rather loosely, the Italian confederation. It had been created by linking the military power of Rome with the economic and commercial strength of Campania. Both parties had derived considerable benefits; for the legions constituted the strongest armed force in the Mediterranean, and the merchants and manufacturers of Campania dominated the whole market from Gibraltar to the Adriatic. However, its very success was a source of rivalry between the partners. For one thing, all important policy was decided in Rome, and statesmen of Capua did not take kindly to having their ambitions restricted to a municipal scale. In addition, the constitution of Capua favored the development of what we would now call left-wing ideas whose supporters—in particular a certain Pacuvius

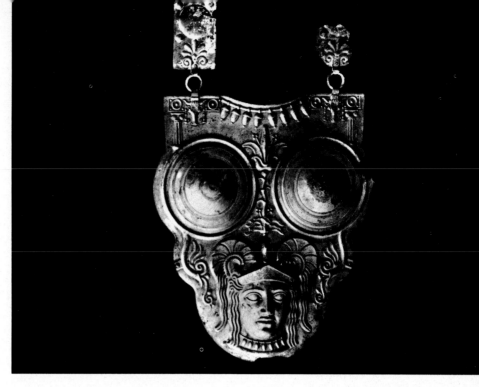

Bronze cuirass belonging to one of Hannibal's soldiers.

Calavius—foresaw the breakup of the union. It is more than likely that these potential secessionists had made a deal with the Carthaginians before the outbreak of the Second Punic War.

If she were to be deprived of southern Italy, Rome would at once lose all her naval power—unequaled in the Mediterranean—and Carthage could have regained Sicily and Sardinia without striking a blow. But no one in any Italian town would dare oppose Rome so long as the legions controlled the country. Therefore a force had to be found that was capable of neutralizing the Roman army. Hannibal thought he might find this force in Gaul. For a long period the Celts had provided mercenaries for the Carthaginians, but no one as yet had the idea of treating these barbarians as a political force and concluding diplomatic agreements with them. One of the greatest errors of the Carthaginian government during the First Punic War had been its ignorance of the profitable use it might make of the Gauls in the Po Valley. In fact the Gauls had remained at peace throughout the war and had subsequently been subjugated by the Romans. Hannibal was determined that the same mistake should not be made again. He sent envoys throughout the Celtic territory, who brought back extremely useful information.

Until this time the Gauls had occupied the center, the east and the north of France, Holland and western and southern Germany. The Rhine ran through the middle of their territory. For several decades, however, the Celts east of the Rhine had been forced by the Germans to fall back toward the west and the south, driving before them tribes who had previously been settled in the west. This large migration had taken place around 230 B.C.; it was then that the Gauls settled and founded their towns, Paris among them. The repercussions of this great upheaval were felt to the limits of the Celtic world. In 225 B.C. the Romans found themselves face to face with bands of Germans mixed with Cisalpine Gauls.

Opposite Iberian warrior, from a sandstone relief found at Ossuna. Hannibal's army included many Iberians, recruited from Andalusia, which his father Hamilcar had subdued a few years before the invasion of Italy.

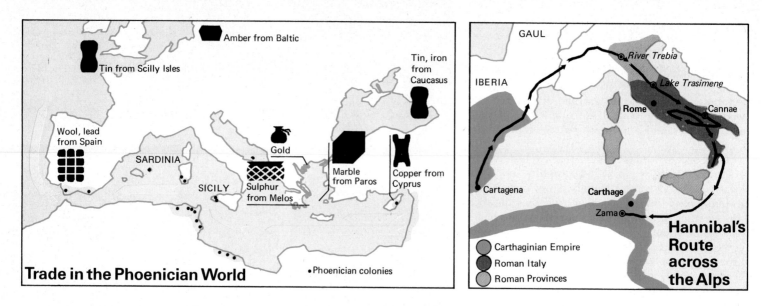

Trade in the Phoenician World

Amber from Baltic

Tin from Scilly Isles

Tin, iron from Caucasus

Wool, lead from Spain

SARDINIA

Gold

SICILY

Sulphur from Melos

Marble from Paros

Copper from Cyprus

• Phoenician colonies

GAUL

IBERIA

River Trebia

Lake Trasimene

Rome

Cannae

Cartagena

Carthage

Zama

Hannibal's Route across the Alps

Carthaginian Empire

Roman Italy

Roman Provinces

For Hannibal this situation offered a double opportunity. For one, there was the possibility of recruiting seasoned auxiliaries from the numerous tribes who had been uprooted. Of even greater importance, the major difficulty facing a Carthaginian expedition from Spain to Italy was overcome. The Mediterranean coasts of Languedoc and Provence had until then been occupied by Iberian and Ligurian tribes who were partly Hellenized as a result of three centuries of trading with the Greeks. The politicians of Massilia could easily have raised from among them numerous opponents to Hannibal's passage. However, at about 230 B.C. the whole area between the Pyrenees and the Rhone had been subjugated by a Celtic tribe,

The prow of a Carthaginian warship; from a Carthaginian stele.

the Arecomican Volsci. Hannibal had only to reach agreement with them to gain not only the right of peaceful passage but also long-term occupation of certain garrisons. By maintaining these, Hannibal could retain his lines of communication with Spain and could receive reinforcements, as was to be the case in 208 B.C. At the same time he could prevent Roman armies from invading Spain by land.

In the light of such considerations it becomes clear that Hannibal's decision to invade Italy by land was not just a bold act of desperation. In fact, he had no other means of surprising an enemy whose defenses were otherwise impregnable. The only important problem that confronted the expedition was that of supply; and Napoleon himself remarked that such obstacles must never stand in the way of strategy. In this case the invading army compensated for its weakness by the factor of surprise. And Hannibal, only too well aware of the importance of propaganda, knew how to exploit the impression his extraordinary venture would make on public opinion. He could not foresee, of course, that this impression was to last for more than twenty centuries. Even today, most people remember Hannibal chiefly because he brought his elephants across the Alps.

We do not know with certainty the route Hannibal took across the Alps. It seems most likely that he crossed the valley of the Isère, through Maurienne and Mont Cenis. This route allows for one of the few authenticated traditions: that Hannibal passed through the Allobroges' territory. However, proof remains impossible.

The destruction of Roman military power and the dissolution of the Italian confederation were accomplished as Hannibal had planned, and with remarkable speed. The battle of Cannae on August 2, 216 B.C., following upon those at Tessin and Trasimeno, deprived Rome of a third of its forces, and that third comprised the youngest and most vigorous elements. Then the large towns of Campania and the Greek cities of Capua, Tarentum and Syracuse defected from Rome, and the Punic fleet was able to come into action.

Suddenly, however, the fortunes of war changed. The reasons for this reversal are much more

Hannibal's ambition thwarted

complex than the reasons for Hannibal's success. Hannibal himself can be absolved from the accusation usually leveled against him, that he lacked decisiveness in failing to make a frontal attack on Rome after the battle of Cannae. In fact the capital's strategic position was so strong, and its perimeter so well equipped with the latest Greek defensive weapons, that a siege would have been extremely hazardous for an army already reduced and encamped in a hostile country. A heavy responsibility, however, must surely rest on the Carthaginian admirals and the leaders of the various rebellions against Rome who failed to coordinate their efforts and thus allowed the Romans to extinguish each outbreak in turn.

Hannibal himself made two bad errors of judgment: he underestimated the capacity for resistance of Rome itself, strongly ensconced as it was on plains surrounded by the mountains of Latium and the Sabine territory; and he overestimated the stability of the Barca kingdom in Spain, which collapsed like a pack of cards in the face of the small army of the Roman general Scipio. On this last point there is no doubt that Hasdrubal had seen the problem more clearly and had recognized the necessity of strengthening the Spanish state before embarking on so hazardous an expedition. In any event, Hannibal was forced to return to Carthage, and at Zama in 202 he was decisively beaten by Scipio. By the terms of the peace treaty of 201, Carthage lost its navy and its empire.

Hannibal was a victim of his Greek education. The successes of Alexander had accustomed men of that time to imagine that history was made and unmade by a few outstanding men helped by a handful of adventurers, and that economic, social and cultural factors or the popular mood could be discounted. The Barcas had hastily imposed a quite artificial political structure on the multitude of small and disparate social groups that inhabited the Spanish peninsula. The Roman state, on the other hand, had grown slowly by a natural process. Those who came to belong to Rome were not even completely aware of having been Romanized, but the process had altered their attitudes and created among them indissoluble bonds. Hannibal's sudden challenge could not interrupt Roman development, but it both modified and furthered the confederation by shattering the framework within which it had operated and allowing Rome to expand throughout Italy and the Mediterranean.

Thus Hannibal must be considered one of the chief instigators of the great revolution that transformed Mediterranean civilization and gave birth to the modern world. It is interesting to note that this view of Hannibal is substantially the same as that held by the Roman historians themselves, who saw the Carthaginians as a divine instrument sent to try the Roman people, purging them through suffering and thus making them more worthy of their divine mission to govern the world.

GILBERT CHARLES-PICARD

Scipio, the Roman general who was chiefly responsible for the defeat of Hannibal.

The ruins of Carthage, in present-day Tunisia.

The expansion of Carthage was brought to a grinding halt when the genius of the Roman general Scipio enabled the Romans to defeat the Carthaginians decisively on their own ground, at Zama in North Africa. Hannibal lived out the rest of his life a haunted exile, forever planning to challenge the might of Rome again, whether on behalf of Carthage or one of the Hellenistic kingdoms.

Rome was now undoubtedly mistress of the western Mediterranean. The dangers that she had experienced at the hands of a Greek leader, Pyrrhus, were not forgotten, so she also determined to keep a watchful eye on the East. She set about systematically forestalling the rise of any potentially dangerous rival in Greece, taking the side of the weaker party against the stronger in political quarrels, to maintain a certain balance of power. Philip v, King of Macedonia, the chief aggressor in Greece, was driven out and a protectorate was set up. Greece was again aided against an "aggressor" when the Syrian Antiochus III, the Great, invaded. He was hounded into Asia Minor by a Roman army, and heavily defeated. Roman influence then rapidly spread over Asia Minor. Pergamum became a client-kingdom, and discord was promoted in Syria so that no strong centralized control remained. In Egypt, the Ptolemaic kingdom was given Roman "protection," and this loose form of protectorate lasted until Egypt became an integral part of the Roman Empire after Actium, the subject of one of our subsequent chapters.

The rise of Rome

From the ashes of Alexander's empire, the foundations of a new empire were rising, as Rome gradually filled the power vacuum left by the disintegrating Hellenistic states. For the first time, the whole Mediterranean area was to be dominated by one state.

Just as the collapse of the Athenian empire had caused Thucydides to ponder on the vicissitudes of political power, so contemporary historians were roused to speculate on the seemingly meteoric rise of Rome to world status. With the perspective of time, we can see the fundamental

Greek warrior

internal instability of the Hellenistic states, with their wandering armies and treasure-seeking princes, as one of the main causes; contemporary historians gave a schematic explanation of Rome's success that is not entirely unrelated. They attributed Rome's rise to the soundness of her constitution. In the neat fashion of Greek political theory, the Greek diplomat and historian Polybius (who had first-hand experience of Rome's expansion in Greece) emphasized its "mixed" character.

With the semi-royal powers of the highest office, the consulship, combined with the oligarchic component of the senate and the democratic component of the people's assembly, Rome had eliminated the potential for strife between oligarchs and democrats, or the dominance of single ruler-kings, tyrants or demagogues. This idealized analysis of Rome's constitution is certainly highly optimistic— as we shall see at Actium, where the Roman state was almost torn apart by a handful of individuals —but it does reflect a measure of truth about Rome's internal stability at this time, and the permanence of her political institutions that allowed her to operate a consistent foreign policy.

Rome's expansion

The immediate question that springs to mind when surveying the hundred-year rise of a small city-state to a position as the leading power in the Mediterranean world is how far, and from when, a conscious policy of expansion was pursued. This has been a favorite question with historians for generations. What one can observe is that the establishment of loose protectorates, rather than permanent administration, would tend to indi-

Grain pits at Ostia

cate that Rome was initially filling a power vacuum for her own protection as much as anything. The advantages of achieving political stability by full-scale annexation could be outweighed by the disadvantages of the cost that it entailed in men and resources. Diplomacy was more feasible for Rome in the latter part of the second century B.C. But where there was an immediate economic "pay-off" Rome might annex territory on a permanent basis. Sicily became a "province"—i.e. under the direct and permanent administration of Rome—after the First Punic War. It was of strategic

value certainly, but its rich grainlands soon played a vital part in Rome's grain supply.

Ships in harbor

The Roman army

The desperate fight against Hannibal had hastened the development of the Roman military machine. It would not be long before this efficient new weapon would be used, not for the occasional skirmish or police-work to back up diplomatic policy, but with a ruthlessness foreign to the war games of the Hellenistic rulers. Roman peace-keeping in Greece took a more aggressive turn. Macedonian influence was effectively broken at the battle of Pydna in 168 B.C., but the Achaean League in central Greece was still causing trouble. The Romans decided to crush Greek resistance once and for all: the consul L. Mummius obliterated the city of Corinth in 146 B.C. This was indeed a bad year for Rome's enemies. The rising tide of opinion in the Roman Senate, which for years had been advocating the destruction of Carthage as the only solution to the danger of Carthaginian expansion, finally won. The Roman general Scipio Aemilianus was given a mandate to destroy the city. He razed it to the ground, so that hardly a trace remained, and is said to have wept when he had finished.

Sarcophagi from Carthage

Frieze from the Great Altar of Pergamum

Italian landscape; a Roman fresco

A by-product of this period of expansion and conquest was the flow of spoils and money from the conquests into Rome. The treasury, which had been drastically depleted by the major war-effort against Hannibal, showed a significant surplus by about 187 B.C. One of the chief economic effects of this influx of wealth was an increase in investment in Italy, much of it going into the purchase of the most solid investment available, land. This was also where the senatorial classes could best spend their wealth, as they were barred from commercial activity. With this growing interest in land came a desire to intensify agricultural production, to take advantage of growing urban markets. This meant there was a need for more labor.

The slave question

The demand for labor was immediate, and there was a much faster and more predictable solution to such a demand than encouraging population growth or attracting the movement of free workers. Slaves could be imported to Italy when and where they were needed.

Traditionally in the Mediterranean world, conquest frequently involved the enslavement of defeated soldiers and local populations. It was a question of business: a captured enemy was worth something, a dead one was not. The idea of a human being as a commodity to be exploited, which is virtually what a slave was, may seem extraordinary and abhorrent today, but in the ancient world, slavery was an accepted institution. Even the most democratic of states, fifth-century Athens, had a large slave population. However,

Rome in the Republican period began to exploit the convention of enslaving conquered peoples on a greater scale than had occurred before. A revolt in Sardinia in 176 B.C. was crushed by a Roman general whose boast was that he had captured or killed some 80,000 people. Most of the captives would have found their way onto the slave market. In 167 B.C., some 150,000 inhabitants of Epirus in Greece were enslaved—the glut in slave labor that such an act must have contributed to can only make one fear for the cheapness of human life under such conditions.

The importation of large numbers of slaves to work on the land in Italy necessitated strict, not to say brutal, control of them. Slaves were worked in gangs, often chained together. The men were often segregated from the women. The Roman writer Cato records the grim reality of such slavery: he maintained that it was cheaper to work slaves to death and replace them, rather than to get less out of them by humane treatment. Slaves

Gladiator fighting beasts

could also be used as raw material for gladiatorial shows, trained and cosseted and fed until the few brief moments in the arena where they died for Rome's pleasure. Spartacus, the subject of our next chapter, was a gladiator.

Not every slave was at the very depths of exploitation. Through the accident of war, highly educated and cultured people might find themselves enslaved. This was particularly true of the Greeks who came into conflict with Rome, and was still the case at the end of the Medieval period. After the fall of the last bastion of Greek culture, the city of Constantinople (the subject of one of our chapters in Volume III), several Turkish businessmen found themselves the somewhat embarrassed owners of

Greek freedmen; formerly slaves of P. Licinius

cultured and indeed noble Greeks, and were perplexed by their courteous deference and superior education. Meanwhile, the children of Roman aristocrats learned the refinements of Hellenic culture from erudite Greek slaves. Roman Senators, barred from commercial activities, made great use of slaves as their deputies in business. Since slaves could not legally own property, the results of their economic activity flowed back into the purses of their masters. A talented slave could also earn enough to buy his freedom eventually. The ties of personal loyalty that bound such slaves to their masters (if sometimes through fear of punishment) made them useful also as instruments of imperial administration under the Roman Empire, and a slave frequently appeared as the Emperor's personal deputy.

Thus slavery, as a legal condition that was the by-product of

conquest, could span a whole range of social classes, according to the historical accident which had made individuals slaves. But as a general economic system operated by the Roman Republic, it involved for the most part the exploitation of the lower classes. The use of slaves *en masse*, as herdsmen, cultivators or gladiators, constituted them as a well-defined

Roman market

social group, and this group-identity of large numbers of hideously-treated people brought about a rebellion within the Roman state which assumed almost catastrophic proportions.

Cloth-merchant's shop

The Slaves' Revolt

As Rome's armies marched victorious across the known world and her fleets patrolled the Mediterranean, hundreds and thousands of slaves were shipped back to Italy as cheap and expendable labor for the vast estates of the rich. Many worked in chain gangs under the lash of brutal task-masters or were sent as shepherds to the wilder parts of the country. Others were put into gladiatorial establishments, where a cruel and bloody death was an almost certain fate. In such conditions revolt seemed inevitable, and after an unsuccessful attempt in Sicily in 135 B.C. a new revolt, under the leadership of the Thracian, Spartacus, exploded in 73 B.C. An army of 40,000 under Crassus was needed to restore order, and 6,000 slaves were crucified as a warning to their fellows. Despite its immediate failure, the revolt hinted that the days of the Roman Republic were now numbered.

One day in June, 73 B.C., seventy-four gladiators broke out of their training establishment at Capua in southern Italy. They armed themselves with weapons stored for training and arena fighting, cut their way through the city and marched across country to Mt. Vesuvius. There near the top they made camp, and soon slaves from the towns and farms joined them. The leaders were the Thracian Spartacus and two Gauls, Crixus and Oenomaus, and their force included a strong contingent of Gauls and Thracians. From the outset Spartacus dominated: it was he who had doubtless organized the breakout from Capua.

The alarmed authorities sent G. Claudius Glaber, a praetor of the year, who tried vainly to surround and dislodge the rebels. But the emboldened slaves came down the slopes and roamed about the south, scattering detachment after detachment of troops. Soon they were masters of the whole south and their ranks were swollen with runaway slaves. Indeed by the spring of 72 they made up two armies, one under Spartacus, the other under Crixus.

In such a large-scale revolt the slaves were in a strong position only while they held together; as soon as they dispersed they were liable to capture or massacre. But unless they could take over the whole of a defensible and self-sufficient area, their only hope was to get back to their own lands. Spartacus knew that his only course was to maintain a massive force until he was safe from attack by Roman armies, then to break out. Once out of the peninsula, he and his men might find refuge in mountainous regions or march out of the Empire altogether. But these plans were impeded by Crixus and his men, who were lured by the plunder available in the rich cities of the south.

The Roman Senate recognized the need for quick, effective action. The two consuls L. Gellius Publicola and Gn. Lentulus Clodianus were each given an army. Crixus was cornered and routed near Monte Gargano, but Spartacus was too good a general to be so easily caught. No longer embarrassed by Crixus, he decided to march north across the Alps. Somewhere in Picenum two battles were fought. Spartacus defeated Lentulus, then turned and smashed Gellius' army. The Senate suspended both generals, as Spartacus again moved north.

By then there were sharp debates in Spartacus' camp. Should they divide into small bands and steal away over the Alps, or hold together in a force that could break the legions? The men resolved to stay united, while still seeking an escape from the trap of Italy. They turned south. Spartacus is said to have contemplated an attack on Rome, although he knew such a venture could not succeed. In Sicily, however, more slaves would join him and he might found a separate state.

The Senate now appointed M. Licinius Crassus, praetor, as field commander. Crassus, a rich, unscrupulous man, had no prestige as a general, and he decided to minimize risks. Gathering the remnants of four legions, he added six more, then set out to bar Spartacus from the Strait of Messina. In the battles that followed, the weight of disciplined troops told: Spartacus was driven down to Rhegium but failed to cross into Sicily. How many men the cautious Crassus had mustered was shown by the extensive fieldworks he then began: a 37-mile-long wall right across the rugged land of Italy's toe, behind which he planned to hem in the rebels and starve them out. But, concentrating his men at one point, Spartacus easily broke through. At last a really capable general, Gn. Pompeius, appeared on the Roman side. Pompey had returned from subduing Spain, and popular pressure made the Senate commission him to go to the aid of Crassus. Spartacus was hoping to seize the port of Brundusium and leave Italy; but his plan was spoiled by the arrival of M. Lucullus with a victorious army from Asia Minor.

Pompey, the great general who did much to complete Roman mastery over the Eastern Mediterranean and to clear the seas of pirates. He was drawn into the campaign against Spartacus on his return from subduing Spain.

Above Two gladiators in combat, with a third standing by ; a relief from Tevere. These two gladiators are similarly armed, but sometimes men with different kinds of armor or weapons were matched—for example, the *retiarius,* with net, dagger, and three-pronged lance, versus a fighter with orthodox sword and shield.

The amphitheatre at Naples, where many gladiators must have died. The wall surrounding the sunken arena was to protect the spectators, especially when wild beasts were fighting. In the distance is Vesuvius, where the first rebel slaves made their camp.

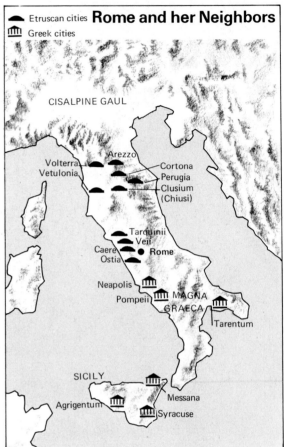

CISALPINE GAUL

Volterra
Vetulonia
Arezzo
Cortona
Perugia
Clusium
(Chiusi)

Tarquinii
Veii
Caere
Ostia · Rome

Neapolis
Pompeii
MAGNA
GRAECA
Tarentum

SICILY
Agrigentum
Messana
Syracuse

Slaves working with a huge windlass; detail of a relief from the Tomb of the Haterii. (Another detail appears on the opposite page.)

Coin showing the sale of a slave.

In their difficult situation, dissensions inevitably broke out among the rebels. Two Gauls formed a force of their own, and Spartacus had to spend more time and thought on rescuing them from the results of their rashness than in building his own campaign. When the two Gauls were defeated in the mountains between Paestum and Venusia, Spartacus turned south again. A slight success roused his men to demand battle in hope of a decisive triumph. Now, however, Spartacus finally was beaten; he was killed in battle, and the revolt was crushed. Six months after his appointment, Crassus was able to carry out the masters' revenge on the slaves who had defied them. Six thousand captives were crucified all along the Appian Way from Capua to Rome—the usual punishment for offending slaves. Pompey arrived only in time to annoy Crassus by helping to round up fugitives.

It was fitting that the last great slave revolt was precipitated and led by men who refused to be gladiators; for it was in the bloody combats of the arena that the most cruel and debasing aspects of the Roman world were concentrated. The fights derived from Etruscan funeral games; but they were taken over and brutally expanded by the Romans.

Though the generalship of Spartacus made his the most serious revolt, there had been earlier large-scale uprisings. The Mediterranean world was undergoing an acute crisis as the system formed by Alexander the Great was collapsing and

Rome was striving to unite East and West in a single empire. As far back as early in the third century B.C. there had been a slave rebellion on the island of Chios, and in 279 came a movement to force the wealthy to give up their property; but the Macedonians, as champions of the *status quo*, intervened. Similar conflicts in Greece led at times to attempts to free slaves for service as soldiers. In 132 came an uprising at Pergamum with a plan for setting up a "City of the Sun," on an egalitarian basis inspired by Stoic thought; but this time Rome intervened.

In Italy, not until the second century, with its vast massing of war captives as slaves, did things become serious. The first warnings came from the wilder regions of the south, in Apulia, where slave herdsmen were gathered. By the nature of their work such men could not be closely superintended; their areas became centers of brigandage.

Then the storm broke, in Sicily. The dates are obscure. We may assume that the revolt proper crystallized from endemic brigandage. Sicily had become a place where slaves could hope to disappear and live by robbery; in about 140 a praetor is said to have sent back 917 fugitive slaves to their mainland masters. The island also attracted criminals and enemies of the Roman order. Jews and Chaldeans, evicted from Rome, seem to have gone there, as did guerrillas from Spain. As bands of desperadoes collected, the countryside became unsafe for unescorted travelers or free villagers.

Wretchedness and brutality provoke revolt

In addition to fugitives and desperadoes and mutinous shepherds, there were large numbers of slaves massed in Sicily for work in the fields; for Sicilian agriculture had grown dependent on slaves. Landlords gave up using free labor and bought slaves, cheap and expendable on account of the wars. To the wretchedness of the latter's living conditions was added the brutality of overseers ready to flog the chain gangs. Often, when war prisoners were bought in bulk, men of the same tribe were gathered together and such groups were liable to breed concerted resistance.

A man who became a focus of slave hopes was Eunus, known at Enna as a magician and prophet. He claimed to see the gods and to have been told the future. Sometimes he breathed fire: historians say he did it by hiding in his mouth a pierced walnut full of burning sulphur and tinder.

At last in 135 a full-scale revolt broke and Enna was stormed. Damophilus, a particularly bad master, was tried in the theatre and spoke in his own defense, but was cut down by two leaders without a formal verdict. The assembly proclaimed Eunus king, and he took the name of Antiochus, calling his people Syrians. The workshops or dormitories of the slave gangs were broken open. We are told that prisoners of the rebels who had shown themselves humane were spared. On the whole it seems that the slaves behaved with modera-

tion; the small freeholders were the ones who were for revenge on the landlords.

Meanwhile western Sicily was also in turmoil. Under the leadership of a herdsman, Cleon, the slaves took Agrigentum. But, contrary to Roman hopes, the two bands did not clash, indeed they may have acted in concert. Cleon accepted Eunus as king and marched with his brother and some five thousand hillmen to Enna. A praetor sent from Rome levied some eight thousand Sicilians but was routed by the slaves. Eunus-Antiochus issued his own coins, with the goddess Demeter on one side, a corn ear on the other. Tauromenium, where the Roman commander had let the walls fall into disrepair, was taken. Lack of supplies forced the slaves to abandon their siege of Syracuse, but they captured a hill fortress, Morgantia.

In 134 one of the consuls took over the Sicilian command but he failed to crush the revolt. Slaves everywhere were stirred by the news of the successful rebellion. In Rome a plot by some 150 was suppressed; severe measures had to be taken against unrest at Minturnae and Sinuessa. In Sicily much confused fighting went on. In 133 a new consul took over; sling-bullets with his name, found at Enna, suggest that he made an assault there. But it was not until 132 that the Romans recaptured Tauromenium and then Enna was besieged; Cleon fell; Achaeus had already

Stele of Gaius Septimius, one of many grave-reliefs or statues that depict middle-class slave-masters whose lives were devoted to money-making. They are executed with a remarkable realism and insight into character which has been called Italian Verism.

Master and slaves; detail from a relief in the Tomb of the Haterii.

Slaves working in the fields, from a mosaic from Bardo in Tunisia. This is one of a series of mosaics depicting the various kinds of farms and villas along the North African coast; these mosaics deal with particular sites and were made to express the pride of the landowner in his estates.

disappeared; Eunus was caught in a cave. Perhaps because of his sacral claims, he was not executed, but was merely shut in a cell to rot. Flying columns of reprisal combed the island, and it is said that some twenty thousand slaves were crucified. Throughout their campaigns the rebels had made no effort to leave Sicily; they had hoped to build there an independent state, and their coins expressed dreams of a fertile earth and a full life.

For a generation things were fairly calm. Then in 104 the shock of the German invasions reawoke unrest. There were slave risings in Nuceria, then in Capua, then near Capua, when a Roman *eques* (of the middle class), ruined by love affairs, armed his slaves. The plebeian general Marius, badly needing men against the Germans, forced the Senate to decree the release of all citizens of allied states held as slaves in the provinces. The Sicilian landowners were infuriated; and after freeing some four hundred men, the governor Nerva refused to comply further. A small revolt in the west was broken by treachery. Then on the south coast the slaves defeated a Roman force, mustered six thousand men, and formed a regular army. Salvius, chosen as leader, took the title of king and threatened Morgantia. The town was saved, but Nerva failed to carry out his promise to free the loyal slaves there, and the latter left to join Salvius. Meanwhile another revolt came in the west under Athenion, who, though defeated,

joined Salvius and remained a considerable threat.

So far, only Roman garrison troops had been involved in Sicily; but the Senate now sent an army of seventeen thousand under the new governor, Lucullus. It included men from as far afield as Thessaly and Bithynia. The slaves, though still outnumbering the Romans, were in the end beaten by the discipline and organization of the legions. Athenion escaped capture by pretending to be dead. But then delays by Lucullus gave the survivors time to regain courage. Lucullus was beaten off, displaced, and finally exiled. Then in 101 the German menace in the north was ended. Manius Aquilius, an energetic and experienced campaigner, was sent to Sicily. Salvius was dead and Athenion was in sole command, but now he too was killed and Aquilius remorselessly rooted out the fugitives. Prisoners, sent to Rome, killed one another rather than be driven into the arena to amuse the mob by fighting wild beasts. There were no more rebellions in Sicily.

But on the mainland unrest grew. By 73 B.C. there were many elements to encourage slaves in thinking an opportune moment had come. For more than half a century the Roman state had been rent by violent inner conflicts. Between 132 and 82, seven consuls, a praetor, and four tribunes of the plebs were assassinated or died fighting other Romans. In 90 came the Social War, a revolt of other Italians demanding fuller rights; in 82 there was civil war that ended in Sulla's dictatorship, with its many proscriptions and legal murders; Sulla's death in 78 brought more political conflicts in Rome.

At the same time there were threats from without. Around the turn of the century came the big German invasions; in Spain sustained resistance was led by Sertorius (murdered in 72); and Pompey on his way to fight there in 77 had to quell a large rising in Transalpine Gaul. At sea there were the wars against the pirates; and in the east, Rome was challenged by Mithridates (not defeated until 66). Further, the free peasantry who had supplied the manpower for the legions was being reduced by war and the encroaching estates of the big landlords, a situation that underlay all the ceaseless social and political conflicts in Rome itself. At such a time slaves might well have hoped to break out of the system and win the wilder parts of Gaul, Thrace, and beyond.

Yet despite the apparently favorable conditions, Spartacus' revolt also failed. A strong and determined body of slaves could begin well, but they had little chance of long resistance to regular troops backed by all the resources of the cities. Their only hope was to move quickly into remote areas; staying in Italy ensured their final defeat.

Did the slaves who rebelled over the years have any social program beyond the desire to become free men? It is argued that in Sicily, by choosing kings, they showed the wish to build the same sort of society that existed elsewhere in their world. But Eunus was a prophetic character; and the

The Ancient World will be transformed

slaves may have used the term "king" to mean no more than leader.

Eunus' coins with their image of farming prosperity suggest an ideal of an earthly paradise that must have inspired his followers, just as his prophecies must have stirred them. The Romans clearly feared his propaganda. In 133 the Senate sent an embassy to placate the goddess Ceres (Demeter) of Enna; and walls were built round the precincts of the temple of Jupiter Aetnaeus, apparently to deprive the slaves of a source of religious enthusiasm.

In the second Sicilian revolt the slaves fought under the aegis of the Palici, Sicilian deities whose shrine had been founded by an early Sicilian patriot. We know from many sources that the lower classes everywhere were stirred at this time by dreams of world-end and world-renovation; and such dreams must have been voiced in Sicily and in the camps of Spartacus. But, no doubt, while some slaves responded to them, others thought only of escape and revenge.

While the slave revolts had few direct political consequences, their social and economic effects were of great importance. Sicily proved that to work the land with large slave gangs was dangerous and more and more landlords turned to tenant farmers rather than slaves for the cultivation of their estates. Columella, writing under Nero, recommended the use of slaves on the home farm, where they could be well supervised. The younger Pliny, a generation later, had much to say of troubles with defaulting tenants and mentioned that he never used slave gangs in chains. The third-century lawyers show the same sort of mixed farming. We get a picture of skilled slaves working on the home farm (attached to a residential villa) at jobs like vine-dressing, with arable farming given over to free tenants.

The slave revolts thus certainly played a large part in the supplanting of the free peasant farmer by the free tenant liable to turn into a share cropper and sink in status. They proved the perils of attempts to till land by slave gangs. And it is perhaps noteworthy that no attempts were made to build up big workshop units of slaves in the crafts and manufactures; it may be significant that in 134 there was much trouble, as we noted, at Minturnae, an industrial town. In the late Empire, with growing insecurity, there was a fall in slave prices, but no effort was made to revive gang work, and the social and economic position of the slaves began to approach that of tenants, who in turn found their lot worsened. Thus the way was opened to developments that slowly transformed the ancient world into the feudal economy of the Middle Ages.

JACK LINDSAY

The amphitheatre at Pompeii; a contemporary painting showing the kind of disorder liable to break out among the excited crowds.

Below Coin issued to commemorate the Social War, when Rome had to face the challenge of the other Italian cities that she was trying to keep in a subordinate position. The chariot represents thanksgiving to the gods for the end of the revolt.

Roman sacrificial procession

The happy judgment of the historian Polybius on the strength of the Roman constitution, because of its mixture of popular, oligarchic and monarchical elements, might certainly appear as an optimistic theorization after the revolt of Spartacus. The Roman state had been shaken by a bitter and violent social disturbance that had only been resolved by two individuals whose power, though technically constitutional, was far too great for the Senate to feel comfortable. Crassus, the multimillionaire, and Pompey, the popular general had succeeded where the regularly appointed consuls had failed, and the "extraordinary commands" with which they had been vested were a *de iure* recognition of the fact that the Roman state was now on the brink of being run by powerful individuals. The existence of such extraordinary commands, continuing until Octavian resolved the power struggle by his victory at Actium (the subject of our next chapter) and set about establishing the Roman Empire, with one individual in permanent possession of autocratic powers, indicates that the needs of the Roman state could no longer be met by using the established constitutional procedure. In the earlier days of the Republic generals had been given special authority in the face of a serious military threat, but the Senate had carefully limited their authority and had been strong enough to keep control. If we look back at the period of Rome's expansion into the Mediterranean we shall see that the Senate had in fact grown in strength, but that its increasing influence in government also brought with it the potential for individuals to influence affairs.

The Roman Senate

During Rome's period of wars and expansion, from the time of the Punic wars onwards, the Senate, composed as it was of men whose experience and status gave

them the ability to judge and make vital decisions in times of acute danger and stress, assumed greater direct responsibility in policy deci-

Roman senators

sions. Since the early days of Rome, the Senate had changed from being a council of men appointed by the consuls (as the successors of the kings) to being a governing body filled by ex-magistrates. The consuls would take their place in the Senate when their term of office was finished: hence a close attachment between these two "elements" of the Roman constitution. Thus the running of the state was concentrated in the hands of an oligarchy—the assembly of the Roman people still voted for magistrates, but had little real choice or influence in matters of government.

Within the Senate, cliques and

Scipio Africanus

power groups tended to form, and aimed at dominating the conduct of government. The great hero against the Carthaginians, Scipio Africanus, was eventually forced to retire from public life because of the success of a coalition of senators hostile to him and his

circle of relations and friends. This coalition indicates the tendency of the Senate to be dominated by groups of the most powerful of the Roman families, a kind of inner circle of old and influential families, the *nobiles* (those families who could claim a consul as an ancestor). The stage was thus set for the emergence of strong individuals, particularly if they had the glamour and popular support which attended a successful general, as Scipio had.

The new army

But, so long as the army of Rome was composed of men from Italy who enlisted for a particular campaign, and were subsequently disbanded,

Plaque of Hermes and Hercules

the loyalty of troops to an individual general was limited. However, Rome found herself almost constantly involved in peace-keeping or in actual wars, and this meant a constant demand for troops. The solution from the military point of view was the creation of a professional standing army, and this was achieved at the end of the second century B.C., under the leadership of a solid

Marius, the Roman general

Italian soldier, who had risen from the ranks to command the armies of Rome, Marius. Once a campaign was over, the troops did not disband and return to their villages and towns as before; they now stayed together as a profes-

Roman soldiers building a fort

sional fighting unit, in need of employment as soldiers, and looking to their leader for guidance. The curse of the Hellenistic age had caught up with Rome: generals and their armies would henceforth face each other on Roman soil, to determine who might control the state. The problem of what to do with a standing army was not even approached until Rome truly became an Empire under Augustus, when he arranged for most of the troops to be stationed on or near frontiers. But it was never solved. The authority of individual emperors, backed up by a willing Senate, kept the problem at bay for the most part in the early Empire. But in the third century A.D. the Empire was to go through a severe crisis, one of whose main causes was the rapid turn-over of emperors made and unmade by the army.

Political reform

The challenge of individual politicians to the collective authority of the Senate did not at first come from within its own ranks, nor yet from generals. The tribunate, originally created by popular pressure to give voice to the demands of the people's assembly and to provide a counterbalance to aristocratic power, provided the vehicle of protest—and almost of revolution, for two brothers, the Gracchi. Tiberius Gracchus attacked serious flaws in the Roman government from his

Roman soldiers marching

Coin of Julius Caesar

Julius Caesar

let the constitution work without the guiding hand of an autocrat. But, for all the semblance of a senatorial revival, and an apparent return to the days when Rome was run along constitutional lines, politics was still at the mercy of individuals, and no issue could really be decided without an army. This was clear when, some twenty years after the reforms of Sulla, the victorious Pompey returned from his campaigning in the East. He had pacified the rebellious territories there, and laid the foundations for their administration as Roman provinces (permanent annexation was replacing diplomacy almost everywhere within the Roman orbit). But his extraordinary command had been voted to him by the people, and since he was not a senatorial candidate, the Senate refused to ratify his arrangements. He could exert no pressure on them because he had disbanded his army, perhaps foolishly under the circumstances. It took pressure from another individual *with* an army, Julius Caesar, to get Pompey's work ratified.

Julius Caesar

Thus the late Republic drew to its end with military power paramount. The years before the battle of Actium, which was finally to resolve the crises of the Republic, were dominated by soldier-politicians like Pompey and Julius Caesar, and then by Antony and Octavian. Their support came not just from their armies (officially legions representing the Senate and people of Rome, but in practice private armies), but intermittently

position as tribune of the people in 133 B.C., calling—among other things—for agricultural reforms to aid the peasantry. In attempting to achieve ratification of his proposals, he managed to get his fellow tribunes deposed, and was labeled by the senatorial opposition as a demagogue seeking autocratic powers. The fear of autocracy (one thinks of the traditional hatred for kingship) among the Romans provoked a violent reaction: Tiberius was killed. So too was his younger brother Gaius Gracchus, who had taken up his dead brother's cause and was campaigning on behalf of the people and on behalf of the equestrian class of citizens (the businessmen of Rome, below the senators in rank), whose interests were not represented politically.

Such violence in politics struck a new and warning note; so did the great wave of popular support which had temporarily carried the Gracchi forward into a position of dominance. The state could be swayed by individuals, and the whole direction of Roman government, despite its apparently solid framework, could be altered. The passionate respect which the Romans of the time had for their constitution, reflecting no doubt their genuine sense of stability, was to limit any attempts at real change. Marius, the Italian soldier-become-general, with the aid of help from an ancient and respectable senatorial family, the Metelli, and the support of the people and his troops, eventually dominated the Roman state. His overthrow was accomplished by a man who was a conservative. who was backed by the Senate, and who set himself up as dictator to patch up the flaws in the Roman constitution. This senatorial candidate, Sulla, produced a solid if backward-looking program of reform before stepping down to

from the people of Rome, whose influence was temporarily—even if not effectively—increased by the political auctioneering that took place. The Senate itself was divided according to the inclinations and interests of its individual members. As a group it gravitated towards support of Pompey against his former ally Caesar, when Caesar in his campaigns and administration of the new provinces in Gaul showed himself to be too successful and clever for the Senate's liking. Caesar proved his superiority by crushing Pompey and his legions in a civil war in Italy itself. He controlled the Roman state for four years, until he was murdered in 44 B.C. for, so his opponents claimed, setting himself up as a

Augustus as a young man

"king" over the Republic. His nephew Octavian inherited his political support, and as we shall now see, finally put an end to the political competitions that were exhausting the resources and vitality of the Roman state.

Roman altar; awaiting the sacrifice

The Battle of Actium

The assassination of Julius Caesar in 44 B.C. initiated thirteen years of bloodshed, during which the people who had plotted his death were hunted down and those who remained in positions of power disputed that power among themselves. Finally the struggle resolved itself into a duel between Octavian, Caesar's grand-nephew and heir, and Marc Antony, his most able lieutenant, in alliance with Cleopatra, Queen of Egypt. In the final confrontation at the naval battle of Actium, Marc Antony and Cleopatra were routed and Octavian became ruler of the world as the Emperor Augustus. Egypt's last bid for world empire had been thwarted. But more important, the work begun by Julius Caesar was continued, and the transition from the anarchy of the end of the Roman Republic to the glory of Empire was completed.

Late in the summer of 31 B.C., the two largest fleets the world had ever seen confronted each other off the northwestern shores of Greece. The four or five hundred warships of Marc Antony, including sixty belonging to Queen Cleopatra of Egypt, faced outward into the Ionian Sea. Against this navy stood another of approximately equal size, which had come with the young Octavian, the future Augustus, from Italy. War had been declared against the foreigner Cleopatra and, by implication, against Antony, her husband in Egyptian though not in Roman law. The crews on each side numbered well over a hundred thousand men.

Behind Antony's ships, on the opposite banks of the narrow channel leading into the Gulf of Ambracia, were posted the two rival armies, each more than eighty thousand strong. Octavian's troops had come from Italy and landed at a port in Epirus, from which they had marched down and seized the northern promontory at the entrance to the Gulf. Only six hundred yards away, across the channel, they could see the troops of Antony stationed on the southern promontory, the peninsula of Actium.

For some years past, the cold, deliberate Octavian had ruled all the Roman possessions west of the Ionian and Adriatic seas—Italy, Gaul, Spain, and much of North Africa. Meanwhile, the more flamboyant Antony—in infatuated alliance with Cleopatra, whose Egypt was nominally independent of Rome—governed the lands that lay eastwards, as far as the Roman frontier on the Euphrates and including the rich territories of Asia Minor. But the conflicting ambitions and personalities of the two men had made a clash inevitable.

To meet Octavian's expected thrusts, Antony had moved his land forces up to positions along the western coasts of Greece, deploying his fleet before them, with his strongest contingents concentrated at Actium. Cleopatra, who saw in the confrontation her great hope of winning the entire Roman world, made the enormous treasures of Egypt available to Antony, thereby providing the bulk of his funds. She persuaded him to fight at sea, not, as some of his generals advised, on land. Moreover, she insisted on taking part in the engagement herself, though the presence of this exotic siren—the target of much hostile propaganda from Octavian—undermined the morale of many of Antony's senior officers. Taking advantage of this situation, Octavian's admiral Agrippa, a superb tactician, had succeeded in weakening Antony's position well before the major battle, by persuading several of his important officers to desert the key points for which they were responsible along the Greek seaboard. Antony's supply lines to Egypt and the east were thus not only threatened but partially cut. Time was against him, and he decided to offer the challenge.

The engagement that followed was one of the decisive encounters in history. Many details have been lost or obscured in a subsequent flood of fragmentary, contradictory accounts, but patient detective work has made it possible to gain some idea of what happened.

Octavian's purpose at Actium is reasonably clear: destruction of the enemy, the conquest of the eastern provinces and seizure of Egypt's revenues. Antony's aims are more obscure. No doubt he, too, hoped to destroy his foes, but, being too good a strategist not to realize that his position had deteriorated, he decided upon an alternative plan. If defeated, he would break through Octavian's line and sail south, and then east into the Aegean. In such an event, his failure to crush Octavian would at least leave him in a position from which he could control his eastern possessions and protect Egypt, the land of his love—and of his financial backing.

In preparation for such a contingency, Antony

Apollo of Actium; a Roman coin issued by Augustus, for whose victory in the battle the god Apollo was held to have been responsible.

Opposite Cleopatra, the queen of Egypt whose fatal attraction for Marc Antony helped to cause the civil war with Octavian, and Antony's decisive defeat at Actium. From a coin of Cleopatra.

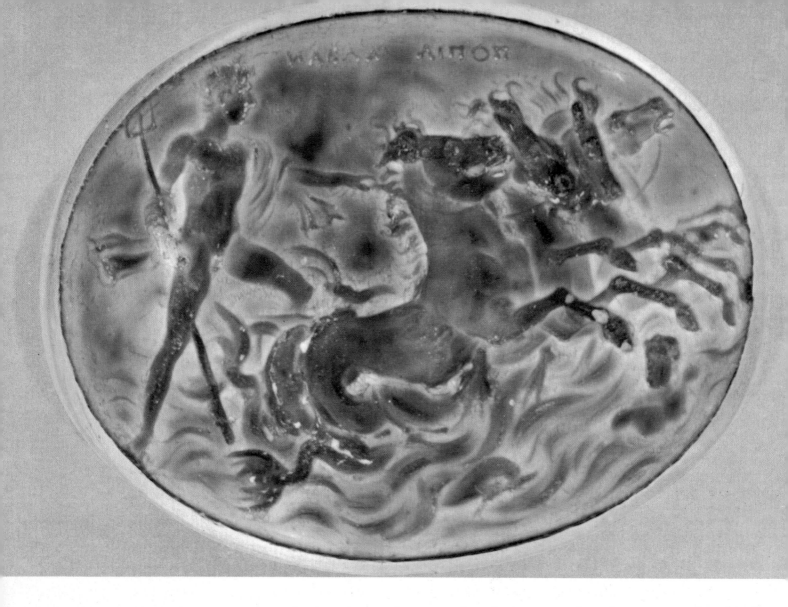

Neptune, god of the sea;
from a Greco-Roman sard.
Neptune was one of the gods
whom Virgil, in the *Aeneid*,
arrays against Antony at
Actium.

gave two unusual orders: the war chest was to be moved from land and lodged on Cleopatra's transport ships, and the entire fleet was to take its sails on board. The secret transfer of the treasury may not have attracted undue attention, but the shipping of the sails had a most disquieting effect on the men. It seemed to them that Antony was already contemplating flight and, although they were no doubt told that the sails were intended solely for victorious pursuit, they could scarcely have been convinced.

After several days of rough weather, September 2 brought calm, and Antony's fleet moved out of harbor. While Cleopatra's well-equipped squadron was kept in the rear—to act as a reserve and to prevent desertions—Antony, at the far right of the front line, directly faced the opposing admiral, Agrippa. Each commander hoped to be able to outflank and turn the other in the afternoon, when a northwest wind usually begins to blow in the Ionian Sea.

The wind shifted and battle was joined. As it raged furiously, Antony witnessed a blood-chilling development: suddenly, three of his six squadrons broke off action and started back to harbor. There is little doubt that this was treachery—the loyalty of the men had been undermined in advance by the enemy to whom they were now deserting. To Antony himself, and to Cleopatra in the second line, the withdrawal posed an immediate and disastrous threat. Now Cleopatra's flagship, with its gold-encrusted stern and purple sails, was seen to get up speed and set out for the open sea, followed by the rest of her squadron. Those who hated the queen interpreted this move, then and later, as cowardice and betrayal.

It is more likely, though, that Cleopatra acted in accordance with a plan prearranged with Antony in the eventuality of defeat. In any case he, too, made the fateful decision that flight was now the only course. His flagship was so heavily engaged that its extrication was impossible, but he managed to transfer to another vessel and, followed by forty or more ships of his squadron, joined Cleopatra in the open sea. As they fled southward toward Egypt, the rest of Antony's ships fought on. Leaderless and without hope, they were all eventually destroyed or captured. Within a week, the army, which had watched these disasters from the shore, capitulated.

Meanwhile, hastening from the scene on Cleopatra's flagship, Antony sat in silence and gazed out to sea. His dream of world rule was over, and so was hers.

Egypt's last bid for world empire

According to Virgil, who was a passionate supporter of the victorious side, the battle had been foretold in mythological times, when the god Vulcan had engraved the principal scenes upon the shield given to Aeneas, the founder of Rome's fortunes:

On one side Augustus Caesar, high up on the poop,
                is leading
The Italians into battle, the Senate and the People
                with him,
His home-gods and the great gods: two flames
            shoot up from his helmet
In jubilant light, and his father's star dawns
            over its crest.
Elsewhere in the scene is Agrippa—the gods and
           the winds fight for him—
Prominent, leading his column: the naval crown
           with its miniature
Ship's beaks, a proud decoration of war, shines on
           his head.
On the other side, with barbaric wealth and motley
           equipment,
Is Antony, fresh from his triumphs in the East, by
          the shores of the Indian
Ocean: Egypt, the powers of the Orient and
          uttermost Bactra
Sail with him, also—a shameful thing—his
          Egyptian wife . . .
Viewing this, Apollo of Actium draws his bow
From aloft: it creates a panic; all the Egyptians, all
The Indians, Arabians and Sabaeans now turn tail.

Although there were, in fact, no Indians in Antony's forces, Virgil and many others saw the battle in terms of the millennial struggle between East and West, with Actium commemorating the resistance of Greece to Persia four and a half centuries before.

The defeated pair did not stop until they came to Egypt. Octavian followed, reaching the outskirts of Alexandria the next summer. In a last desperate attempt to save the city of his queen, Antony resisted Octavian's advance. But in the face of superior numbers, the last of Antony's dwindling troops deserted to the enemy. Returning to the city and hearing a false report of Cleopatra's death, Antony committed suicide. Unopposed, Octavian entered Alexandria, where Cleopatra attempted to

The Emperor Augustus; a Greco-Roman gem:

The triumph of Octavian over Antony represented a victory for the Greco-Roman world over the rulers of the Orient. Two Asiatic prisoners are depicted here on the foot of the sarcophagus of the Pharaoh, Horemheb (*c.* 1300 B.C.) The Egyptians, who held a semi-independent status under Rome before Actium, had themselves been conscious of defending their ancient civilization against barbarians from the east.

Caesar's heir the victor

win him over—as she had so successfully won his great-uncle Caesar, and Antony. But Octavian was not to be wooed, and he actually planned to display his exotic captive in triumph to the Roman crowds. To thwart him and to avoid humiliation, Cleopatra had a snake brought to her and, arrayed in royal robes, put it to her breast. She died of its bite, but in her death there was some victory, for the venom of an asp, according to Egyptian religion, imparted immortality.

Augustan poets generally had no love for Cleopatra, but Horace at least could not withhold his admiration:

> In calm deliberate death too proud
> To freight Liburnian galleys and be shown
> In Triumph, fallen from her throne:
> The mockery of a Roman crowd.

And so Egypt fell into the hands of the ruler of Rome. The kingdom founded by Alexander's general Ptolemy had come to its final end, and the last of the great successor kingdoms of Alexander was no more. First Macedonia had gone, then Pergamum (which had become independent of the Seleucid empire of Syria and the east), then the Seleucids themselves, and now, finally, Egypt. For many years past, it is true, Egypt had not been fully independent of Rome. Cleopatra's father, Ptolemy Auletes, was obliged to call for Roman aid to regain the throne from which the Alexandrians had chased him. But Roman aid came high, and one of those who had to be paid, and paid enormous sums, was Julius Caesar. It was principally in order to collect that money that he went to Egypt and fought the Alexandrian War in 48–47 B.C. He also had the enjoyable experience of meeting Cleopatra, whom he established as ruler of the country. Whether he would have allowed her an empire, however, is doubtful. At any rate, he died while she was in Rome, and Cleopatra returned to Egypt declaring that her child

The prow of a Roman warship, showing warriors probably about to disembark. The crocodile symbol of Egypt indicates that this must be a ship that fought at Actium.

Caesarion was Caesar's, though this claim was, and is, disputed.

Later, supported by the love and troops of Antony, she indeed became an empress. Unprecedentedly placing the head of this foreign woman on his coins, Antony described Cleopatra as "Queen of kings and of her sons who are kings." The defeat at Actium brought the whole dream to an end. Despite some interruptions, Egypt had been a united and independent country for the better part of three thousand years. Now it belonged to Rome.

It was a strange empire that Octavian now ruled. Kings were traditionally unpopular in Rome, and the fate of Caesar had shown that dictators were not wanted either. Yet Octavian guessed that the Romans, eager for peaceful order, would be willing to accept autocracy if Republican institutions were revived. In 27 B.C. he solemnly renounced all extraordinary powers and officially transferred the State to the free disposal of the

Three coins of Antony: *Top* his head on an issue of the Greek east; *below left* one of his warships; *below right* the standard of one of his legions; part of a series issued just before the battle of Actium.

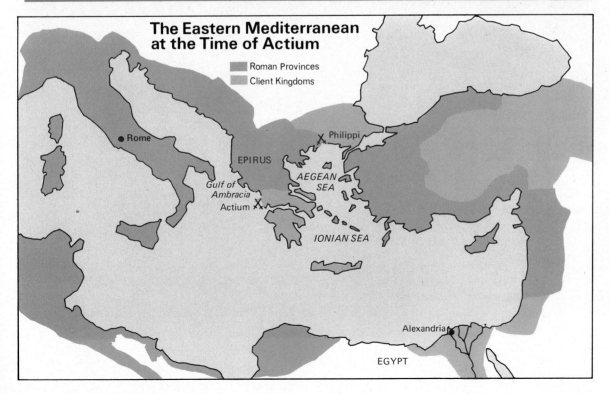

The Eastern Mediterranean at the Time of Actium

- Roman Provinces
- Client Kingdoms

Rome

Philippi

EPIRUS

AEGEAN SEA

Gulf of Ambracia

Actium

IONIAN SEA

Alexandria

EGYPT

Right The Nile in flood; a
Greco-Roman mosaic at
Praeneste (Palestrina).

Below Small Egyptian
mosaics, probably from a
decorative mosaic in a rich
man's house.

Rome's golden age begins

Senate and the people of Rome. Nevertheless, he reserved various means of maintaining control. In the huge group that constituted his special provinces—the greater part of Gaul, Spain, and Syria, as well as the whole of Egypt—he ruled, through subordinates, as supreme governor. He also held, for life, the ancient, democratic-sounding power of the Tribunes, the traditional supporters of the common people's rights. He chose to be designated "princeps," took the venerable name Augustus, and induced first the western, and then the eastern, territories to swear an oath of personal allegiance; an oath which meant more to ordinary citizens than the constitutional fictions that soothed the governing class.

The key to empire was the army. After the battle of Actium, the number of legions (including Antony's, which Augustus inherited) amounted to sixty. The maintenance of so many troops was not only extravagant but perilous to authority, so Augustus reduced the legions to twenty-eight—approximately 150,000 men. Nearly all these professionals were Italians or westerners; a further 150,000 auxiliaries were from less civilized parts of the Empire and usually served in their country of origin.

The army was not the only branch of administration that Augustus transformed to cope with imperial complexities. The Senate was reduced from nine hundred to six hundred members, and the consuls—annually elected chief magistrates—took on important new juridical duties. These duties, performed in collaboration with the ruler, gradually eclipsed the existing law courts. Thus, the old governmental and legal systems that Tacitus described as "incapacitated by violence, favoritism—and (most of all) bribery" were at last reformed. Augustus was helped, of course, in maintaining this great new multiracial system by the senators who governed major provinces in accordance with his wishes.

Egypt, however, was in the peculiar position of having as governor not a senator but a knight. The Order of the Knights had risen to wealth as Rome became an imperial power, and yet, being outside the Senate, had hitherto held no governmental power. Under Augustus the Order was reorganized to provide the beginnings of an Imperial Civil Service. Knights were posted as agents or procurators with such financial duties as tax collection. They could become commanders of the Vigiles, a metropolitan police force and fire brigade of seven thousand ex-slaves; they could serve as generals commanding the Praetorian Guard; and they were entrusted with Rome's vital corn supply.

It was perhaps for this last reason that Augustus put knights in control of the immense wealth he had won at Actium. For Egypt, despite a steady political decline, was an enormously rich country, and its main asset was corn. The Ptolemies had organized a centralized economy which ensured that most of the country's resources remained in their own hands. So determined was Augustus that no one should share the profits he had won that he went to the exceptional length of forbidding any Roman senator to visit Egypt without his permission.

It was not the first time that Rome's financial situation had been transformed by the acquisition of immensely rich territories. Pergamum in western Asia Minor had become a province in 133 B.C., and Syria was won seventy years later by Pompey from the last feeble descendants of Alexander's general Seleucus. Now there was Egypt. Rome itself had become very largely a subsidised city fed from its overseas provinces, and Roman rulers could never for long forget about corn, since their popularity and success depended upon it. Moreover, successive Roman politicians of the previous century had gradually adopted the Hellenistic concept that a great deal of corn must be distributed to the people below the market price—or even free.

Thus Egypt at once became an indispensable bulwark of the Empire. In the centuries that followed, the economic dependence of Rome on supplies from its largest dominions eventually led to the establishment of rival centers of power outside the capital, and there were those who deplored the parasitic condition of the city. Yet, if there were disadvantages to the system, the whole of industry, commerce and communications prospered under Augustus, and the Pax Romana brought new security and freedom of intercourse throughout the Empire. Now for the first time the last bit of Mediterranean shore was under Roman control; to them it had indeed become *Mare Nostrum*, Our Sea.

MICHAEL GRANT

Roman coin issued to commemorate the defeat of Antony and Cleopatra. It is inscribed with the Egyptian crocodile and the words AEGYPTO CAPTA—Egypt captured.

Below Part of a Roman villa at Utica, in Tunisia.

A few weeks after January 1 in the year 29 B.C. the doors of the temple of Janus in Rome were closed. This traditional act symbolized that the Roman state was at peace. The closing of the doors on this occasion

Temple of Janus

was greeted with more than the usual joy and relief that marked the termination of war. Since the murder of Julius Caesar in the Forum in the year 44 B.C., Rome had been plunged, with little intermission, in civil war. From that long agony the state had finally been delivered by Octavian's victory at Actium and the subsequent deaths of Antony and Cleopatra. The Senate and people of Rome were, in consequence, deeply grateful to the man who had brought them this relief, and they were disposed to accept his leadership.

Octavian supreme

Octavian knew this and recognized the strength of his present position. But he was also astute

Augustus with the goddess Roma

and cautious, as well as being a statesman profoundly concerned with the future well-being of Rome. He perceived what were the realities of power, and what were its trappings; and he was careful never to confuse the two.

His uncle, Julius Caesar, of a more flamboyant nature than his own, in the moment of his power had offended Republican principles and had fallen beneath the knives of ardent Republicans. The civil war had taken a heavy toll of these Roman oligarchs; but even in the year 29 Rome was still officially, and by a long and revered tradition, a republic. It would be imprudent to disregard the fact.

Weaknesses of Republican Structure

The civil war, and the struggle between Pompey and Caesar that had preceded it, had revealed the weakness of the Republican constitution. It could not cope with the new power situation that Rome's acquisition of empire had brought. The conquest and control of lands, some of them rich and famous, inevitably meant that the commanders concerned won great fame and acquired immense power. The large armies that they commanded tended to give them personal allegiance. They looked to them for reward rather than to the Senate of distant Rome.

The opportunities afforded by such commands naturally tempted the ambitious. The struggle to obtain them was fierce and expensive. Once obtained, the successful competitor exploited his opportunities to the fullest and sought to extend his term of office. Back in Rome, his enemies prepared for his recall, with accusations of maladministration. And his friends fought to strengthen his position. The perils of such a situation had been demonstrated by the careers of both Pompey and Caesar, and presaged by the earlier struggle between Sulla and Marius. The ambition of Marc Antony, united with that of Cleopatra, had threatened the very sovereignty of Rome itself.

Transfer of Power

The problem that confronted Octavian after Actium was that of a reconstruction of the state that would preserve the semblance of its traditional Republican form yet obviate its manifest weaknesses by investing the reality of power in himself. This he secured by contriving to have various crucial offices assigned to him by the Senate. At the same time he strove to appear as the champion *par*

excellence of the Republic's laws and constitution. Thus in 27 B.C. he dramatically resigned all the offices which he had acquired since 43 B.C. In exchange, the Senate granted him the *imperium* or command over all the armed forces for the next ten years. This also gave him control over those provinces in which armies were located.

Augustus

The Senate also bestowed on him the title of "Augustus." It is difficult to define the exact meaning of this title, by which Octavian has subsequently become known. According to the historian Dio, it signified "as being something more than human." Suetonius reports that there was also a suggestion that he should take the name of Romulus as the second founder of Rome. But this was rejected because Romulus had been a king and Octavian would never be connected with this office or title. Indeed, Octavian was most careful to use no exceptional title for himself. He preferred to call himself *princeps*, in the sense of being the leading citizen of the state. He also kept the military title of *imperator*, which was justified by his command of the Roman armies. In time, as "Emperor," the title became the peculiar designation of the head of the Roman Empire.

Social and religious reforms

Augustus set in motion a number of measures designed to restore the social, moral and economic well-being of the state. In particular, by a series of marriage-laws he sought to increase the true Roman stock which, for a variety of reasons, had been steadily dwindling. He tried also to revive the antique Roman

virtues and improve the moral tone of society by reanimating Rome's ancient religion.

Priesthoods, such as those of the *Flamen Dialis* and the *Fratres*

Roman Archigallus; a bas-relief

Arvales, were reconstituted. New temples were built, including one to Apollo on the Palatine (a tribute to the Apollo of Actium, believed to have given Augustus the victory), and to Mars Ultor, as the avenger of Caesar's assassination. Augustus himself assumed the title of *Pontifex Maximus* (high or chief priest); the title was inherited by successive emperors and finally adopted by the Pope of Rome. It is generally thought that Virgil and Horace supported Augustus in his religious policy through their poetry. Such measures inevitably have the air of a precious antiquarianism. For, although they were punctiliously performed, the vitality of the ancient rites was now beyond recall.

Emperor worship

There was, however, a development in the state-religion at this

Rites of Isis, introduced to Rome from Egypt

Augustus. Eventual decline and fall

Jupiter; from a Roman altar

upheavals of the civil war had prepared the way for a certain change of view. Julius Caesar had been deified after his death, and in the year 29 B.C. a temple had been solemnly dedicated in Rome to him as "Divus Julius." In consequence of this deification Octavian as the heir of Julius had received the title of "Divi filius." His later title of Augustus reinforced the tendency to regard him as having more than human status. However, the association of deification and kingship was probably

Coin of the deified Julius Caesar

time which was destined to have important repercussions later, particularly for emergent Christianity. It had long been the custom in the ancient Near East for divine honors to be paid to kings and rulers: e.g. the Egyptian Pharaoh had been worshiped as the incarnate son of the sun-god Rē. Alexander the Great had regarded himself as divine; and many eastern peoples readily agreed to acclaim as a god one of such stupendous genius and success. In turn, the later Hellenistic rulers expected and were accorded divine honors.

Julius Caesar deified

To Republican Rome such ideas were naturally abhorrent. But the

Temple of Vesta

enough to prevent the veneration paid to him from turning into actual worship in Rome and Italy during his life.

Divus Augustus

But it was otherwise in the provinces. Temples were dedicated to Roma and Augustus in Pergamum and Nicomedia. In 12 B.C. Drusus consecrated an altar at Lugdunum in Gaul to Roma and Augustus. The association of the genius of the city and the Emperor is significant; for the cult of the two came to constitute a declaration of political loyalty. On September 17, A.D. 14, shortly after his death, the Senate decreed that Augustus should take his place among the gods of the state as "Divus Augustus." His golden image was placed on a couch in the temple of Mars to receive divine honors.

Architect of the Roman Empire

Augustus has been called the "architect of the Roman Empire," and there is abundant justification for the title. As he is reputed to have said of his building activity: "I found Rome of brick, I leave it of marble," so he might have said: "I found the Roman state a Republican ruin, I leave it a

The Emperor taking leave of his army after a victory

strong monarchical Empire." Although eschewing the title and trappings of kingship, Augustus had gathered all effective power into his own hands. And, out of the chaos he had inherited, he fashioned the imperial Rome that was to dominate the ancient world for the next four centuries, and the imagination of Europe for long centuries after. But the hands into which such absolute power had been gathered were strong, and the mind which controlled and directed that power was far-seeing and firm.

The Army's power

However, Augustus could not ensure that he would be succeeded by emperors equally sagacious and strong. Moreover, although he succeeded in controlling the power of the army, the fate of Rome always rested ultimately on the army—not only for its defense against the barbarian peoples beyond its frontiers, but also for its own internal stability and well-being. Thus the future of the Empire, and with it the civilization of the ancient world, depended upon two problematic factors: the ability of the Emperor and the efficient loyalty of the army.

Decline and fall

The subsequent history of the Roman Empire is that of the operation and interaction of these

two factors. And its main theme is the growing awareness of the army, or those who commanded its most powerful contingents, that they could both make and destroy emperors. The internecine warfare that resulted, punctuated only by short intervals of peace, gradually sapped both the economic and military strength of the Empire.

The collapse was gradual but inevitable. Rome itself was twice sacked by barbarian armies before the resignation of the Emperor Romulus Augustulus in 476 brought the Western Empire to an end. However, the division of the Empire by Constantine, and the

Battle between Romans and Dacians

founding of Constantinople in 330 as the capital of the Eastern Empire, ensured the continuance of the Roman *imperium* in the eastern Mediterranean lands for another thousand years—indeed until the fall of Constantinople to the Ottoman Turks in 1453.

We will now see how the problem of assimilating conquered peoples became too big for Rome, and how a major disaster limited future expansion of the Empire.

Arminius, Liberator of Germany

By 9 B.C. it seemed that Augustus' ambition to extend Roman territory to the Elbe had almost been achieved. But the Romans overestimated the extent to which they had successfully assimilated their new province. Encouraged by revolts in the Empire, German aspirations to freedom and prowess in arms both found their champion in Arminius, a German by birth but also a Roman citizen. Arminius' knowledge of the terrain made a German victory a strong possibility, and his annihilation of the legions sent to maintain order shook the Empire to its core. Rome was forced to abandon any idea of a province beyond the Rhine, and the implications for the future of Europe were incalculable.

A barbarian holds out a child to the Emperor Augustus, symbolizing Roman responsibility for the dominions of the Empire.

Augustus pushed the frontiers of Roman dominion outward in almost every direction. But during the forty-five years of his sole rule he was forced to fight constant and simultaneous campaigns to maintain the lines he wished to draw on the map of Europe. The frontier between the subject province of Gaul and barbarian Germany was to prove especially troublesome, and the whole might of Rome eventually was to be challenged by one barbarian leader, Arminius, of the Cherusci tribe. But Arminius, whom Tacitus called the liberator of Germany, was not the first German to threaten Rome.

Around the end of the second century B.C., two barbarian tribes, the Cimbri and the Teutons, had gradually migrated southward from the neighborhood of Jutland until they reached the northern frontier of Rome. After pushing the Roman armies as far south as Orange, in the Gallo-Roman province of Narbonensis, they proceeded toward Italy itself. They were stopped, however, by one of Rome's outstanding generals, Marius, who defeated them at Aix-en-Provence in 102 B.C. and obliterated them at Vercelli the following year.

Germanic pugnacity engraved itself upon the Roman mind and tongue: a man of ferocious character was called "Cimber," and the "furor Teutonicus" was spoken of long after the tribe had disappeared. Although there was nothing yet approaching a German nation, Rome remained highly conscious of this mass of Germanic peoples in northern Europe. The line of demarcation between the Celts in Gaul and the Germanic tribes to the east was vague, and though the Celts tended to concentrate west of the Rhine, there was still a lot of German blood and influence in that region.

Then in 58 B.C. Julius Caesar entered the picture. The territory of which he was governor included not only the Adriatic coast and what is now north Italy but also the province of Narbonensis. Caesar picked a quarrel with Ariovistus, a German leader influential in Gaul. He then proceeded to annex all Gaul, establishing the Rhine as the frontier between Roman and non-Roman lands. And so Caesar crystallized the idea of a subject Gaul west of the Rhine and a free Germany east.

Half a century later, Augustus gradually pushed Rome's eastern European frontier to the Danube. But a frontier consisting of the Rhine and the Danube made a very long and devious line, including a right angle along their upper courses. An Elbe-Danube line would be a great deal shorter, communications would be easier, and potentially hostile tribesmen would be safely enclosed within the Empire. So Augustus' younger stepson, Drusus, crossed the Rhine to fight four successive campaigns in Germany. He reached the Weser and finally, in 9 B.C., the Elbe. The Romans built fortresses, and the entire area from the Rhine to the Elbe was regarded as a new Roman province.

The Germans were, for the most part, semicivilized pastoral nomads. Tacitus, in his *Germania*, vividly describes these people with their wild, blue eyes, reddish hair, and hulking bodies—politically unstable tribesmen who loved a fight but disdained work. The Romans hated their new province, "bristling with woods or festering with swamps," but Roman influence gradually seeped in, and modern excavations show that a good deal of trade was conducted.

One Roman governor after another fought laborious campaigns to consolidate the new conquests and frontiers. The greatest weakness lay in the fact that the shorter Elbe-Danube frontier could not be completed until Bohemia (now western Czechoslovakia) was conquered too. This became obvious when an astute German chief, Maroboduus, led his entire Marcomannic tribe on a migration from occupied southwestern Germany into free Bohemia and established authority over the German tribes of Saxony and Silesia. The Roman government decided that it was imperative to put a stop to the expansion of Maroboduus.

The Gemma Augustea, or Vienna Cameo, showing Augustus seated with the goddess Roma ; to one side, the victorious Tiberius steps from his chariot. In the lower register, captive Germans are held by the hair, while Roman soldiers erect a trophy of victory.

Below A barbarian surrenders his standard to the Emperor Augustus ; the reverse of a coin issued by Augustus.

One man challenges mighty Rome

In A.D. 6, therefore, twelve legions were launched in a massive three-pronged invasion under the supreme command of Augustus' elder stepson and heir apparent, Tiberius. But a huge revolt broke out in northern Yugoslavia, putting an end to the campaign against Maroboduus. Nevertheless, the tribal chieftain very sensibly came to terms with Rome and was recognized as a king and friend of the Roman people. Meanwhile, the Yugoslavian revolt, described as Rome's gravest foreign threat since Hannibal, took three years to suppress.

The new province of Germany watched these events with rising excitement. The Romans were not, after all, infallible; they had been compelled to spare Maroboduus. Prolonged resistance to their power was not beyond the bounds of possibility. These were the circumstances when a new Roman governor, Publius Quintilius Varus, reached Germany. Husband of Augustus' grandniece, Varus was among the Emperor's closest friends and had a hard-won reputation for firmness and order. When he arrived in Germany, however, he miscalculated the situation. He regarded the country as already subjugated and believed he could impose civilian methods of control such as were possible in the rich, well-organized provinces he had hitherto governed. The third-century Greek historian Dio Cassius describes the situation:

"The Romans held portions of the country, not entire regions but such districts as happened to have been subdued . . . The soldiers wintered there, and cities were being founded. Gradually the barbarians adapted themselves to Roman ways, getting accustomed to holding markets, and assembling peacefully.

"But they had not forgotten their ancestral ways, their inborn nature, their old proud way of life, their freedom based on arms. As long as they were unlearning their ancient customs gradually and as it were by degrees, they did not protest against these changes in their mode of life, for they were growing different without being aware of it. But when Quintilius Varus was appointed governor of the area and in the course of his official duties attempted to take these people in hand, striving to change them, issuing orders as though they had already been subdued and exacting money as from a subject nation, their patience was exhausted."

Earlier, in A.D. 4, Tiberius, at that time governor of Germany, had given an important West Germanic tribe, the Cherusci, the privileged position of a federated state within the Empire. Members of their ruling class, among them the young prince Arminius, were made Roman citizens. Arminius entered the imperial service as an officer in its auxiliary military forces, gaining the status of a Roman knight.

The Cherusci, whose territory reached almost to the Elbe, played a leading part in the arrangements of Varus. Like his predecessors, Varus proposed to winter on the Rhine and spend the summer at advanced posts far inside the recently conquered province. And so in A.D. 9 he established a summer camp for his three legions (6,000 men each) in Cheruscan territory. Two legions were left behind on the Rhine. His own advance headquarters were on the west bank of the Weser. Varus befriended the Cheruscan chiefs, including Arminius, little realizing that Arminius was even then plotting against him.

Some of the chiefs tried to warn the governor of this impending treachery, but Varus was persuaded to lend the conspirators legionary detachments, which they said they needed to guard certain posts and escort supplies for the Roman army. Moreover, when the time came for Varus to withdraw to the Rhine for the winter, the plotters persuaded him to change his route. He had intended to march back to his winter camp at Vetera by the military road, but the fictitious report of a local rising induced him to make a northwesterly detour through difficult wooded country. The conspirators saw the main army off from their summer camp on the Weser. As Varus took his leave, they asked for and received permission to rejoin their tribes—ostensibly to recruit men to help put down the revolt that they had invented.

The Roman column moved slowly. It was encumbered by a heavy baggage train and large numbers of women, children and servants. As it proceeded through the rough country, felling trees and making paths and causeways, a shower of missiles suddenly descended. There could be no doubt of what had happened. The Germans were attacking. The legionaries were hampered by the wind, rain and mud that had always made them dislike Germany. They were too short of auxiliaries—cavalry, archers and slingers—to strike back effectively. All they could do was press on and hope to reach the nearest fortress, Aliso, which lay somewhere on or near the Lippe River, perhaps two-thirds of the way from the Weser back to the Rhine.

Discipline asserted itself sufficiently for a camp to be pitched for the night on high ground. Wagons and baggage were burned or jettisoned and next morning the march was resumed. The legions started off in better order over open country, but this left them vulnerable to German attacks, and they were again compelled to take refuge in the woods, where they spent a most disagreeable day struggling through obstacles. They suffered heavy losses, some of them self-inflicted because of the difficulty of distinguishing enemy from friend. That night they managed to huddle together in another makeshift camp, with a totally inadequate rampart.

When morning came, it was still raining, there was a biting wind and they could see that the Germans had received reinforcements. The commander of the Roman cavalry lost his nerve and rode off with his regiment in the vain hope of reaching the Rhine. Varus was suffering from wounds and fully realized what the Germans would do to him if they caught him alive. To avoid this fate, he killed himself. Some members of his staff followed his example, and the two generals who were left in charge did not long survive. One mistakenly offered capitulation, which turned into a massacre; the other fell fighting as the Germans broke into the encampment. Except for a few legionaries who escaped under cover of darkness, the entire Roman force, some 20,000 men, was either captured or slaughtered.

Six years later another Roman commander in the area, Germanicus, formed the idea—according to his uncle Tiberius a very demoralizing one—of taking his troops to visit the site. The occasion provided Tacitus with one of his highlights:

Sword of honor with decorated scabbard, probably one of many made for presentation to officers who served under Germanicus in A.D. 17. The upper panel of the scabbard (detail *left*) shows Tiberius welcoming Germanicus on his return.

"Now they were near the Teutoburgian Wood, in which the remains of Varus and his three legions were said to be lying unburied. Germanicus conceived a desire to pay his last respects to these men and their general. Every soldier with him was overcome with pity when he thought of his relations and friends—and reflected on the hazards of war and of human life. Caecina was sent ahead to reconnoiter the dark woods and build bridges and causeways on the treacherous surface of the sodden marshland. Then the army made its way over the tragic sites.

"The scene lived up to its horrible associations. Varus' extensive first camp, with its broad extent and headquarters marked out, testified to the whole army's labors. Then a half-ruined breastwork and shallow ditch showed where the last pathetic remnant had gathered. On the open ground were whitening bones, scattered where men had fled, heaped up where they had stood and fought back. Fragments of spears and of horses' limbs lay there —also human heads, fastened to tree-trunks. In groves nearby were the outlandish altars at which the Germans had massacred the Roman colonels and senior company commanders.

"Survivors of the catastrophe, who had escaped from the battle or from captivity, pointed out where the generals had fallen, and where the Eagles were captured. They showed where Varus received his first wound, and where he died by his own unhappy hand. And they told of the platform from which Arminius had spoken, and of his arrogant insults to the Eagles and standards—and of all the gibbets and pits for the prisoners."

Exactly where the Roman army was annihilated is uncertain—though not for lack of attempts to locate the site. Early in the sixteenth century, when

The Emperor's ambitions thwarted

Right Barbarians besieging a Roman fort; relief from Trajan's Column.

Below A Roman soldier; bronze statuette of the first century A.D.

the story was becoming celebrated, the Lippischer Wald was renamed the Teutoburger Wald, and a monument to Arminius now stands on the supposed site of the battle.

As had been feared, the triumphant Germans swept on toward the Rhine. All the advance forts to the east of the river, except Aliso, fell without resistance. Aliso's commander and a force of archers succeeded in holding out until their stores were exhausted. Then on a dark night, the garrison slipped out—women, children and all—and managed to make its way to the winter camp at Vetera on the Rhine. There they found the province's two remaining legions, which Varus' nephew Lucius Asprenas had hastily brought north from Mainz.

The disaster upset Augustus more than anything in his long life, and he took every counter measure that he could think of. He dismissed all the Germans and Gauls in his personal bodyguard. Determined efforts were made to replace the lost legions, but few recruits of military age were available. Finally a force consisting mainly of retired soldiers and former slaves (who were not normally admitted to the legions) was entrusted to Tiberius, who had rushed back from Dalmatia. He led them to the Rhine to join the remaining two legions and defend the entire line of the border.

The Germans did not, however, manage to approach the Rhine. Deterred by Asprenas and delayed before the ramparts of Aliso, they lost any chance of mounting a surprise attack. Moreover,

an attempt by Arminius to convert his rebellion into a national German revolt came to nothing. Such a revolt was contingent upon the support of Maroboduus, whom Arminius tried to intimidate in a gruesome manner. His men had come upon some of the Romans cremating the body of Varus in the Teutoburg Forest. They seized what was left of the corpse and mutilated it. They cut off the head and sent it to Maroboduus, appealing to him to join the insurrection. But he saw no advantage in harnessing himself to the ambition of Arminius. It seemed wiser to stand by his treaty with Rome. The head of Varus was forwarded to Augustus, who performed the funeral rites.

Five years later Augustus died. Shortly before his death he sent his brilliant young grandnephew, later called Germanicus, to take command on the Rhine. When Tiberius came to the throne in A.D. 14, Germanicus fought three massive and expensive campaigns against the Cherusci. A longstanding quarrel between Arminius and his pro-Roman father-in-law Segestes flared anew, with Germanicus siding with Segestes. Arminius' wife fell into Roman hands, and although Arminius himself was urged by his brother to collaborate with Rome, he refused. And so a great battle between Arminius and the Romans was fought at Idistaviso, probably near Minden. Germanicus claimed the victory, despite the fact that his legions and auxiliaries had been forced to retreat. But the Germans were far from subjugated.

In A.D. 19 Arminius picked a quarrel with Maroboduus, the German who had snubbed him, and a battle ensued. Although the outcome was indecisive, Maroboduus lost much of his power, and soon afterward his Bohemian kingdom lost its independence. But Arminius' end was also at hand, as Tacitus describes:

"I find from the writings of contemporary senators, that a letter was read in the Roman senate from a chieftain of the Chatti, Adgandestrius by name, offering to kill Arminius if poison were sent him for the job. The reported answer was that Romans take vengeance on their enemies, not by underhand tricks, but by open force of arms.

"However, the Roman evacuation of Germany and the fall of Maroboduus had induced Arminius to aim at kingship. But his freedom-loving compatriots forcibly resisted. The fortunes of the fight fluctuated, but finally Arminius succumbed to treachery from his relations.

"He was unmistakably the liberator of Germany. Challenger of Rome—not in its infancy, like kings and commanders before him, but at the height of its power—he had fought undecided battles, and never lost a war. He had ruled for twelve of his thirty-seven years. To this day the tribes sing of him. Yet Greek historians ignore him, reserving their admiration for Greece. We Romans, too, underestimate him, since in our devotion to antiquity we neglect modern history."

Tacitus was justified in calling Arminius the man who had freed Germany. He was not, however, a national chief. "He was only," wrote one historian, "the leader of a faction even among his tribesmen, not a champion of the German nation, for no such thing existed. The very name was of recent date, an alien appellation; there was among the Germans little consciousness of a common origin, of a common interest none at all."

Still, it was thanks to his extraordinary skill and courage that the Romans were excluded, from then on, from Germany across the Rhine. With the exception of a coastal strip and a tract on the upper Rhine and Danube, the province was abandoned. Rome was forced to recognize that annexation was impossible or inadvisable and to treat trans-Rhenane Germany as a client-state, dependent economically, but nothing more.

Had Arminius not frustrated Augustus in his aim to establish an Elbe-Bohemia-Danube frontier, almost the whole of the present Federal Republic of Germany and the Czech area of Czechoslovakia would have been parts of the Roman Empire. Might-have-beens are notoriously unprofitable, but it is likely that in the end these territories, under Roman rule, would have become as docile and Latinized as Gaul. Any idea of the Rhine as a frontier would have been irrelevant and forgotten. The whole concept of Germany would have been unimaginably different, and so, therefore, would every subsequent century of European history.

MICHAEL GRANT

Triumphal Roman arch at Orange, in southern France, probably built by the Emperor Tiberius to commemorate his suppression of a Gallic revolt.

The slaughter of Varus' legions abruptly halted the northward expansion of Rome's power. It also marked the end of the expansion of the Roman Empire as a whole. The Emperor Trajan was to annex the new province of Dacia at the end of the first century A.D., but the period of giant growth which had taken Rome from being a small city-state in the middle of Italy to her position as mistress of the civilized world was effectively ended. The victory of German arms over the might of the invincible legions was also an augury for the later years of the Empire when Rome employed Germans as top military commanders as her armed strength lost its potency.

The victory of Arminius must have brought home the lesson that consolidation was now the most urgent task facing Augustus. The armies of conquest were henceforth armies of territorial defense, deployed at strategic intervals around the vast periphery of the Empire. Within its frontiers, territories conquered by the sword were turned into provinces of the Empire. The establishment of towns with all the accompanying apparatus of Greco-Roman institutions and civilization meant that within a century the uncouth cousins of Arminius could be as Roman as anyone in Rome itself. Roman citizenship was not available automatically to the inhabitants of a province. It was granted to individuals and urban centers thought worthy of the honor and likely to provide a foundation for the actual Romanization of an

Tombstone of Roman centurion

area. The Romans accepted local distinctions—a man from Syria would still be a Syrian even if he were also a Roman citizen. Local characteristics were not usually suppressed, but they were often dropped in favor of appearing more Roman. At least, they were not suppressed while they offered no threat to the power or basic tenets of Roman rule. The assimilation of a measure of Roman culture, and lip-service to the fact of Roman power, were the two things required of provincials. It was clearly easier in some ways to assimilate primitive barbarian Germans. Once their political and military resistance had been broken, the way lay open to the benefits of civilization. They had no strongly rooted cultural traditions and values of their own to conflict.

Rome's problems in the East

The problem that the new Empire faced in its southern provinces was of a different order. On the southern fringes of the Mediterranean, civilizations had existed thousands of years before Rome had appeared on the scene, as we have already seen. Rome was no doubt seen by the Greeks and Jews and other people of ancient stock as just another in a long line of conquerors. Alexander had marched about, subduing many people who were in some cases rather more Greek than he was. Then there had been the Carthaginians, and now the Romans. The imposition of Roman power was just another political domination, not the joyous arrival of a chance to be civilized.

The Emperor Trajan

Arminius may not have been a nationalist leader, but his conflict with Rome involved the clash of two distinct political and racial groups. In a sense, Roman civilization was anti-nationalist in that Romanness overrode any national or local identity. It was only specifically anti-nationalist when faced with nationalism that refused to accept the few basic principles of Roman rule and when any group offered a real threat to Roman rule.

The Jewish people

The Jewish people offered just such a threat. Their religion was decidedly ethnic and exclusive, and rigidly fixed in its orthodoxy. There was no chance that syncretism could accommodate the demands made by official emperor-worship. These very conditions were to bring about the fall of the Temple and the destruction of the Jewish nation, as we shall see. But they were also to determine the development of Christianity, whose dramatic beginning is the subject of our next chapter, for the Christians inherited the Jewish antipathy to emperor-worship, and thus brought upon themselves the fate of martyrs when faced with a test of their loyalty to the Empire.

But for Romans, the life and death of Jesus was not at all significant. In the context of the history of Rome that we have so far explored, Jesus was just another rebellious troublemaker. Thousands of slaves had been crucified in like manner after the revolt of Spartacus. His death was merely one more item in the list of repressions that Rome found necessary to consolidate her power. Let us now look at the background to the emergence of Jesus as a religious leader.

Herod the Great

Jewish history during the four decades preceding the birth of Jesus of Nazareth is notable for the reign of Herod the Great. Herod was descended from the Idumaeans, an Arab people dwelling to the south of Judaea. They had been forcibly converted to Judaism by the Jewish king John Hyrcanus (134–104 B.C.). Herod's father Antipater had been chief minister of the High Priest Hyrcanus II

German couple; from a tombstone

Jupiter (Zeus): a Greco-Roman plaque

Master and pupils; Roman relief

Mummy shroud from Roman Egypt

(75–40 B.C.); his good relations with the Romans had made him the virtual ruler of Judaea.

Herod was appointed governor of Galilee by his father, and quickly distinguished himself by his efficient and vigorous rule. But he soon needed all his ability to survive the turmoil into which Judaea was plunged in consequence of the Roman civil wars, the attacks of Jewish enemies, a Parthian invasion, and the intrigues of Cleopatra of Egypt. From an amazing series of adventures, which were graphically described by the Jewish historian Josephus, Herod eventually emerged in 31 B.C. as King of the Jews. He enjoyed the friendship of Augustus, who admired his ability and appreciated his usefulness. Since Judaea constituted a vital strategic link in the defense of Syria and Egypt, it was important to the Romans that it should be securely held. Augustus found in Herod a client-king whose loyalty he could trust and whose government would be strong and efficient.

Herod's Temple

Herod was undoubtedly the most capable king who ever ruled Judaea. He improved its prosperity, rebuilt many of its cities, made a superb seaport at Caesarea, and encouraged trade. His foreign policy greatly benefited the Jews of the Diaspora. He also rebuilt the Temple at Jerusalem on a most magnificent scale—the wonder which it evoked has been preserved in the *Gospel of Mark*.

Yet, for all his achievement, Herod was hated by the Jews for his Idumaean descent and his

pagan tastes. They hated him also for dark tragedies that clouded his domestic life. His suspicious nature caused him to order the deaths of the leading members of the Hasmonaean family, to whom he was related by marriage but whose position he had usurped. Among those who thus died was his wife Mariamne, whom he dearly loved, and their sons—but in these tragedies Herod's sister Salome had played a sinister part.

Herod's policy

Herod's pagan tastes were really the expression of his Hellenizing policy, which had far-sighted motives. Herod professed the Jewish faith, which he signally patronized by his munificent rebuilding of the Temple. But he

Coin of Herod the Great

knew the innate fanaticism of Judaism, and foresaw the dangers of its ultimate conflict with Rome. He promoted the Greco-Roman

Tombstone of Roman legionary

Egyptian mummy shroud showing the dead person attended by gods

way of life by the building of temples dedicated to Augustus, and theaters, amphitheaters and stadiums. His purpose was probably to acquaint the Jews with this wider culture, without constraining them to adopt it. But it was in vain. When he died in the year 4 B.C. the Jews seemed even more fanatically disposed, encouraged perhaps by their pride in the very Temple which Herod had built for them. They failed to appreciate the fact that Herod's reign had

preserved them for three decades from the grim realities of direct Roman rule. That rule they were soon to experience with baleful consequences. The events of the next few years would ultimately be of significance for the whole world: the Roman Empire, which put to death a religious dissident, would eventually be taken over by the religion that he had founded, as the first chapter in Volume II will show. But first we will look at the beginnings of that religion.

Roman tax-collector

Jesus of Nazareth, Savior God of a New Religion

For Romans alive about A.D. 30 the life and death of Jesus was of no significance whatsoever. In the context of Roman history, Jesus was just another rebellious troublemaker. After the revolt of Spartacus thousands of slaves had been crucified in the same way as Jesus. His death was merely one more item in the list of repressions that Rome found necessary to carry out in order to consolidate her power. And yet in the end the religion founded by Jesus would take over the Roman Empire itself, and eventually make its way all over the world. The consequences for the subsequent history of civilization were incalculable.

Writing early in the second century, the Roman historian Tacitus told his readers how Nero had been suspected of burning Rome in A.D. 64. To free himself from suspicion, the infamous Emperor "fastened the guilt and inflicted the most exquisite tortures on a class hated for their vices, whom the people called Christians. Christus, from whom the name derived, suffered the extreme penalty during the reign of Tiberius on the order of the procurator Pontius Pilate. The pernicious superstition, suppressed for the moment, broke out again, not only in Judaea, the source of the evil, but in Rome itself . . . Accordingly, acknowledged members of the sect were first arrested; then, upon their evidence, an immense multitude was convicted, not so much of the crime of firing the city, as of hatred of mankind."

This significant passage from the *Annales* of Tacitus shows what an educated Roman knew and thought about Christianity some eighty years after its birth. To him it was a dangerous subversive movement whose founder had been executed for sedition by the Roman governor of Judaea; but that had only temporarily checked the movement, and it had spread from Judaea to the underworld of Rome. Nero had found that the Christians were convenient scapegoats for the fire; for people already believed that Christians hated mankind.

We need not accept as accurate this damning estimate of primitive Christianity. Yet it is important historical evidence because it is the earliest non-Christian source; all our other information comes from Christian writings that were inspired by theological, and not historical, interests. This fact constitutes a fundamental problem for the historian of Christian origins, for it is his task to understand how Christianity began as a historical movement. The Christian Gospels purport to give factual accounts of the life of Jesus; but these writings are based on the assumption that Jesus was not just a man, but that he was the Son of God, sent by God into this world to save mankind. This assumption involved some very complex theology; it had nothing to do with historical fact.

These theological ideas, nevertheless, are of historical importance, because they form the basis of Christianity—and the birth of Christianity is certainly one of the most important milestones of history. The historian, therefore, must explain how such ideas originated, and trace how they developed into the religion we know as Christianity. But he must also explain who Jesus was, and what he taught and did as an historical person. There have been thinkers who have denied that Jesus ever existed and have regarded him as a mythical figure. This view is no longer held by responsible scholars. But there is much conflict of opinion about what can reasonably be accepted as historical fact about both the person and career of Jesus.

Ironically, the most certain fact that we know about Jesus is that he was crucified by the Romans for sedition against their government in Judaea. The Roman governor who ordered his execution was Pontius Pilate, who held the office of Governor of Judaea from A.D. 26 to 36. We can be certain of this one fact because the Roman execution of Jesus is recorded not only by the Roman historian Tacitus, but also by the authors of the four Gospels, who might have wished to suppress such damaging evidence. That Jesus had been crucified for sedition was indeed an embarrassing fact. For Christians it meant that their master had been regarded as a rebel against Rome, and that they were likely to be incriminated as well.

The early Christians would probably have preferred to keep quiet about the execution of Jesus, but the fact was too well known to conceal. Instead, they attempted to show that Jesus was really innocent of sedition. A large part of each of the four Gospels is devoted to the trial and crucifixion of Jesus. The Gospel of Mark, earliest of the

An inscription, found at Caesarea in 1961, containing the names of the Emperor Tiberius and Pontius Pilate; the latter is designated "Praefectus of Judaea."

Opposite The Crucifixion, depicted on a Gnostic gem probably made in the third century A.D. It is one of the earliest representations of the Crucifixion, the Church having at first tended to emphasize the glory of Jesus rather than his shameful death.

A criminal executed

Bottom Coin of Tiberius, A.D. 14–37, the "tribute penny."

four, sets the theme for the others by endeavoring to show that the death of Jesus had been plotted by Jewish leaders who hated him. These leaders, Mark points out, condemned Jesus to death for blasphemy in their own court, the Sanhedrin; but they lacked the authority to execute him. Consequently, they handed Jesus over to Pilate, charging him with sedition against Rome. Pilate was not convinced by the charge and sought to release Jesus. His efforts, however, were frustrated by the Jewish leaders, who stirred up the mob to demand the crucifixion of Jesus. Pilate was forced to accede and so, at last, ordered the execution. Hence, according to the Gospels, Jesus was really the victim of the malevolence of the Jewish leaders and the weak character of Pontius Pilate.

The most certain fact we know about Jesus thus entails a problem: Christian evidence admits that Jesus was executed for sedition against Rome; but it also maintains that he was innocent. Can this claim be accepted? This question is basic to all understanding of Jesus as an historical person.

If Jesus were really a rebel against the Roman government in Judaea, he would have been very different from the gentle person Christian doctrine holds him to be. But, at the same time, he would be more intelligible historically, for among the Jews of his time there was a fierce hatred of Roman rule. That rule was an affront to their religion since they fervently believed that they were the Elect People of their god Yahweh and should not be subject to a heathen lord. To them Judaea was Yahweh's holy land, and its produce should not be given in tribute to the Roman Caesar. Many Jews, in fact, refused to submit to Rome and died as martyrs for Israel's freedom. The usual Roman penalty for rebellion was crucifixion. Hence the problem: did Jesus also die as a martyr for Israel's freedom? Or was he obedient to Rome, as the Gospels make out, and was his crucifixion due to the Jewish leaders?

Long and complex research has been devoted to these problems. All we can do here is outline some possible answers.

The Gospel accounts of the trial of Jesus reveal a strong apologetic motivation. The early Christian authors were obviously concerned with transferring the responsibility for the crucifixion of Jesus from the Romans to the Jews. Their purpose in so doing was a result of the situation in which the Christians found themselves after A.D. 70. That year marked the end of a four-year-long Jewish revolt against Rome, and anti-Jewish feeling had grown intense among the Romans. The Gentile Christians, consequently, found themselves in a dangerous and perplexing situation. The Jewish origins of their religion were well known; so, too, was the awkward fact that Jesus had been executed by the Romans as a rebel. To the Roman authorities and people, all Christians were suspected of being sympathetic to Jewish nationalism and to Messianic fanaticism.

The Gospel of Mark deals with this dangerous situation as it affected the Christians of Rome about A.D. 71. But Mark's attempt to turn Pilate into a witness to the innocence of Jesus and make the Jews solely responsible for his death breaks down under critical analysis. This is also the case when the accounts of the trial of Jesus in the other Gospels are examined. We must conclude, therefore, that the Romans crucified Jesus as a rebel because they deemed him to be one.

This conclusion, necessarily summarized here, is confirmed by an abundance of cumulative evidence from various sources.

Something of the career of Jesus as a historical person can be reconstructed from a critical appraisal of the Gospels. A native of Nazareth in Galilee, Jesus was at first associated with John the Baptist. John announced, in the tradition of Hebrew prophecy, the imminence of the kingdom of God and sought to prepare the Jews for this fateful event by a baptism of repentance. Jesus, perhaps after the arrest of John by Herod Antipas, carried on the mission. He achieved a measure of success in Galilee but soon encountered opposition from the Jewish authorities. Jesus then became convinced that it was these authorities who were delaying Israel's preparation for the kingdom of God.

By his followers and by many of the people, Jesus was recognized as the Messiah, God's chosen agent for the redemption of Israel. And he also undoubtedly so regarded himself. At this stage in his ministry, Jesus was probably more concerned with the opposition of the Jewish authorities than

he was with the Romans, for Galilee was then ruled by a Jewish prince, Herod Antipas. Jesus came into direct contact with the Romans only when he visited Jerusalem, which was in Judaea. The Jewish authorities in Galilee, however, were closely associated with the Roman rule of Judaea, for Jerusalem was the religious center for all Jews. The High Priest at Jerusalem was actually appointed by the Roman governor to control "native" affairs and maintain good order among his people. Consequently, both the High Priest and the Sadducean aristocracy, of which he was a member, were suspicious of any popular movement likely to disturb the peace. And the movement led by Jesus appeared to be just such a disturbance.

The priestly aristocracy, headed by the High Priest, controlled the Temple of Yahweh at Jerusalem; their position gave them great authority as well as a rich income. Seeing them as the chief obstacle to Israel's conversion, Jesus finally decided to challenge their control of the Temple. Accordingly, with his disciples and Galilean followers he staged a Messianic entry into Jerusalem at the feast of the Passover. Gathering support, he attacked the trading activities of the Temple. These activities were a profitable source of revenue to the priestly aristocrats, and Jesus' attack was obviously a far more serious affair than the Gospels represent it to have been. It is even possible that Jesus intended to seize the Temple and reform the priesthood, as the Zealots were later to do in A.D. 66. The outcome of

Jesus' bold move is difficult to assess. It would seem that he did not achieve complete success; but his supporters remained too numerous for the Jewish leaders to arrest him publicly.

After this so-called "Cleansing of the Temple," Jesus stayed on in Jerusalem, although he withdrew from the city each night. He seems to have been uncertain of his next move. The question that the historian must now face is whether the action of Jesus in the Temple had been connected with a Zealot operation. We learn from the Gospels that at this Passover there had also been an armed rising against the Romans, apparently led by Barabbas, which seems to have involved the Zealots. That two uprisings, one against the Jewish authorities and one against the Romans, should have occurred in Jerusalem at the Passover is certainly remarkable. The coincidence suggests that there may have been some connection between the two events.

Jesus continued his stay in Jerusalem until the night of the Passover feast, which he ate with his disciples within the city. By then he probably realized that his attempt to challenge the authorities had failed and that it would be wiser to withdraw to Galilee.

Christian tradition records that, in Gethsemane that night, Jesus experienced an agony of indecision. However, the initiative suddenly passed from him to his enemies. One of his apostles, Judas Iskariot, had defected and betrayed his rendezvous to the

Above Ivory plaque showing scenes of the arrest and trial of Jesus; from a reliquary of the fourth century A.D.

Below The crypt of the Convent of the Sisters of Zion on the site of King Herod's Antonia Fortress, which was probably the site of Jesus' trial.

A new religion is born in the East

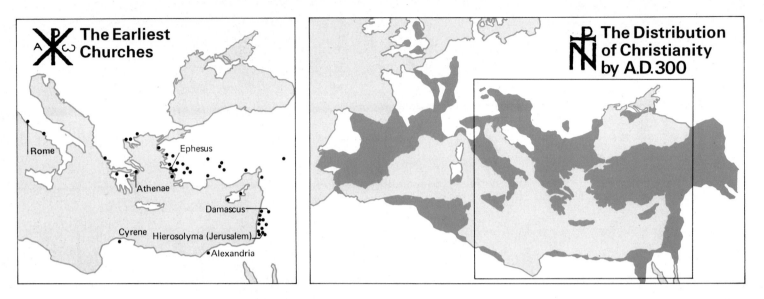

The Earliest Churches

Rome
Ephesus
Athenae
Damascus
Cyrene
Hierosolyma (Jerusalem)
Alexandria

The Distribution of Christianity by A.D.300

Below Pagan caricature of a crucifixion, from a wall of the Palatine Palace, probably dating from the third century A.D. It shows a slave (?) praying to a crucified figure with an ass' head, and the inscription reads "Alexemenus worships his god."

Jewish leaders. Taking no chances, they sent a heavily armed band to arrest Jesus. After an armed struggle in the darkness, the disciples fled and Jesus was taken. During the rest of that night the Jewish authorities interrogated him about his aims and his disciples, so that they could draw up a charge preparatory to handing him over to the Romans. In so doing, the High Priest was discharging his duty to the Roman government.

The High Priest charged Jesus with sedition, particularly for his claim to be the Messianic King of Israel. It is possible that he also accused Jesus of being the real leader of the recent rising against the Romans, thus exonerating Barabbas who was under Roman arrest. In other words, it is likely that Jesus was charged with heading a two-pronged attack: on the Jewish authorities in the Temple, and on the Romans in the Antonia Fortress and Upper City. What is certain is that Pilate condemned Jesus. The *titulus* which he ordered to be placed on the cross above the crucified Jesus, is evidence of the political nature of the charge: "This is Jesus the King of the Jews."

The crucifixion of Jesus as a rebel by the Romans was not an extraordinary event in the light of contemporary Jewish history. Thousands of other Jews similarly perished, either as leaders or supporters of revolt. But from this point onwards Christian tradition makes even more problematic the search for historical fact about Jesus. It was the usual practice for the bodies of executed criminals to be buried in a common grave. According to the Gospels, this did not happen to the body of Jesus. Instead, a disciple named Joseph of Arimathaea obtained the body from Pilate and buried it in a rock-hewn tomb of his own. Three days later, the tomb was found to be empty. Subsequently a series of visions, in which the crucified Jesus appeared to various disciples, convinced his followers that Jesus had risen from the dead. The visions were, significantly, limited to the disciples of Jesus; no one outside their fellowship is recorded to have had a similar experience. According to Christian tradition, these appearances of the Risen Jesus continued for forty days.

It is difficult to evaluate these traditions of the Resurrection of Jesus. Although the physical reality of the Risen Jesus is stressed, it is never asserted that he resumed his life on earth; instead he is said to have ascended to heaven. But, whatever the truth of the traditions about the Risen Jesus, there can be no doubt that from the disciples' faith in it, Christianity was born.

When the original disciples of Jesus became convinced that he had risen from the dead, their faith in his Messiahship revived. But, in the light of their new conviction, they had to adjust their own Jewish ideas. According to contemporary belief, the Messiah would overthrow the nation's oppressors and "restore the kingdom of Israel." But Jesus had been executed by Israel's oppressors: how could he, then, be the Messiah? The disciples soon found a solution in Holy Scripture. The prophet Isaiah had spoken about a suffering Servant of Yahweh, and the disciples applied this prophecy to Jesus. Because of Israel's sins, Jesus had died as a martyr; but God had raised him up. He would soon return, with supernatural power, to fulfill his Messianic role and redeem Israel.

So the Christianity of the original disciples was essentially a Jewish faith. They probably never contemplated that it would lead to a new religion distinct and separate from Judaism.

The transformation of Christianity from a Jewish Messianic sect into a universal salvation-religion, centered on Jesus, was due to Paul of Tarsus. Paul had not been an original disciple of Jesus. In fact, he had at first fiercely rejected Jewish Christianity because it preached a "crucified Messiah"—a scandalous thing to a pious Jew—and helped persecute members of the movement. Suddenly, however, Paul had a profound spiritual experience, which he attributed to the intervention of God. He became convinced that God had chosen him to reveal Jesus to the Gentiles, in a completely different guise from the one presented by the Jewish Christians. The Jewish Christians, in fact, had not even considered their faith in Jesus as being applicable to non-Jews.

Paul's new conception of Jesus drew its inspiration from Hellenistic ideas rather than from Judaism. The Gnostic philosophy, which was widely followed in Syria and Alexandria and farther east, held that all mankind was enslaved by demonic powers and taught how Gnosticism could save men from their subjection to the demonic vein, taught that God had sent Jesus into the world to save men from their subjection to the demonic rulers of the planets.

It was a very esoteric doctrine but one that Greco-Roman society of that time could understand and appreciate. Jesus was presented by Paul as a savior-god, who had died and risen again. Through the sacrament of baptism, Christians were ritually identified with Jesus in his death and resurrection. In consequence, they were reborn to a new risen life *in Christo*.

Paul's new "gospel" was repudiated by the Jewish Christians of Jerusalem. They also rejected his claim to be an apostle, and sent out emissaries to his converts to present their own "gospel" as the true and original form of Christianity. Paul's teaching might easily have been finally discredited and lost, but in A.D. 70 the Mother Church of Christianity at Jerusalem itself perished in the destruction of the city by the Romans. Christianity was thus freed from its primitive involvement with Judaism and Paul's version of Christianity survived and set the pattern for the entire faith.

Before the destruction of Jerusalem, Christianity had already spread outside Palestine. It moved mainly northwestwards, through Syria and Asia Minor, to Greece and Italy, although it was also established at an early date in Egypt. Freed from its Jewish cradle, Christianity quickly adapted itself to the spiritual needs of Greco-Roman society and eventually even survived the downfall of the Roman Empire in the West. The subsequent conversion of the barbarian peoples, who were to form the new nations of Europe, gave the Christian Church immense influence and power. The civilization of medieval Europe was, indeed, essentially the product of Christianity, and the later predominance and diffusion of the European peoples throughout the world made Christianity a cultural force of universal influence.

The Christian system of chronology still proclaims, even in a secular world, the decisive nature of the birth of Jesus—though ironically, it sets the event at least four years too late. By the sixth century, Christians regarded the birth of Jesus as so significant a turning point in world history that they reckoned time from it—the *Anni Domini* (A.D.), the "years of the Lord," that continue to designate our present era.

S. G. F. BRANDON

Houses and churches made by early Christians in the caves of Goreme, in Turkey, with (*right*) the interior of one of the churches.

Herod the Great died in the spring of 4 B.C.; his death sparked off an explosion of the long pent-up feelings of his Jewish subjects. Revolts immediately broke out in different parts of the country under various leaders. The situation was made worse by a Roman procurator, Sabinus, who moved in with troops to secure Herod's very considerable property for the Emperor Augustus. At Jerusalem, crowded with pilgrims for the feast of the Passover, armed conflict soon broke out. The Romans were ordered to withdraw by the rebels, "and not to stand in the way of men who after a lapse of time were on the road to recovering their national independence."

This statement of Jewish aims, which is recorded by the Jewish historian Josephus, is significant. It embodied an ideal, inspired by traditions of the heroic days of David and the Maccabees, which was rooted in the peculiar nature of Jewish religion. Every Jew was brought up to believe—and the belief was reinforced daily by the study and practice of the Torah—that Yahweh, the god of Israel, had given his people the land of Canaan as their Holy Land, where they were faithfully to serve him. This belief implied a conception of the state as a theocracy; Yahweh owned it and was its sovereign lord, and his vice-regent on earth was the high priest. This conception in turn implied the freedom of the Jewish people to devote themselves to the maintenance of this theocracy.

Judaea under Roman rule

The Jewish revolt, which was apparently uncoordinated, was eventually suppressed by Varus, the Roman governor of Syria, who

Roman soldiers; an oil lamp

Terracotta impression of 10th legion

intervened with two legions and ruthlessly crushed the rebels, two thousand of whom he crucified. What was to be the future government of Herod's kingdom was decided by Augustus, the Roman Emperor. He seems not to have regarded any of Herod's sons as being capable of succeeding their father in the sole rule of the kingdom. Consequently, he divided it: one son, Archelaus, was appointed ethnarch of Judaea and Samaria; another, Herod Antipas became tetrarch of Galilee; a third son, Philip, received other territories outside Palestine proper, also with the title of tetrarch. So far as Judaea and Samaria were concerned, this arrangement lasted only till A.D. 6. Archelaus, having proved an incompetent ruler, was deposed, and Augustus put his ethnarchy under Roman rule.

The Prefect and the High Priest

To implement the decision, a Roman governor—called praefect or procurator—was appointed.

Under the new order, the Jewish High Priest was recognized by the Romans as the head and representative of the Jewish people. He was given control of domestic affairs and jurisdiction over his people in matters relating to Jewish law. The Jewish priestly aristocracy, since it was not popular with the people, naturally tended to be pro-Roman in its attitude. The maintenance of Roman rule guaranteed the continuation of its own favored position in the Jewish state.

Roman tribute

One of the first actions taken by the Romans on incorporating Judaea into their Empire was to order a census for the purpose of assessing tribute. The Jews had been accustomed to pay tribute to Herod. They hated Herod; but he was a Jewish king, and their tribute went to the maintenance of a Jewish state. But the imposition of Roman tribute was another mat-

ter; it gravely affected their religious principles.

The fact that it did so was immediately made clear by a rabbi, Judas of Galilee, who was backed by Sadduq, a Pharisee. Judas told his fellow-countrymen that the payment of tribute to Rome would be an act of apostasy towards Yahweh. Obedient to Judas' exhortation and despite the contrary advice of Joazar, the High Priest, that they should submit to the tribute, many Jews rose in revolt. They were rigorously put down by the Romans, and Judas of Galilee and many others perished.

However, the teaching and example of Judas were not forgotten. Many of his followers took to the deserts of Judaea, to wage guerrilla warfare against the Romans. The members of this "resistance" movement, which was led by the sons of Judas of Galilee, were called Zealots, because of their zeal for the cause of Yahweh.

Pontius Pilate

This unpropitious start to Roman rule in Judaea was followed by some twenty years of internal peace. This conclusion is drawn from the fact that Josephus mentions nothing during the period. Perhaps the ruthless suppression of the revolt in A.D. 6 had cowed the Jews. Whatever the cause, trouble started again in 26 when Pontius Pilate was appointed as governor.

Since the public ministry of Jesus and his crucifixion took place during Pilate's term of office (26–36), interest in the happenings of these years is naturally very great. Pilate's involvement with Jesus has already been discussed in the preceding chapter; attention, therefore, can here be given to other aspects of Pilate's government.

For Pilate's career we are completely dependent on the accounts of Josephus given in his *Jewish War* and *Jewish Antiquities*, and on a tractate written by Philo of Alexandria. The accounts of Josephus are intrinsically problematic, because out of the ten years of Pilate's term of office only three events are narrated. Philo's account also raises difficulties, since the incident which he describes is not mentioned by Josephus.

Affair of the Standards

Josephus begins his account of Pilate with an incident that must have happened shortly after his arrival in Judaea. It had apparently been the custom of previous governors, out of deference to Jewish religious scruples concerning graven images, to arrange for troops on garrison duty at Jerusalem to remove the effigies of Roman gods from their standards before entering the holy city. Pilate canceled this arrangement. When the Jews of Jerusalem saw the images displayed on the

A defeated opponent submits to the Emperor; from the Arch of Constantine

Jewish sarcophagus

standards, they were horrified. According to Josephus, they flocked in crowds to Caesarea, to beseech Pilate to countermand the order. Pilate was obdurate, and tried to frighten them into submission. Faced with their readiness to die for their religion, he at last relented. Josephus claims that Pilate was acting on his own malevolent decision in this matter. There is, however, much reason to think that the governor was obeying orders from Rome.

The Aqueduct

The next clash, recorded by Josephus, occurred over the building of an aqueduct. Jerusalem needed more water, so Pilate had the aqueduct built and defrayed the cost from the Temple treasury. Since this money was sacrosanct, there was a great uproar, which Pilate suppressed with heavy Jewish casualties.

The Gilded Shield

The incident related by Philo is curiously similar to that of the standards. This time Pilate placed some gilded shields, dedicated to the Emperor Tiberius, on the Herodian palace in Jerusalem, which the Romans used as their headquarters. The Jews immediately objected. Their reason is obscure. Since the shields bore no images, their offense probably lay in the inscription, which might have mentioned the divinity of the Emperor. After a fierce altercation and a Jewish appeal to Rome, Tiberius ordered the shields to be removed to the Temple of Augustus in Caesarea.

Pilate and the Samaritans

According to Josephus, Pilate's career as governor was terminated by his savage action against the Samaritans. These people, whom the Jews regarded as heretics, met in arms at their sacred Mount Gerizim, stirred up by some Messianic prophet. Pilate, fearing a revolt, promptly intervened with force, and heavy Samaritan casualties resulted. The Samaritan leaders complained to Vitellius, the legate of Syria, who ordered Pilate to Rome for trial. However, before he reached there, Tiberius had died, and Pilate passes out of history into Christian legend.

These accounts of Pilate's relations with the Jews, even allowing for the manifest distortions of Josephus and Philo, are significant. They reveal the basic impossibility of the Jews living ever peaceably under Roman rule. Quite apart from Roman harshness, which many other peoples also resented, Jewish religion made submission intolerable.

Caligula's threat

Jewish suspicions concerning Roman intentions against their religion were not, however, groundless. In A.D. 39 their worst fears were realized. The Emperor Caligula, who was probably mad, believed passionately in his own divinity. Knowing this, the gentile inhabitants of the Jewish city of Jamnia erected an altar to him, for the purpose of offering sacrifice to his divinity. The altar was promptly destroyed by the Jewish inhabitants. Caligula, enraged by

this affront to his divinity, ordered Petronius, the legate of Syria, to prepare a colossal gilt image of himself, in the guise of Zeus, for erection in the Temple at Jerusalem. The Jews were horrified at the projected sacrilege. Petronius procrastinated, fearing that the attempt to set up the statue in the Temple would be met by a fanatical revolt of the whole people. The situation was approaching a crisis when Caligula was murdered in Rome.

Coin of Caligula (obverse)

Roman standards ; coin of Caligula

The Temple seemed thus to have been miraculously saved from most awful desecration—a desecration which paralleled that of the "Abomination of Desolation" erected by Antiochus Epiphanes in 167 B.C. The Jews were profoundly thankful for their deliverance. But the threat from which they had so narrowly escaped remained to haunt them with the fear that it might be renewed by another emperor.

King Agrippa

After the death of Caligula, independence under a Jewish king unexpectedly came to Israel. This sudden change of fortune was due to the gratitude felt by the new Emperor Claudius towards the

The Emperor Claudius

Jewish prince Agrippa, who had helped him to secure the imperial throne. As a reward, Claudius appointed Agrippa King of the Jews. Although he was of Herodian descent, being a grandson of Herod the Great, Agrippa was a pious Jew. His devotion to Judaism won him the approval of his subjects. However, this happy situation lasted only four years, for Agrippa died in the year 44.

Agrippa's death was a bitter blow to the Jews. For Claudius, passing over Agrippa's son on account of his youth, placed Judaea back again under direct Roman rule. The brief interlude of national independence seems to have made the re-imposition of Roman rule even more intolerable. The revolt and fatal consequences form the subject of our last chapter.

The Ark of the Covenant ; synagogue relief

Menorah from Jewish stone sarcophagus

Destruction of Zion

After the death of King Agrippa in A.D. 44, Judaea returned to direct Roman rule, and from that moment Jewish history seemed to take on an air of inevitability. According to orthodox Jewish belief the Holy Land belonged to God and God alone. The presence of a Roman Governor in Jerusalem was in itself an affront to God, and to pay tribute to the Emperor was to give to a non-believer what was God's by right. Tension and disorder steadily increased, stimulated by Roman maladministration, Messianic excitement and nationalist activity. The fatal explosion finally came in A.D. 66. With the resulting loss of their land and the Temple at Jerusalem, the Jews' religion ceased to be a religion that demanded the ritual of sacrifice and the people themselves were scattered abroad without a national home until the present century.

Gravestone of a Roman soldier of the 10th legion, stationed in Palestine and possibly killed during the siege of Jerusalem.

Opposite top General view of Jerusalem.

Jewish ossuary (*below*) of first century A.D. with inscriptions in Greek. The practice of placing bones in ossuaries was against Jewish tradition, but around Jerusalem at this time it was used fairly widely.

In the summer of the year 66 the priests of the great Temple of Yahweh in Jerusalem refused to offer their customary daily sacrifices for the well-being of the Roman Emperor and people. These sacrifices were an accepted token of Israel's loyalty to Rome, and a refusal to continue making them was tantamount to a declaration of revolt. The priests concerned were members of the lower order of the Temple clergy, who subscribed to Zealotism. For sixty years or more, the Zealots had formed the "resistance" against the Romans in Judaea, and their ideas were shared by many other Jews who were not active members of their party.

Behind this refusal of the lower priests lay a complex situation. The higher clergy, who formed a priestly aristocracy, were presided over by the High Priest. This aristocracy supported the Roman government of Judaea because it ensured their own social and economic position; the maintenance of the "loyal" sacrifices was essential to good relations with the Romans. But the policy and attitude of these priestly aristocrats made them unpopular with the people and particularly with the lower clergy, who longed for the freedom of Israel. To control the members of the lower clergy, the High Priest had reduced or cut off their stipends. The fateful refusal to offer the sacrifices, however, was only taken when Eleazar, a young aristocrat and captain of the Temple, defected to the lower clergy. Eleazar's defection provided the malcontents with an able and vigorous leader, and it was he who persuaded them to revolt.

Fighting quickly broke out in Jerusalem. The High Priest and his party, reinforced by troops sent by the Jewish prince Agrippa II, sought to gain control of the Temple. They were fiercely opposed by the lower priests, who were joined by the *Sicarii*, the extreme action group of the Zealots. Meanwhile, Menahem, the surviving son of Judas of Galilee and now leader of the Zealots, had suddenly attacked and destroyed the Roman garrison at Masada, the great fortress by the Dead Sea. Equipping his followers from the armory there, Menahem quickly made his way to Jerusalem and at once took charge of the revolt. The forces of the High Priest and Agrippa were soon defeated, and many of the priestly aristocrats were murdered.

Menahem seems to have assumed royal powers, probably as the Messiah-King, but his reign was short. Eleazar, doubtless jealous of the new leader who had assumed command of the revolt that he had started, plotted to have him murdered in the Temple. Some of Menahem's followers, including a relative named Eleazar ben Jair, managed to escape the ensuing massacre and withdraw to Masada.

The death of Menahem left the revolt leaderless. He had been dynastic head of the Zealot movement and had been at once accepted as the charismatic leader of Israel's revolt against Rome. None of the other leaders of Zealot bands or rebel groups had the prestige or authority needed to command a national revolt. However, the Jews were committed to rebellion, and they continued to wipe out surviving Roman garrisons in Jerusalem and elsewhere. In retaliation the Gentile inhabitants of Caesarea, the Roman headquarters, rose against the Jews and slaughtered twenty thousand of them, according to the Jewish historian Josephus. This massacre provoked Jewish reprisals against many Gentile cities in Palestine and in Gaulanitis, east of the Sea of Galilee. In turn, Jews living as far afield as Syria and Egypt had to pay the penalty for their compatriots' actions.

The procurator of Judaea, Florus, seems to have done nothing effective to maintain Roman authority during the initial stages of the revolt. Josephus claims that Florus actually welcomed the revolt as an opportunity to cover up his own maladministration, which had far exceeded that of any previous governor. Whether or not that was

Above Sixth-century mosaic of Jerusalem from Madaba, south of Amman. The Romans had rebuilt Jerusalem in A.D. 130, calling it Aelia Capitolina.

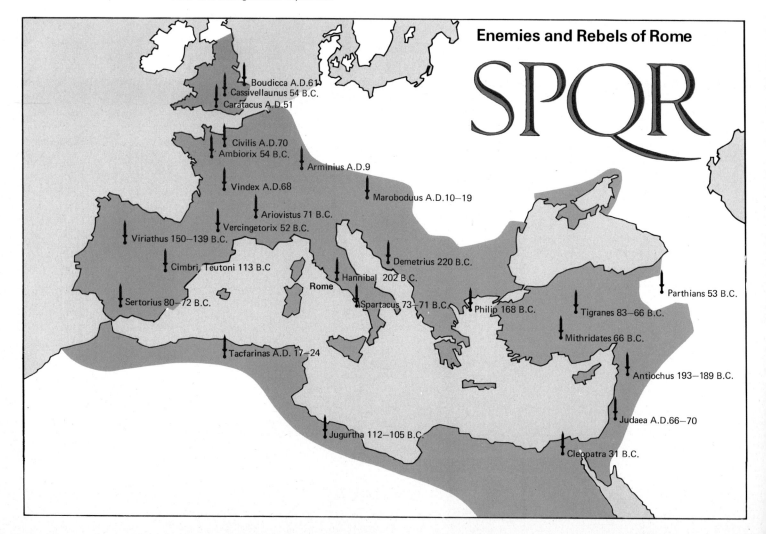

Enemies and Rebels of Rome

SPQR

Boudicca A.D.61
Cassivellaunus 54 B.C.
Caratacus A.D.51
Civilis A.D.70
Ambiorix 54 B.C.
Arminius A.D.9
Vindex A.D.68
Maroboduus A.D.10—19
Ariovistus 71 B.C.
Vercingetorix 52 B.C.
Viriathus 150—139 B.C.
Demetrius 220 B.C.
Cimbri, Teutoni 113 B.C.
Rome   Hannibal 202 B.C.
Parthians 53 B.C.
Sertorius 80—72 B.C.
Spartacus 73—71 B.C.
Philip 168 B.C.
Tigranes 83—66 B.C.
Mithridates 66 B.C.
Tacfarinas A.D. 17—24
Antiochus 193—189 B.C.
Judaea A.D.66—70
Jugurtha 112—105 B.C.
Cleopatra 31 B.C.

Judaea against the might of Rome

the reason for Florus' initial inaction, the situation in Judaea rapidly grew beyond his military resources to cope with it. It was now the duty of the legate of Syria, Florus' superior in the administration of the Roman Empire, to intervene and restore Roman sovereignty.

The Syrian legate, Cestius Gallus, took some three months to assemble his forces for the punitive expedition. His army consisted of one full-strength legion, the twelfth, with other specially selected legionary reinforcements, six cohorts of other infantry, four squadrons of cavalry and some fourteen thousand auxiliary troops. It was a formidable force, well calculated to deal with the disorganized and untrained Jewish rebels.

Entering the country from the north, the Roman army swept aside whatever opposition the rebels had managed to organize in the countryside and laid siege to Jerusalem itself. They soon penetrated the city's fortifications and made preparations for the final assault on the Temple walls. Occupying a commanding position superbly reinforced by massive walls, the Temple constituted the keypoint in the defense of Jerusalem. It was, moreover, the most sacred spot in the Holy Land, and all Jews could be expected to fight fanatically in its defense.

The Jews did, indeed, fight with fanatical courage, but they were no match for Roman military science and professional discipline. They were actually beginning to despair of the outcome of the contest, when Cestius Gallus suddenly and unaccountably ordered the operation to stop and withdrew his troops to neighboring Mount Scopus. The next day the Jews saw the Roman army retiring northwards, evidently breaking off the siege. At first they feared a ruse, but when they realized that the Romans were indeed retreating, their joy and exultation knew no bounds—here truly was proof of the succor of Yahweh, their god. In his honor they had challenged the might of Imperial Rome, and, at the eleventh hour, he had miraculously intervened and put their dreaded foe to flight. The Jews quickly pursued the retreating Romans and caught them as they descended the narrow Beth-horon pass. Only by sacrificing his rearguard and abandoning his heavy equipment was Cestius Gallus able to extricate his forces and struggle back to safety in Syria.

Thus ended the first armed encounter between puny Israel and mighty Rome. The Jewish rebels had trusted to their god and not to their military resources; matched with Rome, their cause was hopeless. But they had won, defeating a legionary army. The very site of their victory, the Beth-horon pass, was portentous—there Joshua had defeated the Amorites, and Judas Maccabaeus had triumphed over the Seleucid army under Seron. Yahweh was the god of battles: he had given victory to their ancestors fighting against enormous odds, and so had he given victory to them. In the face of what appeared to be such a marvelous demonstration of divine approbation, even the

cautious and hesitant were won over to a wholehearted commitment to this struggle for Israel's freedom. Coins were specially struck, expressive of their exultation and faith. They bore inscriptions: "Jerusalem the Holy;" "Deliverance of Zion;" "Redemption of Zion."

The defeat of Cestius Gallus was a serious blow to the Romans, both to their prestige and to their imperial ambitions. Judaea was a vital link in the defense of their Near Eastern provinces and Egypt. There was, moreover, a large Jewish population in Mesopotamia that might rise in sympathy. And Rome's traditional enemies, the Parthians, were always ready to invade at a sign of Roman weakness. The Emperor Nero, whatever his other failings, made a wise choice of commander to restore Rome's dominion over rebel Judaea. He appointed Vespasian, a veteran who had proved his ability in hard campaigning in southwestern Britain. No chances could be taken next time, and Vespasian set about preparing a powerful army of three legions and a strong auxiliary force.

The exact situation in Jerusalem at this time is difficult to determine, because of the historian Josephus' apologetic concern about his own dubious part in the events that he describes. He is our chief source of information, but he is often elusive and obscure about matters in which he was personally involved. From the accounts, sometimes conflicting, in his *Jewish War* and in his *Autobiography*, it would seem that a moderate party endeavored to gain control in Jerusalem and coordinate the nation's forces for the greater struggle with Rome that was sure to come. Josephus claims

Reverse of a coin of Vespasian, issued in A.D. 70 to commemorate the capture of Jerusalem. It is inscribed JUDAEA CAPTA, and shows a Jewish prisoner and the symbolic mourning figure of Judaea.

(1) Bronze coin of Agrippa, A.D. 50–100. (2) Shekel of Bar-Kokhba, A.D. 133. (3) Antioch assarion of Tiberius, A.D. 14–37. (4) Bronze coin of Herod the Great, 37–4 B.C. (5) Shekel of the first Jewish revolt, A.D. 66–70. (6) Dilepton of Mattathias Antigonus, 40–37 B.C.

Rome imposes her presence

Roman civilization was well established in Palestine and the Middle East before the revolt of the Zealots. Great public buildings included the temple at Byblos (*above*) and the theater at Caesarea (*below*).

Below left Aerial view from the south of the rock of Masada, the last stronghold of the Zealots. In the distance is the Dead Sea.

that he was appointed general in Galilee, to fortify its cities against a probable Roman advance from Syria, and he tells how assiduous and ingenious he was in carrying out his task. He also discourses at length on the iniquities of various rebel bands, and particularly on one of the Zealot leaders, John of Gischala. But, as the sequel suggests, there was undoubtedly another side of the story, and it is probable that John already suspected Josephus' loyalty to the Jewish cause.

By the spring of 67 Vespasian was ready to begin his campaign. But the new Roman commander was confronted with a very different situation from that which had faced Cestius Gallus the previous autumn. His route to the insurgent capital was now blocked by a number of fortified towns, which had first to be reduced before he could venture into the barren hills of Judaea for the final siege of Jerusalem. This was a difficult, protracted task, for it meant a succession of sieges of strongly held places. Unable to oppose the Roman legionaries successfully in the open field, the Jews nevertheless excelled at fighting among fortifications; in such operations their fanatical courage and individual resourcefulness matched the discipline and military science of the Romans. But it was a mode of warfare that took a terrible toll of life: not only was the defeated garrison eventually wiped out, but the inhabitants were generally massacred by the Romans, exasperated by long resistance and their own heavy losses.

During the campaign of 67, Vespasian captured a number of Judaean towns. Josephus gives a long account of the siege of one of them, Jotapata, where he was the Jewish commander. To escape death after the final assault on the town, Josephus surrendered to the Romans. Brought before Vespasian, he assumed the role of prophet and foretold that Vespasian would become Emperor of Rome. Whether Vespasian believed this audacious prophecy, we have no means of knowing other than from Josephus' own account. But he kept Josephus a prisoner at his own headquarters instead of sending him to Rome as he had first intended. In 68 Nero died, and from a resulting civil war Vespasian emerged in 69 as Emperor. Josephus' fortune was made. He first served as a liaison-officer on the staff of Titus, Vespasian's son and successor as commander in Judaea. After the successful siege of Jerusalem, Josephus returned to Rome with his imperial patrons and there he wrote his *Jewish Wars* to commemorate their victory over his own people.

The Roman reduction of Galilee seems to have resulted in an internecine struggle for leadership among the insurgents in Jerusalem. Josephus' account of it was inspired by apologetic motives; but it would appear that the moderate party, led by Ananus, a former High Priest, gradually lost control as Zealot groups from Galilee congregated at Jerusalem. The arrival in Jerusalem of John of Gischala gave the Zealots a

capable leader and, supported by a strong body of Idumaean rebels, they finally overwhelmed the moderates, and killed Ananus and other leading figures. The Zealots now had complete control of the Temple, and it is significant that they proceeded to elect a new High Priest by the ancient custom of drawing lots—doubtless an attempt to end the monopoly of the office long exercised by the priestly aristocracy. The Zealots also burned the public archives, containing the money-lender's bonds, an action taken, according to Josephus, to encourage the poor to rise against the rich.

The Roman campaign of 68 was devoted to reducing insurgent centers outside Jerusalem. It was probably during the operations in the area of Jericho that the monastic settlement of Qumran was destroyed. The members of the community had anticipated the attack by hiding their sacred scriptures in adjacent caves, where they remained forgotten until their chance discovery in 1947 and their subsequent fame as the Dead Sea Scrolls.

When Vespasian was elected Emperor, the campaign of 68 ended. It became necessary for him to leave Palestine, with a considerable force, to make good his title at Rome. As fighting ceased,

only the strongholds of Herodium, Masada and Machaerus—outside of Jerusalem itself—remained in Jewish hands.

The suspension of the war in Judaea during 69, however, was of little avail to the Jews. According to Josephus, fierce struggles for mastery still continued among the insurgents in Jerusalem. He charges the rebel leaders with terrible enormities, of which the chief victims were the people of Jerusalem. That his account is distorted by personal interests is certain; it paid him to blame the Zealots to cover up his own betrayal. Indeed, the theme of his *Jewish War* is that of a peaceable people being dragged to disaster by brigands and fanatical desperadoes—namely, the Zealots. He is silent or elusive about the religious ideals of the Zealots; for they clearly had a faith, however fanatical, which he lacked. Josephus was always too mindful of the reality of Roman power to share in the Zealots' whole-hearted devotion to Yahweh.

In the spring of the year 70 the Romans were ready for their long-delayed vengeance on rebel Jerusalem. Vespasian appointed his elder son, Titus, to command the final operations. Titus assembled his army in Egypt and from there

The courtyard of the citadel at Jerusalem, built against the city's western wall on the site of Herod's palace, which was the last stronghold of the rebels in the city.

The end of a nation

marched into Judaea at the head of the most powerful force yet directed against the Jews. There were four legions, including the twelfth, which was intent on avenging its defeat in 66, and they were supported by a large auxiliary force.

The approach of the Romans shortly before the Passover at once united the Jewish factions within the city. John of Gischala and the Zealots held the Temple, and Simon ben Gioras organized the defense of the rest of the city. Jerusalem had three separate strongholds: the Temple; the fortress of Antonia, adjacent to it; and the palace of Herod, defended by massive towers, in the Upper City. Surrounded and subdivided by walls, the city had to be taken piecemeal. From the east it was overlooked by the Mount of Olives; but the steep intervening valley of the Kedron rendered it virtually impregnable on that side. The northern side was its weakest, despite efforts made to strengthen the defenses. And, accordingly, it was from the north that Titus began his attack.

The subsequent siege, one of the most terrible in history, is vividly described by Josephus, who was present on the staff of Titus. From the start the Jewish cause was hopeless. The city was crowded with refugees, as well as with troops, and famine soon became a more terrible scourge than the bombardment of the Roman *ballistae*. Josephus records a case of cannibalism—a mother killed her child and ate it. The Romans completely encircled the city with a wall of their own, built to prevent supplies from entering and refugees from escaping. Jerusalem was, indeed, "kept in on every side," as Jesus is recorded to have prophesied.

The Romans gradually broke their way through the outer and inner walls of the city, but the Jewish patriots fiercely contested every advance towards the Temple, focal point of their resistance. The fighting was extremely savage, and prisoners were cruelly treated by both sides. The reply made by John of Gischala to a Roman offer of surrender on terms shows the spirit of the defenders. The Romans had waited until Jewish morale would be at its lowest; the last lamb had been offered in the Temple, and now the daily sacrifice to Yahweh had to stop. The Zealot commander nevertheless replied firmly that "he never would fear [its] capture, since the city was God's."

At last on August 29 the legionaries broke into the Temple. Its courts were crowded with refugees, hoping to the last for a miracle of divine intervention, and they were butchered by the ferocious legionaries. By accident, according to Josephus, the Temple was set ablaze by a Roman soldier who hurled a firebrand into an inner chamber. Despite the efforts of Titus to save the famous sanctuary, the legionaries could not be stopped in their lust for slaughter and destruction. Thousands of Jews perished in the Temple courts. Many priests retreated to the roofs, where they hurled ornamental spikes down on the Romans and finally plunged to their deaths in the flames of their burning sanctuary. When order was restored, the victorious legionaries erected their standards in the Temple courts and offered sacrifice to them, saluting Titus as Imperator. This act was a strange fulfillment of the prophecy the Jews had long feared—that the "Abomination of Desolation" would be set up in their Temple.

The capture of the Temple marked the virtual end of the revolt. Fierce fighting continued in the Upper City, but by September 26 all Jerusalem was in Roman hands. Most of the city had been reduced to a smoking ruin, and Titus ordered what was left standing to be razed, except the three great towers of the palace of Herod, which he preserved as a monument to the former strength of Jerusalem. Jewish losses during the siege had been enormous—Josephus puts the number at 1,100,000. The figure is surely a gross exaggeration; but the true figure must have been very large, for the siege was long, the famine severe and the

Part of the foundations of Herod's temple revealed near the Wailing Wall by recent excavation at Jerusalem.

fighting fierce and at close quarters. The number of Jewish prisoners taken during the whole war is estimated by Josephus as 97,000, many of whom subsequently perished in the arenas of the Empire.

Titus returned to Rome. There, in 71, Vespasian and Titus celebrated their victory over rebel Judaea in an elaborately staged triumph. The victorious legionaries paraded through the streets of Rome with multitudes of Jewish prisoners displaying the rich booty, including the treasures of the Temple, followed by their proud commanders. The triumph culminated with the execution of Simon ben Gioras, as the chief rebel general, and a sacrifice of thanksgiving to Jupiter Capitolinus for the victory. On the Arch of Titus, in the Forum, two bas-reliefs still commemorate this triumph— the legionaries exulting as they carry the great Menorah of the Temple, the silver trumpets and the altar of shew-bread, while a winged Victory crowns Titus.

Even after the fall of Jerusalem, the Zealots did not give up the struggle. Some escaped into Egypt, where they tried to stir the Alexandrian Jews to revolt. They were rounded up, tortured in an endeavor to make them acknowledge "Caesar as lord" and executed. At Masada, by the Dead Sea, the Zealot garrison under Eleazar ben Jair held out until A.D. 73, when the Roman commander Silva laid siege to the fortress with the tenth legion. By incredible feats of military engineering in that waterless desert terrain, the Romans surrounded the great rocky plateau with a wall, obviously intent on preventing any escape. They also built a great ramp, to bring their battering-rams within range of the fortress walls. But the Zealots

fought back until they saw that further resistance was hopeless.

On the night before the final assault, the Jewish defenders killed their families and then themselves, preferring suicide to surrender. When the Romans broke in the next day, nine hundred and sixty dead bodies, among the smoking ruins of the fortress, testified to Zealot faith and fortitude.

The destruction of Jerusalem in A.D. 70 marked the definitive end of the Jewish national state until its rebirth in 1948. During the intervening nineteen centuries the Jews, scattered throughout the world, were a homeless and persecuted people. In 1967, in the Six Days' War, they finally completed their return to their ancient home by gaining possession of the Temple site. But, in the struggle to resurrect their national state, it has been to the Zealots of Masada that many have looked for inspiration. The excavation of that tragic site has been an act of national piety, which movingly links the new Israel with the old Israel that died there so heroically in A.D. 73.

S. G. F. BRANDON

Top Roman soldiers carrying loot—including the Menorah and altar of shewbread—from the sack of Jerusalem; a bas-relief from the Arch of Titus, at Rome.

Below Titus, the son of the Emperor Vespasian, commanded the Roman expedition that captured Jerusalem from the Zealots.

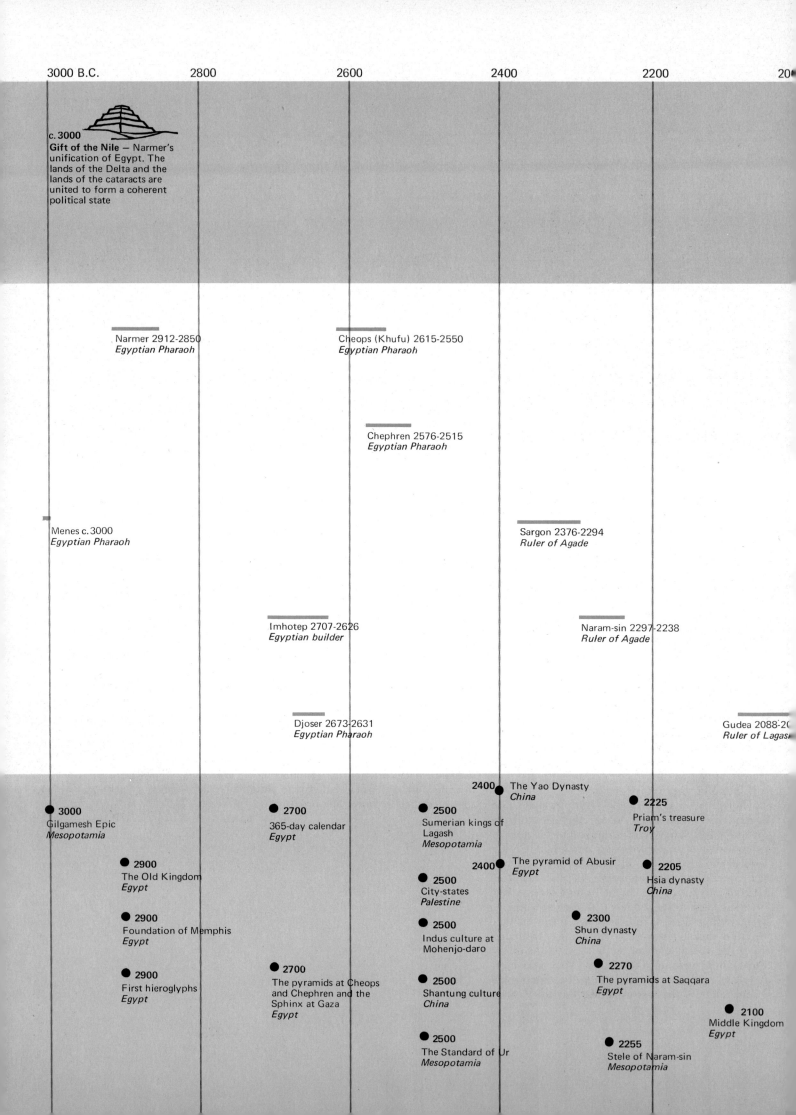

Timeline: 3000 B.C. – 2000 B.C.

3000 B.C.   2800   2600   2400   2200   20•

c. 3000
Gift of the Nile — Narmer's unification of Egypt. The lands of the Delta and the lands of the cataracts are united to form a coherent political state

Narmer 2912-2850
Egyptian Pharaoh

Cheops (Khufu) 2615-2550
Egyptian Pharaoh

Chephren 2576-2515
Egyptian Pharaoh

Menes c. 3000
Egyptian Pharaoh

Sargon 2376-2294
Ruler of Agade

Imhotep 2707-2626
Egyptian builder

Naram-sin 2297-2238
Ruler of Agade

Djoser 2673-2631
Egyptian Pharaoh

Gudea 2088-2(
Ruler of Lagash

2400 The Yao Dynasty
China

● **3000**
Gilgamesh Epic
Mesopotamia

● **2700**
365-day calendar
Egypt

● **2500**
Sumerian kings of Lagash
Mesopotamia

● **2225**
Priam's treasure
Troy

● **2900**
The Old Kingdom
Egypt

2400 The pyramid of Abusir
Egypt

● **2500**
City-states
Palestine

● **2205**
Hsia dynasty
China

● **2900**
Foundation of Memphis
Egypt

● **2500**
Indus culture at Mohenjo-daro

● **2300**
Shun dynasty
China

● **2900**
First hieroglyphs
Egypt

● **2700**
The pyramids at Cheops and Chephren and the Sphinx at Gaza
Egypt

● **2500**
Shantung culture
China

● **2270**
The pyramids at Saqqara
Egypt

● **2100**
Middle Kingdom
Egypt

● **2500**
The Standard of Ur
Mesopotamia

● **2255**
Stele of Naram-sin
Mesopotamia

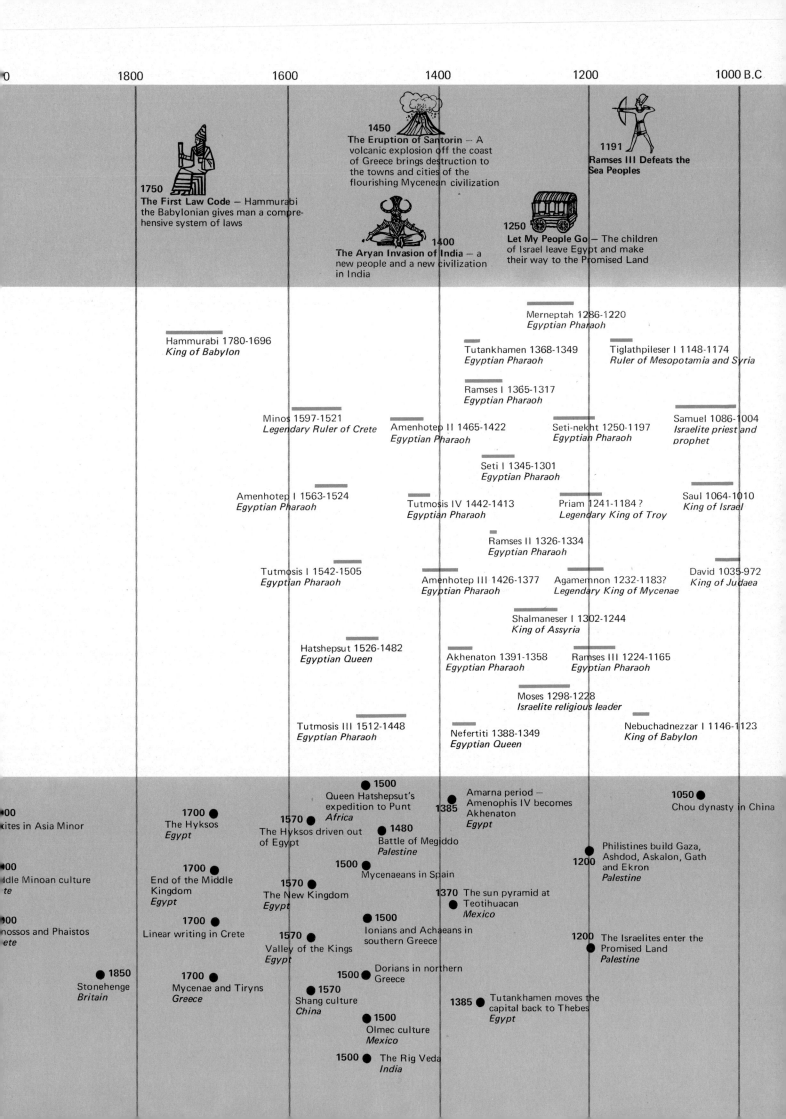

1800 1600 1400 1200 1000 B.C

1450
The Eruption of Santorin — A volcanic explosion off the coast of Greece brings destruction to the towns and cities of the flourishing Mycenean civilization

1191
Ramses III Defeats the Sea Peoples

1750
The First Law Code — Hammurabi the Babylonian gives man a comprehensive system of laws

1400
The Aryan Invasion of India — a new people and a new civilization in India

1250
Let My People Go — The children of Israel leave Egypt and make their way to the Promised Land

Merneptah 1286-1220
Egyptian Pharaoh

Hammurabi 1780-1696
King of Babylon

Tutankhamen 1368-1349
Egyptian Pharaoh

Tiglathpileser I 1148-1174
Ruler of Mesopotamia and Syria

Ramses I 1365-1317
Egyptian Pharaoh

Minos 1597-1521
Legendary Ruler of Crete

Amenhotep II 1465-1422
Egyptian Pharaoh

Seti-nekht 1250-1197
Egyptian Pharaoh

Samuel 1086-1004
Israelite priest and prophet

Seti I 1345-1301
Egyptian Pharaoh

Amenhotep I 1563-1524
Egyptian Pharaoh

Tutmosis IV 1442-1413
Egyptian Pharaoh

Priam 1241-1184 ?
Legendary King of Troy

Saul 1064-1010
King of Israel

Ramses II 1326-1334
Egyptian Pharaoh

Tutmosis I 1542-1505
Egyptian Pharaoh

Amenhotep III 1426-1377
Egyptian Pharaoh

Agamemnon 1232-1183?
Legendary King of Mycenae

David 1035-972
King of Judaea

Shalmaneser I 1302-1244
King of Assyria

Hatshepsut 1526-1482
Egyptian Queen

Akhenaton 1391-1358
Egyptian Pharaoh

Ramses III 1224-1165
Egyptian Pharaoh

Moses 1298-1228
Israelite religious leader

Tutmosis III 1512-1448
Egyptian Pharaoh

Nefertiti 1388-1349
Egyptian Queen

Nebuchadnezzar I 1146-1123
King of Babylon

1500
Queen Hatshepsut's expedition to Punt
Africa

Amarna period — Amenophis IV becomes Akhenaton
Egypt

1385

1050
Chou dynasty in China

1700
The Hyksos
Egypt

1570
The Hyksos driven out of Egypt

1480
Battle of Megiddo
Palestine

1200
Philistines build Gaza, Ashdod, Askalon, Gath and Ekron
Palestine

1700
End of the Middle Kingdom
Egypt

1570
The New Kingdom
Egypt

1500
Mycenaeans in Spain

1370 The sun pyramid at Teotihuacan
Mexico

1700
Linear writing in Crete

1570
Valley of the Kings
Egypt

1500
Ionians and Achaeans in southern Greece

1200 The Israelites enter the Promised Land
Palestine

kites in Asia Minor

Middle Minoan culture te

nossos and Phaistos ete

1850
Stonehenge
Britain

1700
Mycenae and Tiryns
Greece

1500
Dorians in northern Greece

1570
Shang culture
China

1385 Tutankhamen moves the capital back to Thebes
Egypt

1500
Olmec culture
Mexico

1500 The Rig Veda
India

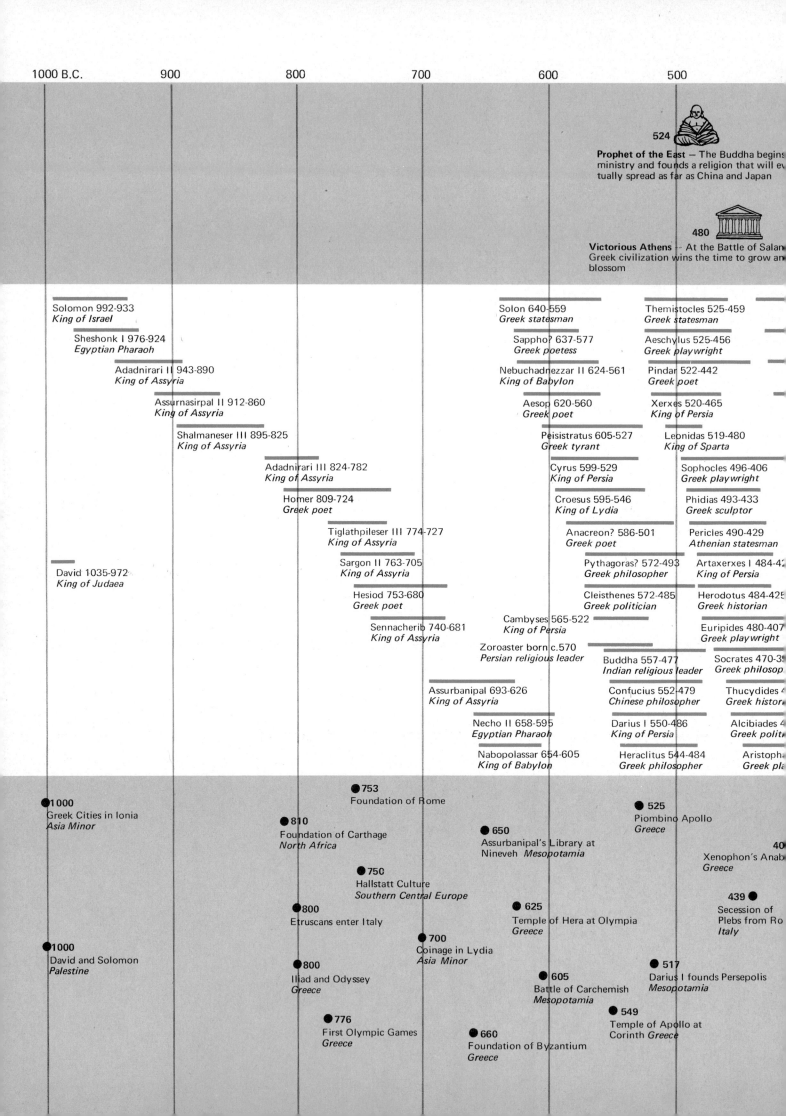

1000 B.C.   900   800   700   600   500

524
Prophet of the East — The Buddha begins
ministry and founds a religion that will ev
tually spread as far as China and Japan

480
Victorious Athens — At the Battle of Salam
Greek civilization wins the time to grow an
blossom

Solomon 992-933
King of Israel

Sheshonk I 976-924
Egyptian Pharaoh

Adadnirari II 943-890
King of Assyria

Assurnasirpal II 912-860
King of Assyria

Shalmaneser III 895-825
King of Assyria

Adadnirari III 824-782
King of Assyria

Homer 809-724
Greek poet

Tiglathpileser III 774-727
King of Assyria

David 1035-972
King of Judaea

Sargon II 763-705
King of Assyria

Hesiod 753-680
Greek poet

Sennacherib 740-681
King of Assyria

Zoroaster born c.570
Persian religious leader

Assurbanipal 693-626
King of Assyria

Necho II 658-595
Egyptian Pharaoh

Nabopolassar 654-605
King of Babylon

Solon 640-559
Greek statesman

Sappho? 637-577
Greek poetess

Nebuchadnezzar II 624-561
King of Babylon

Aesop 620-560
Greek poet

Peisistratus 605-527
Greek tyrant

Cyrus 599-529
King of Persia

Croesus 595-546
King of Lydia

Anacreon? 586-501
Greek poet

Pythagoras? 572-493
Greek philosopher

Cleisthenes 572-485
Greek politician

Cambyses 565-522
King of Persia

Buddha 557-477
Indian religious leader

Confucius 552-479
Chinese philosopher

Darius I 550-486
King of Persia

Heraclitus 544-484
Greek philosopher

Themistocles 525-459
Greek statesman

Aeschylus 525-456
Greek playwright

Pindar 522-442
Greek poet

Xerxes 520-465
King of Persia

Leonidas 519-480
King of Sparta

Sophocles 496-406
Greek playwright

Phidias 493-433
Greek sculptor

Pericles 490-429
Athenian statesman

Artaxerxes I 484-42
King of Persia

Herodotus 484-425
Greek historian

Euripides 480-407
Greek playwright

Socrates 470-3
Greek philosop

Thucydides 4
Greek histor

Alcibiades 4
Greek polit

Aristoph
Greek pl

●1000
Greek Cities in Ionia
Asia Minor

●810
Foundation of Carthage
North Africa

●800
Etruscans enter Italy

●1000
David and Solomon
Palestine

●800
Iliad and Odyssey
Greece

●776
First Olympic Games
Greece

●753
Foundation of Rome

●750
Hallstatt Culture
Southern Central Europe

●700
Coinage in Lydia
Asia Minor

●660
Foundation of Byzantium
Greece

●650
Assurbanipal's Library at
Nineveh *Mesopotamia*

●625
Temple of Hera at Olympia
Greece

●605
Battle of Carchemish
Mesopotamia

●525
Piombino Apollo
Greece

●549
Temple of Apollo at
Corinth *Greece*

●517
Darius I founds Persepolis
Mesopotamia

40
Xenophon's Anab
Greece

439 ●
Secession of
Plebs from Ro
Italy

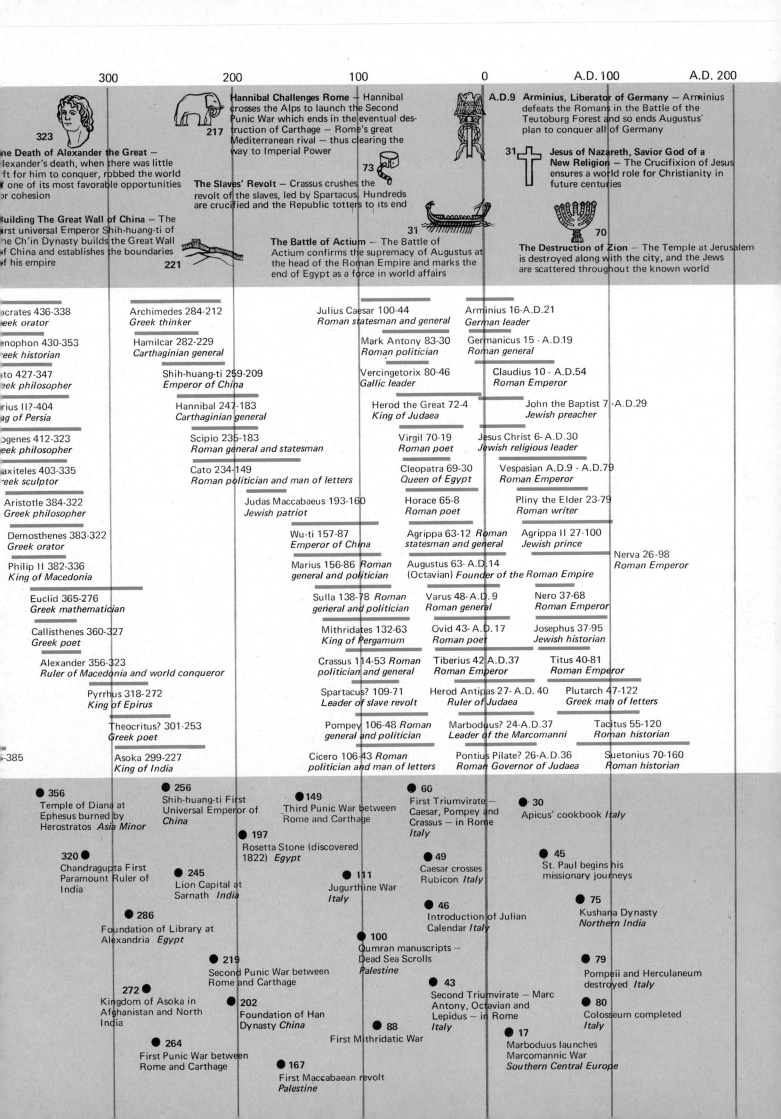

300 **200** **100** **0** **A.D. 100** **A.D. 200**

323

The Death of Alexander the Great — Alexander's death, when there was little left for him to conquer, robbed the world of one of its most favorable opportunities for cohesion

Building The Great Wall of China — The first universal Emperor Shih-huang-ti of the Ch'in Dynasty builds the Great Wall of China and establishes the boundaries of his empire **221**

217 **Hannibal Challenges Rome** — Hannibal crosses the Alps to launch the Second Punic War which ends in the eventual destruction of Carthage — Rome's great Mediterranean rival — thus clearing the way to Imperial Power

73 The Slaves' Revolt — Crassus crushes the revolt of the slaves, led by Spartacus. Hundreds are crucified and the Republic totters to its end

31 The Battle of Actium — The Battle of Actium confirms the supremacy of Augustus at the head of the Roman Empire and marks the end of Egypt as a force in world affairs

A.D.9 Arminius, Liberator of Germany — Arminius defeats the Romans in the Battle of the Teutoburg Forest and so ends Augustus' plan to conquer all of Germany

31 Jesus of Nazareth, Savior God of a New Religion — The Crucifixion of Jesus ensures a world role for Christianity in future centuries

70 The Destruction of Zion — The Temple at Jerusalem is destroyed along with the city, and the Jews are scattered throughout the known world

Isocrates 436-338
Greek orator

Xenophon 430-353
Greek historian

Plato 427-347
Greek philosopher

Darius II?-404
King of Persia

Diogenes 412-323
Greek philosopher

Praxiteles 403-335
Greek sculptor

Aristotle 384-322
Greek philosopher

Demosthenes 383-322
Greek orator

Philip II 382-336
King of Macedonia

Euclid 365-276
Greek mathematician

Callisthenes 360-327
Greek poet

Alexander 356-323
Ruler of Macedonia and world conqueror

Pyrrhus 318-272
King of Epirus

Theocritus? 301-253
Greek poet

?-385

Archimedes 284-212
Greek thinker

Hamilcar 282-229
Carthaginian general

Shih-huang-ti 259-209
Emperor of China

Hannibal 247-183
Carthaginian general

Scipio 235-183
Roman general and statesman

Cato 234-149
Roman politician and man of letters

Judas Maccabaeus 193-160
Jewish patriot

Asoka 299-227
King of India

Julius Caesar 100-44
Roman statesman and general

Mark Antony 83-30
Roman politician

Vercingetorix 80-46
Gallic leader

Herod the Great 72-4
King of Judaea

Virgil 70-19
Roman poet

Cleopatra 69-30
Queen of Egypt

Horace 65-8
Roman poet

Wu-ti 157-87
Emperor of China

Agrippa 63-12 *Roman statesman and general*

Marius 156-86 *Roman general and politician*

Augustus 63- A.D.14 (Octavian) *Founder of the Roman Empire*

Sulla 138-78 *Roman general and politician*

Varus 48- A.D. 9 *Roman general*

Mithridates 132-63
King of Pergamum

Ovid 43- A.D.17
Roman poet

Crassus 114-53 *Roman politician and general*

Tiberius 42-A.D.37
Roman Emperor

Spartacus? 109-71
Leader of slave revolt

Herod Antipas 27- A.D. 40
Ruler of Judaea

Pompey 106-48 *Roman general and politician*

Marboduus? 24-A.D.37
Leader of the Marcomanni

Cicero 106-43 *Roman politician and man of letters*

Pontius Pilate? 26-A.D.36
Roman Governor of Judaea

Arminius 16-A.D.21
German leader

Germanicus 15 - A.D.19
Roman general

Claudius 10 - A.D.54
Roman Emperor

John the Baptist 7-A.D.29
Jewish preacher

Jesus Christ 6- A.D.30
Jewish religious leader

Vespasian A.D.9 - A.D.79
Roman Emperor

Pliny the Elder 23-79
Roman writer

Agrippa II 27-100
Jewish prince

Nerva 26-98
Roman Emperor

Nero 37-68
Roman Emperor

Josephus 37-95
Jewish historian

Titus 40-81
Roman Emperor

Plutarch 47-122
Greek man of letters

Tacitus 55-120
Roman historian

Suetonius 70-160
Roman historian

● **356**
Temple of Diana at Ephesus burned by Herostratos *Asia Minor*

320 ●
Chandragupta First Paramount Ruler of India

● **286**
Foundation of Library at Alexandria *Egypt*

272 ●
Kingdom of Asoka in Afghanistan and North India

● **256**
Shih-huang-ti First Universal Emperor of *China*

● **245**
Lion Capital at Sarnath *India*

● **219**
Second Punic War between Rome and Carthage

●**202**
Foundation of Han Dynasty *China*

● **264**
First Punic War between Rome and Carthage

● **167**
First Maccabaean revolt *Palestine*

● **197**
Rosetta Stone (discovered 1822) *Egypt*

●**149**
Third Punic War between Rome and Carthage

● **111**
Jugurthine War *Italy*

● **100**
Qumran manuscripts — Dead Sea Scrolls *Palestine*

● **88**
First Mithridatic War

● **60**
First Triumvirate — Caesar, Pompey and Crassus — in Rome *Italy*

● **49**
Caesar crosses Rubicon *Italy*

● **46**
Introduction of Julian Calendar *Italy*

● **43**
Second Triumvirate — Marc Antony, Octavian and Lepidus — in Rome *Italy*

● **30**
Apicus' cookbook *Italy*

● **45**
St. Paul begins his missionary journeys

● **75**
Kushana Dynasty *Northern India*

● **79**
Pompeii and Herculaneum destroyed *Italy*

● **80**
Colosseum completed *Italy*

● **17**
Marboduus launches Marcomannic War *Southern Central Europe*

The Fires of Faith

Editor Friedrich Heer

A.D. 312-1204

Introduction

The title of this section is not meant to imply that fires were burning continually from 312 to 1204. Yet fires there were: fires lit by zealous men that consumed the ancient gods, ancient cultures and eventually men themselves.

The rise of Christianity to its position as the official Church of Constantine's Empire was accompanied by fires in which the temples and other treasures of ancient cultures were destroyed—for example, the library at Alexandria. Then the Islamic fires from the desert seemed to consume the gardens of late antiquity, where vases and statues had survived from the age of Hellenism. And at the dawn of our own age, in 1204, the crusaders plundered and set fire to Constantinople and destroyed, for the time being at least, the Empire of the Romans. The Byzantine Empire and in particular Constantinople itself, with its glittering palaces, its baths, its art treasures and its luxury, was coveted as much by the tenth-century Ottonian Germans as by the Franks—the Latin Christians of 1204.

The fires of faith, the bright lights of destruction, the explosions of fanaticism, the everlasting wars and feuds that filled this era—was there even *one* year when there reigned a peace comparable to the *pax romana* that Augustus had envisaged or the *pax mongolica* that the great Mongolian khans created at the height of their power? All the undoubted devastation should not make us forget that the fires of faith brought life as well as destruction. The contents of this volume demonstrate that the dynamic forces that created the western world had their origin in these troubled centuries, and that the foundations of European culture up to the present day were laid over a thousand years ago.

We know both a great deal, and very little, about Constantine, to whom the Church owed its rise to power. Until 1969 the princes of the Roman Catholic Church—the Eminences, Excellencies, Cardinals and Bishops—bore the official titles of the higher bureaucracy of Constantine's Empire. The liturgical vestments of the clergy are still based on the robes of office of the imperial official. We know a great deal about Constantine, his life, his policy and all that this self-styled "thirteenth apostle" did for the Church. Yet we know little about his inner life. He was no doubt pious in his own way, like men who, since the earliest days of humanity, have waited in fear and hope for a sign from the Holy One.

St. Patrick's Celtic mission signified the beginning of a specifically *European* Middle Ages, with the activity of highly individual and highly individualistic monks and missionaries who traveled from island to island, farther and farther northwards, and then conquered the continent of central Europe and northern Italy in one great movement. Europe was becoming Celtic. In contrast to the centralism and uniformity of Rome, "Celtic" Europe was blessed with a multiplicity of highly independent personalities. These men from the British Isles thirsted after freedom; they had lively intellects and were fired with curiosity.

One, Pelagius, became the great opponent of St. Augustine, and the heresy of Pelagianism was considered a great danger by Rome for more than a thousand years. Pelagius saw man as a creature destined by God to freedom and reason, to shouldering the responsibility for what he did with his own life.

Carolingian civilization and the culture created by Charlemagne, his sons and his grandsons, which provided a broad and secure basis for European civilization up to the eighteenth century, would have been unthinkable without the gifted clerics from the British Isles. These clerics were the first *clercs* or intellectuals; they provided the officials and the school teachers for the whole of the European continent.

The Europe that was coming into being underwent a number of major invasions. The battle against the

Introduction

Huns on Campus Mauriacus near Troyes in 451 and the Battle of Lechfeld in 955 have a great similarity, indeed a close affinity, in that they were not, either of them, simply battles in which the West repelled the East—as they have too often been considered. On the contrary, these two great battles showed the extent to which East and West were interwoven. The frontiers were blurred; there were Eastern and Western troops, leaders and politicians in both camps.

The Rule of St. Benedict: possibly nothing has contributed more to the inner peace of Europe and the formation of an inwardly stable race of men than the Benedictine Order. Moderation, a wise balance between physical and mental activity, a renunciation of fanaticism in any form, including exaggerated asceticism: those were the maxims followed in the Benedictine monasteries that spread civilization throughout Europe in the "Benedictine centuries." The humanity of the Benedictines made an irreplaceable contribution to the turbulent, constantly warring Europe of their day.

Mohammed's *Hegira* or emigration (it was not a flight) from Mecca to Medina marked the beginning of the rise of Islam. A new world was created, a self-contained hemisphere reaching from Baghdad to Cordoba and even Toledo. For too long people saw only the "scourge of Allah" over the East; today we see the "sun of Allah" instead. Arabian doctors, technicians, philosophers, scientists and poets (and consequently Jewish ones, too, since the Jews were at the courts of the Arabian princes) created a civilization oriented towards Hellenistic antiquity in the Near East, without which European civilization at the height of the Middle Ages would have been unthinkable. The learned "disputation," the art of dialogue and verbal combat, was an offspring of the "world of the three rings" in the glittering Arabian civilization of the Spanish peninsula. Those three lights of the Christian Middle Ages, Albert the Great, Thomas Aquinas and Dante, were the spiritual inheritors of this Arabic-Hellenistic intellectual civilization.

The year 800 was a particularly important milestone, with the Carolingian Renaissance in the West paralleled by the Japanese Renaissance in the Far East. The political unity of Europe in Charlemagne's Empire was short-lived, but the social, religious and cultural foundations laid with the help of men from Spain, northern Italy, and above all the British Isles, lasted until the French Revolution and Napoleon, who considered himself a new Charlemagne.

What Charlemagne achieved for the Continent, Alfred the Great achieved for England. This truly great man, who won London from the Danes in 886, was the real founder of the English nation. Alfred also created the English navy as a political tool. He founded English literature, in the continuity of a tradition from Latin antiquity. The "scholar," and the essentially English type of education with its "open" tradition derived from ancient humanism (witness Thomas More and even J. H. Newman), were both offsprings of the erudition encouraged by Alfred the Great. Alfred himself translated into English Boethius' *On the Consolation of Philosophy*, which sought to offer mankind a *via media*, a "middle path" and a means of self-assertion between life and early death.

After the Battle of Hastings in 1066, Anglo-Saxon England was linked, through the Normans, to the Continent. An Anglo-French "western hemisphere" was created by the extensive possessions of the English kings in France. French was Richard Coeur de Lion's language, and the language spoken at the English court until the late Middle Ages.

In the "dark ages" of the tenth century, when the Continent was being invaded by Normans, Arabs and Magyars, and Rome seemed likely to collapse under the "pornocracy" of patrician families who used dagger and poison in their fight for the papal throne, Otto I brought about a unification of the ravaged German territories.

The kings and emperors of Otto's time became the great instruments of a reformation in Rome; and the monks of Cluny became their most powerful allies. With the unfortunate Henry IV began a two-hundred-year-long battle in which emperors and popes deposed and execrated each other. The battles over investiture that took place in Germany and Italy in the time of Henry IV and Henry V were destined to be repeated in England and France in the thirteenth and fourteenth centuries. From the protracted conflicts between emperors, kings and popes there developed on the one hand the world state (which then subjugated "its" Church once again), and on the other hand the imperial Church of the Pope. The papacy ultimately defeated the emperors and the Pope was proclaimed "true Emperor, lord over all kings and princes, and commander of the earth." It was not until the Second Vatican Council that the ideology, political aims and claims to power of the papacy were challenged as un-Biblical—mainly by theologians from countries that lay at the heart of the old Holy Roman Empire.

The twelfth century brought to Western Europe a flowering of culture to a degree unknown since the days of classical antiquity. Cities were constructed (chiefly at first in Italy), universities were founded, and the Gothic style was born. France or, to be more exact, the small area around Paris under the direct rule of the French kings, and Provence in the south—the cradle of courtly love, with its own language, a civilization focused on women and love that fostered a refined, cultured existence—became the cultural center of Europe, attracting students and teachers from all over the Continent.

This Latinized Europe of the West was, however, preparing for an explosive confrontation with the East. Nowadays we can define the "East" not only as Byzantium—the political civilization of the East Roman Empire, its intelligentsia, its bureaucracy and its education—but also as Byzantium's close allies, the Islamic princes with their lands in *Outremer*, the Holy Land. The Emperor in Constantinople sent his hearty congratulations to Saladin for his conquest of Jerusalem, the Holy City of Jews, Christians and Moslems. The "Franks" (the name by which western Europeans had been known for hundreds of years in the Middle and Far East), with their crusades, must be considered just as much a continuation of the Viking voyages as a prologue to the colonial expansion of western Europe.

Europe in the year 1200 knew little of events in other continents. Buddha existed in the West only in the legend of Baalaam and Josaphat—disguised as a Christian saint. Mohammed was thought of as a type of devil or antichrist, a fiendish deceiver. China, India and Japan were very remote. The conception of a wider world existed only in visions, dreams and legends. Nevertheless, southwest Europe was already assembling the force that—in the thirteenth and fourteenth centuries—was to send Franciscan monks to Africa, Asia, China, and deep into Mongolia.

This then was Europe—and the world—as it was forged in the fires of faith marking the tumultuous millennium that stretched from Constantine's vision on the road to Rome to the destruction of his city on the Bosphorus by errant crusaders.

FRIEDRICH HEER

In This Sign Shalt Thou Conquer

The Roman Empire, at the end of the third century A.D., *was at the point of collapse. Struggles among rival emperors brought frequent civil wars, while barbarian hordes threatened the borders. Early in the new century, a soldier named Constantine proclaimed himself Emperor and immediately set out to make good his claim in a series of campaigns that took him, by the summer of 312, to the edge of Rome. Constantine had a momentous vision—a vision in which he was told that he would conquer in the sign of the Cross, the symbol of the despised young Christian religion. The warrior's subsequent victory at the Battle of the Milvian Bridge won for Christianity an end to persecution and recognition as a legal religion.*

The third century of the Christian era was a grim, squalid age. For centuries the Roman Empire had maintained peace and fostered prosperity throughout the Mediterranean world, but now it was in decline. Stable central power had collapsed, as a succession of would-be warlords marched their predatory armies up and down the Empire, striving to seize power or to hold it against their rivals. Sometimes the legions actually put the Empire up for auction. At one and the same time there might be three or four self-styled emperors. None of them lasted long.

Meanwhile, the lot of the common man became ever more miserable and uncertain as cities were sacked, the countryside ravaged and wealth confiscated to pay the rapacious soldiery. Debasement of the currency and interruption of trade routes led to a galloping inflation. The urbane, sophisticated culture of the cities sank under a rising tide of philistinism and peasant brutality, as men jettisoned their intellectual baggage in the cheerless struggle for survival.

Faced with the uncertainty of life, people turned to magic and divination in attempts to penetrate the inscrutable will of the power that ruled the universe. Or they embraced religions that promised salvation in the next world to those who performed the right actions or held the right beliefs. A single, all-powerful god more and more replaced in men's minds the consortium of Olympians. Some called him Apollo; some, the Unconquerable Sun; others, Mithras.

Toward the end of the century, the successful soldier-emperor Diocletian tried to stabilize Roman society. To solve the problem of political power, he devised a cumbersome system of joint emperors, the junior succeeding the senior at regular intervals. To solve the economic problem, he tried to freeze all prices; predictably, it did not work. Neither did his arrangements for the succession to power; emperors would not retire at the appointed time—though Diocletian himself did—and rivals turned their armies against one another. Soon there were six or seven self-proclaimed emperors ruling in different provinces, and all seemed set for a return to the chaos of the preceding century.

One of these contenders for power, Constantius Chlorus, ruled in Britain and Gaul. He died in July, 306, in the legionary camp at York. His eldest son, Constantine, had the support of the army and came to terms with Severus, who ruled in Italy and Africa. Their plan to rule as joint emperors in the West was short-lived: in a few months Severus was eliminated by Maxentius, son of Diocletian's old colleague Maximian. Constantine felt his position threatened, and in any case he would never have been content to share power. In 307 he proclaimed himself sole legitimate Emperor in the West.

At first Constantine had to ward off German attacks on the Rhine frontier. After a year or two of marches, battles, sieges and skirmishes, he could be sure of his rear. In 310 he advanced into Spain, defeated Maxentius' forces there and gained control of the provinces. But this was not enough. The key to lasting and stable power lay in Italy, and above all in Rome. Constantine's army was by now a disciplined and confident force, accustomed to victory. In 312 its commander decided to put its fortune—and his own—to the ultimate test by invading Italy.

In the late summer of 312 Constantine marched his army across the Alps. It was not a large force, for he could not risk denuding the Rhine frontier of troops. Although Maxentius' army was many times larger, he was no soldier, and he waited irresolutely in Rome, plying the pagan gods with sacrifices and magic rites. Constantine, as always, was decisive, rapid and driven by an overmastering lust for power. Susa, at the exit from the Alpine pass, was taken by storm. Turin was entered after a cavalry battle. Without resting, Constantine pressed on to Milan. A few days to rest his tired but exultant troops—and he advanced on the strongly fortified city of Verona, which controlled the crossing of the Adige. Before

An allegorical figure on the pediment beneath the colossal head of Constantine in Rome, representing one of the provinces of the Empire.

Opposite Constantine the Great, God's vice-gerent on earth; a contemporary Roman head of colossal dimensions.

Constantine marches on Rome

Right A eunuch-priest of the cult of Cybele (*Magna Mater*), one of the many mystic religious cults prevalent during the early Christian period. He holds the symbols of fertility and is surrounded by the sacred implements of the cult; second-century bas-relief from Latium.

Below The four tetrarchs who succeeded Diocletian in 305 were the last rulers to persecute the Christians in Italy; fourth-century porphyry group from St. Mark's, Venice.

the city walls stood the main force of Maxentius' army in northern Italy. The battle was long and hard-fought, but discipline and leadership told. By evening the plain was strewn with corpses and Constantine held Verona.

The conqueror was now free to march on Rome. His route, through Bologna, across the Apennines to Florence, and southward through Etruria, was that followed today by the Autostrada del Sole. During his march south he had a portentous vision.

This was not Constantine's first vision. A few years earlier, in Gaul, Apollo the sun-god had appeared to him. More than most men of his age, Constantine was alert for the miraculous. Years later he recounted to Eusebius, the Bishop of Caesarea, what he had seen on the road to Rome that autumn day in 312. Eusebius recorded the story:

> He called to God with earnest prayer and supplication that he would reveal to him who he was, and stretch forth his right hand to help him in his present dangers. And while he was thus praying, a most marvelous sign appeared to him from heaven. He said that about noon he saw with his own eyes a cross of light in the heavens, above the sun, and bearing the inscription BY THIS SIGN SHALT THOU CONQUER. At this divine sign he was struck by amazement, as was his whole army, which also witnessed the miracle.

The nature of Constantine's vision has been discussed for centuries. The most plausible explanation is that he saw a solar halo, which is sometimes cruciform. The inscription was probably the product of his own overheated imagination. Be that as it may, Constantine believed that the god of the Christians had revealed himself as the true god and had promised him victory.

As he slept in his tent that night, he dreamed that Christ appeared to him, displaying the same sign and commanding him to make a likeness of it and use it as his standard in battle. At dawn the next morning, he set his artificers to work to fashion the labarum, a Christian version of the traditional Roman military standard with the monogram of Christ set in a wreath surmounting it. It was an overt proclamation that Emperor and army were under the protection of the Christian god. Sure of his destiny, Constantine pressed on to Rome.

As his enemy approached, Maxentius at last bestirred himself. His forces outnumbered Constantine's, but army and populace alike were demoralized by famine and by the capricious barbarity of Maxentius' rule. And, finally, Maxentius was a poor strategist. Encouraged by an ambiguous oracle, which told him that the enemy of the Romans would perish, he stationed his army by the Milvian Bridge where the Via Flaminia crosses the Tiber, about two miles from the walls of Rome. The army thus had its back to the river, always an uncomfortable situation. To make supply and reinforcement easier, he constructed a second bridge of pontoons or boats close by the existing stone bridge.

On October 26, 312, Constantine reached his enemy's position. At once he began the attack, and Maxentius' ill-prepared and unenthusiastic forces

soon cracked. Constantine threw his reserves into the breach, and all along the line Maxentius' men, afraid of being surrounded, turned tail and ran. The rout was complete. Emperor and army fled back to the river, hoping to reach the far bank and the safety of the walls. But as Maxentius was crossing the bridge of boats, it collapsed. Rumor at the time said that, as a trap for Constantine, it had been built to break, but this seems like an explanation after the event. The fleeing soldiers panicked, and in the crush Maxentius was thrown into the river. The next day his body was found, and its head was cut off and carried on the point of a spear into Rome.

There was no further resistance to Constantine. Crossing the Milvian Bridge, he entered the city the next day by the Porta Flaminia, amidst the acclamations of Senate and people. He had united the whole western half of the Roman Empire under his own rule.

Equally important, Constantine felt that the god of the Christians had demonstrated his power by granting him the promised victory. Henceforth he was committed to the support of the Christian Church. And that Church, from being a repressed, poor, and occasionally persecuted minority of low social status, now found itself suddenly raised to the heights of power, prestige and patronage.

After a brief stay in Rome, Constantine returned to Milan. There he had a meeting with Licinius, who held the Balkan provinces. It was in their interest to make common cause against Maximinus, the ruler of Asia Minor and the East. Their alliance was sealed by the marriage of Licinius to Constantia, the sister of Constantine. At the same time the two emperors issued a joint edict on religious toleration, the famous Edict of Milan:

We resolve to grant both to the Christians and to all men freedom to follow the religion which they choose, that whatever heavenly divinity exists may be propitious to us and to all who live under our government.

Further clauses spell out the details of the program of toleration and order the restoration of Christian places of worship that had been confiscated.

The Edict of Milan marked the triumph of Christianity over persecution and put it on the same footing as other legitimate religions. It did not establish the Church as the official religion of Rome, but it was accompanied or followed in the next few years by a series of enactments favoring the Christians. Members of the clergy were exempted from costly municipal duties—and the wealthier classes, upon whom these duties fell, now began to become priests and bishops. Regular payments were made to churches from state funds. Sunday was proclaimed a holiday in the army: for some it was the feast of Christ, for others that of the sun god. The churches were recognized as legal institutions, able to receive legacies and administer property. The decisions of bishops were given the same validity in civil law as those of the courts. Freedom of pagan sacrifice was limited by legislation; some pagan temples were closed and their property sequestered.

Constantine and members of his family gave

The catacombs, galleries hewn out of underground rock, were used by Romans as burial chambers, and by the persecuted Christians for secret meetings and services as well as burials. This fresco from the third-century catacomb of St. Calixtus shows early Christians at prayer.

This early Christian inscription illustrates the symbolism of the early Church, a private code of supreme significance to secret worshipers. The fish represents Christ himself (probably with implicit reference to the miracle of feeding the five thousand) and the laurel leaves are the sign of his promised triumph.

The Milvian Bridge where, in A.D. 312, not two miles from Rome, Constantine fought his most crucial battle. Victory secured him control of the western half of the Roman Empire, but its most significant outcome was the confirmation of his prophetic vision of success and his new-found faith in the Christian God.

A relief from the Arch of Constantine showing the battle of the Milvian Bridge being joined between Constantine's army and the more numerous but demoralized forces that defended Rome under Maxentius.

lavishly for the building of churches all over the Empire. And when the Church itself split into factions, either because of the conduct of individuals during persecutions, as in Africa, or because of doctrinal disagreement, Constantine intervened. He organized synods and councils and put strong pressure on them to reach agreement, and in the last resort he used the arm of the civil power to enforce the decisions of the Church.

Although Constantine never wavered in his espousal of the Christian cause, he was not baptized until 337, when he was on his deathbed. Such deathbed baptism was common at the time: by making it difficult to commit a mortal sin between baptism and death, salvation was guaranteed.

Constantine, who held absolute power in a violent age, had sinned much; his hands were stained with blood, not least with that of his son Crispus, accused by the Empress Fausta of an attack on her virtue. Fausta herself was the next victim, charged with

false accusation, and while the true facts of the case are lost, the executions in both cases were by Constantine's order. His approach to Christianity was gradual and idiosyncratic. In 312 he probably knew little theology and less about the history and organization of the Church. Years later—we do not know exactly when—he was able to preach an Easter sermon in which he touched on many of the thorniest problems of Christian doctrine. He was fond of referring to himself as the bishop of those outside the Church. What he presumably meant was that by guiding the Roman state along Christian lines he ensured divine favor and protection for the Romans as a whole, including those who did not accept Christianity.

Constantine's conversion has fascinated historians and psychologists for centuries. Yet, all is still not clear. The difficulty is twofold. First, the world of ideas of the early fourth century is strange to us, and many of the key facts are unknown. Second, there is the problem of entering into the mind of this unusual man—unusual to his contemporaries as well as to us. Ill-educated but fond of the company of scholars; gentle and humane, yet never hesitating before a battle—or an assassination; superstitious and otherworldly, yet a realistic administrator and a bold and decisive reformer—Constantine was a man of many parts.

Today we know more about the fourth century than scholars did a generation or so ago. And it may be that we have a deeper understanding of psychology in general and religious psychology in particular than they had.

One long-held view can be rejected out of hand. According to this theory, Constantine's conversion was entirely a matter of policy, carefully and cynically calculated, and designed to win for him the support of a numerous and important group in the society of the time. But the Christians were neither numerous nor important, and this was especially true in the western half of the Empire.

It is true that Christians were more numerous in

Constantine's conversion to Christianity

some of the eastern provinces. But in 312 the eastern provinces were not Constantine's problem, and even there Christians were far from forming a majority. It is unlikely that Christians—however we define them —formed ten per cent of the population of the Empire. As for their importance, there were upper-class Christians, of course; but the bulk of the Christian community seems to have belonged to what we call the lower middle class of the cities and towns—traders, artisans, small landowners and petty "rentiers," whose influence on the course of affairs was negligible. Nowhere were the country people Christian. And the army, whose support was crucial for Constantine until the last of his rivals had been eliminated, was and long remained solidly pagan. If Constantine's conversion was a matter of calculation it was an ill-considered one, and with no real bearing on his success.

Constantine was evidently a religious man—in the terms of the early fourth century—in that he was anxious to identify the Supreme Power that ruled the universe and to put himself in the right relation with it. He was also an ambitious man, one determined to concentrate the imperial power in his own person and then pass it on to his sons. He did not seek the personal indulgence that power permits. He was no Maxentius, unable to see beyond extortion and debauchery. He was, in fact, rather austere in his personal life. For him, power meant the ability to impose order upon chaos, to tidy up the appalling mess of the Roman Empire. He wanted to find God, but not in any spirit of humility; he was a man fully conscious of his mission and of his ability to

This roundel from the Arch of Constantine incorporates material taken from an earlier sarcophagus.

accomplish it, if only the power that ruled the universe would help him.

The war with Maxentius had been a desperate gamble. As Constantine marched through Etruria to the decisive conflict at the Milvian Bridge, he must have anxiously hoped and prayed for a revelation. In these circumstances it is not surprising that one was vouchsafed him. He had Christians in his entourage, among them his mother Helen, who was later canonized as a saint. Repudiated by his father for the sake of a dynastic marriage, she was a devout

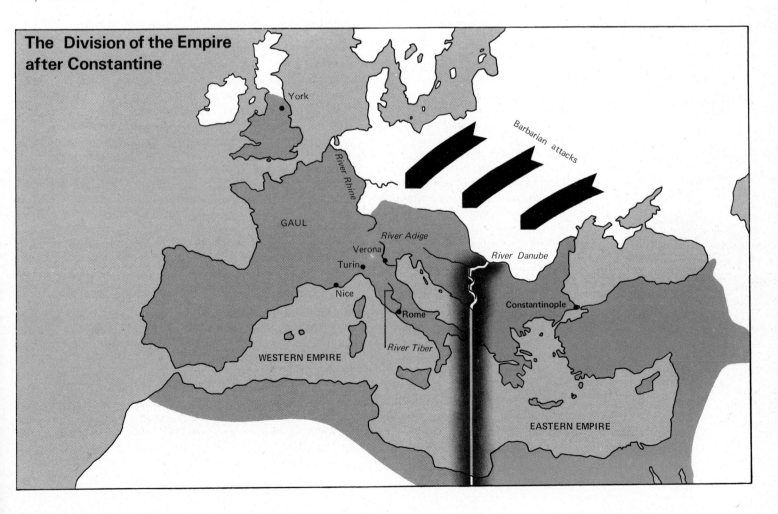

The Division of the Empire after Constantine

York

River Rhine

Barbarian attacks

GAUL

River Adige

Verona

River Danube

Turin

Nice

Constantinople

Rome

River Tiber

WESTERN EMPIRE

EASTERN EMPIRE

Christian who in her old age made a pilgrimage to the Holy Land and there, it is believed, found the True Cross. The god of the Christians was to Constantine one of the candidates for Supreme Power in the universe. In a state of emotional exaltation, he took a natural phenomenon for a divine sign. That his revelation was corroborated by a dream that night also need surprise no one. What confirmed Constantine in his assurance not only that the Christian god was the true god, but that he, Constantine, was his chosen vessel, was the victory a few days later at the Milvian Bridge, a victory that changed the shape of the world.

Constantine lived and reigned for twenty-five years after 312. In 324 he invaded Licinius' territory, confident that he had the protection and support of the Almighty. A naval battle in the Bosphorus and a land battle at Chrysopolis on the Asiatic shore sealed Licinius' fate. Once again the god of the Christians had given victory to his servant, and Constantine now held the whole, reunited Empire.

It was then that Constantine refounded the ancient Greek city of Byzantium, calling it the city of Constantine—Constantinopolis—and designating it the second capital of the Empire, the new Rome. No doubt Constantinople lay on one of the main military roads of the Empire, leading from the Rhine and Danube frontiers to the Persian frontier. No doubt, too, that the economic and demographic center of the Empire lay in its eastern provinces. Yet it was not these considerations that led Constantine to found the new capital and to enrich it with the spoils of the Empire. He said himself that he gave the city its name by the command of God. It was to be the first wholly Christian city in the world, adorned

with magnificent churches built by the Emperor's command, and containing no pagan temple. Constantine surely intended it as a symbol and a memorial of his final victory—won close by—and of the accomplishment of his great design.

Meanwhile, faced in the East with a split in the Church on doctrinal matters, Constantine had once again intervened. The Council of Nicaea in 325, at which the Emperor himself presided, defined the beliefs of the Church. The Emperor ordered that they be adhered to and put the full weight of the State behind the Church authorities in dealing with recalcitrants. To Constantine it seemed his obvious duty to ensure that worship was conducted in a manner pleasing to the Almighty. Thus, though the majority of Romans were still pagans, though Constantine himself still retained the old pagan office of *pontifex maximus*, though pagan symbols still appeared on the coinage, a further step was taken towards the fusion of the Roman State and the Christian Church.

With the vast mass of bullion that his victories had given him, Constantine issued a new gold coin of guaranteed purity, the solidus. This, together with the peace of a united Empire, ended the inflation and encouraged trade and industry.

The administration of the Empire was radically reorganized. Civil and military power were rigidly separated; a mobile strategic reserve was created; and a new hierarchy of officers of state, responsible to the Emperor himself, was established.

Constantine had his sons, Constans and Constantius, brought up as Christians; unfortunately they became religious bigots. Later they were appointed junior co-emperors, and arrangements were made for them to succeed their father on his death. All did not go exactly according to Constantine's plan, but a major struggle for power was avoided. Until 350 Constans ruled in the West and Constantius in the East. From 350 until his death in 361 Constantius reigned as sole Emperor, like his father before him.

As Constantine, at last baptized and a full member of the Christian Church, lay on his deathbed on Whitsunday of 337, he could reflect that he had solved the constitutional, military and economic problems of the Empire and that he had given it a new capital and a new religion.

We might put the emphasis differently today. The Roman Empire Constantine knew soon crumbled. In 410 Alaric the Goth sacked Rome. Soon the western provinces and even Italy itself became barbarian kingdoms. But the eastern provinces, Greek in speech and Greco-Oriental in thought and feeling, survived. With its capital, Constantinople, the Eastern Roman Empire for a thousand years preserved the cultural heritage of Greece and the political heritage of Rome.

Constantine's other innovation is still with us, and without it European civilization would be unrecognizable. It was Constantine who launched Christianity on the path to power. In the half-century between the battle at the Milvian Bridge and the death of Constantius, the Christian Church changed decisively. From being a persecuted, inward-looking minority, it became a confident, sometimes arrogant majority. Not only were Christians far more numerous in 361 than in 312, but they now counted their adherents among the influential upper classes; they had taken over and adapted the intellectual heritage of Greece and Rome; their churches were the most magnificent buildings in the cities and their bishops were the leading citizens. The Church had acquired prestige, riches, power and a network of communications extending to every village of the Empire. Julian the Apostate's attempt in 361–63 to put back the clock failed.

There was nothing inevitable about this. Christianity had a missionary dynamic, but so had other religions. Without the support of a successful ruler, it could not have become the commanding ideology of the Empire. We need only glance at Rome's neighbor Persia to be convinced. There Christians were an active, occasionally persecuted minority. And this they remained until they were overwhelmed by the Arab conquest. No Emperor ever paid much attention to them, let alone gave them his passionate and powerful support.

As we survey the history of the Middle Ages, the Renaissance and modern times, almost everything that we see—from the great cathedrals of Europe, the iconography of our art, and the imagery of our literature, to our systems of education, law and philosophy—owes much of its shape to Constantine's vision on the road to Rome and his victory at the Milvian Bridge.   ROBERT BROWNING

The Emperor Constantine being blessed by Christ is the scene depicted on this sixth-century, late-Byzantine ivory plaque. Constantine's claim to divine authority directly given by Christ was acknowledged by the Pope in Rome and transmitted to a long line of Byzantine emperors.

Below The church of St. Irene in Constantinople was founded by Constantine, and is one of many churches in the city formerly known as Byzantium which Constantine renamed when he chose this meeting-point of Europe and Asia, overlooking the Bosphorus, as the Empire's new capital.

The fourth century, which opened with the triumph of Christianity in the Roman Empire, closed with the beginning of the Dark Ages. Leaders of the barbarian tribes, massing outside the Empire's frontiers, had already infiltrated their agents into the high places of imperial politics. The old order of Roman imperial administration, already severely weakened in the late third century and only partly restored by the reforms of Diocletian, was gradually disrupted during the years following Constantine's death. Thus, the gulf between the East, where the imperial system continued, and the West, where conditions of virtual anarchy came to prevail, can be clearly seen. The breakup of the West into a number of smaller units was already in prospect. The main subject of this passage will be events in Europe and the Eastern Roman Empire, but at the same time things were happening outside Europe—in some cases parallel to European history, in others, dramatically different from it.

The World of the Orient

In the Far East, the once-great empire of Han China had fallen apart in the early third century, and China was long to remain in a state of political turmoil. Then came the establishment of the Tsin dynasty in the year 265, and about this time a new force was beginning to make itself felt in northern China. During the fourth and fifth centuries, meanwhile, the Tsin were to extend their power into the southeast, and a new era in Chinese social and cultural history was inaugurated.

At first the Tsin power in the north had been severely curtailed by the incursion from beyond the frontiers of Hunnic tribes from central Asia. A number of warring barbarian dynasties were established in the north, but they were supplanted in about 430 by the new northern Wei dynasty.

The great unitary Chinese empire seemed a thing of the past. Despite the turmoil that preceded the foundation of the Tsin, the so-called age of the Three Kingdoms in the third century was regarded by succeeding generations as an age of chivalry, commemorated in the great *Romance of the Three Kingdoms*. Moreover, despite the continuation of civil war and foreign invasion, the fourth century witnessed a revival of cultural life and significant technical advance. The

Taoist stele; northern Wei period.

native Chinese religious philosophy of Taoism enjoyed a new vogue, and the pacific cult of Indian Buddhism made considerable advances. It may well have been in a spirit of resignation that people in the war-torn land of China sought refuge in the Taoist ethic, one that rejected personal striving and endeavor and held that it was the function of the ruler to provide the minimum of good government necessary for peace and order. The tenets of Confucianism, based on a fully administered and well-ordered state, were in full retreat.

It was not for many centuries to come that the links of trade between China and Europe were to re-establish a degree of contact between the two civilizations. But it is important to notice that, although remote from one another, both Europe and China suffered the same scourge in the depredations of the Huns. Failing in their attempt to overrun the whole of China, these nomadic warriors retreated to the steppes of central Asia, from which in the fifth century they were to descend on Europe.

The hordes of nomadic barbarian tribes known collectively as the Huns were the scourge of civilization in several areas during the fourth and fifth centuries. Roughly contemporary with their attacks on China were their invasions of northern India, which became intensified during the fifth century. But at first these troubles on India's northern border did not seriously disturb the course of a period of peace, prosperity and unity that may justly be regarded as the golden age of ancient Indian civilization. It was

the age of the Gupta dynasty, which established itself in the north in A.D. 320, just four years before the Emperor Constantine asserted his sole rule over the whole Roman Empire.

In the first fifty years of their dynasty, the Guptas unified the whole of north and northwest India and were soon to gain the homage of the states of the south. The climax of this age of unity and cultural advance came in the reign of Chandragupta II (380–415). The prosperity of his empire is described in the diary of the Chinese Buddhist monk Fa Hsien, who was in India from 405 to 411 to research and collect Buddhist and other religious texts. Chandragupta and his successors promulgated a code of law for the whole subcontinent, and sent embassies as far afield as Rome. This was also a golden age for the arts; it witnessed the beginnings of

Painting of a Boddhisattva from the Ajanta caves.

the mural paintings in the Ajanta caves and the career of the Sanskrit dramatist Kalidasa.

Just as China had been subject to the religious influence of Indian Buddhism, so during the fourth century was her civilization also enriched by contacts with Persian as well as Indian traders. Like India, Persia enjoyed a period of great power and prosperity during the fourth century, under the rule of the Sassanid dynasty. Ever since

The Sassanid King Peroz (459–84) hunting.

the founding of their power and the capture of Ctesiphon in 226, the Sassanids had successfully established their ways throughout Persia and had extended their influence beyond their frontiers, even defeating the armies of Rome. During the reign of Shapur II (309–79), Persia continued to offer a major threat to the eastern frontiers of Rome, which suffered another major reverse when the Emperor Julian the Apostate was defeated and killed in battle in the year 363. The conflict between the two empires, which was centered upon the border state of Armenia, was temporarily resolved by the partition of that country in the last decades of the fourth century. The Armenians had accepted Christianity and consequently were subject to persecution by their Persian rulers, a pretext for the intervention of eastern Rome in the future.

The first century of a Christian Empire

When Constantine followed up his victory at the Milvian Bridge with the Edict of Milan, a new era in European affairs opened. As we have seen, the edict did not make Christianity the official religion of the Empire; but the sturdy and well-organized Christian Church achieved a new status that it fully exploited during the coming century. Constantine used the growing power and influence of his new ally to further his own ends. He saw his own authority encompassing ecclesiastical affairs. After his victory over the ambitious Licinius, which made him the sole arbiter of the Empire, he had convened the Council of Nicaea, the first general council of the Church, which decided many important matters of faith and Church administration. Ex officio, the Emperor had always held the office of *pontifex maximus*, the ultimate authority in the

The deification of the Emperor, from an ivory panel.

As the Church emerged from the shadows of governmental disfavor with the Edict of Milan, it revealed a bewildering number of conflicting views on the nature of the faith and, above all, on the nature of Christ. The most general view was that Christ, despite his human manifestation, was of the same substance as the other members of the Trinity, a mystic and indivisible unity. Yet it was the opinion of an Alexandrian priest named Arius that God the Father had created Christ, the Son who, although the first being of creation, was not equal with the Father. The Arian heresy, perhaps the most serious threat to the faith of Christendom before the Reformation, spread so widely in the eastern parts of the Empire that it endangered civil as well as religious peace. It was to meet this

Fresco from Dura Europos, Syria, one of the earliest surviving Christian churches in the Near East.

threat that Constantine had convened the Council of Nicaea and it was there that Roman Catholic orthodoxy found its champion in the figure of St. Athanasius. But although Nicaea proclaimed the Trinitarian doctrine, Arianism remained strong throughout the century; the barbarians adopted it as they came within the orbit of the Empire, and even some Emperors were among its adherents.

Throughout the centuries of religious dispute, the bishops of Rome held firm in their opposition to Arianism. As early as the reign of Pope Julius I (337–52), they were pressing their claim not only to seniority among the patriarchates of the Church, a claim by the city of St. Peter that was not denied by Antioch or Alexandria, but also to the supreme authority in matters of faith. Their claim was strengthened during the reign of Pope Damasus I (366–84) when Valentinian I, the Emperor of the West, decreed that all religious disputes should go to the Pope, and still more significantly when Theodosius as Emperor in the East officially con-

Coin of Theodosius.

demned Arianism and made belief in the equality of the members of the Trinity the test of orthodoxy.

With Theodosius' decree "De Fide Catholica" of 380, the doctrinal position of Rome was vindicated by imperial authority. But the Church in the West did not in any way accept this as vindicating imperial claims to authority over it. On the contrary, St. Ambrose preached openly that the Emperor was in the Church, and not above it. When, therefore, Theodosius found himself excommunicated for his brutal repression of the citizens of rebellious Salonika, he was obliged to make formal public confession of his "sin" before he could regain admission to the sacraments.

In matters of doctrine and, quite sensationally, in matters of Christian discipline, the Western Church had by the end of the fourth century made good even its most grandiose claims. Although the Arian heresy survived for centuries in the barbarian kingdoms, it had

been branded as heresy and the Roman position had been upheld. Later, in the Middle Ages, the popes of Rome were to find their position threatened by the secular power, but that position and its authority had been unequivocally stated as early as the fourth century. And in the generation of upheaval and turmoil that followed in the West, the spiritual rulers at Rome were to be the only unbroken link with the glories of the imperial past. Thus, when new kingdoms emerged after the barbarian invasions, they received their Christianity, their passport to the new Roman civilization, from the Church. They found themselves confronted by a sophisticated and mature diplomatic and political body in the papal chancery. A body that so controlled the "commanding heights" of civilization could hardly be seriously challenged on its own ground.

Under Gregory I the temporal power of the popes was firmly established. One of his greatest successes was the conversion of England, which Gregory entrusted to St. Augustine. But the light of faith had never, in fact, been completely extinguished in Britain, and the Celtic Church, which survived in Ireland, Scotland, Wales and Cornwall, represented a tradition dating from the first or second century. The Celtic Church kept faith and learning alive, and Celtic culture flourished at a time when civilization seemed, in many places, to be in retreat.

religious affairs of the Empire, and Constantine had no intention of surrendering this important attribute of his predecessors. Yet by linking the hierarchy of the Church to that of the civil administration, Constantine not only reinforced the one by providing it with a powerful spiritual ally, he also strengthened the other by giving it influence beyond its spiritual concerns.

Yet it was in the spiritual field that the Church really exercised her power. By the end of the century it had almost usurped the ancient authority of the imperial *pontifex maximus*. The climax came in the reign of the Emperor Theodosius, who was forced to seek public absolution from St. Ambrose in the cathedral of Milan.

Three points had been at issue: who was to be the final arbiter in matters of faith, Church or Emperor? If Church, was the claim of the bishops of Rome to supreme authority in the universal Church to be allowed? And finally, how was faith to be defined? The Church was involved in a struggle for power with the Emperor, but it was also at odds with itself.

Crucifixion scene from the great Roman church of St. Sabina.

Mission to Ireland

In the spring of 432, Laoghaire, ruler of a petty kingdom in northern Ireland, gathered his court near Tara to celebrate the annual rites of his pagan religion. The Christian missionary Patrick appeared in the midst of the gathering, confounded the King's magicians with a miracle of fire and—on Easter Sunday—converted Laoghaire. Patrick went on to strengthen the fledgling Christian Church in the Emerald Isle and to establish a religious tradition that was to endure for centuries. As Continental Europe slipped into the Dark Ages following the collapse of the Roman Empire, it was the monks of Ireland who kept alive the flame of faith and who—as missionaries—brought that faith back to the lands where it had been lost.

According to the annals of Ireland, St. Patrick arrived there in 432, and died three decades later, in 461. His mission to Ireland had been prompted by a series of dreams or visions, which strengthened an earlier resolve to dedicate himself to God's service. His great work, the *Confessio* (written about 450), is his spiritual autobiography, his account of his dependence upon God for his ability to carry out this resolve. We gather from Patrick's own words that the journey of 432 was made with a set purpose, the evangelization of Ireland. He recognized to the full his natural disabilities, such as teaching and writing in a tongue not his own. But outweighing all these was his unshakable belief that God had dedicated him to be a bishop to the Irish.

When St. Patrick went to Ireland he knew very well what kind of country he was going to. Years before, when he was only sixteen, he had been carried off from his father's home in Bannavem (either in Britain or Gaul) by pirates and taken to Ireland. There he was bound to a master, Miliucc, whose flocks he tended for six years. Then in response to a dream, he traveled two hundred miles to the coast and escaped by ship. He eventually reached his own family, but soon, in another dream, a man named Victoricus appeared to him with letters from the Irish begging him to return to them. Accordingly he set out once more for Ireland.

Patrick appears to have landed on the east coast. But we must leave the saint's own narrative at this point, for he tells us little about his practical life and his work, though we learn something of the insults that he had to endure from unbelievers, something of his converts, and of the sons and daughters of Irish chieftains who, at his urging, became monks and virgins of Christ. Otherwise, he speaks merely of journeying through many perils, even to outlying regions beyond which no man dwelt, and where no one had come to baptize, or ordain clergy, or confirm the people. The *Confessio* concludes with a pious hope that on this account he should never part with his people, and a prayer for perseverance in whatever he should have to endure.

The rest of our information comes from Muirchu, a seventh-century chronicler. Patrick resolved, as his first act, to go to his former master Miliucc with an offer to pay him the ransom that would have been due to him if Patrick had not escaped, and also with the hope of converting him. Muliucc, however, heard of his coming and, the chronicle says, set fire to himself and his house and all within it.

As the Feast of Easter was now approaching, Patrick proceeded on foot to the Plain of Tara, where King Laoghaire and his court were celebrating the great heathen feast of the druids. On his arrival Patrick kindled a fire by miraculous means, confounding Laoghaire's magicians and throwing doubt on their ancient traditions. The king marched out from Tara and summoned Patrick to appear before him. But Patrick, according to the legends, brought a great darkness over the land and the frightened king feigned conversion and returned to Tara. The next day, Easter Sunday, Patrick entered the hall of the king's palace to preach the Gospel, and emerged victorious from all contests with the druids. Patrick then threatened the king with death unless he truly believed. On the king's compliance, Patrick granted him his life, but because of his obduracy he prophesied that none of his seed should be king thereafter.

It is clear that the Easter ceremony is the climax of Muirchu's traditional narrative. The conversion of the king of Tara was, in his view, the apotheosis of Patrick's evangelization of Ireland. Along with it, he laid great emphasis on the keeping of Easter, and on the transition from the heathen to the Christian ceremony. The conversion of Ireland and the adoption of the "Patrician," or Roman, Easter are evidently held to be one and the same thing.

The Tara episode is followed in Muirchu's chronicle by a series of miracles much more briefly told, including the story of the bestowal of the land of Armagh on the saint, and ending with the story of the choosing of the little boy Benignus as Patrick's successor. Most of Book II of the chronicle is devoted to accounts of the saint's death, tidings of

An inscribed stone at County Kerry in Ireland, one of several examples of monuments of pagan Druidic ritual which have been adapted with Christian symbols by early Christian worshipers for their own use.

Opposite A cross from the illuminated manuscript of the Lindisfarne Gospels which shows the force of the Irish Christian mission started by St. Patrick.

Above left A portal dolmen, a monument which would originally have been covered in earth to form a chamber. This one, near Ardara in Donegal, is typical of the Druidic monuments St. Patrick would have encountered in Ireland.

Above right Croagh Patrick, the hill where St. Patrick worked as a shepherd after he was brought to Ireland as a prisoner.

Below The Gallarus Oratory, made of unmortared stone, is still watertight, though probably 1200 years old. It is one of the best preserved early church buildings in Ireland.

which he was said to have received from an angel, and which he sent to Armagh, "which he loved beyond all other places," summoning men from there to assist him to his last resting place. Patrick is believed to have died in 461, and to be buried at Saul, near the present city of Armagh.

Muirchu's *Life* is a chronicle in the form of a biography, but a comparison with Patrick's own *Confessio* reveals at once the tendentious nature of the former document, and above all the change in the gentle and noble picture of Patrick himself to a wonder worker who indulged freely in curses and vengeance.

Muirchu's information about Ireland at that time concentrates on the "high-kingship" because, at the time he was writing, Tara was the political center of Ireland. King Laoghaire was the eldest son of Niall Noígiallach, who had made himself master of the north of Ireland by conquering the ancient kingdom of Ulad, which had formerly stretched across northern Ireland from Antrim to Donegal.

But in Patrick's time, Ireland was divided into a number of *coiced* or small kingdoms, and there was no "high-king." Niall is believed to have conquered the Ulad and destroyed their capital, Emain Macha, which was only two miles from Armagh. He presumably made Patrick his chaplain there, but one can only speculate on the sequence of events that led to this, since he could hardly have liked or trusted Patrick. Niall had raided often in late Roman Britain, and his mother's name was Cairinn (from the Roman, Carina). Late Roman political influence may have helped place Niall in his advantageous position in central Ireland, and may also have influenced the appointment of Patrick.

With Niall we enter a new phase of Irish history, just as with Patrick we enter a new phase of Irish religion. The two came about simultaneously. Niall must have been a very able politician to create and retain his central position, and to retain, in that age, the loyalty of his sons. His influence grew and by degrees he acquired the midlands. His policy can be traced in the work of Muirchu, and in that of another chronicler, Tírechán of Armagh. Under Niall the influence of Patrick's work grew also.

Patrick was not the first to introduce Christianity into Ireland. According to Prosper of Aquitaine, a fifth-century theologian, Palladius was sent to the Irish as their first bishop by Pope Celestine in 431. Little is known of Palladius, but he probably worked in Wicklow in the south of Ireland. Muirchu tells us that his efforts met with little success, that he eventually left, and died in the land of the Picts (Scotland).

The centralization of episcopal authority in the see of Armagh is one of the first signs of Patrick's Roman influence. In Gaul the bishops were centered in the principal towns of the provinces. But in Ireland, where Roman influence was less direct and up-to-date, the bishops were stationed in the monastic centers, the only places of civil organization. For the same reason, the earliest learning of the Irish was centered in the monasteries, and it was the monasteries that acted as distributors of learning to the surrounding districts.

But the change came about very gradually. Ireland had always been an agricultural country, lacking the towns that Gaul possessed and which constituted the framework of her ecclesiastical organization. Ireland had substituted for them monastic foundations with an agricultural economy, where the bishops held a subordinate civil position, the abbots holding the political power. Above all there was no unity such as had been established in Gaul by the Roman political regime. Each monastery was independent of its fellows, and differed in its masses and daily routines.

The Irish habit of wandering was the beginning of the most remarkable missionary work of the early Church, to which Christian Europe owes much. About the year 585 we find St. Columbanus setting out with his twelve companions on his celebrated journey to Gaul and beyond. At the beginning of the Carolingian Age the Irish monk Dicuil tells of Irish *papas*, "clergy," who had been found in Iceland and in the Faroes shortly before his own day. We find Dicuil himself at the court of Charlemagne, and the Anglo-Saxon *Chronicle* reports that three Irish monks had sailed to Britain in a coracle without sail or rudder and with only a limited supply of food, because they wished to be on pilgrimage "they recked not whither." This follows an ancient tradition, in line with the casting adrift of Maccuil by Patrick in chapter 23 of Muirchu's *Life*.

The death of St. Patrick did not mean the end of his see at Armagh. We can see how firmly rooted this was by the fact that it survived till modern times without any obvious diminution of its prestige. About this time, the latter half of the fifth century, the breakdown of Roman authority in Britain was complete, and with the disintegration there was a consequent slowing down of communications between the two countries. Britain closed in upon herself. Ireland was left virtually alone and continued to develop on her own lines.

The carved figures on the wall of the Romanesque church on White Island are taken to represent St. Patrick, King Laoghaire and the abbots of an early-tenth-century monastic settlement.

These lines were now twofold, however. There was first of all the older monastic regime in which each monastery was governed by the abbot, and where the bishop lived in the monastery in a purely spiritual office; and there was the newer regime according to the Catholic Order from Armagh. This second order was under the Meath Dynasty and was gradually changing, while the monastic naturally lasted longer, being more widespread and deeply rooted. The result was a struggle between the two Churches, especially in the North. The gradual change that came about can best be seen in the history of St. Columba of Iona.

Born in Donegal about 520, Columba is said to have been trained for the Church from an early age. He left Ireland about the year 563, at the age of forty-three, and led a migration of some twelve followers from the country of Dalriada in the north of Antrim to Argyll in Scotland. He settled on the island of Iona, southwest of Mull. His biographer, Adamnan, gives no reason for the move save that he

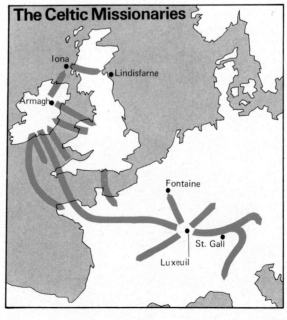

Left An early example of Irish Christian art representing the crucifixion; this cast-iron plaque may have been part of a book cover.

St. Kevin's church in County Wicklow is part of the Saint's sixth-century monastic settlement, and its high pitched stone roof is typical of oratories of that period.

Below A tenth-century carved stone cross, one of many such crosses with which the Irish Christians proclaimed their beliefs and their art.

Bottom Iona Cathedral, part of the monastic settlement on the beautiful, lonely island of Iona off the west coast of Scotland where St. Columba sailed from Ireland in the sixth century.

wished to be a pilgrim for Christ—the old habit of wandering.

Some twenty years later another famous saint, Columbanus, was trained at the monastery of Bangor in County Down. At the age of about forty-five he obtained leave from his abbot to go to the Continent with twelve companions, including St. Gall. Here he proved himself one of the most influential of the Irish monks. He founded three important monasteries in the Vosges Mountains, first in Annegray, next in the chief monastery in the great Luxeuil, and finally in nearby Fontaine. Columbanus' inflexible adherence to the older system of Irish ecclesiastical government and his political views gave offense to the bishops and to Queen Brunhild, and he and his Irish monks were ordered home to Ireland in 610. He was able to escape at the moment of embarking, however, and eventually reached Bregenz on Lake Constance.

From Bregenz, leaving St. Gall behind him in the great monastery that still bears his name, he made his way over the Alps to Bobbio in Italy. He was given land on which to build his famous monastery, which he began in 614. He died there in the following year at the age of about seventy-five. His exacting rule was doubtless the one that he had adopted from his Irish monastery at Bangor. But in spite of its severity, his own activities and those of his disciples gave it a wide diffusion in France, Germany and elsewhere, and were of enough importance for Pope Gregory II in 719 to commission St. Boniface to counteract the Irish influence in Germany. St. Clothair and later kings in Gaul protected and endowed Luxeuil.

Meanwhile the influence of St. Columba's sanctuary on Iona gradually spread. By a curious coincidence, about the time of St. Columba's death, Pope Gregory I sent a mission to Kent under St. Augustine in which the Roman Order was naturally inculcated. Bede tells us that St. Augustine first preached to the King, Aethelbert, who had in fact already heard something of Christianity. His queen was Bertha, of the Christian royal family of the Franks. The King was converted, and baptized in 597. He gave Augustine and his companions residence in his royal city of Canterbury. The next king of England to receive baptism was King Edwin of Northumbria, in 627, and his conversion came about chiefly through his marriage to the Christian princess Ethelberga, daughter of King Aethelbert of Kent. With her to Northumbria went her chaplain Paulinus, through whose zeal and by whose guidance Edwin's subjects soon followed the example of their King and were converted to the Catholic faith.

After the death of King Edwin his immediate successors lost the faith, but it was restored with the accession of Oswald, who had spent his early life on Iona and been trained in the Celtic Order. It was during the reign of Oswald's brother and successor, Oswiu, that the controversy over when the feast of Easter should be celebrated reached its height. At the Synod of Whitby, held in 664, the cause of the Roman Church, quoting the authority of St. Peter

Iona sacked by the Norsemen

and the decision of the Council of Nicaea, was upheld by Bishop Wilfrid of Ripon, and that of the Celtic Church, which preferred the older practice of reckoning Easter in the same way as the Jewish Passover, by Colman, Bishop of Lindisfarne. Oswiu and his people decided in favor of Wilfrid and Rome. In 669 Theodore of Tarsus, consecrated Archbishop of Canterbury by Pope Vitalian, arrived in England. During his archiepiscopate the unity and organization of the Church of Canterbury was secured.

The death of St. Columba did not at all mean that the sanctuary of Iona came to an end. On the contrary it continued to flourish under a succession of Columba's collateral descendants for several centuries till the time of Adamnan; but the gradual extinction came with the repeated incursions of the heathen Norsemen, who sacked it time after time. In 802 the monastery was burned and in 806 some sixty-eight monks were slain. In 825 the whole community perished. At last in 849 the sacred relics were transported to the new church at Dunkeld by Kenneth MacAlpin.

Iona was not the only sanctuary destroyed by the Norsemen. In Ireland, especially, the destruction was great, and traces of heathenism did not finally disappear in Ireland until the end of the ninth century. Monasteries such as Clonmacnois, which had been founded in 548 and which had been virtually a university, were pillaged of their treasures. There was a wholesale evacuation of monks to the Continent, some carrying their books with them but far more carrying with them, as more easily portable, the Latin learning that, especially since St. Patrick's day, they had been quietly absorbing in their monastic libraries. In this matter, Ireland's loss was a gain for Europe. Many a Continental library has been enriched by manuscripts salvaged from the Viking period in Ireland, and by the learning of her refugee monks.

Among the most famous of the scholars who left Ireland for the Continent at this time were Sedulius Scottus and Johannes Scottus. Sedulius was a member of the court of King Charles the Bald at Liège, and may have been a member of a mission of Irishmen that is known to have come in the middle of the ninth century to the court of Charles the Bald from Maelsechlainn, the Irish king. He was one of the most learned men of his time—poet, scholar, scribe, theologian and courtier. He was a precise Latin scholar, and there are hints of Irish sources in some of his writings and some slight knowledge of Greek.

Even more remarkable was Johannes Scottus Eriugena, "John the Irishman." Little is known of his origin or of his early life, but he was also a member of the palace school of Charles the Bald. He must have arrived there at least as early as 845, and remained at least till after 870, probably as a teacher. His learning was wide and precise, including Latin and Greek—the latter a rare accomplishment of his day. Among his many writings, the greatest is the *De Divisione Naturae*.

"It is impossible for the Classical scholar to exaggerate the significance of the part played by the Irish in the work of preserving Classical literature," says Norden. From the earliest period one has only to think of St. Gall and Bobbio, and during the ninth and tenth centuries there had been hundreds of refugee monks who sought the retreats offered by the Irish monasteries of Péronne, Laon, Reims, Fulda, and Würzburg. In the eleventh century Ratisbon was founded by an Irish monk from Donegal on his way to Rome. From Ratisbon foundations were made at Würzburg and Nürnberg, and even at distant Kiev a monastery was founded which lasted till the Mongol invasion in 1241. For three hundred years these abbeys kept in touch with Ireland and drew their monks from them.

NORA CHADWICK

Above The Ardagh Chalice, the most famous piece of early Irish Christian metal work, is of beaten silver decorated with gold and enamel. Among the remarkably delicate engravings are the names of the Apostles and animal symbols. It probably belonged to an eighth- or ninth-century church.

Left The Book of Durrow is the earliest fine illuminated manuscript and it represents in its maturity of style the highest point of artistic achievement in the Irish illumination tradition, particularly in the pages illustrating the symbols of the Evangelists, like the one shown here, in mellow colors.

Ireland before the coming of Patrick

According to the most ancient traditions of Ireland, her history had been linked to that of the Mediterranean world long before the coming of St. Patrick and the religion of Rome. Even after St. Patrick, the history of the country was to remain the preserve of an oral tradition handed down by a

Minstrel harp from a Viking burial.

class of minstrels or bards. In western Europe these minstrels were the latest heirs of an heroic Iron Age society, of which the earliest example known to us was the Greece described by Homer. At the time of Patrick's mission, Ireland was ruled by Celtic kings and her society was by then entirely Celtic. Yet the picturesque and misleadingly precise lays of the bards not only traced the descent of every one of these kings back to the most remote past (genealogies which, after the acceptance of Christianity, were to stretch back to Adam), but also told of four conquerors who had preceded the Celts.

Their origins and their destinies must necessarily be classed as obscure, but we are told that when the original settlers of the island were defeated by the seafaring Fomors, many of them fled to Greece. The next race of invaders, the Tuatha De Danann (in whose name there might be a fossilized form of "Danai"—one of the names by which the ancient Greeks were known), made use of magical powers to assist them in their conquest. However, these arcane skills were not proof against the Milesians —according to the legend the last

conquerors of the island and, if so, a Celtic people. The Milesians, whose name also has an attractively Mediterranean flavor, originally came from Spain. This tradition is neither inherently absurd nor lacking in some archaeological evidence. It is now fairly generally accepted that Phoenician traders from the Mediterranean reached Cornwall in their quest for tin— sufficient indication of the skills of the early seafaring peoples. And more direct links between Ireland and Spain itself may be seen in the remains of megalithic monuments in these two countries, as in other parts of coastal Europe.

Whatever their origins, the Celts were well established in Ireland at the time of the Roman conquest of Britain. Their numbers were swelled by the arrival of small groups of refugees fleeing before the invading army. We know from the account of his son-in-law, the historian Tacitus, that the Roman

Early Celtic head from England, dating from the time of the Roman occupation.

general Agricola had contemplated the conquest of the island—not, it appears, because of military necessity nor in the hope of material gain; but rather as a tactical move of psychological warfare against the Britons themselves, to impress on them the omnipotence and ubiquity of Roman arms. But the demonstration was never made. The conquest of Ireland by Rome, if so it may be termed, did not come until four centuries later, when she received her religion and first literate culture at the hands of a Roman missionary.

During the intervening period, there is evidence of trading with the Empire and also of some raiding by Irish adventurers. Yet for the

Stone fort in the Greenan mountains, Ireland, for centuries the seat of the Kings of Ulster.

most part these centuries were spent in the internecine warfare between seven kings who divided the country among them. During this period the most powerful house attempted to make good their claim to be High Kings.

In many ways Ireland was remarkable among the countries of western Europe in the early Middle Ages, especially for the survival of an ancient Iron Age culture, complete with the institution of kingship. But more important still is the early sense of a unity of culture that surmounted the political divisions of the country and was expressed in the use of a common language and a common legendary tradition. It was this tradition that was so important a feature in the success of missionaries of the fifth century.

Ireland after Patrick

The brilliant story of Christian culture in Ireland and its importance to the civilization of medieval Europe has been touched on. The talents of the Irish in the humane arts were not, however, matched by an equal skill in the business of politics. When the Norse invaders fell upon the country at the end of the ninth century, the Irish were unable to dislodge the intruders. Nor could they sink their differences in order to form an effective counterbalancing power. The reason may perhaps be found in the continuing clannish structure of Irish society. Despite the temporary unifying effect of the reign of Niall the country continued to be divided into warring territories.

The Norsemen brought not only destruction to the thriving cultural

life of the island, but also a new principle of social organization in the towns that they founded— such as Limerick, Wexford and Waterford—and the trade that they conducted. Furthermore, the Norsemen, engrossed in their trading activities and with their overseas territories in Man and the north of England, never seem to have concerned themselves with the outright conquest of Ireland. Thus, unlike their neighbors in England who, in the eleventh century, surrendered independence for a strongly unified state, the Irish were free to continue their interclan rivalry until, during the twelfth century, they too felt the weight of Norman conquest and entered on a tragic period of foreign oppression.

Only once did the situation seem likely to alter. In the early years of the eleventh century, Brian Boru, King of Munster, usurped the high kingship and united the country. On the historic field of Clontarff, in the year 1014, he defeated a great army composed of the Vikings of Dublin, of Man and the Isles, and their Irish allies. The power of the Vikings in Ireland was broken. But in the same year Brian Boru, who had described himself proudly as *Imperator Scottorum*, and who seems to have tried to modify the fragmented nature of Irish society, was killed. The Norsemen's influence was now limited to the important but no longer menacing trading communities. The petty kings and great families of Ireland resumed their age-long struggles, which even the first impact of the Norman conquest in the 1160s did not check. Even the Normans, who never conquered this turbulent country, soon found themselves involved in the complexities of Irish clan politics. In the end it was this very clannishness that enabled the Irish to retain their strong identity as a nation throughout the centuries that followed.

The early history of Scotland

We have seen how St. Columba established an outpost of Irish Christianity on Iona in the sixth century. The island was part of the Scot kingdom in northern Britain that had been founded by settlers from Ireland itself. The original inhabitants of Scotland—the Picts—are one of the more shadowy peoples

Pictish stone slab from Scotland with figures of warriors.

of European history. It seems likely that they settled in the country before the arrival of the Celts in Britain and had received Christianity during the fifth century at the hands of St. Ninnian. At the time the community of Iona was founded, the land we now know as Scotland was divided among several kingdoms: the Picts to the northeast; the Scots; the British in Strathclyde to the southwest; and the Angles in Northumbria to the southeast. During the ninth century a new power established itself in the Hebrides and the mainland districts of Caithness and Sutherland. This was the Norse earldom of Orkney, which all but destroyed the Pictish kingdom. As a result, before the middle of the century the Scottish king, Kenneth I MacAlpin, was able to extend his control over what remained of the kingdom. It was with his house and its successors that the future of Scotland was to lie. In the tenth century they succeeded in winning the lowland areas of Lothian and the Tweed frontier from the English King Edgar. In the early eleventh century, Kenneth MacAlpin's succes-

sors acquired the whole inheritance of the last of the kings of Strathclyde. The power of the earldom of Orkney had gradually been eroded, so that by the end of the eleventh century only the isles and the northeasternmost tip of mainland Scotland was controlled by the Norwegian rulers.

The Vandals in Africa

In 451 Europe was confronted by the menacing power of the central Asian steppes that had so long affected her destiny indirectly. Fear of the Huns had been the force that had driven the first wave of German invaders into the Roman Empire during the fourth century. Gradually, their long trek westwards was to lead the two great confederacies of the Goths to set up kingdoms in the old lands of the Roman Empire. The stories of these kingdoms will be the theme of a later chapter.

The first Germanic kingdom to be established within the Empire was, however, that of the Vandals. They had been settled on the Danubian frontier as early as the third century and had, in the figure of the noble Stilicho, given Rome one of her greatest statesmen. However, Stilicho, like the Roman Aetius after him, was to fall victim to the murky intrigues of the court of the later Western Empire. Among other charges against him was one of having invited the barbarians into the Empire in the fateful year 406.

Crossing the Pyrenees

It is true that the Vandals were among the group of tribes that crossed the Rhine in that year. Unable to find territory in Gaul, they continued to move west, crossing the Pyrenees three years later. In Spain they lived on uneasy terms with the Empire, to which they made nominal allegiance, and with their barbarian neighbors, the Visigoths. However, they were even at this stage showing abilities in seamanship that were later to make them the first barbarian naval power in the Mediterranean. In 429, under pressure from the Visigoths, they were led by their king, Gaiseric, to Africa.

Here again we find contemporaries charging the imperial commander of the province, Boniface, with collusion. But the charge can almost certainly be discounted, and the defeat of Boniface himself was

Mosaic monument to early Christian martyrs in north Africa.

so complete and so rapid that history, as distinct from scandal and rumor, has been denied the opportunity of fabricating any

real explanation of this supposed treachery. Within five years the imperial government had been obliged to recognize the *de facto* power that the ruthless leader of the Vandals had won for himself in Africa. During his long reign of fifty years, Gaiseric (d. 477) not only established a kingdom in Africa, but became a menace to Mediterranean shipping, and seriously threatened the Eastern Empire. In 455, he sacked Rome with legendary brutality. He defeated all attempts to overthrow him and concluded a peace with the Emperor in which Zeno recognized the barbarian power in North Africa and Sicily, Sardinia, Corsica and in the Balearic islands.

The Vandals remained a ruling minority in Africa, settling on the estates of dispossessed Romans. They retained their ancient customs and traditional method of mounted warfare, but gradually succumbed to the unaccustomed life of southern luxury. The Roman citizens of the former province retained their own law courts and continued to serve in the main offices of the civil administration. But in one crucial respect the life of the conquered population was frequently one of bitter oppression. Like Germanic peoples elsewhere, the Vandals were Arian Christians. Persecution of the Catholics, by fines, confiscation and outright cruelty, recurred throughout the Vandal period.

The Moorish onslaught

After Gaiseric's death, Vandal power in Africa was under increasingly severe attack from the Moorish tribes of the interior. Although toward the end of the period some rapprochement was achieved with the Eastern Empire, and the persecution of Orthodox Christians ceased, the last Vandal king, Gelimer, renounced the alliance. The kingdom fell prey to the armies of the Emperor Justinian under the command of Belisarius.

The incursions of Attila were among the more sensational events in the history of Europe during the fifth century, but his Hunnic ancestors had long before set in motion a train of events that had far-reaching consequences for the Empire in the West. The century of Vandal rule in Africa was paralleled by the Ostrogothic domination of Italy, and outshone by the enduring state the Visigoths established in Spain after the Vandals left.

Seal of Alaric II, powerful king of the Visigoths.

Attila, the legendary "Scourge of God," was the force that—curiously enough—helped to hold the tottering Roman Empire together for a few more years. Halfway through the fifth century, the Empire was defended by an array of feuding barbarian tribes enlisted as mercenaries. These tribes were united by a common fear of the Huns, who had left Central Asia to invade India, Persia, Central and Eastern Europe and were now threatening the West. Aetius, commander-in-chief of the Roman army, knew the Huns well and their leader, Attila, in particular—the Roman general had once been a hostage in the Huns' camp. Aetius also knew that the real danger to the Empire came from within, from its disintegrating society. When Attila invaded Gaul, Aetius checked him at a battle fought southeast of Paris. But the Roman "victory" brought only a temporary halt to the inevitable fall of Rome.

On the battlefield of the Campus Mauriacus—to the west of the old Gallo-Roman town of Troyes, some ninety miles southeast of Paris—two armies faced each other in the year 451. In retrospect they might be seen as the forces of two contrasting worlds: Asia against Europe, the civilization of the plains against that of the towns, pagan barbarism against the Christian heritage of Greece and Rome. But this assessment would be superficial.

Arrayed behind the Hun, Attila, was a horde of tribes more or less under his command: not only his own people but also Ruli, Heruli, Gepidae, Ostrogoths, Lombards and others. Opposed to him in defense of the Roman Empire was the last of the great Romans, the nobleman Aetius. Among his forces there were hardly any Gallo-Romans, but a mixture of barbarian peoples whose loyalty was not to be relied on: Franks, Burgundians, Alans, Sarmatae, Visigoths, and even a number of Britons who had been recruited indiscriminately along with the very Germans who had driven them out of their own island territory. What is more, the Visigoths under King Theodoric could well find themselves confronted by their kinsmen, the Ostrogoths, under the command of a Hun. Attila had defeated the Visigoths in a previous battle; he treated the Ostrogoths as run-away slaves. Aetius' forces had only one common bond: their fear of the Huns who had driven them from the steppes of Russia and the plains of Germany and forced them into Gaul.

The defense of the Roman Empire at this time was entrusted to the very people who presented the greatest threat to its peace. Barbarians were enlisted as mercenaries—first in small groups, then whole peoples at a time. German soldiers reached the highest ranks. Both the Vandal Stilicho and later the Sueve Ricimer were to command Roman armies.

Unfortunately, these dangerous allies expected regular payment, which the Empire was no longer in a position to supply. Some of them revolted, and

demanded lands off which they might live; the Visigoths, who had put themselves at the service of the head of the Eastern Empire in 376, ravaged certain Greek provinces and Italian towns under their chief, Alaric. In 410 they sacked Rome herself before crossing the Alps and finally settling in Aquitaine.

In 407, a particularly violent wave of tribes had broken on Gaul. The Alans, Sueves and Vandals had been driven from Persia by the Huns and had made their way across Europe. The Alans had ended up as scattered communities on both sides of the Pyrenees; the Sueves were eventually to establish a kingdom in the region of the Douro in the north of what is now Portugal, while the Vandals made their way from Spain to Africa, where they were to dominate the Maghrib for more than a century.

Peoples who had previously been living between the Elbe and the Rhine followed the example of these enterprising invaders, and ventured forth in their turn. Burgundians, Alamani, and Ripuarian Franks established themselves on the left bank of the Rhine and acquired the status of federate territories. At the same time Angles, Jutes and Saxons were gradually occupying the eastern parts of Britain, from which the kingdom of England was later to emerge.

Behind these German tribes there were the Huns, or rather the various peoples of Hunnish stock who had left their native steppes of central Asia to invade India and Persia on the one hand, and central and eastern Europe on the other.

As soon as he learned that the Huns had crossed the Rhine, Aetius hastily assembled an army from among the barbarian tribes established in Gaul for half a century. This army clearly lacked unity, as Aetius was only too well aware: although there were many reliable troops, the loyalty of the Alans under their king, Sagiban, was not to be relied on.

Attila himself, ruler of the people who occupied the vast plains between the eastern Alps and the

A portrait of Theodosius the Great, ruler and defender of the Eastern Empire from Constantinople.

Opposite An ivory diptych in Monza Cathedral traditionally said to represent Aetius, the defender of Gaul, his murderer the future Valentinian III and the princess Galla Placidia. (Some scholars prefer to identify the portraits as the Vandal Stilicho and his family.)

The weapons of barbarian warriors; a two-edged, gold-handled sword found in France and probably made by a Byzantine craftsman, which tradition attributes to King Theodoric; a silver Moldavian helmet, possibly Hunnish; and the boss of a shield.

Urals, was not interested in territorial gains but rather in military victories; above all he was a man drunk with power and greedy for fame. However, he must not be thought of simply as a brute or a hardened fighting man who never got down from his horse and who ate his food raw. He was a skilled politician and was gifted with a lively intelligence, to which was allied a certain cruelty. He did not conquer merely in order to possess but fundamentally to assert his own greatness and extend his dominion.

The Roman Empire fascinated this barbarian; in fact, he might well have wished to be a Roman. He exchanged ambassadors and hostages with Constantinople, as a guarantee of the mutual desire for peace. He lived in a palace whose rooms, although of timber, boasted rich carpets and where the pleasures of the Roman bath were enjoyed. He held court in the Roman manner, reclining on a state couch, and presided over brilliant banquets at which a wealth of gold plate was to be seen. His chancellery was managed by Roman scribes, and one of his secretaries, the poet Orestes, was to become regent of Italy and father of the last Western Emperor, Romulus Augustulus.

Overweening ambition was the dominant trait in Attila's character. Shortly after the death of his uncle, King Rugila, Attila had his own brother Bleda assassinated so that he should be sole ruler. But this empire was only a brief episode in the history of the Hunnish tribes. In 445 Attila renewed his advance towards the Mediterranean.

Whether war or diplomacy would be required for this advance, the king of the Huns cared little—so long as he was the master. But this crafty Oriental knew when to make a strategic withdrawal. On one occasion he had brought pressure on the Eastern Emperor at Constantinople, Theodosius II, to pay him tribute money. But when the feeble Theodosius was succeeded by a more energetic man, Attila turned his attention to Rome.

On this occasion he came in the guise of a friend, but one whose friendship was mixed with impudence. He demanded the hand of the sister of the Emperor Valentinian III, for whose dowry he thought that half of the Western Empire would be appropriate. Valentinian showed this suitor the door.

What then was to be the next step for a man who was to become the legendary "Scourge of God"? After his repulse by Constantinople and his humiliation by Rome he simply went to seek his fortune elsewhere. In the spring of 451 he was on the banks of the Rhine where he became involved in the internal quarrels of the Ripuarian Franks, and announced that he was going to punish his fugitive slaves, the Visigoths, who were for the time being peacefully installed in Aquitaine.

The man who was governing Gaul at that time probably knew Attila better than anyone else. Aetius, who was the son of a noble family, had in fact spent part of his youth as a high-ranking hostage at the court of Rugila. Attila had been his companion. He understood, better than anybody else,

184

Attila is halted at the Campus Mauriacus

the nature of the Huns. Surrounded by terrified barbarians who trembled at the Huns' approach, only Aetius understood Attila's character. To him fell the task of defending Gaul.

He appreciated the warlike qualities of the Huns. As a nobleman and commander-in-chief of the Roman army, Aetius had enlisted Huns for his personal bodyguard and his picked troops; and it had been with the help of Hunnish auxiliaries that he had subdued the Burgundians in 435.

Aetius realized that Attila was more concerned with his reputation than with acquiring territories for which his nomadic horsemen would find no use. He also knew that Attila lacked persistence. Treves, Metz and Reims were burned, and Attila's hordes passed some distance from Paris, where St. Geneviève urged the people to remain calm and not to flee. In May of 451, Attila besieged Orléans, whose bishop, Aignan, was able to escape in time to seek help. It was at this juncture that Aetius called up the federal troops based in Gaul and marched on Orléans. Thereupon Attila retreated. Once more, in the face of firm resolution on the part of his enemies, he decided to abandon his original plans and explore fresh fields.

At the Campus Mauriacus, however, Aetius caught up with Attila at last. The carnage and ferocity of this battle were to become legendary. Theodoric, the king of the Visigoths, was killed in the fight, but the battle was indecisive: neither the troops of Attila nor those of Aetius were overwhelmed. Attila, however, had been halted in his tracks, and this was sufficient: he had not wished to fight and so once again he turned back and recrossed the Rhine without hindrance. Aetius could easily have pursued the retreating Huns and harassed them, but in fact he did nothing. He made no effort to exploit his victory and he even sent home the barbarian contingents that made up his army.

A great deal of criticism has been directed at this strange decision, which left at the gates of the Roman Empire a potential invader who might at any time renew his attacks. Was it want of resolution? Aetius was not lacking in decisiveness, as his brilliant campaigns in Africa bear witness. It has sometimes been thought that the earlier friendship of the two opponents and their youthful comradeship may have influenced his decision, but it is scarcely likely that Aetius would have let such a sentiment come before the interests of the Empire.

Nor must one forget that Aetius had a profound knowledge of Attila's character: he was ambitious and arrogant, but in the last resort he was less of a menace than his people had been three centuries earlier when they had established themselves north of the Black Sea and dominated all who had not fled. Aetius alone realized that the fear of the Huns was out of all proportion to the real danger they posed.

He also knew that the greater danger that threatened the West was an internal one; the breakup caused by the rivalry of peoples who had only recently established themselves, and the collapse of Roman hegemony. For many years he had fought all over Gaul against the banditry of the Bagaudae, and had kept guard on frontiers that he had no choice but to entrust to the federate peoples. It was only the fear of the Hun that gave these groups a certain degree of cohesion.

The defeat of Attila could only lead to the outbreak of quarrels and revolts among the very people who were defending the Empire. It would therefore be better to leave a man like Attila on the other side of the Rhine, so as to keep the federate peoples in a state of vigilance. This would ensure internal peace and security from external attack. Fear of the Hun was to serve Aetius' purpose in his relations with the Burgundians, Visigoths and Franks.

As always, when checked in one direction, Attila decided to try his luck elsewhere. In 452 he invaded Italy; Aquileia, Pavia and Milan fell into his hands. The Emperor Valentinian III was jealous of Aetius' prestige, and instead of calling upon him for help, fell back on Rome where he proceeded to negotiate with the Hun. Pope Leo I intervened, and a payment of tribute was agreed upon. Attila had humiliated the Western Empire and he retired satisfied.

The death of the king of the Huns in 453 was also the death knell of the dominion that had been founded on his extraordinary character. The subject peoples revolted, and the Huns themselves split up. It was the end of the Hunnish threat—and also the end of the Western Empire.

In spite of Aetius' efforts, the unity of the western world was shattered. The Roman Empire had survived many other revolts, but the object of almost all of these was to usurp power at Rome and acquire the universal domination that went with the title of Emperor. From this time onwards, national wars were to be the common lot of Europe.

There was no central authority that could withstand the forces of disintegration. Valentinian killed Aetius—who he realized would eventually supplant him—only to be assassinated in his turn. In Gaul the Visigoths and the Burgundians gained their

A mosaic from Carthage, c. A.D. 500 shows a Vandal landlord newly settled in as owner of the estate left vacant by a retreating Roman.

The heritage of Rome survives

Barbarian Invasion of Europe

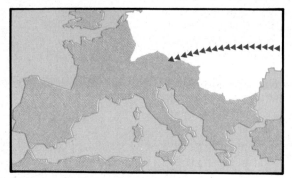

Huns
▶ In the first century they conquered parts of Germany. They provoked the Vandal invasion in 406; tried to invade Gaul in 451 and Italy in 452. Their attacks faded out in the late-fifth century.

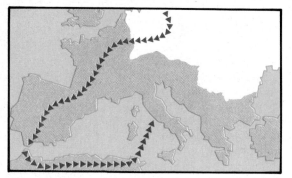

Vandals
▶ Associated with other barbarian peoples, they set up an independent kingdom in Spain, after 410. They were driven out by the Visigoths in 430, when they crossed over to Africa. From this part of Africa now called Tunisia they dominated the whole of the western Mediterranean for a century.

Visigoths
▶ Settled in Illyria in 400 and invaded Italy in 410. They sacked Rome but failed in their attempt to conquer Italy. They settled in southern Gaul from 410 to 415. From there, in 80 years they conquered Spain and south-west Gaul as far as the Loire.

Ostrogoths
▶ Tried in vain to settle in Italy, after their entry into the Empire in 378. Installed after 450 in Illyria they eventually reached Italy where their king, Theodoric, created a mighty barbarian kingdom at the beginning of the sixth century.

Burgundians and Alemans
▶ Fought among themselves. Fleeing from the Alemans, the Burgundians installed themselves in Savoy after 440. Their kingdom slowly spread towards the Massif Central and the Durance until the end of the fifth century.

Franks
▶ Divided into very different groups. They only started moving south after 450. But they played a very big part in the Roman army.

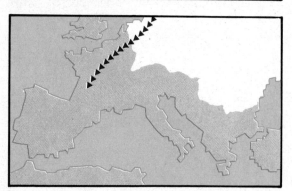

● Extent of Roman Empire

independence and their kings promulgated laws which were binding on the Romans who were now under their authority. They had already forgotten that they themselves were intruders. On the northern frontier the Franks began their slow progress towards Belgium. Soon, the last Emperor in the West, Romulus Augustulus, was to be dethroned by the king of the Heruli, Odoacer. The Ostrogoths, who had formerly been subject to the Huns, made an incursion into Italy at the instigation of the Eastern Emperor, but were eventually to found an independent kingdom.

As soon as Attila disappeared from the scene, a whole new world appeared. The Visigoths, the Burgundians and other federate peoples who had been called to defend Rome had in fact been defending their new lands and their future kingdoms. From this time onward, the West was no longer Roman; it was barbarian, and the barbarians were well aware of it.

They did not, however, make a clean sweep of the civilization that they had found in the Roman Empire. In varying degrees they had all felt the same fascination as Attila. The Ostrogoth Theodoric modeled his administration on the same lines and with the same framework as that of Rome, and staffed it with Romans. He proceeded also to surround himself with men of letters, of whom the most famous was Cassiodorus. The Visigoth Ataulf had donned the woolen toga of the Romans when he married the Roman princess, Galla Placidia, to the sound of a wedding hymn. When his successors were driven from Gaul by Clovis, they established at Toledo a brilliant court. One of Ataulf's successors became a composer of hymns.

Throughout the entire West it was Christianity, the religion of the Romans, that gradually prevailed over that of the invaders, which was either German paganism or Arian Christianity. Mixed marriages, which increased enormously in course of time, were to eliminate many of the differences between Roman and barbarian families.

The Germanic peoples had added their social and cultural heritage to that of ancient Rome, and it would be unjust to ignore it. They contributed a different conception of society and the family, based on the hereditary principle, the contractual obligations of the craft unions and the vested security of public authority. It was due to the influence of German ideas that over part of Europe the conceptions of royal power, class structure and the disposition of property slowly evolved over a thousand years. Although they did not despise the written word as a means of administration, the barbarians made the verbal communication, as evidence or declaration of intention, the fundamental basis of the western juridical system. Because they were warriors and nomads they accepted the idea that service in the army carried greater prestige than work in the fields. The medieval lord was to imitate the German warrior, and not Cincinnatus.

They introduced new technical processes into Europe, notably in metalworking, both for armor

and for jewelry. They also widened the range of artistic conception with their own sources of inspiration and choice of themes.

At the end of the fifth century Clovis extended the kingdom of the Salian Franks in the northern half of Gaul, at the expense of the remaining Roman territory and the other Frankish tribes. In 507 Clovis also subdued the Visigothic kingdom of Aquitaine, and some years later his sons annexed the kingdom of Burgundy. Already, however, the Franks were divided among themselves and engaged in internecine strife. Neustria, Austrasia, Burgundy and Aquitaine were continually engaged in hostilities until the accession of the Pepin dynasty at the end of the seventh century. Either in concert or separately, the Franks joined issue against the peoples of Germany, in particular the Thuringians and Bavarians.

During the same period the Anglo-Saxon kingdoms all aspired to dominate Britain. The fortunes of war gave pride of place first to Kent and then to Northumbria and Mercia.

Within the boundaries of barbarian Europe itself, hostilities were engaged in with equal ardor. Britons and Anglo-Saxons were so antagonistic that missionaries had to be sent from Rome to evangelize England. In Italy, the partial failure of Justinian's attempt at reconquest left unprotected both the citizens of Byzantium and the last arrivals from the German migration, the Lombards, who had established themselves in the north and center of Italy in the middle of the sixth century.

Europe then remained divided. The unity that Charlemagne succeeded in achieving was to last only the length of his reign, and the coronation of Christmas A.D. 800, marks a summit rather than a beginning. The Church itself reflected the political fragmentation. The authority of the Pope seldom prevailed, and the religious synods brought together only the bishops of a single province or kingdom. The Latin language survived and was generally adopted, but each group modified it in its own way. In fact, there was only one unifying factor to act as a link between the Empire of Constantine and that of Charlemagne: the Christian faith. JEAN FAVIER

Above A mosaic in the church of St. Appollinare Nuovo in Ravenna, a church founded by Theodoric, King of the Ostrogoths, and decorated with scenes of his life. This one shows his royal palace.

Left The mausoleum of King Theodoric of the Ostrogoths at Ravenna.

Bottom left A gold lamina plaque from the crown plate of a helmet bearing the representation of King Agilauf the Lombard receiving the homage of his people.

Below The seventh-century votive crown of Recceswinth the Visigoth.

Ironically, the victory on the Mauriac Plain sealed the fate both of victor and vanquished. After his death in 453, Attila's empire broke up not only as a result of the feuds among his heirs but also because of a successful rebellion among his German subjects. For the victorious Roman general, Aetius, the outcome of the battle was still more directly catastrophic. He fell victim to a palace conspiracy of enemies who feared his immense prestige. The Emperor Valentinian III is said to have boasted of the disposal of this powerful and popular rival to a favorite courtesan. Her laconic reply was: "You have cut off your right hand with your left."

With the sack of Rome in 455 by the armies of Gaiseric the Vandal, the weakness of the Western Empire was fully revealed. Thereafter the influence of barbarians in the imperial court, which had been considerable, became supreme. From his victory over Vandal armies in 456 to his death in 472, the Suevian general Ricimer was arbiter of the fortunes of the West. Beyond the Alps, only the territories of Syagrius in northern France remained under Roman rule, and these constituted, because of their isolation, a virtually independent kingdom soon to be destroyed by Clovis. During the brief reign of Majorian (457-61), the best traditions of the Empire were revived by that competent and conscientious ruler, but his growing prestige was a threat to Ricimer, who had him deposed and murdered. For another fifteen years the fiction of a Western Emperor was maintained. But in 476 the auspiciously named but pitiable figure of Romulus Augustulus was wiped

out by the soldiers of Odoacer, another successful German soldier who, like Ricimer, succeeded in wielding the real power in the West.

In the East, thanks to the determined efforts of the emperors, the influence of barbarians in the armed forces and the capital itself was held at bay. Despite the abortive expedition sent by Leo I against the Vandals in 468, the integrity of the eastern half of the Empire was largely maintained. Leo's son-in-law and successor, Zeno, was at first obliged to accept the *coup d'état* of Odoacer; later, he cleverly diverted the Ostrogothic tribes in the Balkans by commissioning them to put an end to Odoacer's regime in Italy.

New Powers: the Visigoths in Spain

It was the Visigothic army that, at the battle of Adrianople in 378, defeated the Emperor Valens; it was the Visigoths under Alaric who sacked Rome itself in 410. Yet, ironically, three centuries later it was the Visigoths who were virtually extinguished in their attempt to defend their Romanized Christian traditions against the invasions of a new wave of barbarians.

By 415, Alaric's successors had led the Visigoths through Gaul to Spain. There, in a series of campaigns fought ostensibly on behalf of the imperial power at Rome, they drove out the earlier Germanic settlers and returned most of the Iberian peninsula to imperial rule. As a reward for their labors, and lest they should become too powerful, they were settled in the large territories of southwest France, later to

be the semi-independent duchy of Aquitaine.

This Visigothic kingdom, free from all allegiance to the Roman Emperor, expanded dramatically. Under its great King Euric (c. 420-486), it extended from the Loire to Gibraltar. It comprised the whole of southern France west of the Rhone and all of Spain save the tiny states of the Basques and the Suevic kingdom to the northwest. It was this mighty power, with its capital at Toulouse, that was overthrown by Clovis and his Frankish army at the Battle of Vouillé in 507. As a result, the Visigoths were, for the rest of their history, confined to Spain, except for a small stretch of territory on the southwest Mediterranean coastline of Gaul. Yet, reluctant to recognize the completeness of their defeat at the hands of the Franks, the Visigoths did not move their capital from Toulouse to Spain until as late as the 540s. The savior of the Visigothic cause in France had been Theodoric, the Ostrogothic king of Italy, who viewed with disquiet the rapid rise to power of the Franks. In addition, Theodoric also acted for a time as regent of the French Visigothic kingdom and did much to lay the foundations of its future.

Visigothic inscription from eastern Spain.

A vital part of the Visigoths' barbaric past, which was in part the cause of their ultimate downfall, was the principle of the elective monarchy. The principle indeed underlay the kingship of all the European post-barbarian kingdoms; but the internal division and weakness caused by elective monarchy were particularly serious in the exposed peninsular kingdom. The success of Justinian's Roman armies in Spain was facilitated by

the divisive rivalry for the Visigothic throne during the middle of the sixth century. The natural preference of the Romano-Iberian population for the religious orthodoxy of the Byzantine Empire as opposed to the Arian Christianity of their conquerors strengthened the Byzantine position, as did the conversion of the Suevi in the northwest to Catholicism. Yet despite this religious antipathy among the subject population, the great Visigothic king Leovigild, who finally established the capital at Toledo, was able to recover much of the territory lost to Rome. Furthermore, Leovigild lessened the effects of the religious conflict by passing legislation in favor of mixed Arian-Catholic marriages. His successor, Reccared, took the process to its logical conclusion: he presided over the third council of Toledo in 589 which, by a majority decision, proclaimed orthodox Catholicism the state religion. Yet the effects of the Arian period continued to be felt.

The king still possessed a decisive voice in religious affairs, a feature of Spanish life that remained prominent. Indeed, in the sixteenth century the notorious Spanish Inquisition was, in effect, an agent of royal policy. Under the Visigoths the regular councils of Toledo formed the great council of an almost theocratic state.

It was one of the great achievements of the Visigoths that, after their acceptance of Catholicism, they succeeded in welding into one people the diverse races of the Iberian Peninsula. A major reason for their success was the immensely significant legal code promulgated by King Recceswinth in the 650s. The code, written in Latin, was not only the first major legal code to be issued by one of the successor barbarian kingdoms, but it also, most significantly, unified into a single legal system the Roman and Visigothic laws of the two populations.

The Ostrogoths in Italy

The Italy St. Benedict knew was that of Theodoric the Ostrogoth, the barbarian ruler who most truly and splendidly continued the traditions of the ancient Rome that he had displaced. Theodoric's exact status within the political environment of the late antique world is not absolutely clear. In a letter written to the Byzantine Emperor Anastasius, he acknowledged the Emperor's seniority and admitted

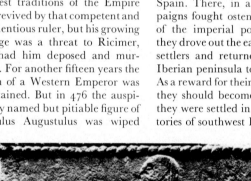

German warriors of the period of the invasions.

that his own court could only attempt to imitate the magnificence of Constantinople. Doubtless, this was true; nevertheless, it is clear from the tone of Theodoric's letter and from an evaluation of his whole policy that the Ostrogoth ruler regarded himself as a free agent throughout Italy and in his dealings with the barbarian kingdoms to the north.

Theodoric had led the Ostrogoths into Italy in the late 480s at the invitation of the Emperor Zeno himself. Zeno's aim was twofold: to free the Balkans of the depradations of the Gothic hordes, and to re-establish in Italy a power that at least recognized the suzerainty of the empire. Since the year 476, Italy had been under the rule of Odoacer. German troops under his command in the north had revolted against the feeble authority of the last of the Western Emperors and demanded land in payment for their services. When their demands were refused, the youthful Emperor, Romulus Augustulus, was deposed. Messengers were sent to Constantinople demanding that Odoacer be recognized as the imperial vicar in Italy. When Odoacer, however, lent his support to a pope who was unacceptable to the Emperor, and then to a rival for the imperial throne itself, his days were numbered. Within five years of Theodoric's arrival in Italy, the troops of Odoacer were defeated. Odoacer himself, after a three-year

resistance in the marsh-girt city of Ravenna, surrendered only to be treacherously murdered.

Theodoric had secured Italy in the name of the Emperor. But thereafter he was to rule—with the assistance of the powerful land-owning bureaucracy and through the coercive power of his Ostrogothic soldiery, whom he rewarded handsomely with land—as King of Italy and Dalmatia.

During the reign of Theodoric, Italy enjoyed a late Indian summer of peace and prosperity. Even a Byzantine historian observed that Theodoric had been a fair and just ruler to all his subjects. Nevertheless, some members of the old patrician class—Orthodox in religion and opposed to the Arian Ostrogoths, nostalgic for the distant past of Roman imperial grandeur and unwilling to lose touch with the representative of that tradition—attempted to open negotiations with the Byzantine court without Theodoric's knowledge. Regarding this as treason, Theodoric ordered the execution of a number of senators, among them his one-time councillor and friend, Boethius.

Boethius' "On the Consolation of Philosophy"

Boethius, the man described by Gibbon as the "last of the Romans whom Cato or Cicero could have acknowledged as their countryman," was a man whose philosophy was to be of seminal importance throughout the Middle Ages. He wrote in the strong tradition of ancient classical and pagan learning. His most famous work, *On the Consolation of Philosophy*, was popular in Europe up to the Renaissance. Written while he was in prison awaiting his execution, it is in the form of a dialogue between Boethius and Philosophy, personified as a decorous and beautiful woman. Boethius, an influential adviser at Theodoric's court, had been consul in the year 510. He lived to see his sons become consuls in their turn. He believed that the false charges of treason, which accused him of plotting with the Emperor Justin for the overthrow of Theodoric for the restoration of the ancient liberties of the senate, had been brought by powerful enemies whom he had offended by his defense of the interests of the poor citizens in his role as consul. Boethius, later to be canonized as a saint, was quite mistakenly regarded as a champion of trinitarian

Baptistry of the Arian church in Ravenna: the interior of the dome.

orthodoxy against the Arian heresy favored by the Ostrogothic court. Indeed it may well have been an imperial edict of Justin against the appointment of pagans, heretics, or Jews to official posts that first awoke the suspicions and anger of the aging Theodoric.

The religious division between the Orthodox Emperors and their Arian Ostrogothic agents in Italy exacerbated the increasingly uneasy relations between the two. On his death, Theodoric was succeeded by his daughter, Amalsuntha, whose admiration for, and loyalty to, imperial Rome was well known. In time, however, her loyalty to the Emperor alienated her from the Ostrogothic nobility; in 535 she was overthrown and murdered. This provided the pretext for which the Byzantines had been waiting: the first campaigns of Justinian's generals heralded the end of Ostrogothic rule in Italy.

The reign of Theodoric was a glorious period in the history of early medieval Italy. At his capital of Ravenna, Theodoric built a palace of considerable splendor

closely modeled in style on Diocletian's palace at Spalato (Split).

Monuments of the Ostrogothic period

Among the great monuments of the Ostrogothic period that have survived to the present are the church of San Apollinare Nuovo, and the superb mausoleum that Theodoric had built for himself. Unusual for its period, the mausoleum was built of stone rather than brick and is roofed with a single circular block weighing over 450 tons. The placing of the roof represents a major engineering achievement in the tradition of ancient Rome. The

Coin of Theodoric the Great.

work of Theodoric's artists, which glorified both the religious doctrines of Arian Christianity and the greatness of the Ostrogothic state, was replaced at Justinian's order with a mosaic scheme based on Orthodox Christianity. In such troubled times, many of the traditions of Roman culture were kept alive in the cells of Benedictine monasteries.

Boethius as consul, from an ivory diptych.

The Three Kings, dressed as barbarian noblemen; part of Justinian's mosaic scheme in St. Apollinare, Ravenna.

The Rule of St. Benedict

On one occasion, it is said, St. Benedict's monks tried to poison him, and they often disregarded his instructions. But monasticism in the West was Benedict's creation. Before he founded Monte Cassino in 520, there were numerous other groups of monks in Europe, all with their own monastic rules. But Benedict's Rule for his followers was the first to achieve general acceptance. It provided an ideal for monasticism that was at once disciplined and possible to achieve and maintain. With its emphasis on the individual monastery, Benedict's Rule was ideally suited to a world degenerating into chaos; and, indeed, it was largely in Benedictine monasteries that classical learning survived during the Dark Ages. Perhaps more than any other single force, the Rule of St. Benedict gave adolescent Europe a message of fairness and a tradition of Christian behavior.

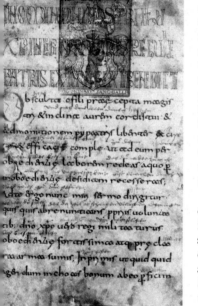

The Rule of Benedict, a page from the St. Gall version of Benedict's code of practical and spiritual monastic behavior which became the basis of monastic life for the Western world.

Opposite St. Benedict carrying a model of his monastery at Monte Cassino; a fresco of the eighth or ninth century.

Some eighty-five miles southeast of Rome, the traveler to Naples sees on the rocks of a towering hill a large, fortress-like building with the cupola of a church in its midst. It is the abbey of Monte Cassino, reduced to dust by the Allied Air Forces in 1944, and now rebuilt in facsimile to replace what was destroyed. In the early sixth century this was a remote region traversed only by herdsmen who were still pagan, and on the summit of the hill was a ruined temple of Apollo, together with a still earlier ruin of a fortress. About the year 520 the abbot Benedict, then some forty years old, arrived at Monte Cassino with a small group of monks. He was attracted to the place perhaps by the solitude of the hill and by the building stone available from the ruins.

Benedict was born into a family in the higher level of society, possibly Roman in origin but then settled in the central Italian province of Umbria. The youth studied first in Rome but left the city with his education unfinished to live first as a hermit and later as the abbot of a group of small monasteries at Subiaco, thirty miles east of Rome. After repeated troubles with insubordinate monks, he left Subiaco and led a faithful group of followers to Cassino. The new monastery prospered and drew the attention of the Gothic king and warrior Totila, who visited Benedict at Cassino in 542. Five years later, the abbot was dead. Neither Benedict nor his contemporaries could have imagined that Monte Cassino, more than a thousand years later, would be looked upon as the cradle of medieval civilization, and that he himself would be hailed by a pope as the "Father of Europe." What assured him lasting esteem was the writing, about 530–40, of his rule, or code of behavior, for his spiritual sons at the abbey.

We must not imagine Benedict's monastery as a large and regularly planned building complex, with church, dwellings, cloister and the rest. It was probably a small group of low, shedlike, contiguous structures, half-stone, half-wood, one of which would have been the chapel, another the refectory, and a third the dormitory. No doubt there was additional accommodation for novices and guests. There was no cloister, and the oratory was a simple room with wooden benches or stools and a stone altar. In the upland valley below the buildings, the monks cultivated vines and olives, with fields of cereals and legumes. The life was that of a small, simple Christian community of devout laymen.

The monasteries of western Europe in 500 lacked firm cohesion at every level. A few, like St. Martin's Marmoutier near Tours in France, were bishops' foundations, but most were outside the regular church organization. The frequent siting of a monastery, and still more a hermitage, in a desert or some other inaccessible spot, far from the sphere of a city bishop, made what links there were to the official church very tenuous. Nor was there any organization into groups or alliances. There was no "order" or "institute." Every monastery, if not a cluster of small communities as at Subiaco, was an independent house under a single abbot. Finally, there was no generally accepted rule. The directories that existed were either mere codes of liturgy, penances and punishments, or idiosyncratic rule books such as the contemporary *Rule of the Master*. Each monastery depended entirely on its abbot, and monks could come and go from house to house, sometimes drifting all through life in this way.

In such a situation the genius of Benedict found its opportunity. Though not a trained writer or theologian, he was familiar with scripture; with the writings of the Desert Fathers and of Basil, Leo the Great, and Augustine; and above all with the *Conferences* and *Institutes* of John Cassian. But the end product of his reading and meditation was a document original alike in its spiritual wisdom, its comprehensive scope and its refined brevity. It is relatively short; indeed, if liturgical instruction and scriptural quotations are disregarded, it is very short. But it established the framework of the whole life of a monastery—disciplinary, domestic and economic—and the whole

The monastery buildings at Monte Cassino, the church in the background. These buildings were completely restored after their destruction by the Allies during World War II.

Subiaco, the small group of monasteries some thirty miles east of Rome, where Benedict was Abbot and from which he drew the monks who followed him to found Monte Cassino.

course of the monk's activities, both external and spiritual. The Rule provides for patriarchal government, which entrusts full authority and responsibility to an elected abbot. The adherents to the Rule are to remain in one place, be obedient and practice monastic virtue. The main function of the monks and the focal point of the community is the Divine Office or succession of services, which inspires the work, study, prayer and meditation with which the rest of the day is occupied. Goods are held in common but there is no specific vow of poverty—a feature of immense importance for the performance of the works of mercy. In addition, room is found for brief but profound instructions that combined common sense with spiritual wisdom. Of this life the abbot and the Rule were the two pillars, and the vow of stability (remaining in one place), which Benedict instituted, gave strength to the whole.

There is no autograph or nearly contemporary copy of the Rule but, as might be expected, the extant manuscripts are very numerous. They probably exceed in number those of any other ancient writing save the Bible. The oldest known manuscript is English, probably from Worcester, written about 700 and now in the Bodleian Library at Oxford. This, however, is not the most trustworthy text. That distinction is acknowledged by modern scholars to belong to manuscript 914 of the ancient library of St. Gall in Switzerland. The distinguished palaeographer, Ludwig Traube, showed in 1898 that the St. Gall manuscript was written about A.D. 817. It is a close, if not an immediate, copy of the manuscript brought from Rome to Charlemagne in 787 to be broadcast throughout his empire. Charlemagne's text is thought to have been a faithful copy of the original. It differs considerably from the smooth "vulgate" text, which removed the vernacular Latin forms and constructions of the original, and became standard from early times to the present day.

Until about 787 the forms and machinery of the decayed imperial system had continued to function, however weak and disfigured they may have been. When the young Benedict was a student at Rome, Boethius, the philosopher and friend of Theodoric, was writing his theological and philosophical treatises and planning to translate the whole of Plato and Aristotle into Latin. For the Roman Church, a golden age of liturgy and musical creation and legal study was just ending. Fifty years later, all this had vanished. Rome still survived, but the old official, educated class was gone, and the papacy and clergy had begun to fill the administrative void. The Rome of the popes had succeeded the Rome of the emperors, and the old literary education and thought had ceased to exist in Italy.

The life of St. Benedict spanned this unique historical divide, and the Rule was actually written

The founders of the Middle Ages

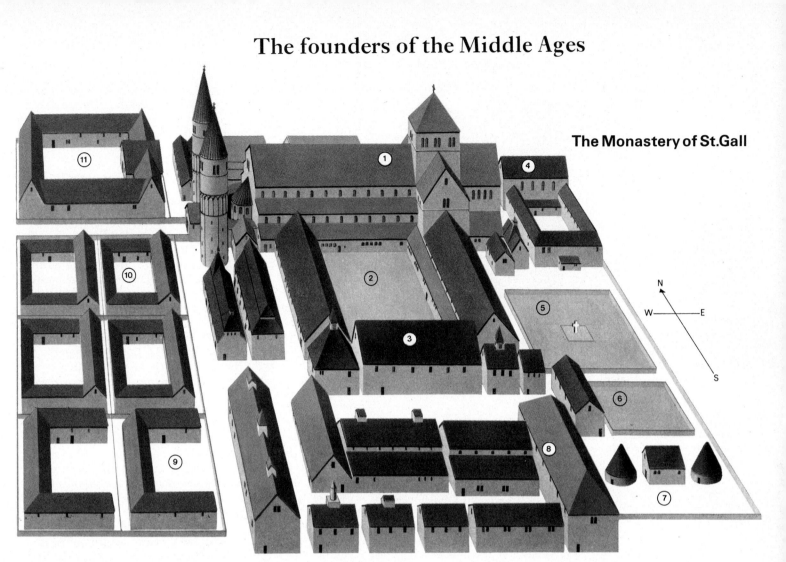

The Monastery of St.Gall

1 The basilican church, with transepts, square tower, an apse at either end, and two detached conical towers at the west end.
2 The cloister, surrounded by monastic buildings; dormitory to the east (*right*) and cellar to the west (*left*).

3 The refectory on the south side of the cloister, parallel with the church.
4 To the east of the church are two cloisters belonging to the novices quarters and the infirmary.
5 The monastic cemetery with a cross in the center.
6 The vegetable garden.

7 Enclosures for poultry.
8 The buildings far south of the church (in the foreground) include the kitchen, bakery and brew-

house, the press, the barn and other workshops.
9 Enclosures for horses and cattle.
10 Further farm quarters.

11 Important buildings including the school, the *scriptorium*, the guest's house and the abbot's house.

while armies were fighting for the control, or the destruction, of Rome. He, along with others of the same historical period, is one of the group known familiarly to historians as "the founders of the Middle Ages." Heirs themselves to the legacy of the past, they transformed and reinterpreted its treasures into a form acceptable to the world that was coming into being. Thus, Benedict summed up in simple form the monastic teaching of Egypt and Asia Minor, already latinized by Cassian. He incorporated the Roman tradition of firm but just government, and gave the entire inheritance to an institution that was to be of great significance for almost a thousand years of European history.

It also happened that in so doing he gave to that institution a viability that it had not hitherto possessed and ensured to it a particular character, both material and spiritual, that was essential to its survival. During his lifetime, the final disintegration of the Roman Empire of the West was taking place.

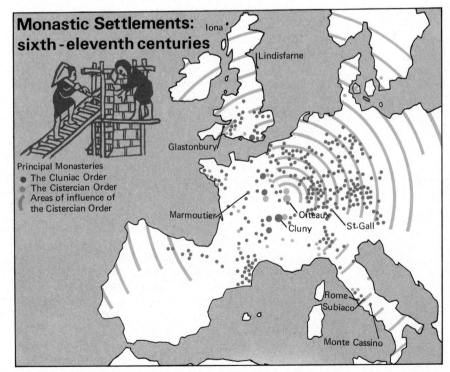

Monastic Settlements: sixth-eleventh centuries

Principal Monasteries
● The Cluniac Order
● The Cistercian Order
Areas of influence of the Cistercian Order

Iona
Lindisfarne
Glastonbury
Marmoutier
Cîteaux
Cluny
St.Gall
Rome
Subiaco
Monte Cassino

A page from the eleventh-century manuscript of St. Gregory's *Life of St. Benedict* written at Monte Cassino, showing the death of the Saint.

Right A monk engaged in his lonely task of manuscript writing; an illustration from a manuscript dating from the period of St. Benedict's life.

Rome, throughout its centuries of dominance, had been the only center of government and administration, of economic and financial life, and to it all talent had flowed. Both literally and figuratively all roads led to Rome, and in the later centuries of her Empire all methods of government, all articles of commerce, from cooking-pots to mosaics, from villas to ampitheaters and forts, were standardized in Rome, blueprinted and mass-produced throughout the provinces. It was this fact that had made the spread both of Christianity and monasticism physically possible.

After the transfer of the capital to Constantinople, and especially after the invasions around 400, all centralizing influences weakened and broke down. Fragmentation replaced consolidation, and the main unit of existence was the self-supporting village or estate. To such a world the monastery of the Rule was perfectly adapted. A compact economic unit, almost entirely self-contained and self-supporting, with its food cultivated by its inhabitants, and with domestic animals, arts and crafts within its ambit, it had a small surplus for market with which to buy a few necessities, such as metalware and salt.

The monastery was also self-contained in its life. The monks lived, prayed and studied in their monastery, and worked in its sheds and gardens. They had no employment or office that took them away from their enclosure, for this, as the Rule said, would be altogether harmful for their souls. They could indeed be sent on errands, to market or on the business of the house, but this was only infrequent, and not to be spoken of when accomplished. They had no superior beyond the abbot, and no alliance with any other community. In the background was the protective and punitive jurisdiction of the bishop, but this was rarely felt as long as all went well.

It was a microcosm of ages and types. Recruitment was of two kinds, the one of adults—some of them possibly clerics or monks from elsewhere, but others from the illiterate native peasantry—the other of children, offered to God by their parents, to be educated in the monastery and then normally to become monks. All ages were therefore present, and all classes from the educated and well-born to the illiterate Goth and ex-serf.

There is no hint in the Rule, as there is in the contemporary scheme of Cassiodorus, a Roman monk who founded monasteries on similar lines, of the function of monks in copying manuscripts and preserving classical literature; but the provision for reading—both private and liturgical—presupposes books, and books presuppose literacy and writing, just as the presence of children made education necessary. If the Rule did not prescribe teaching and learning, it certainly did not forbid them. The careful copying and composition of books, with their lavish binding, ornamentation and illustration, both for the liturgy and for the library, inevitably developed. No doubt many of these activities and tendencies were already present in monasteries in different degrees when Benedict wrote, but in later ages without the Rule all would have depended upon the abbot—who might countenance or command either a stricter, more penitential life with longer prayers, or a less well-knit and self-contained regime.

Contrary to the venerable myth of Benedictine history that pictures the Rule spreading far and wide almost at once, it is certain that its influence was not widely felt for a century. A generation after Benedict's death, Monte Cassino was sacked by the Lombards, in 581, but the story of a group-migration to Rome and the foundation by Gregory the Great of monasteries observing the Rule has no sure authenticity. Pope Gregory indeed knew the Rule and wrote an account of St. Benedict, but there is no other mention of the abbot's name till a century after his death. Such evidence as exists seems to establish that for almost two centuries the Rule was only one of several, used either separately or in conjunction in the monasteries that continued to multiply in Western Europe. It was only by a gradual

The Benedictine centuries

process—the reverse of Gresham's monetary law—that the practical and spiritual excellence of the Rule gradually won for it first a wide popularity and later an exclusive superiority. At last Charlemagne, who was not in fact a great patron of monks, could ask if there were any other rule; and his son, Louis the Pious, endeavored in 817 to impose Benedict's Rule as the sole code for all monasteries of his empire.

Henceforward, save in the Celtic regions, Benedict's Rule was indeed the only rule for two hundred years (800–1000), and when new orders came into being in the eleventh century, most of them—including the greatest, that of the Cistercians—followed the Benedictine Rule while modifying it variously in practice in the direction of austerity, hermit life, or of a wider activity. During the same period the Rule was followed by all organized women religious. So wide was the extension of the monastic order that the years between 600 and 1150 have been called the Benedictine centuries, and it is undoubtedly true that in that epoch almost all the monks followed the Rule and that the particular qualities of the Rule impressed themselves on all monks and, through them, on the whole Western Church. What then were those qualities?

The first, perhaps, was its simplicity. Granted that the monastic life is a valid form of Christian dedication, then the Rule appears as the simple application of the teaching of Christ to that life. Flexible discipline, absence of distractions, and the elementary Christian duties of prayer, self-control, service and mutual help make up the Rule. Such an existence, lived in the spirit of St. Benedict, has the regularity and variety for a successful integration of body and mind.

Beyond and above this are certain positive qualities. It is a rule of life. In contrast to so many religious ordinances, the mention of death is rare, and there are no directions for the last moments and burial of the monk. Benedict is dealing with life, and beyond life with the reckoning that is the sole but solemn sanction proposed again and again as a warning to his all-powerful abbot. Next, there is the stress on mutual love, aid and service. Though the monk has left "the world," he has not left his fellow Christians, and his love of God can be fulfilled and tested by his love of his brethren, who may be frail or unattractive in body or spirit.

Though Benedict did not envisage any external work for others, his monks were, in fact, agents of great power in the development of medieval Europe. As a large majority of the trained and educated minds of Europe were to be found in the monasteries, a majority also of the leading bishops and counselors of emperors and kings were of their number. Inevitably, also, monks were almost the sole missionaries. Most of the priests outside the abbeys were tied to their rural churches as the appointees of the local landowner or group of urban citizens. They were also, for the most part, either married or living a family life with a consort recognized by convention, if not by law. It was left to the monks of Ireland, Scotland, England and Germany—Columbanus,

Aidan, Boniface, Willibald, Anskar, Suitbert and the rest—to carry the Gospel to central and northern Europe. Gradually the monks gave to the whole Church their devout practices and spiritual outlook. Their liturgical arrangements were adopted by the secular clergy and by Rome herself. Lay devotions reflected monastic practice, since to that age the monastic way of life seemed the only perfect form of Christian life. The monks of St. Benedict, in fact, without conscious effort, brought the attributes of monasticism to the whole Western Church. Of the great saints and writers between 1000 and 1200, the majority were monks: Gregory VII, Anselm, Bernard, Abelard, Suger, Eugenius III, Ailred, and a hundred others.

All these were sons of St. Benedict, following the Rule that they had learned by heart as novices and heard each day in their chapter-house; the very name, chapter-house, was taken from the chapter of the Rule read publicly there daily. Throughout their lives they remembered well the passages in which Benedict exchanged the language of the legislator for that of the experienced father of a family, and set out counsels of justice and moderation, humanity and gravity, reminding them that the service and love of Christ must be their only aim, and God's judgment the only criterion of their action. Although historians have not mentioned this, it may well be that the greatest achievement of the Rule of St. Benedict was to give to adolescent Europe a message of fairness, of human feeling, and of civilized and Christian behavior. Such counsels, given to the moulders of opinion and the governors of Europe in the centuries when Western civilization and thought was coming to maturity, were an influence second only to that of the Gospel in furthering the spirit of tolerance and fair dealing as part of the Christian life.

DAVID KNOWLES

The sixth century—in the West a period in which the seeds of a new type of monastic and Church-oriented culture and a fragmented political system were being planted—was for the Eastern Roman Empire and its Persian rival an age of great splendor. Despite the closing of Plato's academy at Athens by Justinian in 529, the tradition of lay classical learning was never broken. Moreover, the Arab civilization emerging in Egypt, Syria and Persia continued and even developed that tradition. The ease with which the Arabs overthrew Persia and conquered great tracts of territory from Rome was largely the result of the fierce religious ardor of their new Moslem faith; but there were also weaknesses within these great empires, to which we now turn.

The Age of Justinian

The Eastern Roman Empire was not unscathed by the turmoil of barbarian invasions, but whereas the Western Empire ceased to exist as a political entity, the East recovered. After a period during which the barbarians in the service of the imperial army had dictated events in Constantinople, there followed the reign of the Emperor Zeno. Although orthodox himself, he was willing to attempt a compromise with the powerful monophysite heresy, a heresy that denied the dual nature of Christ as man and God and claimed that he had only one nature—the divine. Zeno's successor, Anastasius I, restored the failing finances of the Empire and laid the foundations of the greatness of the sixth century. But his monophysite tendencies were marked. His successor, the aging but well-entrenched chief of the imperial guard, Justin, permitted no half measures; his persecution of the monophysites was total; he launched the edict against pagans and heretics that so angered Theodoric, an Arian. But if he was sound on religion, Justin was also very much a soldier and aware of his own limitations. He was virtually illiterate, and he increasingly entrusted the government to his nephew, Justinian, who succeeded him as Emperor in 527.

It was not at all clear to the people at the time that the might of Rome was finally a thing of the past. None of the intruding barbarian kingdoms had produced valid new systems of administration,

Justinian. Mosaic from St. Apollinare, Ravenna.

and both Theodoric and the Frankish ruler Clovis had accepted imperial insignia of office. When Justinian came to the throne, the Ostrogoths in Italy were facing difficulties after the death of Theodoric, and even the Franks were showing signs of chronic internal divisions. Throughout the Mediterranean world, in fact, the upstart regimes seemed ripe for conquest.

Only with the wisdom of hindsight can we see that the universal Roman Empire of antiquity had been irreversibly split and that the populations of Italy, Africa and Spain neither needed nor wanted the government of a distant capital with its dying ideals. Nevertheless, by the end of his reign Justinian, thanks to the talents of brilliant generals like Belisarius and Narses, had not only checked the Persian advance but also had made the Mediterranean once again a Roman lake.

Vandal empires crumble

First to go was the Vandal kingdom of Africa, Sardinia and Corsica; shortly after, Sicily was taken from the Ostrogoths. The conquest of Italy itself was to be delayed, largely by intrigues at the court against the generals in the field. Finally, in the middle of the sixth century, the Roman armies succeeded in recovering southern Spain from the Visigoths. Within its own terms, Justinian's policy, no matter how heavy the drain on the Empire's resources, was successful. However, it must be realized that within a century of Justinian's death the ill-defended Danubian frontier, his major strategic blind spot, had

been breached by Slav and Avar invaders. While they were conquering a large part of the west Balkans, most of Justinian's Mediterranean territories were also being lost. The most completed reversals, of course, were due to the astonishing advance of Islam.

Besides making notable territorial gains, Justinian, drawing again on the wealth of the imperial treasury and imposing increasingly heavy taxes on the old and newly conquered lands, put through a vast

Interior of Hagia Sophia, Constantinople, now a mosque.

program of public works that glorified Rome, Orthodox religion and himself. Chief among these were the church of San Vitale at Ravenna and the great cathedral of Hagia Sophia at Constantinople, one of the most remarkable achievements in the whole history of architecture. The jubilant Emperor is reported to have ridden his horse up the main altar of the basilica and cried out: "O Solomon, I have outdone thee."

Dissension and weakness

It is in the nature of empires to decay. Yet whatever the strictures of later historians, there is no real doubt that for half a century, thanks to the ambitions and qualities of Justinian, the Empire in the East enjoyed one of the most brilliant epochs in the history of empire.

Empress Theodora, from St. Vitale, Ravenna.

But the cracks in the structure were never far below the surface, and they found expression in religious differences. The Emperor as head of both Church and State had to ensure both religious uniformity and the loyalty of heretical territories. Justinian's attempts to strike an acceptable religious compromise led him eventually into heresy himself. Heresy was adopted in frontier religions such as Syria and Egypt as a mark of their opposition to the central government; in its struggle for independence against Constantinople, the patriarchate of Alexandria adopted monophysitism, and the divisions rent even the capital itself.

Opposed to the Orthodox Emperor was the party of Justinian's wife, the beautiful Theodora, who supported the monophysite cause. The factional politics of the late Roman imperial court have given us the phrase "Byzantine politics" as a synonym for intrigue and corruption. Procopius, whose official history is our best source for the period, also wrote the scandalous *Secret History*. In it, himself a representative of the old aristocracy, he attacks the upstart Emperor and his wife, whom he slanders for her humble origins in the world of the actors employed by the circus. Yet Theodora was a woman of courage and political acumen. In a regime where the popular voice was excluded from constitutional expression, the rival sporting factions of the Blues and the Greens of the Hippodrome, focused ostensibly upon the chariot races, acquired some of the characteristics of political parties. The Blues were the party of the Emperor and Orthodox in religion; the Greens were the party of the Empress and were

Scene of chariot races in Constantinople.

monophysites. The two parties were generally rivals, but they united in the famous Nika riots in 532. Justinian would have fled before the fury of the mob, but Theodora and the generals held firm and order was restored.

Corpus Juris Civilis

For subsequent generations this intense, confident and vital period presents a barely credible amalgam of the most diverse elements. But there can be no doubts about its achievements: its greatest monument, the *Corpus Juris Civilis*, a codification of all Roman law, was to exert an immense influence on the West and has remained the basis of all systems of Roman law in Europe today.

After Justinian's death, the Empire's external enemies made severe inroads. The slow but sure progress against these threats by the emperor-soldier Maurice was brought to an end by the usurper Phocas in 602. His overthrow of Maurice served the Persian emperor as a pretext for several highly successful campaigns of conquest, supposedly to avenge his former protector. The Avar advance gained a fresh impetus. In 610 Phocas was replaced by Heraclius, but the counter attack could not be launched for another decade. During this period the Persians took Jerusalem, capturing the most sacred relic of Christendom, the True Cross.

The end of an Epoch

Heraclius began a triumphant but arduous campaign of reconquest which ended in 627 with the capitulation of Persia, Rome's ancient enemy. During the war, the city of Constantinople itself had withstood siege by both the Avar and Persian

forces. But the very year in which Heraclius set out upon his epic campaign, 622, was also the year of the Hegira. Islam thus arose at a time when both Emperor and Empire were exhausted by the depradations and exertions of the previous generation; the hard-won provinces—with them the great Greco-Roman cultural centers of Caesarea, Antioch and Alexandria —were soon lost to the lightning conquest of Islam. The importance of this conquest in shaping the brilliant culture of the Arab World can hardly be overrated.

The Byzantine Era begins

It is usually from the reign of Heraclius that historians date the beginning of the Byzantine Era as distinct from the age in which the Eastern Empire is regarded as merely the continuation of Rome. In social affairs the change is marked by the restructuring of the provinces so that the civil and military authorities, separate since the time of Diocletian, were merged under the military authority. At the same time, something similar to the later European system of feudal land tenure was introduced; each province supported a body of troops and the soldiers received grants of land on condition of military service. Greek rather than Latin became the official language of the Empire; Egypt, Syria, Spain and North Africa were lost and the possessions of the "Roman" Empire in Italy itself were greatly reduced. After the time of Heraclius, in fact, the Eastern Empire took on its medieval aspect.

The last glories of the Sassanids

In the fifth century the Persian Sassanid rulers, the weak and in-

effective successors of Shapur, were forced to pay tribute to the northern barbarian kingdom of the Hephtalites. To this external enemy was added a subversive religious doctrine, preached by Mazdak, who derived many of his ideas from the teachings of Mani, which also had revolutionary social implications of common ownership of property and of women. The doctrine, which struck at the very roots of the hierarchical and aristocratic system of society, was nevertheless taken up by King Kavadh I, possibly as a welcome weapon against the overpowerful nobility and as a counterbalance to the influence of the Magi, the Zoroastrian hierarchy at court. In fact, Kavadh laid the foundations for a revival of the Persian power by combating the anti-monarchist powers within the state, reforming the conditions of peasant life, and restructuring the administration for more effective

Ruins of a Persian Zoroastrian temple.

exercise of royal power. His son, Chosroes I (531–79), brilliantly extended the achievements of his father's reign, and led the newly confident empire in triumphant war against its enemies: the Heph-

talite kingdom was crushed; the northern frontiers were secured against the Huns; while to the south he even brought Yemen under Persian rule. Against Rome, Chosroes was able not only to invade the Syrian provinces of the Roman Empire, but even to sack the mighty city of Antioch. Pretexts for the dispute between these ancient enemies were never lacking. The Christian kingdom of Armenia was a constant source of irritation to the Persian emperors, and both empires maintained client Arab princes in the buffer zone on their Syrian frontier; the internal disputes of these could always be seized upon at will as a *casus belli* by either of the great powers. Nor was the confrontation one between the simple opposites of Christian and infidel; monophysitism was strong within the Armenian church and the Arab tribes of Syria, so that the crucial matter of religious unity was inevitably intertwined with the vexing problem of political allegiance.

After the glorious reign of Chosroes I, symbolized by the rich and splendid monuments and palaces of his capital at Ctesiphon, whose ruins are still to be seen today, there followed a period of civil disturbance and rebellion. It was not until the accession of his grandson, Chosroes II, supported by the Byzantine Emperor Maurice, that the greatness of the Persian Empire seemed to have returned. Yet, exhausted by the ambitions of Chosroes II, crushed by the defeats inflicted by Heraclius and weakened by renewed civil war and internal dissension, the once mighty Persian Empire fell an easy prey to the armies of Islam, which captured the fabled wealth of Ctesiphon in the year 637.

Ruins of the Arch of Chosroes and palace at Ctesiphon.

The Flight to Medina

Hoping to find a more receptive audience for his message, the prophet Mohammed fled from his native Mecca to the neighboring city of Medina. This event of 622, the Hegira, marks the beginning of the new Moslem religion and the beginning of a dynamic new civilization in the Middle East. Mohammed himself proved to be both an inspired religious leader and an astute politician, creating a theocracy and presiding over it as Allah's Messenger. He also was a military leader: Mecca was soon brought into the Moslem orbit and at Mohammed's death in 632 the entire Arabian Peninsula was his. But it remained for his successors, the caliphs, to impose Islamic rule over much of Asia and Africa and to bring a frightening challenge to Christian Europe.

The Moslem era begins in A.D. 622, the date of the Hegira, Mohammed's emigration from his home town of Mecca to the neighboring city of Medina. In fixing the date for the initiation of the Moslem era, Caliph Omar, successor to Mohammed's first Caliph, Abu Bakr, is said to have hesitated between choosing the Hegira, the date of Mohammed's birth, or the date he first accepted the vocation of prophet. When Omar chose the first alternative he no doubt had good practical reasons: the date of the Hegira was better fixed in men's minds than the less spectacular moment when Mohammed was finally convinced of his divine mission, a date that was, in any case, altogether dubious.

Yet the Caliph may also have been quite conscious of the fact that it was the Hegira, even more than the first appearance of the angel Gabriel to Mohammed, that marked the historical epoch of the rise of Islam. In Mecca, Mohammed—a tradesman and previously a caravan leader—had gathered around him a considerable number of followers. Yet, faced with the resistance of the leading families, he was unable to attain political power—despite the fact that the visionary side of his character went hand-in-hand with a genius for affairs and a mastery over men. Having become familiar with Judaism and Christianity, he felt it was his prophetic mission to warn his pagan compatriots of the coming day of judgment and urge them to turn to the one true God—and the ethical duties imposed by him upon man—before it was too late. To the astute politicians of Mecca, Mohammed might have appeared as an impractical dreamer or, as they less politely put it, a madman.

Latent in Mohammed were immense political gifts, which found only limited scope in the role of venerated head of a small and persecuted religious community; of these immense gifts his later career as the founder of a powerful religious state in Medina bears eloquent witness. Having failed to satisfy his political aspirations in Mecca, Mohammed cast about for more promising fields of action in the neighboring town of Taif and among different Bedouin tribes, but without avail. His chance came from the great oasis of Yathrib, north of Mecca, the center of which was also called Medina, i.e. "the city." The oasis was inhabited by several tribes that followed the Jewish religion, and by two others, the Aws and the Khazraj, that were pagans and warred among themselves.

Some Medinians came in contact with Mohammed, and in 621, during the pilgrimage to the pagan sanctuaries near Mecca, a number of them met Mohammed on a mountain pass outside Mecca and accepted his main religious teachings. In the course of the next year, more Medinians adhered to the teaching of the prophet, and at the next pilgrimage the Medinian contingent included a considerable number of Mohammed's followers. At "the second treaty of the pass" they agreed that Mohammed would come to Medina and that they would give him full protection.

After this agreement was reached, Mohammed's Meccan followers began to slip away from the city and find their way to Medina, in anticipation of the eventual emigration of their Prophet. Their empty houses, with their doors thrown open by the wind, made—so the traditional account says—a sad impression upon the Meccans who passed by and expressed their grief at the disruption caused by Mohammed in the life of the city. At last, of the Moslem community only Mohammed himself, his cousin Ali, and Abu Bakr (who was one of the Prophet's oldest adherents and was particularly close to him), and their womenfolk, remained.

By September, 622, Mohammed himself was ready to escape from his native city. The Meccans obviously did not relish the idea of the persecuted community of Moslems finding a new home in Medina and possibly causing trouble to them. Therefore they were determined to prevent Mohammed leaving and joining his followers in Medina; he was forced to flee. Although the word Hegira (or, to render the Arabic more exactly, *Hijra*) does not mean "flight," as it is often translated, but rather

A tile from Asia Minor with a view of Mecca, the shrine of the prophet Mohammed's birth place and holy center of Moslem belief.

Opposite The mosque in Cairo, the earliest surviving example of a place of Moslem worship.

A reward of one hundred camels

"emigration," the circumstances of Mohammed's emigration justify our speaking of his flight.

One September day Mohammed informed Abu Bakr that he was to accompany him. His cousin Ali would be left behind to look after the womenfolk. Abu Bakr took with him all the money he had, amounting to five or six thousand *dirhams*. (*Dirham* was the name of the silver coins current in Mecca, no doubt mainly Persian pieces with the image of the Persian king; the Meccans minted no coins of their own. A *dirham* would be about four grams of silver.) He also arranged with one of his sons to come every day to their hiding place in order to bring news from the city, and ordered a freedman of his, Amir the son of Fuhayra, to graze some sheep in the desert in order to provide fresh milk and meat every night.

The two fugitives left Abu Bakr's house by a back door and hid in a cave of Mount Thawr, an hour's journey to the south of Mecca. This was in the opposite direction to that of Medina, and thus they hoped to evade search parties who would look for them on the road leading north. Mohammed and Abu Bakr remained in the cave for three days, living off the milk and meat of the sheep brought nightly by Amir, and other food brought from Mecca by a daughter of Abu Bakr. In later times, many legends were woven around the stay in the cave, in marked contrast to the sober realism of the earlier accounts, the essential truth of which is confirmed by Mohammed's own reference to the cave in a passage of the Koran (9:40): "If you do not help him, yet God had helped him already when the unbelievers drove him forth the second of two, when the two were in the cave, when he said to his companion, 'Sorrow not; surely God is with us'."

The rulers of Mecca promised a reward of a hundred camels for the return of the fugitives. After three days, when the hue and cry had died down, the two men set out on their journey. The practical Abu Bakr had arranged every detail. He had previously given two camels to a Bedouin called Abdullah, son of Arqat, who was to serve them as guide. The Bedouin now appeared riding his own camel and bringing the two camels for Mohammed and Abu Bakr. Abu Bakr's daughter also arrived with provisions for the journey. The freedman Amir rode behind Abu Bakr on the same camel and served Mohammed and Abu Bakr on the way.

The three men thus made their way through the desert to Medina, after a detour that brought them to the shore of the Red Sea. After a journey of four days, they arrived at Quba, near Medina. Mohammed remained in Quba, as the guest of a local man, for two to four days, or longer according to some accounts. Those days were perhaps spent in making the last negotiations with the various sections of the population of Medina, so that Mohammed would be able to enter the city itself as a guest protected

The rocky terrain between Mecca and Medina across which Mohammed rode on his camel with his companion Abu Bakr to found a new religious state.

by the whole Medinian community. At last (according to the most widely accepted version, on Friday September 28, 622) Mohammed left Quba and, riding on his camel, proceeded to Medina.

In one version of the legend, the various clans of Medina through whose quarters Mohammed made his way vied with one another in offering the Prophet hospitality. But Mohammed left it to the divinely inspired decision of his camel to choose for him the place where he would stay. On the spot where the camel stopped, the place of worship—mosque—was to be built. It was a covered space with a courtyard. Rooms for Mohammed and his four wives adjoined the courtyard, and the land was bought from the guardian of the orphans to whom it belonged.

Mohammed was thus established at Medina and the opportunity was given to him of proving himself as a statesman, as he had earlier proved himself a religious leader at Mecca. He proved equal to the task, and during the remaining ten years of his life accomplished deeds for which his first fifty years had scarcely prepared him; those latent powers rose to the occasion. The Prophet was armed, and he showed, in addition to his gift of spiritual leadership, the great astuteness and lack of scruple of the politician.

First he firmly established his position as the political head of the community: strict obedience "to God and his messenger" was demanded. The

The birth of the prophet Mohammed as it is shown in the *Universal History* of Rashid ud-Din.

Left A scene showing the revelation brought to Mohammed by the Archangel Gabriel, from Rashid ud-Din's *Universal History*.

Below The Dome of the Rock, Jerusalem, the first monument of Islam, built *c.* 691 on the site of King David's altar, the spot from which Mohammed is believed to have ascended to heaven.

The Fall of Mecca

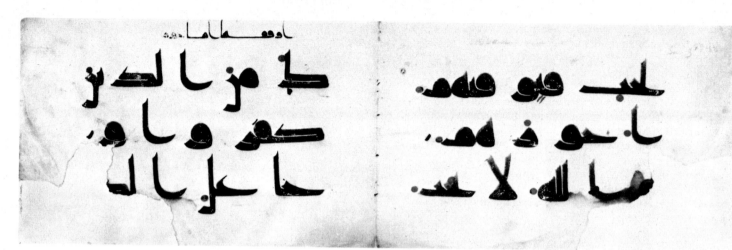

An extract from a parchment Koran, one of the earliest copies in existence of the prophet Mohammed's teachings, the first piece of written Arabic literature.

messenger, Mohammed, became the actual ruler of a theocracy.

During the first years following the Hegira, the war with the Meccans took up most of the energies of the new Moslem state. But opportunities to get rid of the Medinian opposition, branded as the "hypocrites," and the Jewish tribes, who were either expelled or massacred, were not missed.

Soon, however, Mohammed's ambitions went far beyond defending the Moslem refuge in Medina; his new aim was to subject the Arabian peninsula to his rule. Mecca itself was conquered in 630, eight years after the Hegira. Although Mecca's pagan sanctuaries were incorporated into the system of the new religion, and Mohammed's birthplace with its holy Kaaba became the religious center of Islam, the capital remained at Medina. The Bedouin tribes were subdued by force or diplomacy; and by paying the "alms-tax," these nomads acknowledged

the supremacy of the Prophet, even if their religious fervor left a great deal to be desired. Thus, within ten years, the anarchic tribal society of the Arabian peninsula was organized into a semblance of a nation—in itself a stupendous achievement.

Did the Prophet's ambition embrace even wider horizons? Had he, whose mission had originally been the call to preach to the Arabs, hitherto deprived of prophets, come to think himself the bearer of a message to mankind at large? And if so, did he contemplate, as a corollary, the conquest of lands outside Arabia, after having conquered Arabia itself? Before his death in 632, there were skirmishes on the frontier region between the Hijaz and the Byzantine Empire, but it is uncertain whether they were considered as the preliminaries of any large operations. In general, it is difficult to give any definite answer to the question about the Prophet's views of the outside world. If he had any extensive

A thirteenth-century Moslem map of the world by Ibn Said. The spread of Islam was accompanied by the introduction of classical and medieval learning to the Arabs.

plans, he died without having the chance of embarking on their execution. It was his successors (or Caliphs) who founded the Islamic Empire and governed it first from Medina, then from Damascus, and then from the newlyfounded Baghdad.

The Islamic conquests—whether they were planned by Mohammed as a further step in the succession of events inaugurated by the Hegira, or were rather the result of chance successes being exploited and then energetically directed by the Caliphs of Medina—changed the face of a large part of the earth. Within a few years the Persian Empire of the Sassanids was overrun and such important provinces of the Byzantine Empire as Syria and Egypt (followed soon by North Africa) were incorporated into the Islamic Empire. At the beginning of the eighth century, a second wave of conquests added Transoxania, the Indus valley in the east and Spain in the west. They gave Islam roughly the geographical extent it maintained until the eleventh century. (At that time small losses of territory in Spain and Sicily were compensated by large increases in central Asia, India and Anatolia.) Provinces that had formerly belonged to separate states and civilizations were now united within a new empire that developed its own civilization. The political and cultural map of western Asia and the Mediterranean basin had been remade.

For a century and a half, the new Islamic Empire was a centrally governed state, headed by the Caliph, Mohammed's successor as political ruler, but not his successor as prophet. Even after the caliphate began to disintegrate, it still remained a powerful structure for another century, and its ghost haunted the Moslem world long after its real might had disappeared. The office of Caliph was a peculiar creation of Islam: it grew naturally out of the particular circumstances in which the Moslem community found itself after Mohammed's death. In contrast, administrative methods were largely taken over from previous empires, and the bureaucratic system continued the secular traditions of the conquered lands.

The basis of the new Islamic civilization was provided by the economic and social unity of the world it conquered, and this unity lasted even after the disappearance of the political state. Commercial traffic passed easily through the vast tract of land between Transoxania and Spain, and the same (or almost the same) currency was employed; this greatly promoted trade—and with goods traveled social and cultural patterns. Not only merchants but also learned men traveled from one end of the Muslim world to the other and spread a common form of education and culture. Islamic civilization did not grow out of nothing, it assimilated elements of different character.

The Islamic religion itself, the main cementing factor in the new civilization, owed a great deal to preceding religions, chiefly Judaism and Christianity. But the borrowings were used in an original manner and the new religion was more than a new combination of existing elements. Both religious and secular literature was expressed in the Arabic language, and while the vernaculars of the different provinces survived in spoken use, everything—from the simplest letter to the highest literature—was written in Arabic. The Koran, containing the text of the prophecies pronounced by Mohammed in Mecca and Medina, was the first piece of Arabic literature committed to writing, but it was not this fact alone that gave the Arabic language its religious significance. The whole many-branched theological literature created by Islam was in Arabic and was carried by traveling scholars all over the Islamic world.

Secular literature was in the first instance based on the traditional oral literature produced by the tribal society of pre-Islamic Arabia. Its traditional heroic lyric poetry and prose stories were adopted by Islamic civilization; after having been the functional expression of tribal society, this whole literature—reduced to writing by philologists—became the foundation of the humanistic education of urban Islamic society, in the same way as Homer had been the bible of Hellenism. In the Islamic period there developed a courtly urban poetry which, however alien in spirit to the ancient poetry of the desert, was in its style deeply indebted to it. Thus the legacy of

Mosaics from the Great Ummayad Mosque at Damascus, eighth century. The Mosque was formerly a Christian church and still earlier a pagan *temenos*. The most notable mosaic shows the region now Damascus.

The conversion of the Persians

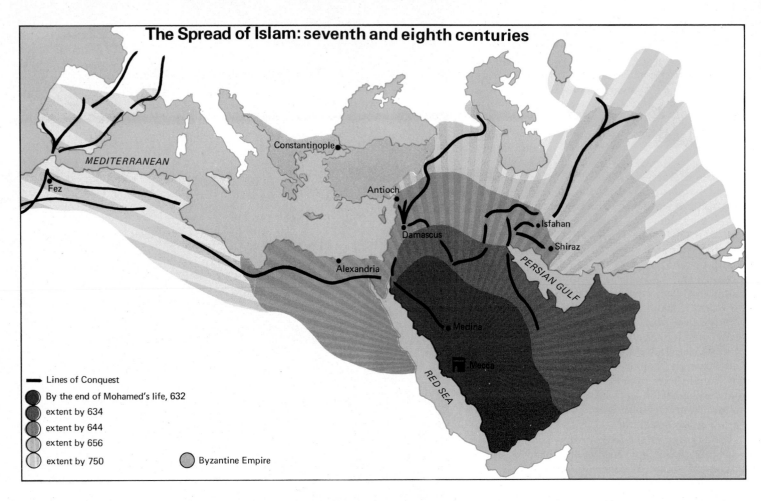

The Spread of Islam: seventh and eighth centuries

MEDITERRANEAN

Fez

Constantinople

Antioch

Damascus

Alexandria

Isfahan

Shiraz

PERSIAN GULF

Medina

Mecca

RED SEA

— Lines of Conquest
- By the end of Mohamed's life, 632
- extent by 634
- extent by 644
- extent by 656
- extent by 750

- Byzantine Empire

Below A distant view of the mosque of Ahmad Ibn Tulun at Cairo. Ibn Tulun was governor of Egypt in 869, and his mosque incorporates the style he brought from Iraq, particularly in its brick and plasterwork.

pre-Islamic tribal Arabia was one of the component elements of Islamic civilization. The other elements came from the ancient civilizations of the territories incorporated into the empire.

The Persians, with an imperial history of more than a thousand years, possessed a strong national sentiment. This tradition had been closely, but not inextricably, connected with their national religion, Zoroastrianism; and even after their conversion to

Islam, the Persians did not renounce their attachment to their secular national traditions. While using Persian as their vernacular, they too wrote in Arabic and adopted the Islamic culture expressed in Arabic; but they introduced into that culture many elements of Persian ideas on statecraft. It was mainly government officials of Persian extraction who were responsible for the promotion of Persian ideas within the world of Islam. Some scientific

Right The Great Mosque at Kairouan, one of the oldest Islamic buildings and the first important one in north Africa.

treatises were also translated from Persian into Arabic; and so were some Indian books, either directly, or through Persian mediation.

In the scientific field, however, the main contribution came from Greco-Roman antiquity. The Christian subjects of the Islamic Empire were in the possession of a large body of scientific and philosophical literature, either in the original Greek or in Syriac translations. (Syriac was the Aramaic dialect used as a literary language by many Christians in the eastern provinces of the Roman Empire, as well as in Persia.) Christian translators rendered these books into Arabic, in which form they became available also to the Moslems, who never mastered either Greek or Syriac. At first their interest in Greek science was mainly practical: they needed physicians to cure them and astrologers to advise them how to arrange their affairs under the most favorable influence of the stars. But soon science and philosophy attracted them for their own sake. Nor were they satisfied with passively studying the writings of the ancients—but reorganized and sometimes even improved upon them.

In general, it would be as wrong to consider the Islamic civilization a mere juxtaposition of existing elements as to consider Islam a mere adding up of Judaism, Christianity and Arabian paganism. By a strange alchemy, the old elements were so fused together and transformed that something quite original resulted. Thus, while Islamic art owes a great deal to the traditions of the previous civilizations, it has a strong character of its own. One of its most individual aspects springs from the prohibition placed by Islam on iconographic representation, with the result that this is virtually nonexistent.

It is obvious, therefore, that Islamic civilization did not come into being in one moment. Nor was it static; it remained—as does everything in history—in continuous flux. The re-emergence of Persian as an Islamic literary language in the tenth century, for example, tended to give the eastern part of the Islamic world a character different from the western part, where Arabic was used exclusively. The foundation of the Islamic Empire—a direct or indirect consequence of Mohammed's Hegira—gave rise to a new civilization. Islamic religion is still very much alive. It is, however, more than doubtful whether Islamic civilization still exists; but for twelve hundred years or so it has undoubtedly shaped the life of a considerable portion of the human race.   S. M. STERN

The Great Mosque of Shah Abbas at Isfahan, showing the rich detail of seventeenth-century faïence work and decorative vaulting.

Overlooking the walls of Fez to the crowded city beneath, typical of the Moslem cities of north Africa.

The siege of Byzantium

During the seventh and eighth centuries, while Europe was in the turmoil of the conflicting dynasties that had succeeded the first generations of barbarian invaders, events of immense importance were taking place on the southern shores of the Mediterranean.

Within a hundred years the armies of Islam had taken the legendary city of Samarkand in the East, while in the West they touched for a moment the banks of the Loire. The successor of the Prophet Mohammed was not to sit on the throne of Constantine until another eight centuries had elapsed, but throughout the seventh and early eighth centuries the threat to Byzantium was a serious one.

By 717 the Arab armies were actually at the gates of the imperial capital. Twice the siege was withstood; twice the Byzantine fleet proved its superiority and the armies of the new faith were driven back.

But although they escaped military conquest, the Byzantines did succumb to the influence of the religious philosophy of their enemies. Within ten years of the first siege of Constantinople, the Emperor Leo III issued the first "iconoclastic" decrees against the

Coin of the iconoclast Byzantine Emperor Leo.

worship of images. For close to a century the Church in the East prohibited images of the saints—the descendants of local deities that Christianity had displaced—and permitted only the barest decoration of its places of worship. The puritanic zeal of Islam infected its rival; and the Emperor Leo, determined to withstand the attack of the infidel, did not hesitate to emulate his virtues. For, like Christianity, the faith of Islam claimed universality; like Christianity, it was exclusive.

Islamic beliefs

Islam, however, differed from Christianity in two important respects. First, belief in a unitary God was absolute and uncompromising —to a Moslem, the Christian doctrine of the Trinity and the inummerable local cults of patron saints inevitably appeared as a thinly veiled polytheism. In the second place, although Islam worshipped one god, Allah, and believed that the full revelation had been given only to Mohammed, his Prophet, it nevertheless recognized parts of the Christian and Jewish canon that Mohammed himself had accepted. This fact reinforced the universal claims of Islam. It may have also been a factor in the welcome that the conquering armies found among the subject populations of the Byzantine and Persian empires.

The faith of the conquerors was not entirely alien and, still more important, they allowed their new subjects to retain their own religious practice only on condition of the payment of poll and land taxes. As we have seen in both the Roman and the Persian empires, religious heresy was often connected with political separatism; for many a provincial of the Near East, oppressed both by heavy taxation and religious discipline from the central government, the armies of Islam appeared as the scourge of God for the sins of an irreligious emperor, or even as their liberator.

The birth of Arab civilization

After the first astonishing wave of Arab conquest had spent itself, the conquerors consolidated their position in their new empire by taking on many of the ways of the Persian monarchy which they had displaced. Already by the time of the fourth Caliph, Uthman, the early ideals and puritan zeal were beginning to fade, and the Caliph was using the semi-sacred office to which he had been elected to buttress his own position and that of his family. In 656 Uthman was assassinated and there followed a disputed succession that was to cause a schism in the faith of Islam which has not been healed to this day. Uthman was succeeded by Ali who, as son-in-law of Mohammed, had been expected by many to follow the prophet himself. In turn, Ali too was overthrown and the new

Decoration from the Ummayad Palace near Jericho.

Caliph, Muawiyah, is generally regarded as the founder of the Ummayad dynasty which held the Caliphate for the next hundred years. While the great body of Islam, the Sunnites, accepted the succession of the first four Caliphs and the laws and traditions (or *sunni*) of the early period, a minority of sectarians (*shiites*) hold that ever since the murder of Ali, the line of the Caliphate has been in the hands of usurpers.

The Dome of the Rock

Under the first Ummayads, the Arabs rapidly enlisted the services of the subject populations and assimilated their skills. Although few monuments survive from this period, they include such architectural achievements as the Dome of the Rock in Jerusalem.

This famous mosque is built over the spot where, according to Arab tradition, Abraham led Isaac to the sacrifice and where Mohammed ascended to heaven. Completed in 691, the Dome of the Rock was built on the orders of Abd al Malik, one of the greatest of the Ummayad Caliphs. He gave a new durability to the empire by introducing a standard coinage, reorganizing the government, improving communications within the empire and making Arabic its official language.

Detail of tiled panels on the Dome of the Rock, Jerusalem.

Although his own campaigns against Islam's external enemies were inconclusive, Abd al Malik prepared the ground work for the resurgence of the eighth century.

The great Oriental civilizations

The art of the early Islamic potters gives the clearest possible evidence that Persian and Arab artisans were very strongly influenced by the high-glazed porcelain wares brought along the trade routes from T'ang China. The T'ang dynasty, established in 618, just four years

A T'ang vase with dragons decorating the handles.

before the Hegira, reached the summit of its glory and power during the seventh century. The short-lived Sui dynasty had reformed the administration and radically improved communications, but the T'ang built on these foundations a brilliant and impressive edifice. T'ang armies extended Chinese power over the neighboring territories of Korea, Manchuria,

Mongolia, Tibet and Turkestan; the art of the potter was brought to the level of high art; and T'ang scholars and poets produced an unequaled flowering in literature.

In the early decades of the dynasty, the influence of Indian Buddhism, which had been a part of Chinese religious life to greater or lesser degrees for centuries past, was powerful. It is from a Chinese Buddhist monk that one of the most interesting documents of the medieval world has come down to us. This is the *Record of the Western World* by Hsuang Tsang, who spent some twenty years researching in Indian Buddhist libraries during the first half of the seventh century. But, although Buddhism retained an important position even under the later T'ang, it was to suffer periods of proscription, and pride of place went to the social and ethical code of Confucius. The Confucian code, with its stress on the right ordering of social relationships, became the official religion of the empire, a role for which it was ideally suited.

The first century of T'ang China was not only a period of foreign expansion but also one of ordered administration, in which centralized government was conducted by a class of officials recruited by a system of examination for merit—a system that was not to be emulated in the West until the nineteenth century. Like all great empires, of course, that of the T'ang was subject to the laws of decay; and already by the middle of the eighth century, the barbarian Uigurs had succeeded in wresting from the Empire considerable tracts of territory on the borders, a situation that was seriously compounded by local rebellions during the ninth century.

Like his homeland of China, the India that Hsuang Tsang visited was enjoying a brief but glorious period of political unity and cultural advance. Under the rule of Harsha, who reigned from 606 to 647, virtually the whole of northern India was brought under the rule of a single government with its capital at the town of Kanauj. Harsha was himself a poet and philosopher. In early life he accepted the tenets of Hinduism, but was converted to Buddhism and became its devout and generous patron. The great Buddhist convocation held at Kanauj in 643, attended by some twenty kings and princes, not only symbolized the king's devotion but also his power. But, after the death of Harsha, India gradually split up again into a series of warring states.

The rise of Japan

We need hardly be surprised that these giant empires of the East enjoyed such comparatively brief periods of unity. The areas that they attempted to control were immense; communications, unless constantly tended, fell rapidly into disorder; and the frontiers were under recurrent attack from barbarian invaders from central Asia. For the much smaller political units of Europe, the road to unity and stability was a long and difficult one. It is therefore all the more interesting to find in the history of at least one empire of this period that the ambitions of the central government were not beyond the possibilities of the situation and its abilities were commensurate with the problems. Although the mountainous geography of Japan encouraged internal divisions, and although these divisions threatened the unity of the state from time to time, nevertheless, from the middle of the sixth century, Japan was to display considerable resilience and survival power as a political entity.

Invasion of Korea

As early as the fourth century, we have records of Japanese expeditions against the mainland kingdom of Korea. At that time much influenced by the culture of China, Korea was to remain an important bridge for the transmission of Chinese influence to the island state. Even before the fourth century, this influence had been felt. The

Japanese probably had knowledge of the Mandarin Chinese system of writing at a very early date and from the fourth century onwards— after what must have been a Herculean feat of adaptation (the two languages are in fact unrelated; Chinese is monosyllabic while Japanese is richly polysyllabic)— the Japanese chancery was using a system of script derived from the Chinese system. The process of assimilating and adapting Chinese culture continued. Thousands of Chinese and Koreans came to settle in Japan, so that by the end of the seventh century a large number of the leading families of the Japanese aristocracy could boast of a mainland ancestry. From China too, in the fifth century, had come the religion of Buddhism. Although it never fully displaced the native Japanese cult system of Shinto, Buddhism quickly gained influential supporters, among them Crown Prince Shotoku Taishi (d. 621). Shotoku is remembered also as the creator of the first truly centralized Japanese administration, which took as its model that of China.

A recurrent feature of Japanese history is the ascendance of the powerful clans which, while recognizing the imperial house, sought to control the effective power of the state. Later, it became common for the emperor to turn over all but his ceremonial functions to another member of the imperial family. This person in turn deputed effec-

Japanese mask of the Nara period.

tive executive authority to ministers of state.

The first important clan to win the ascendance in the state was that of the Soga; but in the middle of the seventh century they were displaced by the Fujiwara family, under the leadership of the great Fujiwara Kamatari. He consolidated and improved on the achievements of his predecessor, Prince Shotoku. And, modeling his work almost slavishly on the example of the T'ang, he set up a centralized administration. In the early eighth century a capital city was built at Nara, which was to emulate the splendors of Ch'ang 'an, the city of the T'ang emperors. But at the end of the century the capital was moved to Kyoto, or Heian-Kyo as it was called, marking the beginning of a new age of elegance and courtly civilization.

Chinese head of a Boddhisattva; seventh century.

Japanese Buddhist triad from the ancient temple of Horyu-ji; seventh century.

Japanese Renaissance

*Since the sixth century, Japan has been ruled by a hereditary imperial family. At first the
Japanese court modeled itself on the Chinese, in its principles of politics, ethics and religion,
in its writing system and in its entire culture. It was not until 794, when the capital was transferred
from Nara to Heian (modern Kyoto), that Japan started to develop a national culture of its
own. About the year 1000, the Lady Murasaki Shikibu wrote the world's first novel,* The Tale
of Genji, *a masterpiece of literary invention that mirrored the life of the brilliant Heian court.
In painting, architecture and the decorative arts as well, there were signs of a growing culture
that was remarkably refined, advanced for its time and—most important—essentially
Japanese in character.*

Tamon Ten, one of the four
guardian demi-gods from the
Kaidan-in Temple; an eighth-
century statue in clay painted
in brilliant color.

Opposite The gateway to the
shrine of the vixen at Kyoto.
The city boasts many such
shrines, all of them restored at
a later date.

Throughout Japanese history, legitimate authority
has resided in the hereditary imperial family which
has been on the throne since the sixth century, but
power lay in the possession of land. Despite seventh-
century measures designed to assert the imperial
title to all land, powerful families amassed vast
estates and in the course of time won immunity from
tax assessment. It is an ironical fact that the power
of the Fujiwara clan lay in precisely this kind of tax
immunity, for eventually it fatally weakened the
imperial (and hence the clan's) authority. Respecting the hereditary principle that was deep-rooted
in all Japanese society, the Fujiwara never attempted to usurp the title of Emperor but instead
acted as regents. The Emperor gave legitimacy to
their regime and was also the fount of honor from
which they could draw the titles and offices to reward
their family and supporters.

This acceptance of a higher if usually ineffective
legitimate authority by the real rulers of Japan was
of immense importance in the country's history. In
all states and at all times palace politics have been
important, but in Heian Japan they were virtually
the sole activity of the regime. Some of the regents
were gifted administrators concerned with the public
interest; but their supremacy rested on their adept
manipulation of palace politics and a subtle and
deep understanding of the intricacies of social and
human psychology. Thus the most powerful men in
Japan were long devoted not to the administration of
the state but to the maintenance of their power base
in a court society that had increasingly little contact
with the country over which in theory it ruled.

For most of the ninth century the Fujiwara were
merely the Crown's most powerful ministers, but
from about 900 to 1068 their power was virtually
supreme. For the next seventy years the "cloistered"
emperors largely bypassed their Fujiwara ministers;
finally, the family was displaced by the military clans
that they had called to their aid. Yet even during
the ascendancy of the Fujiwara, administration
was often threatened by turbulence in the provinces,

only suppressed because the leading military
families were willing to support the regency.

Thanks to external peace, the Empire had no
effective standing army, and there was no force to
stop the encroachments of the great landowners;
thus, by the end of the ninth century most of the
country was virtually controlled by vast tax-immune
manors. Among the many causes of this process, two
were particularly important. First was the oppressive
labor tax, which led many poor men to commend
themselves to their more powerful neighbors. Second
were the large tax concessions granted by the government, theoretically for a limited period, to those
who undertook the development and cultivation of
new land necessary to feed a growing population.
But not only did the government find itself powerless
in the long run to recall these concessions, but the
landowners, from the greatest to the least, "reclaimed" vast tracts of poor or uncultivable land
for the sake of the tax concessions. Here again the
little man, conscious of his weak claims to this kind
of land, commended himself to a more powerful
neighbor, paying him an annual rent for protection
against the central authorities. It was in this environment of insubordination and lawlessness that
the great military clans were born. The central
power was obliged to recruit its own provincial
governors and police forces from the local nobility
and even to call in their aid on occasion to suppress
rioting in the capital.

Fujiwara power depended on the marriages they
arranged for their womenfolk, and even at the height
of their ascendancy the great regents were to base
their claim to power first and foremost on their
relationship to the royal family. In 986, Fujiwara
Yoritada, father-in-law of the emperor who died in
that year, resigned as regent. Since his daughter, the
widowed empress, had produced no heirs, he could
no longer claim connection with the royal family.
Such an act, incomprehensible in Chinese terms,
seems almost inevitable in Japan, where respect for
the hereditary principle was total.

The Phoenix hall, a building of wonderful proportion forming part of the temple of Byodo-in, one of the loveliest Japanese architectural monuments. The temple was originally a villa, built on the outskirts of Kyoto for a wealthy member of the Heian court.

Portrait of Fujiwara Mitsugo. The Fujiwaras rose from the status of courtiers to enjoy supreme power during the tenth and eleventh centuries.

And now we have come to the crucial weakness in the attempt of medieval Japan to graft on to its body politic the principles of Chinese government. Codes embodying these principles were issued and successively revised from the seventh century onward, but realities and the system were out of touch. In Chinese politics the idea of absolute hereditary right was overruled by the doctrine of the mandate of heaven; any new imperial dynasty was vindicated by success—thus it proclaimed the support it enjoyed from the heavenly powers. For the Chinese, the guiding principle of state, as of human life, was that of *Li*, the traditional proprieties by which the harmony between heaven and earth and hence human happiness and political stability were possible. In this system a prime duty of the Emperor was to maintain the correct ritual conduct of his duties and the due observance of *Li*. The Japanese adopted this idea as well as a rigid hierarchy of administration designed for a state where central authority was exercised; it was wildly unsuitable for a country where central authority was virtually unknown. Moreover, the Japanese were unable to take over the one thing that turned the Confucian doctrine of *Li* and the well-ordered state into practical politics—namely, appointment to office on merit and public examination. With such a civil service, the Chinese Emperor could afford to believe that the stability of his power rested on his harmonious balance of the eternal principles of *Yin* and *Yang*.

The Japanese administration—divided between the bureau of Religion and that of State, in which the former was the senior—was dominated by the rulings of its own bureau of *Yin-Yang*, but the men who acted on these rulings were usually well-born courtiers and nothing else. It is important to remember when reading the description of Heian society that follows, that despite its elegance and formality it was surrounded by disorder and danger. Even within the court itself the veneer was thin, and we learn from the diary of Lady Murasaki that the boorishness of Michinaga himself broke through the polite code of etiquette over which he presided. His predecessor was so confident of his position that he would appear in the presence of the emperor stripped to his undershirt for comfort in the heat of midsummer. And this in a society where both men and women dressed with meticulous care, wearing many layers of garments, each chosen for its color, so that even the fringe of the sleeve of an undershirt might be admired! The Heian court was uniquely sensitive to all aspects of human life: to etiquette, to dress, to learning and to the true movements of the heart itself. A lover was expected to conduct his courtship in delicate verses of his own composition and apt quotations from the Chinese classics.

The upsurge in the vitality of native Japanese arts is well illustrated by the architecture of the new capital at Heian. The gridiron pattern of the town plan of Nara had been closely copied from that of the T'ang capital of C'hang-an in China, while the architecture was also essentially Chinese. The rooms were paved in stone, the ceilings supported by painted wood pillars, and the roofs were of semi-translucent glazed green tiles. At Heian a tradition of native Japanese domestic architecture asserted itself. The pillars and other woodwork were in unpainted dark wood, the roofs were covered with

Heian architecture and literature

strips of bark from the *hinoki* cedar tree, while the floors were of wood raised on stilts above the ground, the court returning to the traditional Japanese habit of sitting not on chairs but on rush matting on the floor.

Heian architecture had other distinguishing features. A noble family was housed in a complex of buildings. The *shinden*, or chief pavilion, was surrounded by a number of lesser ones, linked to one another and to the central one by corridors or bridges. The whole was set in a formal park. The garden itself, which at first contained miniature replicas of beloved landscape scenes, came to be subject to strict laws so that it became an object not only of esthetic but also metaphysical contemplation, being viewed from a window and not entered.

Within the interior of Japanese houses, rooms were defined by sliding doors. Free-standing folding screens were also used to vary the space or were placed between the participants in a conversation where etiquette forbade that one should look on the other. The young Genji, in Lady Murasaki's novel, might not see the face of his adored lady until late in a courtship. On one disastrous occasion the lady was so shy that eventually one of her maids answered Genji's gallantries from behind the screen of honor. Delighted by the sweet voice, he pressed his suit; when he eventually did see his princess he was horrified by her plainness!

Genji, however, would at least have been able to entertain himself with the works of the finest painters and poets of the court, for the screens and partitions were decorated with exquisite painting and calligraphy. The artist's inspiration was often a verse or line from Chinese and, later, even Japanese literature. This would be inscribed in a cartouche within the borders of the painting—thus, to the beauty of the painting was added the literary beauty of the text and the quality of the calligraphy. The native Japanese poetic form of the *waka* gradually supplanted Chinese forms. The subject matter also changed: from dealing with idealized landscapes with craggy mountains, so favored by Chinese artists, poets turned to scenes in which undulating hills are decorated with the beauty of the flowering cherry tree and the purple-leafed maple. The subject matter became more urbane and the figures of Chinese legend were displaced by daily scenes in the life of the Japanese aristocracy or of the common people.

It is possible that Lady Murasaki based her description of the early morning in a village on a screen painting rather than her own actual observation of such a scene—the bleacher at work with his mallet or the threshing mills as they begin to grind into action at the beginning of a new day. One tenth-century court poet wrote a series of screen poems on the occupations of the twelve months, or on the character of the four seasons. Other poems were devoted to the description of famous provincial beauty spots; of famous travelers on the road; of the life of the peasants or of nobles indulging in some typically courtly diversion such as hawking or

admiring blossom on the trees. Painters delighted to set people in their landscapes, and in her diary Lady Murasaki records that one of the princesses at the court loved to go out to see the sun go down or the moon fade before the onset of the sun at dawn, or to follow a nightingale through the woods. Indeed, it is remarkable that in a society so essentially wedded to the urbane pleasures of the court and the delights of the capital, city life as such provided poets with little inspiration. Nevertheless, verses survive that poignantly tell of the pains of exile from the capital, for throughout the Heian period exile was the standard punishment for subversion, or even political failure.

Hand in hand with the brilliant flowering of the arts encouraged by the building of the new capital, and with the development of a more truly national style in painting—the so-called *Yamato-e* or "Japanese painting"—went a rise in the status of the painters themselves. Toward the end of the ninth century we find for the first time records of the names of the artists; among the most famous is perhaps Kanoaka—traditionally believed to have been the first to paint real as opposed to imaginary Japanese landscapes.

With the invention of a type of syllabary script in the late eighth and ninth centuries it became comparatively simple to write Japanese. The result was not only that poets tended to abandon Chinese, but they moved toward the development of a prose literature—novels, memoirs and diaries. Great statesmen left diaries written in Chinese, which was

The sophistication of calligraphy was an important aspect of the cultural renaissance fostered by the Fujiwara dynasty from their court at Heian.

An illustration from *The Tale of Genji*, perhaps the world's earliest novel, written *c.* 1000 by Lady Murasaki to mirror Heian court life.

The Tale of Genji

to remain the language of scholarship for centuries to come, but it is in the Japanese novels and memoirs that the brilliant, sensitive—if somewhat artificial—society of Heian Japan lives. These early Japanese works, which are among the most delightful books in world literature, range from the fairy-tale atmosphere of the *Taketori monogatari*, which tells how five noblemen and then even the Emperor himself attempted to woo a beautiful girl only to find that she was a spirit whose home is the moon, to the truly ardent *Genji monogatari*, or *Tale of Genji*. The genre of prose romance reached its highest flowering in the hands of female authors at the beginning of the eleventh century. In addition to the work of Murasaki Shikibu (who wrote a fascinating diary as well as her famous novel), there was the diary of the poetess Izumi Shikibu, recounting her numerous amorous affairs, and the *Pillow Book (Commonplace Book)* of Sei Shonagon, another lady at the court.

Thanks largely to Chinese influence, divination and oracles became a central part of Japanese life. The bureau of *Yin-Yang* and its offices was consulted not only on the auspices for the ceremonies of state, but also by the nobility on the most detailed aspects of life. For the people as a whole there was a large and profitably employed class of diviners and sooth-sayers. Perhaps the strangest of a mass of superstitions was the belief that the spiritual powers walked abroad and that it was unlucky to cross their "directions." Indeed, the world was so thick with dangers that it was safest of all to stay at home. Yet even in this state of total withdrawal, called *monoimi*, one could not be certain of safety indefinitely—on every sixtieth day, the Day of the Monkey, danger could be avoided only by staying watchful all night

and residing in a neutral place. In the year 1104, the cloistered Emperor Shirakawa spent the Night of the Monkey in his carriage at one of the gates of the city—returning to his palace only at daybreak. If a man had to go out on an inauspicious day, he might wear a ticket, called an *imifuda*, in his hat, to warn people with whom he came in contact that they should not approach him. The Japanese delight in ceremonial and display of all kinds was so great that we have contemporary records of great occasions where some of the spectators present arrived wearing their *imifuda*, anxious not to miss the ceremony and protecting themselves against the powers of evil in this way. Some of the most magnificent displays were those put on by the Buddhists.

Buddhism came to Japan during the seventh century. Its immense influence at the capital in the Nara period may have been a factor determining the move to Heian. But Buddhism was to have a deep and lasting effect on Japanese culture. Its broad and non exclusive nature enabled it to accommodate the local spirits and gods of the Shinto cults as the protectors of the Boddhisatvas of Buddhism, and the old faith held its own as an essential part of the religion of the state and the people.

In the early ninth century the sects of Tendai and Shingon arose, both modifications of sects already established in China. The center of Tendai Buddhism was the monastery of Enryakuji, built on Mount Hiyiei overlooking Heian. It was as dangerous to the life of the capital as anything that may have happened at Nara. As the century progressed, both sects became increasingly esoteric, and during the late tenth and eleventh centuries they were to some extent displaced by the cult of the

Detail of a bronze lantern from Todaiji showing the influence of Chinese style.

Above An eleventh-century Buddhist monk on horseback.

Left The great Buddha in the temple of Byodo-in. The sculptor devised the system of assembling pieces of carved wood.

Opposite left Layout of the temple at Todaiji at Nara pre-dating the renaissance of Heian court culture.

Opposite right The statue of the Shinto goddess Nakatsu Hime Zo wearing the robes of a court lady, at the Hachiman-gu shrine in Nara.

merciful Buddha Amida. This cult revolved around belief in immediate rebirth in the paradise of Amida and a very simple devotional system based on repeated invocations of the name of Buddha.

Perhaps the most influential of all the precepts of Buddhism was the belief in reincarnation, and above all the idea of Karma, roughly to be described as the belief in the unavoidable cause-and-effect relation between past, present and future, and the conviction that man's life was affected at every turn by events in his own past lives. Such a belief squared well with the strong streak of fatalism in Japanese thought, and the quietistic aspect of Buddhism constituted a welcome contrast to the violence of life itself. Yet the Buddhist monasteries were far from quietistic in their contacts with the world at large. Rich and tax-exempt, they soon recruited immense bodies of fighting men. These armed "monks" enjoyed a semi-religious status somewhat analogous to the lay brothers of Western monasticism, and their rioting came to be a constant threat to the capital. The civil authorities often showed understandable reluctance to proceed against them.

There were many occasions in the history of Western monasticism when its representatives fell far below the high aspirations of their vocation. But only very rarely do we find accounts of the outright hooliganism that was a recurrent feature in the history of the monasteries around the Japanese capital. Of course, the proximity of Japanese Buddhist monasteries to the cities was an important fact in their development. Nevertheless, at the other extreme, we find examples of asceticism and piety among Buddhist monks which more than equal the most exalted achievements of the West.

It is above all this contrast between extremes that strikes us so forcibly about the society of medieval Japan. A civilization of remarkable sensibility and esthetic achievement was born in a country not remarkably rich in natural resources. Its court was governed by elaborate and elegant ritual and an exquisite awareness of the nuances of social convention and human sensitivities. Yet, as minor but revealing episodes from the history of the period show, the physical conditions of life were often uncomfortable, and the brutal and coarse facts of human nature often broke through the façade of etiquette. In comparison with the situation in Europe during the eleventh century, and indeed for generations to come, however, the civilization of this Oriental culture is breathtakingly advanced.

GEOFFREY HINDLEY

213

Japan during the Heian Period

For some three and a half centuries after the founding of Kyoto, Japan had an imperial court and administration devoted to a refined culture that has shaped the character of the people down to this century. Power was in the hands of the Fujiwara family who intermarried with the imperial house and provided "regents" for a line of boy-emperors, most of whom abdicated voluntarily when they reached adulthood. The Emperor became an idealized figure, protected from the corrupting effects of actual political rule. The sensitive, stylish yet formal spirit of the Heian period under the Fujiwara, who enjoyed their greatest ascendancy from the mid-tenth to the mid-eleventh centuries, is fully embodied in the literary masterpiece *Genji Monogatari* written by a court lady, Murasaki Shikibu, in the early eleventh century.

In sharp contrast to the delicate, almost effete life of the capital was the life on the great semi-independent estates. The large landowners gradually acquired exemption from taxation; thus developed a feudal system with parallels to that in Europe.

As the Fujiwara began to lose their grip on events, civil war broke out between rival factions of the family. In the twelfth century they called two of the powerful military provincial families to their aid. Not surprisingly, when the smoke cleared after a long period of near anarchy, the Fujiwara found that they had been entirely supplanted by their military advisers. In 1166, the Taira family seized power and for the first time in three centuries Japan witnessed political executions; some twenty years later, the Taira were overthrown by the great Minamoto Yoritomo, and in 1185 Japan came under a government controlled by the military. The age of the tea ceremony was succeeded by the age of the samurai: the struggle between the Taira and the Minamoto launched the great period of Japanese chivalry. The principle of military control of the government was to remain at the heart of the Japanese administrative system for another seven centuries.

The Lombards in Italy

Only six years after the founding of Kyoto had marked the beginning of a new epoch in Japan, a still more dramatic turn of events gave new style and pretension to the more backward if perhaps more vigorous civilization of the West. In terms of territorial power, Charlemagne had just claim to the title of Emperor. In a real sense he controlled most of Christian Europe, and the rise of the Frankish power and the house of Charlemagne himself will be an important theme in what follows. But first we must look at events in Italy after the fall of the Ostrogothic kingdom in the sixth century.

Like all the barbarian invaders of the later Roman Empire, the Lombards had originated in north Germany. By the middle of the sixth century they were established in a territory comprising parts of modern Austria and Hungary, where they acted as the allies of Justinian, assisting the imperial armies against another Germanic tribe, the Gepids, who threatened the Danubian frontier. In the late 560s, however, they abandoned their allegiance to the Emperor and crossed into northern Italy where they established themselves within a generation. The capital of the new Lombard state was at Pavia, in the region still known as Lombardy. To the south, the two powerful Lombard duchies of Benevento and Spoleto maintained their independence of the Byzantine emperors and, for a long time, of the Lombard kings of the north as well.

The three Powers

During the seventh and eighth centuries, Italy was divided among three main powers: the Lombards in the north and central areas; the Roman papacy, at first acknowledging imperial suzerainty but soon acting with increasing independence; and the Byzantine exarchate at Ravenna, with additional strong Byzantine presence in the southernmost part of the peninsula and on Sicily.

The Lombards were at first a ruling warrior minority, distinguished from their subjects not only by race and language, but also by religion—those who did adopt Christianity chose Arianism. The independence of Spoleto and Benevento is to be explained not only by their geographical remoteness from the capital but also by the Lombard social order in which the local leaders, or dukes, enjoyed a considerable authority over their following. Indeed, after the death of Alboin, the leader of the original invasion, Italy was ruled for ten years by thirty-six dukes. But the pressures of Byzantine and Frankish armies compelled a return to kingship. Thereafter, the state became increasingly unified, with a system of royal ministers in the provinces. In the middle of the seventh century a code of laws, written in Latin and reflecting both Lombard and Roman practices, was published. Despite the continuing separateness of the Lombard warrior-aristocracy, the increasing influence of late Roman ideas in art and administration is observable. Most significant of all was the gradual ousting of

Jeweled book cover of the great Lombard Queen Theodolinda.

Arian Christianity in favor of Catholicism, and the intermarriage of the Lombard and Roman populations.

The height of Lombard power and prestige came during the reign of Liutprand (712–44), who extended the conquests of Byzantine territory still further and asserted northern Lombard authority over the duchies of Benevento and Spoleto. During his reign, the great Lombard historian Paul the Deacon began his famous history, the earliest of a German people by a German writer, which ends with the reign of Liutprand.

Liutprand's successors, in an attempt to remove the alien corridor between the two halves of the Lombard domain, moved against the lands of the papacy and the remaining territories of the exarchate of Ravenna. But the papacy called in the assistance of its powerful Catholic "sons," the Frankish kings.

On the first occasion of a papal

Contemporary portrait of the commander Minamoto Yoritomo.

Rare example of Lombard art prior to the conquest of Charlemagne; three female saints from a church at Cividale.

The iron crown of Lombardy, one of the most sacred relics of imperial history.

summons, Pepin the Short compelled the Lombards to abandon their conquests and confirmed the papacy's possession of these lands. From this so-called Donation of Pepin may be dated the existence of the papal states as a separate and autonomous territorial unit. Some twenty years later, the Pope called on the aid of Pepin's son Charlemagne. In 774, after his defeat of the Lombard armies, Charlemagne was himself crowned king of Lombardy with the iron crown. From this time on, the successors of Charlemagne were to claim imperial rights in Italy, which was to lead them into many exhausting and largely fruitless expeditions.

Rise of the Franks

While the sun of imperial Rome in the West was setting over the walls of Ravenna, and while the popes at Rome were maintaining themselves as best they could between

Figure of Christ from a casket of Frankish workmanship; seventh century.

the Arian heretic king of Italy on the one hand and the claims of the Byzantine Emperor on the other, a new power was rising north of the Alps early in the sixth century. This was the Frankish kingdom of Clovis and his descendants. With his victory at Soissons over Syagrius in 486, when he was only twenty, Clovis had effectively put an end to the last vestige of Roman rule in Gaul. Over the next twenty years, this leader of a once insignificant tribe overthrew the most powerful barbarian kingdoms, defeating in turn the Thuringians, the Alemanni and above all the Visigoths at Vouille in 507.

In the long vista of history, perhaps the most important event in Clovis' reign was his conversion to Catholic Christianity. By this act he won the support of the indigenous Romano-Gallic population, the support of the Church and the title of consul from the Emperor. In return, Clovis himself protected the Roman Church in Gaul. In the years that followed his death in 511 the Frankish kingdom—although divided among his four sons—continued to expand. The kingdom of the Burgundians, between the Rhone and Loire, was conquered; the duchy of Bavaria acknowledged Frankish suzerainty; and at this early date we find the Franks making expeditions into Ostrogothic Italy as allies of Justinian.

Charles Martel

In the early seventh century a new power structure emerged in Gaul, one dominated by the western kingdom of Neustria, the eastern kingdom of Austrasia, the semi-independent kingdom of Burgundy and the duchy of Aquitaine. In the last twenty years of the century, Austrasia and Neustria—although

nominally ruled by descendants of Clovis, the notorious "do-nothing" kings—were united under the effective rule of Pepin of Heristal, the chief minister or "mayor of the palace" of the king of Austrasia. He was succeeded by his illegitimate son, the great Charles Martel (the Hammer). Martel was not only the ruler of the two northern Frankish kingdoms but also received the submission both of Aquitaine and Burgundy.

At this point the impetus of the second wave of Islamic conquest was by no means spent. Even after the crushing defeat that the Frankish army under Martel inflicted on them at the battle of Poitiers in 732, the Arabs might still have posed a severe threat had it not been for their own internal dissensions. In addition to his achievements as a soldier, which included the pacification of a number of Germanic

tribes on the right bank of the Rhine, Charles Martel did much to unify the Frankish kingdom, both by eliminating the worst excesses of the nobility and asserting the influence of the state in the affairs of the Church. In many ways he laid the foundations for the achievements of his son, Pepin the Short, and his grandson, Charlemagne.

Although Charles Martel did not assume the title of king, the fiction of the Merovingian rule was already difficult to support during his rule. Ten years after Martel's death, Pepin the Short had his deposition of the last of the Merovingians and his own coronation confirmed by the Pope—in return for helping the Pope against the Lombards in Italy. Half a century later, Pepin's son was to accept the consecration of the Church for a still greater honor, that of Emperor, on the fateful Christmas Day of the year 800.

King Pepin III crowned by a divine hand.

A Crown for Charlemagne 800

At a solemn moment during the celebration of Mass in Rome's St. Peter's Basilica on Christmas Day of the year 800, Pope Leo III stopped and turned toward the large man kneeling in front of the altar. Then, in a dramatic gesture that has been the topic of countless historical arguments since, Leo crowned Charles, King of the Franks, as the new Emperor of the Romans. The coronation apparently took even Charles by surprise; and it probably displeased him as well, since it seemed to imply that he received his power from the Pope. Indeed, this may have been Leo's aim, for only a year before he had been driven out of the city by a rebellious population and he was now eager to reassert his authority. Whatever Leo's motives, his action was of momentous significance—in creating a European Christian empire, in continuing the division between East and West, and in sowing seeds of conflict between Church and State.

On Christmas Day in the year 800 Charlemagne heard Mass in St. Peter's in Rome. As he knelt at prayer, Pope Leo III placed on his head a gold circlet in token of an imperial crown: and the Romans proclaimed him Emperor: "To Charles Augustus, crowned by God, the great and peace-giving Emperor of the Romans, life and victory!"

Charlemagne the Frank was a huge man, six feet and four inches tall, and broadly built. He spoke quietly, and was a cheerful, talkative man who enjoyed the debating matches that were popular among the Germanic races. He drank sparsely but ate a great deal, and detested wearing fine clothes made of silk. He favored the shirt and linen tunic of the Franks over tight hose, and in winter a cloak made from the skins of otters or rats. He wore a blue serge cloak and carried a short sword with a hilt of silver or gold. Charlemagne loved hunting, riding and swimming; he loved women, too. Apart from those he was wedded to by Christian marriage, he had some wives under Germanic folk laws and four concubines. Charlemagne valued culture, and the learning of the clerics—he himself understood Latin but probably could not write, since it was only with difficulty that he could form the letters of his name for a signature.

Charlemagne wanted to see ancient Rome reborn in his capital city. In Aix, near the famous hot springs, the imperial chapel was built as an octagon, probably modeled on the Church of the Holy Sepulcher at Jerusalem. Apart from the cathedral and the *sacrum palatium* where the Frankish king intended to live, there was a third building, named the "Lateran." Aix, like Constantinople, was to be a second Rome.

Pope Leo III was made aware of this great project of Charlemagne's when he fled from Rome to the town of Paderborn in Germany in the summer of 799. The people of Rome had driven him out and he sought help from "the protector of the Romans,"

Charlemagne. Rome (*Romanitas*) and Christendom (*christianitas*) were identical to Charlemagne, and for him both concepts were religious. However, "Rome" and "Christendom" had totally different meanings for the Pope and for the Emperor in Constantinople. The latter considered himself to be the only legitimate Roman Emperor, and his Greek Orthodox Church the only true one. The Pope for his part saw himself as the successor of St. Peter, and therefore the one true Roman. His concept of Rome was implicit in his attempt to renew papal Rome as the axis of the Christian world.

Charlemagne's plan to turn Aix into a second Rome could only alarm the Pope, and probably was the basic reason for the coronation of A.D. 800. The idea of transferring the papacy from Rome to Aix must already have taken shape by 799. Once in Aix the Pope would have been only *primus inter pares*, the first of the imperial bishops, in the world's eyes.

At the imperial coronation on Christmas Day, A.D. 800, at least four opposing claims came into conflict: the claims of the Franks, the papacy, the people of Rome and Byzantium. Historians always have and probably always will argue about the correct interpretation of this event, which was both political and religious, and embodied both a sacred and a political constitution for Latin Europe and the West. The argument arises from the conflicts that existed at the time. Charlemagne remained the short-term victor. For him, as for his Franks, his subjects in Lombardy, and the Anglo-Saxons, Irish and Spaniards who were his ideological allies, the imperial coronation of A.D. 800 was a coronation at the hands of God Himself. Charlemagne the king and priest was the successor to the priest-kings of the Old Testament "after the order of Melchisedech." Charlemagne, the "new David," was enthroned in Aix on a sacred imitation of King Solomon's throne. He also saw himself as the successor of Justinian, carrying out and adding to the latter's enactments.

The throne of Charlemagne in the minster at Aachen, seat of Carolingian pretension and a focal point of the cultural heritage of Western Europe.

Opposite Charlemagne the Frank, crowned Emperor of Rome on Christmas Day, A.D. 800; a late-ninth-century bronze statuette portraying the ideal of the monarch as soldier and judge.

A warrior nobleman of the
ninth century, one of a class
whose power Charlemagne
increased and upon whom his
government depended; a
fresco in the Oratory of
St. Benedict.

Below The Frankish talisman
worn by the Emperor
Charlemagne is a phial
mounted in gold and precious
stones which probably
contained relics sacred in
primitive Frankish ritual.

had been transferred from Constantinople to Rome.

Leo's coronation of Charlemagne, which surprised and embittered the latter like an act of aggression, was aimed against the Emperor in Constantinople, against the Frankish king, and against the people of Rome themselves, who were pressed into service for the ceremony by the Pope; they had to chant the ancient Roman acclamation, the ceremonial words of the old imperial liturgy, immediately after the coronation in order to make it legal and binding. The Roman citizens who collaborated with Leo in this act believed that it gave them the right to accept or reject the Pope's choice of Emperor—who might be a powerful ally in the still unresolved conflict of the Romans themselves with their popes. Pope Leo, however, intended their role to be merely one of helpers; the Franks, to their chagrin, were allotted the role of mere onlookers. They were allowed to do or say nothing at the ceremony.

Leo III would have liked to add a second ceremony to this coronation, the first time a Pope had ever crowned an Emperor. He had planned Charlemagne's betrothal to the Empress Irene at Constantinople—but she was deposed before the betrothal could be arranged. If he had succeeded in this, Leo would have achieved that world primacy as head of both Latin and Greek Christendom which the popes as leaders of Europe were to strive for at the time of the Crusades. Hadrian I, Leo's predecessor, had already declared that the Roman Church was *caput totius mundi*—the head of the whole world.

Why did Charlemagne accede to the Pope's plans? Why did he go to Rome at all? Why expose himself to the obvious risk that the Pope would take over the coronation and exploit it for his own ends? One must remember here that Charlemagne's chief aim was to be crowned as Emperor; but he intended

For the Germanic peoples who had been subjugated or won back by Charlemagne's "strong arm," his coronation was the divinely ordained confirmation of the great conqueror's role, since God had first made him "Emperor" on the battlefield.

It is certain that Charlemagne and his advisers did not consider the imperial coronation of A.D. 800 as a papal claim to spiritual and ecclesiastical authority over the rank and office of the Emperor. Charlemagne in any case wanted to avoid an act of provocation against the Emperor in Byzantium.

The Pope, who was the "second victor" of A.D. 800, had quite different intentions. Leo III, a problematical figure whose personality remains obscure, formed part of a great tradition which was to receive new impetus later in the ninth century and which led through Gregory VII to the powerful figures of the twelfth century, Innocent III and Innocent IV.

The popes and their assistants wove the strong web of ideology that later entangled and overthrew the power of the Western Emperors: from Constantine's day, the Pope was the real ruler of Rome; he always handed the imperial office on to *his* candidates, once the majesty of the Emperor

Right Charlemagne in the
ceremonial dress of the Roman
Emperors, a ninth-century
statue at Müstair church,
founded by Charlemagne. The
Carolingian sculptor probably
used a late antique model for
the details of imperial dress in
an effort to represent
Charlemagne's ideal of a
revived Roman Empire.

The protector of Christendom

the coronation to take place on his own territory, after careful preparations by his political and religious advisers. On December 23 of A.D. 800, two days before the coronation, the Patriarch of Jerusalem's legates handed over to Charlemagne a key and a banner, to symbolize that they were handing over to him as master and protector of Christendom the sacred places in the Holy Land.

Charlemagne, as protector of Christendom, believed that the true Christendom was the ecclesiastical Latin Christendom of Rome led by the papacy. The Frankish church was firmly oriented toward Rome. The age-old Roman faith of the Franks was based on the sanctity of St. Peter and was centered on the papacy. Charlemagne was the father of the Latin West, of the traditions that have formed the basis of Western European culture and its schools and universities right up to the present day.

The Carolingian miniscule is the ancestor of modern European printing. It is true that in Charlemagne's Empire Latin, and to a certain extent also Greek, education were better and more productively represented by the English schoolmen than by the decadent, needy scholars of Rome. By Charlemagne's day, Rome had become a cultural and moral desert. It could not be compared in any way with southern Italy, where a rich culture based on ancient Greece still flourished, nor with the civilization of the Lombard kingdom in northern Italy.

The culture acquired by England from the time of Theodore of Tarsus and Bishop Benedict was available to the men of Charlemagne's Empire. The scholars from the Continent had free access to England's schools and libraries. Throughout the whole of the eighth century, England had sent the finest and most educated of her sons across the Channel as teachers and missionaries. From the time of St. Boniface to the time of Alcuin, the Church of the Frankish Empire depended very much on the wisdom and scholarship of British monks.

But these men also acknowledged Rome as their master. For Charlemagne, the laborious work of political and cultural unification of the varied peoples, races and territories of his great Empire could only be based on Roman (and this meant Latin and Christian) belief and culture. His title of *imperator Romanum gubernans imperium*, which he preferred to the less ambiguous *imperator Romanorum*, chiefly signified to him that he was Emperor of all Latin Christendom—the only divinely inspired Christendom, since the Greeks with their contentious discussions were always in danger of heresy.

It was in this context that Charlemagne needed the power of the Roman papacy against the Greeks. His aim was the coexistence of the two empires, and he strived for equality in rank and power with the Eastern Emperor, whose title he recognized as legitimate. He imitated his rival by calling his court "sacral" (*sacer*), following the custom of the Byzantines; and Greek elements were absorbed into the Carolingian civilization. The most obvious example of the imitation of Byzantium occurred in the adoration of Charlemagne by the Pope after the

coronation. Leo III stood to crown Charlemagne, when the latter rose after his prayers, and then threw himself down before Charlemagne in the Byzantine custom of homage and sacral recognition of the crowned Emperor. This seemed monstrous to subsequent popes and was never repeated, for in their conception St. Peter, that is, the Pope, "created" the Emperor.

The coronation of A.D. 800 must be considered from every point of view a decisive step in the development of the great conflict between East and West which has overshadowed Europe from late antiquity up to the present day. It is a conflict between Greeks and Latins, between the Greek and

Below St. Peter receiving the Keys of Heaven from Christ, a ninth-century fresco in Müstair church, demonstrating the belief which was the basis of papal claims to supremacy over Charlemagne's Empire.

Bottom The mosaic over the Imperial door in Hagia Sophia, Constantinople, shows the Byzantine Emperor doing homage before Christ in the attitude of humility which the Pope adopted towards Charlemagne at his coronation.

The Synod of Frankfurt

One of Charlemagne's achievements was the establishment of a stable currency. This silver denier bears the Emperor's head crowned with laurel and surrounded by a title in Roman letters, a style based entirely on imperial Roman tradition.

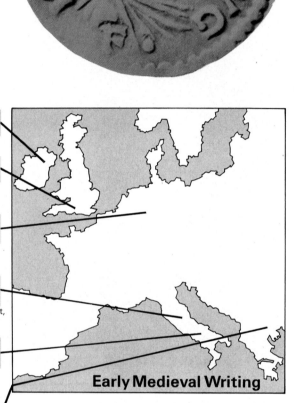

Late-seventh-century Anglo-Irish half-uncials.

Eleventh-century English "Winchester School" writing, a variety of Carolingian miniscule.

Medieval "Gothic" writing still used in Germany well into the twentieth century.

Fourth-century Roman cursive script, the origin of most forms of Western writing.

"Beneventan" script from Monte Cassino, the model for Carolingian miniscule.

The fourth-century *Codex Sinaiticus* in "Cyrillic" script, developed from Greek writing for the transliteration of the Slav languages.

Early Medieval Writing

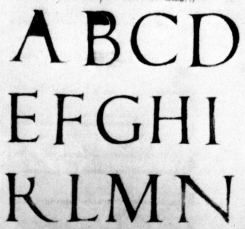

An example of Carolingian miniscules and capitals, a style of writing that developed under Charlemagne from Roman models.

Latin churches, Constantinople and Rome.

The synod of Frankfurt in A.D. 794 was the immediate prologue to the events of A.D. 800. It was an attempt to prove that the Greek Church had departed from the true Christian faith and gone over to the side of evil and the antichrist in its heretical worship of images. The "orthodox council" of Frankfurt represented an attempt to discredit the second synod of Nicaea (A.D. 787). It exploited the material that had been prepared in the *Libri Carolini* by a court theologian, probably Theodulf of Orléans. The Franks accused the Byzantine Church of setting up idols; the conflict over the right degree of worship to be accorded to the holy images in fact continued for centuries in Byzantium.

But the Frankfurt synod's real object of attack was the Eastern Roman emperors—the Byzantine rulers were accused of elevating themselves to the level of false gods in their claim to rule in conjunction with God, and to be themselves divine. It was said that in the evil city of Constantinople people even spoke of the "holy ears" of the ruler. The synod of Frankfurt maintained that far from being equal to the apostles (Constantine the Great was the first to describe himself as "equal to the apostles" and even "the thirteenth apostle"), these emperors were all-too-ordinary mortals in their pursuit of earthly, transient aims.

This attack on the part of the theologians coincided with the objectives of the Roman popes, who were attempting throughout the ninth century to undermine the sacral position of the Eastern emperors. The papacy assumed all the sacral title and claims of the Eastern emperors, and indeed went far beyond them; by the thirteenth and fourteenth centuries the ideologists of the curia were referring to the Pope as *papa-deus*, or "Pope-God."

This rivalry shown by the Carolingian theologians and men of politics with Constantinople was a symptom of the feelings of inferiority the Roman and Latin clerics and theologians experienced when confronted with the far finer civilization of the East. They were greatly inferior to the scholars of the Eastern Church intellectually, spiritually and ecclesiastically; in the fourth century, not a single theologian in the West could follow the subtle intellectual disputations in the Greek church on the question of the Trinity. And if, by the end of the eighth century, the West had caught up to a certain extent, chiefly through the work of the theologians of the British Isles and Spain, there was still no question of any equality between the Franks and the Byzantines in the field of culture and learning. Charlemagne's court theologians were all too aware of this, and knew that they would be considered barbarians in Constantinople.

The Frankfurt synod's goal was nothing less than a demonstration that, now, the Latin Church alone represented the true orthodoxy. The Greeks were denounced as false, heretical, unreliable, evil, gossiping and treacherous; right into the nineteenth century and beyond, such advocates of the Pope's infallibility as de Maistre have repeated this cliché.

This carved ivory book cover showing the Virgin and Child enthroned with St. John on the left and the high priest Zacharias on the right, is from Charlemagne's palace school *c.* 810, and clearly shows the influence of Byzantine craftsmen at Aachen.

The Utrecht Psalter is the outstanding example of the new mode of expression in Carolingian illumination developed from the fusion of Anglo-Saxon, Irish and Frankish techniques under the dominant influence of Byzantine painting. This illustration of uncolored pen drawings has a lively technique and depth of perspective.

If the "one true word of God" had gone over from the East to the West, surely the imperial crown should go as well. An unexpected event now came to the aid of the Carolingian politicians: in 797 the Emperor of Constantinople was deposed, and replaced by a woman. But, according to the masculine theology of the West, which denied equal birth rights to women from St. Augustine's day right up to the twentieth century, Irene was not entitled to rule. Once more Frankish goals coincided with the plans of the papacy. As the *Libri Carolini* expressed it, "the fragility of the [feminine] sex and the fickleness of the [feminine] heart do not permit [a woman] to assume the highest positions in matters of faith or rank, but force her to submit to masculine authority."

However, both "masculine authorities," Pope Leo III and the Emperor Charlemagne, knew that the reality of Byzantine rule could not be overcome with purely theological arguments. Once Charlemagne became Emperor he dropped the issue of

Collapse of the Empire

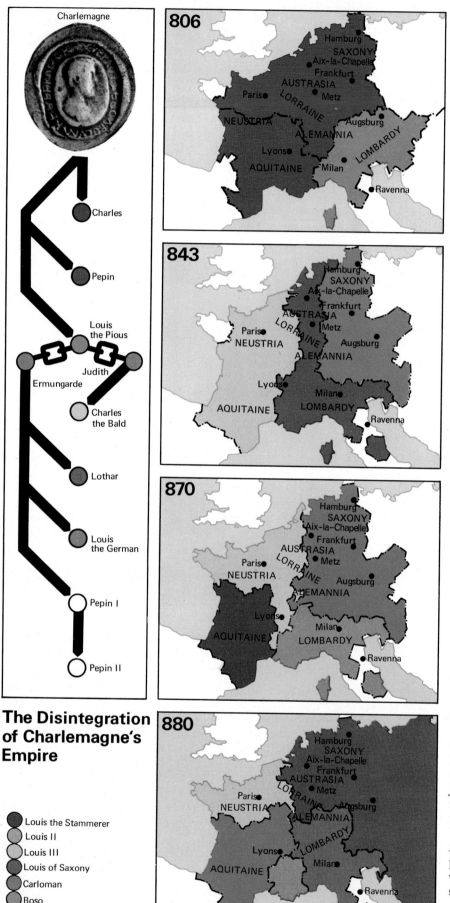

Charlemagne

The Disintegration of Charlemagne's Empire

- Louis the Stammerer
- Louis II
- Louis III
- Louis of Saxony
- Carloman
- Boso
- Charles the Fat

806

843

870

880

image-worship. As Emperor, he set out to establish friendly relations with the Byzantine court. We can safely assume today that an ambassador of Charlemagne's, accompanied by papal envoys, actually traveled to Constantinople to woo the Empress Irene, no longer in her first youth, as a bride for Charlemagne.

The Empress Irene was not unwilling to be Charlemagne's bride, but the powerful patricians of her Empire rebelled. Irene was banished to a remote convent and died a few months after this *coup d'état*, which took place before the eyes of the envoys from the West. Once again a man was Emperor in Constantinople: Nicephorus, formerly the Logothete, or minister of finance. However, the Frankish envoys returned with a Byzantine delegation which was to negotiate the recognition of Charlemagne as Emperor. Two years before his death, a settlement was finally reached: a new Byzantine delegation officially acclaimed Charlemagne as "Emperor"— though not as Roman Emperor. The Emperor of the Romans was to remain the Greek ruler, and he alone. According to Byzantine imperial law there could be any number of nominal emperors; later on, for example, an Emperor of the Bulgarians was recognized.

Charlemagne for his part gave up his claims to extend his dominion over the East. This was the more easily done as he was to be fully occupied until his death in trying to keep the peace among the different races and tribes of his enormous Empire.

The collapse of that Empire began after his death. The papacy at once made a bid to take over the dominant role, as the imperial coronation of Louis the Pious in Rome (A.D. 816) demonstrated. The Pope managed on this occasion to combine the anointing with the coronation for the first time. The Romans, who had been the Pope's adjuncts in A.D. 800, were now completely excluded and their approval disdained. The new, epoch-making liturgy of this imperial coronation made it clear that St. Peter created the Roman Emperor. Rome, the Rome of the papacy, became the focal point of the whole Christian world.

One final point needs to be made about the imperial coronation on Christmas Day, A.D. 800. In the thousand years that were to follow before the downfall of the old Europe, which received its first severe blow in the French Revolution and finally came to an end in World War I, this coronation was remembered by kings, emperors and princes of East and West, North and South alike. Right into the East, into Russia and beyond, and as far as Jerusalem and Baghdad, Charlemagne became the mystical definition of the great ruler, the Caesar and the Augustus, of the Christian world. Napoleon believed himself to be Charlemagne's reincarnation. After World War II, Western politicians spoke of the political and economic coalition of "Carolingian" western Europe which was to withstand the pressures from the East; and Soviet Russian diplomacy reproduced the subtle and devious methods of its "Byzantine ancestor."

FRIEDRICH HEER

Opposite page The *Divisio regni* of 806, Charlemagne's division of his Empire into roughly equal parts to be shared among his sons, avoided the issue of the imperial title. The seal, with the head of a Roman emperor, was used by Charlemagne.

Charlemagne's court at Aachen drew together the different strains of contemporary western culture. These manuscript pages show St. Matthew (*far left*) from the Ebbo Gospels, illuminated *c.* 835 in the Reims school; signs of the Zodiac (*left*) in an astrology text book from Metz, *c.* 840, typical of the survival of classical learning at the Carolingian court; and (*below*) the Anglo-Saxon strain exemplified by the opening pages of St. Matthew's gospel from the mid-eighth-century *Codex Aureus.*

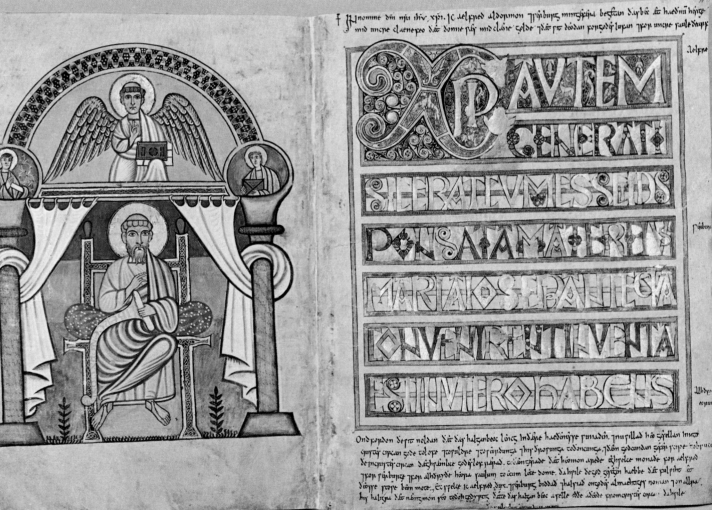

During the ninth century the Empire of Charlemagne dissolved and only the idea of "Europe" survived. And by the late tenth century the eastern and western parts of the Frankish kingdom had coalesced into the dim outlines of the future kingdoms of France and Germany. The Spanish March had disintegrated and been succeeded by the Basque kingdom of Navarre and the county of Barcelona. Italy, broken into a series of ineffectual kingdoms in the peninsula, owed a nominal allegiance to the Emperor (now the King of the east Franks) that was to become gradually less meaningful as the Middle Ages progressed.

After his death in 814, Charlemagne was succeeded by his son Louis I, called the Pious, an amiable

Louis the Pious, from a contemporary manuscript.

but often too compassionate man. Unable to command his unruly subjects or control his quarrelsome family, Louis compounded the faults of his virtues by his indulgence toward his second wife, Judith of Bavaria, and her son Charles. During his reign, Louis was constantly at war with his sons, who finally brought their conflicts to a conclusion with the treaty of Verdun in 843, three years after Louis' death. This treaty—one of the earliest records of the emerging vernacular languages, having both German and French texts—gave the imperial title and capital to the eldest son Lothair, who also received a huge tract of territory stretching from the Low Countries to the plains of central Italy. Louis, called the German, received the eastern lands; and the favorite, Charles the Bald, got the western lands. Verdun was the inevitable consequence of the Frankish prac-

tice of dividing a father's possessions; but in the years that followed the Carolingian house showed a lack of family loyalty and honest dealing that was remarkable even for the times. The settlement of Verdun was crucially revised at the treaty of Mersen in 870, when the

Cup of Tassilo, last great leader of the tribal Duchy of Bavaria.

artificial central kingdom of Lotharingia (present Lorraine) was divided between the western and eastern kingdoms—a division which, for a thousand years, was a fruitful source of conflict between the successor states of Germany and France.

The Empire begins to crumble

The factious rivalries of the Carolingians themselves were compounded by the growing power of the local princes, some of whom had received their lands as the feudal tenants of the royal houses, others of whom claimed the rights of the old pre-Carolingian duchies of Bavaria, Aquitaine and Burgundy, while still others had achieved power as the descendants of the appointed officials of Charlemagne.

The Carolingian Empire in the East came to an end with the reign of Louis the Child, who was succeeded as German king in 911 by Conrad, Duke of Franconia. The chronic divisions of his reign were made worse by the continuing depredations of the Magyars. Throughout the ninth century

Europe suffered constant incursions.

In the year 911 the strength of the Norse invaders was formally acknowledged by the Carolingian king, Charles III, known as Charles the Simple. He granted to their leader, Rollo, territories in the north that were to become the duchy of Normandy. The Carolingians in France had been hampered by the opposition of the mighty nobles; since the late ninth century, the chief contender had been the family of Robert the Strong, whose son Eudes was for a time king. Eudes' son, Hugh the Great, died in 956, virtual ruler of France. The final demise of the Carolingians came thirty years later, when Hugh the Great's son, Hugh Capet, was elected king.

A pattern of allegiance was imposed on the political divisions that emerged during the tenth century, whereby all but a very few of Europe's *de facto* rulers acknowledged their theoretical subordination to some other lord. For, during the ninth century, the socio-political structure of medieval Europe, known to later historians as the feudal system, had taken shape. The term is misleadingly precise since feudal Europe was a patchwork of conflicting allegiances, but generalizations can be made. First, power rested in the possession of land; second, the underlying assumption, whatever the practice, was that power and obligation were inseparable. The lord held his land from the king on the condition that he supply a specified number of armed soldiers to the royal army when called upon. Yet even the king himself—who was also entitled to certain monetary "aids"—was obligated in his turn to be a good lord to his great tenants, and this

contained the seeds of the pretexts for rebellion that were often advanced. In their turn, the great lords might "infeudate" lesser men with lands, subject to similar obligations; while at the lowest level, the peasants either voluntarily or through force of circumstances surrendered their holdings to a great lord in return for his protection both against the central authority and against raiders.

Feudalism was intimately bound up with a system of agriculture, loosely termed the manorial system, in which the land of a village was divided into two or three large open fields, cultivated in common by the villagers, for whom the cost of the increasingly common heavy plough and its valuable ox team was too great for a single family to support. Under this system each peasant household was allotted strips within the common fields and was in return required to do specified days of work on the lord's holding.

Thus by the tenth century, despite near political anarchy, Europe had evolved the base of a political, social and agricultural system that was to provide the framework of history for generations to come.

England before Alfred

Before the reign of Alfred the Great, England was a country of one religion but divided political loyalties.

The central kingdom of Mercia was ruled by the pagan king Penda, whose reign opened in 633 with the defeat of the Christian Edwin of Northumbria. Christianity was restored in the northern kingdom under the aegis of the king, St. Oswald, and the priest St. Aidan, but in 651 Penda again overthrew

Peasant ploughing, from the eighth-century "Utrecht Psalter".

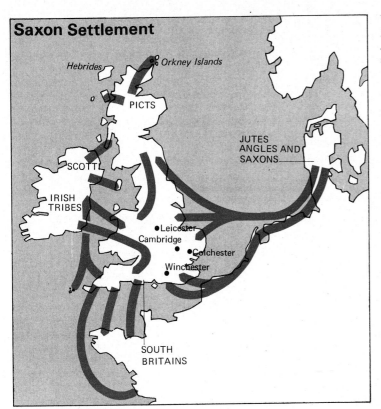

Saxon Settlement

Hebrides
Orkney Islands
PICTS
SCOTT
IRISH TRIBES
JUTES ANGLES AND SAXONS
Leicester
Cambridge
Colchester
Winchester
SOUTH BRITAINS

Venerable Bede. Bede's great work, *An Ecclesiastical History of the English Nation*, can reasonably be considered the only true historical writing in the Middle Ages.

Almost contemporary with this brilliant northern culture, which far outshone anything in Europe and which, through Alcuin of York, was to contribute substantially to the revival of European civilization, the Church in the south of England made major contributions in the field of Church government. After the decision of Whitby, Rome sent a Greek monk, Theodore of Tarsus, to establish the basic structure of the ecclesiastical hierarchy of this new province of the Roman Church. By the time of his death in the early 690s Theodore had succeeded. Although political pressures in the next century were to cause modifications to his scheme, it retained its basic essentials.

Perhaps the most dramatic break in this pattern was the brief period which Lichfield enjoyed as an archiepiscopal see, to satisfy the demands of the powerful King Offa of Mercia. The defeat of Penda had by no means ended the might of the central kingdom. During the eighth century it dominated the political stage under its two great kings, Ethelbald and Offa, whose reigns spanned the eighty years from 715 to 796. Indeed, second only to Charlemagne, Offa was the greatest ruler in eighth-century Europe. He ruled by oppression, yet his code of laws was admired by Alfred; his gold coinage, modeled on that of the Caliphate of Damascus, was the first to be struck by an English king; and his European standing was confirmed by the commercial treaty he signed with Charlemagne.

Viking raids

Nevertheless it was with Wessex that the future was to lie. Under Egbert, who died in 839, the overlordship of Mercia was eventually challenged; the kings of Kent and Essex, for instance, acknowledged the overlordship of Wessex. Yet the kingdom exerted little effective influence to the north, and only bought the acquiescence of its own powerful vassals by extensive concessions to their ambitions. It was, in effect, the Viking raids that brought Wessex to the fore. Only under these attacks, predominantly from the north and east, did the West Country achieve any strategic

significance. And only through the historical chance that produced in Wessex the greatest of all the Anglo-Saxon rulers did that strategic position yield its greatest fruit.

The first raiders on the coast of Wessex landed near Portland in the year 800; taken by the port reeve to be traders, they were told to report to the nearest royal manor; instead, they killed the port reeve and his men. Such attacks soon became commonplace. In 835 a party of Danes landed at Sheppey; a year later Egbert of Wessex was defeated by an army of thirty-five shiploads of Danes. Two years later he defeated the Danes and their Cornish allies at Hingston Down.

Thirty years later the character of the attacks had changed. Instead of merely raiding, the Danes now intended to settle in England. In 865 a great host, led by Ivar the Boneless and Halfdan, sons of the great Viking Ragnar Lothbrok, appeared in East Anglia. In 867 they took York, and using it as their base, terrorized Northumbria

Coins of Offa of Mercia and the Viking invader, Halfdan.

and Mercia for two years. They then moved south, and in 870 established themselves at Reading. In that same year they suffered a great defeat at the battle of Ashdown at the hands of King Aethelred of Wessex and his twenty-year-old brother; but the Danes had recovered their position within a matter of months. Then, in mid-April, the young King Aethelred died. Even as the funeral was being celebrated, news came of another Wessex defeat. The new King Alfred began a reign that was to change the destiny of his nation.

his northern rival. Yet three years later the pagan king himself was overthrown and Christianity was finally established in Northumbria by King Oswy, brother of Oswald.

Northumbria's brittle political achievement was quite overshadowed by the cultural achievements of her churchmen. The aristocratic cleric, Benedict Biscop, made six visits to Rome, and by his foundations of the Benedictine houses at Wearmouth and Jarrow, provided the centers for the brilliant culture that was to follow. St.

Willibrord from Ripon (d. 739) was to be the first of a long line of English missionaries who worked for the conversion of the pagan lands to the east of the kingdom of the Franks. Willibrord's work was magnificently continued by a man from the southwest of England, St. Boniface, who was the first Archbishop of Mainz and was martyred by the pagan Frisians in 754. But the real flowering of Northumbrian Christianity was the work of the scholars and artists who stayed at home, the anonymous artists of the Lindisfarne Gospels and the Book of Kells, and above all the

Part of a Northumbrian manuscript, written for Ceolfrid, early eighth-century bishop of Wearmouth and Jarrow.

Evangelist symbol from the Echternach Gospels, a masterpiece of eighth-century Northumbrian art.

England for the English

Earlier invaders of the British Isles had been assimilated, but the thin veneer of English civilization in the Dark Ages could not withstand the impact of Danish attacks at the end of the eighth century. The fragmented English kingdoms could not seem to unite against this new terror. Then a savior appeared—in the guise of the young prince of Wessex, Alfred. In the first few years after he came to the throne, Alfred fought many battles against the Danes—and lost most of them. Then the tide turned; in 886 Alfred took London. He had won a capital and he had also created a nation. More than just a soldier, Alfred was a scholar determined to foster learning among his people. He translated classical works into the vernacular and issued a new legal code based on the Golden Rule. For this combination of talents, Alfred—alone among English kings—has been awarded the title "The Great."

The Alfred Jewel made of rock crystal over *cloisonné* enamel, set in gold, is inscribed with the words *Aelfred mec heht Gewyrcan* (Alfred ordered me to be made). The base is in the shape of a boar's head with hollow snout. Found near Athelney, the supposed site of Alfred's fort, the jewel is commonly thought to have belonged to that King.

When King Alfred of Wessex captured London in 886, he did more than strike a heavy blow at the Danish invaders. In effect, he became the first King of England and established a new idea of nationhood. His action gave heart to Englishmen all over the land, made them feel that the Danes after all could be defeated, and kindled in them the sentiment of being English, of being members of a nation. Viewing Alfred as their sole overlord, they broke through the lesser loyalties to region and local leader. When Alfred died, he was King of all Englishmen free to give him their allegiance.

In the autumn of 865, a great host of Danes appeared in East Anglia, with many who claimed to be "god-descended" nobles among its ranks. Its leaders were Ivar the Boneless and Halfdan, sons of the great Viking Ragnar Lothbrok. Each autumn the host moved its headquarters; it seized a strong position, fortified it, then ravaged the countryside till the people there bought peace.

The Danes spent a year collecting the horses of East Anglia and forcing the folk to buy peace; then in 866 they moved as a mounted force on York, which they took on All Souls' Day and held unchallenged for four months. Northumbria was at this time embroiled in civil war and it was some time before the rival kings would cooperate. But on March 21, 867, they took the Danes by surprise and broke into York. Quickly driven out again, the two kings, with eight ealdormen, were killed. The Northumbrians bought peace, and the Danes wintered in Mercia, at Nottingham.

Inevitably, the Mercian king made haste to find allies. He was married to a Wessex princess and thus able to call on her kinsmen. He was fortunate; aid came from the King of Wessex, Aethelred, who with his youngest brother came at the head of an army. The Danes avoided battle and the Mercians were able to buy peace.

King Aethelred's young brother, Alfred, was twenty years old in 867. That same year he married Ealhswith, the daughter of a Mercian ealdorman. At the wedding feast he was stricken with illness, and while he recovered from the attack, the same illness was to attack him intermittently for the rest of his life. (It was probably epilepsy, though this has never been verified.)

He rarely enjoyed peace of any kind; he was only married two years when a Danish army invaded his brother's kingdom and made camp at Reading. Aethelred and Alfred summoned their forces and marched on the camp, but their first attack was beaten back.

The host moved on to the great ridge of chalk (then called Ashdown) that runs east to west across Berkshire. The two brothers reformed their forces and followed. The Danes offered battle high up on the ridge in two divisions, one under their kings, the other under the earls. The English army was also ranged in two sections—Aethelred opposing the Danish kings; Alfred, the earls. The Danes fled back to Reading.

A fortnight after this initial success the two brothers, attacking from the marshy meadows of the Loddon, were beaten off by the Danes who fought on firm land. Two months later at Meratun (perhaps Marten, near Marlborough), another hard-fought battle ended with the Danes recovering their ground. Then in mid-April Aethelred died. Alfred was recognized as his successor without opposition.

His start as a king was unlucky. While he was at his brother's funeral at Wimborne, a Wessex force was scattered at Reading; then, a month later, he himself was defeated at Wilton. After a year's exhausting war, he had to buy peace. Ivar the Boneless seems to have disappeared from history at this point and Halfdan was left to command the Danes. In autumn 873 he led his men from Wessex, which had now had four years' peace, to winter in London.

A revolt of the Northumbrian English seems to have drawn them north in 872–73. However, they

Left The Fuller Brooch, a ninth-century Anglo-Saxon silver ornament with symbols of the five senses.

Below A coin minted during Alfred's reign. Alfred's court was an administrative center such as England had not known since the collapse of the Roman Empire.

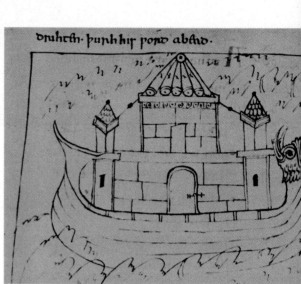

druhtin punh hir pord abond.

wintered at Torksey in Lindsey, then moved to Repton in the heart of Mercia. Burhred, the Mercian king, was defeated; and he left England for Rome, leaving his kingdom at the Danes' mercy. They put a puppet king in Burhred's place, and then divided into two sections which never again united. Halfdan took one group of Danes north to the Tyne and for a year raided the Britons and Picts of Strathclyde. England, long devastated, was losing its value for loot or exactions, and the Danes began to consider permanent settlement. In 876 Halfdan carried out the first of three great partitions which gave over more than a third of eastern England to the Danes; in general, the occupied area was that now covered by the county of York—not till the tenth century was there any large Danish immigration north of the Tees or west of the Pennines. Halfdan left England at this time and was killed in 877, fighting in north Ireland.

Meanwhile, the second section of Danes, under three kings, had gone to Cambridge. They were considering a fresh attack on Wessex. An English force in the fens was keeping watch; but in autumn 875 the Danes slipped away on a dark night and spread across the country. The area around Wareham was laid waste. Alfred had a smaller body of Danes to meet this time; and though he was again obliged to buy peace, he was given hostages. The Danes swore to leave Wessex "on their holy armlet," a more solemn oath than they had so far deigned to swear to Englishmen. They had been a year at Wareham when, despite their oath, they moved off on a night march to Exeter. A storm off Swanage broke a reinforcing fleet; and in summer, they departed for Gloucester, the center of rich lands in Mercia. By the year's end they had cut Mercia in two; one half was held by a puppet-king, the other divided among the army. The area they took included the medieval shires of Nottingham, Derby and Leicester.

But settlement was a long way off—not all the Danish soldiers wanted to become farmers. Early in 878 a group moved south to Chippenham in Wessex, where Alfred often went to hunt. They were led by Guthrum, apparently the last survivor of the three Danish kings. Never before had a Danish army moved during winter, and their unexpected irruption forced much of Wessex to submit. Some West Saxons even went overseas, while Alfred retreated into the rough regions west of Selwood. East Mercia and Northumbria were lost; East Anglia, helpless. Luckily a Danish fleet from Dyfed foundered off Dorset, and Wessexmen won a minor victory at Countisbury Hill. But at Easter, his kingdom overrun and his army decimated, Alfred withdrew to the Isle of Athelney in the Somerset marshes, a thick alder forest with sparse clearings. The Danes held everything now—except the king's person. It seemed that soon Wessex too would be partitioned.

It was a critical time, and one that has passed into the legends of English history. It is only too believable that Alfred would have had the wit and the courage to visit the Danish camp as a bard, and listen to his enemy discussing the plans for attack. And Alfred *could* have done it—he loved music all his life and in that age it would have been essential for such a man to be able to play and sing himself. The famous episode in the peasant's hut probably took place at this period too, assuming that it actually happened. He was probably on the way back to his forest retreat after spying on his foes when, tired and hungry, he sought shelter and a morsel to eat at a humble dwelling. The good housewife, believing him to be an unknown wayfarer, set the bread to bake and promised him food and shelter, and asked him to watch the bread and see that it did not burn. Alfred, worn out with his exertions and preoccupied with the cares of his lost kingdom, of course forgot the bread. He sat there quietly while the poor woman, her batch of bread ruined, unknowingly scolded her king as a useless, idle fellow.

Alfred's courage and tactical skill saved the situation. He went on tackling Danish raiding-parties, and after seven weeks grew strong enough to think about the army itself. Leading the men of Somerset, Wiltshire and Hampshire (west of Southampton

Alfred captures London

Water), he met the enemy at Edington and won a decisive victory.

For a fortnight the Danes resisted in Chippenham, then agreed to have their king baptized and leave Wessex. In the summer of 878, their still powerful host retired to Cirencester in Mercia for a year, then went back to make a final partition of East Anglia.

Wessex alone of the English kingdoms survived the Danish onslaught intact. In what had been Mercia, Northumbria and East Anglia, three large hosts of Danes had settled on the land. The next seventy years were to be taken up with the struggle to reimpose English rule (in the name of the West Saxons) on the lost areas; but nothing could wipe out the social effects of the settlements, all over the larger part of England, that came to be called the Danelaw.

In the autumn of 878, however, a new Danish host entered the Thames and wintered at Gulham. But Alfred had changed the whole situation. In November, 879, the Danes departed for the Low Countries. Guthrum no doubt had no wish to challenge Alfred again. The English were watchful; and when, in late 884, a part of the new host landed in Kent, Alfred drove them away. The Danes tried two more raids, aided by the Danes of East Anglia; and Alfred decided to teach the latter a lesson by sending a fleet into their waters. He managed to capture sixteen Viking ships off the mouth of the Stour, but before he could depart his fleet was beaten by a large Danish force.

It was at this time that Alfred took London, and while the details are scarce, it was an event of the first importance; it was after this victory that he assumed the supreme title. He showed that he meant to respect the traditions of each area coming under his overlordship; since London had been Mercian for some 150 years, he handed it over to Aethelred, ruler of English Mercia, who was henceforth his faithful ally and henchman. The settlement of the 886 war is preserved in a treaty between Alfred and all the counselors of the English people, and all the folk of East Anglia under Guthrum, the Danish king.

The treaty, as between two equal powers, laid down boundary lines. Alfred claimed no supremacy over Guthrum's area, but doubtless felt that the treaty gave him the chance of securing the interests of the English there. His power reached as far as the Humber River in the north.

Peace was not to be had for long. In 892 a great host, defeated in the Low Countries, assembled at Boulogne to invade England. The Danes of East Anglia aided the newcomers, and a protracted war resulted. Alfred realized that he must build a strong navy as well as reconstruct the land-defenses. The shire-levies were no longer adequate, so, by allowing half the peasants to stay at home while the other half campaigned, he was able to assemble a good army which could be held together much longer than before. He also saw to his defenses, and provided refuges for his menaced people; by the early tenth century every village in Sussex, Surrey and Wessex

east of the River Tamar was within twenty miles of a fortress. Thus a coherent system of national defense was built up. Though it was completed under Edward, his son, the scheme was Alfred's and he began its implementation. As for the navy, he ordered the making of warships that were swifter, steadier, and nearly twice as long as those of the Danes; he gave careful consideration to their design and they were constructed to his specifications.

His aim was to prevent the two companies in which the invaders sailed from joining forces; he took up a position between their camps at Appledore and Milton, near Sheppey. First he forced the smaller body at Milton to sign a treaty and leave for Essex; then in late spring 893, the militia under his son Edward met the larger force on land at Farnham and defeated them. The Danes took refuge on an island in the Thames. Meanwhile, Alfred,

The church at Bradford-on-Avon is one of the finest remaining examples of Anglo-Saxon architecture. The chancel is the narrowest in England, and the walls 2 ft. 6 in. thick. It is probably a seventh-century foundation with tenth-century additions.

Alfred dies—but the foundations are laid

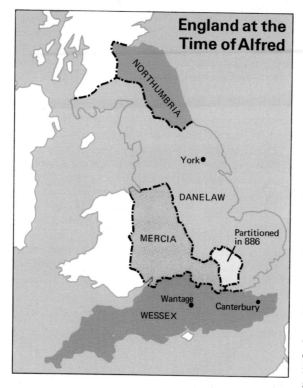

England at the Time of Alfred

NORTHUMBRIA
York●
DANELAW
MERCIA
Partitioned in 886
Wantage●
WESSEX
Canterbury●

moving from the west, was held up by the news that a host from Northumbria and East Anglia was attacking Exeter. But Edward, reinforced from London, managed to hold the Danes on the island till they agreed to retire and join their allies in the east. It gave Alfred a respite, but a dangerously large number of Danes was thus concentrated in Essex.

The struggle that now ensued was the most exacting that Alfred, in a lifetime of war, was ever to face. His resources could not last forever, so he was forced to fall back on a desperate expedient. The Danes, a united host, seized the deserted Roman town of Chester, intending to use it as a base against English Mercia. But they found nothing to sustain

them; Alfred had burned the corn and slaughtered the cattle. They had to withdraw from the scorched earth and turned to Wales, where they stayed until the summer of 894. Then they made their way eastward across England to Mersea, where they established a post some twenty miles north of London. Alfred, not daring to take the smallest rest from the apparently endless fight, managed to dislodge them in the summer of 895—and achieved a resounding success. For the first time, the Danes seemed daunted by the courage and resolution of the English King. They sent their women home, and themselves made a forced march across the country to the Severn. Many of them left England; some made their way back to Danish East Anglia. Alfred could at least feel that a united and peaceful England was a real possibility.

This account of Danish movements is needed to bring out how shifting and varied a threat Alfred had to counter, and the flexible strength he showed in meeting the many threats. A navy had been inaugurated as a matter of settled policy. When he died on October 26, 899, the English were still on the defensive; but a solid basis had been built for checking the Danes and for ultimately unifying the Danish and English areas in a single kingdom.

His greatness appeared as much in his educational as in his military and administrative work. No other king of the Dark Ages had such a desire to master the available culture and hand it on to his people. A personal urgency drove him to explore the problems of fate and free will, to find out how a man came to knowledge and how the universe was ordered. His own long struggles, with their many setbacks and problems, aroused in him a need to grasp the thought of the past so that he could use it in shaping the future; he was stirred with a true reverence for human achievement. By initiating a series of translations from the Latin, he founded English prose literature. In the preface to the first of his own translations he described how low learning had fallen;

"The Mump," the hill on the Isle of Athelney in Somerset where Alfred is thought to have built his fort in 878, at the most critical point in his lifelong wars against the Danes. Also associated with this site is the story of the burned cakes.

230

Alfred expanded many passages, drawing on his own experience and on that of travelers from whom he got information on the peoples of northern and central Europe; as a work of systematic geography the book is remarkable for its time. He then moved from the factual sphere to deeper matters, translating Boethius' *On the Consolation of Philosophy*, the work of a sixth-century statesman awaiting death after an abrupt turn of fortune. He was sympathetic to its creed that a man should rise above fate, convinced that Boethius gave a Christian value to Stoic ideas. Finally, he rendered the first book of Augustine's *Soliloquies* into English.

He thus did more than provide a primary basis for a system of secular knowledge and an outlook on life which, as expressed by Boethius, he felt did much to harmonize ancient thought with northern heroic tradition. He also carried out the difficult task of creating the instrument of English prose. Slowly, the language matured and became capable of expressing a wide range of thought. Moreover, near his reign's end, he issued a legal code into which he introduced the Golden Rule from *St. Matthew*. Though primarily transitional, his code included arrestingly new features for that age: provisions protecting the weaker members of society against oppression, limiting the blood feud, and stressing the bond of man and lord. It strongly aided the transformation of the tribal type of noble into the feudal type. The next two centuries were to see, all over Western Europe, the growth of conditions in which men sought lords and lords sought men: and Alfred's code facilitated this trend in the specific English form in which the national king played a key part. In the code, indeed, we see the unique qualities that marked the national monarchy which Alfred did so much to create. The code appeared at the end of a century in which no other English king had issued laws and the other kings of Western Europe were ceasing to exercise the legislative powers traditionally theirs.   JACK LINDSAY

very few of the clergy south of the Humber knew what their service meant in English or could turn a letter from English into Latin. By 894, when he wrote, there were once more learned bishops and a group of literate clerics, with whom he worked at a considered scheme of education for his people.

His biographer Asser, who had come from St. David's, tells how Alfred's curiosity had been awakened by two visits to Rome before he was seven, and how he set out to learn Latin between 887 and 893. Alfred's own translations began with a work by Pope Gregory the Great, *Pastoral Care*, on a bishop's duties; then came Orosius' history of the ancient world and Bede's *Ecclesiastical History*. In the Orosius,

Ivory plaque of tenth-century Anglo-Saxon workmanship, carved with a crucifixion scene.

The Frank's Casket, a carved whalebone box of Northumbrian Anglo-Saxon origin, *c.* 700. Illustrated here is the lid, which shows a Germanic hero, possibly Wayland's brother Egil, fighting off attackers.

England in the tenth century

As a soldier, Alfred, rightly called the Great, saved his nation; as a legislator, he established the concept of a nationwide law for all the English; as a patron, he not only launched an educational revival but himself translated Boethius' *On the Consolation of Philosophy* and sponsored the Anglo-Saxon *Chronicle*, a major historical source for another two centuries. Although he had consolidated the existence of an English nation, Alfred had been able only to contain the threat of the Danes. Vast territories in the north and east of England remained independent of the kings of Wessex and their client-kingdom of English Mercia.

Alfred's son, Edward the Elder, reigned conjointly with his sister Aethelflaed, the Lady of Mercia. At her death the kingdom was united. During this period the English, basing their defense on the series of fortified towns begun by Alfred, made headway against the incursions of the Scandinavian kingdoms that surrounded them. Even in the midst of a struggle for survival, Alfred had planned for the future. His fortified boroughs provided not only military bases but the foci of local administration and trade. Edward extended the military fortifications but an aggressive counterattack against England's enemies did not come until the reign of Athelstan (924–39).

Brother-in-law of the Carolingian Charles the Simple of France; of Hugh Capet, the greatest man in the French kingdom; and of the German Emperor Otto I, Athelstan mightily defended his position at home. He inflicted the crushing defeat of Brunanburh on the combined forces of the Scots, Irish, Norse and Welsh—a fight commemorated in one of the great epic poems of Old English. The glitter of the medieval English monarchy was at its most dazzling in the subsequent reign of Edgar; at his coronation in 973, eight client-kings are said to have paid homage.

English literature appears

It was in the tenth century that the potentialities of the Old English language, ancestor to that used by Chaucer and Malory, first became apparent. The triumphant song of Brunanburh is paralleled at the end

St. Dunstan kneeling in prayer.

of the century by the tragic and heroic poem on the defeat of the Earl Byrthnoth by the Danes at the Battle of Maldon in 991. Such verse was in the well-established heroic tradition of *Beowulf*, but in the tenth century, English found its primary power as a means of expression in prose. The Anglo-Saxon *Chronicle* itself was of course written in English, while the Church employed English prose not only in its preaching but also in magnificent homilies, lives of the saints, and translations of parts of the Bible.

Among these lives of the saints was one of St. Dunstan, Abbot of Glastonbury, Archbishop of Canterbury, close confidant of King Edgar and church reformer. It was through Dunstan that the great Continental movement in Church and monastic reform, launched by the founding of the Abbey of Cluny in 910, reached England. During a short stay in Flanders in the middle of the century, Dunstan had seen

King Canute and his wife dedicate a cross to Winchester Cathedral.

Islamic armies on the march, from a manuscript of the Baghdad School.

the work of the reformed Benedictines at first hand, and returned to England in order to transform the unregenerate Church there. But in the last twenty years of the century the renewed impetus of Danish invasions plunged the country once again into a dark night of disruption and despair. After the humiliating reign of Aethelred the Redeless—in which neither king nor people displayed the confidence of their ancestors—Britain was only to be saved by the enlightened rule of the great Danish king Canute early in the eleventh century.

The Arab world

Just as the armies of Islam had profited from the religious discontent of the great empires it conquered, so religion provided the pretext for the overthrow of the first Moslem dynasty. The population of eastern Persia, which had accepted the new faith, nevertheless felt aggrieved and discriminated against. The Persians claimed that they did not enjoy the full exemption from taxation that was their right as believers; more important, they resented the alien rule of the distant regime at Damascus. When the central

government ignored their protests, the local nobility of Khorasan, with the aid of discontented Arab colonists, rose against the Umayyads. Abu al Abbas, a descendant of Mohammed, was leader of this revolt. By 750 Abu al Abbas had founded his own dynasty, the Abbasids, and seen all but one of the Umayyad family perish in a sea of blood. Under the Abbasids, the Persian influence in Islam became increasingly marked; within a generation, the Caliphs had founded a new capital at Baghdad, on the banks of the Tigris, which was to become one of the greatest cities in the world.

It was at this time that the great collection of stories, now known as the *Arabian Nights*, first began to be assembled. Despite the Indian origin of many of the tales, they are a monument to the glories of the Arabic language and to the golden age of the Abbasid caliphate under the great Harun al Rashid or Aaron the Upright (d. 809) and his son Al Ma'mum (d. 833). During their reigns, the process of Persianization reached its highwater mark. In addition, under the impulse of Syrian Christian scholars, the Arabs began to discover the treasures of classical Greek philosophy and science, with incalculable consequences for the future of civilization.

Greek influence

Al Ma'mun founded a school at Baghdad for the translation of the classics of Greek philosophy and science. The impact was tremendous; not only was Arab scientific thought advanced, but the tool of Aristotelian dialectic was applied to all fields of thought, including theology. Some scholars aimed to reconcile Greek with Islamic thought, but a rival school opposed such liberalizing tendencies—a similar controversy was to arise in twelfth-century Europe. Greek theory also influenced music, and the scale used in Arab music shows remarkable similarities to that postulated in ancient Greek treatises. But here an equally important influence was that of Persia. Traditionalists opposed the seductions of the "romantic" Persian style on the gounds that it would corrupt the solemn and serene music prescribed by Mohammed; but despite opposition from famous musicians, the Persian style gained ground. Its music became one of the chief glories of Islamic civilization and the esteem in which it was held was reflected in the fame of the great musicians, which sometimes rivaled that of their princes.

The profound impact of the Arab conquests, from the frontiers of China's T'ang empire to Spain, is reflected in the spread of the religion of Islam today. During the Middle Ages the whole of this vast area was linked by a common religion, a common language, and common coinage. It was traversed by heavily frequented trade and pilgrim routes. Like the world of Christendom, it had many vital shared interests and beliefs. The political divisions that soon arose, while provoking more than their share of wars, did not seriously impede the flow of a common culture.

After the establishment of the Umayyad caliphates of Spain in 756, the unity of Islam was further broken. The Aghlabid emirs on the North African coast were plundering the Christian shipping of the western Mediterranean and sending raiding parties far up the rivers of mainland Europe. Farther west, in modern Morocco, a rival Shiite caliphate had arisen. And for the last half of the ninth century the emirs of Egypt, too, asserted their independence. The break-up of the vast Arab Empire was hastened by the fact that the Caliphs at Baghdad, unable to raise an army from the now settled populations of their flourishing empire, had to recruit Turkish mercenaries. After an attempt to weaken the influence of this Praetorian guard by establishing a new capital at Sammarra, the Caliphs were forced to return to Baghdad. As the tenth century progressed, their effective influence progressively waned. In Persia a new national dynasty, the Samanids, revived Persian culture; in Egypt the Fatimid caliphate founded a brilliant independent civilization which survived until the twelfth century; and in Spain the court of Cordova was legendary in Christendom as well as in Islam.

Spain—the legacy of the Visigoths

By the eighth century, the Spanish Visigoths had guaranteed the triumph of Catholicism over Arianism, given the Spanish monarchy a characteristic and continuing controlling interest in ecclesiastical affairs, and presided over the birth of a highly individual and brilliant culture. Spanish culture was eclectic in its inspiration, drawing on barbarian and classical motifs, on the art of Byzantium and, in the field of scholarship, on the tradition of the long-established, though persecuted, Jewish community. The very liturgy of the Church was a unique blend of Roman, Arian and Byzantine Eastern element.

Group of saints from a Spanish Apocalypse of the tenth century.

Brick minaret, c. 850, from the mosque at Sammarra, the largest in the world.

Archbishop Isidore of Seville, of mixed Spanish and Byzantine ancestry, was one of the most remarkable figures in the Europe of the Dark Ages. His writings continued to exert an immense influence through the Middle Ages. In jewelry, sculpture, book illumination and architecture, Visigothic Spain displayed a considerable and refined creative talent. One of the most interesting surviving monuments is the church of S. Juan de Banos, dedicated by the first Catholic king, Recceswinth.

The Visigoths left a lasting imprint on Christian Spain. The much-reduced kingdoms of Asturias and Galicia, on the northern coast, felt themselves the heirs of the Visigothic tradition. And the long-delayed counterattack of the Christian kingdoms, conducted by the Visigoths' successors, Castile, Leon, Navarre and Aragon, was thought of by the Spaniards as the Reconquest.

Moslem rule in Spain began with the landing of a predominantly Berber army under the leadership of the Arab Tarik at Gibraltar in 711. The new rulers recognized the Caliph at Damascus; but in 756 the sole survivor of the Umayyad family, expelled from Damascus by the Abbasids, established himself at Cordova. His family, of whom the greatest ruler was Abd al-Rahman III (912–61), the man who brought Islamic civilization in the peninsula to its highest peak, ruled for another 250 years.

The Caliph of Cordova's Library

It was Europe's most glittering capital: a place where Moslems, Christians and Jews lived, worked, studied and thought. Tenth-century Cordova was as preoccupied with philosophy, poetry and medicine as Paris was to become in the eighteenth century. Spain's intellectual ferment was a product of the recently established Islamic society, but it was also concerned with the old, with preserving the ancient learning of Greece and Rome. Toward the end of the century, the Caliph Al-Hakam II gathered a library of 400,000 books and manuscripts—indisputably Europe's finest collection of writings on history, science and literature. The library was largely destroyed by a fanatical successor, and Cordova's days of greatness drew to an end.

Cordova, under its great caliphs of the tenth century, was the most splendid city of Western Europe. Ash-Shaquandī, the poet who sang the praises of his native al-Andalus (Andalusia) says that he rode for ten miles on end through its well-lit streets. A fine bridge spanned the river, which still bears its Moorish name of Guadalquivir, and on either side stretched the quarters of the dominant Moslem population—Arabs and Berbers from Africa, as well as descendants of Spain's indigenous inhabitants who had embraced Islam, and communities of Jews, Christians (*Mozárabes*) and slaves from Eastern Europe. One traveler counted 300 public baths; another, 600—a number perhaps not excessive for a population of over half a million, though it scandalized medieval Christians.

Cordova's other marvelous sights included innumerable workshops for the production of its famous leatherwork, carpets, ivory caskets and other handicrafts; more than four thousand markets; and many hundreds of mosques in addition to the Great Mosque. Although later converted into a Catholic cathedral, this remains one of the supreme glories of Moslem Spain. There were also the gracious residences of the rich, set amidst lovingly cultivated gardens; and the superb palaces of al-Madīna—az-Zāhira and Medinat az-Zahrā, the latter a great administrative and ceremonial headquarters for the Caliphate as well as a palace of unparalleled magnificence. In view of its subsequent history, however, the Caliph's library built up in the tenth century is of paramount importance.

Cordova was more than the seat of a powerful and prosperous empire. It was also, in the words of ash-Shaquandī, "the center of learning, the beacon of religion, the abode of nobility and leadership; its inhabitants had deep respect for the Law and set themselves the task of mastering this science, and kings humbled themselves before the doctors,

exalting their calling and acting in accordance with their opinions." During his long reign, first as Emir and then as Caliph, Abd-al-Rahmān III (912–61) raised Cordova to its eminence. A great soldier and administrator, he was also a tireless builder and a munificent patron of learning and the arts.

His son Al-Hakam II was still more ardent in collecting manuscripts and attracting scholars to his court. His library was reputed to contain some 400,000 books and manuscripts—an incredible treasure, when one realizes that a few hundred volumes would then suffice to win fame for a Christian monastery as a great center of learning. Al-Hakam's patronage set the example for the nobles and merchants of Cordova, who vied with one another in building collections of their own. There was soon a flourishing book market, where rare and beautifully bound works fetched high prices. One Moslem bibliophile has left an amusing account of his pique on bidding in vain for a choice volume; the book was bought by a rich merchant who wanted it simply as an ornament to fill a gap on his shelves. A host of scribes labored to satisfy the literary appetite of the Cordovans, and are said to have produced between them some 70,000 copies of manuscripts every year.

So great was the power and prestige of Cordova that the rulers of the Christian kingdoms of northern Spain would humbly present themselves at the Caliph's court to solicit help in settling their political or personal problems. Sancho the Fat journeyed there to seek aid both in regaining his kingdom and curing his obesity. Both his petitions were crowned with success, the latter under the care of the Caliph's Jewish physician. Scholars from beyond the frontiers of Spain would come to imbibe knowledge from the learned men of Islam.

There were those among the Moslems, as well as among the Christians, who looked with suspicion

One of the main halls, possibly the throne room, in the Medina Azzahra, a pleasure palace decorated in typically complex and sumptuous style.

Opposite The door in the western façade of the mosque at Cordova, showing the detailed decoration in tile and bas-relief typical of the highpoint of artistic achievement under the Caliphate.

The Caliphate breaks up

upon this passion for learning because it threatened to contaminate the purity of their revealed religion. After the death of al-Hakam in 975, power passed into the hands of a ruler of a very different stamp—Ibn Abī Āmir, known to his people as al-Mansūr, the Victorious, and to the Christians as the dreaded Almanzor. Starting as a chamberlain to al-Hakam's infant son, he rose to become the all-powerful minister and commander-in-chief of a puppet Caliph. Fanatically orthodox in his piety, he led his armies deep into Christian territory, sacking cities as far afield as Barcelona, Leon, and Santiago, yet finding time on his campaigns to transcribe a copy of the Koran with his own hand. As a usurper, he courted the support of the influential *faqihs* (religious mendicants) of the strict Malikite school, and it was to win the favor of those intolerant fanatics that he ordered a purge of al-Hakam's great library. The works of poetry, history and science lovingly collected by the Caliph were thrown out and destroyed; Ibn-Saʿīd of Toledo tells us that "some were burned and others cast into the palace wells and covered over with earth and stones." After the tyrant's death in 1002, there was further destruction. The great military and political machine of the Caliphate began to break up as Almanzor's sons and successors battled for power. Within seven years, Cordova was overrun by an army of Berbers and Castilians and its palaces sacked. The remaining treasures of al-Hakam's library and the many private collections were destroyed or dispersed.

But the eclipse of Cordova did not mean the end of Moslem civilization in Spain. Though fragmented into a mosaic of tiny principalities, each with its own "king," army, and court, the Moors attained a brittle but dazzling brilliance.

Of the many other scholars born in al-Andalus, or attracted to the cultured courts of its princes, three

A Mozarabic patio, now the entrance to the convent of St. Clare Tordesillas. During the Caliphate's unique blend of religious beliefs and decorative styles, the Christians developed a style known as Mozarabic, chiefly characterized by the horseshoe arch, which was widely adopted by the Moors.

A chamber in the mosque at Cordova enclosed within foiled arches, reminiscent of the Mozarabic style, whose tilework carries Arabic inscriptions.

deserve special mention. All were admirers of Aristotle and sought to reconcile the wisdom of the ancients with the truths of Islam. Ibn-Bājja (Avempace) is remembered chiefly as the author of *The Rule of the Solitary*, a critique of the materialism and worldliness of contemporary Moslem society. His ideas were further developed by Ibn-Tufayl, author of a remarkable allegorical novel, which became known to the West through translations into Latin and the vernaculars. Its hero—ancestor of Defoe's Robinson Crusoe, Rousseau's Emile and Kipling's Mowgli—is an infant castaway suckled by a gazelle. The child grows up to attain, through observation and reasoning, not only an understanding of the material world but, through mystical contemplation, an awareness of the Supreme Being. He eventually meets his Man Friday in the form of a Moslem hermit, from whom he realizes that the truths he had discovered by the light of reason were

This early-eleventh-century antiphonary designed for use during Christian worship is decorated with a fine Mozarabic horseshoe arch.

The fourteenth-century synagogue at Cordova carries Hebrew lettering on walls decorated in Moorish style. Under the religious tolerance of the Caliphate, the Jews made a highly significant contribution to the cultural life of the city.

An Arabic inscription in the Cordova mosque dating from the Caliphate.

The earliest part of the great Cordovan Mosque, the twelve naves built by Abd-al-Rahman I; the pillars are of jasper and other fine stones.

one and the same as those taught by revealed religion.

The same theme, the *Harmony of Religion and Philosophy* (to quote the title of a modern translation of one of his works), informs the thought of the greatest of the philosophers of Moslem Spain—Ibn-Rushd. Known to the West as Averroes, he was famous during the Middle Ages for his commentaries on Aristotle. Averroes held both philosophy and religion to be true and strove to reconcile the two in his writings. Because Averroes' works were denounced as impious by the *faqihs*, they found little echo in the rest of the Moslem world. Nevertheless, they came to be eagerly studied, debated, and ultimately condemned in the West as subversive of the Catholic faith, particularly in the great work of St. Thomas Aquinas. Thomas was also influenced by another thinker whose name may be added to those of the Moslem philosophers mentioned above— Maimonides, the Jewish scholar of Cordova who sought to synthesize faith and reason.

In the tenth century, new currents of spirituality from Egypt, Syria and other parts of the Islamic

world brought the first *sufis* (pantheistic mystics) to Spain. "I follow the religion of love," wrote al- Arabī, one of the greatest of them. "Whichever way love's camels take, that is my religion and my faith." The way of the *sufi* sometimes proved remarkably close to that of the great Catholic saints such as St. Teresa.

The first Andalusian *sufi* of whom we hear was Ibn-Masarra, who lived near Cordova under the tolerant reign of the caliphs. His writings have not survived, but he seems to have been influenced by the Greek philosopher Empedocles. He taught doctrines, highly subversive in the eyes of the Maliki jurists, such as free will in place of Koranic pre-destination and the perfectability of the individual through ascetic practices. By the end of the twelfth century, *sufis* were to be found in all parts of Moslem Spain. Al-'Arabī has left us descriptions of 105, more than half of whom lived in al-Andalus, and were at one time or another Ibn-Masarra's spiritual masters. He himself died at Damascus after a lifetime spent in study, asceticism, and strange mystical experiences. Of the 400 or so books that his biographers tell us he

composed, one has left a strong mark on our own Western culture. It furnished precedents for Dante's poetic fiction of a journey through the realms of the afterlife, with its geometrical topography, its glimpses of the bliss of the elect and its beatific vision of the divine splendor.

While the *sufis* were contemplating these mysteries and the Andalusian princelings were indulging their passion for literature, luxurious living and palace intrigue, the warlike Christians from the north were pressing in upon the little Moorish kingdoms. Their tactics were to force an "alliance" on a weaker Moslem prince, extort ever-larger amounts of tribute from him and demand the surrender first of key fortresses and eventually of the throne itself. The princes, no longer possessing the military strength to resist, turned for help to their co-religion-ists beyond the Straits of Gibraltar. It was a desperate choice, for Africa was an inexhaustible reservoir of fanaticism; the tribesmen who answered the call—first the Almoravides and then the Almohades or "Unitarians"—looked upon the sophisticated

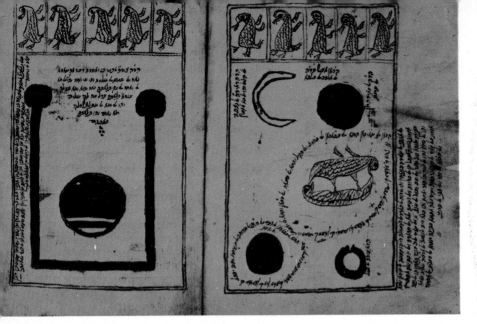

A manuscript in Hebrew on alchemy. Jews, Christians and Moslems collaborated under the Caliphate towards the pursuit of all learning and culture. Alchemy, the basis of modern science, was one of the major preoccupations of these remarkable scholars.

A page from a decorated Arabic treatise on poisons.

Andalusian Moslems as little better than the Christians.

The Christians were repulsed by the Africans and their puppet rulers were ousted, but the invaders themselves came under the civilizing but enervating influence of al-Andalus, until driven out in turn by a fresh wave of fanatics from beyond the Straits. In the process, most of the *Mozárabes*, or Christian minorities, who had been tolerated under the Caliphate but had been increasingly tempted into collusion with the advancing Christians, migrated northwards into Christian territory. So did many Jews, who had likewise lived peacefully with the Moslems but now feared persecution. The population of the expanding Christian kingdoms thus came to include strong elements, both Jewish and Mozarabic,

who were familiar with Moslem ways and impregnated with Islamic culture. This they transmitted to the Catholic communities in which they now lived and to the scholars who came from other parts of Christendom in quest of learning.

The natural center for this work was Toledo, the ancient Visigothic capital situated in the heart of the peninsula and recaptured by the Christians in 1085. Though no Christian kings, until the time of Alfonso the Learned (1221–84), could compare personally with the Moslem princes in intellectual sophistication, they could be tolerant monarchs and enlightened patrons. Alfonso VI, the conqueror of Toledo, prided himself on his title of "Emperor of the Two Religions," while King Ferdinand III, conqueror of Seville and eventually a canonized saint, added a reverence for Judaism and became "King of the Three Religions." At least one church in Toledo seems to have been used interchangeably by Jews, Christians and Moslems for the practice of their respective faiths. One Christian churchman, Archbishop Raymond of Toledo, was an admirer of Arabic learning and the chief promoter of what came to be known as the "School of Translators." This was not an institutionalized body, such as a university or school, but a tradition of practical scholarship in the translation of Arabic texts on all branches of philosophy and science into Latin and later into Spanish. It lasted for more than a century. Toledo was well chosen for such a task. Many of the surviving manuscripts from al-Hakam's great library had found their way there, and a body of scholars competent to translate them resided in the city. The usual method was for the Arabic text to be translated orally into Spanish by a Moslem, Jewish

240

following century, the flow of Greek philosophy and science—the metaphysics and natural science of Aristotle, the medical treatises of Hippocrates and Galen, the works of Ptolemy, Euclid and many other thinkers—enriched by the commentaries and original contributions of the Arabs, began to quicken the intellectual life of a Western Europe that had known them only in scraps or not at all.

The Moors had first been lured to Spain by its wealth and fertility; they stayed on to transmit to the West the riches they had inherited from Greece and the East. After nearly seven centuries they were driven from the peninsula. The Spanish *Reconquista* was a long and complex affair—a tide of Christian conquest ebbing and flowing over the land, but leaving islands where, for considerable periods, Moslems and Christians lived more or less tolerantly together and became influenced by each others' culture. But gradually fanaticism and intolerance were to gain the upper hand until, under the Catholics, Ferdinand and Isabella, at the end of the fifteenth century, religious conformity became the touchstone of national unity.

Granada, the last outpost of Moslem civilization in Spain, was captured in 1492, and there Cardinal Cisneros presided over bonfires of Islamic texts—as Almanzor had once presided over the purge of the Caliph's great library. But long before the spirit of tolerance and cultural interchange vanished in the smoke of the Granada holocaust, the scholars of Spain had fulfilled their mission as the industrious middlemen of culture, and transmitted to medieval Europe the forgotten learning of the ancient world.

STEPHEN CLISSOLD

Above A page of Arabic script from a manuscript on medical studies, a subject of much inquiry at the court of Cordova.

Above left An eleventh-century ivory casket intricately carved in the Spanish-Moorish style.

or Mozarabic scholar, and then to be transcribed into Latin by a Spanish cleric.

The fame of Toledo soon attracted scholars from many parts of Europe. Daniel of Morley tells us that he left Paris in disgust at its obsession with law and the pretentious ignorance of its doctors and made his way to Toledo, where true learning was to be found. The Slav scholar, Hermann of Carinthia, made the same pilgrimage in order to study a manuscript of the *Almagest* by Ptolemy, the second-century astronomer whose theory of the movement of the sun and planets held the field in the Middle Ages until discarded in favor of the Copernican system. Hermann stayed on to study and translate many other works by Greek and Arabic scholars, as did Gerard of Cremona, another student of Ptolemy, who is credited with more than seventy translations on geometry, algebra, optics, astronomy and medicine. English scholars showed themselves particularly active in this field. Notable among them was Adelard of Bath, whose quest for knowledge took him as far afield as Africa and Asia Minor, and whose intellectual curiosity embraced the whole field of human interests from astrology to trigonometry, Platonic philosophy to falconry. Another Englishman, Robert of Chester, collaborated with Hermann of Carinthia and Spanish scholars in translating the Koran, and composed polemical tracts designed to demonstrate the superiority of Christianity to Islam. Michael Scot, who became an astrologer in the Arabicized court of Frederick II of Siciliy, probably acquired his Islamic learning in Toledo. Some Spanish scholars appear to have made the reverse journey to England. Pedro Alonso, a converted Jew from Aragon, played an important part in introducing Arabic astronomy into England and possibly served as physician to King Henry I.

Spain was not the only channel of cultural communication between the Islamic world and Western Europe—Sicily was another intermediary —but it was the most important. Writing in the middle of the twelfth century, John of Salisbury laments the prevailing neglect of mathematics, geometry and logic "except in the land of Spain and the borders of Africa." In the course of that and the

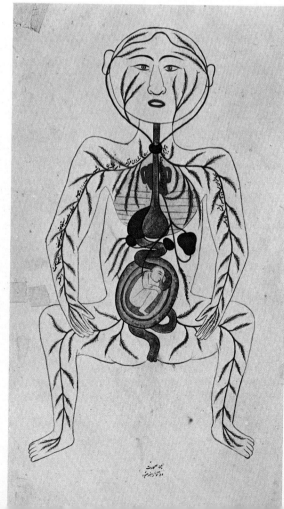

Above An Arabic medicine pot.

Left A diagram from a Persian copy of an eleventh-century Arabic medical text. The physicians of Cordova based their learning upon the discoveries of the ancient Greeks.

After the reign of the great Abd al-Rahmān III, Islamic Spain was increasingly subject to internal division, and the overthrow of the Cordovan Caliphate in 1013 allowed the Christians to capture the great city of Toledo. The Spanish Arabs now called on the newly converted and fanatical North African Berber tribes known as the Almoravides. By the beginning of the twelfth century, these allies, whose empire was based in Morocco, were in control of Islamic Spain. Within seventy years, they in their turn fell to the still more puritanical sect of the Almohades. In 1195 the Almohades inflicted a crushing defeat on the armies of Alfonso VIII of Castile, but this was more than reversed by the great victory of the united kingdoms of Castile, Leon, Navarre and Aragon on the field of Las Novas de Tolosa in 1212.

Islam fails

After that defeat, Islam never recovered its old power in Spain. Under the caliphate of Cordova, both the industry of the Moorish invaders and their religious toleration of the conquered Christians and the formerly persecuted Jews contributed essentially to the great cultural flowering of the period. The *Mozārabes*, Christians who retained their faith on the payment of annual dues, were allowed their own places of worship. And throughout the Islamic period—save for a few years before its recapture—the city of Toledo kept its cathedral, its archbishop and its liturgy. Despite the strict religious principles of the twelfth-century Moroccan rulers and the subsequent flight of numerous *Mozārabes* to the Christian kingdoms of the north, the cultural traditions of earlier ages was strong. It was the works of men like Avempace (*d.* 1138) who drew on the Aristotelian commentaries of the tenth-century Al Farabi of Damascus, and above all his great follower Averroes of Cordova (1126–98) who contributed so essentially to the intellectual ferment of twelfth-century Europe.

Church reform in Europe during the tenth century

The ninth century was a period of fierce rivalry for the control of central authority, of cynical and brutal struggle by lesser potentates for independence from that authority, and of invasions from outside

Europe. Yet gradually, if only by force of custom, lay society was evolving commonly accepted principles of organization and legitimacy that were slowly to gain—during later generations—ever-growing effectiveness.

In terms of power, the ninth century was a secular period. The immense power that the Church was to exercise in European society was a thing of the future, and as the tenth century opened the Church, in all its organs, was at one of its lowest points. Many of Europe's greatest bishoprics were, in effect, the hereditary fiefs of the local great family. If the family did not actually occupy the see, it appointed its own nominees as a matter of course. In other sees, the appointments were made by the king. The bishops themselves shared the ambitions and morals of their turbulent class and were also expected to pay a considerable sum of money to their patrons on entering their office. In feudal terms this was construed as the "relief" that any heir paid his overlord on taking up his inheritance, to clear him of the outstanding obligations of his predecessor and as recognition that he held the fief from a higher power.

Sins of Simony

In ecclesiastical terms such payments amounted to the sin of "simony." The name was derived from the Samaritan sorcerer, Simon Magus, who, according to the account in the *Acts of the Apostles*, attempted to buy spiritual power from Christ's apostles. In practical terms, simony produced a chain reaction: the bishop, who had paid a heavy fee to enter his see, recouped his payment by charging for the rights of ordination to his inferiors, and they in their turn charged the faithful for the very benefits of religion. It is not hard to understand the outrage of ecclesiastical reformers. But to the kings and magnates of early medieval Europe it seemed totally reasonable that bishops, who after all were vast landowners, should accept the same obligations as their lay colleagues.

Not only were the bishops subject to the feudal ceremony for receiving their lands from their lord, but by the ninth century the king was also investing them with the ring and staff, the symbols of their spiritual power. Thus the regular offices of the Church had become almost indistinguishable from the

great secular estates which they often equaled in wealth. The secularization of Church property extended to the lowest levels. The parish church was usually the personal property of the local landowner who disposed of it at will; often the priests—most of whom were married, clerical celibacy being a thing of the future—treated their parishes as hereditary holdings and might well enrich their own families by granting Church lands to laymen in return for payment.

Conditions of Monastic life

Conditions were little better in the monasteries which, springing from the great movement initiated by St. Benedict in the sixth century, were the heirs to a great tradition of piety and retreat from the world. During the course of the centuries, they had grown rich through large endowments which they had received from pious benefactors. In their turn, they became objects of the ambitions of the lay aristocracy. It was not uncommon for the richer monasteries to be controlled by absentee lay abbots who unscrupulously engrossed the revenue of the house to their own uses. In other cases the monks themselves might form themselves into a college of canons, forsaking their monastic vows and the ideals of the life of communal poverty in order to live off the income of the monastery in their own houses complete with wives and families.

When matters had reached this pass, the very nature of the Benedictine Rule contributed to increase rather than mitigate the decline. St. Benedict's Rule had been

merely a rule of conduct not dependent on a central organization. In the past, the autonomy of each monastery in this cell-like structure had been an element of strength, and the monasteries' adherence to the Rule had been ensured by visitations from the local bishop. But in a world where the episcopate was itself in dire need of reform, European monasticism was without a guardian. There are many recorded instances from both the ninth and tenth centuries, and indeed later, of reforming abbots being maltreated and expelled by the inmates of the house they had come to purge.

The respect for the ideals that monasticism had proclaimed was not dead, and pious laymen and ecclesiastics were to be found. But the Church as an organization was desperately in need of leadership from outside to help in putting its own house in order. In the eleventh century, as we shall see, the very papacy itself was to require the strong hand of a pious emperor for its reform.

Monastic reform

In the early years of the tenth century, however, the movement for monastic reform, so important to the Church as a whole, owed its effective beginning to the initiative of a lay ruler. In 910, Duke William I of Aquitaine, called the Pious, founded a monastery at Cluny, in the French province of Burgundy. It is possible that this initiative might have produced few lasting results had it not been for the forceful personality of the second abbot, Odo. During his reign, from 927 to 942, Odo made Cluny the leader of

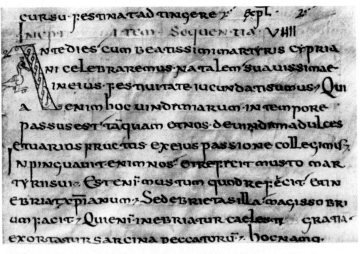

Manuscript from the monastery of Luxeuil, one of the earliest foundations of the Benedictines.

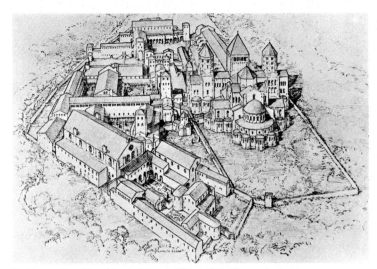
Reconstruction of the abbey buildings at Cluny when this was the greatest church in Christendom.

the movement of reform that was gathering strength everywhere in Europe. However, Duke William had given the new house one priceless advantage, which made Cluny a truly remarkable institution at the time of its foundation. The Duke surrendered, for himself and his heirs, all rights that he had as founder.

Thus from the outset Cluny was freed from the dangerous ties to the lay aristocracy that had brought disaster to so many monasteries in the past. Abbot Odo added to this another great guarantee of independence when he won exemption both for Cluny and her sister houses—both present and future—from episcopal visitation. On these bases, and on that of his own immense reputation, Odo was able to begin a process which, under the autocratic rule of a great line of abbots, was to produce what was in effect a new monastic order. Odo himself was summoned by Hugh the Great, the virtual ruler of France, to reform the house of Fleury on the Loire, and this was to become in its turn a major center of reform.

At the very end of the tenth century began the rule of Abbot Adilo (994–1048). Under him and his successor Hugh (1049–1109), Cluny reached the highwater mark of its influence and wealth. The strength of the reform rested not only on the qualities of these great abbots but, more important still, on the tight organization whereby Cluny itself retained control over all the houses that accepted its reforming agents or were founded under its auspices. Every year the priors of the Cluniac houses, of which there were some two hundred

by the late-eleventh century, met at Cluny under the presidency of the abbot. The effect of this annual convocation was carried through by a well-administered system of visitation, the houses of the order being divided into ten provinces.

Thus within two centuries the prestige of European monasticism, once so low, was immense, and its leaders were men of considerable influence both in the Church and in lay affairs. But it is perhaps not surprising that an organization as

The garden of Paradise; Romanesque sculpture from the abbey of Cluny.

powerful as Cluny began, in its turn, to lose touch with the spirit of the reform. The abbey building of Cluny proclaimed its great wealth; the luxuriant carvings and gold and jeweled church ornaments might be regarded as celebrating the glory of God, but by the critics of Cluny they were looked upon as a betrayal of the monastic vows of poverty. Thus in the early eleventh century Cluny itself was to give birth to a movement devoted to another great reform of European monasticism.

The Saxon kings of Germany

As the body of the Church gained in vigor through the reform of monasticism, the greatest power in medieval Europe, the German empire, was also gathering its strength. Its true founder is generally recognized as being Henry I, known as Henry the Fowler, the Duke of Saxony, who was elected to succeed Conrad I in 919.

During his reign, Henry succeeded in recovering the duchy of Lothairingia, part of the old central kingdom, from its allegiance to France. Then, after having been forced for five years to pay tribute, Henry defeated the Magyars at the

Henry the Fowler, Duke of Saxony.

battle of Riade in 933. In addition, he extended the northern frontiers of Germany at the expense of the pagan Wends in Brandenburg, and he took measures to protect his frontiers with fortified strong points and by introducing reforms into the training of his Saxon army.

Internally he did nothing to hamper the great power of the old duchies, ruling what might almost be described as a federal state. Nevertheless, he secured the recognition of his son, Otto I, as his successor. In 936 Otto I became King of Germany. His position was, however, contested at first by his brother Duke Henry of Bavaria,

Duke Henry of Bavaria, known as the Wrangler.

while Eberhard of Franconia also rose in rebellion. The new king successfully met the challenge and survived another wave of rebellion in the 950s in which his son was involved. In 951 he assumed the title of King of Lombardy, and eleven years later he was to be crowned Emperor.

Otto is often regarded as the true founder of the medieval German Empire. The title had been in abeyance for fifty years when he revived it. Certainly the Ottonian empire was essentially different from its Carolingian predecessor. Geographically, it was virtually coterminous with the kingdom of Germany, though its rulers still retained ambitions in Italy and nourished even more wide-reaching claims.

The monarchy was now in theory elective, and that theory was eventually to have far-reaching consequences. By the second half of the tenth century, the power of the regional German landowners had become so entrenched as to be a permanent danger to the central power. Otto attempted to meet this situation by balancing the power of the lay magnates with that of the great prelates of the Church. Under what has sometimes been called the "Ottonian system," Otto relied increasingly on these ecclesiastical magnates for the chief officers of the administration of the empire. As we shall see in a later chapter, this close involvement of Church and State was to have historic consequences.

At the Lechfeld

On a battlefield littered with corpses and discarded weapons, the victorious Otto I had his cheering troops proclaim him Emperor. Germany had been close to civil war, and rebellious nobles had allied themselves with the barbarian Magyars, who were intent on destroying what passed for civilization in tenth-century Germany. It was Otto's achievement to unite the Germans against both the rebels and the invading Magyars. His new "Roman" Empire differed from the old in its strongly Christian character. Otto was the protector of the Church and constantly encouraged missionary work among the Slavs. His territorial ambitions also lay in the East, but in these he was largely frustrated. Nevertheless, Otto's victory at the Lechfeld in 955 ensured that much of Central Europe would be safeguarded for Latin Christianity. And even the defeated Magyars, who settled in Hungary, became, under their great king St. Stephen, a Christian nation.

Part of the Chalice of St. Udalrich, Bishop of Augsburg, loyal priest and military leader under Otto I, and hero of the battle of Lechfeld against the Magyars.

Opposite Otto II, his Empress Theophano and the future Emperor Otto III pay homage to Christ in Majesty by the traditional Byzantine proskynesis. To the left and right of Christ are St. Maurice and the Virgin.

The battle fought on the Lechfeld outside Augsburg on St. Lawrence's day, August 10, A.D. 955, was highly significant for the whole of Europe. The victory of King Otto I over the Magyars was directly connected with the foundation of his empire—and with the constitution of the German imperial Church as a leading political power—which was to survive till its destruction at Napoleon's hands. The other consequences of Otto's victory were the re-alignment of the eastern frontier of Bavaria with Austria; the foundation of the Hungarian kingdom with the coronation of Stephen as king; and the formation of Germany's eastern policy for the next 1000 years.

On August 8, 955, Udalrich or Ulrich, Bishop of Augsburg, stood at the eastern gate of the town—clad only in his stole and without shield, helmet, coat of mail or sword—while the attack on his beleaguered town was at is fiercest, and exhorted his people to stand firm. When the attack had been fended off, Udalrich spent the night in prayer. While the nuns walked in procession through the city streets praying and chanting, he lay prostrate in devotion on the cathdral floor, beseeching the Virgin Mary to protect his people and liberate the city. On the following morning, he celebrated communion with his people; the Magyars withdrew from the city as Berthold, the son of Arnul, the Count Palatine, brought them the news of Otto I's approach.

These strange and deadly enemies, the Magyars, had already made a deep impression on the peoples settled in the German territories by the time they confronted Otto I's army in 955. Contemporary chroniclers testify to the shock the inhabitants experienced on seeing them; they called the Magyars monsters, fiendish deformities of the human race. According to Widukind of Corvey, Otto I called them "the enemies of God and man" and "the enemies of Christ" before the battle. This gives some indication of the degree of terror aroused by the Magyars, with their Mongolian features, when

they swept into western Europe on their raiding expeditions in the fifty years prior to the Battle of Lechfeld.

Who were the Hungarians or Magyars? They had been settled for centuries in the south Russian grasslands between the Don, Donets and Dnieper rivers until they were driven out in A.D. 889 by the Petchenegs from the region of Atelkuz. They invaded Bulgaria in 894 at the instigation of Byzantium, were repulsed by Simon, and crossed the Veretz Pass to settle on the plains on the other side. Under Arpad's leadership, seven Magyar tribes, and an eighth tribe of Khazars known as Kabars, settled on the banks of the River Tiza and the middle reaches of the Danube. The Hungarian plains served as a gathering ground for these nomads, from which they set out on their raids. After the death of Arnulf of Carinthia in 899, they penetrated into Frankish territory across the Danube and destroyed the empire of Great Moravia. Between 896 and 955 they mounted campaigns into central and western Europe. They made thirty-two raids into east Frankish territory; Bavaria was attacked in 907, Franconia in 918, Lotharingia in 920, and Saxony in 924. In 899, 921 and 947 they penetrated into Italy, burning Pavia and reaching as far as Spoleto. They plundered Burgundy, West Franconia and Swabia in 937 and 951, and reached Spain in 943.

The battle of Lechfeld threw the Magyars back towards Hungary, where they finally became settlers. The young Vajk, son of Arpad's great-grandson Gezá, married Gisela of Bavaria in 995 and was baptized with the name of Stephen, patron saint of Passau. His kingdom survived until Horthy, the imperial regent, gambled it away in World War II.

The Magyars, in fact, had had close acquaintance with Christendom since the sixth century, through their Alanic and Armenian neighbors, their contacts with Byzantium, and some of their countrymen who were Roman mercenaries. In fact in the background to the Battle of Lechfeld was the struggle

The Magyars defeated

between Byzantium and Rome for the religious and political hegemony over central and eastern Europe, the same region that today is the battleground of the conflict between the western world and Russia. In the early part of the tenth century, the Bulgarians went to Rome for help in their fight against Byzantine imperialist designs, while the Moravians went for help to Byzantium out of fear of the Bavarian Latin Church and Carolingian imperialism.

It was a Bavarian nobleman, Berthold, who reported Otto's approach to the Hungarian forces outside Augsburg. The ties between the Bavarians and the Magyars formed the direct prelude to the Battle of Lechfeld, which occurred in the middle of civil war in the German lands, and was its peak and its turning point. In the years before 955, Otto was involved in quarrels with his brothers and then with his sons. In the year 954 the dukes who were in revolt against Otto, and the nobility of Swabia, Bavaria and Lotharingia, were in communication with the Magyars through the intermediary of the Count Palatine, Arnulf. Otto's traitorous son Ludolf provided Horka Bulcsu, the leader of the Magyars, with guides into Franconia and opened the way for him into the heart of his father's territory. In Bavaria, Duke Henry and Ludolf, brother and son of Otto, were fighting each other for power. Widukind wrote that "even the bishops showed themselves not a little irresolute, as they sent envoys to both parties."

Yet King Otto I's greatest victory was won before the battle: in the reaction against the Magyar forces that swept across large areas of Germany in 954, he was able to bring the civil war to an end and unite the Franks, Swabians, Bavarians and Bohemians under his command. The Magyars were surprised to find a powerful coalition ready to meet them since, till then, they had been able to exploit the civil strife dividing Germany. The Saxons took no part in the battle, for they were fighting the Slavs from the Elbe; neither did the Lotharingians, nor Henry of Bavaria, who was still suffering from a wound received in an earlier struggle against his brother, Otto; nor did Otto's son Ludolf, who had been rendered powerless.

Otto's victory at Lechfeld thus secured his kingdom, and according to Widukind's account, he made his troops proclaim him *Imperator*, Emperor, on the battlefield itself. In those days, victory in battle was seen as God's verdict and so Otto's claim was legitimized. His coronation on February 2, 962, in Rome marks the foundation of Germany: a precarious consolidation of the Germanic races who had fought each other for their independence ever since the collapse of the Carolingian Empire. This was the origin of the "Holy Roman Empire of the German Nation" which survived until 1806.

It is true that the adjunct "Roman" originated with Otto II; "Holy" was added in the twelfth century by Frederick Barbarossa; and "of the German Nation" did not come until modern times. Otto I and his successors did not lay claim to Charlemagne's position. As rulers over Germany and the greater part of Italy (and from 1033 over Burgundy too), these German emperors occupied a special position as protectors of the Church and the papacy. The Emperor had a degree of honorary precedence over other western kings (even this was frequently challenged) but no overlordship or power to command.

Once peace was secured in central Germany by the victory of 955, Otto was able to pursue his territorial gains in the south, in Italy, and in the northeast. Italy was still in the power sphere of his Byzantine opponent, who had been the unseen ally of the Magyar Horka Bulcsu on the Lechfeld. And there was still a chance that the Byzantine Church could gain ground in Hungary, Bohemia and Moravia, and in Poland, and thus indirectly gain political support for the Eastern Emperor.

Early in 955 Otto had driven the Slavs back to the Oder with his victory at Recknitz in Mecklenburg, and before the Lechfeld battle began he had sworn to found at Merseburg a missionary bishopric dedicated to St. Lawrence if he were the victor. It seems highly probable that Otto considered it his life's vocation to incorporate the northern and eastern Slavs into his empire. The victory at Lechfeld, which ensured the safety of the southeast, created the necessary military conditions, and Rome was

Left The Holy Lance, sacred symbol of the Ottonian Empire. It represented the Emperor's authority in military and political as well as religious spheres.

Below This illustration of an attack on a fortified town from an eighth-century manuscript reflects the style of battle of the Ottonian Empire.

to provide the spiritual impetus. The emperorship would confer a mandate as guardian of the Church and protector of Christendom, and the papacy would sanction this role.

The most important experiences of Otto's youth had had to do with the Slavs: he had already taken part in the Slav wars of 928–29, he spoke Slavonic, and a Slav princess bore him his son William, later Archbishop of Mainz. Conversion by the sword, the *deus teutonicus* or "German god," proved its worth by success in battle. The war against the Slavs was pursued with utter ruthlessness by the margraves Hermann and Gero, and by Otto himself, from 938 to 950. Widukind testifies to the Saxons' admiration for the enemy's bravery (many of the Saxon nobility were confederates of heathen Slav princes, or even related to them by marriage). The Slavs suffered terrible losses and those who survived defeat in battle were often hanged.

With Otto I began the German expansion towards the East, which penetrated as far as Riga and Reval in the twelfth and thirteenth centuries. In the tenth century, this expansion encountered formidable opposition. The Saxon nobility was opposed to German colonization east of the Elbe because it could not raise as high levies from the Christian German peasants as from the heathen Slavs. (Later on in the Middle Ages the Teutonic Order in Prussia reacted in a similar way). In any case, Germany lacked the population and the economic power for such an undertaking. It was not until more than three hundred years later that settlers from Germany and the West penetrated into the regions that German swords had fought over in vain for so long.

Otto I himself saw his political expansion into Eastern Europe as a missionary obligation to propagate the faith of the Latin Church. In 955, probably immediately after the Battle of Lechfeld, Abbot Hadamar of Fulda was sent by Otto to lay his plan for Magdeburg before Pope Agapetus II. Agapetus entrusted the creation of new bishoprics to the king's judgment. Magdeburg was to become a "German Rome." At the Synod of Ravenna the new metropolitan see was allotted the suffragan bishoprics of Havelberg and Brandenburg, the new bishoprics of Merseburg, Zeitz and Meissen, and the newly founded Polish bishopric of Posnania. Otto even thought of adding Prague. Magdeburg was to rank first among all the churches to the east of the Rhine, and her establishment was to consist of twelve cardinal priests, twelve cardinal deacons, and twenty-four cardinal subdeacons, on the pattern of Rome.

This was a great plan and, if it had been realized, a huge area of Eastern Europe would have come under German domination. But it could never become reality: the German church had too little manpower or spiritual strength to carry the eastern mission through. In 959, Otto had the greatest difficulty even in finding a bishop and a priest for his proposed mission to Russia.

The strongest resistance to Otto's over-ambitious

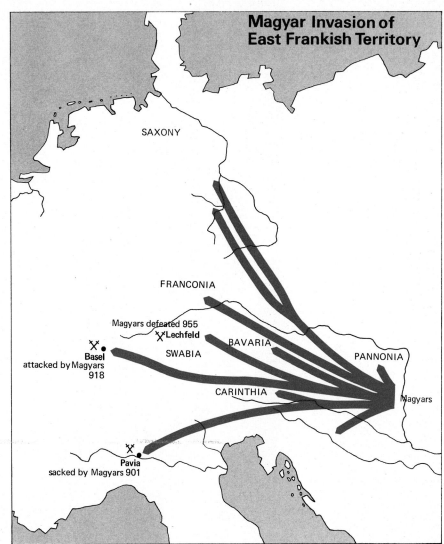

Magyar Invasion of East Frankish Territory

SAXONY

FRANCONIA

Magyars defeated 955
X Lechfeld

X X
Basel
attacked by Magyars
918

SWABIA

BAVARIA

CARINTHIA

PANNONIA

Magyars

X X
Pavia
sacked by Magyars 901

mission to the East came from Mainz and Rome. William of Mainz, the first bishop of Germany and Otto's son by a Slav wife, entered his protest in a letter sent directly to the Pope. According to William, his father's explanation that he was extending the boundaries of Christendom by converting the Slavs to Christianity was simply a cover for his real motive: their political subjugation. The son's attack on the father must have startled the empire—but William maintained this allegation to his death. Then, in 968, Pope John XIII set the boundary of the archbishopric of Magdeburg at the River Oder. In this, the papacy sought to appear as protector and ally of the nations whose previous independence was now threatened by the might of Germany. The Pope, like the Holy Roman Emperor, certainly wanted a Latin Western Europe to oppose the heathen and the Greek Byzantine East; but he was not eager to see it take the form of an eastern German empire.

So the greatest of Otto's plans for the East failed. It was not until several hundred years later that Magdeburg exerted any influence in the eastern territories, and then through its municipal laws and its citizen's rights. The great Slav uprising of 983

A coin bearing the figure of the warrior-Emperor Otto the Great.

A tenth-century German ivory plaque showing Otto the Great bringing a model of Magdeburg Cathedral to Christ. Otto founded Magdeburg as a German Rome which would unite his Empire with Eastern Europe.

repulsed both Christendom and the German rule east of the Elbe. Contemporary witnesses such as Dietmar of Merseburg and Adam of Bremen thought the aggressive behavior of the German princes was the immediate provocation. Dietmar complained further that even Christians were rejoicing over the renewed power of paganism among the Slavs.

At that point, however, Otto the Great's grandson, the young Otto III, had the wisdom to rescue Otto's work and preserve his achievement from complete destruction. His conception of the new Europe gave the victory at Lechfeld and the German mission to the East a more lasting significance.

Otto III had the courage to reject the conception of the empire as a military alliance of a dozen German nobles and more than a dozen German prelates seeking to extend their rule eastwards. He tried to give the empire a reality as a federation of Latin-Christian peoples. Therefore, he named the Polish Duke Boleslaw "brother and colleague of the empire" (*frater et cooperator Imperii*). In the face of the strongest resistance both within Germany and from the papacy, Otto III succeeded—with the aid

of his Slav friends—in converting Poland and Hungary to Christianity, and thus won them for the West. In both countries he founded an independent church. Voytech-Adalbert, Otto III's great friend and the first Czech Bishop of Prague, became the great Western apostle to the Slavs, with support from both the Emperor and Pope. Adalbert founded the Benedictine monastery of Brewnow near Prague and settled it with Roman Benedictines, as a starting point for the conversion of Poland and Hungary.

Adalbert's pupil, Astrik-Anastasius, founded the great Hungarian abbeys of Martinsburg and Pecsvarad; Adalbert baptized King Stephen (who was later canonized); and Astrik became the first leader of the Hungarian Church. Adalbert died a martyr's death at the hands of the Prussians in 997, and his funeral at Gnesen was a moving demonstration of faith. He was buried by Duke Boleslaw in the presence of the Emperor, and his martyr's grave became a rallying point for the foundation of the Polish Church. Gnesen was created an archbishopric in his honor. Otto III's friend, Bruno of Querfurt, set out from Hungary and traveled as a missionary

248

Europe saved for the Latin Church

into the Russian steppes as far as the Volga, coming into friendly contact with the new Christian state of St. Vladimir in Kiev.

As for Hungary, the foundation of the archbishopric of Gnesen as a see independent of the German Church gave King Stephen the legitimate hope that conversion to Christianity need not mean submission to Germany. Shortly after the creation of the see of Gnesen, Stephen married Gisela, sister of the Duke of Bavaria, and they carried through the conversion of Hungary to Christianity together.

Otto III wanted to complete the work begun at the Battle of Lechfeld by his grandfather Otto I, using new, more modern means. To mark the new European status of his Polish "brother and colleague" Boleslaw, Otto gave him a golden circlet and a duplicate of the holy lance (said to have pierced Christ's side on the Cross) which Otto I had borne in the Battle of Lechfeld. Otto III even traveled to Aix—as his grandfather, Otto the Great, had done before him—and descended into the tomb of Charlemagne, opened his grave, took the golden cross from his neck and some of his clothing, drew a tooth from his mouth and clipped his fingernails. In this way he hoped to transfer to himself some of Charlemagne's power and charisma. When he died prematurely in 1002, his successor Henry II buried Otto III's remains in Augsburg, in Udalrich's tomb chapel. The holy power of the bishop who had seen the Battle of Lechfeld, together with that of the dead Emperor, were to help Henry bear his heavy burden of office.

These, then, were the consequences of the Battle of Lechfeld. If the Magyars had won, the Byzantine East would have penetrated with them deep into the heart of central Europe. Otto I's victory made it possible to gain Hungary and Poland and to safeguard Bohemia and Moravia for the West and for its Latin Church. Byzantium gained Russia and came to a halt at the Balkans—where the Roman papacy and the central European powers came into conflict with Russia and the Orthodox Church in 1914.　　FRIEDRICH HEER

Left The crypt of the church at Quedlinburg founded by Otto the Great on his eastern route.

Below left and right The four provinces of the Ottonian Empire, Sclavinia (Slavs), Germania, Gallia and Roma bringing tribute to Otto III in attitudes of total subjection. Otto is shown enthroned and crowned in Imperial majesty.

The birth of Hungary

The battle of the Lechfeld, so important to Western Europe, had an equally profound influence on events in Central and Eastern Europe. The almost total annihilation of their army compelled the Magyars to settle in their new home on the Hungarian plains, and within sixty years they had embraced

The Holy Crown of St. Stephen, King of Hungary.

Christianity. Under King Stephen I (997–1038), who was later canonized, they accepted Christianity from Rome, a process that had been began by Stephen's father, Duke Geza. The new king accepted not only religion but also his royal title and crown from Pope Sylvester II. Although he had to face opposition from some of his pagan nobility, he was able to push through his religious programs and also to lay the basis of a royal administration closely modeled on that of the German empire. During the eleventh century the new kingdom, halted in its westward advance, also lost part of its territory in the southeast to the nomadic Patzinaks. But this loss was balanced for a time by the Hungarian conquest, which gave the new state an important seacoast on the Adriatic.

Thus in the early eleventh century the main contours of medieval Europe had emerged and the political position of the German emperors seemed assured.

Sung China

The empire of Otto and his Saxon successors was roughly contemporary with a renewed period of grandeur and prosperity in the world's largest empire, China. We have seen how in the late ninth century the glories of the T'ang dynasty were subject to internal divisions and attacks over the frontiers by Asian barbarians. After the deposition of the last T'ang emperor in 907, there followed the fifty-year period generally known as the age of the Five Dynasties. The largest single territory was that in the north, which was subject to the fluctuating rivalries of short-lived emperors—some remotely related to the T'ang, others of barbarian extraction. But in fact the true inheritors and preservers of the T'ang civilization were large states to the south—states that had already begun to assert their independence in the last years of the ninth century—for the most part well ordered and free of internal or external strife. In the north this period saw the surrender of a large stretch of territory between the Great Wall and Peking to the nomad tribes of the Kitans. This surrender was to be confirmed by the consolidating and peacefully intentioned Sung dynasty. The area was not recovered for another three centuries, when the whole of China came under the rule of the Mongols.

The Sung dynasty, regarded by some as the most enlightened age of Chinese history, was founded at a time when the Chinese were fully conscious of their national identity, one based on a common written language, an old tradition that the lands of the Middle Kingdom

Palace in a landscape; Sung dynasty painting by Chao Po-chü.

should be governed by no more than one head, and by an administration with a common training and a common devotion to the religious and philosophical teachings known as Confucianism. The turmoil of the Five Dynasties was generally felt to be an unwarranted disturbance of the natural and proper order of things. The Sung came to power through a *coup d'état*, but the first Sung emperor, Chao Kuang-yin, was a man of unusual stamp. Such was the force and moderation of his character that he was able to prevent the massacre of the deposed imperial family, and to free himself of the threat of a military coup by awarding large estates remote from the capital to the chief commanders of his own army who, in exchange, resigned their commands. He then set about restoring the civil administration. Thus began a period marked throughout by moderation and a remarkable concern on the part of a line of outstanding emperors for the arts of government. Within thirty years, the rulers of the southern states had accepted with comparatively little opposition the new dynasty. The eleventh century was to be one of the golden ages of Chinese history.

Buddhism

Ruled by an imperial house whose main concern was the maintenance of peace and the efficient administration of the empire's immense resources, China was free from the rebellions and threats of rebellion that had been all too common under the dynamic yet oppressive rule of the T'ang. The period was one of renewed study of the Chinese classics, and also of an attempt to integrate foreign systems, such as Indian Buddhism, into a single all-embracing universal system based on a radically rethought Confucianism. The advance of scholarship was greatly facilitated by the fact that, even under the Five Dynasties, the classics had been printed for the first time; their resulting diffusion and availability produced an intensity of commentary and study that may be reasonably compared with the impact of the printing of the Christian texts on the age of the sixteenth-century Reformation in Europe.

After an abortive attempt to expel the Kitans in the first years of the eleventh century, the third emperor of the Sung dynasty accepted the situation and agreed to pay a large annual subsidy to those nomadic invaders. The outcome was a century of peace for the Chinese and a century of exposure to civilization for the Kitans themselves. In an age when the settled populations of the Far East were always liable to the depredations of more barbaric and aggressive neighbors, the Kitans were to suffer the fate of the Chinese themselves and fall to the armies of their former subjects, the hardy tribes of the Kin or Chin, the "golden people." Sung China failed to appreciate the gravity of this new threat, and as a result still larger territories to the north were lost.

A Golden Age

Yet despite its reduced state, China, thanks largely to the pacific policies of the Sung emperors, was able to boast a population far in excess of its predecessors and of course far larger than anything beyond its frontiers. It has been estimated, on the basis of the contemporary imperial census of families, that in 1124 the population of China was already at the 100,000,000 mark. The prosperity of the empire was due both

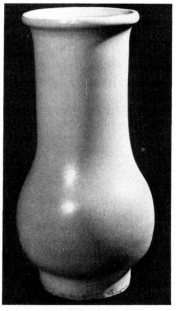

Fine example of a Sung vase.

to the long period of internal peace and also to the enlightened policies of its rulers.

Wang An-shih, the finance minister of the Emperor Shen Tsung (1068–85), believed that the wealth of the Chinese empire derived from the peasants; he aimed at lessening the tribute owed by the provinces to the capital, substituting money taxes for labor obligations and thus weakening the hold of the money lenders.

The "New Laws" were certainly not aimed at social justice but rather at introducing greater efficiency and flexibility into the administration of imperial finances. Wang An-shih belonged to the party of the Innovators; and the political struggles between them and their opponents, the Conservatives, contributed to the weakening of the empire and hastened its capitulation to the Kin. The eventual triumph of the Conservatives, who rested their policy on strict conformity to the precepts of Confucianism and the continuance of the practices of the past, was to color all aspects of Chinese civilization. It certainly mitigated against originality of expression in the established arts, such as bronze-working. However in the relatively new art of porcelain, not discovered until the eighth century, artists enjoyed comparative freedom; and Sung porcelain is generally regarded not only as the first, but also as the finest produced in China.

The Viking World

The explorations of Eric the Red, remarkable as they were, are only a part of the story of Viking conquest and exploration. The raiders from the sea were a fearful and bloody terror to the sedentary populations of Europe, from Scotland to the Mediterranean. The predatory attacks of the Vikings seemed to threaten the new civilization rising from the Dark Ages with utter destruction. The sack of the Holy Island of Lindisfarne off the northeast coast of England in 793 presaged the storm. Adventurers from Denmark and Norway set up kingdoms in Ireland and Man, won control of most of the northern and eastern parts of England, established themselves in northern France, raided in the Mediterranean, and carved a kingdom for themselves in southern Italy.

For centuries, the Scandinavian peoples had been in trading contact with the Roman world, and one of the most important of their routes led down the rivers of European Russia to Byzantium. The famous Varangian Guard of the Eastern Emperors, in fact, was recruited from Norse adventurers. And in the ninth century, Swedish leaders set up a number of "Varangian"

Head of a Viking; carving from the Oseberg burial.

principalities, chief of which were Kiev and Novgorod. Under the semi-legendary Rurig of Novgorod and Igor of Kiev, the traffic in luxury goods going north and slaves and fur going south flourished, and the new states rapidly increased in wealth and power. By the end of the ninth century they had been united under the princes of Kiev and, with the defeat of the Magyars and the Patzinak Turks, the supremacy of the Varangian-Slav principality of Kiev was assured from the Black Sea to the Baltic.

Civilizing influence

Despite their well-earned reputation for brutality and vandalism abroad, the Scandinavians had developed a vigorous and confident tradition of their own. They produced, for instance, a unique and extremely beautiful style of animal carving and some of the world's finest masterpieces of the metal workers' art on their weapons and ships. The ship was central to Viking life; it was not only a mode of transport but also played an important part in the rituals of the dead and the beliefs about afterlife. But to a later age, it is the breathtaking beauty of the lines of these long, rakish yet supremely elegant vessels that catches the imagination. Perfectly adapted to their function of sea voyages followed by periods of river navi-

gation, the Viking ships are in themselves proof of the artistic and engineering skill of this wild, terrible but talented people.

The Scandinavian kingdoms

The Vikings were distinguished from the first wave of Germanic invaders of the fifth century by the rapidity with which they became assimilated with the conquered peoples. In Normandy, Norman England and Sicily the same pattern

Animal head, probably from a Viking ship.

is seen; and in vast areas of Slavic Russia, the adept and probably not very numerous conquerors had soon merged into their surroundings. Barely a century after the arrival of the first Varangian or Swedish princes, the Russian states accepted Christianity. Their leader, Grand Prince Vladimir of Kiev, was in effect a Slav.

Yet the heroic epic of exploration, rapine and conquest, in addition to peaceful trading, which even took the Vikings to the confines of Persia, should not blind us to the evolution of the Scandinavian kingdoms themselves. Under Harold Bluetooth (d. 985), Denmark was already a Christian kingdom. Although there was a short period when Denmark reverted to paganism under his son and successor, Sweyn, the great Canute not only restored the religion but also confirmed earlier conquests. He ruled over an empire that comprised England, Norway and Denmark itself.

The empire fell apart after Canute's death, but his successors were able to assert their independence from their great southern neighbor, the German empire. With the reign of Waldemar, Denmark achieved the frontiers she was to maintain for the rest of the Middle Ages, the southern provinces of Sweden and large tracts along the Baltic coast. Waldemar used the power of the Church to consolidate his rule, finding in Archbishop Absalom an able and willing right-hand man.

At about the same time, St. Eric IX of Sweden was using the pretext of holy war to conquer the territory of the pagan Finns on his eastern frontier. But the first of the Scandinavian countries to achieve a degree of unity was Norway, under Harold Fairhair (d. 933). His successful campaigns against the petty kings of the time led many to flee Norway for Iceland, but the history of the country after his time remained troubled. Many attempts were made to establish Christianity on a firm footing, but it was not until the eleventh century that solid progress was made.

In this period, too, Christianity became the dominant faith in Iceland, although the country had already been settled by Irish monks, themselves driven out by the ninth-century refugees from Harold I's Norway. In the year 930 the oldest surviving European parliament, the Icelandic Althing, was established at Thingvellir.

Voyagers West

A thousand years ago, the Norsemen or Vikings—Danes, Norwegians and Swedes—were terrorizing the greater part of Europe. Their earliest activities were chiefly limited to raiding and destroying, occupations for which their mastery of the sea admirably suited them. But in time they came to settle down—in the British Isles, in Iceland and in Greenland. It was this last, snow-covered and icebound land that was first colonized by Eric the Red—a man so named because of the color of his hair, his fiery temper and the murderous blood on his hands. Eric's son Leif, introduced Christianity to Greenland and in a voyage even farther west came upon a land, rich in grapes, that he named Vinland the Good. The Vikings did not stay long in Vinland and the colony in Greenland eventually expired. But five hundred years later, another voyager west, Christopher Columbus, rediscovered the "lost continent" and the world called it America.

To the eyes of a man born in Norway the western coast of Greenland had perhaps a homelike look. In the year 982, Eric the Red and his small band of Vikings rowed up a fjord—to this day called Ericsfjord—and found, hidden behind the barren cliffs, slopes and valleys where the grass grew lush in the long Arctic daylight.

Eric was not actually the first Norseman to visit Greenland. Some eighty years before, an Icelander named Gunbjorn had sailed along the glacial east coast of the island. Gunbjorn, however, had judged the land uninhabitable. Eric was now testing this verdict and disproving it. He sailed farther west than the boldest of earlier navigators, and spent three full years in systematic exploration.

Only after this long expedition was Eric able to return to Iceland, for his period of banishment was over. He had been called the Red, not for his red hair alone but also for the blood on his hands. Even among a people as quick as the Vikings to take up the sword or battle-axe, Eric and his family were noted for their feuding. When his father was exiled from Norway for a killing, the family emigrated to Iceland. After a couple of his serfs had offended a neighbor and been slain, Eric fought that neighbor and killed both him and another. For this offense he was driven out of the region.

Eric, however, had married a wealthy man's daughter, Thjodhilde, and he moved now to her lands in another and richer part of Iceland. While he was building his house of stone and sod, he entrusted to a neighbor his wooden beams—treasures in a land where wood was scarce. When he wanted them back, the neighbor refused to return them, and in the fight that followed, Eric killed two of his neighbor's sons. At the spring moot—the assembly of free men where cases at law were tried—Eric had the backing of his wife's family and other powerful friends. His punishment for the second double slaying was fairly light: three years in exile.

He used those years in a brilliant feat of explora-
tion. Perhaps even more brilliant was his calling the new island by so deceptive a name. For on his return to Iceland he invited his countrymen to join him in colonizing the fertile valleys of "Greenland," maintaining that "men would be much more eager to go there if the land had an attractive name." Eric was evidently a gifted promotor. He persuaded some five hundred persons to sail, with their cattle and equipment, over perilous seas to establish a colony in a land that they had never seen. Of twenty-five ships that sailed from Iceland that summer, only fourteen arrived. The others were either forced back or lost *en route.*

Yet the Viking ships were probably the finest in the world at that time. Viking craftsmen knew how to shape and fit the narrow planking of the hulls for speed, strength and water-tightness. Though the planking was only an inch thick, and thus light and flexible, it withstood the battering of the Atlantic waves. The shipwrights had iron and steel tools, but no iron was used to hold the vessel together; ribs and planks were joined with pineroot pegs. Wide and low amidships, with deep keels and even deeper side-rudders, these ships could resist the currents of the sea and sail almost directly into the wind. Prow and stern curved high out of the water, surmounted by the gleaming dragon's head and pronged wheel-like dragon's tail that were meant to frighten both human foes and evil spirits.

Members of the colony proceeded in various traditional ways to the "land taking." Some consulted fate by throwing their wooden beams overboard and settling wherever these drifted ashore. Eric, however, made his home on the most fertile spot in the whole country, which suggests that he was a man who left little to chance. He called his farm Brattahlid (Steep Slope), and it became at once a kind of headquarters for the colony.

It was Eric's son Leif who brought Christianity to the Greenland colony. On a voyage to Norway, he drifted off course to the Hebrides, where he stayed a

A gilt-bronze winged dragon, 11 in. long, from the front of a seventh-century Viking shield; part of the treasure found in a buried Viking royal ship at Sutton Hoo in East Anglia.

Opposite A half-excavated Viking boat burial in Denmark, showing the graduation towards the stark prow of the ship tomb. Stones were often used in the symbolic shape of a boat, probably when a real boat could not be spared.

Above left The prow of the royal Viking ship excavated at Oseberg in Norway, which had been used as the tomb of a princess and her attendant, and which displays the very fine wood-carving of a Viking craftsman. The Vikings were the world's best shipbuilders of their time.

Above right The shores of Greenland at the spot (Ericsfjord) where the exiled Eric the Red landed in 982 with his Viking colonists.

The great tenth-century runic stone at Jelling in Denmark, showing the figure of Christ crucified, carved in barbaric style. The stone was set up by King Harald Bluetooth and the inscription reads: "King Harald had this monument made in memory of his father, Gorm, and his mother, Thyri. Harald, who conquered all Denmark and Norway, made the Danes Christians."

winter, fell in love, and perhaps was converted. When he finally reached Norway he was officially baptized at the court of King Olaf Tryggvason, himself a recent convert. Olaf gave Leif a priest to accompany him to Greenland.

Christianity eventually overthrew the Norse gods, but for a long time the old beliefs and the forms of Norse society persisted with little change. The people continued to practice magic, divination and witchcraft. Men seem sometimes to have combined the old beliefs with the new, for tombstones have been found in the shape of the Christian cross, inscribed with prayers asking that the dead warrior may enter Valhalla. In remote Greenland, unconsecrated laymen collected the tithes and even administered the sacraments. Yet, when a man had to be buried without a priest to officiate, "a stake would be set up from the breast of the dead, and in due course, when clerks came that way, the stakes would be pulled up and holy water poured into the place, and a service sung over them."

During its first century as a Christian colony, Greenland was part of the remote German diocese of Hamburg-Bremen. It was not until 1126 that Greenland received a bishop of its own who could consecrate priests there. This first resident bishop, Arnald, taught the Greenlanders how to make sacramental wine (which could also be used for other purposes) from the crowberries that grew plentifully on the high heaths. Arnald built a cathedral at Gardar—and the Greenland colony eventually had no less than sixteen parishes, with many churches, a monastery, and a convent. The churches were built of huge blocks of stone in a Cyclopean style of masonry quite unknown in Norway or Iceland. Apparently the Greenlanders borrowed the technique from the Scots.

Clearly, the colony prospered and achieved virtual self-sufficiency. The people ordinarily lived on fish and on milk and meat from their scrawny livestock, and on such vegetables as they could raise in the short growing season—mainly brassicas, leeks, and radishes. They had great difficulty in cultivating any sort of grain, so they had to do without beer and bread until a trading ship came in from Iceland, England, Norway or Ireland. What attracted traders to them was their walrus ivory and furs and the sturdy frieze cloth woven from the wool of their great flocks of sheep. They took advantage, too, of the one commodity they had in surplus—time; they carved utilitarian objects out of soapstone and wood. They also made miniature walruses and boats, chess pieces, draughtsmen and other playthings.

Trade and communication with the outside world became so vigorous during the twelfth and thirteenth centuries that the colony seems to have grown to two or three thousand people. A population of this size

Leif Ericson discovers Vinland

must have spread out to every pocket of land usable for pasture or tillage. In the twelfth and thirteenth centuries, walrus ivory was a highly valued product. Papal agents traveled all the way from Lucca to Greenland to collect it in lieu of a monetary tithe. By the fourteenth century, however, African ivory as well as English and Flemish cloth were displacing the exports of Greenland. With shrinking demand, trade diminished sharply and communication with the outside world became more and more infrequent. Bishops continued to be appointed to the see of Greenland, but seldom resided there. A papal letter of 1492 said that they had been reduced to venerating the altar cloth, as they had no priest.

That pathetic note is the last mention of the Greenland colony in the archives of Western Europe. What had happened to this community, seemingly so solidly established for five hundred years, to bring about its total extinction? Legends, both of Iceland and of the Eskimoes, tell us of battles with the nomadic hunters of the far north whom the Greenlanders called "Skraelingen." These attacked and destroyed the eastern part of the colony in 1360. According to their own story, the Eskimoes eventually destroyed the western settlement also. The last group of Greenlanders, they say, were burned down in their church.

What had happened and decimated the settlers before this, however, and reduced them gradually to helplessness, was the growing severity of their climate. These last settlers still had some contact with Europe, for fifteenth-century graves reveal that their clothes were in the current European middle-class fashion—long gown, short cloak and hood. Their bones, however, show that their bodies were stunted by malnutrition and scurvy. The glacier, moving into their fjords, had shut them in from marine hunting; the ice rising to a higher permanent level in their soil had destroyed their crops. Nature thus reduced all who did not join the Skraelings in their nomadic life or, as some surely did, emigrate back to Iceland or Norway. In 1540, an Icelander curiously named John Greenlander found on the site of the west coast settlement only the dead body of a man wearing hood and frieze clothes. "By him lay his iron knife, bent and almost worn away." In establishing a colony in Greenland, European man had apparently arrived at his natural limits.

It is one of the ironies of history that in 1492, the very year all communication between Greenland and Western Europe ceased, a Western European rediscovered America. For, as we know, a Greenlander had found the American continent five hundred years earlier. It was Eric the Red's son, Leif, who sailed far to the west and south of Greenland and, about the year 1000, discovered a place rich in grapes, which he called Vinland.

Vinland the Good, the sagas call it. Authorities debate the bearings indicated in the saga, but there is no doubt that Leif had happened upon North America. The first to follow up his exploration was his brother, Thorstein, who reached America three to six years later. Then another chief, Karlsevne,

took a colony to winter in Vinland. For a Greenlander, the new country was closer than Norway. Karlsevne encountered many Skraelings—the Greenlanders seem to have made no distinction between Indians and Eskimos—and traded bright red cloth for their furs. But eventually the colonists and the natives clashed. The Indians descended in a "great multitude of boats," and although the attack was beaten off, the Vikings realized that they were too few in number to conquer a hostile country. They sailed back to Greenland. There is no record of any later settlement, but for some time the Greenlanders continued to visit America for purposes of trade. Perhaps they were mainly seeking wood—some of their coffins were made of larch, which is thought to have come from the American coast.

Both Eric the Red's settlement of Greenland and Leif Ericson's discovery of America seem to have

A carved pictorial stone, one of a series on the island of Gotland *c.* 900, showing a Viking ship probably carrying the dead to the Other World.

The manuscript recording the discovery of Vinland by Leif Ericson, son of Eric the Red in A.D. 1000. The country he found full of vines is now known as North America.

Right A bronze image of the Viking Thor, the Thunderer, the noblest and most powerful of Norse gods, clasping his hammer; found in Iceland.

been curious dead ends. Hundreds of colonists were willing to forsake Iceland for more remote and inhospitable Greenland; it was only a short step to the far more abundant land of Vinland. And yet no permanent colony was ever established there. Our sources are so sparse that the reasons for this cannot be deduced. Certainly the Vikings usually showed no fear of long sea voyages or of hostile populations. Their chief historic role, after all, was that of the last great invaders of Europe.

Some say blandly that "Scandinavia had nothing to contribute to European civilization," and comment on the Vikings' taste for sacking monasteries, which were indeed the richest treasure houses they could find. They were, in their time, as dreadful as the earlier Germanic invaders in theirs. Others have seen the Vikings as shrewd traders, craftsmen technologically in advance of the Christian world; as men who, though illiterate, expressed in their art and epic an ample and creative spirit.

Norwegians began their first incursions into northern England in 787. Thereafter, they or their Danish cousins returned repeatedly. At first the raids came in summer; then the Norsemen built strongholds so that they could winter in the land. Later they took possession of whole districts of England. Other Vikings drove the Celtic hermits out of the far northern and western islands and likewise overran most of Ireland. Dublin and Limerick fell to them, and for a few short years—from 834 to 841—Norsemen ruled a unified Ireland. Central government did not survive, but for a long time the Norwegians kept firm regional control of the country. After 845, the chronicler says "there came great sea-cast floods of foreigners" to Ireland.

In 842, meanwhile, the Danes sacked London and Rochester. They expanded the "Danelaw"— the countries in which Danish law prevailed—until it embraced all England. At the same time other Danes were transforming Frisia and the Netherlands into bridgeheads for deeper incursions into the Holy Roman Empire and into France. They sacked

Utrecht, Nantes, Bordeaux and Paris, to name only some of the major towns. In the 860s, Paris fell again: "The number of ships grows," a chronicler wrote. "The endless stream of Vikings never ceases to increase. Everywhere the Christians are victims of massacres, burnings, and plunderings." The Vikings looted the city, established themselves on an island in the Seine, and were only driven away by other Vikings who had been bribed by French lords. Then in 886, came another siege of Paris: "The town trembles, and horns resound, the walls are bathed in floods of tears, the whole region laments, from the river are heard the horn blasts."

While Vikings thus pushed up the rivers of France from both the North Sea and the Atlantic, laying waste the land and especially the towns, other Norsemen sailed past Gibraltar into the Mediterranean. In 860, Pisa and Lucca fell to them, were

Left A bronze die from Öland, showing a Norse hunter and two attacking bears. These dies were used to make bronze metal plates for helmets and other pieces of armor.

Right Coins used by the Vikings in the eleventh century.

Danegeld—a bribe to keep away

looted and left to their lamentations. Another expedition about the same time plundered Lisbon and Cadiz. Twice the same band of Vikings rowed up the Guadalquivir and sacked Seville. Finally they were driven off with the loss of many ships and men, but the survivors managed to regroup in France and to carry some Moorish captives, "blue men," into Ireland. Meanwhile, the Swedes exploded eastward, to conquer and rule the "land of the cities" that they found flourishing in western Russia along the Neva and Dnieper rivers. "We called them in to settle our quarrels and rule over us," a later Slavic chronicle explains. And it is true that the conquerors' rule first unified this land. In 865 these Swedish princes, known as the "Ros," organized a fleet that sailed down the Dnieper and across the Black Sea to besiege Constantinople. Only a storm, attributed by the inhabitants to the intercession of the Virgin, saved the Eastern capital of Christendom.

The Vikings sometimes agreed to forego pillage in return for regular tribute. As early as 810, Gottfrid of Denmark invaded Frisia with a fleet of two hundred ships and broke down the defenses organized by Charlemagne. He extorted from the local lords a tribute of one hundred pounds of silver. In subsequent raids on the Frankish lands, staggering sums were collected. By 926 the Frankish kingdom had paid thirteen danegelds or tributes. Seven of these payments are known to have amounted to 39,700 pounds of silver. The regular levies of danegeld in England were patterned on the Frankish example. In order to pay off the invaders, the Anglo-Saxon kings imposed on their subjects the first regular tax in English history.

Yet the Vikings could not always be bought off, because often tribute only whetted their appetite. Their kings and chieftains had little control over the young warriors who organized marauding expeditions. Such expeditions formed part of the usual education of the young Scandinavian aristocrat— and often the basis of his further fortunes. Later sagas explain the Viking conquests of England and Ireland as the work of vassals rebelling against the feudal authority of kings at home. But such explanations spring from an age in which feudal ties were more binding. The original movement, in fact, was chaotic and diverse. Norsemen were attracted by the political weakness of the Carolingian empire. In one instance, two of Charlemagne's sons invited them to fight the third. Usually, however, they did not wait for invitations, nor did they obey when their kings commanded peace. In general, the invasions appear to have been the response of a multitude of local aristocrats to land hunger and the pressure of overpopulation. The Viking expansion was a kind of *Völkerwanderung* by sea.

By 875 the Norsemen seemed to have surrounded Europe. They attacked it from every quarter and seemed on the point of conquering the entire continent. The century of raids was followed by a second century during which the invaders settled into the society that they had conquered. In the West

Top The Oseberg cart, a ceremonial object found among the grave goods at Oseberg, is covered with elaborate carving representing scenes from myth and legend.

Above A runic inscription carved on stone, thought by the Germanic peoples to contain occult powers and used for magic and for monuments.

Left The ninth-century pictorial stones on Gotland represent scenes from myth and legend with mounted ships and warriors predominating. This is an unusual piece of carving showing a domestic scene.

Right Buddha-like figure of Hiberno-Saxon origin on the handle of a bucket found in the Oseberg ship burial.

they became lords of Frisia, Flanders, Normandy, and most of England and Ireland. In the East they introduced political unity to Russia by distributing cities among the brothers of a ruling house. They followed the odd practice of rotating the seats of power among the rulers whenever one of the princes died. The Vikings also assimilated the language and much of the culture of the Slavic milieu. By the year 1000, Byzantine missionary work had converted the Norse princes and the Russian populace to Christianity.

In Western Europe, effective resistance to the invasions followed the establishment of centralized governments. New kingdoms were organized independent of the decaying structure of Carolingian authority, and the Norsemen were contained. By driving the Danes back to the Humber, Alfred of Wessex became the only king in English history to receive the epithet of "the Great." Reconquest of much of the Danelaw by Alfred's sons and grandsons permitted the development of an English monarchy that ruled over a mixture of Anglo-Saxon and Christianized Danish subjects. Similarly, in France, Count Oddo of Paris in 887 drove a besieging force of Vikings back to Burgundy. This sort of resistance paved the way for the famous treaty between Rollo the Norman and Charles the Simple in 911. Rollo received all the region of the lower

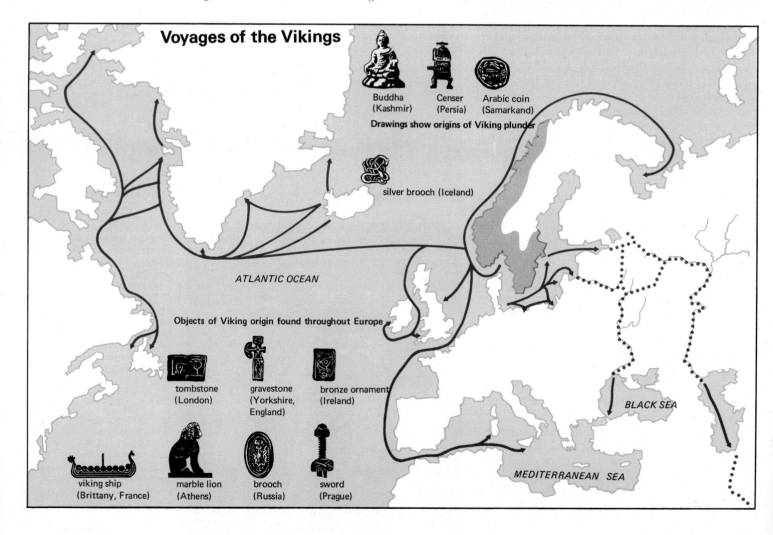

Voyages of the Vikings

Buddha (Kashmir) Censer (Persia) Arabic coin (Samarkand)

Drawings show origins of Viking plunder

silver brooch (Iceland)

ATLANTIC OCEAN

Objects of Viking origin found throughout Europe

tombstone (London) gravestone (Yorkshire, England) bronze ornament (Ireland)

viking ship (Brittany, France) marble lion (Athens) brooch (Russia) sword (Prague)

BLACK SEA

MEDITERRANEAN SEA

The Danes invade England

Seine—henceforth known as Normandy—on condition that his men defend the land, receive baptism and do homage to Charles as their overlord.

The treaty tacitly assumed that the Norsemen would continue their raids on Brittany; the Bretons had to establish a line of defense themselves. The Normans soon acquired the language as well as the religion of their subjects and their nominal overlords. They also acquired outstanding skill as horsemen and as builders of forts and siege machinery. Firmly bound by feudal ties of allegiance, they became in the eleventh century the conquerors of England. In the same period, they sent an expedition into Sicily which, with the blessing of the Pope, seized the island from the Moors and founded a new south Italian kingdom. As in other places, the Vikings native talent for war and government remained in evidence long after they were fully absorbed by the language, the economic system and the culture of their new land. A similar pattern of resistance and assimilation may be seen in Ireland, where in 1014 Brian of Munster defeated the Norse kings of Dublin; after this, the Norsemen became part of the complex tribal society of Ireland and dominated some of its cities, but their role of alien masters had ended.

At this very time, the Danes invaded England once more and almost gave a *pax normana* to England. From 1013 to 1042, King Canute and his sons undid the work of Alfred the Great. They tried to unite what remained of the Danelaw, Anglo-Saxon England, Scotland and Denmark under a single Scandinavian king's rule. Quite different from the old-style Viking raids, this was a unifying operation by a strong monarchy, no longer pagan, but Christian. "Merry sang the monks at Ely as Cnut the king rowed by."

In history, the Vikings remain an experience on the poetic fringe of the European memory. Perhaps because they were the last incursion of an unlettered and pagan people upon the Europeans, they left the impression of a primal tribe of brothers: rapacious, lusty, loyal to their chiefs and to each other, but given also to rebellion and fratricide. Yet they were skillful craftsmen and energetic traders who eventually governed thriving cities. In war they were subject to the madness they considered divine, the "going berserk" that doubles a man's strength and makes him immune to pain.

In the names of our Wednesday, Thursday, and Friday we still do honor to their three chief deities: Odin, Thor, and Frey. Odin: the subtlety and craft that built their ships, guided their merchants, taught their sailors the use of arms and horses and forts. Thor: the thunder god of violence. Frey: the god of fertility who made men rich in kinsfolk and ever poor in land. All are implicit in the three symbols sacred to Thor: the hammer, the battle-axe, and the sacred ring. These gods symbolize forces that drove the Vikings to exploration and conquest, forces not unrelated to the European "restlessness" that ultimately drove men to navigate and conquer most of the globe. — RENÉE WATKINS

Above A carved dragon's head from a sledge found in the Oseberg grave, Norway.

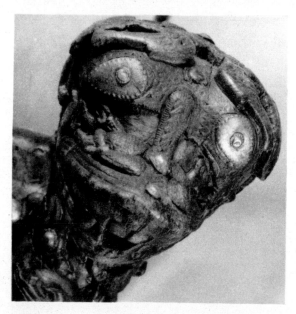

An animal headpost from the Oseberg ship burial; these headposts, intricately carved with zoomorphic designs, were probably meant to protect the dead.

An ornamental Danish axe-head of iron inlaid with silver.

During the eleventh century, a view of world history is dominated by the splendors of the Sung empire in China. Founded in the last decades of the previous century, it reached a peak during the eleventh century that entitles it to be regarded as one of the most brilliant epochs in the history of civilization. The European stage is commanded by the prestige and apparent power of the German empire founded by Otto I and ruled over by his descendants. But both the ambitions of the emperors and the ever-growing power of the great vassals contributed, with other causes, to a decline which even the reign of the great twelfth-century emperor Frederick Barbarossa did not reverse. By 1200, power in Europe was slipping from the hands of the German emperors and was taken up by the central kingdom of France.

The emergence of France as the dominant power in European affairs during the high Middle Ages was by no means a foregone conclusion. To observers of the coronation of Hugh Capet as king in 987 it must have seemed a very unlikely event. It is worth remembering how slow this rise was. Not for another two and a half centuries —centuries of constant struggle— was the French ascendancy to become obvious.

The French monarchy from Hugh Capet to Louis VI

At the time of his coronation Hugh Capet was perhaps the most important man in France. His family, founded over a century before by Robert the Strong, had already provided two kings during the troubled years of the later Carolingians. His lands, grouped around the important towns of Paris and Orléans, were strategically well-placed; among his feudatories were some of the most powerful men in the kingdom; and he himself enjoyed the support of the Church, to which in large measure he owed his election. But there were many houses with more extensive possessions, and at the opening of the eleventh century the map of France dramatically reveals the considerable threat of the provincial powers with which the Capetians had to contend.

In the south, the duchy of Gascony and the county of Toulouse were remote; to the north of them stretched the great duchy of Aquitaine, controlled by the house of Poitou; to the northwest, Brittany, never subdued by Charlemagne, maintained its ancient independence; and still farther north was the powerful duchy of Normandy, which was soon to be transformed into the strongest province of France by the efforts of Duke William. These were the main territories; but as the century advanced, the lands between Normandy and Aquitaine were gradually mastered by the small but dynamic county of Anjou.

Throughout France, the great lords who pressed upon the king were in their turn continually struggling to contain the ambitions of a mass of lesser vassals. Nowhere else in Europe did the full effects of feudal land tenure make themselves felt so rapidly as in France. Amid this multitude of magnates, each already striving to maintain his position within his duchy (the dukes of Burgundy, for example, failed and themselves became little better than bandits), each aimed to strengthen his position at the expense of his neighbors. The kings of the Capetian dynasty were in territorial terms one of the weaker groups in the kingdom. Their advantages were nebulous but, as it turned out, important. The change of dynasty from Carolingian to Capetian did not weaken the respect in which the kingship itself was held. Well aware that their hold on their own vassals was often little stronger than the ties of feudal obligation, the great feudatories were eager to acknowledge the theoretical supremacy of the king from who their own authority ultimately derived.

The king, then, was the suzerain of all and beholden to none save God. Second, the monarchy enjoyed and cultivated the support of the Church, an element to be of increasing importance as the century went by. Third, the dynasty, by a remarkable demographic feat, was able to provide an unbroken line of male descendants for three and a half centuries. Each Capetian was careful to have his son crowned king before his own death. The ancient principle of election, never forgotten in Germany, was gradually, if only by force of custom, displaced by that of hereditary kingship.

Finally, the Capetians, unlike their Carolingian predecessors, were never greatly tempted to assert the full theoretical power of their office. They were content to devote their energies to making themselves absolute masters in their own domains and vassals.

The kings had to tread warily. In the middle of the century, Henry I—attempting to preserve his position in the dangerous wars between his two great vassals, William of Normandy and Geoffrey of Anjou—shifted alliances between them and suffered two humiliating defeats at the hands of William. His son and successor, Philip I (1060–1108), showed more circumspection and wiliness in seizing his

King Philip I of France.

advantage at the most opportune moment. He managed to extend the royal domain with small but significant accessions and to draw some advantage for himself from the civil wars which raged in Normandy between the sons of William the Conqueror.

The tide turns

It was during the reign of Louis VI that the tide finally turned. After a century of acceptance, the Capetian dynasty, whatever its weaknesses, had become the focus of what may be regarded as a nascent national feeling. Louis VI, tireless in his efforts to put down the petty baronage within the royal domain itself and active in asserting his rights as king in France abroad, left to his son a country more firmly governed than ever before. More important still, by marrying the young prince to Eleanor, heiress of the vast lands of Aquitaine, he seemed to have supplied the French

Illustration of the move to hereditary kingship: the eldest son is associated with the king in power.

Eleanor of Aquitaine.

monarchy with a firm base from which to assert its control of the whole country. It is one of the tragedies of French history that the weak and monkish Louis VII was unable to satisfy his passionate wife.

England before the Conquest

The empire of Canute the Great, King of Denmark, Norway and England, fell apart after his death

Page of an Anglo-Saxon royal Bible with an image of St. Ethelreda.

in 1035. For England his reign had been a period of peace and prosperity, but his sons were unable to continue the tradition of their father. In 1042, when the last of them died, the English recalled the senior surviving member of the house of Wessex from exile in Normandy. The son of Aethelred and his Norman wife, Emma, Edward was forty years old when he came to the throne. He had grown to manhood in a foreign land, and he now found himself in a country

where the great families, well-entrenched in the years after Canute, had little interest in a return to a powerful kingship.

Chief among these families was that of Earl Godwin, who was able to force the king to contract marriage with his daughter Edith. The marriage was merely a formality, for Edward seems to have taken a vow of celibacy on religious grounds. Despite a period of exile and disgrace during which the king was able to consolidate the position of his many Norman friends and ministers at court, the house of Godwin returned in irresistible strength in 1052. That same year, Edward made an immensely unpopular move by promising the throne to his cousin, William of Normandy, a promise he did not have the power to enforce. Godwin, who died the following year, and then his sons, soon gained control of the apparatus of government. Thanks to Edward's celibate life within marriage, there was no natural heir to the throne, and all but one of the remaining branches of the ancient royal house of Wessex had died out.

When King Edward himself died in January, 1066, he was succeeded by Harold Godwinson, elected by the Witan with the approval—so it was claimed—of the dying king. Revered during his own lifetime for his saintly character and in a later age beatified and canonized by the Church, Edward the Confessor has as his enduring monument the Abbey of Westminster, which was his foundation and to which he devoted most of the last years of his life.

It is easy perhaps to write Edward

Seal of Edward the Confessor.

off as a weak and ineffectual king, and indeed the facts of his reign reveal him as lacking the wily and aggressive ruthlessness required of a successful monarch during the eleventh century. But we should not forget the powerful position that the English earls had already built up by the time when the new king arrived from overseas to take up a taxing kingship, nor that Edward was then already past his prime. More important, it was Edward, who, by his choice, gave William of Normandy his strongest claim to the throne. Despite the immense power and prestige of the hated Godwin family during the last ten years of his life, Edward never went back on that choice. In fact, he did all in his power to ensure its acceptance by his English earls, to whom the choice was so unpopular. Although it was undoubtedly colored by hatred of the Godwin clan, Edward's decision on the succession was a wise one for England. He chose as his heir one of the most effective rulers in a Europe crowded with overmighty vassals and ineffective kings.

The Danegeld

One of the most remarkable powers of the English monarchy was that of levying a universal tax—called the "Danegeld"—on the population at large; and this was to provide a valuable source of revenue for the first Norman kings. Compared with any other state in contemporary Europe, except possibly the Empire, the England of Edward the Confessor boasted an administrative system and a monarchic potential second to none. It was a tool that the autocratic and gifted William of Normandy knew well how to use. When we add to these advantages the fact that by the very act of conquest William was able to rapidly eliminate the powerful territorial interests of the earls and replace them with chosen men who owed their very position in England to him, we can see that the strength of the Norman English monarchy—so important a factor in medieval English history—was by no means fortuitous.

It was soon demonstrated that, despite the inevitable humiliations and brutalities attendant on conquest, the saintly Edward had chosen his heir with considerable shrewdness. Finally, it is worth noting that Harold, Edward's successor, owed his kingship to election. Without the Norman conquest, England might well have found herself saddled with the divisive effects of an elective monarchy which, in the long run, was to destroy even the power of the mighty German emperors.

Edward the Confessor enthroned at Westminster.

William the Conqueror

The disputed succession following the death of King Edward the Confessor brought new invasions and new wars to England. Then, two great battles fought in the fall of 1066 decided the country's future. At Stamford Bridge, Harold, King of England, defeated his cousin and namesake Harold of Norway. His joy was short-lived; immediately after the battle, King Harold learned that another cousin and claimant to the throne, William of Normandy, had crossed the Channel from France and had landed only one hundred miles away. Overconfident after his recent victory, Harold rushed south with but half his army, and was soundly defeated by William at Hastings. Although undertaken with the blessings of the Pope, William's invasion was in a sense the last great Norse conquest, and ironically it brought England more closely into the orbit of continental Europe.

The sheer white cliffs of the English coast, where William the Conqueror is thought to have landed with his army.

Opposite top The coronation of King Harold at Westminster Abbey; the Bayeux Tapestry *c.* 1100. This tapestry, about 231 ft. long and 20 in. wide, depicts the entire story of the Norman invasion of England and its historical circumstances.

Opposite bottom William, Duke of Normandy, at the head of his army, dressed for battle in chain mail and armor, and exhorting his men to fight with courage; Bayeux Tapestry *c.* 1100.

At about nine o'clock on the morning of October 14, 1066, two armies of approximately equal size faced each other across the valley between Telham Hill and a nameless rise marked by the presence of a "hoary apple tree," close to the modern town of Battle. William, Duke of Normandy, commanded a motley host of Norman retainers, Breton allies and Flemish mercenaries—the majority of them adventurers whom he had persuaded to cross the Narrow Sea for loot and land. William's army has been estimated at somewhere between six and seven thousand men; it was probably nearer the lower figure. Perhaps 1,200 of these were mounted knights who had brought their horses with them in the boats. The rest were infantry, and included an unusually large number of archers. The knights wore heavy hauberks of leather plated with rings of metal, reaching to the knees, and their legs were protected by high leather boots. In battle they used swords and lances. But the ecclesiastics among them, such as William's half-brother Odo, Bishop of Bayeux, wielded maces. A mace could crush a man's skull *sine effusione sanguinis*—without that shedding of blood which the Church forbade to clerics.

Harold of Wessex, King Harold II of England, had perhaps a thousand more men than the Duke, drawn up in tight formation around his two standards: the Dragon of Wessex and his personal banner, the Fighting Man. The nucleus of this force consisted of professional soldiers: Harold's housecarls, who were armored like the Normans. There had been much Norman influence in England since the accession of Edward the Confessor, who had grown up in Normandy—and the armorers of England had learned from their fellows across the Channel. But Harold had ordered his professionals to dismount, in order to stiffen with their shield-wall the levies of inexperienced men hastily assembled from London and the vicinity. The latter were armed with whatever they had: slings, axes, javelins, even hammers and scythes. The housecarls relied on their Danish

pole-axes—fearsome weapons—and on spears used either for throwing as javelins, or as lances to turn charging horses and unseat knights.

Harold's men were tired. They had marched the sixty-odd miles from London in two days and had taken up their positions only the previous night. Harold himself and the housecarls were even wearier than the levies; in the course of the past month they had covered nearly four hundred miles from London to York and back again, and had fought a great battle. For 1066, the "year of the comet," had seen other invasions besides Duke William's expedition.

According to medieval belief, "the star with hair" portended the death of a king or the destruction of a kingdom. Certainly Halley's comet, which shone in the skies over England at the end of April, 1066, justified all such fears. King Edward the Confessor had died at the beginning of January, and Harold Godwinson had been crowned as Edward's successor on the day of his funeral. (Whether you thought this right or wrong depended on whose partisan you were.) There were at least three other strong candidates for the throne. Closest in descent from the English royal line as well as the line of Norman dukes was Edgar the Atheling, but he was still a boy. Another candidate was Harold Hardraada, King of Norway, who had formed an alliance with Harold Godwinson's brother Tostig. Tostig had recently been deposed from his earldom of Northumbria; he seems to have been of a treacherous and vicious disposition and had roused the whole countryside against him. The strongest claimant of all was William the Bastard of Normandy, who was also descended from English kings and who was convinced that King Edward had promised him the succession.

During the last years of Edward's life, however, Harold had been the effective ruler of England. That was why he had been able to seize the throne so quickly; and in the nine months and nine days of his

ROLDO: REGIS HIC RESIDET: HAROLD REX: ANGLORVM: STIGANT ARCHIEPS

HIC WILLELM: DVX ALLOQVITVR SVIS:

King Harold marches south to Hastings

Norman soldiers pillage the English countryside. Here a woman and her child are shown fleeing from a house set alight by soldiers, with the buildings of Hastings close by; Bayeux Tapestry.

reign, he succeeded in consolidating his popularity. To quote one of his supporters, he "abolished unjust laws and made good ones, patronized churches and monasteries, and showed himself pious, humble and affable to all men."

He also proved to be a remarkably good soldier and a foresighted organizer. When—soon after the appearance of the comet—his brother Tostig raided the Isle of Wight and harried the southern coast of England, Harold rushed down to Sandwich from London and drove him away. Then, hearing that William of Normandy was gathering forces to make good his claim to the throne, Harold posted ships and men all along the coast and kept them there through the summer. But few generals or kings in those days could master the logistics of large standing armies. By early September, provisions had run out. Moreover, the danger seemed past; spring and summer was the time when "kings go forth to war." Harold allowed the men of the *fyrd*, the national levy of Anglo-Saxon England, to disband on September 8. He himself returned with his ships to London—disastrously losing many of them in the same storms that were keeping William of Normandy from crossing the Channel.

The dissolution of the army came at the worst possible moment. Barely back in London, Harold learned that his Norwegian namesake, Harold Hardraada, had invaded the north. Tostig had joined forces with him, and in a fierce battle at Fulford the English traitor, the Norwegian king, and a mixed force of Norwegians and Flemish mercenaries had crushed the defending English led by the earls of Mercia and Northumbria. Southern England seemed to be wide open to invasion.

Harold at once set out for the north with his house-carls. He must have gathered up the dispersing *fyrd* as he went, for by the time he reached York he is said to have had an army of "many thousand well-armed fighting men." He covered more than two hundred miles at such speed that he caught the Norsemen and their allies by surprise. On September 25, 1066, the armies met at Stamford Bridge. The Norsemen, though weakened by Fulford, which had been a costly battle for both sides, fought ferociously. But Harold achieved complete victory; both Tostig and King Harold Hardraada were killed and the bulk of the invading force destroyed. The comet had truly foretold the death of kings. But its influence had evidently not yet waned. Harold had also lost many of his best men, and in the midst of his triumph he learned that the Duke of Normandy had landed at Pevensey. With his mounted house-carls, Harold returned to London at top speed, leaving the rest of his army to follow at slower pace.

William of Normandy was at this time approaching his fortieth year. Brutal, avaricious, ruthless, consumed by ambition, he was also a courageous and resourceful leader, a magnificent administrator, a pious Christian, and a good ruler who used tyranny to achieve the ends of stern justice. He had overcome the handicaps of bastardy and a frightful boyhood under savage tutelage and had clawed his way to unchallenged power in a duchy racked by dissension and treachery. Two years before, he had tricked or forced Harold Godwinson into swearing to support his claim to the English throne. As soon as Harold seized the crown, William initiated a skillful propaganda campaign in all the courts of Europe, accusing the new king of perjury. He secured papal

blessing for his expedition to punish the "oath-breaker," and at once began gathering men and building ships for the invasion of England. Unlike Harold, he succeeded in holding his forces together for six dreary weeks, while he waited for contrary winds to change so that he could cross the Channel with his host. His big, heavy ships, built to carry horses and ponderous equipment, were propelled only by sails, not by oars.

Although he did not know it, the delay was providential. Had he embarked when he was ready, he would have encountered an intact English navy and coastal guard and might never have succeeded in landing. As it was, when the wind finally shifted to the south and the Normans disembarked at Pevensey, they met no opposition. By the time Harold, with fatal impetuousness, reached the Sussex Downs with his available men—half his army had not yet come up, one chronicler asserts—William was fully ready for him. Nevertheless, the Normans had the disadvantage of terrain; they would be attacking uphill against the English. And William could not take the risk of avoiding battle, for Harold's army was blocking the road to London. It was clear that the English would only grow stronger with each passing day, for they had vastly greater resources. Good sense could only have urged Harold, for his part, to wait, retreat, draw the Normans deeper into a hostile countryside. But he chose to fight, perhaps from overconfidence after his recent victory, perhaps to save his lands from further pillage.

The story goes—and it is a pretty one, though it may not be true—that the first blow on the Norman side was struck by the minstrel Taillefer, who rode in the van performing juggling feats with his sword

The battle is joined at Hastings between the Anglo-Saxon forces of King Harold and the Norman invaders led by Duke William, a scene of ferocious slaughter vigorously depicted; Bayeux Tapestry.

Left Twelfth-century stone statue of a Norman warrior in chain mail and armor in the church of St. Martial, Limoges.

The tide of the battle turns

The nave of Romsey Abbey in Hampshire illustrates the round arches characteristic of the Norman architectural style, which was preferred by William's newly appointed, high-ranking priests.

Right The abbey at Caen from which Duke William set out to invade England, and where he lies buried, displays the Norman Romanesque style, which William's victory introduced into England.

and "singing of Charlemagne and all his men." (Perhaps he sang an early version of *The Song of Roland*.) The mounted Norman knights formed the center, just as the English had the housecarls in the center of their line. On William's left were the Bretons; on his right, Robert of Beaumont—one of the heroes of the day—with a mixed force of Flemings and French. The infantry advanced first, sending a rain of arrows into the English shield-wall, and receiving all kinds of missiles in return. Then the Norman cavalry attacked. But they were toiling uphill against superior numbers, and the English line stood firm. The terrible slaughter, the ferocity of the hand-to-hand combat, the slain being stripped of their armor in the midst of the carnage—all this is vividly depicted in the Bayeux Tapestry.

After suffering heavy losses, William's forces broke and retreated in confusion. William himself had his horse killed under him (he lost three in the course of the day), and the rumor spread that he was dead. Harold's undisciplined levies broke formation to pursue the fleeing enemy. In this crisis, William snatched off his helmet to show himself to his men. "You are throwing away the victory!" he shouted—and together with his brother Odo, he succeeded in rallying the knights. The mounted Normans, with their superior mobility, quickly surrounded the isolated detachments of Englishmen and cut them down. The incident had given William the key to the battle. Now he ordered his men to feign flight, and twice the ruse succeeded. Then the Norman army resumed its struggle against the thinned English ranks. In the final assault, William commanded his archers to shoot high, so that the arrows flew over the protecting wall of the housecarls' shields. Simultaneously, his cavalry charged. Still the English fought on until Harold himself was killed, perhaps in the melée, perhaps by a fortuitous arrow that struck him in the eye. His two brothers had already fallen, and with their leaders dead the English soldiers lost heart. At nightfall they began to flee in disorder. The battle that decided the fate of England was over.

The Battle of Hastings did not spell the end of English resistance, but it definitely transformed the Duke of Normandy into William the Conqueror. William proceeded to encircle London, cutting the capital off from the rest of the country until the city had no choice but to surrender. By the end of the year, he had entered London. And on Christmas Day (in conscious imitation of Charlemagne's coronation as Emperor on Christmas Day, A.D. 800), he was crowned by the Archbishop of York.

After his victory and coronation, William swiftly consolidated his rule. He rewarded the Norman barons who had fought beside him by parceling out among them the lands formerly held by Englishmen who had died in battle, or who afterwards rebelled against him. As the *Anglo-Saxon Chronicle* bitterly commented: "He gave away every man's land." Within twenty years of the Conquest, nine-tenths of the land of England had changed masters. By scattering the holdings of his new magnates all over the English countryside, he gave the lords wealth but retained the essential power in his own hands. Thus by adroit policy, he established the strongest and most stable monarchy in Europe.

The Conqueror's system of land tenure was strictly feudal. The king himself remained the overlord and landlord of all England, so that even the greatest nobles were his tenants. Starting afresh in a new country, William was able to organize the feudal hierarchy on more logical principles than existed in Normandy, where the land tenure and political and social organization had resulted from haphazard growth. England had been moving toward the development of a feudal society before the Conquest; the general principle of "no man without his lord" was well-established. But the full development of feudalism with all it implied awaited the arrival of the Conqueror and his redistribution of land.

One ironic incidental effect of William's victory was the "return" to England of the Bretons, descendants of families that had been driven across the Channel by the Anglo-Saxon invasion five hundred years before. There had been many Bretons in the Norman army, and they were appropriately rewarded. Men like Alan the Red, Ralph of Gael, and Judhael of Totnes received vast estates, especially in southwest England, where Gaelic was still spoken.

It is curious to find, at a later date, Bretons and Saxons uniting in rebelling against the Normans. For there were rebellions, especially among the Danes of northern England. William suppressed them with an iron hand; in his "harrying of the north" he almost wiped out the population in the Vale of York. Twenty years later, when he ordered virtually every cottage and hide of land in the country to be counted, so that the king could know—and tax—what he owned, the Vale of York was still deserted. That first great medieval survey, incidentally, was so thorough that it was compared to the Day of Judgment; the record came to be known as the Domesday (i.e. Doomsday) Book. The census caused much discontent and local revolts. But William and his successors nevertheless succeeded in winning the confidence of their subjects—so much so that William's son, William Rufus, found he could depend on English levies to defend him against his own Norman barons.

William had come into England with the papal blessing, carrying a papal banner and wearing around his neck at Hastings the holy relics on which Harold had allegedly sworn fealty to him. Once in control of England, he proceeded to introduce into the English Church the principles of Gregorian reform. He attempted to improve the education of the clergy and to enforce the celibacy of priests. Guided by the great churchman Lanfranc, whom he appointed Archbishop of Canterbury, he furthered the internationalization of the English Church, replacing English bishops and abbots by learned Frenchmen and Italians. He separated secular and ecclesiastical courts in order to assure the immunity of the clergy from secular interference—a step that was to have far-reaching and often unpleasant consequences for his successors. William agreed to the payment of "Peter's Pence" to the papacy. But at the same time he strongly rebuffed the efforts of Gregory VII to assert feudal authority over the Crown of England, and he saw to it that control of the English Church remained firmly vested in him alone. Appeals to Rome, or the entry of papal

St. John at Palermo, erected in the early twelfth century in Roger II's Sicilian kingdom, illustrates the way that the Normans preserved the Oriental stylistic traditions of the earlier Arab rulers.

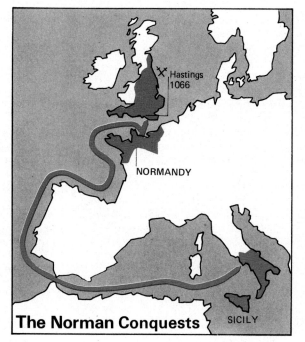

The Norman Conquests

The Norman heritage in England

legates into England, were forbidden without his consent; and he resisted all the Pope's efforts to interfere with his prerogative of appointing high prelates of the Church. His firmness gave England a privileged position which his successors maintained. Because of his policy the full fury of the Investiture conflict that racked Central Europe never burst upon England. A life-and-death struggle between the English Church and the monarchy was delayed for a century. When it came at last, it culminated in the shocking murder of Archbishop Thomas Becket; but the monarchy emerged from that contest with its hold over the English Church basically strong.

In one sense, the Norman Conquest can be considered the crowning accomplishment of that great wave of expansion which carried the sea-rovers of the Scandinavian world to Iceland, Greenland and even the shores of America, and enabled them to found the Russian monarchy and guard the gates of Constantinople for the emperors. For Normandy had, after all, been a Scandinavian settlement, and in the boyhood of William the Conqueror Old Norse was still spoken at Bayeux. But the majority of the Northmen settlers in Normandy had adopted the language and the Latin civilization of their surroundings. What they brought to England, as well as to their far-flung settlements in Sicily and the Holy Land, was French speech and Roman traditions in government, law and church affairs, along with Viking energy and a new organizational talent that seems to have sprung from the amalgam. These descendants of Viking pirates actually put an end to what may be called the Scandinavian period in English history. Until 1042, a Dane had been King

Above St. Albans Cathedral, one of the powerful ecclesiastical seats built under King William in the Romanesque style, near the ancient Roman town of Verulamium.

Below Domesday Book, a survey that William's officers drew up after the conquest of England, listing all the land and buildings of his new domain.

of England; after 1066, England became too strongly centralized a monarchy for further incursions from the north to be possible. Moreover, the union of Normandy and England under one monarch, although it was not destined to last, brought England fully into the orbit of the European world. English history remained, after the Norman Conquest, a process of alternating approach to and withdrawal from the Continent—a process that has continued to the present day. While Scandinavia withdrew for centuries from the main arena of European politics, the English played their part, at first through their Continental possessions, later through Continental dynastic and political alliances.

In the first century after the Conquest, language remained one of the strongest links. Although the Norman nobility rapidly learned the Anglo-Saxon language—which, after all, closely resembled the language spoken by their own grandfathers—they continued using French at court. Literature, which was always directed toward the literate leisure class, ceased to be written in Anglo-Saxon. The *Anglo-Saxon Chronicle* continued to be kept for ninety years after the Conquest, but it ceased with the accession of Henry II.

On the other hand, there was a remarkable outburst of literary creativity in the twelfth century, the consequence of growing wealth and a stabler society. In architecture, too, there was an enormous outburst of vitality; Canterbury, Lincoln, Wells and Salisbury cathedrals, to name just a few, remain witnesses to the Norman style. The generosity of William and his successors also resulted in the building of many monasteries throughout England, and led to a revival of monasticism. The monks reclaimed and cultivated many of the fens and forests of England, thereby adding materially to the wealth of the country. They contributed to the reform of religious life, and often brought from their mother-houses in France the learning of the Continent.

Altogether it can be stated—at the hazard of all such generalizations—that the Norman Conquest, though it caused much suffering, also brought fresh air and an infusion of new energy into a somewhat stagnant society. It reorientated England into the mainstream of European history. As it turned out, William the Conqueror's successors enlarged his Continental domains so greatly that they nearly succeeded in swallowing all of France. The struggle of the kings of France to right the balance of power influenced much of the subsequent history of Western Europe. — RICHARD WINSTON

The Tower of London. The White Tower, built by William to consolidate London's position as the administrative capital of England.

The first seal of William the Conqueror, showing the Norman king enthroned.

The successors of William I

William had ruled both in England and Normandy, but at his death the inheritance was divided. The ancestral duchy on the Continent went to his eldest but feckless son, Robert, and the newly conquered island kingdom to his second son, William Rufus, or William II. For England, despite the subsequent notoriety of William II, the arrangements were beneficial. Whatever his faults as a man and his harshness as a king, William Rufus maintained the royal authority unimpaired, suppressing the baronial revolts which followed the Conqueror's death and holding the northern

morals but, more vehemently, to his refusal to fill vacant sees while channeling their revenues into the royal exchequer. Indeed, much of William's ill repute with posterity stems from the bad press he got from the ecclesiastical chroniclers. William had made Anselm Archbishop of Canterbury during an illness that terrified him with the fear of death. His father had forbade the English clergy to appeal to Rome without royal permission, and his brother who succeeded him was to fight hard—and largely successfully—to maintain the royal claim to invest bishops. William Rufus, by his unyielding opposition to Anselm and the papacy, sturdily upheld the rights of the Crown.

William Rufus was killed while

Duke Robert of Normandy.

part the conquered nation seems to have accepted royal oppression as preferable to the dangers of an uncontrolled baronage. Not only did the young Henry succeed in usurping the claims of his older brother, Robert, to the kingdom, but in 1106, with an army in which the Anglo-Saxon infantry was a vital element, he won final control of the duchy of Normandy at the victory of Tinchebrai. Even so, during the rest of his reign, Henry had to face threats to his position in Normandy.

Growth of central government

In England, with the help of such great ministers as Roger, bishop of Salisbury, Henry introduced a system of financial and judicial administration that was to leave the mark of its reforms on English life for centuries to come. The exchequer, founded under Henry I, exercised a more effective control over the officers and finances of the English king than that enjoyed by any other European sovereign, while the quality of royal justice was such that even members of the nobility were prepared to pay handsomely for it. Once the system of traveling royal judges, "the justices in eyre," was launched, the power of the king's court came to be felt throughout the land.

Yet for all the efficiency and strength of Henry's monarchy, he did not seek to eliminate either the baronage or the Church—the two great mainstays of a feudal monarchy. The quality of medieval government depended on the quality of the king, and when Henry died at the end of 1135, an era of strong government had come to a close. Henry had planned for his daughter Matilda, wife of the former Emperor Henry V, to succeed

him, and had compelled his leading subjects to swear allegiance to her. But Matilda's claim was contended immediately after Henry's death by her cousin Stephen of Blois, a powerful man in England, thanks to lands received from Henry himself. A decisive body of the English baronage, affronted by the prospect of petticoat rule, offended by the imperious and haughty nature of the ex-Empress and no doubt well aware of the pliant good nature of Stephen, renounced their oaths of allegiance to Matilda. In 1136, after he had granted a charter of liberties to the Church far in excess of anything conceded by his predecessors, Stephen was recognized by Pope Innocent II. But Matilda did not abandon her claim, and there followed a decade of civil war which left an indelible mark on the memory of England. Stephen's own weakness and chivalry were delightedly traded upon; and the nobility of England could hardly believe their luck in having on their hands a fully fledged civil war in which the rival claimants were only too eager to bid for their support.

Undoubtedly the gloom of the period is heightened by the paucity and bias of our sources. Nevertheless, it was undoubtedly a difficult period, which only ended in 1147 when Matilda retired to Normandy, which had been taken over by her second husband, Geoffrey of Anjou. In 1153 their twenty-year-old son, Henry, Duke of Normandy, Anjou and Maine, and also of Aquitaine by virtue of his marriage to its duchess, Eleanor, went to England, where he found many supporters. King Stephen, broken by the death

Galilee Chapel in Durham Cathedral. Durham was the greatest of the Norman ecclesiastical border fortresses in the north of England.

frontier with Scotland. In comparison with even the strongest of Continental kingdoms, England enjoyed a priceless advantage in the incontestable position of the central monarchy. In twenty years, William I had made this ever more sure, and his son was strong and intelligent enough to capitalize on it. However, his means to this end and the oppressiveness of his ministers provoked the discontent both of the baronage and the people at large. Yet his position was further strengthened in 1096 when he won control of Normandy when his indigent brother Robert pledged the duchy to the king to finance his participation in the crusades.

William Rufus had no more bitter enemy than the Church, which objected not only to his personal

hunting in the New Forest on August 2, 1100, by an arrow fired by one of his companions; the speed which his younger brother showed in taking advantage of this turn of events has led to speculation that Henry may have been prepared for what happened. Whatever the circumstances of his succession, however, there can be no doubt that the reign of Henry I was of lasting advantage for England. It is a remarkable and crucial fact that for the first seventy years of its existence the Norman kingdom of England was ruled by three strong-willed and efficient kings whose principal enemies were the Church and the discontented elements of their own Norman baronage. Such English resistance as there was, was effectively contained, but for the most

Interior of Canterbury Cathedral built by Anselm, who succeeded Lanfranc as Archbishop.

Geoffrey Plantagenet.

of his own eldest son, acknowledged Henry as heir to his throne. When he died the following year, the crown passed without dispute to a young man who was to prove himself one of England's greatest rulers.

Emperors and Popes before Canossa

Thanks to the hard policy of William I and his successors, England maintained a firm stand against the claims of the reformed papacy, and in 1106 Henry I won a compromise settlement much to his advantage. In the Empire the struggle was both longer and much more bitter, if only because the principles at stake affected the plenitude of papal power in the most obvious way. It was one of the ironical aspects of the events leading up to Canossa that the papacy, which inflicted such dramatic humiliation on the Emperor. Henry IV, had been saved from its own incompetence and corruption only a brief thirty years before by his father, Henry III. The scandalous

corruption of the monastic arm of the Church had been slowly cauterized during the tenth century by the great reform movement launched by the founding of Cluny. But despite this, and despite the rising tide of popular piety throughout Europe, the papacy remained in a parlous state. For the first forty years of the eleventh century, it was virtually the dynastic toy of Roman families. And the sin of simony was not unknown at papal elections.

Lay intervention was essential if reform was to be successful in the body of the secular Church, where bishops and clergy were so closely involved in the secular world itself. The Emperor Henry II, fully aware of his power in church and state, had sponsored a series of synods to spur the Church to reform itself. The movement was interrupted by the reign of the Emperor Conrad II, but under his son, Henry III (1039–56), the problems of the papacy were solved. Henry succeeded in ensuring the election of his cousin who, known to later ages as St. Leo IX, was to be a chief architect of the reformed Church which was soon to challenge the pretensions of the Emperor himself.

The Normans in Sicily

Six years before William Duke of Normandy embarked for his momentous invasion of the Christian island of England, with the papal blessing on his banners, two members of a family of the petty Norman nobility had begun their conquest

of the Moslem island of Sicily, also with papal blessing. Despite their humble origins, Robert and Roger de Hauteville were the founders of a Mediterranean power which throughout the twelfth century was to hold at bay the forces of the Pope and Emperor of the West and prove dangerous enemies to the Emperor of the East.

The Norman presence in southern Italy began in the 1010s when a group of Norman pilgrims were recruited as mercenaries in the perpetual struggle among the last outposts of the Byzantine Empire, the Lombard principalities and the independent cities of which Naples was the leader. By 1030 their leader had received the fief of Aversa from the Duke of Naples. In the 1040s, Robert Guiscard ("The Cunning") of the family of Hauteville appeared in Calabria to begin a career of merciless but brilliant brigandage that by 1059 had forced a reluctant papacy to recognize his position in the treaty of Melfi. Leaving his brother Roger to complete the conquest of Sicily, Guiscard set out in the 1080s on a conquest of the Byzantine Empire itself, but died before his plans could materialize. After his death, his state in southern Italy soon fell apart.

Roger, however, who died in 1101, was able to leave a well-ordered and powerful kingdom in Sicily. This kingdom reached the height of its power and prestige under the rule of his second son, Roger II (1105–54). A true Hauteville in his ambition and in his

Queen Constance with her child, the future Emperor Henry VI.

ruthlessness, Roger nevertheless recognized the realities of power in his island kingdom, in which a small group of conquerors found themselves ruling a motley population in which Catholics from France and Italy rubbed shoulders with Orthodox Byzantine Christians and Islamic Saracens. Throughout their history, the rulers of Norman Sicily, who soon brought the mainland territories into their kingdom, exercised a degree of religious toleration remarkable in Europe. Displaying to the full the Norman talent for assimilation, Roger II not only instituted a harem, but also provided himself with a first-class fleet, which enabled him and his successors to pursue an imperial policy. In the 1130s, exploiting a papal schism, Roger was able to have himself recognized as king—a title which, though it was granted by an anti-pope, he vindicated and later had confirmed by the true Pope.

At his death, Roger II left a seemingly powerful kingdom, one whose eclectic culture was to make a notable contribution to the twelfth-century "renaissance."

Through the silk industry of Palermo, founded by workers captured by raids on Byzantine territories, he brought the secret of silk to Europe. His sensual successor, William I, was swift to put down rebellion, and left the kingdom intact.

William II (1166–89), called the Good because of the degree of internal peace that he maintained, followed the traditional policy of his house against the Byzantine Empire. To further it he married his daughter Constance to the future Emperor Henry VI. William's ambitious policy eventually failed, however, and after his death the kingdom passed to the Empire. The marriage he had arranged was to have fateful consequences for the future of southern Europe.

The Norman King Roger II of Sicily, depicted on a Byzantine-style mosaic.

REX·ROGAT·ABBATEM! MATHILDIM·SUPPLICAT·ATQ;

Humiliation at Canossa 1077

For three days in January, 1077, Emperor Henry IV stood barefoot in the snow outside Canossa castle, waiting to see Pope Gregory VII and to beg him to lift the dread sentence of excommunication. Henry's action was the culmination of a conflict between Church and State that had been brewing for centuries. Medieval rulers had come to regard their bishops merely as feudal nobles who were expected to fill their proper roles in the functioning of their kingdoms. But some of the clergy wished to emphasize the religious office of bishops by removing them from the responsibilities, and the privileges, of civil government. The Pope's victory in forcing Henry to humiliate himself at Canossa did not resolve the conflict, but it did help play down the sacred character of kingship and thus paved the way for the creation of modern secular states.

In January of 1077, Pope Gregory VII was residing at Canossa, a castle on the northern slopes of the Appenines owned by the Countess Matilda of Tuscany. On the 25th day of that month, the Emperor Henry IV appeared in front of the castle as ordered, "and since the castle was surrounded by three rings of walls, he was allowed inside the second ring. His entourage had to wait outside. He stood divested of his royal garments, without the insignia of his dignity, without ornaments of any kind. He was barefoot and fasted from morning to the evening in expectation of the sentence of the Roman Pope. He had to do this for a second and a third day. On the fourth day he was allowed to appear before the Pope and was told that the excommunication would be repealed under certain conditions."

The chronicler to whom we owe this moving description, Lambert of Hersfeld, then tells of the conditions. The Emperor was to submit himself to a thorough judicial examination to determine whether he was to keep his domains; he was to sever his personal relations with certain evil men whose advice had led him to the point at which, a year before, the Pope had excommunicated him. At this, the Pope said Mass, and during the office he declared that in order to prove his innocence of countercharges that had been leveled against *him* (they ranged from murder and adultery to heresy and simony) he would eat one half of the Lord's body and hoped he would be struck down dead if he were not innocent. Having done so, Gregory invited the Emperor to do likewise. But Henry was obviously uncertain either of his own innocence or of the effectiveness of the test—it is impossible to say which. Caught unawares, we are told, he blanched and stammered and sought excuses and eventually begged the Pope not to insist, pleading that since the men who had accused him were not present the test could not possibly be significant. Gregory was won over, the tense moment passed and then the Pope invited the Emperor to share his breakfast. Henry must have sighed with

relief. But when the news of his reconciliation with the Pope was announced to the Italian bishops assembled outside the castle, there was a violent commotion. These men had supported Henry because they were jealous of the Bishop of Rome. They now felt let down and threatened to depose Henry and lead his son, who was still a minor, to Rome and there unseat the Pope. Only with the greatest diplomacy was this outburst of indignation suppressed. In the end, they all agreed to wait for the assembly at which Henry was to place his case before the magnates of the Empire and wait upon their decision.

The day of Canossa appeared to be a great triumph for the papacy and, as such, has become almost proverbial. In fact, the Emperor got the better of the Pope. By doing penance, Henry obliged Pope Gregory VII to lift the excommunication and thus removed the one great obstacle that had stood in his way. Henry could now rally his supporters, and by 1081 he was able to march an army into Italy, appear before Rome and, after lengthy battles, install there a Pope of his own choice, Clement III, the Archbishop of Ravenna.

Pope Gregory held out inside the castle of Sant' Angelo; but Henry was crowned Emperor in Rome on March 31, 1084 by his own Pope. Eventually the Normans from Sicily under their king, Guiscard, came to Gregory's rescue. The fighting in Rome was severe and the city suffered grievously. But no decision was reached and eventually the Normans withdrew, taking Gregory south with them in semi-captivity. He died in Salerno on May 25 of the following year, breathing his last with a somewhat ironical variant of verse 8 from Psalm XIV: "I have loved righteousness and hated iniquity; therefore I die in exile."

The clash between the Emperor Henry IV and Pope Gregory VII was the culmination of a long development that, but for the fiery intolerance of the Pope and the youthful temper of Henry IV, might have had a completely different ending.

Henry IV with his son Henry (the future Henry V) and two clerics. The combined opposition of Church and family pursued Henry to his tragic destiny.

Opposite Henry IV in St. Nicholas' chapel at Canossa asks Matilda of Tuscany to intercede for him with the Pope so that his excommunication (1076) might be revoked. He is supported by Hugh, Abbot of Cluny, in this cunning though bitter gesture of political ignominy.

Charlemagne's idealism fades

The iron crown and cross from the tomb of Henry IV in Speyer Cathedral.

The conflict between Church and State had been developing for centuries. One of the most far-reaching effects of the barbarian invasions of the Roman Empire in the fifth and sixth centuries A.D. was the blow to the Christian churches. The invaders were all Christians, but conversion to the new religion had been for them a mass movement; they followed their king. It had not been associated with spiritual regeneration, nor had it been an answer to a spiritual need. The barbarians needed a new communal ritual to replace the one they had lost when they had left their homesteads. Furthermore, the economic decline of the Roman Empire, which had in fact preceded the invasions but which was further hastened by them, had essentially meant a decline of urban life and culture.

With the advancing ruralization of the imperial territories, there disappeared also the economic and administrative basis of the churches. The urban Christian communities and their bishops declined in number and importance. By the seventh century, bishops were no longer churchmen; they were the owners of large landed estates. They came to share the customs and outlook of the landed magnates, and as such they were soon rendering military service to kings. All this was not so much an expression of declining piety as it was the result of the economic and social changes that took place during the early Middle Ages. With the centers of religious organization dispersed, educational opportunities—essential to a religion based on the knowledge of the Bible and a complex liturgy—declined sharply. Christian pastors of these centuries, in their simple-minded dislike of the pre-Christian, pagan cultures of Rome and Greece, lent an active, if unwitting, hand to that decline by decrying education—for to them education usually meant the study of pagan literature.

The short-lived idealism of Charlemagne (768–814) had no real lasting effect. But in the course of the tenth century, man's innate yearning for transcendence, for spiritual edification, for ascetic morals and ethical guidance began to reassert itself. There emerged, at first in the central parts of the old Carolingian Empire, in the so-called Middle Kingdom comprising the present-day Netherlands, Lorraine and Burgundy, a new monastic movement led by the monks of Cluny. This newly reformed branch of the old monastic order propagated the idea that the religious life was one of seclusion, dedicated wholly to prayer. The influence of Cluny's example was enormous. A vast number of daughter houses were established in Central Europe, and hundreds of new recruits for religion were enlisted. The reform movement also led to the reorganization of old religious houses. By the early eleventh century, a wave of revived religious activity was sweeping across Europe.

One of the innovations introduced by Cluny was the regulation that a reformed monastery should be exempt, no matter where it was situated, from the control of the local bishop. Bishops being potentates, this was an essential factor in the success of the reform movement. By the eleventh century, abbots of both reformed and not so reformed houses, such as Suger of St. Denis, Poppo of Stablo and Odilo of Cluny, tended to replace bishops as the trusted advisers and scribes of kings and emperors. The reason was that kings soon discovered they could benefit from this new movement. If the inhabitants of their kingdoms could be imbued with religious fervor, the kingdoms would receive a spiritual substance as a result.

The first monarch to recognize this was Henry III of Germany (1039–56). Henry's relations with the magnates of his kingdom were unhappy. In 1047 he was almost assassinated while visiting Adalbert, the Archbishop of Bremen and Hamburg. Adalbert was a very able administrator and had sought to turn his archdiocese into a territorial state. The Saxon nobility was highly suspicious of such nonfeudal behavior, and when they discovered that Adalbert had Henry's full support, they conspired against Henry—hence the attempted assassination. Similarly,

Emperor Henry IV; from the shrine of Charlemagne at Aachen Cathedral.

The twelfth-century chronicle of Otto of Freising shows how, after Pope Gregory VII had made peace with him, Henry IV betrayed him by appointing an anti-pope Clement III and expelling Gregory by force from Rome. The death of Gregory (*below*) at Salerno was embittered by his exile.

Conrad, Duke of Bavaria, angered by Henry's close association with the episcopate of Bavaria, rose against him. The rebellion was suppressed, but Conrad escaped and in 1055 organized a major conspiracy to assassinate Henry. Another long-standing rebel was Godfrey, Duke of Lorraine, whom Henry prevented from taking over the whole of his father's inheritance. Godfrey was not content with half and eventually married an Italian heiress in order to compensate himself for his loss of power. The Italian threat which thus emerged was considerable.

Faced with such threats to his authority, Henry turned to the Church for support of his throne. He decided not only to throw his weight behind the re-form movement of the Church, but also to provide it with the administrative framework and centralized direction it would need in order to become truly universal. A shrewd statesman, Henry decided to introduce reform into the see of Rome, the bishopric which was the first see of Christendom.

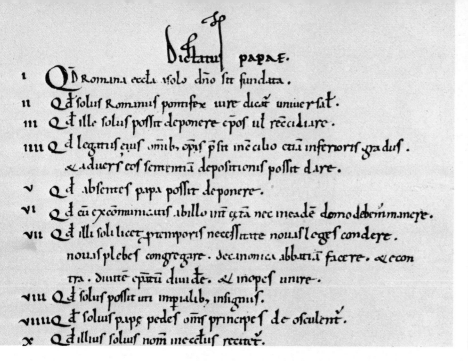

The bishops of Rome, during the century and a half preceding the reign of Henry III, had had neither desire nor opportunity for exercising the functions of the papacy. The office, the leading governmental institution in the city, had become the coveted prize of the aristocratic clans in and around Rome. These parties had fought over the papacy and had removed successful candidates by murder or blackmail. The incumbents who were willing to play along were always scions of these families, their minds and ambitions more on local power than on the welfare of the Church—of which most of them knew only by hearsay and which interested them little if at all.

In 1046, Henry III decided to intervene. He held a synod at Sutri, deposed the reigning Pope Gregory VI, declared several other claimants to the see also deposed and caused, in quick succession, a whole series of "foreign" popes to be installed in Rome. All those who took office under imperial patronage were ardent reformers and came from abroad. Thus the spirit of the reform movement captured the city of Rome, for with the new popes there also appeared a large number of foreign clergy, who supported the reform movement.

With this action, however, Henry III also introduced the possibility of conflict between Empire and Church. His objection to the deposed popes was based on the principle that simony was an evil practice. No man should be allowed to assume a spiritual office in return for material considerations such as money payments or promises of political influence. The reform party was only too happy to seize this opportunity, to capture Rome and to spread their ideas and practices from the central see of Christendom. At the same time, the fact that they owed their position to the Emperor raised an irksome question. It was becoming more and more clearly the object of the reform movement to make the Church independent of laymen and to see to it that in the Church none but canon law prevailed. But insofar as the reform party owed its capture of

Rome to the Emperor, the Church could hardly be said to be independent.

Nevertheless, this was an issue which, given time and thought, could have been settled amicably. After all, the Emperor (and, for that matter, many a king) was not exactly a "lay" person. He was elevated to the throne by unction and wore garments of religious significance—not the least significant, his splendid crown. True, the crown was perhaps only a special kind of helmet, but its splendor of gold and precious stones made it into a symbol of the sun. An anointed ruler was another David and had divine sanction. His ascendancy in the Church and his protection of religion need not therefore necessarily be construed as an act of lay interference.

Under Pope Leo IX (1049–54), the reform movement made rapid progress. He brought a large number of his friends and associates to Rome and spent much time traveling. He used his authority to remove simoniacal bishops and abbots, and granted the vacant sees to adherents of the reform movement. The presence of his supporters in Rome created an institutional background to the reform movement by surrounding the papacy with a suitable clergy who would be likely to elect a suitable successor. A few years later, Pope Nicholas I formally created the College of Cardinals to ensure an orderly election by the presence of an advisory body. Both the prestige and the influence of the papacy rose enormously during this decade, and is reflected in the publication of the new collection of canon law, the so-called *Collection in Seventy-Four Titles,* which gave great prominence to the legal prerogatives of the see of St. Peter.

The death of Henry III in 1056 was a blow to the movement. He was succeeded by his son, Henry IV, a minor. During the necessary regency, Henry became so frustrated and depressed by the unpleasant forms of tutelage exercised over him that he failed to develop a prudent and balanced outlook. But a prudent and mature assessment of the situation was required. The close cooperation between Henry III

276

and the reforming party was based on mutual esteem. But, as we have seen, it had led of necessity to the strong assertion of the primacy of the see of Rome. To assert such primacy in regard to the Church was one thing; a personal clash, and a rivalry between Pope and Emperor could easily turn the question of primacy into one of who was master, Emperor or Pope. Although there were several ambiguous pronouncements on this question, the matter had never been settled. There had been occasions of conflict that in turn had given rise to further ambiguous pronouncements like the famous statements about the two swords—one wielded by the Pope, the other by the Emperor—or like the statement that Church stood to State like soul to body. But there had never yet been a confrontation, and everyone had probably preferred a merciful vagueness to any definite answer.

Henry IV came of age in 1065 and spent the first ten years of his reign subduing the rebellious Saxon nobility. In 1075 he thought he was at last firmly established. In that year there was a dispute over the succession to the archbishopric of Milan. Henry and Pope Gregory VII supported rival claimants. When Henry refused to drop his candidate, he received, on New Year's Day, 1076, a letter from Gregory in which he was tactlessly reminded that he owed obedience to the Pope. Henry, aware of Gregory's somewhat tenuous hold over the city and people of Rome, and made confident by his recent triumph over the Saxon nobility, was determined, after years of frustration, to use the full force of his authority. He wrote back to Gregory, charging him with all sorts of crimes and ordering him to relinquish the papacy. He also invited the people of Rome to rid themselves of their bishop. Gregory replied by excommunicating and deposing Henry.

This situation had been brought about by the temper of the two protagonists. There was some precedent for Henry's deposition of an unworthy Pope. There was none for Gregory's deposition of an unworthy monarch—he was, clearly, behaving in a revolutionary manner. But it needed little stretching of the major points of the reform movement to include among the prerogatives of the Holy See the right to depose kings. And Gregory had fortified himself in advance by adding a formal statement of his rights, the *Dictatus Papae*, to his register. The gist of this manifesto was that the Roman bishop alone, not the Emperor, had universal power. The kings of Christendom, with the exception of William the Conqueror, naturally became wary of Gregory. But needless to say, the nobility of Germany seized the opportunity of the Emperor's difficulties and rebelled against him. Formally excommunicated, Henry could do nothing. And so he humbled himself at Canossa.

Canossa by itself did not become a turning point: Gregory, as we have seen, died in exile; Henry never quite managed to restore peace in his empire. The disputed issue of the primacy of Pope or Emperor was never resolved. But as a result of the long war unleashed by Gregory's invitation to rebellion in Germany, the monarchy became weaker and weaker over the next half century.

For the papacy, the consequences of Gregory VII's actions were more far-reaching and in the long run, equally fatal. Since no subsequent Pope could disavow the reform movement and since the spirit, if not the letter, of the *Dictatus Papae* had become built into the reform movement as a result of the clash between Henry and Gregory, the papacy was launched on a course in which superiority over temporal powers was explicitly claimed from time to time.

Probably the nascent states of late medieval Europe, as well as the princedoms which sprang up within the confines of the old Empire, were indirectly the ultimate beneficiaries. For even if papal superiority over secular rulers could not be clearly vindicated, the status of kingship and of the Empire came to be desacramentalized. The unction became less and less of a sacrament; kings became less and less new Davids. And when the number of sacraments was officially defined as seven, at the Lateran Council in the early thirteenth century, the royal or imperial coronation was not one of them. Cut down to size as secular magistrates, and less and less frequently thought of as quasi-priestly rulers and divinely appointed kings, the new monarchs of Christendom settled down to the task of pragmatic government and utilitarian administration. As such, they all learned to treat their clergy, high and low, as their subjects. They mastered the techniques of taxing them and making the Church in their lands into departments of state. For good or ill, the modern secular state could not have evolved had the popes not taken the initiative towards making kingship less of a sacred office. PETER MUNZ

Left Henry IV investing his son, the future Henry V, with the royal insignia at Aachen in 1099.

Right Henry V receives the imperial insignia at his coronation in Rome by Pope Paschal in 1111. The struggle for supremacy of the Empire between secular and ecclesiastical authority appears to end in victory for the Pope.

A triumph for orthodoxy

The events at Canossa and the condemnation of Peter Abelard under the auspices of St. Bernard of Clairvaux were signal triumphs for the papacy and the orthodox doctrines of Western Christianity. The capture of Jerusalem by the First Crusade, on the other hand, was an exhilarating achievement for European Christendom as a whole. Yet during these sixty-three years new forces emerged, forces that led to questions about the spiritual status of the ecclesiastical hierarchy, and even about the fundamental doctrines of the faith. Meanwhile, the successes of the crusaders diminished and the Latin states that they had established in the Levant fell into a decline in which even Bernard himself was implicated.

Within ten years of the humiliation of Emperor Henry IV, Pope Gregory VII ended his days in exile from Rome, supported only by the Norman army of adventurers that he had called to his aid. Although his great rival was to end his reign opposed by a papist party supported by his own son, that son, Henry V, soon demanded in his turn the rights of clerical investiture

Signature of Pope Calixtus II on the Concordat of Worms.

claimed by his father. The conflict was not resolved until the compromise of the Concordat of Worms in 1122. Its terms approximated the terms won by the Emperor's father-in-law, Henry I of England, some fifteen years earlier. In return for surrendering the right to invest bishops with the spiritual symbols of their office, the rulers won papal recognition of their right to have an effective voice in the election of bishops. But discord between the Church and the secular authorities was to remain potentially explosive for generations to come. Indeed, there were many people in Europe who deplored what they regarded as the worldliness of the Church.

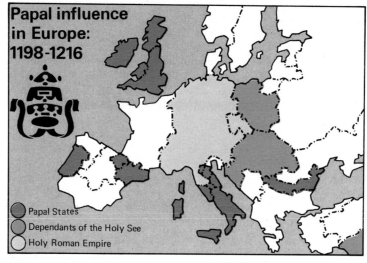

Papal influence in Europe: 1198-1216

- ● Papal States
- ◐ Dependants of the Holy See
- ○ Holy Roman Empire

Arnold of Brescia

During the eleventh century, a movement had sprung up in Lombardy devoted to an ascetic and "primitive" Christianity and known as the *Humiliati*. But the opposition among the public at large to the growing secularization of the Church was most dramatically embodied in the career of Arnold of Brescia.

Probably a pupil of Abelard, and condemned with him at Sens, Arnold preached that only the lay power should own and administer property. In the last years of his life—before his execution at the order of the Pope—Arnold led a republican government in the city of Rome itself. Arnold's ideas, though politically subversive, were not as serious a challenge to the authority of the Church as was the intellectual unrest abroad during the twelfth century, an unrest

Albi, center of the Albigensian heresy; the cathedral.

symbolized by the career of Abelard. Arnold, indeed, had not been killed as a heretic; nor were the *Humiliati*, who after all claimed only to be returning to the teachings of poverty of Christ himself, at first open to charges of heresy. But the case was quite different with the sect known as the Cathari, whose successors were the Albigensians of southern France. The doctrine of the Cathari was less of a heresy within the Christian Church than it was a rival religion. It must therefore be regarded as one of the most serious manifestations of the new ideas abroad in Europe during the twelfth century. The Cathari had originated in the Bulgarian lands of the Byzantine Empire, and their beliefs show the strong influence of Eastern thought, as found in the teachings of the Persian Mani. They saw the world as the battleground of two equally powerful forces of good and evil, and regarded the physical creation of the world as the work of the evil one. Thus rejecting God's role in the creation, they overthrew one of the fundamental doctrines of Christianity. The speculations of an Abelard and the humble aims of the *Humiliati* in no way tended to the extreme anti-Christian position of the Cathari. Yet their searching questions into the substance of orthodoxy could only be regarded as menacing by the ecclesiastical establishment. The Church was in habitual political dispute with the lay power and was constantly on guard against the subversion of heresy.

The threat of Islam

In the twelfth century, religious speculation, as St. Bernard feared and foresaw, was not to be easily stopped. A substantial contributory factor to such speculation was Islamic civilization. It is true that in Spain Islamic culture had flourished on European soil for centuries. But it was only in the newly confident and outward-looking society of the twelfth century that all the conditions were right for Europeans to profit from the rich store of Greco-Arabic learning that had been on their doorstep for centuries. The movement had been gathering momentum throughout the previous century, and now the Arab influence was readily accepted.

The monk Gerbert, who became Pope as Sylvester II, had been the first Westerner to use the "Arabic" numerals, and it was probably he who introduced the astrolabe for astronomical experiments into Europe. At Salerno and then at Monte Cassino, thanks to the writings of men such as Constantine the African, the principles of Greco-Arabic medicine were being studied in Europe. Islamic thought, with its bases in the works of Aristotle and Plato and the science of India, was immensely influential in the early twelfth century at the great school of Chartres. And direct contact with the Greek texts of the ancient philosophers was possible for such Western scholars as James of Venice, who studied at Constantinople. But the main impetus was from Islam and above all from the cosmopolitan courts of newly Christian Spain. There, Arabs, Christians and Jews combined to initiate a revolution in mathematics that was to culminate at the end of the century in the career of Leonardo of Pisa. The much-traveled English scholar, Adelard of Bath, spent many years in Syria and Spain. His numerous important translations include the first Latin version of Euclid. Adelard, in fact, was one of those who introduced

Page from an early Byzantine herbal with later Arabic inscription.

the new Arabic writings on the study of alchemy from which European chemistry was to spring. Europe's contacts with the East and the Arab World were probably also crucial to the development of the Gothic style in architecture.

It is interesting that the impact of Arabic culture on European thought seems to have been at its greatest during the period when the Christian kingdoms of Spain were enjoying their greatest success in the long process of reconquest. Toledo, the ancient Visigothic capital, was recaptured in 1085, and by 1100 the combined kingdoms of Castile and Leon had pushed their frontiers well to the south of the Ebro River. Their advance was slowed during the twelfth century when the Moorish emirates in Spain were united under the Murabit dynasty.

Spain reconquered

The Spanish victories were important, but they were no compensation for the massive blow suffered by the Christian cause in the East at the Battle of Manzikert in 1071. Here the Byzantine Emperor Romanus IV was defeated by the armies of the Seljuk Turks, and the whole of Anatolia, the vital hinterland of Constantinople and Christendom's eastern bulwark, was suddenly put in jeopardy. The defeat in part had been due to treachery, as civil war compounded the troubles of the Empire. Now numbered among her external enemies was a new force, the Norman principality of southern Italy.

The domestic conflict of the Eastern Empire ended with the accession of Alexius I Comnenus in 1081. He was able to foil the Normans by a diplomacy that included an alliance with, and important trading concessions to, the growing power of Venice. But Constantinople itself was threatened by the depredations of nomadic tribes from the Asian steppes. Nevertheless, by the early 1090s, thanks to the Herculean efforts of Alexius, the Empire, although much reduced by the events of the previous twenty years, seemed to have weathered the storm. But a new problem now appeared.

Earlier in his reign, in his search for allies, Alexius had appealed to the West for mercenaries. With the arrival of the crusaders in the European provinces of the Empire in 1095, Alexius found himself with a force that threatened to overwhelm rather than support his realm. Instead of mercenaries, of the kind Byzantium had used for centuries, came a host of landless barons and footloose adventurers inspired with hatred of the Infidel, hope of eternal salvation and little respect for the "schismatic" Christian Emperor of the East. This vast and fervent body of men was under the command of a group of ambitious princes who included Alexius' old enemy, Bohemond the Norman. Nevertheless, the Emperor succeeded in transporting the crusader army away from his capital to Palestine. In addition, he exacted from most of the leaders an oath of homage for any lands that they might recover.

Among those to swear was Bohemond; but his subsequent attempt to hold Antioch as an independent principality led him at one point to call for a "crusade" against the Christian Emperor of the East himself. Such corruption of the spiritual ideals of the crusade was to be a dull thread throughout its history. But even from the outset, the motives and motivations of the crusaders had been mixed. What was the nature of the newly confident and aggressive Europe from which they came?

The Crusaders

Undoubtedly the religious impulse was strong. The crusade was launched by the stirring call to liberate the Holy Places made by Pope Urban II at the Council of Clermont in 1095. While Jerusalem had been controlled by the Arab Fatimid dynasty, access to the city had been comparatively easy for the growing flood of Western pilgrims, who were inspired by the new mood of piety abroad in Europe following the monastic reforms of St. Bernard. But with the conquest of Palestine by the fanatical Seljuks, advancing in the wake of their victory at Manzikert, the pilgrim routes were cut. Although the religious intentions of Urban II need not be questioned, he must have been aware of the massive increase in the prestige of the papacy already high after Canossa, that would follow from the recovery of Jerusalem under his aegis. Urban's call rang throughout Europe and was taken up by itinerant preachers such as Peter the Hermit. Indeed, Peter led a vast but disorderly band of common people to the crusade and, despite his own obscure and humble origins, he enjoyed some prestige with the army. Although the later crusades were to be led by kings and emperors, the first was undeniably a popular movement, even though most of its aristocratic leaders may have had ulterior political ends of one kind or another.

Crucial as religious idealism and land-hungry ambition were to the success of the crusade, underlying both idealism and ambition was the fact that for more than a century the population of the West had been growing at an almost explosive rate—possibly because of improvements in the dietary regime of the whole population. The dynamism and expansionism of European intellectual and political life can be observed, but it is impossible to measure precisely the dimensions of the population expansion that it reflected. We know that during the tenth and eleventh centuries vast new areas of forest

Dedication of the abbey of Cîteaux to the Virgin by its early saintly abbots.

and marsh had been reclaimed for agriculture within the traditional frontiers of Christendom, and that the vast movement of colonization of the lands to the east of the German empire had begun.

The growth and increasing physical vigor of the peasant population that these facts indicate were caused, at least in part, by a revolution in agricultural machinery and techniques. In this revolution there were three vital elements that gradually merged: the development of a new plough, more capable of turning over the heavy and fertile soils of the northern European plain than its predecessor; the introduction of a new system for the rotation of crops, which made for a more efficient use of land and also made possible the introduction of new crops with higher protein content; and the gradual adoption of the horse as a draught animal, in place of the more slow-moving oxen of previous generations. The combination of these three factors created a new situation in northern European agriculture, which has been viewed as the basis of the cultural ascendancy of the north, above all of France, throughout the Middle Ages. There can be no doubt that the new agriculture played an important part in European life of this period.

But in saying this we do not forget that it was the new spirit of inquiry abroad in Europe, that enabled the splendidly vigorous society of the twelfth century to adopt the new learning and evolve for itself a new intellectual orientation.

A crusader receives Holy Communion; sculpture from Reims Cathedral.

Abelard in Paris

Through the early Middle Ages, such teaching and studying as existed in Europe was centered on monasteries and cathedral schools, and theology was the "queen of sciences." The new universities that sprang up across Europe in the twelfth and thirteenth centuries made it possible for other branches of learning to flourish and develop. Groups of questing students gathered around such renowned teachers as Peter Abelard at Paris to form the nucleus for these universities. The dialectical methods introduced by Abelard were to have a profound influence on the thinking of his day and brought him into conflict with the Church—just as his celebrated romance with the lovely Héloïse earned for him the fury and the terrible retribution of her offended family.

The seal of Clare College, Cambridge. The foundation of the Universities of Cambridge and of Oxford was largely caused by the emigration of dissident students from the University of Paris.

Opposite Scenes from student life from the illuminated statute book of the College of Hubant at the University of Paris.

The road from Orleans to Paris was crowded with groups of pilgrims singing psalms, merchants driving pack-animals laden with bundles, horsemen with fine trappings and all sorts of riff-raff. The young student who had been making his way along it for several days saw in the distant hollow of the river, in the glow of the sunset, the bell-towers and roofs of the Ile de la Cité. He urged on his mount: "Paris at last!"

This emotion that Peter Abelard experienced on arriving in Paris was to appear later in his autobiography. Thanks to this work, which Abelard entitled *Letter to A Friend, or the History of My Misfortunes,* we are familiar not only with the quite exceptional restlessness that characterized his life but also with his course of studies and with the intellectual framework of the times.

The reader might well be surprised at the strength of Abelard's emotion upon reaching Paris, considering the city's condition in the year 1100. It was a small town, crammed between the banks of the Ile de la Cité, with houses rising in tiers even on to the bridges—the Petit-Pont on the left bank and the Grand-Pont on the right. It hardly extended any farther than the island; only a few small market towns had grown up in the vicinity of the abbeys of Saint-Germain-des-Prés, Saint-Marcel and Sainte-Geneviève. No one could have suspected that one day Paris would become the capital city. The King resided there only occasionally, and the Bishop of Paris was only one of a number of suffragan bishops under the Archbishop of Sens. And knowledge, like power, had yet to reach any degree of centralization; seats of learning were spread over a wide area like the châteaux of the lords of the manor, and like the towns that came into being and took shape at the same period. The monastic schools of Bec or Saint-Benoît-sur-Loire, and the episcopal schools of Chartres or Reims, were already much better known than the schools of Paris.

But Paris attracted Peter Abelard because of his enthusiasm for the subjects of dialectics. He had learned the elements of it in the various schools he had attended in his native Brittany—where his father was lord of the manor of Pallet, near Nantes—and also at Loches where he profited from the lessons of the celebrated teacher Roscelin. But Guillaume de Champeau, the authority on dialectics, taught in Paris. Thus Abelard decided—when he was about twenty—to go to Paris to hear Guillaume lecture, and through him to perfect himself in the art.

The study of dialectics was pursued with enormous enthusiasm in the student world of the twelfth century, and it is important to know why. It is accepted that traditionally the subjects of learning were divided into seven branches, which we know as the seven liberal arts. Whereas the useful arts encompassed the manual crafts—carpentry, metalwork, etc.—the liberal arts were concerned both with the physical sphere—arithmetic, geometry, music and astronomy (the quadrivium)—and the sphere of the spirit—grammar, rhetoric and dialectics (the trivium). Every student would normally be expected to study these various subjects and to complete the whole cycle. The more gifted ones would then grapple with the "sacred science," to which Abelard later gave the name of theology. Grammar was the field we call letters—literature and the study of ancient and modern authors. Rhetoric, the art of expressing oneself, held then a position of great importance, for the whole of medieval culture was based on the spoken word and gesture. These were to be succeeded at the time of the Renaissance by a civilization based on writing and printing. Finally, dialectics was the art of reasoning; it was, as Rabin Maur wrote as early as the ninth century "the discipline of disciplines ... it is dialectics that teaches us how to teach and teaches us how to learn: in dialectics reason discovers and shows what it is, what it seeks, and what it sees."

Dialectics, then, aroused great enthusiasm in scholastic circles. Its sphere can be compared to that of logic: it showed how to make use of reason in the search for truth. But it also presupposed an exchange of views, a discussion, which was called the "disputation;" logic does not necessarily entail this for it can be carried on by a thinker in the privacy of his own room. The "disputation" took a predominant

Héloïse and Abelard; this sculpture is on a capital at the Salle des Gardes de la Conciergerie in Paris.

place among scholastic exercises. At the beginning of each study, there was a reading from a text, the "lectio." "Reading" was the equivalent of teaching; when later at the University of Paris it was forbidden to "read" Aristotle, this meant that it was forbidden to make use of certain of his works as a basis of instruction.

Whenever a teacher embarked upon the study of a work, he first gave a general introduction. He then made a commentary upon it which was called the "exposition" and was divided into three parts: the "letter," that is to say the grammatical explanation; the "sense," or comprehension of the text; and finally what is called the "meaning," that is the deeper meaning or doctrinal content. The "littera," "sensus," and the "sententia" (meaning) constitute the glossary. There are a great number of manuscripts from this period that reveal this method of teaching, even in their actual layout. Each page comprises one or two central columns of text, while the glossary surrounds the text and fills the top, bottom and sides of the page. A similar layout was to survive in printed books even to the end of the fifteenth century.

When it came to a question of the "sententia" or doctrinal content, a host of questions could be raised that had to be resolved, and it was this that constituted the disputation or "disputatio" which formed such a distinctive part of scholastic exercises. In the following century, there were a great number of works, in particular several parts of the *Summa* of St. Thomas Aquinas, which are given the name of *Questiones Disputate*, that bear witness to the conditions under which they were worked out, i.e. in

the course of those disputations in which both teacher and pupils took part. The disputations that are so much in demand by present-day university students were accepted quite naturally in feudal times and survived until modern times.

In fact, they were so readily accepted that an exceptionally gifted pupil like Abelard found it tempting to take advantage of the fact. He had originally been well received by Guillaume de Champeau, that indefatigable disputant, but in spite of his youth he did not hesitate to attack his teacher's propositions, even to the point of forcing him on two occasions to modify them. This success brought him considerable renown but it also aroused fierce jealousies, as much on the part of his fellow students as of Guillaume himself. Abelard responded to their attacks by opening a school of his own, first at Melun and then at Corbeil; but he had also set his sights on the chair of dialectics in Paris itself, at the school of Notre-Dame. He succeeded in his ambition, and later taught at Mont Sainte-Geneviève just outside the city. His reputation was a powerful magnet to the students of Paris—among them some from the provinces and some from abroad.

The story of his love for Héloïse, the niece of Canon Fulbert of Notre-Dame, is famous, as is the story of Fulbert's fury when he believed that Abelard was about to desert her. The emasculation that Fulbert's hired ruffians inflicted on Abelard in 1118 brought to an end, for the time being, his activities as a teacher. He became a monk and retired to the cloisters of Saint-Denis, where he stayed until 1120.

But the excitement that Abelard had aroused in

The foundations of the University of Paris

no way abated. In 1127 the canons of Notre-Dame, finding that the student body had become far too boisterous, decided to expel them from the cloister which they occupied. The teachers and scholars found hospitality on the slopes of Mont Sainte-Geneviève, under the aegis of the abbey of the same name. Abelard himself taught there, at least from 1133 onwards; and the Englishman, John of Salisbury, has borne witness to the enthusiasm that he aroused. The originality of his teaching was embodied in his use of the resources of dialectics to prove the truth of certain articles of faith. It was a rash position to adopt; he drew upon Aristotle—as yet little known in the West—when making a commentary on certain fundamental dogmas of Christianity, such as the Trinity. This was to arouse distrust and to scandalize certain defenders of the faith, such as St. Bernard of Clairvaux, to such an extent that Abelard was to find his propositions condemned at the Council of Sens in 1140. He appealed to the Pope, who upheld the Council, and Abelard decided to submit to their decision.

The philosopher's life was to reach a peaceful conclusion in 1142 in the shade of the abbey church of Cluny.

Meanwhile, the "student explosion" had determined the physical layout of Paris. The left bank became the home of the intellectuals, and was soon filled with schools which little by little replaced the vineyards; while the right bank, which afforded easy access for river traffic, became the home of commerce. Paris became honored as the "fountain of knowledge" and the "paradise of pleasure" for students all over Europe. In the following century, Alexander Neckham was to write, "it is there that the arts flourish, it is there that divine works are the rule."

Even so, there was still no such institution as a university. When Abelard died in 1142, the methods of teaching had not yet appeared in texts, and there was no organization in this effervescent student life. Teachers and pupils found themselves in the houses that from this time on formed compact rows on the slopes of Mont Sainte-Geneviève and on the approaches of the Petit-Pont. The Rue du Fouarre, in what is now the Latin Quarter, is a reminder of the bales of straw (feurre, fourre) that normally served as seats, and the Rue de la Parcheminerie recalls the material which was after all the medium for the transmission of thought: the humble lambskin, cleaned and degreased to provide a surface for writing. Each of the folio volumes of those times, so reverently preserved in our libraries today, represents a whole flock of sheep.

In general, the teachers lived in a very hand-to-mouth fashion and the question of their salaries was one that gave rise to fierce debate. Was it permissible to disseminate knowledge for financial reward? Peter Abelard openly declared that his pupils owed him both material rewards and honor, but preachers like St. Bernard of Clairvaux argued violently against those who used teaching for their own profit. No problem existed for those who were

Left The seals of the faculties of the University of Paris.

Below The act of foundation of the College of Robert de Sorbon, soon to became the faculty of theology.

The seal of Paris University.

Paris attracts the greatest teachers

A teacher of grammar above the figure of the grammarian Donatus, an allegorical representation, in the masonry of Chartres Cathedral, of the studies pursued at a university.

Top right Plato and Socrates depicted in a book of astronomical tables and prognostications, from St. Albans.

Bottom right A bastion in the city wall at Oxford, the scene of many fierce disputes between representatives of the opposing factions of "town and gown," which were characteristic of university towns in the medieval period.

assigned a benefice by a cathedral church or abbey, and this applied in the case of Abelard, who enjoyed the office of prebendary canon, although this did not mean that he was a priest; nor for those members of the mendicant orders, notably the preaching friars who at the beginning of the thirteenth century had a special duty to teach and were maintained by their orders—despite the opposition of the secular clergy.

The bond that linked this sphere of activity to the bishop upon whom in principle it depended was somewhat tenuous. It was the bishop who in the person of his chancellor granted throughout his diocese the *licentia docendi*, the permission to teach from which arose the term "licenciate" that is still in use. The abbot of Sainte-Geneviève, however, claimed the right to do this throughout the area under the jurisdiction of his abbey.

We learn from a bull of Pope Innocent III, dating from the end of 1208 or the beginning of 1209, that a number of disputes arose about the year 1200. Teachers and pupils of Paris then united in a single association and nominated a commission of eight members from among themselves whose responsibility it was to draw up statutes by which they would be governed. Thus there came into being the *Universitas Magistrorum et Scolarium Parisiensium*, the University, that is to say the association in a united body of the teachers and scholars of Paris. The Pope ratified its autonomy and denied the bishop and his chancellor the right to refuse a licence to whomsoever the teachers nominated as qualified to teach. In 1215 the papal legate Robert de Courçon confirmed the rights of the University by approving the statutes that freed both teachers and students from the tutelage of the bishop. At the same period (to be exact the year 1200) the King of France had of his own accord freed the University from the jurisdiction of the royal courts, and it was now answerable only to the ecclesiastical courts. Judicial autonomy was thus added to administrative autonomy; the world of thought and knowledge became the epitome of freedom.

In the thirteenth century, the University of Paris was to earn a great reputation, with teachers like Albert le Grand from Germany, Thomas Aquinas from Italy and Roger Bacon from England. But for all that, its existence was marked by unruliness and agitation. The strike of 1229–31 was triggered off by a brawl which had broken out between some students and innkeepers of the Faubourg Saint-Marcel one Shrove Monday. But the royal troops put down the disturbance rather too rigorously. And there was the well-known struggle waged by the secular teachers against the friars of the mendicant orders whom they wanted to ban from teaching in their universities.

From this time onward poor students found board and lodging in colleges. The first of these was founded in Paris in 1180 by a middle-class Londoner named Josse. Similar foundations were to spring up: the college of Saint-Thomas du Louvre in 1186 and the college of Bons-Enfants in 1280. But all those were

to be eclipsed in the future by the one established in 1257 by Robert de Sorbon, the chaplain to Louis the Pious. He founded a college in a house that the King had given him, situated in the Rue Coupe-Guele, which is now the Rue de la Sorbonne. In fact, although the colleges started off as hostels for poor students, they became in time centers of teaching; for example, the College of Robert de Sorbon was the headquarters of the Faculty of Theology of the University.

Although Paris remained famous for its teaching of the liberal arts, as in Abelard's time, the curriculum was nevertheless distinguished by the inclusion of medicine and theology. From the end of the twelfth century, the students at Paris formed various distinct groups according to their place of origin, in other words, "nations." There were four nations represented at the University of Paris: French—that is to say, natives of the Ile-de-France—Normans, Picards and English. At the end of the Middle Ages, because of the wars between France and England, the English nation was replaced by the German. Each one had its own statutes. One could discern in these spontaneous groups of students a foreshadowing of the nations that were born in the course of the wars of the fifteenth century.

It was in this period, however, that the University of Paris went into a complete decline. The scholastic methods founded upon Aristotelian logic, which had been introduced to the West through the Arab thinkers, particularly Avicenna and Averroes, became set from the beginning of the fourteenth century onwards in formulae which were to offer an easy butt for the skits of François Villon. Under Philippe-le-Bel and then under Philippe de Valois, the University had begun to adopt a political role, and its power in the state seemed to grow in proportion to the decline in the quality of its studies.

And it was no longer the only university; its organization had inspired various other foundations during the thirteenth century.

University foundations were to multiply in the fourteenth and fifteenth centuries, but it was a period of the spread of learning rather than any advance or renewal of intellectual or technical research. The only progress in this period was seen in the science of armament and military equipment, with the introduction of gunpowder.

But at this period, the University of Paris was discredited because at the time of the wars between France and England it took sides with the invader. The Sorbonne, the Faculty of Theology, succeeded in maintaining its reputation under the *ancien régime*, even when the University as a whole went into decline. The brilliance and freshness of Abelard, and his enormous influence, had played a decisive part in establishing this reputation. Through his lectures, even more than his writings, Abelard brought reason to the traditional mystery surrounding faith and an independent intellect to the elaborated system of logic. In no small measure he laid the foundations for the advent of humanism.

REGINE PERNOUD

Students at Paris are shown carrying books and in other activities pertaining to the life of the University in the illuminated statute book of the College of Hubant.

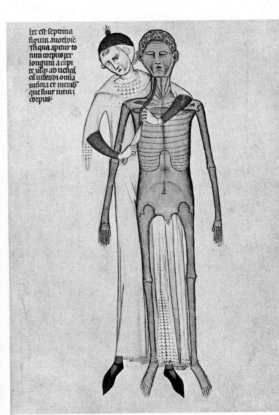

Left Fourteenth-century astrolabe, an instrument for astronomical measurement, and one of the many mathematical instruments that medieval European scholarship took from earlier Arab examples.

Right A mid-fourteenth-century medical manuscript of Guy of Pavia. Some of the greatest medical centers of medieval Europe were in France and Italy, their learning based directly on Arab sources.

The cult of courtly love takes root ar

The glory of Chartres

In the glories of its new cathedral, the town of Chartres provided the fullest single expression of vigor and inspiration of twelfth-century Europe. The school of Chartres itself had been in the forefront of the revival of Neoplatonist philosophy that marked the intellectual ferment of that glorious century. Like other important centers, it had been receptive to the intellectual stimulus provided by that century's full discovery of Greco-Arab learning. Chartres also symbolized the cultural and political hegemony that northern France was to exercise throughout Europe during the thirteenth century and after. This hegemony was prepared for in the work of the great Abbot Suger, churchman, statesman and inspired patron of the arts, whose church of the Abbey of St. Denis provided both a fitting shrine for the French monarchy and the seminal building of the Gothic Age. Paris, as the home both of the kings of France who were to come into their own during the thirteenth century, and of the great new university, was to dominate Europe in the coming generations. Yet during the twelfth century itself, national leadership was located in the south, the home of the rich Provençal culture. Before turning to Provence, let us first look at the other strangely "un-European" society which had sprung up in Outremer, the lands "over the sea," in the Holy Land.

Outremer, heir to the Crusades

The fruits of the First Crusade had been the city of Jerusalem itself and several Christian principalities, representing roughly the modern states of Israel, Lebanon and parts of modern Turkey and Syria. Despite the mixed motives behind the crusading movement, popular religious sentiment had been strong. Throughout the first half of the twelfth century, the newly founded Frankish kingdoms in Outremer and the crusading orders of knights, the Templars and the Hospitalers, received occasional reinforcements in the shape of militant pilgrims from Europe anxious to defend the gains of Christendom in the Holy Land. But the recapture of the inland northern county of Edessa by the sultan Zangi in 1144 sounded the death knell of the

Christ in Majesty, from Vézelay, where Bernard of Clairvaux stirred Conrad III and the French King to embark on the Second Crusade.

Christian states in the Middle East. By the end of the century, they had been reduced to a thin coastal strip. Thanks to the stirring oratory of St. Bernard, two mighty armies under the command of the aging German king Conrad III and the pious but inexperienced Louis VII of France set out on the ill-fated Second Crusade of 1147.

From the outset the venture was weakened by divided councils, while animosity and distrust soon developed between the Westerners and the Byzantines. For Byzantine survival, and thus ultimately for the survival of the Christian cause in the East, Moslem disunity was crucial. Yet few things could be better calculated to unify Islam than the concerted attack of powerful Christian armies. The situation grew still worse when, as was the case, the objectives were ill-defined and ill-coordinated. Reluctant to assist his Christian allies for such reasons, the Emperor Manuel was dismayed at the ease with which the unruly crusading armies pillaged the Byzantine lands through which they passed. When the Germans finally met the Infidel, however, they were easily defeated and dispersed. When King Louis of France, with his beautiful and headstrong wife Eleanor, arrived at Antioch, he was urged to strike at Aleppo, the seat of power of the sultan Nur ed Din. The plan was sound, but Louis was suspicious of the very close liaison between Eleanor and her uncle, the Count

Raymond, who had suggested the strategy to him. Anxious to visit Jerusalem, Louis instead left Antioch for the Holy City. From Jerusalem the Christians attacked Damascus, a potential ally against their main enemy, Nur ed Din. In fact, the army was forced to abandon the siege and the crusade did nothing but demonstrate the vulnerability of the western crusading effort.

To the Provençal ladies of Queen Eleanor's train, the semi-Oriental court of Antioch must have been a magical world, and the soldiers were often reluctant to quit the ease and comfort of these rich cities for the battlefield. But still they could not accept the ease with which their cousins had adapted themselves to the mores of the East. The astonished northerners found themselves in a supposedly Christian and crusading society—yet one where even the pleasures of the harem were not unknown, and where princes often conducted diplomatic negotiations in Arabic. For their part, of course, the second-generation crusaders were living in a political environment that made the simple equation of Christian versus Infidel an impossible recipe for continued survival. Inevitably, as the rival civilizations of Islam and Christianity came to know one another at first hand, they discovered that the religious-political tags that made them enemies could not obscure the fact that they were all men. We have touched on the eagerness of

Christian scholars in Spain to learn from Islam, but in the Norman kingdom of southern Italy an even greater degree of cultural miscegenation made itself apparent. In Outremer the fusion was complete; they were, of course, potential enemies, as the kings of France and England were enemies, and both sides found it advantageous when calling up help from outside to emphasize the element of the religious war. But if Outremer shocked the northern crusaders, the vibrant and revolutionary principles of the culture of southern France threatened them—and it was closer to home.

The culture of Provence

The political rivalry between the kings at Paris and their many powerful vassals was of long-standing, and the most serious threat was posed by the virtually autonomous dukes of Aquitaine and the counts of Toulouse. Southern France was also a separate area

Carving of a troubadour.

Miniature of lovers, and a majestic head of the Virgin, which exemplify the the eleventh-century cult of woman.

Brutality and murder typical of the Albigensian crusade.

or, in the far north, the mythological hero, Beowulf. The poetry of the troubadours instead dealt with love between man and woman, and a unique and revolutionary love at that. Suddenly woman became an object of respect in the male society of the Middle Ages. The cult of courtly love was the cult of woman, which in religious terms was paralleled by the equally sudden appearance of the cult of the Virgin during the twelfth century; Chartres itself was the first great church to be dedicated to the Virgin. As the thirteenth century progressed, the two cults approached and sometimes merged into one another. In a characteristic medieval musical form, the polyphonic motet, a piece based on a fragment of plainsong from an antiphon to the Virgin might use the text of a French love song in the upper part. Furthermore, at a time when marriage was explicitly a matter of dynastic policy and brides were regarded as counters on the diplomatic chess board and wives as pieces of property, the notion of love was certainly not connected with the marital state. To some extent the cult was a game and known to be a game for, ironically, the objective of the poets, who were almost exclusively men and usually landless younger sons, was to win a rich and landed wife and thus join the system they were supposed to be fighting.

In some ways, the cult of courtly love was an ideal rationalization of a society centered upon the castle of a great lord thronged by landless adventurers and presided over during the lord's many absences by the great lady. But the game was taken to extraordinary lengths; for example, at the court of Eleanor of Aquitaine. First at Angers then at Poitiers, Eleanor held courts of love, presided over by the ladies. The cult even had its own bible or legal code in the shape of the Code of Love in thirty-one articles. Written for Eleanor's daughter by her chaplain, the Code of Love was regarded by the orthodox members of the old society as one of the most subversive, as it was certainly one of the most influential, books of the time.

We have seen Eleanor on crusade with her husband, Louis VII of France. The crusade, attended by many great ladies and their troubadours, was itself something of a romantic episode. Yet, angered by his wife's infidelity and disturbed by her inability to produce sons, the French king finally yielded to the urgings of St. Bernard to rid himself of this "she devil" and sought a dissolution of the marriage. The Pope, himself persuaded by Bernard, granted the dispensation. For Eleanor—who said of her husband "I thought to have married a king but found I am wed to a monk"—the event could only be considered as a "happy release." But the divorce had disastrous consequences for France and the history of Western Europe. Five years later she married Henry Plantagenet, heir to England and the duchy of Normandy.

Heresy and separation

We have already touched on the impact of the Catharist heresy in Europe; by 1167 it had reached such proportions that the Cathari (their name comes from the Greek word meaning "pure") held their own ecclesiastical council. Sixty years later, the whole rich flowering of Provençal culture was obliterated in the bloody and vindictive Albigensian crusade launched with the Church's blessing and conducted by soldiers and adventurers from the north. The Cathars, like many reforming sects since, held that the Church had been corrupted by its involvement in the world ever since its adoption by Constantine in the fourth century. Only their own pure and simple living, they held, came close to that of the primitive Church. To the rebellious and aristocratic society of the south, it had a double appeal, both as the religious equivalent of that society's political separatism and as a truly aristocratic religion. The small elite of the Catharist *Perfecti*, for instance, exerted a deep fascination on the aristocratic ladies who dominated Provençal society. Indeed many of these ladies publicly embraced Catharism.

The Cathars proclaimed the wickedness as well as the irrelevance of war and even of the crusades. The Church was thus obliged to produce apologists of its own who advanced the argument of the just war. Yet the crusades had in their favor the facts that they hastened the Christianization of the worst excesses of the martial element in feudal society and fostered the evolution of the concept of Christian chivalry. After the twelfth century warfare was as bloody and brutal as ever, but the concept that war was subject to the laws of God and civilized behavior had arisen, and the code of knightly chivalry had been born.

linguistically, and it was culturally separate, with a virtually unbroken tradition stretching back to Roman Provence. Moreover, there was close contact with the Arab World, and, as the twelfth century progressed, the separatism of the south was reinforced by the rapid spread of the Albigensian religious heresy.

The heralds and agents of this new civilization were the troubadours. Their verses, probably influenced by Arabic models, survive from the eleventh century; the earliest troubadour known to us by name is Duke William of Aquitaine (1071–1126). The most distinctive features of Provençal culture, when compared with that of other European regions, are the active participation of a cultured aristocracy and the development of a specifically court culture as opposed to a Church culture. Vernacular lyric poetry may be said to have been born in Provence during this period; forms that were invented by the Provençal poets continued to be used down to the Renaissance and indeed beyond More important, however, than the forms was the subject matter.

Until then the main subject of court poetry had been the heroic deeds of great emperors and warriors—of Charlemagne and Roland

St. Dominic, who led the crusade against heresy in the eleventh century.

The Palace of the Virgin

*With its clusters of columns, its soaring arches, its superb stone carvings and its matchless
stained-glass windows, the cathedral of Notre-Dame de Chartres is perhaps the finest achievement
of the Gothic movement that swept Europe in the thirteenth century. A disastrous fire of 1194 left
little more of Chartres' old cathedral than the western towers and the crypt. In a great burst of
energy and artistic creativity, the reverent people of the small French town rebuilt their
"palace of the Virgin" in the remarkably short span of twenty-five years—and for this reason
Chartres Cathedral shows more unity of design than most Gothic cathedrals. Notre-Dame de
Chartres has been called a Bible for those who cannot read: the saints appear immortalized in
stone at the portals ; the glorious windows present Old and New Testament stories ; and the
arches and columns carry men's eyes—along with their thoughts—heavenward.*

On June 10, 1194, the cathedral of Notre-Dame de
Chartres, rebuilt in the eleventh century by Bishop
Fulbert, was destroyed by fire. Only the crypt, the
narthex, the two western towers and the Portail
Royal—built early in the twelfth century—were
spared in the disaster, which also engulfed a great
part of the small city, some fifty miles southwest of
Paris. From this catastrophe there arose a cathedral
that, in its architectural design, its sculptures and
its stained glass windows, constitutes one of the
outstanding proofs of the Gothic genius and one of
its most original in expression.

Thanks to the religious faith of the Middle Ages,
Notre-Dame de Chartres was largely rebuilt in a
quarter of a century. The *Book of the Miracles of
Notre-Dame* tells us of the enthusiasm of the enormous
number of staunch Christians who took part in the
rebuilding of the cathedral. They transported the
materials across the flat country of Beauce, and even
harnessed themselves to the heavy wagons of lime,
timber and stone.

Everything favored the immediate rebuilding of
the cathedral, which was achieved through the
generosity both of anonymous believers in the diocese
of Chartres and the whole of northern France, as well
as the munificence of French and foreign rulers.
Among the royal patrons of Chartres was Richard
Coeur-de-Lion who, although he was at war with
Philip Augustus, was eager to make his offering and
to contribute to the restoration of this famous
cathedral dedicated to the Virgin Mary. Christian
unity was not yet an empty phrase.

From 1210 onwards, services could be held in the
new nave. On January 1, 1221, the choir was handed
over to the cathedral chapter. Between 1230 and
1235 the transepts were finished, and in 1260, with
the solemn consecration of the rebuilt cathedral,
the work had virtually been completed.

Perhaps the brilliant but anonymous architect
responsible for the plan of the new cathedral came
originally from Laon or Soissons, that is to say, from

northern France, where Gothic art had recently
emerged with such striking innovations. The consecration of the abbey church of Saint-Denis on
June 11, 1144, had ensured the transmission of the
Gothic style to the whole of France, and its influence
at Chartres can be seen in the transverse ribbing of
the cathedral towers, and even more in the Portail
Royal, which was inspired by Saint-Denis and
escaped the fire of 1194.

The second half of the twelfth century had been
an age of rich and promising architectural experiments. Cathedrals were planned and built with
widely differing plans—Laon with its single aisles,
Paris with its double aisles, Sens with no transepts,
Noyon with the ends of the transepts semicircular
in form, and Senlis with an ambulatory surrounded
by chapels. With the exception of Sens, all these
cathedrals have great galleries or triforia above
their aisles, and all of them, including Sens, have
sexpartite nave vaults.

The architect of Chartres had no wish to copy
these designs, splendid as they were. To understand
his intentions, one must bear in mind the existence
of the great crypt built in the eleventh century by
Bishop Fulbert, and the considerable limitations
this imposed on the ground plan. But the architect
was sufficiently ingenious to overcome all these
practical problems—in fact they provided him with
inspiration. The interior of the building, which is
some four hundred and thirty feet long, has a complete unity of conception because of the speed with
which it was built, apparently with no second
thoughts or regrets. The nave, fifty-four feet across,
is wider than that of any other cathedral because of
the Romanesque foundations of the existing crypt.
It is divided into seven bays, not counting those
between the two towers on the west front, and is
flanked by single aisles which are repeated again in
the transepts. The transepts, over two hundred
feet long, almost form a second cathedral at the
center of this vast church. The choir has four

The Angel of Chartres looks
out from its pinnacle on the
east end of the choir.

Opposite The cathedral of
Notre-Dame de Chartres,
rebuilt after its destruction by
fire in 1194. The cathedral is
a symbol of the medieval
Christian unity, and is one of
the greatest expressions of
the Gothic genius.

Below left The diagram of Gothic architectural development shows : (1) barrel vaulting ; (2) the development of the pointed arch and rib vaulting ; (3) the stress taken by a buttress ; (4) the Gothic development of the flying buttress ; (5) a section of a Gothic cathedral to show buttresses supporting the roof and the thin tracery of windows and pillars.

Below right The north window at Chartres, a magnificent piece of stained glass, depicting the Virgin Mary enthroned as the Mother of Jesus. It is one of many windows, some donated by local trade guilds, by which the glory of the cathedral was enhanced.

rectangular vaults and a semicircular apse with seven bays. It has also a double ambulatory with seven shallow apsidal chapels.

Had it not been for the exceptional width of the main structure, the architect would almost certainly have given the cathedral greater height. As it is, the main vault is about one hundred and twenty feet high, surpassing those of Senlis, Laon and Paris. Chartres itself was soon to be surpassed by Reims, Amiens and, above all, Beauvais—the most daring structure ever attempted by Gothic architects. Thanks to the unknown architect of Chartres at the end of the twelfth century, the way was opened up for a new style which most of Europe eventually embraced.

It was a vital turning point both from the esthetic and the spiritual point of view, a decisive flowering that was to dominate all others. It was the master builder of Chartres who designed the pure Gothic style. He discarded excessively wide spans covered by sexpartite vaults and built the main structure

Gothic Architectural Style

"Cathedrals inevitably remain unfinished . . ."

with rectangular quadripartite vaults. He abandoned the triforia, which reduced the amount of light in other buildings. At Chartres, the simple and graceful arcades are above the great archways of the nave and choir, and in the clerestory he replaced the small, timid windows of the early Gothic period with two large vertical windows surmounted by a rose, thus reducing the wall at this point almost entirely to glass. He also replaced the cylindrical columns such as may be seen at Laon, Durham or Paris by shafts divided into small columns which foreshadowed the later column clusters of Amiens, Reims and Beauvais. Finally, on the exterior he was the first architect to devise a systematic use of the flying buttress, to withstand and counterbalance the forces exerted by the vaults.

The whole building was as sound as it was daring. This new predominance of void over solid was used in an equally masterly fashion on the façades of the transepts, which were pierced with five large lancet windows surmounted by glowing rose windows. This feature was derived from Laon, developed at Chartres, and soon afterwards brought to even greater magnificence in Paris. It was from Laon, too, that the architect of Chartres took the idea of a multiplicity of towers. He had inherited from the Romanesque period the two towers on the western façade, but this was not enough. He began the construction of further towers on either side of the façades of the transepts. In addition, and following a Carolingian tradition, two further towers were erected at the springing of the apse. Both are incomplete. If one adds the lantern doubtless intended above the crossing, there would eventually have been nine towers soaring above the city. No one had the courage to complete this imposing project. "Cathedrals," said Auguste Rodin in a later age, "inevitably remains unfinished. . . ."

Nevertheless, the "Classic" cathedral had been born and now imposed itself on the Christianity of the thirteenth century. The ceaseless craving for light sprang into life at Chartres, and what Chartres symbolizes above all—with boldness, but not recklessness—is the victory of the spiritual over the material. The time was not yet ripe for the next leap forward: time was, in every accepted sense of the term, at a stop, a divine moment within which the whole spirit of the century of St. Louis was embraced.

More than any other cathedral, that of Chartres is the living proof of the magnificence which the Church of the thirteenth century wished to confer upon the house of God. The Abbé Suger, a century before, had declared his intentions without ambiguity at the time of the reconstruction of Saint-Denis; and in this he was faithful to the explicit instructions which he had been given by the Order of St. Benedict to which he belonged, and even more precisely to the policy laid down by Hugues de Cluny. "The spirit in its blindness strives towards the truth through the medium of material things, and upon seeing the light recovers from its previous despondency." These words of Suger were carved on the very portal of his abbey church, and in this way he repudiated that latent craving for austerity which was sometimes carried to the point of schism or even to the heresy of iconoclasm—which had always been condemned by Rome but which had held so much attraction for successive Church reformers.

This magnificence, which transformed the cathedral of the thirteenth century into a forerunner of the heavenly city, had its most obvious manifestation in the glory of its stained glass windows. The Abbé Suger had, once again, been the innovator, but the introduction of stained glass was also a direct consequence of the technical achievements of Gothic architects. The windows and rose windows of the cathedrals of the thirteenth century never ceased to increase in surface area. Walls were constantly lightened and reduced to a simple tracery of stone, and so the stained glass window acquired supreme importance. This tendency had already been foreshadowed at Saint-Denis but first came to fruition and made its greatest impact at Chartres. The attenuation of the masonry reached its ultimate

Opposite The sculptures on the south portal of the cathedral are noble representations of the saints, central figures of the medieval Church as intermediaries between God and men.

The apse and broad transepts of Chartres, conceived by the master builder, expressed a new concept of space, simplicity of line, and light.

perfection in St. Louis' Saint-Chapelle at Paris, which was consecrated in 1248. But it is impossible to comprehend this quest for translucency without examining Notre-Dame de Chartres.

The stained glass was not simply a form of decoration but was also a history book of religious teaching. There was nothing superfluous in this feature which was directed, as Gerson says, "to those who cannot read what they should believe." In the entrance portals at Chartres, the Old and New Testaments are strictly interpreted as evidence of the fulfillment of the divine promise. The stained glass windows above the choir are devoted to the mysteries of the Virgin, the patron saint of Chartres; just as in those of the north rose window, the Virgin Mary is honored as the Mother of Jesus, and is acclaimed by the kings and prophets of the ancient law. The prophets, symbolically carrying the evangelists on their shoulders, also appear in the south rose window, which presents the eternal Christ as described in the Apocalypse of St. John. Finally, the lives of the saints occupy a prominent place.

Many of these legendary windows, particularly those in the aisles where they are more easily seen in detail, were donated by the city guilds: blacksmiths, furriers, bakers, innkeepers, money-changers—donors from all walks of life who were anxious to play their part in the building of the cathedral, just as in their daily lives they dedicated their work to God. In accordance with religious teaching and with the time, their donations were contributions towards the achievement of redemption.

Details of sculpture from Chartres: (*above*) One of the kings of France;
(*top right*) A man helping in the construction of a church, carries two doors on his back;
(*right middle*) A knight in mail leads two captive kings;
(*right bottom*) A craftsman with his tools.

The cathedral of the thirteenth century was the product of enthusiastic and sustained cooperation, a house of God above all, but in that very capacity a house of the people of God. It was the result of a degree of "participation," in the full sense of the term, that the twentieth century is anxious to reinstate. In the heyday of Christian Europe in the Middle Ages, on the other hand, the term "participation" was applied quite literally by the administrators of Chartres, Paris, Amiens, Reims, Bourges and Strasbourg, and by all those who appointed themselves pioneers of the Gothic message beyond the confines of the kingdom of St. Louis.

In fact, the thirteenth century was above all an age of synthesis—theological, philosophical, historical, literary and esthetic. The cathedral was the material and spiritual embodiment of all the scholastic *summa* of men like Thomas Aquinas and Albertus Magnus, of that "universal mirror" of a Vincent de Beauvais that brought together in a single group, dedicated to God, the riches of nature, the achievements of thought, the victory of virtue over vice and the divinely inspired development of mankind from the ancient law to the new. This then was the cathedral, an epitome of all the wonders of the world, a torchbearer for that medieval humanism which devoted itself to finding a common ground between nature and reason—an ethic that could only come into being on an esthetic basis. And it was this basis that the Gothic genius was to embody in full measure.

The cathedral was a creation of theologians who

292

Asserting the unity of Christian dogma

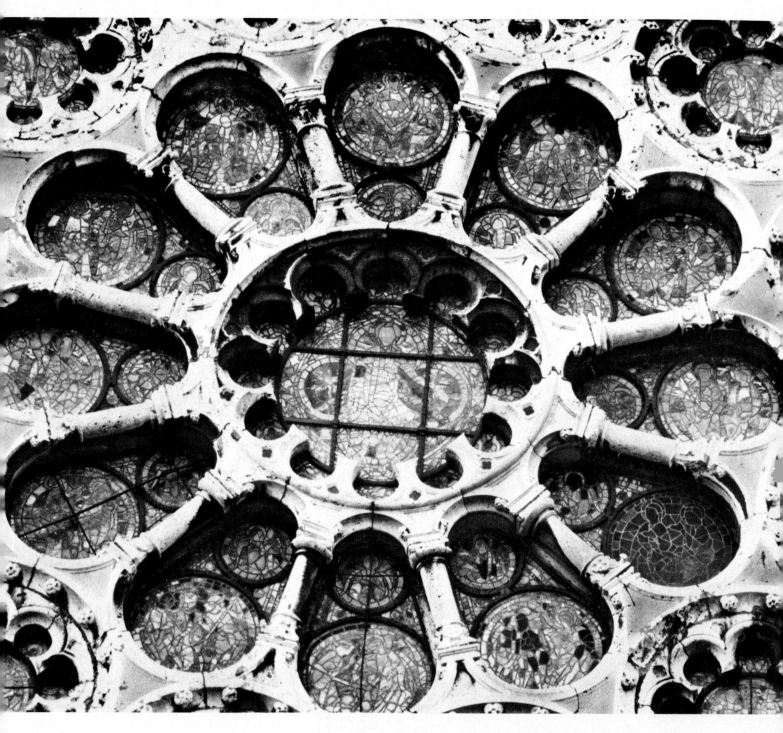

strove above all to uphold the orthodox faith against all the outbreaks of heresy. The whole of its presentation was intended to assert the unity and permanence of Christian dogma. If it was aggressive, it fought only to reaffirm the truth. Its aim was to afford proof, and if in the end it proved attractive too, it was because it had succeeded in proving the goodness and beauty of truth—two ideas that from then on became inseparable.

In the comprehensive iconography of its portals, the builders of the cathedral—which was conceived as the home of divine majesty and its omnipotence—dwelt inexhaustibly on the solemn theme of the Last Judgment, with which is associated the glorification of the Virgin Mary, her death, assumption and crowning. It is worth noting that most of these figures were originally colored in an attempt at realism designed to emphasize to the faithful the truths of dogma. (The sculptures of the Parthenon were similarly treated in the Athens of the fifth century B.C.) But the medieval cathedral was equally intended to cater to human weakness in the most humble aspects of the daily round, and in those seasonal occupations of the lives of men, as God had first decreed. When extolled by St. Francis of Assisi, nature revealed herself in all her beauty and pristine freshness: in the sculptor's repertoire of decorative motifs—watercress, oak, ferns, strawberry plants,

The rose window in the west front at Chartres, in the Romanesque "wheel" style.

293

Political life begins in the cathedral

The vines on a capital in Reims Cathedral are typical of the interest that Gothic builders showed in natural motifs, particularly those connected with the everyday life familiar to them, rather than the common emblems of classical sculpture.

The great porches of Reims Cathedral, showing clearly the influence of Chartres Gothic.

vines and wild roses—replaced the conventional acanthus derived from antiquity and taken over by Romanesque artists. If images of the saints appear on all sides, between God, who is omnipresent in the cathedral, and man, it is because they are the essential intermediaries—the Church Triumphant opening the way for the bodies and souls of the Church Militant.

By derivation, religion means a bond. The cathedral is the material link of this bond, established by God for all time. Nothing in it is comparable to a pagan temple or even a Jewish temple, which were almost exclusively reserved for the divinity and his priests. The cathedral is the heart, soul and brain of the Christian city, and although it is above all a temple, it is also a refuge. In a cathedral one might pray, weep or laugh, for it embraced all aspects of life. The cathedral church was the scene of performances of the liturgy, the seat of power of the bishop and the place for his *cathedra* or throne, and was not only a sanctuary for the clergy but also for the whole diocese. What is more, as a result of the tendency toward universality that marked the thirteenth century, the cathedral was ready to gather under its aegis all those who—although outside the limits of the diocese—nevertheless looked upon it as theirs, and had considerable respect for its celebrated relics or for the pilgrimages that set off from it. The enormous size of the medieval cathedrals—and some of them were quite disproportionately large in relation to the towns they towered over—cannot otherwise be explained. The cathedral was an offering to God and an offering to his people.

Nor was this all. Inseparable as it was from religious life proper, political life had its first burgeonings in the cathedral, and it was in the cathedrals as a whole that corporate life became aware of the part it had to play. It was under the vaulted roofs or in front of the cathedral portals that the arts of drama and music were reborn and that popular art had full play. It was in the shadow of the cathedrals too that intellectual life had new beginnings. As a prelude to the rise of the universities, the newly established church schools were, little by little, brought to perfection. The cathedral was at once a Christian church, a national temple, the scene of festivities, the asylum of the sciences and a refuge for suffering humanity. It was the true communal house, the very heart of the city. It was the Arc of the Covenant, and its support.

Later ages termed the cathedral style, given such impetus at Chartres, Gothic art. There was, of course, something critical in this name. The term "Gothic," in the derogatory sense of barbarian, was the product of the Italian Renaissance, which created a new type of humanism to replace that medieval humanism of which the cathedral was the embodiment. Gothic art was an art of the cities. From the middle of the twelfth century onwards, Europe was being completely transformed economically and socially. The reign of the middle classes was beginning. As Pierre Gaxotte has put it: "The old social orders were becoming distorted

before they finally broke up. The great estates lost their importance, the bonds of country life were being loosened and the towns were being reborn." The lay clergy exhibited a spirit of enterprise which equalled that of the growing towns, and the bishops who rebuilt the cathedrals were men of discernment and ambition. It would not, however, be true to assert that the age of monasticism had passed: apart from the Cistercians, to whom in large part Gothic art owes its international influence, the Franciscans and Dominicans began a great age of expansion in thirteenth-century Europe. Nevertheless, the established order of things, which had held sway during the Romanesque period, was during the Gothic era successfully challenged by secular power. Such was the new state of things.

A papal legate of the thirteenth century declared: "France is the oven where the intellectual bread of humanity is baked." Gothic art was more than a French art, it was international; and such was the universality of its message that all the nations of Christendom modified it and interpreted it according to their own traditions and temperament—from Canterbury to Lincoln and Westminster, from Marburg to Cologne, from Toledo to Leon, from Genoa to Siena and Orvieto, from Nicosia to Famagusta and Jerusalem, to the very limits of those hard-fought regions where, as a result of the Crusades, the Cross had prevailed over the Crescent.

The thirteenth century had achieved in the esthetic and spiritual spheres that sense of unity for which the twentieth century is still groping. As a permanent reminder of its technical virtuosity and perfection of form, the cathedral with its subtle blend of realism and idealism, with its lyrical qualities and its luminous sense of mystery, bears witness to a "period of greatness comparable to that which Greece experienced at her zenith." It would serve as a model for us if we could still believe in the return of a Golden Age.   YVAN CHRIST

The birth of the New Byzantium

The first decade of the thirteenth century was a critical period for civilization. In the West, the Europeans, in the tradition of their barbarian ancestors, sacked the world's greatest city; while in the East, the Mongol chieftan Temujin held a congress to lay plans for the conquest of the world, adopting the terrible name of Genghis Khan, "lord of the world."

In the 1260s, Genghis Khan's successors conquered Sung China, and in 1242 the Christian states of Russia had come under Mongol sway. Two centuries earlier, the

The Byzantine Emperor receives the envoys of Vladimir of Kiev.

Russian princes had been converted to Orthodox Christianity in the reign of Grand Prince (later Saint) Vladimir of Kiev (980–1015), who married the sister of the Emperor Basil II. Kiev became the metropolitan see of Russia, and under Grand Prince Yaroslav (1019–54) enjoyed a golden age whose brilliance reflected the splendors of Byzantium. Yaroslav's son married the daughter of Harold of England and one of his daughters became Queen of France.

After Yaroslav, however, the advances of the Turkish Cuman tribes on the Russians' southern frontier, and the treaties between Byzantium and Venice, severely weakened the trading position of Kiev. The descendants of Yaroslav were to· establish a number of principalities, but the grand prince, first of Kiev then of Vladimir, for a variety of reasons retained a more than theoretical ascendancy. The major principalities were Kiev itself, Novgorod in the north, and the principality of Suzdal. During the eleventh and twelfth centuries, Russian society stabilized into the recognizable divisions of the aristocracy, the merchant class whose richer members were able to join the ranks of the aristocracy, and finally the peasants. This increasingly well-articulated social structure, in which the ecclesiastical hierarchy played an important part, produced conflicts of interest between the states, conflicts that often reinforced the dynastic policies of the princes.

Meanwhile, the chroniclers inveighed against the internecine wars between the Christian rulers and urged them to unite against the pagan enemies on their frontiers, such as the Cumans or the powerful state of the Volga Bulgars. The opening of new trade routes to the north and the gradual emergence of different distinguishable nationalities—the Great Russians in the north, the White Russians in the west and the Ukrainians around the lands of Kiev—further emphasized the differences among the principalities.

In the mid-twelfth century, the declining state of Kiev was overrun by the armies of the prince of Suzdal, who sacked the city, retained his own capital of Vladimir and took over the old Kievan claims to supremacy. Henceforth, the grand princes of Vladimir, later called Muscovy, were to maintain their claim to the leadership of Russia.

The merchants— a new power

In Novgorod, although the theoretical supremacy of the princes of Vladimir was recognized, the effective rule lay with the merchant aristocracy. Novgorod was the natural *entrepôt* of the intersecting trade routes from the altic to Asia, and from the north down the river system of European Russia to Kiev.

Twelfth-century church of St. Demetrius at Vladimir, capital of the Muscovite Empire.

Furthermore, it was largely isolated from the depredations of the Asian nomads by the states to the south and by its own wild hinterland stretching to the White Sea—a land too sparsely inhabited to raise a political threat, but one nevertheless rich in walrus ivory and furs. The merchant oligarchy was further stimulated in its independence by connections with the German merchants of the Hanseatic League.

The great and growing wealth of the Italian cities—and above all those inveterate rivals, Venice and Genoa, was based on their exploitation of the riches of Byzantium. And throughout Europe, the power of the cities was growing. London was a flourishing trading center in the twelfth century, but more significant was the ascendancy that the German merchants of the Hanseatic League established in the Baltic, and the growth of the trading activities and wool industry of the Flemish cities. The commercial life of Europe now came to be a major aspect of the life of the Continent, polarized around two centers to the north and the south. Trade routes between them met at the great fairs of the towns of Champagne.

With this commercial wealth and power went a political drive by the governing oligarchies of the towns to rid themselves of the interference of their aristocratic overlords. In Italy the towns won a notable victory. The Emperor Frederick Barbarossa's ambitions led him into conflict with the Pope, who excommunicated him, and provoked the determined opposition of the north Italian towns—eventually even those with imperialist sympathies. The imperial army was defeated by the Lombard League, and Barbarossa came to terms with the Pope and met the demands of the cities. His son, Henry VI, maintained and extended his father's imperial aims, conquering the Norman kingdom of Sicily and defeating the papal allies. After Henry's premature death in 1197 and the temporary successes of his son, Frederick II, no future Emperor was ever again to exercise effective authority over the communes of north Italy.

New kings, old struggles

In 1187, the forces of the kingdom of Jerusalem were crushed in the Battle of Hattim by the armies of the dashing and brilliant Saladin. The city was lost and the kingdom

Emperor Henry VI leading his knights at the siege of Naples.

itself reduced to a coastal strip. For one last glorious moment, Christendom witnessed the armies of the Emperor and the kings of England and France embarking on a crusade to recover the cradle of their faith. The aging Emperor, Frederick Barbarossa, set out with a magnificent and well-disciplined army, which rightly struck fear into Saladin. However, differences between Barbarossa and the Byzantine Emperor soon became apparent, and the German threat finally was dissipated when Barbarossa died on the campaign.

In 1191, Richard I, the Lion Heart, of England arrived with his army at the besieged town of Acre, where his bitter rival Philip Augustus of France had been encamped for some months. Vitalized by the reinforcements and heartened by the inspired generalship of Richard, the Christian armies won a series of victories that seemed to bring them within reach of Jerusalem. But Richard was forced by the military realities of the situation and by political affairs at home to return to Europe. Richard spent very little time in his kingdom and showed none of the abilities of his father, Henry II, as a ruler. His far more talented brother John was also unhealthily ambitious, and during Richard's absence on crusade intrigued for the throne. Finally, troubles at home were compounded by threats abroad. Philip Augustus of France, who laid the foundations of his country's greatness in the later Middle Ages, was determined to recover the Angevin lands in France. He had exploited both the conflict between Henry II of England and his sons, and John's disloyalty to Richard, to good effect. But in five years Richard won back almost all Philip's gains, and confirmed England's presence in France with the building of the mighty fortress of Château Gaillard in Normandy. The art of military

A courtly tournament.

fortification had advanced considerably during the twelfth century and Richard was perhaps the greatest military architect of his age. With his death in 1199 and the growing discontent of the English barons with fighting the dynastic wars of the Angevins abroad, the kingdom was greatly imperiled. Compared to the disaster on the Bosphorus in the same year, the capture of Château Gaillard by the French in 1204 was of marginal significance in European affairs, yet it precipitated the loss of most of the English possessions in northern France to the French king.

Chivalry in the West

Richard I's defects as a man and as a ruler have been forgiven him by posterity for the aura of military glamour that surrounds his name. In these terms, his career was the fitting conclusion to a century in which the concept of knightly chivalry began to emerge from the bloody business of self-interested warfare. In the face of the slowly developing sophistication of society at large, the turbulent nobility of Europe—whose scope for private warfare was in any case being limited as the feudal monarchies

grew in power—began to accept the idea of rules to govern warfare. More and more, they channeled their aggressive urges into the causes of their sovereign, into the religious crusade, or into the military sport of the tournament.

At first, tournaments had been little more than wars to the death between friends, so to speak. In theory the vanquished were taken prisoner, but the weapons and conduct of the fight were genuine and men were often killed. Those who were captured could expect to pay heavy ransoms and the world of the tournament provided the opportunity for many a landless younger son to make his fortune. William the Marshal, the elder statesman of John's England, was the prime example; but even before his death the institutions were changing. Royal authority saw itself threatened by these violent gatherings of its vassals, and the wealthy landowner was less and less willing to chance his fortune to this military lottery. Furthermore, such old-world piracy hardly accorded with the new aura surrounding the chivalry of the institution of knighthood.

The idea of the Christian warrior in the service of the just war was partly inspired by the ideals that continued to cling to the crusade. Still more important were the romantic legends surrounding that greatest of all Christian warriors, the Celtic hero King Arthur.

Profits in the East

The Byzantine Empire was restored to an aggressive posture by Alexius I (d. 1118), who had not only recovered much of Anatolia from the Seljuk Turks after the disaster of his predecessor at Manzikert, but had also contained the ambitions of the first crusaders and restored the finances of the Empire. His successor, John II, successfully held the position; but Byzantium was embattled against strong and determined enemies. The Turkish victory at Myriocephalum in 1176 over the Emperor Manuel I, although it involved them in heavy losses, put an end to all hopes of a Byzantine recovery in Anatolia. At the moment, however, the real threat lay in Europe. Successive Norman rulers of Sicily had attempted to conquer the Christian Empire in the East, and in 1195 the Emperor Henry VI had prepared an expedition which only his death

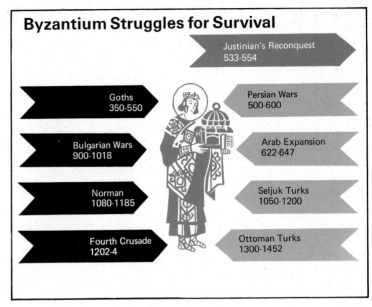

Byzantium Struggles for Survival

- Justinian's Reconquest 533-554
- Goths 350-550
- Persian Wars 500-600
- Bulgarian Wars 900-1018
- Arab Expansion 622-647
- Norman 1080-1185
- Seljuk Turks 1050-1200
- Fourth Crusade 1202-4
- Ottoman Turks 1300-1452

prevented. But quite apart from these military threats was the running sore of Venetian trading privileges within the Empire.

These privileges had been granted by Alexius I in his alliance with Venice against the Normans. They gave the merchants of Venice an even more privileged position than the Greek traders themselves. The Empire lost the carrying trade of its own merchandise and the revenue of the former tolls. The attempts of the Emperors to break loose (in 1171 Manuel I had all Venetians imprisoned and their goods impounded) only provoked a determined counterattack; and the Fourth Crusade has been called the greatest commercial coup of all time. But despite the declining political situation from the middle of the century, Byzantine art and letters enjoyed a remarkable flou-

The Christ mosaic in Hagia Sophia, mid-twelfth century, one of the supreme works of Byzantine art.

rishing during this period, including a marked revival in classical Greek scholarship and literature which paralleled the brilliance of the twelfth-century "renaissance" in Europe.

Seeds of autocracy

A rapid survey of twelfth-century society impresses us first with its vitality and second with the clear signs of new institutions in embryo. The town evolved systems of internal government and inter-city federations, but the guilds and the Hanseatic League later developed protective and monopolistic tendencies which hampered rather than directed growth. Chivalry, an excellent means for the taming and civilizing of aggression, soon became a meaningless game, and even in the realm of the intellect the same process can be observed. Vitality and restless inquiry were gradually institutionalized. The statutes drawn up by a papal legate for the University of Paris in 1215 heralded an age when the great centers of intellectual activity, once so free, not only gained powers for governing their own members but also became more easily subject to the control of outside authorities. The old universal institutions of empire and papacy were challenged not only by the emergence of new, more tightly knit political units but also by powerful "lobbies" for the interests of separate social groups. In the event of conflict with Church or king, such institutionalization made the target of official displeasure easier to identify.

The Fall of Constantinople

The crusaders from the West had taken an oath to free the Holy Land from the Moslems, but now they were stranded at Constantinople—unable to pay the Venetians for the ships that were carrying them eastward. Easily deflected from their religious mission, the knights and nobles of the Fourth Crusade agreed to help the deposed Byzantine Emperor regain his throne. And thus, in the spring of 1204, the walls of Constantinople—never before breached by an enemy —fell to the crusaders. The sack of the city, culmination of this senseless war of Christian against Christian, lasted for three days and when it was over Christendom's most splendid city lay in ruins. All Europe was shocked by this rapacious diversion of the crusading movement, and the breach between Eastern and Western Christianity widened to a permanent split. In the succeeding centuries, this fatal division could only work to the advantage of the Moslem Turks advancing from the East.

A portrait of the Emperor John II Comnenus, twelfth-century Byzantine Emperor.

Opposite A crusading knight mounted and in full armor.

During the winter of 1203–4, a large army of crusading knights, brought by a Venetian fleet, was encamped around the city of Constantinople. Their ultimate purpose was to reconquer the Holy Land, but since they did not have the necessary money to pay the Venetians for the ships, it had been agreed that the crusaders should postpone their conquest of the Holy Land and first use their armed might to accomplish a task dear to Venice: that was to place Alexius, the son of Isaac Angelus, on the throne of Byzantium. Alexius and his father had been the victims of a palace revolution: the Emperor Isaac was dethroned by his brother—another Alexius— and blinded, in the Byzantine fashion, to render him helpless. He was then thrown into prison with his son. But the son, Alexius, managed to escape and make his way to the court of his brother-in-law, Philip of Swabia, King of Germany. He made good use of his connections and when it became known that the crusading army, for lack of money, was stranded in Venice, Alexius seized his opportunity. He promised to pay the crusaders' debt to the Venetians if he were placed on the throne of his father in Constantinople.

The Venetians and crusaders had carried out their side of the bargain. In July, 1203, they laid siege to Constantinople. The usurper, Alexius III, fled and his officials released the old Emperor from his prison. On August 1, his son was solemnly crowned as Alexius IV in the church of Hagia Sophia.

Installed on the throne, Alexius IV soon discovered that he could not pay the Venetians. The crusaders were therefore still stranded in Constantinople. As time went by, their relations with the Byzantines became more and more strained, and when the crusaders presented an ultimatum in February, 1204, another palace revolution took place and Alexius IV was deposed. The crusaders now decided to install one of their own leaders as emperor. They stormed the city and in the middle of April made their first successful landing on the Golden Horn. A fire in the city, started by accident or treachery, made defense impossible. The members of the imperial family, many nobles and the Patriarch fled, and before long Enrico Dandolo, the Doge of Venice, and the other leaders of the crusaders entered the Great Palace. The rank and file were allowed to sack the city.

The sack lasted for three days. Neither the Venetians nor the crusaders, coming from the West, had seen such riches before. Drunk with greed and lust they let themselves go. They seized everything that seemed precious and carried it away; the rest they destroyed. They ransacked palaces and dwellings; they killed, raped and looted; and countless books and works of art were destroyed—until Christendom's largest and most splendid city lay in ruins. On May 16, Count Baldwin IX of Flanders and Hainault was made Emperor of Romania, as the Latins chose to call it, but his power was negligible. Constantinople was in ruins and his power over the princes who established themselves in the western parts of old Byzantium became nebulous, for they only owed him some kind of feudal allegiance, whereas many of the outlying parts of the old Empire rallied to various members of the former imperial family.

The plan to continue the crusade, meanwhile, was abandoned and the papal legate, Peter of Saint-Marcel, absolved all crusaders from their oath to fight for the delivery of the Holy Land from the Moslems.

The city of Constantinople had been founded by the Roman Emperor Constantine in A.D. 328–37. It had been consecrated on May 11, 330, as the new Rome, a city that contained no traces of ancient paganism. The site was chosen for its strategic importance, at the spot where Asia and Europe meet on the Bosphorus—the significance of which had been obvious to Herodotus in the fifth century B.C. A great many churches were built and the city was

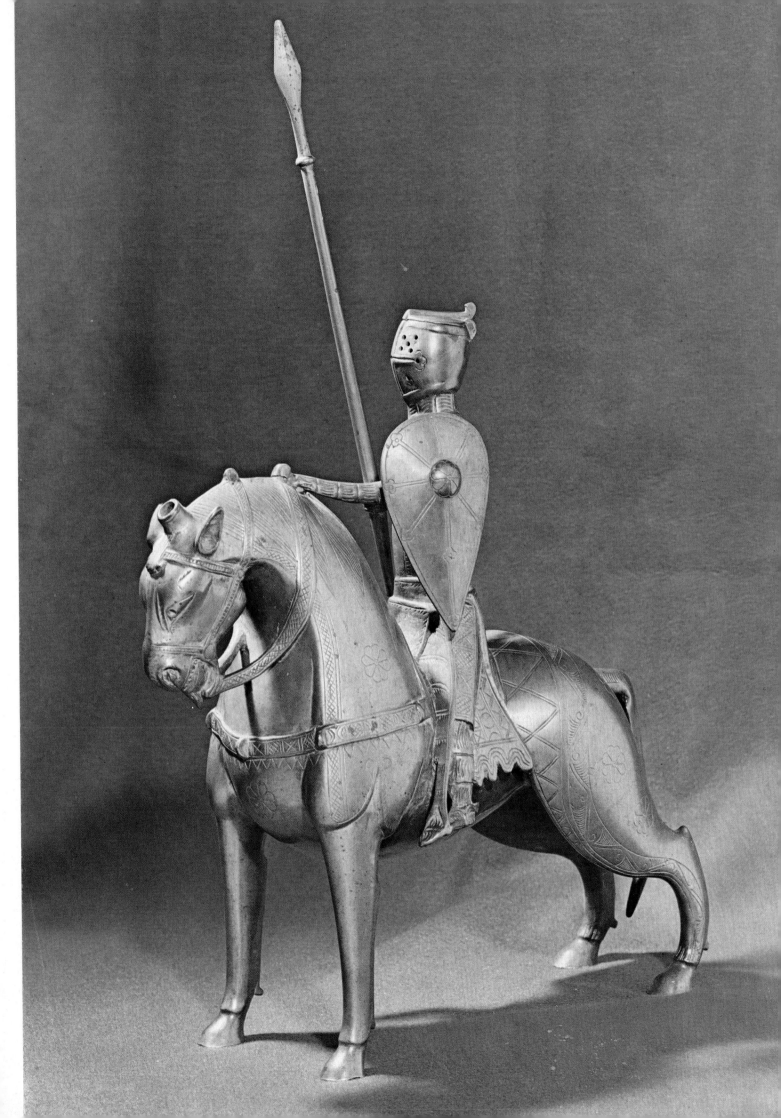

The Imperial center moves East

Right The Emperor Frederick Barbarossa dressed as a crusader, a probable reference to the Third Crusade begun by Frederick in 1189 after the fall of Jerusalem.

Above Saladin, Sultan of Egypt and Syria 1137–1193, a Moslem leader of remarkable gifts, and one of the crusaders' most formidable enemies.

The figure of Richard Coeur de Lion on his tomb at Fontrevaux Abbey.

richly endowed with fountains and statues and soon became the administrative and commercial center of the Eastern Roman Empire.

Less than a hundred years after the founding of the new Rome, the city on the Tiber was sacked by the barbarian invaders of the Western Empire and, from then on, Constantinople alone carried on the traditions of Roman government.

The transfer of the capital to Constantinople was, of course, an explicit admission of the fact that the ancient Roman Empire was becoming orientalized. In the East, the Greek language was predominant, and eventually the reigning culture of Constantinople and its Empire became an amalgam of

Oriental and Greek influences. It was inevitable that in the eastern half of the old Roman Empire the form and content of Christianity should develop along lines different from those followed in the West. And the Patriarch of Constantinople, presiding over his Church under the immediate eye of the Emperor, in a city vastly richer and more alive than medieval Rome, naturally became the head of the Eastern Church and became more and more reluctant to concede any claims the Bishop of Rome advanced as the successor of St. Peter. It is impossible to define the differences between Eastern and Western Christendom in one single principle; but in the East, Semitic traditions of uncompromising monotheism and of objection to religious imagery frequently came to the fore, and there were strong Oriental currents of cosmic mysticism apparent in the shape of the liturgy and even in the shape of the Cross, which in the East came to have four equal arms.

When the imperial center was shifted to Constantinople, the threat from central Europe was only peripheral. When it became stronger in the fifth century, Byzantine diplomats took steps to direct the invaders westward, away from Constantinople, into Italy and Spain. But when Byzantine influence in the West was completely extinguished in the seventh and eighth centuries, it became apparent that a threat far greater than that of the Teutonic invaders was about to engulf the Eastern Empire. The Teutonic invaders had not only displayed a certain respect for Roman traditions but had actually accepted Christianity. Their invasions of the Roman Empire therefore laid the foundations for an eventual assimilation. But in the eighth and ninth centuries, the Arabs—newly converted to Islam—erupted from the interior of their peninsula into the Mediterranean regions and swiftly conquered Egypt, Syria and Palestine—seriously weakening the power of Byzantium.

Islam was a religion even more fiercely prophetic and missionary than Christianity, and there was no possibility of assimilation. The Emperors in Constantinople had to watch their dominions shrink; they fought valiantly, however, and as long as they

straddled the Bosphorus they kept a firm hold on Greece in the west and Asia Minor in the east. But in the course of the eleventh century another wave of Asian invaders came forward: the Seljuk Turks— a horde of nomads from the steppes of Turkestan— seeking their fortune by pillage. They conquered Syria and Palestine, and though they dealt a heavy blow to the power of the Moslem caliphs, they soon accommodated themselves with their Arabic subjects because they, too, embraced Islam. They advanced into Asia Minor and were confronted by a Byzantine army—which they defeated decisively on the field of Manzikert in Armenia in 1071. The whole eastern wing of the Byzantine Empire immediately collapsed.

Ten years later, a palace revolution in Constantinople brought to power Alexius I Comnenus, an intelligent and enterprising new Emperor—the first of a dynasty that was to rule for over a century. As part of his program of internal as well as external restoration, he wrote a letter to Pope Urban II asking for military help from the West in order to assist with the defense of Eastern Christendom against the Moslems. At that time the papacy was experiencing the full swing of the Gregorian reform movement; Urban eagerly welcomed this opportunity of leadership and promptly appealed to the newly stimulated religious fervor of the masses.

Naturally enough, the papal invitation to go on a crusade—issued at Clermont, France, in November, 1095—was not intended to rescue Alexius I Comnenus and support the tottering edifice of Byzantium.

The purpose of the crusade launched by Urban's appeal in 1095 was, therefore, different from Alexius' purpose when he had written for help. The crusaders were to fight the Moslems, not to save the dynasty at Constantinople but to conquer the Holy Land. The two purposes were, of course, not necessarily incompatible. But the differences in emphasis were strong enough to lead to deep mistrust and to ultimate dissension between Alexius and the crusaders.

As it was, the papal appeal met with enthusiastic response from all classes of people. Christians in Europe had never before experienced the liberating zest of religious evangelism. Religion had meant, if it was not an invitation to monasticism, the worship of relics and a certain amount of communal ceremonial in the shape of the Mass. There was hardly any clergy capable of giving spiritual nourishment and no popular edification of any kind. Hence the papal appeal, carried by countless preachers into every corner of Christendom, stimulated the pent-up religious enthusiasm; and people rushed to save Jerusalem. The reconquest of the Holy Land was indeed a stimulating goal; but it received substance from the papal idea that to go on a crusade meant to "take the Cross" and was, therefore, an act of penance: a crusader's vow would assure eternal salvation.

The idea of a pilgrimage to the Holy Land in expiation of sins was a very old Western tradition, even though the Moslem conquest of Jerusalem had made such pilgrimages very hazardous. Now the tradition

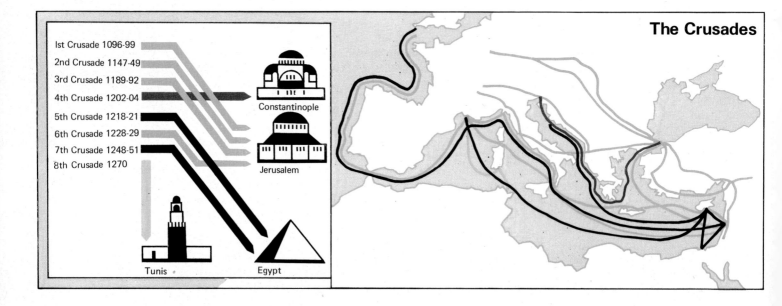

The Golden Gate and the walls of Constantinople around which the Venetian army encamped and laid siege to the treasure-laden city in 1203.

received not only a new vitality, but a new emphasis. The crusading pilgrim was also a fighter for God and the old pilgrimage was turned into a holy war.

The First Crusade, which departed for Jerusalem in 1096, made its way down the Balkans. It was a large number of poor people following an inarticulate religious sentiment. There were camp-followers and beggars, vagabonds, brigands, harlots and last, but not least, a large number of professional warriors—knights newly educated in the ideals of chivalry which now received a religious sanction. But religious fervor does not provide by itself much of a basis for a military expedition. The trains of people that set out eastwards were without provisions, without leadership and without discipline. The

enthusiasm of the poor tended to diminish as they were apprehended and set upon by people from whom they had pillaged. Their sufferings were enormous and most of them died on the way. The knights were in a more advantageous position, but they were subject to an odd mixture of religious fervor and material greed: they clearly bore in mind the possibility of carving out landed estates for themselves in the East, and the violence they displayed in foreign parts came to be a mixture of acquisitiveness and religious intoxication.

All in all, it is surprising that the First Crusade achieved its purpose. In crossing Asia Minor, the crusaders reconquered the littoral from the Turks and allowed Alexius to repossess himself of some of

Jerusalem captured in 1099

the major cities. Eventually, the knights invaded Syria and Palestine: they captured first Antioch and finally, in 1099, Jerusalem. With the opening of the Levantine ports to Christian trade, Italian ships started to arrive. The Mediterranean was once again opened to merchants from Christian lands.

But the relations with Byzantium went from bad to worse. Alexius owed a debt to the crusaders. But, alternately, they owed a debt to him for supplies, advice and guidance. Once established in Jerusalem, however, the Western knights refused to hand back the regained territories to Alexius. Instead, they set up the Latin kingdom of Jerusalem, received a papal legate, and obliged the Christian inhabitants of their new kingdom to withdraw from the Greek ritual. If Alexius felt relieved at the cessation of Moslem pressure, he soon realized that the expedition had not really helped to restore his Empire. On the contrary, owing to the close personal relations of many of the crusading knights with the Norman knights who, in the preceding century, had invaded southern Italy, he was now forced to resign himself to the loss of territory in Italy, and to recognize the independence of the kingdom of Jerusalem and several other principalities which the crusading knights had carved out for themselves in the East.

Apart from the political and ecclesiastical ill will prevailing on all sides, there were also powerful social and cultural forces at work in promoting tension. The crusaders had carried to Jerusalem their primitive military and political feudalism. The kingdom they set up in Palestine and Syria resembled England after the Norman Conquest much more than it did the centralized bureaucracy of Byzantium. And the theological and liturgical differences served to underline the rift. Early in the twelfth century, the Latin West was as yet largely innocent of dialectics and scholasticism; and the theological assertiveness of the Roman Church struck the Byzantine theologians, trained in the subtler traditions of Greek scholarship, as mere boorish presumption.

Eventually, however, the nemesis of power began to overtake everybody. The Christian knights in their Jerusalem kingdom eagerly availed themselves of the Oriental luxury that surrounded them. They tended to become acclimatized. At the same time, Moslem power began to recover from the shock of its first defeats. The crusaders' victory had been the stimulus needed for reorganization. Zanghi of Mosul conquered Aleppo and Edessa; his son, Noureddin, Damascus and Egypt. And Saladin finally won the victory of Hattin in 1187 and

Above A coin from Constantinople shows the personification of the city holding a cornucopia or horn of plenty.

Detail of the Pala d'Oro, the altarpiece at St. Mark's in Venice, which incorporates part of the looted treasure that the crusaders brought back from the sack of Constantinople.

Above The crusader castle of Krak des Chevaliers in Lebanon. Many crusader fortifications are still standing today.

Below A crusader's map of Jerusalem marking the holy places of the city.

regained Jerusalem for Islam from the Christians.

Appeals for more aid were sent to the West. The Emperors of Byzantium became more and more reluctant to help, because they reckoned that they had been duped by the crusaders. Italian merchants were willing to provide ships—at a price. But the new crusading recruits who came over from the West were shocked to find their relatives and companions installed in palaces of Oriental splendor, with food and spice , incense and precious clothes, which were neither reminiscent of their austere castles in Flanders and Lorraine nor particularly expressive of religious zeal.

If the Byzantines were displeased with the outcome, they at least benefited for the time being because the attention of the Moslems was directed against the Kingdom of Jerusalem instead of against their Empire. In Europe itself, the growing threat to that kingdom stimulated further efforts which in turn were nourised by the Apocalyptic fears current in the twelfth century. In 1147, St. Bernard of Clairvaux preached a new crusade and fired people's imagination by fanatical sermons that exhibited a curious combination of bloodthirsty aggressiveness and a desire for moral purification. The immediate effect of his activities was the Second Crusade led by the Emperor Conrad III and by King Louis VII of France. The expedition was a complete failure; and most knights perished in Asia Minor before they even reached the endangered Holy City. After the battle of Hattin and the fall of Jerusalem, the Emperor Frederick Barbarossa set out in 1189 on a third crusade and was supposed to be joined in the Holy Land by Richard the Lion Heart of England and Philip Augustus, King of France. This time the most elaborate preparations were made. Crusaders were recruited in order to serve their Lord Jesus as vassals—a marked departure from the earlier, indiscriminate religious enthusiasm and the blank promise of eternal salvation for taking the Cross.

The Turks are poised to strike at Europe

After a long march down the Danube, the crusaders crossed safely into Asia Minor during Easter, 1190. But Frederick himself was drowned in the Saleph River and a great many crusaders died from hunger and thirst as well as from fighting the Turks. Only a remnant of the army reached Antioch, and they failed to reconquer Jerusalem.

If the new organization and official royal leadership had introduced a more serious kind of military planning, it had also shifted the perspective. With kings in the lead, a crusade was more clearly a political than a religious venture. And kings, in the nature of things, had dynastic ambitions. Already, in 1190, when forced to spend the winter in southern Greece, Frederick Barbarossa had been under great pressure to conquer Constantinople. Many of his knights felt that it was better to have a bird in the hand than two in the bush. It had taken all of Frederick's determination to force them to desist, and his own determination drew great strength from his conviction that his expedition to Jerusalem was a necessary part of the Apocalyptic vision of the universe according to which, at the end of time, the last Emperor had to go to Jerusalem in order to hang up his shield and lance on the barren tree on the Mount of Olives.

After Frederick's death and the removal of his influence, dynastic ambitions gained the upper hand. Richard the Lion Heart was an irresponsible adventurer and Philip Augustus had concerns closer to home: the mutilated trunk of the Kingdom of Jerusalem received no help from either of them. In the early years of the thirteenth century, Pope Innocent III, full of his own prestige, sought to revive the idea of a crusade. But though his appeal met with an enthusiastic response and a large army of knights assembled in Venice to take ship to the East, the political issues had gained the upper hand. Lack of money for the passage placed the crusaders at the Venetians' mercy. And since King Philip of Germany was married to the sister of Alexius, the fugitive claimant of the Byzantine throne, the whole expedition—as we have seen—was eventually diverted to the conquest of Constantinople with the avowed aim of placing Alexius IV on the imperial throne. Alexius himself had played cleverly on the crusaders' lack of money: he promised ample rewards from the coffers of Byzantium. But the crusaders' rewards did not come in the manner envisaged by Alexius.

The fall of Constantinople and the installation of the Latin kingdom of Romania there fatally weakened the great bastion that had sheltered Europe from the East. None of the Byzantine successor states in Asia Minor, nor the restored dynasty of the Paleologi in Constantinople in 1261, were militarily viable. As a result of the enfeebled state in which Constantinople was left, the Turks advanced from strength to strength. By the middle of the fifteenth century, they had surrounded the imperial city on the Golden Horn and pushed forward into the Balkans as well as into the Aegean Sea. Finally, in 1453, Constantinople itself fell, and the Turks were at last poised to strike at the heart of Europe.

PETER MUNZ

Mosaic pavement in the Basilica of St. John the Evangelist at Ravenna, 1213, depicting episodes from the Fourth Crusade.

Tomb of a crusader in Dorchester abbey. Medieval England, like the other nations of Christendom considered a crusader killed in battle worthy of the highest honors of the Church.

312

In This Sign Shalt Thou Conquer — Constantine defeats Maxentius at the battle of the Milvian Bridge aided, he believes, by the Christian God.

432

Mission to Ireland — St. Patrick arrives in Ireland, converts it, a establishes monastic stronghol of learning.

Origen c. 181-253
Christian teacher at Alexandria

Caracalla 186-217
Roman Emperor

Cyprian (St.) 202-58
Christian teacher

Plotinus 204-70
Greek philosopher

Aurelian c. 214-75
Roman Emperor

Shapur I c. 215-72
King of Persia

Manes c. 215-75
Persian founder of new religion

Pappus c. 230-300
Greek mathematician

Zenobia c. 230-73
Queen of Palmyra

Porphyry c. 232-304
Greek philosopher

Diocletian 243-316
Roman Emperor

Constantius Chlorus c. 250-306
Roman Emperor in Britain and Gaul

Anthony (St.) 251-c. 356
Egyptian hermit

Arius c. 258-336
North African philosopher

Eusebius 263-339
Bishop of Caesarea

Iamblichus c. 265-330
Syrian Neoplatonic philosopher

Constantine c. 280-337
Roman Emperor 306-37

Constantius II c. 288-361
Roman Emperor: East 337-50; whole 350-61

Athanasius c. 295-373
Eygptian theologian

Ermanrich c. 305-70
King of the Ostrogoths

Maxentius d. 312
Roman Emperor

Shapur II 309-79
King of Persia

Ulfilas 311-83
Translator of Bible into Gothic

Martin of Tours (St.) d. 397
Missionary in Gaul

Basil the Great (St.) c. 330-79
Greek Father of the Church

Gregory Nazianzen (St.) c. 330-89
Cappadocian theologian and writer

Julian the Apostate c. 331-63
Roman Emperor

Ambrose (St.) 340-97
Latin Father of the Church

Jerome (St.) 340-420
Latin Father of the Church

Theodosius c. 346-95
Roman Emperor in the East

Kalidasa c. 352-420
Sanskrit dramatist

John Chrysostom (St.) c. 347-407
Greek Father of the Church

Augustine (St.) 354-430
North African Christian teacher

Gratian 359-83
Roman Emperor

Stilicho c. 365-408
Vandal; Roman general

Alaric c. 374-410
King of the Visigoths

Pelagius c. 375-435
Irish Monk

Chandragupta II c. 380-415
Gupta King, India

Cyril of Jerusalem c. 381-444
Bishop of Alexandria

Nestorius c. 386-451
Syrian theologian

Gaiseric 390-477
King of the Vandals

Patrick (St.) c. 391-461
Irish missionary priest

Aetius c. 397-454
General of Western Empire

Yazdegerd I
King of Persia 399-420

Fa Hsien fl. 399-414
Chinese Buddhist monk

Leo I the Great c. 399-46
Pope

Ricimer d. 472
Roman general of Sueve

Theodosius II 401-50
Emperor of the East

Attila c. 410-53
King of the Huns

Priskus c. 411-74
Historian

Theodoric I
Visigothic King 419-5

● **212**
Full citizen's rights for all free inhabitants of Roman Empire

● **220**
End of Han Dynasty: China divided into Three Kingdoms

● **224**
Persia united under Ardashir: Sassanid Dynasty ousts Parthians

● **250**
General persecution of Christians in Roman Empire

● **250-69**
First Gothic War: Goths pushed back to Black Sea by Emperor Claudius II

● **265**
Tsin Dynasty *China*

● **270-90**
Incursions by Germanic tribes in Italy and on Rhine and Danube repelled by Rome

● **292**
Diocletian divides Roman Empire into four parts

● **296**
Third Persian War: Romans routed by Persians at Carrhae

● **307**
Constantine declares himself sole legitimate Emperor in the West

●
Gupta Dynasty established unites *North India*

● **324**
Constantine conquers Licinius

● **325**
Council of Nicaea

● **330**
Constantinople declared capital of the Empire

● **c. 375**
Hunnish inroads into Europe

● **378**
Battle of Adrianople: Romans defeated by Goths

● **384**
Partition of Armenia between Persian and Roman Empires

● **385**
Buddhism enforced by Wei Dynasty *China*

● **390**
Theodosius excommunicated, then publicly absolved

● **391**
Library at Alexandria burned

● **403**
Capital of Western Empir moved to Ravenna

● **405**
St. Jerome completes "Vulg translation of Bible

● **407**
Avars found first Mongol empire throughout Mong

● **410**
Alaric sacks Rome

● **429**
Gaiseric establishes Van Kingdom in Africa

● **c. 43**
Wei Dynasty established *North China*

622

Scourge of God
ampus Mauriacus (Chalons)
s turns back Attila at the
of the Empire; but Western
is shattered.

520

The Flight to Medina —
The establishment of the Moslem
religion brings with it a unifying
Islamic civilization, new yet
preserving ancient scholarship.

The Rule of St. Benedict — It
provided a framework in which
monasteries became self-sufficient
communities where learning
could survive.

ntinian III 419-54
eror of the West

Totila c. 513-52
King of the Ostrogoths

Uthman c. 588-656
Caliph

Willibrord (St.) 657-739
English missionary

c. 426-91
eror of the East

Columba of Iona (St.) c. 520-97
Irish missionary to N. Scots

Chosroes II d. 628
King of Persia

Boniface (Winfrid) 673-754
Anglo-Saxon missionary

acer c. 433-93
g of the Heruli

Gregory of Tours c. 538-94
Frankish historian

Harsha c. 590-647
Ruler of N. Indian Empire

Bede 673-735
English historian

eodoric the Great c. 455-526
rogothic King

Gregory I the Great 540-604
Pope

Theodore of Tarsus c. 602-90
Archbishop of Canterbury

Leo III 675-740
Byzantine Emperor

Romulus Augustulus c. 459-98
ast Roman Emperor

Columbanus (St.) c. 540-615
Irish missionary to Gaul

Ali c. 602-61
Caliph, Mohammed's son-in-law

Abd al Malik
Caliph 685-705

Clovis 466-511
King of the Salian Franks

Augustine of Canterbury (St.) d. 604
Roman apostle of England

Aidan (St.) d. 651
Apostle of England

Charles Martel c.688-741
Ruler of Austrasia and Neustria

Kavadh I c. 470-531
King of Persia

Alboin c. 541-72
King of the Lombards

Rothari 605-52
King of the Lombards

John of Damascus 690-754
Orthodox theologian

Mazdak c. 475-531
High Priest of Zoroastrianism

Aethelbert c. 560-616
King of Kent

Fujiwara Kamatari c. 605-80
Japanese statesman

Liutprand
Lombard King 712-44

Tribonian c. 475-545
Eastern jurist

Isidore of Seville c. 560-636
Bishop and man of letters

Hsuan-tsang 605-64
Chinese Buddhist traveler in India 625-48

Pepin the Short 714-68
Frankish king

Narses c. 478-567
Byzantine courtier

Yang Ti 560-618
Founder of Sui Dynasty

Moawiyah c. 609-80
First Ummayad Caliph

Boethius c. 480-524
Philosopher

Mohammed 570-632
Founder of Moslem religion

Caedmon c. 617-82
English Christian poet

Benedict of Nursia (St.) c. 480-547
Italian monk

Li Yuan 570-636
First T'ang Emperor, China

Tenji 626-72
Emperor of Japan

Justinian 482-565
Eastern Emperor

Shotoku Taishi 572-621
Ruler of Japan

Pepin of Heristal 635-714
Mayor of Austrasia and Neustria

Procopius c. 490-562
Eastern historian

Abu Bakr 573-634
First Moslem Caliph

Musa c. 640-716
Moslem general

Belisarius c. 505-65
Eastern general

Heraclius I 575-641
Byzantine Emperor

Oswy d. 670
King of Northumbria

Theodora 508-48
Eastern Empress

Omar 582-644
Arabian Caliph

Isperich c. 652-700
Khan of Bulgaria

Chosroes I c. 511-79
Persian King

Reccared
Visigothic King 586-601

Recceswinth d. 672
Catholic King of Visigoths

● 455
me sacked by Vandal
iseric

● 534
Vandal kingdom in North Africa
overthrown by Belisarius

● 616
Compulsory baptism of
Jews *Spain*

●664
Synod of Whitby

● 720
Arabs cross Pyrenees into
Aquitaine *France*

● 476
End of the Western Empire

● 546
Rome ravaged by Totila the
Ostrogoth

● 618
T'ang Dynasty founded *China*

● 732
Battle of Poitiers: Franks
defeat Arabs *France*

● 486
Clovis defeats Syagrius at
Soissons: end of Roman
rule in Gaul

● 563
Hagia Sophia cathedral
consecrated at Constantinople

● 627
Persia defeated by Heraclius

● 493
Theodoric defeats Germans,
kills Odoacer

● c. 585
St. Columbanus sets out from
Ireland to Gaul

● 630
Mecca captured by
Mohammed *Arabia*

● c. 500
Talmud receives definitive
form *Babylon*

● 597
King Aethelbert converted
by Augustine at Canterbury
England

● 637
Ctesiphon captured by
Islamic armies *Mesopotamia*

19
ain occupied by Angles,
ons and Jutes

● 507
Clovis drives Visigoths out
of Gaul at Battle of Vouillé

● 606
Civil service examination
system established *China*

● 658
Moawiyah establishes
Ummayad Dynasty at
Damascus *Syria*

450
ndagupta beats back
te Huns (Ephthalites) *India*

● 534
Justinian's legal code Corpus
Juris Civilis

● 614
Capture of the True Cross
in Jerusalem by Persians *Palestine*

750	800	850	900	950

794
Japanese Renaissance — A national civilization follows the removal of the capital from Nara to Heian (Kyoto)

800
A Crown for Charlemagne — The conflict between West and East defined; the struggle for dominance between papacy and emperors begun.

886
England for the English — By capturing London from the Danes, Alfred the Great established his claims as supreme national leader.

950
The Caliph of Cordova's Library — The great libraries of Cordova become centers of scholarly inquiry, and ultimately preserve Greco-Arabic learning for medieval Europe.

955
At the Lechfeld — To defeat the Magyars at Lechfeld, Otto I united the Germanic peoples and established his Empire's claim to be defender of the Roman Church.

982

Paul the Deacon c. 720-800
Historian of the Lombards

Abu al Abbas 723-54
Founder of Abbasid Dynasty

Alcuin c. 735-804
English scholar

Charles the Great (Charlemagne) 742-814
Frankish King and Emperor of the West

Irene 752-803
Byzantine Empress 797-802

Offa II
King of Mercia 757-96

Harun al Rashid c. 766-809
Abbasid Caliph

Eginhard 770-840
Frankish historian

Louis I the Pious 778-840
Emperor of the West

Al Ma'mun 786-833
Abbasid Caliph

Leo III d. 816
Pope

Lothair I 795-855
Emperor of the West

Egbert
King of Wessex 802-39

Louis the German 804-76
King of Germany

Johannes Scottus Eriugena c. 814-77
Irish Scholar

Charles the Bald 823-77
King of France, Emperor

Kenneth I MacAlpin d. 858
King of united Scotland

Arpad c. 834-907
Magyar leader

Charles the Fat 839-88
King of France, Emperor

Alfred the Great 849-99
King of Wessex

Arnulf of Carinthia 850-99
German Emperor

Harold I Fairhair c. 850-933
King of Norway

Aethelred
King of Wessex 866-71

Halfdan d. 877
Viking leader

Al-Farabi c. 870-950
Scholar of Damascus

Henry I the Fowler 877-936
German King

Rollo (Robert I of Normandy) 878-931
Norse leader

Charles III the Simple 879-929
King of France

Conrad I d. 918
Elected King of Germany

Abd-al-Rahman 890-961
Caliph of Cordova

Edward the Elder d. 924
King of England

Al Mutanabbi 905-65
Arab poet

Otto I the Great 912-73
German Emperor

Al-Mansur 914-1002
Regent of Cordova

Bogomil c. 914-61
Bulgarian priest

Athelstan d. 939
King of England

Widukind of Corvey 924-98
German historian

Firdausi 932-1020
Persian poet

Harold Bluetooth c. 935-85
King of Denmark

Hugh Capet c. 938-96
King of France

Vladimir the Great (St.) 940-1015
Grand Prince of Kiev

Edgar c. 943-75
King of England

Gerbert of Reims 943-1003
Pope Sylvester II

Chao Kuang-yin d. 975
Chinese Emperor

Sven I Forked Beard c. 960-
King of Denmark

Al-Hakam II
Caliph of Cordova 961

Brian Boru c. 962-10
King of Munster, Irela

Fujiwara Michinaga 966-
Japanese Regent

Leif Ericson 967-
Norse discoverer

Stephen I (St.) c. 972-1
King of Hungary

Mahmud of Ghazni 976-1
Persian conqueror of Punj

Aethelred
King of Englan

Yaroslave the Wi
Grand Prince of K

● **756**
The Donation of Pepin establishes Papal States

● **756**
Ummayad caliphate established at Cordova *Spain*

● **762**
Baghdad founded as capital of Abbasid caliphs

● **774**
Charlemagne crowned King of Lombardy

● **778**
Defeat of the Franks at Roncevalles *France*

● **787**
First Viking raids on England and Ireland

● **788**
Independent Shiite caliphate *Morocco*

● **794**
Synod of Frankfurt

● **799**
Pope Leo III flees Rome and seeks Charlemagne's help

● **816**
Imperial coronation of Louis the Pious at Rome

● **843**
Treaty of Verdun

● **865**
Massive Viking attacks on East Anglia

● **870**
Treaty of Mersen: Lotharingia split

● **872**
Samanid Dynasty at Bokhara

● **c. 875**
Viking attacks throughout Europe

● **878**
Peace of Wedmore: partition of England into Danelaw and Alfred's kingdom

● **889**
Magyars expelled from Atelkuz by Petchenegs

● **907**
End of T'ang Dynasty *China*

● **907-54**
Magyar depredations in Germany

● **910**
Cluny Abbey founded *France*

● **911**
Rollo granted territories by Charles the Simple: *Normandy*

● **960**
Sung Dynasty establish *China*

● **962**
Lombardy under Ger rule

● **968**
Synod of Ravenn

● **969**
Egypt conquered Fatimids: Cairo ca

● **987**
Accession of Capeti Dynasty *France*

● **995**
Baptism of Magyar Va as Stephen; foundatio Kingdom of Hungary

1066
William the Conqueror — Under a strong monarchy, England fully enters the orbit of the European world.

1100
Abelard in Paris — The Council of Sens confirmed Church resistance to Abelard's application of Aristotelian logic to matters of faith.

1204
The Fall of Constantinople — By sacking the Byzantine capital and setting up there the Latin Kingdom of Romania, the knights of the Fourth Crusade fatally weakened the greatest bastion against the Turks.

agers West — Eric the s discovery of Greenland the conquests of Normandy, and and Sicily, an example orse expansionism.

1077
Humiliation at Canossa — By humiliating Henry IV and making the conflict an open one, Gregory VII ultimately strengthened the independence of medieval monarchies.

1194
The Palace of the Virgin — Chartres Cathedral as rebuilt after the fire of 1194 was intended as an epitome of the wonders of the world and served as torch-bearer for medieval humanism.

edeless
016

Somadeva c. 1035-82
Indian poet

Nr ed Din 1118-74
Ruler of Syria

Henry VI 1165-97
German Emperor

054
of Russia

Urban II 1042-99
Pope

Manuel I Comnenus c. 1120-80
Byzantine Emperor

Philip II Augustus 1165-1223
King of France

cenna 980-1037
bian scholar

Alexius I Comnenus 1048-1118
Byzantine Emperor

Louis VII c. 1120-80
King of France

Dominic (St.) c. 1170-1221
Castilian preacher

Hazm 994-1063
ish statesman and writer

Henry IV 1050-1106
German Emperor

Frederick I Barbarossa c. 1122-90
German Emperor

Francis of Assisi (St.) c. 1182-1226
Italian itinerant preacher

te 995-1035
of Denmark and England

Philip I 1052-1108
King of France

Eleanor of Aquitaine c. 1122-1204
Wife of Henry II of England

Frederick II of Sicily 1194-1250
German Emperor

gar of Tours 1000-89
h theologian

Bohemond I c. 1056-1111
Norman Prince of Antioch

Averroes c. 1126-98
Spanish Moslem scholar

Ferdinand III 1199-1252
King of Castile and Leon

IX (St.) 1002-54
e and Church Reformer

Henry I 1068-1135
King of England

Ibn Tufayl c. 1127-85
Spanish Moslem scholar

ard the Confessor 1002-66
of England

Peter Abelard 1079-1142
French Scholar

Waldemar I the Great 1131-82
King of Denmark

Robert Guiscard c. 1013-85
Norman conqueror of S. Italy

Avempace (Ibn Bajja) d. 1138
Spanish Arabic philosopher

Henry II 1133-89
King of England

Henry III 1017-56
German Emperor

Suger c. 1081-1151
Abbot of St. Denis

Maimonides 1135-1204
Jewish scholar in Spain

Gregory VII (Hildebrand) 1020-85
Pope 1073-85

Louis VI the Fat 1081-1137
King of France

Saladin c. 1137-93
Sultan of Egypt

Wang An-shih 1021-86
Chinese minister

Bernard of Clairvaux (St.) c. 1090-1153
French churchman

Eric IX (St.)
King of Sweden 1150-60

Harold Godwinsson c. 1022-66
King of England

Arnold of Brescia c. 1095-1155
Italian Church reformer

Yoritomo Minamoto c. 1147-99
Japanese military dictator, Shogun

William I the Conqueror c. 1027-87
King of England

Roger II 1097-1154
Norman Count of Sicily

Alfonso VIII the Noble 1155-1214
King of Castile

Alfonso VI 1030-1109
King of Leon and Castile

Genghis Khan 1155-1227
Mongol ruler

Roger I c. 1031-1101
Norman Count of Sicily

John of Salisbury c. 1115-80
English political philosopher

Richard Coeur-de-Lion 1157-99
King of England

Anselm 1033-1109
Archbishop of Canterbury

Thomas Becket 1118-70
Archbishop of Canterbury

Innocent III 1161-1216
Pope

1000
Ericson sails to North erica ("Vinland")

● **1046**
Emperor Henry III deposes Pope Gregory VI in favor of reform popes

● **1106**
Henry I settlement with the papacy
England

● **1167**
Oxford University founded
England

000
nd converted: allegiance ct to Rome

● **1071**
Battle of Manzikert: Byzantium loses Asia Minor to Seljuk Turks
Turkey

● **1122**
Kitan territory seized by Kin tribes *China*

● **1169**
Kiev conquered by Andrei Boguliubski of Suzdal
Russia

001
mud of Ghazni begins nder and conquest of jab *India*

● **1085**
Toledo recaptured from Moors *Spain*

● **1122** Concordat of Worms
Holy Roman Empire

● **1187**
Saladin defeats crusaders at Battle of Hattin *Palestine*

1004
g Empire buys off ans with annual tribute na

● **1086**
Almoravids annex Moorish Spain

● **1144**
Franks expelled from Edessa by Zanghi of Mosul

● **1192**
Feudal military rule under shogunate: Kamakura period
Japan

● **1013**
Fall of Caliphate of Cordova
Spain

● **1099**
Capture of Jerusalem by First Crusade
Palestine

● **1145**
Almohades conquer Moorish Spain

● **1042**
End of Danish rule in England

● **1167**
The Taira seize power from the Fujiwara
Japan

The Expanding World of Man

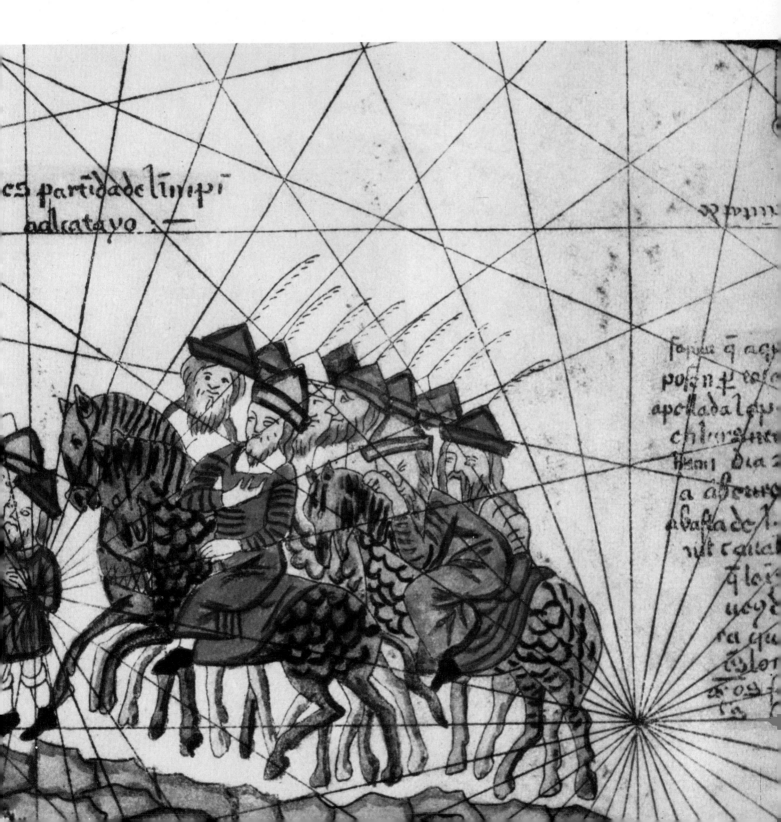

Editor Neville Williams

1215-1588

Introduction

Sixteen milestones of history—all of which occurred between the early thirteenth and the late sixteenth centuries—are authoritatively discussed in this section. Together they provide a comprehensive picture of nearly four hundred years of world history. Any increase in the number of contributions would diminish the significance of each chosen event; while any reduction in the number of selections, by focusing on a few "epoch-making" battles, would eliminate the spiritual, artistic and scientific achievements of the era.

Although European events dominate the first half of Part Three, the theme of the whole—as the title makes plain—is *The Expanding World of Man*. Accordingly, milestones in the history of Russia, China, the Americas and India have been included. And despite Sir Edward Creasy's assertion—in his 1852 study entitled *Fifteen Decisive Battles of the World* —that all milestones of history are necessarily military or naval actions, no more than seven of the sixteen essays in this part are primarily concerned with warfare.

The Peasants' Revolt in England is considered a milestone in history despite the fact that it failed—for the English rising led to similar rebellions in France and Flanders and, collectively, those outbreaks altered the social structure of feudal Europe. In much the same way, it was subsequent interpretations of Magna Carta, coupled with the constitutional and historical significance ultimately attached to the document, that elevated the signing of the Great Charter to an event of singular importance. Some of the milestones included in this volume have more than a single claim to attention. In the field of cultural history, for instance, Dante's *Divine Comedy* stands as one of the half-dozen finest works of poetry in all of Western civilization—yet we learn more about the Christian spirit of the Middle Ages from Dante's masterpiece than we do from any other single source.

The Expanding World of Man is concerned with more than simply the discovery of new continents and the interaction of civilizations. From the mid-thirteenth century, man's intellectual horizons were also expanding. The philosophical treatises of Roger Bacon and the subsequent development of humanism —which affected art, letters and every aspect of human life—paved the way for the Renaissance. The rediscovery of Greece added a new dimension to classical scholarship, which had hitherto been limited to the civilization of Rome. The humanist outlook, which embraced a fearless search for truth and beauty, questioned the fundamental purpose of man. That search led, inescapably, to dispute with authority, especially the authority of the Church. The new theology of Luther, Zwingli and Calvin was as much an "expansion" of man's world as Columbus' voyage or Copernicus' theory of the universe were— and the renewed theology of Catholicism, born at the sixteenth-century Council of Trent, was itself an expansion of the medieval system perfected by St. Thomas Aquinas. Erasmus' detachment from theological controversy and Montaigne's quizzical open-mindedness in matters of faith both exemplify a broadening of outlook that would have been considered heretical in the age of Innocent III (1198–1216).

With the beginning of the Age of Discovery, Europe ceased to be a Mediterranean continent. There was a shift of emphasis to northwestern Europe and to the development of Antwerp—not merely as the commercial capital of the world but as the center of banking and finance as well. The new capitalism of the Antwerp Exchange and of such great European banking houses as the Fuggers of Augsburg is certainly an expansion of the system of

313

Introduction

medieval credit built up by Jewish money lenders and the banks of Florence. Never before had society been so fluid: careers in the service of monarchs like Louis XI of France or Henry VIII of England were open to talented members of all classes.

The sixteen essays in this section are not presented in isolation; the unique events with which they deal are placed in historical context by means of narrative passages that link each essay to its successor. These linking passages make no effort to cover world history with textbook comprehensiveness. Instead, their function is to provide this volume with a greater cohesion than would otherwise be the case, and to offer a general survey of *The Expanding World of Man* in these four remarkable centuries.

Each linking passage deals with the events, the people and the achievements that set the stage for the "milestone" that follows. There was more to the High Renaissance than the Sistine Chapel, and more to the Continental Reformation than Luther's Bible—and the essays that describe those events are amplified by the narrative links that precede and follow them. These linking passages describe the characteristics of the epoch (such as chivalry or anti-clericalism), the tendencies and movements that underlay it (the rise of the universities and vernacular literature, humanism and the demand for Church reform), the economic changes that gave it shape (decline of feudalism, apogee of Venetian trade with the Levant), and the developments in art and architecture that gave the era its unique style.

In general, the links discuss events that were of great moment in the history of a particular country but are of insufficient importance to rank as "milestones" in world history. For example, the execution of the accused heretic John Huss at the Council of Constance (1415) was a seminal date in the rise of Bohemian nationalism, but Huss' martyrdom had little long-term effect on the development of Europe. Other seemingly significant lives and events have been rejected as "milestones" and relegated to the linking passages for similar reasons: the legacy of the remarkable Holy Roman Emperor Frederick II, whose contemporaries dubbed him the "Wonder of the World," was purely negative; the life's work of Pope Boniface VIII proved basically unconstructive; and even Henry Tudor's victory at Bosworth Field was no more than a domestic event ensuring a change of dynasty on the English throne.

In their own fields, Tycho Brahe's charts of the heavens and Vesalius' anatomical studies of the human body were tremendously important, yet none can be described as epoch-making in broad historical terms. Such achievements are accordingly described in the linking passages.

With the closing of the Middle Ages the pace of change quickened. The globe was shrinking as rapidly as man's knowledge of the universe was expanding. In the maelstrom of the Reformation both art and science strove to escape from the straitjacket of clerical control—and Christendom came under attack from within as well as from without. National states hardened under the rule of strong kings, and Europe was plunged into a series of dynastic wars that lasted until 1763.

As a result of those developments, the history of the sixteenth century is richer and more varied than that of the previous era. Consequently, three essays each have been assigned to the thirteenth, fourteenth and fifteenth centuries, while the sixteenth century—with full justification—has been treated in seven separate essays. This imbalance creates an unevenness in the time span covered in each of the linking passages: there is half a century between Marco Polo's arrival at Peking and Dante's writing of the *Divine Comedy*, and half a century between the Peasants' Revolt and

Joan of Arc's death—but only ten years separate the Copernican theory from Luther's Bible, and the Battle of Lepanto and Akbar's entry to Gujarat occur within two years of one another. Nonetheless, it is fair to say that no individual of importance or event of significance has been omitted.

In the ensuing pages the reader can trace the changing facets of Christian experience from St. Francis of Assisi and St. Louis through Wycliffe, Thomas à Kempis, Savonarola and the Protestant reformers to St. Francis Xavier and St. Ignatius Loyola; he can observe the evolution of the papacy from the time of Innocent III through the pontificate of Sixtus V; and he can survey the politics of the West from the accession of Henry III of England through the assassination of Henry IV of France. As the essays progress, the reader moves gradually from a world of monastic chronicles, written in Gothic script and beautifully illuminated, to an age in which printed books with elaborate woodcuts are a commonplace. Warfare persists: crusades against the Turk, the Hundred Years' War between England and France, the wars of religion and frequent civil wars—all fought during this period—suggest that sophisticated Europe was basically no more politically advanced than India or Persia, China or Japan. Those conflicts are fought against a background of changing tactics on land and sea, and with increasingly efficient weapons.

Dynasties fall, boundaries change, enterprise supplants the chivalric ideal, and written languages take shape in this era. There is a new urgency about man's quest for fulfillment as he attempts to explore the unknown, exploit his environment, understand the purpose of life and come to terms with reality—and in so doing, "expand" the world of man.

NEVILLE WILLIAMS

Agreement at Runnymede 1215

In the summer of 1215 King John of England affixed his seal to Magna Carta, a crude bill of rights drawn up by his rebellious barons, and thus unwittingly hastened the decline of omnipotent, "divine-right" monarchs not only in England but in Europe as well. The "firm peace" that was reached at Runnymede proved to be an enduring one: the Great Charter survived subsequent civil wars, numerous rewritings and even annulment by the Pope. In ensuing generations, Magna Carta was reinterpreted and expanded to the point where it became the "irrepealable fundamental statute" of English law. And five and a half centuries later the personal liberties guaranteed by the Charter served as the basis for the Bill of Rights of the United States Constitution.

On June 15, 1215, a remarkable confrontation took place at Runnymede, a meadow located a mile or so to the west of the Thames-side town of Staines and twenty miles southwest of London. This unusual assembly, a formal meeting between King John of England and a party of his subjects who had been in rebellion since the beginning of May, had been called to settle the dispute concerning the King's rule and the general conduct of the government. As such, the gathering at Runnymede was unprecedented in English history.

When the antagonists met on June 15, the broad terms of agreement had already been settled through official envoys. The confrontation at Runnymede was the final stage of a long and complex series of negotiations begun by representatives of the beleaguered King and his rebellious barons on May 25, 1215. On June 19, a final settlement, described in the records of the meeting as a "firm peace," was finally reached.

Nonetheless, King John and his opponents continued to meet at Runnymede through June 23, for the King was compelled to fulfill immediately some of the concessions he had promised. From June 15 to 23, therefore, John and the rebel lords rode out to Runnymede daily; the King and his supporters from his castle at Windsor, the rebel party from the town of Staines.

The rebel party, made up of a group of barons and their supporters, was dominated by England's most powerful landowners, who held title to their estates in return for military and other forms of feudal service to the King. The final settlement therefore assumed feudal characteristics that now seem antiquated and inadequate: the rebels renewed their homage and fealty to the King; the King and his leading supporters swore a solemn oath to observe the terms of the settlement; and the execution of the agreement was secured by a treaty that placed the barons in charge of London, the capital of the realm. The terms of the settlement were written in a charter, one that came to be known, because of its large size, as Magna Carta, or the Great Charter.

At the time, the charter form seemed the most suitable vehicle for the terms of peace. Charters were frequently used in the early 1200s to record grants of land, rights or privileges; they were the most solemn and formal documents available for such transactions. In 1215 England had no statute laws and but a rudimentary concept of legislation. Hence this part of the settlement took the form of a solemn concession, an apparently voluntary act of self-restraint, whereby John promised to right the wrongs alleged against him and to limit both his own and his successors' actions in the future. Magna Carta was traditional and familiar in form, a fact that seemed to give it strength and permanence.

King John did not actually affix his signature to the Charter; instead it was sealed with the impression of the Great Seal and witnessed by the Archbishop of Canterbury and other great men. The document, written in Latin and which later came to be divided into some sixty numbered chapters, originally was written without such aids to reference and ranged haphazardly over most aspects of government.

First, Magna Carta sought to regulate the feudal relationships between the Crown and its immediate tenants by laying down rules about payments due on the succession to estates, about the custody of wards and their lands, and about the marriage of heiresses. Second, it provided for regular justice in central and local courts and sought to ensure that the King would only act against his subjects by recognized legal procedure. The most famous and most significant chapter of Magna Carta, Number 39, states:

> No free man shall be taken or imprisoned or deprived or outlawed or exiled or in any way ruined . . . except by the lawful judgment of his peers or by the law of the land.

Third, the Charter attempted to regulate the King's financial power, seeking to control his right to tax and the manner in which his officers collected debts or sought to increase royal revenues. Fourth, it demanded that the King restore rights and property

Pope Innocent III, at first John's enemy, but later his ally against the barons.

Opposite King John, from his tomb at Worcester Cathedral.

An attack on tyranny

King John; Magna Carta attacked his power.

that he had seized or acquired by unjust agreements. Fifth, it arranged for the election in every county of juries of knights who were to inquire into the activities of the sheriffs and other local agents of the Crown. Finally, the Great Charter established a body of twenty-five barons—originally twenty-four of the rebel leaders and the Mayor of London—who were to hear and adjudicate complaints and claims against the King under the terms of the Charter.

In all, Magna Carta was a radical, indeed a revolutionary document. "Why," King John is purported to have asked, "do they not demand my kingdom?" The Charter had been inspired by deep and bitterly felt grievances, focused for the most part on King John himself. Unlike his brother and predecessor, Richard I, who spent most of his brief reign (1189–99) fighting abroad, John (1199–1216) was largely resident in England, and was personally responsible for his government. John was an active and inventive monarch, but he was faced with several major problems. The Continental empire accumulated by his father, Henry II (1151–89), was breaking up; Normandy, England's remaining Continental holding, had fallen to the French in 1204.

John responded to his problems with energetic defiance, mustering all the resources of his realm for military and diplomatic victory on the Continent; war plans and war finance dominated his policies. He achieved a settlement with the Pope in 1213, but failed in a great counterattack against King Philip of France in 1214. This defeat led immediately to the outbreak of a rebellion which had been developing in England for some time. The opposition exploited the King's failures abroad—soon after the loss of Normandy he was nicknamed John Softsword—but it fed on the resentment produced by his policies at home. This welling discontent was caused by the King's financial demands, by his exploitation of feudal relationships for his own political and financial interests, and by his increasing readiness to inject political and personal considerations into his exercise of justice. John's subjects were further outraged

Chateau Gaillard, a great English stronghold in France, which John lost to Philip Augustus of France.

by his use of patronage, which sharply distinguished those in from those out of favor, and by his reliance on a number of skilled foreign advisers who came to England from the lost lands on the Continent and enjoyed increasing influence and reward as sheriffs, custodians of castles and husbands of native heiresses.

Magna Carta dealt with all these injustices and inequities, but it was not concerned with them alone. King John's transgressions were not novel, and many of the grievances that the Charter dealt with considerably antedated John's reign. Richard I, the King's brother, and Henry II, their father, had also found the task of defending England's Continental possessions to be demanding and expensive; they too had been forced to muster armies and levy heavy taxes. Nor were John's policies really new. He and many of his most important officials had been brought up in the administrative traditions of Henry II's court, and for the most part they simply adhered to those traditions.

The political theories and assumptions that the Charter embodied were likewise issues of long standing. In the course of the twelfth century men had become increasingly familiar with two notions, both of which they owed in large measure to the increasing law and order provided by the Crown. One assumption derived from a growing readiness to accept and expect regular justice according to routine procedures in a court of law; from that notion emerged the idea of an established custom of the realm. The other concept derived from the fact that kings sold, and subjects bought, rights and privileges. Local communities—first towns and then counties—had rapidly acquired privileges in this way, possessing and defending them in common, and chartered liberties held by individuals or groups had become common features of English feudal society. Magna Carta, which sought to equate the custom of the realm with the rights of all free men, summarized both these trends. English law and political thought were profoundly affected by the Charter, which

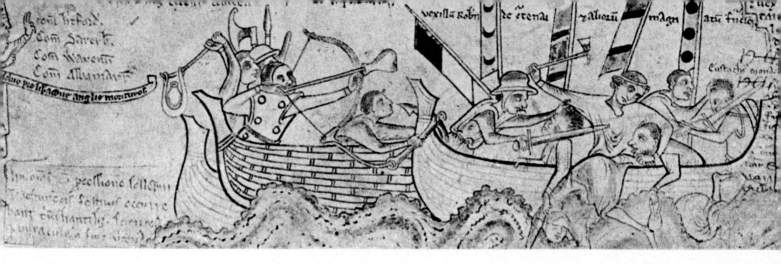

equated law with liberties and ultimately law with liberty.

The rebellion of 1215 marked a new departure. It was not simply another example of feudal anarchy, but rather a political and legal program, a statement of general rather than individual aims. As the crisis deepened in the early months of 1215, the argument turned increasingly on defining the customs of the realm, and upon erecting a largely fictitious "ancient custom" to challenge the innovations of Henry II and his sons. Out of these arguments grew a list of preliminary demands, which the rebellious nobles submitted to their king in April. John failed to meet the baronial demands, and in May of 1215, the barons went to war. On May 17, the rebels seized London, and the King was forced to open negotiations at Runnymede.

However, the June settlement was only a temporary one. On the one hand, it was a compromise that failed to satisfy the most intransigent of the King's opponents; on the other, it was equally unacceptable to the King himself. In time, inquiries into local government provoked outbreaks of lawlessness. The restoration of lands and privileges to individuals revealed a number of irreconcilable cases soluble only by force of arms. By September the country was drifting into a new civil war. The Charter itself provided the King with a rationale for attack, for although its text asserted that the Charter had been freely granted, the supporters of the document knew that their demands had been exacted by force. On these grounds, Pope Innocent III, to whom both parties had appealed for arbitration, annulled Magna Carta on August 24, 1215. The civil war that ensued was a bitter affair that continued for a year after John's death in October, 1216. Although the war ultimately involved the French, Magna Carta remained the central issue. Peace was secured only by reissuing the Charter in November, 1216, and November, 1217. These versions owed a great deal to the approval of the Pope and his agents in England. They omitted many of the purely temporary sections of the Charter of 1215 and abandoned the court of twenty-five barons and many of the provisions concerned with financial administration. With John dead and the new king, Henry III—a boy of nine at his accession—less of a threat to the barons' power, these chapters were no longer as essential. It was the 1217 version, slightly amended in 1225, that was incorporated into the law of the land. The 1217 and 1225 versions of the Great Charter were accompanied by a Charter of the Forest specifically concerned with the administration of the royal forests. In subsequent confirmation the two were usually associated.

The Charter's transformation was both curious and unique. Originally, Magna Carta was simply part of a settlement to end a civil war; it was in force only during the summer months of 1215, until its annulment by Pope Innocent. Yet it became, in the works of the great legal historian, F. W. Maitland, "the nearest approach to an irrepealable fundamental statute that England has ever had"; nine of its chapters still stand on the statute book. This transition from peace treaty to "fundamental statute" makes Magna Carta significant.

England was not alone in having such a charter of liberties; they were common features of European politics in the thirteenth and fourteenth centuries. Hungary had the Golden Bull (1222); Germany had both the Confederation with the Ecclesiastical Princes (1220) and the Statute in Favor of the Princes (1232); Aragon, the General Privilege (1283) and the Privilege of the Union (1287); and France, the charters of privileges of Normandy, Burgundy, and other provinces (1315). All these concessions sprang from situations analogous to that of England in 1215: war, financial pressure, harsh administration and discontent. No contemporary would have selected the English Magna Carta as the one most likely to survive, and yet it did while the other charters were soon defunct.

Magna Carta survived and flourished because it became inextricably linked with the processes of English government and political life. As early as 1215, careful measures were taken to ensure its full publication—a copy was sent to each shire, and the

A battle at sea between the English and the French.

Philip Augustus unhorsed at the Battle of Bouvines (1214) —one of the series of battles in the endemic war between France and England.

"The Charter walks abroad"

The sufferings of prisoners arrested without trial. This was banned by Magna Carta.

Magna Carta; an attempt by the barons to increase their power at the expense of the King became in time the foundation stone of constitutional liberty.

sheriff was ordered to read it out in the county court. This procedure was repeated in 1216, 1217, 1225 and again in 1253. As time passed, even greater emphasis was given to publication: a twice yearly reading in the county courts became law in 1265, a twice yearly reading in the cathedrals followed in 1297, and a reading four times a year in the county courts was decreed in 1300. On this last occasion, English was specified as the appropriate language, apparently for the first time. As a result, the Charter was well known, and copies proliferated in monastic or cathedral archives, in legal text books, and even

in the hands of the knights who did much of the work of the county courts.

However, the story of the Charter did not end with the feudal politics and law of the thirteenth century. Its longer survival depended on two features of the original document that were preserved in all subsequent reissues: first, the Charter was a grant in perpetuity intended to last for all time; and second, it stated broad general procedures and principles rather than detailed and transitory points of law. Thus each generation could reinterpret the Charter to fit new circumstances. Between 1331 and 1363 Parliament passed six statutory interpretations of the famous Chapter 39, which developed it in directions unimagined in 1215. These interpretations equated the "lawful judgment of peers" with trial by jury, a process that scarcely existed in thirteenth-century England; they identified the "law of the land" with "due process of law," a phrase that would have been all but incomprehensible in 1215; and they replaced the words "no free man" of the 1215 version with "no man whatsoever estate or condition he may be," a change that extended Magna Carta's protection to the villeins, or the majority of the population, who were thus brought within the scope of a provision from which they had been hitherto excluded.

Such reinterpretation became common and was extended to other chapters, particularly in the seventeenth century. Even in contemporary times, lawyers have appealed to the chapter of Magna Carta that states that widows are to have their dower and marriage portion without delay in order to secure the prompt payment of a widow's pension, and to the chapter that permits free entry and exit from the realm in order to challenge the requirement of a passport for foreign travel.

Lawyers have been encouraged in this practice by the peculiar prominence that Magna Carta has acquired in English common law. The Charter was always given pride of place as the first item in the printed collection of statues published in the sixteenth century, and by the late thirteenth century—at a time when men were first becoming acquainted with the notion of statute law—Magna Carta already figured prominently in the manuscript collections of statutes that lawyers were then beginning to compile as books of reference. In a sense, Magna Carta became the origin of statute law. In 1215 this was unintended, at least by the rebel barons; their legal theory did not carry them beyond the idea of chartered privileges. Nevertheless, the 1215 charter contains a number of provisions concerned with the detailed administration of the law that do not seem to have been part of the rebels' demands, and which were probably inserted by the lawyers of the Crown simply in order to reform existing laws. The reissues of 1216 and 1217—particularly the latter—contain additional and more important material of the same kind, concerned with the conveying of land and the sessions of local courts. Much of the Charter of the Forest is made up of similar detailed regulations. Each of these successive documents show progressively better drafting, and all are marked improvements as legal drafts on the 1215 petition, known as the Articles of the Barons, in which the King's opponents first stated their demands.

These revisions of the original Charter were the work of men experienced in the administration of the courts, who used the Charter as a means of legal reform. Hence, Magna Carta was both a program of rebellion and a statement of law. The former characteristic was the more prominent in 1215, the latter in the revisions of 1217 and 1225. The former characteristic led to the demand for its confirmation in later crises; the latter made it a starting point for a growing body of legislation in the thirteenth century. The Provisions of Merton of 1236, the Statute of Marlborough of 1267, and the Statutes of Westminster of 1275 and 1285 were all in part concerned with points of law first formulated in Magna Carta, and as a result the Charter has become embedded in English history as a fundamental law. In the constitutional conflicts of the seventeenth century, Magna Carta was the obvious weapon to use in defending Parliament and the common law courts against the prerogative of the Stuart kings. "I shall be very glad to see," Sir Benjamin Rudyard declaimed in a Commons debate on the Petition of Right in 1628, "that old, decrepit Law Magna Carta which hath been kept so long, and lien bed-rid, as it were, I shall be glad to see it walk abroad again with new vigour and lustre..."

In the hands of Sir Edward Coke, first the Chief Justice and then the bitter constitutional opponent of the Stuarts, the Great Charter was used to attack royal monopolies, prerogative taxation and the prerogative court of the Star Chamber. All these Coke denounced as injurious to the freedom of the individual or to established judicial process. Others used the Charter to justify the principle of habeas corpus and the claim, advanced in the Petition of Right, that there should be "no arrest without cause shown." Coke was the first to equate the "liberties" of the Charter with the liberty of the individual, and it was the legal writings of Coke that carried the Charter to North America and planted the principles that he had found in Chapter 39 in the constitutions of the early colonies and ultimately of the United States. By this time, the Charter was considerably altered; the feudal liberties of the thirteenth century had given way to liberty as conceived by Coke and the American Founding Fathers, but some of the characteristics of the original charter still remained. Coke and his fellows regarded Magna Carta as a statement of fundamental, incontravertible law which itself went back beyond 1215 to the days before the Norman conquest of England. The men of 1215 had made no claim as bold and precise as that, although they had maintained, somewhat falsely, that their program was but a statement of ancient custom. Indeed, it was their myth that provided the foundation for Coke's modern legal structure—which continues to influence much of British, and American, legal thought today.   J. C. HOLT

Parliament in the reign of Edward I; the growth of parliamentary liberties sprang from Magna Carta.

Henry III and later successors of John reissued Magna Carta.

321

Five months after King John was forced to grant the Magna Carta at Runnymede, Pope Innocent III—who was then at the height of his power—opened the Fourth Lateran Council in Rome. As a young man, Innocent had mastered Scholastic philosophy at Paris and canon and civil law at Bologna, but his pontificate (1198–1216) revealed him to be a man of action as well. In 1215, the fifty-four-year-old Pope seemed likely to dominate Europe for years to come. "The Lord left to St. Peter the governance not of the Church alone, but of the whole world," Innocent proclaimed—and he appeared bent on putting this claim into effect. "Princes have power in earth, priests over the soul, and as much as the soul is worthier than the body, so much worthier is the priesthood than the monarchy," he preached.

The unity of Christendom was Innocent's cherished ideal. To this end he inspired the Fourth Crusade, demanded rigorous treatment of the Albigensian heretics, and summoned 1,500 archbishops and other dignitaries to Rome to hear his plans for Church reform. The decrees that Innocent required the Lateran Council to endorse—almost without discussion—emphasized the universality of the Church and the significance of its sacraments, redefined dogma, and laid down detailed rules for episcopal elections, monastic life, the qualifications of the clergy and theological instruction. The Pope expected that those decrees would pitch spiritual life in a higher key, leaving no man in doubt of what the Church required of him. The Council, which ended in 1216 with the summoning of another crusade, capped the career of the greatest of the medieval popes—for Innocent died shortly after the Council dispersed.

Francis of Assisi

Through his patronage of both the Franciscans and Dominicans, Innocent associated the papacy with the new spiritual movements. The wisdom of Innocent's alliance with those new orders cannot be underestimated, for through the genius of Francis of Assisi (1182–1226) the religious life of the West was to be completely transformed. St. Francis, born Giovanni Bernardone, was the son of a wealthy Tuscan merchant. His childhood companions nicknamed him Francis ("the Frenchman") because of his penchant for French romances and troubadours' songs.

While in his twenties, Francis experienced a sudden conversion and told his friends that he intended to marry "a fairer bride than ever you saw, who surpasses all others in beauty and excels them in virtue" —the Lady Poverty. He renounced his possessions to lead a life of prayer and poverty in the hills—and soon attracted a substantial band of followers. In ragged habit and bare feet, he tended lepers, collected alms for the poor, preached the brotherhood of man and animals, and put the message of the Gospels in the language of the troubadours. Holy poverty seemed to bring a gaiety of spirit to the Franciscans, earning the Tuscan mendicants the nickname "God's jesters."

Detail of a reliquary of St. Francis.

Pope Innocent gave his cautious approval to the Order of Minorites (or Gray Friars) and Francis returned to Assisi to organize additional groups of friars in the area. Such religious groups were soon established throughout the West. Francis traveled widely—even arguing his case before the Sultan of Egypt—before relinquishing the rule of his Order to Brother Elias of Cortona in 1220 in order to devote himself to simpler tasks.

One of Francis' final tasks was to draw up a Rule for his friend St. Clare and her "Minoresses." These female counterparts of the Gray Friars, known as the "Poor Clares," were similarly dependent on alms, but like all other orders for women— and unlike the Franciscans—they were strictly enclosed. Two years after his death, St. Francis was canonized and his followers began to formulate plans for a great church at Assisi. Ironically, it was to be richly endowed and superbly decorated by the greatest artists in Italy—which was supposed to honor the apostle of poverty.

The Dominicans

In these same years the Order of the Dominicans, or Friars Preachers, was founded by the Spaniard Dominic de Guzman (1170–1221), who had been sent to Provence to help convert the Albigensian schismatics. If heresy was to be combated, he argued, there was an imperative need for an educated, preaching ministry in the towns; therefore, study was to be an integral part of the Dominican's vow. While St. Francis spurned possessing so much as a crucifix of his own, St. Dominic insisted on books for all his brothers.

Albigensian Heretics

The Albigensian heretics of Provence—who took their name from the town of Albi on the Tarn River —professed a total disregard of all authority, spiritual and secular. They classified believers into two groups: "the perfect," who renounced property, marriage and the world at large and on death passed directly to a state of glory; and "other believers," who could live as they chose, provided they received before death the sacrament of the *Consolamentum*, an act of absolution which could be performed only once in a lifetime, however, and those who recovered from their death beds were expected to commit suicide. The sect quickly took root in Provence.

The Albigensians did not attract much attention until Count Raymond VI of Toulouse joined the movement. Zealous priests were sent to wean the Albigensians from their errors, but their descriptions of the Christian life smacked too much of asceticism for those nurtured on Provençal vernacular literature. When his priests' arguments failed, Innocent III obliged Philip II of France to proclaim a crusade against the Albigensians, whom he called "heretics worse than the Saracens." Raymond soon submitted and restored Provençal churches to orthodox use, but many of his subjects held out.

The young Henry III

Henry III was only nine at the time of his accession to the English

An elephant that was presented to Henry III, from Matthew Paris' *Chronicles*.

throne and control of the government was placed in the hands of William, Earl of Pembroke.

Upon Pembroke's death, the papal legate Pandulph was appointed regent. Archbishop Langton soon persuaded the Pope to recall Pandulph, however, and power passed to Hubert de Burgh, England's chief justice, who was anxious to restore strong government and free England from interference by foreigners. After coming of age, Henry III dismissed Hubert and attempted to rule England alone. He foolishly appointed the Frenchman Peter des Roches as chief justice, and Roches promptly appointed his kinsfolk to high office. His actions provoked the English barons to renounce their fealty to Henry and threatened his position. Following in the steps of Stephen Langton, the saintly Archbishop Edmund Rich warned the king that his attempt to rule the realm without the cooperation of his barons would end in disaster. Henry wisely expelled the French officials.

Henry found fulfillment for his religious ideals and cultured tastes in his buildings at Westminster. The reconstructed Abbey, which housed the relics of Henry's mentor, Edward the Confessor, was the first building in England with double

The head of Henry III.

tiers of flying-buttresses and bar-traceried windows. "As the rose is to other flowers," ran an inscription on a tile in the Chapter House, "so is this house to other buildings." The nearby Palace of Westminster was no less splendid. Its *tour de force* was the Painted Chamber, an enormous, richly decorated room that the king ordered his clerk of the works to have finished by a certain date, "even though you have to hire 1,000 workmen a day."

Curiously, in the business of

The seal of Philip Augustus.

government proper, Henry showed no such drive. His rival, Philip II of France, on the other hand, was an energetic and forceful king. During his long reign (1180–1223) the kingdom of France tripled in size (largely as a result of Philip's conquest of Normandy and Poitou from John of England). Philip thoroughly reformed the financial and judicial administration of his realm by employing a corps of professional officials. By playing off one great feudal landowner against another, he likewise reduced the powers of the barons. In consequence, French feudalism became firmly established, and military obligations to the Crown were reaffirmed. Philip walled and paved Paris, built the original Louvre (as a fortified palace) and endowed the Cathedral of Notre-Dame. Indeed, the layout of the capital remained much as he left it until the age of Napoleon III.

This was also the age of French romances, of courtly love and chivalry. It was the age of the fables of Chretian de Troyes of Champagne, of the *Chanson de Roland* and of troubadours improvising their songs as interludes between recited passages of prose (the lay, vernacular counterpart to the monks' Latin plainsong, which was sung between the spoken prayers of divine offices). The schools of Paris, now in their prime, produced drinking songs as well as disputations on Scholasticism. And contemporary crusades—

even in the Age of Faith—were as much adventures on the frontiers of Europe as campaigns against the dreaded Infidel.

Frederick II and the Holy Roman Empire

The sudden death of Emperor Henry VI in 1197 plunged Germany into fourteen years of civil war. The struggle for the throne was resolved in 1211, when the German princes deposed the already excommunicated Guelf emperor Otto IV, and invited the eighteen-year-old Frederick, a Hohenstaufen, to be their king. Frederick, the son of Henry VI and Constance of Sicily, had been under the guardianship of Pope Innocent III since his mother's death.

Despite his early pledges that he would not attempt to unite the Empire with his inherited kingdoms of Sicily and Naples, Frederick did precisely that—and the resulting confederation hemmed in the Papal States. Moreover, Frederick refused to confirm the enormous privileges over the German Church that Otto had granted to Rome—and he created additional friction by his crusading. At his coronation in Rome in 1220, Frederick renewed his pledge to deliver Jerusalem from the Infidel, but he found political conditions in Naples and Sicily such that he was forced to restore order there before launching his first crusade. In 1227 he set sail for the Holy Land but was obliged to return to port a few days later when he became quite sick. Alleging that Frederick's illness was feigned, Pope Gregory IX excommunicated him.

Frederick II's successful operations in the Holy Land and his command of the Arabic language enabled him to extract a ten-year truce from Malik-al-Kamil, the Sultan of Egypt, a truce that granted him control of Jerusalem, Bethlehem and Nazareth. On Gregory's orders, the Patriarch of Jerusalem refused to celebrate religious services in Frederick's presence. In defiance, the Emperor, who had married the daughter of the late king of Jerusalem four years earlier, crowned himself king in the Church of the Holy Sepulcher.

Frederick's feud with the papacy became even more bitter when Innocent IV replaced the aged Gregory IX in 1243. Fearful of his life, Innocent fled to Lyons where, in 1245, he gathered a synod, demanded Frederick's removal and

put forward his own candidates for Emperor. Despite the Emperor's offers of reconciliation, the Pope would not retract his demands and even went so far as to preach a crusade against him.

Known as *Stupor mundi*, the wonder of the world, Frederick II amazed his contemporaries and leaves posterity puzzled. Some have called him "the first modern man to occupy a throne," and certainly his remodeling of his Italian kingdom, with its remarkable code of laws, and his passion for science foreshadow the autocratic princes of the Renaissance. Yet Frederick left Germany much as he found it: a conglomeration of feudal principalities utterly divided on the nature of the Empire and the person of the Emperor.

A brilliant linguist with a real passion for scholarship and the arts, Frederick was as much at home with the philosophy of Aristotle as with the study of natural science. He wrote a remarkable book on hawking, translated Arabic works and found a niche for the Provençal poets expelled during the Albigensian crusade. After his own crusade, he installed Saracen garrisons in Italy and his court was exposed to the esthetic influences of Moslem civilization; the courtyards of his palace were decorated with fountains, the rooms were luxurious with cushions and colorful silk hangings, perfume and exotic fruits. He turned his court into a university, noting that "science must go hand in hand with government, legislation and the pursuit of war." He founded the University of Naples, the first university to owe its origin to royal initiative, and endowed a medical

Frederick II with a hawk.

Marienburg, headquarters of the Teutonic knights.

school at Salerno, which admitted women as well as men.

The Emperor's patronage of the Teutonic Knights, whom he reorganized as a crusading, military order in 1226 to combat the Mongol invasions, led to German colonization beyond the eastern frontiers of the Empire, notably in Prussia. The flag followed the Cross and resulted in a considerable German migration towards the northeast.

Mongol incursions

From the steppes of Central Asia in the eleventh century came the Mongol Tartars, who were to dominate Russia for 250 years. After a prolonged struggle for supremacy, the chieftain Temusin was acknowledged Genghis Khan, or "Very Mighty King," by an assembly of the leaders of Mongol tribes at Karakorum in 1206. Genghis Khan led his nomadic followers into northern China and northern Persia, and even penetrated as far west as Bokhara in southwestern Russia. Led by Subotai, the Great Khan's chief of staff, the Mongols swept on across the Caucasus and onto the steppes of Polovtsk. The prince of Kiev and the rulers of southern Russia hastened to the aid of the Polovtsi, but were defeated at the battle of the Kalku River in 1223. By the time of his death in 1227, Genghis Khan had consolidated his empire in North China, and ten years later Genghis' grandnephew Batu began a systematic conquest of southern and central Russia. He took Kiev in 1240, and marched on Novgorod, a city then ruled by the Grand Duke Alexander Nevski.

The Russian Giant Stirs

The thaw of 1238 was a particularly heavy one in northeastern Russia and flood waters accompanying it forced the apparently invincible Mongol chieftain Batu to withdraw to the steppes of Central Asia. Batu's retreat saved the city of Novgorod from certain sack and spared its adolescent Grand Prince, Alexander. The significance of Novgorod's escape became apparent two years later when Russian troops led by the young Prince defeated the vast armies of King Erik of Sweden on the banks of the Neva River. In rapid succession, Alexander (who had added Nevski to his name to commemorate his initial victory) routed the Germanic Knights of the Teutonic Order and turned back a Lithuanian invasion. Having secured Russia's frontiers, Alexander devoted the rest of his life to interceding with the Tartars on behalf of his people. His selfless diplomacy led to Alexander's canonization in 1380.

The Archangel Michael; the Orthodox faith alone held Russia together in the thirteenth century, when it was attacked from all sides.

Opposite St. Boris and St. Gleb : these national saints appeared to Nevski's army in battle and scattered the enemy.

Russia began to emerge as a European power shortly after the middle of the ninth century A.D. The Grand Duchy of Kiev, cradle of the Russian empire, was founded during that century by Normans and Slavs—men of Indo-European rather than Asian origin—who built their city along the river route that leads from the Baltic to the Black Sea. Around Kiev arose a great cluster of principalities that were eventually united under the house of Rurik. This powerful dynasty of Scandinavian origin married its daughters to the kings of France, Hungary, and Norway, and to the Emperor of Germany, while contracting other family alliances with the Byzantine Emperor and the King of England. Converted under Vladimir the Saint, the Kievian state became a bulwark of Christendom against the nomads of the steppes. Linked with the great European commercial centers by her flourishing trade routes, "the Mother of Cities," as the Russians fondly called Kiev, rapidly became one of the most active and civilized metropolises on the Continent.

A Mongol invasion at the beginning of the thirteenth century put an end to Kiev's promising development, and for the next two hundred years the Russian nation was dominated by Asiatics. After the devastation of Kiev and the banks of the Dnieper by Mongol hordes, or armies, a large part of the population scattered to the north and east, where the virgin forest remained impenetrable to the enemy. The Grand Duke of Kiev, a descendant of Rurik's dynasty, transferred the center of government to the region of the Upper Volga and the Oka rivers, to the principalities of Rostov, Vladimir and Suzdal.

As a result, the whole aspect of national life was transformed. Intermarriage among the colonists and the indigenous Finnish tribes gradually produced a race of Great Russians—bearded, snub-nosed men of sober habits, the hard-working builders of the future empire. With the exception of Novgorod, a great commercial city in northwest Russia that was allied with the German Hanseatic League, the towns of the Suzdal, remote from the stream of commerce, preserved a clearly provincial character. The princes of the Suzdal appeared as nothing more than wealthy landowners, principally concerned with the administration of their large estates. Eschewing the incessant competition for the succession that preoccupied their relations and neighbors, the Suzdal princes transformed their own possessions into hereditary fiefs, a move that greatly strengthened their power.

Nonetheless, these princes were threatened from all sides by the gravest dangers. They had become vassals of the Mongols, and each of them was obliged to appear before the lieutenants of the Great Khan, who were established in the Lower Volga region, to make humble application for their investiture. In addition, the power of the Grand Duke was scarcely recognized over the immense territory—extending from the Gulf of Finland to the approaches to the White Sea—which belonged to the free city of Novgorod. Rich merchants, the real rulers of this patrician republic, chose and dismissed their local princes as they saw fit, with the sole purpose of ensuring the defense of their frontiers—although they generally gave preference to the increasingly powerless descendants of the Grand Duke of Kiev. Only a definite threat from without caused the merchants to request the aid of the younger sons of the house of Suzdal. To all this was added the increasingly strong pressure exerted on Russia by her western neighbors, the Swedes and the Teutonic Knights, who were representatives of more developed civilizations, which were capable of wiping out the last traces of the Russian national idea.

Alexander Nevski stands out in great clarity against the somber background of this tragic period of Russian history. In his spiritual and physical beauty, the clearness of his gaze and the purity of his soul, he represented the archetype of the princely saint as envisioned by Russians in the Middle Ages. In him the themes of patriotism and Christianity

Victory at the Neva

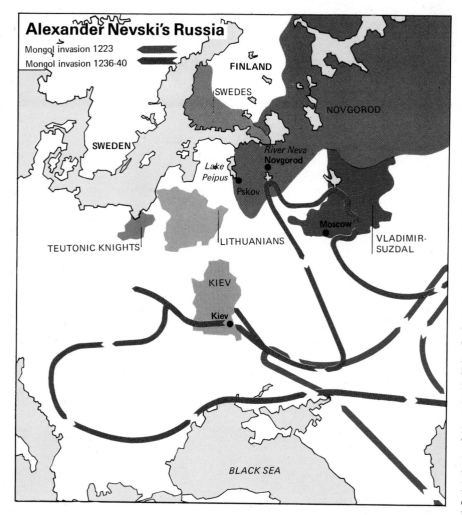

Alexander Nevski's Russia

Mongol invasion 1223
Mongol invasion 1236-40

FINLAND
SWEDES
NOVGOROD
SWEDEN
River Neva
Lake Peipus
Novgorod
Pskov
Moscow
TEUTONIC KNIGHTS
LITHUANIANS
VLADIMIR-SUZDAL
KIEV
Kiev
BLACK SEA

A copper cross of thirteenth-century Russian origin.

became interwoven and eventually merged into one another.

Alexander was born in May, 1219, at Pereyaslavl, a fief that was owned by his father, who was of the house of the Grand Prince of the Suzdal region. He spent the first years of his life in this small city, which stood on the shores of a lake among trees and meadows and was defended by a simple wooden palisade. He was scarcely three years old when his father was elected Prince of Novgorod and resettled some six miles away from that ever-unruly city in order to preside over its fortunes.

At the age of nine Alexander and his elder brother Theodore were left alone at Novgorod under the guardianship of certain nobles. Their father, who had grown disgusted with his office, rarely returned to Novgorod after 1228, and during a subsequent civil crisis, the children were obliged to flee the city under the leadership of a tutor. Theodore died prematurely some years later, and when his father, in 1236, became Grand Prince of Kiev—that is, the ruler of all Russia—Alexander fell heir to the fief of Novgorod.

The adolescent found himself faced with terrible responsibilities. A great Mongol invasion of the north of Russia occurred the following year. Led by Batu, grandson of Genghis, the invaders swiftly defeated the Volga Bulgars and swept into northeastern Russia. By March of 1238, the barbarians had advanced to within sixty miles of Novgorod. Alexander's fief appeared doomed when Batu, fearing that imminent spring thaws would trap his forces in the heavy forests around Novgorod, suddenly withdrew to the steppes.

Alexander's memorable reign at Novgorod lasted for sixteen years. Alexander made it his business to combat the separatist tendencies of the city, to strengthen its links with the central power, and to weaken the economic and political power of the *boyars*, or local grandees. In 1239 he married the daughter of the Prince of Polotsk, a feudal neighbor. During the next few years Alexander frequently enjoyed the pleasures of the chase, and hunted bear armed only with a sling—but such diversions never swayed him from his administrative duties.

Alexander's first military victory, won in 1240 on the banks of the Neva, had world-wide repercussions and earned him the name of Nevski. In an attempt to conquer those parts of Russia that had not fallen under the dominion of the Tartars—and to cut off Novgorod's sole outlet to the Baltic Sea—King Erik of Sweden gathered together a great army and placed it under the command of his son-in-law Birger. The Swedish sovereign derived some encouragement in this undertaking from a bull issued by Pope Gregory IX in 1237, and addressed to the Bishop of Uppsala. That edict summoned the Swedes to a crusade against the Finns, who had abandoned their Catholic faith under the influence of their neighbors the Russians. King Erik's interpretation of this papal message was clearly somewhat forced, but it appeared to furnish him with some justification for his aggression against Russia.

Alexander had foreseen the danger, and in 1239 he had organized the defense of the routes from Novgorod to the sea, and had placed sentries on both sides of the Gulf of Finland. Pelguse, the chieftain of the local tribe and a convert to Christianity, warned Alexander that a Swedish army was disembarking on the banks of the Neva, and the Prince hastened to meet the enemy. Reviewing his troops before their departure, Alexander uttered the phrase—an allusion to the Psalms—that has remained his most famous: "God is not on the side of force but of the just cause, the *Pravda.*" The word *pravda*, employed in modern times as the title of the most important Soviet newspaper, is not easy to translate; it means at the same time "truth," "justice," "social equity," and "just cause"—and embodies, even today, the deepest aspiration of the Russian people.

In order to engage the enemy, Alexander's troops were forced to march over marshy land, a region around modern Leningrad that still presents a rather gloomy appearance. Pressing on swiftly, Alexander's army arrived at the mist-shrouded banks of the Neva several hours after dawn. There, according to Russian legend, the local chieftain Pelguse had witnessed a curious vision as the sun rose. He saw a boat bearing several mysterious ghosts coming slowly down the river. As the vessel drew near, the shades

were revealed to be two holy princes, Boris and Gleb, and their heavenly oarsmen, who were coming to the aid of their "brother Alexander."

The battle, which began a short time later, caught the Swedes unawares; they were convinced that the Novgorod forces, deprived of the assistance of a Suzdal army recently destroyed by the Mongols, would be in no position to offer them resistance. Birger, the King's son-in-law, and many of his knights were installed in a gold embroidered tent, but the main body of the Swedish army had not yet disembarked. The Russians carried out their attacks with lightning-like rapidity; while Alexander himself wounded Birger with a blow from a spear, his men-at-arms cut the bridges joining the boats to the river bank. Panic seized the Swedes, who fled in utter disorder. According to legend, archangels swept down from Heaven and wiped out the Swedish knights on the opposite shore of the Neva.

Similar scenes occurred in the following year, when Alexander inflicted total defeat on the Knights of the Teutonic Order, a German crusading force that had acted in concert with the Swedes. The Knights had seized Izborsk, and broken the Truce of Pskov by burning the outskirts of that city before the boyars could open the gates to them. Having crushed the Swedish offensive, Alexander made ready to go to the aid of Pskov. Prevented by the boyars from carrying out this plan, Alexander withdrew to his father's estate at Pereyaslavl. It was not long before he was recalled by his subjects, who had at last realized the true extent of their danger. Alexander returned with regiments raised in the territory of Suzdal, and set off for the western frontier at the head of the

combined Russian forces.

Sergei Eisenstein's film classic *Alexander Nevski* has made the public in the West familiar with this battle, in which the steel-clad Teutons initially drove a wedge through the Russian lines, forcing them to retreat out onto the ice of Lake Peipus. There the Russians regrouped, attacked the enemy on two flanks and brought down or put to flight hundreds of German knights. Alexander's victory was complete, and the German advance was arrested for centuries. The battle, which salvaged the very existence of the Russian nation, was supposedly joined by heavenly armies, similar to those that had brought aid to Prince Alexander at the Neva.

Alexander's father, the Grand Prince Yaroslav, died on his way back from the Mongol camp at Karakorum, where he had been summoned by the Great Khan. Russian chroniclers, whose assertions agree with the testimony of Plano Carpini, the famous Italian traveler, suggest that Alexander's

Genghis Khan, the Mongol chief whose death in 1227 saved Russia from annihilation.

Above left Alexander Nevski leads the Russians into battle.

The city of Novgorod in the thirteenth century.

Medieval cathedral of Peroslave with the nineteenth-century statue of St. Alexander Nevski.

Bear hunting: a favored occupation in thirteenth-century Russia.

father was poisoned. The matter of the succession could not be settled without further intervention of the Tartar leaders. For reasons that remain unknown, it was not the deceased prince's eldest son, Yuri, but Alexander who was summoned, together with his brother Andrew, to appear before the Asiatic overlords.

Alexander was now faced with a tragic dilemma. Was the hero of the Neva and Lake Peipus to adopt the attitude of a humble vassal and recognize openly the loss of Russian independence—thus insulting the death-under-torture already suffered by some of Alexander's near relations? A Western knight might not have submitted to such a sacrifice of his honor, but Alexander was a Russian knight—an Orthodox prince—and, thinking solely of the good of his people, he preferred to submit to the Divine Will, and took counsel of the higher clergy. The metropolitan Cyril—head of the Russian Orthodox Church—gave his approval to Alexander's decision to leave for the Mongol camp on the condition that he worship no idols and not deny his faith in Christ.

Collaboration with the Tartars was, at that moment, a historical necessity. The term "collaborator" has been somewhat discredited in recent times, and has become synonymous with treachery. We consider it a patriot's duty to continue the struggle, as long as the slightest chance of success remains— but there was no chance for Russia in 1246. The nation could count on no help from outside, for the attitude of neighboring countries was entirely hostile.

328

The Prince becomes a monk

Moreover, Russia's armies, which had been sufficient to confront enemies as courageous as the Swedes or the Teutons in equal numbers, could offer no defense against the nomad hordes, who carried all before them as they advanced by tens, or even hundreds of thousands.

Subsequently, the Russians have recognized the great service that Alexander rendered them by sacrificing his pride for the sake of the Fatherland. The Mongols themselves were profoundly impressed by the conduct of this man, whose reputation had reached them some time beforehand; they granted him the honors due to his rank and spared him both the ordeal by fire and worship of the idols. Nevertheless, they did oblige Alexander to undertake the interminable journey through the deserts of Asia to Karakorum, and only allowed him to return to his native land after three years' absence. In the years that followed, Alexander returned to his masters' camp, situated north of the Azov Sea, on three occasions, to arrange current affairs and to implore the Mongols' mercy for his people.

Alexander's eldest brother was dead, and his second brother, Andrew, had taken to flight after an attempted rising, which ended—as could be foreseen—in terrible reprisals. Alexander thereby became the Grand Prince of Russia. It was his concern now to prevent further invasions, to inspire the Great Khan with confidence, to serve as intermediary between him and the Russian people, and to prevent rash insurrections even at the price of painful concession.

This superhuman task was made no easier by fresh attacks from Sweden, against which, in 1258, Alexander was obliged to conduct a new and similarly victorious campaign. Incessant unrest in Novgorod assumed an especially serious character when, in 1259, the Tartars exacted a tribute from the population of the land.

In 1262, when the exactions of the Tartars provoked another popular uprising, Alexander undertook his fifth journey to the Tartar headquarters, in an effort to ward off a punitive expedition. For a whole year he struggled to pacify the Great Khan and his henchmen, and eventually succeeded in dissuading the Tartars from their plan of raising Russian regiments for a war against Persia. But Alexander had come to the end of his strength. On the return journey, over roads made difficult by the autumn rains, he fell ill, and was taken to a monastery, where he died in November, 1263. Before drawing his last breath, Alexander gave up his princely rank and put on the habit of a monk.

In subsequent years, numerous miracles occurred at Alexander's tomb, which led to his being canonized locally in 1380, and by the whole Russian Church at the Council of 1547. Five centuries after Alexander's death—after the victorious outcome of his successor's war against Sweden—Peter the Great caused the relics of St. Alexander Nevski to be transferred to the new capital of St. Petersburg (Leningrad), where they lie today at the monastery that bears his name. CONSTANTINE DE GRUNWALD

The dormition of the Virgin Mary: an icon of the Novgorod School.

St. George and the Dragon, representing the triumph of good over evil.

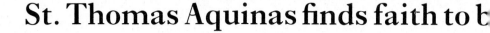

St. Louis of France.

Frenchmen look back upon the reign of Louis IX (1226–70) as one of the golden ages of the French monarchy. Few kings of France were as dearly loved by their subjects or achieved as high a reputation among contemporary monarchs as Saint Louis. His austere upbringing by Blanche of Castille (who was queen-regent of France during her son's minority) and his natural piety led Louis to model his life on the ideal of Christian knighthood—and consequently his reign was dominated by crusading ventures against the Infidel. His strategic ability did not match his enthusiasm, however, and his campaigns proved disastrous.

The Seventh Crusade

In preparation for his first campaign, the Seventh Crusade (1248–54), Louis IX laid out the port and town of Aigues-Mortes on an estuary of the Rhone in Languedoc. The French army, which sailed from Louis' new port, easily took the Egyptian city of Damietta, but when Louis advanced on Cairo he was captured and his army was massacred. The French king paid the Sultan of Egypt an enormous sum to ransom himself and many other Christian captives. Upon his release, Louis made a prolonged pilgrimage to Jerusalem, postponing his return to France for four years. The objectives of Louis' second crusade—officially, the Eighth Crusade, made in conjunction with Edward I of England in 1270—were changed at the last moment, probably at the insistence of Louis' brother Charles of Anjou, and the French monarch found

himself leading his followers across the sands of Tunis. The Anglo-French force was struck by dysentery and Louis died, still convinced that he could convert the Emir. Almost at once reports began to circulate of miracles being wrought by the agency of the King's relics, and before long he was canonized.

As Christendom's holy knight, Louis had been the chief promoter of peace in Europe. He had, for example, yielded the districts of Limousin and Perigord to Henry III of England on the condition that Henry become his vassal for the attenuated duchies of Aquitaine and Gascony and renounce all English claims to Normandy, Maine, Anjou and Poitou. Unhappily, the Treaty of Paris (1259), which confirmed this arrangement, contained the seeds of the Hundred Years' War.

Men and nations turned to Louis as the natural arbitrator in their disputes. He advised on the succession to the throne of Flanders and in 1264, by the *Mise of Amiens*, adjudicated in favor of Henry III against the English barons. Royal power and administration increased in France during his reign, but the country was pushed to the verge of bankruptcy. Louis, who brought tremendous prestige to the French monarchy, was able to follow the Cross only because his grandfather Philip II had established a strong royal administration.

English Gothic

While Henry III was lavishing more money than he could readily afford on a shrine for St. Edward the Confessor at Westminster, bishops and priors throughout the country were collecting benefactions from the rich and humbler offerings from pilgrims in order to transform the country's Norman cathedrals and churches into truly English edifices. In time, masons and glaziers altered the pointed arches and vaulted roofs of those cathedrals

beyond recognition. The west fronts of Peterborough and Wells cathedrals, the transepts of Durham and York, and the chapter houses at Lichfield and Lincoln were erected in this period—demonstrating both the range of craftsmanship and the wealth that could be tapped to finance operations on such a grandiose scale. Salisbury Cathedral, perhaps the finest example of English Gothic architecture, was completely rebuilt in the comparatively short period between 1220 and 1258. In this formative age of religious festivals and mystery plays, pilgrimages—to Becket's shrine at Canterbury, to St. Hugh's tomb at Lincoln, to St. Alban's, Bury and Winchester—were commonplace.

Universities come of age

The thirteenth century saw the consolidation of the universities, which had grown from uncertain origins to become key institutions of the medieval state. The Paris schools had outshone all others in the days of Peter Abelard (*d.* 1142), but it was not until 1200 that the University of Paris received a royal charter, incorporating its guild of masters. (By contrast, Bologna, already the fountainhead of legal studies, was organized as a guild of students.) Paris was soon recognized as the home of theological study and there, in 1257, Robert de Sorbon, Louis' confessor, founded the Sorbonne, a college where both professors and students pursued courses in Scholastic theology. Young men from all over Europe flocked to the Sorbonne to sit at the feet of such renowned lecturers as Guillaume de St. Amour and Pierre d'Ailly.

Oxford had already become a *Studium Generale*—a home of doctors, faculties and students from all quarters—by the time that Henry II's dispute with Becket closed the Paris schools to Englishmen. A scholarly quarrel at Oxford in 1209 led to the establishment of a second

university community at Cambridge. There, as at Oxford, the Franciscan friars played a leading role. The first rector of the Oxford Franciscans was Robert Grosseteste—chancellor and later Bishop of Lincoln, the diocese in which Oxford lay—who became a staunch defender of the university's liberties against the king, barons and townsfolk.

After a seven-year apprenticeship, a student at either English university attained the rank of master. As public proof of his ability he gave a specimen lesson—and was then licensed to teach anywhere. In this era before collegiate foundations, there was a notable freemasonry among Europe's wandering scholars' life, for political events occasionally forced an entire teaching faculty to migrate to another center of learning for a season. When Walter de Merton founded his college at Oxford in 1266, he took the precaution of acquiring property at Cambridge also, for use in the event of just such a migration.

In the middle years of the thirteenth century the first collegiate foundations—William of Durham's

The library at Merton College, Oxford's oldest college.

Great University Hall (later University College), Balliol and Merton at Oxford, and, in 1284, Peterhouse at Cambridge—were established. They proved to be of great benefit to scholars, Church and King.

St. Thomas Aquinas

The Italian St. Thomas Aquinas (1224–74), the most respected of medieval philosophers, entered the Dominican Order to study at Paris under Albert of Cologna. Aquinas, who spent most of his life teaching at Paris, and at Rome and other Italian cities, dominated Scholastic philosophy with his encyclopedic

The west front of Salisbury Cathedral: perhaps the finest example of English Gothic.

knowledge and incisive mind. His principal work was to build an elaborate structure reconciling pure philosophy with Church dogma and substituting Aristotelianism for Platonism as the most specifically Christian philosophy. Although he eliminated from the Latin version of Aristotle's texts the errors perpetrated by commentators through the centuries, his acceptance of Aristotle was uncritical.

The core of Thomism was that philosophy and theology were independent disciplines within their own bounds: the task of philosophy was to examine the natural order in the light of reason, while that of theology was to investigate the supernatural order as revealed in God's world. For Aquinas, faith and reason were separate phenomena that the orthodox thinker must satisfactorily reconcile—he was personally convinced that faith was rational; and reason, divine.

In his *Summa Theologica (Sum of All Theology)*, he attempted to create a perfect, all-embracing system, unfolding all that was known of the relationship between God and man. Aquinas' literary method was that of dialectical disputation, the familiar form of argumentation at the universities. He began by asking such questions as whether God existed, whether He was perfect, whether He was eternal. He painstakingly resolved all objections to each answer before passing from one point to the next.

The *Summa*, a monumental work that was impressive for its scholarliness and force of argument, irrevocably united philosophy with the medieval Church. As a result Aquinas came to be regarded as the most representative and the most balanced of the "Schoolmen."

Roger Bacon and medieval science

A systematic thinker of a very different kind was the English Franciscan friar Roger Bacon (1214–92). "Suspected novelties" in his lectures at Paris and Oxford led to his being disciplined by his Order. Indeed, the significance of Bacon's work lay in the very modernity for which he was disciplined. He gave up teaching the philosophy of Aristotle in order, as he said, "to acquire knowledge of all the sciences and their use in the field of theology," and for twenty years he labored in pursuit of that great design. During that time Bacon spent nearly five thousand dollars

on "secret books, different kinds of instruments, tables and other things." For him mathematics was "the alphabet of philosophy," and experiment, not speculation, was the keystone of science. Although Bacon did not actually invent eyeglasses, he did experiment with the use of convex lenses for correcting defects of vision, and although he is no longer honored as "the inventor of gunpowder," his contributions to scientific thought, as embodied in his great encyclopedic treatises, make him unique among medieval writers.

While Bacon's contemporaries were engaged in metaphysical disputations, he was describing and defining what he called "experimental science." "Experimental science alone," he wrote, "can ascertain to perfection what can be effected by Nature, what by art, what by fraud. It alone teaches how to judge all the follies of the magicians, just as logic tests argument." Bacon paid a high price for his role in the transmission of Greek and Arabic knowledge into Western scholarship: for many years he was obliged to work in strict secrecy; his superiors accused him of practicing "the black arts"; he was barred from England and he lost his family's financial support. Pope Clement IV ultimately recognized the friar's genius, however, and he was allowed to return home.

Germany after Frederick II

Meanwhile in Germany, Frederick II had died, leaving the Empire to his son Conrad IV, and Sicily to his illegitimate son Manfred. Both Germany and the Italian kingdom were soon plunged into war. Manfred later succeeded in regaining southern Italy and Sicily but in 1266 Charles of Anjou, brother of Louis IX, eagerly accepted a papal offer of the Sicilian crown.

Even more disastrous was the "great interregnum" in Germany (1254–73), for it spelled the doom of the Empire as an effective political organization. The bizarre "double imperial election" of 1257 —which resulted in the rival candidates, Richard, Earl of Cornwall (Henry III's brother) and Alfonso X of Castile, each claiming a majority of the seven electoral votes—discredited all concerned. Alfonso never set foot in Germany, while Richard, glorying in his title "King of the Romans," failed to establish his authority even where support

Rudolf I: the first Hapsburg Emperor.

was strongest. The 1257 election did fix the number of electors at the arbitrary number of seven, however, and in 1273 those electors united in choosing Rudolf I of Hapsburg, a weakling prince who was no threat to them. For the next two hundred years the Emperor was a meaningless figurehead, while the German potentates, lay and spiritual, ruled their districts as they chose.

Simon de Montfort and the first parliaments

During his struggle with the Hohenstaufen, Pope Alexander IV had offered the Kingdom of Sicily to Henry III for his second son, Edmund "Crouchback," in return for a considerable sum. The "Sicilian business" proved a fiasco, but the Pope insisted on payment. Before he was permitted to raise taxes to pay the Pope, Henry had to agree to his barons' demands to be brought into partnership with him in the government of the realm. Their plan of reform was embodied in the Provisions of Oxford (1258) with "parliaments" meeting three times a year to discuss affairs and redress grievances. However, implementation of the barons' plan proved impossible while personal animosities remained. Louis IX's

arbitration in favor of Henry was rejected by the city of London, and civil war broke out. The leader of the baronial opposition, Simon de Montfort, defeated his royal brother-in-law at the battle of Lewes in 1264, and for fifteen months was virtual ruler of England. In 1265 he called a parliament composed of two knights from each shire and—in a revolutionary step—added two burgesses from each previously unrepresented borough. Lord Edward, Henry's elder son, led the conservative barons against de Montfort at Evesham later the same year, and Henry III was returned to the throne. The events that occurred after the Provisions of Oxford were signed permanently affected the development of English government, however. And when Edward I succeeded Henry, one of his first acts as king was to summon a parliament similar to the one called by his uncle, de Montfort.

The seal of Simon de Montfort, virtual ruler of England for a year.

Fighting in the East

In the middle of the thirteenth century there were also decisive battles in the Near and Far East. The Mongol chieftain Hulagu, grandson of Genghis Khan, captured Baghdad in 1258, executed the Caliph and established the rule of the Il-Khans in Persia. Hulagu next took Aleppo, and seemed likely to overrun Syria until his advance was checked by the Mameluke of Egypt at Ain Jalut in 1260 and the Moslem state was saved. The Mameluke's warriors took Jaffa and Antioch in 1268, and there held the forces of the Eighth Crusade at bay. News of his accession reached Edward I at the Crusader's camp before Acre, "the sink of Christendom," in 1272. A year earlier, a caravan of Venetian merchants had passed through Acre on its way to the Orient.

When East Met West

Thirteenth-century Europe was only vaguely aware that its imported silks originated in a land to the east called Cathay. China, for its part, knew about the West but was not especially interested in it. Then, in the summer of 1275, three travelers from Venice reached the court of Kublai Khan, China's Great Lord of Lords. The brothers Niccolò and Maffeo Polo and Niccolò's son Marco lingered in the Far East for twenty years, and when Marco returned to Italy he set down his impressions of those years in a book entitled, somewhat grandiosely, Description of the World. *Marco Polo's travel narrative fascinated generations of readers; two centuries later it stirred the ambitions of another seeker of Cathay, Christopher Columbus.*

Every year at the beginning of June, Kublai Khan, Great Lord of Lords, "the mightiest man that ever was in the world since Adam our first parent," was accustomed to leave his winter palace in Peking for a three-month-long vacation at his summer palace in Shangtu ("Xanadu"). This princely pile of "marble and other ornamental stones, marvelously embellished and richly adorned, with gilded halls and chambers" stood at the entrance to a spacious game-park which provided food for the imperial falcons. In a pleasant grove, in the midst of the park, stood another large palace—a portable structure of split bamboo poles, held in place by more than two hundred silken cords. This palace was "reared on gilt and lacquered pillars, on each of which stood a dragon entwining the pillar with his tail and supporting the roof on his outstretched limbs."

Here it was that Kublai was visited, one summer day in the year 1275, by three travelers from far to the west—the brothers Niccolò and Maffeo Polo, merchants of Venice, and Niccolò's son Marco. The elder Polos were no strangers to the Khan. Some ten years earlier they had journeyed to his court in the train of an envoy sent by Kublai's brother Hulagu, Il-Khan of Persia. The Polo brothers had been assured that Kublai had never seen a "Latin" and was very anxious to meet one. They had been royally received and plied with questions "about the emperors, the government of their dominions and the maintenance of justice; then about kings, princes and nobles; next about the Lord Pope and all the practices of the Roman Church and the customs of the Latins." Then, because the Great Khan's curiosity was still unsatisfied, the elder Polos had been sent back to Europe on a special mission to the Pope, with a request that "he should send up to a hundred men, well versed in the seven arts and skilled to demonstrate to idolaters and others by clear reasoning that the Christian religion is better than theirs."

Support for a missionary enterprise on such a grandiose scale was scarcely to be expected from any Pope. However, after some delay—caused by the two-year electoral deadlock that followed the death of Clement IV in 1269—his successor Gregory X gave the project his blessing and ordered two learned Dominican friars to undertake the task of converting the Mongols. Unfortunately, the friars' resolve failed soon after the expedition set out, and the Polos went on alone. If no attempt was to be made to convert the Great Khan to the Christian faith, at least he would not lack for instructors in the benefits of East-West trade—and if Kublai was disappointed at this imperfect response to his appeal, he was too polite to show it. We are told that, after the ceremonial preliminaries in 1275, Niccolò presented Marco, then a lad of twenty-one, with the words: "Sire, this is my son and your liege man." To which the Khan replied: "He is heartily welcome."

This episode, like all else that we know of the Polos' travels in the East, is described in Marco Polo's ambitiously conceived narrative, *Description of the World.* Marco dictated his account to Rustichello of Pisa, a professional writer of romances, while both men were being held as war prisoners in Genoa in 1298. It is disconcerting but not surprising to discover that the court scene described above reproduces, almost verbatim, an earlier account that Rustichello had written on the presentation of Tristan to King Arthur at Camelot. There are other passages in the book that can be ascribed with some probability to the romance-writer rather than to the traveler, but the work as a whole carries conviction, not only by its wealth of detail, much of it fully supported by contemporary Chinese evidence, but by its sheer matter-of-factness. Much of Polo's narrative is little more than a catalogue—but a catalogue whose items include a dazzling profusion of gold and rubies, silks and sables, perfumes and spices, exotic customs and mysterious arts. Written in French, the traditional language of romance, and extensively copied and translated, *Description of the World* implanted an enticing and indelible image of "the gorgeous East" in the mind of Europe.

By the thirteenth century, Europeans had been vaguely aware for some time that the silks that they

Kublai Khan, Emperor of China and grandson of Genghis Khan; Marco Polo spent twenty years at his court.

Opposite The Venice from which Marco Polo set out on his journey.

"A ruler surpassing the Caesars"

Niccoló and Matteo Polo receive missionary instructions from Pope Gregory X.
Missionary enterprise went hand in hand with commercial effort and exploration.

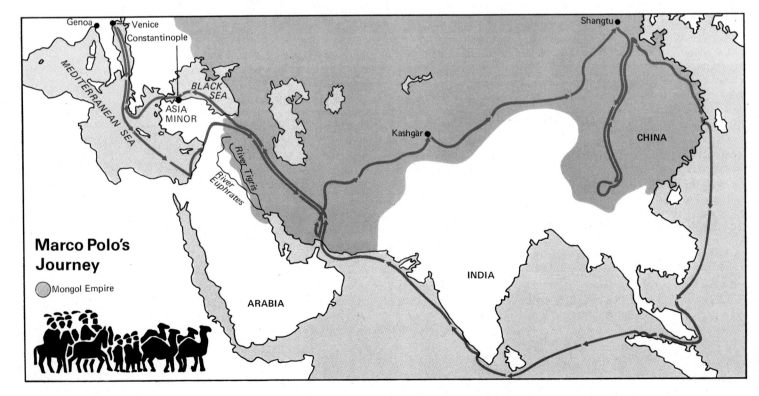

Marco Polo's Journey

Mongol Empire

imported from the East originated in the land of the *Seres*. Since 1127, when northern China came under the rule of a nomad people, the *Kitai*, Europeans had taken to calling the lands to the east by the name *Cathay*. But neither of these names conveyed an image of the country or its inhabitants. The Chinese, probably thanks to Arab traders, were better informed about the West, particularly the Byzantine Empire, but they were not especially interested in it. Such trade as did trickle between the two regions passed through the Islamic states of the Middle East and Central Asia, and those nations deliberately interposed a barrier to direct commercial intercourse. The people most interested in penetrating the barrier were the merchant adventurers who formed the ruling class in the republic of Venice. Since the capture of Constantinople in the Fourth Crusade (1204), the Venetians had dominated the trade of the Black Sea and established a factory at Sudak in the Crimea. Their opportunity for further eastward expansion came with the meteoric rise of the Mongols.

Before 1206, the Mongols were inconspicuous among the numerous turbulent nomadic tribes of the Asiatic steppes whose periodic eruptions had vexed their settled neighbors since the days of Attila (A.D. 406?–453) and before. In that year, at a time when a social and economic upheaval had disrupted ancient tribal loyalties, the Mongols produced a leader with the genius to weld a miscellaneous band of hard-riding, sharp-shooting bowmen into an invincible army, whose numbers swelled with every victory. Assuming the title of Chinghiz (or Genghis) Khan, this Mongol leader conquered northern China ("Cathay") and then set out, in the words of Marco's *Description*, "to conquer the whole world."

By 1259, when the title of Great Khan devolved upon Genghis Khan's fourth successor, Kublai, the Mongol dominions extended from the Pacific on the east to the Mediterranean and the Black Sea on the west. The western territories were ruled by three subordinate khans—headquartered in Russia, in Persia, and at Bukhara in the heart of Asia—who soon became virtually independent. The European nations found themselves for the first time in direct and alarming proximity to an empire based in the Far East.

Marco describes Kublai as "the wisest man and the ablest in all respects, the best ruler of subjects and of empire and the man of the highest character of all that have ever been in the whole history of the Tartars." (Tartar was the current European name for the Mongols.) A Persian historian, Wassaf, declares that Kublai's reputation as a ruler "surpasses all that history tells of the Caesars of Rome." Even the Chinese annals, naturally prejudiced

Above A Mongol archer.

Above left Defeated Mongol troops retreat from Persia; from a Persian manuscript.

Elephants as well as infantry and cavalry were used by Mongol warriors.

335

Twenty years in China

against a foreign conqueror, praise him as a wise judge of men, a patron of letters, and one who truly loved his subjects. Under Kublai's protection the Polos were free to travel at large through China, all of which came under Mongol rule in 1279. Marco and the two elder Polos were able to observe at close hand a civilization far older and technically far more advanced than that of Europe—although as members of an alien ruling class, they never entered fully into the cultural life of the Chinese people.

What the Polos actually did during their twenty years' sojourn in the Far East is hard to say. No authentic references to them have been found in Chinese sources, and the few personal details given in the *Description* include some claims (perhaps added by Rustichello rather than Marco) that cannot be accepted as literally true. But Kublai, who could not afford to be wholly dependent on the loyalty of his Chinese subjects, employed many foreigners in positions of trust and authority, and there is no reason to doubt that Marco's extensive travels within the Great Khan's dominions, and beyond as far as India and Ceylon, were undertaken in an official capacity, even if we suspect an element of exaggeration in the language of the *Description*:

He had seen and heard more than once, when emissaries whom the Khan had dispatched to various parts of the world returned to him and rendered an account of the mission on which they had been sent but could give no other report of the countries they had visited, how their master would call them dolts and dunces, and declare that he would rather hear reports of these strange countries, and

of their customs and usages, than the business on which he had sent them . . . So Marco paid close attention to all the novelties and curiosities that came his way, that he might retail them to the Great Khan . . . Accordingly the Khan used to entrust him with all the most interesting and distant missions . . . and was so well satisfied with his conduct of affairs . . . and showed him such favor and kept him so near his person that the other lords were moved to envy.

Already we find a Venetian developing those special talents that were, at a later date, to make the reports of Venetian ambassadors one of the historian's most reliable and interesting sources.

Presumably the Polos did not forget that they were merchants, or that their mission had been intended to serve a religious purpose; and there are faint indications that they may have met with some success in both areas. Friar Odoric of Pordenone, who visited China soon after 1320, asserted that he knew of many people in Venice who had actually seen *Kinsai* (i.e. Hangchow, the former capital of Southern China). And the *Merchant's Handbook* of Francesco Pegolotti (1349) makes the startling claim that the overland route to Cathay was then "perfectly safe, whether by day or by night." Marco's interest in Chinese Christianity is shown by his numerous references to Nestorian churches and his lively account of a supposedly Christian sect investigated by him and his uncle Maffeo in Foochow. This interest must have helped to encourage the beginnings of Western missionary enterprise, leading up to the appointment in 1307 of Giovanni di Monte

Marco Polo's journey, from a Catalan Map.

oppressive tactics of their Hapsburg overlords. Emperor Rudolf I first recognized the privileges of the Uri, but it was from neighboring Schwyz that the future federation of cantons, "Switzerland," took its name. In 1291 the three communities formed a Perpetual League (perhaps as an extension of an earlier alliance) for self-defense against would-be aggressors.

The Schwyz took advantage of the disputed imperial election of 1314 (in which Lewis of Bavaria successfully challenged the Hapsburg candidate Frederick) to seize the great abbey of Einsiedeln. Frederick placed the rebels under the ban of the Empire, but Lewis

A mail shirt of about 1300, probably English.

removed the ban. In November, 1315, Frederick sent an army of 20,000 men, led by his brother Leopold, against the Swiss, but a confederate force of 2,000 routed the Emperor's picked troops at Morgarten. As a contemporary noted, their encounter was not so much a battle as a massacre—"like a herd driven to the shambles by these mountain people." In December the victors formed a new league: the confederates were to be "as one person, like man and wife"; they were to respect their overlords, but they were permitted to withhold their services if those lords acted unjustly. Members were made to swear that they would not make treaties with outside powers without consulting the Confederation at large. This new league was solemnly recognized by Lewis IV.

France loses Sicily

After the death of Manfred, King of Sicily, in 1266, his daughter Constance, whose husband was the heir to the throne of Aragon, assumed the title "Queen of Sicily." She was not, however, in any position to substantiate her claim. Hohenstaufen rule had ended with the execution of her cousin Conradin, but bloodshed continued as Charles of Anjou put to death many of Conradin's supporters. As the papal nominee, Charles could do no wrong in Italy, where—in addition to being Duke of Provence and Anjou and King of Sicily and Naples—he was "senator" of Rome, imperial vicar of Tuscany and lord of many Lombard cities. Charles consolidated his rule in these considerable territories by outright oppression—then turned his ambitious eyes eastward to Constantinople. He persuaded the Pope to proclaim a crusade against the Byzantine Emperor.

While Charles was assembling a great fleet in Messina harbor during the spring of 1282, Peter III of Aragon, who was in close touch with the Greek Emperor, was making preparations for an invasion of Sicily. Peter's plan appealed to the merchants of Barcelona, who were so eager to supplant the Genoese in Sicilian trade, that they gladly rented ships to him.

It now became evident that Charles had sown dragon's teeth in Sicily. He was detested by the Sicilians, and his French soldiers were hated for their insolence. On Easter Monday, 1282, a French sergeant accosted a young married woman outside the Church of the Holy Ghost in Palermo and was stabbed by her husband. The people of Palermo rose as a man, crying "Death to the French!" And while the church bells rang for Vespers, they massacred the garrison. News of the "Sicilian Vespers" spread to other towns and they too proclaimed communas. At the end of April Charles' fleet mutinied, but it was not until August that a deputation from Messina and Palermo was able to reach Peter III in Algiers to offer him the crown of the Two Sicilies.

Venice and Genoa: trading rivals

While the French and the Spanish fought for the Two Sicilies, Venice and Genoa continued their struggle for exclusive trading rights in the Levant and the Black Sea. Genoa's concordat with the Byzantine rulers (which granted their merchants freedom to trade throughout the Eastern Empire, as well as possession of Smyrna and special privileges in Constantinople) was balanced by Venice's favorable treaty with the Turks.

In 1294 the Genoese closed the Dardanelles, but the Venetians forced the passage and sacked Galata. After capturing the Aegean islands of Chios and Phocaea from the Venetians, Genoese adventurers attacked their rivals at Curzola in 1299. Marco Polo, home from the East, was captured during that engagement and spent his imprisonment writing the tale of his travels. A peace treaty arranged through the mediation of Milan put an end to military operations in the eastern Mediterranean but the commercial rivalry of the two Italian states persisted.

At the turn of the century, the Venetians began building great galleys, which they intended to use in trading with northwest Europe, and in 1317 this fleet made its first voyage to Flanders. To their surprise the Venetians found the Florentines already well established in the capitals of northern Europe. Florence, once torn between Guelf and Ghibelline factions, had developed into an oligarchy of bankers. The "florin," first coined in 1252, had become the standard currency of international finance and members of the great Florentine banking houses financed government debts in England, France and Germany.

Florence

Florence rapidly became the artistic and cultural capital of the West. It produced Giotto, who broke away from the Tuscan-Byzantine school of "flat" painting and made his figures real and three-dimensional, and Dante, the poetic genius of the Middle Ages. Both men had artistic forerunners in Florence. Giotto's teacher Cimabue painted frescoes in the churches of Assisi and wrought a splendid mosaic in the apse of Pisa Cathedral. Giotto himself achieved much greater dramatic power than his master, however, and he can fairly be termed "the founder of modern painting." His fresco cycle of the Legend of St. Francis at Assisi and his decorations of Florentine chapels—all commissioned by successful bankers as a peace offering to the Church for having charged usurious rates of interest—show both a novelty of composition and a remarkable technique. In a passage on the brevity of human glory, Dante observed that "Cimabue thought that he held the field in painting, but now Giotto is acclaimed and the former's fame obscured."

Giotto's *Flight into Egypt* from the Capella degli Scrovegni all'Arena.

The Divine Comedy

Banished from his native Florence during a period of civil turmoil, Dante Alighieri composed his renowned allegory, The Divine Comedy, *to express his resentment and frustration over the enforced exile. The stanzas of his Christian epic contain scornful references to contemporary political figures, well-known clerics and personal acquaintances—but Dante's masterpiece is more than a catalog of grievances. In eschewing classical Latin for colloquial Italian, Dante gave new dignity to the vernacular and made his epic accessible to a vast new audience. And in tracing the Poet's journey through Hell and Purgatory and into Paradise, the Florentine genius provided a synthesis of contemporary political and theological ideologies that is unparalleled in world literature.*

Dante's political enemy, Pope Boniface VIII, consigned to the eighth circle of Hell—although he did not die until 1305, three years after Dante completed the *Inferno*.

Opposite Dante and Virgil, his guide through Hell and Purgatory.

On Good Friday in the year 1300, Dante Alighieri, a citizen of the thriving Italian city-state of Florence, found himself lost in a dark wood. Fleeing from its terrors, he encountered the ghost of his favorite author, the Latin poet Virgil. The poet told Dante that he could escape from the forest only by taking a road that led down into Hell and through it to Purgatory and Paradise. With Virgil as his guide, Dante crossed the river Acheron and began the terrible descent. Hell was a huge, funnel-shaped pit with ledges circling its sides, on which the ghosts of the sinful suffered pains appropriate to their offenses.

As Dante climbed down those tiers, he recognized both unimportant Florentine contemporaries and figures of Christian and classical history, such as Caiaphas—the Jewish High Priest who presided over the council that condemned Jesus to death—and Ulysses, the wandering hero of Homer's epic. At each level of their downward journey, Dante and his ghostly guide encountered sinners of greater guilt. At the lip of the funnel they found those who were merely lustful, but as the two journeyed onward, they passed heretics, seducers, perjurers, and traitors—and finally came to Judas, the betrayer of Christ, and Brutus, the betrayer of Julius Caesar, both of whom were being tormented by Satan himself at the cold center of the earth. Virgil led Dante through a tunnel past this final horror, and they emerged at the other side of the world.

The two eventually came to the foot of the mountain of Purgatory, which was in form the exact opposite and complement of Hell: a peak rising up into the skies. Like Hell, the mountain was a series of circles inhabited by those who had succumbed to various classes of sin: those guilty of the more destructive sins, such as Pride, were found near the bottom, those guilty of the more trivial, such as Lust, were at the top. Unlike the lost souls in Hell, the inhabitants of Purgatory were all working, with certainty of ultimate success, for release from the effect of their sins. When Dante emerged at the summit, he could see, across the river Lethe, the Earthly Paradise that

man had enjoyed in his original innocence. The pagan Virgil could not pass into this region, and he was replaced as guide by the shade of Beatrice, a woman whom Dante had known and loved as an adolescent in Florence, and who had remained a symbol of perfection ever since. After rebuking him severely for his life of sin, Beatrice led Dante into Paradise.

Once in the celestial regions, Dante's progress became a weightless ascent through realms of air and light. With Beatrice at his side, he passed through the levels above the earth that contained the planets, the sun and the stars, meeting souls whose earthly lives had embodied a hierarchy of virtues. He was carried before the apostles Peter and John, who examined his understanding of the Christian virtues of Faith, Hope and Charity. Finally the Florentine was admitted to the Empyrean of God and the Saints, where he acquired a new guide, St. Bernard. He was then led before the Virgin Mary, by whose intercession Dante was permitted to look into the light of the Trinity.

Such, briefly, is the story told in Dante Alighieri's *Divine Comedy*. The work itself is one of the most important epic poems and one of the greatest Christian allegories in literary history. Its one hundred cantos are divided into three equal sections: the *Inferno*, which concerns Virgil and Dante's descent into Hell; the *Purgatorio*, which deals with the two poets' ascent of Mount Purgatory; and the *Paradiso*, which describes Dante's voyage through the heavens, culminating in his arrival at the Empyrean of God.

Despite its length and weighty philosophical content, the *Divine Comedy* was an enormously popular work. That success was due in part to the fact that Dante had composed his materpiece in the vernacular, Italian, rather than Latin—a choice that scandalized many of the poet's scholarly contemporaries, but made the epic accessible to a far larger audience. In addition, the *Divine Comedy* was studded with topical references—to members of the papal court, Florentine officials, friends, and

A pictorial version of Dante's Hell by Orcagna.

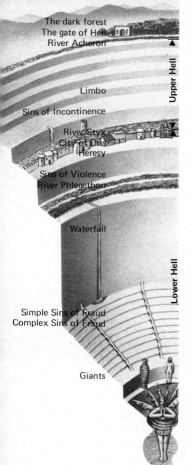

Dante's Hell

The dark forest
The gate of Hell
River Acheron

Upper Hell

Limbo

Sins of Incontinence

River Styx
City of Diss
Heresy

Sins of Violence
River Phlegethon

Waterfall

Lower Hell

Simple Sins of Fraud
Complex Sins of Fraud

Giants

local reprobates—which made the work lively reading. That liveliness was further enhanced by Dante's use of *terza rima* verse form, a rhyme scheme (aba, bcb, cdc, ded, . . . yzy, z) that linked each stanza to the one that followed and gave the *Divine Comedy's* narrative an easy flow.

Stylistic considerations aside, the *Divine Comedy* was, before everything else, the record of the author's own conversion, of his movement from Hell to Heaven. In the *Purgatorio*, Dante portrayed himself as a penitent, shedding the stains of his sins as he climbed through the levels of successful repentence. The Roman poet, Virgil, and Dante's contemporary, Beatrice, were the inspirations of his real life as well as the poetic symbols of Natural Reason and

Divine Grace. Thus Dante was, in one sense, compressing much of the anguish of his earthly career into the few days of his spiritual odyssey. We do not know much about the author's conversion, although, by comparison with his literary equals, Homer and Shakespeare, Dante's public life is rather well documented. The known facts give us some hints of the reasons why Dante fused the account of his own central religious experience with both an elaborate expression of a comprehensive religious and moral outlook and a commentary on the great men and events of his lifetime.

Dante was born into a middle-class Florentine family in 1265. He grew up—and no doubt expected to spend his entire life—in that great city, one of the

Art, politics and finance in Florence

most exciting, affluent, colorful, and turbulent metropolises of Europe. As a young man he became a good lyric poet, and composed a large number of love poems in the new style of Italian versifying that was becoming fashionable. He also fell in love with a girl named Beatrice, who married somebody else and died when Dante was twenty-five. About that time Dante began to lose interest in love poetry and became more interested in philosophy and theology.

Dante recognized and accepted the responsibilities of his class and, while in his thirties, took a reasonably prominent part in the politics of Florence, which was an independent republic run, for the most part, by its more well-to-do citizens. For anyone with principles, the political world was a dangerous one. Dante's period of political activity, which started in 1295 when he was thirty, was a period of bitter strife between the Black and White factions of the Guelphs, the dominant political power in Florence. It was also the period of the pontificate of Boniface VIII, one of the most aggressive of the medieval popes, who interfered in Florentine affairs on the side of the Blacks. In 1302, while Dante, who was a White, was absent on a peace mission to the Pope, the Blacks seized control of the city. Dante was one of those banished for life, and he spent the last twenty years of his life—years of increasing fame—condemned, as he said of himself, to "exile and poverty," "a ship without sails or rudder" wandering from one northern Italian patron or court to another.

Most of Dante's important writings were composed during his exile. It is not surprising, therefore, that the political circumstances of his age—circumstances of which Dante was so conspicuously a victim—should figure prominently in his great poem. Florence in his lifetime was at the summit of its material greatness. The thirteenth century had been a prolonged period of spectacular economic expansion all over Europe, and the great Italian commercial centers had played a role in this expansion not unlike the one that England would play in the nineteenth century. They had provided the western world with its textile industry, its great merchants and bankers, and—in 1252—with the florin, the first gold coin to be minted in Western Europe since the fall of the Roman Empire. Dante himself did not belong to a great mercantile clan. In fact, he looked back rather nostalgically to the days of his ancestor, Cacciaguida, who had lived in the simpler Florence of the twelfth century. Beatrice's husband, on the other hand, was one of the Bardi, famous merchants who trafficked with England and France.

The cloth industry and international trade had enabled Florence and several other larger Italian cities to become independent republics and to re-create the city-state spirit of ancient Greece and Rome. By the end of the thirteenth century, the traders, master-craftsmen and shopkeepers of Florence had largely established their freedom from the influence of the local noble families, who still retained a foothold in both the city and the country. This development was confirmed, about the time Dante entered politics, by the Ordinances of Justice (1293), a kind of constitution that based city government on the guilds, or trade associations of ordinary citizens.

Popular government inevitably involved faction. Throughout the thirteenth century, Florence had been torn by the strife between "Guelfs" and "Ghibellines"—broadly speaking, supporters of the Pope and the Emperor, respectively. This feud was traditionally traced back to 1215, when a member of one family mortally offended a member of the other by breaking his engagement to a girl of the latter's house. But for that, as Dante's forebear Cacciaguida

Dante and his poem by
Domenico de Michelino,
with Florence on the right.

said, "many would have been happy who are now sad." Rivalry between the Guelfs and the Ghibellines became an inseparable part of Florentine life. By the end of the century, the Ghibellines had ceased to be a serious threat to civil stability, but feuding between Black and White Guelf elements—which supplanted the original quarrel—led to the catastrophic turning point in Dante's career.

The Italy outside Florence, in which Dante spent his years of exile, was, in his eyes, a political "hostel of woe, a ship without a pilot in a great tempest . . . a brothel." Unlike other parts of Europe, which had been absorbed into such geographically large political units as the monarchies of England and France, northern Italy had no dominant power. The region was a mass of petty states, ruled either by republican cities like Florence or by lords like Can Grande de la Scala, the hospitable ruler of Verona to whom Dante dedicated the *Paradiso*. From our perspective, the political chaos of Italy seems one of the preconditions of the Renaissance, necessary to the

free and diverse development of life and thought; effective unification of fourteenth-century Italy would probably have been stultifying. But to Dante, who had suffered so much from the effects of that disunity, the vision of a stable order imposed from above was overwhelmingly attractive. There was no power in Italy with the resources or prestige to impose unity, and so Dante, like many of his contemporaries, turned hopefully to the German Emperors.

For several centuries the rulers of Germany, claiming to be the successors of the Roman emperors, had been trying intermittently to establish their authority in Italy. In former times several had been partially successful: Frederick Barbarossa, in the twelfth century, and Frederick II, in the thirteenth, had wielded a good deal of power in the peninsula. But the economic expansion of Italy made it increasingly unlikely that a backward German warlord would be anything but a tool of local politicians if he brought his retinue over the Alps. In this hope, as in other things, Dante was a romantic. While he was in exile

344

Italy: "a hostel of woe"

he wrote a book on monarchy, in which he argued, with references to philosophical and historical matter drawn from his classical reading, that men ought to accept the authority of a single ruler, the divinely ordained Roman Emperor.

The chief opponents of the German imperial claims in Italy were, of course, the popes, particularly Pope Boniface VIII (1295–1303), whose supporters in Florence were responsible for Dante's exile. In the *Divine Comedy*, which is set in 1300, Boniface is already expected in the eighth circle of Hell, three years before his death. This bit of literary revenge is part of the highly critical view of the papacy as an institution that permeates Dante's work. Earlier medieval popes, although greatly venerated as the successors of St. Peter, had not been very powerful, and the transition from claimed powers to exercised powers took place largely in the century before the *Divine Comedy*, when the fortunes of the papacy were roughly the reverse of those of the Empire.

At the beginning of the thirteenth century, the popes had become the effective rulers of a state in central Italy. More remarkable perhaps, they had acquired control over many aspects of the Christian Church beyond the Alps. The popes played an increasingly substantial part in appointing northern European bishops and rectors, whom they were then able to tax in order to subsidize their political ambitions at home. Boniface VIII was a particularly ambitious pope, who belonged to one of the great Roman families, Gaetani, and was an expert canon lawyer. He asserted the authority of the pope to correct all Christians, including kings, in a Bull published in 1302, which begins with the ringing words "*Unam Sanctam*—One holy, catholic, apostolic Church . . ." Boniface's whole career embodied the conception of the Church as a militant, temporally powerful institution—a conception that Dante denounced.

The papacy was not the only institution that was building up its power at the turn of the century. The most powerful man in Europe at that time was Philip

the Fair, King of France, and his ascendancy was indirectly to affect Dante's life.

One of the most significant movements of the poet's lifetime was the developing connection between the papacy and the French monarchy, a compound of attraction and rivalry between the two institutions with the largest claims to real influence over the Christian world. Pope Boniface invited Charles of Valois, brother of King Philip, to bring an army to Italy, and it was while the Pope's supporters in Florence were strengthened by the temporary

Pagan and Christian art contrasted: *Strength* (*left*) by Niccoló Pisano, and *Faith* by Giotto.

The Church Triumphant by Martini: Pope Benedict XI (1303–4) negotiates a peace treaty between Philip IV of France and Edward I of England, with Florence in the background.

The hierarchical universe of "The Divine Comedy"

presence of Charles' army that Dante was exiled. The poet therefore had every reason to hate the royal house of France—and he took the opportunity to denounce it when he met their remote ancestor, Hugh Capet, in the *Purgatorio*.

More spectacular events were to come. Boniface eventually was forced to devote much of his pontificate to a fierce struggle with Philip the Fair—a contest that became the central theme in the political history of Europe at this period. The Pope's claims to powers of taxation and jurisdiction in northern Europe brought him into conflict with the pretentious and ruthless French King. Boniface issued the famous papal Bull, *Unam Sanctam*—which was plainly directed against Philip. An exasperated Philip retaliated by sending a small expedition to Anagni, the Pope's birthplace and residence outside Rome. In 1303, the Pope was taken prisoner by the French king's troops—an atrocity that seemed, even to such an enemy of Boniface as Dante, to be the work of a new "Pilate," who was crucifying Christ's vicar.

Before Dante completed the *Divine Comedy*, the power of the French monarchy had led to the election of a French pope, Clement v, and the establishment of the papal court at Avignon, in southern France, where it was to remain until 1377. Whether this was an advantage or a disadvantage for the papacy is a question for debate, but there is no question that the "Babylonian Captivity" left Italy even more destitute of political leadership. The exiled Dante greeted with enthusiasm the election,

The ideal of *Good Government* in the city by Lorinzetti.

in 1308, of a German emperor, Henry VII, who was reputedly just and magnanimous, and ambitious to take control of the peninsula. Henry came to Italy in 1310 and remained for three years. His ambitions were ground down by the impossibility of overcoming opposition from various quarters—notably from Florence—and he died of a fever in 1313. It is ironic and rather disconcerting that Dante's political idealism, expressed in his book on monarchy and reaffirmed in the *Paradiso* (where Henry VII was promised a place in the Empyrean), should have attached itself to this last, feeble representative of a barbaric tradition of Germanic power.

Although circumstance drew him into the cockpit of Italian politics, it is not as a politician or political commentator that Dante interests us chiefly, but as the most superb exponent of medieval ideas. Dante had the ideas of the era at his fingertips; he was a superhuman amateur who mastered a dozen disciplines. The *Divine Comedy* is the work of a man driven by a lifelong need to make sense of the world, who has, at great cost, succeeded. For this reason, the *Divine Comedy* is a textbook of medieval attitudes.

The physical world in which the poem is set, for example, is an extremely careful and accurate picture of the universe as it was conceived by medieval man before the Copernican revolution. The earth is at the center; the moon, planets, sun and stars move in fixed orbits around it, and the angelic and celestial regions lie beyond. This attractively unified world picture was not merely of physical importance, for the

ascent from earth to heaven was both a physical and a spiritual ascent.

As a young poet and scholar, Dante had already opened himself to the most advanced philosophical influences of his day. The resultant paradox in his intellectual make-up—which was the paradox of contemporary European civilization as well—was that Christian faith was combined with an intense admiration for pagan classical writings. In choosing Virgil as his guide for the journey through Hell and Purgatory, Dante was acknowledging the value of natural reason, unillumined by Christian revelation, as it was used by the noblest pagans. It would be difficult to say whether the general scheme of the *Divine Comedy* owed more to the Christian story of Christ's descent to Hell and ascent to Heaven, or to the descent into Hell that is the central episode in Virgil's *Aeneid*. During the thirteenth century Christian thought had been nearly overwhelmed by the effects of a renewed acquaintance with the writings of Aristotle, which covered, in a masterly fashion, nearly every aspect of natural knowledge—physics, biology, politics, ethics, logic and so on—and made a very deep impression on Europe's foremost scholars. When Dante looked for rational explanations of perennial problems (such as the influence of the stars or the origins of political life), he turned to the writings of the philosophers of Paris, notably Albert the Great or St. Thomas Aquinas, or to the pagan philosophers themselves, carefully choosing arguments from their works for his own synthesis.

Dante's house in Florence.

The thirteenth century had also seen astonishing innovations in religious life, chiefly associated with the creation of the new orders of friars. St. Francis and his followers, who founded the Franciscan order about the time the Magna Carta was sealed, aimed to live a life of utter poverty, in imitation of the life of Christ and his apostles. The Franciscans rejected conventional worldliness, not by retreating to the isolation of a monastery but by living humbly among the common people. The friars did not make much of a mark outside the universities in northern Europe, but in Italy they became as much a part of the texture of life as Wesley's successors were to be in industrial England. In Dante's day, many of the Franciscans were revolutionary critics of the Church, hunted and persecuted by the ecclesiastical authorities. Dante sided with these radicals, who provided him with his vision of an apostolic Church, truly devoted to the original purposes of Christianity, and set against the Church of Boniface VIII—which, in Dante's view, had "fallen into the mire" in attempting the impossible combination of spiritual functions with political power.

The *Divine Comedy* did not reflect a generally accepted thirteenth-century philosophical, political and religious synthesis—precisely because no such synthesis existed. Its inclusiveness is quite personal, the result of Dante's incomparably wide sympathies. The souls whom the author has placed in the Heaven of the Sun, for example, include not only the great orthodox doctors of the Church, but also Siger of Brabant and Joachim of Fiore—who were commonly regarded as dangerous heretics. Thus, the *Divine Comedy* makes an excellent introduction to thirteenth-century thought, but it does not really reflect the temper of the age.

Unlike the impersonal analyses of contemporary scholastics, the *Divine Comedy* is a highly personal work of art, and—despite Dante's hatred of the Florentines—it is also a product of that city, not of the cloister. It cannot help but remind us of Michelangelo's Sistine ceiling—a similar attempt to make sense out of everything that the Christian and the pagan worlds offered. The desire to achieve such a synthesis was one of the central and recurrent aims of Florentine Renaissance minds. Dante Alighieri's *Divine Comedy* was the first attempt to create that synthesis, and, because every educated Florentine knew Dante's work intimately, it became the constant inspiration for the others.   G. A. HOLMES

Warfare dominated Europe after 1320. Edward I pursued an imperialist policy designed to bring the whole of Britain under his sway, and the success of his Scottish campaigns led to a firm alliance between France and Scotland that persisted until 1560. The intervention of Welsh princes in English politics reached its peak during the Barons' War. Llewelyn the Great was recognized as Prince of Wales and overlord of the Welsh magnates under the Treaty of Shrewsbury in 1267. But he refused to pledge his fealty to the new King of England and in 1277 Edward was forced to invade North Wales.

Scotland's vacant throne

When Alexander III of Scotland died in 1286, his granddaughter, a young Norwegian princess, succeeded to the throne. It was Edward's hope that his son Edward of Carnarvon would marry her and thus unite the two crowns, but the "Maid of Norway" died on her journey to Scotland in 1290, leaving ten claimants to the vacant throne. To avoid civil war, the Scots accepted Edward's adjudication that John Balliol should succeed the princess. Balliol's nobles soon deprived him of power and formed an alliance with Philip IV of France, with whom England was currently at war over conflicting claims to Gascony, a region in southwestern France. Edward led an army north in 1296 to subdue the Scots, and at his orders the sacred Stone of Scone, on which Scottish kings were customarily crowned, was removed to Westminster Abbey. Once Edward's armies withdrew, there was a series of popular risings in Scotland. The rebels, ably led by William Wallace, threw off the English yoke. Scotland's independence was short-lived, however: Wallace was defeated at Falkirk in 1298, and forced to flee to France. In 1304 Edward resumed his Scottish campaign and Wallace was captured and executed.

Robert Bruce, the grandson of one of the claimants of 1290, put spirit into the Scots' revolt—and was crowned King of Scotland in 1306. Edward I died shortly thereafter, on the eve of yet another expedition against the rebels, and in the next few years Bruce reconquered most of his kingdom, regaining all the castles garrisoned by the English except Stirling. When Stirling also fell, Edward II

at last stirred himself to lead a great army against Bruce. On June 24, 1314, at Bannockburn, a few miles south of Stirling, the Scots won a decisive victory, assuring their independence.

The disaster of English arms at Bannockburn left the worthless Edward II at the mercy of his barons, but after the fall of Thomas of Lancaster in 1322, none of them were able to dominate the government. The baronial opposition, which had originated with an attack on the King's favorite, Piers Gaveston, concentrated in the later

The Battle of Crécy where the English won a great victory.

stages of Edward's reign on the removal of the new favorites, Hugh Despenser and his son. Queen Isabella, accompanied by Edward, her eldest son, departed for her native France, where she allied herself with the exiled Roger Mortimer, Earl of March. In 1326 they landed in England to avenge Lancaster's death; the Despensers were slain, Edward II was imprisoned and his son was recognized as king by Parliament. A year later the deposed monarch was cruelly murdered in Berkeley Castle and power passed to Isabella and her paramour Mortimer.

Edward III

Edward III was only seventeen when he dismissed Mortimer, excluded his mother from state affairs and became the effective ruler of England. Energetic, and eager to shine on the battlefield as well as on the tournament ground, Edward soon became the most popular of all medieval English kings, a warrior who led his people to national glory. Although the English monarch's long-range ambition was to enlarge the English duchies in France, he

first avenged the English humiliation at Bannockburn by defeating the Scots at Halidon Hill near Berwick in 1333. Edward restored Balliol to the throne and insisted on the cession of considerable territory. Robert Bruce's young son David, the rightful king, escaped to the French coast, where Philip VI openly took his part.

The Hundred Years' War

The perennial cause of friction between England and France was the anomalous position of Gascony, the last Continental fief of the English kings. Edward III refused to abandon his patrimony, and the successors of St. Louis continued to agitate for the expulsion of the English from southwestern France. From this conflict arose the Hundred Years' War, which lasted, truces notwithstanding, from 1337 to 1453.

At the time of Charles the Fair's death in 1328, successive Capetian kings had provided a direct male heir to the French throne for three and a half centuries; Charles failed to do so, and the Crown passed to a cousin, Philip of Valois, the nephew of Philip IV. Within a decade Edward III claimed the French Crown as the son of Charles IV's sister —and Philip VI retaliated by confiscating Gascony. Edward secured alliances with the Flemish princes and with the Emperor, while Philip recruited Italian mercenaries. The English heralds delivered a challenge to Philip to appoint a day for the battle, but Philip, who had been warned by the renowned astrologist Robert of Sicily not to engage the

English army while Edward was in command, stalled.

Edward invaded Normandy in the summer of 1346. His army marched up the left bank of the Seine from Rouen toward Paris, where Philip had amassed a great army to defend his capital. The English were forced to retreat, closely pursued by the confident French. At Crécy, however, Edward won a decisive victory; using tactics learned in the wars with Wales and Scotland, English archers equipped with longbows slew the French cavalry. The sixteen-year-old Prince of Wales, who commanded the vanguard, was accoutered in the black armor that was to give him the chivalrous name "The Black Prince." The victory at Crécy won immediate fame for English soldiers; the flower of French aristocracy had been cheated of what seemed like certain victory by English yeomen armed with the weapons of Robin Hood.

Philip's Scottish allies, who invaded England in 1346, were defeated at Neville's Cross, and David II, who was promptly captured in the fighting, was not ransomed until eleven years later. Edward next laid siege to Calais, which held out—largely through the determination of its governor, Jean de Vienne—for over a year before it was finally starved into surrendering. The King agreed to spare the town, provided that its leaders would come before him barefoot and with ropes around their necks to present him with the keys to the city. The lives of the six valiant burghers who volunteered for the humiliating task were spared through the intervention of Queen

Edward III with the burghers of defeated Calais.

John II of France, who was taken as a prisoner to London.

Philippa, and before long Calais became the leading town for the English wool trade—a function that it continued to perform until the French recaptured the city in 1558.

Battle of Poitiers

John II, who succeeded his father Philip IV in 1350, was forced to debase French coinage to pay for his coronation at Reims, and in the following year he was forced to issue no less than eighteen ordinances announcing further devaluations. John was eager to achieve a chivalrous victory over the Black Prince, and he led an immense French army against him in Gascony. In a pitched battle at Poitiers John very nearly achieved his goal; the French fought desperately, but they failed to appreciate that the English were employing virtually the same tactics that they had used at Crécy. John's force lost the day when Gascon troops circled around behind the French and attacked them from the rear. The French monarch, his son and his ally, the King of Bohemia, were all captured, and many of his chief nobles were killed.

John was transported to London in 1356 and his son, the future Charles v, became regent. The most powerful individual in France at this time was Etienne Marcel, provost of the Paris merchants, who dominated the meetings of the Estates-General that were called in 1357 to stabilize the country's finances.

The Jacqueries

At this juncture a group known as the "Jacqueries" emerged on the French political scene. The movement took its name from the derisive nickname, "Jacques Bonhomme," that the French nobility had given to the peasants because of their patience in enduring all oppressions —such as crippling feudal dues.

The cry "Death to a gentleman!" was raised, and the peasants began to arm themselves. Atrocities occurred throughout the country. Marcel tried to use the Jacqueries to assist him in reducing the power and prestige of the nobles, only to be murdered himself on July 31, 1358, as he was about to welcome Charles of Navarre to Paris. The Dauphin then returned to Paris, suppressed the uprising and prepared to sue for peace with England. Edward III had failed to take Chartres when the French refused to fight a pitched battle against him, and both countries were exhausted. A peace treaty was signed at Bretigny near Chartres. By the terms of the treaty Edward abandoned his claims to the French Crown, contenting himself with the Duchy of Aquitaine and its dependencies, Calais, Ponthieu and Guisnes. The French agreed to pay three million gold crowns for King John's ransom. Yet the Peace of Bretigny was no more than a truce; Frenchmen everywhere echoed the words of the citizens of La Rochelle: "We will acknowledge the English with our lips, but never with our hearts." During the first stage of the Hundred Years' War the ideal of chivalry came to dominate Western society. It had its own unwritten codes of behavior, its own orders of knighthood (such as Edward III's Order of the Garter), and its own literature. In essence, chivalry implied that responsibility went hand in hand with privilege. It inculcated an ideal of social service that was both unpaid and unservile—service of the weak (especially womenfolk) by the strong, of the poor by the wealthy, and of the lowly by those of high estate.

The German succession

War was the norm in Europe during the fourteenth century. Germany was the scene of periodic strife between the Hapsburg anti-king and the Bavarian Emperor Louis IV. Pope John XXII declared Louis deposed in 1327, and his act led to a violent pamphlet war between the Pope and two adversaries, Marsiglio of Padua and William of Occam, both of whom supported the deposed Emperor against the Avignonese Pope. It was only through a papal alliance that another candidate, Charles IV of Luxemburg, finally succeeded in obtaining his election as Holy Roman Emperor in 1347.

Revolt in Rome

On Whitsunday, 1347, Cola di Rienzi, an innkeepr's son who had become a notary, led a revolution against the nobles of Rome. Marching into the capital, Rienzi summoned a parliament, abolished senatorships and had himself proclaimed tribune and liberator of the Holy Roman Republic. Rienzi, a dictator with extravagant ambitions, sought to bring the whole of Italy under his sway—not by conquest (as Robert of Sicily had attempted) but through the consent of the people. Representatives of various municipalities assembled at Rome to celebrate the "Feast of Italian Unity" and Rienzi declared that Rome would establish a new "imperium" in the West, giving voice to the dreams of Dante and Petrarch, Pope Clement VI urged

The city of Rome, from a gold seal of Ludwig of Bavaria.

the exiled Roman patricians at Avignon to depose Rienzi, but the tribune, aided by a Hungarian army, defeated the expatriates' troops. Yet at the end of the year Rienzi abdicated and asked Emperor Charles IV for protection. He was tried and condemned at Avignon but his life was spared.

Granada

The Moorish kingdom of Granada managed to maintain a vigorous independent existence despite internal factions and envious neighbors. Under the Nasride dynasty the fortified palace of the Alhambra —named for the Arabic adjective that described the color of its reddish, sun-dried bricks—slowly rose on the plateau of Monte de la Asabica in Granada.

The Hanseatic League

The consolidation of the Hanseatic League and the kingdoms of Poland and Bohemia occurred in this same period. The absence of a firm government in Hamburg, Lubeck and the seaports of northeastern Germany allowed those ports to acquire independent status, and they soon drew together to form an association (*Hansa*) for mutual security and the protection of their trading rights. They enjoyed extensive privileges in various countries —in England, for example, members of the Hanseatic League paid lower customs rates than other aliens. The Hansa towns first formed into a league in 1344, and those governments that would not accept their monopoly on Baltic trade found themselves cut off from supplies of naval timber.

Casimir III of Poland

In Poland, Casimir the Great's prudent foreign policy not only saved his kingdom from partition, but increased its stature. He gained from Bohemia the right to a free hand in Silesia and made a satisfactory peace with the Teutonic Knights—thus providing Poland with defensible frontiers. Casimir codified the law, reformed the administration and encouraged trade (notably by granting the Jews privileges). Having no direct heir, he decreed that his throne should pass to his nephew, Louis I of Hungary, upon his death.

By the time he ascended the Polish throne in 1370, Louis had already built up a reputation as soldier, autocrat and patron of learning. He had avenged the murder of his brother Andrew, consort of Queen Joanna of Naples, by overrunning that kingdom in 1347, but the Pope had refused to sanction his coronation. His long struggle against Venice, which lasted from 1345 to 1358, brought him control of many towns on the Dalmatian coast.

Meanwhile, in Buda, Cracow, Granada, the Hansa cities, Paris, London, and Florence, the Black Death was taking a heavy toll.

The Black Death

By 1345 the shipping lanes between Europe and the Levant were regularly plied by merchant vessels carrying cargoes of spices, silks, fine porcelains—and plague. Rats on board those ships harbored fleas on their hides, and those fleas in turn harbored **Pasteurella pestis,** *the bacillus that causes bubonic plague, in their stomachs. Within a decade after the first outbreak of plague in Europe, some 33,000,000 people—roughly one-third of the Continent's population—had succumbed to the dread disease. Medieval physicians were powerless to check the plague's spread, and clerics convinced their followers that the disease was divine retribution for unnamed sins. By the time the plague had run its course, it had decimated Europe and doomed its feudal social structure.*

The sailing vessels that plied the trade routes linking fourteenth-century Europe and the Levant were invariably rat-infested—and those rats were usually flea-infested. As a result, sailors, dockworkers and port dwellers of the era frequently developed severe skin infections, worms and typhus. Flea-borne diseases rode the caravan routes and shipping lanes in the early 1300s, and minor epidemics were common.

Within the stomach of each flea lurked *Pasteurella pestis*, the bacillus that causes bubonic plague. Infection followed these host rats westward: by 1346 the plague was rampant in Asia Minor and by early 1348 it had reached Sicily and the mainland of Europe.

To fourteenth-century Europeans, the Black Death—as the first great epidemic was later called—was a God-sent punishment for their sins. The plague itself was occasionally said to be visible—as a cloud of mist or a pall of black smoke—but it remained mysterious in its origins and its workings. Doctors were powerless to control it. They prescribed a variety of arcane treatments for its prevention and cure, but most physicians had as little confidence in the efficacy of their prescriptions as did their patients. That mutual lack of confidence was more than justified; it would have required powers of diagnosis far beyond the range of the medieval doctor for him to identify the three lethal strands of pure plague—bubonic, pulmonary and septicemic. Indeed it is only within the last few decades that techniques have been evolved to check and stamp out such an epidemic.

Once launched on the mainland, the plague spread with awesome speed. It must have seemed to contemporary Europeans that nothing would stop the disease until the last man had died. Indeed, the only medical mystery that remains today is why the bubonic plague did *not* consume the whole population.

Villages in the third category were all but impossible to find in Italy, the first country on the Continent to be overwhelmed by the Black Death. Florence, one of the greatest cities of Europe, possessed somewhere between ninety and a hundred thousand inhabitants in 1348. Of these, according to one contemporary chronicler, "not one in ten was left alive" when the plague had run its course. In a memorable description of the plague contained in the prologue to the *Decameron*, Boccaccio claims that a hundred thousand Florentines died during the epidemic. Such statements were not intended to be taken as precise estimates; rather they were hyperbolic expressions by eye witnesses of the enormity of their experience—as meaningless statistically as an assertion made by the Pope's advisers that the Black Death cost the lives of 42,836,486 people throughout the world.

From Italy, the plague spread both overland and, on shipboard, along the European coastline. On land, where the advance of the disease was governed by the motion of rats or infected men, the progress was laborious. It is noteworthy, for instance, that the Black Death reached Moscow from the Crimea by way of Italy, France, England, and the Hanseatic ports—not by moving overland. Germany, on the other hand, was assailed principally by land, as the plague moved up the Mosel valley, through Bavaria and through the Balkans.

The fearful suffering was made worse by the ferocious persecution of the Jews that accompanied it. Medieval men felt a desperate need to blame his tribulations on some scapegoat, and the Jews were a convenient minority group, already unpopular for economic and social reasons. A few unfortunates were tortured into confessing that they had poisoned local wells, and instantly the whole race was inculpated. In Germany the Black Death also produced the Flagellant Crusades. In an attempt to take upon themselves the sins of the world, long processions of penitents literally whipped themselves into a frenzy at services held in every town they visited.

Marseille seems to have been the first French town to be infected. The plague soon reached Avignon,

Boccaccio, whose *Decameron* describes the horror which the Black Death aroused, by Andrea del Castagno.

Opposite Death Riding Triumphant, from Palermo Cathedral.

A military operation in the West Country

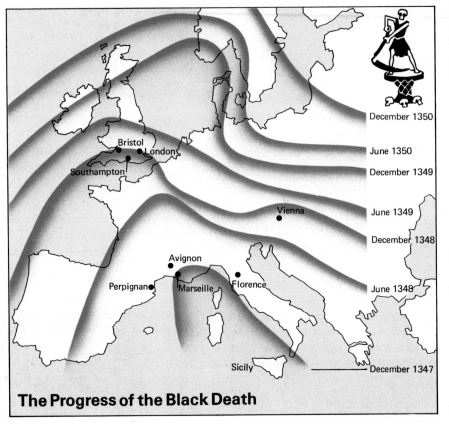

The Progress of the Black Death

December 1350
June 1350
December 1349
June 1349
December 1348
June 1348
December 1347

where it spared Pope Clement VI—who retreated to his chamber and took refuge between two enormous fires—but treated the populace with particular severity. The Pope's immunity was not exceptional, however. Although many men of importance perished throughout Europe, the rich—who could flee the cities and take shelter in their spacious and relatively hygienic manors—suffered conspicuously less than their poorer contemporaries.

In France, as elsewhere in Europe, little pinpoints of reliable data about the plague's course stand out from the mists of uncertainty and vagueness. In Perpignan, for instance, records show that, out of 125 scribes and legists active before the Black Death, only 44 survived; seven of the town's eight doctors and sixteen of its eighteen barbers and surgeons also disappeared.

The first case of bubonic plague in England almost certainly occurred at Melcombe Regis in Dorset in June or July of 1348. Other ports, however, vie for the doubtful honor of being the first victim, and Bristol and Southampton must certainly have been infected within a few weeks of the outbreak of the epidemic. It is possible to visualize the plague's spread, in the first months, as a kind of military operation: the initial attack on the Dorset ports, followed by a bold thrust across the country to the north coast, seaborne landings at scattered ports to outflank the defense, slow mopping-up operations in Devon and

View of a city by Amrogio Lorinzetti; the plague, brought by boat, from the East spread rapidly due to crowded and unhygenic living conditions.

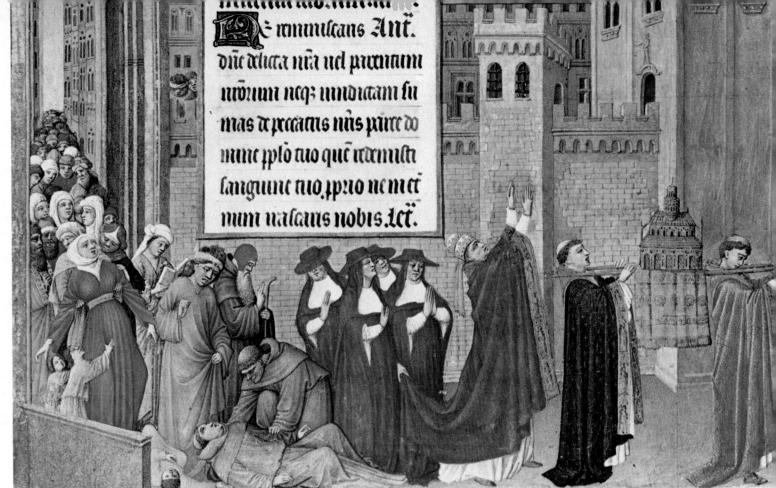

Cornwall, and then a final thrust up the Thames valley towards London. After March, 1349, the campaign analogy can no longer be pursued; the disease poured forward in a hundred different directions and sprang up simultaneously in a hundred different spots. By the end of 1350, virtually every village in England, Scotland, and Wales had suffered casualties.

It is possible to chart the progress of the Black Death in England with greater accuracy than elsewhere because of a wealth of manorial and ecclesiastical records. It is, of course, dangerous to argue that because only twenty-five per cent of the beneficed clergy died in the deanery of Henley, while forty-three per cent died in the deanery of Oxford, the same ratio applied to the general population in those areas. There is, however, enough evidence to establish a general pattern: East Anglia and the West Country were probably the worst afflicted areas; London, where the Black Death raged throughout the whole of 1349, seems to have lost between twenty and thirty thousand people out of a total population of some seventy thousand—a stark figure, although modest in comparison with the lurid estimates of contemporary chroniclers and some nineteenth-century historians.

By December, 1350, the epidemic had blanketed the whole of Europe—and by December of the following year it was virtually at an end. Certain areas—Bohemia, large sections of Poland, a mysterious pocket between France, Germany and the Low Countries, and tracts in the Pyrenees—had largely escaped the effects of the plague.

Attempting to establish any overall estimate of mortality is hazardous and speculative. There is a better chance of doing so in England than elsewhere, yet even in England's case calculations differ widely and must be hedged around with a multitude of qualifications. Reliable sources have estimated that England's mid-century population of 2,500,000 to 4,000,000 persons had been reduced by 50 per cent by 1400. As a rule of thumb, the statement that "roughly 33 per cent of the population of Europe died of the plague before it had run its course" is reasonably reliable. That figure could conceivably have been as high as 45 per cent or as low as 23 per

The Church's pleas for forgiveness and an end for the plague are ignored as Death strikes a friar during a papal procession; from the *Tres Riches Heures du Duc de Berry.*

Medical knowledge was as powerless as religion to help victims of the Black Death.

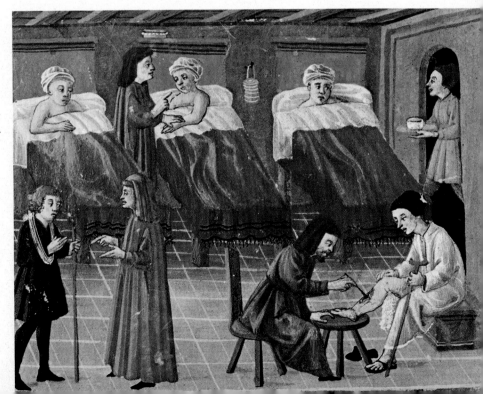

The social structure of Europe shattered

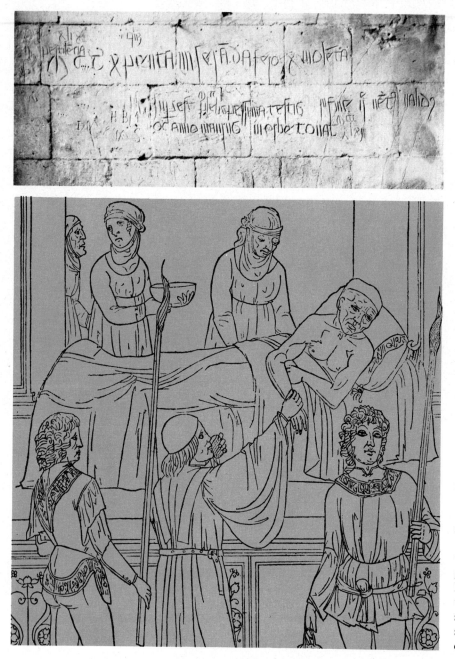

cent—but those are certainly the outside limits.

It is impossible to eliminate one-third of a continent's population over a period of some four years without desperately dislocating that continent's economy and social structure. In Europe in the mid-fourteenth century, that blow was buffered by the fact that the Continent was suffering from over-population—or rather from a surplus population that current agricultural techniques could neither feed nor employ. Vast economic expansion in the thirteenth century had already given way to mild recession, and the population of Europe in 1345 was probably only slightly above what it had been in 1300—that is, in the neighborhood of 100 million persons.

Chronic underemployment remained widespread, however, until the plague struck. The sudden disappearance of roughly one-third of the labor force inevitably altered the relationship between employer and employee, and radically modified the relationship between landlord and tenant. To maintain his available labor supply, or to bribe reinforcements away from neighboring employers, the manorial lord was now frequently forced to pay greatly increased wages. To ensure that his cottages were occupied, he had to accept reduced rents or modified labor services.

In theory, the movement of labor was controlled; tenants should not have been able to dictate terms to their masters. But in the chaos produced by the plague, such regulations could not be enforced. Economic realities asserted themselves within this feudal framework: prices of manufactured products soared in England, as canvas, iron, and salt all more than doubled in cost between 1347 and 1350. At the same time, livestock—such as cows, sheep and oxen—fell disastrously in value. The result was that the typical landlord was paying more for his purchases, getting less for his farm-produce, and less as rent for his cottages, and was at the same time being forced to give higher wages for whatever labor he could secure. Most found themselves in grave economic straits. A common remedy was to reduce the extent of the land that a landlord farmed himself, and to

Top "Miserable . . . wild . . . distracted, the dregs of a people alone survive to witness." Graffiti on the walls of England's Ashwell Church, dating back to 1350, show the horror that the living continued to feel when the plague was over.

A doctor protects himself with a pomander and by burning herbs as he takes the pulse of a plague victim.

Burying plague victims at Tournai, Belgium.

rent vacant tenements, and this profoundly affected the structure of rural society.

Thus the Black Death created striking modifications in the social structure of the European countryside. Its influence upon the Church was perhaps even more dramatic, however. Among the lower ranks of the clerical hierarchy particularly it is almost literally true to say that anyone who did his duty conscientiously had barely one chance in ten of survival. Where the most infectious, pulmonary form of the disease was in question, continued contact with the sick was almost sure to prove fatal. In such circumstances, only a priest who shirked his responsibilities could reasonably hope to see out the epidemic; in England and Germany—and probably in the other countries of Europe as well—roughly half the clergy proved that they knew how to do their duty. But even though the clerics suffered more severely than the laity, they somehow contrived to leave their contemporaries with the impression that they were behaving with something less than nobility. The reputation of the Church fell almost as rapidly as the death roll of priests mounted. By 1351 the Catholic Church in Europe had been stripped of its ablest members.

G. M. Trevelyan has claimed that the Black Death was as significant a phenomenon as the Industrial Revolution, and that the latter was actually less striking in its effect because it was not, like the plague, "a fortuitous obstruction fallen across the river of life and temporarily diverting it." "The year of the Black Death" wrote Friedell, even more emphatically, "was . . . the year of the conception of modern man."

Today one feels less certain that the years of the Black Death were in fact so marked a watershed. For one thing, it should never be forgotten that the plague of 1348 was only the first of a series of epidemics that sputtered throughout Europe until the beginning of the eighteenth century. Bubonic plague returned to England in 1361, 1368–69, 1371, 1375, 1390 and 1405.

In addition, it is hard to identify with precision any major trend that was initiated by the Black Death, rather than simply reinforced by it. The substitution of wages and cash rent for labor services was certainly given striking impetus by the depredations of the plague, but this was a process that was already far advanced in some areas before 1347—and the next half century by no means witnessed continued and uninterrupted progress toward the disappearance of the feudal relationship. It was unquestionably easier for a tenant to desert his manor during the immediate aftermath of the Black Death, but that right had already been tacitly conceded by many landlords during the years of surplus labor that preceded the plague. The dearth of available manpower that followed the plague often made it more, not less difficult for the peasant to choose his place of work and move his home. Even in such fields as architecture—where it has often been accepted as dogma that the shortage of skilled workmen after the

Above left Flagellants try to drive off the plague by whipping themselves.

Above Our Lady of Mercy protects the faithful while plague strikes down its victims with arrows.

355

The birth of Perpendicular architecture

plague led to the substitution of the Perpendicular for the Decorated architectural style—the seeds of change had actually been sown long before the first workman died. The transept and choir of Gloucester Cathedral—the very cradle of the Perpendicular style—were completed as early as 1332.

The Black Death may not have been a conspicuous innovator of new trends, but its influence on the second half of the fourteenth century was nonetheless considerable. For one thing, the position of the tenant was permanently strengthened in relation both to his landlord and to the wage scale, which never fell back to the rates prevailing before the plague. The Black Death was the most significant among the factors contributing to the turmoil that marked the end of the fourteenth century. The insurrections of the Jacquerie in 1358 and of Tuchins in 1381, the rising of the weavers in Ghent in 1379, the Peasants' Revolt in England in 1381, all arose from social and economic conditions that would have existed even if *Pasteurella pestis* had never left its home in Central Asia. But it is highly unlikely that conditions in Europe would have reached a point of desperation as rapidly as they did if the plague had not occurred. The Peasants' Revolt, for example, was at least in part a reaction to the Black Death. Attempts by labor-hungry landlords to wrest from their tenants many of the rights that the latter had won over the preceding decades did much to create a climate of discontent in England.

The real "contribution" made by the Black Death was far less precise. By the second half of the fourteenth century, the disintegration of the manorial system was already far advanced. The Black Death aided the process immeasurably by exacerbating

existing grievances, heightening contradictions and making economic nonsense of a situation that previously had seemed outmoded but still viable. It is not even absolutely certain that the plague "caused" the Peasants' Revolt or the similar uprisings in other countries. It cannot even be said that, but for the epidemic, the Revolt would have taken a substantially different form. What can be asserted is that

The smell of death overcomes the pleasures of the hunt from Orcagna's *Triumph of Death*.

if there had been no Black Death, bitterness would never have risen by 1381 to the level that it did.

In the same way, it can be argued that although the Black Death did not "cause" the Reformation, it did create the circumstances that made such ecclesiastical reform possible. "The plague not only depopulates and kills," wrote Neibuhr, "it gnaws [at] the moral stamina and frequently destroys it entirely." Paradoxically, the decades that followed the plague saw not only a decline in the prestige and spiritual authority of the Church, but also the growth of a new, radical, questioning religious fervor, based upon disillusion and even despair. In Italy, those decades marked the great period of the Fraticelli, Franciscan rebels who once had been denounced as heretics by the Pope and now deemed the Pope himself a heretic. In England that era was the age of Wycliffe and of Lollardy, a period of new and aggressive anti-clericalism that drew its strength from the discontent and doubts of the people at large. The age was one of spiritual unrest, or pertinent questioning of the value and conduct of the Church, and of disrespect for established idols.

Such a spirit would have been abroad even if bubonic plague had never visited the shores of Europe. The Black Death can hardly be made responsible for the growth of doubts about the doctrine of the Transubstantiation—but it did create a state of mind in which doctrines and dogmas were more easily doubted. Wycliffe was a child of the Black Death in the sense that he belonged to a generation that had suffered terribly and learned through its sufferings to question the premises on which the Church and society were based. The Church itself became a victim of the Black Death; large numbers

St. Roch, the plague saint.

of its dedicated ministers perished, and its reputation and authority began to decay. The Reformation was inevitable, but it might not have come so quickly and so violently if the walls of establishment religion had not first been undermined and outflanked by the visitation of the plague.

Can it truthfully be said, then, that "the year of the Black Death was the year of the conception of modern man?" Such colorful generalizations must be viewed with suspicion; eras seldom end and new generations rarely begin with such convenient tidiness. However, the Black Death—especially when considered as a series of epidemics rather than an isolated phenomenon—did unquestionably hasten the decline of values and the breaking down of behavior patterns that had stood firm over many centuries. It opened men's minds, dispelled their illusions and awoke their doubts. It played a crucial role in the phenomenon that can be most conveniently described as "the ending of the Middle Ages."

PHILIP ZIEGLER

A German *Pestblätte* for protection against the Black Death.

357

After Louis II's deposition in 1346, the German princes chose Charles of Bohemia, the Pope's candidate, to be the next Holy Roman Emperor. Charles had been brought up at the French court, where he met Clement VI and earned himself the nickname "the priest's Emperor." True to Clement's wishes, he repealed his predecessor's anti-papal legislation and undertook not to interfere in Italian affairs. Indeed, the principal event of Charles IV's reign was the publishing of the *Golden Bull*. The effect of that papal decree, which was promulgated at the Diet of Metz in 1356, was to devalue imperial power, leaving the government of Germany in the hands of the electors.

The establishment of a poorly-conceived imperial electoral college during the preceding century had resulted in "double elections," anti-kings and civil wars. The new constitution fixed the number of electors at seven. They included the Archbishops of Mainz, Trier and Cologne, the King of Bohemia, the Count Palatine of the Rhine, the Duke of Saxony and the Margrave of Brandenburg. The Pope was excluded from German politics—and although Innocent IV protested, he was forced to acquiesce. Even more significant was the fact that the other German princes had been deprived of any say in the choice of their Emperor.

Thus the successor of Charlemagne had become in effect an elective president, dependent upon three spiritual and four temporal rulers. As a result a later Holy Roman Emperor would describe Charles IV as "the stepfather of the Empire, but the father of Bohemia" —for as the electors had hoped, Charles concentrated his efforts and attention on his native duchy. During his reign, Charles acquired Lower Lusatia and Brandenburg and in 1348 founded Prague University, the first seat of learning in Central Europe. On his death in 1378, his son Wenceslas inherited both Bohemia and the Empire.

The Avignon Papacy

The popes at Avignon found that their expenses increased considerably during their exile, for they were obliged to finance a series of wars in Italy to safeguard the remnants of papal territorial possessions there. To gain the revenues necessary for those campaigns, the fiscal machinery of the Church had to be overhauled throughout Europe. New dues such as annates and clerical tenths were imposed, and Avignon became the center of an intricate network for controlling appointments. All the Western states were in the process of developing new administrative and financial machinery at this time, but the papacy set the pace. More money was raised than had seemed possible, and the residence at Avignon grew in splendor; the cardinals, who were growing in importance under the reorganized Curia, lived in greater luxury than their predecessors at Rome ever had.

All the Avignon popes were born in the south of France, and Frenchmen dominated the College of Cardinals (113 out of the 134 were French). In these circumstances there was no chance of a Pope's being able to act as mediator in the Hundred Years' War.

Many contemporary rulers urged the Pope to return to Rome, among them Emperor Charles IV himself. Catherine of Siena, who encouraged Gregory XI to consider the matter impartially, reminded him that "it is more needful for you to win back souls than to recover your earthly possessions." Gregory summoned up his courage and entered Rome in 1377, but his life was in constant danger. Upon his death a year later, Charles IV tried his utmost to ensure the election of a pope who was not French, and while the conclave of cardinals met in the Vatican, the Roman crowd outside chanted "We want a Roman, or at least an Italian." Urban VI, who was elected by the conclave, was both an Italian and indisputably anti-French. The French cardinals withdrew from Rome to Naples, declared Urban deposed and chose the Bishop of Cambrai as antipope.

Charles died before he could alert Christendom to the dangers of two rival popes. The Great Schism —a line of Italian popes at Rome and a rival succession of French popes at Avignon—lasted for forty years, and the scandal was only ended by the Council of Constance. The Schism literally split Christendom, for France, her ally Scotland, Spain and Naples supported Avignon, while the Emperor, England and the northern kingdoms supported Rome.

Rivalry between Venice and Genoa

In Eastern waters the struggle between Venice and Genoa continued. The Genoese admiral Luciano Doria sailed into the Adriatic, defeated the Venetian Vittorio Pisano at Pola in Istria and blockaded Venice. The city, which was dependent upon imported food, was threatened with starvation. With the Genoese fleet already inside the lagoons, Venice's days as a great sea power seemed numbered. Suddenly Pisano seized the channel leading from the lagoons to the sea. His masterly stroke turned the tables on the Genoese, who suddenly found themselves threatened with starvation. In June, 1380, the Genoese surrendered. Genoa never recovered and Venice became undisputed master of the Levantine trade.

The Ottoman Empire

The westward expansion of the Ottoman Empire became a matter of grave concern for the nations of Central Europe when, in 1345, Turkish troops crossed into Europe and settled on the Gallipoli Peninsula. When the city of Adrianople fell in 1360, the Turks made it

A portrait of the poet Petrarch by Andrea del Castagno.

their capital. In that same year the corps of Janissaries—the spearhead of both army and government— was organized and those warriors soon conquered much of Bulgaria and Macedonia and began raiding eastern Greece and Albania.

Petrarch

If Wycliffe was "the Morning Star of the Reformation," Petrarch (1304–74) was most certainly the Morning Star of the Renaissance. As a young man this remarkable Florentine spurned a legal career in order to devote himself to humane letters. He turned to the classics as an escape from his own age, which he found repellent. At age twenty-two, Petrarch took minor orders. The benefices found for Petrarch by the Colonna family supported his activities and enabled him to travel widely.

There were two sides to this remarkable man: he was both an independent scholar, who assembled a library of classical authors and wrote about Cicero and St. Augustine, and a noted vernacular poet, who made public his love for Laura in the matchless lyrical verse of the *Canzoniere*. Several colleagues openly criticized Petrarch's Italian verses—implying that it was vulgar to write poetry in colloquial language —and occasionally students caught reading the *Canzoniere* were disciplined. Petrarch's vindication came in 1341, when he was awarded

Emperor Charles IV with his son and Charles V of France at a state banquet.

the poet's crown by the Senator of Rome. Classical authors would no longer be revered for their every utterance; Petrarch had questioned the deadweight of authority with a fresh mind, and his work had a powerful influence in the revival of classical scholarship.

Boccaccio

One of Petrarch's last compositions was a Latin version of Boccaccio's story of Griselda. Giovanni Boccaccio (1313–75) was a born storyteller whose *Decameron* followed the path

The Alcazar at Seville, begun by the Moors and finished by Peter the Cruel of Aragon.

of the authors of earlier romances. He was the father of Italian prose and, perhaps, the first author to gain fame during his own lifetime as a result of his writings alone. He was not a politician like Dante or a civil servant like Chaucer, but a professional author. He spent his idle hours with Maria, the illegitimate daughter of Robert, King of Naples, and she served as his model for Fiammetta, the presiding genius of the feasts that form the setting for the *Decameron*.

Charles V of France

In France, Charles v (1364–80) showed himself to be a progressive statesman. He was determined to seize control of the financial machinery that had been set up by the Estates-General and to use the increased revenue provided by the salt and the hearth taxes for reform

and consolidation, and also for the formation of a professional army.

Spanish Civil War

Growing conflict between the Castillian supporters of Peter the Cruel (1350–69) and those of his stepbrother, Henry of Trastamara, ultimately led to a civil war that was to involve both France and England. French "free companies" commanded by Bertrand du Guesclin forced Peter into exile at Bordeaux, a region ruled by the Black Prince. The Prince, sympathetic to Peter's cause, invaded Castille and defeated the pretender and his French allies at the battle of Najera in 1367. Peter was restored to the throne, but he soon fell out with the English and Henry returned to Castille in 1369 to reign undisputed. The sole legacy of Peter's reign was the completion of the Alcazar at Seville, the palace begun in 1181 during Moorish rule.

Second phase of the Hundred Years' War

In 1369 nobles of the Court of Armagnac in British-held Aquitaine appealed to Charles v to rid them of the Black Prince, and when the Prince refused to appear in person at the king's court, the Hundred Years' War was resumed.

In his last months, the Black Prince promoted overdue reforms in the Good Parliament and secured the impeachment of Lords Lyons and Latimer for war-profiteering. John of Gaunt, Edward's fourth son and the outstanding political figure in England, made his Palace of the Savoy into the finest residence in England with his wealth from the wars. Gaunt almost certainly aimed at succeeding to the throne.

The Black Prince's ten-year-old son Richard ii came to the throne in 1377 and John of Gaunt ruled England as regent.

Wycliffe and Church reform

Gaunt's circle included two of the most remarkable Englishmen of the Middle Ages, John Wycliffe and Geoffrey Chaucer. Wycliffe was rector of Butterworth, a parsonage in Gaunt's patronage, but he spent most of his life at Oxford, where he dominated university life. He found the prosperous Church completely out of touch with the great changes that were taking place in the

structure of society; on all sides men were crying out for Church reform, yet the smallest change was prevented by the innate conservatism of the institution itself. The Oxford don provided his own remedy for a decaying faith by gathering together a band of "poor preachers," scholars who spent their free time preaching the Gospel in market places and on village greens, as the friars had in their heyday. Wycliffe studied the era of primitive Christianity in the *Acts of the Apostles* and in Paul's epistles. By contrast, the fourteenth-century Church, with its rival popes living in great splendor at Avignon and Rome and its English bishops too occupied with state affairs for pastoral work, seemed to have overreached itself. Wycliffe preached a return to Biblical simplicity with an enthusiasm that was to prove infectious. One of his greatest achievements was to inspire a translation of the Bible—known as "The Lollard Bible"—into the English tongue. Wycliffe's views on the sacraments brought about his downfall. He attacked the practice of auricular confession and denied the orthodox doctrine of transubstantiation in the Mass, and his enemies—who had tried unsuccessfully to bring him to trial in 1376—found their chance to do so during the Peasant's Revolt. Like Luther in the 1520s, Wycliffe was dis-

credited by the popular movement.

Geoffrey Chaucer (*c.* 1340–1400), the first English poet of consequence, was a Londoner who spent

King Richard II of England from the Wilton Dyptich.

his life as a diplomat and later as a customs officer in the King's service. His first major work, *Troilus and Creseyde*, which embroidered upon the ancient tale of Troy in the medieval tradition, was largely based on Boccaccio's *Il Filostrato*. Chaucer came into his own with *The Canterbury Tales*, a verse *Decameron* about English pilgrims. All English society except the aristocracy was faithfully observed in the *Tales*, which described such deftly-drawn characters as the Knight, the Man of Law, the Franklin, and the Wife of Bath.

Chaucer reciting *Troilus and Creseyde*.

Wat Tyler "Captures" London

For decades English peasants had been forced to contend with residual feudalism, intermittent warfare, spiraling taxes and recurrent plague. In late May of 1381, the oppressed peasants of Kent and Essex rose in simultaneous, spontaneous rebellion against the Crown. An army of incensed tenant farmers marched on London in early June of that year, and King Richard II's helpless ministers took refuge in the Tower. The apparently doomed government was saved by the fourteen-year-old King's bravura: crying "Sirs, will you shoot your King?", Richard rode out to meet his assembled subjects. And by the time the Lord Mayor of London had rallied a force to "rescue" the King, Richard had made peace with the peasants. His actions averted civil war but they could not stem the popular tide; similar risings erupted across Europe in the next decade as peasants everywhere demanded a voice in their government.

Domestic scene from *The Occupations of the Months.*

Opposite Richard II, whose courage destroyed the Peasants' Revolt.

At the end of May, 1381, some villagers at Brentwood in Essex roughhoused a tax collector. There was nothing unusual in their action: the age was a turbulent one in which disputes led readily to violence, even among respectable members of the community. A visit from some awe-inspiring officer of the law was usually sufficient to quell any local disorder. But in the early summer of 1381 the usual did not happen.

No less a person than the chief justice of the King's Bench went down to Essex to hold an inquiry and punish the Brentwood rowdies. The justice found himself surrounded by an armed multitude who drove him off after making him swear on the Bible never to come their way again. Manhandling a tax collector was one thing; mishandling a royal justice was quite another—and infinitely more serious. However, instead of taking to the woods as outlaws or fleeing the country, the villagers appealed for the support of their neighbors, and insurrection spread rapidly throughout the county.

These events appear to have taken the government by surprise, although they were simply the sudden boiling over of an already seething mass of discontent that had been brewing in the countryside for several months. Now that some had openly defied authority, countless peasants left their homesteads and took to the roads. Dissidents in Kent made their way to Maidstone, and there chose as their leader Wat Tyler.

Nothing is known for certain of Tyler's origins or background. Some said that he was a highway robber, others that he was an artisan from Deptford who had slain a tax collector for insulting his daughter. It was reported at various times that he was a disbanded soldier from the war in France, and that he was the wayward younger son of a respectable Kentish family. It is clear from the way Tyler impressed himself upon contemporaries and chroniclers—and hence on posterity—that he had a strong personality and a gift for leadership. Yet Wat Tyler was never anything more than the leader of the rebels of Kent. There was no single "Peasants' Revolt" with a single leader, but rather a number of uprisings, each with a separate identity and separate leader (if it had any leader at all). What gave Tyler prominence, and turned his share in the revolt into a dramatic political event, was the decision made by the men of Kent to combine with those of Essex, on the other side of the Thames, and march on London. On June 11, these two great peasant armies began to converge on the capital.

When the news filtered through to the King's ministers at London, disbelief gave way to despair. The revolt was the culmination of a decade of troubles. The war against France had faltered ever since the Black Prince, heir to the throne, had contracted a recurrent fever. The Prince died in 1376. His aged father, King Edward III, followed him the next year and was succeeded on the throne by a ten-year-old grandson, Richard II. Aristocratic factions competed for control of the government and for the spoils of office.

When the war had begun back in 1337, the English economy was booming, with a rising population that made even the cultivation of marginal land profitable. But the boom was already weakening when, in 1348, the bottom was knocked out of the economy by the arrival of the Black Death. Competition for increasingly scarce labor pushed up wages. Landless laborers, hitherto the lowest stratum of the village community, were suddenly quite well off, for they could offer their services to the highest bidder. Some of those who had steady jobs on a yearly contract gave them up to work for higher daily wage rates somewhere else.

Above A bullock-drawn plough from the Lutrell Psalter.

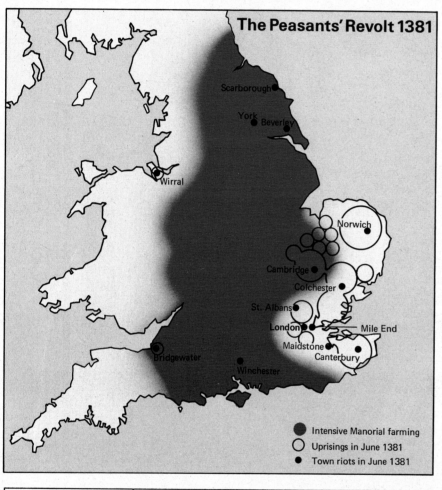

The Peasants' Revolt 1381

Scarborough

York
Beverley

Wirral

Norwich

Cambridge
Colchester
St. Albans
London — Mile End
Maidstone
Canterbury
Bridgewater
Winchester

● Intensive Manorial farming
○ Uprisings in June 1381
● Town riots in June 1381

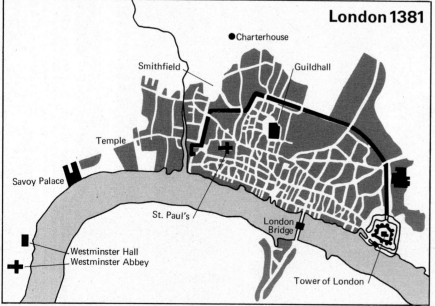

London 1381

● Charterhouse

Smithfield
Guildhall

Temple

Savoy Palace

St. Paul's

London Bridge

Westminster Hall
Westminster Abbey

Tower of London

The more established peasants on the other hand —those who held land and paid for it in rents and labor services to their landlord—found themselves in an invidious position. Caught in an economic squeeze, the landlords raised rents while exacting every ounce of old-fashioned labor services (which did not have to be paid for, and were hence much more valuable than they had been when labor was cheap).

It was this economic crisis that made Parliament all the more reluctant to grant taxes—and all the more ready to believe that the men who controlled the government in the King's name were incompetent and spend-thrift. The situation was becoming desperate and the Commons very truculent, when, in January, 1380, the Archbishop of Canterbury, Simon Sudbury, a fair-minded man and a sound administrator, offered to take over as Chancellor. With another prominent churchman, Robert Hales, the prior of the Knights Hospitaler, acting as treasurer, there was a fair prospect that the country would at least be governed honestly.

Unfortunately, Parliament failed to provide Sudbury and Hales with a proper revenue; instead of a tax graduated according to people's ability to pay, the Commons would agree only to the levy of a flat-rate poll tax—of one shilling per head of the population over sixteen years of age. This was both inadequate and iniquitous.

For some reason, the government did not attempt to disperse the rebels who gathered outside London on June 11. It probably hoped that the peasant armies would break up of their own accord when they became weary and short of food—but the rebels proved to be much better organized and better disciplined than anyone had anticipated. By the evening of Wednesday, June 12, the men of Essex had reached the outskirts of London and had camped at Mile End. The main body of the Kentishmen encamped at Blackheath, while an advance guard pushed on to the south suburbs. The only bridge across the Thames was closed against them, but many sympathizers from London crossed over by boat to join the rebels, who broke open two prisons at Southwark and sacked the Archbishop's palace at Lambeth. The King and his ministers, gathered at the Tower of London, caught sight of flames in the distance and knew for certain that the uprising was serious. They could not make much sense of it, however, and sent envoys to ask the rebels' purpose; the peasants replied that they were loyal subjects of the King who wished to ask him to take action about

"All men were created equal"

the misgovernment of the realm by John of Gaunt.

That night at Blackheath, a priest named John Ball preached a now famous sermon to the assembled multitudes. In the beginning, he said, all men were created equal, and it was only the contrivances of the wicked that had reduced some men to servitude. Englishmen now had the chance, if they would seize it, of casting off the yoke that they had borne so long, and winning the freedom they had always desired.

Early the next morning, the fourteen-year-old King attempted to speak to the rebels from a boat lying on the river at Gravesend, while his listeners crowded the banks. They clamored for him to come ashore, but his ministers took fright when the rebels abused them as "traitors," and made the rowers pull away. As the royal party retreated to the Tower, the rebels poured into the city. It proved impossible to defend the gates against the insurgents, who had many supporters among the urban proletariat, and the houses and property of unpopular ministers, foreigners, and lawyers (against whom the rebels showed a special animosity) went up in flames.

That night the young King held council in the Tower. Opinions were divided: some were for an immediate show of force; others said that attempts should first be made to calm the mob down by negotiation. Siding with the latter, King Richard had it proclaimed throughout the city that everyone should come to meet him the following morning, June 14, beyond the city boundary at Mile End. Part of the plan was to draw the rebels away from the Tower, allowing unpopular ministers a chance to escape, but the plan misfired when some of the rebels remained on watch.

The Mile End meeting went well. The rebels were courteous and the King conciliatory. He agreed to free everyone from the burdens of serfdom, and set his clerks to work preparing charters. As to the alleged traitors, he said that the rebels could do as they wished with them—but only after their guilt had been proved by due process of law. (Meanwhile, some of the rebels had decided to settle this matter for themselves. While the King was at Mile End,

they broke into the ill-guarded Tower, dragged out Archbishop Sudbury and Robert Hales, and beheaded them on Tower Hill.)

Some of the rebels were satisfied with the Mile End meeting and the execution of "traitors" and began to disperse; but many remained, including the more militant leaders of the Essexmen and the Kentishmen who followed Tyler. Later on that Friday, June 14, the rebellion degenerated into a reign of terror, and attacks on property gave way to the slaughter of anyone the mob disliked. In an effort to regain control of the situation—by dividing peasant protest from the passions of the London mob—King Richard called another meeting for Saturday at the Smithfield cattle market, just outside the city wall.

Riding up to the King at Smithfield, Tyler added several new and impossible demands to those made at Mile End. He insisted that all men should be equal, and admit no lordship save that of the King, that the estates of the Church should be confiscated and distributed to the laity, and that all bishoprics should be abolished save one. The King kept up a show of sympathy, but Tyler's studied insolence provoked a member of the royal party to denounce him as a notorious highwayman and thief. Tyler drew a dagger and lunged at the enraged noble. The mayor of London, William Walworth, intercepted Tyler and struck him down from his horse, and one of the King's squires ran a sword through the rebel leader.

The peasants let out a great cry and strung their bows, but Richard rode toward them crying, "Sirs, will you shoot your King? I will be your leader, follow me." For one perilous moment the peasants hesitated—and then followed Richard out to the field of Clarkenwell. Mayor Walworth hurried back into the city to raise every armed man who could be trusted—but when he and his party returned to rescue the King, they found him talking at ease with the rebels. Richard would not allow force to be used, but granted the peasants his pardon and sent them away to their homes.

Events in London provided the most dramatic story, but risings elsewhere were no less important. There were disturbances at York, Scarborough, Beverley, and Winchester—although whether these were anything more than town riots of a kind familiar in the fourteenth century is difficult to say. At towns in eastern England, however, there was clear evidence of opposition to merchant oligarchies and monastic landlords. At St. Albans the townsmen forced the abbot to grant them the sort of municipal self-government that towns of comparable size elsewhere had long before achieved, and at Bury St. Edmunds there was a violent assault on the abbey that owned the town lands.

Meanwhile, the royal government had taken the offensive. Proclamations announced the death of Tyler, repudiated concessions extorted by force, and called on local officials to establish order. Dismay among the peasants in Essex revived insurrection—but this time the government was prepared, and the rebel forces were cut down by troops at Billericay.

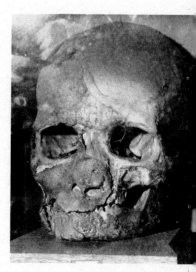

A thief at work.

Below left Feeding the barnyard cock—and sparrows.

The head of Archbishop Simon of Sudbury, from Sudbury Parish Church, Suffolk.

Rebellion: the only resort for the unenfranchised

Peasants reap corn under the direction of a reeve.

Rebel leader John Ball leads his "army" into London. The banners are those of England and St. George.

Judicial commissions were set up to search out and punish offenders, and a hundred or more were executed before the government relented and banned capital punishment. In the Parliament of November, 1381, a general amnesty was granted to all except 287 named offenders who had committed serious crimes.

Any account of the peasant uprisings of 1381 must attempt to explain why they were concentrated in eastern England. If peasant misery, provoked to rebellion by an iniquitous tax, were the only cause, it is surprising that there were no risings in midland England, where the manorial economy was most strictly organized and the burdens of serfdom most severe. Peculiarly, Kent, the center of rebellion, was the one part of England where there was little if any servile tenure; it was a county inhabited by both peasant smallholders and numerous wage laborers, and it was one of the few places where the Statute of Laborers was enforced effectively. Freeholders were common in East Anglia, but there were also many serfs—tied to the soil and obliged to render services and special payments to a landlord. Unlike the great estates of midland England, the manors there tended to be small—too small to be economic-

ally viable agricultural units—and most lords allowed the peasants to farm the tenements in their own way. Some landlords had freed their serfs, relying instead on rents, but others retained their legal hold over the peasants in order to exploit their labor as well as their prosperity.

It was this contrast between free and unfree, between the good fortune of some and the ill luck of others, that apparently lay behind the discontent in East Anglia. Moreover, both there and in Kent there was a distinctive social custom; when a peasant died, his holding was divided equally among all his sons. This policy had subdivided and ultimately impoverished peasant holdings. The Black Death was therefore a blessing in disguise, for it gave the survivors new opportunities for prosperity, provided they were prepared to work hard and build up a little capital to invest in vacant holdings. Too often, however, those opportunities were whittled away by exacting landlords; savings were reduced by rising rents, and hard-won capital drained away in unfair taxes. Thus, the basic cause of the Peasants' Revolt was mounting frustration—the poll tax was simply the last straw. England's peasantry resorted to evasion, and rebelled against pertinacious attempts to collect the infamous head-tax.

On the whole, the rebels were remarkably moderate in their demands. They were simply seeking a fair deal—all they asked for at Mile End was abolishment of the remaining burdens of serfdom. Instead of demanding an end to rents, they merely asked for the reasonable rent of fourpence an acre. And instead of seeking an end to taxation, they asked only for the sort of taxes "which our forefathers knew and accepted."

Fearful monastic chroniclers made much of the element of communistic equality revealed by Wat Tyler at Smithfield, but there is little evidence that such sentiments were widespread. The peasants were rebels against the iniquities of an economic system, not revolutionaries attempting to overthrow it. Indeed, nothing is more remarkable in the English rebellion of 1381—in contrast to contemporary peasant uprisings on the Continent—than the infrequency of attacks upon landlords themselves. There was astonishingly little bloodshed during the English rising—until the rebellion began to degenerate into anarchy. Even then, most of the bloodletting was in the towns, where personal animosities were sharper. The houses of the gentry were invaded and plundered (probably for food as much as for anything else), and their manorial accounts and legal records destroyed, but the gentry and their families were unharmed. Those individuals who suffered did so because they were the agents of central or local government, or because they were lawyers. The hostility shown toward lawyers is particularly significant—it was they who were taken as the chief symbols of obstruction to free enterprise and self-help, rather than the landlords, who were considered victims of economic circumstance.

The nobles and gentry could voice their discontent in Parliament, but rebellion was the only pos-

sible resort for the unenfranchised. The rebels voiced no demand—at least no articulate demand—for a share in Parliament or government, but the political consciousness of the rebellion was strikingly manifest. Admittedly, that consciousness was crude and shallow: the rebels demanded the heads of supposed traitors—but in murdering Sudbury and Hales, they murdered men who were honestly, if feebly, trying to improve the situation. Sudbury and Hales became the scapegoats for a decade of political ineptitude. Many of the gentry would have sympathized with the rebels' disdain for the ruling clique. But in the rebels' unswerving loyalty to King Richard and their insistent claim that they were "his true Commons," they were criticizing the failure of the knights and burgesses, as well as the magnates in Parliament, to serve the country properly. It was a forcible reminder that the upper classes could no longer treat political affairs as if they alone were concerned.

In their distrust of central government, and in their hankering after what they fondly imagined were the good old days in matters of rents and taxes, the rebels were manifesting a very conservative form of discontent—a discontent that fastened upon mismanagement rather than upon the structure of society. In demanding the abolition of restraints upon peasant free enterprise, the rebels were, of course, asking for economic change—but their actions do not indicate that they wanted social re-

volution. Thus, John Ball's famous sermon concentrated more on democratic freedom than on socialist equality, and in this way may be said fairly to reflect the aspirations of his listeners.

Those who rose in rebellion achieved little for themselves, but they did for the first time reveal the power and determination of the lower orders. The story, garbled and simplified in the telling, of how Wat Tyler "captured" London remained to fortify the courage of individual peasants and frighten the ruling classes. Some of the consequences were unfortunate: upper-class fears manifested themselves in a renewed insistence on order and conformity, new ideas were made synonymous with subversion, and criticism—such as Wycliffe's criticism of the Church —was driven underground. But beneath that show of upper-class solidarity, change went on nevertheless. There was a tacit understanding that the clock could not be put back, or the lower classes disregarded, and as economic developments made peasant free enterprise seem good sense, landlords relaxed their insistence on ancient customs and found more acceptable ways of exploiting their tenants' prosperity. English peasants eventually gained their freedom—without having to resort again to armed rebellion. Perhaps this was because they had not made the mistake of asking for too much or waging a class war. On the Continent of Europe, the story was a different and far more bitter one.

W. L. WARREN

A double view of the Revolt: on the left Wat Tyler is killed while Richard II looks on; on the right Richard addresses the mob.

The Peasants' Revolt in England was paralleled by risings in France and Flanders. Languedoc rose in protest against the rapacious Duke of Anjou, who quashed the insurrection at Montpellier and then sent two hundred men to the stake, two hundred to the gallows and two hundred to the block, while depriving 1,800 others of their property. When new taxes were proclaimed in Paris in 1382, men stormed the Hotel-de-Ville, armed themselves with mallets and made a bid for control of the city.

France after Charles V

These outbreaks and the manner of their suppression owed much to the early death of Charles v. The monarch's death in 1380 left his young son Charles vi (1380–1422) and his kingdom at the mercy of "The Princes of the Lillies," as the royal dukes of Anjou, Berry and Burgundy were called. The Princes, who had intervened in the rebellion in Flanders, defeated the Flemings in a pitched battle at Roosebeke on November 27, 1382, and crushed resistance in Ghent.

When the Count of Flanders died in 1384, his son-in-law, Philip the Bold of Burgundy, inherited his lands. The death of the Duke of Anjou later that same year left Philip in a position of enormous power in France. In 1388, however, Charles vi reached his majority. He restored his father's councilors and then turned to his brother Louis of Orleans.

In 1392 Charles had an attack of insanity and, as his malady became gradually permanent, the government passed to Philip the Bold of Burgundy. When Philip died in 1404, his son John the Fearless made a bid for the throne, but he was opposed by the mad king's licentious brother, Louis of Orleans, with whom Queen Isabella was openly living. Each mustered armies, fortified his Paris residence and prepared for civil war. It appeared that disaster had been averted in November, 1407, when the Duke of Berry brought Burgundy to the bedside of the ailing Orleans—but three days later Orleans was assassinated on Burgundy's orders.

The foundation of New College

Within five years of Wycliffe's death, Oxford University entered on a new phase of its existence: William of Wykeham's scholars moved from their temporary quarters to the new buildings of St. Mary College of Winchester, familiarly known as New College. Wykeham, Bishop of Winchester and Lord Chancellor, designed his college to house a warden, seventy poor scholars, ten chaplains and sixteen choristers—and to ensure that his benefaction was not wasted, he established a grammar school at Winchester where boys were given instruction in Latin (an essential preliminary to the university course). After a two-year probation at New College, those students qualified as perpetual fellows. Statutes minutely regulated the lives of Wykeham's scholars, who were the first in Europe to have study rooms to themselves. The buildings, no less than the statutes, were planned by Wykeham with great care and set the standard for collegiate buildings in England for centuries to come.

John Huss

Through Richard ii's marriage to Anne of Bohemia, a close connection had developed between Prague and Oxford universities, and numerous Bohemian students had come to Oxford to hear Wycliffe lecture and had returned with copies of his works. John Huss (1369–1414) was too young to have sat at the doctor's feet, yet he became Wycliffe's greatest convert.

After 1401 Huss was recognized as the leading figure at Prague University and the leader of the

John Huss, condemned as a heretic by the Council of Constance, and burnt.

Slav Party in the Empire. He was thought to be a natural choice to lead a nationalist movement in the wake of the anti-German risings of the previous decade. The contingent of German scholars at Prague succeeded in condemning Huss' views, but King Wenceslas, who needed the Slavs' support in his efforts to end the Great Schism, overturned the Germans' ruling and changed the constitution of the University to make the Slavs supreme. The Germans accordingly withdrew and formed a rival school in Leipzig. In 1409 Huss again became rector at Prague, and a year later the archbishop held an inquiry into his doctrines and pronounced him a heretic. The city of Prague rose in protest and was itself placed under an interdict.

Relying on a safe-conduct issued by the Emperor, Huss obeyed the Pope's summons and journeyed to the Council of Constance. Upon his arrival Huss, who had come to debate with the cardinals, found himself on trial for heresy. He was condemned not for heresy, but for refusing to abjure: "I may not offend God and my conscience by saying that I hold heresies that I have never held," he maintained—and on July 6, 1415, Huss was burned at the stake.

Bohemia was in an uproar over Huss' betrayal by the Emperor Sigismund, and Hussite doctrines became the central plank in the Slav Party's program. The Slavs refused to recognize Sigismund as their king, and Pope Martin v, whose election at Constance had officially ended the Great Schism, proclaimed a crusade against them in 1420. Under the resolute leadership of John Ziska and an extremist named Procup, the Slavs defeated every German army sent into

New College and Wadham College, Oxford, with doctors and scholars.

Bohemia. Finally at the Council of Basel (1431–35) the Hussites accepted a compromise: under the *Compactata*, Bohemians and Moravians were permitted to receive both kinds of Communion, provided that the sacraments were administered only by ordained priests. Free preaching was to be tolerated so long as the bishops' authority was recognized. These arrangements satisfied the majority of the Hussites, and Sigismund entered Prague in 1435. The memory of Huss had been vindicated.

The Cathedral at Prague. Prague was a center of discontent until the Czech people were given partial independence.

Council of Pisa

Heresy was only one of the problems facing the Church at the beginning of the fifteenth century. In past centuries ecclesiastical crises had been overcome through a series of general councils, each of which was summoned by a reigning pope. But with rival popes at Avignon and Rome, this method was out of the question. Instead, a council was summoned over the heads of both popes. Paris University persuaded Charles VI of France to withdraw his support of Benedict at Avignon and, with the additional support of the Emperor and Henry IV, Charles convened the Council of Pisa in 1409. At this gathering, which was attended by ecclesiastics from all over Europe, both popes were deposed. The conclave then elected a Franciscan as Alexander V, and upon Alexander's early death settled on an Italian clerical

The Emperor Sigismund, the leading spirit at the Council of Constance.

brigand, who became John XXIII.

The two deposed popes refused to resign, however, and a threefold division of the Church replaced the Schism. Pisa had failed to end the Schism and, more importantly, it had failed on the issue of Church reform, the matter foremost in the minds of the Paris theologians.

End of the Great Schism

In 1414, the Emperor forced John XXIII to convoke the Council of Constance. Sigismund of Hungary presided over this three-year-long enclave, which was attended by princes as well as prelates. Pope John, who came to Constance hoping to exploit the divisions of the Council, was deposed by the Emperor and Gregory XII in Rome resigned. Shortly thereafter the Avignonese pope, Benedict XIII, was abandoned by his supporters, leaving the field free for the election of Odo Colonna as Pope Martin V in 1417. The Great Schism was at last ended.

Portuguese independence

In Portugal John I, illegitimate son of Pedro I, succeeded to the throne in 1385 after leading a popular revolt to drive the Queen Regent and her daughter Beatrice from the country. At the time of the coup, Beatrice was betrothed to John, Prince of Castile—and the Castilians promptly invaded Portugal and besieged Lisbon, only to be decisively defeated at the battle of Aljubarrota in August, 1385. After centuries of insecurity, the independence of Portugal from Castile was finally assured. As a further

guarantee, John I signed the Treaty of Windsor in 1386. That agreement, by which Portugal and England became permanent allies, was secured when John married the daughter of John of Gaunt. (John of Portugal's remarkable son, Prince Henry the Navigator, encouraged voyages of exploration eastward around Africa, and set the Western powers on the course of much more extensive discoveries.)

Far East

There were significant changes in the Far East during this period. A Shogun named Yoshimitsu ended the civil war between northern and southern Japan in 1392 and brought the country under firmer rule than it had ever known. His mission over, Yoshimitsu resigned his shogunate to his son and retired to an estate near Kyoto. There he built the Golden Pavilion, to which he attracted a remarkable group of artists and dramatists. In neighboring China, a revolutionary monk named Chu Yüan-chang (1368–98) founded the Ming dynasty and, after seizing Nanking, built up an army powerful enough to expel the Mongols from his homeland.

In Persia, the Mongol vizier Timur the Great (or Tamerlane, 1369–1405) seized power in his native Samarkand and soon overran Khorasan, Afghanistan and Kurdistan. He defeated the Mongol Golden Horde in 1391, conquered Mesopotamia and, in 1397, invaded India, devastating the kingdome of Delhi. Timur defeated the Ottoman Turks at Ankara in 1402 and was planning a campaign against China in the months before his death.

English victory in France

Like Edward III, Henry V was primarily a soldier. With Parliament's blessing he revived the English claim to the French throne and landed an army at Harfleur in Normandy in the summer of 1415. After the port surrendered, the English monarch marched north along the coast, where he eventually encountered a considerable French army encamped between the villages of Agincourt and Tramecourt. There, on October 25, English archers wrought havoc upon the French cavalry. Henry proceeded in triumph to Calais and then returned home. Two years later he led

a second expedition to France, this time with the intention of systematically extending his conquest of Normandy. In 1419 the fortress of Rouen, last stronghold of the French army, surrendered. Through Burgundian pressure the French finally came to terms.

The Treaty of Troyes, signed in 1420, virtually ceded France to Henry V. By its terms he was to marry Catherine, daughter of the insane Charles VI, to govern France as regent during his father-in-law's life, and thereafter to succeed him as king. Paris and the north rejoiced at these arrangements but in southern France the Dauphin continued to be recognized as the true heir. As the thirty-eight-year-old English ruler prepared to embark upon a third expedition to France, he suddenly died, leaving an infant of nine months to succeed him as Henry VI.

The English Parliament appointed the infant King's uncle John, Duke of Bedford, as Protector of England, but when Bedford also became Regent of France, power in England passed to his brother Humphrey, Duke of Gloucester. Difficulties with England's Burgundian allies and dissension in the Council between Gloucester and Cardinal Beaufort hindered Bedford's progress in the field. It was not until 1428 that he was ready to launch an attack on the territory south of the Loire that had openly declared its preference for the uncrowned Charles VII. Bedford opened his campaign with the siege of Orleans, the gateway to the south, but the city, and with it the Valois cause, was miraculously saved by Joan of Arc, the "Maid of Orleans."

A monument to Pope Martin V in St. John Lateran, Rome.

The Maid of Orleans

The peasants of southern France believed that she was a saint, and followed her into impossible battle; the English insisted that she was a witch, and ultimately burned her at the stake. Footsoldier and foe alike were certain that some supernatural force guided the peasant girl from Lorraine who called herself Joan of Arc. No mere mortal could have rallied the vanquished troops of the deposed Dauphin as the Maid had done—nor could any commander alive have led such a motley force against the English siege troops that surrounded Orleans and routed them in less than a week as the Maid had done. Joan's "voices" saved France and restored the Dauphin to the throne, but they doomed her in the process. As she went to the stake on May 30, 1431, a penitent onlooker exclaimed "We have burned a saint!"

On February 12, 1429, a French army led by Jean d'Orleans, natural half-brother of the King's cousin, Charles d'Orleans, was ignominiously routed by a mere supply train of the English army. The Bastard of Orleans' humiliating defeat left the King despondent, the court stunned and the French citizenry thoroughly discouraged. It seemed that nothing could halt the English army's advance; Orleans, cornerstone of the kingdom and the gateway to central France, appeared doomed. The country braced itself to face the final English onslaught—but as it did, word began to spread through the French countryside of an extraordinary girl from Lorraine who claimed that she brought the King help from God.

Like most of Europe, fifteenth-century France was still suffering from the aftereffects of the Black Death, and according to contemporary chroniclers Charles VII's kingdom had not yet recovered its former strength. In France as elsewhere, there had been a rash of popular risings following in the wake of the plague, and these recurrent civil disturbances had further undermined the precarious French monarchy. France, therefore, was unprepared to counter the English invasion when it came; the young Dauphin's troops could offer only token resistance to the invasion launched by their former allies.

In 1340, nearly a century earlier, the King of England had openly proclaimed himself King of France. Intermittent fighting had ensued, but by the end of the century peace had been re-established. In 1392 the unhappy King Charles VI of France had become so unbalanced that he could no longer rule his kingdom effectively. Like the regular reappearances of the plague, Charles' insanity recurred intermittently after 1392, but the internal weaknesses of his kingdom did not become fully evident until the night of November 23, 1407. On that fateful night the King's brother, Louis d'Orleans, was assassinated by John the Fearless, Duke of Burgundy. In the political vacuum created by Charles' incapacity, the royal princes engaged in a bitter struggle for power—their feuding soon developed into civil war.

In an attempt to restore order to the faction-torn country, several rival claimants asserted their uniformly dubious claims to Charles' throne. Among them was King Henry V, scion of the Lancaster dynasty, which had recently seized the English throne from the last Plantagenet, Richard II. On August 14, 1415, Henry V disembarked on the beach of Saint-Adresse near Le Havre. Less than three months later his small expeditionary force brought an imposing French army to its knees on the field of Agincourt. In a battle that almost defies description, the English lost some four or five hundred men, the French almost 7,000. The nobility of France was decimated. Thousands fell on the battlefield and nearly fifteen hundred others were taken prisoner and transported to England. Among the captives was Charles d'Orleans, leader of the "Armagnacs" and foremost opponent of Henry V's French ally, John the Fearless, Duke of Burgundy. (After Agincourt, Henry's "Burgundian cousin" made it clear that his interests enlisted him on the side of the victorious young King of England.)

Henry began the methodical reconquest of Normandy, an ancient English possession, in 1417, and a year later Paris was delivered into the hands of the English and their Burgundian allies. The luckless Charles VI of France became a mere puppet and his son, the Dauphin Charles, barely escaped a Burgundian plot to take him prisoner. The Dauphin attempted to secure support for his projected campaign against the English through negotiations with Henry's wavering ally John the Fearless, whose immense territories stretched from Burgundy to the North Sea. On September 10, 1419, the two met on the bridge at Montereau, a village located at the junction of the Yonne and Seine rivers in northern France. The interview—and the Dauphin's ambitions—were cut short when one of the Dauphin's overzealous followers assassinated the Duke of Burgundy. The Duke's murder drove his son Philip

Joan and her banner; a marginal drawing from the *Register* of Parlement.

Opposite Joan of Arc; a symbolic painting from Antoine du Four's *Lives of Famous Women*.

The Dauphin—known as the King of Bourges

Charles VII, the weak Dauphin whom Joan made King of France; by Jean Fouquet.

A letter from Joan to the people of Reims, March 12, 1430.

the Fair into firmer alliance with England, and the Dauphin was obliged to abandon Paris and take refuge south of the Loire.

The notorious Treaty of Troyes, signed on May 21, 1420, officially recognized England's claims to the French Crown. Henry V sealed the pact by marrying Catherine, daughter of Charles VI of France, and the French Crown was officially entailed upon him. The Dauphin was formally excluded from the succession, and his mother, Queen Isabella of Bavaria, further discredited his candidacy by encouraging suspicions about his legitimacy. The University of Paris, which had played a major part in drawing up the Treaty of Troyes, warmly welcomed the handsome young English King, and a gold coin, struck by Henry to win the confidence of the French merchants, was symbolically named *le salut*—the salvation.

Two years later a brace of events occurred that no one had foreseen: Henry, who was in the prime of life, died suddenly on August 31, 1422—and two months later, on October 21, Charles VI followed him. The succession was left to two rival claimants, the Dauphin Charles and Henry and Catherine's nine-month-old son, the infant Henry VI. In accordance with the provisions of the Treaty of Troyes, the Crown of France rightfully belonged to the infant King. To secure Henry VI's claim, his uncle, the Duke of Bedford, assumed the title of Regent of France, subdued Normandy and the Ile-de-France and established the court at Paris. Disowned by his mother, the Dauphin could lay claim to no more than the southern half of France, and he became known by the derisive title of King of Bourges.

In 1428 Bedford judged that his hegemony north of the Loire was sufficiently well-established and he undertook a major offensive against the Loire-side city of Orleans. Bedford's target was a city of primary strategic importance, for it controlled the roads to the south. Its capture would enable the Regent to link up northern France with the English fiefdom of Guienne (Aquitaine) in the southwest of France.

Joan of Arc at the court of Charles VII.

Directly controlled by English
Burgundian territory
Anglo-Burgundian territory
Lands loyal to Anglo-Burgundian alliance
Controlled by French monarchy
Fiefs of France
new French territory

France 1420

BRITTANY
ANJOU
BERRY
BURGUNDY
Rouen
Paris
Reims

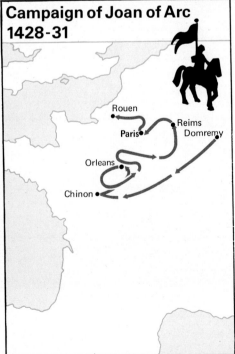

Campaign of Joan of Arc 1428-31

Rouen
Paris
Reims
Domremy
Orleans
Chinon

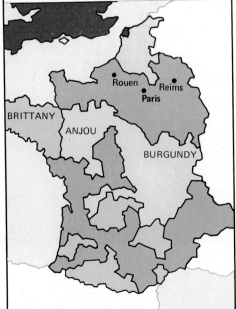

France 1453

BRITTANY
ANJOU
BURGUNDY
Rouen
Reims
Paris

"You shall be crowned King at Reims"

John, Duke of Bedford, leader of the English army in France, from the *Bedford Hours*.

Philip the Good, Duke of Burgundy, England's major French ally.

Below The castle of Chinon, commanding the confluence of the Loire and the Indre, captured from the English by Joan.

The siege of Orleans, therefore, was mounted with deliberation. Bedford's commanders, employing a strategy that had proven effective ten years before at Rouen, encircled the town with a temporary barricade to prevent egress. The population, completely surrounded by allied troops and undermined by famine, could expect no help from the Dauphin, who was without resources, without initiative and moreover without much confidence in his own cause. It was at this point that the peasant girl from Lorraine first sought an audience with the Dauphin.

After keeping Joan waiting for two days, the King finally consented to receive her. By all accounts, the peasant maid's first words to her sovereign renewed the Dauphin's flagging hopes: "Fair Dauphin, I am called Joan the Maid. The King of Heaven sends you word by me. You shall be crowned and consecrated King in the city of Reims, and are to be the viceroy of the King of Heaven, who is King in France." Furnished with arms and a small company of men—all that the Dauphin's utmost efforts could raise—Joan set out for Orleans, and on April 29, 1429, she succeeded in getting a relief convoy into the beleaguered city. She entered to the tumultuous acclaim of the townspeople, who "felt as if the siege were already raised," according to an eyewitness.

Astonishing as Joan's feat was, it was less dramatic than the events that followed. To the astonishment of the Dauphin's supporters and the stupefaction of

The coronation of Charles VII at Reims.

Below Joan leads the French attack on Paris.

Bottom The capture of Joan of Arc by Burgundian troops at Compiègne.

the allies, the siege of Orleans was raised after only three engagements. On Wednesday, May 4, the English fortifications at Saint-Loup were taken and the Loire-side gate to the city was liberated. On May 6, a skirmish took place on the opposite bank of the Loire—and when it was over, the English had lost the fortifications of Les Augustins. A day later the fortifications of Tourelles—which guarded the approach to the city's main bridge—were also taken. The left bank of the Loire was now open; Orleans had been relieved.

Realizing that his cause was lost, the English commander raised the siege a day later, on May 8, 1429. Joan forbade her men to pursue the enemy or to engage in further combat, for May 8 was a Sunday—a day of truce. The brief campaign was over; in less than eight days, a city invested for more than six months had been liberated.

The Dauphin and his advisers were uncertain as to the best way in which to utilize their unanticipated victory. Their quandary produced a temporary lull in the campaign, and Joan was forced to intervene. She urged Charles to advance upon Reims, where, the maid insisted, he would receive the consecration of his kingship.

From a strategic point of view, the march to Reims—deep within the Anglo-Burgundian zone—was extraordinarily daring, and it was undertaken in circumstances of the utmost improbability. The first English fortifications on the Dauphin's invasion route had to be taken by storm, but Joan's troops were equal to the task: Jargeau fell on June 10, Meung on June 15, and Beaugency two days later. The first decisive encounter of the campaign took place on Saturday, June 18, when the French King's army clashed with a force led by Bedford's commanders Talbot and Falstaff. The unpremeditated engagement was a stunning victory for the Dauphin: the English lost two thousand men and Talbot was captured, while French losses were negligible. (Some

"We have burned a Saint"

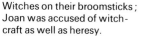

contemporary chroniclers speak of two French deaths, others of three.) Continuing northward virtually without opposition, Charles reached Reims and was crowned there on Sunday, July 17.

Such a reversal of circumstances was all but unparalleled in the annals of history and it is not surprising that the highly superstitious English at once suspected that their opponents had been aided by supernatural forces. In a letter written at the end of July, 1429, Bedford himself called Joan "a hound of the Evil One," and the University of Paris was not slow to express a similar view. A year later Joan was captured by a Burgundian force at Compiègne, and while the spineless Dauphin stood by, the Maid of Orleans was ransomed by the English, imprisoned and subjected to a farcical ecclesiastical trial at Rouen. In the course of that inquest, the simple dignity of Joan's replies disconcerted the most able of her interrogators, and their charge of sorcery could not be made to stick. In the end, it was on the very minor charge of wearing men's clothing that the chief prosecutor, Pierre Cauchon, succeeded in having Joan condemned. Cauchon, a member of the University of Paris who had been made a bishop for his active part in drafting the Treaty of Troyes, ordered the Maid's death.

Before she was led to the stake on May 30, 1431, Joan repudiated the confession that had been tormented out of her, and as the flames leaped around her an observer exclaimed, "We have burned a saint!" Less than two years after the coronation ceremony at Reims, the hostility of the English, the opposition of the universities and, above all, the defection of her associates had conspired to martyr the Maid of Lorraine. The Dauphin, now Charles VII, hastened to dissociate himself from the peasant girl to whom he owed his crown, and truth about the trial and condemnation of Joan of Arc was not established until almost twenty years later.

On November 10, 1449, eighteen years and six months after Joan's death, French troops entered Rouen, freeing the city after thirty years of English occupation. During those years the resumption of Anglo-French hostilities had turned to Charles' advantage: in 1430 the Duke of Burgundy had been forced to surrender Compiègne, and in 1435 he had been obliged to sign a separate peace treaty with his cousin Charles. A year later Arthur de Richemont, the Constable of France, entered the liberated city of Paris, and within a decade tentative overtures of peace were being made. That new atmosphere of amicability was officially acknowledged through the marriage in 1444 of Henry VI and Margaret of Anjou, a close relation of King Charles. Years of foreign domination had made the French citizenry aware of their own aspirations, however, and in 1449 a popular insurrection drove the English governor from Rouen and forced the King of France to renew military activity in the region. It is noteworthy that one of the first things that Charles did after he recovered Rouen was to order an inquiry into the matter of Joan of Arc.

Witches on their broomsticks; Joan was accused of witchcraft as well as heresy.

Lawyers and judges at Joan's trial.

The results of that inquiry, which was based upon the transcript of the trial and the testimony of surviving witnesses, seemed to justify another, lengthier investigation, and a second inquiry—this time a full ecclesiastical one—took place in 1452. Not until three years later, after a trial authorized by Pope Calixtus III, was Joan finally cleared of the charge of heresy. On July 7, 1456, the martyred Maid was solemnly rehabilitated.

In the course of their long conflict, France and England established their reciprocal independence and achieved internal unification. By 1456, England was ready to assert her insular destiny and France was ready to undertake the development of a centralized monarchy. Elsewhere in Europe, other nations began to assert their autonomy. Each sought to establish for itself a precarious national equilibrium, one that could survive the personal ambitions of individual princes and the economic rivalries of their subjects.

At a time of such confusion and uncertainty, the career of Joan of Arc had a remarkably decisive impact upon the course of European history. In much the same spirit as the townspeople of Orleans —who once welcomed her as a heroine and a saint— historians and the general public alike acknowledge Joan of Arc's exceptional contribution to world history.   REGINE PERNOUD

The burning of Joan at Rouen.

Left Pope Calixtus II who rehabilitated Joan, thirty years after her death.

The English assumed that the "spell" cast by the sorceress of Orleans had been lifted when she was executed, and they anticipated that their conquest of France would swiftly follow. As an essential preliminary to recovering England's Continental holdings—and to discredit the illicit coronation of Charles VII at Reims—Cardinal Beaufort crowned the child Henry VI in Paris in December, 1431. Within a year the strained alliance between England and Philip, Duke of Burgundy, began to founder.

At the same time, intrigues initiated by Humphrey, Duke of Gloucester, were undermining Bedford's authority at home and he was forced to return to England. France rallied in his absence: English influence in northern France was soon confined to Normandy and Paris. Despite Bedford's courageous leadership, the second campaign was a disaster and Philip, deciding to abandon the English alliance, summoned a general peace congress at Arras. Philip then agreed to recognize Charles VII as King of France in return for the cession of several Somme towns held by Charles' supporters. Charles in turn acknowledged Philip's sovereignty. The terms of the *entente* humiliated Charles, who soon broke the spirit of the agreement. Philip had expected to become Charles' principal councilor and greatest feudatory, but the French King remained deeply suspicious of him.

The Congress of Arras offered England the whole of Normandy and extensions to the Duchy of Gascony if she would agree to sign a treaty recognizing Charles VII as King of an attenuated France. Bedford, ever hopeful that the fortunes of war would shift in his favor, refused the Congress' terms. When Bedford died a year later, English authority in France crumbled, and Charles entered Paris. Almost at once he had to face a rebellion led by the great nobles— Brittany, Alençon and Bourbon— who supported the Dauphin (the future Louis XI). The English took advantage of French dissension to reconquer Harfleur, but the Duke of York, the English regent in Normandy, failed to exploit his success, and French troops reconquered most of Gascony. By 1444 both sides were too exhausted to pursue the fighting, and a truce was signed at Tours. The truce led to the marriage of Henry VI and Margaret, daughter of the Duke of Anjou.

France captures Bordeaux

Five years later England was on the verge of civil war, while France had broken the brief truce and reclaimed the whole of Normandy. Fighting resumed, and Charles VII's military reforms soon began to tell: the French soldiers were much better disciplined and more effectively led than their opponents —and they were determined to rid their homeland of foreign troops. Bordeaux fell in June, 1451, but the town's inhabitants—who had been privileged subjects of the King of England for decades—had little love for French taxes and military obligations, and the following year they invited the English army to take over the town. Margaret of

The chapel of King's College, Cambridge, founded by King Henry VI.

Anjou then instructed John Talbot, Earl of Shrewsbury, to bring the whole province under English rule. A massive French army counterattacked in the spring of 1453, and in July of that year Castillon was besieged. Chanting their war cry "Talbot, Talbot, St. George," the British garrison marched out to attack the French camp, but in a day of heavy hand-to-hand fighting they were overwhelmed. Talbot himself was slain and his men fled.

Charles VII was able to enter Bordeaux in triumph on October 19, 1453—an event that marked the effective end of the Hundred Years' War. It had taken a century of almost constant warfare to convince England's kings that it was

not feasible for them to administer dominions in France. The English were, however, permitted to retain only Calais and a few neighboring towns. Charles VII, "le Bien Servi," had indeed fulfilled the prophecies of Joan of Arc, the heretical peasant girl from Domremy.

Henry VI of England

Henry VI was an unhappy child who grew up amid the incessant rivalry between Humphrey, Duke of Gloucester, leader of the war party, and Cardinal Beaufort and his brothers (the legitimized descendants of Gaunt), who were anxious for peace. He had no talent for government and longed to withdraw from the world. (His piety found expression in his foundations at Eton and King's College, Cambridge.) Gloucester's wife, in the full knowledge that her husband was next in the line of succession, attempted to practice witchcraft on the King in 1441.

The unpopularity of the match that Cardinal Beaufort had arranged between Henry VI and the high-spirited Margaret of Anjou, coupled with the reverses in France, reflected on Beaufort and weakened the prestige of the Crown. With the deaths of both the Cardinal and his old rival, Duke Humphrey (who spent his last days in prison as a suspected traitor), power passed to the Duke of Suffolk. Parliament promptly laid the disasters in France at his door and impeached him for maladministration and corruption. The weakling King turned on his favorite minister:

Suffolk was banished in 1450 and was assassinated at Calais.

Violence continued to dominate domestic politics in England. In 1450, in what was known as Cade's Rebellion, 30,000 men from Kent and Sussex marched on London to demand the head of Lord Chancellor Say and the restoration of Richard of York to the Council. Government had effectively broken down throughout the realm.

Philip the Good of Burgundy

Under Philip the Good (1419–67), Burgundy was consolidated as a powerful "middle kingdom," between France and Germany. With Flanders and Artois—which Philip inherited—as a nucleus, the Prince forced one of his cousins to surrender her lands in Holland, Zeeland, Hainault and Friesland. He annexed Brabant upon the death of another cousin. Philip achieved his design of centralizing the government of this collection of provinces by compelling the vigorous municipalities in each region to submit to his rule. For years Ghent opposed him, but he crushed its independence in 1453. Though the Treaty of Arras had not brought him the national influence that he had anticipated, Philip remained a ruler to be reckoned with. His court set new standards in ceremony and etiquette—many of which were adapted by future kings of France and England. He established the Order of the Golden Fleece in honor of a mistress whose tresses "had been the object of many pleasantries."

The library at Oxford founded by Duke Humphrey.

Flemish Mysticism

The mid-fifteenth century was a period of intense interest in Flemish mysticism. It marked the second generation of the "New Devotion" movement, which stemmed from the work of Gerard Groot (d. 1384), a Carthusian monk who founded the houses of "the Brethren of the Common Life." The rule of the Brethren and their mystical theology provoked criticism—the Dominicans maintained that certain of their practices were heretical—but the Council of Constance approved their way of life. Thomas à Kempis (c. 1380–1471), trained to follow the ideals of Gerard Groot, was sent to the new Augustinian Convent of Mount St. Agnes at his native Kempen. To support the convent, he spent his days copying missals and devotional works. He wrote many edifying tracts and sermons, culminating in his *Imitation of Christ*, which reveals in the simplest language the life of the spirit. In the next several centuries, his treatise would be read and reread more frequently, perhaps, than any other volume except the Bible.

The Flemish School

At different times both Hubert van Eyck and his brother Jan worked at the Burgundian court, developing a uniquely Flemish school of painting that was rich in detail and color. Much of their work reflected the splendor of Philip the Bold's court, yet their religious paintings demonstrated a depth of feeling that forms a counterpart to the writings of Thomas à Kempis. The van Eycks' finest achievement, on which each in turn lavished his genius, was the large and complex polyptych of the *Adoration of the Lamb* in the Church of St. Bavon in Ghent. Jan, the younger brother, developed a novel technique of painting in oils with varnish that helped to preserve his brilliant colors for posterity.

Cosimo de' Medici and Florence

The fortunes of the Medici Bank had long been linked with papal finances, and Giovanni de' Medici (d. 1429) reaped enormous profits from the Council of Constance. Four years after Giovanni's death, his son Cosimo urged the powerful Albizzi family of Florence to wage

Prince Henry the Navigator, who tried to reach Japan by sailing eastward.

war against Lucca. When the Florentines came off badly in the campaign, Cosimo joined the populace in decrying the war—and was exiled for his duplicity. The Albizzi soon found that they had killed the goose that laid the golden egg, however, for the Medici Bank alone could provide the funds that were necessary to finance their government. In September, 1434, the newly elected signory of Florence ordered Cosimo's recall.

Cosimo de' Medici succeeded in banishing all possible rivals to his authority. Although he never took the title of prince, Florence was his city and until his death in 1464 he ruled it through a series of docile administrators. Cosimo, who ruthlessly suppressed conspiracies in 1444 and again in 1457–58, took considerable care to appear as the friend of the peasant and the artisan. He used his considerable wealth as a patron of art and letters, encouraged Marsilio Ficino and other philosophers and supervised a great collection of manuscripts; his library was the first private library ever opened to the public. He built the Church of St. Lorenzo, enlarged St. Mark's, and supported Donatello and Ghiberti.

Artists and scholars living in Italy during the middle of the fifteenth century enjoyed the richest patronage in history. The Medici in Florence and the Sforzas in Milan vied with each other and with successive popes for the services of Italy's greatest artists. Architects and artists were commissioned to beautify palaces and churches, and poets were paid to sing their praises.

Naples and Sicily united

As successor to the amorous Joanna II, the last of the Angevins in Italy,

Alfonso the Magnanimous, King of Aragon, acquired Naples in 1435—thus reuniting the crowns of Naples and Sicily. He made Naples the hub of his Aragonese empire in the Mediterranean and turned his court into a remarkable center of art and humanism.

Prince Henry the Navigator

Prince Henry the Navigator founded a new school of seamanship at his residence in the Portuguese capital of Algarve. His aim was to establish a sea route to the East that outflanked the Moslem world. To achieve that aim, Henry harnessed the crusading zeal of the medieval world to the enterprise of discovery. Each year his expeditions penetrated farther down the west coast of Africa. By the time of Prince Henry's death in 1460, Portuguese navigators had explored the Senegal and Gambia rivers and the Cape Verde Islands—and had brought gold and slaves home to Lisbon. The European world had entered a new era of discoveries.

Council of Basel

A reformist party at the Council of Basel succeeded in asserting that it was heresy for a pope to contradict the decrees issued by a general council. Pope Eugenius IV (1431–47) took immediate exception to the Council's decree, and divisions hardened concerning negotiations for reunion with the Greek Church. In 1434 a revolutionary movement in Rome drove Eugenius to Florence, where he remained for nine years under Cosimo de' Medici's protection. The despotic Cardinal Vitelloschi ruled as Eugenius' viceroy for several years, only to be murdered by another cardinal. In an effort to break up the anti-papal Council of Basel, Eugenius convened a council at Florence in 1438, but the prelates at Basel refused to adjourn until their mission had been accomplished.

The stock of the papacy had rarely been lower than it was at the mid-point of the fifteenth century. Lorenzo Valla had recently proved that the Donation of Constantine, the document on which the papacy's claim to lands around Rome was based, was a forgery. In France a national synod had endorsed the Pragmatic Sanction of Bourges, a document embodying many of the

anti-papal reforms decreed at the Council of Basel. In addition, the Sanction limited the revenues that the papacy could collect in France. A year later, Germany followed suit: the Diet of Mainz drew up a similar Pragmatic Sanction that abolished payment of annates and papal provisions to benefices in the Empire. The decline in respect for the papacy was eventually reversed by the skillful diplomacy of Aeneas Sylvius Piccolomini (the future Pius II). The Concordat of Vienna negotiated by Piccolomini and signed in 1448 by the new Emperor Frederick III, won back Germany for the Pope.

The Orthodox Church

John VIII, Emperor at Constantinople, traveled to Italy in 1439 to

Frederick III giving the future Pius II the poet's crown.

discuss the basis for a reunion of the Eastern and Western Churches. Before departing he accepted the Pope's conditions for ending the schism between Byzantium and Rome that had persisted since 1054. John and his successor found it impossible to enforce the union in the face of popular resistance, however, and Orthodox bishops in lands conquered by the Turks continued to regard the Sultan with greater respect than the Roman Pope.

Nicholas V (1447–55), perhaps the greatest pope of the fifteenth century, was a Tuscan scholar who planned to make Rome the imperial capital of art and literature and wanted to harness the Renaissance to the services of the Church. Coincidentally, Nicholas' chief antagonist, the Sultan Mahomet II (1451–81), was also a patron of learning and the arts.

Le siege du grant turc auec ij deles pricipaulx conseilles
Le siege du capiteine gnal de la turquie

The Fall of Constantinople   1453

The Eastern Roman Empire had endured for eleven centuries, but now it was reduced to little more than the city of Constantinople itself. Another Constantine—the last to sit on the Byzantine throne—ruled the decaying city and nervously watched the Ottoman Turks inexorably advancing from the east. Eastern and Western Christendom were split over doctrinal disputes— and there would be no help coming from Europe. Overtures to the Turkish Sultan were dramatically rebuffed; Constantine's ambassadors of peace were beheaded as they arrived. On Easter Monday, 1453, the Sultan's advance guard was sighted and the gates to the city were closed. The Greeks heroically resisted the Turkish siege, but it could have only one outcome. As the Turkish victors streamed into the fallen city, they were witnessing the end of one long and brilliant chapter in man's history—and the beginning of another.

The traveler from the West, seeing Contantinople for the first time during the early decades of the fifteenth century, would have been saddened—even possibly horrified—by what lay before him. Brought up on tales of this golden metropolis—second only to Rome itself in splendor, and seat of an Empire that had lasted more than a thousand years and could boast the longest chain of unbroken monarchy in the history of Christendom—the traveler would have found instead a crumbling ruin of a city, half-deserted and shot through with despair. "Its inhabitants are few," wrote Pedro Tafur, a young Spaniard who arrived in 1437. "They are not well-clad, but miserable and poor, showing the hardship of their lot . . . The Emperor's palace must have been very magnificent, but now is in such a state that both it and the city reveal the evils which the people have suffered and still endure . . . Inside, the building is badly maintained, except for those parts where the Emperor, the Empress and their attendants live, and even these are cramped for space. The Emperor's state is as splendid as ever, for nothing is omitted from the ancient ceremonies; but, properly regarded, he is like a Bishop without a See."

Tafur's description was accurate; the once-glorious Empire of the East, which had formerly stretched from Italy to the borders of Mesopotamia, now extended little farther than the walls of Constantinople itself. For centuries the Empire had stood as a bulwark against the tide of Islam, allowing Christianity time to put down deep roots in Eastern Europe—and even after the loss of the Anatolian heartland to the Seljuk Turks in the eleventh century, the Empire had remained rich, powerful and—ostensibly—prosperous. The quays of Constantinople were crowded with the shipping of three continents, and merchants from every land and clime thronged its bazaars. City wharves and warehouses overflowed with silks and spices, ivory and gold, while beneath the mosiac-encrusted cupolas of its thousand churches lay some of the holiest relics of Christianity.

Constantinople's prosperity aroused increasing envy and cupidity among Western Crusaders throughout the twelfth century, and it was perhaps inevitable that they should make their own bid for control of the Greek metropolis. The seizure of the city, on Good Friday, 1204, by that exercise in unmitigated piracy still ludicrously known as the Fourth Crusade, stripped Constantinople of its treasures and condemned it to fifty-five years of misrule by Frankish thugs occupying the throne of the Byzantine emperors. The city was left weak, desperately impoverished and well-nigh naked to its enemies.

Not long after Michael VIII Palaeologus rode back into his shattered capital in 1259, a new dynasty sprang up in the Turkish-held lands across the Bosphorus: the house of Osman—or, as we now prefer to call them, the Ottomans.

Under Osman and his successors, Turkish conquests came swiftly. By 1340 virtually all of Asia Minor was in their hands; in the next twenty-five years they crossed the Dardanelles, set up their capital at Adrianople (modern Edirne) and made themselves masters of western Thrace. Their victory at Kosovo in southern Yugoslavia in 1389 won them Serbia and the Balkans. By that time the Byzantine Emperor, surrounded by enemies, plagued by palace revolutions, his morale further shaken by the Black Death, had been forced to acknowledge the Turkish Sultan as his overlord. Only one hope now remained: a grand Christian alliance to deliver the Empire and save Europe—while there was still time—from the Moslem invader.

The possibility of such an alliance was dim. The Eastern and Western Churches had long been in schism, and it seemed unlikely that the Pope would declare a Crusade for the rescue of schismatics who did not even recognize his primacy. The Catholic princes of the West, blind as ever to political realities, tended to look on the Turkish conquests as divine retribution for those who had rejected the Christian

A janissary by Giovanni Bellini: the janissaries were a corps of highly trained troops from Christian families who formed an elite corps in the Sultan's army.

Opposite The siege of Constantinople by the Turks, showing Turkish boats being dragged across land behind the suburb of Pera: from the *Voyage d'outremer de Bertandon de la Bronuiere.*

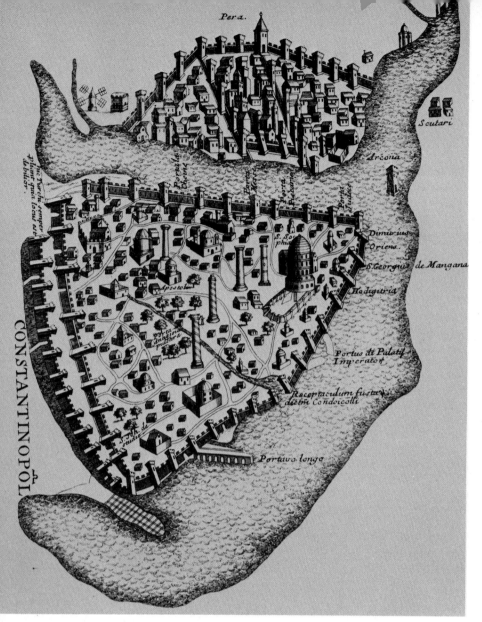

The city of Constantinople.

Truth. Was Constantinople worth a Mass? Its Emperor thought so; and in 1439, at Florence, the emissaries of John VIII Palaeologus accepted papal authority. In theory the Churches were now reunited, but in practice the schism survived. "Better the Sultan's turban than the Cardinal's hat," declared the Byzantine minister Lucas Notaras—and the majority of his compatriots agreed with him. When John died in 1448, he left his brother Constantine an embittered and divided city.

We know very little about this last and most tragic of all the Byzantine emperors. At the time of his accession he was forty-four. Although no reliable portraits have come down to us, he seems to have been tall and rather swarthy—a little unimaginative, perhaps, but straightforward and absolutely honest, an able administrator and, above all, a brave soldier. It was just as well. Before Constantine had been three years on the throne, the Turkish Sultan, Murad II, died of apoplexy at Adrianople. By the standards of his time, Murad had been a peaceable ruler, prepared to live on friendly terms with his Christian subjects. His successor was a young man of a very different stamp.

Though still only twenty-one, already Mehmet

II had given proof of a character to be respected and feared. An intellectual who spoke six languages —including excellent Latin and Greek—he was by nature introverted and morose, almost pathologically secretive and possessed of a streak of cruelty that terrified his subordinates. From childhood Mehmet had hated all Christians, and as he grew older this hatred had been transformed into a single, burning idea: to capture Constantinople. Now that he was Emperor, he intended to lose no time in realizing that ambition.

When the Greek ambassadors came to congratulate him on his accession, however, the young Sultan affirmed his peaceable intentions and blandly promised to respect Byzantine territory. But within a matter of months he had summoned architects and masons from all over his dominions, and on April 15, 1452, the first stones were laid in the construction of a great castle on the European side of the Bosphorus, a few miles north of Constantinople, where the straits are at their narrowest. Neighboring churches and monasteries were razed to provide building materials, and just four and a half months later, on the last day of August, the fortress—now known as Rumeli Hisar—was completed. Constantine sent ambassadors to ask Mehmet his intentions, although he must have known them only too well. Mehmet's answer was clear: as each ambassador arrived, he was immediately beheaded.

And still Europe would not understand. The Pope was genuinely concerned, but could stir no enthusiasm for a relief expedition; the Western Empire was a broken reed. In November a Venetian ship that refused to stop when hailed from Rumeli Hisar was sunk by Turkish cannon, its crew was decapitated and its captain publicly impaled—but the Most Serene Republic, which was doing good business in Ottoman ports and had no wish to become involved in an expensive war, chose to ignore the incident. Genoa took a similar line. The whole district of Pera to the east of the Golden Horn was a Genoese colony whose best hope of preservation seemed to lie in coming to an agreement with the Turks rather than in taking up arms against them. France and England were still exhausted after the Hundred Years' War, and England was further handicapped by a King, Henry VI, whose apparent saintliness was insufficient to conceal his undoubted imbecility. From all the other monarchies of Europe the response was equally unpromising. By March of 1453, when the immense Ottoman army—well over a hundred thousand strong—began to move from Adrianople toward the Bosphorus, it was clear that the city's survival was going to depend on its inhabitants alone.

The Emperor now ordered a hasty census of all able-bodied men—including monks—who were capable of bearing arms. The results were even worse than he had feared: after nine successive visitations of the Black Death in less than a century, Constantinople had lost some 40 per cent of its already dwindling population. There were, however, more than a thousand foreign residents of the city, including almost the entire Venetian community, who pledged

A mighty three-fold rampart

their support—and these had recently been joined by a Genoese contingent led by a famous soldier of fortune, Giovanni Giustiniani Longo. Disgusted by the apathy of his government, Giustiniani raised a private army of seven hundred on his own. Constantine gave them an enthusiastic welcome, but even with foreign reinforcements he had less than seven thousand men to defend fourteen miles of walls.

Those walls were for the most part in excellent repair. The ramparts that ran along the Golden Horn needed little defending, since the harbor could be closed by stretching a chain across its mouth from Acropolis Point, the southern tip of the Horn, to the shores of Pera on the north. The Marmara walls, south of the city, rose straight out of the sea and were protected by treacherous shoals—making them equally inaccessible. The weight of the Turkish attack therefore was expected to come from the landward side. Here a great three-fold rampart ran for some four miles in an unbroken line across the neck of the peninsula on which the city stood, joining the imperial palace at Blachernae in the north with the Marmara walls at Studion in the south. It was, and still is, a magnificent fortification—and it had never been breached since its construction by the Emperor Theodosius, one thousand and six years before.

On Easter Monday, 1453, the advance guard of Mehmet's army was sighted by the Byzantine lookouts. At once the Emperor ordered all the gates to the city closed, the bridges across the moats destroyed and the boom laid across the Golden Horn. Within three days, the Turkish army was drawn up along the whole length of the land walls. At the center was the red and gold tent of the Sultan himself, surrounded by his picked corps of Janissaries. The defenders saw for the first time what they would have to face—and on the following day they felt it. Mehmet

prided himself on his cannon—a comparatively new weapon, which he planned to use on an unprecedented scale. Three had already been employed to considerable effect from Rumeli Hisar, but the Sultan had brought several others from Adrianople. These had been specially made for him by a renegade Hungarian engineer, and included one twenty-seven-foot-long monster, capable of hurling cannonballs weighing half a ton for a mile or more. But the walls held against the bombardment.

The walls of Constantinople.

Rumeli Hisar, which controls the Bosphorus. Built by Mehmet in 1452, this was the first sign that he intended to capture the city.

When Christ deserted Constantinople

At sea, too, the long battle had begun. The Ottoman navy had sailed up through the Dardanelles and the Sea of Marmara, and now lay at the entrance to the Bosphorus, about a mile away from the mouth of the Horn. Mehmet's navy was not doing well. Repeated efforts to force the boom had been beaten back by an effective combination of arrows and "Greek fire," an incendiary invented by the Byzantines that burned on the surface of the water. And on April 20, three Genoese galleys and an imperial transport had actually managed to smash their way through the enemy and, under cover of darkness, had slipped into the harbor.

This reverse infuriated Mehmet. He immediately ordered the speeding-up of a plan he had formulated during the first days of the siege: the construction of a huge causeway up the valley that led from the Bosphorus shore, over the hill of Pera, behind the Genoese colony and down again to the waters of the Horn. On Saturday, April 22, Constantinople witnessed what was possibly the most extraordinary scene in all its history, as countless teams of oxen dragged some seventy ships on wheeled cradles over

Constantine VIII Palaeologus the penultimate Byzantine Emperor: from the *Journey of the Magi* by Benozzo Gozzoli.

a two-hundred foot ridge and then slowly lowered them down the other side into the harbor. The Greeks' amazement must have been darkened by despair—they could no longer rely on a safe anchorage for their fleet. Yet, more important, they now had another ten miles of wall to defend. The Genoese colony of Pera, whose benevolent neutrality had hitherto been an invaluable source of information on Turkish movements, was surrounded.

Another month went by, during which food supplies began to run short. The defenders struggled valiantly on, but the walls were beginning to crumble under the incessant pounding of the cannon, and Constantine was finding it increasingly difficult to maintain his subjects' morale. Then, on May 23, came a last, shattering blow to Christian hopes. During the preceding winters, the Venetians in the city had sent an urgent appeal to their republic, begging Venice to intervene on Constantine's behalf. At last in early May, they had secretly dispatched their fastest brigantine to look for the relief expedition. The ship had searched the Aegean, but found no trace of an Italian fleet. The crew, knowing that their return to Constantinople meant almost certain death, had nevertheless insisted on doing so. The Emperor wept as he thanked them. Only Christ, he murmured, could save the city now.

To many, however, it seemed that Christ too had deserted Constantinople. On May 24 the moon went into eclipse, and while the city's holiest icon was being carried in procession through the streets it suddenly slipped from its platform. Hardly had it been replaced when a hailstorm burst over the capital—a storm of such fury that the whole procession had to be abandoned. And the next day men awoke to find Constantinople shrouded in a dense fog—a phenomenon unheard of at the end of May.

Five months earlier, a service of reunion with Rome had been held in Hagia Sophia, and since that time the church had been avoided by the Orthodox faithful. But now, in this final hour of trial, doctrinal differences were forgotten. On the evening of May 28, when it was plain that Mehmet was preparing for his final assault on the land walls, the Emperor joined his people in the great church where, with Orthodox and Roman priests officiating side by side, the Christian liturgy was celebrated for the last time in Constantinople.

At half-past one in the morning the Sultan gave his order to attack. The sudden noise, bursting out of the stillness, was immediately answered by all the bells of the city, rallying every able-bodied defender to the walls. Though each man must have known that the cause was lost, all still fought magnificently; two successive Turkish charges, the first by the irregular *bashi-bazouks*, the next by a wave of fanatical Anatolians, were driven back—and a third, by Mehmet's own regiment of Janissaries, fought hand-to-hand for an hour or more without making any appreciable headway. Suddenly Giustiniani fell, mortally wounded. Seeing their leader carried from the walls, the Genoese soldiers panicked and fled, leaving the Greeks to face the enemy alone.

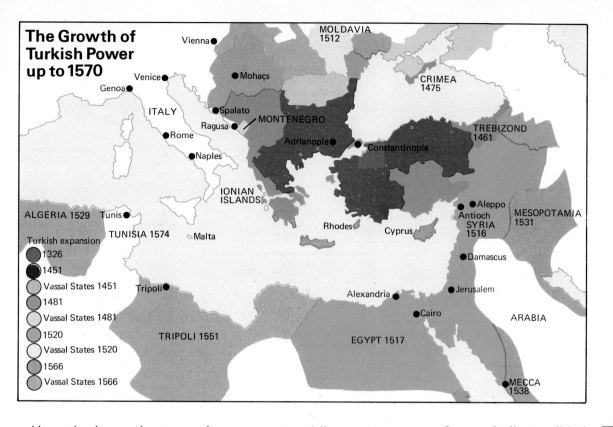

The Growth of Turkish Power up to 1570

MOLDAVIA 1512

Vienna

Venice
Genoa
ITALY
Rome
Naples

Mohaçs
Spalato
Ragusa
MONTENEGRO
Adrianople
Constantinople

CRIMEA 1475

TREBIZOND 1461

IONIAN ISLANDS

ALGERIA 1529   Tunis
Turkish expansion
○ 1326
● 1451
○ Vassal States 1451
○ 1481
○ Vassal States 1481
○ 1520
○ Vassal States 1520
○ 1566
○ Vassal States 1566

TUNISIA 1574   Malta
Rhodes   Cyprus

Aleppo
Antioch
SYRIA 1516

MESOPOTAMIA 1531

Damascus

Tripoli

Alexandria   Jerusalem

Cairo

ARABIA

TRIPOLI 1551

EGYPT 1517

MECCA 1538

Almost simultaneously came another, even greater catastrophe. At the northern end of the walls, where they joined the imperial palace, was a tiny postern gate, through which the defenders had been making occasional sorties to harry the Ottoman flank. By some mischance the gate had been left unbarred; the Turks fell upon it and burst through.

The Byzantine Empire was finished. The Emperor, seeing that all hope was gone, seized his sword and ran to where the fighting was thickest. He was never seen alive again. Much later, his body was identified among the piles of corpses. It had no head, but on its feet were purple buskins, embroidered with the imperial eagles of Byzantium.

As the victorious Turks streamed across the walls and through the streets, the massacre and carnage became appalling. Moslem tradition permitted three days of rapine and looting after the storming of a city, but the Sultan restricted his soldiers to one. He himself seems to have been strangely calm and subdued in the hours of his supreme triumph. Not till late afternoon did he enter Constantinople. He rode slowly to Hagia Sophia where, before the high altar, he touched his turban to the ground in thanksgiving.

Thus the Byzantine Empire gave place to the Ottoman. The news of its fall was received with horror among the peoples of the West, who suddenly felt profoundly guilty—as well they might. For it was Western Europe, with its Fourth Crusade, that had inflicted the first mortal wound upon the Eastern Empire; the Turks had merely administered the *coup de grâce*. Even at the end, the Christian princes, by firm and concerted action, might have delayed the inevitable; but they did not choose to do so. Instead, they argued and prevaricated—and while Europe dithered, Byzantium died. The Empire's life had been long, brilliant and glorious.

Taken as an isolated event, Constantinople's fall was not a matter of as much direct political significance to Europe in general as was at one time believed. Many of the great developments for which the city has been wholly or partly credited—events that mark the end of the Middle Ages—were already under way. Explorers and navigators had long since begun seeking out and mapping new trade routes to the Indies. In Italy the Renaissance had run half its course, and Byzantine scholars there had been revealing the mysteries of Greek culture for fifty years and more. Nor can it be argued that Mehmet's victory opened up Europe to Turkish invasion, for the Turks had already gained a European foothold.

For the Greeks and Turks, however, the events of May 29, 1453, are still annually commemorated—by the former as their greatest tragedy, by the latter as their most shining triumph. And it is right and proper that they should, for on that day the histories of both peoples were radically changed. The Greeks entered upon nearly four centuries of subjugation, during which their Church provided the only focus for their national aspirations. The Turks, for their part, saw the defeat of their arch-enemy as the confirmation of their European Empire.

After five centuries, the rest of us can afford to take a dispassionate view. We can applaud the way the new capital soared, phoenix-like, from the ashes of the old, and we can accept the events here related as just another proof that the dominions of this world, even that of God's vice-regent on earth, cannot last forever. But we too owe a debt to Byzantium—which preserved and cherished the Greek spirit for a thousand years while Western Europe was groping its way through the Dark Ages, and which somehow combined that spirit with a new religious awareness, to form a technique of expressing spiritual values in visual terms that is without parallel in Christian art. When Constantinople fell, the world was diminished.

JOHN JULIUS NORWICH

Sultan Mehmet II, conqueror of Constantinople, by Giovanni Bellini.

383

The fall of Constantinople enabled Mehmet the Conqueror to press his attack on Eastern Europe. Believing that he was a modern Alexander, the Sultan led his troops into Bosnia, Albania and Serbia, where John Hunyadi's heroic defense of Belgrade in 1456 finally checked the Turkish advance. (Hunyadi's troops had been aroused by a nationalist crusade preached by John, the friar of Capistrano.) The Peloponnesus fell to the invaders, ending the rule of the Palaeologi in Greece, and in 1461 the Turks conquered the Empire of Trebizond, the last independent Greek state still in existence.

Mehmet's troops then turned their attention to the Genoese and Venetian stations in the Aegean, and an alarmed Pope Pius II (1458–64) urged the rulers of Christendom to join him in the mightiest of all crusades. In the years before he took holy orders, Pius had charmed the courts of Europe with his brilliant verses and his witty, immoral plays. Emperor Frederick III had crowned him poet laureate of Germany. But now, "forsaking Venus and Bacchus," he preached the moral duty of fighting the Turks. Only Hungary and Venice heeded his words and, as an example to the rest, Pius himself took up the Cross. Curiously, neither his crusading zeal nor his sudden death moved the conscience of the West.

The Turkish fleet soon wrested Scutari and Euboea from the Venetians and by 1478 their raiders had reached the outskirts of Venice. The desperate Republic signed a peace treaty with Mehmet in 1479, surrendering most of their posts in Albania and undertaking to pay a yearly tribute for the privilege of trading in the Levant. Mahomet's forces attacked southern Italy, raided Styria and Carinthia, and besieged Rhodes, which was held by the Knights of St. John. It was only Mehmet's death in 1481 (and the ensuing dispute over his successor) that saved the Balkans and Italy. Renewed attacks were launched in 1512, which led to the conquest of Syria and Egypt under Selim I.

Greek Scholarship revived

The Greek scholars who fled to Italy and Central Europe as the Sultan's armies advanced into their homeland brought with them precious manuscripts hitherto buried in the libraries of Byzantium. During the next half-century or so,

the study of all aspects of classical Greek culture was revolutionized. The Humanist approach to art and letters—the fearless search for truth and beauty once limited to the civilization of Rome—gained a new dimension through the rediscovery of Greece. The Humanist outlook, which affected every aspect of life and questioned the very purpose of man's existence, was bound to lead to disputes with authority, especially the authority of the Church— the invention of printing made the results of that intellectual ferment known throughout the West.

Lorenzo the Magnificent

Under Cosimo de' Medici (d. 1464) the government of Florence passed

A bust of Lorenzo the Magnificent.

from an oligarchy to an autocracy. Lorenzo the Magnificent, who held the reins of power from 1478 to 1492, prided himself on being merely "a private citizen," although he made a princely marriage to Clarice Orsini. Lorenzo survived a 1478 plot in which his brother was assassinated, and skillfully used the occasion to increase both his position and his popularity. Greeted as the "savior of Florence" after concluding a favorable treaty with Naples, he effected a reform of the constitution and established the Council of Seventy, a body completely under his control. Lorenzo was respected throughout the peninsula for his masterful diplomacy— in his last years he effectively kept Italy at peace.

Lorenzo's regime appears liberal by comparison with the reigns of contemporary tyrants in Naples and Milan. The unscrupulous Ferdinand I, King of Naples (1453–94), struggled throughout his reign to preserve his doubtful title to the throne and to keep one step ahead of his barons' incessant intrigues. The history of the Sforza family of

Milan (1450–1500) is one of oppression, usurpation and assassination. Lodovico Sforza, who ousted his nephew from the duchy in 1479, remained insecure in spite of his ruthlessness, and his fears eventually involved all Italy in a war with the French. Curiously, despite such uncertain and oppressive political conditions, the Italian Renaissance flourished.

England after the Hundred Years' War

The defeat of the English army at Chatillon and the death of Commander Talbot in 1453 ended the fighting in the Hundred Years' War. Nothing but Calais remained of Eleanor of Aquitaine's inheritance. The Continental conflict was finally settled, but fighting soon resumed—this time in England itself. Richard, Duke of York and heir apparent to the weakling Henry VI, raised a private army, and in 1453, when Henry became temporarily insane, York was appointed protector. Henry recovered and Margaret produced an heir, but York was determined to fight for the throne.

Wars of the Roses

York's supporters defeated those of the Queen and Edmund Beaufort at St. Albans in 1455. The Wars of the Roses—a long series of short campaigns between Lancaster and York—had begun. Lack of "governance" and the utter breakdown of feudal society had made civil war inevitable, and the numerous soldiers of fortune who were returning from France (where they had been accustomed to the spoils of warfare as much as to the prowess of arms) took readily to the only profession they knew. Fundamentally, Richard of York stood for the restoration of law and order—and against the incapacity of the Crown.

Edward IV, by an unknown artist.

He received more support from the Commons than did his opponents, but most of the population remained indifferent to the strife.

York claimed the throne in 1460, but died soon thereafter at the Battle of Wakefield. His son Edward, Earl of March, then rallied the Yorkists to victory at Mortimer's Cross, marched south to join the Earl of Warwick (who was known as "the kingmaker"), and took the capital. At the age of nineteen, March became King Edward IV. He defended his title at Towton in Yorkshire, and Henry and Margaret fled to Scotland. The imbecile Henry was able to make a pathetic return to nominal kingship in October, 1470, when Warwick shifted his support to the Lancastrian camp, but his restoration was short-lived. On Easter Day, 1471, Edward IV won a decisive victory in the mist at Barnet—and with the subsequent defeat of Margaret's Welsh army at Tewkesbury and the brutal murder of Henry VI, Edward was at last secure on the throne.

For the next dozen years Edward IV proved himself a strong monarch, eschewing corruption and acting much as Sir John Fortescue had recommended in his tract, The Governance of England. But the legacy of treachery was not yet spent: Clarence, Edward's elder brother,

Henry VII, England's first Tudor king.

was executed in 1478 for plotting against the King; and when Edward died in 1483, his younger brother Richard dethroned Edward's son, Edward V (and probably ordered his—and his brother's —murder in the Tower). Richard III's days were numbered, however, and in 1485 Henry of Richmond— who represented the Beaufort-Lancastrian line through his mother, the widow of Owen Tudor —defeated the hunch-backed King on Bosworth Field.

Elizabeth of York, wife of Henry VII.

Henry Tudor strengthened his doubtful claim to the throne by marrying Elizabeth of York, daughter of Edward IV, to form a union of the Red and White Roses that settled the disputed succession. The old feudal nobility had been decimated by years of internecine strife, and Henry VII was determined to maintain his supremacy.

France strengthened under Louis XI

In many ways, the first of the Tudors took as his model the French King Louis XI (1461–83). As a prince, Louis' taste for rebelliousness had led to his banishment to Dauphine, where he enjoyed the protection of the Duke of Burgundy. His vigorous administration of that principality proved invaluable training and earned Louis the nickname "The Spider" for his diplomatic cunning. There was no nonsense about him; he worshiped hard facts and spurned opinions. During his coronation banquet he amazed the courtiers by removing his uncomfortable crown, but they soon accustomed themselves to his ungainly figure, his coarse language and his penchant for ambling about the realm in shabby clothes and an old felt hat. Here was a Renaissance

Louis XI.

tyrant ruling by decree, who was very different from the princes of Italy. He frowned on the wearing of silk, considered gilding a wasteful luxury and lacked money for patronizing art—yet he felt that it was provident to keep the Church's good graces, and he showed himself to be a man of religion.

Louis' achievement lay in curbing the great feudatories of France, ending anarchy and freeing the country from intervention by England, Burgundy and Spain. He enlarged the frontiers of France, made it a unified kingdom (with the exception of Brittany and Lorraine) and brought it prosperity. Administration was overhauled and talented men of humble origin replaced the nobility in many governmental posts.

France conquers Burgundy

Charles the Bold (1467–77), son of Philip the Good of Burgundy, envisioned a kingdom that stretched from the North Sea to the Mediterranean, but Charles proved to be no match for Louis XI, who formed a coalition against him. By purchasing England's neutrality, Louis eliminated Charles' natural ally and negated the usefulness of the upstart's marriage to Margaret of York, Edward IV's sister. Charles curbed the city of Liège and successfully incorporated Gelderland, but he overreached himself in 1473 when he occupied Alsace-Lorraine and declared war on the Swiss cantons. In January, 1477, the Swiss pikemen vanquished the Burgundian cavalry at Nancy and Charles was slain. Louis immediately annexed the duchy of Burgundy proper and occupied Franche-Comté. Charles' Flemish possessions, fearing French annexation, compelled Charles' twenty-year-old daughter Mary to safeguard their local privileges under such humiliating terms that she gladly married Maximilian of Austria—and thereby inaugurated an era of Hapsburg domination of the Netherlands.

Hapsburg Empire

By the time that Frederick III, the second Hapsburg Emperor, was crowned by Nicholas V in Rome in 1452, he had already reigned for a dozen ineffectual years—and he was to survive for another forty-one. Upon his return from Italy,

the feud between Frederick and his brother Albert was renewed and the Emperor was eventually driven from Vienna. The imperial electors would have gladly deposed him—except that they were unable to agree upon a successor.

Frederick's son Maximilian took over the government in 1486—against the Emperor's will—and the deposed monarch retired to Linz to study astronomy, alchemy and botany. He was obsessed with a belief in the future greatness of his house, an obsession that was epitomized by his monogram A.E.I.O.U. (*Austriae est imperare orbi universo*). Frederick's vision became a reality in 1477 with Maximilian's marriage to Mary of Burgundy.

Matthias of Hungary

Matthias Hunyadi was elected King of Hungary in 1458 at the age of fifteen. In the aftermath of his elder brother's murder, the country was deeply divided and likely to fall to the Turks; few observers gave Matthias more than a few years as King, but he proved to be a good patriot, a competent soldier and an able administrator. He formed a regular army (known from the color of its armor as "The Black Brigade") created the Magyar Hussars, which became the best disciplined troops in Europe, and equipped his army and his fleet on the Danube with cannon. Thanks to his vigorous leadership the Turks failed to

conquer Hungary, the Czechs were expelled from the north of the kingdom and the Hapsburgs from the west. Matthias patronized artists, built up a great library and, in 1467, founded Pressburg University. His codification of the law in 1486 earned him the name "Matthias the Just."

The art of printing

Marco Polo's diaries, published at the end of the thirteenth century, were the first Western texts to note the existence of printed paper currency in China. At the time, the technique of printing was unknown in Europe. A century later, woodblocks were being used to reproduce playing cards and portraits of saints in Venice and in the Low Countries. The decisive step in the development of printing came with the invention of movable type around 1454. That discovery is generally attributed to John Gutenburg (c. 1400–68), a goldsmith.

The first Italian press was set up at Subiaco in 1466. By that time William Caxton, an English textile merchant who resided in Bruges and translated French romances as a hobby, had become fascinated by the new art. In 1477 he shipped a press home to England and set it up at Westminster. The first book that Caxton printed in England was *The Dictes and Sayengs of the Philosophers*, the first copy of which he presented to Edward IV.

Caxton presents a book to Edward VI.

Landfall at San Salvador

The patent from Spain's Catholic Kings gave the Genoese sea captain the mission to "discover and acquire islands and mainland in the Ocean Sea." When he set out across the unknown Atlantic, Christopher Columbus was seeking to establish the western route to Japan and China—the Cipangu and Cathay of Marco Polo's tales. Most men recognized that the earth was round; from various sources one could calculate the distance to Japan as only 3,000 miles (it is actually 10,000 miles); and no one—least of all Columbus—suspected the presence of an intervening continent. Thus, the historic landfall of October, 1492, was not immediately recognized as the great discovery it was—and Columbus died believing he had reached the Orient. Columbus' error was soon detected, of course, and the impact of Europe on America—and America on Europe—was profound and enduring.

A ship, thought to be Columbus' *Santa Maria*.

Opposite Christopher Columbus, the discoverer of America.

According to popular myth and many textbooks, Christopher Columbus, a Genoese in the service of the Spanish court, sailed with three ships from the River Odiel, crossed the Atlantic, and discovered America in 1492. In truth, Columbus' voyage revealed to contemporary Europe the existence of islands and a continent that were already inhabited—and had been for many centuries by peoples who had crossed the Pacific.

Of the people who first migrated to the Americas from Asia by crossing the Bering Strait, we know next to nothing. They were, no doubt, primitive hunters and gatherers who carried very little in the way of cultural baggage with them. They almost certainly developed their characteristic cultures independently in the Americas. They may, conceivably, have been reinforced by subsequent transpacific migrations, but there is no real evidence.

Thus, Columbus was not the first man to land in the Americas. In fact, he was not even the first European commander to land in the Americas: Icelanders and Greenlanders preceded him by nearly five hundred years, and it is possible that fishermen from English west-country ports, fishing off Newfoundland, may have sighted land before 1492. Columbus, then, did not discover a new world; he established contact between two worlds, both already old.

The significance of historical events, nevertheless, must be measured by their consequences. The discoveries of the Norsemen were all but forgotten by 1492, and those of the Bristol fishermen, genuine or not, got no publicity; but all Europe heard about Columbus. He made his voyage at a time when recently developed ships and navigating instruments made it possible to maintain contact with the discovered lands. His expedition was the first transatlantic voyage to have immediate, significant and permanent results; from that time, people, plants and animals flowed in a steady stream from the world of Europe to the world of America. Christopher

Columbus—not Leif the Lucky or some nameless fisherman from Bristol—made the voyage that brought the Americas firmly within the range of European action.

The precise objects of Columbus' first voyage have never been satisfactorily resolved. By the terms of his agreement with the Spanish monarchs, Columbus was to "discover and acquire islands and mainland in the Ocean Sea." This standard formula would obviously include the legendary island of Atlantis or Antilla, if such a place existed; but the phrase "islands and mainland" was almost certainly also understood to mean Cipangu and Cathay, the names by which Marco Polo had described Japan and North China some two centuries earlier.

In theory, at least, there was nothing fantastic about a proposal to reach eastern Asia by sailing west. Men recognized that the earth was round, and no one suspected an intervening continent; getting to Asia was a matter of winds, of currents and above all of distance. Could a ship, her crew and the stores she carried endure so far? Columbus apparently thought they could. What he proposed to do if he actually reached Cathay, he never explained. His ships were almost unarmed, carried few trade goods and no presents for princes. He bore a letter for the "Great Khan", but once Columbus arrived in what he believed to be the general neighborhood of Cathay, he made no serious attempt to find and enter its harbors. Instead, he wandered among the islands looking for gold and eventually, having lost his flagship, set sail for home.

Columbus returned to Spain in 1493, convinced that he had found outlying islands in the archipelago of which Japan was supposed to form a part—and such an archipelago is indicated on the German cartographer Martin Behaim's 1492 globe. Columbus supported his contention by combining Marco Polo's estimate of the east-west extent of Asia—which was an overestimate—and Polo's

Insula hyspana

Woodcut of Columbus' landing on what he thought was the coast of Cathay.

A practicable western sea route to Asia not only promised an immensely valuable trade in silk and spices—it also evoked a wide range of cherished dreams.

Was Columbus to be believed? The King of Portugal and his advisers, who knew more about exploration than most people, apparently thought not. Had they believed Columbus, they could have made more diplomatic fuss than they did. They were already deeply committed to an attempt to reach India by the route around Africa, and so therefore had strong motives for discrediting Columbus. On the other hand, they also wanted to keep the Spaniards out of the eastern Atlantic, and were delighted to see them pursuing chimeras to the west. The Portuguese therefore kept their own counsel; they laid half-hearted claims to Columbus' discoveries, but made no trouble.

Columbus' arguments were not entirely implausible; they were supported by—or, with a little ingenuity, could be reconciled with—respectable and respected authorities. Columbus himself was a self-taught and extremely persuasive geographical theorist, a capable sea commander and a careful, although somewhat old-fashioned, navigator. He had also shown himself to be a hard-headed negotiator—to picture him as an impractical mystic is mere caricature.

Spain's regents, Ferdinand and Isabella, were sufficiently impressed by Columbus and his reports to undertake a considerable outlay in money and diplomatic effort. The Bull of Demarcation of 1493 assured them of papal support, and the Treaty of Tordesillas, signed by Spain and Portugal in 1494, guaranteed Portuguese acquiescence, at a price which—as later appeared—included the renunciation by Spain of both the eastern route to India and all claim to Brazil. Meanwhile, Columbus was sent off again with a powerful fleet and a numerous company to settle Hispaniola and its gold "mines"—and to pursue his search for Cipangu and Cathay.

Thus early, and as a result of Columbus' arguments, there appeared an ambiguity in Spanish colonial policy: were the new "Indies" to be developed as possessions, valuable in themselves—or were they to be treated as ports-of-call in a maritime drive to reach the commercial centres of the East? Columbus' insistence, after his second voyage, that Cuba was actually a promontory of mainland Cathay, deceived no one. Subsequent voyages—by Vespucci, by Columbus himself and by many lesser discoverers—revealed a landlocked Caribbean to the west of Cuba, and a great continental land mass to the south. Nowhere, on islands or mainland coast, were there kingdoms remotely resembling those described by Marco Polo or his fellow Venetian, Niccolo de' Conti.

The new territories had their attractions for settlers, however: free land, abundant labor, gold in the islands and on the Isthmus and pearls off Cumaná. And as the settlements grew, so did the revenue that accrued to the Crown. Maritime expeditions in search of Asia by a westward route, on

report of the distance from Japan to the Asian mainland—1,500 miles, another overestimate—with Ptolemy's estimate of the circumference of the earth, which was an underestimate. Columbus next assumed the length of an equatorial degree of longitude to be 10 per cent shorter than Ptolemy had taught—or 25 per cent shorter than the true figure. By this calculation, the westward journey from Spain to Japan was less than 3,000 nautical miles (the actual great circle distance is 10,000 nautical miles). Thus, according to Columbus' reasoning, Hispaniola and Cuba were near to where Japan ought to be, and the east coast of the mainland of Cathay was within reach. Columbus clung to this belief with passionate insistence to the end of his life.

Long-lived Christian legends—such as those of Prester John and of St. Thomas in India—appealed to those who sought an ideal of Christian perfection, now lost in Europe, that had existed long ago and might be found again, surviving far away.

The Westward search for the Orient

the other hand, were costly in lives and money—and for many years produced nothing but disappointment. There seemed to be no way of sailing round, or breaking through, the vast barrier that men now called "America." Spanish attempts to reach Cathay were consistently disastrous; meanwhile the Portuguese were fighting and trading in all parts of the Orient, and making Lisbon one of the greatest spice markets of Europe.

The events of 1519–21 posed this Asia-American dilemma in clear and unmistakable terms. In 1519 Magellan left Spain on his great voyage around the world, in the course of which he proved that an all-sea western route to Asia was feasible—but long, dangerous and scarcely economic. Magellan's expedition also revealed that the South Pacific was no mere gulf, but an ocean wider than the Atlantic.

In the same year that Magellan established a long-coveted Spanish outpost in the Moluccas, or Spice Island, Cortes set out from Cuba to conquer Mexico. The Aztec empire was unlike any the Spanish had encountered in the New World, and its immensely greater population, and sophisticated culture and economy made Mexico a prize that was seriously comparable with the kingdoms of the East. The riches of the Aztec nation invited systematic campaigns of conquest instead of random marauding.

Cortes hoped, in the Columbus tradition, to

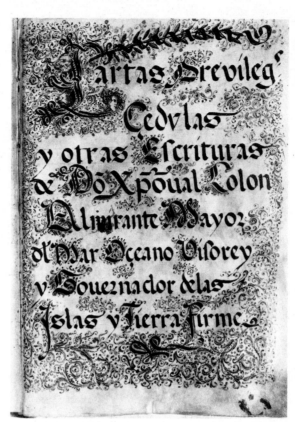

The beginning of the *Book of Privileges* granted to Columbus by Ferdinand and Isabella of Spain, and Columbus' coat-of-arms as Admiral of the Ocean.

Amerigo Vespucci, after whom the American continents are named.

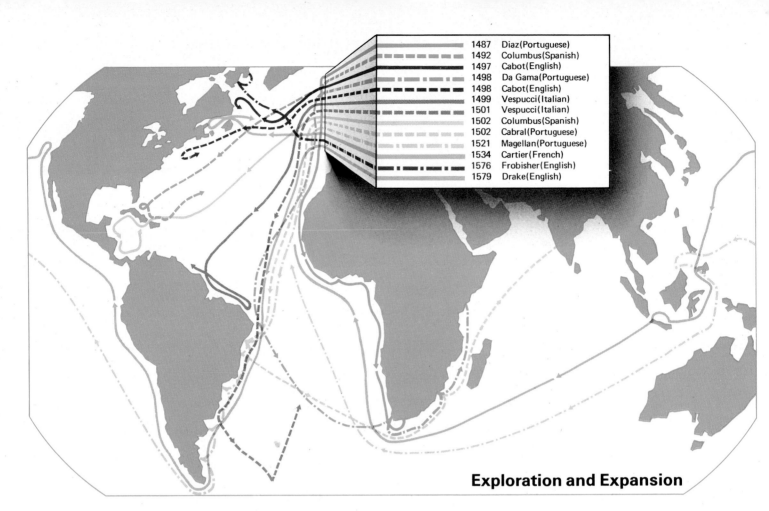

1487	Diaz(Portuguese)
1492	Columbus(Spanish)
1497	Cabot(English)
1498	Da Gama(Portuguese)
1498	Cabot(English)
1499	Vespucci(Italian)
1501	Vespucci(Italian)
1502	Columbus(Spanish)
1502	Cabral(Portuguese)
1521	Magellan(Portuguese)
1534	Cartier(French)
1576	Frobisher(English)
1579	Drake(English)

Exploration and Expansion

A mid-sixteenth-century
Genoese map showing con-
temporary ideas of the world.

pursue the search for Eastern trade, in ships built on the Pacific coast. But in 1527—six years after Cortes delivered Mexico to Spain—Charles v decided to abandon Spain's claims to the Spicery. The distances and the hazards were too great, and the Portuguese were locally too strong. In 1529, by the Treaty of Saragossa, Charles sold out to the Portuguese.

Fresh developments in the "Indies" seemed to confirm the wisdom of his decision. During the 1530s, a second and greater native empire—the Inca, in Peru—was discovered, conquered and laid under tribute. In the 1540s, immensely productive silver veins were found both in Mexico and in Peru. Within a decade, streams of bullion were flowing into Spanish coffers, and the pepper profits of Portugal seemed insignificant by comparison. By mid-

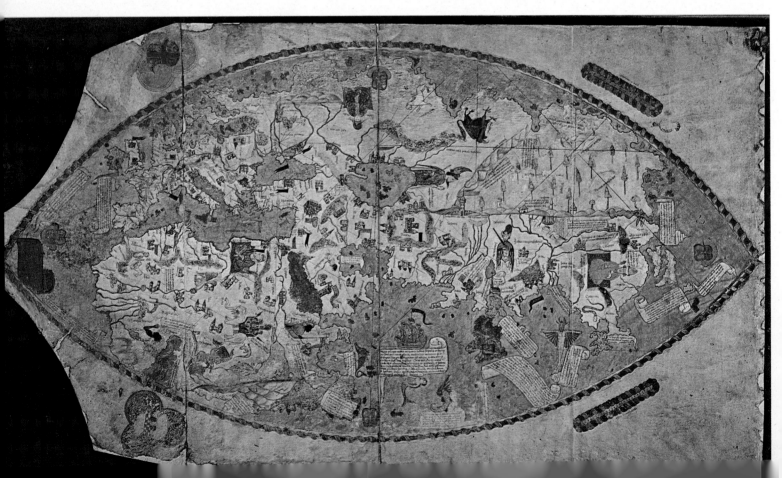

Silver and the search for Eldorado

encircling visions of Columbus and Cortes and other explorers.

In another and more general sense, the stories of the East and West Indies were also connected, for in the course of the seventeenth century, the Portuguese monopoly of European-Asian trade was invaded—and the volume of that trade greatly increased—by Dutch, English, French and other European trading companies. Since few European goods were salable in the East, the companies exported silver to pay for their purchases of spices, silks, calicoes and, later, coffee and tea. Much of this silver came directly or indirectly from America, and the impact of American silver upon the monetary and price systems of western Europe is well known: it made Spain, for a time, the economic envy and commercial terror of Europe. The use of American silver outside Europe is not as well known, and its effect is often overlooked. It is noteworthy, therefore, that throughout much of the seventeenth and all of the eighteenth centuries, Spanish or Mexican *piasters*, or pieces of eight, were the coins most commonly used and most readily accepted in business dealings between Asians and Europeans throughout the Orient. Piasters flowed to the East not only across the Pacific and through Manila, but also across the Atlantic and around Cape Horn, having played their part in European commerce on the way. Without this flow of silver, the successes of the various East

The Holy Roman Emperor, Charles V, whose economy depended on huge shipments of silver from the New World.

Ferdinand and Isabella, the Catholic Kings of Spain, entering Granada Cathedral.

century, the decision seemed final. Spain's overseas interest was to be concentrated on an empire of territorial dominion, tribute and mineral exploitation in the New World—not on an empire of commercial profit in Asia.

Spain's initial settlements in America had been outposts in the race to reach the East; Spain, in losing the race, gained an empire. Spheres of influence had been delimited, a sensible, strategic withdrawal had been made, and a fair compensation had been received. Yet the interwoven stories of the European colonization of the East and West Indies were not so easily separated. The Treaty of Saragossa, backed by Portuguese pugnacity, kept Spaniards away from the Moluccas, but the Portuguese made no particular protest when Miguel López de Legazpe landed in the Philippines in 1564 and seven years later founded Manila as a Spanish colony. Chinese junks and Portuguese ships from Macao were soon trading there, and Manila became a unique back door to the closed, self-sufficient, xenophobic half-world of late Ming dynasty China, linking a society in which silver was in high demand with one in which it was cheap and plentiful. The Spanish ships that carried silver from Acapulco to Manila returned with silk, porcelain, jewelry and drugs—some for sale in Mexico, some for transshipment to Peru (the source of much of the silver), some for re-export to Europe. At its height, the Manila trade equaled in value the official transatlantic trade of Seville. The Manila galleons maintained their hazardous but profitable sailing until 1815—a long-lasting reminder of the world-

Geographical knowledge enlarged

India companies would have been difficult, perhaps impossible. Columbus and Cortes were intuitively right, in ways that they could not have dreamed of—for the exploitation of the New World was a necessary condition of the eastward spread of European trade and influence in the Old.

Silver was not the only New World product that altered the course of Old World history. European settlers used the apparently limitless land of the Americas to raise the products with which they were familiar—sugar, wheat, cattle—and in so doing vastly increased the world's supply of food. At the same time, traders brought native American crop plants to Europe, Africa and Asia, and some of these took root and spread. Potatoes, originally grown in a limited area in the high valleys of the Andes, became an indispensable staple throughout temperate Europe. Maize, which originated in Central America and spread both north and south in the centuries before Columbus' arrival, quickly established itself in southeastern Europe, West and Central Africa, and—perhaps most significantly of all—in China. It was an essential factor in the rapid growth of the Chinese population in the eighteenth century, particularly in inland provinces where rice could not flourish. Even the humble cassava, an insipid staple of the native peoples of northern South America and the Antilles, was carried to West Africa by slavers, where it became the chief food of millions of natives. Thus, the establishment of transatlantic contacts—which in the Americas led to demographic catastrophe and the destruction of whole civilizations—made possible the support of immensely greater populations in Europe, Africa and Asia.

Along with new food crops, Europe acquired new luxuries and new social habits from America. Cacao—chocolate—had been a royal food and drink, a means of exchange, and the basis for social ritual in ancient Mexico. In seventeenth-century Europe, it became a fashionable fad, and Venezuelan planters made fortunes growing cacao beans in the eighteenth century for the European market.

Tobacco too had a profound impact on the Old World. An indigenous American plant, it was used by the natives in almost all the known ways—powdered as snuff, infused, and smoked in pipes, cigars, and cornhusk cigarettes. It made the circuit of the world within a century of Columbus' landfall, and aroused choruses of curiosity, enthusiasm or indignation wherever its use became prevalent. Vice or solace, drug or poison, it has probably made more men's fortunes than all the silver of the Indies.

The impact of all this upon the economic fortunes of Europe can hardly be exaggerated. It began to be felt within a few years of Columbus' first voyage. Moreover, the impact of discovery was not only economic, but intellectual and imaginative as well. In the space of a hundred years, European seamen achieved an enlargement of geographical knowledge that was unparalleled in its extent and in the speed of its discovery.

In addition, those explorers had encountered curious animals, unfamiliar plants, and strange natural phenomena in such variety that the purveyors of fabulous tales were suddenly unable to compete with the truthful narratives of sober adventurers. The knowledge they brought home, which was subsequently spread by the new device of printing, affected every aspect of European life and thought. Geographical exploration is the most empirical of all forms of scientific inquiry, the most dependent upon eyewitness experience. Practical navigators put the theories of revered authorities in cosmography to the test, and often proved them wrong. Inevitably, men of inquiring mind were encouraged to question, by observation and experiment, accepted authorities in other fields of knowledge. Unknown lands, and the social behavior of their supposedly simple inhabitants, caught the imagination of philosophers, poets and painters.

This new appreciation of the number and diversity of human societies led Europeans to look with fresh and critical eyes at their own society and institutions. Slowly, hesitantly, the idea grew in the minds of a few outstanding men, that there might be a new realm of learning and understanding beyond the horizon of the classics, ancient philosophy and the teachings of revealed religion. Magellan, contemplating the immensity of unknown oceans, prepared the way for Kepler, to whom the round earth itself was "of a most insignificant smallness, and a swift wanderer among the stars." J. H. PARRY

Cardinal Cisneros lands in Africa; the conquest of the New World and North Africa was seen in religious terms.

The thirty years between Columbus' discovery of America and Magellan's voyage around the globe were crowded with the achievements of other navigators. Columbus himself made three additional voyages, in the course of which he established a colony on Hispaniola and discovered Cuba, Puerto Rico, Jamaica and Trinidad. John Cabot, a Genoese living in England, persuaded Henry VII that he was capable of reaching "the Island of Brazil," and in 1497 he sailed westward under royal instructions "to discover and settle new lands across the Atlantic." Cabot's voyage was made in defiance of Pope Alexander's Bull of 1493, which reserved the new continents for Spain and Portugal. The intrepid Genoese reached Cape Breton Island and sailed south along the coast of Newfoundland. Cabot was convinced that he had found "the land of the Great Khan," but English commercial interest in Cabot's ventures faded as soon as it became clear that there was no spice trade in the region.

The Portuguese were more successful. Bartholomew Diaz rounded the Cape of Good Hope in 1487 during a storm which was so severe that Diaz' crew forced him to return immediately to Lisbon. A compatriot, Vasco da Gama, set out ten years later to retrace Diaz' steps and find a sea route to India. He reached Calicut on the Malabar Coast in May, 1498, and thus achieved, within the space of two generations, the ambitious scheme of Prince Henry the Navigator. A year after Vasco da Gama's return, Cabral assembled a fleet and established regular trade with Portugal's newly-discovered outposts. He sailed first to Brazil, where he stayed for ten days, and then made for the Cape of Good Hope and the Indian Ocean. He loaded his thirteen ships with pepper and other spices in Malabar and brought them safely home to Portugal. By 1503—thanks to the new sea route—the price of pepper in Lisbon had dropped to a fifth of what it was in Venice.

Spanish and Portuguese explorers in the New World continued to investigate the coasts, estuaries and islands of Central and South America. In 1501, a Spaniard named Amerigo Vespucci undertook a voyage for the King of Portugal which convinced him that the Brazilian coast was part of a "New World"—and not an outlying portion of Asia. The German geographer Martin Waldseemüller proposed that the new continent should be named "America" after Amerigo Vespucci.

Two other feats round out these years of intensive discovery: on September 26, 1513, Balboa crossed the Isthmus of Panama and sighted the Pacific Ocean, and six years later Magellan circumnavigated the globe—a voyage that took him from Spain to Brazil, down the South American coast to the straits that now bear his name and into the Pacific. Although Magellan was killed in the Philippines, one ship from his fleet continued westward, and reached Spain in 1522.

Central Italy

The monarchs of Europe concentrated their attention on Italy during this era, for the cradle of the Renaissance remained a conglomeration of warring states that were ripe for plunder. The death of Lorenzo the Magnificent in Florence in 1492 removed from the Italian scene the one ruler capable of maintaining peace, and the election of Rodrigo Borgia, Lorenzo's longtime rival, as Pope in that same year virtually ensured that Italy would be plunged

Pope Alexander VI Borgia.

into turmoil. Pope Sixtus IV (d. 1484) had already weakened the papacy's moral authority by promoting his nephews in order to strengthen his territorial power. His successor, Innocent VIII, was a corrupt nonentity, and Cardinal Borgia's election as Alexander VI—achieved through wholesale bribery—opened the most scandalous chapter in papal history.

Alexander VI swiftly established Borgia rule in central Italy by securing sinecures for the seven children born him by a succession of mistresses. His second son, Cesare, became an archbishop at the age of sixteen and a cardinal two years later; his daughter Lucretia changed her husbands as policy dictated.

Poisoning became a standard political weapon as, by sheer ruthlessness, the head of the Church subdued the great houses of Orsini and Colonna in Rome. Moved by the murder of his son, the Duke of Gandia, Alexander appointed a committee of cardinals to plan reforms, beginning with the Curia itself. He soon thought better of the idea and abandoned it.

Living in great splendor at Rome as a secular monarch, the Pope spent a fortune patronizing the arts. Alexander decreed that the year 1500 was to be celebrated as a jubilee year of the Church, and the pilgrims who flocked to Rome—to be fleeced by papal collectors—saw for themselves the level to which the Church had been reduced by the House of Borgia.

Savonarola

The most outspoken critic of Alexander VI was Girolamo Savonarola (1452–98), the prior of San Marco in Florence. In sermon after sermon he denounced the corruption of the papacy, the shortcomings of Medici rule in Florence and the paganism of the Renaissance. When the Florentines banished Piero de' Medici in the aftermath of the French invasion of 1494, they turned to Savonarola. He refused an office in the Christian republic that he devised, but remained its guiding spirit nonetheless. The administration of justice was remodeled and poor-relief introduced.

Savonarola then demanded that the Augean stables of Rome be cleansed: he implored Alexander to call a general council to reform the Church, but his call went unheeded. The prior disobeyed a summons from the Pope and was excommunicated. Alexander persuaded the Signory of Florence to execute Savonarola.

Savonarola by Fra Bartolommeo.

Machiavelli

Niccolo Machiavelli (1469–1527), a Florentine who rose to become chief secretary of the republic, was led by his experiences in Renaissance politics to write *The Prince*, a manual of statecraft. Diplomatic missions had brought him into contact with Cesare Borgia, tyrant of the Romagna. Machiavelli admired Borgia's political realism without qualification—and indeed it is Cesare who is the hero of the

Bronzino's portrait of Machiavelli.

Florentine's book. *The Prince* taught rulers the means of maintaining themselves in power.

France invades Italy

After 1494, war became the norm on the Italian peninsula. Piero de' Medici, who had succeeded Lorenzo the Magnificent in Florence, signed a secret treaty with Ferdinand of Naples in 1492. The signatories planned to despoil Milan, which was ruled by Lodovico Sforza, and Sforza in self-defense invited Charles VIII of France to press his own claims to Naples. After Ferdinand's death in January, 1494, Charles prepared for war. Charles invaded Italy, marched on Florence and Rome and, in February, 1495, entered Naples.

Louis XII continues the Italian Wars

Upon Charles' death in 1498, his cousin the Duke of Orleans—last of the direct line of the House of Valois—succeeded him as Louis XII. After safeguarding his position within France by marrying Charles' widow, Anne of Brittany (thereby securing the duchy of Brittany for the Crown), Louis launched a second invasion of Italy. He laid claim to Milan as the grandson of Valentin Visconti, and with Spanish

hom all knowledge was his province

help he succeeded in driving Lodovico Sforza out of Milan in September, 1499. Lodovico briefly regained the duchy with the aid of Swiss and German mercenaries, but he was soon captured and taken to France as Louis' prisoner.

Louis XII next made a treaty with Ferdinand of Aragon for the partition of Naples, but the allies subsequently fell out over the division of the spoils, and Spain regained control of Naples in 1504. For another half-century the Italian peninsula remained a battleground of the great powers.

Ludovico Sforza by Leonardo.

Leonardo da Vinci

Leonardo da Vinci was perhaps the most characteristic of the giants of the Renaissance—a "universal man" who took all knowledge as his province. He combined superb artistic skill as a painter and sculptor with remarkable scientific insight—to a degree that no single man had ever achieved. Born at Vinci in the Arno Valley in 1452, he joined the artists' guild of St. Luke in Florence and trained under Verrocchio before moving to Milan, where his many-sided genius developed under

The Recyell of the Historie of Troye, Bruges 1474.

the patronage of Lodovico Sforza. Leonardo made elaborate drawings for a bronze equestrian monument to Francesco Sforza, Lodovico's father, during this period. His project never advanced beyond the clay model stage.

After completing the *Virgin of the Rocks*, Leonardo painted the *Last Supper* on a wall of the refectory of the Convent of Santa Maria della Grazie at Milan. Working on the plaster in oil instead of fresco, Leonardo created an entirely original painting that became, for Christians the world over, the standard representation of Christ with his disciples. When Louis XII saw the finished work in 1499, he was so moved by it that he asked whether it could be removed from the wall and transported to France.

Throughout these years Leonardo filled his notebooks with meticulous drawings that showed his power as a creative thinker. Those sketches exemplified his acute observations of nature, his inventive genius and the extraordinary range of his interests. He drew daring flying machines, a helicopter which he developed from his studies of birds in flight, armored fighting vehicles and a submarine. He studied anatomy and optics and the formation of rocks, and his head was full of ideas

Leonardo's study for the Sforza monument.

for constructing irrigation works and fortifications. In his paintings he put into practice his theories of perspective, light and shade that he had worked out in his journals.

For most of Leonardo's active life, Italy was the cockpit of war. Leonardo spent a season with Cesare Borgia in the Romagna as a military engineer, and in 1507 he was appointed painter and engineer-in-ordinary to the King of France. He ultimately settled in France.

Revival of classical scholarship

New printing presses were being opened each year in Italy, Germany, France, the Netherlands and England—and the most notable among them was the Aldine Press, established in Venice by Teobaldo Manuci. Before 1493 there were scarcely any Greek texts in print, other than Homer's ever-popular epics. Manuci therefore gathered together a band of distinguished scholars—his "Academy"—to advise him on the choice of texts and to edit them. Before he died in 1515, Manuci produced editions of twenty-eight Greek and Latin classics, notably the works of Aristotle in 1495 and the writings of Plato in 1513. His editions made the philosophy of ancient Greece available for the first time to Western scholars. After 1498 Manuci also printed octavo editions of the classics.

The revival of classical scholarship spread far beyond Italy. New universities sprang up at Aberdeen and Wittenberg, while Jesus, Christ's and St. John's colleges were established at Cambridge. Erasmus became Professor of Greek at Cambridge in 1511, and Lady Margaret Beaufort, the mother of Henry VII, founded professorships of divinity at Oxford that same year. In London the Humanist Dean Colet founded St. Paul's School and in Edinburgh the Scottish Parliament made schooling from the age of eight compulsory for the sons of "substantial householders."

Tudor power consolidated

Serious challenges to Henry VII's title were ended with the routing of the Yorkist supporters of the pretender Perkin Warbeck in 1497. The Tudor King consolidated his power by marrying his eldest son, Arthur to Catherine of Aragon and his daughters to the kings of Scotland and France. Two of those marriages had far-reaching effects: Margaret's marriage to James IV of Scotland in 1502 led to the eventual union of the two countries. And upon Arthur's sudden death, his brother Henry, new heir to the throne, was obliged to marry Catherine.

Maximilian strengthens the House of Hapsburg

Under the Emperor Maximilian I (1493–1518), the House of Hapsburg strengthened its hold on Germany by reforming imperial administration and extended its power in Europe through a series of dynastic marriages. In 1495, at the Diet of Worms, Maximilian abolished private warfare in the 240 principalities that comprised his Empire.

Through his marriage to the daughter of Charles the Bold of Burgundy, Maximilian acquired the Netherlands and the key city of Antwerp, and in 1496 he married his only son, Philip the Handsome, to Joanna of Castile. After the death of Isabella, Queen of Castile, in 1506, Philip and Joanna traveled to Valladolid to claim Castile from Ferdinand of Aragon.

Papacy defeats France

The renewal of the papacy owed much to Julius II (1503–13). As a soldier, he led an army against Perugia in 1506 and, with French aid, conquered Bologna. As a diplomat, he joined the League of Cambray, which had been organized for the express purpose of dismembering Venice and her holdings. With the French victory at Agnadello in 1509, Julius gained Rimini and Ravenna. He then sided with the Holy League to expel the French from Italy. The French recaptured Bologna in 1511 and destroyed Michelangelo's statue of Julius, but a year later Milan surrendered to the League and the Pope was called "Deliverer of Italy."

Frescoes for Pope Julius

*Insisting that he was a sculptor, not a painter, Michelangelo Buonarroti reluctantly mounted
the scaffolding that his assistants had erected inside the Sistine Chapel and began the task of
covering more than one thousand square yards of plaster with frescoes. For more than three years,
from late in 1508 until 1512, Michelangelo labored under the Sistine's vaulted roof.
Working almost singlehandedly, he covered the vast ceiling with some three hundred Biblical
figures. The task was a staggering one, and took its toll: in a letter to a friend, Michelangelo
complained in verse that "the brush endlessly dripping onto my face has coated it with a
multi-colored paving." When he finished, the Florentine was, by his own description,
"bent as a Syrian bow"—but his masterwork was lauded as a triumph of Renaissance art.*

A portrait of Michelangelo
by Jacopino del Conte.

Opposite Adam and Eve are
dismissed from the Garden
of Eden after eating of the
fruit of the Tree of
Knowledge of Good and
Evil, one of Michelangelo's
paintings from the
Sistine Chapel.

When he yielded to Pope Julius II's insistent pleas
and returned to Rome in 1508 to paint the frescoes
on the vaulted ceiling of the Sistine Chapel, Michelangelo Buonarroti was accepting a unique and
hazardous artistic challenge. The thirty-three-year-
old Florentine was already recognized as the foremost sculptor of the age. His *Pietà* had been on
display in St. Peter's in Rome for nearly a decade
and his colossal *David* had dominated a central
square in Michelangelo's native Florence for four
years. And although he had worked on a number of
paintings—including the *Doni Tondo* (the Holy
Family) and the *Battle of Cascina*—Michelangelo had
always preferred sculpture to painting. (Months
later, when he was totally absorbed with his work
in the Sistine Chapel, the artist complained "I am
neither working in a pleasant environment, nor am
I a painter").

After resolving a longstanding quarrel with
Julius, Michelangelo returned to Rome in the spring
of 1508. At that time the sculptor still hoped to be
given permission to start work on the gigantic
mausoleum that he and the Pope had planned several
years earlier. Michelangelo intended to ornament
Julius' tomb with a series of powerful figures—slaves,
victories and prophets—and he had already begun
work on several of those statues. But now the Pope
had another scheme in mind; he wanted Michelangelo to paint the vaulted Vatican chapel named
for Pope Sixtus IV. That ambitious project had
been suggested to Julius by the treacherous Bramante, the architect in charge of the reconstruction
of St. Peter's.

Bramante disliked Florentines in general and he
was particularly jealous of Michelangelo. The
latter's return to Rome acutely displeased the
architect, and he did his best to provoke another
quarrel between Michelangelo and the Pope by
persuading Julius to ask the Florentine to paint the
Sistine ceiling. The cunning architect suspected that
Michelangelo would refuse, and he knew that the
sculptor's refusal would exacerbate the already

precarious truce between the two men. If, on the
other hand, Michelangelo accepted the commission,
Bramante felt sure that he would botch it, since the
project was alien to the sculptor's temperament.
Such a failure would almost certainly force the
Florentine artist to leave Rome—and Bramante had
already arranged to have his friend and distant relation, Raphael, take over the work on the Sistine
Chapel.

The professional risk that Michelangelo was
taking in accepting Julius' offer was compounded by
the fact that Raphael was just beginning to paint a
series of frescoes in a number of smaller rooms in the
Vatican. It was inevitable that the Florentine's
Sistine frescoes would be compared with Raphael's
stanze. Moreover, his work would have to compete
with the scenes from the life of Moses and Christ—
painted by the finest fresco artists of the *Quattrocento*—that already decorated the walls of the Sistine
Chapel and were much admired.

Michelangelo had every reason to refuse the commission; instead, he accepted Julius' offer with
apparent relish—and immediately set about com-
plicating his task. He discarded the Pope's rather
unpretentious plan to add the twelve apostles to the
arch-stones of the vault while decorating the central
section with grotesques, and he obtained Julius' permission to replace it with a far more ambitious composition consisting of three superimposed schemes.
That revised design called for a series of panels
depicting the Biblical story of *Genesis*. To them,
Michelangelo planned to add portraits of Christ's
blood ancestors, and the prophets and the sibyls who
announced his coming on Earth. The third element
of Michelangelo's composition was to be a series of
Ignudi (nude youths), whose function was to provide
a dynamic link between the Biblical scenes and the
intermediate panels.

Not surprisingly, Michelangelo soon found himself faced with several significant problems. He arranged to have a number of his students come south
from Florence to assist him, but he soon realized

The Temptations of Jesus: one of Botticelli's paintings in the Sistine Chapel.

A detail from Perugino's Baptism of Christ from the Sistine Chapel.

that they were not equal to the task. He sent some of them back to Florence and employed the others at menial tasks, while undertaking most of the painting himself. In addition, the already overtaxed artist was obliged to contend with the Pope's impatience to see the work finished and to deal with the ambitions of Raphael, who longed to take Michelangelo's place. Moreover, he ran into technical trouble, particularly with mildew. These dilemmas were minor ones, however; the artist's greatest problem was that he had to paint three hundred figures and roughly one thousand square yards of plastered surface while lying curled up under the ceiling. Michelangelo described the curious torture that he endured while carrying out his task in a poem to a friend:

> My stomach is thrust towards my chin,
> My beard curls up towards the sky,
> My head leans right over onto my back,
> My chest is like that of an old shrew,
> The brush endlessly dripping onto my face
> Has coated it with a multi-colored paving.
> My loins have retreated into my body,
> And my buttocks act as a counter-weight.
> I tread blindly without being able to see my feet,
> My skin stretches out in front of me
> And shrinks in folds behind.
> I am as bent as a Syrian bow.

Apart from anything else, Michelangelo's feat was one of sheer physical endurance. The Florentine began work on his frescoes at the end of 1508 or the beginning of 1509, and did not finish them until November of 1512.

Michelangelo's frank and generous character led him to adopt a totally different approach to fresco painting from that taken by his predecessors, who had sought to camouflage the shape and mass of the vaults they were painting. In contrast, Michelangelo deliberately emphasized the massive appearance of his figures by framing them with painted *trompe-l'oeil* architecture. Within those monumental structures, the artist created a vast, interlocking masterwork that so overwhelmed the other fine murals decorating the walls of the Chapel that they were completely forgotten.

The natural manner in which the human figures were portrayed, the high quality of the drawing, the use of perspective and the outstanding combination of coherence and movement embodied in Michelangelo's Sistine frescoes so enchanted contemporary critics that for centuries observers failed to realize that Michelangelo had shown himself to be a very fine colorist as well. Unfortunately, subsequent restorations—undertaken in 1565, 1625, 1710, 1903–5 and again in 1935–36—have dimmed the freshness of the original frescoes. During the eighteenth century, the panels were varnished with glue in a well-intentioned attempt at restoration that deadened the frescoes' colors. The accumulation of dust, the infiltration of water and the smoke from wax candles have also contributed to the ceiling's deterioration—to the extent that today they are darkened and cracked. Nevertheless, a careful

St. Peter's Montorio, Rome, designed by Bramante.

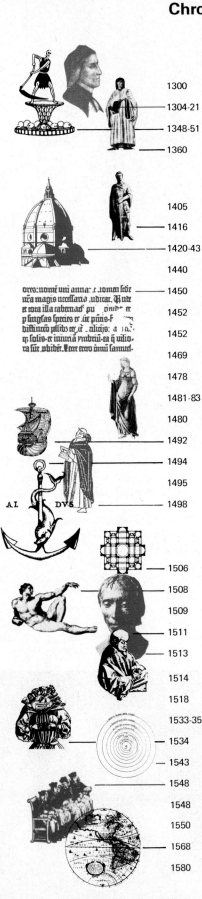

Chronology of the Renaissance

1300	Giotto working in Assisi
1304-21	Dante Alighieri publishes *Divine Comedy*
1348-51	Black Death devastates Europe
1360	Boccaccio publishes *Decameron*
1405	Aretino translates Plato
1416	Donatello casts statue of St. George
1420-43	Brunelleschi builds cupola of Florence Cathedral
1440	Nicholas of Cusa publishes *On Learned Ignorance*
1450	Gutenburg perfects moveable type
1452	Piero della Francesca paints murals at Arezzo
1452	Alberti publishes *On Architecture*
1469	Lorenzo di Medici becomes ruler of Florence
1478	Botticelli paints *Primavera*
1481-83	Leonardo paints *Virgin on the Rocks*
1480	Beginning of Spanish Inquisition
1492	Columbus discovers America
1494	Aldus Manuci prints first pocket books
1495	Leonardo paints *Last Supper*
1498	Execution of Savonarola
1506	Bramante begins to rebuild St. Peter's
1508	Michelangelo paints ceiling of Sistine Chapel
1509	Raphael paints frescoes in Vatican
1511	Erasmus publishes *In Praise of Folly*
1513	Machiavelli publishes *The Prince*
1514	Castiglione writes *The Book of the Courtier*
1518	Titian paints *The Assumption of the Virgin*
1533-35	Rabelais publishes *Gargantua* and *Pantagruel*
1534	Luther publishes German Bible
1543	Copernicus' book on Astronomy
1548	Council of Trent begins
1548	Tintoretto paints *The Miracle of the Slave*
1550	Vasari publishes *Lives of Painters*
1568	Mercator's world projection
1580	Montaigne publishes *Essais*

The *Pietà*. Michelangelo preferred sculpture to painting, and was reluctant to paint the Sistine Chapel for Pope Julius.

Medal of Pico della Mirandola, expressing the philosophy of love in the words "Beauty, Love and Pleasure."

examination of the Chapel ceiling reveals richly orchestrated colors that are a far cry from the stony, monotonous palette so often attributed to Michelangelo.

From the beginning, Michelangelo was faced with an esthetic and theological dilemma that was as great as any of his technical quandaries: his frescoes clearly had to relate both in theme and order to the two series on the lateral walls. Those works, painted by the great artists of the *Quattrocento*, represented the history of humanity *sub lege* (that is, under the law of Moses) and *sub gratia* (during the life of Christ). Michelangelo decided, therefore, to concentrate mainly on the history of the world *ante legem* (before Moses received the Ten Commandments)—and he filled the center of the vault with nine great Biblical scenes. To illustrate the announcement of the coming of Christ through the ages Michelangelo added the ancestors of Jesus, starting with Abraham, and the soothsayers.

Michelangelo also had to take into consideration the fact that his predecessors, in accordance with an ancient Christian tradition, had started painting their frescoes from the altar and worked their way toward the main door. Consequently, the same chronological order had to be preserved in the ceiling

Love, Sacred and Profane by Titian.

400

The Fall of Man and Neoplatonism

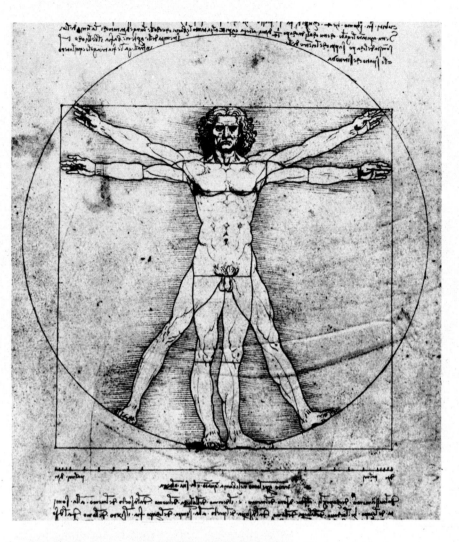

frescoes, which began with a scene depicting the first day of Creation (*God Dividing the Light from the Darkness*), painted above the altar, and ended with the *Drunkenness of Noah* at the far end of the Chapel.

That constant reference to the Scriptures lent a strong Christian flavor and religious fervor to the Sistine frescoes, one that is not apparent in Michelangelo's earlier works. The Christ of the St. Peter's *Pietà*, for example, is depicted as a kind of Apollo put to death, while the *David* looks more like a beautiful Greek youth than the ancestor of Jesus. The naked fauns lurking behind the Holy Family in the *Doni Tondo*, like the figures in the *Battle of the Centaurs*, Michelangelo's first work, reveal the esthetic and artistic influence of the Greeks and Romans—not the Bible—upon Michelangelo's early work. The paintings on the ceiling of the Sistine Chapel, on the other hand, are grounded in the concept of Original Sin and represent an impassioned call to the Redeemer.

The theme of the Fall of Man was not a uniquely Christian one, however, and Michelangelo's fervor may have been aroused as much by his Neoplatonic background as by his heightened Christian awareness. Indeed, Michelangelo spent his formative years in Florence at a time when Neoplatonism was rapidly becoming the favorite philosophy of the

Leonardo da Vinci's Vitruvian Man.

Above left A poem by Michelangelo, with a drawing of himself painting the Sistine Chapel.

The title page of Marsilio Ficino's treatise *On the Immortality of Souls*.

401

Michelangelo's *Universal Guide*, from the Sistine Chapel.

The Delphic Sybil.

The Flood.

intellectuals. He was profoundly influenced by that trend and at least one eminent scholar has called Michelangelo the only Renaissance artist "to adopt Neoplatonism in its entirety, and not just certain aspects of it."

It is, in fact, possible to interpret the Sistine frescoes in Platonic terms, starting from the main door instead of from the altar. According to that interpretation, the first scene to be observed, the *Drunkenness of Noah*, represents the imprisonment of the soul within the body and the fetters of an earthly existence. The next painting, the *Deluge*, symbolizes the despair of humanity enslaved by the passions of a mundane world, and the panel that follows it, the *Sacrifice of Noah*, reveals the moment when the soul first becomes aware of its own existence and tries to communicate with God by offering Him a gift. That awareness of self implies an awareness of sin— which is illustrated in the next painting, the *Fall of Adam and Eve*. When studied in inverse order, the other Biblical scenes on the ceiling—the *Creation of Eve*, the *Creation of Adam*, *God Dividing the Waters*,

The Soul rising to a final state of Grace

the *Creation of the Sun, Moon and the Planets*, and *God Dividing the Light from the Darkness*—illustrate the ascent of the human soul from earthly, material existence to a final state of grace.

Neoplatonism is one of the keys to understanding the apparent paganism of many Renaissance art works, for despite their outer charm and pagan worldliness, most of those works are grounded in ascetism. Indeed, an invitation to ascetism can be found at the core of Platonic philosophy. According to Neoplatonist doctrine, the soul can remember only God and can attain grace only by breaking the chains that bind man to the earth. Ficino's *Theologia platonica*, one of the classic books of the Renaissance, states that "the life of the body is a sickness of the dreaming, tortured soul. All our movements, actions and passions are nothing more than the twisting and turnings of sick people, the nightmares and delirium of the insane." It is essential, the author insists, to banish all temptations produced by the senses. "The desire of the senses, which draws us towards everything that is material, massive, dull and shapeless . . . is not love but merely a pointless, stupid hunger, degrading and hideous." That doctrine, which permeated the whole of the Renaissance, rejects all sensual pleasure but glorifies earthly beauty, which is seen as the first step up the "miraculous ladder" that ascends to God. Thus, Michelangelo's *Ignudi*, which created something or a stir when the Sistine ceiling was unveiled on August 14, 1511—and which led to the aforementioned accusations of paganism—were in fact symbols of truth and purity. (Michelangelo also expressed the Neoplatonic creed in one of his poems. "My eyes which are in love with beauty and my soul which is in love with salvation," he wrote, "can only ascend to heaven by the contemplation of all the beauty surrounding me.")

It is vitally important to appreciate the degree to which the Renaissance evolved its own philosophy of art—for if the Renaissance had not developed its uniquely "religious" and fundamentally optimistic conception of beauty, many superb works of art might never have been produced. Neoplatonism equated beauty and goodness with godliness. Its disciples maintained with absolute assurance that beauty was the "flower of goodness," and that it was through beauty that goodness was revealed to us. "We would not know the meaning of goodness," wrote Ficino, "nor would we seek it, since it is so well concealed, if we were not guided to it by the signs and marks of beauty and of love which accompanies it." Some fifty years later, in 1528, Castiglione took up the same theme in the *Cortigiano*:

It is very rare for an evil soul to inhabit a beautiful body. For outer beauty is the true sign of inner goodness . . . Beauty and goodness are more or less the same thing. This particularly applies to the beauty of the human body, whose main function, it seems to me, is to reflect the beauty of the soul. The latter, aware of the true beauty, which is that of God, glorifies and beautifies everything it touches.

In the light of these—and other—fervent declarations, it is not surprising that the Renaissance produced such poetic wealth and artistic originality. Or that Michelangelo produced such exuberant, inspiring, and fundamentally Christian frescoes for the ceiling of Julius' renovated Chapel.

JEAN DELUMEAU

The Creation of Man.

One of the *ignudi*, used for decoration at the corners of the main pictures.

Leo X, son of Lorenzo the Magnificent, by Raphael.

Pope Julius II envisioned Rome as the artistic capital of the world, but it was his successor, Leo X (1513–21), son of Lorenzo the Magnificent of Florence, who achieved Julius' vision. In doing so, Leo faced stiff competition from Europe's secular princes: Isabella D'Este of Mantua invited "the best painters in Italy" to decorate her palace, Francis I enticed Leonardo da Vinci to France and the Emperor Charles V appointed the Venetian, Titian, as his court painter.

Raphael, who was a generation younger than Leonardo and eight years younger than Michelangelo, received numerous papal commissions and rapidly became the leading exponent of the High Renaissance. While Michelangelo was completing the ceiling of the Sistine Chapel, Raphael was working on the frescoes in the Stanza della Segnatura at the Vatican and painting the *Sistine Madonna*.

A very different exemplar of High Italian culture was Ariosto's *Orlando Furioso*, which was published in 1516 after a dozen years of steady composition. That poetic romance, which dealt with the epic struggles of the Christians and the Saracens, had two secondary themes: Orlando's madness and his eventual cure, and the love between Ruggero and Badamante.

Three young kings

In England, France, Spain and Germany the old guard was changing, and the European scene was soon dominated by three youthful kings. Henry VIII succeeded his father in 1509 at the age of eighteen, and six years later the nineteen-year-old Duke of Angouleme

became Francis I of France. Charles of Ghent inherited the throne of a united Spain in 1516 when his grandfather Ferdinand I died, and in 1519 he succeeded his paternal grandfather, Maximilian I, as Holy Roman Emperor. Personal rivalries between these three young monarchs—each of whom looked upon himself as the embodiment of Renaissance chivalry—and the relations of each to the papacy were to dominate European politics for thirty years.

England joins the Holy League

Henry VIII entered Euorpean politics in 1511 when he joined Pope Julius' Holy League to drive the French out of Italy. The Royal Navy, reformed and consolidated at Henry's express wish, commanded the English Channel during this

Francis I of France by Clouet: after his victory at Marignano the defeat at Pavia shattered Francis' Italian hopes.

period and frequently put men ashore to burn French coastal villages. In 1513 Henry signed an offensive alliance with Spain that called for the invasion of France. The King led his army out to join the Emperor's troops, but in so doing he missed the only engagement of the short campaign. That clash, known as the Battle of the Spurs, took its name from the hasty retreat of the French cavalry.

Battle of Marignano

In the summer of his accession, Francis I set out for northern Italy with an army of 110,000 men. His immediate objective was to capture the Duchy of Milan, but he expected to subdue all Italy and sweep onward speedily to Constantinople. So he avoided a battle with the

Swiss by not using the orthodox route through the Mont Cenis Pass, marched into Italy and routed the Milanese at Villafranca. A few days later the Swiss infantry attacked Francis' camp at Marignano. They pressured the French relentlessly, but Gian Trivulzio, the French general, maintained his ground and when reinforcements arrived from Venice, the combined forces were able to defeat the Swiss mercenaries. The Battle of Marignano was the end of an epoch in European warfare—until that clash, Swiss troops had been invincible in battle.

One immediate result of Francis' first campaign was the signing of the Concordat of Bologna in 1516. The Concordat entitled Francis to appoint French bishops and abbeys. It freed the French Church from close papal control in return for the payment of annates to Rome—a system called the "Gallican Liberties," which were not abolished until the nineteenth century.

Charles V of Spain succeeds to the Hapsburg dominions

Before his death in January, 1519, Maximilian I readied his grandson, Charles I of Spain, for the Hapsburg succession. Francis I was determined to contest the election, and both Pope Leo X and Henry VIII initially pledged him their support (although the latter later announced that he would stand as a candidate himself). To insure Charles' election, his agents in Germany used vast sums of money—advanced them by the great German bankinghouse, the Fuggers of Augsburg—to influence the imperial electors. At the last moment the Pope abandoned his opposition to Charles and the seven electors—who were uniformly anxious to exclude Francis I from interfering in the Empire—elected Charles in June of 1519. Placing Spain in the care of his old tutor, Adrian of Utrecht, the Emperor-elect departed for the Netherlands—and on October 23, 1520, he was crowned at Aachen.

As the most powerful sovereign in the world, Charles V ruled the Empire, Spain, Sicily, Naples, Sardinia, the Netherlands, the Hapsburg dominions centering around Austria and most of the newly discovered continents across the Atlantic. The tension evoked by the prolonged election contest ultimately led to war, both with the French and within Germany itself.

The Field of the Cloth of Gold

The imperial election campaign postponed the long anticipated meeting between the kings of England and France, each of whom had sworn that he would not shave until he had seen the other. The arrangements for the meeting were in the hands of Thomas Wolsey, who had been both Lord Chancellor of England and a cardinal since 1515. Wolsey, who cast himself in the role of arbiter of Europe, devised the Peace of London, an agreement that he hoped to get England, France, the Empire, Spain and the papacy to sign. The Field of Cloth of Gold was intended as a "summit meeting" between the two kings to guarantee the peace of Europe. By the summer of 1518, 6,000 English workmen were busy preparing King Henry's quarters—including a huge banqueting hall—at Guisnes, and the French were no less active at Ardres. Midway between Guisnes and Ardres was the Val d'Or, the spot selected for the meeting. Pavilions and galleries had been erected nearby, overlooking a tournament ground.

More than 5,000 people accompanied Henry on his Channel crossing and rode with him to Val d'Or. The two kings, supported by the greatest nobles in their realms, rode to opposite edges of the field and then, as trumpets sounded, the sovereigns galloped forward to the appointed place and, still mounted, embraced three times.

Clement VII crowns Charles V as Emperor, by Vasari.

The Field of Cloth of Gold where Henry VIII and Francis I met but could not agree.

Thus opened the Field of Cloth of Gold, a prelude to three weeks of jousting, banquets, dancing and pageantry that ended with a High Mass, celebrated in the open by Wolsey and sung to music especially composed by Robert Fairfax. Many contemporaries considered the program of events the Eighth Wonder of the World, for it enshrined the rebirth of chivalry. Most remarkable of all was the fact that the sovereigns of two countries that had been enemies from time immemorial should at last meet on such cordial terms. At the end of the festivities a treaty was signed that proposed marriage between the infant Mary Tudor and the Dauphin, and ended French interference in Scottish affairs. Both before and immediately after the Field of Cloth of Gold Henry VIII met with Charles V at Dover and Gravelines. There is no evidence to convict the English King of duplicity, however, for Charles found that he could not draw Henry into an alliance with him against France.

Erasmus of Rotterdam

Erasmus of Rotterdam (1466–1536), the greatest Christian Humanist of the age, sought to serve God by advancing knowledge. He had been ordained in 1492, but he soon found monastic life as uncongenial as he was later to find life at court. When he met John Colet at Oxford at the turn of the century, Erasmus promised to devote himself to studying theology. He sought out the best teachers of Greek in Europe and began to prepare for the task of editing the Greek text of the New Testament. Much of this work he undertook while lecturing at Cambridge, and his edition, with full notations, was published in Basel in 1516.

Erasmus profoundly hoped that once theologians had access to accurate editions of the Scriptures, religious contention would cease. Instead his efforts provoked further theological controversy, for his text showed Christendom that the Latin Vulgate was not infallible. It is in this sense that the adage, current in his own life-time, that "Erasmus laid the egg that Luther hatched," rings true. A return to scriptural evangelism spelled trouble for the Church.

Erasmus had not hesitated to ridicule medieval Scholasticism or lampoon popes and prelates in his *In Praise of Folly*, yet his loyalty to the Roman Church was never in question. He regarded Luther as a dangerous prophet and at the end of his life he wrote "I abhor the Evangelicists, because it is through them that literature is everywhere declining." It was as a man of letters, universally admired for his tolerance, wit and prodigious output, that Erasmus towered over his contemporaries. The breadth of his interests and the height of his scholarship are best seen in the great number of surviving letters that he wrote to such fellow Humanists as Sir Thomas More, to kings, popes and to a lively circle of friends. Apart from his editions of the Early Fathers and his work on the Latin New Testament, he produced two volumes of commentaries embodying his liberal philosophy—the *Adages* in 1500 and the *Colloquies* in 1524. Both were "best-sellers" and dominated teaching in schools and universities for a century.

Luther and the Reformation

In 1517 a papal hireling named Johann Tetzel came to Saxony to raise funds for the rebuilding of St. Peter's in Rome by selling papal indulgences. This practice—whereby a subscriber purchased the release of souls from purgatory and bought grace for himself with hard cash—was a time-honored instrument of Church finance. Tetzel, who went about his business with unprecedented effrontery, gravely provoked Martin Luther, and on October 31, 1517, Luther nailed his ninety-five *Theses*, denouncing the sale of indulgences, to the door of the palace church at Wittenberg. His action, the normal way of giving notice of a public disputation, was the beginning of the Continental Reformation that was to tear Germany apart.

Martin Luther (1483–1546) entered the Augustinian monastery of Erfurt at the age of twenty-two, but he soon transferred to Wittenberg to study Scripture. In 1512, while he was lecturing on the Epistle to the Romans, Luther discovered, in St. Paul's teachings, what he considered to be the key to all Christian doctrines: man's salvation by faith in Christ alone. Further consideration of Paul's writings led Luther to deny the sanctity of works. At this stage the monk had no intention of severing ties with the Church.

The posting of Luther's *Theses* brought matters to a head. Tetzel had recently proclaimed that it was through the grace of the indulgence that man was reconciled with God. He insisted that there was no need for repentance, provided a man paid what he could afford, and he assured his listeners that they could even buy the right to sin in the future. The idea that "everything might be done for money" was anathema to Luther, and he responded with the *Theses*. Complaints about his outburst reached Pope Leo X, and the ecclesiastical controversy that the Wittenberg monk stirred up soon expanded to include many more issues than merely the sale of indulgences.

Luther's act coalesced a general sentiment that had been gathering strength in sixteenth-century Europe, and many beliefs fused in the Reformation, which produced different results in each country.

Turkish expansion

Under Sultan Selim I (1512–20), the Turks renewed their westward advance. Following a struggle for the succession, Selim forced his father, Bayazid II, to abdicate and then turned upon his neighbor, the Shah of Persia, who had supported a rival contender for the Turkish throne. In 1514, Selim won a great victory at Chaldiron in the Euphrates Valley. He then overran Anatolia and Kurdistan, and would have penetrated deeper into Asia Minor except for the threat of Kansu, Sultan of Egypt. Selim returned to Syria, where he defeated Kansu through the skillful use of artillery. The towns accepted Selim's rule. But Egypt refused to accept Turkish suzerainty and Selim conquered it.

Moguls in India

One of the most remarkable monarchs of the age was Baber (1483–1530), founder of the Mogul dynasty

Erasmus of Rotterdam, humanist, intellectual and biblical scholar.

in India. At the age of twelve Baber succeeded to the throne of the tiny kingdom of Fergana in the mountains of Turkeshar. In ensuing years, he survived plots, mutinies and defeats in battle by courageous military leadership alone. In 1504 he led his army across the snow-capped Hindu Kush to capture Kabul, the capital of Afghanistan. As hope of regaining his captured kingdom faded, Baber found himself drawn to India, much as his ancestor Timur the Great had been in 1397. After preliminary raids on Lahore, he defeated Ibrahim, Emperor of Delhi at Panipat in 1526. By 1527 Baber was master of north India.

The Conquest of Mexico 1521

Like many a Spanish youth of his generation, Hernando Cortes was stirred by tales of the New World being explored and colonized by his countrymen. At the age of nineteen, he reached the Antilles; fifteen years later he was the wealthy proprietor of several estates in Cuba. But the rumors of fabulously rich kingdoms—always just beyond the next island or over the next mountain—were persistent, and early in 1519 Cortes set out at the head of an expedition to Mexico. By an incredible combination of luck, ingenuity and courage, Cortes and his small force overwhelmed the awesome Aztec empire. Horses and firearms—both unknown to the natives— were the keys to Cortes' success; and this easy triumph of European skill and technology over Indian brute force set the pattern for succeeding generations of conquerors—and foredoomed America's native population.

At the dawn of the sixteenth century, Western civilization stood on the threshold of a new age—an age of discovery and challenge, of bursting frontiers and distant, undreamed-of horizons that has had no parallel until our own day. America had been discovered, but the continent remained virtually unexplored.

The pattern was to change in 1519, with the appearance on those shores of a man of very different stamp from any who had gone before him. His name was Hernando Cortes and in less than three years— through a combination of brilliant leadership, superhuman courage and almost incredible good luck— he was to achieve the downfall of the Mexican empire and of its emperor Montezuma. His story is one of special significance, for it marks the first direct confrontation, in all their power and might, of the Old World and the New.

Cortes, the son of a humble country squire of Estremadura in southern Spain, had left home at the age of sixteen to seek his fortune. Three years later he arrived in Hispaniola. In the years that followed he acquired several large estates in Cuba and became, by local standards, a rich man.

Despite its pleasures, life in Cuba ultimately began to pall, and in 1518, Cortes talked, intrigued and bribed his way into the command of a new expedition to the west. On February 10 of the following year the expedition set sail. It had two main objectives, one material and one spiritual. The material one, as always, was gold—a subject never very far from the minds of the conquistadors. But the spiritual purpose was equally real and even more important; the conquistadors might be despoilers, but they were missionaries as well.

The Spanish commander's resources were small— eleven ships, carrying less than seven hundred men —but he possessed two secret weapons unknown to the American natives: firearms, including several small cannon, and sixteen horses. Cortes used both weapons in his first clash with the mainlanders. In a battle fought near Tabasco in southeastern Mexico, terrified Maya Indians bravely stood their ground against the cannon, but the horses proved too much for them. At the outset they actually imagined horse and rider to be a single animal—some monstrous centaur bearing down upon them—and they soon fled. Cortes, striding over to a nearby tree, struck it a great blow with his sword and claimed the whole territory for Spain. The conquest of Mexico was under way.

The next morning, the Tabascans sent peace emissaries to the Spanish camp bearing rich gifts for their conquerors. Among these gifts was a young native maiden named Marina. This girl, whom Bernal Diaz describes as good-looking and intelligent, was probably the greatest godsend that Cortes ever received—not because she eventually became the conquistador's mistress and the mother of his child, but because she spoke both Mexican and Maya. Cortes already had a Spanish-Maya interpreter, so that from the moment Marina joined him, his language problems were at an end.

Other problems were only just beginning, however. The Spaniards' next landfall, some two hundred miles north of Tabasco, lay within the frontiers of the warlike Aztec empire of Montezuma.

When the Aztecs went to war they did so not to kill but to take prisoners for sacrifice—and they could never take enough. During the four-day consecration of the great temple at Tenochtitlan, no less than 80,000 victims met their deaths on the sacrificial altars. Throughout the carnage, the method of dispatch never varied: the victim's breast was ripped open with an obsidian knife and the still-palpitating heart was torn out and offered to the gods.

Among these gods was one named Quetzalcoatl, the Feathered Serpent. A recounting of his legend reveals a fantastic series of coincidences that makes the history of the conquest sound more like a fairy tale. Long ago—ran the legend—Quetzalcoatl had

Hernando Cortes, the conqueror of Mexico; by N. Medellin.

Opposite Xochipilli, the Aztec god of poetry, music, theater and dancing.

A view from the *Florentine Codex*. In the background an Indian sights the Spanish ships; left, the Spaniards unload supplies; right, questioning an Indian.

Mask of the sun god, Tonatiun.

the Rich Town of the True Cross—thus neatly reflecting the two preoccupations of the Spanish colonial mind—gold and the Gospel.

While preparations were being made for the great march to the interior, another group of Indian emissaries arrived at Vera Cruz. These friendly members of the Totonac tribe invited Cortes and his men to visit their city of Cempoala, twenty-odd miles to the northwest. Explaining that they had recently been conquered by the Aztecs and were presently being crushed by the savage tribute wrung from them by their hated overlords, the Totonacs asked to accompany the Spaniards on their campaign. Cortes accepted their invitation and agreed to take them with him on the condition that they give up their own predilection for human sacrifice and embrace the Cross.

Before setting forth, Cortes made a decision that, for sheer cold-blooded courage, must rank as one of the most remarkable of his life: he bribed a few of his sailors to puncture the hulls of his ships with holes and then, on the pretext that they were worm-eaten and unseaworthy, deliberately run them aground. Henceforth, whatever happened, there could be no retreat.

Thus, in August, 1519, this extraordinary young man set off without maps across an unknown country, against an empire of apparently limitless power, wealth and savagery, never knowing what lay beyond the next hill except that he would probably be encountering armies many times stronger than his and almost certainly hostile. On this trek, Cortes was accompanied by about five hundred Spanish musketeers (a sizable garrison had been left behind at Vera Cruz), thirteen horses, a few pieces of light artillery and perhaps a thousand Totonac irregulars.

Now there was hard fighting in store for them. The people of Tlaxcala, a town located roughly halfway between Vera Cruz and Tenochtitlan, rejected the Spaniards' peace overtures and put up an impassioned and heroic resistance. Only after three weeks and four major battles (in which they suffered immense losses) did the Tlaxcalans admit defeat and allow Cortes into their capital. Then, however, they too offered him their friendship—and proved as good as their word. Henceforth, they became his most trusted allies, and a large number of them accompanied Cortes on the next stage of his journey, which brought him to the holy city of Cholula.

Although the natives offered no overt opposition as the Spaniards entered Cholula, the conquistadors were immediately suspicious. Many of the streets had been barricaded, and piles of stones were visible on the rooftops. Most ominous of all, there were no women or children anywhere. It was the faithful Marina who first discovered the truth: the Cholulans intended to ambush Cortes' entire army the next day and to carry it off to Montezuma for sacrifice. Cortes laid his plans quickly but carefully. Early the following morning he gathered all the Cholulans he could muster within the Spanish stockade. Then, through Marina, he told them that he knew all that was in their hearts—and pronounced sentence. As he

come down to earth in human from, white-skinned and black-bearded; then after twenty years he had sailed away to the east. It was said that he would return one day, dressed in black, to re-establish his rule. His homecoming would occur in a "One-reed Year," and would bring much tribulation and suffering in its train. According to the Aztec calendar, a "One-reed Year" fell only once in every fifty-two of our years. There had been one in 1415, and another in 1467; the next fell in 1519.

Thus, Montezuma had reason to be anxious even before he learned of the coming of Cortes—and when his spies reported sighting a band of mysterious strangers, led by a man with an unusually pale face and a black beard—and dressed in black from head to foot—the emperor's direst suspicions seemed confirmed.

Believing that there was a faint chance that "Quetzalcoatl" might be bribed not to come to the capital, Montezuma sent ambassadors down to the coast with propitiatory gifts. The move was a fatal one. These gifts, every one of which was of gold, convinced Cortes that he was indeed on the threshold of El Dorado; and he resolved to lead the puny force under his command against Montezuma's huge empire. Cortes knew that the authorities in Cuba would never countenance so dangerous an enterprise before he established a secure and independent colony on the mainland. Therefore, on the very spot where he had first received the Aztec ambassadors, the conquistador founded a new Spanish colony. In honor of his Good Friday landing he named the settlement Villa Rica de Vera Cruz—

A Temple "worse than any Spanish slaughterhouse"

did so, Spanish musketeers opened fire from the surrounding rooftops; by Cortes' own admission, more than 3,000 men died in the next two hours. It was a massacre, and he has been bitterly condemned for ordering it. Yet it is difficult to see what else Cortes could have done. He was not normally a bloodthirsty man—never once in the whole campaign did he resort to force unnecessarily.

The journey from Cholula to the capital—a fifty-mile-long march that led the conquistadors up between the twin volcanoes that guard the southeastern approaches to the city and over a pass 12,000 feet high—must have been the most grueling of all. On the other side of the pass, the road began to descend, and the Spaniards suddenly found themselves gazing down on a huge lake that sparkled in the sun. In the midst of that lake, linked to its shores by three slender causeways, was the city of Tenochtitlan.

On November 8, 1519, Hernando Cortes led four hundred tired and bedraggled soldiers along the southern causeway into the Aztec capital. Another, different procession approached from the opposite direction: the emperor himself, in his golden palanquin, was riding out to meet his god. The scene must have been a strange one.

The great Montezuma descended from his litter, and the other great chieftains supported him beneath a marvelously rich canopy of green feathers, decorated with gold, silver and pearls . . . And there were other great lords who walked before the great Montezuma, laying down cloaks so that his feet should not touch the earth. Not one dared to raise his eyes towards him.

Dismounting from his horse, Cortes strode smiling toward the emperor—and now for the first time, the Old World and the New stood face to face.

This first encounter with Montezuma made a deep impression on the Spaniards—as did the emperor's address of welcome, in which he greeted Cortes as a king and a god, spoke of promises and prophecies and seemed virtually to be offering the Spanish leader the throne of Mexico. Despite Montezuma's effusive greeting, Cortes remained on his guard; although he was being treated as an honored guest, he had not forgotten that he was on an island fortress in a distant land, with only a handful of men and no lines of communication to the outside world. He followed Montezuma to a great palace that had been prepared for his reception.

At the age of fifty-two, Montezuma was tall and slim, with fine eyes and, as Bernal Diaz put it, "an expression that was at once tender and grave." In the weeks that followed, the Spaniards grew to love and respect the Aztec ruler, not only for his prodigious generosity but even more for his extraordinary natural grace and charm. Montezuma soon knew the conquistadors by name, and they in turn treated him in a manner befitting his rank. Cortes had, meanwhile, told Montezuma of his own Emperor, Charles v—the sovereign to whom the Aztecs were henceforth obliged to acknowledge their allegiance. They seemed to accept this condition readily enough; it was when the conversation turned

to religion that Montezuma's jaw seemed to tighten. Nonetheless, he willingly agreed to Cortes' request to be allowed to visit the great temple.

That visit was a nightmare that none of the members of Cortes' party ever forgot. "The walls of the shrines," wrote Bernal Diaz, "were so caked with blood, and the floor so bathed in it, that the stench was worse than that of any slaughterhouse in Spain." In the topmost sanctuary, before the idols, lay five human hearts, still warm and steaming; around the altar, their long hair matted with gore, stood the priests who performed the sacrifices and who afterwards ceremonially ate the limbs of their victims.

Montezuma, who seemed unable to comprehend his guests' revulsion, remained gentle and dignified amid those charnel horrors. Cortes saw that however ready the Aztec ruler might be to pay lip-service to the throne of Spain, he had no intention of forsaking his old gods. Somehow his authority would have to be undermined, while the Spaniards' own security was increased. Cortes therefore took a step that, in so precarious a position, few but he would have dared —he made Montezuma his hostage. As Cortes was careful to explain when he broke the news to Montezuma, the emperor was not a prisoner. His "captivity" would amount to nothing more than a change of residence; the day-to-day business of government would still be in the emperor's hands alone.

By the beginning of the year 1520 the conquest of Mexico might have seemed over. But suddenly Cortes' luck changed: the Spanish authorities in Cuba, infuriated by his insubordination and frantic with jealousy at his successes, dispatched a punitive expedition which Cortes destroyed.

Meanwhile, disaster had struck in the capital. In May, during an annual religious festival, Alvarado had suddenly suspected a plot against his garrison. Losing his head, he and his men had charged into the temple precinct, killing every Indian present.

An Aztec priest's knife, with a handle of wood set with mosaic.

Fighting in Tenochtitlán: Spanish cavalry and infantry with their Indian allies attack the temple.

The death of Montezuma

Spanish gunman firing a crude arquebus; from the *Florentine Codex*.

Right A friar describes the ceremonial of the province of Mexico to the Viceroy, De Mendoza, while native priests look on.

The title page of the *Codex Mendoza*.

More than a thousand natives, including the flower of the young Aztec nobility, were slaughtered, and within an hour the whole city was up in arms. Since that time the Spaniards had been blockaded in their palace. Thanks to Montezuma's intervention there had been no further bloodshed—but Montezuma's influence was waning. An opposition party, resolved to rid Mexico of the Spaniards once and for all, had arisen. And on the very evening that Cortes returned to the capital, a specially convened Aztec Council of State had deposed the emperor from his throne and selected his nephew Cuauhtémoc as his successor.

By morning the atmosphere had changed from passive sullenness to active hostility. For four days the Spaniards defended themselves as best they could against incessant Indian attacks, but on the fifth, seeing that the situation was hopeless, Cortes sent to Montezuma and asked him to negotiate a truce. The Spanish envoy found the ex-emperor sunk in despair. There was nothing he could do, he claimed—his friendship for Cortes had cost him his crown, and his people would no longer listen to him. He agreed to make one final effort, however, and for the last time he donned his robes of state and stepped out onto the terrace above the great square.

As Montezuma emerged, the howling mob below fell silent in a spontaneous surge of sympathy for the deposed monarch. Then, suddenly, a volley of stones was launched at the emperor. One of them struck Montezuma on the head, and he fell to the ground. The Spaniards carried him to his quarters, and Cortes himself hastened to the battered ruler's side. The wound did not seem particularly grave, but Montezuma had apparently lost the will to live. By nightfall he was dead.

Montezuma had been a noble and a tragic figure. He had foreseen, in a way that Cortes had not, that the fall of his empire was to be inevitable and total. Although mistaken in his belief that Cortes was a god, Montezuma could no more have prevented the conquest than if it had been divinely ordained.

His friendship with Cortes—for whose sake he ultimately gave both his throne and his life—was founded not on cowardice but on wisdom, for he had understood that violence could not prevail. Little more than a year after his death, Montezuma's premonitions were to be proved correct.

Cortes' last hope of remaining in the city perished with Montezuma. He knew that he must retreat—and fast. That night, when the crowds had dispersed, he and his soldiers slipped silently from their quarters and began their march along the western causeway (which was shorter than the southern one, and promised to be less well guarded). The Aztecs had not been deceived, however. The silence was suddenly shattered by the blast of a conch-shell trumpet. Suddenly the waters on each side of the causeway were alive with war-canoes, whose occupants showered arrows on the retreating Spaniards. In the chaos and carnage that followed, Cortes lost more than half his soldiers—many of whom died not from wounds but by drowning, weighed down by the pocketfuls of Aztec gold that they had been unable to resist carrying off with them. That dreadful night, June 30, 1520, was afterwards known as the *Noche Triste*—the Night of Sorrow.

Spanish sufferings did not end when what was left of the shattered column reached dry land. It was another two hundred miles and twelve agonizing days—during which the survivors were atttacked by a huge Aztec army at Otumba and, miraculously, routed it—before they at last reached Tlaxcala and safety.

Few other commanders, after such a debâcle,

would have dreamed of continuing the campaign, but Cortes was still determined to re-enter the capital in triumph. He immediately set about the task of re-building his soldiers' strength and morale and collecting reinforcements. The *Noche Triste* had taught Cortes that he could never trust the causeways again. Therefore, at Tlaxcala, two hundred miles from the sea and 7,000 feet above it, he began to construct a fleet of thirteen shallow-draft brigantines, specially designed so that they could be dismantled into easily portable sections and reassembled on the shores of the lake surrounding Tenochtitlan. By Christmas all was ready; and on December 28 Cortes led some 550 Spaniards—roughly the same number as had accompanied him on his first expedition, but this time augmented by some 10,000 Indian allies and forty horses—back into the valley of Mexico. A base camp was set up at Texcoco, on the eastern shore of the lake, and while the brigantines were being prepared for action, the Spanish leader sent messages across the water to the new emperor, Cuauhtémoc, calling on him to surrender.

As Spanish strength had grown, so the Aztecs' had declined. Their capital had suddenly been struck by a new and dreadful scourge almost certainly introduced by the invaders—smallpox. Having no hereditary resistance to it, the Indians had perished by the thousands.

The final assault on the Aztec capital began in April, 1521. Victory proved far more elusive than the Spaniards had expected. The brigantines were invaluable, but they could not be everywhere at once, and attack after attack was driven back across the causeways. At last Cortes saw that there was only one solution—the slow, systematic annihilation of the city—and he therefore ordered his men to destroy the houses and the streets one by one, using the rubble to fill in the canals. The Aztecs fought on, but by the end of July the southern half of their city was a heap of ruins. The southern and western spearheads of the Spanish attack, led by Cortes and Alvarado respectively, met in the great marketplace of Tlatelolco. Bernal Diaz again described the scene:

> On the way we passed through a small square, where there were wooden poles on which they had impaled the heads of many of our Spaniards whom they had killed and sacrificed during the recent battles. Their hair and beards had grown much longer than they were in life; which I never would have believed if I had not seen it.

Next to the marketplace was the high temple through which Montezuma had guided Cortes less than two years before. A party of Spaniards climbed to its top, set the shrines on fire, cast the idols down the steps and planted their banners. When the Aztecs saw the eagles of Spain fluttering from their highest pyramid, they knew that they had lost—yet the twenty-six-year-old Cuauhtémoc refused to surrender. Instead he made a valiant effort to escape to the mainland to continue his resistance from there, and it was only when the fastest of the brigantines overtook him that he finally gave himself up.

Bernal Diaz summed up the siege of Tenochtitlan:

During the whole ninety-three days of the siege there was the unceasing noise of their accursed drums and trumpets, and their melancholy battle-drums in the shrines and on the temple-towers. But after Cuauhtémoc's capture all of us soldiers became deaf—as if all the bells in a belfry had been ringing together and then suddenly stopped.

Thus, on the evening of August 13, 1521, the city of Tenochtitlan finally fell—and with it fell the Aztec empire. Men still argue over the rights and wrongs of the conquest, some maintaining that imperialist aggression can never be condoned, others, insisting that Mexico was enriched by her Spanish colonial experience, and that Cortes was justified in eliminating the bloodiest civilization the world has known.

There is no statue of the conqueror in modern Mexico City, but in the Square of the Three Cultures, the spot where Cuauhtémoc acknowledged the end of his empire, a marble plaque provides what is perhaps the wisest epilogue of all:

It was neither a victory nor a defeat. It was the painful birth of that commingled people that is the Mexico of today.
                                    JOHN JULIUS NORWICH

The death of the Aztec leader, Montezuma, from the *Codex Mendoza*.

411

Cardinal Wolsey falls from power as Henr

The entry of Hadrian VI to Rome, a detail from his tomb.

Optimists in Europe believed that a forceful pope would be able to bring peace to Italy, settle the religious issue in Germany and inspire the West to stand firm against the Turk—and when Adrian of Utrecht was elected as successor to Leo X in 1523, men's hopes were renewed. Adrian VI brought to Rome a reputation for statesmanship and scholarship. As tutor to the future Charles V, Adrian had succeeded Cardinal Ximenes as effective ruler of Spain. His election to the papal throne surprised but did not frighten Adrian, who immediately set about planning a series of long overdue reforms which would end the abuses that had made Renaissance Rome synonymous with corruption.

The Italian cardinals did not take to the Dutch professor of divinity, a northerner whom they considered indifferent to artistic beauty and classical antiquity. Their distaste was obviated by Adrian's death only a few months after he was elevated. The loss was an especially unfortunate one, for Adrian's personal qualities were such that, had he lived, his pontificate would surely have been a remarkable one. His successor, Clement VII (1523-34), was a Medici, brought up in the household of the great Lorenzo. Clement had come to dominate the College of Cardinals during the pontificate of his cousin, Leo X, and had proved to be an efficient second-in-command. As Pope, Clement revealed his Medici blood. He seemed more concerned with the salvaging of his temporal possessions than with the salvation of Italy.

A fundamental problem of contemporary politics was the future of French power in Italy. Prospero Colonna brought an imperialist army to Italy in 1522 to drive the French from Milan and restore the Sforza family to power. The French

army's defeat only encouraged Francis I to launch additional campaigns to regain his lost holdings. In subsequent undertakings, the French King's greatest handicap was not a lack of funds to finance those expeditions but the defection of the Duke of Bourbon to Charles V. When an army led by Admiral Bonnivet and the Chevalier Bayard invaded Lombardy in 1524, Bourbon routed them, laid waste to Provence and put Marseille under siege. That winter, the undaunted Francis I crossed the Mont Cenis Pass, easily took Milan and opened the siege of Pavia.

In February, 1525, Bourbon led a well-disciplined army of Spaniards and imperialists to Pavia's aid. The French and their Swiss allies were routed, and casualties exceeded those inflicted in the battle of Marignano some ten years before. Roughly 14,000 men were slain, including Richard de la Pole, pretender to the earldom of Suffolk and the throne of England. Many of the deaths were attributed to the fact that the Spanish infantry used muskets for the first time in the history of warfare. Francis was taken prisoner and transported to Madrid, where months later he had to purchase his release by sur-

Pope Clement VII, more interested in Italian politics than in theology.

rendering the Duchy of Burgundy.

Fearing Charles' domination of Italy, Pope Clement VII soon formed the League of Cognac, an offensive alliance designed to undo the harsh Treaty of Madrid. The League hoped to force Charles to give Francesco Sforza independent sovereignty over Milan and its members planned to press for recognition of the ancient liberties of several other Italian states.

All eyes were on Rome in August, 1526, as Cardinal Pompe Colonna plundered the city and forced the Pope to take refuge in the Castle of St. Angelo. In May, 1527, imperial troops under the Duke of Bourbon's command mutinied, looted the city's treasures and killed 4,000 Roman citizens. Bourbon himself was slain and it was nine months before fire, bloodshed and pillage gave place to order. The second sack of Rome marked the end of an epoch: the age of Renaissance Rome as the center of learning and of the arts was over.

The Pope was in as much danger as his city. Besieged in the Castle of St. Angelo for six months, he at last agreed to the Emperor's terms, which included crowning Charles and calling a general council of the Church to deal with the Lutheran problem in the Empire. A day before his scheduled release from St. Angelo, Clement escaped to Orvieto, and in June, 1529, he finally came to terms with Charles V. They agreed that the Medici would be permitted to return to Florence and the Sforzas to Milan—and that Charles would attempt to encourage towns in the Papal States to return to Clement's obedience. Six months later France signed the ignominious Peace of Cambrai, nicknamed "The Ladies' Peace" because it was negotiated by Charles' Aunt Margaret and Louise of Savoy, the Queen-Mother of France. That treaty confirmed Hapsburg rule in Italy, and required Francis I to renounce his claims on the peninsula and his sovereignty over Flanders and Artois in the Low Countries.

Thomas Wolsey

By 1520, Thomas Wolsey was preeminent in England. His power was symbolized by his two residences, Hampton Court and York Place (later Whitehall), both of which were built out of ecclesiastical revenues and the fat fees that he received as Lord Chancellor.

His palaces were the envy of every Englishman, including the King. No Englishman had ever wielded such authority, for Wolsey was both King Henry's chief minister and the Pope's legate—an unprecedented combination of powers. His high-handed rule weakened the Church's resistance to subsequent royal demands—and consequently lay people became antipapal, if not also anti-clerical.

In 1527 Wolsey had become ensnared in negotiations with the

Cardinal Wolsey, who dominated English politics for fifteen years, and fell from power when he proved unable to obtain an annulment of Henry's marriage.

Pope about the validity of Henry's marriage to Catherine of Aragon. Catherine had failed to give Henry a legitimate male heir, and the King was bent on divorce, legally sanctified by Rome. But because Charles V was Catherine's nephew and—unprompted—took her part, the chances of obtaining a favorable ruling from Clement VII, the Emperor's puppet, was remote. For one brief moment, when Clement was seriously ill, Wolsey had hopes of becoming pope himself, but Clement recovered and Wolsey, who knew Henry only too well, realized that he could not remain his chief minister much longer. For all his claims to having influenced events in the courts of Europe, the Cardinal had failed to achieve Henry's wishes. In 1525 he presented the King with Hampton Court and in October, 1529, he gave him York Place as well. Wolsey had fallen from power—and Parliament was as determined as Henry had been to seek revenge. Stripped of all his offices except the Archbishopric of York, Wolsey retired to the north. Within a few months he was arrested as a suspected traitor and he died on the way to London.

Henry VIII was to achieve his divorce by uniting in his own person —as King and Supreme Head of the Church—the same powers that Wolsey had accumulated as Lord Chancellor and Cardinal-legate.

Peasant Revolts

In June, 1524, warfare of a different kind broke out in the West as peasants living on the estates of Count von Lupfen in the Black Forest took up arms to abolish serfdom, feudal services and enclosures, and the payment of tithes. The movement spread rapidly into the Rhineland, Swabia and Franconia and later reached Bavaria, the Tyrol and Alsace. Manifestoes were drawn up which lent an air of respectability to the looting and slaughter that followed. Thomas Munzer, a prist from Saxony who signed orders "The Sword of the Lord and of Gideon," attempted to impose some sort of order on the rebels. But after several initial successes, the peasant army was encircled at Frankenhausen, and in May, 1525, Munzer was executed. Martin Luther, who had disowned the rebels' challenge to secular authority, preached against their political attitudes.

Zwingli of Zurich

Shortly after Luther published his *Theses* in Wittenberg, a very different sort of reformer began to revitalize the life of Zurich. After studying at Vienna University, where he was disciplined for rowdyism, Urich Zwingli (1484–1531) took holy orders and developed his own approach to Humanism. The publication of Erasmus' Greek New Testament added a new dimension to Zwingli's theology, and by the time that he was appointed priest of the Great Minster at Zurich he had grounded his faith on the Bible.

Despite his weak voice, Zwingli was a remarkable preacher. He denounced the sale of indulgences, fasting, the celibacy of the clergy and the use of mercenary armies (in which so many men from the Swiss cantons served). His 1523 dispute with the Bishop of Constance led Zwingli to draw up a set of fundamental articles of religion and to promote disputations on them. Zwingli converted the citizens of Zurich, who demonstrated their faith by removing all images from their churches and refusing to accept episcopal jurisdiction. In 1525, Zwingli completed his liturgical reforms, supplanting the Latin Mass with a service stressing the commemorative nature of the Lord's Supper.

As leader of Zurich, Zwingli envisioned his city as the cornerstone of a wide evangelical confederation—and in 1529 he founded the Christian Civic League as a first step toward achieving that goal. Berne, Basel and Constance joined the league immediately and Strasbourg joined a short time later. In 1529 the League went to war with the Catholic Forest Cantons, which were defeated and forced to abandon their alliance with Austria. That same year Zwingli journeyed to Marburg at the invitation of Philip of Hesse and took part in a disputation with Luther. Philip hoped to effect a reconciliation between the two reformers, but the chasm proved to be too deep.

Zwingli's militancy provoked a second war with the Catholic cantons in 1531, and at the decisive battle of Kappel he was killed. The subsequent peace treaty divided the Swiss Confederation into Protestant cantons—principally Zurich, Berne, Geneva and Basel—and Catholic cantons—notably Lucerne and Freiburg—and that division persisted. As a Catholic soldier noted on the battlefield at Kappel, Zwingli was "a rotten heretic, but a good confederate."

The Reformation reaches Scandinavia

By comparison, the Protestant Reformation made rapid strides in Scandinavia. The kings of Denmark still claimed to rule the three Scandinavian kingdoms under the terms of the Union of Kalmar (1396), but opposition to Danish rule in Sweden had become persistent. The Danish kings imposed a heavy tribute on the Swedish nobility in an effort to force the Swedes to recognize their claims to that country's throne. Christian II, who succeeded to the Danish throne in 1513, was determined to press his claim by force. He defeated a Swedish peasant army on the ice of Lake Asunden in January of 1520. Ston Sture, the leader of Swedish resistance, perished in the battle but his widow, Christina, defended

Catherine of Aragon, who was divorced by Henry VIII.

Stockholm for eight months before surrendering. Christian promised the city amnesty, but after his hurried coronation he summoned an assembly to Stockholm Castle and, with the assistance of Swedish Archbishop Gustavus Trolle, took action against Christina Sture, many nobles, two bishops and the chief burgesses of the city. Trolle was anxious to revenge himself on the nationalist party (which had deposed him in 1517) by extracting a heavy fine—but Christian was out for blood. On November 8, 1520, after a mock trial for heresy, some ninety leading Swedes were executed in the city's market place. The event, known as "The Stockholm Bloodbath," earned its instigator the name "Christian the Tyrant."

Sweden was rescued from Danish tyranny by Gustavus Vasa, a rebel whose father and other relations had been slaughtered at Stockholm. A year before the "Bloodbath," Vasa had launched a campaign to sever Sweden from the Union of Kalmar. He had fallen into Christian II's hands but escaped.

But in January, 1521, Vasa returned to the province of Dalarna —long a center of nationalist resistance—and was promptly elected to lead the peasant army that began the reduction of castles in Danish hands. Increasing numbers of prominent Swedes came over to Gustavus, but Stockholm held out. Fortunately for Gustavus, a rebellion—provoked by Christian's heavy taxation and his quarrel with the Church—broke out in Denmark at this point and the King was deposed in favor of his uncle Frederick. In June, 1523, a fully representative Rikstag unanimously elected Vasa King of Sweden.

Gustavus was the creator of modern Sweden. For years the independence of his state had to be vigorously defended against its Scandinavian and Baltic neighbors —and even from Emperor Charles V. The outstanding event of Gustavus' reign came in 1527, when he severed Sweden's ties with the Church and adopted Lutheranism. The Swedish monarchy had always been elective, but Gustavus feared that his cherished work might be endangered by faction, and in 1544 he established the Vasa dynasty. Gustavus left to his successor an independent nation state, solvent, effectively administered and defended by a superb army. The new Sweden was soon to become an important factor in European politics.

Titian

Titian (1490–1576), the greatest of all Venetian artists, is often considered the founder of modern painting. His contemporary fame was based on the *Bacchanals*, which he painted for the Duke of Ferrara, and on the outsize painting of *The Assumption* in the Frari Church in Venice. Titian eventually aban-

Ulrich Zwingli, who converted Zurich to Protestantism.

doned religious themes for those of classical mythology and for portraiture. The friend of kings and popes, he established what subsequent generations would come to regard as "the official portrait" concept. Titian's later style, with its disregard for contours, was in some respects "Impressionistic," and his technique was equally remarkable. The master constantly revised his canvases and, according to one of his pupils, if he "found something in a painting that displeased him, he went to work like a surgeon."

A Bible for the Masses

The astounding thing about the vernacular version of the New Testament that appeared in Germany in the fall of 1533 was not that it was an able and often forceful translation, but that it existed at all. The translator, the controversial Wittenberg monk Martin Luther, had recently been excommunicated by the Pope—who recognized only the Latin Vulgate Bible—and had been banned by Emperor Charles V. The printer and publishers of "Luther's Bible"—the first complete translation of the New Testament into any vernacular tongue—were therefore taking grave risks in backing the outspoken monk's enterprise. Their gamble paid off handsomely, however; Hans Lufft, Luther's printer, sold nearly 100,000 copies of the monk's Bible. In one bold stroke, Luther had reached the largest lay audience in history—and in so doing, had proved the power of Europe's fledgling popular presses.

During the last days of September, 1522, an extraordinary book was published in Wittenberg, Saxony, a German town of three thousand inhabitants. The volume's short title, printed in highly ornamental Gothic letters, was *Das Newe Testament Deutzsch— Vuittemberg (The German New Testament—Wittenberg)*. No publication date was given, and the name of the translator was not mentioned. The name of the printer, Melchoir Lotter the Younger, and the names of the publishers, the painter Lucas Cranach and his partner Christian Doering, were also omitted. The format, a smallish folio, included twenty-one woodcuts created in the workshop of Lucas Cranach and devoted exclusively to the last section of the book, *Revelation*. The edition appeared in 3,000 copies, each priced at half a gulden, approximately the weekly wage of the best-paid craftsmen of the age.

The printing and publishing of this undated vernacular version of the New Testament had been undertaken in great haste and in full secrecy; the translator, the Wittenberg monk and professor Martin Luther, was under the ban of Emperor Charles V—in addition to his excommunication by the Pope. Names had been omitted for fear that the imperial edict, which threatened anyone who assisted the condemned heretic, might be applied to the printers or to the entire community. Despite those fears, the edition, the first full translation of the New Testament from the original Greek into a vernacular tongue, was soon sold out and a reprint with corrections was issued in December of the same year. At the same time, a pirated edition came out in the Swiss city of Basel, the greatest center of printing and publishing in Europe.

During the next several years, Luther published parts of the Old Testament, which he translated from the original Hebrew with the assistance of collaborators. In 1534, the first complete German-language edition of the Bible was printed in Wittenberg by Hans Lufft, who was to serve as the main printer of the work for decades and who as a result became one of the richest men in the town. Luther himself never received any remuneration for the nearly 100,000 copies of the "Luther Bible" that Hans Lufft printed.

In addition to Lufft's editions, authorized and unauthorized versions of Luther's translation abounded. Pirated editions outnumbered legitimate ones by at least four to one. A form of copyright, granted by special privilege of a local prince, was in existence at the time but in Luther's case this protection was valid only for the dukedom of Saxony— or, to be more precise, for that half of Saxony ruled by the Elector, Luther's patron. In the other half of the country, which was controlled by Luther's enemy Duke George, the monk's books were banned and his Bible was immediately supplanted by another edition. The text of that version, purportedly written by the court-chaplain Emser, was taken without compunction from the Lutheran translation, with some added "corrections." Many other Catholic editions of the time made use of this procedure.

The Holy Roman Empire was without a central authority in the early sixteenth century. The division of the Empire into self-governing principalities— imperial free towns and countless independent possessions held by archbishops, bishops, prince-abbots and mere counts, each eagerly defending his rights or what he called his "liberties"—made it possible to set up printing presses everywhere and to publish almost any book, however dangerous or seditious it might be. Ecclesiastical as well as temporal censorship did indeed exist, but they could be applied only locally; a book suppressed at one place would soon appear at some other place, often in a remote town where the printer was on good terms with his magistrate. This state of affairs, although politically lamentable, accounted for the rapid spread of printing in sixteenth-century Europe. In particular, Bible printing became commonplace, although vernacular versions of the Bible were still

Title of Luther's translation of the New Testament—the first Bible to be translated into German, published in 1522 by Melchior Lotter.

Opposite A woodcut of Luther, 1520, while he was still an Augustinian.

A printing shop in the late-fifteenth century, from a *memento mori*.

Below right The church at Wittenberg where Luther posted his ninety-five theses on October 31, 1517.

regarded as dangerous by ecclesiastical authorities.

Luther himself enjoyed the huge success of his translation and wrote only: "It is easy to plough a field that has been cleared. But no one wants to uproot the forest and tree trunks and put the field in order." He did become irritated, however, when his qualifications as a Biblical scholar were questioned. He retorted: "You are doctors? So am I. You are theologians? So am I. But I can expound the Psalms and the Prophets. You cannot do this. I can translate. You cannot do this." And when incorrectly printed and garbled editions of his work began to appear in rapid succession, he exclaimed: "They do that snip-snap: Money, that's what they are after."

Luther could indeed translate, and in time his work was recognized as the decisive event in the development of the modern German language.

During his own lifetime, Luther's Bible became the cornerstone of the Reformation. It was Luther's belief that Scripture should be the sole guide, the supreme authority in matters of faith. This view was in direct opposition to the tenets of the Roman Catholic Church, which, in Luther's words, "places the Pope above Scripture and says he cannot err."

This principle of "sola scriptura"—Scripture alone—had been Luther's guide and weapon from the beginning of his rebellion against Church stricture. In 1521, one year before the publication of his New Testament, Luther journeyed to the German city of Worms, where, at the invitation of the Emperor, he defended his views before an assembled Church Diet. In his famous final declaration before Charles V and the assembled prelates, Luther declared: "Unless I am convinced by testimony from the Holy Scriptures . . . I am bound by my conscience and the Word of God." The enraged Emperor issued an imperial edict banning Luther as a heretic and rebel against authority. His decree, the most comprehensive edict of general censorship in modern times, also imposed strict supervision of all printed productions, including leaflets, posters, woodcuts and pictures; no one was permitted to "compose, write, print, paint, sell, buy or secretly keep such productions." Luther's answer was the publication of his Bible.

On his return from Worms, Luther was intercepted by the emissaries of his patron, the Elector of Saxony, and brought in secret to Wartburg. There he wrote the first draft of his translation.

A few words must be said about the extraordinary circumstances under which a work of such magnitude and difficulty was undertaken. Luther labored

almonefrpe athpn Black Letter
perle feffe & proftei Aldus Roman
ueftibulum fauise Aldus Italic

Aldus Manutius (Manuci)   Johann Froben   Geofroy Tory   Robert Estienne

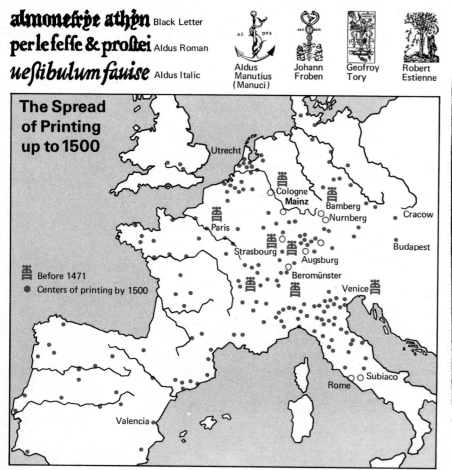

The Spread of Printing up to 1500

Utrecht

Cologne
Mainz
Bamberg
Nurnberg
Cracow

Paris

Strasbourg
Augsburg
Budapest

Beromünster

Venice

Rome
Subiaco

Valencia

🏛 Before 1471
● Centers of printing by 1500

without aid from the outside. He had only a handful of books at hand, and he did not have access to any libraries other than his own meager one. During this period, Luther disguised himself as a Junker. He sported a beard and carried a sword at his side. To the great annoyance of his protector and his entourage, who wanted him to keep quiet, Luther wrote numerous letters and tracts from his hiding-place.

Only during the last weeks of his seclusion did the fugitive start on his great translating task. He had nothing to work with except the Greek New Testament published by Erasmus of Rotterdam eight years earlier, the Latin Vulgate, the only officially recognized version of the Bible (which Luther had known more or less by heart since his monastery days), and perhaps two or three books more. It took the monk no more than ten weeks to finish his translation; a mere copyist would have been pressed just to copy the entire text from an existing original in this amount of time, at the standard rate of ten pages a day. Speed was crucial, for Luther was extremely eager to return to Wittenberg, where serious disturbances had arisen among his followers.

Luther therefore broke out of his prison—in defiance of the express order of his protector—and went to Wittenberg, where he corrected the rough draft of his manuscript with the help of his friend, Philip Melanchthon, a twenty-five-year-old professor at the university who was already recognized as one of the most eminent classical scholars of the age. In the midst of the dissension that was shaking the little town to its foundations, the monk's text went into print on three presses at the same time. Luther's concern over such minutiae as the typography of his volume led him to replace his slovenly former printer with Melchoir Lotter, who did his work so well that the list of errata at the end of the first edition of Luther's Bible contained only a handful of minor errors. (There were no major printer's errors like the one contained in the English Bible of 1631. That version, called the "wicked Bible," omitted the word "not" from the Seventh Commandment.)

In the eyes of the Church, Luther's grave and unforgivable error was in undertaking his task in the first place. The Latin text of the Vulgate was the only accepted one, and to translate it into the vernacular was considered an act of willful interpretation, dangerous and possibly heretical. The fight to make the Bible available in the "vulgar tongue" had indeed attached itself to great schismatic movements throughout the centuries of Church history. The Waldensians and Albigensians, heretical sects that sprang up in southern France at the end of the twelfth century, had their own translations of the Bible—and both were equally condemned by the Church.

The first German translations of the Bible were produced in Bohemia during the fourteenth century. These manuscripts were written in secret and distributed clandestinely under threat of death; to be found in possession of a vernacular Bible was often

The burning of John Huss after his condemnation by the Council of Constance in 1415.

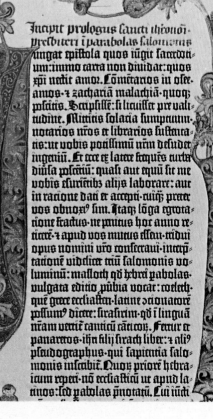

Part of a page of Wycliffe's Bible: those who translated the Bible into the vernacular were always suspected of heresy.

The first impact of printing on the masses

The title page of Luther's Latin Bible with his handwritten notes and his signature.

sufficient evidence to condemn a man to the stake. The smell of burning hangs on each surviving copy of these Bibles. No Albigensian translations have been preserved, but in spite of severe suppression, more than two hundred manuscript versions of Wycliffe's translation, as well as other medieval versions, are still extant.

The publication of each of these editions was a religious, social and political event of the greatest consequence. The masses—the poor to whom Wycliffe sent out his "poor priests"—wanted to have access to the Word of God in their own language. The fifteenth-century Hussite movement presented the Church, and governments as well, the frightening spectacle of a great rising of the common people, under the banner of Biblical inspiration combined with strong national and social aims. Luther was, therefore, initially accused by his adversaries of being a "Bohemian," a "second Hus."

Persecution of religious dissenters was rampant throughout Europe. William Tyndale, the first to translate the Bible into modern idiomatic English, printed his work at Cologne and Worms in 1524, two years after Luther's New Testament first appeared. Tyndale, whose translation was strongly influenced by Luther's model, perished at the stake. Only a pitiful single fragment of his first edition of the New Testament has been preserved. Later reprints, brought over to England from Antwerp, were publicly burned at Paul's Cross. The list of "Bible-martyrs" is a long one, as is the list of strict prohibitions against the printing or reading of those martyrs' translations. In Spain, all translations in the "vulgar tongue" were placed on the first Index printed by the Inquisition in 1551. Shortly after Luther's death, the Spanish representatives at the Council of Trent described all renderings into the vernacular as "mothers of heresy."

Luther's undertaking had another important meaning, as the crowning achievement of the great Humanist movement. "*Ad fontes*"—back to original sources—had been the watchword of Renaissance scholars. The phrase, applied at first to the Greek and Latin classics, later came to include the greatest

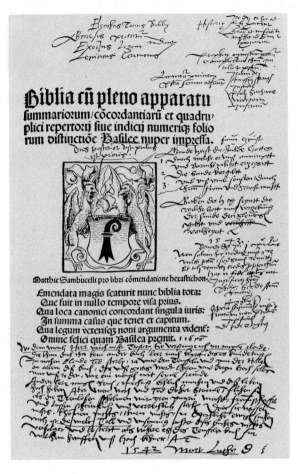

monument of antiquity, the Bible. It was known, of course, that the Bible had originally been written in Hebrew and Greek, but only the Latin Vulgate, derived from a translation made by St. Jerome in the fourth century, was officially recognized by the Church. By 1500, scholars had grown dissatisfied with this state of affairs. Italian Jews printed the Hebrew text of the Old Testament, and in 1516 the Dutch scholar Erasmus published his Greek New Testament. The Dutchman's move was a bold and dangerous one, and only the considerable prestige enjoyed by the man universally recognized as Europe's greatest living scholar saved Erasmus from prosecution. As criticism went further, many differences between the original text and the Latin translation were detected, indicating how corrupted the official version of the Bible had become in the course of more than a thousand years.

From the Church's point of view, however, every single word of the Vulgate remained sacrosanct and unalterable; it was still the basis of Church dogma and of the body of usages, including the smallest details of the worship service. Interpretation of ecclesiastical law, based on the Vulgate, was conducted exclusively by the appointed doctors of the Church, and subject to final sanction by the Pope. Any textual criticism was considered an attack on Church tradition, rather than a philosophical exercise. Indeed, the official revision of the old Latin text of the Vulgate itself, reluctantly recognized as inevitable, was only undertaken at the end of the

The title page of the first translation of the Bible into German, 1534. Copies of this edition are usually in bad condition due to its enormous popularity.

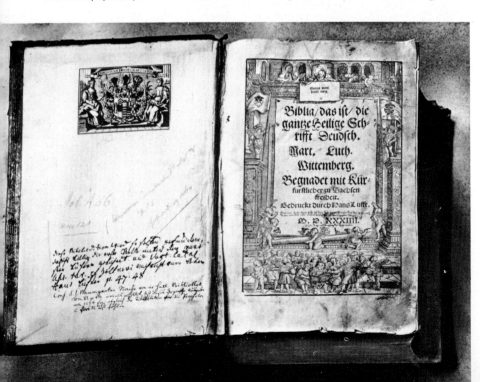

St. Luke painting an icon : a picture from Luther's German edition of the Bible, 1540.

sixteenth century. In some instances, arguments regarding the placement of a single comma in the revised Vulgate raged for years.

Luther was not concerned with commas. He translated the Latin text to the best of his ability and with considerable command of Biblical scholarship. The style and sweep of his language has been admired even by his enemies, and his powerful German has been marveled at—particularly since Luther had been educated, from boyhood onwards, exclusively in Latin. During his long years in the monastery and his first academic career, the monk had been obliged to express himself in that language; how he acquired his rich and flexible German vocabulary therefore remains a mystery. It was only in his thirty-fifth year that Luther suddenly broke out of the prison of an alien language—and into the freedom of his native speech. His little tract entitled "On Indulgences and Grace," which followed immediately upon the steps of his *Ninety-five Theses*, was Luther's first German-language publication. It was immediately reprinted, and twenty different pirated editions were soon being sold.

Historically speaking, the publication of Luther's Bible marked the first time that the medium of printing had made a profound impact on the masses of the people. With one bold stroke, Luther had reached a public of incomparably larger dimensions than any former revolutionary or reformer had dreamed of. He continued the fight with his well-

Luther's friend and ally Melanchthon, by Dürer.

Left An engraving of Desiderius Erasmus of Rotterdam, one of the leading humanists of the sixteenth century, by Albrecht Dürer.

419

The teaching of Christ compared with the teaching of Antichrist; a Lutheran attack on the Roman Church.

Luther with Melanchthon's version of the Bible in Greek and Hebrew: an illustration by Cranach from Luther's translation of the Bible.

known pamphlets and books, and it has been estimated that during the first decade of his public struggle, nearly a quarter of the works published in Germany came from his pen.

Despite the futile edict issued by Emperor Charles v at Worms, printing increased by leaps and bounds in those years. In addition to pamphlets, broadsides, tracts and books, pictorial propaganda became a very powerful weapon as well. It was aimed at the still largely illiterate public, a very large proportion of which was converted to Lutheranism by this means of communication. The papal nuncio, who had been sent to Worms to deal swiftly with the heretical Wittenberg monk, wrote home in near-despair. He counseled the Pope that almost nine-tenths of the Empire had become Lutheran, and that the rest cried out against "Roman tyranny." The publication of Luther's Bible was unquestionably the greatest and most lasting achievement of this period, and therefore that date of September, 1522, may be regarded as no less important than those of such well-known historical events as the publication of Luther's *Theses* in 1517 or his stand at the Diet of Worms in 1521.

Statistical figures about book sales do not tell the whole picture, however. It is not true, as has been repeatedly said, that the Bible was, for all practical purposes, "unknown" before Luther's version appeared. The Latin text of the Bible had been printed on the presses of Gutenberg and his companions at Mainz, in 1450–55, and many editions had followed. There had even been earlier unauthorized German translations, printed during the fifteenth century. More than a dozen of these works, mostly taken from texts printed in the previous century, were in existence. Extracts from Biblical texts, homilies and commentaries abounded.

Nevertheless, the demand for the whole text, the clear and unfettered Word of God, printed in the language of the people, remained and became irresistible. The older editions, written in Latin or in out-dated and halting vernacular, were not read by the people; they were intended for scholars, well-to-do persons or great libraries, and their cost was forbidding (the price of a single volume amounting in earlier times to the value of a good-sized town house). It is significant that a large number of these books have been preserved in excellent condition. By contrast, very few copies of the early printings of Luther's Bible are still extant, and those often badly mutilated from constant re-reading.

In those countries where the book was admitted, Luther's Bible became the great formative influence over the next centuries. The imposing figures regarding distribution of the Scriptures that were published by the great Bible societies in the nineteenth century pale almost into insignificance if compared with the number of old family Bibles in the sixteenth and seventeenth centuries. These volumes were, more often than not, the only book in the house, the only family possession of value, bequeathed from one generation to the next, and consequently bearing the family tree on the fly-leaf. No statistical figures will tell us how often those editions were read aloud to the whole household, servants included. One could, however, design a map of sixteenth-century Europe that divided the Continent into Bible-reading and non-Bible-reading regions. In central France, for instance, the Catholic Church continued to struggle with the stubborn, Bible-reading Jansenists, long after the Huguenots had been thoroughly eliminated.

Bible reading was not an unmitigated blessing. The Roman Church had reservations about individual interpretations of the Scriptures, and Luther himself was forced to struggle, from the time he printed his first draft, with what he called the "heavenly prophets" who interpreted the text in their own light, according to inspiration they claimed to receive from above. Many sects and movements, such as the Spiritualists and the Anabaptists, evolved during this period. Some of these groups developed valuable versions of their own. Bible reading, no longer restricted to matters of faith and religion, became the basis for studies of social and political developments. It was not displaced until the eighteenth century, when secularization arrived in the wake of the Enlightenment.

RICHARD FRIEDENTHAL

Above One of a series of woodcuts on the papacy by Cranach.

Below Luther's meeting with Pope Paul III, by Salviati.

The Spanish adventurers who explored the western coast of South America in the early 1500s returned to Panama with tales of an empire of untold wealth located in Peru. Those explorers found a ready

Francisco Pizarro, conqueror of Peru.

listener in Francisco Pizarro (1470–1541), a soldier of fortune who had settled in Darien, a port city on the Pacific side of the Isthmus. He and Diego de Almagro patiently explored the coastline of Peru for four years before Pizarro felt that he had sufficient evidence to convince Charles v of the importance of conquering the Incas. He arrived at Charles' court while Cortes was being feted for his victories in Mexico, and the latter's presence insured Pizarro of a fair hearing. The Emperor readily agreed to Pizarro's proposals, and appointed him governor and captain-general of Peru.

Pizarro set sail from Panama in 1530 with one hundred and eighty men, twenty-seven horses and two cannon, and he soon established a settlement on the Peruvian coast. He found the country in the final stages of a war of succession in which Atahualpa, one of the contenders, ultimately defeated his rival, moved the capital from his opponent's stronghold at Cuzco, to Cajamarca in the central plateau, and had himself crowned Inca, or emperor, of Peru. Under the ruse of conferring with Atahualpa, the tiny Spanish force surprised Cajamarca and took the Inca prisoner on November 16, 1532. Incredibly enough, Pizarro's tiny army had conquered the Inca kingdom in the course of a single afternoon.

During the 1530s other Spanish expeditions founded Cartagena in New Granada, conquered Yucatan, colonized La Plata (later Argentina) and settled Buenos Aires.

Spanish attempts to colonize Florida were less successful. Armed with an imperial patent that empowered him to establish settlements on the Gulf Coast, Hernando de Soto (1499–1542) landed in Florida in 1539. He discovered the Mississippi, Arkansas and Oklahoma.

A more persistent attempt to colonize Florida was made by the French in 1564. French fishermen had visited the Newfoundland coasts in the earliest years of the century, but the first planned expedition to the Americas was that of Giovanni da Verrazano, whom Francis I sent out to explore the coast between Cape Fear and Newfoundland in 1524. Ten years later Jacques Cartier made the first of three voyages to the New World.

Calvin at Geneva

By the time that Luther's Bible was published John Calvin (1509–64) had already settled in Paris and experienced what he called a "sudden conversion."

At the age of twenty-six he completed the first draft of his *Institutes of the Christian Religion*, a work expanded over the years from six to eighty chapters. Calvin's work was to have as profound an influence on the direction of the Reformation as Luther's Bible. His style was incisive, and his familiarity with the works of the Early Fathers was complete. Calvin gave a new twist to the doctrine of predestination enunciated by St. Augustine by arguing that a strict moral code was the basis for Christian life. In Calvinistic theology, discipline was fundamental.

In Geneva Calvin was able to put into practice his plans for

John Calvin, father of Presbyterianism.

completely re-organizing religious life. Under a theocratic government, the town became "the most perfect school of Christ." The state was restructured to establish the supremacy of the Christian Church.

Calvin was the most distinguished Biblical scholar of his generation and his teaching was infectious.

The Anabaptists

Lutherans and Catholics alike found a common enemy in the Anabaptists, the extreme left wing of the Reformation movement. Protestantism's radical left was composed of a variety of sects that were collectively dubbed "Anabaptists" by their detractors because they all rejected infant baptism. The Anabaptists believed that baptism was a personal, adult act of repentance. (Indeed, the mass baptisms performed in Amsterdam in the early 1500s astounded Luther and Pope Clement as much as they did the Anabaptists.) Such novel doctrines threatened the very foundations of authoritarian religion, and those who believed in them were mercilessly persecuted.

To escape such treatment, numbers of the Leyden sect settled in Münster in Westphalia. Their leader, John of Leyden, captured control of the city in February, 1534, and established a "communist state," whose excesses—admittedly grossly distorted in contemporary reports—were nonetheless remarkable. Because women outnumbered men four to one in Münster, John of Leyden made polygamy lawful—and he personally took sixteen wives. Attempts to unseat John were repulsed with considerable bloodshed, but in the spring of 1535, a joint expedition of Catholic and Lutheran princes forced Münster to surrender. The sect's leaders were executed and the Bishop of Münster was recalled.

Henry VIII's divorce

Henry VIII's envoys at Rome could make no progress with "the King's great matter." Henry's pleas for special consideration (as one whose attack on Luther's doctrines had earned him the papal title "Defender of the Faith") were ignored, and the opinions favoring his divorce that Cranmer had canvassed from European universities were dismissed by Pope Clement VII. Henry convinced himself that Catherine

of Aragon's inability to provide him with a son was divine punishment for his having married his deceased brother's wife. It was up to Thomas Cromwell to persuade Henry that his divorce did not need papal sanction, but could be effected by the King himself in Parliament. Meanwhile, Anne Boleyn waited in the wings.

In 1531, the English clergy, led by Archbishop Warham, sued for pardon for the offense of praemunire, paid an enormous fine and acknowledged Henry to be their supreme head "as far as the law of Christ allows." A year later—in a move calculated to convince Clement that his determination

Archbishop Thomas Cranmer.

was unfeigned—the King confiscated benefices customarily paid to the Pope. Henry then began undermining the powers of the Church courts, which were already highly unpopular. In 1533, Parliament passed an act that restrained appeals to Rome—and ended the Pope's interference in English affairs. As soon as the act became law, Thomas Cranmer, Warham's successor as Archbishop, opened a court of inquiry into the validity of the King's marriage with Catherine. Their marriage was soon declared void, and Henry was at last free to acknowledge his union with Anne Boleyn (who gave birth to Princess Elizabeth five months later). The final break with Rome came in 1535 when Henry assumed the title Supreme Head of the Church. The clergy, peers, members of Parliament and officials were required to take oaths of loyalty to the King, and Henry VIII became virtual pope in England.

The hopes of England's religious zealots notwithstanding, Church doctrine changed little after 1535. The Six Articles of Religion, a 1539 act that was designed to "abolish diversity of opinions," restated the ancient faith, including the doctrine of transubstantiation—but only after the King had intervened in the debate in the House of Lords to argue with the reforming bishops. The pressures of militant Protestantism soon overcame such reactionary legislation, however, and Archbishop Cranmer found himself swimming with the tide.

Sir Thomas More

The voice of conscience in those times was that of Sir Thomas More (1478–1535), a Humanist and lawyer whom Henry VIII had chosen to succeed Wolsey as Lord Chancellor. More's father had removed Thomas from Oxford when he discovered that his son was learning Greek, a subject that the elder More regarded as one of dangerous modernity. Thomas had been placed at Lincoln's Inn to read law and to prepare himself for the King's service. In his *Utopia* More condemned the abuse of power and preached toleration, and as Speaker of the Commons in 1523 More proved a forceful opponent of Wolsey. His home at Chelsea epitomized the New Learning in England. Erasmus, an occasional houseguest, noted that "in More's household you would realize that Plato's academy was revived, except that in the Academy the discussions concerned geometry and the power of numbers, whereas the house at Chelsea is a veritable school of Christian religion."

More had accepted the position of Lord Chancellor on the understanding that he would not be required to play a part in Henry's divorce, but by 1532 that issue so dominated politics that Sir Thomas felt obliged to resign. He repeatedly refused to take the oath of supremacy to Henry that was required by statue—although he swore to be loyal to the King and the succession—and as a result he was imprisoned in the Tower of London for a year. At his trial, Sir Thomas denied that Parliament could make the King Supreme Head of the Church, and he was executed as a traitor in July, 1536.

English Reformation

While More was still in prison, Henry VIII appointed Thomas Cromwell to be his vicar-general and ordered him to visit England's religious houses and discover the extent of their wealth. As a result of Cromwell's report, 376 houses with property that earned under $480 a year in rents were dissolved and the Crown acquired lands that earned a yearly total of $76,800 in rents. Those lands were soon parceled out by grant to courtiers and by lease to gentry in the shires. The dispossessed monks were granted pensions, and many of them found benefices as secular clergy.

The Pilgrimage of Grace was a conservative protest against Henry's breach with Rome and his confiscation of monastic property, but it was also a reaction against the centralized rule of the Tudor monarchy. Robert Aske, a Doncaster lawyer, recruited thousands of peasants to march under his banner of the Five

Thomas Cromwell.

Wounds of Christ. Their attempt to reverse the course of English domestic policy had no chance of success, however, for the rest of the country, in particular the populous, prosperous south, was solidly behind the King.

In 1539, Henry ordered the dissolution of the greater monasteries, and most surrendered without protest. The abbots of Reading and Colchester had been executed some years before, for denying the king's supremacy and the Abbot of Glastonbury had been martyred for refusing to resign his rule. England's more politic abbots swiftly surrendered their property, and Crown revenues more than doubled. Iconoclasm accompanied the ending of monasticism in England, and St. Thomas Becket's tomb at Canterbury—the focal point of medieval pilgrimages—was pilfered.

The Convocation of Canterbury petitioned Henry VIII for an authoritative version of the Scriptures in English and he was eventually persuaded by Cranmer and Cromwell that Miles Coverdale's translation—the first complete Bible in the English tongue—contained no heresies despite the fact that it had been prepared on the Continent and printed in Zurich. "If there be no heresies," announced the monarch, "in God's name let it go abroad among our people"—and a 1536 injunction required a copy of the Bible to be placed in every church.

Tyndale's New Testament

A few weeks later William Tyndale was burned as a heretic in Antwerp. His tract, *Obedience of a Christian Man*, had prophetically outlined the cardinal principles of the English Reformation: the supremacy of the ruler and the authority of the Scriptures. Tyndale had found it dangerous to continue his work of translating the Bible while living in his native England, and in 1526 he emigrated to Worms, where his English New Testament was printed. Many copies of Tyndale's New Testament were smuggled into England and some of those were seized and burned by the common hangman. Archbishop Warham even sent agents to Europe to buy and destroy copies of Tyndale's work. Ironically, his New Testament, coupled with Coverdale's version of both Testaments, formed the basis of the official "Great Bible" that was prepared under Cranmer's guidance in 1539.

William Tyndale Bible translator.

As a result of the labors of Coverdale and Tyndale, the English became known as "The People of the Book." Later English-language versions of the Bible embodied many of their cadences.

Advances in Science

Scholar-scientists began to examine facts for their own sake, and many of them were prepared to criticize accepted explanations and to pursue new methods without seeking higher justification. The most notable scientific advances were made in surgery and anatomy. Paracelsus (c. 1493–1541) published the first manual of surgery in 1528, and Vesalius transformed the study of anatomy by advocating and practicing dissection. Two books marked the progress of technology: Biringuccio's *Pirotechnia* discussed the manufacture of gunpowder and glass, and Agricola's *De re metallica*, described all aspects of mining ores. But in astronomy there were still greater advances.

Sir Thomas More, author of *Utopia*, painted by Holbein.

The Earth Dethroned

By September of 1543, it had become obvious to the citizens of Frauenburg, Poland, that their beloved physician, Nicholas Copernicus, would not live out the year. The good doctor's failing health was a matter of special concern to his brash young disciple, Georg Joachim, who had long urged his mentor—a noted amateur astronomer—to publish his observations on planetary motion. After months of pleading, Joachim had at last been given permission to deliver Copernicus' manuscript to a local printer—and a copy of the published text reached the doctor on his deathbed. That volume postulated the first really new theory of planetary motion in almost two thousand years. Copernicus' insistence that the sun—not the earth—was the center of the universe helped usher in an epoch of broad scientific inquiry that earned the modest astronomer the title "Father of the Scientific Revolution."

A copy by Lorman of Berlin of a contemporary portrait of Nicholas Copernicus.

Opposite A room in the house at Frauenberg that Copernicus inherited from his uncle, and where he carried out most of his astronomical work.

Nicholas Copernicus, the Polish astronomer whose theory of planetary motion helped revolutionize scientific thought in the late sixteenth century, was born on February 19, 1473, at Torun, a Hanseatic community that had fallen under the protection of the King of Poland.

Little is known of Copernicus' childhood. His father died when he was only ten, and Nicholas, his brother Andrew and their two sisters were adopted by their maternal uncle. Lucas Watzelrode (or Waczenrode). A scholar and Roman Catholic priest, Watzelrode was consecrated Bishop of Ermland six years after he adopted the Koppernigk children. At that time, the See of Ermland was virtually an autonomous state, almost encircled by lands controlled by the Teutonic Knights. It owed nominal allegiance to Poland, but the Bishop served as both temporal ruler and spiritual head of the See. His palace was located at Heilsberg (about thirty-nine miles south of present-day Kalingrad, Russia) and his cathedral was located in the coastal city of Frauenberg, some forty miles to the northwest.

In 1491, when Nicholas was eighteen, he and his brother were sent to the university at Cracow, where young Copernicus pursued an interest in astronomy that he had first demonstrated while a schoolchild in Torun. The university of Cracow, one of the first institutions of higher learning in northern Europe to be influenced by the rediscovery of Greek science, was renowned for its high intellectual standards and was consequently attended by numerous foreign students. Copernicus studied mathematics and astronomy at the university.

While still a student, Copernicus began to assemble a collection of astronomical books that he was to keep by him for the rest of his life. The young student's interest in astronomy was looked upon with favor by the Church, which was at that time much concerned with the possible reform of the calendar. When Copernicus left Cracow, his uncle wanted to have him installed in a canonry in Frauenberg,

but until a suitable vacancy occurred, the Bishop felt that his nephew might profitably seek a degree in ecclesiastical law. Accordingly, Nicholas departed for the famous law school at Bologna in 1496.

While in Bologna, Nicholas lodged at the home of Domenico Maria de Novara, a professor of astronomy. The two men observed the heavens together, and spent many hours discussing possible improvements that they felt could be made in the prevailing theory of planetary motion. Nicholas remained in Bologna for three and a half years and then journeyed to Rome for the celebrations attending the 1,500th anniversay of Christianity. He lingered in the city for a year, and during that time made some celestial observations, particularly of an eclipse of the moon, and gave informal lectures on astronomy and mathematics.

During the years that he was in law school, a canonry became vacant at Frauenberg and Nicholas was elected to fill it. On July 27, 1501, he was duly installed—and promptly was granted further leave of absence so that he might go to Padua to study medicine and complete his law studies. Nicholas chose, however, to graduate in ecclesiastical law at Ferrara, and in 1503 was made a Doctor of Canon Law there. He then returned to medical school at Padua.

In Italy, as elsewhere in sixteenth-century Europe, medical training was largely theoretical. The teaching of medicine was based on certain rules attributed to Hippocrates, a Greek physician who lived in the fifth century B.C. Those rules, coupled with the writings of the Roman surgeon Galen (circa A.D. 200) and those of the eleventh-century Arabian chemist and physician Avicenna, composed the bulk of contemporary medical lore. Practical treatment involved the study of astronomy, because the current belief was that the celestial bodies exerted an influence on the human body and on the herbal drugs that were prescribed as cures.

When Copernicus, by then in his early thirties,

appointed, Copernicus returned to Frauenberg. The astronomer's final years were spent tending not only the Bishop and his successors, but also the town's poor, who grew to love him. Indeed, in Copernicus' own lifetime, it was for his medical skill and not his astronomical theory that he was noted.

Copernicus carried out his astronomical work whenever he was freed of his other duties. Initially, he had become dissatisfied, as many astronomers of his day were, with the generally accepted theory of the universe. That concept, based on the teachings of Greek philosophers, placed the Earth, fixed and immovable, at the center of the universe. Around it, in order, orbited the moon, Mercury, Venus, the sun, Mars, Jupiter and Saturn. Beyond Saturn lay the sphere of the fixed stars, which supposedly rotated once every twenty-four hours. Heaven lay beyond this starry sphere.

The problem with this theory—one that still troubled astronomers in the sixteenth century—was how to account accurately for the movements of the sun, moon and planets. To resolve this dilemma, ancient astronomers had evolved three basic provisos: first, that motion took place about the Earth; second, that such motion was uniform in speed; and third, that movement must be in a circle. The great difficulty was that the sun, moon and planets did not move across the sky evenly; they moved faster at some times than at others, and, worst of all, the planets appeared to perform loops in the sky as they wandered across the background of the stars.

Throughout antiquity solutions designed to explain some or all of these observed effects had been proposed, and in the second century A.D. the Alexandrian astronomer Ptolemy had worked out a comprehensive scheme of planetary motion that was still in use in Copernicus' day. Ptolemy explained planetary motion by using a collection of circular motions devised in the fourth century B.C. by Apollonios of Perga. Basically, each planet was conceived of as orbiting in a small circle, known as an "epicycle." The epicycle, in turn, moved at a regular rate around the circumference of a larger circle, known as a "deferent," at whose center lay the Earth. Ptolemy ingeniously modified this system not only to account for the planet's orbital loops, but also to account for changes in the apparent distances of given planets from the Earth, and for unevenness in their motion. He did this by offsetting the deferents from the center of the Earth, by allowing the deferents and epicycles to rock, and by using more than one epicycle for each planet. It was a brilliant system, and it remained in use (in modified form) for nearly 1,400 years.

By Copernicus' time, Ptolemy's system had been interwoven with the ideas of Aristotle, who had conceived of the universe as composed of a series of concentric spheres, with the Earth at the center. Many sixteenth-century astronomers thought of Aristotle's spheres as real, although transparent, and made of the purest crystal. According to Aristotle's generally accepted laws of physics, celestial bodies

returned to Heilsberg in 1506, he was appointed medical attendant to his uncle (with whom Nicholas shared certain governmental duties). In March, 1512, Watzelrode died, and by June of that year Copernicus was installed at Frauenberg cathedral. Nicholas' gratitude for all that the old man had done on his behalf was expressed in a book that he published in 1509, three years before the Bishop's death. The work, a Latin translation of some Greek verses by Theophylactus, was dedicated to Lucas Watzelrode.

At Frauenberg, Copernicus carried out a number of ecclesiastical and temporal duties. He lived in the modest style expected of canons, possessing but two servants and three horses. He set up his own astronomical observatory. In 1514 he was invited to Rome to assist in the reform of the calendar but felt it necessary to refuse, believing that the proposals were premature and that more research was needed into the motion of the sun and moon. Two years later he moved about fifty miles from the cathedral in order better to administer several of its large estates. Copernicus was now forced to spend long periods away from his observatory, and his absences grew more frequent when war broke out between Poland and the Teutonic Knights in 1519.

When, at the end of the war, a new Bishop was

426

Dissatisfaction with Ptolemy's ideas

were eternal and composed of a heavenly material—quite different from anything on Earth—whose natural place was the sky. Heavy bodies fell to the ground, Aristotle taught, because their natural place was the center of the universe (which was, of course, the center of the Earth). These laws were to have an important bearing on the acceptance of Copernicus' proposals.

While still a university student, Copernicus had had grown dissatisfied with the views of Ptolemy. He decided to read the Greek authors for himself to see whether he could find a clue to any other explanation of planetary motion. To seek new ideas from ancient writings was not unusual: for one thing, it was commonly held that the Greek philosophers had special knowledge of scientific matters; and for another, appeals to ancient authority—to the Scriptures, the teachings of the Church or some other early source—were customary. In his reading of Greek authors, Copernicus discovered that several did not accept the geocentric view of the universe. At least one bold thinker had even gone so far as to suggest that the Earth and planets orbit the sun—and it was this view that Copernicus eventually revived.

The resurrection of some unusual and unfamiliar Greek speculations would not have been enough—by itself—to make Copernicus famous, had he not spent years perfecting the mathematics of his new view, computing future planetary positions and making observations to provide additional evidence. He prepared a carefully reasoned argument in support of his theory, using arguments somewhat similar to those adopted 1,800 years before by Aristotle, but reaching a different conclusion. In 1530, while Copernicus was at work on his theory but before he was ready to set down his views in detail, the astronomer issued a manuscript that contained the essential facts. The manuscript was called *Commentariolus (The Litttle Commentary)*, and although it boasted no diagrams or detailed descriptions, it aroused considerable interest. Indeed, in 1533 John Widmanstad, the Papal Secretary, lectured to the Pope and some of his cardinals on the views it contained. At this time, such religious opposition as there was to Copernicus' theory of a moving Earth came from the Protestants, who believed it to be contrary to a literal interpretation of the Scriptures.

Copernicus was urged to publish his theory in full, but claimed that he was not ready. Indeed, he might never have agreed that his facts and figures were sufficiently complete had it not been for the efforts of George Joachim, a young Protestant scholar who came to see him in the spring of 1539. Better known by his Latinized name Rheticus, Joachim remained with Copernicus for almost three years, and it says much for the characters of both men—and for the stimulation that their scientific study provided—that in an age torn by religious dissension, the two men worked harmoniously together.

In 1540 Rheticus persuaded his host to publish a summary of his views, which was subsequently printed in Nürnberg under the title *Narratio Prima (A First Narrative)*. Not content with this, Rheticus continued to urge Copernicus to draw up his theory in detail. In the end he prevailed, and in 1543 a complete manuscript was delivered to Johann Petrejus, the Nürnberg publisher who had printed the *Narratio Prima*. Unfortunately, Rheticus moved to the University of Leipzig soon after delivering the manuscript, and he was forced to leave the technical details to his old tutor, Johannes Schoner, and a Lutheran divine, Andreas Osiander.

Osiander, worried about religious opposition to Copernicus' work, gave the publication a title without consulting Copernicus. (Copernicus had left his manuscript untitled, and was therefore partly to blame.) The book appeared as *De Revolutionibus Orbium Coelestium (On the Revolutions of the Celestial Spheres)*, although it is clear that Copernicus himself did not believe in the reality of Aristotle's spheres. More significant, however, was the fact that Osiander inserted an unsigned preface, disclaiming any physical reality to the movement of the Earth and explaining that Copernicus' theory was no more than an ingenious way of computing future planetary positions. The book appeared in 1543, and tradition has it that a copy reached Copernicus on his deathbed in October of that year.

Copernicus' theory as set out in *De Revolutionibus* places the sun firmly at the center of the universe, with the planets orbiting around it. The Earth is dethroned from its privileged position in the midst of all creation and is relegated to the role of mere satellite, orbiting the sun and rotating once on its axis every twenty-four hours. (It still acts as the body

The Lutheran divine, Andreas Osiander, who gave Copernicus' book its misleading title, and explained away many of his ideas in order to reduce opposition to Copernicus' theories.

The Copernican solar system as depicted by Thomas Digges in the 1576 edition of his father's *Prognostication Everlasting*.

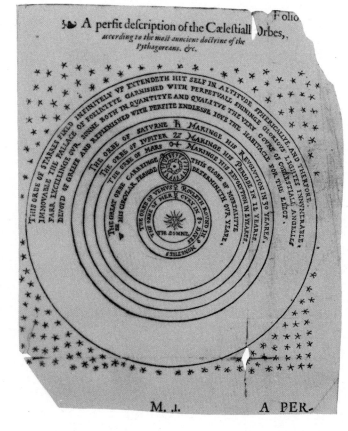

Opposition to Copernicus—scientific and religious

Sixteenth-century astrolabe used to tell the altitude of stars and planets.

about which the moon performs its monthly orbit, however.) The epicycles and deferents of Ptolemic astronomy are retained, and no changes are made in Aristotelian physics. Copernicus could not free himself from the ancient Greek beliefs that the heavens were incorruptible and that celestial movements must be circular and regular. Yet his system did possess regular motion centered on the sun, instead of off-centered motion about the Earth, which Ptolemy had advocated.

To Copernicus, this new scheme seemed virtually a moral victory, for it kept the true spirit of the Greek belief in circular motion. Moreover, his system was more elegant mathematically—as contemporary mathematicians were quick to realize—and it appeared to give more accurate results when used for computing the future positions of the planets. The tables in *De Revolutionibus* were used by the mathematician Erasmus Reinhold to prepare, under the patronage of Duke Albert of Prussia, a new set of tables of future planetary positions. These *Prussian Tables*, as they were called, were more precise than any previously published.

In England, the new theory received considerable support, particularly from Thomas Digges, a distinguished Elizabethan mathematician. Digges followed up a new consequence of the Copernican theory, which he realized affected all commonly held assumptions about the extent of the universe. Aristotle and other Greek philosophers had argued that since the sphere of the stars rotated once every twenty-four hours, that sphere must be finite in size —for if it was infinite, it would have to rotate at an infinite speed to complete a revolution in the same period. Digges appreciated that in a heliocentric

universe, where the Earth turned on its axis while orbiting round the sun, this argument was no longer valid. In an astronomical handbook published in 1576 and titled *Prognostication Everlasting*, Digges proposed an infinite universe of stars, each similar to our sun; his proposition completely refuted the idea of a spherical universe.

But if the Copernican theory met with support in England and much of Germany, it also faced some opposition. That opposition was of two types— scientific and religious. The former was based on arguments founded on Aristotle's physics: how could so heavy a body as the Earth be thought to move? Why, if it moved, should bodies still fall to the ground and the moon remain with it in space? How could it rotate once a day without setting up tidal waves and hurricanes as it rushed around in the surrounding air? Another significant scientific argument was based on observation: If the Earth orbited the sun, then at one time of year it would necessarily be nearer to some stars than to others, and as it moved, the nearer stars would be replaced by others. Some change in star positions ought, then, to be observable, but the most careful examinations of the sky showed no change at all. Copernicus, who had foreseen this argument, countered it by saying that the stars were too far away for any change to be observed. This deduction was perfectly correct, as we now know, but in the sixteenth century, it seemed insane to assert that God had made a universe with an immense gap between the planetary orbits and the stars. Only telescopic observations made from 1600 onwards, coupled with the gradual rejection of Aristotle's physics, removed these objections.

A page from the original manuscript of Copernicus' *De Revolutionibus,* and the title page of the first edition.

A celestial globe of the
mid-sixteenth century.

Some Protestants rejected the theory from a religious point of view, citing Biblical passages which asserted that the Earth stood still. There were others who were less committed to so literal an interpretation, however; Copernicus had dedicated *De Revolutionibus* to Pope Paul III, and the Roman Catholic Church had raised no objections to the theory. Copernican astronomy was strongly advocated by Giordano Bruno, who learned of it while on a visit to England in 1583. Bruno, a former Dominican, had found much to criticize in his Church and had published many contumacious books attacking it. In these books, which supported a magical form of anti-authoritarian government, Bruno extolled the Copernican view of a heliocentric universe (although not for scientific reasons) and it was this, more than anything else, that led to *De Revolutionibus Orbium Coelestium* being placed on the Index of Prohibited Books in 1616.

Although his detailed descriptions of planetary motion were to be superseded within the next 150 years, Copernicus' theory was nonetheless a profound break with scientific tradition—the first dramatically new view of the universe in almost two thousand years. Copernicus' work acted as a powerful stimulus to future scholars, encouraging them to re-think the principles underlying the behavior of the universe. The new laws of planetary motion described by Johannes Kepler between 1609 and 1621, and something of Galileo Galilei's mathematical physics published in 1638 and his earlier observations with a telescope, owe a debt to the spirit of *De Revolutionibus*. The publication of Newton's *Principia* in 1687 culminated an era of intense scientific enquiry of which Nicholas Copernicus had been one of the pioneers.

COLIN RONAN

429

A great spiritual revival lay at the heart of Rome's reply to Wittenberg and Geneva, for in truth the Counter-Reformation was already under way when Luther posted his *Theses*. The calling of the Lateran Council in 1512 and the program of reforms drawn up by Adrian VI some eleven years later were more than straws in the wind. Early in his pontificate Paul III (1534-49) appointed a Reform Commission and, despite his own conservatism, he was persuaded by his cardinals to call a general council. The council, which met at Trent in 1545 to determine policy and restate doctrine, concluded its work under Pius IV in 1562-63. But it was new religious orders, rather than general councils, that gave impetus to the Counter Reformation.

A number of new orders were established at this time, principally in Italy. Paoli Giustiniani, a Venetian of noble birth, embraced poverty in 1528 and founded the Capuchins, an order dedicated to working among the sick and needy. In 1535, Angela Merici formed the Ursuline Order, as an association of lay women pledged to a life of good works. And in 1540, Philip Neri (the future apostle of Rome) founded the Congregation of the Oratory.

The most significant of the new orders was the Society of Jesus, founded by Ignatius Loyola. Loyola (1491-1556) was a Spanish soldier and courtier who underwent conversion and wrote his *Spiritual Exercises*. While studying at Paris in 1534, the young Spaniard and his friends renounced wordly possessions and pledged to dedicate their lives to God's Word. They ultimately intended to undertake a barefoot pilgrimage to Jerusalem, but in the interim Loyola's followers worked in Italy. The Jesuit Order

Pius IV's Bull recalling the Council of Trent, 1560.

Ignatius Loyola, founder of the Jesuits.

was formally recognized by Paul III in 1540. Their Rule involved unquestioning obedience to the Pope —and almost from the beginning they served as the Church's shock troops, propagating the faith wherever they were sent. Their task was to reconvert the lands lost to Protestantism and to convert the heathen.

As Spaniards, both Loyola and his compatriot, Francis Xavier, were more at home among the heathen in the Moslem world than among Lutherans in North Germany. Their plans for missions to India, Brazil and the Congo received enthusiastic support from John III of Portugal and in 1542 Xavier set out for Goa. Meanwhile, in Europe the Society of Jesus quickly won a reputation as a teaching order with high standards in both classical studies and theology. The Jesuits established their first college at Padua, but their most famous was the College at Rome, which was founded in 1551.

To combat heresy, Paul III established the Inquisition in Rome in 1542 and issued the first papal Index of Prohibited Books some fifteen years later. The decrees of the Third Session of the Council of Trent further revitalized Catholicism and a new breviary was issued. Work on the dome of St. Peter's proceeded according to Michelangelo's plan and masses composed by Palestrina, director of music at St. Peter's, were sung in the Great Nave of the Cathedral.

Henry VIII

After executing Anne Boleyn in 1536 for adultery and incest, Henry VIII married Jane Seymour, who gave the King his longed-for son before dying in childbed. Henry's 1540 marriage to Anne of Cleves was arranged by Thomas Cromwell as part of a grand alliance with the German Protestant princes. The

union lasted only six months, and as soon as Henry had shed Anne, the Duke of Norfolk, who had ousted Cromwell on a charge of treason, cemented his position by marrying his niece Katherine Howard to the King. Katherine eventually trod the same path to Traitor's Gate that her cousin Anne Boleyn had walked, and Henry ended his matrimonial adventures in 1543 by marrying Katherine Parr, a widow of scholarly tastes— who managed to survive him.

Henry's unslakable thirst for military glory squandered his resources. The King's victory over the Scots at Solway Moss in November, 1542, was overshadowed by his disastrous campaigns in France. Charles V came to terms with

Henry VIII; Tudor despot.

Francis I without consulting his English ally, and all Henry could salvage from his conquests was Boulogne. Yet for all his excesses, Henry VIII laid the foundations of a strong national state. To Europe's considerable astonishment, he had defied the pope and had brought both Church and State under his forceful rule in England and Wales.

Defying the arrangements that had been made for Edward's minority, the prince's uncle, Edward Seymour, seized power as Lord Protector, took the title of Duke of Somerset, and unleashed a doctrinal Reformation. A prayer book compiled by Cranmer was forced upon the Church in 1549 by the Act of Uniformity, and the West Country rose to demand the restoration of the Catholic liturgy. Before the rising was put down, Robert Kett led a revolt in Norfolk in protest at the enclosure movement. John Dudley (who was soon to become Earl of Northumberland) defeated Kett and conspired to replace Seymour. In October, 1549, Seymour was ousted and Northumberland assumed effective control of the government; he was to rule England for the remainder of Edward's reign. In 1552 a second, more radically Protestant prayer book was approved.

To remain in control of the

government and to insure the survival of a Protestant England after the sixteen-year-old King's death, Northumberland married his son Guildford Dudley to Lady Jane Grey, eldest claimant to the throne in the Suffolk line of the succession. He prevailed upon the dying King to bestow the crown on Lady Jane rather than on Princess Mary, the rightful heir. Against her will, Jane was proclaimed Queen in July of 1553, and she reigned for thirteen days. Meanwhile, Mary's supporters rallied in East Anglia, and when an army sent to engage them deserted or disbanded, Northumberland surrendered.

Mary I's Spanish marriage

Queen Mary (1553-58) reintroduced the Roman Mass and, as the child of Catherine of Aragon, reconciled England with the papacy. Protestant bishops—among them Cranmer, Latimer and Ridley— who refused to recant were burned and others took refuge in Zurich and Geneva. In 1554, Mary married Philip of Spain, son of Charles V, but when Parliament opposed his plans to secure an English crown, Philip left the country. He returned only once, to insure that England would join Spain in her war against France—a war in which the English lost Calais, the last English foothold on the Continent. The seizure

Mary Stuart, Queen of Scots.

of Calais in 1558 ended Philip's hope of succeeding to the throne.

Mary, acknowledging at last her inability to produce an heir, became reconciled with her sister, Elizabeth, who succeeded the barren Queen on November 17, 1558. Protestants regarded Elizabeth's accession as the dawn of a new age, but Elizabeth I was determined to find in religion, as in politics, a moderate course—to heal the wounds inflicted by extremists.

James V and Mary Queen of Scots

Buttressed by interlineal marriages, Scotland maintained the "Auld Alliance" with France until 1560. Within a year of the death of his first wife, Madeleine of France, James V married Mary of Guise. Continuing border strife with Henry VIII's troops culminated in the Scots' defeat at Solway Moss in 1542. James V, who was mortally wounded in the battle, left as his successor a six-day-old daughter, Mary Queen of Scots. She was betrothed to Edward Tudor under the peace treaty of Greenwich in July, 1543, but after Cardinal Beaton's bid for the regency, the treaty was repudiated by the Scottish Parliament. Protector Somerset invaded Scotland again in 1547 and captured Edinburgh in a vain effort to reimpose a marriage treaty that would unite the two kingdoms. The young Queen of Scots, who was already betrothed to the Dauphin, was whisked away to France, leaving the rule of Scotland to her mother. The "Auld Alliance" had never appeared as menacing to England as it did in the years that Mary of Guise ruled a Scotland garrisoned with French troops while her brothers, Francis, Duke of Guise and the Cardinal of Lorraine, dictated French policy.

The growth of Protestantism north of the border altered the entire situation. Enflamed by Cardinal Beaton's persecution of heretics, the Protestant party assassinated him in 1546, and in 1555 John Knox returned from Geneva to preach reform of the Scottish Church. The first Covenant was signed in 1557, and Knox urged the Protestant Lords of the Congregation to rebel. In 1559 they sacked religious houses, seized Edinburgh and deposed Mary of Guise. Elizabeth answered the Scottish lords' appeal for help by sending troops and ships north to drive the French from Scotland. The following summer she signed the Treaty of Edinburgh with the Protestant Council of Regents, thus ending the endemic strife between the two kingdoms that had persisted for centuries. The Parliament in Edinburgh abolished papal jurisdiction and approved a Calvinistic Confession of Faith, drawn up by Knox, that established the Presbyterian Church of Scotland.

The Dauphin, whom Mary Queen of Scots had married, succeeded his father as Francis II in 1559, but reigned for only eighteen months. Mary, who claimed the throne of England as the granddaughter of Henry VIII's elder sister Margaret, regarded Elizabeth as a usurper and never ratified the Treaty of Greenwich. After Francis' death she returned to Scotland. She longed for a meeting with Elizabeth and an assurance that she would inherit the throne of England, but her claims and her search for another husband exasperated Elizabeth, The beautiful, imperious and impulsive widow outraged her own subjects by her devotion to Catholicism, and the gaiety of her court at Holyrood House angered Church elders, who soon questioned her fitness to rule.

Mary married the worthless Lord Darnley in 1565. Darnley was soon discredited for his complicity in the murder of David Rizzio, the Queen's Italian favorite. He was assassinated in Edinburgh in 1567 on the orders of James, Earl of Bothwell, who then seized Mary and married her. In a matter of weeks

Francis II of France.

the Lords of the Covenant had routed Bothwell's supporters at Carberry Hill, placed Mary in Lochleven Castle and forced her to abdicate in favor of her infant son James VI. Mary's step-brother, the Earl of Moray, was named regent. In May, 1568, Mary escaped to England, where she expected to find support for her efforts to regain the Scottish throne. Elizabeth, who feared Mary's influence among English Catholics and was wary of her designs upon the kingdom, decided to keep her in captivity.

Europe after 1540

The European scene changed rapidly after the mid-1540s. Luther,

Henry VIII and Francis I died in rapid succession. Emperor Charles V, the lone survivor, seemed to be at the height of his power when, in April, 1547, he won the decisive Battle of Muhlberg and ended his struggle with the Schmalkaldic League. Within a few years, however, his vast Empire began to collapse.

Fearing Hapsburg domination, the Empire's Protestant princes formed a defensive league. Henry II of France joined the League on the condition that he receive the bishoprics of Metz, Toul and Verdun in exchange for subsidizing a campaign against Charles. Henry occupied the bishoprics in 1552, and Maurice of Saxony invaded southern Germany at the head of a French army. The Emperor was forced to flee from Innsbruck, barely escaped capture and rode across the Brenner Pass to Villach. He made a last attempt to regain his Empire in 1554 with the aid of the Duke of Alva and the unpredictable Albrecht Alcibiades. The latter's defeat at Schwarzach in June ended the fighting and Charles, empowering his brother the Archduke Ferdinand to settle the religious question at the Diet as best he could, left Germany to her fate.

Thirty-eight years after the publication of the Wittenberg *Theses*, Germany finally acknowledged Lutheranism at the Peace of Augsburg in 1555. Charles was forced to abandon his hopes that his son Philip would be permitted to succeed him in the Empire, for both the princes and Archduke Ferdinand were opposed. Philip formally renounced his claims at the Diet of Augsburg and in September, 1556, Charles abdicated in favor of Ferdinand I. Charles had previously resigned the government of the Netherlands, Milan and Naples to Philip at a grand ceremony in Brussels, and in 1598 he surrendered the Empire and returned to Spain.

A general peace treaty was signed at Cateau-Cambresis in April, 1559. By the terms of that treaty France retained Calais and the bishoprics of Metz, Toul and Verdun. Piedmont was returned to Savoy—although both France and Spain kept garrisons at various key points —and Spanish possession of Franche-Comte was confirmed. During a tournament celebrating the end of Hapsburg-Valois strife, Henry II of France was accidentally killed, bringing Francis II, husband of Mary Queen of Scots, to the throne.

Upon returning to Spain in 1558, Philip II established Madrid as his capital and began building his great palace of the Escorial in the solitary foothills of the Sierra de Guadarrama. For forty years Philip ruled from the Escorial—directing policy, weighing reports, annotating despatches and making calculations.

Mary Tudor, Queen of England, and Philip II, King of Spain.

By 1558 both France and Spain were on the verge of bankruptcy, despite the seemingly inexhaustible resources of the New World. The riches of Mexico were being systematically exploited, and the silver mines that had been opened at Potosi, Peru, in 1545, were operating under the able administration of Francis de Toledo, the greatest colonial administrator of Spain's golden century. Yet each sailing of a treasure fleet to Europe added a new spiral to the price revolution.

Philip II, as his nickname "the Prudent King" implies, was sufficiently realistic to place politics before religion when the two interests clashed. Though a devout Catholic, much of his policy was distinctly anti-papal. He was never so happy as when national interests coincided with crusades against heretics and infidels—and his long struggle against the Dutch Calvinists, his eventual war with England, his cruel suppression of the Moriscos in Spain and his ending of Turkish supremacy in the Mediterranean were all undertaken for political as well as religious reasons.

In the last months of his reign, Suleiman the Magnificent embarked on another campaign in Hungary, took Belgrade and opened the siege of Szigeth. The fortress fell three days after the Sultan's death, and Emperor Maximilian II, whose army had melted away, came to terms with the new Sultan, Selim II (1566–74). Selim then turned his attentions to a naval war against Venice.

Cutting the Sultan's Beard

On September 16, 1571, a mammoth fleet composed of some three hundred ships weighed anchor in the Sicilian port of Messina and sailed for the Levant. Pope Pius V, who had summoned that navy and blessed its undertaking, hoped that the combined might of his Holy League fleet could strike a crippling blow against the Ottoman Empire. The Turks' increasing boldness on both land and sea threatened not only Venetian trading rights in the eastern Mediterranean but the Pope's none-too-secure empire as well. Pius himself chose Don Juan, natural brother of Philip II of Spain, to lead the Holy League against the Infidel—and he chose well. In an epic sea battle that pitted the Christian fleet against the combined navies of Ottoman Emperor Selim II and his Near Eastern allies, Don Juan captured or sunk more than two hundred Turkish vessels and inflicted some 25,000 casualties. His stunning victory ended Turkish incursions into Europe for decades.

The victor of Lepanto, Don Juan of Austria, bastard son of Charles V, from a portrait by Alonso Sánchez Coello.

Opposite Bruno del Priore's picture celebrating the victory at Lepanto. The figures in the lower left-hand corner represent the Republic of Venice, Philip II of Spain and Pope Pius V, while on the right, Death, with his scythe, mows down the Turks.

The first of July, 1571, was a day of rejoicing in Barcelona, Spain's principal seaport. On that scorchingly hot morning, a fleet of forty-seven war galleys lay at anchor in the harbor, and the city rippled with gaiety and excitement. Don Juan of Austria, half-brother of Philip II, the King of Spain, had just gone aboard the *Reale*, the flagship of the fleet, to introduce himself to its crew. The *Reale*, built in the shipyards of Barcelona, was painted red and gold—Don Juan's colors—and was bedecked with elaborate carved emblems. Multicolored pennants hung from the ship's rigging, and rose-colored velvet was draped over the planking.

Curiously, this day of triumph was to end with a humiliating rebuff for Don Juan. Upon returning to his quarters in the viceroy's palace, the young prince found a letter waiting for him from his half-brother, Philip II. The letter curtly ordered him to refrain from calling himself by the title of Highness and to confine himself to the title of Excellence, as befitted his station. Philip's note was a blunt reminder that Don Juan was illegitimate; he was the natural son of Charles V and a Flemish washer-woman, Barbara de Blomberg—and he was, therefore, a bastard. Don Juan began his proud reply to the King with the words: "God has made me the brother of Your Majesty. . . ."

In the eyes of history, Don Juan of Austria was the triumphant victor at Lepanto, but he was not the only actor in the drama by any means. Other personalities were to play equally important parts before, during and after the battle.

At the time of the Battle of Lepanto, Philip II was at his most powerful, and Spain was at the height of her glory. The Spanish regent had not inherited the great European hegemony that his father, Charles V, had conquered and subsequently relinquished. Nevertheless, Philip reigned over a completely independent Spain, which was no longer just another province of the Holy Roman Empire. In addition,

he controlled the Netherlands and Spain's profitable New World possessions, Mexico and Peru. As the ruler of Milan, Naples and Sicily, Philip also controlled nearly the whole of Italy—with the notable exception of Venice, which had maintained its independence ever since the ninth century, experiencing both prosperous and difficult times during that period.

The history of Venice has the rich, colorful texture of silk about it, and the flavor of Oriental spices. The Venetian merchants, creators of the sturdy *galeazza de mercanzia*, the huge trading vessels that were to prove their worth at Lepanto, were expert in the art of importing and exporting. For centuries they had been the custodians of the great international markets, and the principal suppliers of merchandise from the Orient to the Western countries. And from time to time the Venetians had found it necessary to defend their flourishing trade by force of arms. In the fifteenth century, Venice—which already ruled a Mediterranean empire that stretched from Istria and the Dalmatian coast to the Ionian islands and Crete—adopted a policy of territorial as well as maritime expansion. The Sultan of Turkey granted the Venetians exclusive trading rights within the Ottoman Empire, and in 1489, Venice annexed the island of Cyprus.

In Turkey, Selim II had succeeded his father, Suleiman the Magnificent, to the Ottoman throne. The new Sultan was very concerned about the annexation of Cyprus by Venice, for it hindered the free passage of Turkish ships across the waters lying within the vast Ottoman Empire. He determined that the Venetians had to be driven off Cyprus; if they refused to cede the island of their own free will, the Turkish fleet would have to intervene. Needless to say, the Venetians found the demands of the Sultan totally unacceptable, and when the Doge of Venice presented Selim's proposals to the Senate, they were angrily rejected as being contrary to the

Don Juan: an admiral chosen by the Pope

Philip II of Spain regarded Lepanto as a minor victory; he was more interested in stamping out heresy and crushing the Berbers. He was also jealous of the reputation of his half-brother, Don Juan.

The palace of the Escorial, the center of Philip II's vast empire.

peace treaty signed some years earlier with the Sublime Porte (the Ottoman government in Constantinople).

While the Venetians were trying to preserve their territorial possessions in the Mediterranean, Philip II of Spain was organizing an expedition to conquer the coastal strip of North Africa. Consequently, although there was little love lost between Spain and Venice, events combined to make a military alliance between the two states mutually beneficial. This community of interests needed only a moral justification, pronounced by some supreme and undisputed authority, to transform it into a true pact. The logical person to serve as this authority was Pope Pius V, and it was he who fashioned the Venetians' war of reprisal against the Turks into a religious crusade against the Infidel. Pius' creation, the Holy League, was ably supported by the fanatical Catholicism of Philip II.

The Holy League was confirmed by a treaty drawn up between Venice and Spain and approved and promulgated by the Pope, who was also one of the signatories. It consisted of a common declaration of war against the Turks and the Moors in Algeria, Tunis and Tripoli. It laid down the terms and conditions of intervention by the respective parties, and detailed the military contributions and the division of expenses between the two states and the Papacy. It was agreed that the conduct of the war should be under the leadership of three commanders: a Venetian, a Spaniard and a representative of the Papacy. However, in accordance with the wishes of the Holy Father, one paragraph of the treaty stipulated that Don Juan of Austria should become commander-in-chief of the joint forces.

The Holy League treaty was drawn up and signed in Rome on May 20, 1571. Two months later, on July 11, a convoy of eleven galleys, a protective vanguard for the main Spanish fleet, raised anchor and set sail from Barcelona. Nine days later, a second convoy, consisting of thirty-seven ships and led by the *Reale*, weighed anchor. It too was bound for Genoa. Don Juan stopped only briefly at this Italian port before pressing on to the Sicilian port of Messina, the assembly point for the allied squadrons.

The *Reale* reached her destination on the evening of August 23. By that time more than three hundred ships, thirty thousand soldiers, and fifty thousand rowers and sailors were gathered in Messina. Galleys and troops from Venice, Genoa, Naples, Sicily and the Papacy had joined Don Juan's fleet. Savoy and the Knights of Malta sent their contributions.

Don Juan carried out a lengthy, careful inspection of the force under his command. On board the *Reale*, he held meetings with his chief officers: the Genoese Andrea Doria, the Venetians Sebastiano Venier and Agostino Barbarigo, the Pope's delegate Marco Antonio Colonna, the Spaniards Santa Cruz and Requesens, and Alexander Farnese, Don Juan's childhood companion. The ships' captains received precise and secret instructions as to the order of battle and their own special duties.

The Turks, meanwhile, had left a trail of blood and fire behind them in Cyprus, where they occupied the main town of Famagusta, and in Corfu, which they destroyed. The city was in ruins when Don Juan stopped there on September 28. Two days later, he gave orders for his fleet to set sail for the Bay of Gomenitza, on the Albanian coast, for Don Juan had discovered that the enemy fleet was lying not far from the Turkish base of Lepanto, at the mouth of the Gulf of Patras in western Greece. The enemy fleet was composed of two hundred and eight fighting galleys, sixty-six galliots, or small galleys, and eighty-eight thousand men, twenty-five thousand of whom were soldiers.

On October 3, the Christian fleet left Gomenitza, and sailed south past the island of Corfu. Three days later, it passed the fortress of Preveza on the eastern shores of the Ionian Sea. During the night of October 6, the fleet moved south toward the island of Cephalonia, and anchored off Lepanto, north of the Gulf of Patras and close to the Cape of Actium (where Octavius and Marc Antony had fought their famous battle for control of the Roman Empire). At dawn on Sunday, October 7, Don Juan of Austria carried out a final inspection of his fleet. Everything seemed to be in order, and the prince felt confident, particularly when a light westerly breeze sprang up, giving the Christian fleet the advantage. At 11:45 A.M., Don Juan gave the order for the white banner of the Holy League to be hoisted on the mast of the *Reale*. The guns were fired, and the battle was on.

The Christian fleet, which consisted of two hundred and eight fighting galleons, six large galleys, and one hundred and two smaller craft carrying twelve to seventeen oars, formed a rectilinear front. Barbarigo was in command of the left flank of the fleet, and Doria of the right flank; the *Reale* lay in the center, surrounded by the galleys of Colonna and Venier. A relief galley, belonging to Requesens, lay next to the flagship, so close that the two were almost touching. Behind them, a fourth division, under the command of Santa Cruz, was waiting in reserve. The six huge Venetian *galeasses*, each weighing six hundred tons and each armed with 180 guns, were lined up in front of the main fleet. These enormous ships which were so ponderous that they had to be towed into position by galleys, were manned by a crew of one thousand men and four hundred and fifty rowers, eight men to each oar.

The Ottoman ships were spread out in a crescent-shaped formation facing the battle fleet of the Holy League. Scirocco, Pasha of Alexandria, and Ulüch Ali, Dey of Algiers, were in command of the right and left extremities of this curve, while the center of the formation was occupied by Pertev and Ali Pasha, whose flagship, the *Sultana*, lay opposite the *Reale*.

The two fleets joined battle, attacking each other with great violence. The Christian and Ottoman commanders-in-chief eyed each other warily from the two opposing flagships, separated by a distance of not more than five yards. Ali Pasha was wearing a caftan made of white brocade embroidered with precious stones, and on his head was a turban, wound around a steel helmet. He was surrounded by three hundred janissaries and a hundred archers. The two flagships collided with a tremendous crash. Drums were beating; bugles were blowing. The bright sun lit up the vivid yellows, greens and reds of the Moslem flags and glittered on the helmets of the Christian soldiers. Don Juan, standing on the forecastle of his galley, raised his sword high into the air, made the sign of the cross and plunged into the attack. Four hundred leather-booted Spaniards followed close behind, brandishing their halberds.

The battle lasted for five hours, and until the very end the outcome remained uncertain. Both the *Reale* and the *Sultana*, symbolic prizes in the contest, were invaded by the opposing side and then almost immediately abandoned. Turks and Christians alike displayed extraordinary valor: Alexander Farnese single-handedly captured the galley in which the treasure of the Turkish fleet was stored. A party led by Ulüch Ali, taking advantage of a breach in Doria's division, plunged forward to attack the galleys of the Knights of Malta, strangled the thirty knights, and captured the black flag of their Order. It looked as though the battle would go in favor of the Turks until the Holy League's reserve division, under the command of Santa Cruz, intervened.

Late in the afternoon, Don Juan himself managed

Andrea Doria of Genoa, who, acting on secret orders from Philip II, refused to fight. This unsuccessful attempt to reduce the effect of Don Juan's victory was part of Philip's campaign to subjugate the Republic of Venice.

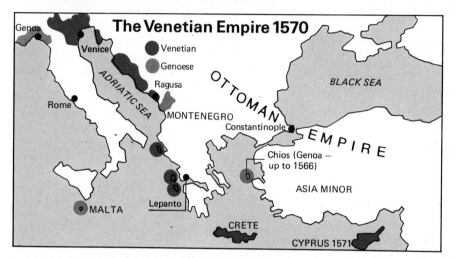

The Venetian Empire 1570

Venetian
Genoese

Genoa
Venice
ADRIATIC SEA
Ragusa
Rome
MONTENEGRO
Constantinople
OTTOMAN EMPIRE
BLACK SEA
Chios (Genoa — up to 1566)
ASIA MINOR
MALTA
Lepanto
CRETE
CYPRUS 1571

to set foot on the deck of the *Sultana*. Just as he was about to capture Ali Pasha, the Turkish commander was struck in the head by a shot from an harquebus and fell dead. A Spaniard cut off the fallen leader's head and offered it to Don Juan. It was then stuck on the end of a pike and displayed to all the combatants. The air was filled with cries of joy from the Christians and cries of despair from the Turks at the sight. From that moment, the Holy League was assured of victory. Colonna succeeded in disengaging the *Reale* from the Turkish galleys that were hemming it in, and the battle deteriorated into a massacre. The Turkish galleys, inexorably blasted by the guns of the Christian ships, were set on fire, sunk or captured. The strength of the Christians, combined with the superiority of their armaments, was too much for the Moslems, despite the fact that the latter were more skilled at maneuvering their ships. By five o'clock in the afternoon it was all over; at the masthead of the Turkish flagship, the *Sultana*, the crucifix had replaced the flag of the Prophet.

A total of twenty-five thousand Turks were killed and five thousand taken prisoner—a total loss of thirty thousand men. Twelve thousand Christian slaves were freed from the captured galleys.

Not surprisingly, the whole of Christendom was filled with joy at the news of the victory at Lepanto. The Turks had suffered a spectacular and decisive defeat, at least when judged solely from the number of casualties sustained and ships lost. The Turkish fleet had not been wholly destroyed, however; the Algerian Ulüch Ali had managed to escape with forty ships. According to Pertev, the comrade-in-arms of Ali Pasha, the Christians' victory "had only

Alexander Farnese, a childhood companion of Don Juan, who was one of the leaders of the expedition.

A breathing-space for Christendom

A coin struck by Pope Pius V to celebrate Lepanto. The motto reads "O Lord, Thy right hand destroyed the enemy."

cut off the beard of the Sultan." His taunt implied that the beard would grow back again.

Nevertheless, the Republic of Venice had been saved for the time being from the danger of further attacks by the Ottomans, who had been menacing its frontiers, laying waste to its possessions and massacring its subjects. But for this setback, the Sultan might well have conquered Venice itself. All the same, Venice had lost the flower of its young nobility and a substantial portion of its fleet. Moreover, it had managed to maintain its political independence, but it was gradually losing its commercial supremacy. During the years that followed the Battle of Lepanto, Venetian galleys, driven out of the Levant, found that they no longer had any call to sail to northern ports. The British, unable to obtain the merchandise from the Mediterranean that they had grown to expect, decided to get it for themselves. They sailed through the Straits of Gibraltar, and soon established commercial relations with the Christian trading stations located in the eastern Mediterranean. They then went a step further, and opened trade negotiations with the Sultan, who badly needed tin for his guns. Thus, only ten years after Lepanto an English fleet of merchant ships flying the flag of the Levant Company was plying the Mediterranean. They sold English metals and manufactured articles to the Ottoman Empire and, in exchange, bought silks and spices from the Turks. These English traders were soon joined by Dutch merchants, who established commercial relations with the Sultan.

In this way, Venice was deprived of both its suppliers and its clients at the same time—to the benefit of the Turks. For the first time in history, northerners were trading in the Mediterranean, a sea that until then had been reserved for Mediterranean peoples. Venice, which suffered a great loss of economic prestige, grew apprehensive, for it still feared the possibility of a Turkish attack. To rectify this situation, Venice concluded a separate peace treaty with the Ottoman Empire several months after the Battle of Lepanto. The terms of the treaty were relatively honorable, but Cyprus became a Turkish possession once again.

The breaking of the pact of the Holy League by the Venetians, through their separate treaty with the Turks, did not anger Spain, as might have been expected. It had quite the contrary effect, for this move served Spain's interest admirably. And those interest were synonymous with the interests of Philip II, who had complete political control over the country. The personal policy he adopted in regard to the Lepanto expedition was so riddled with secret, subtle intentions that it often seemed to run counter to the national interests. For instance, when the Genoese Andrea Doria, who was in command of the right flank of the Christian fleet, abandoned his position and withdrew his forces—thus allowing the Algerian Ulüch Ali to penetrate the League's formation—this move was not in fact a miscalculation, but a positive decision not to fight. Nor was this refusal to fight a voluntary action on the part of

The Battle of Lepanto, by an unknown artist.

Doria—it was carried out on the secret orders of the King of Spain himself, without the knowledge of Don Juan of Austria. Philip II wanted a victory over the Turks, but he did not want this victory to be too spectacular. He wanted to save Venice only so that he could later annex it.

Although Philip II had seen to it that he did not become too deeply involved in the Lepanto expedition, he was prepared to pay the larger part of the expenses. The Spanish treasury had not merely run dry, but was also heavily mortgaged by costly loans contracted with the bankers of Genoa. However, the King of Spain refused to permit financial worries to divert him from his main objectives: crushing the Berbers and stamping out heresy. He expelled the Moriscos and Marranos from Spain—the Moslem and Jewish inhabitants who had been converted to Christianity—because he doubted the sincerity of their conversion and feared especially that the Moriscos might be the vanguard of an eventual Islamic invasion of Spain. Philip had good reason to fear the Moslems; less than a century had elapsed since Ferdinand and Isabella, Philip's great-grandparents, had succeeded in driving the Moors from Iberia. The King's religious zeal concealed a more practical motive, however. By confiscating the possessions of the Moriscos and Marranos, he was able to replenish the empty coffers of Spain.

Taking advantage of the psychological effect of Don Juan's victory over the Turks, Philip II sent him off forthwith to conquer Tunis, in an effort to regain

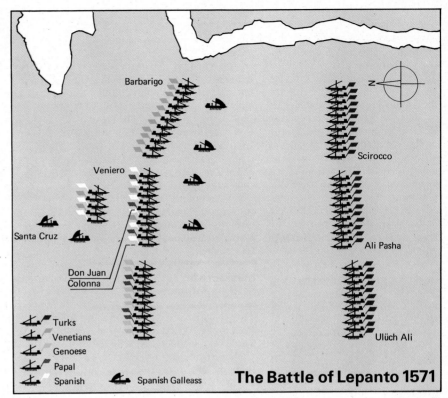

The Battle of Lepanto 1571

the Protectorate, which had been under Arab rule for many years. Within a month, Don Juan had captured Tunis; he begged leave of Philip II to be proclaimed king of it, but his request was refused. In any case, Don Juan's victory was only temporary: a year later, Ulüch Ali retook Tunis and the fort of La Goletta and exterminated the eight thousand Spaniards living there. Thus, Spain's military gains as a result of the Battle of Lepanto were negligible. Nevertheless, since he was at last safe from the menace of a Turkish attack, Philip II was able to turn his attention and energies to Great Britain and the Netherlands.

In short, the real victory of the Battle of Lepanto was gained by Christendom. The powerful Ottoman Empire suffered a decisive defeat in the waters of the Ionian Sea, a defeat that was to put an end to its territorial expansion. If there had been no Battle of Lepanto, the whole of Europe might have fallen into the hands of the Turks. Italy might have suffered the same fate as that of Greece, and Western Europe might have disintegrated in much the same way as the Roman Empire did during the fifth century. Moreover, the psychological and moral effects of Lepanto were profound, for this victory destroyed once and for all the myth of the invincible Turk.

JEAN DESCOLA

A mid-sixteenth-century Turkish quiver and arrows.

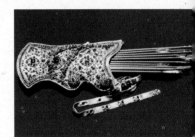

Three thousand Protestants are murdere

By the middle of the sixteenth century, many prominent French nobles and a substantial portion of the middle class had adopted Protestantism—despite continued threats of persecution. As regent for her son Charles IX, Catherine de' Medici attempted to achieve a balance of power between the Catholic supporters of the House of Guise and the chief Huguenot nobles. In January, 1562—the month that the final session of the Council of Trent opened—Michel L'Hopital, the moderate constable of France, promulgated the Edict of St. Germain. For the first time, the Huguenots received official recognition. In the face of this threat to French Catholicism and to stable

Claude de Lorraine, Duc de Guise.

government, the Duke of Guise, the Cardinal of Lorraine and the Duke of Montmorency created a militant league to renew persecution of the Protestants. The Guises ordered the massacre of 1,200 Huguenots at Vassy in 1562, an action that provoked the first of seven Wars of Religion. Those clashes, which continued intermittently until 1580, led in turn to a war of succession. In 1598, after thirteen years of dynastic war, Henry of Navarre was able to achieve a lasting peace. His Edict of Nantes, promulgated in 1598, granted Huguenots equal political rights with Catholics and insisted upon limited toleration of their worship.

By the turn of the century, France had been a battlefield for thirty-six years. Incessant civil war, broken by periodic, uneasy truces, had claimed the flower of her nobility. In the beginning Conde, the Huguenot commander, had pinned his hopes for military victory on English support, but the army that Elizabeth I sent to garrison Le Havre was decimated by the plague in 1563, and thereafter English aid took the form of

subsidies. John Casimir of the Palatinate was one of a group of German soldiers of fortune who had answered the Huguenot summons and marched his mercenary armies into France. The modest concessions that the Huguenots and their allies secured through the Peace of Amboise in 1563 and by the Treaty of Longjumeau, some five years later, satisfied neither side. The terms of the Peace of 1570, which ended the third war, were more encouraging for the Huguenots, who were granted amnesty, liberty of conscience and permission to retain their strongholds in La Rochelle, Montauban, Cognac and La Charité.

Massacre of St. Bartholomew

Two years later, in August, 1572, Paris prepared for a royal wedding. Margaret of Valois, Charles IX's Catholic sister, was to wed Henry, Duke of Bourbon and King of Navarre, who had become the leading Huguenot in France. In a more mature age, the marriage of a Catholic princess and a Protestant king might have healed the divisions of the realm, but the atmosphere of Paris in 1572 was too explosive. Four days after the wedding Admiral Coligny, the Huguenot commander-in-chief, was wounded by an assailant who

Gaspard de Coligny, Protestant leader.

was working for the Duke of Guise. Catherine de' Medici, the Queen Mother, fearing Huguenot reprisals on the royal family, proposed an immediate massacre of all Huguenots in the capital. Catherine's weakling son Charles IX agreed—and lists were swiftly compiled.

The massacre of St. Bartholomew's Day.

Henry of Navarre was spared in the Massacre of St. Bartholomew, but the Duke of Guise personally executed Coligny and some 3,000 other Protestant Parisians were slaughtered. The massacre touched off similar attacks in the provinces—notably in Bordeaux, Orleans, Lyons, Rouen and Toulouse—in which an additional 10,000 Huguenots died. Deprived of their generals, the Huguenot army withdrew to La Rochelle and other strongholds. Many civilians emigrated from France at this time, and refugees by the thousands poured into England and Germany. In general the Huguenots, many of whom were skilled craftsmen, were welcomed in the lands to which they fled.

The events of 1572 drove the Center Party, which was composed of moderates such as L'Hopital, to support the Huguenots. Navarre, the future King Henry IV, feigned conversion to Catholicism to save himself during the massacres, but four years later he abjured Catholicism and was recognized as head of the Huguenot Party. Protestant Europe was shocked by the massacres, which left it more vulnerable than ever to militant Catholicism. Coupled with Don Juan's victory at Lepanto and the success of Alva against the Dutch rebels, events in France made the future of Protestantism look very bleak.

Philip II and "The Beggars"

Charles V had begun his life as Charles of Ghent—and despite his Spanish crown and imperial office, he had been regarded with affection by his subjects in the Low Countries. Those same subjects looked upon Philip II, Charles V's son, as an interfering Spaniard—and not without reason. One of Philip's first acts as ruler of the Netherlands

was to introduce the Jesuits, and when he returned to Spain he left his natural sister Margaret, Duchess of Parma, as regent. During Margaret's rule, Dutch policy was directed by Cardinal Granvelle, Bishop of Arras, who provoked disturbances in Holland and Zeeland by establishing new Catholic bishoprics. The northern provinces—those that eventually formed the Dutch Republic—were already strongholds of Calvinism, and they protested Granvelle's actions through a series of risings. Margaret was forced to call in the Spanish army to suppress the rebels. The Nationalist Party, headed by Count Egmont, persistently demanded that the Spanish soldiers leave, Granvelle be replaced and the provinces be left to enjoy their ancient liberties—and in 1564 the Cardinal was dismissed.

In 1566, Prince Louis of Nassau, brother of William of Orange, and Philip of Marnix organized the lesser Dutch nobility into a confederacy—soon nicknamed *Les Gueux* (the Beggars)—which demanded that the Inquisition be withdrawn and freedom of worship reinstated. Margaret of Parma promised concessions, but these failed to satisfy the Dutch extremists. In August there were violent waves of iconoclasm in Hondschoote, Valenciennes, Antwerp and Groningen: some four hundred churches were sacked, statues and images were broken and abbeys were burned. Those spontaneous outbreaks, as much social as religious in nature, forced Margaret to withdraw the Inquisition; yet she retaliated by raising an army of German mercenaries that annihilated 2,000 reformists near Antwerp.

Philip chose his ablest general, the Duke of Alva, to bring the Netherlands to heel, and Alva arrived at Brussels in August, 1567, with an army composed of 20,000 seasoned

Spanish and Italian soldiers. As military governor, Alva established the Council of Blood, a tribunal that instigated a reign of terror, and Margaret handed the office of regent over to him. Calvinist refugees began to leave for England and Germany, and their numbers increased after counts Egmont and Hoorn—who personified resistance to Spanish rule—were executed for high treason.

In 1568 the outlawed William of Orange, who was destined to be the savior of the Dutch, defeated the Spanish with a mercenary force raised in Germany. That action at Heiligerlec marked the outbreak of the Revolt of the Netherlands, a conflict that was to dominate European politics until the close of the century. Out of the long struggle with Spain emerged an independent Dutch Republic composed of the Protestant northern provinces. The Catholic southern provinces—the future Belgium—remained under Spanish rule.

The Spanish dominated mid-sixteenth-century Italy with the exception of Savoy, which was restored to Emmanuel Philibert by the Treaty of Cateau-Cambresis. Emmanuel, who succeeded his father to an apparently empty title and sought fame as a general of Philip II, proved to be the lone Italian ruler capable of building an independent, centralized state. His victory over the French at St. Quentin in August, 1557, earned him the lost provinces of Savoy and Piedmont at a subsequent peace conference. (France was permitted to retain her garrisons in Turin and Pignerolo, however, and Spain continued to hold Asti.) The wars had devastated the duchy to such an extent that there were "no citizens in the cities, neither man nor beasts in the fields." Emmanuel Philibert inaugurated a series of reforms, stabilized the currency and formed a standing army that was the envy of his neighbors. After initially repressing the Protestant Waldenses in the valleys of Piedmont, he was persuaded to grant them religious toleration.

Brahe's "new" star

The Danish astronomer Tycho Brahe (1546–1601) was a curious contradiction. The modernity of his instruments and calculations was balanced by the reactionary nature of his intellectual outlook—Brahe regarded astronomy as a

Tycho Brahe in his observatory.

"divine" science and rejected the Copernican theory of a heliocentric universe. While studying chemistry at Augsburg, he made a nineteen-foot quadrant and a celestial globe five feet in diameter, and when he returned to Denmark his noble uncle encouraged him to build a laboratory in his castle. From that vantage, Brahe observed the "new" star Cassiopeia on November 11, 1572. Brahe's discovery brought him unprecedented royal patronage: Frederick II granted the astronomer the island of Hveen, on which Brahe built his Uraniborg Observatory in 1576. Brahe designed his own instruments and with them achieved new standards of accuracy, but his fame rests primarily on the voluminous observations that he recorded in great detail. Those records form the basis of modern astronomy.

Ivan IV of Russia

The excesses of the Glinski and Shuiski factions in Russia during Ivan IV's minority were a disastrous preparation for his eventual rule (1547–84). Until her early death, his consort Anastasia had a restraining influence on the Tsar, but for most of his reign he acted like a possessed monster, plunging the country into unprecedented carnage that earned him the name "Ivan the Terrible." His early campaigns against the Tartars enabled him to annex Kazan in 1552 and Astrakhan in 1556, and gave the Tsar complete control of the Volga River. Ivan fought a long and costly war with Livonia between 1557 and 1582, but he failed to acquire his objective—an outlet on the Baltic. English adventurers under Chancellor arrived at Archangel in

1553 and established trading privileges in Moscow, but for the most part Ivan's contacts with the West were less numerous and less significant than his predecessor's had been.

Ivan's cruelty was legendary. He left Moscow in 1564—to escape from a boyar rising led by Prince Kurbski, and upon his return he inaugurated a reign of terror that lasted for the rest of his life. The Tsar murdered his eldest son in a fit of rage in 1580; and when he was overcome by the beauty of the new Cathedral of St. Basil in Moscow, he put out the architect's eyes—to prevent him from being able to design another so great. Ivan personally directed the Massacre of Novgorod, in which some 60,000 men and women were slaughtered in the streets for contemplating an alliance with Ivan's enemy, Livonia.

Ivan the Terrible.

"I am your god and God is mine," Ivan thundered, and his people came to accept their Tsar's violent nature as readily as they accepted his near divinity.

Japan

The early history of Japan is a chronicle of prolonged anarchy. The country was devastated by wars of succession and lives were sacrificed on a Muscovite scale. The arrival of Portuguese ships in 1542 brought Japan into contact with the West for the first time, and in 1549 St. Francis Xavier and two companions landed at Satsuma and set about converting the inhabitants. The princes of Japan were more interested in muskets than in missals, however—and it seemed likely for a time that the importation of more sophisticated methods

of warfare would lead to unprecedented carnage. The country's eventual recovery from endemic civil war and its emergence as a unified state in the late sixteenth century resulted from the efforts of three remarkable leaders, Ota Nobunaga, Hideyoshi and Ieyasu.

Nobunaga, who seized power in Kyoto in 1568, soon managed to impose his rule upon the central provinces and gradually weakened the power of the Buddhist monasteries (notably the military community on Mount Hiei). Profiting by Western methods learned from the foreign traders who came to the free port of Nagasaki, Nobunaga built Japan's first castle on the shores of Lake Biwa.

In 1582, Nobunaga was assassinated by one of his generals, who also destroyed the castle on Lake Biwa. Upon his return from campaigning in western Japan, Hideyoshi avenged Nobunaga's death—and in the next few years he overcame all opposition and became the virtual dictator of a unified Japan. When, in 1592, the Koreans refused to permit Hideyoshi's troops to pass through the peninsula on their way to China, he invaded Korea. Confronted by a huge Chinese army, Hideyoshi was forced to retreat. The dictator's last years were clouded by the persecution of Christian missionaries, whom Hideyoshi accused of seeking to divide his people in preparation for a conquest by European powers.

Persia

While Akbar was consolidating the Mogul Empire, Shah Abbas I (1587–1629) was establishing a strong personal rule in Persia. In order to expel the Uzbeks from Khorasan, he came to terms with the Turks and surrendered Tabriz and Georgia to them. His army then won a decisive victory near Herat, ending the long series of Uzbek depredations. Abbas the Great resumed the war with Turkey in 1602 and regained Tabriz, Shrivan and subsequently Baghdad. His successes continued and, by the time of his death, his kingdom stretched from the Tigris to the Euphrates. Although cruel to his own family and subjects, Abbas was remarkably tolerant of foreigners. He profited greatly from the advice of two Englishmen, Anthony and Robert Shirley, who came to his court on a diplomatic mission and remained in his service.

A New Empire for India

In February, 1573, following a protracted siege, the Afghan stronghold of Surat capitulated to the Mogul Emperor Akbar. The Indian monarch's victory added the textile-rich province of Gujarat and its busy ports on the Arabian Sea to Akbar's burgeoning Empire—and it effectively ended decades of internecine strife in northern India. A generation earlier, Akbar's father, Humayun, had captured and briefly held Gujarat before launching an impetuous and disastrous campaign in the east. Akbar's reconquest of the province consolidated his holdings and radically diminished both internal and external threats to the Mogul throne. From this secure power base, Akbar was able to quell further outbreaks, promote amicable Moslem-Hindu relations, promulgate a new religion and lay the groundwork for a truly pan-Indian nation.

In the traditional view of Indian historians, the Mogul Empire in India was established in 1526 when Baber, a descendant of Genghis Khan, defeated the Afghan prince Ibrahim Lodi in the First Battle of Panipat. After the great Sikandar Lodi's death in 1517, the old Delhi sultanate—which dated from the first Moslem conquest at the end of the twelfth century—had been split up among contending members of the Lodi family, each of whom was supported by a different Afghan tribe. Disputes over the succession had raged for nearly a decade when Baber intervened in 1526. His action was clearly prompted by hopes of personal gain and not out of any sympathy for the squabbling Afghans, for Baber had already extended the boundaries of his central Asian empire of Farghana into parts of Afghanistan, and he was eager to acquire the Punjab and Delhi itself. The deeper Baber advanced into India, the less secure his own northern possessions became and he was obliged to wage a continual struggle to convert his implicit sovereignty over the Lodi into actual domination.

By the time of his death in 1530, Baber had become master of Delhi and Agra, moved down the Ganges to establish himself in Jaunpur, secured his western frontiers against the martial princes of Rajasthan and extended his sway in the east down to the border of Bengal. The conqueror established little more than his sovereignty in those regions, however; Baber introduced no new cultural or administrative ideas, developed no Indian "policy" and built no distinguished public structures. From the natives' point of view, one foreign ruler had been replaced by another; the difference was only one of tenancy of the Delhi sultanate.

Baber's son, Humayun, was even less effectual as an emperor. He assigned the government of the Punjab, Kandahar and Kabul to a brother in order to be free to direct the continuing Indian campaigns. Those campaigns were numerous and sizable, for both the Hindu kings and the Moslem rulers of India opposed Humayun. The beleaguered monarch was also at odds with his kinsmen the Mirzas—descendants of the great conqueror Timur (Tamerlane)—a turbulent lot who were only too anxious to grab for themselves any convenient slices of the cake that Baber had carved out of India. The Mirzas' hostility was ironic, for Baber had deliberately brought them to India to strengthen his hold over northern India.

In the course of his campaigning, Humayun defeated Bahadur, the Sultan of Gujarat, drove him out of the province, and then abandoned the chase to launch a vigorous assault against an Afghan force in the east. That Afghan army was led by Sher Shah of the Sur tribe—a man who was one of India's ablest sovereigns. While Humayun was preoccupied with Bahadur, with the Mirza rebellion and with safeguarding his western lands against his ambitious brother, Sher had established a trained army in southern Bihar and had extended his personal control into Bengal by defeating its sultan in 1538. Alarmed by Sher's welling strength, Humayun marched into the Bengal capital—only to find the city empty. Sher had withdrawn—and his army was sitting astride Humayun's sole line of communication with Delhi. The outgeneraled Mogul ruler was hounded back to his capital, and in 1540 he was driven out of India. The Delhi sultanate had a new ruler.

Sher Shah's accession marks the first great turning point in sixteenth-century Indian history, for Sher did much more than simply assume sovereignty over Humayun's former possessions. He retook Malwa, which Humayun had given up, established his authority in Rajasthan, and—more than any other contemporary Indian ruler—inspired a nationalistic following.

The keystone of Sher's reforms was a new revenue system: he abolished the old hit-and-miss system of crop-sharing in favor of a system based on the crop-bearing potential of measured areas, and employed

A portrait of Akbar, Mogul Emperor.

Opposite Building the city of Fathpur Sikri as part of the celebrations for the birth of Akbar's son.

Baber, Humayan and Akbar, the first three Mogul emperors of India.

into the system, but the fundamental structure of the Mogul revenue system—devised by Sher Shah—remained unchanged throughout the whole Mogul period. Indeed, Sher's reforms put India on a stable economic footing that lasted long beyond his own short reign.

After Sher Shah's death in 1545, political turmoil broke out afresh in northern India. Sher had left no one to succeed him, and Afghan tribal groups rallied to the support of a number of nobles of the Sur tribe. By 1554 the empire had been divided among three such nobles, each of whom was calling himself sultan. In the midst of the confusion Humayun—who had managed to recapture the Afghan capital of Kabul after fifteen years of wandering—marched on India to regain his lost kingdom. He defeated a Sur army at Sirhind in the Punjab in 1555 and went on to occupy Delhi without opposition. Within six months he died and his son Akbar—born during Humayun's exile and not yet fourteen years of age—succeeded to the somewhat precarious Mogul throne.

The affairs of Mogul government were initially well served by a council of regency, and the council in turn was blessed with competent generals. The three Sur pretenders to the throne were defeated, as was a former minister of one of the Sur "sultans." Hemur, a low-born man with a natural head for soldiering, was perhaps the most dangerous enemy of the Mogul state. He actually managed to occupy Delhi in 1556, but was killed in a clash between his followers and the Mogul forces at the Second Battle of Panipat. With these dangers removed, the Mogul generals soon recaptured Gwalior and Jaunpur.

In 1562, Akbar married the daughter of a Hindu rajah. Such interfaith marriages were by no means unknown, but in Akbar's case there was one outstanding difference: by the Moslem ruler's decree, his wife's Hindu relatives were regarded as members of the royal family, were frequently appointed to high office and were permitted to practice their own religious rites. This policy, which earned Akbar the support of the Rajput princes, was continued by his successors during the heyday of the Mogul dynasty. It is noteworthy, however, that the rigid orthodoxy of Aurangzeb, Akbar's great-grandson, lost the Mogul Empire the support of its Hindu population and contributed to the Empire's decline. Akbar's decree was the first of many steps taken by the Mogul Emperor to make himself the ruler of all his people, Hindu as well as Moslem.

During the 1560s, the young ruler gradually rose to a position of strong personal power. Akbar's armies invaded Malwa and held the region despite some reverses; the Gond kingdom in east central India was annexed; Mogul armies captured Bihar, where there had been another attempt at Afghan resurgence; and military supremacy over the Rajputs was won. The Rana of Chitor, acknowledged head of the Rajput clans, had remained haughty and aloof during the early 1560s. He had spurned all contact with the Moguls, and had indicated his readiness to take up arms against them at any time.

a well-drilled civil service to conduct the necessary surveys, collect the revenues and maintain the accounts. Chief administrative officers were appointed in each district to insure that the revenues were collected, to settle cases of injustice in the system and to make sure that the cultivators were not being subjected to any form of oppression. The civilian population was further relieved from anxiety by a rigorous campaign against organized brigandage and other crime. "An old woman with a basketful of gold," says a contemporary historian, "could sleep safe out doors at night without a guard."

Sher Shah's achievements were a source of embarrassment to later Mogul historians, who sought to credit their own rulers with the achievements of his reign. The administrative measures that he introduced were later attributed to Baber's grandson Akbar by his sycophant-biographer, Abu'l Fazl. It is true that in 1571 Akbar's revenue minister, Todar Mall, eliminated some abuses that had crept

Suppressing rebellion in Gujarat

sultans who were installed as puppet rulers. Suspicious nobles plotted against one another and against the best interests of the state, faction was rife and the ambitious Portuguese were a constant menace on the coasts.

The Portuguese, who had been established at Goa since 1510, were masters of the western seas. (Gujarati sailors were competent enough as coastal pirates, but naval warfare was scarcely known in India.) The foreigners sacked and burned more than one town on the Gujarat coast and—most disturbing of all to the Moslem powers of India—they were able

Rejoicing at the birth of Akbar's child.

While watching an elephant fight, Akbar is told that his wife has had a baby.

The successful campaign against Chitor, personally led by Akbar (who had already distinguished himself on the field against Malwa), was followed in 1569 by the fall of two other great Rajput strongholds. Akbar's paramountcy was assured, but he was still forced to contend with rebellious parties at home. In the middle of the decade there was a revolt by an Uzbek faction that tried to set up Akbar's cousin as the ruler. The cousin—and the Uzbek instigators of the rising—were suppressed, but rebellion persisted. The Mirzas, who had received small assignments of land during the Mogul restoration, invaded Malwa and made their way to Gujarat.

At the time, Gujarat was in the midst of severe troubles. Sultan Bahadur had been assassinated through Portuguese treachery in 1537. His nephew, the ruler of the neighboring state of Khandesh, had died within weeks of receiving his summons to the Gujarat throne, and from that time the Gujarat sultanate had been held by a succession of minor

The central pillar of the Diwan-i Khassat at Fathpur Sikri, the city built by Akbar to celebrate the birth of his son.

to menace the peaceful pilgrim traffic to Mecca and the Hejaz.

The Gujarat state, which by the 1560s was little more than a polite fiction, was not strong enough to contain its own nobles, much less foreign aggressors. Gujarati nobles parceled out the land among themselves, and they were joined in their depredations by the Mirzas and by the local Habshis—a nominally Abyssinian group, which had been brought to India as slaves, soldiers and palace guards, but had risen to considerable local prominence. The nominal regent of Gujarat during this time of civil strife was I'timad Khan, a converted Hindu. Powerless and desperate, he invited Akbar's intervention.

Akbar had, in the meantime, grown disturbed by his failure to produce an heir. A visit to a Moslem mystic and recluse in the village of Sikri, twenty-three miles southwest of Agra, had given him hope, however, for the mystic, Shaykh Salim Chishti, had prophesied the birth of three sons. In 1569, Akbar's Hindu wife, sent to Sikri to live under the Shaykh's protection, gave birth to a son (who was later to succeed his father as the emperor Jahangir). In his delight, Akbar decided to build a vast mosque at Sikri in the Shaykh's honor, and to transfer his court to the city that he planned to build there. Construction began in 1571, and the spacious and varied structures bear witness to Akbar's taste. In general the styles owe more to Hindu tradition than to Moslem; only the mosque and the tombs show the influence of the builders and masons of Gujarat and Malwa. It was from Sikri in 1572 that Akbar set off in response to I'timad Khan's invitation.

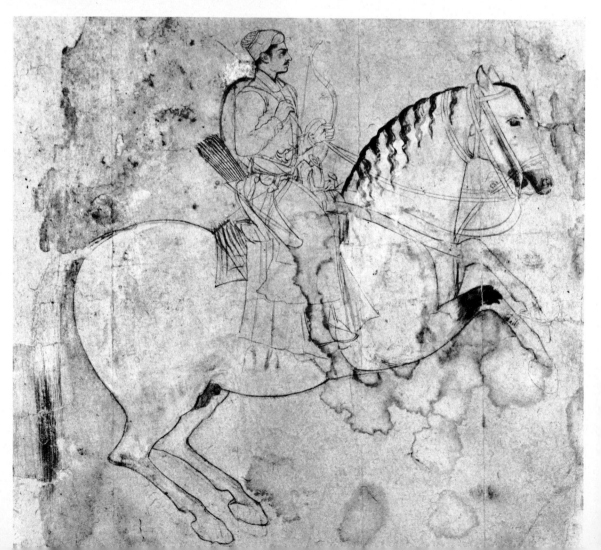

A Mogul officer on horseback.

Akbar expands his Empire

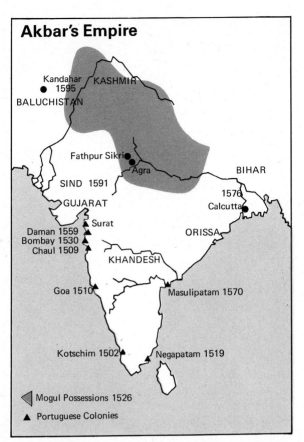

Akbar's Empire

Kandahar 1595
BALUCHISTAN
KASHMIR
Fathpur Sikri
Agra
BIHAR
SIND 1591
1576
GUJARAT
Calcutta
Daman 1559
Bombay 1530
Chaul 1509
Surat
ORISSA
KHANDESH
Goa 1510
Masulipatam 1570
Kotschim 1502
Negapatam 1519
Mogul Possessions 1526
▲ Portuguese Colonies

The monarch's reception at Patan and Ahmadabad—where he received the submission of the Gujarati nobles—was more of a triumphal procession than a campaign. There was little resistance in the disheartened north, and what opposition there was came from the southern section of Gujarat, where the Mirzas and the rebellious Habshis formed a resistance party. They were defeated in battle by the Mogul forces at the end of 1572, and a protracted siege of the rebel stronghold at Surat ended in a Mogul victory in February, 1573. Akbar returned in triumph to Sikri, and Gujarat became a province of the Mogul power. In commemoration of the victory, the city of Sikri received the new name of Fathpur, "town of victory," and Akbar built a vast portal on the south wall of the mosque as a triumphal arch.

Moslem historians have probably attached too much importance to the "conquest" of Gujarat, for the victory over the province was by no means hardfought. But although we can scarcely consider the conquest of Gujarat one of the decisive battles of history, the acquisition of the province did mark a new phase in Mogul affairs. Gujarat was a rich country, famous for its textiles and other valuable commodities such as indigo, saltpeter and salt.

Another province was soon added to Akbar's Empire: Bengal fell to the Moguls in 1576. By this time the Mogul ruler's attitude had outgrown the old concept of the Delhi sultanate, and had attained many of the qualities of an *imperium*. Akbar, who ruled a wider range of subjects than any of his forbears, soon set about organizing and unifying his Empire. He introduced a series of administrative reforms.

After his return from Gujarat, something happened that provoked Akbar's curious mind: a Moslem divine expressed the hope that Akbar might become his people's spiritual as well as their temporal ruler. Within seven years Akbar acted upon that suggestion. A document was issued that gave the ruler authority to pronounce on any question pertaining to the religion of Islam. In addition, Akbar initiated discussions on theological questions —and through those discussions it became increasingly obvious that the Emperor was entertaining doubts about the sufficiency of Islam. From 1579, representatives of faiths other than Islam were summoned to the debates, and a dispatch was sent to Goa asking that priests be sent to the court to satisfy Akbar's curiosity about the Christian faith. By the time that the two Jesuit missionaries arrived in Fathpur Sikri, Akbar's revisionist ideas had led him to forbid mention of the prophet Mohammed's name in public prayers. His partiality for the Jesuits, and for the Jains and Parsis that he invited to the court, alarmed his orthodox subjects and brought about the most serious crisis in his reign.

"Islam in danger" had more than once been a rallying cry in Moslem India, and it was invoked again in 1580. Aided by Akbar's half brother, Mohammed Hakim, who advanced on the Punjab, discontented Afghan settlers in Bihar launched an open rebellion against Akbar's Christianized

The Great Gate at Fathpur Sikri.

Akbar's siege of a fort in Rajputam, 1568.

445

Above A late-sixteenth-century carpet from Lahore.

Left Akbar receives a Western embassy.

administration. A false step would have meant Akbar's ignominous disappearance from the Indian scene. He sent his most competent generals to deal with the rising and prepared an overwhelming force to counter his half brother's advance. The embattled Emperor's display of power terrified Mohammed Hakim, and Akbar soon subdued the traitor. The Emperor's generals dealt severely with the rebels in the east, and when Akbar returned to his capital at the end of 1581, he had overcome all obstacles.

In 1582 he renounced Islam and promulgated a rather naive syncretistic eclecticism, known as the *Din-i Ilahi*, or "Divine Faith," as the official religion of the Empire. Akbar became the supreme spiritual power in his realm, and the Jesuit mission withdrew. The Portuguese remained a threat in the west, but elsewhere his Empire continued to grow: Khandesh fell to the Moguls in 1577, Kashmir capitulated in 1586, and Sind, Oriss, Baluchistam and Qandahar succumbed within a decade. Repenting its earlier submission to Akbar, Khandesh resumed its independent status, only to be reoccupied in 1601, at the same time that the provinces of Ahmadnagar and Barar were added to Akbar's rapidly burgeoning Empire.

In relation to the world as a whole, the crucial years of Akbar's reign were those during which the sultanate expanded into an empire through acquisition of the wealth and commerce of Gujarat, the establishment of contacts with Europe through the Jesuit missions, and the painstaking reform of the administration. Essentially, those were Akbar's years at Fathpur Sikri—years in which Akbar first conceived of Moslem India in pan-Indian terms.

J. BURTON-PAGE

A celebration: the costumes show the strong Western influence that Akbar encouraged.

A lion hunt.

Henry of Navarre decides "Paris is worth

In the years between the Battle of Lepanto and the defeat of the Spanish Armada the center of gravity of European politics shifted from the Mediterranean to the Netherlands—and the sea power exemplified in those key naval actions was of fundamental importance in the Dutch struggle for independence from Spain. William of Orange had issued letters of marque to the "Beggars of the Sea," nationalist free-booters whose small craft plundered Spanish shipping in the Channel. The Beggars initially worked out of English harbors, and when these facilities were closed to them they captured Brielle, a Dutch seaport fourteen miles west of Rotterdam, and used it as their base. In 1572 William was elected Stadtholder, or governor, by the provinces of Holland, Friesland and Zeeland. He promised to rid the Low Countries of Fernando Alva, Charles v's commander-in-chief, and led a Dutch army into the field. Although Haarlem fell to the Spanish, Alva failed to take Alkmaar. Finding his advance checked, the general asked Philip II to recall him. The Dutch rebels regained Zeeland in 1574 and saved Leyden by opening the dikes. A year later Don Louis Requesens, Alva's successor, cut communications between Holland and Zeeland, and a desperate William of

Part of the *Entry of Henri IV into Paris* in 1594 by Gerard.

William the Silent of Orange-Nassau.

Orange offered the sovereignty of the Netherlands to Elizabeth I, who sensibly refused his offer.

The Orangemen's war of independence was becoming an international affair: English adventurers were fighting in William's army, while the Duke of Anjou, heir to the French throne, and John Casimir of the Palatinate were both leading mercenary forces against the Spanish. Philip II appointed his half brother, Don Juan of Austria, victor of Lepanto, as military governor of the Netherlands. Before Don

Henri III of France.

Juan could reach his new command, the Spanish army—unpaid for many months as a result of financial crises in Spain—mutinied and sacked Antwerp. Before a month was out, representatives of all seventeen Dutch provinces had signed the Pacification of Ghent, a document which demanded that Philip recall his soldiers and grant religious toleration in the Netherlands.

Differences between the Flemish southern provinces and the Dutch northern provinces had grown steadily as a result of conflicting religious allegiances, and in 1579 matters came to a head. By the Union of Utrecht, Holland, Zeeland and the five other "Dutch" provinces banded together to defend themselves against Spain. William of Orange was so dismayed that the Union excluded the southern provinces that he delayed adding his signature. The Union, ratified, in 1581 by the Act of Abjuration (which renounced all

allegiance to Philip II), was in effect the constitutional beginning of the Dutch Republic.

The Duke of Parma, greatest soldier of his day, was gradually making headway against William of Orange during this period. The Catholic Duke of Anjou, abetted by Elizabeth I (to whom he was betrothed), fought episodic campaigns in the south, but was chiefly concerned with carving out a principality for himself. In 1583 his troops sacked Antwerp with such violence that their action became known as the "French Fury." A year later Anjou died and Parma liberated Ypres and Ghent. On July 10 of that year William, the hero of the revolt, was assassinated at Philip II's instigation. Parma captured Antwerp in August, 1585.

War of the Three Henry's

With the death of the Duke of Anjou in 1584, the Huguenots' struggle for recognition became merged with the war of succession, for the heir to that throne was the Protestant Henry of Navarre. The House of Guise united the various Catholic factions into a league to oppose Navarre's claim, and Philip of Spain agreed to support their candidate, Henry, Cardinal of Bourbon, in return for territorial concessions. Henry III capitulated to the Guises' demands for revoking all religious toleration and France was plunged into another war. That conflict, known as the War of the

Three Henrys, was more extensive than earlier campaigns.

Henry III at last stirred himself against the Guise, only to have the Duke of Guise make himself master of Paris on May 12, 1588, the Day of Barricades. The King escaped, and from exile agreed to the Catholic League's terms for summoning the States General. When the congress met at Blois in December, Henry arranged for the assassination of both the Duke of Guise and the Cardinal of Guise and had the Cardinal of Bourbon and others arrested. "At last am I King of France, no more a prisoner and slave," he remarked. In truth, Henry was far from independent.

Catherine de' Medici did not live to see her third son's assassination at Blois, nor to witness the accession of her fourth. During her forty years as Queen Mother, Catherine had tried in vain to dictate policy to four equally mindless kings of France, but she had found events too complex for her and the House of Guise more than a match for the House of Valois. Catherine had as great an interest in self-preservation and as great a taste for intrigue as Elizabeth I, but she failed to match the English Queen's successes.

Parma's death robbed the League of its greatest resource, and although Catholic troops continued to hold Paris, Navarre won ground steadily. In 1593, Navarre became a Roman Catholic, and the following year he was crowned Henry IV at Chartres and entered Paris.

Catherine de' Medici, mother of four kings.

Gregorian Calendar

In 1582 Pope Gregory XIII promulgated a reformed calendar, which was adopted in all Catholic countries in place of the Julian Calendar. Under the Gregorian Calendar, October 4, 1582 was followed by October 15—to compensate for the days lost over the centuries through the use of the inaccurate Julian Calendar. Most Protestant countries gradually realized the folly of continuing with the Julian system, but Holland held out until 1700, Great Britain until 1752, and Russia until the 1917 Revolution.

If Gregory left his mark on chronology, Sixtus V (1585–90) left his on history. He rid the ecclesiastical estates of bandits and made his rule respected, overhauled the Church's administrative system, limited the College of Cardinals to seventy members and set higher standards for men who hoped to be elevated to the cardinalate. In his short pontificate he built roads and bridges, laid out the Lateran and attempted to drain the Pontine marshes. His lack of historical sense led him to use the ancient Roman columns of Trajan and Antoninus as pedestals for statues of St. Peter and St. Paul, but he did give Rome a new grandeur. He demanded that the dome of St. Peter's be completed, and employed six hundred men working around-the-clock to finish the work in twenty-two months.

Germany and Western Europe

Germany, like France, suffered from inadequate leadership in the sixteenth century. Emperor Rudolf II (1576–1612), a scholarly man with a predilection for astronomy and astrology, seemed to be a throwback to Frederick III. He was incapable of government and was eventually forced to resign most of his responsibilities. Rudolf patronized the Jesuits and under their direction the Counter Reformation gained ground in all the Hapsburg lands. The seeds of the Thirty Years' War germinated during Rudolf's long reign.

In 1572 Sigismund II—the last of the Jagellon dynasty that had ruled Poland since 1386—died and the Estates declared the monarchy elective. Through Catherine de' Medici's intriguing, her son Henry was elected King on the condition that he would neither marry nor declare war without the Estates' consent. After a year as a constitutional monarch, Catherine's son returned to France to succeed his brother as Henry III. In Henry's absence the Poles deposed him and elected Stephen Bathory to be their king. Bathory, an intrepid soldier, ended Russian encroachments.

Sebastian I of Portugal invaded Morocco and was killed at the Battle of Alcazar in 1578, leaving his throne to Cardinal Henry of Guise, who was already an old man. Following the Cardinal's death in 1580, five claimants to the throne emerged. Alva was hastily summoned home to command the invasion of Spain's kingless neighbor, and he defeated the supporters of Don Antonio, Prior of Crato, at Alcantana, near Lisbon. As a result of Alva's campaign, Philip II doubled his colonial empire.

Elizabeth I of England

Queen Elizabeth I realized that it was necessary to enforce religious conformity to achieve national unity—and by promoting a broad, national church she hoped to end the religious uncertainties of the previous two decades. Elizabeth regarded herself as the instrument of "God's Providence," but she did not consider it part of her mission to introduce Calvinistic theology or the Presbyterian system of church government to England. She stressed the continuity of the Church of England and the medieval Church by emphasizing the similarity of their episcopal governments.

Initially, Elizabeth had fewer problems with those who opposed her church settlement than with those Puritans and Catholics in Parliament who pressed her to settle the succession and marry. But she steadily refused to name her successor, claiming that within a month of doing so, she would find herself in the Tower. The Queen knew from her experience during Mary's reign that an heir apparent inevitably became the focus of opposition. Proposals of marriage came from various princes, and Elizabeth embarked upon a series of lengthy courtships—first with the Archduke Charles and later with Francois, Duke of Alençon (and later Anjou). The latter genuinely fascinated Elizabeth, but the difficulties of selecting a Catholic husband proved insuperable. If Robert Dudley's wife, Amy Robsart, had not died under suspicious circumstances, Elizabeth might well have married Dudley. He remained her favorite, although his position was successively challenged by Raleigh, Hatton and Essex.

For most of Elizabeth's reign England was isolated in a hostile Europe. The Queen stretched her friendship with Catholic Spain as far as she dared, permitting her seamen to harry Spanish shipping. Those incidents did not provoke an outbreak of hostilities—but the seizure of three Spanish treasure ships that had taken refuge in Plymouth did. Spain severed all commercial relations with England for six years (1568–74), and in the spring of 1572, Elizabeth signed a defensive treaty with France. That treaty proved to be a durable one: it survived the St. Bartholomew's Massacre, Elizabeth's imprisonment of Mary Queen of Scots and England's subsidies to the Huguenots—all events that exacerbated already tense Catholic-Protestant relations. In July, 1585, the Guises overturned the alliance, but its existence had postponed the day of reckoning with Spain for more than a decade.

Sir Francis Drake's maraudings along the Spanish Main opened a new chapter in the history of privateering. In 1573 he brought home $96,000 from raids upon

Robert Dudley, Earl of Leicester.

Nombre de Dios, and four years later Drake became a national hero when he circumnavigated the globe. His raids on Spanish settlements in the New World and his capture of a hoard of Peruvian silver from the *Cacafuego* netted Drake's investors a return of 1,400 per cent on their initial investments. And when the *Golden Hind* put in to Deptford, after its globe-girdling voyage, Elizabeth knighted "her pirate."

In 1585 Drake sailed to the Caribbean and sacked Santo Domingo and Cartagena. The Queen provided $24,000 in cash and two of her ships for the undertaking. Her action constituted a declaration of war against Spain. Drake's leaving Plymouth on an obvious errand of plunder provoked the confiscation of all English shipping in Spanish ports. That same year, through Sir Water Raleigh's initiative, an English expedition under Grenville and Lane planted England's first colony in the New World. They named the ill-fated colony Virginia, in deference to the Queen.

The problem of a successor was heightened by Mary Queen of Scots' arrival in England in 1568, for despite her obvious disadvantages, Mary was fundamentally a more suitable successor than any representative of the Suffolk claimants. The Northern Rebellion, a last attempt to reverse the course of England's religious and political development, coupled with the Duke of Norfolk's treason in the Ridolfi plot, insured Mary's continued captivity, while Pius V's 1570 Bull (which deposed Elizabeth and absolved her subjects from their allegiance to her) brought a spate of penal legislation against the English Catholics. Catholic opposition to Elizabeth's regime grew increasingly desperate under these circumstances: they now conspired for nothing less than Mary's release, and Elizabeth's assassination.

Walsingham's discovery of the Babington Plot, which implicated Mary in plans for Elizabeth's murder, led to the Scottish queen's trial in 1586. Mary was found guilty of treason and duly sentenced, but Elizabeth—who had often saved Mary from the militant Puritans in Parliament—could not bring herself to sign the warrant for her execution until February, 1587. She ultimately accepted the argument that she could never feel safe while Mary—the center and soul of every plot against her—was alive and she sent Mary to her death.

The Invincible Armada

There was a time when England and Spain seemed destined for a firm alliance if not an outright political union, but the differences between the Protestant island kingdom and the Catholic monarchy to the south proved irreconcilable. By early 1588, Spain was arming the mightiest naval force ever assembled. The Armada's commander, the Duke of Medina Sidonia, was totally ignorant of naval warfare, and had a distressing tendency to seasickness—yet, pressed by King Philip II, he led the Enterprise northward that summer. A nervous England waited—Queen Elizabeth unhappily contemplating the costs of a large standing army to defend her realm against invasion; the English seadogs eager to have at the Spaniard. The first clashes were inconclusive; then—according to hallowed English legend—"God breathed" and winds dispersed the invading fleet.

Lord Howard of Effingham, Earl of Nottingham, Lord High Admiral. His knowledge of naval tactics was as limited as that of the Spanish commander, the Duke of Medina Sidonia.

Opposite A symbolic picture of the triumphant Elizabeth.

A long peace between England and Spain seemed assured with the marriage, in 1554, of the Catholic Queen Mary and the Hapsburg Prince Philip, soon to be King Philip II of Spain. But within four years Mary died, childless, and was succeeded on the throne of England by her half-sister, the decidedly Protestant Elizabeth. Initially the new queen remained at peace with Philip II, but two decades later she reversed herself and entered an alliance with the people of the Low Countries, who were trying to throw off the Spanish yoke. In 1585 Elizabeth sent an army led by Robert Dudley, Earl of Leicester, to fight alongside the Dutch rebels against Philip's troops. The fiction of peace with Spain, further jeopardized by the privateering raids of John Hawkins and Francis Drake against Spain's New World possessions, could no longer be maintained.

Philip II confiscated all English ships docked in Spanish ports, and plans for a combined naval and military expedition against England were drawn up by the Marquis of Santa Cruz. When news of the execution of Mary Queen of Scots reached Spain, Philip ordered preparations to go forward speedily. A grand fleet was collected and outfitted, and supplies were gathered for the 8,000 mariners and 22,000 soldiers who were to be transported to Calais, a French seaport across the Channel from Dover, to rendezvous with the Duke of Parma's army. The meeting with Parma required perfect timing, if the expedition were to succeed. Philip anticipated that the combined Spanish forces would be welcomed as liberators by some 25,000 English Catholics. Pro-Spanish sentiment was indeed high in certain regions, and long-range culverins or heavy cannon, made in Sussex and Gloucestershire in 1587, were smuggled to Spain by unpatriotic iron-masters.

England prepared for the anticipated invasion by training county militia and by establishing along the coastal headlands a system of beacons to warn of the enemy's approach. Sir John Hawkins, prudent treasurer and comptroller of the Royal Navy, assured Elizabeth that the fleet was ready for action, but the Queen, who could not afford to keep her "wooden walls" permanently in commission, was obliged to defer mobilization until the last moment. At the time, attack seemed the best method of defense, and in the spring of 1587, Sir Francis Drake boldly led twenty-three vessels into Cadiz harbor, where they destroyed some thirty Spanish ships. On the way home, Drake's fleet captured and burned thousands of empty barrels and other cooper's stores that were being shipped to French ports for use in victualling the Armada. Drake's raid, dubbed the "singeing of the King of Spain's beard," prevented the Spaniards from launching an invasion that year.

European seers had long been predicting that 1588 would be a year of disaster, encompassing the fall of empires and perhaps the Armageddon itself. An early setback for Philip, the death of his admiral Santa Cruz, seemed to confirm those portents. Philip chose the Duke of Medina Sidonia, a thirty-eight-year-old grandee from Castile, as Santa Cruz' successor. Although ignorant of naval warfare and prone to seasickness, Medina Sidonia was a brave and level-headed commander, and he accepted the post against his will. The new commander found the preparations for the invasion inadequate, the vessels poorly equipped and the victualling arrangements deplorable (water casks made of green wood had been substituted for those burned by Drake's raiders, and the water supply was tainted). Medina Sidonia held out for more time, but Philip, usually reluctant to move, insisted on pushing ahead. The fleet now consisted of thirty-two first-line ships: twenty galleons; four Mediterranean galleys (which later found Atlantic conditions so impossible that they turned back); four galleasses, crosses between galleon and galley that used oars when the wind dropped; and four armed merchantmen. These warships, organized in squadrons, were supported by

CORONO

EXHILER

ELIZA, TRIVMPHANS

Guilielmus Rogerus sculp. P. 1589

Two admirals with no knowledge of seamanship

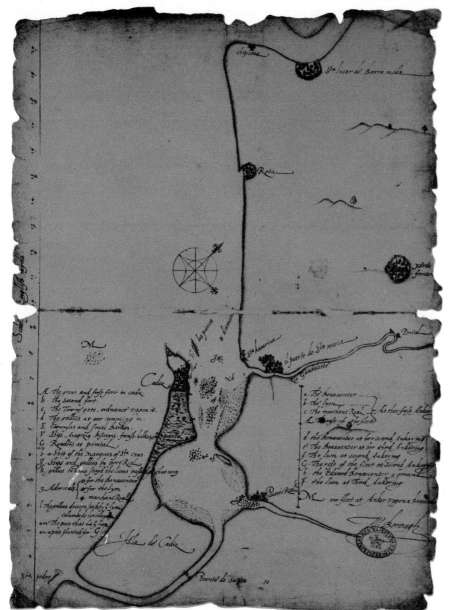

Above Cadiz Harbor with the positioning of the Spanish and English ships at the time of Drake's bold attack in 1587.

Below Part of Drake's letter to Queen Elizabeth, describing his action at Cadiz.

forty merchantmen, twenty-three freighters and two dozen pinnaces, which were used as scout ships.

Pope Sixtus V had blessed the Spanish Enterprise although he had withheld his financial support, and on April 15, 1588, the banners to be carried in the crusade against the heretic Queen were hallowed in Lisbon Cathedral; and every man in the expedition took the Sacrament. By April 30, the fleet was ready to leave, but gales delayed the actual sailing until May 20. Progress up the coast was painfully slow and the weather treacherous, and on June 9 Medina Sidonia anchored at the Spanish seaport of Corunna to wait for stragglers. Finding storm damage extensive and supplies low, he wrote to Philip asking whether he should continue. The King was adamant, and on July 12 the Armada left Corunna. The invaders were in good spirits, but even pro-Spanish Frenchmen were laying 6 to 1 odds that the Armada would never pass Ushant, an island off the Brittany coast.

The English fleet's first line was composed of eighteen large galleons and seven smaller vessels. Elizabeth's ships were more heavily armed than their Spanish counterparts, and their longer and more slender hulls gave them greater maneuverability. Privately-owned armed merchantmen and small pinnaces brought the fleet's total to 197 vessels.

In December, 1587, Elizabeth had appointed Lord Howard of Effingham to command her fleet. Like his Spanish opponent, Lord Howard was an aristocrat and—despite his administrative office of Lord High Admiral of England—he had little knowledge of naval tactics. Yet he was able, by force of his strong personality, to impose obedience on the unruly English captains Drake, Hawkins and Frobisher. Initially, Lord Howard's fleet was based at Queenborough, to defend the Thames; Lord Henry Seymour, based at Dover, patrolled the Straits, while Drake's Plymouth-based fleet stood ready to scour the western approaches to the Channel. In May, 1588, Howard moved his main fleet to join Drake's in Plymouth Sound, but the Queen refused to permit the combined force to go marauding—partly because of the cost of stores, and partly because she feared that the Armada might elude Howard and enter the Channel unopposed.

When word reached England in early July that the Spaniards were at Corunna, Howard received fresh authority for loading victuals—and a hint from Elizabeth that he might now seek out the enemy in their own port. An English fleet of ninety ships left Plymouth in haste on July 7 and raced towards Biscay on a strong northeast wind. As Howard's ships neared the northern coast of Spain, the wind suddenly shifted to the south and the fleet was forced to return to Plymouth, reaching port on July 12, the very day Medina Sidonia left Corunna. A week later the captain of an English scouting ship brought news that some Spanish ships were off the coastal Scilly Islands with their sails struck, waiting for stragglers. The English left the Sound by the night tide, and anchored in deep water. The following morning, Saturday, July 20, Howard led fifty-four

The Ark Royal, flagship of Elizabeth's fleet.

ships to leeward of the Eddystone Rocks and sailed straight south—a brilliant move that enabled him to double back on the enemy.

Medina Sidonia formed his fleet into a great crescent, with the strongest galleons at the points and flanks and the weakest in the middle, so that they appeared to Howard as an imposing enemy "with lofty towers, castle-like, in front like a crescent moon." This defensive formation limited the English to an attack on the Armada only where the Spanish were strongest.

The English needed to maneuver into a position in which their cannon could be used effectively, while the Spanish needed to close in with grappling-irons and board the enemy. Grand sea duels between fleets composed of ships-of-the-line were unheard of in warfare, and the tactics were as yet unwritten. The stalemate continued as the fleets moved up the Channel; English attacks on the points of the crescent failed to draw blood, and the only Spanish casualties in the five days of sailing were two ships lost in accidents. The Spanish had wasted 100,000 cannon balls with nothing to show for their fusillades, and the English were also running short of shot.

Though the Cornish beacons had been lit on July 19, not until the Armada was off Portland Bill, four miles south of Weymouth on the southern coast, four days later, did the order go out for the main army to assemble at Tilbury and for the second army, which was to defend the Queen's person, to go to St. James's. On that day, July 23, 1588, Leicester was named lieutenant-general for the defense of the realm, and from all over England the mustered levies began converging on the southeast. Booms were improvised across the Thames to prevent a Spanish raid on London.

Medina Sidonia anchored off Calais on July 27, only to discover that Parma had no flat-bottomed boats available to transport 18,000 men camped between Dunkirk and Nieuport out to the Armada. Howard, too, was in a quandary, for he could not get within gunshot range of the Spanish. He called a council of war, and it was decided to attempt to break up the Spaniard's formation by sending a fleet of large fire ships into the Armada's midst.

Drake volunteered his own ship, the 200-ton Thomas, and seven other owners proffered theirs as well. The vessels were filled with anything that would

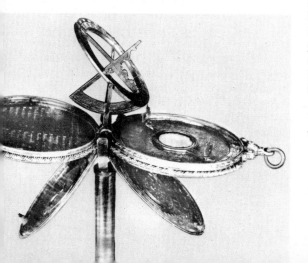

"Drake's dial," a sixteenth-century navigational instrument used by Drake.

Fire ships—England's secret weapon

The English attack the Spanish off Calais. The use of fireships threw the Armada into confusion from which it never recovered.

burn and their guns were double-shotted so that they would explode from the intense heat. The Spanish had feared a secret weapon—and here it was. Soon after midnight the fireships, lashed together, approached the anchorage, cutting through the cordon of pinnaces. In great confusion the Spanish galleons slipped their cables and stood out to sea. None of the Armada's vessels caught fire, but the impregnable crescent had been broken.

At dawn on July 28, Lord Howard divided his squadrons to deal with the scattered enemy. Drake, in the *Revenge*, was to lead the fight and, aided by

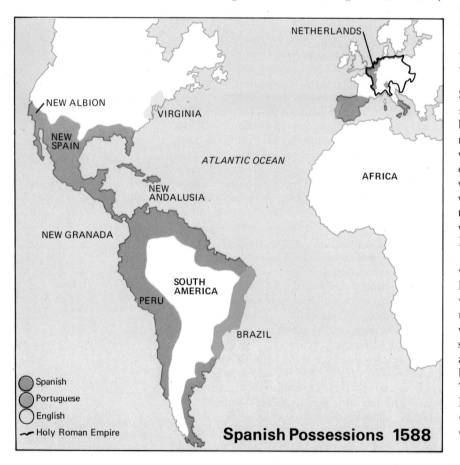

Spanish
Portuguese
English
Holy Roman Empire

Spanish Possessions 1588

Frobisher and Hawkins, he pounded the Spanish flagship, whose defenders were reduced to using muskets. Howard had driven the rudderless *San Lorenzo* ashore, and in the four hours of close fighting that ensued the Spanish suffered major casualties. The duel at Gravelines, a French port fifteen miles southwest of Dunkirk, clearly demonstrated the superiority of the English in handling their vessels—but Medina Sidonia still would not give in. Squalls and blinding rain saved the Spanish from certain defeat; when the weather cleared, the English discovered that the Spanish had drifted out of range and reformed the old crescent formation. Two Spanish ships had sunk, however, and most were leaking. His ammunition nearly spent, Howard could not repeat the attack—but he pursued the enemy north along the Netherlands coast.

Early on July 30, when it seemed certain that the Spanish fleet would be driven on the perilous lee shore of the Zeeland sands, the wind suddenly backed to west-southwest, enabling the Spanish to maneuver into the deep waters of the North Sea. At a war council on board the *San Martin*, casualties and damage were reported and it was agreed that if the wind changed again, the Armada would fight its way through the Straits of Dover and attempt to take an English harbor. If the wind held, the fleet would have to sail westward around the British Isles.

The wind did not change, and Medina Sidonia, who had already lost seven of his first-line ships, knew he must at all costs bring the rest of his limping vessels home. The long, hazardous voyage around the Orkney and Shetland islands and west of Ireland would have to be made on meager rations. Seventeen ships broke away from the fleet in a desperate attempt to secure food and water in Ireland, and all but two were wrecked. The remainder battled on. Their fight was now only with the elements, for Howard had given up the chase north of Berwick, on the Scottish border, on August 2, when it became clear that the enemy would not attempt a landing.

The Queen, hedged in by her guards at St. James's,

The Armada Portrait of Queen Elizabeth.

felt left out, and decided to visit the coast. Leicester politely forbade the journey, so Elizabeth then decided to visit Tilbury. The Earl did not have the heart to disuade her, and she went by barge on August 8 to inspect the men. A steel corselet was found for her, and the Queen rode through the ranks "like some Amazonian empress." She stayed nearby and returned to the camp the next day to review the troops and make the speech that, Leicester said, "so inflamed the hearts of her poor subjects as I think the weakest person among them is able to match the proudest Spaniard that dares now land":

. . . Let tyrants fear. I have always so behaved myself that under God, I have placed my chiefest strength and goodwill in the loyal hearts and goodwill of my subjects; and therefore I come amongst you, as you see, at this time, not for my recreation and disport, but being resolved, in the midst and heat of the battle, to live or die amongst you all; to lay down for God, my kingdom and for my people, my honour and my blood, even in the dust. I know I have but the body of a weak and feeble woman;

Sir Francis Drake, pirate, explorer and naval captain. Legend obscured history and made Drake the hero of the campaign against the Armada.

455

England saved—by a Protestant wind

One of a pack of playing cards produced to celebrate the victory of 1588: the king of hearts represents the army of the Earl of Leicester, Lieutenant-General for the Defense of the Realm.

King

The Army of 1000 horse, and 22000 Foot, which ye Earle of Leicester comanded when hee Pitched his Tents att Tilbury

The Armada, a contemporary engraving showing the crescent formation of the Spanish fleet.

but I have the heart and stomach of a king, and a King of England too, and think it foul scorn that Parma or Spain, or any Prince of Europe, should dare to invade the borders of my realm; to which, rather than any dishonour should grow by me, I myself will take up arms . . .

Elizabeth assured her troops that they would be paid for their services and asserted that she did not doubt that they would shortly have a great victory. The cheers were thunderous. During dinner in Leicester's tent that night, news came that Parma was embarking from Dunkirk and would cross on the spring tide. Those eager for action were disappointed, however: Parma's chances had been dashed eleven days before, when the British fireships scattered the Armada.

Lord Howard was later criticized for not having destroyed more ships—although the English had not lost a single ship and no more than one hundred men in the whole engagement. Little was heard about the crews still on shipboard—many of whom died like flies from typhus while their officers quarreled about their pay. The significance of the Armada's defeat soon pierced the haze, and court and capital celebrated. The captured flags were placed in St. Paul's, and the Queen journeyed to London on November 24 to attend a Thanksgiving. John Piers, Bishop of Salisbury, preached on the "Protestant wind"—the same wind that had wrecked Pharaoh's chariots in the Red Sea—and his impassioned oratory earned him promotion to the Archbishopric of York.

To mark the English fleet's victory, Elizabeth took the novel step of issuing various medals, with

her bust on the obverse and a suitable engraving of the storm on the reverse; "God breathed and they were scattered," ran one of the inscriptions. She sat for a special portrait that included views of the English galleons proudly returning from Calais and of the Spanish ships foundering, and Sir Thomas Heneage gave her "the Armada jewel," a brooch that incorporated a miniature of herself by Hilliard. The following year, Elizabeth asked Burghley to draw up an honors list including six earldoms, but they both thought better of the idea before the peerages were announced. In 1597 she belatedly advanced Howard to the Earldom of Nottingham; his patent described his brilliant service in 1588.

By the time the Spanish flagship *San Martin* reached Santander on September 13, many on board had died from scurvy or typhus and Medina Sidonia himself was delirious from dysentery. Among the thousands who later died were the Spanish commander's stalwarts, Recalde and Oquendo. The sick Admiral was unable to organize relief for his men; he never returned to sea and never lived down the obloquy of the campaign that was unfairly heaped on him. Philip II took the defeat with dignity, never realizing that the Armada had been set an impossible task, with inadequate provisions and ammunition. No one praised Medina Sidonia for succeeding in bringing home sixty-seven battered ships.

Legends soon obscured history: Drake became the hero of the campaign, and the Queen was credited with the idea of the fireships (which purportedly actually burned some galleons). Above all,

The medal struck to celebrate the victory of 1588: the Spanish fleet is scattered and destroyed.

the wind was made "God's instrument" in England's victory—when, in truth, the weather had favored the Spanish all along.

The campaign did not cause Philip II to sue for peace with England or lead him to recognize Dutch independence, nor did it end England's fear of invasion. The action was decisive primarily in that it checked the colossus of Spain—which had grown considerably since the Battle of Lepanto and the conquest of Portugal. The fact that the Enterprise had been a holy crusade—and an unsuccessful one—shows that the Counter-Reformation, no less than Spanish prestige, had passed its apogee. French Huguenots no longer felt that the world had ended with St. Bartholomew, or Dutch Calvinists that hope had been buried with William the Silent. The events of 1588 put new hearts into the Protestant cause.

NEVILLE WILLIAMS

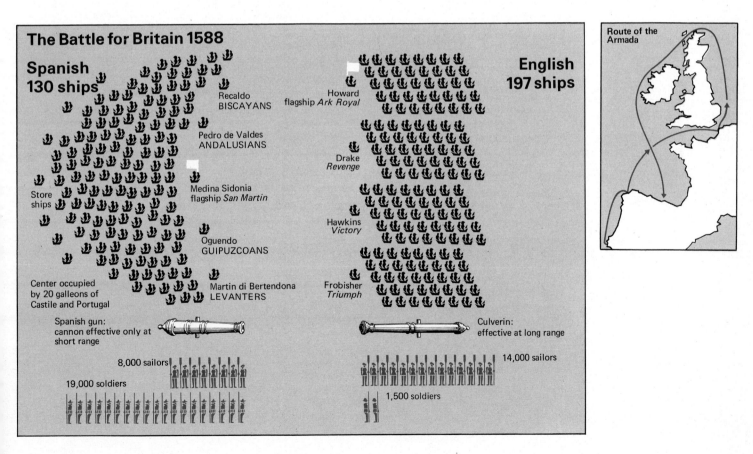

457

1215
Agreement at Runnymede — England's King John signs Magna Carta, and unwittingly speeds the decline of "divine right" monarchs

1240
The Russian Giant Stirs — The victories of Alexander Nevski help a great nation take shape on Europe's eastern borders

1275
When East Met West — The travels of Marco Polo, recorded in a famous book, arouse Europe's curiosity about the mysterious Ori

Gregory IX 1145-1241
Pope

Simon de Montfort the Elder
c, 1160-1218 *French Crusader*

John c. 1167-1216
King of England

William Marshall, Earl of Pembroke d. 1219
Regent for Henry III of England

Robert Grosseteste c. 1170-1253
Oxford Franciscan scholar

Edmund Rich (St.) c. 1170-1240
Archbishop of Canterbury

Snorri Sturleson 1178-1241
Icelandic politician and writer

Saadi 1184-1283
Persian poet

Hermann von Salza d. 1239
Grand Master of Teutonic Knights

Hubert de Burgh d. 1243
Justiciar of England

Blanche of Castile c. 1185-1252
Queen of France

Innocent IV d. 1254
Pope

Batu d. 1255
Leader of Mongol Golden Horde

Louis VIII 1187-1226
King of France

Albert the Great (St.) 1193-1280
German scholar at Paris

Raymond VI
Count of Toulouse

Ferdinand III 1199-1252
King of Castile

Birger Magnusson d. 1266
Swedish jarl (earl), regent

Haakon IV c. 1204-62
King of Norway and Iceland

Henry III 1207-72
King of England

Simon de Montfort c.1208-65
Leader in English Barons' War

Louis IX (St.) 1214-70
King of France

Roger Bacon c. 1214-94
English scholar

Kublai Khan c. 1215-94
Mongol Emperor

Hulagu 1217-65
Il-Khan of Persia

Rudolf I of Hapsburg 1218-92
German Emperor

Alexander Nevski (St.) 1219-63
Prince of Novgorod and Vladimir

Niccolo Pisano c. 1220-80
Italian sculptor and architect

Alfonso X the Learned c. 1221-84
King of Castile

Michael VIII Palaeologus 1124-82
Byzantine Emperor

Thomas Aquinas (St.) 1224-74
Italian philosopher

Charles of Anjou 1226-85
King of Naples

Manfred c. 1230-66
Hohenstaufen King of Sicily

Otakar II 1230-78
King of Bohemia

Boniface VIII 1235-1303
Pope

Peter III c. 1239-85
King of Aragon

Edward I 1239-1307
King of England

Cimabue c. 1240-1302
Florentine painter

Alexander III 1241-86
King of Scotland

Llewelyn the Great d. 1282
Prince of Wales

Philip III the Bold 1245-85
King of France

John Balliol 1249-1315
King of Scotland

Marco Polo c. 1254-1324
Venetian traveler

Osman I c. 1259-1326
Turkish Sultan

Meister Eckhart c. 1260-1328
German theologian

Sciarra Colonna d. 1329
Ghibelline leader in Rome

Guillaume de Nogaret c. 1265-1
Chancellor of France

Clement V 1265-13
Pope

John Duns Scotus c. 1265-1
British scholastic philosophe

Dante Alighieri 1265-132
Italian poet

Giotto 1266-1337
Florentine painter

Philip IV the
King of Fran

● **1214**
Battle of Bouvines: French conquer Normandy and Poitou

c. **1200** ●
University of Paris founded

Albigensian crusade begun ● **1208**

Fourth Lateran Council ● **1215**

Genghis Khan takes Peking ● **1215**

Indus valley and Afghanistan ● **1221**
conquered by Mongols

● **1226**
Order of Teutonic Knights reorganized by Frederick II

Cordova, Moorish capital, ●
taken by Castile　**1236**

Golden Horde established ●
in southern Russia by Batu **1242**

1244 ●
Jerusalem taken by
Egyptian Moslems

Seventh Crusade, led by ●
St. Louis　　　**1248**

1253-99 ●
Venetian-Genoese struggle over trade in the Levant and Black Sea

Florin first coined **1252** ●

1258
Sack of Baghdad by
Mongol Hulagu

● **1265**
De Montfort's "G
Parliament"

● **1266**
Battle of Benever
Charles of Anjou
Sicily from Germ

● **126**
St. Thomas Aqu
Summa Theolog

● **12**
Battle of Tagliac

1264-5 ●
Barons' War in England
against Henry III

1320
"The Divine Comedy" — In composing his epic poem, Dante gives expression to new ideologies and helps create the modern Italian language

1381
Wat Tyler "Captures" London — England's boy King averts civil war, but cannot ignore his subjects' demands for a larger voice in Parliament

1351
The Black Death — Trading vessels returning to fourteenth-century Europe from Asian ports carry a new and deadly cargo: bubonic plague

Petrarch 1304-74
Italian poet

Timur the Great c. 1336-1405
Mongol conqueror

John Huss 1369-1415
Czech religious reformer

Etienne Marcel d. 1358
Provost of Paris merchants

Charles V 1337-80
King of France

John Ziska d. 1424
Czech military leader

Stephen Dushan c. 1308-55
King of Serbia

Jean Froissart c. 1337-1410
French chronicler

John the Fearless 1371-1419
Duke of Burgundy

Casimir III the Great 1310-70
King of Poland

Philip van Arteveld 1340-82
Leader of Flemish weavers' rebellion

Isabella of Bavaria 1371-1435
Queen of France

Edward III 1312-77
King of England

Gerard Groote 1340-84
Dutch Monastic reformer

Lorenzo Ghiberti 1378-1455
Florentine sculptor

Giovanni Boccaccio 1313-75
Italian writer

John of Gaunt 1340-99
Duke of Lancaster

Thomas à Kempis (St.) c. 1380-1471
German monk

Cola di Riezi 1313-54
Roman tribune

Geoffrey Chaucer c. 1340-1400
English poet

Procup d. 1434
Taborite leader

Charles IV of Luxemburg 1316-78
Holy Roman Emperor

John 1340-1416
Duke of Berry

Eugenius IV 1383-1447
Pope 1431-47

Urban VI c. 1318-89
Pope 1378-89

Philip the Bold 1342-1404
Duke of Burgundy

John Hunyadi c. 1385-1456
Hungarian national hero

John II 1319-64
King of France

Catherine of Siena (St.) 1347-80
Italian Dominican nun

John of Capistrano (St.) c. 1385-1456
Italian preacher

Peter I the Cruel 1320-67
King of Portugal

John Ball d. 1381
English preacher

Donatello c. 1386-1466
Florentine sculptor

3-1314

Bertrand Du Guesclin c. 1320-80
Constable of France

Wat Tyler d. 1381
Leader of English Peasants' Revolt

Henry V 1387-1422
King of England

iam Wallace c. 1272-1305
ttish rebel leader

William of Wykeham 1324-1404
English churchman and educationist

John I c. 1357-1433
King of Portugal

John of Lancaster 1389-1435
Duke of Bedford, Protector of England

ert Bruce 1274-1329
of Scotland 1306-29

Louis I the Great 1326-82
King of Hungary

Wenceslas 1361-1419
German Emperor

Cosimo de' Medici 1389-1464
Ruler of Florence

Diniz 1279-1325
King of Portugal

John Wyclif c. 1328-84
English religious reformer

Richard II 1367-1400
King of England

John VIII Palaeologus 1390-1448
Byzantine Emperor

Edward II 1284-1327
King of England

Chu Yuan-chang 1328-98
Founder of Ming Dynasty China

Henry IV (Bolingbroke) 1367-1413
King of England

Humphrey Duke of Gloucester 1391-1447 *Son of Henry IV of England*

Ludwig IV of Bavaria 1287-1847
German Emperor

Edward the Black Prince 1330-76
Prince of Wales

Charles VI 1368-1422
King of France

Henry the Navigator 1394-1460
Portuguese prince

Marsiglio of Padua c. 1290-1343
Italian political philosopher

Gregory XI 1330-78
Pope

Martin V 1368-1431
Pope

Alfonso V the Magnanimous 1396-1450 *King of Aragon, Sicily and Naples*

William of Occam 1290-1349
English philosopher

Charles II the Bad 1332-87
King of Navarre

Sigismund 1368-1437
German Emperor

Philip the Good 1396-1467
Duke of Burgundy

Philip VI 1293-1328
King of France

Henry II of Trastamara c. 1333-79
King of Castile and Leon

Yoshimitsu d. 1395
Japanese Shogun

Nicholas V 1397-1455
Pope 1447-55

1276
er manufactured in
y

English Parliament **1297** acquires right to approve taxation

Hundred Years' ● War begun **1337**

Adrianople Turkish ● capital **1360**

Turks conquer Serbia and ● **1389** Balkans at Kossovo

● **1314**

● **1391**

● Yuan (Mongol) Dynasty
280 established in China
(Peking)

Scots rout English at Bannockburn

Jacquerie peasant ● revolt in France **1358** **1340** ●

Venetians definitively ● defeat Genoese **1380**

Golden Horde defeated by Timur

● **1282**
cilian Vespers: French
se Sicily to Aragon

1315 ●
Battle of Morgarten:
Ludwig IV recognizes Swiss confederation

Asia Minor controlled by Turks

Russians defeat Mongols ● at Kulikovo **1380**

1396 ●
Union of Kalmar: Sandinavia under Danish rule

● **1291**
Turks capture Acre

First Venetian trading ● expedition to Flanders **1317**

Formation of Hanseatic ● League **1344**

Ming Dynasty established in China **1368**

1381 ●
Venice cedes Dalmatia to Louis I of Hungary

Battle of Crecy **1346** ●

Resumption of Hundred ● Years' War **1369**

1385

1397 ●
Delhi sacked by Mongol Timur.

● **1307**

Naples overrun by Louis I of Hungary **1347**

Battle of Aljubarrota: ● Portuguese independence

cession of Rudolf I as
peror ends German
erregnum (since 1254)

Papal court moved to Avignon

● **1325**
Aztec Empire established in Mexico at Tenochtitlan

1356 ●
Poitiers: John II of France captured by English

1378 ● Bolingbroke deposes **1399** The Great Schism Richard II of England ●

1431

The Maid of Orleans — Saint or witch, a peasant girl from Orleans sways a nation — and is burned at the stake for fulfilling her mission

1453

The Fall of Constantinople — The inexorable advance of the Ottoman Turks spells the end for the once-brilliant Roman Empire of the East

1492

Landfall at San Salvador — Seeking the elusive Orient, Christopher Columbus happens upon America and opens a new world to Europe

John Gutenberg c. 1400-68
German printer

Francesco I Sforza 1401-66
Condottiere of Milan

Murad II 1403-51
Ottoman Sultan

Charles VII 1403-61
King of France

Constantine XI Palaeologus 1404-53
Byzantine Emperor

Pius II 1405-64
Pope

Richard Duke of York 1411-60
Pretender to English throne

Joan of Arc (St.) c. 1412-31
French national heroine

Sixtus IV 1414-84
Pope

Frederick III 1415-93
German Emperor

Henry VI 1421-71
King of England

William Caxton c. 1421-91
English printer

Louis XI 1423-83
King of France

Richard Neville 1428-71
Earl of Warwick, "Kingmaker"

Mehmet II 1429-81
Ottoman Sultan

Alexander VI 1431-1503
Pope

Charles the Bold 1433-77
Duke of Burgundy

Marsilio Ficino 1433-99
Florentine humanist

Ivan III the Great 1440-1505
Prince of Muscovy

Edward IV 1442-83
King of England

Matthias I Corvinus c. 1443-90
King of Hungary

Julius II 1443-1513
Pope

Sandro Botticelli c. 1444-1510
Florentine painter

Lorenzo de' Medici (the Magnificent) 1449-92 *Florentine ruler*

John Cabot c. 1450-98
Italian explorer for England

Bartholemew Diaz 1450-1500
Portuguese navigator

Francisco de Almeida c. 1450-1510
Portuguese admiral

Aldus Manucci 1450-1515
Venetian printer, humanist

Isabella I 1451-1504
Queen of Castile and Leon

Christopher Columbus c. 1451-1506
Italian discoverer

Ludovico Sforza "Il Moro" 1451-1508 *Duke of Milan*

Richard III 1452-85
King of England

Girolamo Savonarola 1452-98
Italian religious reformer

Ferdinand V the Catholic 1452-1516
King of Aragon

Leonardo da Vinci 1452-1519
Italian artist and inventor

Ferdinand I d. 1494
King of Naples

Alfonso de Albuquerque 1453-1515
Portuguese admiral

Amerigo Vespucci 1454-1512
Italian discoverer

Henry VII 1457-1509
King of England

Maximilian I 1459-1519
Holy Roman Emperor

Jacob Fugger 1459-1525
German merchant prince

Vasco da Gama c. 1460-1524
Portuguese navigator

Louis XII 1462-1515
King of France

Pico della Mirandola 1463-94
Italian humanist

Desiderius Erasmus c. 1466-1536
Dutch humanist

Selim I 1467-1520
Ottoman Sultan

Paul III 1468-1549
Pope

Niccolo Machiavelli 1469-1527
Florentine statesman

Charles VIII 1470-98
King of France

Francisco Pizarro 1470-1541
Spanish conquistador

Albrecht Durer 1471-1528
German artist

Thomas Wolsey c. 1472-1530
English cardinal and statesman

Lukas Cranach 1472-1553
German painter

Nicholas Copernicus 1473-1543
Polish astronomer

Leo X 1475-1521
Pope

Michelangelo 1475-1564
Italian sculptor and painter

Cesare Borgia c. 1476-1507
Italian ruler

Titian 1477-1576
Venetian painter

Clement VII 1478-1534
Pope

Thomas More, Sir 1478-1535
English humanist and statesman

Montezuma c. 1480-1520
Mexican Emperor

Ferdinand Magellan 1480-1521
Portuguese navigator

Charles, Duke of Bourbon 1480-
Constable of France

Christian II 1481-1559 (deposed 1
King of Denmark, Sweden, Norwa

Raphael 1483-1520
Italian painter

Babar 1483-1530
Founder of Mogul Empire

Martin Luther 1483-1546
German religious reformer

Ulrich Zwingli 1484-1531
Swiss religious reformer

Thomas Cromwell c. 1485-1540
English statesman

Hernán Cortés 1485-154
Spanish conquistador

Atahualpa d. 1
Last Inca of Pe

Thomas Cranmer 1489
English prelate

Ignatius Loyola (St.) 1491
Spanish founder of Jesuits

Henry VIII 1491-
King of England

William Tyndale 1492-15
English humanist and refo

Paracelsus c. 1493-
Swiss physician

Francis I 1494
King of France

Suleiman I the Magn
1494-1566 *Ottoman*

Gustavus I
King of Sw

Ed
c. 150

● **1414-17**
Council of Constance: end
of Great Schism

● **1415**
Battle of Agincourt

● **1402**
Turks defeated by
Timur at Ankara

● **1419-35**
Hussite Wars

● **1420**
Treaty of Troyes

● **1415**
Huss burned for heresy

● **1410**
Baghdad captured by Turks
(from Timurid Mongols)

● **1436**
Gutenberg's invention of
moveable type for printing

● **1439**
Council of Florence
attempt to end East-West
schism

● **1435**
Treaty of Arras: alliance
of Charles VII and Philip
of Burgundy

● **1431-35**
Council of Basel

1455-85 ●
Wars of the Roses

● **1456**
Turks checked by
Hungarians at Belgrade

● **1453**
Castillon: end of Hundred
Years' War

Inquisition established in ●
Spain   **1478**

Venetian-Turkish peace ●
treaty   **1479**

End of Tartar rule in ● **1480**
Russia

Battle of Nancy: **1477** ●
Burgundy annexed to
France

●
Leonardo's Last Supper **1495-**

1489 ● Venice anne
Cyprus

Diaz rounds Cape of ●
Good Hope

1487-88 ●   ●
1492
Granada taken: Moors a
Jews expelled from Spa

Cabot discovers ●
Newfoundland 14

Treaty of Tordesillas ●
divides world between **1494**
Spain and Portugal

Diet of Worms abolishes ●
private warfare in Germany **1495**

1512
escoes for Pope Julius — Michelangelo's
iumphant achievement in painting the ceiling
the Sistine Chapel marks a high point of the
alian Renaissance

1533
A Bible for the Masses — Martin Luther's
secretly-published vernacular translation of the
New Testament proves the power of the popular
press in Europe

1543 The Earth Dethroned —
Copernicus' theory of planetary
motion—making the sun and not
the earth the center of the
universe—inaugurates a scientific
revolution

1573
A New Empire for India — By
conquering the province of Gujarat,
the Mogul Emperor Akbar lays the
foundation for a pan-Indian nation.

1521
he Conquest of Mexico — Luck, ingenuity and
ourage— and the skillful use of horses and
rearms—enables Cortes to topple the mighty
ztec empire

Cutting the Sultan's Beard — Two vast navies—
one Christian, one Moslem—engage in a sea duel
that determines the course of trade in the
eastern Mediterranean

1571

1588
The Invincible Armada — As
Spain's mighty naval force
approaches, England seems
doomed—but "God breathes" and
the island kingdom is spared

John Calvin 1509-64
French Protestant leader

Philip II 1527-98
King of Spain

Mary Stuart 1542-87
Queen of Scots

Robert Devereux, Earl of Essex 1567-1601
English nobleman

Humayun d. 1556
Mogul Emperor

Emmanuel Philibert 1528-80
Duke of Savoy

Maurice of Nassau 1567-1625
Dutch national leader

Gerard Mercator 1512-94
Flemish cartographer

Louis I de Condé 1530-69
French Protestant leader

Akbar the Great 1542-1605
Mogul Emperor

Felix Lope de Vega 1562-1635
Spanish dramatic poet

Mary of Guise 1515-60
Wife of James V of Scotland

Ivan IV the Terrible 1530-84
Tsar of Russia

Tokugawa Ieyasu 1543-1616
Japanese Shogun

Jahangir 1569-1627
Mogul Emperor

Mary I 1516-58
Queen of England

Robert Dudley c. 1532-88
Earl of Leicester

Francis II 1544-60
King of France

Johannes Kepler 1571-1630
German astonomer

Henry II 1519-59
King of France

John Hawkins 1532-95
English privateer and slavetrader

Alexander Farnese 1545-92
Duke of Parma and Piacenza

Francis of Lorraine 1519-63
Duke of Guise

William of Orange (the Silent) 1533-84
Leader of Netherlands revolt

Tycho Brahe 1546-1601
Danish astronomer

6-1560
French Protestant admiral

Gaspard de Coligny 1519-72
French Protestant admiral

Stephen Báthory 1533-92
King of Poland

Don Juan of Austria c. 1547-78 *Spanish
admiral, Governor General of Netherlands*

ip Melancthon 1497-
man humanist 1560

Catherine de' Medici 1519-89
Queen of France

Miguel de Cervantes 1547-1616
Spanish novelist

rles V 1500-58 *Holy Roman
eror and King of Spain*

Sigismund II 1520-72
King of Poland

Michel de Montaigne
1533-92 *French writer*

Charles IX 1550-74
King of France

ohn III 1502-57
ing of Portugal

Sixtus V 1521-90
Pope

Henry of Lorraine 1550-88
Duke of Guise

dinand I 1503-64 *Archduke,
German Emperor*

Count Egmont 1522-68
Flemish leader

Elizabeth I 1533-1603
Queen of England

Medina Sidonia 1550-1615
Commander of Armada

n Knox c. 1505-72
ttish religious reformer

Margaret of Parma 1522-86
Regent of the Netherlands

Ota Nobunaga 1534-82
Japanese warlord

Henry III 1551-89
King of France and Poland

Pius V 1505-72
Pope

Selim II c. 1524-74
Ottoman Sultan

Rudolf II 1552-1612
Holy Roman Emperor

Louis II 1506-26
King of Hungary

Ali Pasha d. 1571
Ottoman general

Toyotomi Hideyoshi c. 1536-98
Japanese dictator

Walter Raleigh, Sir c.1552-1618
English statesman

mour, Duke of Somerset
d Protector of England

Charles of Guise 1525-74
Cardinal of Lorraine

Francis Drake c. 1540-96
English admiral

Henry IV (of Navarre) 1553-
1610 *King of France*

Francis Xavier (St.) 1506-52
Jesuit missionary

Giovanni Palestrina c. 1525-94
Italian composer

Francis, Duke of Alençon and Anjou
c. 1554-84 *French prince*

nando, Duke of Alva 1508-82
nish general, Regent of Netherlands

Maximilian II 1527-76
Holy Roman Emperor

El Greco c. 1541-1614
Cypriot painter in Spain

Abbas I the Great 1557-1629
Shah of Persia

● **1509**
yptians and Indians
uted by Portuguese in
dian Ocean off Diu

● Diet of Worms: Luther
1521 under Imperial ban

● Suleiman invades Hungary
1541

● Adoption of 39 Articles
1562 and establishment of
Anglican Church

● **1541**
Calvin organizes Geneva
as theocratic state

1525 ●
French defeated
at Pavia

● **1530**
Antwerp: new Bourse
financial hub of Europe

● **1555**
Peace of Augsburg:
Lutheranism tolerated
in Germany

● **1572**
St. Bartholemew's Day
Massacre in France

rignano: Francis I
kes Milan **1515**

● **1521-9**
War between France
and Spain

● **1542**
Inquisition established in
Rome

● **1557-82** Russian-Livonian war

● **1585-98**
French War of Succession

1516-17 ●
urks conquer Syria and
gypt

● **1534**
Foundation of Jesuit Order

● Silver deposits
1545 discovered
at Potosi, Peru

● **1568**
Revolt of the Netherlands

Luther's 95 Theses ● **1517**

● Mogul Empire established
1526 in North India by Babar

● Treaty of Cateau-Cambresis:
1559 end of Hapsburg-Valois strife

● **1590**
Unification of Japan
under Hideyoshi

● **1519**
Magellan's circumnavigation

● Mohacs: Turks defeat
1526 Hungarians

● **1545-63**
Council of Trent reforms
Roman Catholic Church

● **1562-80**
French Wars of Religion

Twilight of Princes

Editor Christopher Hibbert

1601-1789

Introduction

Before the French Revolution every major European state except Venice was a monarchy, and every monarch except the King of Poland succeeded to his throne by right of birth. It was the Age of Absolutism; it was an age in which a monarch could claim—as Louis XIV is alleged to have done—*"L'état c'est moi"*—"I am the state;" it was an age in which an autocrat might, in his will, bequeath his country to his sons as though it were his own personal property. It was, moreover, an age in which a monarch might bestow vast estates and innumerable peasant-slaves upon his favorites—as Catherine the Great did when she retired her violent lover, Count Grigori Orlov, with a fortune of 17 million rubles, a marble palace and estates staffed by 45,000 serfs.

Yet by the beginning of the eighteenth century there were indications in Europe and throughout the civilized world that the long era of the hereditary despot— even of the enlightened despot who considered himself, in the words of Frederick the Great, "the first servant of the state"—was drawing to a close. No future Emperor of China was to govern with such serene confidence as Ch'ien-lung, Son of Heaven; no future King of France was to shine as brightly as the Sun King; and no future King of Sweden was to lead victorious armies through the plains of Germany as did Gustavus Adolphus.

In the two centuries covered in Part Four, the slow process of transforming the fractured territories of medieval Europe into a relatively small number of powerful, centrally governed states was finally completed, and Europe's dominant position in the world— foreshadowed by the skills and daring of the early navigators—was firmly established. During those centuries of gradual consolidation, the map of the world was transfigured: some states grew, others shrank, and a few were altogether effaced. In the Levant the ancient Ottoman Empire began to crumble; in India

and North America the French and British fought to control and expand new colonies; in the South Pacific a whole new world was discovered; and in China a foreign dynasty vastly extended the frontiers of the empire by driving the Gurkhas from Tibet, conquering Turkistan and reducing the Burmese to suzerainty.

When thirty years of religious wars were ended by the Treaty of Westphalia in 1648, Europe's public law seemed settled and its national frontiers seemed securely fixed. Yet by the close of the following century —an era that Goethe considered the dawn of a new age in the history of the world—the well-trained armies of the old order had been turned aside by the massed forces of revolution, public law had been flouted time and again, and almost every frontier had been obliterated and redrawn by Europe's ruling dynasties as they pursued their conflicting ambitions.

The Turks, thrown back from Vienna in 1683, lost Hungary to Austria and the Crimea to Russia, and ceased to be a threat to the Christian world; Spain's European empire disintegrated as Sardinia fell to the House of Savoy, Franche-Comté to France, and the Netherlands to the growing power of Austria. Sweden's power had been eclipsed; Poland, soon to be entirely dismembered, was already being cut up by her neighbors; and two new powers—which later became the most powerful in all Europe—had emerged with ruthless force. Those two were Russia, which had pushed southward to the Black Sea and westward to the Baltic, and Prussia, which had been created by the vigor of the House of Hohenzollern. Of the great maritime powers of Western Europe, France had not yet recovered the glory that the later years of Louis XIV had so sadly tarnished; Holland's power was in decline through competition with larger states; and England —now known as Great Britain—was creating the strong outlines of an overseas empire that was to decide the fate of North America and Australia and to

Introduction

leave its indelible mark on the subcontinent of India.

The drive and forcefulness of the despot were decisive in transforming those frontiers and effecting those transfers of power in Europe. "Kings are absolute lords and have full authority over all people," wrote Louis XIV, whose practical example deeply influenced the rulers of eighteenth-century Europe. His opinion was shared by Peter the Great and Frederick the Great, different though their concepts of autocracy were. It was Frederick the Great's belief that "a well-conducted Government must have a system as coherent as a system of philosophy, so that finance, police and the army are coordinated to the same end, namely the consolidation of the state and the increase of its power. Such a system can only emanate from a single brain, that of the sovereign." Catherine the Great, who continued Peter's work in modernizing and westernizing Russia, insisted in her *Instructions to the Commissioners for Composing a New Code of Laws* that while all men were equal before the law, the sovereign was absolute: "The extent of the empire necessitates absolute power in the ruler. Any other form of government would bring it down in ruins."

The effective exercise of absolute power required immense resources of energy and application. Catherine the Great, though she delighted in good food, good conversation and good lovers, would often work for fifteen hours a day, beginning at five o'clock in the morning. Frederick the Great also got up at five, and allowed himself no more than two hours a day for relaxation. "I rise at five in the morning," said Charles III of the Two Sicilies, who "thought himself the most absolute monarch in Europe" according to the British ambassador. Following the death of Maria Theresa of Austria, her son, Joseph II, threw himself into his work with such astonishing avidity that he was able to issue more than six thousand long decrees on all manner of subjects in the ten years before his own death. Louis XIV, whose life appeared to revolve around the choreographic ceremonial of an enervating court, had a real talent and taste for administration: his ministers were forbidden to seal anything without his order or to sign anything without his consent. His successor, Philip, Duke of Orleans, who ruled as regent for eight years after Louis' death, worked all day and—in the opinion of more than one observer—simply wore himself out.

But although they stride across the years with such vitality, setting their mark for good and ill upon the history of their times, those absolute monarchs provide but one fitting title for their era—*Twilight of Princes*. For the Age of Absolutism was also the Age of Reason, the Age of Enlightenment and the Age of Scientific Revolution—an age in which Newton's discoveries were more important than the conquests of Frederick the Great, and Diderot's *Encyclopédie* was more influential than the triumphs of Louis XIV. It was the age of French *philosophes* as well as French despots; an age in which the new scepticism was disseminated and the secularization of society and thought were all but completed; an age in which thoughts of international revolution were already in the air, and in which the princes, moving slowly into the twilight, were ultimately brought to their end.

CHRISTOPHER HIBBERT

A Play for All Seasons

The tragic legend of Denmark's Prince Amleth had fired the imaginations of European storytellers long before England's famous playwright, William Shakespeare, began work on his Revenge of Hamlett Prince of Denmark *in 1600 or 1601. In fact, the tale of Hamlet's bloody demise was already a familiar folk legend when Saxo Grammaticus, a Danish scholar, first committed it to paper in 1186, and its popularity had not diminished four centuries later when Thomas Kyd produced his melodrama based on the tale. Drawing heavily upon Kyd's action-filled but otherwise inconsequential drama, Shakespeare created what is certainly his most famous tragedy and quite possibly the most famous play in world literature. In the centuries since* Hamlet *was first performed, its title role has been coveted—and attempted—by nearly all leading actors.*

No play has had a more enduring impact on the world than Shakespeare's *Hamlet*. It has been acted in every country where there is a serious interest in the theater, and leading actors the world over have been eager to play the part of the melancholy Prince. In the chronicles of writing and performance for the stage, *Hamlet* has become a part of world history.

The saga of the Danish Prince Amleth was first recorded in the twelfth century by the Danish scholar Saxo Grammaticus, but it has its origins in Scandinavian legend. In Saxo's story the murder of Amleth's father by his uncle is common knowledge. Amleth pretends to be insane to save his own life until he can avenge the murder. Revenge, when it comes, is bloody and violent: while the members of the court are celebrating a false report of Amleth's death, Amleth tricks them into drunkenness, sets fire to the hall, kills his uncle and proclaims himself king.

In the late sixteenth century an English play about Hamlet appeared in London. That play, which was probably written by Thomas Kyd, was a bloody, old-fashioned melodrama, complete with a ghost that went about wailing "Hamlet, revenge." The play was in the repertory of the Chamberlain's Men—one of London's two leading acting companies—for some time. In fact the type of melodrama it represented was spoofed in another play produced by the same company:

> A filthy whining ghost
> Lapt in some foul sheet, or a leather pilch,
> Comes screaming in like a pig half sticked
> And cries, *Vindicta*–Revenge, Revenge!

This English *Hamlet* was the play that Shakespeare rewrote in creating his own play.

Documented records of Shakespeare's tragedy begin in 1602, although the exact date of its composition is unknown. The date 1601 is usually given, but the author may have begun work on the play in 1600. In July, 1602, "a booke called the Revenge of Hamlett Prince Denmarke, as it was latelie Acted by the Lord Chamberlayne his servantes" was "entered" at Stationers' Hall in London. The practice at the time was for new books, including the texts of plays, to be sent to the headquarters of the Stationers' Company, whose members—all the booksellers and most of the printers in London—had the sole right of publication.

The application for the right to print *Hamlet* did not give the author's name. It did, however, clearly indicate that the play was already popular, and it identified the company of actors performing the play as the Chamberlain's Men. Of this troupe or "fellowship" Shakespeare had been a leading member and a shareholder for eight years. Shakespeare's writing skill—more of an asset than his acting—and the great ability of Richard Burbage, the troupe's leading player, had won renown and prosperity for the Chamberlain's Men. They were favored by Queen Elizabeth and had the acclaim of the general public. A rhymed epitaph that appeared after Burbage's death in 1618 named "young Hamlet" as one of his principal roles.

Thus we know that the most famous of Shakespeare's tragedies started with every advantage. Its author had been well established by his histories and comedies, and by the tragedy *Romeo and Juliet*. Further, the play was performed by a renowned company headed by Burbage.

It became immediately apparent that *Hamlet* was one of those rare works of art with nearly universal appeal. The play was great melodrama, with blood and violence and pageantry. But it was much more, for Shakespeare had taken an old, familiar plot and had shifted the emphasis from external events to Hamlet's character. And the man he revealed— paralyzed by gloom and indecision, torn between the flesh and the spirit, with shifting moods, uncontrolled passions, sharp insights and haunting fears—proved frighteningly real not just to seventeenth-century audiences but to every later generation.

Yet, while *Hamlet* has impressed and gripped audiences down the centuries, it is nonetheless a play of its own period. It is the first of the four great

The Globe Theater in London: for many years the home of the Chamberlain's Company, of which Shakespeare was a leading member.

Opposite The print of Shakespeare used as the frontispiece to the First Folio edition of his plays, published in 1623.

Elizabeth I at
Blackfriars, surrounded by
her guard of honor.

The Earl of Essex, one-time
favorite of Elizabeth I.

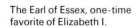

Shakespearean tragedies that reveal an increasingly dark and pessimistic view of human nature. Shakespeare was to write light romantic pieces after that phase, but he never returned to the old gaiety of his "high fantastical" comedies, which had their happiest, finest—and final—hour in *Twelfth Night*, which was almost certainly produced in 1601.

The first years of the seventeenth century in England were dominated by the twilight of the reign of the great Queen Elizabeth. The glory of Gloriana was being dimmed by her years, and her heart had been bruised, if not broken, by a shattering event. In February, 1601, her former favorite the Earl of Essex had led a foolhardy rebellion. With him was a clique of malcontents, including Shakespeare's early patron, the Earl of Southampton.

The challenge to the Queen's sovereignty found little public support and failed miserably. Essex was convicted of treason and beheaded; Southampton, lucky to escape with his life, was imprisoned in the Tower of London. Some of the insurgents had paid Shakespeare's company a special fee to revive *Richard II* at the Globe Theater, and even—as the Queen later alleged—to play it in the streets. Their purpose was to show that the deposition of a monarch could be successful—and it was absurdly stupid of the players to accept their bribe. There was an official inquiry into the company's conduct, but they were not penalized and they were quickly returned to royal favor. A subsequent remark of the Queen's —"Know ye not that I am Richard the Second?"— indicated that the wound had been deep.

Elizabeth's death came in March, 1603. The nation mourned and wondered. The Protestant succession was assured—there would not be a revival of civil and religious war to ravage public life with blood and hatred. But none could be sure how King James VI of Scotland would behave when he became also King James I of England. Doubts and fears gathered, and thus *Hamlet* was born in stormy weather, in a country under a cloud.

Even amid the eager, ardent and creative energy of the Elizabethan Age there had been a cult of melancholy. It had been more of a fashionable pose than a considered philosophy, but during the reign of the new king there was a growing wave of bleak pessimism. In his *History of the World* Sir Walter Raleigh noted that "the long day of mankind draweth fast towards an evening and the world's tragedy and time are near at an end." Raleigh was a prisoner—and probably knew that he was doomed —when he wrote his *History*, but bishops and clerics who were not in danger also preached decay and disaster. In one of his sermons, John Donne, dean of St. Paul's, told his listeners that the sun was "fainter and languishing, men less in stature and shorter lived. No addition, but only every year new sorts of worms and flies and sicknesses which argue more and more putrefaction." Other divines urged the saving of souls before the darkness thickened.

Those dismal forebodings came after *Hamlet* was written. By then Shakespeare had entered a period in which his despair about human character and

The smell of corruption in the English air

destiny was far more prominent than his faith in charity and the saving power of mercy. That view is found in his last plays. If something was rotten in the state of Denmark, there was also a smell of corruption in the English air—and Hamlet's bitter commentary on life anticipate a generally felt insecurity.

The settled philosophy and faith of the Middle Ages had cracked. To question authority in Church and State once had been strange and sinful; it was now familiar and fashionable. The stage of national life had become full of questioning Hamlets.

Had *Hamlet* been no more than a projection of sad scepticism, it could never have pleased as it did. It has lived by the dramatic values of its fast-moving story and still more by the character of the Prince, so quicksilver in his moods, so sharp of wit, so profound in reflection, and, above all, so ready with the perfect phrase and the perfectly chosen word. Whatever were the failings of the new reign and the degradation of court life, the English language reached its summit of power and richness in the Authorized Version of the Bible, which was suggested by and dedicated to King James. The old Anglo-Saxon or Anglo-Norman English had a special strength, and the classical culture of the Renaissance brought new

Above left James I: he took the Chamberlain's Company under his patronage and plays were often performed at court.

Above right The Third Earl of Southampton, an early patron of Shakespeare.

Pirated versions of "Hamlet"

The title page of the Second Quarto of *Hamlet*.

Far right William Kemp, a famous Shakespearian comedian, from a woodcut of 1600.

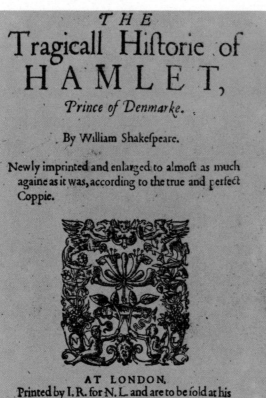

Richard Burbage, the leading player of the Chamberlain's Company. He was the first actor to play the role of "Hamlet."

decoration to its sinewy frame. Hamlet is a university student with a gift of golden words. He commands a thundering eloquence in his parley with the ghost. He can be as brief as poignant: "The Rest is silence." And he dies with a sigh, not a swan song. His part was written in the dusk of Elizabethan glory, and in the high noon of the English language.

There is no question that the play pleased its audiences. In fact, *Hamlet*'s reception was so gratifying that a "pirated" version was thought to be worth printing in 1603. There was then no copyright of plays, and the manuscripts were keenly guarded by the companies for which they were written in order to prevent performance by rivals. If a piece were popular, a bogus text could usually be dishonestly obtained by bribing one of the minor players. Such players were known as "hired men" to distinguish them from "sharers," who took the chief roles. The hired men's wages were very low, and they could be bribed to provide rough scripts based on memories of parts taken by themselves or others. There were also shorthand writers who took surreptitious notes at performances in order to get out a text.

The pirated version of *Hamlet*, a truncated travesty of the play, was known as the First Quarto. The Quarto named Shakespeare as the dramatist, and therefore either he or his company decided to print the full and genuine text. Doing so involved the risk of its being used by other teams of players, but since the play had been published with a text grotesquely unfair to the author, it was decided to issue a correct version. In 1604, therefore, the Second Quarto—which described the play as "Newly imprinted and enlarged to almost as much againe according to the true and perfect Coppie"—was issued. There were two reprintings in 1611.

In 1623 John Heminges and Henry Condell, Shakespeare's fellow sharers in the Chamberlain's Men, printed a slightly abbreviated form of the Second Quarto, omitting four hundred lines out of four thousand. They were probably using a play-house text in which some cuts had been marked, for the complete version occupies the stage for nearly four hours—or nearly double "the two hours' traffic of our stage" mentioned by Shakespeare in his prologue to *Romeo and Juliet*. Uncut, *Hamlet* is the longest of Shakespeare's plays.

The unauthorized first edition of the text stated that the play had already been performed both in and out of London, and it is certainly true that *Hamlet* appealed not just to the regular playgoers or to the students at Oxford and Cambridge. In 1607, when Captain Keeling of the East India Company's ship *Dragon* was sailing east with two other vessels, *Hector* and *Content*, they were becalmed off Sierra Leone. There Keeling recorded in his diary that he entertained Captain Hawkins of *Content*. There was a fish dinner and then he had "Hamlet acted abord me: which I permitt to keepe my people from idlnes and unlawful games, or sleepe." That they managed to improvise a stage on the tiny ships of the period is remarkable. So is the fact that the Captain had taken a copy of *Hamlet* with him. The performance by the crew, organized for the sake of discipline rather than in devotion to drama, must have been extremely crude. The impact of *Hamlet* had indeed been wide.

There is no record of command performances of *Hamlet* at court, even though King James constantly made requests to see other plays. If *Hamlet* was never in demand at court, that is understandable. James had married a Danish wife, and neither the story of the murder and revenge nor the remarks about the drinking habits of the Danes were complimentary to the Queen's nation. But the play remained in the repertory of the King's Men (the name the Chamberlain's Men had taken upon the accession of James I).

English actors frequently toured in Europe, where

they had a high reputation. As early as 1586, the Earl of Leicester had taken players with him when he was with an army in Holland, and the Shakespearean clown William Kempe was among them. Fynes Moryson (1566-1630), a Cambridge scholar and traveler, met English actors at Frankfurt. "The Germans," he wrote, "not understanding a word they said, flocked wonderfully to see their gesture and action." The English standard of performance was thought exemplary. In 1626 an English company led by John Green played *Hamlet* in Dresden. They used a shortened version: *Der Bestrafte Brüdermord, Prinz Hamlet ans Dannemark*.

English theaters, closed by the Puritans for nearly twenty years during the civil war and the Commonwealth, were reopened after the restoration of the monarchy in 1660. *Hamlet* was one of the first plays to be revived. The diarist Pepys noted that Thomas Betterton played the Prince "beyond imagination" in "the best part I believe that man ever acted."

In recent years classics have been subjected to the whims of directors who want to prove their ability by giving old plays a new look. *Hamlet* has been dressed in the costumes of many periods, including our own. It has received new interpretations and been staged according to strange theories. Through all that, it has held its position at the summit of English drama, continually examined by scholars while continually fascinating the general public. More than any of Shakespeare's plays, it has justified Ben Jonson's promise of the author's survival, "not for an age but for all time."   IVOR BROWN

Thomas Betterton, a well-known actor after the Restoration of 1660. *Hamlet* was one of his favorite roles.

Left The title page of John Donne's *Sermons*, published in 1640.

John Donne, poet and divine.

473

While *Hamlet* was being performed for the first time in London, an impoverished fifty-six-year-old Spaniard who had once been a soldier and had lately been in prison was writing "just such a book as might be begotten in a jail." The Spaniard's name was Miguel de Cervantes Saavedra and the book was *Don Quixote*, the first modern novel. Cervantes' work was in the tradition of the picaresque romances that had been popular in Spain since the middle of the sixteenth century, when the anonymous *La Vida de Lazarillo de Tormes y de sus fortunas y adversidades* was published. *La Vida* had been followed by the equally popular works of Mateo Alemán, Agustín de Rojas, and Francisco López de Úbeda, whose *La Pícara Justina* appeared in 1605. Indeed, the Spaniards have been credited with inventing the picaresque novel —a genre that takes its name from the Spanish word for rogue, *pícaro*.

Don Quixote was much more than a picaresque novel, however: Cervantes' work was soon recognized as the greatest social romance of the early seventeenth century. The Spaniard's highly moralistic masterpiece succeeded not only in ridiculing the picaresque novel and its chivalric sentiments, but also in demonstrating the follies of prejudice and the real dangers behind an exaggerated contemporary regard for pure blood and nobility of birth—a regard that was coupled with widespread disdain for work.

Cervantes himself led a hard and vigorous life. He joined the army in 1568 and served in Italy, where he was badly wounded at the Battle of Lepanto in October, 1571. On his return to Spain he was captured by Barbary corsairs and taken to Algiers, where he was sold as a slave to a Greek renegade. Ransomed after five years, Cervantes returned to his homeland in 1576. He tried and failed to make a living as a playwright and eventually found employment as a collector of provisions and stores for the Spanish Armada of 1588. After the fleet's defeat, he was retained as an ill-paid and overworked commissary to the galleys—but his unbusinesslike methods soon led to his imprisonment. Out of that experience grew Cervantes' great literary panorama of Spanish society, *Don Quixote*, which was published in 1605. In 1614 a spurious sequel to *Don Quixote* appeared, and a year later Cervantes himself published an authentic second installment.

On April 23, 1616, Cervantes died in Madrid; on that same day Shakespeare died in Stratford, England. Like his contemporary, Shakespeare may also have been a soldier—and may even have fought against Cervantes' countrymen in the Netherlands. Indeed, Spain and England were at war for most of the two authors' lives, and the rivalry between the two countries was not over at the time of their deaths.

Cervantes: soldier, slave and author.

Spain under Philip II

Although the Spanish Empire was far less extensive than it had been in the splendid days of Charles V (1500-58), it was still the largest and most widespread empire on earth. Apart from her rich possessions in Italy and Sardinia, Spain still retained several key European possessions — including Franche-Comté and the Netherlands — whose feudal estates had come into Spanish hands through purchase, marriage, treachery and violence at the beginning of the fifteenth century. Spain still held her rich empire across the Atlantic, and she had extended her dominions in Western Europe and America.

In 1581, Philip II, son of Emperor Charles V, forcibly annexed Portugal after declaring himself heir to the decrepit and scarcely sane Henry II, who had died leaving no direct heirs. There were four other claimants to the Portuguese throne, all of whom were grandchildren or great-grandchildren of King Emanuel I. The strongest claim was that of the Duchess of Braganza, whose father was one of Emanuel's younger sons. All the other contenders— with the exception of Don Antonio, Prior of Crato, who was illegitimate —were descended through the female line. The Church favored

union with Spain, as did several prominent members of the Cortes, or parliament — and when the Duchess of Braganza was won over to their side by large grants of land and by the promise that her husband would be made King of Brazil when Philip II became King of Portugal, the success of the Spanish party seemed assured. In order to forestall the Spanish, Don Antonio proclaimed himself King and occupied Lisbon. But a Spanish army commanded by the great Duke of Alva invaded Portugal and soon overwhelmed Don Antonio's forces at Alcantara.

Sixty years of captivity

After his coronation as King of Portugal, Philip promised to recognize the constitutional rights of the Portuguese people, particularly those of the influential *hidalgos*. He agreed to summon the Cortes regularly and to create a Portuguese privy council with responsibility for Portuguese affairs. The country's possessions in Brazil, Africa and Asia were to be held by Portugal, which was to be considered not as a conquered province but as a separate kingdom, joined with Spain in a mutually profitable political union.

Few of Philip's promises were observed: the Cortes was summoned only once; the government of the country was left to the grasping favorites of the Spanish court; and the union with Spain—known in Portugal as the "Sixty Years of Captivity"—led to incessant involvement in wars with Spain's maritime enemies. There were two serious insurrections in the 1630s, and in 1640 the lazy Duke of Braganza, grandson of the Duchess whose claims had been bought out by Philip II, rode a wave of national discontent to the throne. As King John IV, he expelled the Spanish garrisons from his country.

The empire crumbles

Despite the size of her empire, Spain's power at the beginning of the seventeenth century was already in decline. The defeat of the Armada in 1588 had exposed the incompetence of the Spanish navy and had given Spanish self-esteem a severe shock. Since that time it had become increasingly clear that Spain no longer had the strength to maintain the position she had presumed to occupy in the world. The con-

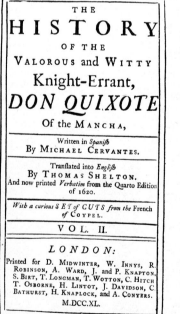
Don Quixote: more than a picaresque romance.

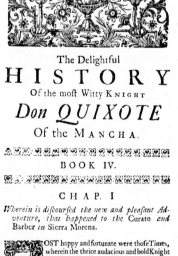

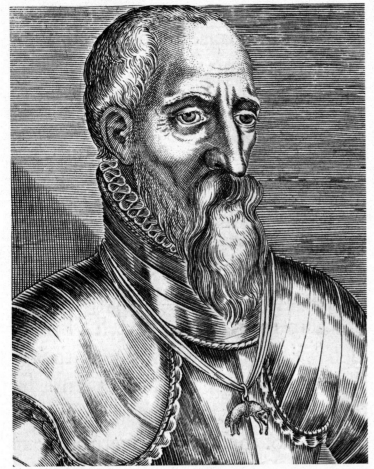

The Duke of Alva, who almost destroyed the Dutch revolt.

Philip III

Philip II died at the Escorial a few months after the Treaty of Vervins was signed and he was succeeded by his son Philip III, a pious, extravagant, incapable monarch who was content to leave the government in the hands of the worthless Duke of Lerma. The unscrupulous Duke encouraged the King's extravagances while acquiring a vast personal fortune and involving his impoverished country in disastrous foreign entanglements. Fearing that they might support a Mohammedan invasion of Spain, Lerma expelled the Moriscos, or Spanish Moors, from the country. His move was almost as damaging to Spain as Louis XIV's expulsion of the Huguenots would later be to France; for the half-million Moriscos whom Lerma forced into exile were among the most skilled members of the community.

Hoping to strike a blow against England in 1602, Spain landed an army in Ireland to bolster the cause of the Earl of Tyrone. The intervention was wholly unsuccessful; and by the time Don Juan del Aguila, the Spanish general, had evacuated Kinsale, Spain's finances were all but exhausted.

The accession to the English throne of James I, who "naturally loved not the sight of a soldier nor any violent man," saved Spain from further expensive involvement with England; for Elizabeth's successor achieved a peace settlement between the two countries in 1604. Thereafter, despite the strength of anti-Spanish feeling in England, relations between Madrid and London became more friendly. Philip's skillful diplomat, the Count of Gondomar—whose task was to keep James from aiding the Protestant states in their quarrels with Spain and to prevent English attacks on Spanish possessions in America—helped maintain this amicable relationship. Negotiations were eventually entered into for a marriage between James I's son Charles and the Infanta Donna Maria, sister of the Spanish King.

Spain had been saved by the pacific policies of James I and the skills of Count Gondomar—but nothing could save her from the loss of her possessions in the Netherlands, where Dutch rebels, supported by England and subsidized by France, had been resisting all attempts to crush them for over thirty years. On April 9, 1609, a treaty was signed that recognized the Dutch Republic as an independent state.

tinuing war with England was but one of the constant strains on her resources.

Toward the end of his reign, Philip II added to his country's fiscal burden by intervening in France in support of the Catholic League, a group that sought to unseat Henry of Navarre. The Duke of Parma was ordered to march across France to help raise the siege of Paris, and Don Juan del Aguila was directed to land in Brittany at the head of two thousand men. The siege of Paris was successfully raised, as was the siege of Rouen; but Parma, Philip's most valued servant, was wounded during an attack on Caudebec and died on December 2, 1592. Subsequent Spanish victories—the capture of Doullens and Cambrai by the Count of Fuentes, Parma's successor, and the reduction of Calais and Amiens—counted for little when weighed against Henry of Navarre's superior diplomatic skill. And by the Treaty of Vervins, signed in May of 1598, Philip was obliged to recognize the failure of his schemes in France and to return all his conquests except Cambrai.

The Escorial, capital of a world empire.

HAERLEM

Revolt of the Netherlands 1609

The revolt that erupted in the Spanish Netherlands in 1568 pitted a small band of vastly out-numbered, militantly Protestant Dutch nobles against the armies of Spain's Catholic King, Europe's mightiest monarch, Philip II. The contest was a lopsided one, and Philip's victory over the Dutch troops led by William of Orange should have been a swift one. Instead, the fighting dragged on for forty years before a temporary truce was agreed upon in 1609. William of Orange had been assassinated in 1584 and Philip died in 1598—but the dream of an independent Dutch state lived on. Sporadic fighting continued for forty years after the truce, however. Not until 1648, by the terms of the Treaty of Munster, was the former Spanish possession divided into the independent Dutch Republic in the north and the "obedient" southern provinces (later known as Belgium).

The Dutch nation achieved its independence through a war that lasted for eighty years—from 1568 to 1648. If a single day can claim to be the turning point in that long struggle, it is probably April 9, 1609, the day when Spain was compelled to sign a twelve-year truce with the Dutch rebels and thereby recognize that the war had reached a state of complete deadlock. The truce acknowledged, *de facto*, what forty years later was to be recognized *de jure*: that the Dutch Republic was an independent state. Before the final Treaty of Münster was signed in 1648, there were to be military threats to that independence from Spain and more serious threats from France. Frontiers were to be adjusted by military action but subject only to these relatively minor changes in territory and law, 1609 marked the emergence—through political revolt and armed conflict—of a new state in Europe, unique in its constitution, its social structure and its economy.

In its earliest phase, the resistance to Philip II of Spain, who had succeeded his father Charles V as sovereign of the Burgundian Netherlands in 1555, came from the great aristocrats. Charles had scarcely abdicated when the trouble began. The high Netherlands nobility resented Philip's assumption that he "ruled" their territories and could treat them as he liked. They protested against the presence of Spanish troops on Dutch soil, the enforcement of the Inquisition by persecuting Edicts, the rationalization of the Netherlands bishoprics and the general disregard of their traditional feudal rights and privileges. Of the three leaders, Egmont, Hoorn and William, Prince of Orange, it was the latter who rapidly developed the habit of command and the exercise of authority. Yet even Orange, desperately trying to maintain reasonable relations with Philip and also—after the King's departure for Spain in 1559—with his regents and deputies, could not prevent the spread of more violent protest. Some five hundred lesser nobles banded together in a league that was by no means inclined to moderation. Neither

were the fanatical Protestants who went on a wild spree of iconoclasm in the churches of Antwerp and other cities in 1566.

Philip's answer was to send the Duke of Alva to suppress the revolt in 1567. Orange fled, Egmont and Hoorn were executed, and thousands were burned or killed. Alba subsequently proposed a turnover tax, known as the "Tenth Penny," that turned the powerful merchant class in cities like Antwerp, Ghent and Bruges against Spain. Nevertheless, Alba's brutal measures seemed to be working when, in 1572, a band of Dutch rebels—ordered out of Dover harbor by Queen Elizabeth I—fell upon the Dutch port of Brill and succeeded in capturing it. These "Sea Beggars" then went on to take the nearby communities of Flushing, Middelburg and Zierikzee. They swiftly established control over the entire Scheldt estuary and the approaches to Antwerp. That region was not only the center of Spanish government in the Netherlands but also the largest commercial entrepôt in the world. And although Alba successfully laid siege to Haarlem, the dogged resistance of Leyden and Alkmaar led to the liberation of most of Holland and Zeeland.

In 1573 Alba retired to make way for two successors, Luis de Requesens and Don Juan of Austria. Neither succeeded in quelling resistance nor in stemming the growing mutinies among the 60,000 unpaid Spanish troops stationed in the Netherlands. Between 1578 and 1579—amid growing Spanish confusion—Orange consolidated the rebel forces and strengthened their grip on the northwestern Netherlands. Unfortunately for him, religious quarrels between Dutch Catholics, moderate Erasmians and extreme Protestant groups like the fanatical Calvinists of Ghent made national unity impossible; the Prince's opportunity for an early victory was lost amid factional squabbling.

In 1577 Philip sent Alexander Farnese, later Prince of Parma, to join Don Juan. Farnese was not only one of the greatest military commanders of the

Obyt Anno 1592. 3 Decemb.

Alexander Farnese, Prince of Parma and Governor of the Netherlands; he was one of the military geniuses of his age, but was unable to hold Spain's northern possessions together.

Opposite Spanish soldiers executing Dutch rebels in Haarlem, from *de Leone Belgica* by Francis Hogenberg 1585.

477

century, he was also an adroit diplomat. By military genius and skillful bribery, Farnese reunited a large part of the south and east for Spain, and in 1579 he signed the Treaty of Arras with the leaders of the southern provinces. That treaty was, in effect, an answer to the Union of Utrecht—an accord signed by most of the northern and some of the southern provinces and towns that is regarded as the foundation charter of the Dutch Republic.

From 1578 to 1589 Farnese pushed north, recapturing most of present-day Belgium—including the great cities of Ghent, Bruges and Antwerp—for Spain. He reached the region where the Rhine, Maas and Lek rivers cross the Low Countries from east to west before his progress was checked by Philip's orders to divert troops to the 1588 invasion of England. Just before Antwerp fell, the rebels' great leader, Orange, was struck down by an assassin. Orange was succeeded by his son Maurice, who proved to be an even greater military commander. With the political help of another republican leader, Jan van Olden Barneveldt, Maurice regained much of the territory to the south and east that Farnese had captured, but he could not break the siege of Ostend. Its surrender to Spinola, another brilliant Italian commander in the pay of Philip II, ended the first half of the war and made the truce of 1609 inevitable.

Little of real consequence happened after hostilities were resumed in 1621. In a protracted and dreary struggle, the Dutch, under Maurice's successor, Frederick Henry, managed to capture 's Hertogenbosch, Maastricht and the surrounding country. Neither a French alliance nor the marriage of Frederick's daughter Mary to James, Duke of York, enabled them to do more. The 1648 Treaty of Münster irrevocably divided the Netherlands into

the obedient Provinces of the South, which remained loyal to Spain, and the Dutch Republic, which became a monarchy in 1813.

Nineteenth-century historians assumed that the rebellion was Protestant and liberal, and that there was something about the ethos of the "Teutonic" north that predestined it to lead the Netherlands out of the decadent, Catholic, persecuting Spanish Empire. The explanation is obviously defective. In the early stages—and indeed as late as 1578—the revolt drew much of its strength from the south: the southern city of Ghent was, from the beginning, a violent, unrepentant center of Calvinism—and Calvinism itself entered the Netherlands from the south (from France, via the Walloon provinces). The original center of Orange's resistance movement was in

A difference of social structure

Brabant, or Brussels, a city that lay far south of Holland and Zeeland. The Sea Beggars drew much of their strength from Flanders, Brabant and Wallonia, and many southern Catholic nobles were as strong in defense of their privileges as their poorer northern neighbors—until they were bribed back into loyalty by Farnese.

Such obstinate facts caused the most famous twentieth-century historian of the revolt, Peter Geyl, to reject the religious or "racial" explanation of the rising in favor of a quite different one. The Netherlands, he argued, had already formed a natural cultural unity before the revolt; the country was on its way to becoming a political unit before the fighting began. Thus the revolt began as a medieval, feudal, noble protest and ended as a conquest of the north by Protestant forces working through the Sea Beggars. The north was able to fight off Spanish attempts at reconquest because it was protected by a defense line of great rivers that even Farnese failed to breach.

Geyl's interpretation has become virtual orthodoxy, although after forty-odd years it seems oversimplified. Unquestionably the rebels were helped by geography. Yet other factors must be taken into account. For one, the era was one of siege warfare, not mobile warfare. Southern cities like Ghent, Bruges and Antwerp were well fortified and capable of self-defense. For another, the pattern—even in the north—was inconsistent: the northern city of Haarlem fell, but Amsterdam remained pro-Spanish and Catholic until 1578, when it fell to the rebels by an internal coup d'état. The truth is that Antwerp and the other southern cities succumbed through muddle, bribery and loss of morale—rather than through absolute indefensibility.

Nor should one ignore another important feature of the revolt that does not fit Geyl's theory of a united Netherlands disrupted solely by Spanish military force. The fact is that even before Philip's accession there were marked differences of social structure between south and north. The south was more prosperous, more commercial, more industrial—and yet more subject to feudal, aristocratic influence—than the north, which was a poorer society, dependent upon shipping and fishing. From the beginning of the revolt in 1567, merchants, manufacturers and workers began to move north, sensing that the north was likely to be safer and less exposed to the risk of princely or aristocratic looting than the south was. Perhaps ten per cent of the southern population—and a far higher percentage of its most dynamic members—emigrated during this period, and by the 1590s they were prominent among the professors, printers, artists, bankers, clothiers, silk spinners, shipbuilders and overseas traders in Amsterdam, Haarlem, Leyden, Middelburg and many other ports and cities of the north.

The southern aristocracy, immobilized by their investments in land and property, could contribute little to the revolt. Shamefaced, they stayed put and allowed themselves to be bribed into renewing their loyal pledges to Spain. On the other hand, there can be no doubt about the fanatical sincerity of the

Frederick Henry, Prince of Orange; it was ironic that Holland's struggle for liberty should be led by German nobles such as the princes of Orange.

southern Calvinists, most of whom came from the lower or middle classes.

There was little homogeneity among the classes that supported the revolt, and it is difficult to determine the motives that drove them on. Simple hatred of Spanish occupation and Inquisitional persecution was widespread among the middle and upper classes. (Among other things, persecution, war, dynasticism and all the costs that accompanied them were bad for business—and Dutch society was already a business society.) At the other end of the scale, frustration and mistrust were increased by a new phenomenon of the age: unprecedented inflation, which afflicted aristocracy and working men alike. Nobles living on incomes derived from more or less fixed rents found themselves caught between rising costs and falling receipts at a time when court jobs and army appointments were going to Spaniards. And as industry deserted the old guild-dominated towns for the Flanders countryside, a growing force of workers found itself turned adrift, workless and starving. As a result, the extremes of Dutch society were united in their discontent and unanimous in their support of both political and religious dissent. They were soon joined by the potentially less vulnerable and certainly more circumspect middle class, whose members were disturbed by the prospect of damaging and unlimited Spanish taxation. This class took control of the new Republic.

It is that combination of social classes and political motives which distinguishes the revolt of the Netherlands from the feudal protests, Protestant rebellions and peasant uprisings that occurred in France, England, Germany, Italy, Spain and Scandinavia in the late sixteenth and early seventeenth centuries. The Dutch revolt represents the one successful rising of a mercantile republic against the centralized,

Francis Gomarus: leader of the Calvinist extremists.

A Dutch merchant with his wife in Java. The Dutch colonial empire, like that of England, grew during the seventeenth and eighteenth centuries, while those of Spain and Portugal stagnated.

Right The Mayor of Delft. Dutch domestic life, after independence was officially acknowledged by Spain, became far more prosperous than it had previously been.

The Rise of the Dutch Republic to 1648

- ○ Holy Roman Empire
- ● United Provinces
- ○ Remained Spanish Netherlands

Dutch open dykes 1573
Alkmaar
Amsterdam
Haarlem
Besieged by Alba 1572-73
The Hague
Assassination of William the Silent 1584
Rotterdam
Brill
Leyden
Utrecht
Zutphen
Defeat of Sir Philip Sidney 1586
Delft
Breda
Bruges
Ghent
Antwerp Sacked 1576
Maastricht
Nieuwport
Brussels
Louvain
Liége
Mons
River Rhine
Cateau-Cambrésis
FRANCE

monarchical absolutism typified by the states of early modern Europe—Spain, France, England and Prussia. Curiously, the Dutch example did not spread. (John Adams, scraping the bottom of the barrel for money to finance the American Revolution, appealed to the spirit of comradeship between the American "federation" and its Dutch "originals" —and got nowhere.)

The chronicle of the Republic's economic and cultural history is an altogether different story. Before the 1590s the northern provinces were poorer than their southern neighbors, but after 1590 they rapidly overtook them. Amsterdam soon replaced Antwerp as the world's foremost entrepôt, and the Dutch *fluit*—an unarmed, cheap, sea-going barge—introduced a technological revolution in shipbuilding. The Dutch *fluit* fleet soon established a virtual monopoly on the trade in grain, timber and naval stores from the Baltic to Europe.

In the early seventeenth century Dutch merchants opened new markets in Russia, Greenland, Newfoundland, India, Java, Sumatra and Australasia. At New Amsterdam (renamed New York after its capture by the English) and at the Cape of Good Hope, the Dutch left colonies that helped to shape the character of future settlements. In India, Ceylon and the East they founded a great trading company, the East India Company. And in North and South America and the West Indies the Dutch West India Company flourished for a time.

Dutch colonial history has been emphasized in Western history books, yet statistically it was never as important as Dutch trade within Europe. The

"new drapery"—carried by Belgian emigrants from Ypres to Leyden, and then to Norwich and Colchester—revolutionized Europe's textile trade, replacing old, heavy, expensive cloths with bright, light, cheaper textiles. Antwerp silk weavers and linen bleachers carried their skills to Amsterdam and Haarlem, and cohorts of merchants and bankers followed King William and Queen Mary to England. In ensuing decades, Dutch bankers helped to shape the structure and finance of the Bank of England, and the loans by which England financed her wars—including the American Revolution—were underwritten by men named Vanneck, Van Notten, and Capadose.

Almost every country in Europe profited from Dutch immigration. From London to Rome and Danzig to Warsaw, Dutch settlers used their engineering skills to clear swamps and marshes and to build dams, locks and canals, water works and pumping systems. Colbert employed Dutchmen in Bordeaux to reclaim land and build textile factories, and in Sweden Dutch immigrants negotiated contracts with the Crown that gave them a virtual monopoly of iron and copper mining, the manufacture of munitions, the cutting of timber and the export of tar, hemp and rope. Export of Dutch capital and skill to less-developed economies is a recurrent feature of economic life in the seventeenth century.

Along with the economic tide went ideas, philosophy and works of art. Grotius was the spokesman, advocate and historian of the patrician governing class, but his principles—among them *mare liberum*, or freedom of the seas—were adopted by England and later by the entire civilized world. (Indeed Grotius' claim to the title Father of Modern International Law has never been challenged.) Philosophers like Descartes, Spinoza and Locke took refuge in the relatively tolerant climate of Holland.

Rembrandt, the greatest of the hundreds of Netherlands artists whose works have become part of Europe's cultural heritage, lived not far from Spinoza in Amsterdam's Jewish quarter. Dutch art, like many Dutch innovations, grew up under strong Italian influence, yet it developed its own unique and unmistakable style. Seascapes, domestic interiors, flower paintings, portraits, landscapes—all demonstrate a miraculous absorption of detail into broad and satisfying patterns that has rarely been equaled before or since.

The capacity for combining detailed observation with significant generalization links seventeenth-century Dutch artists with their scientific contemporaries—men like Leeuwenhoek, Boerhaave, Huyghens and Stevin—who brought scientific methods to microscopy, biology, zoology, medicine, astronomy, architecture, ballistics and navigation.

Economic decline set in with the eighteenth century, as competition from larger states, high defense costs and heavy taxation combined to check Dutch prosperity and diminish Dutch power. But in their heyday, Dutch capital, Dutch enterprise and Dutch technology—all by-products of the Dutch revolt—served as a powerful driving force, propelling a predominantly agrarian, semifeudal Europe toward industrial revolution and socio-economic modernity.

CHARLES WILSON

The ratification of the treaty of Münster, 1648, which finally gave Holland independence from Spain.

The perverse fragmentation

While Spain was signing a truce with the Dutch rebels in 1609, King James of England was entertaining vague but grandiose notions of peacefully uniting the whole of Europe and establishing himself and the Pope as joint presidents of a great council of the Church. James' ambitious design far exceeded his rather limited talents and powers, however, and seventeenth-century Europe remained as perversely fragmented as it had been at any time in its history.

In the south, the unwieldy Ottoman Empire, slowly recovering from the shattering defeat of its navy at Lepanto, sprawled across the southern shore of the Mediterranean from Algiers to Egypt and Syria, and stretched northward across Anatolia and the Bosphorus —through Greece, Bulgaria and Hungary—to the Black Sea and the Crimea. This vast empire was ruled by Sultan Ahmed I, a sickly king who was to die before he was

James I welcomes his son Charles home after his visit to Spain.

thirty. Ahmed's decadent and corrupt Empire had long since lost the vitality that had made it the terror of Christendom in the days of Suleiman the Magnificent. Nonetheless, its confidently predicted

demise was to be postponed for more than three centuries.

Beyond the Empire's northern boundaries were the three largest states in Europe—Poland, Russia and Sweden. Of these, Sweden— under the stern military rule of the aggressive Charles IX—was by far the most powerful. By 1609 she had seized Estonia, and with the conquest of Livonia and Ingria she pushed Poland out of the eastern Baltic.

Barbarous Russia

Russia, shut out of the Baltic by Sweden, cut off from the Black Sea by the Turks and engaged in interminable disputes with Poland, was reckoned of small importance in European affairs. "If a man consider the natures and manner of life of the Muscovites, he will be forced to allow that there cannot be anything more barbarous than that people," a German visitor decided. "They never learn any art or science or apply themselves to any kind of study; on the contrary they are so ignorant as to think that a man cannot make an almanack unless he be a sorcerer, nor foretell the revolution of the moon and the eclipses unless he have some communication with devils."

The few schools that existed in the primitive, thinly populated country were in the hands of superstitious and narrow-minded monks; there was no parliament; there was no justice worthy of the name; there was no freedom of thought, no intellectual life, no economic development. Instead there was sloth and prejudice, corruption, violence and wholesale drunkenness. Ivan the Terrible—the Grand Duke of

Muscovy who had bestowed the title of Tsar upon himself and who had ruthlessly imposed an autocratic government of the most oppressively despotic kind upon the Russian people—had died in 1584, leaving a weak and pious heir who was content to place the administration of the country in the hands of his brother-in-law, Boris Godunov.

Godunov — who gained wide popularity among the landowning class by forbidding peasants to move from one estate to another, thus placing them at the mercy of their masters and accelerating their debasement into serfs—had himself chosen as his brother-in-law's successor. In 1598 he became Tsar of All the Russias. The accession of a

Ivan the Terrible: his death threw Russia into turmoil.

mere boyar aroused the anger and jealousy of the nobles, who conspired to overthrow Godunov. And thus, while the nobles plotted, while gangs of bandits terrorized the countryside, while hundreds of square miles were devastated by plague and famine, while an impostor who called himself Dimitri, the younger son of Ivan the Terrible, mustered an army in Poland —a disturbed Russia entered the seventeenth century.

To the west of Poland lay a conglomeration of over three hundred German states, all of them under the nominal protection of the ill and indolent Austrian Hapsburg Emperor, Matthias, who had succeeded his brother in 1602.

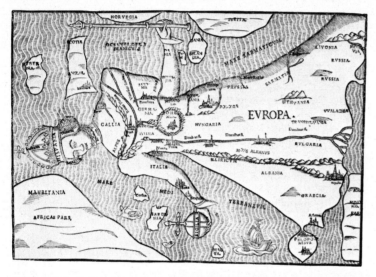

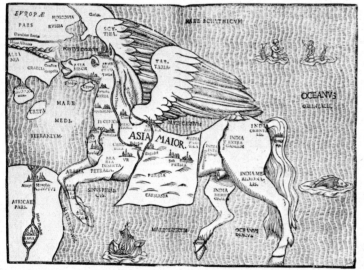

Europe and Asia through the eyes of the early-seventeenth century.

Italy—a geographical expression

Like Germany, Italy was what Metternich would later call "*ein geographischer Begriff*" — "a mere geographical expression." In the northeast lay the Republic of Venice, whose lands stretched from Bergamo to Istria and down the eastern shores of the Adriatic. (Overseas they also included Crete, which was not to fall into the hands of the Turks until the end of the seventeenth century.) South of Venice were the Papal States, which cut Italy in half from Ancona to Rome and extended as far south as Terracina, sixty miles north of Naples. Naples itself was the capital of a kingdom that included Sicily and Sardinia and formed part of the vast possessions of the King of Spain.

The extensive Duchy of Milan was also part of the Spanish Empire. Milan's neighbors — aside from Venice to the east and Switzerland to the north—were the Duchy of Mantua, ruled by the Gonzaga family; the Duchy of Modena, governed by the House of Este; the Duchy of Parma, which was in the hands of the Farnese; the Republic of Genoa, to which Corsica belonged until it was sold to France in 1768; and the Piedmontese possessions of the House of Savoy. Victor Emmanuel III, a descendant of the King of Savoy, was to become the first king of a united Italy in 1861.

France's ascendancy

France, to whom the House of Savoy would one day lose both Savoy and Nice, was ruled by Henry IV, the most remarkable ruler of his time. The son of the

The execution of Henry IV's murderer Ravaillac.

Duke of Vendôme and Jeanne d'Albret, Queen of Navarre, he was educated as a Protestant and distinguished himself in the religious wars in France. On the death of his mother in 1572 he became King of Navarre, and following the assassination of Henry III in 1589 he became King of France.

Ten years of fighting intervened before Henry, who had become a Catholic convert, could claim his inheritance. From that time on, Henry, aided by his friend the Duke of Sully, concentrated his considerable talents upon restoring the fortunes of France. Riding over all opposition and ignoring all criticism, Henry drove through reforms of the administration, finances, industry and the army, and gave Paris new buildings of great beauty.

In his efforts to weaken the power of the Hapsburgs, the French King entered into a series of alliances with the Protestant princes of Germany, the King of Sweden, various Italian states, the Swiss cantons and the Duke of Lorraine. After the death of his first wife, Margaret of Valois, sister of Henry III of France, Henry married the formidable

Marie de' Medici, and thus gained the favor of her uncle, the Grand Duke of Tuscany. By the time of his assassination in May, 1610, Henry had prepared France for the fulfillment of her great destiny. Cardinal Richelieu, minister to Henry's son and heir Louis XIII, and Richelieu's successor, Cardinal Mazarin, were to achieve that destiny.

While France was rising to domination in Europe, Spain was becoming ever weaker. She was internally exhausted: her economy was unstable, her treasury was ruined, and the American gold that poured into her ports was grossly ill-distributed. In no country in Europe was there so marked a contrast between the magnificence of the rich and the abject poverty of the poor. The American colonies were also proving a liability to Spain.

England, for her part, had as yet made little attempt to colonize America. Her sixteenth-century voyagers had been more concerned with discovery, adventure and plunder. In 1583 Sir Humphry Gilbert had taken possession of Newfoundland in the name of Queen Elizabeth, and in 1584 a fleet sent out by Sir Walter Raleigh to explore the American seaboard north of Florida had occupied the district known as Virginia. But even such men as Richard Hakluyt, whose *Principal Navigations, Voyages and Discoveries of the English Nation* was published between 1598 and 1600, believed that a colony's main uses were as a promoter of trade or as a penal settlement. It was not until 1609, with the founding of Jamestown in Virginia, that the age of English colonization really began. Eleven years later, an even more significant landfall was made in New England.

Henry IV of Navarre and France: enemy of the Hapsburgs.

Marie de' Medici, widow of Henry IV, with her son Louis XIII.

The Pilgrims at Plymouth   1620

Unlike their predecessors, who settled in Virginia at the end of the first decade of the seventeenth century, the religious dissidents who boarded the Mayflower *in September 1620 had no patron and no significant financial backing. Those expatriate Englishmen—most of whom had recently sought—and failed to find—ecclesiastical equanimity in Holland—sailed without a royal charter and without commercial backing. Their voyage was undertaken amid considerable uncertainty and at long odds—and when half the 102-man company died within six months of their arrival, Plymouth Colony appeared doomed. Indeed, the Colony never did prosper, and it was ultimately absorbed into the thriving Massachusetts Bay Colony—but not before America's most famous colonists had firmly established religious diversity and, to a degree, religious toleration as a fact of life in the New World.*

From September 6 to November 9, 1620, the merchant ship *Mayflower*, usually employed in the Anglo-French wine trade, sailed west across the Atlantic Ocean toward the coast of North America. On board were 102 men, women and children bound for a new life in a new world. (According to William Bradford, leader of the *Mayflower* company and first governor of Plymouth colony, the original passenger list totaled 102. Two children were born during the voyage.)

The *Mayflower*'s passengers were predominantly poor men, drawn from the ranks of small craftsmen, artisans and petty tradesmen. Many of them came from Leyden, Holland, where they had made a meager living in and around the cloth industry. All were English—and although they were poor, their main reason for leaving Europe was not to improve their economic lot but to secure religious freedom. They had emigrated from England and settled in Holland to escape religious persecution, seeking and finding in Holland the right to organize their own church. But in Leyden other vexations had arisen: the immigrants feared that their children would quickly absorb Dutch ways, lose their attachment to the English community and abandon the "Pilgrim's" church.

The Pilgrims were a community centered upon a church. Like many other Englishmen of their time, they had grown discontented with the Church of England. The majority of its critics had remained within the Anglican Church, pressing for reforms; the Pilgrims were part of a small, weak minority which had decided that it could no longer profess allegiance to a corrupt Church. Following the lead of their ministers, a number of persons from Scrooby, in Nottinghamshire, had separated themselves from their parish churches and formed their own congregations. Their act was blatantly seditious—a challenge to Church and State alike—and rather than risk prosecution, the separatists had fled to Holland in 1607. Holland too had posed problems, and the

immigrants had therefore boarded the *Mayflower*, hoping that they would soon be beyond the reach of the English government—yet free to remain English in the New World.

In early November of 1620, the *Mayflower* reached Cape Cod. New England was not the Pilgrims' intended destination; their original plan had been to settle themselves in a remote and empty part of Virginia, which was already an English colony. The settlers attempted to sail free of the New England coast and proceed south, but the currents and winds hindered them and they returned to Cape Cod. On November 11, their ship lay safely at harbor. The Pilgrims had decided to settle in New England.

Winter was near, and the settlers were justifiably apprehensive about its coming and about the desolate look of the nearby coasts. William Bradford, their great leader and chronicler, noted in his journal the "violent and savage hue" of the "wilderness." Reconnoitering parties were put ashore to search for a suitable place to begin the long business of building a new settlement, but it was several weeks before such a place was found. The *Mayflower*, cruising down the inner coast of the Cape, reached a sheltered harbor. The inlet was safe for shipping, and its shores had "divers cornfields and little brooks"; all in all, "a place fit for situation." There the settlers would establish Plymouth Colony.

The long search for a suitable site for their future colony had been only one of the Pilgrims' troubles. Since they were outside the jurisdiction of Virginia, some of the passengers—those recruited in London, who were not members of the Leyden church—claimed that no government existed and that no one could exercise authority over them. Bradford and the other Pilgrim fathers resolved that dilemma by drafting the famous Mayflower Compact. In signing that document, the vast majority of the adult males on board the *Mayflower* pledged their obedience to an elected governor and to any laws on which they might agree. In effect, control was given to the

The seal of the Plymouth colony: it was used on official documents.

Opposite A reconstruction of the Plymouth Colony as it appeared in 1627.

485

The first Thanksgiving

English Emigrants to America

Boston

Cambridge

Greenwich

Southampton

Plymouth

Main emigrant areas

Secondary emigrant areas

William Laud, who became Archbishop of Canterbury in 1633. His rigid intolerance of Puritanism caused a wave of emigration to New England.

Below left The port of Southampton: one of several ports on the south and east coast of England from which emigrants set sail for America.

Below right The *Mayflower*, the ship in which the Pilgrim Fathers sailed to the New World.

Leyden group, the dissenting faction was suppressed, and the colony's chances of survival were enhanced.

Unity was necessary. The first years of the colony's existence were hard and cruel ones, as famine, disease and privation—all potential invitations to anarchy—overtook the little society. Half the *Mayflower's* original passengers were dead by the spring of 1621, and the colony did not achieve even the most modest sort of security until two years later. Yet its internal life proceeded smoothly. The religious community of the Pilgrims acted as a stabilizing force, and so did their social homogeneity. After a few years the colony became a self-governing settlement—one in which there was a simple and unself-conscious legal and political equality.

During those first difficult years, the struggling colony received immeasurable assistance from several indigenous Indian tribes, notably the Wampanoag. Their chief, Massasoit, signed a mutual aid pact with the settlers in 1621. Legend credits Squanto, sole survivor of the Pawtuxet Indian nation, with teaching the colonists how to catch and dry herring, tap maple groves for their sugar, and plant the native corn—Indian style, four kernels to a mound. Squanto had been captured by an English slaver in 1614 and sold to a Spanish master, had escaped to England and, in 1618, had returned to his homeland—to find all the members of his tribe wiped out by a smallpox epidemic. Squanto's transoceanic travels had given him a knowledge of the English language and English customs that was to prove of inestimable value to Bradford and his company.

The Pilgrims, touched and astonished by the Indians' aid, reciprocated by inviting Squanto and ninety-odd members of Massasoit's tribe to the most famous alfresco buffet in American folklore—the first Thanksgiving dinner. That feast, held in mid-October of 1621 to celebrate the completion of the colony's first harvest, featured native turkey, duck, geese, deer, corn bread and wild berries. The Indians, obviously caught up in the spirit of the occasion, stayed for three days.

The Thanksgiving celebration was the lone bright spot in a year otherwise noted for famine, skirmishes with unfriendly Indians and uncontrolled epidemics—known collectively as the "General Sickness." The *Mayflower* passengers were not unique in their sufferings, however; Virginia's early settlers (1584 and 1607 at Jamestown) had had similar experiences. It was the radical nature of the Pilgrims' religious attitudes, their poverty and their lack of support from England that set them apart from other early American colonists. Virginia was the creation of English gentry and merchants, who financed voyages of colonization and supported New World colonies for commercial reasons. Massachusetts Bay, the third English colony in North America, had both a royal charter and financial backing from several quarters. Plymouth Colony, on the other hand, was the only North American settlement to be established with little aid from England and no influential friends.

Plymouth never became a particularly thriving colony. It remained a society of traders, small farmers and fishermen—poor and unpopulous. In 1630 the colonization of Massachusetts by the Puritans began in earnest, and that colony soon surpassed Plymouth in size and importance. In 1691 the Pilgrim colony was absorbed by its large and powerful neighbor (more or less willingly, since the two shared similar religious and political systems). The memory of Plymouth's founding remained a vivid one, however, and the story of those poor and humble settlers—who sailed three thousand miles across the storm-tossed Atlantic to find religious freedom and suffered in the wilderness to build their new homes—became a not unimportant part of American legend.

By the end of the seventeenth century, that legend had already become a politically useful tool in New England. The Pilgrims and the Puritans were frequently depicted as a poor, harassed minority that had fled the persecution of kings and bishops to secure freedom in the New World. There, at their own expense, they had built simple but godly societies that were antipathetic to monarchs—unless they were good Protestant ones who left them alone—and

to bishops, of any religion whatsoever. New England was naturally sympathetic to Cromwell, to the Parliamentary side in the English civil war and to the nonconformists exiled upon the return of the Stuarts. Their plight corresponded perfectly with the Anglo-American nonconformist tradition—a tradition that had its roots among the middle classes, was suspicious of ecclesiastical hierarchy, aristocracy and monarchy, and was devoted to representative assemblies that opposed any flavor of absolutism or princely power, whether exercised by kings or their ministers.

New England was only one region of America, and the Plymouth settlers were only part of a much larger migration of Englishmen to the New World—one that rapidly produced settlements along the entire Eastern seaboard. For the most part, those migrants were humble people: indentured servants, young men and women from the lower sections of

Colonists landing in Virginia: In 1607 the first permanent English colony in the New World was established at Jamestown in Virginia.

Left Indians celebrating a victory: in the early years, the Pilgrim Fathers received invaluable assistance from local Indian tribes.

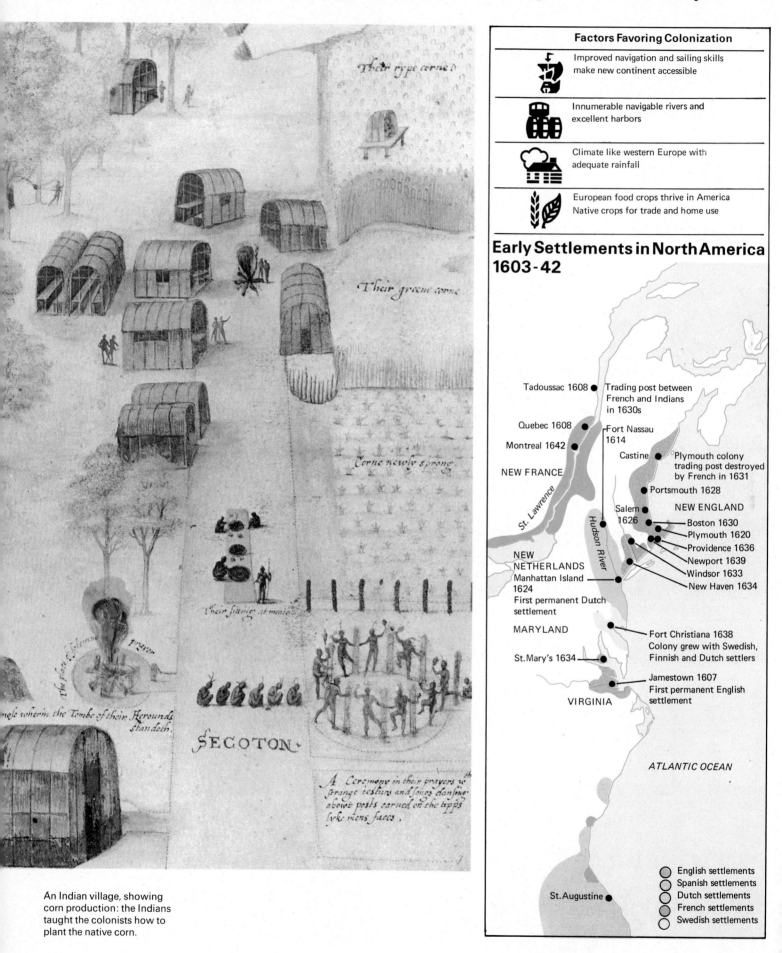

An Indian village, showing corn production: the Indians taught the colonists how to plant the native corn.

Factors Favoring Colonization

Improved navigation and sailing skills make new continent accessible

Innumerable navigable rivers and excellent harbors

Climate like western Europe with adequate rainfall

European food crops thrive in America Native crops for trade and home use

Early Settlements in North America 1603-42

Tadoussac 1608 — Trading post between French and Indians in 1630s

Quebec 1608

Fort Nassau 1614

Montreal 1642

Castine — Plymouth colony trading post destroyed by French in 1631

NEW FRANCE

St. Lawrence

Portsmouth 1628

Salem 1626 — NEW ENGLAND

Hudson River

Boston 1630
Plymouth 1620
Providence 1636
Newport 1639
Windsor 1633
New Haven 1634

NEW NETHERLANDS
Manhattan Island 1624
First permanent Dutch settlement

MARYLAND — Fort Christiana 1638 Colony grew with Swedish, Finnish and Dutch settlers

St. Mary's 1634

Jamestown 1607 First permanent English settlement

VIRGINIA

ATLANTIC OCEAN

St. Augustine

English settlements
Spanish settlements
Dutch settlements
French settlements
Swedish settlements

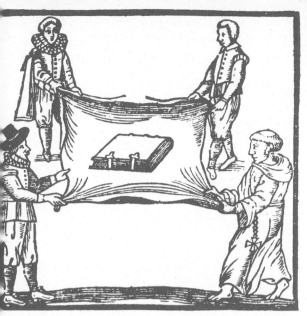

society, artisans and craftsmen. The hopelessly poor and degraded did not come. Nor—naturally enough—did the aristocracy, the gentry and the great merchants. A few men of property made the long voyage, but the colonial upper classes were largely recruited from within. In the process, many of the practices and institutions linked to the privileges of the European and English upper classes disappeared. Hereditary aristocracy was never introduced, nor was the concept of a professional army. Land tenure was simple in America, for the feudal complexity of European practices was rejected. Entailed estates were all but nonexistent, and attempts to introduce "quit rents" (rents paid in lieu of feudal services) and to link landownership to institutional privileges were unsuccessful.

The most remarkable alteration of all occurred in the area of religious toleration. During the first decades of the seventeenth century, the New World witnessed the breakdown of the concept of religious uniformity, a dream that was still cherished in most of the monarchies of Europe. European states had largely acted to choke off the proliferation of religious sects after the early years of the Reformation, but in the seventeenth and eighteenth centuries religious groups sought and found great opportunities in America. Maryland was settled by Catholics from

Protestant England; New England, of course, was colonized by Puritans and Separatists; Pennsylvania by Quakers fleeing Anglican repression; and Nova Scotia by Huguenots seeking security from French religious absolutism.

That massive migration was a remarkable phenomenon. By the end of the eighteenth century it had given America a reputation for profound and widespread religious tolerance. Such tolerance had not always been there—it was the growth of sects that forced its emergence. And grow they did—for once relieved of the weight of effective established churches, the original denominations rapidly splintered and multiplied. Old and New Light Congregationalists and Presbyterians, Baptists, Separate Baptists, Rogerenes, Methodists, Shakers and Quakers, Dunkers and Amish, Huguenots and Anglicans—all testified to the disintegration of European ideas of religious orthodoxy. The multiplication of sects evidenced the weakness of institutionalized religion and also lessened the formal influence of ministers and priests in government.

Diversity was also noticeable in the population of the New World. The French and the Spanish had their own national settlements—the former in Canada and the Ohio Valley, the latter in Florida and the Caribbean—but these were weak and fail-

An illustration from a discourse of 1636 outlining the heresies of two weavers.

Above left A seventeenth-century cartoon showing wrangling sects tossing a Bible in a blanket.

Below left The first church in Salem: Salem was founded in 1626 by discontented members of the Plymouth Colony.

Detail from a Puritan tombstone at Dorchester, Mass. The heavy symbolism of death reflects the tradition of Puritan religious severity.

ing. After 1620, non-English settlers came to the English colonies in increasing numbers. The Ulster Scots—called Scotch Irish in America—and the Germans—known as the Pennsylvania Dutch—were the two largest groups; by 1790 they comprised eighteen per cent of the colonial population. Catholic Irish, French Huguenots, Swiss and Salzburger Protestants, Jews from Southern Europe, Lowland and Highland Scots, and the remnants of early Dutch and Scandinavian colonists made up another twelve per cent. All these foreshadowed the variety of national groups that flooded into nineteenth-century America.

By the eighteenth century, colonial society was moving in the direction of struggle and protest—conditions that normally release social energies and,

for a time at least, increase political opportunities for all classes. England had allowed her American possessions large political freedoms while trying to enforce a certain degree of economic control, and that policy had produced strong local political institutions. Those institutions naturally opposed Britain's restrictions on colonial economic development, and for decades the royal governors of each colony were forced to contend with strong and restive representative assemblies.

The growth of the representative assembly was an essential American development—one that could trace its origins back to the Mayflower Compact. Springing from privileges given to the early colonies in their charters (which were intended to grant a limited form of municipal self-government), the

Half a million black slaves

The South East Prospect of The City of Philadelphia By Peter Cooper *Painter*

assemblies had gradually arrogated parliamentary rights and immunities. Many of their members were fully conversant with the most extreme and advanced theories of eighteenth-century English politics and were as capable of using them as any English radical.

The final struggle came after 1763, when the British Crown, suddenly aware of the need for a revised colonial policy, decided to increase its regulation of American governments. The result was an intensification and universalization of the conflict between autocracy and personal liberty that had prompted the emigration of the Pilgrims more than a century earlier. Americans claimed to stand for the rights of man against the crimes of tyrants—for the people, and against their kings.

The largest non-English immigrant group shared none of the freedom or opportunity that the New World supposedly offered. That group consisted of more than half a million black slaves, nearly twenty per cent of the total population of North America in 1790. The economies of the southern colonies—and their profitable crops of tobacco, rice, indigo and cotton—were supported by the labor of men and women who were regarded as chattel and whose numbers were augmented each year by a thriving slave trade.

Henceforward the rhetoric of Americans would emphasize the differences between Europe and America. The Reverend Ezra Stiles proclaimed that Divine Providence "was making way for the planting and Erection in this land the best policied Empire that has yet appeared in the World. In which Liberty and Property will be secured." That empire, he asserted, would be renowned for "liberty civil and religious" and for "Science and Arts."

His opinion won widespread support among Europeans, for with the American Revolution, the New World had taken its place on the stage of history. Its institutions, and the prevailing opinions of its statesmen, placed it firmly in the "party of humanity"—the camp of the Enlightenment. Given time, the Old World might even catch up with the New.

OLIVER LEVY

Philadelphia. The territory of Pennsylvania was granted to William Penn in 1681, and Philadelphia rapidly grew to be the leading town and port.

Left The first Quaker temple in Philadelphia. Most of the early settlers in Pennsylvania were Quakers.

Quakers being tortured in London in 1656.

For several years after the sailing of the *Mayflower* in 1620, few Englishmen were adventurous enough to make the dangerous and fearfully uncomfortable Atlantic crossing. The prospects on arrival were bleak, and only those whose religious faith was certain, whose sense of adventure was acute, whose ambition was intense or whose debts were overwhelmingly pressing chose to hazard their future by making the long journey. As the colonies prospered, however, new companies were founded and new charters were granted. And as the determination of William Laud to impose uniformity upon the Church of England increased in intensity, the number of emigrants also increased. By the mid-1630s depopulation had become a serious social problem in several areas of England, and the government was obliged to issue proclamations against emigration. Those edicts notwithstanding, more than 60,000 people left England between 1630 and 1643, and a third of them settled in New England.

At first the English government and the Church were glad to see the Puritans leave the country, taking their heresies with them. America was thought of as a useful depository for tiresome, nonconforming Protestants who would otherwise stir up trouble at home. The American colonies, in the words of Peter Heylin, the Archbishop's influential High Church chaplain, were "like the spleen of the natural body, not unuseful and unserviceable to the general health by drawing to it so many sullen, sad and offensive humours."

Within twenty years of the *Mayflower*'s departure, that spleen had

Tradesmen were leaders of heretical protestant opinion in England.

become too full. There was a real fear in England that the offensive nature of the religion practiced in the American colonies—which had previously aroused little interest and had consequently gone unchecked—would spread to the home country. It was decided that an

Complaints against Puritan laws banning selling on Sundays.

Anglican bishop would have to be dispatched to New England and that troops would have to go with him to force the colonists to mend their ways and join the one true Church. The drastic proposal came to nothing, however, for there were troubles enough at home.

But even if a bishop had been dispatched, there can be no doubt that his mission would have met with small success, for Puritanism was by now an essential element in New England life, and New England was becoming increasingly independent of London. The New England Company, which had been organized in London in 1628 to provide a refuge for discontented Puritans as well as a profit for the shareholders, had been transformed into the Massachusetts Bay Company shortly thereafter. Within a matter of months the government of the extensive territories controlled by the Company was transferred from England to America, and it was soon established that no one could aspire to the privileges of a freeman unless he accepted the Puritan creed and conformed to Puritan morality. And since it was only freemen who could name "assistants"—the men who in turn named the governor — political power was lodged in Puritan hands from the beginning. It would have taken more than a lone Anglican bishop to wrest it from them.

Religious intolerance in America

Although the emigrants had gone to America to seek religious freedom, they had, upon arrival, been remarkably intolerant of those who

would not accept their own faith. Moreover, their elected leaders had been less than indulgent in their treatment of the sinners in their midst. Baptists were penalized, and in all of the New England colonies acts were passed to exclude or punish Quakers. The death penalty or various forms of mutilation were imposed for idolatry, blasphemy and adultery. A man who denied the existence of the Devil might have a hole bored in his tongue with a hot iron, and offenses as venial as smoking and wearing unseemly clothes were also considered crimes.

Yet cruel and absurd as their intolerance now seems to us, neither the Puritan colonists nor the zealots from whom they had fled were in conflict with the commonly held views of their time. Religious toleration was considered scarcely more acceptable in the first half of the seventeenth century than it had been in the days of Erasmus and Montaigne, for religion was not thought of as a private matter between God and a man's conscience, but was inextricably bound up with society and politics. It kept a king's subjects in obedience—and because it did so it became the direct concern of the State. (Such a view was not unique to England and the American colonies; it applied with even greater force on the Continent, where the fundamental issues had not yet been resolved.

The issue was not simply one of conflict between Roman Catholics and Protestants. On the Catholic side, for example, there were two rival defenders of the Church of Rome, two forces propagating the Counter-Reformation from different standpoints. There were the

The Orthodox true Minister,   the Seducer and false Prophet.

A seventeenth-century contrast: the orthodox true minister (left), and the seducer and false prophet.

Townspeople fleeing to avoid the plague in 1530: England's troubles were exacerbated by this plague.

Capuchins, an order of friars who had broken away from the Franciscans and were particularly influential in France; and there were the Jesuits, members of the Society of Jesus founded by the Spaniard, Ignatius Loyola, in 1534. On the Protestant side there were also two movements, the Lutherans and the Calvinists. Those rival factions were as essentially different as the two men from whom they took their names—the earthy, ebullient, neurotically self-critical German monk and the austere, polite, reserved French scholar. John Calvin's teaching represented more than a new theology; indeed, what Calvin proffered was a new political theory. He envisaged a theocratic state in which the full privileges of the Church were reserved for those of proved godliness, a society in which pastors and laymen alike were subject to scrutiny and control by a council representative of the community and answerable to no one but God. It was a teaching that formed a direct challenge to monarchic government, one that allied itself entirely

with the growing forces of Republicanism. Its followers were natural enemies of popery—and if there was one thing they detested as much as a papist it was a Lutheran. From the beginning of the seventeenth century the quarrel between Protestant and Catholic had been threatening to erupt into war, and when war did come at last, the reciprocated antipathy of the Calvinists and the Lutherans added to its protracted bitterness and tragedy.

Religious war in Europe

The inevitable battleground was Central Europe, where the Roman Catholic Hapsburg dynasty, still boasting—with good reason—that it was the greatest power in the world, maintained a weakening hold over a vast empire in which Protestants were growing in numbers, power and ambition. Several times in the early years of the century war seemed imminent. In 1608 there was an ominous riot in Donauwörth, a free city on the Danube northwest of Munich, and

in its wake the *Reichshofrat*, a council of imperial advisers empowered to adjudicate in disputes within the vassal states, deprived Donauwörth of its rights and decreed that its church, which had been taken over by the Protestants, should be handed back to the Catholics.

War threatened again in 1610, when the death of the childless Duke of Cleves-Jülich left various provinces along the upper Rhine without a ruler. To prevent a clash between the two Protestant contenders for the dukedom, the Emperor sent in an occupying force—whereupon one of the contenders became a Catholic and the other declared himself a Calvinist. Eventually they agreed to divide the territories between them, and war was once more averted. But no one could doubt that another crisis would soon arise elsewhere.

That crisis seemed to be approaching in 1617, the centenary year of the Protestant Reformation, when, in an effort to increase religious ferment, the Archduke Ferdinand of Styria announced his claim to the Bohemian throne of

his cousin, Emperor Matthias, who was dying without an heir in Vienna. Ferdinand, who had been brought up in a Jesuit college, was known to detest Protestants and to have done all he could to root them out of Styria. He was a friendly, fat, good-natured man with a red face and a passion for hunting—the most improbable of zealots. But a zealot he was, and a politician of both cunning and determination.

The elevation of this devout Catholic to the throne of Bohemia aroused the fear of every Protestant in the country. In 1609 a threatened uprising of Bohemian Protestants forced Ferdinand to grant them a measure of toleration, but they had reason to complain that the toleration accorded them in theory was denied them in practice, and that the disabilities from which they suffered under Matthias were becoming persecutions under Ferdinand. Led by Count Thurn—a nobleman who had been educated in Italy and who, having once been a Catholic, was now more Calvinist than Lutheran—they decided on rebellion. They demanded the execution of two leading Catholic ministers, Jaroslav Martinitz and William Slavata, and called for the immediate establishment of an emergency Protestant committee.

Martinitz and Slavata sent an urgent appeal to Vienna for help, but before their messenger reached the capital the Protestants seized control of Prague. A mob marched on the Hradshin palace, seized the two ministers, dragged them toward a high window, and threw them down into the palace courtyard. With the "Defenestration of Prague," the Thirty Years' War began.

The siege of the Huguenot city of La Rochelle by the French fleet in 1627.

Frederick of Bohemia and Elizabeth: "the Winter King and Queen."

The Rape of Magdeburg

Defying their Catholic Emperor's edict of 1629, the Protestant residents of the fortified Prussian city of Magdeburg refused to cede control of their community to Ferdinand II's son, Leopold. The enraged Emperor promptly laid siege to his arrogant fief, hoping to take by force what he had been unable to win by fiat. His actions provoked a Continental religious war that ultimately involved Sweden, France and Bohemia, as well as the German princes of Hesse, Saxony and Brandenburg. England, Denmark, Spain and the Netherlands were eventually drawn into the struggle—and long after Magdeburg fell, the political conflagration that had been kindled there was still raging. The religious antagonisms that the struggle provoked ended all hopes for a wider Counter-Reformation, divided Germany for decades and shifted the European balance of power.

A German soldier of the mid-seventeenth century.

Opposite Gustavus Adolphus, "the Lion of the North." German Protestants came to rely increasingly on Swedish armies to help them against their Catholic rivals during the Thirty Years' War.

The attack by the imperial German army on the Prussian city of Magdeburg began in the last days of March, 1631. The city, which guarded a crossing point on the river Elbe, was strongly fortified on its land side and was further protected by islets in the river. As one of the richest cities in Prussia, it was believed to be adequately supplied with gunpowder and generously provided with food.

Originally, Magdeburg had been a Roman Catholic archbishopric, but during the Reformation it had fallen into the hands of Lutherans and had acquired a Protestant administrator (or bishop). In 1629 the Catholic Emperor Ferdinand II—victor of the German civil war that began in 1618—issued an imperial edict calling for the restitution of former Roman Catholic properties. The wealthy archbishopric of Magdeburg was assigned to Ferdinand's young son, Leopold. When the city refused to accept the edict, Albrecht von Wallenstein, then the imperial commander-in-chief and an extraordinary soldier and Bohemian tycoon, received orders to occupy Magdeburg on Leopold's behalf.

For seven months in 1629 Count Wallenstein, leading six thousand men, laid siege to the city. His efforts were in vain; the 30,000 citizens of Magdeburg successfully defied their Emperor. Wallenstein, unpopular because of the independent attitude he adopted toward the Emperor, withdrew and was later dismissed. Johan Tserclaes, Count of Tilly, the septuagenarian general of the army of the Duke of Bavaria, took over the command of all the imperial armies. He was an experienced and victorious general who had not only defeated the Elector Palatine at the battle of White Mountain in 1620 at the outset of the German civil war, but had also easily defeated the King of Denmark, Christian IV, when the King came to the aid of the German Lutherans. As a boy, Tilly had been intended for the priesthood, but he had elected to become a professional soldier instead.

In the decade after White Mountain the military scene changed completely. By 1630, peace no longer

reigned in Germany; the siege of Magdeburg rapidly ceased to be an isolated military operation and became part of a general war. On June 26, 1630, King Gustavus Adolphus of Sweden landed in Pomerania and announced that he was coming to the rescue of his fellow Protestants. While Gustavus Adolphus strengthened his base on the Oder River in northern Germany and reinforced his troops, Christian William, the Protestant administrator of Magdeburg who had temporarily taken refuge in Sweden, reentered the city at the end of July, 1630. Supported by Swedish soldiers, he declared that he would defend the archbishopric with the help of God—and the King of Sweden—against all his enemies. But the ultimate safety of the city depended on the coming of the King of Sweden himself, since Magdeburg lay isolated among the neutral territories of John George, Elector of Saxony, and George William, Elector of Brandenburg. Although they were Protestants, these electors had never declared war on their Emperor.

Count Tilly was assigned the task of stopping the Swedish advance into Germany. The aging Field Marshal regarded it as important not merely to secure the strategic Elbe crossing at Magdeburg but, because his Roman Catholic army was short of supplies in this largely Protestant area of Germany, to lay hold of the ample provisions said to be stored in the city. Nevertheless, he was torn between concentrating on confining Gustavus Adolphus to his bridgehead on the Oder and storming the isolated fortress of Magdeburg, which had declared itself to be the first Swedish ally. Thus, in November, 1630, Count Gottfried zu Pappenheim, Tilly's second-in-command, began a renewed investment of Magdeburg, while the Field Marshal himself led darting attacks on the lines of the Swedish King.

Gustavus Adolphus recognized his responsibility for the safety of Magdeburg, but he believed (early in 1631) that the city could hold out without his army's assistance for several months. It was, after all, well fortified and well supplied, and the King had sent one of his ablest subordinates, the fanatical

Above The siege of the town of Bautzen in 1620.

Below The Battle of Lützen, fought on November 6, 1632, where Gustavus Adolphus was killed.

No eagerness among Magdeburg's defenders

Lutheran Dietrich von Falkenberg, and a garrison of 3,000 men to organize its defenses. Meanwhile Gustavus Adolphus himself, with a trained and equipped army of about 13,000, advanced up the Oder, assaulting the important city of Frankfurt and conquering the nearby town of Landsberg.

The burghers of Magdeburg were far from eager to defend their city to the death against the overwhelming forces now assembled before them. They had already withstood over a year's investment by the imperial armies, and they were not particularly loyal to their Protestant administrator from Brandenburg. (Indeed, the burghers had recently looked to the more powerful electorate of Saxony for a ruler.) But they were obliged to yield to the pressure of Dietrich von Falkenberg, who was utterly determined to hold the city until his Swedish master came to the rescue.

Pappenheim, however, was as determined to capture Magdeburg as Falkenberg was to defend it. On May 7, the islets having already been occupied by imperial forces, Pappenheim attempted to storm the city from the river side. By May 9 the situation had grown desperate for the defenders, and the burghers were clamoring for surrender. Early in the morning of Tuesday, May 10, Falkenberg addressed the city fathers, urging them to fight on. But it was too late: Pappenheim, without orders from Tilly, renewed the assault—and this time he was successful.

According to the laws of war in those days, a city that had refused a summons to surrender could be put to the sword—and some 25,000 citizens perished as Magdeburg was pillaged by the imperial soldiers. It was impossible for Tilly to restrain his mercenaries, but he did see to it that the cathedral itself—which harbored thousands of refugees including the wounded Protestant bishop Christian William—and five other city churches were preserved from destruction. The rest of the city caught fire—apparently by accident—and was burned to ashes. Four days after

the assault Tilly was at last able to call off the plundering, and the bodies of the dead were thrown into the river to prevent plague. But whatever booty his men may have acquired amid the dreadful scenes of fire, rape, and slaughter, the immediate military object of the siege was not attained. For Tilly did not obtain the provisions he sought to feed his army.

Gustavus Adolphus and his army were sixty miles

Wallenstein, who began the siege of Magdeburg for the Emperor.

The assassination of Wallenstein, which took place after he had been dismissed from the Emperor's service.

497

A thrill of horror sweeps Protestant Europe

A cavalryman of the seventeenth century, from a series of prints on equestrian exercises.

Above right A cartoon showing the "Lion of the North" scattering Tilly's "Jesuits" at the Battle of Leipzig, 1632.

The rewards of the defeated, from *Les Malheurs de la Guerre*.

away at Potsdam when word of the sack of Magdeburg reached him. After his successes on the Oder, he had gone to Berlin to compel his brother-in-law, George William, Elector of Brandenburg, to join him as an ally. With the help of Brandenburg he had hoped to save Magdeburg. Now it was too late.

The thrill of horror that swept through Protestant Europe at the news of the sack of Magdeburg was tempered by fear in Germany. Whereas those princes more distant from the scene were inclined to look upon the King of Sweden as their only savior, the neighbors of Magdeburg were impressed by the ruthless efficiency of the imperial army.

Tilly himself had misgivings about his success. "Our danger has no end, for the Protestant Estates will without doubt be only strengthened in their

hatred by this," he reported to one of his masters, the Duke of Bavaria. Gustavus Adolphus at once recognized the advantage of the situation. In January, while on his way to Frankfurt, he had signed an open treaty of alliance with Catholic France. The French government had agreed to subsidize the Swedish army; in return, Gustavus Adolphus promised to respect freedom of worship for Roman Catholics in Germany.

Meanwhile, the King—part dreamer, part astute statesman—was making up his mind about future policy. He aimed to create a league of German princes who would be politically and militarily subordinate to him. As the head of such a league he could dominate northern Germany and humiliate the Emperor. The immediate question, however, was

how to deal with the recalcitrant electors in the north.

John George of Saxony had been attempting for some time to create a third force in Germany—one capable of mediating between the Swedes and the Emperor—and early in 1631 he summoned a convention of Protestant rulers to his capital, Leipzig. The convention agreed to raise an army and issued a manifesto to the Emperor Ferdinand outlining the Protestant grievances.

John George, who possessed the only army of any size in northern Germany, had refused to go to the aid of Magdeburg or to ally himself with the Swedish King; George William of Brandenburg was not made of such stern stuff. Even before the fall of Magdeburg he had allowed the Swedes to encamp on his territory and had permitted them to use the fortress of Spandau. Now, within a month of the sack of Magdeburg, he submitted to a series of ultimatums from his brother-in-law, Gustavus Adolphus. On June 11, he signed a treaty placing the resources of Brandenburg and the fortresses of Spandau and Küstrin at the disposal of the Swedes.

Throughout the war in Germany the position of Saxony was of decisive importance. If Gustavus Adolphus could persuade John George to abandon his idea of becoming a third force, all the Protestants would enroll themselves in the Swedish camp. Gustavus Adolphus realized that in order to make the right impression and efface the memory of Magdeburg he must now move forward from his base and seek a victory. On June 24, he decided to advance from Spandau toward the Elbe. Pappenheim had 13,000 men at Magdeburg, but the Swedish army had been substantially reinforced. Gustavus Adolphus crossed the Elbe some fifty miles north of Magdeburg and took the town of Tangermünde; he then withdrew north along the Elbe, since he was not yet prepared to fight Tilly. A clash between the two armies took place in the neighborhood of Werben (north of Tangermünde) at the end of July. After the

two sides had engaged in a cannon duel, Tilly drew off. The Swedes had won a moral victory, and several more German Protestant princes hastened to ally themselves with the invader.

The victory at Werben left John George, the great neutral, even more isolated, his electorate threatened by warring armies on two sides. In the middle of August Tilly sent the Elector an ultimatum ordering him to join the imperial army with his troops. Refusing those demands, John George reluctantly turned to Gustavus Adolphus for help, and on September 3, an alliance was signed. The Elector of Saxony promised to join Gustavus Adolphus on the Elbe, to provide food and quarters for the Swedish army in his territory, and to make no separate peace without him. The treaty was a compromise, for John George retained his political independence and promised to submit his army to the orders of the Swedish King only as long as the emergency continued. But whatever the reservations, the Saxon-Swedish alliance was decisive for the future of the war.

Two days after the signing of that treaty Tilly stormed Leipzig, the Saxon capital. Twenty-five miles to the north the armies of Gustavus Adolphus and John George joined forces for the march south, and on Wednesday, September 8, their troops engaged the imperial army in the battle of Breitenfeld. After two hours of thunderous struggle, the Saxons retreated, but the imperialists were annihilated by the Swedes. Nearly 20,000 of Tilly's men were killed or taken prisoner, and the Empire never recovered.

The destruction of Magdeburg was, therefore, a "milestone" in what modern historians call the Thirty Years' War. That war had begun in 1618 as a revolt of Protestant nobles in Bohemia against the Hapsburg crown: Ferdinand II had been ordered deposed, and Frederick V, the Elector Palatine, had been called to the throne of Bohemia. The Bohem-

Tilly at the siege of Magdeburg.

499

Magdeburg under siege: the fall of the town heralded the great international wars that were to rend Europe and its colonies apart.

Below right Tilly, who succeeded Wallenstein as the leading imperial general.

A mid-seventeenth-century German gun.

ians took this revolutionary step because they considered that their liberties—and in particular the freedom of the Protestant churches inside the kingdom—had been menaced. The Emperor Ferdinand II, who had been brought up by Jesuits and was determined to extend the influence of his Church throughout Germany, was undeterred. He expelled the Elector Palatine from Bohemia and deprived him of his hereditary lands, which were ultimately transferred to the Duke of Bavaria, the leader of the German Roman Catholics. Kings James I and Charles I of England and the King of Denmark were eventually dragged into the contest, but up to 1630 the struggle in Germany remained primarily a civil war. And by 1630 Ferdinand appeared to be winning. It seemed likely that a new Counter-Reformation, supported by the secular arm of the Holy Roman Emperor, would spread throughout Germany.

At this point, however, other European states became directly or indirectly involved. For over sixty years the United Netherlands had been struggling to secure its independence and religious freedom from the formerly formidable empire of the Spanish Hapsburgs, who were considered the senior branch of the Hapsburg family. Because Spain now reckoned that she was owed a debt by Ferdinand II, she pressed for German intervention on her behalf in northern Europe. If peace prevailed inside Germany, the Emperor's powerful army could strike northward and give his Spanish cousins the aid they needed.

After Christian William fled from Germany to seek succor from Stockholm, Sweden and France entered the scene. King Gustavus Adolphus had long contemplated intervention in Germany, although whether he was essentially a Protestant crusader or merely an ambitious king has been disputed by historians. Whatever his motives, he capitalized on the religious ardor kindled at Magdeburg.

As for France, for some thirty years—ever since

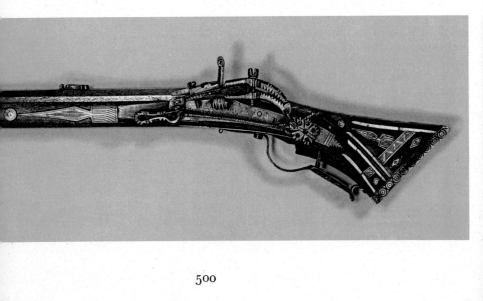

the Bourbon Henry IV had succeeded to the throne of France—a tremendous struggle for power had been waged in Europe between the Bourbons and the Hapsburgs. Henry IV had been determined to end the stranglehold that the two Hapsburg dynasties had exerted over the French kingdom. His successor, King Louis XIII, sustained by his great minister, Cardinal Richelieu, had pursued this policy by every means at his disposal. But Louis was a Roman Catholic, and it was difficult to justify intervention against fellow Roman Catholics in Germany when they were being confronted by Protestant revolts. Richelieu attempted to bribe the Duke of Bavaria, head of the Catholic League in Germany, to fight against his Emperor, for the Bavarian dynasty had always been rivals of the Hapsburgs. But the Duke and his general, Count Tilly, had thrown in their lot with the Emperor and had been promised rich rewards, so Cardinal Richelieu reluctantly turned to the Lion of the North, the Protestant hero Gustavus Adolphus.

Gustavus Adolphus was no man's fool. He was not going to be Richelieu's pawn to humiliate the Holy Roman Emperor. He insisted that the Franco-Swedish treaty (signed at Bärwalde in January, 1631) should be an open treaty; the French were thus obliged to commit themselves in Germany. By the terms of the treaty they agreed only to become the paymaster of the Swedish armies, but after Gustavus Adolphus perished at the battle of Lützen the French were obliged to send an army into Germany.

The period that followed the fall of Magdeburg heralded the beginning of great international wars. At the same time the fall enflamed religious antagonisms in Germany. The signal humiliation of the German Protestants by Count Tilly rallied all the Protestants of northern and central Germany against their Emperor, enabled Gustavus Adolphus to claim to be their rescuer, and gave him the opportunity to advance from the Oder to the Elbe and to destroy the imperial cause at Breitenfeld and Lützen. Thus, the fall of Magdeburg created the conditions that led to a Protestant resurgence and ensured the division of Germany for many years to come. Protestant Brandenburg, the reluctant ally of the Swedes, was in fact to be the focus of a Lutheran-dominated German empire.

The siege of Magdeburg was significant because it helped bring Europe into Germany. In the end the Calvinists as well as the Lutherans achieved religious equality in those parts of Germany where they predominated. The prospect of a wider and fuller Counter-Reformation was brought to an end. Sweden and her paymaster, France, emerged victorious from the war, having inflicted terrible punishments upon the German people. Revolutions took place in England, France and Spain partly as the consequences of this long, expensive and grueling war. Franco-German enmity was ensured for hundreds of years, and the face of Europe was changed, with the center of power shifting to the west.

MAURICE ASHLEY

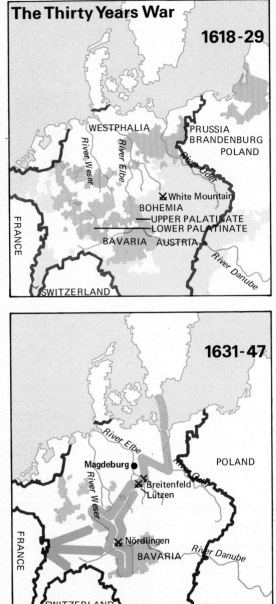

The Thirty Years War

1618-29

Frederick, the Elector Palatine and leader of the Protestant Union, was defeated by Bavaria and Austria in 1620 at the Battle of the White Mountain, having had no help from other Protestant states. The Bavarian army, under Tilly, and the Hapsburg army, under Wallenstein, were then supreme in Northern Germany.

- Protestant Union of 1608
- Catholic League of 1609
- Hapsburg Territories
- Boundary of Holy Roman Empire
- Intervention by Sweden
- Intervention by France

1631-47

The Protestant princes and France, alarmed at the Emperor's successes, persuaded Gustavus Adolphus, King of Sweden, to champion the Protestant cause. He defeated Tilly at Breitenfeld (1631) and Wallenstein at Lützen (1632). Gustavus Adolphus was killed at Lützen and without him the Swedish army was unsuccessful. It was finally routed at Nördlingen (1634).

France then declared war on the Austrian and Spanish Hapsburgs. Condé defeated the Spaniards at Rocroi (1643) and Turenne was victorious against the Emperor.

Treaty of Münster 1648

Germany was by now in ruins, with two-thirds of her population dead, and peace was finally made. The Treaty of Westphalia or Münster (1648) gave Eastern Pomerania, Minden and Magdeburg to Brandenburg; Western Pomerania to Sweden; the bishoprics of Metz, Toul and Verdun and parts of Alsace to France; and Bavaria gained the Upper Palatinate. The Holy Roman Empire was forced to acknowledge the independence of the United Provinces and Switzerland.

- Gained by Brandenburg
- Gained by Sweden
- Gained by France
- Gained by Bavaria
- Gained by Saxony

In February, 1613, King James I's pretty, high-spirited daughter Elizabeth married Frederick V, the Elector Palatine, one of the foremost Protestant princes of Germany. Two years later, in defiance of the Austrian Emperor, Frederick rashly accepted the crown of Bohemia from the Protestant rebels of Prague—and thereby involved England in the Continental dispute known as the Thirty Years' War.

Elizabeth, who was admired for her beauty and vitality and revered as the "Queen of Hearts," was extremely popular in England. And when the Emperor's troops marched against her husband's troops in Prague, her plight aroused the country's deepest sympathy and led to loud demands for her protection. The defeat of Frederick's troops at the Battle of White Mountain in winter, 1620, was followed by the fall of his former capital, Heidelberg, and he and Elizabeth were obliged to seek shelter in The Hague at the court of Prince Maurice of Orange. Demands for action on behalf of the Palatine's misused champion of Protestantism and his unfortunate young wife grew increasingly clamorous in England. There were demonstrations in favor of Elizabeth and against the Hapsburgs, and crowds marched through the streets calling for war against the Emperor. Parliament—when it was summoned in 1621 to provide funds for the government's foreign policy — urged a declaration of war against Spain, whose troops had joined forces with the Austrians.

Ignoring the saber rattling of Parliament and the warlike temper of his people, the English King — who had always turned in horror from the thought of war—persuaded himself that he could better serve his son-in-law by coming to terms with Spain. James was sure that he could restore order in Europe by marrying his son Charles to the Infanta Donna Maria of Spain and by inducing her brother Philip IV to use his influence to restore Frederick and Elizabeth to their palace at Heidelberg. The King's policy, unrealistic as it was and fruitless as it proved to be, was abhorrent to Parliament. The members wanted a Protestant alliance, not a Catholic one, a war against Spain and an immediate end to the marriage negotiations.

James, who had already dissolved a difficult Parliament in 1614—remarking as he did so that he was surprised that his "ancestors should

have permitted such an institution to come into existence"—thus came into direct conflict with the Commons once again. He refused to acknowledge their right to question his policy or to interfere with his inherited prerogative powers. "The state of monarchy," he told them, "is the supremest thing upon earth; for Kings are not only God's lieutenants upon earth, and sit upon God's throne, but even by God himself they are called gods. . . . Kings are justly called gods for that they exercise a manner or resemblance of divine power upon earth. … So it is sedition in subjects to dispute what a King may do in the height of his power."

In James' opinion, it was indeed seditious for Parliament to meddle in matters of State; foreign policy was the King's affair and upon the King's grace did their privileges depend. When the Members entered in their journal a protest that their privileges did not depend upon the King but were the "ancient and undoubted birthright of the subjects of England," James was so angry that he tore the protest from the book with his own hand, dissolved Parliament and ordered the arrest of those members whom he took to be the chief troublemakers. The long contest between the Stuart kings and their Parliaments had begun.

Buckingham

The failure of the negotiations for the Spanish match delighted the English people, and on the return of the Prince of Wales and his friend, the Duke of Buckingham, from the fiasco of their courtship of the Infanta in Madrid, the two young men found themselves suddenly and intoxicatingly popular. To consolidate his triumph, the Duke of Buckingham urged the King to call a Parliament to impeach the unpopular Earl of Middlesex who, as Lord Treasurer,

The Duke of Buckingham in his garter robes.

was the most influential of Buckingham's critics and one of the leaders of the pro-Spanish party in the country.

"My God, Steenie, you are a fool and will shortly repent this folly," James told Buckingham—and added prophetically, "You are making a rod with which you will be scourged yourself." But James was old and ill, helplessly in love with Buckingham, and so delighted to have him back that he gave way. A Parliament was called; Middlesex was swept from power; the entire foreign policy of the country was reversed; and the principle that Parliament had no right to discuss foreign affairs—a principle that the King had vehemently defended three years before—was abandoned. The advice of the Commons was sought as to whether diplomatic relations with Madrid should be broken off.

With Buckingham, the Prince of Wales, Parliament and the country all demanding war, the King could no longer resist—and in preparation for the forthcoming war, alliances were negotiated with the Dutch and with France. (The young French princess, Henrietta Maria, daughter of Henry IV and sister of Louis XIII, was now seen as a bride for Prince Charles.) But although the Commons declared themselves resolved on a campaign in Europe, they declined to vote the money necessary for its proper prosecution. Consequently, the Spanish war—which dragged on for four years and was waged by English rogues, vagabonds, drunkards and cripples—was a tragic disaster. By the time it was over King James was dead and his son, King Charles I, was showing himself to be a monarch ill-suited to meet the challenge that faced the royal house.

Henrietta Maria's entry into London.

Ships of Buckingham's fleet, 1627.

Charles I

Exasperated by Charles' refusal to explain what his foreign policy was intended to achieve or how the money he demanded would be used, the Commons allowed the new King only a fraction of the funds he needed. To make matters even worse, Parliament refused to grant the King the lifetime right to collect customs duties. Charles' predecessors had been granted that right for life; he was obliged to reapply annually. The most formidable orator in the House, an emotional, excitable, vehement West Country squire, Sir John Eliot, protested in his loud, harsh voice that he and his fellow members were not creatures of the King, elected merely to grant him money and to approve his policies, but men with individual consciences and a duty to act only in accordance with what they knew to be right. He condemned the government's policies—and above all he condemned the Duke of Buckingham who, as Lord High Admiral, had sailed across the Channel in 1627 in command of a disastrous expedition intended to support the Huguenots of La Rochelle in their rebellion against the French King.

nd civil war breaks out

Eliot demanded Buckingham's impeachment, just as Buckingham himself had demanded the impeachment of the Earl of Middlesex —and Charles panicked. He ordered Eliot arrested and imprisoned in the Tower, but when the unintimidated Commons refused to do any further business until their champion was released, the King capitulated. Eliot returned to the attack with increased invective, and in an attempt to spare his friend further humiliation, Charles dissolved Parliament. The impetuous young monarch decided to raise the money he so desperately needed without Parliament's help,

Sir John Eliot, leader of
the parliamentary opposition
to King Charles.

to collect the customs duties previously denied him and to impose a capital levy. Those who refused to pay that levy were imprisoned.

The Petition of Right

Yet for all his determination to exist without Parliament, Charles found it impossible to do so. The extraordinary expense of the war against France obliged him to summon Parliament once more. The King hoped the recalled Commons would prove more tractable; lamentably, they proved even less so. Led by Sir John Eliot, they strongly condemned taxation without parliamentary consent and imprisonment without due cause. In 1628 they set out their grievances in a Petition of Right, and they refused to discuss the matter of supplies until the Petition had achieved royal assent.

The period that followed the King's acceptance of the Petition of Right was but a truce in a continuing duel. In January, 1629, a new House of Commons changed the direction of its attack. The archenemy, Buckingham, had been

removed by an assassin's knife at Portsmouth a few months before, but Eliot saw that the general principle of the Commons' right to criticize the King's ministers might be gained if demands for political changes were allied to the growing force of Puritan enthusiasm in the country. He and his supporters therefore launched an attack on the King for having appointed various High Church clergymen to important livings, chaplaincies and bishoprics, and they refused to grant Charles his traditional customs duties until they had debated a resolution that "the affairs of the King of Earth must give way to the affairs of the King of Heaven." Parliament's move was too much for Charles, who was devoted to the Church of England and firmly convinced that the administration of its affairs had nothing to do with Parliament. He sent orders to the

John Pym, Parliamentary leader.

Speaker, commanding him to tell the House to adjourn, but its militant members refused to do so. Shouting "No! No!" in the Speaker's face, they passed resolutions against both the payment of the customs duties and the religious policy of the government.

Charles was appalled. Bursting out in indignation against the "undutiful and seditious" behavior of the Commons and those "vipers" chiefly responsible, he once again ordered Eliot's arrest. And this time he refused to release him. Even when Eliot became fatally ill, the King continued steadfast in his refusal, and upon the "viper's" death at the age of forty, Charles turned down Eliot's son's request that the corpse be laid to rest in the Cornish courtyard where his family and ancestors lay. "Let Sir John Eliot be buried in that parish wherein he died," Charles decreed.

For eight years after Eliot's death, Charles contrived to pay his way without calling a Parliament

The Earl of Strafford.

by restoring to a number of devices for raising money—some of doubtful legality, all of them unpopular. But when the people of Scotland took up arms in 1640 in defense of their Kirk against the Anglican innovations of Archbishop Laud, Charles was forced to recall Parliament. That Parliament proved no more willing to grant the King money for his war against the Scottish rebels than its predecessor had been to vote money for the war against France. Its members declined to vote any supplies until the country's complaints had been satisfied.

Charles responded, as he had done in the past, by dissolving Parliament—but the humiliating outcome of an attempt to subdue the Scots with an underpaid and ill-supplied army led to the assembly of yet another Parliament. That Parliament, the last of his reign, was to force the King to accept an act prohibiting its dissolution without its own consent.

The new Parliament lasted for twenty years. It began by impeaching the King's stern and gifted

minister, the Earl of Strafford, whose execution Charles tearfully accepted for the sake of his family and to avoid further bloodshed. Parliament went on, in increasing confusion and excitement, to impeach twelve bishops and to threaten to impeach the Queen. In his anger and alarm, Charles—who had previously attempted to stem the tide of Parliament's demands by promises and prevarications, by standing his ground as long as he could and then gracelessly giving way, and by alternating between compromise and fitful displays of determination—made a rash and disastrous move. On January 4, 1642, he marched to the Commons with a squad of soldiers, intending to arrest five of its leading members. Those members, warned in time of his approach, escaped from Westminster by boat down the Thames to the City, London's financial district. The King, whose personal courage was never in doubt, followed them there and demanded that they surrender to him. When they refused, he returned to his palace at Whitehall through streets filled with crowds shouting "Privileges of Parliament! Privileges of Parliament!"

A few days later the five members came out of hiding and proceeded in triumph up river to Westminster, where they were met by cheering citizens and beating drums. There were shouts for war against the King and his supporters, and as the placard-bearing crowds passed Whitehall they pointed with excitement and satisfaction to the curtained windows of the empty palace. The King had fled from London the day before. When he returned there it was to his death.

The execution of Strafford.

"A Cruel Necessity"

On January 27, 1649, "Charles Stuart, Tyrant, Traitor, Murderer and Public Enemy" was condemned to death by England's highest court. Oliver Cromwell, leader of the Puritan Revolution, labeled the execution of Charles I "a cruel necessity." Cruel it certainly was—but there were many who doubted its necessity. The King's death effectively terminated a long and bitter struggle between Cromwell and the Crown, but it did not solve the Protector's problems. In the decades before his trial, Charles had dissolved four Parliaments for refusing to grant him his legal revenues —and each time he had been forced to recall the Members. After eliminating the King, whom he called a meddlesome "Man of Blood," Cromwell discovered that Parliament could no more exist without the King than the King without Parliament. A decade after Charles' execution, his fugitive son returned to England to reclaim the throne.

"I fear not death," said Charles I, King of England, as he dressed on the morning of the day on which he was to die. "Death is not terrible to me. I bless my God I am prepared."

Throughout his trial, Charles' courage and his spirit had impressed all who had seen him. His sunken cheeks, shadowed eyes and gray hair had made the forty-eight-year-old monarch look tired, old and worn, but he had walked briskly into Westminster Hall, had sat quietly before the president of the court, and had gazed calmly, almost aloofly, at the judges in front of him and at the spectators behind him as counsel for the prosecution read out the crimes with which he stood charged. When instructed to answer the charges, he spoke with clarity and confidence—and quite without the stammer that normally hampered his tongue—insisting in his Scottish accent that the court had no right to try him. Neither on that day nor on the two following days of the trial could he be induced, by any manner of persuasion, to betray the trust committed to him by God—and "by old and lawful descent"—to make answer to this "unlawful authority."

He was their "*lawful* King" he reminded his judges, and he demanded that they show him a "legal Authority warranted by the Word of God, the Scriptures, or warranted by the constitution of the Kingdom." Since they had no such legal authority, he could not and would not answer them. And he still had not answered them when, on January 27, 1649, as "Charles Stuart, Tyrant, Traitor, Murderer and Public Enemy," he was condemned to be put to death "by the severing of his head from his body."

Shocked by the abrupt ending of the trial, Charles called out, "Will you hear me a word, Sir?"

"You are not to be heard after the sentence," the president of the court insisted.

"No, Sir?"

"No, Sir, by your favor, Sir. Guard, withdraw your prisoner."

"I may speak after the sentence—by your favor, Sir, I may speak after the sentence. By your favor, hold! The sentence, Sir—I say, Sir, I do—"

For the first time in the trial he was incoherent; but as the soldiers closed around him to withdraw him from the court, he regained his former composure. "I am not suffered for to speak," he said with resignation. "Expect what justice other people will have."

Only once during the few days he had left to live did Charles again seem on the verge of losing control of his emotions. That moment came when the doomed King said good-bye to the two of his children who still remained in England. Having blessed them both, he walked quickly away to his bedchamber and with trembling legs fell down upon his bed.

On his last morning he was tranquil, almost serene, assuring the attendant who brushed his hair and fixed the pearl earrings in his ears that this was his second marriage day, that by nightfall he would be espoused to his blessed Jesus. When an army officer came to inform the King that it was time for him to leave, he knelt for a few moments in prayer and then, taking the hand of Bishop Juxon, who had been allowed to stay with him to the end, Charles said in a firm voice, "Come, let us go." As he walked out of Whitehall Palace toward the Banqueting House, his faithful dog Rogue gamboled after him.

The scaffold had been draped in black, and on it, surrounded by lines of helmeted soldiers with pikes and halberds, stood two army colonels, a group of reporters and the executioner and his assistant, both of them masked and disguised with false hair and beards. The King spoke to them all briefly. Then, tucking his long hair up into his white satin nightcap so that it would not deflect the edge of the executioner's blade, he looked up at the sky, said his last prayers, and lay down with his neck on the block.

The axe fell; the head was severed in a single stroke; and "at the instant whereof," said a young spectator, "I remember well there was such a grone by the Thousands then present as I never heard

Charles I's wife, the French princess, Henrietta Maria, whose Catholicism made her unpopular in England.

Opposite A memorial locket of Charles I, containing a piece of linen stained with the King's blood.

The final breach between King and Parliament

The execution on Tower Hill, London, in 1643 of William Laud, Archbishop of Canterbury, the King's most able supporter.

Charles I's family, with the future Charles II in the center.

before and desire I may never hear again."

Curiously enough, there were no disturbances. The execution had taken place outside the Banqueting House instead of on Tower Hill, for the square in front of Inigo Jones' imposing building was small and easily guarded. But the guards were scarcely needed, and although there was a scramble around the scaffold as men and women ran forward to dip handkerchiefs in the spilled blood, the square was soon cleared by mounted troops and London fell into silence.

To Oliver Cromwell, an East Anglian farmer of modest estate who had become the most influential man in England in the years following the civil war, the execution of Charles I in January, 1649, was a cruel necessity. Cromwell had been a member of Parliament during much of the long conflict between that body and the King that is known as the Puritan Revolution. Although it derived its name from the fact that the King and his followers supported the

Church of England while his opponents were on the whole Puritan, the Revolution involved much more than religion. Part of the conflict was constitutional—a dispute between a King who believed in his divine right to rule and a Parliament that wanted a constitutional monarchy. There were also economic issues, for the middle-class gentry and merchants who made up the bulk of the parliamentarian party were fighting for a greater role in determining financial and commercial policies.

The struggle intensified as Parliament sought to find new ways to limit the King's power. In retaliation, Charles tried to rule without a Parliament, but he found that he could not raise money by himself, and financial pressures forced him to reconvene Parliament several times. In 1640 the so-called Long Parliament began its session. Its demands, and the King's rejection of them, ultimately led to civil war.

When the final breach with the King came in 1642, Cromwell, who had been active in the Puritan cause, rushed home from Westminster. Out of his slender resources he equipped and paid a troop of horsemen to fight for the "preservation of the true religion, the laws, liberty and peace of the Kingdom." After the battle of Edgehill—in which Parliament's cavalry were driven from the field by Prince Rupert's Cavaliers (as the King's supporters were called)—Cromwell raised and trained a far larger force of cavalry. His new troops scattered the royalists on Marston Moor "like a little dust," securing the north for the Roundheads (the name given the supporters of Parliament). At Naseby, Cromwell's cavalry, which formed part of Parliament's professional, regularly paid and well-disciplined New Model Army, once again proved its sterling quality. And at Stow-on-the-Wold, on March 21, 1646, Charles' last army in the field was defeated.

Parliament and the army soon fell out among themselves, however, and in their quarrel the captured King sought and failed to find his own salvation. The quarrel began in a religious dispute. Cromwell had urged Parliament, after both Marston

Moor and Naseby, to remember that the soldiers had risked their lives not only for the political liberty of their country but for religious toleration as well. The one cause was, after all, just as fundamental to the issues over which the civil war had been fought as the other. But the Presbyterians in Parliament, rigid in their orthodoxy and not content with persecuting those who, like the King, were devout members of the established Church of England, were insisting that Baptists should be subjected to life imprisonment, that laymen should be prohibited from preaching in public, and that all Independents should be dismissed from the New Model Army. Further, they attempted to disband the army without back pay.

Cromwell attempted to act as mediator in the increasingly bitter quarrel between Parliament and the army. He urged Parliament to be more tolerant and attempted to dissuade the army from falling under the influence of those wilder spirits who were preaching universal suffrage and radical reform. Cromwell himself was far from being a radical. He had nothing against the monarchy as an institution and earnestly desired to come to terms with the King. With the idea of a settlement in mind, he begged Charles to consider the "Heads of the Proposals," a moderate offer based on wide toleration.

Van Dyck's triple portrait of Charles I, designed to help the Italian sculptor Bernini execute a bust of the King. On seeing the portrait Bernini said that the features were those of a doomed man.

Prince Rupert of the Rhine, a brilliant but erratic general, whose undisciplined enthusiasm cost the King dear.

"Heads of the Proposals"

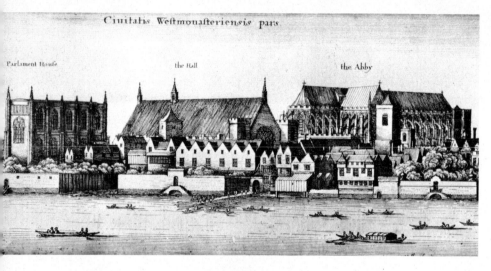

Ciuitatis Westmonasteriensis pars

Parliament House   the Hall   the Abby

The proposals envisaged the use of the English Book of Common Prayer for those who wanted it, a limited form of episcopacy, and an end to Parliament's sequestration of the estates of Cavaliers—a punitive measure that eventually caused the royalist squires to develop an irreconcilable hatred of Puritanism.

There was nothing in these proposals that Charles could not in all honor have accepted, and his more sensible advisers strongly urged him to agree to them. "A crown so near lost was never recovered so easily as this would be," one of them informed him. But Charles believed that by playing off one side against the other he could solve all his difficulties and return to Whitehall in triumph. And thus he preferred to dissemble, prevaricate and intrigue. Although he was a man of high moral character, Charles had no

A view of Westminster in the mid-seventeenth century, by Wenceslas Hollar. One of the centers of opposition to the royal government was the House of Commons.

Below A playing card attacking the "rump Parliament," a small group of militant members of the House of Commons who refused to allow Parliament to be dissolved.

Right Oliver Cromwell, the Lord Protector, as the Savior of England.

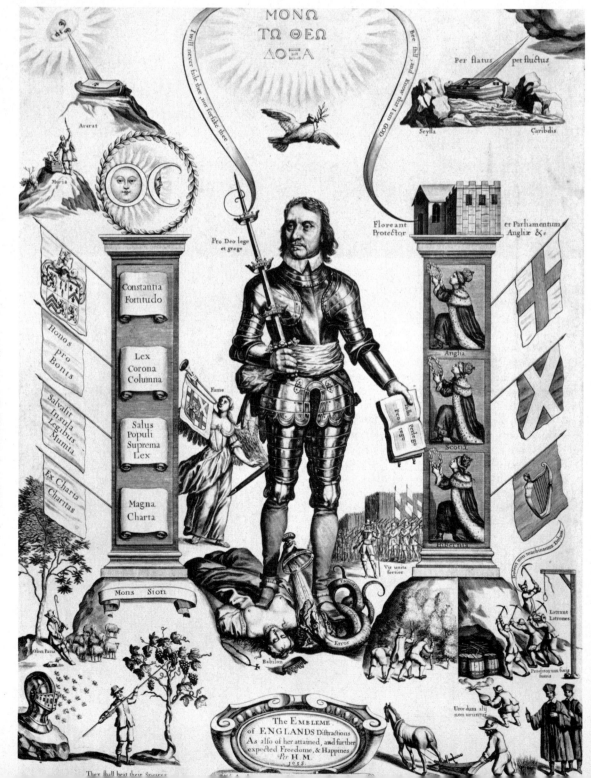

Cavalry exercises in the seventeenth century.

political scruples—and although he was in some respects a learned man, he was not an intelligent one. He was a fine judge of art and horses, but he had little understanding of the human character. He tried to deceive the army, he intrigued with Parliament, and he came to a secret understanding with the Scots that led to a brief new outbreak of the war.

By this time Cromwell had completely reversed his attitude toward the King. He had become convinced that Charles Stuart must be regarded as "a Man of Blood," and that the only hope for peace and order in the country was to bring the King to that justice which his underhanded and traitorous dealings so richly deserved. "I tell you," Cromwell cried out to the hesitant commissioners appointed to try the King, "I tell you, we will cut off the King's head with the crown on it."

Cromwell, his clever, earnest son-in-law, Henry Ireton, and those other regicides whose actions were not prompted by malice or desire for personal gain were all sincerely convinced that the execution of the King could alone prevent the country from falling into anarchy. So long as Charles lived, it was impossible to carry on government by consent; with his death it would become possible to rule by force. And by force they had to rule, or they too would perish.

Although there had been no disturbances in London after the execution, the mood of the country at large was alarming. To many Englishmen, the killing of the King was a sacrilege that God would surely punish, and republicanism was an evil system of government that would arouse His deepest wrath. To others, the new leaders of the country were as unworthy of trust and respect as the dead King himself had been—"silken gentlemen" who would soon prove their fundamentally conservative, not to say reactionary, nature.

Royalists who had fought for the King and Presbyterians who had fought against him joined in condemning the new government. The domestic situation deteriorated rapidly, as economic distress and social unrest were added to political uproar and religious dissent. Beggars roamed the streets; highwaymen by the hundreds infested the roads; the navy, grown mutinous, abandoned the control of the seas to royalist privateers under the direction of Prince Rupert; Scotland and Ireland looked eagerly to the day when Prince Charles would return in triumph to his father's throne; and the monarchies of the Continent looked upon England as a country beyond the pale—convicted and doomed.

Yet the rulers of the country were at first inspired rather than intimidated by the problems that beset them on every hand. Once the new republic, known as the Commonwealth, was established in 1649, they acted quickly to abolish both the office of King and the House of Lords, thus giving to the House of Commons the supreme legislative and executive power in the state. Very soon afterwards they set up a council of state of forty-one members whose duty it was to administer the country's affairs.

Within four years of its establishment, this council

Cavalry exercises in the seventeenth century.

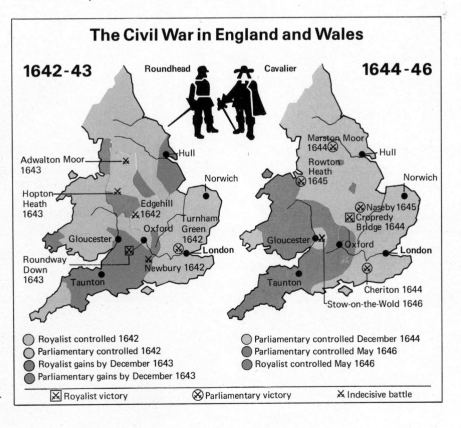

The Civil War in England and Wales

1642-43

Roundhead   Cavalier

1644-46

Hull
Adwalton Moor 1643
Norwich
Hopton Heath 1643
Edgehill 1642
Turnham Green 1642
Oxford
Gloucester
London
Roundway Down 1643
Newbury 1642
Taunton

Marston Moor 1644
Hull
Rowton Heath 1645
Norwich
Naseby 1645
Cropredy Bridge 1644
Gloucester
Oxford
London
Taunton
Cheriton 1644
Stow-on-the-Wold 1646

○ Royalist controlled 1642
○ Parliamentary controlled 1642
○ Royalist gains by December 1643
○ Parliamentary gains by December 1643

○ Parliamentary controlled December 1644
○ Parliamentary controlled May 1646
○ Royalist controlled May 1646

⊠ Royalist victory   ⊗ Parliamentary victory   ✕ Indecisive battle

509

Dissolution of the Rump Parliament

had overwhelmed its enemies. Ireland was subjugated with exceptional ferocity—the garrisons of Drogheda and Wexford were slaughtered without mercy at Cromwell's orders—and two-thirds of the Irish lands were transferred to English ownership.

The council next turned its attention to Scotland. On September 3, 1650, Cromwell destroyed a Scottish army at Dunbar, and thus united Scotland to England in a single British Commonwealth.

Overseas, an overhauled, strong and efficient navy and the talents of Admiral Robert Blake, a seaman of genius, combined to make England the greatest naval power in the world. Prince Rupert's privateers and the Barbary pirates of the Mediterranean were attacked and defeated; war was waged against England's leading commercial and naval rivals; Jamaica was captured; and the Spanish fleet was crippled at Tenerife.

The cost of those wars led to heavier and heavier taxation and to the disruption of trade, and consequently to the increased unpopularity of Cromwell's government. Despite the benefits that its advocates prophesied, the kind of republicanism that

Cromwell's council imposed upon the nation did not recommend itself to the people; the majority of them were pleased when, in 1653, Cromwell forcibly dissolved the Rump Parliament (a group composed of those who had survived Colonel Thomas Pride's 1648 purge of unsympathetic, anti-military members). The members of the Rump Parliament had shown themselves jealous of their powers, addicted to interminable debate, and capable of enacting a statute that made adultery punishable by death. But the Nominated Parliament that followed it—and that in turn persuaded Cromwell to assume the title of Lord Protector—was no more capable of winning the people's trust than its predecessor had been.

The division of the country into eleven districts, each commanded by a major general, contributed more than any other factor to the disesteem in which the people held Cromwell's government, for these major generals were required to assume the duties of guardians of public morality as well as those of tax collectors and policemen. They suppressed horse races and cock fights, prohibited the performance of plays, closed brothels and gambling dens, enforced

The Royal Martyr; the frontispiece of *Eikon Basilike* (Image of a King). Charles' ineptitude as a ruler was only equaled by his piety as a man.

the laws against drunkenness and blasphemy and closed down numerous alehouses.

Aware that the only hope for the future lay in a return to the constitutional rule that he had unwillingly abandoned and to the civil legality that had been suppressed, Cromwell turned to the constitutionalists and legalists in an attempt to release himself from his dependence upon the army. Some of his advisers suggested that he take up the Crown of England and restore to the country the benefits of monarchy. Although at first inclined to do so, Cromwell ultimately rejected the suggestion in deference to the views of those Puritans he most admired. But by the time of Cromwell's death in September, 1658, there was no doubt that most Englishmen longed for a return to the traditions of monarchy—and so it was that, eighteen months later, the return of Charles' son as King Charles II was achieved not merely without bloodshed but with acclamation.

The Great Rebellion had not, however, been in vain. The period of the Commonwealth and of the Protectorate (the years from 1653 to 1659 when England was ruled by a Lord Protector), though rich in political debate and constitutional experiment, has been described as "an interlude in the domestic history of the British people." But it was more than that. It is true that most of what was achieved in the interregnum did not survive the Restoration, and it is true that Cromwell was unable to rule either with parliaments or without them, being compelled by the force of events to carry on a military government that flouted the sentiments of the British people as well as his own conservative instincts and preferences for constitutional rule. Yet it is also true that the experiences that the English people underwent in that era confirmed their hatred of military rule and of the kind of stark Puritanism with which it was associated. In the next decades Parliament suppressed Puritanism with vigor.

For the future, the English monarchy was to develop along peaceful and constitutional lines. In 1688, Charles II's brother and successor, the Roman Catholic James II, attempted to coerce the nation and he was replaced by his Protestant nephew, Prince William III of Orange, in a Glorious Revolution that was bloodless and quick. The power of Parliament, asserted by the execution of Charles I, was finally confirmed.

Henceforward, the English were to experience nothing to correspond with the absolutism prevalent on the Continent in the eighteenth century. Having undergone their Reformation in the sixteenth century and their Revolution in the seventeenth, the English were finished with much of the work that elsewhere remained to be done.

Nevertheless there was still a great deal to do in England: despite local regulation and private philanthropy, social conditions in many areas were appalling; the penal code was ferocious; nonconformists were discriminated against—although not so fiercely that they lived without hope of amelioration or that they emigrated to America in the numbers that had left under the persecution of the High-Church Archbishop Laud in the 1620s and 1630s—and Roman Catholics were subjected to unjust discrimination. Nonetheless, foreigners felt that the English were the most enviable of people and that their government and institutions were worthy of the highest praise and the closest imitation. Montesquieu pointed to their system of government as a model; and in his *Philosophical Letters* Voltaire expressed a widespread opinion when he wrote, "The English nation is the only one on earth which has succeeded in regulating the power of its kings by resisting them; and which after repeated efforts has established that wise government under which the prince, all powerful for good, is restrained from doing ill." CHRISTOPHER HIBBERT

The execution of the King: an imaginary reconstruction.

The Juxon Medal, the gold medal that Charles gave Bishop Juxon (later Archbishop of Canterbury), just before his execution.

511

The rule of Mazarin

The day after Cardinal Richelieu died, on December 5, 1642, King Louis XIII issued a circular-letter to France's leading officials, ordering them to send their future reports to another cardinal, Jules Mazarin. Mazarin, who was originally Giulio Mazarini, was the son of a Sicilian father and a mother who was related to the ancient Roman family of the Colonnas. He was born in the Abruzzi in 1602, educated by the Jesuits in Rome and at the University of Alcala in Spain, and before he reached the age of thirty he had distinguished himself as a diplomat in the service of Pope Urban VIII. In 1634 Mazarin became papal nuncio at the French Court, where his ingratiating charm and brilliant intellectual attainments so recommended themselves to Cardinal Richelieu that he was persuaded to

The death of Cardinal Richelieu.

Anne of Austria, Regent of France, by Rubens.

enter the service of Louis XIII and to become a naturalized Frenchman. He was elevated to a cardinalate in 1641 (after his triumphant success in establishing Louis XIII's sister, the Duchess of Savoy, in the regency of Savoy after the death of her husband), and a year later, at the age of thirty-nine, he succeeded Richelieu as chief minister of France.

Mazarin was an ambitious, avaricious man—cunning, devious and intuitive. Well aware that the sickly and lethargic Louis XIII did not have long to live, the Cardinal concentrated on winning the trust and affection of the King's wife, Anne, daughter of Philip III of Spain. Anne was a neglected wife as well as an attractive and responsive

woman, and Mazarin had no difficulty in winning her trust and, indeed, her devotion. Upon her husband's death in 1643 she was appointed Regent, and Mazarin's position as supreme minister remained secure.

Mazarin continued Richelieu's policies with skill and determination. He maintained the campaign against Austria and guided France expertly through the Thirty Years' War, avoiding its worst dangers and profiting by the opportunities it presented. And when the War ended in 1648, he was able to negotiate a settlement that could scarcely have been more favorable to French aspirations in Europe.

Yet Mazarin was distrusted and hated in France, where he was vilified as a foreigner, condemned as a profligate and gambler, censured as the new and evil power-behind-the-throne (his influence over the unpopular Queen Anne was purportedly due to his gratification of her unnatural physical passions), detested by the nobles—who could gain places at Court only through his influence—and above all, execrated by every class as the man responsible for insupportable war taxes. When the Thirty Years' War drew to an end, France was on the verge of revolution—and in their universal condemnation of Mazarin's financial policies the nobles, the people and the *parlement* of Paris united in an attempt to overthrow the Cardinal and destroy his autocratic power in France.

Mazarin provoked that outburst by levying a tax on the judicial officers of the *parlement* of Paris. When his demand was met by blank refusal—and by counterdemands

for constitutional reforms—he ordered the leaders of *parlement* to be arrested. Parisians rushed out into the streets, built hundreds of barricades, and—by slinging stones

Cardinal Mazarin: hated in France.

through the windows of known supporters of Mazarin—gave the incipient civil war its name—the *Fronde* ("sling").

Condé and the court

These events took place in August, 1648. The Treaty of Westphalia had not yet been signed, and the government's troops, commanded by the Prince of Condé, had not yet returned home from their recent victory at Lens. The Court was therefore powerless to meet the

Prince de Condé: his arrogance and mannerlessness matched his ability as a military leader.

threat of the *frondeurs*. Releasing prisoners and promising reforms, Mazarin and the Queen fled from Paris. Two months later, Condé's troops were released from further operations by the signing of the Treaty. They promptly marched home and laid siege to Paris—and on March 11, 1649, they imposed the Treaty of Rueil upon the *frondeurs*.

Although he had saved the Court, the Prince of Condé soon became estranged from it. Condé—a man of enormous wealth and proven military ability, the acknowledged head of the French nobility and the owner of vast estates—was at the same time utterly unlikable and intolerably arrogant. He was equally contemptuous toward the Queen and toward the low-born Mazarin, who deeply regretted the necessity of having to call upon the Prince for help against his enemies.

Part of a satirical series attacking Mazarin.

The Second Fronde

In an action that was every bit as daring as sudden and as provocative as his arrest of the leaders of the *parlement* of Paris, Mazarin ordered the arrest of the proud and famous Prince and his leading supporters (who included the Prince's brother, Conti, and his brother-in-law, the Duke of Longueville). The country was immediately plunged into the Second *Fronde*, a period of tumult, discreditable intrigues, and disgraceful humiliations. The Prince's supporters attempted to release the captives from their prison at Havre; the Duchess of Longueville entered into negotiations to secure military help from Spain; and Marshal Turenne, whose successes in the recent war had rivaled those of Condé himself, invaded Picardy at the head of a Spanish army—a move prompted as much by the Marshal's desperate love for the Duchess of Longueville as by his support of the revolt.

The history of the Second *Fronde* was one of plots and counter-plots, deceptions, conspiracies and betrayals. It was at once a tragedy and a farce, for there were no heroes, merely characters who did not themselves understand the succession of events in which they had become involved. For a time it appeared that the rabble-rousing priest Paul de Gondi would overthrow the government, but de Gondi was won over to Mazarin's side by the promise of a red hat and the bellicose Cardinal de Retz took his place. Marshal Turenne's invading army was defeated at Rethel, and Turenne also succumbed to a bribe (only to emerge as the commander of the government's forces some months later). Cardinal Mazarin, living in exile at Brühl, appeared at one point to have lost his influence—but by January of 1652 he was back at Court, his power confirmed and his confidence increased.

When Mazarin returned to Court, his enemy, Condé, was still rampaging about the countryside with a motley band of disaffected nobles and an army of recruits, half of whom were French and half of whom were Spanish. In July, 1652, the tiresome Prince reappeared at the gates of Paris, and once again Mazarin wisely withdrew into exile for a short time.

Although Condé entered Paris in triumph, Mazarin knew that the victory was really his, for the people were exasperated by the antics of the rebellious nobles, by the continual disruptions of trade, and by Condé's effrontery in having brought in Spanish soldiers to patrol the streets of Paris. Realizing that the tide of opinion was running against him, Condé withdrew from the capital at the end of that summer and accepted a high command in the Spanish army.

A new enemy

The Second *Fronde* was over. Mazarin could now concentrate on the destruction of Condé and the defeat of Spain. Like his mentor Richelieu, who had been willing to accept allies wherever allies could be found, Mazarin joined forces with Cromwell's Republic in a war against their common enemy, Spain. In 1658 an English army

Marshal Turenne: admirer of Cromwell.

landed in Normandy to fight with the French—led by Turenne—against the Spaniards who were led by Condé. Turenne soon developed a deep respect for the discipline and bearing of the English troops, and he reassured Mazarin that they were "the finest soldiers possible." The Marshal was confident of victory, and his confidence was not misplaced. At the Battle of the Dunes in July, 1658, the Spaniards were soundly defeated. And by the Peace of the Pyrenees, signed in November, 1659, they were obliged to abandon Dunkirk to the English and large tracts of lands in the southeast and along the Netherlands frontier to the French.

Condé, no longer a threat to the French throne, was granted a pardon and withdrew into a quiet retirement that lasted for the rest of the Cardinal's life. Mazarin concentrated his remaining energies upon winning the Spanish Netherlands for France by arranging a marriage between Maria Theresa, the eldest daughter of Philip IV, and her cousin Louis XIV, who celebrated his twenty-first birthday on September 5, 1659.

Louis XIV

Louis married Maria Theresa in June, 1660, and made his state entry into Paris at the end of August. As he rode past the balcony where Cardinal Mazarin stood watching the procession with the Queen Mother, he raised his white plumed hat and bowed low in his saddle to them both.

Mazarin, who was not yet sixty, was a dying man. In constant pain from gout and gallstones, he existed on a diet of milk, broth, game and opium. He had hoped to succeed Alexander VII as Pope, but it was too late for that ultimate ambition to be fulfilled. He was obliged to be content with having completed Richelieu's work, with having brought peace to France, with having accumulated both art and jewel collections of surpassing splendor and an immense fortune of incalculable millions of *livres*.

During his last illness he urgently advised the young King: "Govern. . . . Let the politician be a servant, never a master. . . . If you take the Government into your own hands you will do more in a single day than a minister cleverer than I could do in six months."

It was advice that Louis willingly accepted.

"L'état c'est moi"

With the death of Cardinal Mazarin—who was officially the godfather of Louis XIV and actually the ruler of France during the Sun King's minority—the full power of the state passed to the untested twenty-two-year-old monarch. Acting with astonishing self-assurance, Louis ordered his court into full mourning for the Cardinal, summoned a meeting of his highest ministers—and bluntly informed them that he wanted the benefit of their advice only when he asked for it. Mazarin's pupil had learned his lessons well: the country, threatened by internal rebellion and foreign intrigues, needed an absolute ruler and the young King was determined to be precisely that. Insisting that he was *the state, Louis XIV lifted France to the apogee of her glory and stamped his name on an age.*

In early February, 1661, an outbreak of fire at the Louvre Palace forced the seriously ill Cardinal Mazarin to leave for Vincennes. There he continued to meet frequently with his godson and disciple, Louis XIV, the young King of France. On March 3, the First Minister's condition grew more grave, and the disconsolate young monarch was seen weeping as he left Mazarin's room. That evening Louis convened the Council for the first time since the Cardinal's illness, but he hardly spoke during the meeting.

On March 8 it was clear that the Cardinal was dying, and that night a watch was kept over him by Pierrette Dufour, Louis' former nurse. Early the next morning Pierrette informed Louis that Mazarin had died sometime between two and three o'clock.

Louis ordered the Court to go into full mourning, an honor usually reserved only for members of the royal family. (Some historians claim that Louis' action was proof of a secret marriage between Mazarin and the Queen Mother. It seems more likely, however, that the contrary was the case; if a marriage had taken place, the King certainly would not have advertised it in this way.)

On the following day, March 10, at seven o'clock in the morning, Chancellor Séguier, the ministers and the secretaries of state assembled in the Louvre Palace. The eight politicians gathered dutifully around the King, and with a mixture of fear and curiosity they studied the face of that twenty-two-year-old man whose expression reflected his cold, enigmatic and determined personality.

The King addressed the Chancellor in the tone of a man who was "master of himself and of the universe"—a manner he was to maintain throughout his life:

Sir, ... up to the present time, I have been content to leave the governing of my affairs in the hands of the late Cardinal Mazarin. However, the time has now come for me to take over the reins of government myself. You will kindly assist me by giving me the benefit of your advice *when I ask you for it* ... From now on, Mr. Chancellor, you will not make any decision or sign any paper except on my orders and not before having discussed the matter with me, unless, of course, you are brought these orders directly from me by one of my secretaries of state. As for you, sirs, as my secretaries of state, I forbid you to sign anything at all, not even a safe-conduct pass or a passport, without my prior approval.

Louis' words were received in stunned silence. Yet even those seasoned politicians did not realize that the King's speech ushered in a new and revolutionary phase in the history of France and of the world.

What led this seemingly timid, inexperienced young man to make such a momentous decision— a decision that amounted to a coup d'état? Fortunately, Louis' *Mémoires* provide much of the answer: Mazarin had advised him "not to appoint a First Minister," and Louis had decided to follow his advice "since nothing is more shameful than to see all the functions of the state collected together on the one side while, on the other, there is only the title of king." Louis was devoured by a passion for glory: "In my heart, I desire, more than anything else, more than life itself, an illustrious reputation. ... The one emotion which overpowers all others in the minds of kings is the sense of their own greatness and glory."

France in 1661 required strong leadership. The country was exhausted by the excesses of the Fronde, the armed rebellion of the nobility that had lasted from 1648 to 1653. Louis recognized that fifty years of civil and foreign wars, financial chaos and court intrigue had left France in a deplorably weakened state. He was conscious of the weight of his new responsibility, for "when one holds such a high rank, the slightest error of judgment can lead to the most unfortunate consequences." Yet an unshakable belief in his own divine authority gave him complete self-assurance. That belief was to be the cornerstone of his government: "When God appointed kings to rule over men, He expected them, as His lieutenants, to be shown the respect due to them. Only He has the right to question the conduct of kings."

It was only after 1789 that revolutions were

Cardinal Mazarin, who built up the power of the throne which Louis XIV inherited.

Opposite Louis XIV, the Sun King: he said "L'état c'est moi."

Louis XIV visiting the tapestry factory of Les Gobelins. Louis was a patron of the arts.

associated with movements whose aim, at least in theory, was to further the interests of the masses. Therefore, the sudden change in government that Louis XIV inaugurated after the death of Mazarin was not fully appreciated by his contemporaries. A conventional monarch who respected ancient traditions would not have behaved as Louis did. He was acting on his own initiative, in the style of a Julius Caesar. Although his conception of kingship had its roots in Mazarin's theories, Louis himself developed it into a new and original philosophy. According to his view, a monarch should possess virtually dictatorial powers, the like of which had never previously been seen in France.

Unlike a twentieth-century dictator, who has to maintain his position of power through frequent, spectacular achievements, an absolute ruler such as Louis had nothing to fear from the fickleness of public opinion. Therefore he could rule with the serene self-assurance of one who knows that he is part of a divine, eternal pattern of life.

Like Napoleon, Louis XIV tried to impose his will not only on the French government but on every aspect of national life. He controlled everything—from the order of precedence at Court to troop movements and theological controversies. Nothing—from an important marriage to the building of a road—could be arranged without his approval. King and country eventually became synonymous, and it was no longer possible for Frenchmen to imagine the separation of the two without a sense of anguish and

disorientation. In fact, it was unthinkable that anyone should dare to replace Louis—the divine king who had been empowered by God to rule over his people. Louis created an excellent intelligence service and founded the modern police force, but his authority was never based on a system of police terror. He succeeded in stifling the various factions, destroying the parties and wiping out ideological divisions with the general approval of the people and without resorting to violence.

The France of Louis' time, like the France of today, was a mass of contradictions. Theoretically, there were no limits to Louis' authority, but in practice he was continually confounded by traditional customs and franchises. Feudalism survived in many forms throughout the country, and the *parlements* still claimed to be the arbiters of power. Although individual liberty was unknown, various groups possessed collective liberties and privileges that obstructed the work of the central government. Even civil servants were not directly answerable to the state—having purchased their positions, they were immune from transfer or dismissal. The King had no control over education, and the economy was in a complete state of chaos, hemmed in by a mass of restrictions and anomalies.

Louis set out to correct these deficiencies with a tenacious will and determination. The people were clamoring for law and order, and he intended to give it to them. But he had something even more precious to offer them: he was the personification of a nation

516

France: a mass of contradictions

at the height of its powers, overflowing with vitality and health, a nation that longed for magnificence.

Louis XIII, an austere, reserved monarch, had been respected from a distance by his subjects, while they had loathed Richelieu and despised Mazarin. Their joy and relief were unbounded when they discovered that their new King was a proud, handsome young man, as yet untarnished by corruption and dishonesty. France was soon infatuated with Louis. The nobles, fresh from their rebellion, and the masses, including the forerunners of the angry revolutionaries of 1789, did not submit passively to absolute rule—they were carried away on a wave of enthusiasm for and devotion to Louis. Their obedience was not forced on them but grew out of their state of mind and the particular needs of the moment.

Voltaire commented that during the first half of Louis XIV's reign, he had proved "that when an absolute monarch wants to do good, he can achieve anything he sets out to do." Indeed, with the support of both nobles and commoners, Louis' untried government was able to transform the country in an astonishingly short space of time.

Jean Baptiste Colbert, Louis' Finance Minister, embarked on a systematic economic policy of mercantilism with the object of promoting France's industrial and commercial prosperity. He created new manufactures, encouraged a higher birth rate and methodically set about mobilizing the labor force. During his ten-year term of office, he supervised a major reorganization of the economy: new

Genius at its peak of brilliance

roads were built, canals dug and abandoned ports reconstructed. Colbert created a merchant marine and increased the number of warships from a mere twenty to three hundred. The army was modernized, while the administration was streamlined and carried on with a high degree of efficiency.

Culturally, Louis' reign marked a new high for France. Paris was transformed and monuments were built in every major city. The Louvre, the Tuileries and Saint-Germain were given a new look, and masterpieces of architecture were created: Versailles, the Trianon, Marly. The French genius was at the peak of its brilliance.

Louis XIV cannot be personally credited with these extraordinary achievements. Yet he did preside over a galaxy of talented men—statesmen, generals, engineers, artists, writers, preachers and philosophers, who were the envy of Europe—like an orchestra conductor, carefully controlling them, maintaining harmonious relations among them and, when necessary, manipulating them to serve his own ends.

At the end of twenty years, France, the absolute monarchy and Louis XIV himself were at the height of their glory. The palace of Versailles epitomized the splendor of France and served as a magnificent setting for a king who was universally acclaimed as the greatest monarch of the day and who fully justified the title "The Sun King." No European state dared to fire a gun or make a move without first consulting Louis. Virtually singlehandedly, France under Louis' rule had held the powerful coalition of European powers that opposed her in check, had been victorious on both sea and land, had annexed Flanders, Franche-Comté and Strasbourg, occupied Lorraine and dictated terms to her defeated enemies. Overseas, the French flag was flying in Africa and America.

Other monarchs were quick to appreciate and profit from Louis' example. Since the Renaissance and the Reformation, two distinct currents of political thought had developed in Europe. Catholicism and autocratic centralized monarchy had prospered in the Mediterranean countries. (Long before the accession of Louis XIV, Philip II ruled as absolute monarch over Spain's vast empire.) The political life of the northern regions, on the other hand, had moved in various directions: in England, a constitutional monarchy had been established; in the Netherlands, democracy. Germany, in a state of anarchy, was broken up into a number of small states. Some of these states were ruled by an autocratic monarch, notably the newly created state of Prussia which the Hohenzollerns governed despotically. In the same way, in Russia, Peter the Great had established an autocracy after crushing the boyars, while Catholic Austria was ruled by the Hapsburg dynasty.

A similar situation might easily have arisen in Great Britain, for the Stuarts were only too eager to

Louis XIV establishing the Academy of Sciences.

rule as absolute monarchs in spite of the unfortunate fate of their predecessor, Charles I. The Stuarts' designs were thwarted by the simultaneous growth of commercial capitalism and utilitarian individualism, which eliminated governmental control over private property—a control that was considered a natural and essential function of absolute monarchy. When William of Orange landed in Great Britain in 1688, he brought with him not only 15,000 soldiers—symbolizing protesting, Protestant Europe—but also the English philosopher, John Locke, who had been in exile in the Netherlands. Locke believed that absolute power was incompatible with civil society. "The law of nature," wrote that philosopher of the new thinking, "has instituted political law in order to prevent the natural rights of man from being threatened in the course of his daily life." Locke's political theories triumphed in 1697: Louis XIV was forced to recognize William as King of England and, for the first time, "divine right" gave way to the "natural rights of the people." Divine right was again discredited in 1713 after the War of the Spanish Succession, when Philip V was forced to relinquish all rights to the French throne.

Meanwhile, the absolutist system had already revealed some grave weaknesses. The most serious—the fundamental mistake of Louis XIV—was the expectation that an absolute monarch could successfully shoulder responsibilities beyond the capacity and endurance of a single individual. By vesting all the powers of the state within himself, Louis had exposed absolutist monarchy to the frailties of nature. As he grew older and his faculties began to fail him, so France gradually and simultaneously declined.

The successors of the Sun King were not equal to the task he left them. Louis XV, contrary to general belief, was an extremely lucid, intelligent and hardworking man, and would have probably made an excellent constitutional monarch. Because of his timidity and lack of decisiveness, however, two

Above The Battle of Rocroi, 1643, at which the Duc de Enghein, who was to be better known later as the Prince de Condé, won a great victory over the Spanish army.

Below A corner of the Throne Room at Versailles, Louis' great palace fifteen miles from Paris.

Versailles under construction.

Below A symbolic drawing showing how heretics will be driven from France by the Sun King.

opposing protest movements developed during his reign, both in revolt against the concept of absolutism: the popular movement, based on the ideas of the *philosophes*, and the revolt of the privileged classes, which, from generation to generation, fundamentally opposed the power of the monarchy. The clash of these two revolutionary movements eventually produced the final explosion that became the French Revolution.

Louis XVI, on the other hand, committed a fatal error of judgment when he tried to extricate himself from chaos and confusion by attempting to preserve an obsolete system. He was a scrupulous and virtuous man, but he totally lacked the qualities of leadership. It is said that when he succeeded to the throne, he cried out in desperation: "What a responsibility! I have the feeling that the whole world is going to topple over on top of me!" These prophetic words were to come true in 1789.

Before the final collapse of the absolute monarchy, however—while it was being attacked on all sides, by the *philosophes*, by the *parlements* and by a large

Louis XVI supports the American colonists

number of the aristocrats—France enjoyed an unparalleled success in Europe. Paradoxically, the European nations that had been at loggerheads with Louis XIV during his lifetime began to emulate him after his death. Now that he could no longer dictate to and control them, the European monarchs began to adopt the French way of life with mounting enthusiasm. Every king and prince had to have his own palace of Versailles and his own court etiquette modeled after that of the Sun King. French became the language of diplomacy and was adopted by the world of culture. Thus, absolutist monarchy had not only transformed France into a modern, prosperous country but had also served as a model for Western civilization.

Louis XVI supported the American colonists in their fight for independence, and in so doing, he bankrupted the French treasury. Thus, ironically, the American colonists may be held largely responsible for the downfall of the monarchy in France and for the preservation of the monarchy in England. If the Americans had lost the war, the trend toward authoritarianism in England would inevitably have been accelerated and the English would most likely have reacted violently against it, as they did at the time of the Stuarts. Because George III was defeated, however, he had no choice but to revert to constitutional and parliamentary rule.

The revolution of 1789 swept away the absolutist monarchy in France, but it was a long time before absolutism disappeared from the rest of Europe. In Austria, Germany and Spain, the ruling monarchs reluctantly accepted constitutions, although the rulers managed to retain quite a large share of power —the power that had formerly been theirs by "Divine Right."

Up to 1914, Kaiser Wilhelm II of Germany, Franz Josef of Austria and Tsar Nicholas I of Russia ruled over their empires despotically. It was the disruptions of World War I and the revolutionary movements that developed out of it that finally put an end to the system of absolute monarchy conceived by the young King Louis XIV at the deathbed of Mazarin.   PHILIPPE ERLANGER

Louis XIV and his family: the King's ambitions for his relations were the cause of struggles that involved most of the countries of Europe.

521

A naval nation

When Louis XIV assumed absolute power in France, William, Prince of Orange, who was to become one of Louis' most formidable enemies, was still a boy at school. Twenty years earlier, William's father, the Dutch Stadtholder, had married Mary, eldest daughter of Charles I of England and his French wife Henrietta Maria. The fourteen-year-old bridegroom died ten years later, in 1650; his son Prince William was born a week later.

William grew up in a world dominated by the rivalry between England and Holland, the two great maritime powers of northern Europe. From the earliest days of the Republic, the energy and expertise of Dutch seamen, shipbuilders and merchants had won the Dutch Republic international renown. In Asia the successes of Dutch

St. Paul's Cathedral, rebuilt by Sir Christopher Wren after the Fire of London.

their shared Protestantism united the English and Dutch. In 1588, for example, a Dutch fleet lying off Dunkirk had prevented the Duke of Parma from joining the Spanish Armada's final assault on Elizabeth's England. Since that time, the Dutch had twice demonstrated

The scandal of the Downs

Although they did not regret Spain's collapse, the English viewed the rise of Dutch naval power with concern. The Battle of the Downs

had actually been fought in English waters, and Tromp had arrogantly used those waters as his own. As a result, outraged Britons referred to the sea clash as "the scandal of the Downs." Fortunately for the Dutch, the English, who were on the verge of civil war, were in no state to punish the pretensions of "the damnable Dutchmen." While an irate but impotent England watched, Dutch seamen pushed their way into overseas markets that had formerly been English preserves.

The end of the English civil war, the execution of the English King and the rise to power of Oliver Cromwell, England's energetic and patriotic Protector, opened the way for English resentments to find expression in war. To British regicides, war with the Dutch seemed additionally appropriate, for the young Prince of Orange was the grandson of the traitor they had put to death in 1649.

William of Orange and Mary, daughter of England's Charles I: parents of William III, who later became King of England.

traders and of their East India Company were the envy of the commercial nations of the West; in Australasia, Dutch explorers opened up vast tracts of territory to settlement and exploitation; and in Europe Dutch engineering skills, administration and economy were much admired.

The hustling, aggressive, sometimes ruthless enterprise of the Dutch naturally brought them into conflict with Britain and Spain, and much of what happened in Europe before the Dutch economy began to decline can be seen in terms of the conflict between these great rivals.

There had been a time when

their prowess at sea in brilliant style. In the 1639 Battle of the Downs, Marten Harpertszoon Tromp, a native of Brill, had roundly defeated a strong Spanish fleet under Admiral Oquendo in a naval engagement that confirmed the eclipse of Spanish power in Europe and dealt a blow to the Spanish navy from which it never recovered. And in 1640, at Itamarca (off the coast of Brazil), another Dutch fleet decisively disposed of a Hispano-Portuguese armada that had crossed the Atlantic in a last desperate bid to remove the upstart Protestants from their South American empire.

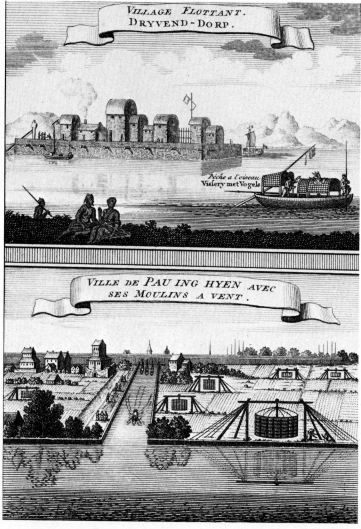

Dutch commercial enterprise in the Far East.

Anglo-Dutch wars

The opening shots in the Anglo-Dutch wars were fired by the English, whose Navigation Act of 1651 had forbidden the importation of all Asian, African and American goods in non-British ships. (The Act also forbade imports from Europe that did not arrive in British ships or in ships belonging to the country of origin.) Since the English did not have enough ships to break the Dutch monopoly themselves, the Navigation Act was more of a petulant

Admiral de Ruyter led Dutch attacks on the English fleet.

challenge to the Dutch than a real threat to their carrying trade. But when the English backed up their challenge by asserting their right to board Dutch ships and to search them for French goods, war was inevitable. For fifty years the Dutch

A Dutch attack on Sheerness, 1667.

had ruled the northern seas, and they could see no reason to observe the outmoded practice of saluting the British flag. They refused to do so, and they opened fire on the English.

It was a bitter and costly war in which first one side and then the other seemed to have the advantage, a war in which the British admiral Robert Blake and the Dutchman Tromp proved themselves to be among the greatest commanders in the history of naval warfare. And when the war ended in 1654, the rivalry was not yet settled; the English continued to regard the Dutch with that mixture of envy, admiration and distaste which they generally reserved for the French.

Open war was touched off again in 1663, when a British squadron sailed to West Africa to support the Royal Africa Company in their quarrel with Dutch West African merchants. The fleet seized various Dutch possessions—all of which the Dutch admiral Michiel de Ruyter immediately recaptured—and the ensuing years of war were as costly and indecisive as those of the 1650s had been. The continuing power of the Dutch Navy was forcefully demonstrated in 1666, the year of London's Great Fire when Admiral de Ruyter trounced the English in the Channel, inflicting nearly eight thousand casualties. (The corpses of countless English sailors were left floating in the sea, clad in the civilian clothes that they had been wearing when the press gangs marched them off.) The next year the Dutch barged through the boom and into Chatham harbor in Kent, burned

Catherine of Braganza, wife of Charles II of England.

four ships of the line, bombarded the docks and crowned their achievement by towing away the largest vessel in the English fleet.

On July 31, 1668, a treaty was signed at Breda, and the second Dutch war came to an end. This treaty settled some vital differences between the two nations, but their quarrels were not yet over. Although mutual fear of the ambitions of Louis XIV brought England and the Netherlands into temporary alliance against France, Louis had little difficulty in persuading Charles II that the Dutch, not the French, were his real enemies—and in 1670 an alliance was signed between England and France that provided for an attack upon Holland, the destruction of its commercial power and the partition of the country.

The Republic alone

The Dutch Republic displayed remarkable resilience and resource in the face of such formidable opposition. The English again failed to defeat the Dutch navy, and the French failed to reach Amsterdam when the Dutch opened the dikes and flooded the countryside. The war continued for six years, and at its end Holland remained as real a commercial rival to England as she had been before it began. During that period she became a dangerous rival to France as well, for her new ruler, William, Prince of Orange, a harsh, brilliant, unattractive, asthmatic soldier, was the leading opponent of Louis XIV's aspirations and the chief architect of the European alliances against him. By the time the European wars were finally over, England had achieved most of her ambitions and had greatly increased both her share of world trade and the power of her navy. Holland emerged from the conflict immeasurably weakened; she was never able to regain her former position as a world power.

The Scientific Revolution

In the course of Holland's economic decline, her people lost nothing of their earlier genius. Her artists continued to guide European trends in art and her universities continued to make their own distinctive contribution to what was to become known as the Scientific Revolution. One of the precursors of this Revolution, a leading pioneer of the scientific method, was

René Descartes, "the father of modern philosophy."

Francis Bacon. Bacon's *Advancement of Learning* was published in 1605, his *New Atlantis* appeared in 1627, and his reiterated call for "minds washed clear of opinions" became the rallying cry of the age. Ten years after the appearance of *The New Atlantis*, René Descartes—the rationalist philosopher, mathematician and inventor of coordinate geometry who has become known as "the father of modern philosophy"—published his *Discours de la méthode*, in which the celebrated Cartesian principle of "systematic" doubt was propounded. The age of Bacon and Descartes was also the age of Johannes Kepler, the German astronomer and mathematician, and of Galileo Galilei, the marvelously versatile Italian astronomer, lecturer and inventor, who perfected the refracting telescope (which had been invented by the Dutch in 1608). With the help of that telescope Galileo was able to demonstrate the essential truth of the Copernican theory.

In 1666 the scientific discoveries of the first half of the seventeenth century were given a deeper meaning when a Cambridge scholar, Isaac Newton, discovered the law of universal gravitation.

Cambridge's Young Genius

In the same year—1665—that Isaac Newton graduated without distinction from Trinity College, Cambridge, the Great Plague struck England. The colleges at Cambridge closed, both scholars and faculty dispersed, and Newton went home to Woolsthorpe. Two years later, mathematician Isaac Barrow's shy and unpromising protégé returned to Trinity—where he promptly astounded his master with the results of his independent experiments. In two short years, Newton had laid the groundwork for discoveries in the fields of geometry, optics and planetary motion that were to revolutionize those disciplines and radically alter man's conception of his universe. Indeed, Newton's studies of motion and gravitation—summarized in his monumental 1687 work, Principia Mathematica—*and his experiments with light and color—detailed in* Opticks, *which Newton published some seventeen years later—are the basis for modern physics.*

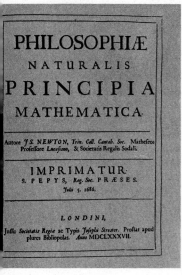

The title page of the first edition of Newton's revolutionary work, *Principia Mathematica*, with Pepys' *imprimateur* on behalf of the Royal Society. The *Principia* explained Newton's ideas about gravity.

Opposite Newton's reflecting telescope: until the development of radio astronomy in the mid-twentieth century, the reflecting telescope remained the usual design for large telescopes, such as that at Mount Palomar, in California.

Isaac Newton, perhaps the greatest intellectual giant among scientific men, is remembered primarily for his theory of universal gravitation, which was published in 1687 and which opened a new chapter in the scientific revolution. Newton demonstrated that the force of gravity could account precisely for the motions of bodies on earth and in space—motions that had previously been considered essentially different, and that had defied mathematical analysis. Newton also developed novel mathematical techniques—particularly the calculus—discovered the nature of white light and colors and designed and built the first practical reflecting telescope.

Newton was born at the small manor house in the village of Woolsthorpe in Lincolnshire on Christmas Day, 1642. Although sickly as an infant, Isaac grew sturdier each year. He was enrolled at a local grammar school to prepare him to manage the small family estate, but Newton was no farmer. He was more interested in making model waterwheels than in minding sheep, and his mother was persuaded by the headmaster of the grammar school to allow her son to attend a university. Newton went to Cambridge in June, 1661. The family finances were limited, however, and he entered Trinity College as a subsizar—which meant that he would pay his own way by waiting on his tutor and doing other tasks.

Neither at grammar school nor at the university did Newton show any particular intellectual brilliance, but in 1663 he came under the influence of the remarkable scholar and mathematician, Isaac Barrow. Barrow recognized something of Newton's abilities, although when he examined the young man in 1664 he found that his young protégé's knowledge of geometry—in those days one of the most important of mathematical studies—was poor. Under Barrow's guidance Newton began to develop and to take an increasing interest in light and the behavior of lenses. When he took his B.A. in 1665, however, he passed without any distinction.

The year 1665 saw the advent of the Great Plague,

first in London and then, less virulently, at Cambridge. The university closed and the scholars dispersed to their homes. Newton returned to Woolsthorpe, and there, in the quiet and isolation of his home, he began to make the first attacks on the problems that he was later to solve so brilliantly. He developed his mathematical skills and began to lay the foundations of a method for calculating quantities that depend upon one another in ways that are never the same from one moment to the next—what has since become known as the calculus. His optical work was concerned first with grinding glass lenses and experimenting with them to try to improve the telescope, and second with investigating the way in which sunlight ("white" light) is broken up into colors by a prism. The latter led him to devise crucial experiments which showed that while white light could be dispersed into colors by one prism, a second prism would disperse each color no further but, if turned upside down, could cause the colors to recombine to form white light. Newton therefore decided that white light was really a mixture of the light of all colors, a view different from those then in general currency, which supposed each color to be a mixture of white light and darkness in different proportions.

The idea of gravity—the attractive power of the earth on objects—was much discussed at this time, and also the behavior of the planets as they orbited the sun. Newton was naturally intrigued by these problems. (His niece, Catherine Barton, first recounted the well-known story of how an apple fell at Newton's feet while he was sitting under a tree at Woolsthorpe, causing him to question whether the earth's gravity, which had pulled the apple downward extended out as far as the moon. Newton felt that without gravitational pull, there was nothing to keep the moon from moving straight out into space, and that only a "fall" toward the earth could change a straight path into a curved one centered on the earth. But although Newton at this point made some

A meeting of the Royal Society, with Newton in the chair.

Working at the Royal Mint. Newton became Warden of the Mint in 1696 and Master in 1701.

calculations—and although he said as an old man that they answered the facts "pretty nearly"—recent scholarship indicates that he was still very far from his final theory when he was at Woolsthorpe.

Using the extremely accurate observations of planetary positions made by the Danish nobleman Tycho Brahe between 1576 and 1597, the German astronomer Johannes Kepler had analyzed planetary motions and come to the conclusion that the planets orbited the sun in elliptical paths, not in circular orbits as hitherto believed. Kepler also found that the time taken to complete an orbit depended on a planet's average distance from the sun, and that the motion of a planet was not uniform but accelerated as the body approached the sun.

These three "laws" of planetary motion had been published between 1609 and 1621; there is evidence, however, that Newton did not know of the law of changing planetary velocities when he was at Woolsthorpe or, indeed, for some years later.

In addition to accepting Kepler's teaching on planetary motion, the scientific world of the 1660s much favored the general picture of the universe that René Descartes had published in 1644. This was particularly so at Cambridge, and there is no doubt that Newton was familiar with every detail of Descartes' theory; it seems certain that Descartes' ideas also exerted considerable influence on Newton during his first years of research. Descartes thought that the universe was completely filled with material that was collected together into giant vortexes. At the center of each vortex lay a star, and around it orbited planets carried by the whirling material of the vortex. The theory concerned itself too with the nature of matter and of other physical aspects of the universe, including light. It was broad in scope and exercised immense influence for a time, and when Newton was at Woolsthorpe turning the question of gravity over in his mind, it is almost certain that he was doing so within the context of Descartes' theory.

That context is especially significant, because although Newton later claimed that he reached his main conclusions about gravitation while at Woolsthorpe, he made no announcement of what he thought until almost twenty years later. It is usually accepted that during his Woolsthorpe years Newton did not know the size of the earth—and thus the moon's distance—with sufficient accuracy, nor could he prove that the earth attracted bodies in space as if its power of gravitation were concentrated

Newton constructs a new telescope

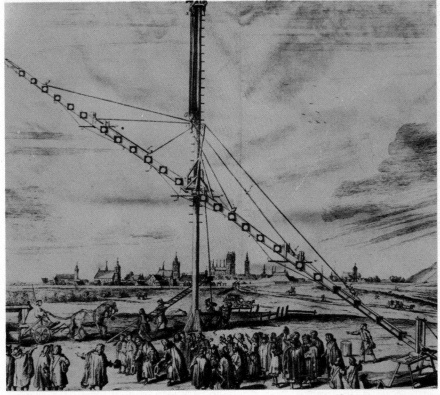

at its center. Scholars have always felt that neither of these difficulties would have prevented Newton from bringing his ideas to a reasonable state of completion. It seems highly probable, however, that Newton's acceptance of Descartes' idea of vortexes prevented him from being able to calculate his answers with complete precision.

Newton returned to Cambridge late in March, 1667, and received his M.A. a year later. He worked with Barrow, helping him to compile a book on optics, but made no reference to his own experiments at Woolsthorpe. Because Newton was shy and feared controversy, he never went out of his way to publicize his achievements. Indeed, Barrow might never have known of his pupil's independent work had he not mentioned Nicholas Mercator's success in calculating the area under a hyperbola. Newton replied that he himself had already done that, and he showed Barrow his notes. It was clear that he had indeed done so—and before Mercator. Barrow soon made Newton's mathematical genius known, and in 1669 he resigned his chair at Trinity in favor of his protégé.

In the seventeenth century a professor of mathematics included in his purview such physical subjects as light and optics, and Newton frequently lectured on those topics. The lectures appear to have created no great stir, but Newton also spent some time constructing a reflecting telescope, and rumors about his work in that area did move outside his immediate circle. Contemporary telescopes were of one type: refracting instruments that consisted of a large lens at the front and a small eye lens at the rear. Such telescopes had several notable defects: they displayed colored fringes around objects and they had a very small area of sharp focus. To obtain even

limited results, telescopes had to be as much as 150 to 200 feet in length. Newton's Woolsthorpe experiments had convinced him that a refractor could never be cleared of its colored fringe images. In this he was wrong, but the mistake led him to consider the construction of reflectors, in which a curved mirror at the back replaced the lens at the front. James Gregory, a Scottish mathematician, had published a design for a reflecting telescope in 1663, but no one had constructed the instrument, which Newton felt had many faults. He therefore designed his own instrument and built a small model, which, although no more than six-and-one-quarter inches long, was as good as any refractor a dozen times larger.

For some years Newton remained at Cambridge, but in 1677 Robert Hooke—one of his sternest critics —became an honorary secretary of the Royal Society and wrote to try to mollify Newton. After Newton agreed to discuss scientific matters again, Hooke began trying to draw him out on the still unsolved question of planetary motions.

Hooke was not alone in trying to find a solution to the movements of the planets. In London Sir Christopher Wren, architect and onetime astronomer, and the astronomer Edmond Halley also discussed the question with Hooke. But although they were all convinced that the planets kept in their paths because the sun attracted them, and that the force of this attraction became less with distance in a particular way, they could not prove their point. The mathematics defeated them. Halley decided to consult Newton and in August, 1684, visited him at Cambridge. Newton agreed that Hooke, Halley and Wren were correct in their surmise about the law of

A refractor telescope made by Hevelius in 1673. Newton's invention of a reflector telescope meant that more satisfactory results could be obtained from a far smaller telescope than was previously possible.

Above left Newton's house in London, off Leicester Square.

John Flamsteed, Astronomer Royal. Newton's insistence that Flamsteed should publish the results of his work as soon as possible led to a quarrel between the two men.

of two printers to overcome any delay, and it was published in London in 1687, with the title *Philosophiae Naturalis Principia Mathematica (The Mathematical Principles of Natural Philosophy)*. Known ever since as the *Principia*, it ran to three editions in Newton's lifetime and brought its author undying fame.

The book is amazingly comprehensive. It deals first with the motions of bodies, both on the earth and in space. Both are controlled, Newton shows, by the three laws of motion: first, a body is either at rest or moves forever in a straight line unless acted upon by external forces; second, the change in such motion is proportional to the external force and the direction in which it is applied; third, to every action there is always an equal and opposite reaction. Newton extends and develops these laws into a whole theory of planetary motion. He then considers the difficult problem of the motion of bodies in a resisting medium such as air or water. Finally he moves on to practical applications of his theoretical assertions.

Revolutionary though the *Principia* was, and widely read as it was, it took time before the teachings it contained were fully accepted. This was true especially in France, where it was primarily due to the efforts of Voltaire that opinion turned in favor of Newton's theory of universal gravitation. Further, writing the book had cost Newton much mental strain. After it was finished, he turned more to other interests, in particular to his studies in chemistry and alchemy. He also turned to theology, for Newton was a Unitarian who spent a great deal of effort on Biblical exegesis to support his views.

In 1693, the strain told: Newton suffered a nervous breakdown. After his recovery he spent very little time and concentrated effort on science, and when recoinage of the currency was agreed on by Parliament, Newton's friend and supporter Charles Montagu obtained the post of Warden of the Mint for him. Newton held the position from 1696 until he was appointed Master of the Mint three years later. During the recoinage the work of Warden was arduous.

In 1701 Newton resigned his chair at Cambridge.

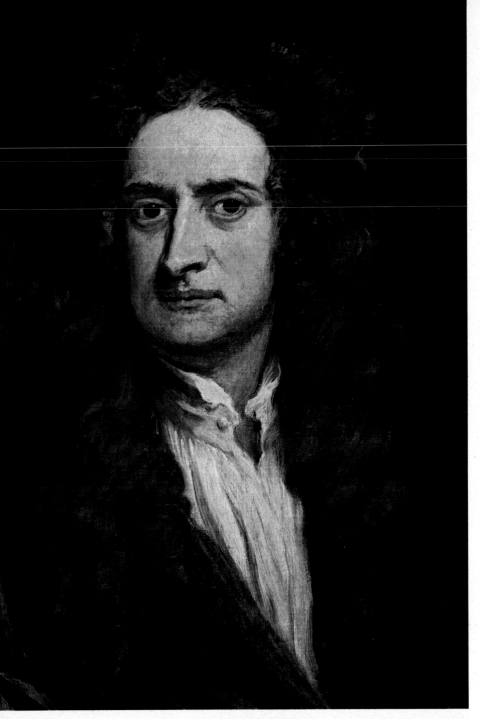

Newton by Kneller, painted in 1702.

Right The Cottage at Woolsthorpe where Newton was born.

attraction, because he had proved it. But he could not find his proof and promised to rework the mathematics and send the results to Halley. When Newton's proof arrived, Halley realized that the significance of what had been achieved was much broader than mere planetary motion. He therefore persuaded Newton to summarize his ideas of motion and gravitation in the form of a book and he obtained the Royal Society's agreement to act as publisher. As it turned out, the Society was unable to meet the publishing costs and Halley defrayed these out of his own pocket.

Halley had more than costs to worry about in getting the book published, for when Hooke raised a question of acknowledgment while Newton was writing, Newton decided to write no more. It took all Halley's powers of persuasion to make him continue. Halley nursed the volume through the hands

528

The discovery of the law of gravity

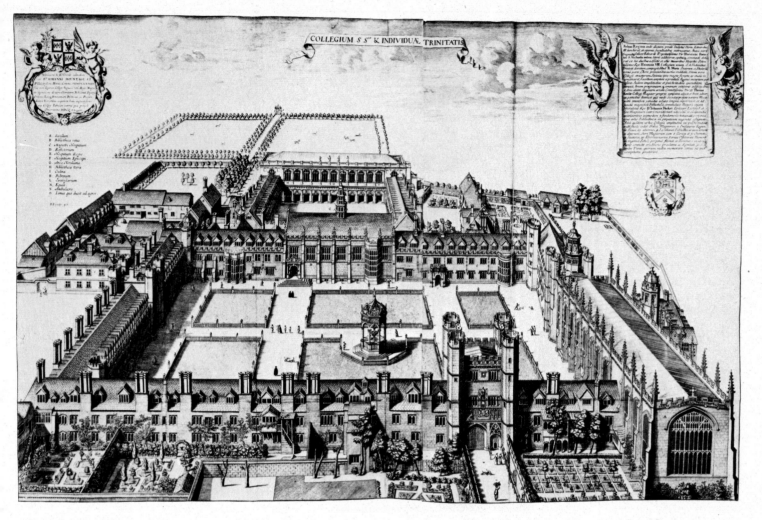

COLLEGIUM Sᵗˢ & INDIVIDUÆ TRINITATIS

Two years later he was elected president of the Royal Society, an honorary position that he held for the rest of his life. It is unfortunate to record that during his presidency, Newton was the center of two bitter controversies, one with the first Astronomer Royal, John Flamsteed, the other with the German mathematician Gottfried Leibniz. The trouble with Flamsteed arose because, although he had been appointed Astronomer Royal in 1675, he had not published any observations. Since he had to supply his own observing instruments, Flamsteed claimed that the observations were his own property and that he would publish when he had them as correct as he could make them. Newton and many others disagreed, and in the end Newton obtained a royal grant for publication and placed Halley in charge of the material that Flamsteed deposited—under duress—with the Royal Society. In 1712 the results came out. Flamsteed had unquestionably been uncooperative and stubborn, but Newton himself behaved in a high-handed way throughout.

But if Newton had personal failings, his scientific contributions make these pale to insignificance. In 1704, after the death of Hooke, he allowed his book *Opticks* to be published. In it he set down not only his theory of colors, but also his view that light was caused by minute particles, a view that allowed him to explain all optical phenomena then known. In 1705 he received the first knighthood to be awarded for science. So immense was his reputation that when he died he was buried in Westminster Abbey.

Newton's greatest monument is his work. Vindicated time and again after his death, first by Halley and then by others, his theory of universal gravitation has acted as a foundation for vast areas of scientific development. It lies behind present space technology and has acted as a beacon to those who have followed his voyages into what he once called "the great ocean of truth."

COLIN RONAN

Above Trinity College, Cambridge. Newton's rooms are between the Chapel and the Gate: the Library is in the rear.

Below left Isaac Barrow, Master of Trinity, who gave up his Professorship so that Newton could succeed him, and who persuaded Wren (*below*) to design the Library without charge.

529

While central and northern Europe were fighting their religious, dynastic and civil wars, Europe south of the Po and the Danube remained relatively quiet—but not entirely at peace. Increasing numbers of travelers were crossing the Alps and sailing into ports on the coasts of the Adriatic and Tyrrhenian seas at that time, and those travelers returned home with ideas and tastes that were to have a profound effect on the character of the north in the next century. The Grand Tour had, in fact, already become an integral part of the seventeenth-century aristocratic culture. The tour was not without its dangers, however, and foreign travelers were often advised to alter their routes in order to avoid local insurrections.

Spain remained the dominant power in Italy until the beginning of the eighteenth century, when she was replaced by Austria. The Kingdom of Naples and Sicily—which comprised the whole of Italy south of the Abruzzi—was ruled by viceroys appointed by the Spanish King. The oppressive character of their government provoked repeated uprisings, among them the 1598 rebellion in Calabria that was led by the philosopher Tommaso Campanella. His unsuccessful attempt to free Naples from Spanish tyranny was put down with great severity, and

Tommaso Campanella: imprisoned for twenty-seven years for attacking Spanish rule in Naples.

Campanella spent the next twenty-seven years of his life in prison.

In 1647 there were widespread riots in Sicily that forced the Spanish Viceroy to flee from Palermo, and that same year there was a revolution in Naples that obliged the Viceroy there to seek safety in Castelnuovo. The Neo-

The Amalfian fisherman, Massaniello, who became Captain-General of the Neapolitan rebels, but was murdered in 1647.

politan rebels—who had been provoked to violence by a new tax on fruit, the staple food of the poor—elected a fisherman from Amalfi to be their captain-general. And when the tumult spread beyond the walls of the city and into the villages and towns of the hinterland, the Viceroy gave way and granted all of the rebels' demands. The fruit tax and all other oppressive taxes were removed, various concessions were granted and the citizens were given permission to remain in arms until the treaty was ratified by the King of Spain.

On July 16, 1647, however, the rebel leader was murdered while haranguing his followers in the marketplace. When the tumult broke out afresh, the Viceroy was again compelled to seek refuge in the Castelnuovo, and a new revolutionary leader was found in Gennaro Annese. When he learned that reinforcements had been dispatched from Spain, Annese appealed to France for help, and in response to the rebel's appeal, the Duke of Guise landed in Naples with an

expeditionary force. Following the unpopular Viceroy's recall, order was restored by his wily successor, Count d'Ognate, who promptly came to terms with Annese—and then had him and all the other ringleaders executed.

Revolt in Sicily

Thirteen years after this popular revolution had almost ended Spanish control over Naples, there was a similar uprising in Sicily. Like the Neapolitans before them, the Sicilians called upon the French to help them drive the Spanish out—and the Spanish, unable to quell the revolt, turned to the Dutch. Both countries responded: a French fleet commanded by the Duke of Vivonne and a Dutch fleet under de Ruyter both sailed for Sicily.

By the 1678 Peace of Nijmegen, Louis XIV abandoned the Sicilian rebels to the persecution of the Spaniards, however, and it was not until 1707 that the Spaniards were at last driven out of Naples.

Even then, it was an Austrian army, not a Neapolitan army, that drove the Spaniards off. By the terms of the Treaty of Utrecht, which was signed in 1713, the Spaniards were obliged to abandon Sicily, which was handed over to Duke Victor of Savoy. Five years later Sicily, like Naples, became an Austrian possession.

Northern Italy

North of the Kingdom of the Two Sicilies lay the Papal States, which had recently increased in size through the reversion of two important fiefs, Ferrara and Urbino, to papal jurisdiction. Urban VIII's attempt to expand his holdings further by attacking the Duchy of Parma was checked by Tuscany, Modena and Venice, and after the 1648 Treaty of Westphalia no hope of extending the papal territories could be entertained. They remained notoriously ill-governed and financially embarrassed until the advent of Napoleon.

The extensive Duchy of Milan had been a dependency of the Spanish Crown since the death of Francesco Sforza ended his family's reign in 1535. Like the Spanish possessions in the south, Milan was handed over to Austria at the close of the War of the Spanish Succession. Tuscany, a neighboring state, was ruled by a succession of grand dukes, all of whom were members of the Medici family and all of whom were incompetent. Upon the death of the last Medicean Grand Duke in 1737, it was agreed that the state should be given to Francis, Duke of Lorraine and husband of Maria Theresa of Austria.

Although repeatedly at odds with their more powerful neighbors, the dukes of Savoy managed to retain their independence. By the 1669 Treaty of the Pyrenees (which ended the war between Spain and France), Charles Emmanuel II was permitted to reoccupy most of the towns that the French had captured. And at the end of the War of the Spanish Succession—during which Prince Eugene of Savoy decisively defeated the French at the 1706 siege of Turin—the Duke of Savoy received the Kingdom of Sicily, which was exchanged for Sardinia in 1718. Thereafter, the rulers of Savoy became known as the kings of Sardinia.

The other principal states of

aly into turmoil

The signing of the Treaty of Nijmegen, 1678, by which Louis XIV gave up his support for the rebels of Naples.

northern Italy were Modena and Parma. The former, governed by the Este family, was transformed by France into the Cispadine Republic during the reign of Hercules III and thereafter became a dependency of Austria. The Duchy of Parma remained in the possession of the Farnese family until 1731, when, upon the death of Duke Antonio, it too passed into the hands of the Austrians.

The Demise of Venice

By the turn of the century, the Republic of Venice had lost most of its former power and vitality—and after years of war with the Turks and repeated quarrels with its jealous neighbors, it had lost most of its overseas possessions as well. In 1570 a 60,000-man Turkish army led by Selim II had landed on the island of Cyprus, which the Venetians had held since 1489. The invaders soon occupied most of the

island, took the city of Nicosia and slaughtered over 20,000 of its inhabitants. Famagusta held out for nearly a year, but in August of 1571 it too was forced to capitulate. The Turks, breaking the terms of the capitulation, flayed the governor alive and dispatched his skin, stuffed with straw, to Constantinople.

A few months after the conquest of Cyprus, the Turkish navy was soundly defeated at Lepanto. The Venetians derived no lasting benefit from their triumph, however, for in 1645 the Turks turned their attention to Crete, which had been a Venetian possession for four centuries. In 1646 they landed an army of 50,000 men, occupied Canea and took Retimo, and two years later they laid siege to Candia. The siege lasted for more than twenty years, but Candia eventually fell—and in September, 1669, the whole island passed into the hands of the Turks.

There was a brief resurgence of

Venetian power under Francesco Morosini, who was appointed commander-in-chief of the Republic's army in 1684 amid renewed hostilities with Turkey. With the help of German mercenaries, Morosini reconquered Dalmatia and the region of southern Greece known as the Morea. The septuagenarian commander was elected Doge, but after his death, the territories that he had reclaimed reverted to the Turks and the Republic ceased to be a threat to the Turkish Empire.

Kitchen to Court

From 1648 to 1687 the Ottoman Empire was ruled by Mohammed IV. His Grand Vizier, an able and vastly energetic Albanian named Mohammed Kuprili who began his career as a scullion in the imperial kitchen, was largely responsible for the resurgence of the Empire's power. Kuprili restored the fleet, recaptured the islands that had been taken by the Venetians and put down revolts against his harsh regime with severity. In 1661 he was succeeded by his son, Fazil Ahmed Kuprili, a more humane

but equally able administrator.

In 1663 Ahmed Kuprili attacked Austria, which represented a far greater threat to Turkey than the Venetian Republic. Following a succession of victories, Ahmed's troops were overwhelmed at the Battle of St. Gotthard Abbey and he was forced to conclude the Treaty of Vasvar on August 10, 1664. A twenty-year truce was imposed—and for eight years the Sultan observed it. Then, in 1672, Turkey declared war on Poland's King Michael Wisniowiecki (who had set himself up as champion of the Sultan's rivals in the Ukraine). And this time Ahmed Kuprili was more successful: his army captured Kamenets, Lemberg and Lublin—and Podolia, the area between Moldavia and the Ukraine, was ceded to Turkey by the Treaty of Buczacs.

Led by John Sobieski, Poland set out to retrieve her fortunes: war against Turkey was resumed, and on November 11, 1673, John Sobieski won his first great victory at Choczim. He was soon to win another more momentous victory at Vienna, one that foreshadowed the collapse of the Turkish Empire.

Disposing of the dead and fumigating houses during a seventeenth-century cholera epidemic in Rome.

John Sobieski: determined to revive the greatness of Poland.

Vienna Under Siege

Vienna—capital of the Hapsburg Empire, cultural hub of Austria's golden age and gateway to the heart of Europe—became the object of an enormous Turkish siege operation in July of 1683. By August of that year the city appeared doomed: its bastions were in ruins, its garrison was decimated by dysentery and cannon fire, and its supply line to Poland was threatened by a Hungarian-Turkish army. Mustering a relief force of more than 60,000 Polish and German troops, John III Sobieski, King of Poland, marched south to save the embattled city. Sobieski's followers arrived in Vienna on September 7, and five days later they met the Turks at Nussdorf in a bitterly contested battle that turned back the "invincible" Ottoman armies. The Sultan's forces would not threaten Europe again.

Suleiman I, whose victory at the battle of Mohacs in 1526 created the threefold division of Hungary that still existed in 1683.

Opposite Mohammed IV's siege of Vienna: the high point of the Turks' advance into Europe.

At the battle of Mohacs in 1526, Suleiman the Magnificent, the most famous of the Ottoman sultans, crushed the medieval kingdom of Hungary. The King of Hungary was killed in that battle, and his country fell under Turkish domination. The Hapsburgs of Vienna laid claim to the slain King's crown, and a long contention between Austria and the Ottoman Empire ensued. During the reign of Sultan Suleiman, three distinct Hungaries emerged: Ottoman Hungary, centered around the great fortresses of Belgrade, Buda and Esztergom on the middle Danube; Transylvanian, to the east of the Tisza and under the control of a prince dependent on Istanbul; and Hapsburg, the territories located to the far north and west of the realm. This threefold division was to undergo little change after Suleiman's death.

In 1664 the forces of the Hapsburg Emperor Leopold I overcame the Ottomans at St. Gotthard on the river Raba. That campaign was the first major field battle that the Christians had ever won against the formidable might of the Ottoman Turks. Despite his victory, the Emperor made peace with the Sultan at Vasvar in 1664 on terms unfavorable to himself. He surrendered several fortresses and recognized an Ottoman nominee as Vaivode of Transylvania.

The situation prevailing in the Emperor's Hungarian territories led the statesmen at Vienna to accept the agreement made at Vasvar. The Hungarian magnates and nobles in Leopold's domain were divided into a pro-Hapsburg element and a faction suspicious of the policies emanating from Vienna. Many of the nobles feared that the Hapsburg desire to impose more centralized administrative and political control would mean the loss of their own large privileges. There was friction, too, on religious grounds. Calvinism had won much success in Hungary, and the forces of the Counter-Reformation sought to end that Calvinist allegiance.

In 1678 Imre Thököly, who was to become a leader of Hungarian resistance to the Hapsburg regime, assumed command of a rebel army.

Thököly turned to Istanbul for aid, and the Grand Vizier Kara Mustafa Pasha sent some assistance to the Hungarian rebels in 1681. At this same time the Emperor, hoping to placate the malcontents, summoned a Hungarian Diet to meet at Sopron. But Kara Mustafa Pasha induced Thököly to repudiate Leopold's concessions and began to give the rebels much more active support.

Leopold I and his ministers, who seemed to be listening to the latter group, concentrated on the activities of Louis XIV. To the government in Vienna, nothing was more unwelcome than a renewal of conflict with the Ottoman Turks—and it was this outlook that led the Emperor to seek from the Sultan a prolongation of the Vasvar settlement, due to expire in 1684. The Austrian ambassador at Istanbul sought to achieve this aim in 1681, but without success. Nor was Albert Caprara, a special envoy sent from Vienna in 1682, able to secure a continuation of the peace. Kara Mustafa Pasha, the Grand Vizier, had now in fact reached the moment of decision. In August, 1682, Thököly received the title of King from Sultan Mohammed IV—a clear indication that the Grand Vizier had chosen war, not peace.

In October, 1682, the Grand Vizier left Istanbul for Edirne (Adrianople). The preparations for a great campaign continued throughout the ensuing winter. At the end of March, 1683, the Ottoman forces set off from Edirne for Belgrade, arriving there at the beginning of May and encamping at Zemun on the northern bank of the Sava. Rain and the need to repair the great bridge across the marshes at Osijek hindered their subsequent advance; not until late in June did the Ottomans reach Szekesfehervar. There the Grand Vizier revealed to a council of war his determination to attack Vienna; there, too, Tartar horsemen from the Crimea joined the army. By the beginning of July, Kara Mustafa had reached Raab, one of the few Hungarian fortresses still under Hapsburg control.

No effort was spared to secure aid from abroad. In January, 1683, the Elector of Bavaria agreed to

Vienna during the siege.

Right An allegorical picture of the Emperor Leopold, who had reduced Ottoman pressure on Europe by his victory at St. Gotthard in 1664.

Atti Bassa, the Governor of Buda, who was to be killed when the Christians recaptured the city, 1686.

send troops to assist the Emperor. More important still was the compact negotiated with Poland. The activities of Thököly and his rebels in the Carpathians, and the resulting suspicion that the Ottomans might be contemplating an attack on the lands around Cracow, induced the Polish King, John III Sobieski, to reach an agreement with Emperor Leopold in the autumn of 1682. The terms of the agreement were clear and simple: Austria would seek to hold the Ottomans on the Danube, and Poland would attack them in the Ukraine. If the Ottomans moved against Cracow, the Emperor would send troops to its assistance; the Polish King would perform a like service should the Ottomans decide to besiege Vienna.

In the spring of 1683 Charles of Lorraine concentrated his forces at Pressburg, and then moved down the Danube to the region of Raab and Komarno. He hoped to reach either Nove Zamky or Esztergom, two important fortresses under Ottoman control, but a divided high command, inexplicit orders from Vienna and a shortage of supplies and fodder doomed his campaign. Lorraine had to fall back toward Raab, and then still farther in the direction of Pressburg. Soon all prospect of holding back the Ottoman advance was gone. A messenger

534

Poland attacks the Ottomans

was sent to Sobieski on July 5, telling him that Vienna was beyond all doubt the objective that Kara Mustafa Pasha had set for himself.

On July 7, the Emperor and his court withdrew westward to Linz and thence to Passau, leaving Commandant Ernst von Starhemberg to hold Vienna. Lorraine, with his cavalry, reached the capital on July 8 and most of his men encamped in the suburb of Leopoldstadt or on the islands in the Danube. His infantry, under General Leslie, began to arrive in Vienna on July 10. To defend the capital, Starhemberg would have eleven thousand regular troops and a number of civilian auxiliaries, amounting to perhaps five thousand additional men. On July 13 the embankment before the walls of Vienna was cleared of buildings that might give protection to the Ottomans. On the following day, Lorraine began to pull his cavalry out of Leopoldstadt, breaking down the bridges across the Danube and retiring to a new position north of the river. On that same day Grand Vizier Kara Mustafa Pasha reached Vienna. The long siege was about to begin.

The defenses of Vienna comprised a banked earthen grade behind which was a counterscarp with palisades and a covered road along its summit. That road was divided into sections, each defensible as a self-contained unit. To the rear of the counterscarp was a dry moat. Additional defenses—in the form of entrenchments and blockhouses—had been erected on its floor. Behind the moat lay the actual walls of Vienna, strengthened with large and formidable bastions. The main Ottoman assault was to be launched against the southern flank of the fortress. On their right wing the Ottomans faced the Burg bastion; their center stood opposite the Burg ravelin, located within the moat; and their left was over against the Löbel bastion.

The Ottoman siege works—an elaborate system of deep trenches covered with timber roofing and provided with gun emplacements—would later receive high praise from the Christians. Kara Mustafa had brought a considerable number of medium- and light-caliber cannon with him, but no large siege guns. The main instruments of attack would therefore be trenches and mines.

The Ottomans began digging their approach trenches on the night of July 14-15. Along the slopes behind these trenches the Ottoman batteries opened fire on the morning of the fifteenth. Kara Mustafa, eager to complete the encirclement of Vienna, sent a strong force across the "canal"—the southern arm of the Danube—with orders to seize Leopoldstadt and the islands in the river. From that vantage batteries soon came into action against the northern walls of the fortress. At the same time the Ottomans established bridges across the Danube, above and below the Viennese fortifications. It was now possible for the Turks to cut off the flow of supplies down the river.

On July 23 the first Ottoman mines exploded along the sector between the Burg bastion and the Löbel bastion. A whole series of assaults and counteroffensives followed thereafter. By August 3 the Turks had broken through the counterscarp opposite the Burg ravelin.

The Ottomans next directed their attack downward against the entrenchments and blockhouses in the moat. After nine days of furious conflict the Turks reached the edge of the ravelin. Starhemberg was forced to withdraw his large guns from the threatened area to the actual walls and bastions of the fortress. On August 12 the Ottomans fired a mine of exceptional size and launched a violent assault that secured them a lodgment on the ravelin itself.

The fighting continued stubborn and bitter throughout the second half of August. Nothing that the Christians could do sufficed to halt for more than a brief interval the steady advance of their foe. On September 3 Starhemberg abandoned the ravelin. Worse was to follow: on September 4 a great mine brought down some of the Burg bastion, and on September 8 two more mines inflicted serious damage on the Löbel bastion. Dysentery and battle wounds reduced the Viennese garrison to perhaps four thousand effective soldiers. If help did not come soon, the city would fall to the Ottomans.

Meanwhile, events of importance had been taking place outside the fortress. Upon the arrival of the Ottomans, Charles of Lorraine had left Leopoldstadt and withdrawn to Jedlesee. There news reached him that Imre Thököly and a mixed force of Hungarians and Turks were thrusting westward along the north bank of the river. That movement, if unchecked, might cut the lines of communication linking Vienna with Poland. It would also diminish the area still capable of providing supplies and forage for the Hapsburg troops in the field. Lorraine, recognizing the danger, advanced eastward to Pressburg and there, on July 30, drove back Thököly and his

Charles of Lorraine, the leader of the Christian army which fought the Turks.

A view of the Siege of Vienna by de Hooghe.

The Siege of Belgrade, 1690. The defeat of the Turks at Vienna did not immediately shatter their hopes of making further conquests in Europe and they recovered much of the territory they had lost during the next few years, but the great threat to Europe was much diminished.

men. At Stammersdorf, on August 24, Lorraine was able to repel a second Turkish-Hungarian advance. The routes along which aid might come from Poland and the German lands remained free.

And at last help was indeed arriving for the relief of Vienna. Toward the middle of August some 11,000 Bavarian troops reached the area south of Krems. Soon about eight thousand soldiers from Franconia and Thuringia joined them. At the same time regiments that had hitherto been serving the Emperor

on the Rhine began to appear at Krems.

Meanwhile, the news had reached John Sobieski on July 15 that Kara Mustafa was moving against Vienna. Orders went out for troops from northern Poland to concentrate at Cracow, as well as forces from the Ukraine, experienced in warfare against the Turks from their service in the Podolian War. The Polish King entered Cracow on July 29; the Podolians, led by Nicholas Sienawski, arrived there on August 2, and the contingents from the north, under Stanislas Jablonowski, on August 8. Time was needed at this juncture to decide which routes should be followed through Silesia, Moravia and Austria, and to arrange with the representatives of Emperor Leopold for the procurement of supplies adequate to maintain the Poles during their advance toward Vienna. But by August 20 all the Polish forces stood waiting at Tarnowski to begin the great campaign. The march southward began on August 22. Nine days later, on August 31, Sobieski met Charles of Lorraine at Oberhollabrunn. Here the German troops also had been brought together—Bavarian, Hapsburg and Franconian, soon to be strengthened through the arrival, on September 6, of a Saxon contingent over 10,000 strong.

By September 7, all the relief forces (numbering more than 60,000 men) were concentrated south of the river near Tulln. On September 9 the fateful advance began eastward across the Wienerwald. On the Christian left stood the Hapsburg troops and the Saxons; the Bavarians and other German contingents held the center; on the right wing rode Sobieski with the Polish forces. By September 11 the army was on the Kahlenberg ridge, only five miles from Vienna.

Kara Mustafa Pasha had begun to suspect that all was not well on his western flank. On September 8-9 he held two councils of war, at which he decided to withdraw from the siege about six thousand infantry and a considerable number of guns. To these troops he added some 20,000 horsemen. It was a belated measure designed to make good a situation

The Decline of Turkey's European Empire

- ● Hapsburg Empire in 1683
- — Frontier of Ottoman Empire in 1683
- ● Poland in 1683
- ● Acquired by Hapsburg Empire in 1699
- ■ ■ Frontier of Ottoman Empire in 1699
- ● Acquired by Poland in 1699
- ● Acquired by Venice in 1699
- ● Acquired by Hapsburg Empire in 1718

SILESIA

POLAND

Cracow

MORAVIA

RUSSIA

AUSTRIA

PODOLIA

Linz   Pressburg   HAPSBURG
        Krems   HUNGARY
Vienna   Raab
Heiligenstadt
        Budapest   River Tisza
                Esztergom   TRANSYLVANIA
OTTOMAN HUNGARY

Mohacs
Karlowitz
Belgrade
        Passau

River Danube

Adrianople

Istanbul

Vienna saved from the Turks

now becoming critical. For Kara Mustafa had committed a number of grave errors in the deployment and use of his forces. He had neglected patrols in the Krems-Tulln area, watches over the routes across the Wienerwald, occupation of the Kahlenberg and adequate defenses for the protection of the Ottoman encampments before Vienna. The price demanded for this negligence was high.

Vienna was saved on September 12, 1683. An Ottoman attack in the region of Nussdorf, below the Kahlenberg ridge, led to a stubborn and complicated battle in broken terrain. Most of the fighting, until noon, was on the left of the Christian line. The Ottomans at length withdrew from Nussdorf, leaving the road toward Heiligenstadt open. On the right the Polish advance was less rapid, but at last Sobieski and his men came out on the slopes above the Alsbach stream. Ahead was more level ground, not two miles distant from Vienna and from the headquarters of Kara Mustafa Pasha near St. Ulrich.

The Christian forces now formed themselves into two lines. It was the moment for a supreme effort. The Hapsburg and Bavarian troops, pushing forward on the left against a strong resistance, swung toward the right. So, too, did the Saxon and German troops attacking in the center. The whole tide of battle surged toward the south and east. And now Sobieski and his horsemen struck hard against the Ottoman center. The Turkish defense held out for a while, then weakened and degenerated almost at once into a total collapse.

Only a rapid pursuit would draw the fullest advantage from the new situation. The difficulties hindering such a pursuit were serious enough—the shortage of supplies at Vienna and the ravaged state of the lands lower down the Danube. Nonetheless, Lorraine and Sobieski wanted to press forward. On September 17 the campaign was once more in motion. By September 23 a bridge had been reconstructed over the Danube below Pressburg. Now the Christians would have access to the supplies and forage available in the district of Schütt. The advance continued thereafter toward Parkany, where a bridge to the great Ottoman fortress of Esztergom crossed the Danube. On October 9, at Parkany, the German and Polish troops, amounting perhaps to 25,000 men, confronted an Ottoman force some 16,000 strong. The Turks made a wild attack, failed to break through and found themselves driven to the bank of the river. A portion of the bridge over the Danube, weakened by the fire of the Christian guns, fell into the water. Unable to escape, about nine thousand Ottomans lost their lives. By October 19, pontoon bridges had been brought into position for a crossing of the Danube. On October 22 the Christians laid siege to Esztergom. The Turkish garrison, seeing no hope of relief, surrendered on October 27. This event brought to an end the operations of 1683.

The siege of Vienna was a great and famous event, celebrated throughout Europe. On the level of individual success or failure it raised men like Starhemberg, Charles of Lorraine and Sobieski to the summit of their personal fame, while to Kara Mustafa it

Turkish troops in the mid-seventeenth century.

brought death, at Belgrade, on the order of the Turkish Sultan.

Its consequences were more notable still in the realm of politics and war. At Linz, in March, 1684, a "Sacra Liga" was formed between Austria, Poland and Venice against the Ottoman Empire. The war thus begun was not to end until 1699, at the peace of Karlowitz. It brought to the Hapsburgs almost all the Hungarian lands; Venice received the Morea (only to lose it to the Ottomans in 1718); Poland acquired Podolia; and Russia, a late participant in the conflict, was given Azov.

It is debatable whether the relief of Vienna saved Europe from an Ottoman conquest. It can be argued that the last Turkish offensive that might perhaps have led to the subjugation of Austria occurred in the bitter conflict of 1593-1606, a war that underlined the fact that the Ottoman Empire had reached the viable limits of expansion. Now, problems of time and distance, of terrain, climate and logistics rendered dubious any enlargement of the already extended frontier.

Even in the realm of warfare, the tide of events was adverse to the Ottomans. Technological advance in Europe had brought about the elaboration of tactical systems which the Turks would find hard to meet. The Ottoman war machine might still be formidable in sieges—witness the assault on Candia in 1667-69 or even on Vienna itself in 1683. On the field of battle, however, the outlook for the Ottomans was grave. Further, the Austria of 1683 was not the Austria of 1526—it stood now on the verge of a golden age as one of the great powers in Europe.

Yet Kara Mustafa had almost achieved the conquest of Vienna. This simple fact will serve to explain how it was that Sobieski, only twenty-four hours after his cavalry had cut through the Ottoman defense, could write to Pope Innocent XI, on September 13, in a spirit of immense and pardonable jubilation, "we came, we saw and God conquered." So must other men have thought on that memorable September 12, 1683.

V. J. PARRY

Barbarossa, one of the most capable sixteenth-century Turkish generals, who led an earlier but also unsuccessful attack on Vienna, 1529.

537

While the Holy Roman Emperor's attentions were diverted by the Turkish invasion of Austria, the French army was making inroads along his western frontier. Louis XIV had ample reason to be proud of this army: composed of 200,000 well-trained officers and men—mostly infantry armed with wheel muskets, bayonets and fourteen-foot pikes—it was well equipped and harshly disciplined. The name of one of its officers, Jean Martinet, a military engineer and renowned tactician, was to give a new word to the English language. The army's strength and efficiency was

Vauban, the most distinguished military architect of the seventeenth century, whose ideas formed the basis of fortifications for two hundred years.

the work of Louis' war ministers, Michel le Tellier and Tellier's son, François Michel le Tellier, the Marquis de Louvois. Marshal Vauban—whose fortresses, built as a cordon around France between 1678 and 1688, are masterpieces of the craft—was responsible for the army's outstanding skill in engineering and siege techniques.

The army had already captured Dunkirk, the Franche-Comté and extensive territories along France's disputed eastern border with the Low Countries—whose towns, Louis confessed, were ever before his eyes. Those victories were confirmed in the 1684 Truce of Regensburg. The Truce ratified French possession of a string of fortified Flemish towns—Luxembourg, Alsace and Strasbourg—as well as the Franche-Comté.

France under Louis XIV

The France of Louis XIV was at the height of its power, but the King had even greater ambitions. In 1683 death removed the restraining counsels of his great minister, Jean Baptiste Colbert, who had restored the country's finances and built up its powerful navy—and Louis' thoughts again turned to war. His opportunity came in 1685, when the Elector of the Palatinate died childless. Louis immediately claimed the country for France.

This claim aroused Europe against him and led to the formation of the League of Augsburg (an alliance composed of Austria, Sweden, Holland and several small German states) in 1686.

England did not join the League, for its Roman Catholic king, James II, was committed to continuing his brother Charles II's policy of maintaining good relations with France. That policy was so unpopular with the English people—indeed, the French ambassador informed Louis that Charles and James were his only English friends—that only French money enabled the last two Stuart kings to avoid war with France. Peace could be

kept only as long as James remained King, but in the Glorious Revolution of 1688 he lost his crown to his Protestant rival, William of Orange—largely because his determination to force Catholicism on his people by unconstitutional means forced his subjects to turn to William for protection.

William of Orange

William's claim to the English throne was twofold: he was the son of Charles I's eldest daughter Mary, and he was the husband of Princess Mary, daughter of James II. On November 5, 1688, William landed at Torbay in Devon with a combined English and Dutch army of 15,000 men. The people welcomed him, James fled to France, and Parliament declared the throne vacant. William and Mary were proclaimed King and Queen on February 13, 1689.

Louis might have prevented the accession of William, his most dangerous enemy, by attacking him in the Netherlands before he could sail across the Channel. Instead, Louis hurled his armies against the Palatinate, thus declaring war on the League of Augsburg. The members of the League were

James II, after his flight from England, meets Louis XIV.

joined in war against France by Spain, Savoy and, of course, England.

War of the League of Augsburg

Despite the number and strength of his enemies, the war went well for Louis. The Duke of Luxembourg, a worthy successor of Condé and Turenne, decisively defeated the allied armies under the Prince of Waldeck at Fleurus in 1690 and under William III of England at Leuze the next year. Mons was captured in 1691 and Namur was besieged and occupied in 1692. The Duke of Luxembourg won further victories over William at Steenkirk in 1692 and at Neerwinden in 1693. Meanwhile, Marshal Catinat captured Nice and overran Savoy, defeating Amadeus II, Duke of Savoy, at Staffarda and Marsaglia. At sea, the navy that Colbert had developed with such care forced the English and Dutch to retreat in disorder off Beachy Head in 1690—and although the French Admiral Tourville lost fifteen ships at the Battle of La Hogue, he inflicted a crushing defeat on the allies in the Mediterranean in 1693.

Despite these early victories, the war had so exhausted France's resources that Louis was compelled to bring it to an end in 1697. By the Treaty of Ryswick, he surrendered nearly all the German territories (except Strasbourg, which he had conquered earlier). Louis was compelled to allow the Dutch to garrison the frontier towns of the Spanish Netherlands and to recognize not only that William of Orange was King of England, but also that William's staunchly Protestant niece, Princess Anne, daughter of James II, should succeed him.

War on heresy

Louis had made another mistake in the 1680s—apart from his decision to go to war. His Queen, Marie Thérèse, had died in 1683, the year of Colbert's death, and left him free to marry Madame de Maintenon. The new Queen, granddaughter of the distinguished Huguenot, Théodore Agrippa d'Aubigné, had been converted to Catholicism and was a devout member of the Church. She did not bear as much of the responsibility for Louis XIV's religious policies as her contemporaries supposed, but she could not conceal her satisfaction when those policies induced the Protestants to recant. She was a pious woman and felt it her duty to convert those who had strayed.

Although not a deeply religious man, Louis was scrupulous in his observances: he heard Mass nearly every day of his life. As a Christian king and head of the Catholic Church in France, he believed that one of his principal duties was to induce all his people to accept Catholicism and to carry out the promise that had been contained in the coronation oath since the

Madame de Maintenon: blamed for the massacres of Protestants that took place after she became Louis XIV's second wife.

time of Henry IV: "seriously to endeavor to extirpate all heretics, so branded by the Church, out of my land."

To achieve that ambition, a campaign was mounted against

the country's million Protestant Huguenots. Missionaries were sent into Normandy, Languedoc and Poitou—areas where the Huguenots were particularly numerous—and proclamations were issued excluding Huguenots from holding public office.

Violence was proscribed, but orders for the billeting of troops in the houses of Protestants inevitably resulted in bloodshed. The poor could not afford to feed and lodge the soldiers; the rich could not bear rough troops ruining their homes. Reports reached Paris of dragoons driving Protestants to Mass, forcing them to listen to the missionaries and sprinkling them with Holy Water.

These methods were strikingly successful: the populations of some towns, following the example of the leading Protestant families in the districts, were converted to Catholicism en masse. Other towns lost nearly all their Protestants by conversion or emigration. By the end of 1685 there were only a quarter of a million Protestants in France. They remained obdurate in their faith, clinging stubbornly to their church councils and schools. They relied on the protection of the 1598 Edict of Nantes, which guaranteed their religious freedom and granted them a recognized position.

Revocation of the Edict of Nantes

Louis determined to eliminate the remaining Protestants and fulfill his pledge of "uniting to the Church those who had strayed from her" and "wiping out all memory of the

A Protestant prayer meeting being broken up by soldiers of the Duc de Guise, after the Revocation of the Edict of Nantes.

troubles, confusion and evil caused in our Kingdom by the progress of that false Religion." On October 18, 1685, he signed the Revocation of the Edict of Nantes: Protestant churches were to be demolished, Protestant schools closed, and children born into Protestant families to be baptized Catholics.

The Revocation was welcomed throughout France by the majority of Catholics since it meant the end of religious wars. The hated Huguenots, so hardworking, prosperous and intolerant of laxity, would have to go. Madame de Sévigné declared that a king had never done and never would do anything more beautiful, and Jacques-Bénigne Bossuet, the Court preacher who had converted the Huguenot Marshal Turenne, compared Louis to Constantine, Theodocius and Charlemagne.

Greeted with such pleasure in France, the Revocation was condemned throughout the Protestant world as an act of unpardonable cruelty. It was also one of the greatest political blunders of Louis XIV's reign. Over 200,000 Huguenots—including many of France's most valuable citizens, talented scientists, financiers and businessmen—chose to emigrate rather than renounce their faith. Settling in England, Holland and Denmark, they established industries in direct competition with those of France, and represented a permanent reminder of the Catholic King's iniquity.

Thirteen years after the Revocation, Louis XIV, who had done so much for France, celebrated his sixtieth birthday. In that year, in Moscow, another, younger ruler promised to do as much for Russia.

William and Mary, whose joint rule ensured the Protestant succession.

A Window on the West

The Grand Embassy that set out from Moscow in 1695 was officially led by François Lefort, tutor to Russia's young Tsar, Peter I. Lefort's entourage included a twenty-three-year-old soldier of imperial mien who called himself Bombardier Peter Mikhailov. Mikhailov—as every member of the Embassy and every crowned head in Europe knew—was Tsar Peter himself. Traveling "incognito" through Western Europe, the young ruler obtained interviews with the Emperor of Austria, the kings of Poland and England, and numerous German princes. As the Embassy made its slow circuit of Europe's capitals, Peter studied Western industries at first hand—and by the time he returned to Moscow he had mastered fourteen special technical skills. His extensive knowledge of European technological advances enabled Peter to Westernize his nation and his army in less than a decade—and helped him achieve the age-old Russian dream of "a window on Europe."

At a time when London, Paris, Rome and Vienna were already flourishing capitals, Moscow was little more than a small village, lost in the forested wilderness of northern Russia. The city is first mentioned in official chronicles in 1147; a century later it became the fief of Prince Daniel, younger son of the famous Alexander Nevski. Under his descendants the small princedom was transformed—through treaties, marriages and territorial sales—into a powerful state whose rulers, the grand dukes, succeeded in shaking off the yoke of the Mongols. Assuming the title of tsar, the Muscovy princes organized a centralized government which eventually administered a vast area that included part of Siberia.

The period of troubles that began with the extinction of the house of Rurik in 1598 and ended with the election of the new dynasty of the Romanovs only temporarily interrupted the evolution of a young and already promising nation. But during the period of Asiatic domination (1223-1380) there had been little contact between Russia and the civilization of the West, and during the troubles that occurred early in the seventeenth century, Muscovy was deprived of all access to the sea. It remained an underdeveloped, feudal country, populated by some 10 million pious but ignorant peasants and dominated by an autocratic monarch who considered himself an heir to the Byzantine emperors. These tsars found only feeble supporters in a fanatical clergy and in a class of indolent noblemen, the boyars. The West remained as much a closed book to them as it did to their subjects. Nevertheless, national defense and urgent commercial considerations dictated a closer connection with the feared and despised West. The idea of an outlet to the sea began to haunt the best minds of a nation that, until then, had kept its eyes fixed on the steppes. Peter the Great, the tsar-reformer, was the man who realized that dream.

Born in Moscow in 1672, Peter led a stormy childhood amid dynastic quarrels, clan rivalries and popular uprisings. His father, Tsar Alexis, pious

and easygoing, had two unpromising sons by an earlier marriage: the sickly Fëdor and the partially blind and feebleminded Ivan. When Alexis died in 1676, Fëdor inherited the throne. His reign lasted only six years, and upon his death the incompetent Ivan and ten-year-old Peter were proclaimed joint sovereigns of all the Russias under the regency of their half sister Sophia, an intelligent and ambitious virago of fifty. Although she was frequently compared to Elizabeth I of England—and although she consciously modeled herself on the Empress Pulcheria of Byzantium—Sophia was unable to maintain order in her own country. Relegated to the background, the adolescent Peter witnessed scenes of bloodshed that gave him a horror for the atmosphere of the Kremlin and for the traditional habits of the old Muscovy.

The young prince was brought up by his mother, Natalia Naryshkin, in a country setting on the outskirts of Moscow. There he supplemented an adequate education through contacts with the humble foreign artisans who lived in the nearby German quarter. Peter, who had a passion for soldiering (a list of his early toys includes pistols, carbines, bows and arrows, drums and cannon), organized his companions—gentlemen's sons, stableboys and street ragamuffins—drilled them and learned with them how to handle arms. Other boys joined the ranks, and the games grew more ambitious. Using boats, they mounted a full-scale assault on a small fortress that Peter had had built on a little island not far from his home. At the end of a few years he had two well-trained battalions of several hundred men each. With this nucleus of what was to become a famous army, he executed a coup d'état in 1689 to free himself from the hampering tutelage of Princess Sophia, put an end to her dangerous intrigues and take over actual power.

At this time two remarkable men became his tutors in the military profession and in the art of Western living: an old mercenary, Patrick Gordon,

The Empress Natalia Kirillovna, mother of Peter the Great.

Opposite Emperor Peter the Great as a shipbuilder at Deptford during his stay in England. His interest in the sea led him to attack the Turkish port of Azov, so that Russia would have an outlet to the sea.

541

The "Grand Embassy" visits Europe

Peter the Great as a child with his elder half-brothers, Fedor and Ivan, patriarch Adrian and a Metropolitan.

scion of an illustrious Scottish family, and young François Lefort, another soldier of fortune and a native of Geneva. Under the influence of these two friends Peter revived the old dream of giving Russia access to the sea. In 1695 he flung himself into a war against Turkey and captured Azov at the mouth of the Don. But even in the moment of victory he realized that his land and naval forces were inadequate to gain him mastery of the Black Sea. He decided to send a "Grand Embassy" to various Western countries, not only to secure the help necessary to continue the war or to conclude an advantageous peace, but also to build up a corps of specialists by initiating young representatives of his nobility into European science.

To everybody's astonishment Peter himself joined the embassy, traveling incognito. For eighteen months the Tsar of All the Russias traveled with his apprentices through the Baltic countries, the German states, Holland and England, vainly attempting to escape notice under the borrowed name of "Bombardier Peter Mikhailov." Officially, the embassy was led by François Lefort, seconded by two Russian dignitaries. But all eyes were naturally turned to the young sovereign, taller by a head than any of his companions, who distributed lavish gifts and was received at every court.

At Königsberg he met the Prince-Elector of Brandenburg; at Koppenbrugge, the princesses of Hanover. In Holland he had his first interview with William of Orange, King of England, whom he was to meet again in London. In Vienna he was on intimate terms with Emperor Leopold of Austria. And on his way back to Russia, at Rawa Ruska, he made friends with Augustus of Saxony, who had just been elected King of Poland.

Diplomatically, the results of Peter's Grand Embassy were rather slight, since none of the European cabinets was ready to support the Russian plans for a crusade against the Turks. But the royal traveler had other interests. His goals included developing his naval building program, organizing a powerful artillery, inviting selected specialists—from among the captains, seamen and engineers he met—to Russia, and building up a corps of his countrymen instructed in the most recent scientific and technological methods. He wanted to superintend the apprenticeship of the young noblemen that he had brought with him, and he cherished the ambition of serving as their model. His biographers never fail to point out that he ended by mastering fourteen skills, not counting that of statesman: at various times he functioned as engineer, cannoneer, carpenter, boatman, armorer, drummer, blacksmith, joiner and tooth-puller.

Peter even spent a week with his old friend Gerrit Kist (who had been a blacksmith in Moscow) in the little Dutch village of Zaandam, working in Master Rogge's yard under the name of Master Peter, exploring the canals and visiting the local spinning mills, sawyards and oil works.

In Amsterdam, where he was to spend more than four months, the Tsar concentrated on increasing his knowledge of shipbuilding. Although he slighted neither the museums nor the laboratories nor the dissecting rooms, he spent the greater part of his time in the East India Company shipyards. But it was in England, in the yards of Deptford and the arsenals of Woolwich, that he completed his apprenticeship and became an accomplished master of the art of shipbuilding. "If I had not come here," he was to say later, "I should never have been more than a plain carpenter." He also perfected the technique of navigation, spent hours rowing and sailing, attended

The *streltsy* fighting Peter's troops, who are led by Patrick Gordon. The *streltsy* were regarded by Peter as his chief enemy as they supported the Regent, Princess Sophia.

A boyar or Russian noble.

Left An Easter procession outside of the Kremlin in Moscow.

Below Cutting the boyars' beards: Peter's reforms affected the lives of all his subjects, but the beard cutting was of symbolic importance.

the maneuvers at Spithead and revived the courage of British sailors during a storm by asking them: "Have you ever heard of a tsar being drowned?" Later, remembering this period in his life, he often said to his courtiers, "The life of an English admiral is infinitely happier than that of a ruler of Russia."

When he was not on the water, Peter inspected the collection of weapons at the Tower of London; visited the Mint and the Greenwich Royal Observatory; went to a masked ball, the theater, a bear fight and a cock fight; paid court to an actress; and incidentally wrecked the elegant house that he and his party were living in. He even found a moment to watch, through an attic window, the opening of Parliament (thus giving a wit the chance to remark: "Today I saw something unique in the world—one sovereign on the throne and another on the roof").

A few months later, as Peter was finishing his conversations in Vienna, he was suddenly obliged to return to Moscow because of an uprising of the *streltsy*, the undisciplined, turbulent and reactionary local militia guards. The *streltsy* were survivors of the old Muscovite regime. Armed with muskets and sabers, unadapted to modern warfare, they occupied separate quarters near the capital and in frontier towns. They had been partisans of Princess Sophia, had participated in all the recent upheavals and were prepared to fight to the last for the maintenance of the old order of society, which they felt was being menaced by an "ungodly tsar" who had gone abroad for unknown reasons. Determined to reestablish Sophia on the throne and to exterminate the nobles and the boyars, they had marched on Moscow—and nothing but the courageous intervention of General Gordon had prevented the success of their plan. With remarkable speed he had dispersed isolated detachments of the *streltsy* before they had had time to concentrate, had encircled their main forces and had

Peter declares war on Sweden

Moscow on August 25, 1698, there was nothing left for him to do but to act as judge.

Peter returned to his country the possessor of intellectual and technical equipment such as no Russian before him had commanded. He knew that his nation was at the crossroads, and that it would be unable to maintain its role in the world without the radical reforms that he was prepared to accomplish. The *streltsy* were barring his way and he considered it his duty to finish with them once and for all. He subjected them to terrible reprisals, participating personally in the interrogations that took place in torture chambers. Three hundred and forty-one rebels were condemned to death, brought in carts to Red Square and hanged from the crenelated walls of the Kremlin, where their emaciated skeletons remained exposed to the horror of passersby.

More executions followed during the ensuing weeks; the number of victims finally reached 799. The sixteen *streltsy* regiments were disarmed and disbanded; the families of the condemned men were turned out of their homes. Princess Sophia, considered responsible for the whole upheaval, was deprived of her rank and obliged to take the veil.

At last Tsar Peter was free: he had broken with the past and was now prepared to lead his country into a gigantic military and reforming enterprise. The horrors of the executions were soon overshadowed by the glory of his victories and of his reforms.

On August 8, 1700, Peter made his historic decision to declare war on Sweden, in order to open a road from Russia to the West by the conquest of the Baltic littoral. He had secured the collaboration of Poland and Denmark, but his alliance with these two rivals of Sweden was to prove ineffectual. With nothing to rely on but his own forces, Peter was defeated at Narva by the valiant Swedish King, Charles XII. Refusing to be discouraged by this defeat, Peter raised and equipped new armies; he put immense effort into creating a good artillery; he worked with his own hands on the construction of the frigates that were to give him mastery of the

Above right Bust of Peter by Rastrelli.

Baltic. Then his disciplined and well-trained regiments seized the mouth of the Neva and entrenched themselves along the coveted littoral. On June 27, 1709, in a battle at Poltava, he put his great adversary, Charles XII, to flight.

To achieve this brilliant success, Peter had been obliged to subject the entire structure of his country to a basic transformation. In a certain sense Russia emerged completely "Europeanized" and "Westernized." Even before venturing into war, Peter had undertaken to change the outward aspects of his fellow countrymen or, more precisely, of his own entourage. During his journeys in Western Europe he had observed how ridiculous the long medieval gowns and long beards of the Muscovites looked to the outside world. The day after his return from abroad, Peter received the boyars who came to greet him with a large pair of scissors in his hand—and chopped off the beards of the most eminent among them. At a banquet later in the same week, the Tsar's jester (an ancestor of the novelist Turgenev) circled the table and cut off the beards of all the

Eudoxia, wife of Peter the Great. The Czar did not get on with his wife who was the daughter of a Court official.

Below right A plan of a battle between Denmark and Sweden: Peter's keenness to have an outlet on the Baltic led him into continuous wars with Sweden, in which the Danes were usually his allies.

One of the *streltsy* soldiers.

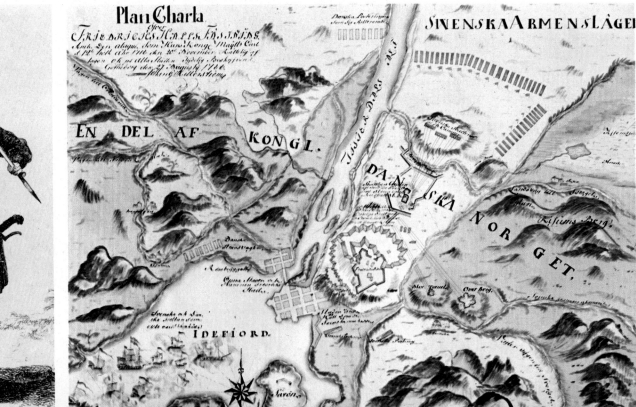

guests who had not yet adopted the new fashion. Three days later nearly all beards had disappeared from the court. Within a few months Peter was also wielding the scissors on the exaggeratedly long sleeves of his attendants. "With these full sleeves," he said, "accidents are always happening: sometimes they get dipped in the soup, sometimes they break windows."

Resistance, of course, was greater in the case of more serious reforms, but Peter nonetheless had his way. He established conscription as a means of recruiting a permanent and regular army with an adequate number of specialists, and he did the same for the fleet. He subjected a recalcitrant Church to his authority by replacing the all-powerful patriarch by an ecclesiastical body, the Holy Synod, which was given strictly limited functions. He replaced the hereditary aristocracy by a "nobility of service" open to all deserving officers and functionaries. And to put an end once and for all to the old customs and habits, he left Moscow and the Kremlin and moved his residence to a swampy, deserted region at the mouth of the Neva, newly conquered from Sweden. There he built his new capital, St. Petersburg (renamed Petrograd in World War I and Leningrad by the Communists in 1924)—"a window on Europe," as he put it.

Permanent connection with the West—the final goal of all his efforts—was not easily established. For long years the cabinets of Europe turned a cold shoulder to the upstart Tsar who took no interest in the great Spanish problem then in the limelight, and who persisted in fighting the "invincible" King of Sweden in what was considered a perfectly "useless" war. Russia's prestige was very low at Versailles, Vienna and The Hague. It was only after the victory of Poltava that all Europe turned its eyes to the East.

Following Poltava, the French cabinet expressed interest in a rapprochement with Russia and in acting as mediator between Russia and Sweden. Peter set off for Paris immediately and soon entered into a friendship with the French regent. His second appearance in the countries of the West was as pregnant with consequences as the first had been. By directing his ministers to sign the Amsterdam Agreement with France and Prussia in 1717, Peter inaugurated a system of interchangeable alliances that was to be employed by his successors on a great scale. By submitting to the admiration of the Parisian populace, by showing a charming affection for the boy king, Louis xv, and by visiting Madame de Maintenon, Louis xiv's durable mistress, Peter laid the foundation for his fame throughout the world.

In Russia that fame was marred by Peter's treatment of his son and heir, the Tsarevich Alexis. The two men could hardly have been more different: while Peter was creating a new Russia, Alexis preferred the old Russia, with its indolent quietism and its horror of innovation. Incapable of leading a revolt himself, he became—quite without premeditation—a symbol around whom all the malcontents in Russia rallied. The contest between the two came to a climax in 1718 when Peter imprisoned Alexis and appointed a supreme court that condemned him to death. It was one of Peter's few—but lasting—blunders.

As the years wore on, he had many victories. The surrender of the Swedish fleet after the naval battle of Hangö in 1714, the military occupation of Finland, and two raids into Skane in southern Sweden led to the signing—on August 30, 1721—of the Treaty of Nystad. That document ceded Russia all of Estonia, Livonia, Ingria and Karelia, and part of Finland, including the fortress of Vyborg.

Peter's triumph was complete. He had conquered the Baltic littoral, his coveted objective. He had further succeeded in establishing a sort of veiled protectorate over Poland and in setting up a series of duchies along the western Baltic. On October 22, 1721, three years before his death, he was proclaimed "Emperor of All the Russias," and the senate bestowed upon him the title of "the Great."

Like a warship launched from the ways, Russia had made her entrance into Europe to the clang of hammers and the thunder of guns.

CONSTANTINE DE GRUNWALD

Peter the Great Square and the Senate in St. Petersburg. Peter built St. Petersburg as a new capital for his kingdom, perhaps because of its proximity to the sea.

Above left The Battle of Poltava, 1709, at which Russia won a decisive victory over the Swedes. This victory secured for Peter Livonia and Estonia as well as a Baltic foothold.

545

Russia's entry into European affairs coincided with the downfall of Sweden. During the reign of Gustavus Adolphus (1592–1632), Sweden had become a first-class power. With the help of French financing, Sweden had emerged from the Thirty Years' War with an outstanding military reputation, a seat in the German Diet and undisputed control of the Baltic. As a champion of Protestantism, Gustavus Adolphus had taken his army south in the Thirty Years' War. His presence had prevented the Austrian Emperor from acquiring any outlet to the Baltic and had thereby eliminated a potentially dangerous rival sea power.

Sweden retained her commanding position in northern Europe during the reign of Queen Christina, Gustavus Adolphus' strange and gifted daughter, who came to the throne when she was eighteen. But the wayward, extravagant and self-centered Christina soon wearied of government. Aware of the unrest that her unusual personal behavior was causing in Sweden, she abdicated in 1654 in favor of her cousin, Charles Gustavus, who became King Charles x.

Within a year of his coronation,

INGRESSO SOLENNE IN ROMA DELLA MAESTA DELLA REGINA DI SVEZIA IL DI XXIII FEB MDCLV.

The entry of Christina of Sweden into Rome after her conversion to Catholicism.

Charles persuaded the *Riksdag* that a campaign against Poland was to Sweden's advantage. Leading an army of 50,000 men into Poland in July, 1655, he occupied Warsaw, forced the Polish King John Casimir to seek refuge in Silesia, and captured Cracow. The brutality of Charles' troops—most of whom were mercenaries—the arrogance of his rapacious officers and his own ill-concealed contempt for national and religious feelings aroused the Polish people. Charles lost Warsaw and more than half his troops in a protracted campaign against large bands of guerrillas and a reorganized Polish army led by John Casimir. Only by buying the help of the Elector Frederick William of Brandenburg was his combined Prussian-Swedish army able to reoccupy Warsaw and defeat the forces of the Polish King. The Poles refused his peace terms, and war was resumed. In June, 1657, the Danes gave Charles an excuse to extricate himself from his exhausting and profitless war by declaring war on Sweden.

Charles' early military successes against Denmark were astonishing: a powerful thrust carried him across Jutland to Fredericksodde, and across the frozen expanse of the Great and Little Belts to Zeeland. Although the treaties of Taastrup and Roskilde in 1658 ceded almost half of Denmark to Sweden, Charles was still greedy for more territory and greater military renown. He resumed the war, but met with little success due to the intervention of Holland, France and England—who feared the obliteration of Denmark by an increasingly powerful Sweden. Upon the King's premature death in 1660, the Council of Regency signed two peace treaties. By the terms of the Peace of Oliva, Sweden's possession of Livonia was confirmed but the Elector of Brandenburg acquired the Duchy of Prussia; by the Peace of Copenhagen, Sweden gained the three Scanian provinces from Denmark in return for giving up the island of Bornholm.

Charles XI

During the years of Charles XI's minority, Sweden's strength rapidly declined, war with Denmark broke out again and the Swedish army was defeated by Brandenburg at Fehrbellin in 1675.

When the young King came of age in 1672, he set out to revive Sweden's power. Boorish and ill-educated—but determined and brave—Charles followed the advice of his shrewd minister Johan Gyllenstjerna. He reorganized the national armaments and his demoralized army, recovered the alienated crown lands, deprived the corrupt *Riksdag* of its control over finance and administration, and converted the government of Sweden into a semi-absolute monarchy. The treaties of Nijmwegen and St. Germain in 1679 ended the wars and confirmed Sweden's possession of Finland, Ingria, Estonia, Livonia, numerous islands in the Baltic and large parts of present-day Denmark, Germany and Poland. Those vast territories were poor and sparsely populated by a variety of races with their own languages and customs. More than three-quarters of Sweden's 3 million people were peasants, most roads were no more than tracks, and few cities were worthy of the name—yet Charles XI made the army a powerful, well-equipped and well-trained one once more.

Charles XII

When Charles XI died in 1697, his fourteen-year-old son, a clever, precocious and austere boy, succeeded him as Charles XII. The *Riksdag*, jealous of the power of the regents, offered him full sovereignty the following year. Charles accepted, and proceeded to attack a coalition that had been formed by Denmark, Poland and Russia to dismember the empire his father and grandfather had built. Charles first advanced on Denmark—whose army had invaded Holstein—landing his troops in Zeeland, a

Gustavus Adolphus, the Protestant King of Sweden.

—battle for supremacy

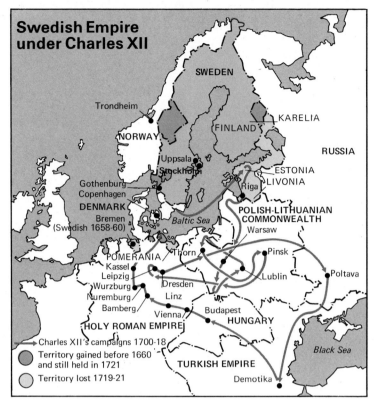

Swedish Empire under Charles XII

→ Charles XII's campaigns 1700-18
● Territory gained before 1660 and still held in 1721
○ Territory lost 1719-21

few miles north of Copenhagen, in August, 1700. Two weeks later, by the terms of the Peace of Travendal, Charles gained a large indemnity and a guarantee that Denmark would make no further hostile moves against Sweden.

Charles then turned his attention to Russia. Against the advice of his generals, he took his army on a week's march through Ingria to attack the Russian fortified camp at Narva. On November 20, 1700, in a heavy snowstorm, his troops overwhelmed a Russian army four times their size in one of the most decisive victories of modern times. Charles captured eighteen generals and 145 cannon. His losses were light—nine hundred men—while Russian casualties were more than nine thousand.

Charles could have marched on to St. Petersburg, but fearful of the enemies who lay undefeated behind him, he turned back to attack Poland. Charles was determined to depose Augustus the Strong of Saxony, who had recently secured his election as Augustus II of Poland, and to replace him with his own candidate, Stanislas Leszcznski. He entered Warsaw in May of 1702, and on July 2 defeated a large army of Poles and Saxons at Klissow. Three weeks later he captured Krakow. In 1703 Sweden won another victory at Pultusk and seized the fortress of Thorn. Finally, in July, 1704, soon after the King's

twenty-second birthday, Stanislas Leszcznski was elected King of Poland in Augustus II's place.

Supremely confident, impulsive and unstable, Charles seemed addicted to the excitement of war. His schemes became ever more ambitious and increasingly ruinous to the finances of his country. In August, 1707, he again attacked Russia, marching on Moscow at the head of an army of 44,000 men. Unfortunately for Charles, while he had been "immersed in the Polish bog," Peter the Great had

had time to reorganize his armies and reoccupy the Baltic provinces.

After a battle on the Warbis River, the Swedes forced Peter's army to retreat. In the appallingly cold winter of 1708—the most bitter Russian winter in a hundred years—the Swedes pursued their retreating foe across a burned and desolate countryside. By the time they caught up with the Russians on the Vorskla River, the Swedish force had been reduced to 20,000 men. At the Battle of Poltava on June 27, 1709, the vastly superior Russian army overwhelmed the Swedes. Charles, who had been wounded on June 7 and was too feverish to lead the battle himself, rode south to seek refuge in Turkey with a small force of cavalry, leaving behind an all but annihilated army.

Charles stayed in Turkey for four years and persuaded the Sultan to declare war on Russia three times, with inconclusive results. In 1715, after an absence of fourteen years, Charles returned to Sweden. Aided by his powerful minister, Baron Görtz—who shared his belief that Sweden was still a great power—Charles raised another army and attacked Norway, hoping to capture enough territory to give him a strong hand in negotiating with his enemies. It was his last campaign: on December 11, 1718, while laying siege to the fortress of Fredriksten, Charles was shot.

In reality, the fate of Sweden and the outcome of the Great Northern War had been decided nine years earlier, at Poltava. By the terms of the Treaty of Nystadt in 1721,

Sweden lost her empire, Denmark moved into Holstein and Augustus II regained the Polish throne. Russia replaced Sweden as the controlling power in the Baltic.

Charles XII, who became King of Sweden at fourteen. His military ambitions proved financially ruinous.

While Charles XII was campaigning in Russia, Charles II of Spain died and bequeathed his possessions to Louis XIV's grandson, Philip—thus plunging Europe into the War of the Spanish Succession. The victories of the Duke of Marlborough, commanding the English armies, and Prince Eugene of Savoy, commanding the Austrian, were followed by the Peace of Utrecht.

The Battle of Poltava, 1709, at which Charles' army was destroyed by the Russians.

Twilight of the Sun King

Louis XIV's claim to the Spanish Netherlands was a tenuous one at best—and all Europe was incensed when the French monarch's troops occupied the Low Countries in 1667. Forty-six years, two inconclusive wars and one inconsequential treaty later, the territorial ambitions of the Sun King were finally curbed and peace was restored to Europe. The treaties signed at Utrecht in 1713 and at Rastatt a year later established a new balance of power among the nations of Western Europe—one that was to last for nearly a century. The militarily humbled French Empire was shorn of several of its overseas possessions; Holland, already weakened, was reduced to second-class status; and Russia, Prussia and England emerged as the dominant European powers. More important, the defeat and subsequent death of Louis XIV ended the Age of Absolutism in Continental politics and inaugurated an epoch of enlightened despotism.

Philip V of Spain. After the Treaty of Utrecht he renounced his claim to the French throne.

Opposite Marlborough and his staff at the battle of Blenheim. This battle ended sixty years of French invincibility—a fact formally acknowledged nine years later by the Treaty of Utrecht.

The treaties concluded at Utrecht in 1713 and at Rastatt in 1714 finally ended the long years of European wars that had resulted from Louis XIV's efforts to extend French hegemony. They also established a new European balance of power that was to survive until the French Revolution.

From the moment Louis XIV took control of the French government in 1661, he was intent on providing France with the best army in Europe—and then using that army, in conjunction with the skilled French diplomatic corps, to make France the most powerful nation on the Continent. Until 1688 it seemed that he would succeed. In 1668 Louis marched into the Spanish Netherlands, using as a pretext Spain's failure to pay the dowry promised him when he married Marie Thérèse, daughter of Philip IV. When the Dutch Republic formed a defensive alliance with England and Sweden, Louis made plans to punish the insolent little nation and at the same time destroy the Dutch as trade rivals. In 1672 he invaded the Republic, thus beginning the first of his great wars. The Dutch managed to keep the French army from advancing on the province of Holland by opening the dikes and inundating the land, and by 1678 Spain, England and the Holy Roman Emperor, Leopold I, had joined the Dutch against France. The war was a stalemate.

The anti-French coalition only temporarily checked the French drive toward supremacy in Europe, however. During the next ten years Louis turned from war to diplomacy and nearly succeeded in making himself master of Europe. He annexed several cities, including Strasbourg, on flimsy legal grounds, and fear of France once more led to the formation of a defensive alliance. Known as the League of Augsburg, that alliance centered around Leopold I and ultimately included most of the German states, Sweden, England, Spain, the Dutch Netherlands and Savoy. From 1688 to 1697 the League—also known as the Grand Alliance—waged a dreary, indecisive, exhausting war with France.

The war ended with the treaty of Ryswick in 1697, but nothing was really settled.

The threat of French hegemony had not been the only irritant to European stability before 1697. Maritime rivalry between France and Spain on the one hand and England and Holland on the other, and ideological differences between the Catholic and the Protestant countries had also been sources of conflict. Now a further element was added: the question of who would succeed to the Spanish throne. Louis had claimed that throne on behalf of his grandson Philip of Anjou; Leopold I had claimed it for his grandson Charles.

Louis, exhausted by the War of the League of Augsburg, was quite ready to renounce in part his claims to the Spanish throne, and to put an end to hostilities by coming to terms with the maritime powers. In 1700, however, Charles II of Spain died, bequeathing to Philip of Anjou his great inheritance. Louis accepted on behalf of his grandson, and from that moment onward war was virtually inevitable.

The War of the Spanish Succession was to last ten weary years. Right from the start, the participating powers spent as much time in negotiations as in fighting. The coalition against France was led by a "triumvirate" consisting of England's Duke of Marlborough, Prince Eugene of Savoy and Antonius Heinsius of the Dutch Republic. It was in the interests of all three of them to prolong the war until France was finally forced to surrender. In 1710, however, Marlborough fell into disgrace and the Tories, who took over the English government from the Whigs, were in favor of making a reasonable peace with France. A year later Emperor Joseph I died, leaving his throne to his brother Charles VI, who was also the Austrian pretender to the Spanish throne. England, which felt just as threatened by an alliance between Austria and Spain as by one between France and Spain, withdrew from the war and signed a preliminary treaty with France on October 8, 1711.

The Treaty of Utrecht was finally brought to a

Charles VI capitulates at Rastatt

Spanish America. She was allowed to send one "authorized ship" annually to trade in Spanish waters, and she secured a monopoly of the slave trade for the next thirty years.

Holland, on the other hand, derived very little benefit from her efforts, apart from the fact that France renounced all claims to the Low Countries, which came under Austrian rule. Spain had to give up all her European possessions outside the Iberian Peninsula to Austria and to the Duke of Savoy, who had been proclaimed King of Sicily.

Surprisingly, the English reacted unfavorably to the Treaty of Utrecht. The opposition was led by the Whigs, who were critical of the Treaty for several reasons. First, they were bitter because they had lost power scarcely twenty years after the Glorious Revolution of 1688 (which had led to the deposition of the Catholic monarch James II and the accession of William and Mary to the English throne). The Whigs of course had brought about the Revolution and, not surprisingly, they had hoped to reap the benefits from it. They therefore opposed the peace treaties, at least in part, simply because they had been drawn up by their opponents, the Tories. More fundamentally, they felt that the whole spirit of the Glorious Revolution had been betrayed by a peace treaty that had preserved the French monarchy practically intact and that had not interfered with the Spanish overseas possessions. Finally, they pointed out the striking contrast between the ever-growing popularity and influence of English ideas on the Continent and the Tory leaders' meek attitude toward two Catholic monarchs who, for all intents and purposes, had been defeated.

It was quite another story on the Continent, especially in France. Although the failing Louis XIV persisted in his rigid absolutism, French thought and writing was becoming more and more permeated with the subtle influence of English science and rationalism. From the year 1715 on, the regent,

Charles XII of Sweden, whose eventual defeat heralded the arrival of a new power in Europe—Russia.

Right Prussia, led by Frederick William I, built up the finest army in Europe, thus laying the foundations of the German military tradition.

successful conclusion after Philip of Anjou—now Philip V of Spain—had renounced all rights to the French throne on July 8, 1712. Even then Charles VI was reluctant to give up his rights to the Spanish throne and delayed signing the peace treaty until the following year at Rastatt.

Those treaties marked the end of French expansion in Europe; they also represented a great victory for England. Louis XIV was forced to recognize the Protestant succession in England and to expel the Stuart pretender, the son of James II, from French soil. Philip V's renunciation of all rights to the throne of France and the French princes' renunciation of the Spanish succession were declared to be inviolable law. Moreover, Louis XIV ceded to England Hudson Bay and Strait, Acadia, Newfoundland and the island of Saint Christopher in the Lesser Antilles. The port of Dunkerque was to be filled up and its fortifications demolished. Britain received Gibraltar and Minorca from Spain and, far more important, she was granted certain exclusive trading rights with

Philippe of Orleans, and his minister Cardinal Dubois adopted a pro-English policy, encouraging more cordial relations between the two countries. (Later on, the Whig Minister, Sir Robert Walpole, was to support that entente.) During that period, the intellectual links between the two countries grew much closer. Montesquieu and Voltaire, in particular, were profoundly influenced by English life and literature. The England of John Locke, George Berkeley, Daniel Defoe and Jonathan Swift set the trend for the age of the *philosophes*.

In short, England now represented the country of freedom, the land where the popular press and partisan pamphlets played a decisive role in the political arena. People on the Continent knew all about the political pamphlets written by Swift and Defoe in

the course of the fiery polemic that had developed as a result of the Utrecht peace talks. England seemed to be the only country where public opinion was sometimes a decisive factor in influencing governmental decisions. Her economic prosperity seemed to be a fitting recompense for her liberal and enlightened government.

Clearly, that contemporary concept of England was based partly on illusions. The corruption so vividly denounced by Hogarth was completely ignored, while enormous interest was shown in the progress of industry and trade, in the amazing discoveries of Isaac Newton, in the promotion of new ideas by the National Academy of Sciences (the Royal Society), and in the predominant role played by the London Stock Exchange. The Treaty of Utrecht brought England a lasting prestige on the Continent, both with her former enemies and with her former allies. The eighteenth century was dominated by England in the way that the preceding century had been dominated by France and the sixteenth century by Spain.

The Treaty of Utrecht reshuffled the European powers into a new pattern of relationships that was to remain in force for nearly a hundred years. Further, the consequences of the adventurous policy of Charles XII of Sweden in northern Europe, and the victories of Prince Eugene over the Ottomans affected the European balance of power just as much as the Treaty of Utrecht. With the final defeat of Charles XII a new major power appeared on the eastern horizon: Russia, whose Tsar Peter revealed his intention of taking an active part in European affairs from that time on.

Russia's emergence as a major power came at the time of the decline of two other formerly powerful states: Poland, which had been weakened as a result of internal anarchy, and Sweden, which had been reduced by the actions of Charles XII to the status of a second-class nation. The Ottoman Empire was

Left Prince Eugene of Savoy who, together with Marlborough and Heinsius, formed the "triumvirate" against France.

Below left George I, first of the Hanoverians, came to the English throne the year after the Treaty of Utrecht. During his reign the Monarchy took the form it retains today.

Claude, Duke of Villars. The greatest French general of the eighteenth century, who defeated Eugene of Savoy at Denain.

Prussia—Germany's emerging giant

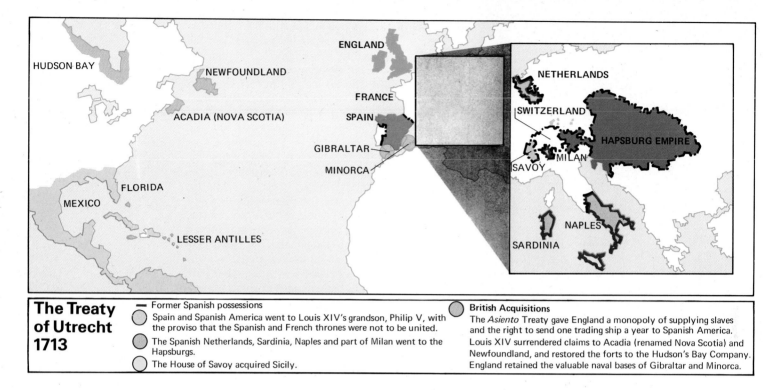

The Treaty of Utrecht 1713

— Former Spanish possessions

◯ Spain and Spanish America went to Louis XIV's grandson, Philip V, with the proviso that the Spanish and French thrones were not to be united.

◯ The Spanish Netherlands, Sardinia, Naples and part of Milan went to the Hapsburgs.

◯ The House of Savoy acquired Sicily.

◯ **British Acquisitions**
The *Asiento* Treaty gave England a monopoly of supplying slaves and the right to send one trading ship a year to Spanish America. Louis XIV surrendered claims to Acadia (renamed Nova Scotia) and Newfoundland, and restored the forts to the Hudson's Bay Company. England retained the valuable naval bases of Gibraltar and Minorca.

another great power that was in a state of decline during that period. Although it still ruled over vast territories, it no longer constituted a serious menace to the Austrian states. Prince Eugene's Austria, on the other hand, had been victorious against both Louis XIV and the Ottoman Sultan and was far more solidly established on the banks of the Danube than it had ever been before.

In Germany, the new kingdom of Prussia was emerging as the heir to the former Swedish territories. The nebulous concept of a loosely knit group of German states, deliberately fostered by the treaties of Westphalia, was in the process of becoming clarified and condensed, while the German people, having recovered from the disasters and ruin of the Thirty Years' War, were becoming aware of their identity. At the time, Prussia was still only one of several powerful states within Germany. Saxony and Bavaria were equally powerful German states, but the former was hindered rather than strengthened by the enormous dead weight of Poland, while the latter was growing progressively weaker, without any apparent gains, as a result of its abortive, imperialist ambitions. Prussia, on the other hand, had a history of strong rulers who had developed the Prussian army into the best in the world. That army was the base on which Prussia rose to great power during the reign of Frederick William I (1713–40).

In Italy, the north and central regions were dominated by Austria, while the Republic of Venice was falling into a fatal state of decline. Neither the Papal States nor the Kingdom of Naples were in a position to play a decisive role in the affairs of the country. The newly created Kingdom of Sardinia, on the other hand, had its eyes fixed more and more determinedly on the fertile plains of the river Po in the north. At the same time, it was playing off the

Bourbons of France against the Hapsburgs of Austria —a diplomatic game that had proved most successful up to that time.

Spain, now that her European possessions had been taken away from her, had turned her attention to internal reforms, as well as to the development of her vast overseas empire. Geographically almost as isolated as England from the European continent, and in possession of a powerful fleet of ships, there was nothing to prevent Spain from becoming a great maritime power. Unfortunately, a nostalgia for her former Italian possessions, combined with the ambitions of Elizabeth Farnese, the second wife of Philip V, diverted Spain from her main course into a fruitless attempt to bring about a revision of the Treaties of Utrecht and Rastatt. Elizabeth's ambitious scheme,

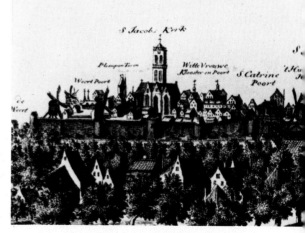

which was supported by both Charles XII and the Stuart pretender, was to prove disastrous for all.

France was equally split by memories of past glories and concern for the future. She soon recovered from the exhaustion of the long wars, but a violent division of opinion still existed: on the one side were those people who held the traditional anti-Austrian views, dating back to the time of Francis I and Richelieu, and who were now reinforced by supporters of the new enlightened thought; on the other side, the Ultramontane Catholics were hoping for a reconciliation between the Catholic Bourbons and Hapsburgs. The policy of the latter group was to be triumphant with the Family Compact, a series of alliances between the French and Spanish branches of the Bourbons. The former attitude involved

France in the War of the Austrian Succession and reappeared during the French Revolution in the policy of the Girondists, who in 1792 succeeded in having war declared on Austria. Everyone in France was agreed, however, that England was their greatest rival.

While the Continent was busy solving its immediate problems, England had quietly arranged the disputed maritime and colonial affairs to her own advantage. For although the Treaty of Utrecht had placed her in a relatively favorable position in general, it had failed in these areas to give England the decisive victory that the Whigs had hoped for. On the surface, England seemed to be even more divided on the right policy to adopt than the Continental powers were, but that dissension was more

The announcement of the Treaty of Utrecht in the streets of The Hague ten days after it was signed.

Left top The allies meeting during the treaty negotiations to discuss peace terms.

Left above The exchange and signing of the treaty.

An engraving of the city of Utrecht produced to celebrate the signing of the Treaty on May 12, 1713.

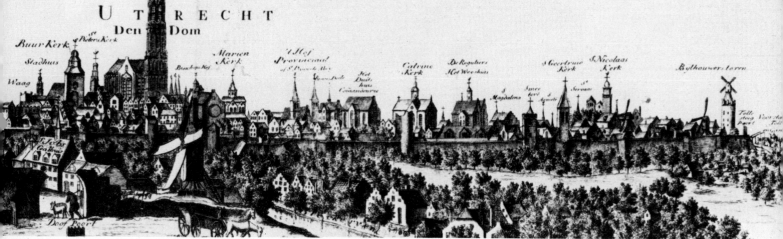

553

apparent than real. The English knew very well that the future of their country lay on the high seas rather than on the European Continent. After the middle of the century they took no further interest in European affairs, except when it was a question of weakening French naval power.

The confrontation of two opposing political views all over Europe was more striking after the Treaty of Utrecht than perhaps at any other time in modern history. On the one side were the traditionalists, who stubbornly persisted in views that very often dated back to the wars of religion. On the other side were the supporters of a new, enlightened policy whose only concern was the reality of the present. Public opinion, when it existed, was equally divided between these two currents of thought.

Cabinet decisions in the eighteenth century, although they did not neglect material interests or ancient traditions, paid little attention to the aspirations of the common people. During the War of the Spanish Succession, the Catalans had demonstrated heroic loyalty toward the Austrian pretender, mainly because they hated the centralist policy of the Castilian government. The people of the German Tyrol showed a similar loyalty toward the Hapsburgs when they were invaded by the Bavarians. Such actions were ignored during the peace talks, however. At that time, the people were still treated like herds of cattle, to be exchanged at the will and convenience of princes and kings, who did not consider the peoples' own wishes on the matter. For example, Sicily was given to the Duke of Savoy, only to be taken away from him a few years later, in exchange for Sardinia; Lorraine was given by Louis xv to his father-in-law, Stanislaus i, ex-king of Poland, as compensation for the loss of the Polish throne. There were numerous similar examples.

John Churchill, first Duke of Marlborough, whose victories over the French at Blenheim, Ramillies, Oudinarde and Malplacquet convinced Louis of his inability to join the thrones of France and Spain.

Right Blenheim Palace, designed by Vanbrugh, was given to Marlborough by a grateful nation after his victory.

A new generation of philosophers

It is worth noting, however, that one of the colleagues of the French representative at the Utrecht peace talks, Cardinal de Polignac, was the same Abbé de Saint-Pierre who published, in the very year that the Treaty was signed, his *Projet du Paix Perpétuelle*. That project was considered for many years to be nothing more than a pleasant utopian dream, a revival of the ideas expressed in the *Mémoires* of Sully. Yet by writing his book, as well as by founding, some years later, the *Club de l'Entresol*, the Cardinal was ushering in the new generation of economists and philosophers who believed that the best antidote to war was the general prosperity of the country. Their influence spread far beyond the frontiers of France and England, the most advanced countries of the day. Saint-Pierre drafted a program for "enlightened despotism" which, although it was not directly concerned with the wishes of the people, at least showed an interest in their well-being, since it encouraged the creation of greater prosperity.

Thus the Treaty of Utrecht not only put an end to a series of wars that had proved disastrous to all concerned, it also marked the opening of new perspectives that were totally alien to the spirit of domination reflected in the absolutism of Louis XIV.

JACQUES MADAULE

Above left Louis XIV, whose ambition of uniting the thrones of Spain and France was finally frustrated by the Treaty of Utrecht.

Above Louis XV taking his seat in *Parlement* for the first time, from a contemporary engraving.

Queen Anne with Knights of the Garter. Under Queen Anne's rule, and particularly as a result of the Treaty of Utrecht, Britain's colonial territories increased.

555

Corneille, whose independence was crushed by his subservience to Cardinal Richelieu.

The almost continuous wars that were fought in Europe throughout the seventeenth century did not prevent its being an age of unparalleled advancement in the development of art and in the improvement of standards of living. And although most of the countries of Europe had, at one time or another, been ranged in conflict against France, French culture had not suffered in the esteem of the civilized world.

The genius of the French dramatists of the seventeenth century was indeed undeniable. Pierre Corneille, whose early comedy *Mélite* was enthusiastically received in Paris in 1629, produced a succession of plays that included *Le Cid*, a masterly piece that marks the beginning of the greatest period in French drama, and *Le Menteur*, a comedy of remarkable originality.

For a time Corneille was one of Richelieu's "five poets" and was obliged to produce plays on themes presented to him by the Cardinal. Corneille, awkward and independent, was quite unsuited to such profitable but restricting work, and soon offended Richelieu by declining to follow his master's schemes. Jean de Rotrou, the only one of the five poets worthy of comparison with Corneille, died of the plague at the age of forty—but by then he had produced an extraordinary number of plays, of which four (*Le Véritable Saint Genest, Don Bertrand de Cabrère, Venceslas* and *Cosroès*) are acknowledged masterpieces.

While *Cosroès* was being performed in Paris, a popular theatrical company was touring the provinces. One of its number was Jean Baptiste Poquelin, whose stage name was Molière. Molière had already proved his gifts as a comic writer, but it was not until his *Précieuses Ridicules* was published in 1659 that he achieved his first real success. Kindly, overworked, anxious and painstaking, Molière was an authentic genius. A most fertile and inventive comic dramatist, he was an inspiration to successive generations of writers for the theater, none of whom were able to match his mastery as a creator of artificial comedy and of scintillating dialogue. Although suffering from serious lung disease, Molière insisted upon taking the part of the *malade imaginaire* in the seventh presentation of his play by the same name.

Jean Racine, whose earliest play, *La Thébaïde ou Les Frères ennemis*, was acted by Molière's company at the Palais-Royal in 1664, was as supreme a tragic poet as Molière was a comic dramatist. Racine retired from dramatic work at an early age, writing nothing for the stage after 1677 apart from two religious pieces for Madame de Maintenon's schoolgirls at Saint-Cyr. His best work was written between 1667—when *Andromaque* appeared—and 1677—when *Phèdre* was first presented.

While Racine was writing in France, the English theater—closed during the Commonwealth—reopened in London. It was no longer a national theater, as it had been in Shakespeare's time; indeed, until the civil war the most notable

Molière, France's leading comic dramatist, as *Le Bourgeois Gentilhomme.*

productions of the English stage were court masques—stylized, allegorical and spectacular pageants on which Ben Jonson and Inigo Jones lavished their respective talents as poet and scenic designer.

Apart from Thomas Shadwell, who was far more prolific as a comic writer than as a playwright; Thomas Otway, whose greatest work, *Venice Preserved, or a Plot Discovered*, appeared in 1682; and John Dryden—English writers for the theater in the Restoration period were more successful in comedy than in tragedy.

Racine, who despite his education among the theater-hating Jansenists, became France's greatest tragic playwright with a reputation exceeding that of his older contemporary Corneille.

Rise of the Opera

Earlier, in Italy, the first genuine operas had been performed. Jacopo Peri and Giulio Caccini had paved the way with *Dafne* and *Euridice*. Claudio Monteverdi, who spent the last thirty years of his life as director of music at St. Mark's in Venice, applied and extended the ideas of the *Nuove Musiche* (new music): his *Orfeo*, first performed at Mantua in 1607, marks an important advance, and his *Il Ritorno d'Ulisse* and *L'Incoronazione di Poppea* are further developments of the genre. Henry Purcell, who was clearly influenced by the new Italian masters, further developed the operatic form with his *Dido and Aeneas*, written in 1689.

The first opera house was opened in Venice in 1637, and others followed: the London opera opened in 1656, the Paris opera in 1669, Rome in 1671 and Hamburg in 1678. As the performances improved, so did the skill of the instrument makers. At Cremona in

northern Italy, the Amati, Guarneri and Stradavari families began making string instruments, particularly violins, of unprecedented quality.

Art on the Continent

Painters as well as musicians drew their inspiration from Italy. Dutch art in particular developed under powerful Italian influences (although with its own distinction and beauty and its own concern for detail). Not only Frans Hals and Rembrandt van Rijn, but Terborch, Pieter de Hooch, Jan Vermeer, Karel Fabritius, Jakob van Ruysdael, Aelbert Cuyp and Meindert Hobbema all belong to this astonishingly fruitful period. So do Rubens, Jordaens and Van Dyck.

Spain's artistic genius, El Greco, died in 1614, but Francisco de Herrera, Francisco Pacheco, Velasquez and Murillo continued to produce canvases until mid-century. In France, the highly individual work of the Le Nain brothers, Antoine and Louis, was as prized as the delightful work of Nicolas Poussin, Gaspard Poussin and Claude Lorrain—all of whom were French landscape painters working in Rome.

Art in England

The persecution of Protestants in the Spanish Netherlands—and the patronage accorded them at the English Court—brought many Dutch and Flemish painters to England. Daniel Mytens served as Sergeant-Painter to James I, and Cornelius Johnson held the same post under Charles I. Van Dyck and Rubens also found a valued and astute patron in Charles—and Van Dyck's English pupil, William Dobson, succeeded him as Sergeant-Painter to the King. During the Commonwealth, the only painters of note were Samuel Cooper and Peter van der Faes (better known as Peter Lely), who had come to London to follow the example of Van Dyck. After the Restoration, Lely's success at court was emulated by Godfrey Kneller, whose portraits hung on the walls of almost every great house in the country.

The most fashionable of these houses were built in the Palladian style that Inigo Jones introduced to England after a lengthy tour of

Congreve (*left*) whose comedies shocked and delighted Restoration England; and John Dryden, one of England's few successful tragic writers of his time.

Italy. (The work of the great Italian architect, Andrea Palladio, filled Jones with admiration, provoked him to open imitation, and inspired a tradition that was carried on in England by Roger Pratt.) After the Great Fire of 1666, Christopher Wren—who had already been responsible for fine work at Oxford and Cambridge—undertook to rebuild many of the City's churches and St. Paul's Cathedral.

If St. Paul's is England's great monument to the genius of the age, Versailles and the Paris of Louis XIV are monuments to the genius of the French. Jules Hardouin Mansard designed the Grand Trianon and other buildings at Versailles, the château of Marly, the Places des Victoires and the Place Vendôme. The gardens of Versailles were laid out by André Lenôtre, father of French landscape gardening.

Law's system

For all the elegance of the more fashionable parts of Paris, France at the end of the War of the Spanish Succession was on the verge of financial ruin. The country had rich resources, but its government was without credit and it could raise loans only at enormous cost. The government's financial position was such that a declaration of national bankruptcy was seriously considered.

Among the French Regent's distraught advisers was a Scotsman, John Law, who appeared entirely confident that if a proper fiscal system were adopted, the crisis could be resolved. Law, the adventurous, attractive and keenly intelligent son of an Edinburgh goldsmith, had led a dissolute youth in London and had fled to Holland in 1694 after killing a man in a duel.

Since that time he had traveled widely, studied the operations of the banks of Europe, lived by gambling and speculation, and endeavored to persuade various governments to adopt his schemes. His contention was that finance was a science, resting on fundamental principles and able to support a coherent policy. He assured the Regent that France's troubles were entirely due to past financial mismanagement, that trade depended upon money, and that the solution lay in creating a supply of money to meet its present scarcity—a supply that would never be hoarded and could never become scarce. What Law meant was that paper—or, in other words, the credit of the State—must henceforth be used for money.

Impressed by Law's confidence and ingenuity, the Regent allowed him to found a private bank with the right to issue notes. The bank was immediately successful; its notes combined the advantages of fixity of value with convenience. A decree, issued on April 10, 1717, ordered tax collectors to receive them as payment and to exchange them for coins.

Having successfully established his bank, Law was permitted to set up a commercial company, the *Compagnie de la Louisiane ou d'Occident*, for the purpose of colonizing and commercially exploiting that North American region. In December, 1718, Law's bank became *La Banque royale*. Its notes were guaranteed in the King's name and made legal tender throughout the kingdom. Branches were opened in five principal French towns. Law's company rapidly amalgamated with other companies, and under its new name, *La Compagnie des Indes*, it developed a virtual monopoly of French foreign trade. To exploit its opportunities, capital was needed—and 50,000 shares

of company stock were therefore issued at 500 *livres* each. The price of those shares rose rapidly, another issue of 50,000 shares was made, and two annual dividends of 6 per cent were promised. Speculation in the company's shares naturally increased.

Law now proposed to take over the national debt and to manage it on terms advantageous to both the government and the *Compagnie des Indes*. The Company agreed to lend the bankrupt French government 15 million *livres* at 3 per cent interest, and financial transactions involving huge sums of money followed. Immense fortunes were made as the price of the five-hundred-*livres* shares rose to 12,000 and then to 20,000 *livres*. For months the rage of speculation continued. Provincial families sold all they had and came to Paris to play the market. John Law became, in Lady Mary Wortley Montagu's words, "absolute in Paris."

In March, 1720, the title Superintendent of Finance was revived, and promptly bestowed upon the Scotsman. By that time, Law's System was already in decay. It was clear that the prosperity was artificial and that the Company could not conceivably pay the dividends expected. Men began to sell shares to invest in property and coin, the price of the shares fell and the worth of paper money depreciated. By declaring dividends as high as 40 per cent, the Scot endeavored to stimulate the circulation of the Bank's notes, but in May it was decreed that their value should be reduced by half. Confusion became panic: the police dispersed speculators in the Paris streets as the Bank, the Company and the System collapsed in ruins.

John Law's initial success in manipulating credit encouraged the launching of a similar scheme in London, one that was soon to collapse as dramatically and devastatingly as had the *Compagnie des Indes*.

John Law, France's Superintendent of Finances, who caused a financial crisis similar to England's South Sea Bubble.

DOMINE

IN TE

SPERAVI

Sarga finissima de Inglaterra
Nº de la Primera Fabrica
Con Yards

RIO DE LONDRES

S & E
S O
N

The South Sea Bubble

In January of 1720, a newly formed English trading corporation known as the South Sea Company issued stock worth £31,000,000—enough to cover England's enormous war debt, which the Company absorbed. Shares of Company stock sold at first for £128 each; by July of the same year the Company's enterprising directors had pushed the value of those shares to £1,000. Generous bribes to high government officials, coupled with equally generous loans to investors (loans that enabled those investors to reinvest their original cash outlays in subsequent issues of Company stock) fed a dangerous inflationary spiral—and led to the Company's inevitable collapse. The bursting of the "South Sea bubble" toppled the government, bankrupted countless small investors and eventually altered England's financial structure.

At nine o'clock on the evening of September 17, 1720, sixteen of the most important men in England met at the General Post Office in London. Their chairman was James Craggs, England's Postmaster General and a senior member of the government that was led by Stanhope and Sunderland. Craggs was joined by five other ministers: his son James, Secretary of State; William Aislabie, the Chancellor of the Exchequer; the Duke of Kent, who was Lord Privy Seal; and two politicians who had recently joined the ministry (following the settlement of a rift in the Whig party), Robert Walpole and Charles Townshend. The other men present were leading members of the governing bodies of the Bank of England and of the South Sea Company.

The meeting lasted six hours. Its purpose was to consider a way to stave off the impending collapse of the market in South Sea stock. From a modest 128 pounds per share—the asking price at the beginning of the year—that stock had soared to nearly 1,000 pounds per share by July of 1720. On September 1 it had sunk to 775, and on the day of the meeting it was being quoted in Exchange Alley at 520. (By the end of the year it would be back to 155.)

Much the same thing was happening that same autumn in Paris, where the elaborate financial "system" constructed by John Law had expanded to encompass the whole of the French national economy, including its currency. Indeed, the growth of the "South Sea Bubble"—as that stock's inflationary spiral was dubbed—was not an isolated incident in British economic history but rather was part of a wave of speculation that swept over Western Europe in the second decade of the eighteenth century. Its influence was felt in Portugal and Switzerland, Hamburg, Vienna and Amsterdam. Much of the dealing, in fact, was international and competitive: the canton of Berne invested in South Sea stock, and Law, speculating on a fall in price, tried to mount a "bear" operation against it by dumping thousands of shares on the market.

The South Sea Company had been founded in 1711 by Harley's Tory government, which had swept into power by promising to wind up the wars waged by Marlborough and, if possible, to dispose of the legacy of debt that had resulted from them. (The discovery that wars could be fought on credit had enabled Marlborough to finance his victorious campaigns at Blenheim and Malplaquet. It had also left the country deeply in debt.) Harley's scheme was a relatively simple one: he created an impressive-looking trading company with power to issue stock, and then invited the holders of certain government debts to exchange them for stock. In return the company received an annual payment from the Exchequer that was more or less equivalent to the interest on the debt that the company had taken over. Although the company was said to have commercial prospects, the scheme was not much more than a camouflaging of the war debt to make it more acceptable to the squires who formed an important part of Harley's majority in Parliament.

It may well have been John Law's stupendous success in manipulating French credit that encouraged the South Sea Company to launch the scheme that culminated in the extraordinary South Sea Bubble of 1720. The leading member of the group of financiers that controlled the Company was John Blunt, a blustering Baptist who had long been jealous of the financial privileges of the Bank of England. The Bank of England was traditionally Whig, and there was more than a hint of Tory reprisal in Harley's decision—based on Blunt's counsel—to create the rival South Sea Company. In any case, the mainspring of the promotion was the ambition of Blunt and his associates.

Early in 1720 the South Sea Company obtained an act of Parliament under which virtually the whole of the outstanding national debt of 31 million pounds could, at the option of the holders, be converted into South Sea stock. In theory, that act authorized the company to create one hundred pounds' worth of stock for every one hundred pounds' worth of debt that it took over. In practice, the rate

Sir Robert Walpole who gained power in England's House of Commons as a direct result of the South Sea Bubble scandal, and during his period in power created the British premiership.

Opposite The trade label of the South Sea Company.

559

A gift of seven million pounds

John Law, the Scot whose financial innovations in France led to speculation similar to that in the South Sea Company.

at which debt was exchanged for stock was left to the Company—and it was no secret, from the very beginning of the scheme, that the stock would be issued at a premium. That action would create a stock surplus (because the Company would be able to issue more shares than it needed for the exchange operation) and that surplus—said the promoters—could then be sold for the Company's benefit. The stock's promoters therefore urged debt-holders to exchange their government bonds at a rate that clearly favored the Company. They argued that such a move would actually increase the debt-holders' profits because the Company in which they had become shareholders would have more surplus stock to sell. So great was the confidence of the promoters that they undertook to make the national Exchequer an outright gift of 7 million pounds out of proceeds from the sale of surplus stock. This huge public bribe was necessary to outbid the Bank of England, for the Bank's directors, seeing their privileged position threatened, had also made proposals for taking over the national debt and converting it into Bank stock. Parliament, in fact, held a kind of auction between the two great financial institutions to decide which of them should wield the great, new and ill-understood engine of credit.

In those days the stock exchange, which revolved around Garraway's Coffee House and the little maze of lanes in which it stood, was a smallish affair and largely unregulated. There were already licensed brokers in existence, but the stocks that they quoted were limited—until the South Sea Year—to government issues and to the stocks of the East India Company, the South Sea Company, and the Bank of England and a few issues bearing the names of companies that had survived the great turn-of-the-century enthusiasm for joint stock promotion. Such companies had originally operated under charters entitling them to carry on a specified enterprise, but by 1720 almost all of them had been con-

verted into "shells"—companies that had ceased the activity for which they had been incorporated—by financial syndicates.

The triumph of the South Sea Company in the spring of 1720 had not gone unopposed in Parliament. It had been fought by a determined group of supporters of the Bank of England—notably Robert Walpole—and its path had been eased by large bribes to certain ministers and parliamentarians. Those bribes characteristically took the form of stock in the South Sea Company, nominally transferred to the legislators at market prices and actually delivered free on demand. The value of the bribes was thus, ironically, proportionate to the success of the scheme. Among those probably bribed in this fashion by Blunt and the South Sea Company's cashier, Robert Knight, were Aislabie, the Chancellor of the Exchequer; Charles Stanhope, the Secretary to the Treasury; the two Craggs; and the Earl of Sunderland who, with James Stanhope, was the government's leading minister. Through Aislabie, King George I, who was titular governor of the Company, also benefited—and so did his two mistresses, the Duchess of Kendal and the Countess of Darlington.

At first matters went well enough. The actual conversion began in May at the rate of 375 pounds' worth of debt to secure only 100 pounds' worth of stock, and large quantities of stock were then marketed at vastly inflated prices. (By August, the going rate for a block of stock purchased at 100 pounds in May had risen to the sum of 1000 pounds.) To promote additional speculation the Company interspersed its issues of stock with loans to purchasers of stock, thus constructing a kind of financial pump by which the same limited supply of cash was used over and over again to force the price of stock to ever greater heights.

The South Sea directors had never expected a boom on this scale, and they did their best to damp down competition. They even obtained an act

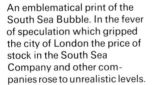

An emblematical print of the South Sea Bubble. In the fever of speculation which gripped the city of London the price of stock in the South Sea Company and other companies rose to unrealistic levels.

Change Alley where dealing in stocks and shares took place.

against unauthorized joint stock companies. (That piece of legislation, the so-called "Bubble Act," remained on the statute book until 1825 and severely restricted joint stock enterprise throughout the eighteenth century.) Their efforts were to no avail, however, and by September of 1720 it was evident to the entire English financial community that the South Sea Bubble was about to burst. Many factors contributed to the crash: the collapse of Law's financial system in France, the panic induced by the arrival of a fresh epidemic of plague, and the sudden realization that even a guaranteed dividend of fifty per cent—which the Company's desperate directors promised their stockholders in August—gave the stockholder who had bought at one thousand only five per cent on his money. But the chief reason for the slump was that a mountain of short-term credit had been extended during the preceding months of intense speculation—and that credit could not be supported by those who had incurred it.

This was the problem that Craggs and the group at the Post Office confronted on the evening of September 17, 1720. They were unable to solve it, and by the end of the year trade was virtually at a standstill and there was widespread unemployment. A parliamentary inquiry was set in motion and it soon began to dredge up the murky story of the passage of the South Sea Act. Blunt became a willing witness against his fellow directors but not before his colleague Knight—of whom the Committee "found it proper to observe that it has appeared to them, throughout their examination, that Mr. Knight, the cashier of the South Sea Company, was principally concerned in their most secret transactions"—was able to abscond to the Netherlands.

During the spring of 1721 the ministry evaporated in a cloud of death and disgrace: Postmaster General Craggs committed suicide; his son, the Secretary of State, died of smallpox: Stanhope, the Prime Minister, burst a blood vessel while defending his government in the House of Lords; and Aislabie, the Chancellor, was expelled from the House of Commons.

The country was in an uproar. "They are *Rogues of Prey*, they are *Stock Jobbers*, they are a *conspiracy of Stock Jobbers*, a name which carries along with it such a detestable deadly image, that it exceeds all humane

A satirical "bubble card" showing "headlong fools" plunging into frenzied investment and eventually into the water.

The House of Commons in
George I's reign, by
Tillemans; a number of
members of the House were
involved in the South
Sea Company.

Sir James Craggs, Postmaster
General, who kept the House
informed of developments
during the crisis.

invention to aggravate it," screeched one anony-mous publicist, the author of *Cato's Letters*. Soothing that tempest, which had destroyed the government and shaken the Hanoverian settlement itself, was Robert Walpole's supreme achievement. Walpole, who succeeded to the perilous office of First Lord of the Treasury upon the resignation of Sunderland in April, 1721, confronted, opposed and finally defeated the "party of revenge" during the next three months.

The Age of Walpole—and of the Pelhams after him—is one of the longest periods of political and economic stability in British history, an era that witnessed the establishing of certain traditions that have survived to this day. The consolidation of power in the House of Commons, the heritage of mistrust of overt collaboration between government and busi-ness, and the concept of the importance of a basic continuity in affairs of state—all date from the long period of calm that succeeded the shock of the South Sea Year. So too does the enduring domination of the country's finances by the Bank of England. Sir Gilbert Heathcote, speaking for the Bank at the Post Office meeting, made it a condition of the Bank's collaboration that in the future the South Sea Com-pany's account should be kept by the Bank of England and by no one else. The Bank and the Treasury justified the confidence they demanded. British public finance, from Walpole's time, became the best managed and the soundest in Europe, and its techniques steadily improved. The fact is of incalculable importance for the history of the next 250 years.

Walpole achieved domestic stability not through the offices of the Bank of England but by falling back on the landowners, and their interests and prejudices

were to remain uppermost in the minds of British politicians for the next hundred years. It is true that British commerce continued to grow, that London supplanted Amsterdam as the financial capital of Europe, that business families made marriages with the landed gentry and that the importance of trade to the country was everywhere lauded, but business in England never achieved equality of respect with landed wealth. A landed estate remained the ideal security for an Englishman. The former great com-mercial powers—Florence, Venice, Amsterdam—had been dominated by merchant princes; England lacked them, even in the period of her greatest com-mercial power.

England's social structure hardened during this period. The absurd inequities of the unreformed House of Commons—to which members were re-turned on the decision of a single magnate or a tiny caucus of electors—were perpetuated by a series of eighteenth-century decisions concerning the right to vote and the respect paid to landed property. The "Venetian oligarchy" denounced by Disraeli, the system of patronage by which progress in life depen-ded primarily on influence, and the deep conserva-tism that allowed almost no change in social or constitutional law between 1720 and 1780—all these are marks of this remarkable era of stability. Its saving grace was that it was a diffused not a central-ized stability. The rights of individuals and, above all, the rights of corporate bodies—be they local authorities, colleges, charities, or guilds—are the stuff and tissue of eighteenth-century English society.

To some extent the period following the South Sea Year can be called stagnant as well as stable. It contrasts vividly with the preceding thirty years, during which the enduring outline of the British con-stitutional settlement had been established. The conquest of Ireland, the union with Scotland, the Hanoverian succession, the supremacy of Parliament and the shape of ministerial government were all achieved in the generation following the Revolution of 1688. It was a period of greatness and promise, not only in politics but in economics, science, and letters. It was an age of new vitality that accompanied Britain's emergence as a great European power. The tendency, unquestionably, was toward political stability, but in another sense the chaotic South Sea Year was a culmination of effervescence.

The succeeding years fell short of the promise of the first twenty of the century. Except in the field of agriculture, technology was slow to find application, despite the earlier progress of scientific theory. For reasons which have never been satisfactorily ex-plained, even the rate of growth of the population decelerated until about 1740, when it resumed a sharper upward trend. It is not unreasonable to attribute some of this slowing down of progress to the recollection of the almost insane burst of optimism which had ended in the disaster of 1720.

That disaster can perhaps best be explained as the impact of new, barely understood financial techniques upon an economy that was still predomi-nantly agricultural. It was in part the penalty that

A system in need of reform

THE BRABANT SKREEN

The Brabant Screen, a satirical print of 1721: on the right behind the screen three directors of the company are hiding, on the left the South Sea Company Treasurer, Knight, receives a letter from a royal favorite, authorizing him to flee to the Low Countries. The pictures on the screen attack the morality of the directors and the Treasurer. It was thought at the time that royal patronage was used to hush up the crisis, as members of the royal family were involved in the Company and its ruin.

Old Custom House Quay in London during the 1720s: the immense expansion of trade that accompanied the growth of Britain's foreign empire was one of the factors that caused the South Sea Bubble.

England paid for becoming the first nation-state to assume the commercial leadership of Europe. The later period of comparative stagnation—the age of Walpole and the Pelhams—can be seen as one in which the new nation-state, still led by its landed gentry, gradually assimilated its new role in Europe and the world.

The contrast between the aftermaths of the speculation in London and Paris is not insignificant. In Paris, an effort was made to wipe away the memory of Law and his system, and huge piles of paper—representing the era of credit—were publicly burned. Law's real success—for he had succeeded, during his five years of power, in revitalizing the French economy as well as inflating the currency—was lost in an almost religious revulsion for high finance that swept the country. France settled down to a long period of backward-looking despotism that was relieved only by her native sons' essentially critical intellectual brilliance. In England, where many had been ruined (and more cheated of wholly imaginary gains) and an extensive reconstruction of the South Sea Company had been necessary, there was no bankruptcy. In the end, the Company's obligations to its shareholders were honored and South Sea annuities remained a feature of the British national debt until Gladstone abolished them upon becoming Chancellor in 1854. The period of stagnation that followed the slump was an age of digestion rather than decay. The commercial and constitutional vitality of the early years of the century was checked, but not destroyed. JOHN CARSWELL

Europe after Louis XIV

When the South Sea Bubble burst, Louis XIV had been dead for five years and his nephew, Philip, Duke of Orleans, was ruling as Regent for Louis' five-year-old great-grandson. In defiance of the Treaty of Utrecht, Philip V of Spain—first of the Bourbon kings and Louis XIV's grandson—had also claimed the regency, but with the help of England and Holland, which had sworn to guarantee the Utrecht treaty, the Duke had thwarted Philip's designs. Undaunted, Philip invaded Sardinia and Sicily in 1717 at the insistence of his wife, Elizabeth Farnese, who wanted a secure inheritance for her sons. His provocative act led to the Quadruple Alliance of Austria, England, France and Holland—and when a French army crossed the Pyrenees and an English fleet under Admiral George Byng destroyed the Spanish fleet off Messina, Philip was forced to make peace and to renounce his claims to the former Spanish possessions in Italy.

Philip's ambitions were further thwarted when Louis XV—who came of age in 1723—rejected the hand of his Spanish cousin, the Infanta, and married Maria Lezczynska, daughter of the former King of Poland. Delegating responsibility for most of the country's affairs to Cardinal André Hercule de Fleury, Louis devoted himself to hunting and to a succession of mistresses, of whom Madame de Pompadour, the dominant figure at Versailles for almost twenty years, was by far the most remarkable.

The year before Louis XV ascended to his great-grandfather's throne, Queen Anne, daughter of James II and the last of the Stuart monarchs, died. Not one of her numerous children had survived, and the crown passed to James I's great-grandson, the Elector of Hanover, who was crowned King George I of Great Britain and Ireland according to the Act of Settlement of 1701. During the reign of George I, the policy of the British government was dominated by the necessity of maintaining the Elector's family on the throne. As a result, the Whig oligarchy became entrenched in power and those Tory squires who might otherwise have supported a restoration of the

Voltaire, the embodiment of the Enlightenment.

ment, arrived in England during Walpole's premiership in 1726 and was profoundly impressed by what he saw. Voltaire was thirty-one at the time, and he had already achieved notoriety in France as a poet and dramatist—and as a satirist who had been banished from court and eventually imprisoned for lampooning the Regent. He had been forced to seek refuge in England after rashly challenging the Chevalier de Rohan-Chabot to a duel, and he arrived bitterly indignant at the tyranny and injustice he had left behind him in France.

The French government that Voltaire railed against had failed to impose an equitable system of taxation—and in an effort to win the support of various sections of the community, exemptions had been granted to whole classes of the

Stuarts were kept occupied in local affairs.

The government's success in maintaining domestic tranquility and in restoring confidence after the South Sea panic owed much to Sir Robert Walpole. As leader of the administration from 1721 to 1742, Walpole established the system by which England has since been governed, a system that made the Cabinet collectively responsible for the government's policy and established the supremacy of the First Lord of the Treasury as Prime Minister in both Cabinet and the House of Commons. The Cabinet—a group of ministers who were all members of Parliament, dependent upon the favor of Parliament and collectively answerable to Parliament for their actions—had not been envisaged in the Revolution Settlement of 1689. Nor had the office of Prime Minister. But under Walpole both Cabinet and Prime Minister evolved and developed in answer to the country's needs. There was no written constitution; nor, apparently, was there a need for one.

Voltaire and Montesquieu

Walpole's system of government aroused deep admiration among foreign observers of the time. Voltaire, who came to be recognized as the very embodiment of the eighteenth-century Enlighten-

Montesquieu: full of praise for England's liberal political system.

people. Not only the nobles and the clergy, but a large proportion of the middle classes had been exempted from the *taille*, or property tax, and entire provinces had been granted other forms of relief. Even worse, the French government appeared totally incapable of reforming that system.

Upon Louis XIV's death, the *Parlement* of Paris was restored to its former authority, but its members (and those of the twelve Provincial *Parlements*) were blind to the need for reform and totally opposed to any proposal that might lead to it. A more representative legislative assembly, elected by the people and responsible to them, was so out of keeping with French tradition that the idea was never even proposed with any sort of conviction. And even those writers who had found cause to criticize the autocracy during the later

Sir Robert Walpole talking to the Speaker in the English House of Commons.

years of the King's reign suggested a return to ancient methods of government rather than a progression to new ones.

To Voltaire, the Englishman's freedom seemed so refreshing as to be an inspiration. In England the press was free, there was a measure of religious toleration inconceivable in France, and there was parliamentary government. Torture, arbitrary imprisonment and arbitrary taxes were evils of the past. The Frenchman's *Lettres sur les Anglais*, a work that increased the disfavor in which Voltaire was held at the French court, provided his countrymen with a glimpse of a society that was much more fortunate than their own.

Charles de Secondat, Baron de la Brede et de Montesquieu, whose *Lettres persanes* was a biting satire of French society, arrived in England in 1729 to study political and social institutions. His verdict was every bit as favorable as Voltaire's had been. "It was the freest country in the world," he decided. "I make exception of no republic. And I call it free because the sovereign, whose authority is controlled and limited, is unable to inflict any imaginable harm on anyone."

Locke on liberty

Both Montesquieu and Voltaire studied the writings of John Locke, the founder of philosophical liberalism. Locke's ideas had deeply influenced the course of the English revolution and his works had provided the eighteenth century with its most worthwhile and durable analysis of the intellectual revolution of the seventeenth. His *Letters on Toleration* defended religious liberty; his *Treatises on Government* upheld political liberty; and his *Essay Concerning Human Understanding* insisted upon intellectual liberty.

For all the enthusiasm that the English constitution aroused in foreign observers, however, it had far more serious defects than they were willing to recognize. For one thing, religious toleration was severely limited: nonconformist dissenters were excluded from both Parliament and the universities of Oxford and Cambridge, and until 1779 Roman Catholics were forbidden to practice their religion in public. For another, the government of England was still an aristocracy, and that aristocracy

The Battle of Culloden at which "the Butcher" Duke of Cumberland, with his redcoats shattered the hopes of the Jacobites.

controlled Parliament. Many of the members held their seats through family influences and bribery, and under their rule social injustices continued unchecked. Moreover, although it was often mitigated in practice, the penal code was ferocious. There was

The entrance to Newgate Prison, London. Despite England's reputation for liberty, more crimes were punishable by death than in any other European country.

scarcely another country in Europe where so many crimes were punishable by death—and the number of capital statutes was increasing. Thirty-three new capital offenses were created in the reign of George II alone—or roughly one for every year of the monarch's reign.

Yet despite the miseries of the unheeded and largely unseen poor, England was a happy country. The Industrial Revolution had not yet brought the tragic problems of the dark, satanic mills to the north, there were few slums in the small towns, and farmers prospered. In the provinces, the power of the Tory squire to govern the life of his tenants and dependents went unquestioned. All in all, life in early Georgian England was stable, placid and self-satisfied. In 1715 and again in 1745, the Jacobites, supporters of the exiled Stuart kings, attempted to overthrow the House of Hanover, but they failed to arouse the English people, who refused to imperil the safe, Protestant monarchy by rallying to the cause of a romantic pretender. At Culloden, on April 16, 1746, Jacobite hopes were dispelled forever by the army of William Augustus,

Duke of Cumberland, the second son of George II. By 1765, Horace Walpole could write that Jacobitism was extinct.

By the middle of the eighteenth century, English optimism was shared by the political writers of France. For all their burning anticlericalism and lost faith in the doctrines of the Church, French intellectuals had not lost their faith in the dignity of man. Man was innately good—and good legislators could make him infinitely better. He could also be made better, and his environment improved, by increasing his knowledge—and it was with a view to increasing man's knowledge that Denis Diderot set about the task of compiling his great *Encyclopédie* in 1741. "The aim of an encyclopedia," as he put it, "is to assemble the knowledge scattered over the face of the earth; to explain its general plan to the men with whom we live, and to transmit it to those who will come after us, so that the labors of past centuries may not be useless to future times; so that our descendants, by becoming better informed, may in consequence be happier and more virtuous . . ."

An Encyclopedia for the Enlightenment

The task assigned to Denis Diderot in 1742 by a consortium of leading Parisian publishers was a relatively simple one: to translate Quaker Ephraim Chambers' single-volume Cyclopedia *into French. Diderot's immediate, ambitious revision of his employers' assignment led to the publication of a thirty-five volume* Encyclopedie *that both summarized and exemplified the Age of Enlightenment. The process took twenty-five years and was conducted semiclandestinely, without the approval of government censors. The series, which was suppressed by the State Council and expressly condemned by the Church, numbered among its contributors the greatest names of the Age of Reason: Rousseau and Voltaire, Quesnay and D'Alembert. The encyclopedia's influence on the courts, councils, and cognoscente of Europe was profound. In France itself, Diderot's work was quoted at court to settle arguments—and was quoted elsewhere, by opponents of the King, to stir a revolution.*

Many of Diderot's friends wrote articles for his encyclopedia: Rousseau for example wrote on music.

Opposite Diderot, who developed the original idea of a translation of Chamber's *Cyclopedia* into French.

Soon after the publication of Diderot's *Encyclopédie*, a book of pirated selections was advertised as containing "the most interesting, the most pleasant, the most piquant, the most philosophical articles of the Great Dictionary," intended to attract all kinds of readers, "and in particular men of the world." The advertisment indicates something about the reading public of the *Encyclopédie*. Men of the world, including the crowned heads of many countries, did indeed have the volumes in their libraries. The Sultan in Constantinople instructed his engineers to make use of the illustrative plates to improve his gun foundry, and learned people all over Europe used the articles to better their knowledge and to write refutations. Army officers, lawyers, economists and clergymen are found on the various lists of subscribers. No other book has had such a dramatic impact on so widespread and influential an audience.

The great French *Encyclopédie* of Denis Diderot and Jean Le Rond d'Alembert is a landmark in the story of the human mind. It is a whole library, and its long list of contributors includes the most famous names of the age. The entire French literature of the eighteenth century is represented in these volumes—not only belles lettres, but also writings on philosophy, natural history, economics, politics and many other subjects. What is still more important, all the contributors were united in the task of creating a new and revolutionary way of thinking, in contrast to the still dominant traditions of the Church in politics and nearly all ways of life. New light was to be shed, and the term "Enlightenment" became the watchword for the whole epoch. The *Encyclopédie* was not the sole instrument of that great movement, but it was by far the most powerful and decisive vehicle.

The war on tradition had begun in the seventeenth century, when scientists and philosophers began attacking what for centuries had been the traditional patterns of European civilization: a divine monarchy; a privileged Church and hereditary aristocracy; a formally maintained, stratified social hierarchy; a legal system that favored the group rather than the individual; and decentralized state government that accounted for considerable local variety and regional autonomy. Both religion and the social order had been accepted on faith, unchallenged.

In addition, the seventeenth century saw new scientific discoveries—particularly Isaac Newton's investigations of motion—bring about startling changes in thought. Newton's investigations and the thinking of Descartes, Francis Bacon and John Locke helped develop a belief in natural law and a universal order. Most important, they developed the confidence that human reason, using the scientific method, could discover truth. Skepticism replaced blind faith, all the old orthodoxies were questioned, and the belief in change and progress replaced the commitment to stability. Nature, the new rationalists believed, was mechanical, ordered and subject to unvarying laws; man, through the use of reason, could discover these laws. Progress and perfection were possible on earth.

By the eighteenth century the Enlightenment—or the Age of Reason, as it has been called—was in full swing. The new ideas had by then become widely disseminated, popularized by the *philosophes*, who addressed themselves to the general public. Those *philosophes* were the men who contributed to the book that became the bible of the Enlightenment, Diderot's *Encyclopédie*. That great work epitomized the rationalism and skepticism of the age, recording scientific achievements, the advance of industrial technology and the reorientation of thoughts. Its

Button making, a typical illustration from the *Encyclopédie* which dealt with practical matters as well as ideas. The first volume of plates was published a year after the first volume of the *Encyclopédie* itself.

point of view was that of the most enlightened, and it challenged sacred and hitherto impregnable institutions. Typical of its attacks was this veiled comment on the French monarchy: "A sovereign, absolute though he may be, has no right to touch the established law of a state, no more than its religion....He is, besides, always obliged to follow the laws of justice and reason."

D'Alembert, in his now famous introductory essay, the "*Discours Préliminaire*," gave full recognition to

The many faces of Voltaire: uncrowned king of the Encyclopedists.

the debt the *philosophes*, or Encyclopedists, owed to their predecessors. He began with Francis Bacon, "born still in the deepest darkness" of the Middle Ages, the first who had broken the chains of scholasticism and metaphysical speculation and had placed empiricism firmly on the map. Empiricism was indeed the watchword of the Encyclopedists. It meant to explore not only the mind but all branches of knowledge and human activities: the arts, geography, zoology, botany, economics, agriculture, chemistry, architecture—even grammar and semantics. The *Encyclopédie* was truly universal, at least in its aims.

The beginnings had been very modest. Originally no more was intended than the French translation of the Quaker Ephraim Chambers' *Cyclopedia*, which had been published some decades before in London and had since been reprinted in several editions. A one-man work with modest aims and much useful information, it had shown that a public existed for this kind of dictionary. A small consortium of leading Paris publishers decided on a French edition and hired as editor Denis Diderot, who had already made himself known to the publishers as a translator of other English reference books and an author of books on mathematical problems, natural history and like subjects. Diderot at once changed the publishers' plan completely—substituting the very ambitious scheme that became the foundation of the *Encyclopédie*, and, in fact, the model for all future encyclopedias. A prospectus was printed, approved by the censor, and distributed. The response from the public was highly satisfactory, and the first virulent critics were shrugged off.

The main task for Diderot, as for any editor of an undertaking of that scope, was to find collaborators. D'Alembert, a leading mathematician who had been internationally honored with memberships in many academies, was willing to take over the section on mathematics besides contributing articles on other subjects. Other friends joined the venture: Jean Jacques Rousseau would be the author of articles on music; Baron Paul Henri Holbach would contribute articles on mining and geology; Voltaire promised his collaboration and delivered a few articles. Dr. François Quesnay, the court physician, wrote on economics, his private hobby. Quesnay proved to be one of the most valuable members of the team; his name now figures in all textbooks on the history of economics as the influential forerunner of Adam Smith.

But the *Encyclopédie* was by no means a mere repository. It was highly original in many places, and it paved the way for further development—not only in political and religious thinking but in such seemingly modest fields as veterinary science (then in its infancy and most important for a predominantly agricultural country). Almost no subject was overlooked. Articles in the form of "letters to the editor" came in as the work progressed, and they were gratefully accepted. An anonymous lady even provided highly professional information about frills and ribbons. Diderot, son of a master cutler and deeply interested in all arts and crafts, provided an article on stockings and the method of knitting them using improved machinery.

In 1751 a first volume appeared in Paris under the title *Encyclopédie, ou Dictionnaire Raisonné des Sciences, des Arts et des Métiers*. It was in folio format, printed in double columns and comprising nearly a thousand pages. The title page mentioned Diderot as the general editor and d'Alembert as responsible for the mathematical entries. The volume carried on the title page the official line of approval by the censor: "*Avec Privilège du Roi.*" Another volume—well received by the public and fiercely criticized by powerful representatives of the Church and tradition—followed shortly. Then the first battle was lost: the censor intervened, permission was withdrawn

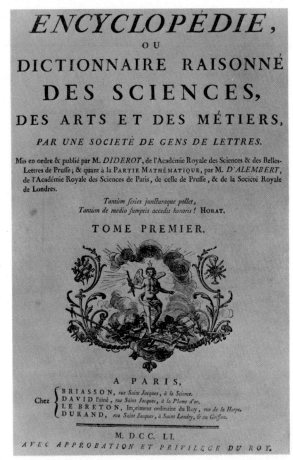

The title page of the first edition of the *Encyclopédie*, published in 1751.

Above The French dramatist Beaumarchais.

Voltaire presiding at a philosophical dinner: others present include d'Alembert, Diderot and Condorcet. The Encyclopedists were regarded by their enemies as a group of dangerous conspirators.

D'Alembert, by Quentin de la Tour. D'Alembert shared the editorial work for the *Encyclopédie* with Diderot.

A copy of the *Encyclopédie* lying on the table of Madame de Pompadour, whose benevolent neutrality helped the Encyclopedists: by de la Tour.

and the entire work was banned under order of the King.

Half a year later, however, the great work was continued, although without official permission and on sufferance, because the chief censor and director of all publications, Chrétien de Malesherbes, sympathized in secret with the undertaking. And so the next five volumes came out. The number of subscribers reached four thousand, a colossal figure for the time, especially taking into account the very high price of subscription.

In 1757 the next battle was joined—and it ended in near catastrophe for the editors. The attorney general denounced the work as dangerous and subversive from the point of view of religion as well as of politics and morals. The State Council gave the order for suppression. Worse still, some of the most important contributors deserted. D'Alembert resigned as joint editor. Jean Jacques Rousseau, who as a friend of Diderot had contributed numerous articles, attacked his former comrades-in-arms in public. The faithful band who had carried the great undertaking to such a spectacular success broke up and was scattered.

Diderot alone remained at his post and decided to continue. Many well-wishers advised him to transfer the *Encyclopédie* to some safer place, such as Berlin or

St. Petersburg, since both Frederick the Great of Prussia and Catherine the Great of Russia had taken considerable interest in the work and sympathized with its views. But Diderot stuck to Paris and his contract with the original publishers. Under his editorship, the final ten volumes of text were completed and printed in Paris. On the title page, however, Diderot's name was replaced by an anonymous "Mr.——"; an obscure firm in the possession of the King of Prussia was listed as printer.

When the final set of volumes came out, Diderot discovered that the publisher, Le Breton, had secretly employed a censor of his own who had eliminated many lines and paragraphs that seemed too dangerous. Le Breton had also taken the precaution of destroying the manuscripts and the corrected proof sheets. Diderot could do nothing but rage and curse. Nonetheless, because he wanted to see his work finished, he began editing a further set of eleven volumes containing engraved illustrations of the industrial arts. Those finely engraved plates, covering the whole field of technical development known at the time, served not only to inform the reader but also to instruct and encourage owners of factories to introduce new methods.

In 1772, after twenty-five years of almost uninterrupted effort, the *Encyclopédie* was finished. Several volumes of supplements and plates followed, and in the end the whole work comprised thirty-five large folios and filled a fairly substantial bookcase. But Diderot refused to work on the supplements or on new editions. In fact he published no more books. The great dialogues and novels of his later years were published only after his death

The fact that Diderot's *Encyclopédie* was published

The benevolent neutrality of Mme. de Pompadour

in spite of solemn public condemnation by the Church and the highest legal authorities and an official ban by the State Council was puzzling to his contemporaries, especially to the enemies of the great undertaking. One explanation for the work's successful appearance is suggested by an anecdote: One day, it was said, a discussion about powder making was going on in the salon of the Marquise de Pompadour, the King's all-powerful favorite. Since nobody knew anything of the process, some well-wisher of the *Encyclopédie* produced the appropriate volume, which had a full and highly instructive article on the topic. The text was read out and generally applauded. There was general consensus that so useful a book should not be banned but should be in the hands of anybody interested in information. The King, the indolent Louis XV, agreed, although he did not see fit to lift the official order. According to another version, the article dealt not with the making of face powder, Madame de Pompadour's sphere of interest, but with the fabrication of gunpowder, which appealed to the King, a great hunter. The story, although apocryphal, is significant: the practical usefulness of the work was certainly directly related to its success—and to the limited tolerance accorded its distribution.

The Marquise de Pompadour's actual role in protecting the publication remains rather obscure. It may be best described as "benevolent neutrality." Yet even that attitude—when held by the de facto ruler of the country—was invaluable. In one of her portraits, painted by La Tour, the Marquise saw to it that among numerous objects displayed on a table to attest to her cultural interests and gifts was a volume of the *Encyclopédie*.

Another and far more powerful influence was the fact that the battle against the *Encyclopédie* took place at the same time as the great campaign against the Jesuit order. Waged by the main Roman Catholic countries—Portugal at first, then Spain and France —it culminated in the final suppression of the Society of Jesus by the Pope. After the ban on the first two volumes of the *Encyclopédie*, there had been elements at work to seize the papers and continue the work under the supervision of the order. The chief censor, Malesherbes, prevented this intrigue by taking the papers into his personal custody and returning them after some time to Diderot. Six years later, when the *Encyclopédie*'s continuation appeared almost hopeless, the Society of Jesus suffered an equally heavy blow: all activity of the order and its members was forbidden in France. The most active adversaries of the Encyclopedists were thereby eliminated from the scene.

Enemies remained, however: churchmen, satirists, defenders of the holy rights of absolute monarchy and the traditional moral standards (although the actual morals of the time, as everybody had to admit, did not exactly conform to the time-honored precepts that were being preached). The fight continued long after the publication of the original edition and finally merged with the ferment of the French Revolution. The *Encyclopédie* has often been described as

Experience Areostatique faite a Versailles le 19 Sept.bre 1783 en presence de leurs Majestes et de la famille Royale par Mr. de Montgolfier avec un Balon de 52 pieds d'hauteur sur 41 de Diamettres. Cette Superbe machine a fond d'asur avec le Chiffre du Roi pesant 900 livres. Ce balon a ete enlevé avec toutes l'applaudissement de tout les Spectateurs et a tombé dans le Bois de Vaucreßon

one of the dominant intellectual influences paving the way to that great event.

The Encyclopedists were widely regarded as a faithful band of brothers or suspected as a sect, or a church of their own, or a dangerous underground conspiracy. But they were by no means as united a movement as they appeared later. They had their personal squabbles, enmities and ambitions. Voltaire, as the uncrowned king of this movement, sent out exhortations and quasi-military instructions from his safe, strategically located stronghold on the border between France and Switzerland: "Form a square, gentlemen! Unity, O brethren!" However, he could not offer much more than praise for Diderot's work and diligence, although he did advise him to transfer the whole undertaking to a safer place, in Switzerland or perhaps Berlin, when the position in Paris seemed hopeless.

Yet history's view of the Encyclopedists as a movement of the greatest consequence is justified. The work came at the right time and it found the right people as collaborators. The names of the antagonists are rightly forgotten and can be found only in very detailed historical surveys of contemporary pamphlets, skits or dramatic productions of the most ephemeral kind. The Church was very poorly served; the monarchy and all traditional powers fared even worse. Half a century later, writers of caliber and standing—members of the generations that had gone through the school of the Encyclopedists— appeared in defense of traditional values. The half-century that preceded them belonged to the *Encyclopédie* and its friends.

RICHARD FRIEDENTHAL

Montgolfier's balloon: the publication of the *Encyclopédie* coincided with scientific advances in aviation and electronics.

Malesherbes, the writer and lawyer who, as Chief Censor, confiscated Diderot's papers.

The upbringing of Frederick the Great

The French *philosophes* revered no monarch in Europe as highly as Frederick II, King of Prussia. Jean Le Rond d'Alembert, the philosopher and mathematician who contributed numerous articles to Diderot's *Encyclopédie* and edited part of it, wrote that Frederick was "a prince greater even than his fame, a hero at once *philosophe* and modest, a king worthy of friendship, in fact a true sage on the throne."

Frederick, the first son of Frederick William I, was born in

Frederick the Great under whose enlightened despotism Prussia developed into Germany's leading state.

January, 1712. The child's father was a harsh, narrow, boorish man whose eccentricities verged on insanity and whose tastes for order, regularity and the military life were reflected not only in the government of his country but in the architecture of his capital. Determined that his son should be a hardy, practical soldier, Frederick William devised a system of education for him that excluded from its curriculum all studies that he considered peripheral to that goal. And when his son displayed a keen interest in learning those very subjects that had been specifically denied him, the King looked upon the boy as an idle wastrel whose character must be molded by stronger and stronger discipline.

Frederick William's disappointment in his son soon turned to dislike—and then to positive hatred. The King did not trouble to hide his enmity, which he frequently voiced in public. He customarily referred to his offspring with contemptuous disdain—and

before the boy was twenty he had decided to run away and to seek protection at the English court. The plan was discovered, and a young friend who had been implicated in it was condemned to death. The execution took place outside Frederick's window, and Frederick William—who conceived that the experience might awaken his son's sense of responsibility—forced young Frederick to watch.

"The whole town shall be his prison," the King wrote after the execution, upon learning that his son had promised not to disobey his commands in the future. "I will give him employment from morning till night in the departments of war and agriculture and of the Government. He shall work at financial matters, receive accounts, read minutes and make extracts.... But if he kicks or rears again, he shall forfeit the succession to the crown, and even, according to circumstances, life itself."

His future thus threatened, Frederick devoted himself to his duties with so much conscientious application and such marked talent that his father's attitude toward him began to change. The young prince's interest in poetry and philosophy and his correspondence with Voltaire were not likely to arouse Frederick William I's unqualified approval, but the practical mind that Frederick brought to the business of government assured the King that he did indeed have an heir of whom he need not feel ashamed.

Frederick comes of age

For his part, Frederick recognized that his father—whom many dismissed as a violent martinet—was in fact a dutiful, economical sovereign who had done much good for his country. Indeed, Frederick William had provided Prussia with an adequate treasury, sound schools, a strictly organized system of taxation and a large and well disciplined army.

"Prussia's entire government was militarized," Frederick wrote. "The capital became the stronghold of Mars. All the industries which served the needs of armies prospered. In Berlin were established powder mills and cannon foundries, rifle factories, etc.... The military character of the Government affected both customs and fashions. Society took a military turn." After he succeeded to

Empress Maria Teresa; the Pragmatic Sanction failed to secure the succession for her.

the throne of Prussia in 1740, Frederick had good cause to thank his father for the strong army and sound finances that Frederick William had bequeathed him.

In truth, Frederick William I was not solely responsible for that legacy. Prussia had begun its climb to power in Europe in the seventeenth century under Frederick William, the Great Elector of Brandenburg and Duke of Prussia, whose efficiency in the government of his possessions was celebrated all over Europe. The Elector's son, Frederick I, obtained the Emperor's permission to adopt the title of King of Prussia, and he placed the Prussian crown on his own head in the cathedral at Königsberg in January, 1701. At that time the territories governed by the royal House of Hohenzollern were all but separate entities: Brandenburg, where Frederick's forebears had been established since 1417, lay at the center and had its capital at Berlin; to the east was Prussia, which had been won by Brandenburg in 1660; to the west, beyond

the Elbe, were the isolated duchies of Cleves, Mark and Ravensburg.

It was young King Frederick II's determination to unite and extend those hereditary possessions, and thereby to make Prussia a mighty force in European affairs. His first opportunity came within five months of his accession when, on October 20, 1740, Emperor Charles VI died without a male heir. By a document known as the Pragmatic Sanction, all the leading European powers except Bavaria had agreed to recognize the right of Charles' daughter, Maria Theresa, Queen of Hungary, to succeed him. When the time came, however, Maria Theresa's army was weak and her treasury impoverished. She was in no position to enforce the recognition of her rights if good faith were lacking and chivalry were shown to be dead.

Silesia and the Sanction

Frederick II was the first to act: in late autumn of 1740 he invaded Silesia. The Hohenzollerns' claim to Silesia was a weak one, and Frederick himself confessed that his invasion was merely "a means of acquiring reputation and of increasing the power of the state." After some initial setbacks, he was entirely successful: his armies defeated the Austrians at Mollwitz in the spring of 1741, and after further Prussian victories at Chotusitz, Hohenfriedberg, Soor, Hennersdorf and Kesseldorf, Maria Theresa was forced to concede the rich territories of Silesia—and a million German subjects—to Prussia.

Frederick, still in his early thirties, now set about the task of

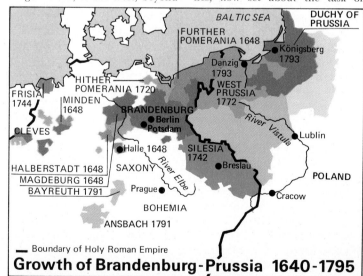

Growth of Brandenburg-Prussia 1640-1795

building Prussia into a powerful and respected state, economically stable and militarily strong. His formidable talents in many fields earned him envy as well as admiration, while his caustic wit—which was frequently directed at the leading women of Europe, the Empress Elizabeth of Russia, Madame de Pompadour and Maria Theresa—earned him their undying detestation. "The King of Prussia," the Hanoverian King of England declared, voicing a popular opinion, "is a mischievous rascal, a bad friend, a bad ally, a bad relation, and a bad neighbor, in fact the most dangerous and ill-disposed Prince in Europe."

Because so many European rulers agreed with the English King, Maria Theresa experienced little difficulty in organizing a coalition of states to crush the Prussian upstart—a coalition that Russia, France and Saxony all willingly joined. Learning (through the treachery of a clerk in the Saxon Foreign Office) of the clandestine measures that were being taken to destroy him, Frederick attempted to forestall his enemies by advancing to the attack himself. In the summer of 1756 he marched into Saxony at the head of his army, provoking the outbreak of the Seven Years' War. In that war, Prussia found herself surrounded by enemies: France (in unnatural alliance with Austria), Russia, Saxony and Sweden. Frederick found one useful ally in England, where William Pitt—recognizing the importance of Prussia in England's challenge to France—subsidized Frederick's army and supported his one powerful ally on the Continent, the Duke of Brunswick.

Fortunes of war

The war in Europe remained Frederick's responsibility nonetheless, and the loneliness and weight of that responsibility all but overwhelmed him. There were times when it seemed that nothing could save him from crushing defeat. After victories in Saxony and Bohemia, he was driven from the field by the Austrians at Kolin, and as his enemies moved in to what seemed the certain kill, he contemplated suicide. But within weeks he and his forces had rallied, and at Rossbach, in November, 1757, he surprised and overwhelmed a French army led by the

A satire on the Treaty of Paris, 1763, which ended the Seven Years' War.

Frederick meeting the Emperor Joseph II in 1760: the two men, despite their hostility, admired each other.

Prince de Soubise. A month later Frederick's army—weak in numbers and tired out by its long campaigning—achieved an equally stunning victory over the Austrians at Leuthen.

Leaving Ferdinand of Brunswick to keep the French occupied in the west, Frederick then turned upon the Russians, whom he defeated at Zorndorf. He was less fortunate

against the Austrians at Hochkirch, and he fared so badly against the combined armies of the Russians and Austrians at Kunersdorf in August, 1759, that he became as gloomy and disheartened as he had been two years before. "All is lost," he reported to Berlin. "The consequences of this battle will be worse than the battle itself. I shall not survive the ruin of the Fatherland. Adieu for ever."

The crestfallen monarch soon recovered his spirits, however, and at Liegnitz and then at Torgau he reversed the tide of his fortunes. Nonetheless, by the end of 1761 it once more seemed that Frederick's cause was doomed. His countryside had been ravaged by Russian troops, towns had been occupied and all but destroyed, his army had suffered terrible losses, and he himself was worn out by the long and tragic war. His enemies watched eagerly for his final collapse—only to see him saved by the death of the Russian Empress Elizabeth. Elizabeth was succeeded by Peter III, who was one of Frederick's most zealous admirers, and the Russians withdrew. With the loss of Russia's support, with the Turks threatening her borders in the southeast, and with Frederick's final victory over her army at Freiberg, Maria Theresa was forced to agree to the Treaty of Hubertusburg in February, 1763. The Treaty of Paris had been signed a few days before; the war was over.

The year before that war began, a disastrous event had occurred in Europe—an event that seemed even more terrible than war itself, and one that brought an age of optimism suddenly to an end. That age, reflected so complacently in Alexander Pope's 1733 *Essay on Man* and based so contentedly on what Voltaire called the *tout est bien* philosophy, ended in November, 1755, when a shattering earthquake destroyed one of the oldest and richest cities in Europe.

Alexander Pope, poet of the age of optimism.

Disaster Strikes Lisbon

November 1, 1775 was All Saints' Day in Lisbon, Portugal's bustling capital city and principal port. Thousands of Lisbon's faithful jammed the city's numerous churches to celebrate the Holy Day—and thousands of them died in their pews shortly before ten in the morning as a series of earth tremors sundered the city. Cathedral vaults collapsed, church walls cracked and buckled inward, and fires—many lit by holy candles—swept the city. As few as 10,000—or as many as 40,000—persons died in the holocaust that followed, and as Lisbon's dazed citizens began the task of rebuilding their devastated city, scientists and seers alike attempted to explain the disaster. The former could offer no answer; the latter were certain that the quake was Divine Retribution for Portugal's collective sins. Both groups recognized that the earthquake had irrevocably shattered an age of optimism.

The Marquis of Pombal who, after the earthquake had wrecked the city, took command of the situation and headed the commission that rebuilt Lisbon.

Opposite The Church of Carno which was damaged in the earthquake and remains today as it appeared in 1755.

After the event there was talk of signs and omens, of crossed swords appearing in the sky and prophesies, but on that momentous November 1, 1755—a religious holiday—the weather was perfect and an unusual stillness in the air and a certain nervousness among the animals passed almost unnoticed. No one was worried about such things on that glorious morning of All Saint's Day, a day filled with the sounds of ringing church bells, the hurrying of the faithful to the churches and the lively bustle of the town and port of Lisbon.

King Joseph and the court had gone to Belém to attend Mass at the monastery of the Jeronimos, and certain wealthy middle-class families had their own chaplain say Mass for them in their private chapels. The majority, however, preferred to go to the Carmo or the San Roque, where they sang the long Masses. All the churches were packed to overflowing.

Suddenly, just a few minutes before ten o'clock, while the Service of the Holy Ghost was being celebrated, there were three violent shocks, one after another, accompanied by a terrifying uproar. All over the city the ground was splitting apart, walls were cracking and vaults were collapsing. A blinding curtain of dust clouded the sky and tongues of fire began to curl upward from the first fires; wax candles overturned on the altars and set fire to the hangings and the gilded woodwork, and stoves vomited forth their burning embers. A strong wind arose, blowing the smoke in all directions and fanning the flames.

Those who had not been buried under the ruins or swallowed up by the crevices in the ground rushed toward the river Tagus, hoping to escape from the scene of the disaster in one of the many boats moored in the estuary. To their horror, they saw that the waters of the Tagus were rapidly receding and that the boats were breaking up, their hulls crashing into one another and becoming stuck in the oozing mud. Then, just as abruptly, the waters began to rise again and came rolling onto the banks in a rushing tidal wave that carried corpses and debris alike as far as the center of the Lower Town.

Thus, within the space of a few minutes, the four elements had joined together: the earth splitting open like an overripe fruit, the wind swirling violently through the air, fire springing up in a thousand places at the same time and the waters angrily barring the way on all sides.

It was a merciless disaster, and terror reigned supreme. No one ever established the exact number of victims, although a total of 100,000 was first suggested. The figure was later reduced to 40,000, and that too was probably an overestimation. But even if one accepts the lowest estimate, of around 10,000 victims, the Lisbon disaster was still a great tragedy.

The 1755 earthquake affected all of Europe. Its tremors had shaken the whole of the Iberian Peninsula and had reached as far as Scandinavia, affecting the springs there. More important, however, was the fact that it had destroyed a city that served as a center for European trade. It seemed that Lisbon had been especially chosen—or cursed—by God, who had used the quake to reveal His wrath toward the whole of Christianity. Such a belief was enough to provoke the less fearful into a serious examination of conscience, while the more credulous were plunged into a state of total religious hysteria. Everyone was afraid, confessed his sins and did penitence. King Louis XV of France went so far as to promise his confessor that he would break off relations with the Marquise de Pompadour; she, in turn, vowed she would give up the wearing of rouge as an atonement.

King Joseph, his family and his court—as well as the monastery and tower of Belém—had escaped the catastrophe. The pathetic King, who was concerned only for his own personal safety and the salvation of his immortal soul, abandoned the task "of burying the dead and taking care of the living" to the man who already wielded the real power behind the throne: his minister, Sebastião José de Carvalho, who was to become famous in the annals of history as the Marques de Pombal.

In 1755, Lisbon was the prosperous capital of a poverty-stricken country. Travelers who came there

A city stultified by wealth

were dazzled at the sight of so many palaces and by the treasures they contained: the rarest of goldware, silks and porcelain, paintings by Rubens and Titian and precious books. (Seventy thousand volumes and many priceless documents were destroyed when the royal palace was burned.)

The churches of the city were even more ostentatious, with their giant organs, their gilt woodwork, their panels of *azulejos* (glazed tiles) and their ciboriums and tabernacles of massive silver encrusted with precious stones.

By 1755 the huge Portuguese Empire had begun to disintegrate. Joseph's predecessor, John V, the last great king of Portugal, had squandered all the gold that he obtained from Brazil by building churches, clothing his prelates in purple and decking out religious ceremonies with pagan ostentation.

Lisbon suffocated under the weight of this inert wealth. The whole country was paralyzed by the King's narrow, pious attitude and by his total indifference to his subjects' interests. Thus paralyzed, Portugal fell without a struggle into the hands of its powerful ally, Great Britain, and was devoured alive. Indeed, the turn-of-the-century Treaty of Methuen, which laid down the terms for trading between the two countries (roughly speaking, Portuguese wines in return for British wool), was such that every Englishman who came to Portugal enjoyed a king's privileges.

A sudden shock, a violent emotion, can sometimes cure a paralyzed person. Pombal had a presentiment that the earthquake might serve as such a shock, reviving the energies of the Portuguese people and rousing the country from its state of hopeless apathy.

In attempting to restore order in Lisbon, Pombal was faced with many urgent and acute problems, all of which had to be dealt with immediately. One section of the city had been completely destroyed. The remainder was tottering on the verge of collapse, endangered by the earth tremors that followed one after another for many months, unpredictable in their timing and their volume. In spite of the rain, the discomfort and the bands of looters, the inhabitants of Lisbon who had not already fled into the country preferred to camp outside, to sleep in the open air under the stars or under any temporary form of shelter that came their way, rather than stay in the city.

With remarkable coolness and clarity of vision, Pombal immediately took the necessary steps to deal with the emergency. The dead were buried or unceremoniously thrown into the river, panic was allayed, famine averted and looters were severely and publicly punished. The complaints of the English merchants, who had lost their stocks as well as money owed to them, were coldly received. They were told that nothing prevented them from returning home to England; none of them did so, however. The situation soon improved, for Pombal had a very clear idea of both the difficulties and the resources of Portugal.

Pombal decided to rebuild the city on exactly the same site that it had occupied ever since its foundation (which, according to legend, dated back to Ulysses). Two months after the catastrophe, the plans for this new city of Lisbon had already been drafted, revealing a boldness of conception, a practical genius and a clear vision of the future.

Pombal made no attempt to reconstitute Lisbon

The waters of the Tagus at first receded, but then returned in tidal waves which smashed the ships lying in the harbor. A contemporary etching showing the disaster.

LISABONA

in its former medieval style, with one section of the city clustered around the port and the rest scattered between the convents and the properties of the nobles. On the contrary, he commissioned a plan for a modern city with wide, well-drained streets laid out at right angles to each other. The façades of the buildings were uniform but dignified in style. They were constructed out of prefabricated sections for the first time in the history of town planning, and they were enhanced by beautiful wrought-iron lanterns and balconies and by the harmonious lines of their mansards and roofs.

Pombal's new Lisbon was dedicated to trade—of vital importance in his plans for the future prosperity of the country—as well as to industry, the growth of which he tried to stimulate. Such a policy soon met with the strong disapproval of the nobility—who considered Pombal an upstart—and of the Church. How could Pombal concern himself with such mundane preoccupations at a time when Divine Wrath had struck down Lisbon as a warning to others? The only thing that mattered was to obtain God's mercy by repentance and resignation. Pombal's detractors wanted more public confessions, processions of penitents, mortifications of the flesh and hymns of praise to ward off even greater evils. They were all agreed that they had deserved to be punished, but at the same time they were quick to point out the guilt in others. Thus the priests were accused of simony, the nobles of corruption, the middle classes of religious apathy and avarice, and the masses of lubricity. Fanatics, acting as Jeremiahs, predicted new catastrophes and cast curses on Lisbon, which they believed should remain a city in ruins like Sodom and Gomorrah.

Pombal had the utmost difficulty in persuading people that the disaster had been caused by a natural phenomenon. His difficulties were aggravated by the fact that science—which for some years had been accepted throughout Europe as the source of all truth—found it almost impossible to provide an explanation for this phenomenon. Famous scientists suggested that the quake might have been caused by the influence of the moon, or by fire and water that had become overheated in the center of the earth or by the little known force called electricity. None of the explanations was satisfactory. People preferred to listen to the oracles and to sermons.

In defiance of Pombal's orders, the Jesuit Malagrida wrote and distributed his *Judgment on the True Causes of the Earthquake*. According to Malagrida, Lisbon—the sixteenth-century center of operations for the Jesuits—had been punished for having sought to deprive the Jesuits of the Maranhão, an area of land claimed by both Brazil and Paraguay. Malagrida was a religious visionary who had great powers of fascination. He was considered a prophet, and he might have reduced Lisbon to a state of superstitious terror had he not been banished to the port city of Setubal. He was soon surrounded by a nucleus of loyal supporters, including some of the most illustrious families of the kingdom, who hatched a plot to kill King Joseph and thereby rid themselves

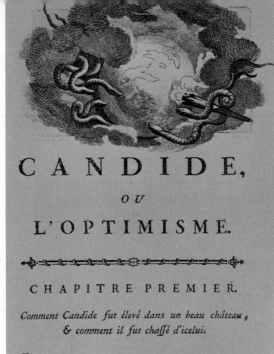

The city of Lisbon was almost totally destroyed. This picture shows how even the strongest buildings had crashed to the ground after the series of tremors.

of his first minister. The plot was discovered, however, and Pombal took advantage of the opportunity to bring all his enemies, aristocrats and Jesuits alike, to trial at the same time. The prisons were filled with them for the next twenty years; the Inquisition condemned Malagrida to be garroted and burned at the stake and many of the most illustrious heads in Portugal rolled beneath the executioner's blade.

Pombal's hands were red with the blood of his enemies, but at last he was free to do what he wanted: set up a government of technocrats. He founded the *Compagnie Royale* in order to wrest control over the vineyards that produced Port wine from the English. Moreover, he sent to France, Italy and Germany for specialist craftsmen to start up or revive such local industries as ceramics, silk, cutlery and smelting

577

The royal palace
at Lisbon.

The statue of King Joseph,
a timid and ineffectual
ruler who fled in terror
during the earthquake.

works. He was a great believer in technical progress, in individual effort and in hard work, and he overcame all obstacles impeding his plans. The Society of Jesus had become progressively weaker and lacking in authority and finally was driven out of the country altogether. An ambitious, active and dedicated middle class did its best to carry out the great aims of Pombal. Before he fell into disgrace, Pombal saw Lisbon rise once again out of the ruins and saw the statue of his master erected in one of the most beautiful squares in the world, a plaza dedicated to commerce. But Pombal was to die a slandered, ruined man, and with his death all the fragile structure of his work collapsed. For the next 150 years, Portugal sank into oblivion, disorder and decadence.

The deadly earth tremors that had destroyed Lisbon had shaken the world. It was not only buildings that had collapsed, but also beliefs; the cracks carved out abysses not only in the ground, but also in the minds of the most well-balanced men.

It was true that this misfortune, befalling a country that could count on few friends at the time, was viewed very severely by many people. The Protestants saw in the earthquake a just retribution for popish idolatry; the Jansenists were overjoyed that the "cradle of the Jesuits" was destroyed; others believed that the crimes committed by the Inquisition had been expiated in this way.

Even compassion tended to be condescending. Emergency aid was generous to begin with, but soon people grew irritated with Pombal's claim that his country was capable of recovering by its own efforts and would soon take its place again alongside the other European nations. The scientists felt resentful toward Portugal because they had been asked to find an explanation for a phenomenon that was beyond their comprehension.

The philosophers, too, were troubled. The Lisbon disaster was a deadly denial of the complacent optimism that had reigned during a century when science served merely as a diversion for the government, and when religion was a pleasant way of making sure of a place in the next world. After all, the finest minds of the time had established, mathematically, that everything was "for the best in the best of all possible worlds." God had been proven infallible as well as just and good.

Why then had God struck down so pitilessly the innocent at the same time as the guilty? Where was His justice, His goodness? If, on the other hand, He had not wanted such a catastrophe to happen—if the phenomenon had been fortuitous—how could He be the Almighty, the wisest of all? What about the perfection of His creation?

People were reluctant to accept the doctrine of collective responsibility that so carelessly sacrificed innocence in its cause. Their belief in God was shaken. They began seriously to question Divine Providence. Man became bitterly aware of his own insignificance, of the precariousness of his existence. Prayer no longer sufficed to reassure him.

Just after the event Voltaire wrote a passionate poem that is one long cry of despair, pity and revolt. Rousseau, although he did not go quite so far, declared that man, and man alone, was responsible for his own misfortunes. If he had lived as a "noble savage" in the midst of nature, instead of crowding together in the cities for sordid motives of profit, there would never have been so many lives sacrificed. Goethe, then a child, was terrified at the thought of the blind wrath of Almighty God that struck indiscriminately at both the good and the wicked. If God were not just, if there were no mercy in Heaven, if, as Voltaire had cried so passionately, "evil is in this world," then there was no longer any joy in living.

Thus, a complete way of life, of thought, of hoping had disappeared, to be replaced by a new approach to existence. Menaced by the hostility of a cruel world, man had to accept the responsibility for his own actions. Pombal had shown him how he could conquer his fear, and tackle with courage the task of rebuilding a city to make it more beautiful and prosperous than the one that had been so cruelly reduced to ashes.

A Portuguese poet advised people to "stay at home in their villages and tend their sheep"—in

Pombal's reconstruction of the capital

other words, to concentrate on making the most of their own resources without depending on others or interfering in their affairs. This philosophy still prevails in Portugal today. Man must fend for himself without expecting God's help; the existence of Heaven is doubtful.

While all these ideas were merging and blending one with another, the old established order was gradually falling apart. Like the decrepit, worm-eaten old palaces and gilded churches of Lisbon, the world was crumbling down to its very foundations. New currents of thought emerged as a result of the traumatic shock that had swept across the whole of Europe: Choiseul expelled the Jesuits from France, the Pope dissolved the Society of Jesus, and the education of young noblemen—which up to that time had been in the hands of the Jesuits—henceforth changed direction. Daring new ideas, no longer contradicted or forbidden, began to circulate.

The Lisbon disaster, by causing man to doubt the wisdom of Divine Providence, marked the end of an era, an era dominated by faith and respect for the established authorities: the head of a family, the king and God. The senseless cruelty of the disaster had not only aroused compassion, Christian solidarity and simple human love, it had also led to objective, nonmaterialistic speculation and to a disdain for individual life, which, although still precious and unique, was subordinate to larger goals. This concept was to lead directly to the conclusion that "the end justifies the means." Without a Divine Justice to separate good from evil, man was responsible for his own actions and had a perfect right to sacrifice the liberty or dignity of others in order to achieve his aims.

The reactions and shock provoked by the Lisbon earthquake in the eighteenth century can perhaps be compared to everything that man experiences in face of the horrifying reality of modern warfare: his confusion in face of the annihilation of the individual, the iciness weighing down his spirit, the despair that finds no relief in understanding. Today, as then, man's anguish is perfectly expressed in Voltaire's lines:

What am I, where am I, where am I going to and from
                              where did I come,
A thinking atom, an atom whose eyes,
Guided by thought, have scanned the heavens?

SUZANNE CHANTAL

The Inquisition in session. For twenty years after a plot to murder Pombal was discovered the Inquisition executed the most able men in Portugal, and thus helped establish Pombal's position.

A picture painted at the time of the earthquake showing the dead and wounded inhabitants of Lisbon lying in the streets while fires rage throughout the city.

For months after the Lisbon earthquake the theory that Lisbon had been destroyed by God's anger was propounded in countless tracts, sermons and moralizing poems. Such pamphleteering was particularly rife in France, where the Chevalier Joseph Cuers de Cogelin wrote that he recognized God's terrible hand in the city's destruction. According to the Chevalier, Lisbon had simply been too proud, too rich. Several French writers contended that France, like Portugal, had grown too proud and too rich, and that some terrible calamity would soon befall her. Among those prophets were some who saw the will of a jealous God reflected in the course of events in India.

In that country, the dissolution

Robert Clive, who became Governor of Bengal and Commander-in-Chief of the East India Company's Army in India.

of the Mogul Empire had provided opportunities for both France and England to extend their influence and power. The trade of the English East India Company, which had bases at Calcutta and Madras, eventually grew to be considerably greater in bulk than that of the French (whose bases at Chandernagore and Pondicherry were less advantageously placed), but in the earlier rounds of the struggle it was the French who were more successful. The talents of the French sailor Mahé de Labourdonnais and those of the brilliant governor of the French East India Company, Joseph François Dupleix, contrasted sharply with the meager talents of Nicholas Morse, the English governor of Madras who surrendered his town to the French in 1746 after a few days' half-hearted resistance. In the summer of 1748, the British attemp-

ted to recoup their losses by launching an abortive siege operation at Pondicherry, only to be obliged to withdraw.

By the Treaty of Aix-la-Chapelle, Madras was given back to the British in exchange for Cape Breton —but French prestige was greatly enhanced by her conduct of the war and French garrisons were greatly strengthened against the time of its continuance. After 1748, however, the French grip on India began to loosen. Dupleix extended French influence in southern India by manipulating numerous Indian alliances, and he set up puppet governments in the Carnatic, in the Deccan and in Hyderabad. But by 1754 he had overreached himself and all but exhausted his finances. Dupleix was recalled to France—and as he departed, another figure of remarkable talents appeared on the Indian scene. This man was Robert Clive, the eldest son of a Shropshire gentleman of modest means.

Clive had migrated to Madras at the age of eighteen to become a writer in the East India Company, and he was there—homesick and miserable—when the town was captured by Labourdonnais in 1746. He entered the army a short time later and greatly distinguished himself during the siege of Arcot (where rival claimants, supported respectively by France and Britain, were contesting for the position of Nawab). By 1756 Clive had become governor of Fort St. David and a lieutenant-colonel in the British army. He took up his post as governor on the day that the young Nawab of Bengal, Suraj-ud-Dowlah, captured Calcutta.

Like his predecessors, Suraj-ud-Dowlah had originally been on

Suraj-ud-Dowlah, Nawab of Bengal, who captured Calcutta from the East India Company.

friendly terms with the British East India Company. But when the British governor refused to remand a rich fugitive who had fled to Calcutta to escape the new Nawab's extortionate demands, Suraj-ud-Dowlah had advanced on Calcutta with an army of 40,000.

The town's defenses had been much neglected during those peaceful years, and the garrison numbered only 250 men. At the approach of the Nawab, both the governor and the military commander of Calcutta fled to the safety of the British ships anchored in the river, and the garrison was left to its fate. It surrendered on June 20 and that night—a night of stifling heat—146 prisoners were locked up in the small punishment cell of the fortress, the Black Hole of Calcutta. All but twenty-three of them died before dawn.

Clive at Calcutta

Although war with France was considered imminent, it was decided that the British forces in the area must concentrate on the immediate recapture of Calcutta. Supported by Rear-Admiral Charles Watson and five men-of-war. Clive set out from Madras with 900 European troops and 1,500 native troops. On February 4, 1757, he overwhelmed the massed ranks of the Nawab's immense army. A treaty was soon concluded, and Suraj-ud-Dowlah was forced to restore all the territory that he had taken from the British.

The long-anticipated clash finally erupted, and Clive was urged to return to Madras. He refused the summons, however, believing it was more important to capture Chandernagore, the base of the French East India Company in Bengal. He succeeded in achieving his objective only after the gallant French defenders of that city had been driven into submission by Admiral Watson's determined onslaught from the river.

Suraj-ud-Dowlah, who was known to be supporting the French, had actively sought to renew his attack on the English while they were engaged at Chandernagore, and a conspiracy was therefore arranged to replace the Nawab with Mír Jafar, a noble who was more acceptable both to the English and to his own people. While the conspirators were plotting his dethronement, Suraj-ud-Dowlah took the field with over 50,000 fighting men and more than 50 pieces of

heavy ordnance served by French artillerymen. Clive moved out of Chandernagore to meet the renegade with just over a thousand Europeans, two thousand native troops and nine field pieces. The two armies met amid the mango groves of Plassey, a few miles out-

A coin commemorating the Battle of Plassey.

side Murshidabad. Clive hesitated to move against so large an army with so small a force—but after initially voting against an immediate attack, he changed his mind. On June 23, 1757, he defeated the Nawab in one of the most fateful battles of the modern world. Suraj-ud-Dowlah fled from the field on a camel, Mír Jafar was installed as a puppet ruler in his place, and the British were masters of Bengal.

The Dutch, appalled by the sudden triumph of their rivals, responded by dispatching several armed vessels to the Ganges. When these Dutch warships seized some English merchant ships, Clive's response was immediate and determined: seven Dutch ships were

Count de Lally on the ramparts of Pondicherry.

Tortures inflicted by the Dutch on English East India Company employees.

captured and the Dutch army was defeated by one of Clive's best officers, Francis Forde. The Dutch were allowed to retain their settlement in Bengal, but the terms upon which they did so removed the threat of Dutch competition on the subcontinent.

The War in the South

The British were equally successful in southern India, where the French general Count de Lally, the son of an Irish Jacobite, vainly endeavored to prosecute an aggressive war against the British settlements with insufficient money and supplies. In December, 1758, Lally advanced against Madras, which was ably defended by Major-General Stringer Lawrence and Lord Pigot, the city's governor. Lally and his unpaid, ill-supplied and mutinous troops were forced to withdraw. A well-equipped army led by Colonel Eyre Coote defeated Lally at Wandiwash in January, 1760, and Coote went on systematically to attack the French forts in the Carnatic. By September Lally had been forced back to Pondicherry. The arrival of a British fleet ended his beleaguered force's hope of resupply, and in January, 1761, he was obliged to surrender. His surrender marked the end of French dominion in India.

Clive, who had left India the year before at the age of thirty-five, had established the base of British power. In the process, he had become an extremely rich man. He was not home long enough to enjoy the pleasures that his fortune could buy, however: in May, 1765, he returned to India as Governor of Bengal and commander-in-chief of the Army.

Corruption in the company

In Clive's absence Bengal had been notoriously governed by a succession of administrators. (Clive's own behavior had unfortunately set the precedent for such conduct.) Mír Jafar had been deposed in favor of his son-in-law Mír Kasim, from whom the Bengal Council accepted £200,000 worth of gratuities. Indeed, the whole of the English East India Company had become corrupted by the commissions and gifts its servants had grown accustomed to expect. It was to be Clive's duty to carry out extensive reforms, and he did so with a dispatch that was widely resented by those who felt that Clive himself was largely responsible for the tradition that money should be extracted from the natives through fear of Britain.

Clive raised the Company's salaries so that its employees had less reason to accept bribes; he forbade the acceptance of gifts and the participation of the Company's employees in private trade; and he reformed the army. Above all, he secured from the Emperor of Delhi —whose forces had recently been defeated by Major Hector Munro at Buxar—a document that granted the Company the provinces of Bengal, Behar and Orissa. Clive thus became the virtual ruler of 30 million people and the recipient of nearly 4 million pounds a year.

Clive left India for the last time in 1767, and on November 22, 1774, he killed himself in one of the fits of depression to which he had always been subject. Clive's work was continued by Warren Hastings, who became Governor of Bengal in 1772 and Governor-General of India in 1773. Hastings reformed

the government of Bengal; supported the Nawab of Oudh against the Rohillas, who led plundering raids against his northern frontiers; and saved British India when a renewal of the French war in 1778 led to its being threatened by a coalition of Indian princes supported by France. By the time Hastings arrived back in England in 1785 (to face charges of impeachment for his supposedly ruthless conduct as Governor-General), he had succeeded in extending the East India Company's influence over even larger areas of India.

In 1784 Parliament passed William Pitt's India Act, which transferred the control of much of the Company's power to the British

Warren Hastings, Governor-General of India.

government. Responsibility for Indian affairs was given to a board of six Privy Councillors appointed by the King.

India was but part of a huge and growing English empire. Lally's 1761 surrender at Pondicherry—which marked the end of French dominion in India—was soon followed by other French territorial losses. The French and Indian War (1756–1763) had not gone well for France. In 1745 and again in 1746 the brilliant generalship of Maurice de Saxe had resulted in French victories (at Fontenoy and Lauffeld), and in the French and Indian War she had enjoyed several initial successes. But in 1759 her Mediterranean fleet had been severely damaged at Lagos and her Atlantic fleet all but destroyed in Quiberon Bay. And on the Plains of Abraham outside Quebec, her noble general, Montcalm, had been killed by a shot from a British gun. Quebec had been taken and North America lost. By the Treaty of Paris she was forced to recognize England's right to most of her former empire.

France was not the only country to be affected by England's burgeoning imperial designs. In 1768 an expedition set sail for the South Pacific that was to add a whole new continent to the Empire.

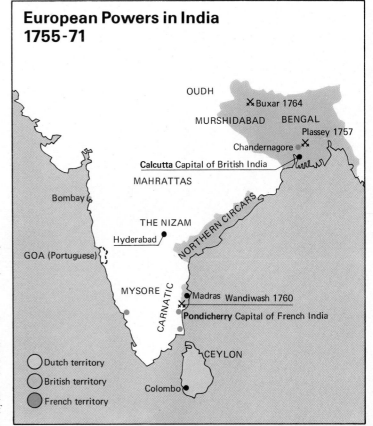

European Powers in India 1755-71

OUDH

✕ Buxar 1764

MURSHIDABAD   BENGAL

Plassey 1757

Chandernagore ✕

Calcutta Capital of British India

MAHRATTAS

Bombay

THE NIZAM

Hyderabad

GOA (Portuguese)

NORTHERN CIRCARS

MYSORE

CARNATIC

Madras   Wandiwash 1760

Pondicherry Capital of French India

CEYLON

◯ Dutch territory

◯ British territory

◯ French territory

Colombo

"Terra Incognita"

Captain James Cook was only one of dozens of eighteenth-century Englishmen who firmly believed that an undiscovered continent lay somewhere in the South Pacific. Cook was convinced that the "Great South Land" had to exist—to balance the known land masses in the northern hemisphere and thereby preserve the earth's orbital stability. Dutch and Portuguese navigators had purportedly touched the shores of Terra Australis Incognita *in the preceding century, but the continent remained virtually unexplored when Cook sailed south from Tahiti in 1769. On April 19, 1770, a crewman aboard Cook's ship, the* Endeavour, *sighted a low promontory on Australia's southeast coast—and before returning to England, Cook investigated and mapped most of the new continent's eastern and northern coastlines. The captain's journals aroused considerable interest at home and led, less than half a century later, to England's annexation of the entire continent.*

It was originally a matter of stargazing that led James Cook to the shores of Australia. A rare occurrence called the "transit of Venus" was to take place in 1769. (During a transit, Venus passes directly between the earth and the sun and appears projected on the sun's disk as a small black dot. Important deductions—such as the scale of the solar system and the distance of the earth from the sun—can be made from its passage.) Astronomers' charts recorded only two previous transits, the first of which had occurred in 1639. The next had taken place in 1761, but observation of the 1761 phenomenon had been unsuccessful and it was therefore of particular importance that the 1769 event be properly charted.

The Royal Society, which was devoted to the cause of natural enlightenment, took a lively interest in the coming transit and petitioned King George III not to neglect the chance of furthering the fame of British astronomy, "a science," the members pointed out, "on which navigation so much depends." Several European nations, among them Russia, wanted to establish points of observation, and England, the Society argued, should certainly do the same. The Royal Society was considered the world's most distinguished scientific body, and its petition carried weight with the King, who was particularly interested in science and exploration.

Because it was essential that the observers follow the transit from a point south of the equinoctial line, the recently discovered island of Tahiti was suggested as a suitable place. The idea of sending an expedition to the Pacific appealed to the King. He promptly gave the project his approval, and the Royal Society approached the Admiralty for a ship and a competent man to sail it. James Cook, a forty-year-old British naval officer who had already surveyed the coasts of Newfoundland and Labrador, was chosen to command the H.M.S. *Endeavour*.

In 1768 the expedition set out. Sailing with Cook were Joseph Banks, a young naturalist of twenty-five with an independent fortune who was later knighted by the King; Charles Green, an astronomer; Doctor Daniel Charles Solander, a Swede who had been Linnaeus' favorite pupil; and two artists, twenty-five-year-old Sydney Parkinson and Herman Dierich Spöring, another Swede who joined the ship at Capetown and seems to have acted as Banks' secretary. In his journal Cook always referred to Banks and members of his party simply as "the gentlemen."

The transit of Venus was successfully observed from Tahiti, but it proved to be a task of secondary importance to the expedition, for Cook had been given secret instructions by the Admiralty. After exploring Tahiti and the neighboring islands, he was to search for the Great South Land that was supposed to exist in the South Pacific. Known as the *Terra Australis Incognita*, it was a shadowy area sketched in around the South Pole on many old charts.

Geographers had been struck by the fact that, unlike the northern hemisphere, the southern Pacific had no large land masses. Having accepted the spherical nature of the earth, they came to the conclusion that in order for the earth to keep its stability, the amount of solid land in the two hemispheres must balance. Hence there must be a great unknown continent in the southern part of the Pacific. Dutch mariner Abel Tasman was supposed to have touched it when he sailed along the western shores of New Zealand, and many believed that Portuguese navigator Pedro Fernandes de Queiros had seen yet another part of it when he landed on Espiritu Santo in the New Hebrides in 1606—but no one was quite certain. Beyond these tentative probes, nothing definite was known about the mysterious continent.

Cook and Banks between them had an extensive geographical library on board, and among the books was Charles de Brosses' useful *Histoire des Navigations aux Terres Australes*, published in Paris in 1756. In his work de Brosses explained, "I call Austral lands all that is beyond the three southern points of our known world in Africa, Asia and America." Accompanying

An engraving of a kangaroo from Banks' *New System of Geography*. Kangaroos were first sighted on Cook's first expedition on the coast of Australia.

Opposite A Wedgewood cameo portrait of Captain Cook made in 1784.

Attacked by natives

The *Endeavour*, after narrowly escaping shipwreck, is laid up on the banks of the Endeavour River in New South Wales.

the text were maps by the celebrated French cartographer Robert de Vaugondy.

In one of his maps, Vaugondy marked out Tasman's discoveries: the southern part of Van Diemen's Land (now Tasmania) and the western coast of New Zealand's North Island. The imaginary eastern coast of New Holland (the early name for Australia) was shown by vague hatchings and was joined to the discoveries of de Queiros, which were displaced westward. Van Diemen's Land was also shown connected to the mainland.

These, then, were the geographical uncertainties that faced the crew of the *Endeavour* as the ship left Tahiti. Cook sailed from the Society Islands in August, and by the end of March of the following year, 1770, he had already charted New Zealand and had circumnavigated its two islands, thus disproving any continental connection. By April 1 he had turned northwest toward Tasmania, but strong southerly gales drove the *Endeavour* north, so that the English arrived at the southeast corner of Australia

itself. Had the weather been fair, Cook would almost certainly have discovered Bass Strait, which separates Australia from Tasmania.

On Wednesday, April 18, certain birds were spotted—a sure sign, Cook noted, of the nearness of land. The following day Lieutenant Hicks sighted a low hill and Cook named the point after him. (Few modern maps bear Hicks' name; the British ship's landfall is known today as Cape Everard.) Sailing northward, the *Endeavour* hugged the shore, looking for a safe anchorage. The calm, noble landscape that they saw had a certain haggard beauty of its own—green and wooded, but with a shore of white sand. Dark figures could be distinguished against the glare. Smoke curled up through the dusty green hanging foliage of the eucalyptus, only to be lost against a pale sky. At night fires pricked the flat shoreland.

Cook, Banks, Solander and Tupaia, a Tahitian chief whom Banks had persuaded to join the expedition, tried to land in a yawl but were prevented from doing so by the heavy surf. Banks noted the parklike

584

aspect of the land, the trees separate from each other "without the least underwood." Passing within a quarter of a mile of the shore, he was surprised at the total lack of interest that their presence had aroused in the natives; they did not seem to notice the passing of the yawl, although an old woman who was gathering sticks and was followed by three children "often looked at the ship but expressed neither surprise nor concern." On Sunday, April 29, the *Endeavour* stood into Botany Bay and anchored off the south shore. Midshipman Isaac Smith, Mrs. Cook's cousin (and later an Admiral of the British Fleet), was the first to land. Young Isaac, eighteen at the time, later recalled how Cook, on the point of stepping ashore, said, "Isaac, you shall land first." Cook was forced to fire a musket loaded with small shot between two natives when a party of them threatened the explorers with spears.

Cook originally called their anchorage Sting Ray Harbor, "occasioned by the great quantity of these sort of fish found in this place." Banks' and Solander's prodigious haul of new plants later provoked him to change the name to Botany Bay. The plants were kept fresh in tin chests, wrapped in wet cloths, while Parkinson and Spöring drew them. (Parkinson worked with such alacrity that he averaged seven meticulous drawings a day.) Banks, who preserved his specimens by spreading them out on sails to dry in the sun, wrote that the aborigines "seemed never to be able to muster above fourteen or fifteen fighting men." He seemed undecided about their actual color—"they were so completely covered with dirt, that seemed to have stuck to their bodies from the day of their birth"—and on one occasion he spat on his fingers and tried to rub it off. His actions altered the color very little, and he judged their skin to be chocolate-colored.

The *Endeavour* remained at Botany Bay just over a week. On May 7 Cook resumed his voyage. A few miles north he passed present-day Sydney Harbor, which he named Port Jackson in honor of one of the

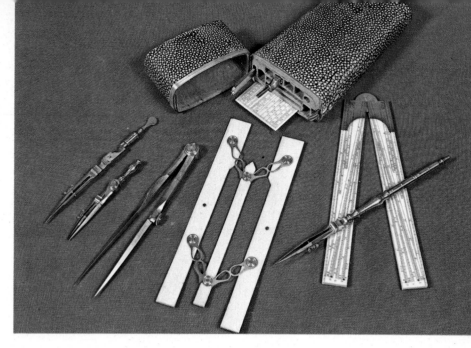

Above Navigational instruments used by Cook on his voyages.

A model of the *Endeavour*, the ship in which Cook made his first expedition in 1768–70.

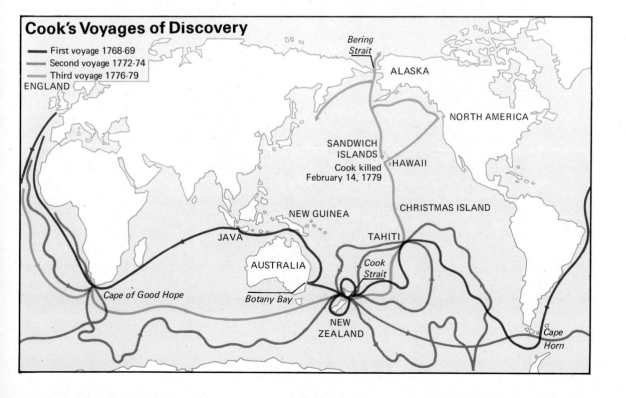

Cook's Voyages of Discovery

— First voyage 1768-69
— Second voyage 1772-74
— Third voyage 1776-79

ENGLAND

Bering Strait
ALASKA
NORTH AMERICA
SANDWICH ISLANDS
Cook killed February 14, 1779
HAWAII
CHRISTMAS ISLAND
NEW GUINEA
JAVA
TAHITI
AUSTRALIA
Cook Strait
Botany Bay
NEW ZEALAND
Cape of Good Hope
Cape Horn

Colonizing Botany Bay

secretaries of the Admiralty. Cook slowly worked his way north, charting the coast. He frequently landed, and he never sailed very far without sending boats ahead to cast shoreward and seaward and take bearings.

As they neared the northern end of the island continent, the voyage nearly came to an abrupt end when the ship grounded on a coral reef twenty miles from land. Cook's seamanship was, however, equal to the occasion: the *Endeavour* was freed and, much damaged and leaking severely, was guided up the estuary of a small nearby river, where she was banked and careened. There the men saw their first kangaroo, which Cook described as "an animal something less than a greyhound, of a mouse color, very slender made and swift of foot." During Cook's stay, natives came to the camp, but they always left their women on the opposite bank of the river. Banks, busy with his glasses, commented on their nudity, noting that they "did not copy our Mother Eve even in the fig-leaf."

Although repairs on the ship finally were finished, a strong wind further delayed Cook's departure. Eventually he managed to creep out and slowly threaded his way through the tortuous mazes of the Great Barrier Reef. Inch by inch the group advanced to the northern point of Australia, which Cook named Cape York in honor of the King's late brother. Sailing west, they rediscovered Torres Strait, and before departing for Batavia and England they landed on a small island off the coast of Cape York. Cook made no claim regarding the strait, but he did claim the land. Accompanied by Banks and Solander, he made for the island and climbed the highest hill—from which he saw nothing but islands to the northwest.

Cook admitted that to the west he could make no new discoveries "the honor of which belongs to the Dutch navigators; but the east coast I am confident was never seen or visited by any Europeans before us." He had already claimed several places along the coast; now he "once more hoisted the English colors and in the name of His Majesty King George III took possession of the whole eastern coast," christening it New South Wales. Three volleys of small arms were fired, and they were answered by a like number from the ship. Why, one asks, did Cook pick on so improbable a name? It has been suggested that since there already was a New England and a Nova Scotia, and since Cook wanted to associate the recent discoveries with his own country, he decided on New South Wales.

The most immediately striking aspect of early maps of Australia is the marked Dutch flavor of their nomenclature. The earliest explorers—before Cook's time—had been Dutch captains serving the East India Company, and rather naturally they perpetuated their sightings by their own names or those of their employers or ships. Some fifteen different landings took place during the first half of the seventeenth century. The first was made in 1606 by the *Duyfken* under the command of Willem Janz, who sighted the present Cape York Peninsula and advanced down the west shore as far as Cabo Keer-Weer, or Cape Turn-Again. Ten years later Dirck Hartog, sailing from Amsterdam in the *Eendracht*, entered present-day Shark Bay, which he named after his ship. Hartog left a pewter plate nailed to a post to commemorate the event; the plate, crudely carved with the men's names and the date, still exists.

Other landfalls followed in quick succession. In 1619 Jacob Dedel came in sight of the mainland in

The island of Huahine, one of the Society Islands, from Banks' *System of Geography*.

the vicinity of Perth, and in 1622 the *Leeuwin* discovered Australia's westernmost point. Later came Tasman's two voyages. His second, in 1644, proved the most rewarding: he sailed along the whole north coast from Cape York to the North West Cape, some three thousand miles—a greater distance even than Cook's northward passage up the eastern side.

By the middle of the seventeenth century three-quarters of Australia's actual coast had been mapped, and one wonders why it took another century and a quarter before Cook completed its outline. The answer is simple: the Dutch regarded this enormous island, about the size of the United States, as completely valueless. No place had been found where they could revictual their ships, and more often than not the crews, in their searchings for water, had been obliged to dig in the sand, unearthing only an evil brackish fluid. From the reports of the time one pictures a low, desolate shoreline dotted with burning fires but otherwise apparently uninhabited. On the rare occasions that the aborigines did make their appearance, they were judged to be "a race of savages more miserable than any creatures in the world." Further discoveries would cost money, and the expeditions had brought in no returns. It was obvious that to establish colonies in a land of this size would be a prodigious undertaking, more than the East India Company or even the Republic of Holland could manage. It was thought best to drop the whole matter.

William Dampier, the first Englishman to visit Australia, agreed with the Dutch about the inhospitable nature of New Holland's shores. A merchant-sailor as well as a privateer, Dampier had visited Australia twice—once in the *Cygnet* in 1688, and again in the *Roebuck* ten years later. Both times he had touched the country's arid northwest shore, and his two celebrated books, *A New Voyage Around the World* (1697) and *A Voyage to New Holland* (1703), did nothing to excite the British government's curiosity. No one in London thought much about Australia until Captain Cook's expedition discovered the well-watered, attractive eastern coastline seventy years later. His report was far more favorable and it led to the British taking possession of the continent.

The first suggestion for establishing a Pacific colony in Australia was made by Joseph Banks before a committee of the House of Commons in 1779. In 1776 the United States had declared its independence, and the loss of her American colonies meant that England could no longer send her convicts across the Atlantic. Nevertheless, English judges continued sentencing convicted persons to transportation, and jails were overcrowded; a new outlet for offenders had to be found.

It was at this point that Banks enthusiastically recommended Botany Bay for that purpose. "The proportion of rich soil was small in comparison to the barren," he noted, "but sufficient to support a very large number of people ... The country was well supplied with water. There were no beasts of prey," and the natives were peaceful when compared with those in New Zealand. Banks did make the proviso

Sir Joseph Banks, a naturalist, accompanied Cook on his first voyage in 1768.

A drawing of a breadfruit or Uru by Sydney Parkinson, a naturalist-artist who worked for Banks on his voyage with Cook.

587

A picture of many of the natives discovered by Cook during his expeditions.

War-boats on the island of Ulietea, one of the Society Islands.

"The finest natural harbor in the world"

that any body of settlers going to the country must take a full year's allowance of such things as victuals, raiment, tools, seeds and stock. Cook, in his journals, had stated similar views. "We are to consider that we see this country in the pure state of nature, the industry of man has had nothing to do with any part of it and yet we find such things as nature hath bestow'd upon it in a flourishing state. In this extensive country it can never be doubted but what most sorts of grain, fruit, roots etc. of every kind would flourish were they once brought hither."

By 1786 Lord Sydney, the Secretary of State, had appointed forty-nine-year-old Captain Arthur Phillip, a man with a fine naval record, to lead a fleet to Botany Bay. His fleet consisted of six transports, three storeships and two ships of war, carrying a total of 1,138 people, of whom 820 were convicts.

When Captain Phillip sailed into the bay, he realized that it had an exposed situation with an indifferent supply of water, and that settling there could lead only to disaster. Instead, exploring a few miles to the north, he entered Port Jackson, the future Sydney, an infinitely more satisfactory location—"the finest natural harbor in the world," according to Phillip, "in which a thousand sail of the line may ride in the most perfect security."

At this point Great Britain, still under the belief that New South Wales might be separated from what the Dutch called New Holland, did not lay claim to the whole of Australia, but just to the eastern coast and all the islands adjacent in the Pacific. But by 1815 Australia's entire perimeter had been examined—and by 1820 Britain had formally annexed the entire country.

Thus the ultimate result of Cook's exploration of the Australian coast was to give Great Britain a whole new continent. But this was not his only achievement in the southern hemisphere. The 1768 expedition had proved that New Zealand was an island group and had closed off Australia's missing coastline—but it also disproved the existence of one enormous southern continent to counter-balance Europe and Asia.

Cook's second voyage, begun in 1772, settled that question once and for all: in the three years Cook was absent, he sailed between 60,000 and 70,000 miles and made vast sweeps in hitherto unexplored parts of the Pacific. He traveled in a giant, irregular zig-zag, penetrating as far south as 70° 10′ latitude, a record not bettered until 1823. During that voyage he made numerous major geographical discoveries, one of them being New Caledonia, the largest island in the South Pacific after New Zealand. Ironically, it was what Cook did *not* discover that was to count as his most important contribution on that voyage: his conclusive proof that there was no great southern continent put our knowledge of the South Pacific on a sound basis. Indeed, maps of that part of the world remain essentially as Cook left them.

RODERICK CAMERON

The death of Captain Cook. Cook was killed by natives on the island of Hawaii on February 14, 1779.

589

Catherine the Great, Empress of Russia, ambitious and dominating, who succeeded her poisoned husband.

While England continued to expand her empire overseas, Russia was extending her frontiers in Europe. Aided by Austria, Russian troops invaded Prussia during the French and Indian War (1756-1763), inflicting an overwhelming defeat on Frederick the Great at Kunersdorf. The Russians captured Colmar, advanced as far as Frankfurt-on-Oder and Berlin, and occupied Prussian Pomerania. Frederick's tenacity (despite the fact that by the end of 1761 his army was reduced to a meager 30,000 men)—combined with Russia's inability to coordinate plans with the Austrians—spelled doom for the Russian campaign. With the death of the Empress Elizabeth and the accession of her half-German nephew as Peter III in 1761, Russian troops withdrew from Prussia.

Catherine the Great

The new Tsar, a weak and incompetent ruler, was poisoned within a few months of his accession by supporters of his dynamic German wife, Catherine, who succeeded him to the throne. A worthy successor to Peter the Great, she is also known to history as "the Great." Catherine's determination to modernize and Westernize Russia was clearly influenced by

the ideas of the French *philosophes*. Indeed, the Empress claimed that Voltaire was her master and Diderot's *Encyclopédie* her bible. But the vast size of her empire, the political power of the nobles and her own determination to extend Russia's frontiers blocked any full attempt to implement the ideas of the Enlightenment. When Diderot (whose library she bought) pressed Catherine to institute more reforms, she retorted: "You only work on paper, while I, poor Empress, work on human skin which is much more ticklish."

Catherine did succeed in abolishing most of the state monopolies and in reforming the provincial administration of Russia. She increased the number and efficiency of the *gubernii*—local authorities administered by a governor and elected councils—and she subordinated the Orthodox Church to the State by secularizing Church lands and granting religious freedom to non-Church members. When Pope Clement XIV's bull, *Dominus ac Redemptor*, dissolved the Society of Jesus in 1773, she refused to expel the Jesuits from Russia.

Compared with her over ambitious and liberal *Instructions to the Commissioners for Composing a New Code of Laws*—most of which she plagiarized from Montesquieu's *Spirit of Laws* and Beccaria's *Crimes and Punishments*—the legal reforms that Catherine actually instituted were minor: the establishment of a new system of courts and the separation of civil from criminal cases. The Empress had more success in reforming the educational system. She established free

Pugachev, an illiterate peasant who claimed to be Tsar Peter III.

public primary schools in the towns, extended the scope of Peter the Great's Academy, and set up a College of Medicine.

Peasant discontent

Despite the benefits certain sections of Russian society gained from her rule, Catherine did little to improve the lot of the serfs. In fact, she increased their number—not only by giving estates to discarded lovers but also by introducing serfdom into new territories conquered by her armies. The extent of peasant discontent was dramatically revealed in 1773. An illiterate Cossack named Pugachev, pretending to be the murdered Peter III, announced that he was marching to St. Petersburg to punish his wife and place his son Paul on the throne. Pugachev gained so much support from the salt miners, Cossacks and peasants of the lower Volga that he was able to capture and pillage several towns, and to hang hundreds of priests, officers and government officials before his eventual defeat. Captured in 1775, he was taken in an iron cage to Moscow, where he was executed for his crime of lese majesty.

The discontent that generated Pugachev's revolt was to last throughout Catherine's reign and was, in fact, to be exacerbated by her aggressive and extremely expensive foreign policy. Determined to expand Russia both west and south, she used the Duke of Courland's refusal to allow Russian troops returning from the French and Indian War to pass through his territories as a pretext to invade his duchy. She replaced the Duke, a son of King Augustus III of Poland, with her own nominee. The death of Augustus himself in 1763 gave Catherine the opportunity to interfere directly in Polish politics. She chose her former lover, Stanislas Poniatowski, to succeed Augustus—and by spending a fortune in bribes and by threatening military action, Catherine obtained his unanimous election in September, 1764.

The French government, which was disturbed by Russia's territorial ambitions and alarmed by the friendship between Catherine and Frederick of Prussia, persuaded Turkey to attack Russia. The Turkish Army was overwhelmed on the Dnieper in 1768 and the Russians occupied Bucharest; the

Stanislas Poniatowski, a former lover of Catherine of Russia, who was elected King of Poland.

Turkish Navy was defeated off Chios and the Russians moved into the Crimea, occupying Moldavia and Wallachia. By the terms of the 1774 Treaty of Kuchuk Kainardji, Turkey ceded Azov and Kertsch to Russia, thereby extending its frontiers to the Black Sea and the lower Danube. Victory in a second Turkish war confirmed Russia's earlier annexation of the Crimea and secured her hold on the Black Sea.

Catherine's success in Turkey was made possible by her role in the War of the Bavarian Succession. Upon the death of the Elector Maximilian Joseph in 1775, the Emperor Joseph II claimed Lower Bavaria for Austria, offering to compensate the Elector Palatine Karl Theodore, the legal heir to the throne, with money and titles for his illegitimate children. But Frederick the Great, having persuaded Karl Theodore's nephew

Gustavus III, King of Sweden, who built up Sweden's strength to avoid Poland's fate.

and legitimate heir, the Duke of Zweibrücken, to reject the Emperor's arrangement, invaded Bohemia. The Treaty of Teschen, which ended the war, guaranteed the rights of the Elector Palatine and the Duke of Zweibrücken in Bavaria, and gave Austria only a small slice of Bavarian territory. Russia, having acted as mediator in the dispute, was in a position to influence Austrian affairs. She obtained the support of Joseph II in her designs on Turkey. Thwarted in his attempt to add Bavaria to his Empire, Joseph decided that an alliance with Russia might win him parts of Turkey's possessions. As we have seen, Russia's gains in the war were considerable, but Joseph's ill-led and disease-ridden army was defeated.

Partition of Poland

Meanwhile, Catherine's protégé in Poland, Stanislas Poniatowski, was

Emanuel Swedenborg.

hampered in his attempts to rule as an enlightened monarch by a constitution that inhibited his initiative. This constitution was guaranteed by both Catherine and Frederick the Great, neither of whom wanted the resurgence of a healthy Polish state.

Early in 1772, Catherine and Frederick agreed that the time had come to partition Poland, and in August of that year they signed the First Treaty of Partition. Russia took the area known as White Russia, east of the Düna and Dnieper rivers; Prussia took West Prussia; and Austria, which had already seized Zips—the Polish enclave to the north of Hungary—took Galicia. Although the King of Poland declared that his country was not "a nation near its fall," a Second Partition Treaty was forced upon him less than a year later. Russia acquired another vast area of eastern Poland, from Polozk to the Dniester, and Prussia absorbed Danzig and a large area in western Poland.

Reduced to about a third of her

Partitions of Poland

- - - Frontiers of Poland before partitions

⬤ Territorial gains of Prussia

⬤ Territorial gains of Russia

⬤ Territorial gains of Austria

1772

BALTIC SEA
EAST PRUSSIA
Dnieper
Danzig
Niemen
PRUSSIA
Warsaw
Cracow *Vistula*
RUSSIA
Kiev
Lvov
AUSTRIA
HUNGARY
MOLDAVIA

1793

EAST PRUSSIA
PRUSSIA
Thorn
Warsaw
Cracow
AUSTRIA
RUSSIA
BUKOVINA
1775 Bar
HUNGARY

1795

EAST PRUSSIA
Riga
Vilna
PRUSSIA
Warsaw
Cracow
AUSTRIA
RUSSIA
BUKOVINA
HUNGARY

Poland partitioned by Catherine of Russia and Frederick of Prussia.

former size, Poland bravely rose in revolt against her oppressors. Under the leadership of General Kościuszko, the Poles won several battles against the Russians and recaptured large tracts of territory. Warsaw and Vilna were liberated and Kościuszko was proclaimed dictator. Prussia then joined the Russians to suppress the patriots. And after Kościuszko's defeat at Maciejowice and the fall of Cracow and Warsaw, the last Polish field unit capitulated in November, 1794. The final partition of Poland came in 1795. Russia moved still farther west, occupying what remained of Lithuania; Austria moved farther north, beyond Cracow and up to the river Bug; and Prussia swallowed the rest, including Warsaw. Thus, Poland ceased to exist as a nation, but for generations it remained an area of dispute among Austria, Prussia and Russia.

Sweden

Frederick the Great and Catherine planned to partition Sweden as well. When Gustavus III succeeded to the throne in 1771, Sweden was close to anarchy. The previous fifty years had been a period of remarkable artistic and scientific achievement. Societies of science, painting and sculpture flourished; the great botanist, Carl von Linné, known as Linnaeus, published his *Species Plantarum* in 1753; Anders Celsius, professor of astronomy at the University of Upsala for fifteen years, invented the centigrade thermometer; Emanuel Swedenborg,

the Swedish philosopher, inventor, scientist and mystic, also studied at Upsala and began his work there. But this intellectual ferment coincided with ruinous political party rivalry. In a forceful yet bloodless coup d'état, Gustavus III arrested the Council, dissolved the Diet, and promulgated a new constitution. He pushed forward reforms in agriculture, commerce, administration and law, encouraged the study of science, and built up a powerful and well-equipped army and navy. Gustavus thus demonstrated to Prussia and Russia that Sweden would not submit passively to Poland's fate.

By 1787, Gustavus' forces were strong enough for a full-scale war. Suspecting that Catherine was subsidizing his enemies, he attacked her while the Russian army was heavily engaged in the second Turkish war. Gustavus' navy did well, and his army was preparing to march on St. Petersburg when an attack by Denmark—from which Gustavus wished to wrest Norway —forced him to withdraw his forces to defend Göteborg. Peace was finally achieved through the mediation of Prussia and England—both of which feared Russia's growing power in the Baltic.

To Gustavus—and to his enemy, Catherine the Great—England's own power, which had appeared irresistible in 1763, seemed irretrievably weakened. The empire England had so recently carved out for herself was crumbling: Wolfe's capture of Quebec in 1759 preceded by only sixteen years the convening of the second Continental Congress at Philadelphia.

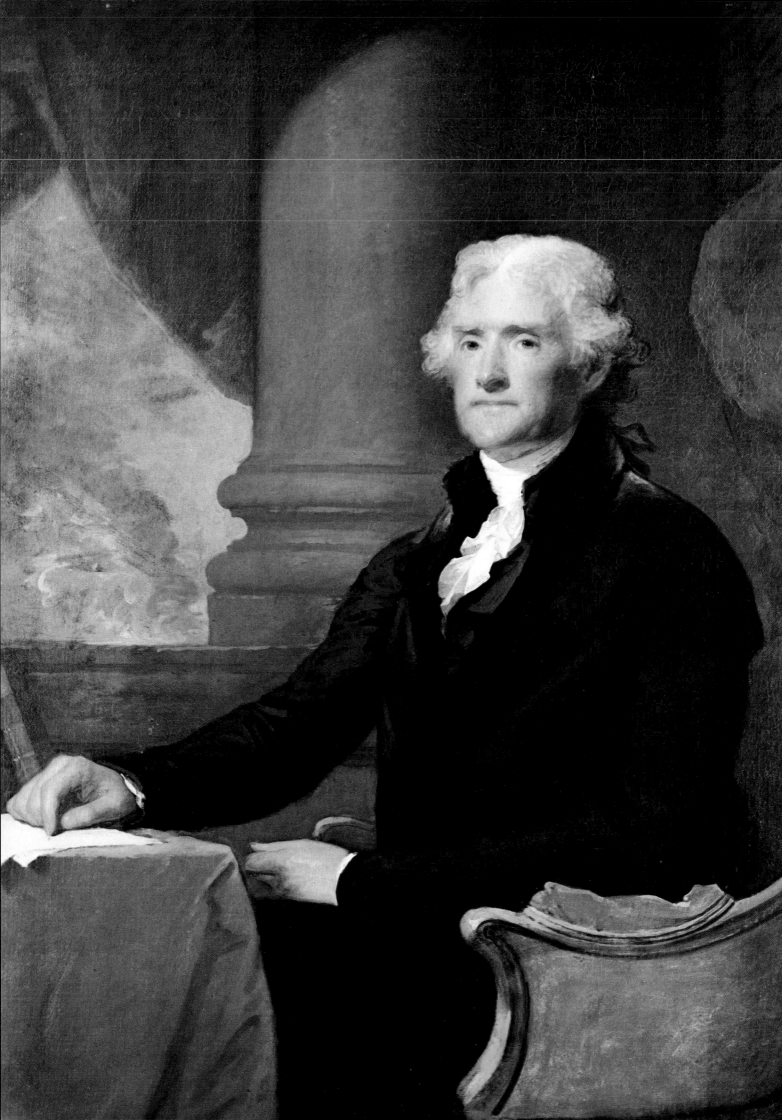

The Declaration of Independence

The angular and garrulous delegate from Virginia seemed an unlikely candidate for the vital task of drafting the Second Continental Congress' proclamation of independence. At thirty-three, Thomas Jefferson was one of the youngest of the representatives who had gathered in Philadelphia —and he was a notoriously ineffective public speaker. Yet Jefferson single-handedly drafted a declaration that not only evoked patriotic fervor in American readers but voiced the rebellious colonies' grievances with consummate diplomatic skill. So artfully worded was Jefferson's document that even the supremely autocratic King of France was able to support it. Ignoring the lanky Virginian's declaration that "governments derive their just powers from the consent of the governed," Louis XVI openly assisted the colonists—and in so doing, ensured the spread of the revolutionary spirit that toppled his own government twelve years later.

The Declaration of Independence, unlike the United States Constitution and most other such famous documents of history, is the work of one man. John Adams of Massachusetts and Benjamin Franklin of Pennsylvania suggested a few changes in the wording, but the responsibility for phrasing the sentiments expressed in that momentous manifesto fell to Thomas Jefferson, a gentleman from Virginia who possessed, to a greater degree than any of his colleagues, what John Adams termed "a happy talent of composition."

Jefferson had arrived in Philadelphia in June, 1775, as one of Virginia's delegates to the Second Continental Congress. The Second Congress was far more radical than the First, which had met in Philadelphia from September 5 to October 6, 1774, to protest Britain's colonial policy. The First Congress had sent several petitions of grievances to King George III, and it had formed the "Continental Association" to boycott British imports into the colonies and bar colonial exports to the Empire. But although the First Congress called for a thorough revamping of the Empire, few of its members contemplated a complete break with England when the Congress was adjourned.

By the time the Second Congress convened in May, 1775, however, England had rejected the petitions of the First Congress and had decided to end the rebellion with force. Armed skirmishes between colonial militia and British troops already had broken out at Lexington and Concord, and as the radicals in the Congress gained support, the delegates adopted measures that moved them inexorably toward the final break with the mother country. A Continental Army was formed; diplomatic feelers were sent to France; American ports were opened to foreign shipping; and finally, in June, 1776, a committee was appointed to draft a formal declaration of independence from Great Britain. The committee was composed of Adams, Franklin, Roger Sherman of Connecticut, Robert Livingston of New York and Jefferson.

Tall, sandy-haired, loose-jointed, Jefferson had not made a good first impression upon his arrival in Philadelphia. He seemed awkward. His clothes were ill-fitting and his talk was as loose and rambling as his gait. At a time when the ability to sway an audience counted heavily, he revealed himself as an ineffective public speaker. Fortunately for the cause of independence, he was blessed with other qualities. If he did not shine in public debate, he did show himself to be well informed, outspoken and incisive in committee work. Obviously the reputation he had made for himself in the House of Burgesses at Williamsburg was well earned.

Intellectually and physically the thirty-three-year-old delegate, one of the youngest men in the Congress, was a curious blend of the Old World and the New. Although he had grown up on the fringe of western settlement—which accounted for his fierce opposition to a government that fostered rank and privilege—he inherited from his mother, Jane Randolph, a member of one of the most distinguished families in the province, a taste for the good things of life. A lover of good books, good music and good wine, and at the same time an accomplished linguist, architect, farmer, naturalist and administrator, the extraordinarily versatile Jefferson could have made a name for himself in any one of half a dozen different professions.

There may have been a grain of truth in the wry comment of one critic that Thomas Jefferson was "a martyr to the disease of omniscience." But if like so many men of varied talents he flitted too easily over too many fields of knowledge, for at least once in his life—in the month of June, 1776—he was utterly and

A five shilling stamp of 1765. The Stamp Act of 1765, requiring almost every paper document to have an official stamp, created anger among all sections of the community.

Opposite Thomas Jefferson, author of the Declaration of Independence and third President of the United States.

An address to the civilized world

George III. He unnecessarily alienated his colonial subjects.

Lord North, British Prime Minister from 1770 to 1782. He tried to limit the freedom of the colonists and thus provoked them to oppose British authority by force.

exclusively engrossed in the task that had been assigned to him. Robert Livingston and Roger Sherman agreed with Adams and Franklin that the wording of the Declaration had better be left to the young delegate from Virginia. Jefferson retired to his lodging on Market Street and was not seen again until June 28, when he emerged with his first draft.

As he sharpened his quill, he may well have reminded himself that the primary purpose of the document over which he was laboring was not so much to declare independence as to proclaim to the world the reasons for declaring it. Jefferson's colleague, Richard Henry Lee, already had submitted a resolution to the Continental Congress on behalf of the Virginia delegation, declaring that "these United Colonies are, and of a right ought to be, free and independent States, that they are absolved from all allegiance to the British Crown, and that all political connection between them and the State of Great Britain is, and ought to be, totally dissolved." But before Congress would pass Lee's resolution, it had appointed the drafting committee to prepare a justification for independence.

Conscious that he was addressing not just the people of England and America but the whole civilized world, Jefferson began his justification with a lofty statement of purpose:

When, in the course of human events, it becomes necessary for one people to dissolve the political bands which have connected them with one another, and to assume among the powers of the earth the separate and equal station to which the laws of nature and of nature's God entitle them, a decent respect to the opinions of mankind requires that they should declare the causes which impel them to the separation.

There is nothing of the passionate rebel in this statement; indeed Jefferson would have denied that the colonists were rebels at all. On the contrary, they were a free people maintaining long-established rights against a usurping king.

Jefferson was writing with one eye on France, from whom it was essential that the colonists should get supplies if they were to make good their assertion of independence. For if the colonists seemed to be rebelling against rightful authority, no state in Europe would deal with them. Jefferson therefore had to persuade readers of the Declaration that the act of separation was legitimate—and more than that, he had to excite sympathy for a downtrodden people who had submitted for many years to the oppression of an unnatural tyrant. Sympathy for the downtrodden and indignation against the oppressor would, he hoped, culminate in active French support of the American cause. While it was too much to expect a king of France to smile upon the strange theory that "governments derive their just powers from the consent of the governed," it was possible that Louis XVI and his ministers might ignore what they did not like in the Declaration in view of the pleasing prospect of taking a hand in the disruption of the British Empire.

In the second paragraph of the Declaration, Jefferson set out to formulate a general political philosophy upon which to rest his case.

We hold these truths to be self-evident: that all men are created equal; that they are endowed by their Creator with certain inalienable rights; that among these are life, liberty, and the pursuit of happiness; that to secure these rights, governments are instituted among men, deriving their just powers from the consent of the governed; that whenever any form of government becomes destructive of those ends, it is the right of the people to alter or to abolish it, and to institute new government, laying its foundations on such principles, and organizing its powers in such form, as to them shall seem most likely to effect their safety and happiness.

The reader of the Declaration of Independence must even now be on guard against the haunting cadences with which Jefferson beguiled his readers. The truths that he called self-evident were not self-evident at all, either to his contemporaries or to later generations. As for the notion that all men are created equal, posterity is still wondering just what Jefferson meant by those words. Certainly men are equal in the eyes of God and in the eyes of English common law, but in every other way they are obviously and distressingly unequal. Even assuming that Jefferson did not include Negroes as men, he would have done better to have adopted the phrase used by his friend George Mason in the Virginia Bill of Rights—"all men are born equally free."

Yet, while it is easy to cavil over certain statements in the Declaration, we must remember that Jefferson was inspired by an ideal that he believed could be attained, for the first time in history, by the people for whom he was speaking. He was trying to harmonize the conduct of human affairs with what he believed to be the laws of the moral universe. However, like all great statesmen he was at the same time a shrewd, practical politician. The Declaration must also be regarded in another light, therefore, as a propaganda document whose purpose was to invigorate the rebellion. Its utterances must be viewed not only as a noble affirmation of the rights of man, but also as a political platform. Taken together they represented an ideal to which the writer and his party aspired.

Having affirmed the right of revolution under certain conditions, and having set forth the theory upon which the colonies would base their republican government, Jefferson moved from the abstract to a specific justification for exercising the rights enumerated in the first part of the document. Namely, he set forth a long list of grievances—not against Parliament, as might have been expected, since the dispute between the colonies and the mother country had

Above The Boston Massacre. This incident was exaggerated to arouse the colonists' discontent.

Below The attack on Bunker Hill and the burning of Charlestown in 1775.

The Declaration of Independence, signed by delegates from the thirteen states.

A satire on the Boston Port Act of 1773, by which the port Boston was closed as a result of the Boston Tea Party: in the picture Lord North pours tea into the mouth of America.

always centered on the question of parliamentary authority—but against the King. The reason for transposing the odium from Parliament to the King was that Congress had decided that Parliament was the legislative body only of Great Britain.

Jefferson cited the King's interference with representative government in the colonies, the harshness with which he administered colonial affairs, his restrictions on civil rights, his stationing of troops in the colonies and his restrictive tax and trade policies. The list also included some grievances that were not very serious, and others that were untrue—in particular the charge that George III had encouraged the slave trade against the wishes of the colonies.

Congress was only too happy to blame King George for every sin in the calendar, but considering that the slave trade was carried on by New England shipowners and supported by Southern purchasers, it would have seemed better not to mention it in the Declaration. John Adams, who acted as Jefferson's spokesman on the floor of Congress, fought hard for

A slave-holding devotee of freedom

the retention of the passage on slavery, but Congress decided against him and the offending passage was struck out. The word "slavery" therefore does not occur in the final text. There was perhaps an indirect reference to it in the charge that the King had deliberately fomented domestic insurrection in America—a charge that might have been taken as referring either to Indians or to Negroes. To have been more specific would have been embarrassing. Slavery was not a topic to be discussed in a document whose keynote was human freedom.

It was especially curious that Jefferson had inserted the section on slavery in light of his own attitude toward the institution. He never denied that slavery was a great evil, as harmful to the white man as to the Negro, but there was a vein of complacent optimism in Jefferson that allowed him to think that slavery would die a natural death. It was already dying out in the North, and in God's good time it would disappear in the Southern states as well. That he owned from one hundred to two hundred slaves, while at the same time maintaining as a self-evident truth that all men are created equal, does not seem to have disturbed him. He was a kind master, and his slaves were devoted to him, which may explain why he was so unconcerned by the equivocal role he continued to play, from July 4, 1776, to the day of his death exactly fifty years later, as a slaveholding devotee of freedom.

The debate in Congress over the provisions of the Declaration was an agonizing ordeal for the author. His committee had been very complimentary; they made only a few changes, which Jefferson promptly incorporated into a new draft. But the other members of Congress were not so easily satisfied. They cut out a quarter of what he had written, altered about two dozen words, and made two insertions in the peroration—references to a "Supreme Judge" and a "Divine Providence." Jefferson had already mentioned the Deity twice, but Congress wanted God in the peroration as well.

Lee's resolution of independence was approved on July 2, but the debate over the wording of the Declaration lasted another two days. Jefferson himself said nothing—he was busy making notes on the weather and on his current expenses. On July 3, the temperature was 76 degrees Fahrenheit—not a hot afternoon for Philadelphia in July. On that same day Jefferson spent 103 shillings, most of which went toward a thermometer. He also bought seven pairs of women's gloves and gave one shilling and sixpence "in charity." On the evening of July 4, the debate was closed, and all the members present with the exception of John Dickinson of Pennsylvania signed the Declaration. The thirteen colonies now became thirteen independent states.

Jefferson had succeeded in imparting a quality of timelessness and universality to what might otherwise have been merely a national document. His colleagues in Congress sensed they were doing far more than repudiating a king: they were founding a new order of society that had as its cornerstone the rights of free individuals. Jefferson had based his ideal of government on the philosophy of natural rights. According to that philosophy, man originally lived in a state of nature without benefit of civil authority. Possessing the right of life, liberty, property, and the pursuit of happiness, each man enforced those rights as best he could. Since the strong often took advantage of the weak, the time came when men were glad to surrender the state of nature for the civil state. In other words they acknowledged their inability to enforce their natural rights themselves, but in so doing they did not surrender them to anybody else. Those precious rights, frequently identified with God's will, no ruler could take from them. Implicit in this contract theory of the origins of civil authority were the doctrines of the consent of the governed and the right of revolution.

American colonists maintained that their philosophy was part of their inheritance, that it had come down to them in the writings of John Milton and John Locke. So obvious was that line of reasoning to the Founding Fathers that John Adams, who as he grew older was sometimes irritated by the eulogies that Fourth of July orators lavished on Jefferson, complained that there was not an idea in the Declaration "but what had been hackneyed in Congress for two years before." Jefferson did not deny it. He was not aiming at originality of principle or sentiment. The essential thing, he said, was "to place before mankind the common sense of the subject in terms so plain and firm as to command their assent, and to justify ourselves in the independent stand we are compelled to take."

Above A notice calling a meeting which resulted in the famous Boston Tea Party, when all the tea aboard the East India Company tea ships was dumped into Boston harbor.

Below Thomas Paine, author of *The Rights of Man*. In 1774 he went to America and took up the cause of the colonists.

Left Messengers ride through the thirteen states in July, 1776, reading the Declaration of Independence to the colonists.

597

The cause of all mankind

John Adams, delegate from Massachusetts, appointed a member of the committee to draft the Declaration of Independence.

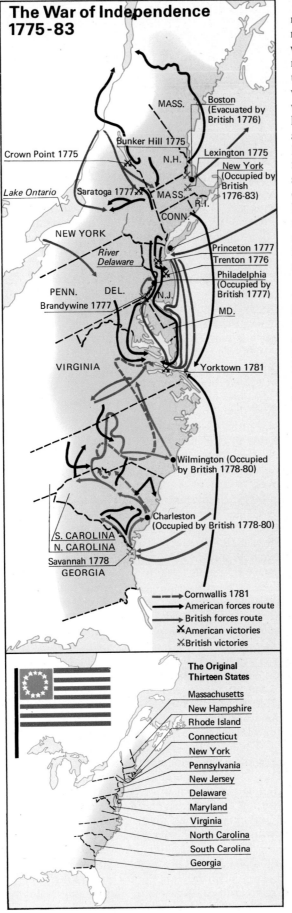

The War of Independence 1775-83

Boston (Evacuated by British 1776)
MASS.
Bunker Hill 1775
Crown Point 1775
Lexington 1775
N.H.
New York (Occupied by British 1776-83)
Lake Ontario
Saratoga 1777
MASS.
R.I.
CONN.
NEW YORK
River Delaware
Princeton 1777
Trenton 1776
Philadelphia (Occupied by British 1777)
PENN.   DEL.
N.J.
Brandywine 1777
MD.
VIRGINIA
Yorktown 1781
Wilmington (Occupied by British 1778-80)
Charleston (Occupied by British 1778-80)
S. CAROLINA
N. CAROLINA
Savannah 1778
GEORGIA

- - -> Cornwallis 1781
——> American forces route
——> British forces route
✗ American victories
✗ British victories

The Original Thirteen States

Massachusetts
New Hampshire
Rhode Island
Connecticut
New York
Pennsylvania
New Jersey
Delaware
Maryland
Virginia
North Carolina
South Carolina
Georgia

While Jefferson was right in insisting that the chief merit of the Declaration lay in its expression of commonly shared beliefs, both he and John Adams were wrong in assuming that the Declaration did nothing more than state what everyone was thinking, in the tone and spirit called for by the occasion. Even those who agreed with Jefferson—and there were many who did not—must have been aware that the truths he proclaimed as self-evident were far from being as axiomatic as he supposed. In substituting "life, liberty, and the pursuit of happiness" for the familiar formula, "life, liberty, and property," he made a significant departure from John Locke and all the other philosophers from whom he is said to have borrowed. No other state paper had ever suggested that one of the essential functions of government is to make men happy, or that one of man's natural rights is the pursuit of happiness. That was indeed a revolutionary doctrine.

It may be argued that the "pursuit of happiness," whatever it may be meant to include, is already implicit in "liberty." If a man is secure in life and liberty he can pursue anything he pleases. To many of Jefferson's contemporaries, the pursuit of happiness may well have seemed too cheap a thing to mention in a proclamation of human rights. As Aldous Huxley once put it, "happiness is like coke—something you get as a by-product in the process of making something else." Evidently Jefferson did not think of happiness as a by-product, but whether we agree with him or not, there is no question but that in specifying the pursuit of happiness as one of man's inalienable rights he launched America on uncharted seas. Today young people, not only in America but all over the world, are taking Jefferson's dictum more seriously than he may have intended.

In at least one other respect the Declaration was startlingly original, not in what it said but in what it omitted. It made no mention of the rights of British subjects. This was a significant omission, since throughout the entire controversy between the colonies and the mother country, beginning with the imposition of the Stamp Tax in 1764, those rights had been the mainstay of the American case. "No taxation without representation": Parliament had no right to tax British subjects without their consent. While his colleagues were still fighting it out along that line, Jefferson had shifted his ground. In his diatribe against George III he pointed out that the King had committed a worse crime than violating the rights of his subjects. He had violated the rights of man. Jefferson was now appealing to a higher court. Mankind in general might not be vitally interested in a controversy between Great Britain and her colonies involving intricate questions of constitutional law. There must be a more inflammable issue than that, and it was part of Jefferson's genius to identify it and present it as he did.

Possibly he was influenced by Thomas Paine, an Englishman recently arrived in America who had taken up the cause of the colonists with all the ardor of a convert. In his pamphlet *Common Sense*, Paine had pointed out that "the cause of America is in a

great measure the cause of all mankind." Many were won over by his eloquence, but Paine was essentially a rabble-rouser; Jefferson, of course, was not.

The argument that Jefferson made before the bar of world opinion has been attacked again and again, either in anger or contempt, by friends as well as enemies of the American Revolution. The critics have in general agreed with Rufus Choate, one of the great lawyer-statesmen of the nineteenth century, that the famous Declaration was after all nothing but a series of "glittering generalities." Jefferson's champions have been no less insistent and no less vocal than his critics. Perhaps the most famous is Abraham Lincoln. In 1861, on his way to Washington to take up the Presidency, Lincoln said:

I have never had a feeling politically that did not spring from the sentiments embodied in the Declaration of Independence. .. Something in that Declaration giving liberty, not only to the people of this country, but hope for the world for all future time....And that all should have an equal chance.

In those words, spoken in Independence Hall, Philadelphia, where the Declaration was signed, Lincoln suggests why it is that all leaders of nationalistic movements and all champions of liberal reform inevitably hark back to the Declaration of Independence. To them it stands for hope:

"till hope creates
From its own wreck the thing it contemplates."

Jefferson may have been overoptimistic when, in his old age, he wrote to John Adams that "the flames kindled on the fourth of July, 1776, have spread over too much of the globe to be extinguished by the feeble engines of despotism; on the contrary, they will consume those engines and all who work them. . . ." Unfortunately, the "engines of despotism" and those who work them have not yet been consumed, but wherever they still exist, and wherever they may appear in the future, they will always have to withstand the challenge of Jefferson's devastating rhetoric.   ARNOLD WHITRIDGE

The Battle of Yorktown, 1781. Britain's defeat at this battle made it finally clear that she must accept America's independence.

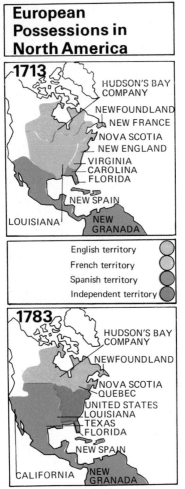

European Possessions in North America

1713

HUDSON'S BAY COMPANY
NEWFOUNDLAND
NEW FRANCE
NOVA SCOTIA
NEW ENGLAND
VIRGINIA
CAROLINA
FLORIDA
NEW SPAIN
LOUISIANA
NEW GRANADA

English territory
French territory
Spanish territory
Independent territory

1783

HUDSON'S BAY COMPANY
NEWFOUNDLAND
NOVA SCOTIA
QUEBEC
UNITED STATES
LOUISIANA
TEXAS
FLORIDA
NEW SPAIN
CALIFORNIA
NEW GRANADA

The Peace of Versailles, signed in January, 1783, recognized the independence of the American republic and renounced colonization on the American mainland. The Earl of Shelburne, whose position as England's Prime Minister had made him responsible for the conduct of the negotiations, had been anxious to keep America within the British sphere of influence. Shelburne hoped to see Britain and America become partners in Atlantic commerce, with America assuming the expensive responsibilities of governing North America and Britain becoming the accepted link between the United States and the Continent. He had consequently striven to obtain the Americans' goodwill and to provide them with an extensive market for British goods by granting them all the territory they wanted. Such largesse angered the Prime Minister's critics, who failed to understand its economic implications. Shelburne countered their attacks by pointing to the relatively small concessions that he had made to England's other enemies in the recent war—and considering the country's fortunes in that war and

the exhausted state in which it had left her, those concessions did indeed seem slight.

The war between England and her American colonies had been welcomed in France. Louis XVI's foreign minister, Charles Gravier Vergennes, hoped that the struggle would reverse the advantages that England had gained from the French and Indian War and provide a fitting retort to the Treaty of Paris. By the time that General John Burgoyne was forced to surrender to General Horatio Gates at Saratoga on October 17, 1777, the French were already supplying the Americans with muskets and gunpowder; the following year, war was formally declared

The widening war

France was but one of England's enemies. The League of Armed Neutrality—which was established in 1780 to prevent British ships from searching neutral vessels for contraband of war—eventually included Russia, Sweden, Austria, Prussia, Denmark, Spain and Holland in addition to France. And of those powers, Spain and Holland

actively joined in the hostilities against their traditional rival. Spain declared war on England in June of 1779 (after obtaining guarantees of French assistance in recovering Gibraltar and Florida) and immediately laid siege to Gibraltar. England declared war on Holland in November, 1780, in a vain attempt to prevent her from joining the League.

The British Navy—faced with the problem of relieving Gibraltar, supplying the army in America, fighting the French in the West Indies and guarding the Channel —was strained to the limit of its resources. The Caribbean island of St. Vincent fell to the French on June 20, 1779 (two days after Spain declared war on England), and Grenada capitulated a fortnight later. In January, 1780, Admiral George Rodney defeated a Spanish squadron off Cape St. Vincent, temporarily relieving Gibraltar and offering the British some respite. But later on that year the British fought three indecisive naval engagements with the French in the West Indies, and in April, 1781, the French, under the Marquis de Grasse-Tilly, captured Tobago. A French fleet led by

Pierre-André de Suffren Saint-Tropez prevented England from seizing the Dutch post on the Cape of Good Hope, and later captured a Ceylonese port that the Dutch had recently surrendered to the British. In July, 1781, the Spaniards captured Pensacola, Florida, and on October 19 Lord Cornwallis' forces at Yorktown surrendered to George Washington.

By February, 1782, the British seemed to be on the verge of collapse. The Spaniards followed up their victory in Florida by capturing Minorca on February 5, and a week later the French captured the West Indies island of St. Christopher. On February 22 a parliamentary motion that was harshly critical of the continuing war in America was defeated by only one vote—and a month later the Prime Minister, Lord North, handed in his resignation.

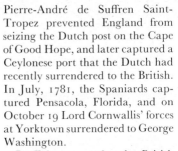

Tom Paine, the prophet of revolution.

Back from disaster

Late in 1782, however, the tide began to turn. Admiral Rodney defeated the French in the April 12 battle of The Saints, captured de Grasse and saved the West Indies. Seven months later, Admiral Lord Howe relieved Gibraltar. Within a year, Benjamin Franklin, the American minister in Paris, John Jay, who was to become Secretary for Foreign Affairs in 1784, and John Adams, the future President of the United States, were all in

Nelson at the Battle of St. Vincent, 1797.

Paris to negotiate a peace settlement.

By the Peace of Versailles, England recovered her West Indian possessions and retained Gibraltar; France, while saving her trading posts, agreed to abandon her other ambitions in India. She retrieved St. Lucia and gained Tobago in the West Indies, added Senegal and Gore in Africa and secured fishing rights off Newfoundland. Spain regained Florida and Minorca. Holland, in accordance with the terms of a separate treaty, retrieved all her former possessions, including the Ceylonese port of Trincomalee, but granted the British the right of navigation among the Dutch spice islands.

Age of achievement

In the year that the Peace of Versailles was signed, Ludwig van Beethoven published his first composition, Wolfgang Amadeus Mozart published his Mass in C Minor, William Blake his *Poetical Sketches*, Immanuel Kant his *Prolegomena zu einer jeden Künftigen Metaphysik*, William Herschel his *Motion of the Solar System in Space*, and Moses Mendelssohn his *Jerusalem*. The quarter-century that elapsed between the Treaty of Paris and the outbreak of the French Revolution—a quarter-century that was divided into two almost equal halves by the War of American Independence—was extraordinarily rich in artistic achievement, philosophical debate and scientific discovery.

Those years saw the ascendancy not only of Voltaire, Rousseau and Diderot, but of Sterne, Smollett, Goldsmith, Burns, Cowper, Johnson and Boswell. In Germany, Goethe and Schiller were rising to prominence. Johannes Ewald was writing for the Danish theater, Beaumarchais for the French, Alfieri for the Italian and Richard Brinsley Sheridan for the theaters of London. Guardi, Greuze and Fuseli were painting in Italy, Chardin, Fragonard and Boucher in France, and Reynolds, Romney and Gainsborough in England. Thomas Rowlandson and James Gillray had begun to lift the caricature into the realm of high art. Bach, Haydn, Beethoven, Gluck and Mozart were composing music for the churches, concert halls and operas of the world. Robert Adams and William Chambers were transforming the architecture of

Gluck, whose music broke away from the Italian tradition.

London, and Jacques Ange Gabriel was altering the face of Paris. In London, George Hepplewhite, Thomas Sheraton and Thomas Chippendale were providing exquisite furniture for the houses of the well-to-do.

The Royal Academy was founded in London in 1768, the Royal Academy of Sciences was established in Lisbon in 1779, and a national theater was set up in Stockholm in 1773. In 1780 Sebastien Erard made the first pianoforte in France; the first gymnasium was opened at Breslau in 1765; and the first carriage-traffic crossed the Brenner Pass in the Alps in 1772. In 1770 a Scottish explorer named James Bruce reached the headstream of the Blue Nile; in 1773 James Cook set out upon his third voyage into the Pacific; in 1783 the Montgolfier brothers ascended in a fire balloon at Annonay and the Marquis Jouffroy d'Abbans sailed down the Saône in a paddle-wheel steamboat; in 1785 Jean Blanchard and John Jefferies crossed the English Channel in a balloon; and in 1787 Horace de Saussure reached the summit of Mont Blanc.

Developments in science during the period were equally remarkable. Between 1764 and 1775 James Hargreaves invented the spinning jenny, Joseph Priestley published his *History of Electricity*, Richard Arkwright set up his spinning machine at Preston, Daniel Rutherford discovered nitrogen, Joseph Priestley discovered oxygen, and James Watt perfected the steam engine.

Revolution!

In the midst of all this intellectual ferment, the threat of international revolution arose: there were several uprisings outside France before 1789, and in 1775 there was a serious peasant uprising in Bohemia. In 1780 London experienced the worst riots in English history when Lord George Gordon, the unbalanced and vehemently Protestant son of the Duke of Gordon, led an angry mob of some 50,000 men to the House of Commons to protest a recently passed act that granted some minor relief to Roman Catholics. In several days of wild rioting at least seven hundred people lost their lives, and the damage done to property was incalculable. Many of the targets of the mob's fury were Irish immigrants, but the outbreak was essentially a revolt of the poor against authority, and it is possible to detect in the riots the first symptoms of the quasi-revolutionary movement that was to end the political system of George III.

There was unrest in the United States and the Low Countries as well during this period. In 1786 a Continental Army veteran named Daniel Shays led a rebellion against the United States government. Shays' Rebellion found widespread support among the people of Massachusetts, who were dismayed by the evident incapacity of both the state and federal governments to solve the economic ills of the territory and to lessen the crippling taxation. In September Shays and roughly a thousand followers converged on Springfield to prevent

the Supreme Court from convening, and the insurrection was not quelled until the Governor had raised an army of 4,400 men.

In Holland, the objects of resentment were the weak and unpopular Prince of Orange and his wife, the intensely disliked Frederika Wilhelmina of Prussia. Holland's commerce had been severely weakened by the recent war against England, and the peace that followed greatly strengthened the influence of the anti-Orange or Patriot Party. The insulting attitude of the Patriots toward the Prince and Princess, whose position by 1787 had become impossible, induced the Princess' uncle, the King of Prussia, to invade Holland, to place William V firmly back on the throne by force and to dissolve the Patriot Party.

There was trouble too in the Austrian Netherlands where there was passionate opposition to the Austrian Emperor's high-handed attempts to reform the Church and the administration without reference to the susceptibilities of the Flemings and the Walloons, and to his contempt for the "antediluvian rubbish" of the people's treasured rights and privileges. In 1787 their feelings burst out into violent riots which forced the Emperor to give way.

Two years later there was trouble in Sweden where Gustavus III, increasingly autocratic, established a new constitution by the Act of Unity and Security (February 17, 1789), thus granting to himself almost absolute powers.

But it was in France in the summer of 1789 that the revolution for which Europe had been waiting began.

Riots in London: three hundred prisoners were released from Newgate in 1780.

"Liberté, Egalité, Fraternité"

In the decades following its conversion into a prison, the crenelated confines of the Bastille served the political whims of four French kings. In the process, the fourteenth-century fortress became the detested symbol of France's arrogant and arbitrary autocracy. Its unfortunate inmates were arrested on lettres de cachet *issued by the King, spirited through the streets of Paris in closed carriages and incarcerated without trial. Not illogically, the ancient fortress became the focal point of anti-royalist ire during the popular risings of July, 1789—and when the fort's entire garrison surrendered to a mob of armed Parisians on July 14, the profound weakness of Louis XVI's government was at last revealed. The King had lost the support of his army—which would not fire upon the citizens—and from that moment, both he and his dynasty were doomed.*

Louis XVI and his son while they were in prison.

Opposite The attack on the Bastille. The prison was thought of as the main bastion of injustice.

Sunday, July 12, 1789. The best of summer was still to come. The day was fine but showery with a hint of coolness in the air. In Paris huge crowds were making their way to the bridges of the Seine. People were saying that Necker—who had been the commoners' favorite minister from the time he persuaded Louis XVI to double the number of deputies representing the Third Estate in the States-General—had been dismissed. What was going to happen next? Already there was a shortage of corn and the price of bread was higher than it had ever been within living memory. Did the enemies of the people—the aristocrats—want to starve French citizens in order to force them to give in? Or was the state on the verge of bankruptcy? Would the States-General, which had been convened on May 5, be dissolved before it even had a chance to debate the situation?

Instinctively, the crowd hurried to the Palais-Royal, a favorite meeting place for eighteenth-century Parisians. Inside, in the gardens, there were so many people crushed together that it was almost impossible to move. Self-appointed orators were standing on the tables, haranguing the crowds with inflammatory speeches. In order to hear the speakers, some of the onlookers had perched themselves precariously on the branches of chestnut trees.

In spite of his stammer, one particular orator seemed to be holding the attention of the crowd, and he had attracted a large group of interested listeners:

Do you realize that, although the Nation demanded that Necker should be kept on as a minister, they threw him out all the same! How much more insolently can they defy our wishes? They will stop at nothing after such behavior! Who knows whether they may not even be planning, arranging, at this very moment, a new Saint Bartholomew's Eve for all patriotic citizens! To arms! Let us all wear the green cockade, the symbol of hope. No doubt, the wretched police are present among us here! Well, let them watch me, listen to me, observe me carefully,

for it is I who proudly urge my brothers to seek their liberty!

At this point, the orator—an unemployed lawyer named Camille Desmoulins whose name was being whispered by everyone in the crowd—drew a pistol from his pocket and shouted: "At least, they will never take me alive! I shall die a glorious death! My one fear is to see France become enslaved!"

Chanting "To arms, to arms!" the crowd swarmed out of the Palais-Royal. A huge procession surged through the streets of Paris to the theaters, and demonstrators went inside and stopped the performances. Joined by the theater audiences, the crowd pressed on to the Musée Curtius, where waxwork figures of the most famous personalities of the age were exhibited. Some of the demonstrators went inside, only to emerge shortly afterward carrying the busts of Necker and the Duke of Orleans.

They continued on to the Tuileries gardens, where an enormous, frenzied crowd was shouting "Long live Necker!" and "To arms!" Suddenly there was pandemonium. People ran off in all directions, shouting that the "Royal Allemand" cavalry regiment had entered the gardens and was charging the crowd. At that moment it became obvious that if the people were to defend themselves, they had to be armed. It was rumored that a militia was to be formed, and that the district committees in Paris would be distributing arms and ammunition on the following day. The militia would be able to force the King and his evil counselors to recall Necker.

Very early the next morning, Jean-Baptiste Humbert—a watchmaker who eventually recorded his experiences during the turbulent days of July, 1789—went to his district committee headquarters in the parish of Saint-André-des-Arts, only to find that the group had already distributed the small quantity of firearms at its disposal. Nevertheless, Jean-Baptiste volunteered to join the citizens' militia

The opening of the States-General in 1789. Popular feeling was expressed at the assembly that led to outbreaks of revolt.

Below The Fall of the Bastille on July 14, 1789. The event was seen by many as a symbol of liberty.

Revolutionary Paris

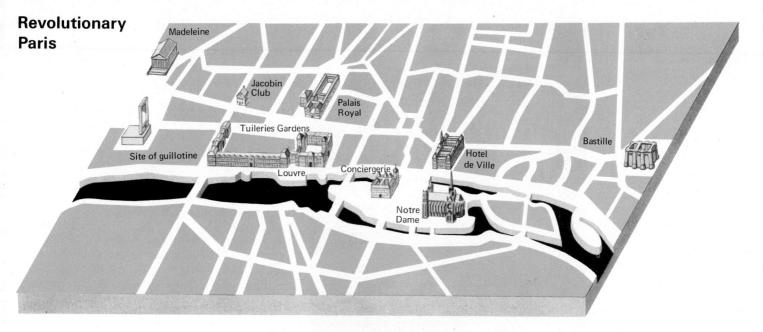

Releasing a prisoner from the Bastille.

Below The Bastille in September 1789. During the summer demolition work on the prison began.

that was being formed. The "electors"—men chosen by each district assembly to elect the deputies representing Paris in the States-General—had decided that every district of the city should raise two hundred men. According to their plan, a total force of 12,000 men could be recruited from the sixty districts of Paris. Those men were badly needed, for news had just come that during the previous night the majority of the customs posts at the gateways to the city had been pillaged and burned down.

It was vital to prevent any repetition of such scenes, and the unarmed watchmaker spent the whole day patrolling the streets of his district. In the evening, the local committee received orders to recruit an additional six hundred men. The anxious electors had decided that the citizens' militia must be increased to 48,000 men. But how were they going to arm all these volunteers? Where could they find the firearms and ammunition?

When daybreak came at last, Humbert and the other exhausted members of his patrol returned to the Assembly. After a short rest, Humbert rose and went out into the street, where he learned that firearms were being distributed at the Invalides. He immediately rushed off to find Monsieur Poirier, the commander of the local militia, and asked him to lead the members of his group to the Invalides. Poirier, pestered with thousands of questions, seemed in no hurry to leave. Impatiently, Humbert seized him by the arm and, followed by five or six other citizens, escorted the reluctant commander to the Invalides.

An enormous crowd had collected on the parade ground in front of the building, and it proved impossible to remain together. Humbert soon found himself separated from his companions, and he entered the huge building by himself. Following the surging crowd through the corridors, he eventually reached the cellars where the weapons and ammunition were stored. As he gained the bottom of the staircase, Humbert caught sight of a man holding

The Bastille surrenders

The Petit Trianon at Versailles, where Queen Marie-Antoinette played at being a milkmaid.

Below The march to Versailles in October 1789. Officers of the Royal Guard who tried to prevent the march were decapitated and their heads carried on pikes by the marchers.

two muskets. He seized one of them and turned to the stairs—only to find that it was impossible to move. The crowd had become so dense that anyone trying to climb up the stairs was pushed down again. It became almost impossible to breathe and terrible shrieks and cries could be heard above the tumult. In desperation, some of those who had obtained muskets advanced with fixed bayonets on the others, forcing those who still had no arms to clear a passage.

Humbert lost sight of his companions in the chaos. He left the Invalides on his own and returned to the Hôtel de Ville, where powder was purportedly being dispensed to the citizens. The watchmaker succeeded in obtaining a quarter of a pound of powder but no musket balls. The clock struck three. Suddenly, the sound of shooting was heard coming from an easterly direction. "They must be fighting at the Bastille," someone said. Humbert rushed into a nearby grocer's shop and bought some little nails, which he planned to use as projectiles in his musket. As he emerged from the shop, a citizen announced that the Hôtel de Ville had finally received a supply of ammunition. Humbert therefore turned back, and was given six pellets of buckshot. Equipped with ammunition, he hurried off to the Bastille.

It was half-past three by the time that Humbert arrived. The outer drawbridge had already been pulled down by the attackers, who were now trying to drag two cannon into the outer courtyard. Humbert gave them a hand and soon found himself in the front of the crowd. Cannon were placed in position at the main gate of the fortress, the drawbridge was raised and the firing began. Humbert fired six rounds of ammunition. As he did so, a hand appeared through a small oval opening on one side of the gate, waving a piece of paper. One of the citizens fetched a wooden beam from a nearby carpenter and placed it across the moat. A man began to walk across the plank but lost his balance and fell. Another man followed him, grasped the paper and read it out loud: "We have about twenty thousand pounds of gunpowder, and we intend to blow up the garrison and the whole district if you do not capitulate. The Bastille, 5 p.m., July 14, 1789."

The note, which was signed by de Launay, the commander of the fortress, did not produce the desired effect. On the contrary, it provoked unanimous shouts of "Lower the drawbridges! We shall never give in!" The citizens began to reload the cannon, and they were on the point of firing when the drawbridge was suddenly lowered. (Later on it was learned that the Invalides soldiers, who formed part of the garrison in the Bastille, had forced the commander to open the gates.) The crowd poured into the fortress; Humbert was in the vanguard. Nine hundred and fifty-four craftsmen, shopkeepers and common citizens, all of whom lived in Paris but many of whom had come from the provinces, earned themselves the title of "conquerors of the Bastille."

The building of the Bastille had been started in 1370, during the reign of Charles v. By the seventeenth century, the fortress had lost most of its importance as a citadel of defense, and Cardinal

ROI ET DE SA FAMILLE À VARENNE LE 22 JUIN 1791

ation du Roi a eu lieu à Varennes, à cinq lieues de France, vers une heure après u moment où l'on venait d'en être prévenu par M. Drouet, maître de poste de nehoull, qui a rendu un service essentiel à la France, qu'elle surprise pour les se voir arrêtés au milieu de la nuit, par deux braves gardes nationaux

LA RECOMPENCE ACORDÉE A Mr DROUET EST DE 30 MILLE LIVRE ET A Mr SAUCE 20 MILLE LIVRE

qui ont bravé les menaces d'un détachement de hussards, qui avoit été commandé par traître Bouillé ! M Sauce, Procureur de la Commune, a invité le Roi d'entrer ch lui et de s'y reposer lui et sa famille Le généreux citoyen de Varennes n'a poi accepté les offres du Roi, disant qu'il devoit tout à sa patrie.

Richelieu, the chief minister of Louis XIII, had converted it into a prison. The Bastille was no ordinary prison, however—it was a state prison. The old fort's unfortunate inmates were not being held for crimes or offenses committed under the common law. They had—without exception—been summarily arrested on *lettres de cachet*—in other words, at the direct and arbitrary order of the King.

In Richelieu's time the Bastille housed as many as fifty-three prisoners, but the number of arrests made by *lettres de cachet* had decreased, and under the reign of Louis XVI the prison held an average of only sixteen prisoners a year. Indeed, on July 14, 1789, the day the Bastille was captured, the victorious citizens found only seven prisoners inside. Moreover, these prisoners had a fairly easy time of it. A prisoner with private means was allowed to send for his own furniture, servants and meals. Poorer prisoners received enough money to provide themselves with the necessities of life. In the eighteenth century the cells were furnished by the state, although prisoners were allowed to add their own personal articles. The food, supplied by the prison, was good, and on occasions prisoners were invited to dine with the warden. It is true that there were some damp, unhealthy dungeons underground—as well as prison cells exposed to bitter cold in winter and the heat of summer, located at the top of the towers of the fortress—but none of them had been used since 1776.

Nevertheless, the Bastille remained an object of great hatred. It symbolized the absolutist authority of the King in its most despotic form. Moreover, its operation was shrouded in secrecy. Prisoners were arrested clandestinely and driven to the Bastille in closed carriages. The soldiers on guard duty were obliged to stand with their faces to the wall, and the prison warders were forbidden to have any conversation whatsoever with the prisoners. Moreover, the

latter were not interrogated when they were arrested and never knew how long they were going to be imprisoned in the Bastille. They might be released several weeks, several months or even several years after they were arrested, upon receipt of another *lettre de cachet* from the King.

By the end of the eighteenth century, most of the prisoners in the Bastille were writers who had publicly denounced various corrupt practices of the regime. Voltaire spent a year in the Bastille in 1717–18, and was incarcerated for another twelve days in 1726. The Abbé Morellet, one of the leaders of the *Parti Philosophique*, was imprisoned for six weeks in 1760. The journalist Linguet remained there from

The arrest of the Royal family at Varenne in 1791. The failure of Louis' attempt to escape led to his execution.

A "religious procession" under the Directorate. Despite anti-clerical feeling in France, religious rights and ceremonies remained popular.

The army supports the populace

Louis XVII as the Dauphin.

The trial of Marie-Antoinette. Although her life had estranged her from the people, many were impressed by her courage during the trial.

1780 to 1782, and during that time he wrote *Mémoires sur la Bastille*, which he published upon his release from prison. For those who believed in free speech, free thinking and free writing, therefore, the Bastille represented everything that was shameful in the *ancien régime*.

Those reasons do not fully explain why the storming of the Bastille should have brought about the capitulation of the monarchy and the victory of the French Revolution. For an explanation of why the government toppled, one must examine a remarkable result of the capture of the old fort. The fall of the Bastille served to illustrate—better than any other event during that stormy period—a fact that was both obvious and almost incredible: the army

did not want to fight against the revolutionaries. On June 24, two companies of "Gardes Françaises" had refused to go on duty. They were followed on June 28 by other companies of soldiers, who laid down their firearms and ammunition and joined the people assembled in the Palais-Royal, assuring the crowds of citizens that they would never fight against the Parisians. Fourteen grenadiers, believed to be the ringleaders, were put in prison, only to be released by the demonstrators. Seventy-five members of the Swiss regiment of Salis-Samade deserted to the citizens' side during the first fortnight in July.

The army's reluctance to fight was graphically demonstrated on the morning of July 14, when the crowd attacked the Invalides and seized the 40,000 muskets that were stored there. Five thousand well-armed soldiers were encamped some four hundred yards from the Invalides at the time. Their commander, the Swiss general Besenval, intended to defend the Invalides. In fact, as soon as he received word that the rioters had arrived, he sent for his corps commanders—who informed the general that they could not rely on the cooperation of their men. According to one witness, the Count of Salmour, "from that moment onwards, the generals were agreed that it was impossible to subdue Paris and that the only prudent course of action was to withdraw." Thus, when de Launay surrendered the Bastille, he did so for two reasons: first, because the Swiss soldiers who garrisoned the Bastille refused to fight, and second, because he knew that he could expect no help from the army outside the fortress. In truth, the fall of the Bastille was due far more to the defection of the troops stationed in Paris than to the enthusiasm and bravery of the attackers. If the 30,000 troops that Louis XVI had concentrated in and around the capital had made the slightest attempt to stop the citizens from attacking, the Bastille would never have been taken. But the defection of the soldiers and their fraternization with the revolutionaries was a clear indication that they too were infected with revolutionary zeal. From that day on, the French monarchy, deserted by its defenders, had no choice but to capitulate.

The fall of the Bastille served as the perfect symbol of royal surrender. The Duke of Dorset, British ambassador to Paris, wrote to the British foreign secretary on July 16: "So, My Lord, the greatest revolution ever known in the history of mankind has just taken place and, relatively speaking, taking into consideration the results as a whole, it has cost very little in the way of bloodshed. At this moment we can consider France as a free country, the King as a monarch whose powers are restricted and the nobles as being reduced to the level of the rest of the nation." In explaining the situation to President Washington, Gouverneur Morris, the new United States ambassador to Paris, noted: "You may now consider the revolution to be over since the authority of the King and the nobles has been utterly destroyed."

The consequences of the fall of the Bastille soon made themselves felt. On July 17, Louis XVI visited Paris in person and was forced to recognize the

Louis XVI is separated from his family. The Royal family were accused of conspiring with foreign countries against the French people.

Permanent Committee, or new revolutionary municipal council, as well as the citizens' militia known as the National Guard. Before July 14, revolutionary municipal councils and citizens' militias had been formed in some of the provincial towns of France. After the fall of the Bastille, this revolutionary movement spread like wildfire. In the country, the peasants attacked the chateaux and destroyed the ancient charters that recorded the peasants' feudal obligations to their masters. In the towns, the bourgeois seized power from the King's representatives and formed National Guard companies to defend themselves. In order to keep the people calm and under control, the States-General, which had become the constituent national assembly, proclaimed the abolition of the "feudal regime." On August 26 they published a "Declaration of the Rights of Man and of the Citizen" that laid the foundations for the new regime: liberty, equality and the sanctity of property.

The movement grew in violence, and soon reached the point of no return. On October 5 the citizens of Paris, fearing fresh counterrevolutionary action on the part of the King, marched on Versailles and took Louis XVI and his family prisoner. The constituent assembly gave France a new constitution and new institutions, based on the rational ideas and beliefs that the French *philosophes* had been developing since the beginning of the century.

The revolutionary fervor soon spread to other countries, including the United States, Great Britain, the Netherlands, Germany, Switzerland, Italy, Hungary and Poland. At the same time, the forces of reaction and conservatism began to organize a counterrevolutionary movement. The clash between revolution and counterrevolution proved disastrous for Europe. From April 20, 1792 onward, that clash took the form of an international war—one that was to last for twenty-three years almost without a break. The counterrevolution's apparent triumph at Waterloo in 1815 proved to be an illusion. In reality, revolutionary ideas, principles and institutions had taken firm root not only in France but in all Europe, and in North, Central and South America.

JACQUES GODECHOT

A revolutionary committee meeting during the Terror. Until Napoleon restored firm central government, France was in danger of sliding into anarchy.

A Play for All Seasons — William Shakespeare's reworking of a familiar folk legend gives the stage its most famous tragedy

1601

1609

Revolt of the Netherlands — Aft eighty years of determined resistance, the Dutch win their independence from Europe's mightiest monarch, Philip II of Spain

Jan van Oldenbarneveldt 1547-1619
Dutch statesman

William Laud 1573-1645
Archbishop of Canterbury

William Bradford 1590-1657
Governor of Plymouth Colony

Louis XIII 1601-43
King of France

Charles IX 1550-1611
King of Sweden

Inigo Jones 1573-1652
English architect

Duke of Buckingham 1592-1628
Favorite of James I

Jules Mazarin 1602-61
Italian cardinal and French minister

Boris Godunov 1552-1605
Muscovite boyar, later Tsar

Peter Paul Rubens, Sir 1577-1640
Flemish painter

John Eliot 1592-1632
English statesman

Abel Tasman c. 1603-59
Dutch explorer

Richard Hakluyt 1552-1616
English geographer

Christian IV 1577-1648
King of Denmark and Norway

Shah Jahan 1592-1666
Mogul Emperor

John IV 1603-56
King of Portugal

Francisco, Duke of Lerma 1552-1625
Spanish minister

Philip III 1578-1621
King of Spain

Thomas Wentworth, Earl of Strafford
1593-1641 *English statesman*

Philip IV 1605-65
King of Spain

Matthias 1557-1619
Holy Roman Emperor

Ferdinand II (of Styria) 1578-1637
King of Bohemia, Holy Roman Emperor

Gottfried von Pappenheim 1594-1632
Imperial general

Rembrandt van Rijn 1606
Dutch painter

Johann, Count of Tilly 1559-1632
Imperial general

William Harvey 1578-1657
English physician

Gustavus II Adolphus 1594-1632
King of Sweden

Pierre Corneille 1606-84
French dramatist

Jacobus Arminius 1560-1609
Dutch theologian

Frans Hals 1581-1666
Dutch painter

John Hampden 1594-1643
English statesman

Anne of Austria 1607
Queen, Regent of Fran

Duc de Sully 1560-1641
French statesman

Albrecht Wallenstein 1583-1634
Imperial general

Frederick V "the Winter King" 1596-1632
Elector Palatine, King of Bohemia

Michel de Ruyter 1607
Dutch admiral

Francis Bacon, Earl of Verulam, 1561-1626
English philosopher and statesman

John Pym c. 1583-1643
English Puritan leader

Michael Romanov 1596-1645
Tsar of Russia

George Monk 1608-7
English general

William Shakespeare 1564-1616
English dramatic poet

Hugo de Groot (Grotius)
1583-1645 *Dutch jurist*

René Descartes 1596-1650
French philosopher

John Milton 1608-
English poet

Galileo Galilei 1564-1642
Italian astronomer

Axel Oxenstierna 1583-1654
Swedish Chancellor

Marten Harpertzoon Tromp
1597-1653 *Dutch admiral*

John Casimir 1609-
King of Poland

James I 1566-1625
King of England (James VI of Scotland)

Frederick Henry 1584-1647
Prince of Orange, Stadholder of Netherlands

Giovanni Bernini 1598-1680
Italian sculptor

Henri Turenne 1611-7
Marshal of France

Count of Gondomar 1567-1626
Spanish diplomat

Cornelis Jansen 1585-1638
Dutch Catholic theologian

Anthony Van Dyck 1599-1641
Flemish painter

Henry Vane 1613-63
English Puritan administra

Claudio Monteverdi 1567-1643
Italian composer

Duc de Richelieu 1585-1642
French cardinal, statesman

Oliver Cromwell 1599-1658
Lord Protector of England

André Lenôtre 1613-17
French landscape garde.

Ambrose, Marquis de Spinola
1569-1630 *Italian general*

Mohammed Kuprili 1586-1661
Turkish Grand Vizier

Robert Blake 1599-1657
English admiral

Cardinal de Retz 1614
French politician

John Donne 1572-1631
English poet and clergyman

Gasper de Guzmán, Count Olivares
1587-1645 *Spanish minister*

Diego Velasquez 1599-1660
Spanish painter

Ben Jonson 1572-1637
English dramatic poet

Thomas Hobbes 1588-1679
English philosopher

Charles I 1600-49
King of England, Scotland and Ireland

Marie de Medici 1573-1642
Queen of France

Ahmed I 1589-1617
Ottoman Sultan

Pedro Calderón 1600-81
Spanish dramatist

1600
Tokugawa period in Japan: capital Tokyo

1609
Invention of microsc (or ? 1590)

1602-18
Persian-Turkish War (Persian territorial gains in war with Turkey)

1610
Assassination of Henr of France

1611
Brandenburg acquir Prussia

1605
Gunpowder Plot: failure leads to Catholic persecution in England

1
Accession of Roma dynasty in Muscovy

1598
Edict of Nantes

1609
All Moriscos expelle from Spain

The Pilgrims at Plymouth — An intrepid band of expatriate Englishmen establishes a new atmosphere of religious diversity in the New World

1620

1631

The Rape of Magdeburg — The Protestant citizens of Magdeburg defy their Catholic Emperor and spark a religious war that engulfs the Continent

1649

"A Cruel Necessity" — Decades of bitter dissension between Parliament's Puritan radicals and England's fumbling monarch culminate in the execution of Charles I

1666

Cambridge's Young Genius — One of Trinity College's least promising graduates, Isaac Newton, lays the foundation for modern physics

"L'état c'est moi" — Declaring that he *is* the state, Cardinal Mazarin's astonishing pupil, Louis XIV, guides the French nation through its golden age

1661

angzeb 1618-1707 *ul Emperor*   Christiaan Huyghens 1629-95 *Dutch mathematician and physicist*   Sheng Tsu - K'ang Hsi Emperor 1654-1722 *Manchu Emperor of China*   Frederick Augustus the Strong 1670-1733 *Elector of Saxony, King of Poland*

rge William 1619-40 *tor of Brandenburg*   Charles II 1630-85 *King of England*   Jean Racine 1639-99 *French tragic poet and dramatist*   Charles XI 1655-97 *King of Sweden*   John Law 1671-1729 *Scottish financier in France*

ce Rupert of the Rhine 1619-82 *eral and admiral*   John Dryden 1631-1700 *English poet*   Leopold I 1640-1705 *Austrian Emperor*   Edmond Halley 1656-1742 *English astronomer*   Peter I the Great 1672-1725 *Tsar of Russia*

n Baptiste Colbert 1619-83 *nch statesman*   Jan Vermeer 1632-75 *Dutch painter*   Sophia Alexeyevna 1657-1704 *Regent for Peter I of Russia*   Philip Duke of Orleans 1674-1723 *French Regent*

derick William "the Great Elector" 0-88 *Elector of Brandenburg*   John Locke 1632-1704 *English philospher*   Mehemmed IV 1641-91 *Ottoman Sultan*   Frederick I 1657-1713 *First King of Prussia*

de La Fontaine 1621-95 *ch poet*   Christopher Wren, Sir 1632-1723 *English architect and mathematician*   Michel de Louvois 1641-91 *French statesman*   George I 1660-1727 *King of Great Britain*

Masaniello (Tommaso Aniello) 622-47 *Neapolitan rebel leader*   Isaac Newton, Sir 1641-1727 *English physicist*   Charles II 1661-1700 *King of Spain*

Charles X 1622-60 *King of Sweden*   Antony van Leeuwenhock 1632-1723 *Dutch natural historian*   Robert Harley, Earl of Oxford 1661-1724 *English statesman*

Jean Baptiste Molière 1622-73 *French Comic dramatist*   Charles V of Lorraine 1643-90 *General in Imperial service*   Mary II 1662-94 *Queen of England*

Blaise Pascal 1623-62 *French scientist and philospher*   Baruch Spinoza 1632-77 *Portuguese Dutch philospher*   William Penn 1644-1718 *English Quaker*   George Byng 1663-1733 *English admiral*

John III Sobieski 1624-96 *King of Poland*   James II 1633-1701 *King of England*   Prince Eugène of Savoy 1663-1736 *Imperial general*

George Fox 1625-91 *Founder of Society of Friends*   Jules Hardouin Mansart 1645-1708 *French architect*   John Vanbrugh 1664-1726 *English dramatist and architect*

Christina 1626-89 *Queen of Sweden*   Marshal Vauban 1633-1707 *French military engineer*   Giulio Alberoni 1664-1752 *Italian minister to Philip V of Spain*

Marie de Sévigné 1626-96 *French noblewoman, writer*   Ahmed Kuprili 1635-76 *Turkish Grand Vizier*   Gottfried Leibnitz 1646-1716 *German mathematician and philospher*   Anne 1665-1714 *Queen of Great Britain*

Sivaji Bhonsle 1627-80 *Maratha leader*   John Churchill, Duke of Marlborough 1650-1722 *English general and statesman*   Ivan V 1666-96 *Joint Tsar of Russia*

Jacques-Bénigne Bossuet 1627-1704 *French preacher and historian*   Marquise de Maintenon 1635-1719 *Second wife of Louis XIV*   Jonathan Swift 1667-1745 *English satirist*

olas Fouquet 1615-80 *nch statesman*   John Bunyan 1628-88 *English writer*   Johan Gyllenstjerna 1635-80 *Swedish minister*   William III (of Orange) 1650-1702 *King of England*   William Congreve 1670-1729 *English dramatist*

olomé Murillo c. 1617-82 *ish painter*   Duke of Luxembourg 1628-95 *French general*   Maria Teresa 1639-83 *Queen of France*   François de la Mothe Fénelon 1651-1715 *French writer, theologian*

cesco Morosini 1618-94 *etian commander and Doge*   Alexis 1629-76 *Tsar of Russia*   Louis XIV 1638-1715 *King of France*   André Hercule de Fleury 1653-1743 *French statesman*

18 ● Defenestration of Prague: beginning of Thirty Years' War

● 1631 Franco-Swedish Treaty of Bärwalde

1644 ● Mandarin dynasty established in China

Swedish ambitions curbed by **1660** treaties of Oliva and Copenhagen

● 1670 Secret Treaty of Dover between Charles II and Louis XIV against Holland: formation of Whig party in England.

● African slaves first brought **1619** to North America

● Galileo condemned **1633** by the Inquisition

Peace of the Pyrenees **1659 ●** between France and Spain

Turkish-Venetian War **1645-64 ●**

● Acute Anglo-French rivalry **1664** in India begins

1622 ● English take Hormuz and gain influence in declining Persian Empire

1640 ● Portugal gains independence from Spain (Braganza Dynasty)

● 1648-53 Fronde revolt in France

1658 ●

Battle of the Dunes: French and English defeat Spanish

● 1673 Test Act: Catholics excluded from **1660** public office in England (till 1828)

1621 ● tavus Adolphus quers Livonia

● 1624 Foundation of New Amsterdam (New York)

1648 ● Peace of Westphalia: end of Thirty Years' War

1652 ● Capetown founded by Dutch settlers

1657 ● English cripple Spanish fleet off Teneriffe

Stuart Restoration

● 1667 Peace of Breda ends second Dutch-English War

1621 ● esumption of utch War of dependence

● 1624 Virginia becomes royal colony

1630 Treaty of Madrid ends Anglo-Spanish War

1630 Massachusetts colonization begun

● 1629-40 Charles I of England rules without Parliament

Treaty of Münster divides Netherlands **1648**

● 1641 Dutch capture Malacca and establish supremacy in East Indies for 150 years

1655-7 Swedish-Polish War

1651 ● First Navigation Act gives English shipping monopoly and opens Dutch-English War (-1659)

1664 ● Treaty of Vasvar: twenty year Austrian-Turkish truce

● 1669 Aurangzeb prohibits Hinduism in India: Maratha rising under Sivaji till 1707

1621 ● flict between English and ch East India Companies

1675	1690	1705	1720

1683

Vienna Under Siege — Kara Mustafa leads the "invincible" armies of the Ottoman Sultan in a final — and nearly successful — assault on Vienna

A Window on the West — Traveling incognito through Europe, Peter the Great learns technological skills that enable him to Westernize his empire

1698

1713

Twilight of the Sun King — The treaties of Utrecht and Rastatt curb the Sun King's territorial ambitions and restore peace to Europe

1720

The South Sea Bubble — The spectacular collapse of the South Sea Company ruins thousands of stock speculators and topples the English government

Alexander Pope 1688-1744
English poet

Nadir Shah 1688-1747
Turcoman Shah of Persia

John V "the Magnanimous" 1689-1750
King of Portugal

Charles de Montesquieu 1689-1755
French political philosopher

Elizabeth Farnese 1692-1766
Queen of Spain

François Marie Voltaire 1694-1778
French philospher

Robert Walpole 1676-1745
English Whig statesman

Maurice de Saxe 1696-1750
French general

Stanislas Leszcznski 1677-1766
King of Poland

Joseph François Dupleix 1697-1763
Governor of French East India Company

Joseph I 1678-1711
Austrian Emperor

William Hogarth 1697-1764
English artist

Charles XII 1682-1718
King of Sweden

Antonio Canaletto 1697-1768
Italian painter

Philip V 1683-1746
King of Spain

Mahé de Labourdonnais 1699-1753
French naval officer

George II 1683-1760
King of Great Britain

Sebastian Pombal 1699-1782
Portuguese statesman

Charles VI 1685-1740
Austrian Emperor

Anders Celsius 1701-44
Swedish astronomer

Johann Sebastian Bach 1685-1750
German composer

John Wesley 1703-91
English preacher

George Berkeley 1685-1753
British philosopher and bishop

Benjamin Franklin 1706-90
American statesman and scientist

George Frederic Handel 1685-1759
German-English composer

Linnaeus 1707-78
Swedish botanist

Anthony Heinsius d. 1720
Grand Pensionary of Holland

Georges Buffon 1707-88
French naturalist

Emanuel Swedenborg 1688-1722
Swedish theological writer

Francis I 1708-65 *Austrian Emperor, Duke of Lorraine and Tuscany*

Frederick William I 1688-1740
King of Prussia

William Pitt the Elder 1708-88
English statesman

Elizabeth 1709-62
Empress of Russia

Louis XV 1710-74
King of France

David Hume 1711-76
Scottish philospher

Louis-Joseph de Montcalm 1712-58
French general

Jean Jacques Rousseau 1712-78
French philosopher

Frederick II the Great 1712-86
King of Prussia

Denis Diderot 1713-84
French philospher

Christoph von Gluck 1714-87
German composer

Charles III 1716-88
King of The Two Sicilies, then of Spain

Maria Theresa 1717-80
Queen of Bohemia and Hungary

Jean d'Alembert 1717-83
French mathematician and philosopher

Charles Vergennes 1717-87
French statesman

Etienne de Choiseul 1719-85
French statesman

Antoinette de Pompadour 1721-64
Mistress of Louis XV of France

Adam Smith 1723-90
Scottish economist

John Burgoyne 1723-92
British general in North America

Joshua Reynolds 1723-92
English painter

Ahmed Shah 1724-73
Afghan ruler

Immanuel Kant 1724-1804
German philosopher

Robert Clive 1725-74 *British soldier serving East India Company*

James Wolfe 1727-59
British soldier in Canada

Anne Robert Jacques Turgot 1727
French economist and statesman

Thomas Gainsborough 1727
English painter

John Wilkes 1727-97
English politician

Peter III 1728-62
Tsar of Russia

James Cook 1728-79
English navigator and explorer

Gotthold Lessing 1729
German writer

Robert Adam 1729
English architect

Catherine II the Great 1729
Empress of Russia

Edmund Burke 1729-97
British historian and statesman

Stanislas Augu 1732-98 *King*

George Washington
American general

Jacques
French

Joseph Priestley
English chemist

1678-79
Peace of Nijmegen ends Franco-Dutch War, confirms Swedish territorial gains

1685
Revocation of the Edict of Nantes: persecution of French Huguenots

League of Augsburg **1686**
against France

Glorious Revolution **1688**
in England

1679
Habeas Corpus Act: protection against arbitrary arrest in England

Bill of Rights gives **1689**
political supremacy to Parliament in Britain

1690
Battle of the Boyne: conquest of Ireland by William III

1694
Gold discovered in Minas Gerais, Southern Brazil

1694
Bank of England founded

1697
Treaty of Ryswick: Louis XIV recognizes defeat by League of Augsburg

1700-21
Great Northern War

1701
Elector of Brandenburg becomes King of Prussia

1699
Treaty of Karlowitz: Austria obtains Hungary, Poland regains Podolia from Turks

1701-14
War of Spanish Succession

1703
Methuen Treaty between England and Portugal, giving England commercial advantage

1707
Act of Union (with Scotland) creates Great Britain

1713
Asiento Treaty gives Britain monopoly in supplying African slaves to Spanish colonies

1713
Pragmatic Sanction reserving Hapsburg succession to Maria Theresa

1717-20 Rise and fall of John Law's financial system in France

1721-42 Rise of Walpole and establishment of cabinet government in Britain

Sicily becomes Austrian
1718 possession: Duke of Savoy obtains Sardinia in exchange

Afghan-Persian War: Persia
1722-30 dismembered by Turks and Russians

1721 Treaty of Nystadt, Russia gains control of Baltic littoral and unofficial protectorate over Poland

1724
China closed to Westerners: missionaries expelled

An Encyclopedia for the Enlightenment — Hounded by government censors and condemned by the Church, Denis Diderot edits his thirty-five volume encyclopedia **1751**

1755

Disaster Strikes Lisbon — When a series of earth tremors shatter Lisbon, mystics insist that the disaster is Divine Retribution for Portugal's sins

1771

1776

The Declaration of Independence — Thomas Jefferson drafts the American colonies' proclamation of independence to justify rebellion and win French support

"Terra Incognita" — Certain that an undiscovered continent lies somewhere in the South Pacific, James Cook sets out in search of the "Great South Land"

1789

"Liberté Egalité Fraternité" — The French monarchy is doomed when troops garrisoning the Bastille refuse to open fire upon a mob of armed citizens

2-99
ident

Thadeus Kościuszko 1746-1817
Polish general

ker 1732-1804
ker and statesman

Johann Wolfgang von Goethe 1749-1832
German writer, statesman and scientist

3-1804

James Madison 1751-1836
U.S. President

n Adams 1735-1826
. President

Camille Desmoulins 1760-1827
French revolutionary

es Watt 1736-1819
ttish inventor

o Tsung — Ch'ien Lung Emperor 1736-96
nchu Emperor of China

igi Galvani 1737-93
lian scientist

Louis XVI 1754-93
King of France

lward Gibbon 1737-94
glish historian

Ludwig van Beethoven 1770-1827
German composer

homas Paine 1737-1809
litical writer and theorist

William, Earl of Shelburne 1737-1805
British statesman

Charles Cornwallis 1738-1805
British general

Wolfgang Amadeus Mozart 1756-91
Austrian composer

George III 1738-1820
King of Great Britain

Joseph II 1741-90
Austrian Emperor

Alexander Hamilton 1757-1804
American statesman

oseph Banks, Sir 1743-1820
British naturalist, promoter of African exploration

William Blake 1757-1827
English poet and artist

iatowski)
nd

Thomas Jefferson 1743-1826
U.S. President

Friedrich Schiller 1759-1805
German writer

tings 1732-1818
eral of India

William Pitt the Younger 1759-94
English statesman

2-1809

Antoine Lavoisier 1743-94
French chemist

2-92

John Jay 1745-1829
American statesman

2-92

Gustavus III 1746-92
King of Sweden

● **1740-48**
r of the Austrian Succession

● **1745**
Prussia gains Silesia by Treaty of Dresden

● **1739-41**
glo-Spanish War Jenkins' Ear

French naval defeats — ● **1759**
loss of Canada to Britain

Battle of Plassey: British ●
gain control of Bengal **1757**

British defeat Emperor of Delhi, obtain ●
control of Bengal, Bihar and Orissa **1764**

Gustavus III's coup d'état ●
and reforms in Sweden **1772**

First Polish partition by ●
Russia, Prussia and Austria **1772**

● **1774**
Placatory Quebec Act ensures Canadian loyalty to Britain

● **1787-92**
Second Russian-Turkish War: Russia's possession of Crimea confirmed

1784 ●
Pitt's India Act: East India Company's power transferred to British Government; interference in native affairs forbidden

French capture Madras ● **1746**

1750-77 ●
Pombal institutes administrative reform in Brazil and promotes trade

● **1747**
Afghanistan under Ahmed gains independence from Persia

● **1739**
ir Shah of Persia defeats hans and sacks Delhi

Imposition of Stamp Tax ●
in American Colonies **1764**

Invention of spinning jenny ●
by James Hargreaves **1764**

Clive's reforms in India **1765-66** ●

Stanislas Poniatowski placed on ● **1764**
Polish throne by Catherine the Great

Seven Years' War **1756-63** ●
(French and American War) **1759** ●
British Museum opened

1773 ●
Jesuit Order dissolved by Pope Clement XIV

● **1774**
Treaty of Kuchuk Kainardji: Russia obtains Azov Kertsch and navigation rights in Turkish waters

1773 ● **1774**
Boston Tea Party Continental Congress: American grievances presented in petition to George III

Pugatchoff rebellion in Russia **1773-75** ●

● **1768-73**
James Bruce's exploration along Nile promotes British interest in Ethiopia

● **1775**

● **1775-83**
American Revolutionary War

● **1778-79**
War of Bavarian Succession

● **1783**
Peace of Versailles: recognition of American Republic: France renounces India

Sydney founded as first Australian penal settlement

● **1787** United States Constitution

● **1788**

● **1788-90**
Gustavus III of Sweden attacks Russia

Watt's steam engine

Age of Optimism

Editor Alan Palmer

1803-1897

Introduction

The character of the nineteenth century was shaped by four movements of momentous change: (1) a political revolt that threatened to topple archaic institutions in the name of nationality and common citizenship; (2) a technological revolution that began with the adoption of iron machinery in factories and continued with the application of steam power to industry and communications; (3) a freeing of the intellect from the artificial discipline of Classicism and the restraints of religious bigotry; and (4) a contraction of world society by which the manners and habits of five continents were integrated, under European dominance, into a single Occidental culture.

None of those four developments was entirely new. The idea of "Liberty, Equality, Fraternity" was broached long before it became a slogan of the Parisian revolutionaries. John Kay's flying shuttle, the first of the textile inventions, was patented as early as 1733 (although it did not come into general use for another thirty years). The mid-eighteenth-century writings of Rousseau anticipated some aspects of Romanticism, while the work of his contemporary, Diderot, successfully challenged obscurantist thought. And for more than three centuries the successors of Columbus and Magellan had been sailing the oceans in a quest for new harbors where settlers might assuage the growing land hunger of Western Europe and traders might make fortunes in silks, spices, tobacco or slaves.

The unique feature of nineteenth-century civilization was the way in which such familiar warps of history were spun into a single fabric. Advances in technological science enabled the pride that people felt in identifying themselves with a nation to be transformed into a belief in imperial greatness as an end in itself. The triumph of retrospective emotion over reason—which was the essence of the Romantic Movement in its first decades—led to the adulation of bronzed heroes planting the tricolor flag on the banks of the White Nile or the Stars and Stripes on the Cuban Sierra. Improvements in medicine and sanitation made Europeans proliferate as never before, even if the principal reason for the increased population was a lowering of the deathrate rather than a higher birthrate. Better communications so encouraged migration overseas that the number of people of European stock living in other continents multiplied almost tenfold between 1801 and 1900. Those "extra-Europeans" were secular missionaries who carried to every segment of the globe the outward trappings of a Westernized society, even though many were seeking to escape from the tedium of its gray respectability. If "progress" destroyed formal slavery and combated illiteracy, it also substituted top hats and frock coats for the colorful costumes of the Japanese samurai and made white collars and sober ties a symbol of social standing in the towns of southeast Asia. The nineteenth century was the Age of European Primacy, a span of four generations in which the smallest of continents molded the world in its image—barely noticing, in its aggressive ebullience, that in so doing it was selling its soul to industry and materialism.

In 1801, when the century opened, the leadership of France was hardly challenged in politics or culture. The young Republic had survived an ill-conducted invasion in 1792 and the more insidious menace of corruption and inefficiency under the Directory (the government that ruled from 1795–99). General Bonaparte assumed power as First Consul four weeks after he returned to Paris from Egypt in October, 1799. In short order he stamped out civil war in Brittany and the Vendée, gave France a constitution and a legal code, restored public confidence in the country's finances, and went on to smash his enemies in the Second Coalition by defeating the Austrians at

617

Introduction

Marengo and Hohenlinden and inducing them to seek peace at Lunéville in February, 1801. Even the British, the most obdurate of Bonaparte's adversaries, wavered in their resolution. On March 14, William Pitt, "the Atlas of our reeling globe," as one of his colleagues wrote in despair, resigned the premiership he had held for seventeen years. His successor, the amiably undistinguished Henry Addington, sought an end to the war with France and, after twelve months of intermittent negotiations, concluded the truce of exhaustion known as the Peace of Amiens. With Savoy, Piedmont, Westphalia and Belgium annexed to metropolitan France and with satellite republics in Holland, Switzerland and Italy, the First Consul was the master of more territories than Louis xiv or any other French king had ever been—and he had not yet reached the plenitude of his power.

The success of Bonaparte's armies was matched by the universal respect shown to France in the arts of peace. Englishmen flocked to Paris during the fourteen-month Peace of Amiens seeking to rekindle the flame of culture in the galleries of the Louvre or in the auditorium of the Odeon. (Their instinctive assumption that what was French was fashionable survived the renewal of the war.) The influence of France extended well beyond her new frontiers. Thomas Jefferson, who became President of the United States in March, 1801, had returned from his European travels with a boundless admiration for French Classicism in the domestic arts, and when the American Congress sought a well-planned capital on the banks of the Potomac it seemed natural to entrust the enterprise to a French engineer, Major Pierre L'Enfant. Jefferson was confident that the Frenchman would conjure up from the wilderness of red clay and alder bushes a city graced with the dignity of the Invalides, the Palais Royal and the Place Louis xv. Even in Moscow people of distinction wore clothes cut in the French manner, used French perfume, consumed French wine, employed French chefs and preferred to make their confessions in French to the abbé of a French church, abandoning their Orthodox faith in a quest for social standing.

Yet the guillotine remained in the center of Paris and Bonaparte himself declared "I am the Revolution." In a sense, he was—for the structure of French government was more decisively changed in the five years of the Consulate than in the decade that preceded it. But the political and social edifice that Bonaparte erected in France and exported in the baggage train of his conquering armies bore little resemblance to the ideas of 1789. When Camille Desmoulins incited the revolutionary crowd to storm the Bastille, he had declared that he would rather suffer a glorious death than see his country enslaved. Napoleon Bonaparte was not a tyrant but a paternal despot who gave the French people an orderly and centralized administration, a disciplined system of national education, and a Church obedient to the State. The Napoleonic Codes, which emphasized the sanctity of property and uniform equality before the law, benefited millions of Europeans inside and outside the old frontiers of France: the Jewish ghettos of Venice, Mainz, Rome and Frankfurt were swept aside by Napoleon's armies, and when his empire reached its zenith in 1811 the Jews of Hamburg, Bremen, Lübeck and Mecklenburg enjoyed full civil rights in a Gentile state for the first time. But these liberties, like the national recognition accorded to the Italians and the Illyrians, were achieved at the cost of almost endless war. "Power is my mistress," Napoleon once confessed; it was certainly the one infatuation to which he remained constant.

There were many who were disillusioned by Napoleon's triumphant progress. Charles James Fox, the tempestuous English champion of liberty, gave up his life in politics rather than support Britain's war with the French Republic. During the Peace of Amiens he hurried across the Channel, but after three months of adulation in Paris he returned to London disturbed by General Bonaparte's love of military display and complaining that freedom was sleeping in France. In July, 1802, William Words-worth, once intoxicated by the promise of the Revolution, set out for Calais in a mood of enthusiasm. Soon after reaching France he heard that Napoleon had been granted the Consulship for life. Indignant, the poet hastened back from a Europe "yet in bonds" to "Kent's green vales," and by autumn of that year his sonnets were invoking the shade of Milton to alert his countrymen to their peril.

War did indeed seem imminent once again. A dispute over the status of Malta, which the British had occupied in 1800, led to new tension between London and Paris. On May 16, 1803, the war was resumed, and the most feared of British admirals, Horatio Nelson, took command of H.M.S. *Victory* at Portsmouth. Throughout that summer the British people awaited the anticipated invasion with a blood-curdling self-confidence that was never put to the test.

As the French Consulate moved resolutely toward the dignity of Empire, others besides Fox and Words-worth changed heart. Across the Continent, in Hapsburg Vienna, a musical genius named Ludwig van Beethoven became increasingly certain that he was shattering the old disciplines of composition even as the First Consul was sweeping aside the accumulated dust of feudal institutions. But his ideals, too, were soon to be shattered.   ALAN PALMER

Sinfonia grande
Louis van Beethoven
Sinfonia
Op: 55

Allegro molto

Beethoven's Rededicated Masterpiece

On December 2, 1804, Napoleon Bonaparte crowned himself Emperor of France. His action incensed the young German composer Ludwig van Beethoven, who had recently added a dedication to Napoleon to the written score of his newest symphony. Declaring that Napoleon had become "a tyrant," the thirty-three-year-old composer ripped the dedicatory page in half and discarded it. Later that same year, Beethoven's rededicated symphony—which he called the Eroica—was performed for the composer's patron, Prince Franz Josef von Lobkowitz. The fascinating but bewildering new work was altered slightly in the next two years (in response to critical appraisals), and a final, authorized score was published in 1806. The vast scale of the Eroica—which was twice the length of Beethoven's earlier compositions—dwarfed the works of Beethoven's contemporaries and set a new standard for future composers.

Ludwig van Beethoven was thirty-three when he began to sketch out a new symphony in E flat major, the *Eroica*, in 1803. Throughout his life he had been interested in politics, and thus it was natural that the activities of Napoleon Bonaparte should have occupied the composer's thoughts. Several contemporaries tell us that Beethoven intended the new symphony to center on the fascinating and controversial Corsican.

Beethoven's attitude changed, however, when Bonaparte crowned himself Emperor in 1804. The composer's pupil, Ferdinand Ries, gives us an interesting description of his teacher's reaction:

Not only I but several other intimate friends saw this symphony, already written down in score, lying on his table, and on the title page there was the word "Bonaparte" way at the top and way at the bottom "Luigi van Beethoven," not a word more. If and how the gap was supposed to be filled, I do not know. I was the first to bring him the news that Bonaparte had declared himself Emperor, whereupon he was enraged and cried, "He is not anything but a man like the rest of us! Now he will trample all the rights of man and only indulge his own ambitions; now he will put himself above everyone else and will become a tyrant!" Beethoven went to the table, took the title page at the top and tore it in half, throwing it on the floor. The first page was written again, and now the symphony got its title: *Sinfonia eroica*.

This autograph manuscript has disappeared, but we do have a nineteenth-century manuscript score with many corrections and additions in Beethoven's own hand. The title page of this score contains Beethoven's autograph and the dedication to Napoleon, which has been vigorously scratched out. This early copy, now owned by the Gesellschaft der Musikfreunde in Vienna, is dated 1804, the year in which Beethoven probably completed the first version of the symphony. When the symphony was published the title page read, *Sinfonia eroica composta per festeggiar il sovvenire d'un grand uomo* ("Heroic symphony composed to celebrate the memory of a great man").

As always, Beethoven worked long and hard before arriving at the final form of his new composition. In recent years a big sketchbook containing many pages of *Eroica* sketches has been discovered in the Soviet Union and published in facsimile. Many of the principal themes and other parts of the work are contained in these Russian sketchbooks, but not all appear for the first time. Beethoven constantly reshaped his material to make it more telling and very often more concise. One of the principal themes in the *Eroica*'s finale turns up in two other Beethoven compositions produced in 1801: a set of contredanses and the ballet *Die Geschöpfe des Prometheus* ("The Creatures of Prometheus"). Beethoven also used the theme as a subject for piano variations. But interesting though the use of the theme in these other works is, the *Eroica* seems to place it in a new context, which gives it a new dimension.

Because this was a period in which the composer was most inadequately protected by copyright laws, Beethoven conceived a scheme whereby he gave the exclusive right of performance of large-scale works to some wealthy patron for a year or two. In the case of the *Eroica*, the patron was Prince Franz Josef von Lobkowitz, a talented amateur musician (a contemporary newspaper describes him as having a "bass voice of rare beauty") at whose beautiful winter palace in Vienna the first performances of the *Eroica* took place some time in 1804.

We have only very fragmentary reports of the symphony's reception at these semiprivate performances, but two contemporary reports illustrate something of the shock with which this new,

A sketch of Beethoven.

Opposite above The title page of a contemporary manuscript of the *Eroica*, signed by Beethoven. *Below* A page of the score from the same manuscript.

"Piling-up of colossal ideas"

Pierre Jean David, court painter of the Napoleonic Empire.

Napoleon's coronation at Notre-Dame, painted by David. When Napoleon became Emperor, Beethoven, furious that his hero had proved himself ambitious and fallible, changed the inscription of his third symphony.

towering masterpiece was received. One is related to us by Ferdinand Ries. He tells us of the horn dissonance just before the recapitulation in the first movement, wherein the horn announces the beginning of the theme in the tonic while the tremolo strings are still in the dominant. It is even now a terrific dissonance. Ries reports: "At the first rehearsal of this symphony, which was ghastly, the horn player came in correctly. I was standing next to Beethoven and I thought he [the horn player] made a mistake and said: 'That damned horn player! Can't he count? It sounds monstrously wrong!' I think I was very near getting my ears boxed. Beethoven did not forgive me for a long time."

Another reaction came from the cultivated and charming Prince Louis Ferdinand of Prussia, who visited Vienna about this time and was at a concert given by Lobkowitz's private orchestra, at which the *Eroica* was performed. The Prince, himself a virtuoso pianist and a talented composer, was stunned by Beethoven's new composition and at the end asked to have the whole thing repeated.

The new symphony fascinated but also bewildered contemporaries. Georg August Griesinger, the friend and biographer of Joseph Haydn, who was Saxonian legation secretary at Vienna and who was in constant correspondence with the publishers Breitkopf & Härtel in Leipzig, wrote on February 13, 1805, from Vienna: "This much I can tell you, that the symphony was given in two concerts, one held at Prince Lobkowitz's and the other by a hardworking amateur called Wirth, and was received with much success. I hear both admirers and opponents of Beethoven praising it as a work of genius. The one group says, here is more than Haydn and Mozart, the symphonic ideal has been brought to a higher plane! The others [opponents] miss a certain overall roundness, they object to the piling-up of colossal ideas."

The first public performance took place on April 7, 1805, at a benefit concert by the violinist Franz Clement in the Theater an der Wien. (It was for Clement, a child prodigy who had played with Haydn in England, that Beethoven later composed his violin Concerto in D, Op. 61.) The critic of the *Allgemeine Musikalische Zeitung* must have summed up the general opinion when he wrote about the work as follows:

This long, highly difficult composition is actually a very widely conceived, bold and wild fantasy. In it we do not miss original and beautiful passages in which one must recognize the energetic, talented spirit of its creator. ...The reviewer certainly belongs to Beethoven's sincerest admirers; but with this work he must admit that he finds all too many harsh and bizarre effects as a result of which it is difficult to preserve an overall view and its unity almost entirely disappears.

In a review after the second performance of the *Eroica*, the same correspondent tells his readers that the symphony lasted a whole hour. In those days, the first part of the opening movement's exposition was repeated, an idea that Beethoven later abandoned. The correspondent suggests:

. . . the Symphony would greatly gain . . . if Beethoven could bring himself to shorten it and to introduce more light, clarity and unity into the whole . . . instead of the *Andante* there is a Funeral March in C minor which later receives fugal treatment. But that fugal section sinks from organized order into apparent confusion: and if after repeated hearing one misses an overall conceptual line even when one listens most attentively, this fact must appear curious to any unprejudiced lover of music. Also there is much missing in order that the symphony could please generally.

As was frequently the case with his most important compositions, Beethoven took his time about the *Eroica*'s first publication. No doubt many of the changes in the Gesellschaft der Musikfreunde copy of the score were made as a result of early performances.

It was not in fact until the autumn of 1806 that Beethoven allowed the work to be published. As was the custom in those days, the first edition was not of the score but of the individual parts. The work was dedicated to Prince Lobkowitz and contained the following interesting note on one of the pages of the first violin part:

This Symphony, having been expressly conceived as longer than customary, should be performed rather at the beginning than at the end of a concert, shortly after an overture, an aria, or a concerto; for if it is placed on the program later it will lose its proper and intended effect for the listener, who will have been tired by the previous numbers. The part of the third horn has been so conceived that it may be executed at will either by a first or second horn player.

Beethoven himself held the *Eroica* in high esteem. After he had written the Fifth Symphony, but before he had written the Ninth, he and a friend went to Nussdorf to dine at a favorite restaurant. Beethoven was in a particularly good mood, and the friend asked the composer which of his symphonies he preferred. "Ha, ha, the *Eroica*," said Beethoven in great good humor. His friend: "I would have thought the C minor [No. 5]." Beethoven: "No, the *Eroica*."

The symphony as Beethoven found it was a highly developed and beautifully symmetric work of art. It had begun in Italy in the early eighteenth century as a *sinfonia* or operatic overture with three movements: fast-slow-fast. Then the Austrians and Germans had taken over the form and turned it into a concert symphony.

In 1740 a minor Austrian composer, G. M. Monn (1717–50), added a minuet as a penultimate movement. After some vacillation as to whether the minuet should be the second or third movement, and after some indecision as to whether it should be included at all, the minuet soon became an integral part of the symphonic structure.

Some of the early Austro-German productions were large-scale affairs with trumpets and drums, but others, particularly the Austrian, were chamber symphonies with a small orchestra generally consisting of oboes, horns, and strings. By the middle of the century the symphony was a well-developed art form flourishing all over Europe, particularly in Paris, which was then the center of the musical world and also the center for music publishing.

Although the early eighteenth-century symphony had much to recommend it—it was a highly civilized, formally subtle and neatly orchestrated affair—it could not be said that it plumbed the emotional depths. Audiences expected to hear bright and gay music, and such melancholy as there might be was generally confined to the slow movements and had a mild benevolence about it, rather like the Italian winter. Obviously this lack of emotional depth must have struck more than one composer, and it is interesting to observe that in the second part of the 1760s there seems to have been a kind of musical revolution all over Europe. Suddenly elegance was simply not enough. In

Above Beethoven in middle age. Despite his growing deafness, Beethoven continued to compose.

Below left The courtyard of the house in which Beethoven was born.

Below right The organ on which Beethoven played from an early age.

The Old Court Theater in the Michaelerplatz in Vienna. Beethoven studied under Haydn, at Vienna, center of the musical world.

Paris, we find Franz Beck, a contemporary of Haydn and a pupil of Johann Stamitz, writing symphonies with a new spiritual depth and a strength that often borders on real violence. The minor key now assumed a different emotional concept. Before, Italians such as Vivaldi had often treated minor keys in much the same manner as major ones. In this new revolutionary language, the minor key became the vehicle for an agonizing reappraisal.

In Vienna a whole group of interesting young composers, foremost among them Joseph Haydn, began to experiment with turbulent symphonies in the minor key. We find G minor symphonies by Haydn, Johann Christian Bach and the impressionable young Mozart, whose so-called *Little* G minor Symphony (K. 183) was composed as a result of a trip to Vienna in 1773. Some of the Haydn symphonies of this period achieve a disturbed emotional violence that is unique not only in Haydn's oeuvre but also in the whole eighteenth century. And not only symphonies were affected by this new and forceful language: we find it in sonatas, operas, and especially in the new string quartet form, such as Haydn's Opus 20 quartets of 1772. (These Haydn quartets also reintroduce large contrapuntal forms, including full-fledged fugues, into the sonata form. Beethoven was much impressed by the fugal finales in Haydn's Opus 20 and copied at least one entire movement for study.)

This musical movement has been allied to a similar movement in German literary circles known as the *Sturm und Drang* ("storm and stress")—a philosophic concept that took its name from a now nearly forgotten play by Friedrich von Klinger

written in 1776. The musical revolution, however, took place a few years before this German literary movement of the 1770s, which included Goethe and Schiller among its members. In any case Haydn himself to some extent repudiated his *Sturm und Drang* style, and his later symphonies returned to a better balanced, if emotionally less exciting, world.

Meanwhile Mozart had burst upon the scene, and while he did not write very many symphonies after his arrival in Vienna in 1781, those he did write caused a profound impression on thinking musical people. In particular the last four Mozart symphonies—the *Prague* in D, K. 504 (1787); in E flat, K. 543 (1788); in G minor, K. 550 (1788); in C, K. 551 (1788)—created a new atmosphere that was in part just as emotionally disturbed as the *Sturm und Drang* symphonies composed twenty years earlier. The G minor, K. 550, pushes the eighteenth-century symphony as close as possible to a frightening new world in which the ordered scheme of things sometimes appears almost to disintegrate: at the beginning of the second section in the symphony's finale, Mozart grimly flirts with what would in future be known as the twelve-note system.

Haydn's last twelve symphonies, written between 1791 and 1795, followed Mozart's, and in some respects they go even further formally and in pure brilliant force than Mozart's. Beethoven felt very much in awe of this grandiose symphonic tradition when he came to Vienna to study with Haydn in 1792, and although it would have been an expected move for Beethoven to write a symphony, he did not do so until 1799.

Beethoven's First Symphony was dedicated to Gottfried van Swieten, Haydn's and Mozart's

Beethoven: Classicist or Romanticist?

patron and the author of the librettos for Haydn's *The Creation* and *The Seasons*. Chronologically, the symphony crosses the bridge to the nineteenth century but it is still very much an eighteenth-century work. Although it is beautifully executed and orchestrated by a master, it nevertheless does not penetrate into any new world. Nor does Beethoven's Second Symphony, a work of great brilliance and effect composed in 1802. The fast scherzos that Beethoven inserted in place of the traditional minuet derive from Haydn's late quartets of Opus 76 and especially Opus 77, in which are found the one-in-the-bar fast scherzo archetype that from then on was to become standard. Beethoven's orchestration is also that of late Haydn and Mozart: pairs of woodwinds, brass and kettledrums.

It is significant that after 1795 Haydn himself never wrote another symphony and even resisted attractive offers from Paris and elsewhere to do so. Obviously, he considered his concept of the symphony to be completed with his last three works of 1795. In a sense there was nothing other composers could do, if they were to remain within the boundaries established and perfected by Haydn and Mozart, except to write variants of what already had been done so brilliantly.

When Haydn returned from London in 1795, he turned his attention to large-scale choral music and produced the six last masses and the enormous oratorios *The Creation* (1798) and *The Seasons* (1801). Obviously Haydn had become interested in large-scale forms for which he felt the symphony was not fitted. We know from Beethoven's own words that he assiduously studied Haydn's late masses, and the complicated broad forms found in Haydn's *Schöpfungsmesse* (1801) and *Harmoniemesse* (1802) must have excited Beethoven's attention. Such a movement as the *Kyrie* in the *Harmoniemesse*—a long and involved slow movement that formally opens up a whole new world to conquer—may have suggested to Beethoven that a symphony might well be composed along similar lines.

It is interesting that the *Eroica* is twice the length of not only Haydn's and Mozart's symphonies but also Beethoven's earlier efforts in the form. Quite simply, there are ideas on a vast scale that are better suited to grandiose movements. After all, no one had laid down the rule that it was necessary to write symphonies with Haydn's conciseness; and indeed, one of the very principles of Haydn's symphonic art is the at times violent telescoping of ideas such as that found in the first movement of Symphony No. 102. And if Haydn himself turned in his old age to broader ideas and larger form, it was clear that the symphony might be reorganized along such lines.

There has been much discussion as to whether Beethoven was a Classicist or a Romanticist. Nowadays we tend to think of him as the culmination of the Classical period. After all, Beethoven was deaf after about 1810 and can hardly have heard many of the new works of the budding German Romantic composers. There is one point, nevertheless, in connection with the *Eroica* that is worth making. Hitherto, composers' personalities to a certain extent tended to be subordinate to the concept and form of the art work they produced. If there is anything Romantic in Beethoven's treatment of the symphony, it is that the force of his towering personality is felt throughout the four movements. Here the listener feels that the personality has absolute command over form and content.

As far as the finale is concerned, this was perhaps the movement of the eighteenth century that was the most stereotyped. Naturally Haydn and Mozart wrote all sorts of different finales, some rondos, some in sonata form, and some in a brilliant combination of sonata and rondo. In one of the biggest Haydn finales (Symphony No. 101, 1794) there is a brilliant double fugue that enters in the middle of a sonata-rondo. And Mozart's fabulous *Jupiter* finale (K. 551, 1788) pointed the way to the finale's becoming much more than a witty and sophisticated conclusion. There is one characteristic insert in the *Eroica* finale that serves greatly to enlarge the horizon: the slow section that comes just before the final coda, and that not only broadens the size of the movement but introduces us to the innermost secrets of Beethoven's heart. Here was a man larger than life—here indeed was a soul expanded to greatness; here was one of the major milestones in the history of music.

From this point, indeed, the symphony never was the same; it never could go back to its eighteenth-century size and scope. Just as nothing in painting was ever the same after Masaccio and nothing in literature after Shakespeare, music was now ruled by the Beethoven stamp. Future composers would measure their efforts against his mighty ones. Johannes Brahms, composing his First Symphony in C minor, was to say: "I feel his giant steps behind me." Schubert, Dvořák, César Franck, Bruckner, Mahler—all looked back to 1803, when, in a peaceful suburb of Vienna, the symphony was reborn.

H. C. ROBBINS LANDON

Mozart as a child. Mozart's influence, like Haydn's, is apparent in much of Beethoven's work.

Beethoven's death mask.

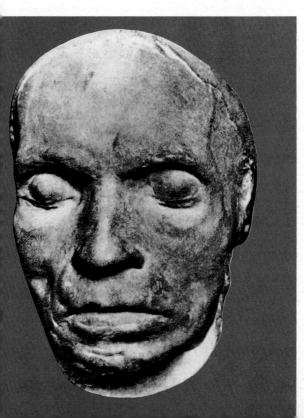

Napoleon's Empire

On May 18, 1804, the senators of France issued an official proclamation which declared that, subject to the verdict of a later plebiscite, "the Government of the Republic is entrusted to a hereditary Emperor." Within the space of a few weeks the French people gave their all-but unanimous assent to establishment of the Empire, and on December 2, 1804, Napoleon assumed the imperial crown in a dramatic ceremony in the Cathedral of Notre-Dame. Lest any devout legitimist mock the credentials of the revolutionary dynasty, the Pope himself had been induced to travel to Paris to sanctify the solemn pageant by his presence and benediction.

The meeting of Napoleon and the Tsar at Tilsit in 1807.

Sir Walter Scott, creator of the historical novel.

Napoleon thus became symbolic successor to Charlemagne, who received his crown from Pope Leo III in A.D. 800. The young lieutenant who watched a republican mob batter down the Tuileries gates in August, 1792, had come a long way in the intervening twelve and a half years.

Napoleon's coronation completed the alienation of many of his earlier admirers. It seemed to Beethoven to stultify the revolutionary spirit—yet in essence it corresponded with the mood of the times. The Romantic revolt against the Age of Reason had begun by evoking Greco-Roman themes, and, appropriately, Napoleon wore the laurels of a Roman conqueror during the ceremony at Notre-Dame. By 1804 the Romantics had fully "discovered" an idealized medieval past as well. In that year Schiller published *Wilhelm Tell*, and British readers began reading Walter Scott's first collection of border ballads. Therefore it was no surprise that Napoleon's coronation ceremony also consciously echoed the ritual of the "Empire of the West," the heroic age of the legendary *chansons de geste*.

Within a decade, Romanticism was to inflame Germany and other lands with a nationalistic passion that sought liberation from the Napoleonic yoke, but it would be a mistake to antedate that mood of patriotic emotionalism. In 1805—and even as late as the summer of 1812—the Emperor could still stir the imagination of young conscripts with the thrill of participation in some great adventure. "We are going to Greater India. It is three thousand miles from Paris," wrote a nineteen-year-old fusilier, as he set out for Moscow and the agony of the Berezina. The rhetoric of the imperial bulletins, which identified the armies of the present with the victorious hosts of the past, encouraged a sense of marching with destiny. So long as Napoleon himself could hail "the God of War and the God of Success" as comrades-in-arms, the peoples of his Empire felt no need of a nostalgic quest through the centuries for national identity. The Romantic Movement flourished as a liberating force in politics only when fortune turned against Napoleon and exposed the emptiness of his ideal. And yet, curiously enough, within a decade of Napoleon's death that same movement was to react against the frustrations of the Metternich era and serve as midwife at the renaissance of the imperial legend. Romanticism, the most irrational of all cultural creeds, was consistent only in its inconsistencies.

The early years of the Empire were a long cavalcade of victory. In the autumn of 1805 Napoleon marched against the most powerful of his enemies, Russia and Austria. On November 13 his troops entered Vienna, and one week later the first performance of Beethoven's *Fidelio*, an opera passionately exalting the ideals of 1789, was attended by an audience that consisted exclusively of the Emperor's officers. On the first anniversary of his coronation, Napoleon smashed the combined armies of Austria and Russia at Austerlitz. In the following October he humbled the Prussians at Jena, and in June, 1807, he wiped out another Russian army at Friedland. Tsar Alexander I of Russia, for two years France's implacable foe, sued for peace. Napoleon and Alexander met on a raft in the Neman River at Tilsit, and the Tsar was soon flattered into friendship and alliance. A grandiose plan for partitioning Europe into a western sphere of influence (under the domination of France) and an eastern sphere (under the domination of Russia) made Tilsit the apogee of Napoleon's career. The Grand Army was still to gain other triumphs—it was to take Vienna for the second time in May, 1809, and it was to see the golden cupolas of Moscow glinting under the September sun of 1812—but only at Tilsit did Napoleon hold the map of Europe in the palm of his hand. "The world begged me to govern it," he was to say amid the uncertainties of later years.

England's war effort

The British remained obstinately disinclined to make peace from the breakdown of the Peace of Amiens until the final collapse of the Empire in 1814. Their military contribution to the campaigns of those years was slight, however. In the summer of 1808 a force of 15,000 men under General Sir Arthur Wellesley (who was to become the Earl of Wellington in February, 1812, and a Duke in 1814) landed in Portugal to check the inroads of General Junot's army in the Iberian Peninsula. For six years Wellesley's men tied down the French in the dusty red hills of Cantabria and Castile, thereby succoring the insurgent Spanish guerrillas, whose national insurrection was the first to challenge Napoleon's imperium. The fighting in Spain was to be immortalized by Goya's paintings and Napier's prose, but despite the fact that Wellington crossed the Pyrenees and reached Toulouse before the Emperor abdicated, the Peninsular Campaign remained essentially a sideshow, a second front that never became a decisive arena of battle. The "Spanish ulcer" may have weakened Napoleon, but it did not destroy him.

The principal British war effort was at sea. French mastery of the English Channel was essential if the soldiers of Napoleon's Grand Army were ever to land in Kent and Sussex. The French naval squadrons were divided between the bases of Brest and Rochefort in the Atlantic and Toulon in the Mediterranean, and for two years after the resumption of war in 1803 the Royal Navy kept close watch on each of those bases. Three-decker ships of the line—floating batteries of a hundred cannon—and single-decker frigates mounted with two or three dozen guns braved Biscay gales and Mediterranean squalls to batten down the Franco-Spanish squadrons.

Despite the British Navy's vigilance, Admiral Missiessy managed to slip out of Rochefort, and Admiral Villeneuve managed to evade the blockade of Toulon early in 1805. The French admirals sought to carry the war to the West Indies, where they hoped to evade the British patrols and double-back up a denuded channel. Missiessy successfully raided Martinique, but he was eventually forced to return to Rochefort; Villeneuve was chased by Nelson for five months before he finally found refuge at Cadiz.

Trafalgar

On October 21, 1805, Villeneuve put to sea again. He was intercepted by the British off Cape Trafalgar and lost eighteen of his thirty-three ships. Some 4,408 French and Spanish sailors perished in that battle and the storm

Nelson, Britain's greatest admiral.

that followed it; the British lost 449 officers and seamen, among them Nelson himself. Consequently, the news of Britain's greatest naval victory was received not with jubilation but with mourning.

The battle at Trafalgar confirmed the supremacy of British sea power, and although Napoleon rapidly rebuilt his fleet (he

achieved more for the French Navy than any administrator since Colbert), British command of the high seas was never seriously challenged for the remainder of the nineteenth century. Naval maneuvers in the decade following Trafalgar consisted primarily of blockade operations and the interception of commercial shipping. It was a war of attrition, expensive and exhausting. Conditions of service in the Royal Navy were grim: more than twelve times as many British seamen died from disease in the Napoleonic Wars as were killed in battle. Since numbers could be kept up only by impressment, it is hardly surprising that there were ten thousand more desertions than deaths. The hardy veterans who survived were famous for their jollity and good cheer: with two shillings and sixpence a week in pay, a diet of salt beef and maggoty biscuit, and the threat of fifty or more lashes for disobedience, they certainly needed a merry temperament if they were to remain sane!

Once the danger of invasion receded in 1805, the Napoleonic Wars made little direct impact on the people of the British Isles. Jane Austen's novels, most of which were written in that period (while her brothers were serving as naval officers in the Mediterranean and the Atlantic), are vignettes of a comfortably peaceful society. The Wars did not constitute a serious drain on manpower. Wellington's total casualties in the Iberian Peninsula were lower than Kutuzov's losses in ten hours at Borodino in 1812. Indeed, fewer than 54,000 British sailors and soldiers died from enemy action in the eleven years between the resumption of

hostilities and the abdication of Napoleon—6,000 fewer than were killed on the first day of the Battle of the Somme in 1916. Moreover, the population of Britain continued to increase rapidly. It rose

Jane Austen, whose novels, written during the Napoleonic wars, are vignettes of a peaceful society.

from 10.5 million in the 1801 census to almost 12 million ten years later, beginning the process by which it doubled in size over the first half of the century. Medical science and hygiene were prolonging life, and thoughtful men in authority ruminated gloomily on the callous doctrine of the Reverend Thomas Malthus, whose *Essay on the Principle of Population* argued that wages should be kept at subsistence level in order to counter the natural prolificacy of the laboring masses.

Reaction and reform

There was, indeed, little sympathy in those years between the social classes in Britain. The English country gentlemen profited from the war as more and more land was enclosed in order to meet the demand for corn (which could not

One of Goya's horrifying depictions of the Peninsular War. Spain was devastated by both the British and the French.

be imported so long as Napoleon kept the Continent closed to English ships). Manufacturers, too, benefited from the continued hostilities: the need to clothe and equip the armies of Britain and her allies artificially stimulated the new factory industries. In fact, only the working population fared badly: prices were high, food was scarce, and hours of work in the mines and heavy industries were long. There were waves of anti-Jacobin hysteria among the landowners, who used the emergencies of war to justify action against demonstrations of social and political discontent. In 1799 and 1800 all radical associations were suppressed by acts of Parliament, and workmen's "combinations" (which sought improved conditions from employers) were declared illegal. Ironically, a similar prohibition of workers' associations, the "Loi le Chapelier," had been introduced into the French National Assembly in 1791 and was retained, in a modified form, in the Napoleonic Code. But in Britain incipient trade unionism was regarded as a symptom of the revolutionary virus from beyond the Channel.

Political liberty was increasingly curtailed in England and Scotland as the war with France dragged on. Reformers were silenced or prosecuted for preaching "sedition," and in 1810 William Cobbett, the most patriotic of radical pamphleteers, was imprisoned for two years for protesting the flogging of local militiamen by German mercenaries. "The mass of the people have nothing to do with the laws but to obey them," Bishop Horsley of Norwich had declared in 1795. That uncompromising mood prevailed among the Tory governing class for a quarter of a century, culminating four years after the war had ended in the notorious Six Acts of 1819 (which blocked free speech, free assembly and freedom of the printed word).

It was only when men like Peel and Huskisson, the voices of commerce and trade, began to pierce the inner ring of Tory legislators in the 1820s that sanity returned to political life. Only then was it seen that what was haunting the land was not the specter of revolution but the misery of hunger and insecurity. Industrialism had changed the face of England too speedily for its people to accept or its rulers to comprehend. In retrospect that was clearly the tragic message of the Luddite riots of 1811–13.

"General" Lud's Army

Ned Lud, a Leicestershire laborer whose name became synonymous with industrial sabotage in the first decades of the nineteenth century, was an unlikely candidate for even so dubious an honor. "General" Lud, as he was sometimes called, was a feebleminded "stockinger" whose isolated act of industrial anarchy took place some thirty years before the general outbreaks of 1811. Those outbreaks were perpetrated by roving bands of jobless textile workers who called themselves "Luddites" and who operated under cover of darkness. Their acts of vandalism, although directed at the new labor-saving machines that had robbed many of them of their livelihood, were inspired by discontent over living conditions and inflationary prices as well. Little more than a decade after the first Luddite riot, trade unions were formed to redress workers' grievances.

Cotton workers in 1813.

Opposite John Bull and his burden, a cartoon of 1819 lampooning the social structure of England.

From early 1811 until early 1813, during the turning point of the Napoleonic Wars, three regions of England were disturbed by a series of industrial riots involving the destruction of machinery: the Midland hosiery and lace-making districts of Leicestershire, Derbyshire and Nottinghamshire; the West Riding of Yorkshire; and the cotton areas of Lancashire and Cheshire. It eventually became necessary to employ a force of 12,000 soldiers—a larger army than the one with which Wellington had started his Peninsular campaign in 1808—to suppress the riots. Some thirty years earlier, Ned Lud, a laborer from Leicestershire, had smashed two lace frames belonging to his employer and in the process gave a name—"Luddism"—to the whole phenomenon.

The anger of the rioters vented itself largely against textile machinery of various kinds. For that reason it was generally assumed that the immediate cause of the riots was the introduction of new labor-saving machinery into the affected industries. This view is a far too simple one of a complex situation. Only to a limited extent did the riots of 1812 have as their main objective the destruction of labor-saving machinery, for such labor-saving machinery was not new. The immediate causes of the disturbances were the high price of foodstuffs, the collapse of the British export trade to the United States after February, 1811, and the effects of Napoleon's Continental System, which aimed at the exclusion of British goods from Europe.

Both at home and on the Continent, 1811 and 1812 were bad harvest years. By August, 1812, the price of wheat in Britain had reached the shockingly high price of 160 shillings a quarter (the average for 1792 had been as low as 43 shillings), and the prices of such coarse foodstuffs as oatmeal and potatoes also rose as the masses began to substitute them for wheat in their diet. In February, 1811, the United States, which had been trying desperately to avoid entanglement in the Napoleonic Wars, announced that the Non-Importation Act of 1809 would henceforth be enforced against Britain only. (That act had originally prohibited all trade between the U.S.A. on one hand and Britain and France on the other.) The measure cut down British exports to the U.S.A. from 11 million pounds sterling in 1810 to less than 2 million in 1811. Textile areas were particularly affected by this cutting off of their largest market.

Luddism is best understood by examining what went on in each of the three districts. In 1811 the counties of Nottingham, Derby and Leicester contained about 90 per cent of all stocking and lace frames in the kingdom. Those frames, which were used for knitting cotton, woolen and silk fabrics, were spread widely through the villages as well as the towns, but the preponderance were found in the Nottinghamshire countryside. The industry's entrepreneurs were wealthy merchant hosiers who owned the frames and supplied cotton, woolen and silk yarns to the journeymen stockingers and lace knitters. The merchant hosiers organized the collection of the finished articles through agents, middlemen, or "bagmen," and then sold them to the London wholesale houses. Those merchants also collected frame rents from the stockingers, usually one shilling a week per frame.

Following the collapse of both home and export markets in 1811, warehouse stocks accumulated rapidly and soon one-fifth of the knitting frames in the Midlands stood idle. Many other stockingers were only partially employed, and they often had to accept payment in kind at unfavorable rates. Those stockingers, caught between the double misery of high food prices and unemployment, grew increasingly irate over the use of wider—and therefore more productive—frames in the workshops where they were employed. They also objected to using knitted fabric produced on those wide frames to make cheap and inferior "cut-up" articles. Stocking shapes, for example, could be cut out of a large piece of knitted fabric and those shapes could then be sewn together in pairs to make stockings.

628

Pub.d Dec.r 15 1819 by J. Tegg 111 Cheapside London

The growth of rioting

Rioting broke out in Nottinghamshire in March, 1811, spread to Leicestershire and Derbyshire by the following November, and finally died down in February, 1812. Gangs of young stockingers, organized and paid by the older men in the trade, roamed the Midlands countryside at night and demanded admittance to cottages and knitting sheds so that they could smash up the wide frames. The stockingers who had the custody of those frames put up very little resistance; the frames, after all, were owned by the merchants, not the weavers. The rioters claimed to be acting in the name of "General" Ned Lud, the apprentice stockinger of Leicester. (According to folklore, when Lud was reprimanded by his master for bad work, he took up a hammer and beat some knitting frames to pieces.) The participants in those nighttime raids took an oath of secrecy when they were initiated—or "twisted-in" —to the organization. Old narrow frames—those that could not be used to produce material for cut-ups—were generally left intact, and the mobs

Rawfold's Mill, where William Cartwright beat off an attack of 150 Luddites in 1812. This incident formed the basis for Charlotte Brontë's *Shirley*.

Bottom Luddites shooting Mr. Horsfall, by Phiz.

RAWFOLDS MILL.

seldom stole anything except firearms. In all, some one thousand frames were destroyed by workers who directed their anger not so much against the new machines as against a new use to which old but recently improved machines were being put. Only after numerous regiments were drafted and sent into the Midlands did the troubles gradually cease; in the aftermath seven men were sentenced to terms of transportation—but no one was hanged.

In Yorkshire, Luddism broke out only in the region known as the West Riding, and it flourished mainly in the district north of Leeds and in the Huddersfield area. In those areas the trouble was confined to that section of the woolen cloth industry that had to do with the raising of nap on rough cloth and its subsequent close shearing. Two labor-saving machines, the gig-mill and the shearing frame, were gradually coming into use for those purposes. The gig-mill consisted basically of two large rotating cylinders covered with hundreds of teasels, and it raised the nap on cloth much more expeditiously than hand-teaseling. With such a machine, a man and a boy could do the work of seven skilled men, and the gig-mill's use spread in Yorkshire during the 1780s and 1790s. Once the nap had been raised, the shearmen or croppers trimmed it off with a pair of shears weighing between thirty and forty pounds, leaving the surface regular and smooth. A mechanical shearing frame had been invented during the eighteenth century, and it further economized the industry by rendering five skilled men out of six unnecessary. There had been riots against the shearing frame in Wiltshire and Somerset between 1797 and 1802, but by 1807 about fifteen hundred frames were at work in the north of England. Thus the riots in the West Riding were more specifically against the introduction of labor-saving machinery —but hardly against *new* machinery, for gig-mills and shearing frames had been known for years.

Had the times been more propitious, the triumph of the machines would probably have taken place without much public disturbance, but in the West Riding, as in the Midlands, the distress of 1811 and 1812 set off a violent reaction. In January, 1812, small bands of men (similar to those in Nottinghamshire) moved about the affected areas, smashing gig-mills and shearing frames with large sledgehammers. Many of the small manufacturers stopped using the machines temporarily; others—those with greater resources and more guts—defied the Luddites. Two mills near Leeds were successfully attacked in March, 1812, and on April 9 some 300 Luddites sacked and fired Joseph Foster's cloth mill at Horbury. In the same month, however, William Cartwright of Rawfold's resolutely beat off an attack by a mob of 150 Luddites, killing 2 of them. (Charlotte Brontë's *Shirley* is based on that episode.) During the summer of 1812, the Continental System collapsed, trade revived, and the troubles died down. However, seventeen of the rioters were sentenced to death by hanging at York Assizes in January, 1813.

In the third Luddite area, Lancashire and

Cheshire, the movement showed itself to be less an antimachinery movement than a series of food riots that led, almost by accident, to attacks on cotton mills. In those shires, competition between power-loom weaving and the handloom had not yet reached serious proportions. In the Manchester-Stockport area, less than 2,400 power looms were in operation in 1813—at a time when handloom weavers in the district numbered in the tens of thousands. In Manchester itself the worst riots took place in the potato market when mobs of women, having failed to get the farmers to bring down their prices, seized the loaded carts and either sold the potatoes at a low rate or looted them. At Oldham a mob of miners from the Hollinwood coal pits—men who worked in an industry largely untouched by machinery—went around to the food shops enforcing a list of maximum prices. Then, almost as an afterthought, they launched a couple of unsuccessful attacks against Daniel Burton and Sons' power-loom factory at Middleton. These and other riots in Lancashire and Cheshire led to death sentences for twenty-three people.

The next major outburst of machine breaking occurred in April, 1826, when large-scale riots involving the destruction of power looms took place in East Lancashire. Attacks on power-loom factories in Manchester itself proved generally unsuccessful. Once again, a close connection existed between the riots and the state of trade. The great economic boom of 1824–25 had been followed by a severe recession in the winter of 1825–26, causing great distress in the manufacturing districts. As a result of the new series of riots, ten persons received

death sentences, but all ten were eventually transported for life instead of being executed.

Surprisingly enough, the final spasm of machine breaking took place in agriculture—where the degree of mechanization was low—rather than in industry. The riots that erupted in the agricultural counties of southern and eastern England in 1830 were sparked by a hard winter. The prices of food-stuffs had risen rapidly throughout 1830, and riots raged from the September to the December of that year, with November as the peak month. The rioting agricultural laborers directed their main efforts against threshing machines, which robbed them of the labor of hand-threshing during the long winter months. The threshing machine, worked at first by horses and later by small steam engines, had proved increasingly popular in Scotland, northern England and North Wales during the Napoleonic Wars.

After the peace of 1815 the prosperous farmers in the wheat-growing counties of eastern and southern England rapidly adopted the threshing machine, despite the fact that labor was now abundant. A newly invented portable threshing machine proved very popular, particularly in Suffolk, and laborers watched the progress of mechanization with increasing alarm. Threatened with the prospect of being thrown onto the public charity of the poor law during the winter months, mobs attacked farm-houses, burned hay ricks and destroyed the threshing machines on a large scale. Some farmers deliberately left their machines out in the open—where the laborers could destroy them more easily—in the hope that their action would divert the mob's attention from more vital property. (The

The Peterloo massacre: the Manchester and Cheshire Yeomanry breaking up a meeting in favor of universal manhood suffrage in 1819. Unrest, both industrial and political, was endemic in early-nineteenth-century England.

Charlotte Brontë, whose novel *Shirley* describes the Luddite troubles.

The "Plug Plot" riots

Home Office roundly condemned this practice as a surrender to the blackmail of illegal force.)

The next large-scale outbreak of rural rioting—which occurred in 1843–44—was much tamer and less violent. The 1830 riots, however, appear to have delayed the progress of farm mechanization only to a limited extent; the intervention of the threshing machine and the mechanical reaper was not permanently halted. Emigration overseas and the drift to the towns over the next forty years solved the problem of the labor surplus on the land more effectively than agrarian violence.

In the eighteenth century (and indeed well into the nineteenth), the major output of British industry—with the exceptions of coalmining, iron-making and shipbuilding—was produced under various forms of what has been labeled the domestic or "putting-out" system. The essence of that

system was that the producer, often assisted by members of the household, worked at home on material that he either bought himself or was entrusted with by a merchant manufacturer or middleman. In the latter case, the material—yarn, iron or leather, for example—remained the property of the merchant. Sometimes, as in woolen weaving, there was partial mechanization. (Cloth had to be taken to a water-driven falling mill to be cleaned and thickened, for example.) In the Black Country and the Sheffield area, the nail makers and other workers in metal labored in their own homes or in lean-to sheds at the sides of their houses. In the textile trades, which were spread widely over the countryside, the spinning of woolen, worsted and cotton yarns was carried out in the household until the last two decades of the eighteenth century, when spinning rapidly changed into a factory industry, powered by the water wheel and the steam engine. Weaving of all kinds was carried on under the domestic system until the first decades of the nineteenth century, although loomshops containing as many as a dozen looms and their attendant weavers could frequently be found.

Relatively small but complicated machines presented few problems for the domestic system, despite the fact that the looms themselves were frequently extremely complex affairs to operate and service, depending on the quality and nature of the fabric woven on them. The stocking knitting frame, originally invented in 1589, was perhaps the most complicated machine in use in British industry in the early eighteenth century, yet many thousands had been installed in the workers' homes. Increasing complexity brought other problems than those of installation and servicing, however. Laboring families could easily afford cheap and simple spinning wheels, and even in the eighteenth century looms were usually owned by the weavers who operated them. The more complex and expensive stocking and lace-knitting frames—which cost between £10 and £30 at a time when a skilled worker might earn only £30 in a whole year—tended to be owned by the merchant hosier, and the journeymen stockingers

A FREE BORN ENGLISHMAN!
THE ADMIRATION of the WORLD!!!
AND THE ENVY of SURROUNDING NATIONS.!!!!

A coal works in Coalbrookdale, Staffordshire. The growth of industrialization was at the heart of Luddite and later complaints.

paid weekly or monthly rents for the privilege of using them.

The fact that materials and machines were lent out put hostages into the hands of the workers: embezzlement of raw material was a constant problem and legislation against both theft and the detention of work for long periods went on as long as the domestic system lasted. Refusal to complete webs in the loom and the slashing of unfinished pieces of cloth must have been fairly common as early as the sixteenth century, to judge by the legislation against those offenses. A riot among the woolen workers of Melksham in Wiltshire began in 1738 with the cutting of all the warps in the looms of a merchant clothier named Coulthurst who had lowered the piecework prices for cloth. Luddism was foreshadowed as early as 1675 when a mob of London weavers attacked immigrant French weavers for using ribbon looms, called "Dutch engines," that enabled one weaver to weave sixteen or more ribbons at the same time. Moreover, industrial sabotage and destruction were not confined to the domestic trades. In the northeastern coalfields, rioting miners burned down pit-head machinery in the 1740s and set coal stocks on fire in pursuance of demands for higher wages. The eighteenth-century statute book contains frequent Acts of Parliament directed against arson in coal pits, and as late as 1831 striking miners at Bedlington in Northumberland wrecked pit-winding gear.

The great strike movement of 1842—known as the "Plug Plot" riots—marks the beginning of a change in tactics. During those riots in Lancashire, Cheshire and north Staffordshire, the strikers concentrated on stopping, rather than wrecking, the mills by removing the lead safety plugs in the steam engine boilers. Their conduct, although extreme by modern standards, compares favorably with the excesses of Luddism. It presented itself as a method of attempting to force a rise in pay and indicates the extent to which some sections of the workers had come to terms with the new industrial capitalism by 1842.

The economists—among them Dr. Andrew Ure, whose *The Philosophy of Manufactures* was published in 1835—labored to explain the necessity for the rapid introduction of improved machinery to enable mass-produced British goods to remain competitive in the world's markets. Ure also stressed the futility of opposing the adoption of inventions designed "to abridge labor," and he cited Richard Roberts' "self-acting" mule of the 1820s as a prime example. (Roberts' invention had been specially commissioned by the master cotton spinners to put an end to continued demands for higher wages from the aristocracy of the cotton workers, the fine mule-spinners.) Ure's propaganda coincided with the beginnings of improvement in both industrial relations and living standards. Trade unions, which had been wholly illegal from 1799 to 1824, received a grudging recognition from Parliament, the law and society from the latter date. By 1851 the first of the new and increasingly respectable New Model trade unions—the Amalgamated Society of Engineers—had been formed from a coalition of older bodies. Those new amalgamated societies placed their prime emphasis on the thorough seven years' apprenticeship to skilled crafts (which had the effect of raising wages by restricting the number of adequately trained workers). To some extent such apprenticeships were a subtler form of Luddism, but they did assure the artisans employed in such developing industries as engineering, ironfounding, printing and shipbuilding a share in any profits accruing to capital investment in new machinery. Such tactics could hardly be employed by workers in the semiskilled and unskilled trades, however, and they began to organize in unions from the 1870s onward. Here cautious and restrictive working rules of various kinds had to be employed at shop floor level.

Luddism therefore survived as a frame of mind, occasionally expressing itself in acts of sabotage during industrial disputes, but more generally acting as a silent brake not only on the introduction of new and more productive machinery, but also on speedier methods of working and better works organization.   W. H. CHALONER

The War of 1812: Britain and America figh[t]

Economic warfare

Shortly after five o'clock on the afternoon of Monday, May 11, 1812, the Right Honourable Spencer Perceval, who had been Prime Minister of Great Britain for two and a half years, was assassinated in the lobby of the House of Commons by a recently bankrupted commercial agent, John Bellingham. The eminence of the victim and the location of the crime made Bellingham's act unique in

Spencer Perceval, the only English premier to be assassinated.

the records of murder. It also emphasized the despair felt by a large section of the business community over the burdens imposed upon them by a never-ending war —for although Bellingham was mentally deranged, his conviction that the government was responsible for the acute economic recession was held, less violently, by thousands of impoverished manufacturers and laborers.

English morale was lower in the winter of 1811–12 than at any other moment in the Napoleonic Wars. Those were the months in which machine breaking spread northward from the Midlands to reach an angry climax in Lancashire and Cheshire. And factors other than the Luddite hysteria were also contributing to the general malaise. After two bad harvests, food was scarce, and in the spring of 1812 wheat was selling at three times the prewar price. Moreover, the Napoleonic Wars that had once stimulated industry were strangling it. Napoleon had responded to the British naval blockade by instituting the Continental System (which sought to close all Northern and Western Europe, except Portugal, to British goods). The British had retaliated by cutting off trade not only with Napoleon's Empire but with any

state that broke the blockade. As both combatants sought to regulate Europe's trade, manufacturers in England and France began to feel the strain. The most drastically affected areas were regions in England where the Wars had earlier brought quick profits. In the new industrial towns of Lancashire and Yorkshire warehouses were filled with exports for which there were no markets. Factories began to close and unemployment spread. In August, 1810, no less than five Manchester firms went into liquidation, and shock waves of bankruptcy continued to trouble the northern counties for more than a year.

On the afternoon of May 11, 1812, John Bellingham stepped out of the drab uniformity of frustration that had gripped England and entered the margin of history. By that time, the British government had already decided to repeal the trade restrictions known as the Orders in Council. The Orders had imposed a disastrous economic burden on English manufacturers and, by encouraging the Royal Navy to search American ships for contraband, they had so alienated the United States that President Madison was threatening the British with another war across the Atlantic. Perceval's assassination delayed the announcement of repeal until the new Prime Minister, Lord Liverpool, had formed his

James Madison, who started the war of 1812 between the U.S. and Britain.

government, but on June 16, 1812, it was finally announced in the House of Commons that the Orders in Council would be withdrawn. But it was too late to avert war.

The port of Liverpool, hub of Lancashire's industrial boom and the center of British trade with the U.S.

War of 1812

The London newspapers, elated by Wellington's successes in Spain, tended to deride the United States and minimize the significance of Madison's action. But the American Republic in 1812 was a far larger and more developed state than the embryonic Confederation that had won recognition of its independence in 1783. The wise counsel of President Washington and Alexander Hamilton had both increased the interdependence of the individual states and fostered their "infant industries." It is true that under President Thomas Jefferson (1801–9) the states had jealously preserved their rights and their fundamentally agrarian economies, but Jefferson had also been responsible for the biggest land deal in history, a measure that doubled the size of the Republic. By the Louisiana Purchase of 1803 the nominally French territories that stretched from the Mississippi Valley westward to the Rockies were sold to the United States. For the nominal sum of 15 million dollars the Americans had acquired a piece of real estate four times as large as metropolitan France.

The population of the United States had grown from 5.3 million when Jefferson took office to some 7.5 million in 1812. New roads pushed the line of settlement westward through the Appalachians, and explorers crossed the newly acquired territory to the Pacific. Textile mills spread industry across New England and indirectly gave "the peculiar institution" of slavery a new life as a means for producing more and more cotton. The first steamboat, Robert Fulton's *Clermont*, sailed up the Hudson River from New York to Albany in 1807, and work had started on a canal to

link the Hudson and Lake Erie and open up the farmlands of the Ohio Valley.

Under such circumstances, war with England was welcomed by some Americans, for an American victory would secure even more territory for settlement by hardy pioneers. Canada's rich farmlands sorely tempted the "war hawks" who felt that the nation's honor was being insulted by the British Navy—particularly because it was believed that the British had incited the Shawnee Indian warriors of Tecumseh to rise against the Americans along the Ohio.

The war hawks' enthusiasm notwithstanding, the Anglo-American War of 1812 was a mistake, as many of the Federalists in New England perceived from the start. On paper, the United States should have been able to achieve the hawks' prime objective, the subjection of Upper Canada. Statistically, Americans outnumbered Canadians fourteen to one, and as long as the British were committed in Europe against Napoleon little military assistance could be ferried across the Atlantic. The Americans had three major problems, however: (1) geographical conditions in the Great Lakes hampered communications; (2) the British fleet in the western Atlantic outnumbered the U.S. Navy; and (3) there was opposition to the War from individual American states (which refused to allow their militia to fight outside state boundaries).

The War was characterized by a series of naval duels—the most famous of which was the encounter of the two frigates, *Chesapeake* and *Shannon*, in January, 1813—and by inept and poorly coordinated land campaigns. American attempts to invade Canada from Detroit, Niagara and Lake Champlain failed in 1812, but U.S. troops gained a victory between Lakes Huron and

Erie in October, 1813. Most of the fighting in 1813 consisted of punitive raids: the Americans successfully set fire to the capital of Upper Canada (which was then called York and is now known as Toronto), and the British burned Buffalo.

After Napoleon's abdication, British veterans of the Peninsular Campaign were shipped to Canada. Those troops made two attempts to strike southward toward the Hudson; on each occasion they were repulsed. In June, 1814, a British expeditionary force was embarked at Bordeaux and conveyed directly to Chesapeake Bay. Meeting little opposition on landing, it advanced on the city of Washington and set fire to the Capitol and the President's residence (not yet known as the White House), and other administrative buildings. The British then attempted a similar raid at Baltimore, where they were finally repulsed by the guns of Fort McHenry. On Christmas Eve, 1814, a peace treaty was signed at Ghent that restored relations between the two countries without reference to the issues that had brought them to war. News of the peace treaty did not reach the United States until seven weeks after its signature, and during the intervening period General Andrew Jackson won a resounding victory for the Americans at New Orleans. Such operations reflected no credit on the strategic thought of either of the combatants, although there were many acts of valor. The only gains for the United States were the making of a popular hero at New Orleans and the inspiring of a national anthem by Francis Scott Key at Fort McHenry.

In a sense, the War of 1812 reversed American foreign policy. When George Washington retired from the presidency in 1797 his farewell message advocated isolation from Europe's affairs. That policy had been followed by his successor, John Adams (despite the opposition of Hamilton and the

James Monroe, who steered the United States away from the whirlpool of European affairs.

Federalists), and with occasional lapses by Thomas Jefferson. Madison, on the other hand, had allowed the war fever of back-country congressmen to stampede him into a conflict whose resolution depended ultimately on the course of battle on the mainland of Europe. Had the Peace of Ghent represented a real victory for either side,

the Americans might have become involved in Europe's affairs for several generations. Instead, the treaty admitted—by its very silence—the folly of the war's causes, and consequently Madison and Monroe (his Secretary of State and successor as President) were able to steer the Republic away from the whirlpool of European affairs.

Napoleon's "ally"

Napoleon, of course, had welcomed the rupture of Britain's relations with the United States in 1812. Eighteen months before the War, a dictated note to the American Minister had declared "His Majesty loves the Americans"—and throughout the dramatic winter of 1812–13, Napoleon was constantly seeking news of American victories from his Foreign Minister. But although the Anglo-American War and the War of the Fourth Coalition ran parallel to each other in time, they were totally different in character and objectives. (In fact, the Russians' victories over Napoleon were publicly celebrated in Georgetown, D.C., twelve months before the army of Russia's ally burned Washington, D.C.) For Napoleon America remained a sanctuary to which he might one day escape: it could never have been a source of military assistance.

By the early summer of 1812 it had become clear that war was returning to the great plains of Eastern Europe. Half a year earlier,

on December 19, 1811, the Emperor's librarian had received a request for "good books with the best information about Russian topography" and "the most detailed account in French of the campaign of Charles XII [of Sweden] in Poland and Russia." For four months Napoleon remained in Paris, meticulously studying maps and reports. He dictated lengthy instructions for his garrisons, indicating how the Army of Italy was to be moved northward across the Alps to the sandhills of Pomerania, how the Imperial Old Guard was to break off its engagements with Wellington in the Sierra de Gata and march seventeen hundred miles through Spain, France and Germany in order to reach the River Vistula by the last week in May, how six thousand horses were to be transported from the Jutland Peninsula to East Prussia, and how rice supplies were to be speeded eastward from Hamburg. All was planned in detail.

The finest military machine in the world had throbbed into action once again. Marshal Berthier, who had learned his staff work as a young officer assisting the Americans in their struggle for independence, immersed himself in logistic problems. Louis Nicolas Davout, the most methodical of Napoleon's marshals, peered through specially designed spectacles at the muster rolls in his army corps—70,000 men from six nations. General Eblé, the incomparable military engineer, worked out details of pontoon bridges to be thrown across the Neman, the sluggish stream separating Prussia from Russia. The paladins of Napoleon's Empire—the red-haired Ney; Murat, magnificent in exotic uniforms; Oudinot, with saintly face and tyrant's temper; and many others—journeyed eastward to the woods of birch and pine along Europe's eastern border. No one could doubt that Napoleon regarded the forthcoming campaign against Russia as the climax of his military career. He left Paris on May 9, 1812, held court at Dresden for his brother sovereigns and allies from Vienna and Berlin, and reached a Polish village on the banks of the Neman in the late evening of June 21. Moscow lay five hundred miles to the east. "I am embarking on the greatest and most difficult enterprise I have so far attempted," he had told one of his counsellors as he set out from Paris.

The White House, burnt by the redcoats in 1814.

Retreat from Russia

Death and desertion had thinned the ranks of Napoleon's vast Grand Army by the time it reached Smolensk in August of 1812, but even these difficulties had failed to dampen the Emperor's optimism. "Within a month we shall be in Moscow; within six weeks the war will be over," he declared. Time was to prove him half right. By September the Corsican's troops had indeed conquered Moscow—but the war was far from over. Because the Tsar refused to negotiate a peace treaty, Napoleon was faced with the prospect of retreating or attempting to quarter some 700,000 troops in the gutted capital through the oncoming—and legendarily severe— Russian winter. The Emperor chose to retreat—over the same scorched earth that his army had trod little more than a month earlier. By the time the army reached France, all but 30,000 members of the original force were dead or missing, and Napoleon's Grand Empire was toppling.

On June 24, 1812, Napoleon Bonaparte crossed the Neman River in command of the most powerful army that had ever existed in Europe. Every allied and vassal country was represented: Italy, Belgium, the Netherlands, Switzerland, Austria and Prussia. The Army of Twenty Nations, as it came to be known, was a microcosm of Napoleonic Europe.

A few nights earlier, the orderly officers sleeping near Napoleon's room had been astounded to hear him singing some verses of a patriotic song, the *Chant du Départ*. Now the Emperor was playing with his riding whip while humming another tune to himself. This show of gaiety, however, may have concealed a certain anxiety. Napoleon had just declared war against Russia.

The Treaty of Tilsit, which had been concluded between Tsar Alexander I and Napoleon in 1807, was already verging on collapse when the two rulers held a meeting at Erfurt. After the signing of the Treaty, Russia had reluctantly joined in the Continental System, a scheme of economic warfare aimed at closing the European markets to British goods. As a result of these measures, however, the Russian textile industry had suffered from a shortage of cotton, while the cessation of exports of wool and hemp to England had created enormous difficulties for the wealthy landowners. Thus the Franco-Russian alliance was unpopular in Russia, and a pro-English party was plotting to overthrow Alexander I. The Tsar too was exasperated by the meager advantages he had gained from the Tilsit agreement. Although he had obtained Finland, Bessarabia and a section of Galicia, he was still waiting for Napoleon to implement the plan to divide the Ottoman Empire between them. Moreover, some of his conquests were in jeopardy. The presence in Stockholm of Bernadotte, the heir presumptive to the Swedish throne, represented a threat to Finland. Also, Napoleon's creation of the Grand Duchy of Warsaw was a step toward the reconstitution of the ancient Kingdom of Poland, of which Galicia had been a part. Finally, when the Emperor annexed the Duchy of Oldenburg, which belonged to a relation of the Tsar's, the alliance broke down.

Napoleon too had decided on a direct confrontation with the Tsar. The extremely ambiguous attitude of Alexander during the Emperor's Austrian campaign in 1809 had persuaded Napoleon that the Franco-Russian alliance would not work. In 1812 he believed the right moment had come to attack his rival. His alliance with the Hapsburgs through his marriage to Marie Louise made him optimistic about German support. Furthermore, he knew he could count on a second front, since war had broken out again between Turkey and Russia in 1809.

Napoleon considered Russia a threat to Europe, and he saw himself in the role of defender of civilized Europe against the Russian invasion. In fact, he aspired to be the successor to the Roman emperors and drive back the northern barbarians as far as the plains of Central Asia. Napoleon is reported to have told his confidant Narbonne, "Marius created Caesar. The extermination of the Cimbri [a German tribe] was the first step toward the foundation of the Roman Empire; and by steeping itself in the same blood, or similar blood, the Empire renewed its strength during the reigns of Trajan, Aurelian and Theodosius." Then, considering the problem within a contemporary context, he added, "Remember Suvorov and his Tartars in Italy—the only solution is to drive them back beyond Moscow, and what better moment than now for Europe to do this—under my leadership?"

Although Napoleon believed that the campaign would be a short one, he made extremely careful and detailed preparations. He ordered the War Office to draw up the most accurate maps possible of the Moscow and St. Petersburg regions, and he collected a vast mass of information about the Tsarist Empire. Nonetheless, he was convinced that the Russians would soon collapse in the face of his

Alexander I, Tsar of Russia. He ordered that Moscow should be left deserted for Napoleon's troops to capture.

Opposite Napoleon as First Consul.

Dreams of a world empire

Napoleon at the Battle of Wagram in 1809—one of his many victories.

Right The emperors of Russia (Orthodox) and Austria (Roman Catholic) and the King of Prussia (Lutheran) give thanks to God after the Battle of Leipzig, 1813, in which the French were decisively defeated.

The French Army flees through Leipzig after its retreat from Moscow.

attack and that the maps and statistical information would not be needed.

Napoleon explained his plan to Narbonne:

The barbarians are superstitious people with simple ideas. A deadly blow aimed at the great, sacred city of Moscow, the very heart of the Empire, will gain for me in a single stroke this blind, inert mass of people. I know Alexander. . . . Perhaps he will acknowledge defeat at the mere sight of the unparalleled stockpile of armaments that I am building up and at the huge European army which I shall display for inspection at Dresden.

The Emperor was planning even further ahead. He still cherished the old dream that had haunted him ever since the Egyptian campaigns: to strike at India, the very source of British power and wealth in Asia. He confided to Narbonne:

Supposing Russia is defeated, tell me whether a great army of Frenchmen and auxiliaries, setting off from Tiflis, would not be able to make their way directly overland as far as the Ganges and then whether one touch from a French sword would not suffice to destroy the whole structure of the great British mercantile system throughout India.

A total of 700,000 allied troops were engaged in the Russian campaign, divided into three corps and

a reserve force. In the Russian camp, 200,000 men under Prince Mikhail Barclay de Tolly had been divided into three armies. The huge, unwieldy size of Napoleon's army was to be his downfall. Communications and transportation were most inefficient, and military headquarters was soon in a state of chaos.

It is incorrect to claim that the Russians deliberately planned their strategy to draw Napoleon into the heart of Russia, thus allowing the vast spaces of the countryside and the rigorous climate of the Russian winter to destroy him. In fact it was more a lack of coordination among the Russian generals, combined with their fear of being confronted with the Emperor, that drove them into retreat. The idea of making use of space and climate occurred to them only afterward. The Prussian officer Karl von Clausewitz, who later was to write a famous treatise on warfare and who was in the service of the Tsar at that time, was quite categorical on this point: "The Russian retreat was not the outcome of a carefully thought-out plan; but resulted from the fact that each time they were about to join battle with the enemy, they decided that they were still not strong enough to confront him."

Prince Barclay de Tolly eluded Napoleon at Vilna, abandoning that town on June 28. Here Napoleon received the Tsar's envoy, who had brought him a letter. When Napoleon asked him how to get to Moscow, the envoy replied: "One can choose one's own route to Moscow. Charles XII went there via Poltava."

Napoleon next hoped to catch the main Russian force unawares at Smolensk, but once again Barclay de Tolly eluded him. At Smolensk several of his advisers urged Napoleon to take up winter quarters until the following spring. More than half of the cavalry were already dismounted, and the number of deserters was continually growing.

Napoleon, however, was not to be swayed from his purpose. "Within a month we shall be in Moscow; within six weeks the war will be over."

The Russians, however, could not allow Napoleon to enter Moscow, their sacred city, without putting up a fight. On September 7 they joined battle with Napoleon's Grand Army at Borodino. Entrenched behind strong defenses, Field Marshal Mikhail Kutuzov, who had succeeded Barclay de Tolly, repulsed the French attack at first but finally was forced to retire. Napoleon, however, by refusing to engage his Imperial Guard, lost a great opportunity to destroy the Russian Army. The French casualties were very heavy: forty-seven generals and one hundred colonels were killed.

As a result of the Russian retreat at Borodino, Napoleon's Army entered Moscow on September 15. "The whole of this empty, uninhabited town was filled with a deep, mournful silence," noted General Armand de Caulaincourt. "Throughout our long march through Moscow, we did not come across a single person." The following day, fire broke out in the capital. The Emperor was visibly upset. One witness has described the scene:

He walked slowly down the steps of Ivan's Tower, from where he had been watching the fire, followed by the Prince of Neuchâtel and some of his officers; then, leaning on the arm of the Duke of Vicenza, he crossed over a small wooden bridge leading to the quayside of the Moskva River; there, he found some horses.

Despite the conquest of Moscow, the Tsar refused to negotiate peace terms. Napoleon was faced with a dilemma: he thought of launching an attack on St. Petersburg, but this idea was frowned on by his colleagues. A number of staff officers suggested that it would be better to remain in Moscow, where they were well provided with supplies. At the same time, the Grand Army was in danger of being cut off from its bases by Russian reinforcements.

The retreat from Russia was hindered by the cruelty of the winter weather, which decimated Napoleon's army.

Left Joachim Murat, Marshal of France and King of Naples.

Arthur Wellesley, later Duke of Wellington. Wellesley's brilliant campaigns in the Iberian Peninsula were a major factor in upsetting Napoleon's carefully prepared campaigns.

639

General Frost shaveing Little Boney, a cartoon published in 1812.

After a month of procrastination, Napoleon finally made up his mind to withdraw, and on October 19 the Grand Army evacuated Moscow. It was already getting late in the year, and the first frosts had appeared. Napoleon's plan was to withdraw along the road leading to Kaluga, which lay farther south than the route they had followed on their way to Moscow and thus would afford a milder climate as well as more abundant supplies. Kutuzov, however, barred his way to Maloyaroslavets on October 24. The Emperor was forced to take the road to Smolensk, through the devastated countryside where everything had been destroyed by the Russians or by French pillagers. In addition to famine and the terrible cold (the thermometer fell as low as −30°F.), the retreating army had to contend with guerrilla attacks carried out by the bands of Cossacks pursuing it. The withdrawal turned into a complete rout, and soon Napoleon's Grand Army had deteriorated into a shapeless, undisciplined mass of troops who abandoned vehicles, guns, and frozen corpses in their wake.

When they finally reached the Berezina, Napoleon's forces had been reduced to 30,000 men and an unending procession of stragglers. Moreover, the survivors nearly lost their lives in the Berezina, the ice of which had broken during a sudden thaw. They were saved, however, by the heroism of General Eble's *pontoniers* who bravely worked away in the frozen water and built two bridges, one for the soldiers and the other for vehicles. Sergeant Bourgogne has described the scene vividly: "The foot soldiers dragged themselves painfully along, nearly all of them with frost-bitten legs swathed in rags and

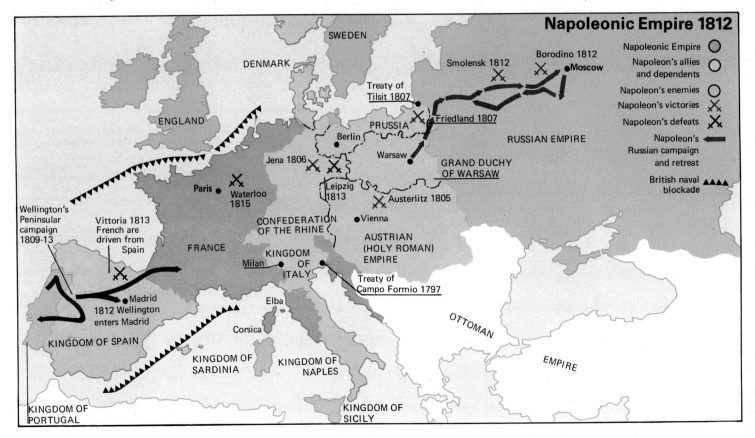

pieces of sheepskin, and dying of hunger." These were the remnants of the Imperial Guard. Then came Napoleon: "The Emperor was on foot and carried a stick in his hand. He was enveloped in a large cloak lined with fur, and wore a purple velvet cap on his head with a band of black fox fur." Bourgogne includes this description of a veteran of the Old Guard who was watching the scene: "I saw large tears rolling down his cheeks into his moustache from which icicles were hanging."

Finally, in the middle of December, the remnants of the Army of Twenty Nations recrossed the Neman.

Earlier, however, (on December 5) Napoleon had handed over the command of the survivors to his brother-in-law Murat and had hurriedly returned to Paris on hearing of the conspiracy of General Malet. The General had attempted to take over power in the French capital by spreading the false rumor that the Emperor had been killed outside Moscow. Napoleon left behind him in Russia 400,000 dead and 100,000 prisoners. Never before had an army experienced a disaster of such great magnitude.

The fall of the Grand Empire dates from the time of the Russian defeat. At the beginning of 1812, the Empire included not only France but also Belgium, Holland, the Hanseatic cities of Bremen and Hamburg, the left bank of the Rhine, Catalonia, northern Italy, Rome and the Papal States, and the Illyrian provinces. Napoleon ruled over three political formations: the Kingdom of Italy, the Swiss Confederation, and the Rhine Confederation, which included nearly the whole of Germany apart from Austria and Prussia, as well as the Grand Duchy of Warsaw. This vast area constituted nearly half of Europe and had a population of 71 million inhabitants. War against England lay at the root of the Grand Empire: Napoleon had become involved in a series of conquests in order to close the Continent to English goods and to ruin the pound sterling by an effective blockade. This was, however, never effective.

Under his rule, the Empire became unified. The Civil Code was introduced in every country. New judicial principles of social equality and civil liberty replaced the old feudal system. Napoleon wrote to Joseph Fouché, his Minister of Police: "What I want is a European Code, a European Supreme Court of Appeal, the same currency, the same weights and measures, the same laws for everyone." To the Council of State he declared, "If you unite every country as far as the columns of Hercules, as far as Kamchatka, the laws of France must be introduced there."

There were many additional unification projects. The highway became the chief coordinating factor in Napoleonic Europe, just as it had been in the days of the Roman Empire. The great Simplon and Saint Gothard highways were constructed at this time. Vast works were undertaken that changed the face of the ancient capitals (in Rome, for instance, the Pontine Marshes were drained). Nationalities intermingled in the army. Even the arts were not exempt from this desire for unification. Henceforth it was in the Louvre that the works of Rubens of Antwerp or the masterpieces of Italian or Spanish art could be admired. It was even planned to

Napoleon's study at Fontainbleau.

Blockading "the nation of shopkeepers"

The Battle of Smolensk, where Napoleon, on the way to Moscow, defeated the Russians.

transfer the archives of the subjugated countries to Paris. And Napoleon created the Order of Reunion to replace the old European decorations, symbolizing the fusion of different countries into the Empire.

Would this Napoleonic Europe have been a workable system? Even at the time of the Russian expedition, cracks were already beginning to appear in its structure. In 1810 Napoleon had modified his concept of the Continental System. Because he was unable to prevent smuggling with England, he decided to become a smuggler himself. He authorized the importation of English goods under a system of licenses. (The high duties he levied on these goods enabled him to finance the Russian expedition.) This limited trade with England was restricted to French ports, which later redistributed the products imported from Great Britain to the rest of Europe. At the same time Napoleon stepped up the campaign against smuggling in the allied and subjugated nations, especially in Germany, where English merchandise worth millions of francs was burned in Frankfurt.

Europe, already reluctant to put up with the shortage of sugar, coffee and cotton imposed by a blockade that also was proving economically disastrous, was even more reluctant to suffer these privations when it saw that France was exempt from them. Indeed, by his system of licenses and by the restrictions imposed on industrial development in certain countries such as Italy, Napoleon planned the creation of a gigantic market in Europe for the benefit of French businessmen and manufacturers. "My ruling principle," he stated, "is that France comes first." The blockade, which started as a means of attacking England, became from 1810 onward the instrument with which to maintain French economic hegemony over the rest of Europe.

But Napoleon lost his reputation of invincibility in the snows of Russia, and Europe took advantage of the French Emperor's failure to rise up against him. The revolt began in Prussia, where poets, academics and politicians inspired the growth of a patriotic movement that spread throughout Germany. Thousands of volunteers joined in the fight for

642

The Battle of Borodino, which laid open the route to Moscow.

freedom and wore the black, red and gold cockade. Austria allied itself with Prussia and Russia, and in October, 1813, they defeated Napoleon at Leipzig. From then on Germany was lost to the Emperor.

Holland was the next to revolt. On November 15, 1813, the Dutch drove out the French occupation troops and invited the Prince of Orange to rule them. In the meantime, the Swiss Confederation had withdrawn from the French sphere of influence and had proclaimed its neutrality. The raising of troops for the Russian campaign had depleted the French forces stationed in Spain, and in June of 1813 British forces under Wellington defeated them in a bloody battle at Vitoria, driving them out of the Iberian Peninsula with the help of the Spanish.

Thus the disastrous Russian campaign speeded up the disintegration of the Empire by bringing to the surface all the discontent with French domination that had been felt for a long time in Europe. All those countries that had been merged into the Continental System regained their former independence. The Emperor himself was forced into exile, first on Elba and then, after escape and the abortive attempt to regain power that ended at Waterloo, on St. Helena.

The Congress of Vienna, called in 1814 to remake Europe after Napoleon's collapse, was a major effort at European cooperation. Yet the victors, obsessed by their own interests, ignored the nationalist movements that had begun to emerge at the time of the Russian campaign. These violent nationalist movements, especially in Germany and Italy, were to provoke a long series of revolutions and wars. Thus the collapse of Napoleon's Empire marked the beginning of a long period of division in Europe.

The Napoleonic balance sheet was not totally negative, however. The Russian disaster did not jeopardize the radical changes that the Emperor had introduced into Western Europe, particularly the destruction of feudalism. Moreover, although he envisioned a united Europe that would exclude both Russia in the east and England in the west, Napoleon had simplified the map of Europe to a large extent and had broached the idea of European unity—a concept that had lain forgotten since the time of Charlemagne.   JEAN TULARD

Above Metternich, who led the Austrian peace delegation in 1813 and presided over the Congress of Vienna.

The Congress of Vienna, which redrew the map of Europe after the Napoleonic era.

The Russian campaign and the fall of Napoleon

On March 31, 1814, Tsar Alexander I of Russia, resplendent in gilded stirrups, gold epaulets and a golden collar, became the first foreign conqueror to enter Paris since Henry V of England in 1420. The Tsar was accompanied by the insignificant King of Prussia, Frederick William III, and was followed a fortnight later by the Emperor Francis I of Austria. Thus all three allied sovereigns were in residence in Paris on May 4 when Louis XVIII, brother of the Bourbon King who was executed in 1793, claimed a throne that was his by inheritance rather than by the will of his subjects. Metternich and Castlereagh (the foreign ministers of Austria and Britain) and Wellington, who had commanded the allied troops in Portugal and Spain, watched the return of the Bourbons with apprehension, for all three suspected that the French people would never take this fat and forgotten representative of the old order to their hearts. "It made a most painful impression upon me," Metternich later wrote in his memoirs.

While Louis XVIII was being crowned in Paris, Napoleon—still an Emperor in name—departed to rule the tiny island of Elba off the coast of Italy. It was anyone's guess how long he would play out the parody of power.

The downfall of Napoleon had meant far more than a change in regal personalities, for the Emperor had transformed Europe more rapidly and more comprehensively than any sovereign for a thousand years. It became the task of the victors not only to dismantle the imperial apparatus of government but to control the national aspirations stimulated throughout the Continent by the years of revolution and warfare. At the same time, it was essential for them to build up a lasting settlement that would be safe both against renewed aggression by France and against any attempt by one of the allied powers to establish a military dominance over its neighbors. The settlement came just in time: the Russians' successful eastward thrust in 1813–14 had already cast a heavy shadow over the deliberations of the Austrians, the Prussians and the British. Their suspicions were fanned by Talleyrand who, in the last months of war, had shifted his

allegiance from Napoleon to Louis XVIII and now exercised his talent for diplomatic negotiations on behalf of the Bourbons.

By the first Peace of Paris (May 30, 1814), the territory of France was limited to the frontiers of 1792, with minor adjustments. It took far longer to determine the character of the new Europe. The task of doing so fell upon the Congress of Vienna, a gathering of six emperors and kings, two dozen German princelings, and a host of plenipotentiaries and diplomats who

Louis XVIII: crowned King of France in 1814 in place of the banished Emperor Napoleon.

met in the Austrian capital from September, 1814, to June, 1815. A spate of formal entertainment and the gossip of an overcrowded city won the Congress a dubious reputation for frivolity and scandal—much of which was unjustified. The statesmen worked hard to achieve their principal objective, the "general repose of the European Continent," and although there was a major rift between Russia and her western allies, they were successful. Europe was given the opportunity to convalesce for a decade.

The Treaty of Vienna

The Congress' final act (which is generally known as the Treaty of Vienna of June, 1815) set up three new political entities and two subject kingdoms. The territorial creations were: a united kingdom of the Netherlands (Holland, Belgium and Luxemburg), a German confederation of thirty-nine loosely linked independent states with no central government, and a free city in the ancient Polish university town of Cracow. The subject kingdoms were: Lombardy-Venetia, which was ruled by the Austrian Emperor, and Congress Poland (the area around Warsaw), which was ruled by the Tsar of Russia.

The Treaty also called for the Swiss confederation to be re-established and given a guarantee of permanent neutrality; the pre-Napoleonic dynasties in Spain, Piedmont, Tuscany, Modena and Naples to be restored; and Norway, which had previously been linked to Denmark, to be handed over to Sweden. Prussia obtained new territories in the Rhineland, an area of great future significance both because of its untapped mineral resources and because of its strategic importance as a launching pad for the invasion of France. The British, more interested in colonies than in Europe, secured Malta, Heligoland, the Cape of Good Hope, Tobago, Mauritius and Ceylon. They were also given a protectorate over Corfu and the Ionian Islands (which remained under British administration until 1863).

These territorial decisions inevitably paid scant regard to national rights, for European rulers still thought primarily in dynastic terms, and they equated "nationalism" with "revolution" as a cause of upheaval. The German and Italian peoples were particularly disappointed by the settlement, and so, in time, were the Poles and Belgians. But as an exercise in the statecraft of reciprocal compensation, the Congress was without a parallel in the history of diplomacy. The principle of a balanced "concert of Europe" that the Congress established lasted for the remainder of the nineteenth century. No great

powers fought each other for almost forty years after the Treaty of Vienna, and there was no war involving all Europe for ninety-nine years.

Not all the credit for the long peace rests with the statesmen in Vienna. For example, it can be argued that the opening of other continents lessened the likelihood of a long and exhausting war in Europe. But there is no doubt that the delegates to the Congress were conscious of the need for some international order that would curb the anarchy of competing states. They accepted, for the first time, the principle of free navigation on the great inland waterways (the Rhine and the Moselle, in this instance) and they settled the delicate questions of ambassadorial precedence and privilege, an essential preliminary to the establishment of any regular system of diplomatic negotiation. In addition the Congress issued two declarations concerned with fundamental human rights: a condemnation of the slave trade and a recommendation that the liberties of the Jewish people should be broadened, especially in Germany. In retrospect it is clear that the Congress of Vienna—although universally execrated by men of liberal sentiment —was not without moral dignity.

Escape from Elba

The last months of the Congress were disturbed by a dangerous

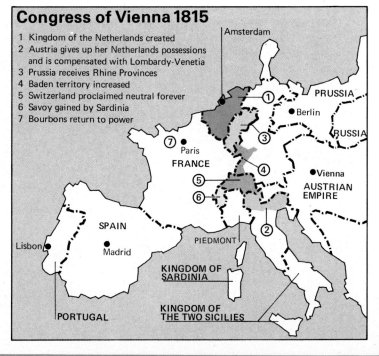

Congress of Vienna 1815

1. Kingdom of the Netherlands created
2. Austria gives up her Netherlands possessions and is compensated with Lombardy-Venetia
3. Prussia receives Rhine Provinces
4. Baden territory increased
5. Switzerland proclaimed neutral forever
6. Savoy gained by Sardinia
7. Bourbons return to power

Wellington at the Battle of Waterloo, where Napoleon was finally defeated by Britain and Prussia.

threat to the new settlement. In February, 1815, Napoleon escaped from Elba. Three weeks later he was back in Paris, Louis XVIII was in exile, and French loyalties were swiftly shifting back to the Emperor. Once more the European statesmen formed a coalition against "the international outlaw." Wellington left Vienna to command an Anglo-Dutch force in Belgium; Marshal Blücher concentrated a Prussian army on the lower Rhine; and the Austrians and Russians slowly mobilized. On June 18, Wellington defeated the French at Waterloo (ten miles south of Brussels). The Emperor might still have defended France from the joint Anglo-Prussian invasion (fresh troops were being raised to replace his losses), but the politicians of Paris lost their nerve, and Napoleon was induced to abdicate. Once again allied troops entered Paris. The fallen Emperor was conveyed to St. Helena, a tiny granite outcrop in the South Atlantic, where he died in May, 1821.

The immediate consequence of Napoleon's Hundred Days was the Second Peace of Paris (November 20, 1815), which redrew French frontiers as they had been in 1790 and imposed a war indemnity of 700 million francs on the French people. The terms of the treaty further stipulated that allied troops were to occupy France for a period of from three to five years.

An indirect consequence of the Second Peace of Paris was a new endorsement of the need for international cooperation to safeguard the whole Vienna settlement. Both Castlereagh and Metternich believed such cooperation could best

be achieved through a system of "diplomacy by congress," and a legal basis for such conferences was provided by a clause in the Quadruple Alliance that was signed in November, 1815, by Austria, Britain, Prussia and Russia.

Tsar Alexander favored an even more elevated concept—a "Holy Alliance of Justice, Christian Charity and Peace"—to which he induced most of his brother sovereigns to subscribe (although both Metternich and Castlereagh regarded it with considerable cynicism). Unfortunately, the Tsar chose to inform the world of his Holy Alliance at a review of the Russian Army of occupation in Paris and his alliance became the particular butt of Europe's liberals. Within a few years the term Holy Alliance was being applied to the whole policy of repression followed by the three Eastern autocracies, Russia,

Marshal Blücher: commander of the Prussian troops against Napoleon at Waterloo.

Prussia and Austria. The Tsar's original ideal, a muddled and mystical call for something more exalted than mere reactionary government, had been lost.

At first, the Congress System favored by Metternich and Castlereagh functioned effectively. Unlike the League of Nations or the United Nations, the Congress System had no permanent secretariat, but was a genuine experiment to test the possibility of international administration. The first meeting, held at Aix-la-Chapelle in 1818, was highly successful. But a fundamental difference separated Britain from her old allies at the remaining congresses. The Austrians and Russians believed that the great powers had a right and a duty to intervene if other states were threatened by internal unrest. The British refused to associate themselves with repressive measures against liberal revolutionaries in Spain and southern Italy. The congresses at Troppau in 1820 and at Laibach in 1821 were inconclusive, and when the British withdrew from the Congress of Verona in 1822 the whole system fell apart.

The sick man of Europe

Long before Britain's insistence on nonintervention killed the Congress System, there were signs of a deep rift between the two main champions of repression, Russia and Austria. Ever since the first sessions of the Congress of Vienna, Metternich had tried to avoid discussions about southeastern Europe. The weak and incompetent government of the Turkish Empire had been challenged by a major revolt in Serbia in 1804, and there were powerful movements for national independence in the other Balkan States as well. Metternich knew that the Russians were eager to benefit from the increasing feebleness of the Sultan's Empire, and he feared that if Turkey-in-Europe broke up into small national states the process of disintegration would also affect the Austrian Empire (for many of the submerged historic nationalities in southeastern Europe were subject to both Austrian and Turkish rule). Friedrich von Gentz, who was Metternich's chief adviser in foreign affairs, wrote in 1815: "The end of the Turkish monarchy could be survived by the Austrian for only a short time." This prophetic warning was to prove accurate at

the end of World War One.

So long as the principal challenge to Turkish rule came from Serbia, Metternich had some hopes of maintaining "a state of repose" in the Balkans, for there was bitter feuding between the leading Serbian families (one faction of whom favored cooperation with the Sultan). But a new spirit of national

Skulls on a tower at Nis in Yugoslavia commemorating the first Serbian uprising.

cultural regeneration was at work among the Greek communities, not only in the Aegean but in the Turkish ports on the Black Sea and even in Constantinople. The prospect of a revolt in Greece appealed to the Tsar because of the close links between the Russian and Greek branches of the Orthodox Church. And there were others besides the Russians who felt kinship with the Greeks. The romantic spirit, harnessed to a classical education, ensured that if Greece sought her independence, the echoes of her struggle would resound throughout Western Europe and even beyond the Atlantic.

On April 6, 1821, Archbishop Germanos of Patras called on his compatriots to free themselves from Turkish rule. The Greek War of Independence had begun. Metternich, who deemed the move a catastrophe, complained that the headquarters of the European revolution could never have shown more cunning than in selecting Greece as the center from which the whole Continent would be set aflame. The Greek revolt rallied Europe's liberals—and from among the philhellenes, democracy was soon to find its martyr-hero.

Death of a Poet

Insurrection engulfed the Ionian Peninsula in the early spring of 1821 as a determined band of Greek patriots attempted to free their homeland from Ottoman oppression. Their cause found widespread international support—particularly in England, where John Hobhouse, a close friend and traveling companion of Lord Byron's, founded a committee to assist the insurgents. Byron, England's foremost Romantic poet, found the rebels' cause a particularly compelling one, and on July 13, 1823, he sailed for the strife-ridden peninsula. In his youth Byron had toured Greece with Hobhouse, and he remembered the country as a place of unending beauty. Instead, he encountered inclement weather, earthquakes, riots and mutiny. Discouraged and embittered, Byron lingered at his headquarters in Missolonghi until April of 1824. On the ninth of that month, the poet-soldier caught cold while riding; ten days later Lord Byron, the personification of Romanticism, was dead.

Byron's signature carved on a column at the east end of the Temple of Poseidon at Cape Sounion in Greece.

Opposite Byron in Albanian national dress. Byron's sympathy for the Greeks was largely based on romantic ideas.

In mid-May of 1824, dispatches from the Gulf of Corinth reached London announcing that a month earlier, on April 19, George Gordon, Lord Byron, had died at Missolonghi. The first to open the dispatches was Byron's friend Douglas Kinnaird, who immediately forwarded their contents to another old friend, John Cam Hobhouse. "I can scarcely write to tell you," Kinnaird said, "yet delay is absurd and I know not how to soften what your own fortitude alone can make you bear like a man— Byron is no more...." The news, Hobhouse noted in his diary, threw him into "an agony of grief." No less agonizing were the emotions of Augusta Leigh, the ill-fated sister who had loved Byron far too well. A cousin reported that even Lady Byron, his former wife, was "in a distressing state," and that "she said she had no right to be considered by Lord Byron's friends, but she had her feelings." Of Byron's one-time Italian circle, the widowed Mary Shelley remembered him with especially deep affection. "Albé," she recorded in her journal, "the dear, capricious, fascinating Albé—has left this desert world! God grant I may die young!"

Meanwhile the story of Byron's death had "come upon London like an earthquake" and had reverberated throughout the length and breadth of England. To the generation that was then emerging from childhood, it seemed as if some tremendous natural calamity had shaken the framework of the universe. In Lincolnshire, fifteen-year-old Alfred Tennyson hurried down to the cold little stream that ran below his father's garden, and scratched the momentous phrase "Byron Is Dead" upon the surface of a sandstone rock. Jane Welsh wrote to her stern young suitor, Thomas Carlyle, that she had heard the report while she was surrounded by a crowd of people. "My God, if they had said that the sun or the moon had gone out of the heavens, it could not have struck me with the idea of a more awful and dreary blank in the creation...."

Nor were Byron's only mourners his friends, or those who had eagerly studied his works and passionately admired his genius. At Belvoir, the Duke of Rutland was entertaining a large party of jovial country neighbors. When the news was brought to him as he sat at the dinner table, he stood up and commanded silence. "Gentlemen," he exclaimed, "Lord Byron is dead." And without discussion, the company rose from their chairs, called for their servants and carriages, and quietly made their way home.

Few great men, in any country or period, have left behind them so acute a sense of loss. Yet only eight years earlier, on April 26, 1816, Byron had said good-by to England, an exile and a social outcast who appeared to have realized in life the tragic predicament that he had frequently portrayed in literature. He was as solitary as his own *Childe Harold*, the subject of as many alarming legends as the Corsair or the Giaour. Over his head hung a heavy cloud of scandal, and on his journeyings he was to be pursued and harried by a crowd of hostile English tourists. They scrutinized him impudently if they encountered him face to face, or followed his daily round, however pedestrian it might be, with the help of opera glasses. Once, in Switzerland, some tablecloths happened to have been hung out from the windows of the Villa Diodati; his fellow English travelers naturally imagined that what they saw was an array of petticoats belonging to the women of his harem.

Byron, it is true, did not always discourage such legends. The course of debauchery into which he had plunged after settling in Venice in 1817 was just as outrageous as any of the exploits with which the most spiteful gossips credited him. The easy-going Venetians themselves had sometimes looked a little grave, murmuring that milord was a *giovane stravagante*, indeed a very wild young man. True, he had tired of his random sexual adventures, but the

646

The Romantic poet par excellence

Lady Byron, engraved by Freeman.

damage was already done. And his association at Pisa and elsewhere with the notorious atheist, Percy Bysshe Shelley, and other English expatriates of the same kind did not do much to improve his reputation.

Yet he remained the Romantic poet par excellence, the artist who had caught and fixed the vague imaginings and the restless, unsettled desires of his literary and social age. Keats and Shelley were still seldom read; the powerful influence of Wordsworth and Coleridge was confined to a relatively small group. In Byron alone did English writers and critics find a full-blooded personification of the new Romantic mode of feeling that, having begun to take shape as a self-conscious literary movement during the second half of the eighteenth century, had reached its climax with the appearance of *Childe Harold* and the series of highly dramatic and brightly colored verse tales—*The Giaour*, *The Bridge of Abydos*, *The Corsair*, *Lara*, *The Siege of Corinth*, *Parisina* that Byron had written, usually at breakneck speed, during the last three years before he left England.

Nothing could dim the renown of *Childe Harold*. But once Byron had settled down in Italy he embarked upon a very different type of epic, and some of his admirers, Hobhouse included, began to grow a trifle restive. Byron himself considered that *Don Juan*, written in Italy, was a much more important production than any of his earlier poems—it gave a far less distorted view of his own protean personality. But readers who had enjoyed his romantic panache were shocked by the "quietly facetious" tone (an astringent mixture of wit and lyricism) that he now applied to solemn subjects. Further, they were often bored by the elaborate blank-verse dramas that Byron always persisted in regarding as his finest and least perishable works. The reception of his dramas was somewhat lukewarm; and after his foolish Italian mistress, the Countess Teresa Guiccioli, had voiced her disapproval of *Don Juan*, which hurt her idealistic

conception of love. Byron decided he must cut the poem short.

In 1823, Byron was living in Genoa, a lonely, bored and disappointed man. At thirty-five, he felt old; he believed that his popularity was waning; moreover, he had long since fallen out of love with Teresa Guiccioli, though she remained an inseparable companion. He sometimes considered deserting Italy and seeking a new refuge beyond the Atlantic Ocean, perhaps in the United States (though he distrusted Americans, whom he regarded as members of a coarse-minded race), or possibly in Venezuela. The South Americans, he thought, might suit him excellently. "Those fellows," he told Hobhouse, "are as fresh as their World, and fierce as their earthquakes. . . ."

Then, in the early days of 1823, he received a heartening piece of information, which gave his thoughts a much more cheerful turn. Hobhouse and other English liberals had recently set up a committee to assist the cause of the insurgent Greek patriots. For nearly two years those Greeks had been conducting a desperate struggle against the armed forces of the brutal Ottoman Empire. What Byron heard of the committee and its aims immediately aroused his interest; and when delegates, on the way to Greece, arrived at Genoa in April, he not only welcomed them and was delighted to discuss their plans, but "even offered to go up to the Levant in July, if the Greek provisional Government think that I could be of any use."

His motives were mixed. For Byron, "dearly beloved Greece" had a profound emotional significance. In no other country, he declared, had he ever been completely happy. Greece symbolized youth and love, sensuous gaiety and the carefree life of action. In his gloomiest moments, Byron's imagination constantly turned back to its rocky, sunlit islands and its dangerous, white-capped seas. He would sometimes talk of the "grey Greek stone" under which, once he had finished his wanderings, he hoped he might be laid to rest.

Thus Byron's attitude toward the Greek cause was both emotional and altruistic. On one hand, he saw the opportunity of reliving an old dream and throwing off his lassitude. On the other, all his most generous instincts were excited by the idea of human freedom. In *Childe Harold* he had delivered a poetic message to the Greek people, bidding them remember their splendid past and reassert their ancient dignity. Now he considered the practical side of the problem: what the insurgents were most likely to need (money, ammunition, medical stores) and what he himself could supply. At the end of April he learned that he had been elected to the Hobhouse Committee, and early in June he decided that he would definitely undertake the expedition. On July 13, 1823, he boarded the *Hercules*, accompanied by Teresa Guiccioli's brother, Pietro Gamba; that strange ruffian, Edward John Trelawny; his personal physician, Dr. Francesco Bruno; two servants; his English valet, William Fletcher; and Tita, his Venetian gondolier. On the fifteenth, after some

Byron and Marianne. Byron's reputation as a philanderer scandalized London high society.

exasperating delays, the *Hercules* set sail for Greece.

When Byron reached the Ionian Islands at the beginning of August, 1823, Greece was hopelessly divided among a half-dozen warring leaders, of whom the most conspicuous were Alexander Mavrokordatos, a wily Phanariot politician; Colokotronis, head of the provisional government; the gallant brigand Odysseus; and Marco Botzaris, a chieftain of the savage Souliot tribe. Each was eager to secure the Englishman's support—and each was equally determined to lay hands upon the committee's well-stocked war chest. Byron was obliged to remain on the island of Cephalonia until the year had almost ended before he was able to sort out their conflicting claims and make plans for his future movements. Finally, he decided to join Mavrokordatos and his allies on the north shore of the Gulf of Corinth. After escaping many dangers (once his light vessel was nearly shipwrecked; once it narrowly avoided capture by a watchful Turkish frigate), he landed at the dismal little town of Missolonghi early in January, 1824.

During the three months that he spent at Missolonghi, Byron's life was purgatorial. He had remembered Greece as a place of unending beauty. But his new headquarters, located in a ramshackle house, looked out over a shallow and stagnant lagoon that was divided from the sea by a ridge of sand and mud. Beyond the dilapidated town itself stretched gloomy and unhealthy marshes. Byron, however, had come to Missolonghi as a soldier, not as a tourist. He immediately made himself at home in his uncomfortable lodgings where he received his guests seated, like a Turk, upon a mattress and a cushion, a heavy cloak wrapped around his shoulders. In his bedroom—the only room where this fastidious and oversensitive being could enjoy a few hours' solitude—he kept his books, his uniforms, and one or two treasured possessions.

Far worse than the petty discomforts of his life was the atmosphere of dissension against which Byron had to contend almost as soon as he reached the mainland. Alexander Mavrokordatos was an earnest and high-minded patriot; but this subtle Levantine gentleman, with his commonplace European clothes, his gold-rimmed spectacles, his drooping moustaches and long untidy locks, was not the perfect fellow warrior, and Byron presently discovered that Mavrokordatos had little real control over the forces he was supposed to lead. Much more picturesque were the kilted Souliot tribesmen, hung round with weapons and silver ornaments, from whom the poet had recruited his private body-

guard. These "rude soldiers" had been quartered at Byron's house, where they stacked their guns and played noisy games of cards in a spacious outer room. Unfortunately, they were a greedy, disloyal crew. As early as January 18, they raised a murderous riot; and on February 19, they once again mutinied and shot down a foreign officer. Byron met the crisis with "calm courage."

Meanwhile, every military scheme miscarried. Byron and Mavrokordatos had planned to assault Lepanto, the Turkish fortress farther up the gulf. Byron himself meant to march at the head of the Souliots, and he eagerly awaited his first taste of action. But unfavorable weather—rain had been falling almost incessantly since his arrival at Missolonghi—the defection of the Souliot contingent, and the hurried departure of most of the

Above left Missolonghi, with its shallow stagnant lagoon. Here Byron spent three purgatorial months.

Byron at Missolonghi with his huge Newfoundland dog, Lyon.

The east front of the Parthenon, as it was in Byron's day.

Frustration in Greece

Lady Caroline Lamb, one of Byron's mistresses.

The cremation of the poet Shelley, showing Byron in attendance.

'Tis time this heart should be unmoved,
Since others it hath ceased to move:
Yet, though I cannot be beloved,
      Still let me love!...
The Sword, the Banner, and the Field,
Glory and Greece, around me see!
The Spartan, borne upon his shield,
      Was not more free...
Tread those reviving passions down,
Unworthy manhood!—unto thee
Indifferent should the smile or frown
      Of Beauty be.
If thou regret'st thy youth, *why live?*
The land of honourable death
Is here:—up to the Field, and give
      Away thy breath!...

Critics have sometimes been puzzled by the poet's reference to his "reviving passions" and to the "smile or frown of Beauty." Yet even at Missolonghi he could not shake off love; the habit of loving was too deeply rooted. There seems no doubt that the object of Byron's last passion was his sixteen-year-old Levantine page, Loukas Chalandritsanos, a youth of "a most prepossessing appearance," as an observant member of his suite noted. Byron's solicitude for his page had long been obvious; and on the voyage to Missolonghi, when they seemed likely to fall into Turkish hands, he declared that he "would sooner cut him in pieces and myself too, than have him taken out by those barbarians ... for you know what his fate would be."

Further significant evidence of his affection for Loukas is provided by a second poem, which was found among his papers after his death but was allowed to remain in manuscript until 1887. The poet begins with a recital of the dangers through which he has stood beside his friend, but adds:

Thus much and more; and yet thou lov'st me not,
And never wilt! Love dwells not in our will.
Nor can I blame thee, though it be my lot
To strongly, wrongly, vainly love thee still.

English mechanics whom he had relied on to produce the artillery he needed brought his hopeful plans to nothing. By February 15 he was almost at breaking point. That evening, when he had withdrawn to his room in an anxious and dispirited mood, he suddenly collapsed with what his attendants believed must be an epileptic seizure.

Nothing is so remarkable about Byron's behavior at Missolonghi as the proud stoicism with which he faced and surmounted the incessant troubles of his daily life. These included the Souliot mutinies, a violent earthquake, the escape of a stranded Turkish brig that had seemed to offer such an easy prize, and the pitiless torrents of rain that lashed down into the muddy streets. On January 22, Byron had celebrated his thirty-sixth birthday; the occasion inspired him to produce some verses that he described as "better than what I usually write":

At Missolonghi, Byron, who in the past had so often succeeded in love, evidently discovered what it was to fail.

Byron's seizure on February 15 had left him weak and shaken. He began to abandon hope, and by the end of February he decided that his situation was "intolerable." All that he could do was to retain his post; and throughout the month of March he hung on grimly, doling out supplies, arguing and advising, and, as often as the weather allowed him, making a brave attempt to raise the Greek morale by riding forth with his attendants and bodyguard into the open country that lay beyond the lagoon. During one of these expeditions, on April 9, Byron appeared to catch cold. Although he was feverish, he rode out again on the next day. Afterwards he retired to his sofa, where he suffered from "shuddering fits" and "wandering pains." He then summoned Dr. Bruno, who was joined by Dr. Millingen. Both were inexperienced physicians who hopelessly mismanaged the case. Although their patient at first refused to be bled, he gave way as his strength declined and submitted to a disastrous regime of bleeding and purging, which further weakened his resistance. By April 15 his life was clearly in danger, and his mind was growing clouded.

During his lucid moments, he once spoke of consulting a witch—he could not forget a gypsy soothsayer's prediction that his thirty-sixth year was bound to be perilous, and imagined that he might be a victim of the evil eye. However, Dr. Millingen records that he "did not hear him make any, even the smallest, mention of religion." Indeed, he seemed to reject such thoughts, muttering that he would not "sue for mercy." But memories of his past life haunted him; and on Easter Sunday, April 18, he called William Fletcher to his bedside and struggled to impart some crucial message which Fletcher, he insisted, must carry back to Lady Byron. The message, alas, was unintelligible. Later those who gathered around him could distinguish only a few broken phrases: "Why was I not aware of this sooner? Why did I not go home before I left for here? ... Poor Greece—poor town—my poor servants, *Io lascio qualche cosa di caro nel mondo.*" On April 19, as darkness approached, a peal of thunder rolled across the gulf. Soon afterwards, at a quarter past six, Byron opened his eyes, then closed them for the last time.

As he had prepared to leave Italy for Greece, Byron had remarked, both to his friend Thomas Medwin and to his last female admirer, Lady Blessington, that he did not expect that he would return from Greece. A fatalist whose character had always included a strongly self-destructive strain, he had hoped to find in death the justification of a life that had ceased to afford him either pride or pleasure. Though he was unprepared for the physical accident of death, it completed the moral pattern that he had already laid down. Not only did it redeem his personal credit and ensure him a lasting place in the hearts of his contemporaries; but it advanced, as nothing else could have done, the cause of Greek and European freedom. Like the far-famed pursuit of happiness, nationalism—the right of every country to determine its own destiny—is an essentially Romantic concept; and Byron was among the first, and certainly not the least effective, of the great Romantic liberators.

PETER QUENNELL

The Massacre of Scios, Delacroix's picture of Greek sufferings.

Left Greece Expiring by Delacroix, symbolizing the struggles of Greece during the rising against the Turks.

The statue of Byron, intended for Westminster Abbey. The Dean and Chapter refused to accept any memorial to such a notorious profligate, and the statue is now in the Wren library of Trinity College, Cambridge, where Byron was educated.

651

Glory and Greece

In December, 1822, a renowned public figure declared: "The mention of Greece fills the mind with the most exalted sentiments and arouses in our bosoms the best feelings of which our nature is susceptible." The speaker was James Monroe, the fifth President of the United States, and his declaration formed part of his State of the Union address. Monroe's words fell on sympathetic ears: enthusiasm for liberty and the democratic ideal was boundless among the citizens of the proud young Republic, and they were well aware of the struggle being fought in Greece, nine thousand miles from their eastern seaboard. Philhellenic societies had been founded in all the larger cities, and a new settlement along the Michigan frontier had been named Ypsilanti to commemorate one of the earliest heroes of the Greek War of Independence. In Tennessee the principal town in territory that had been recently ceded by the Cherokee Indians was honored with no less a name than that of Athens.

The American people did not fully understand the delicate questions of power politics unleashed by the Greek revolt. They believed in resistance to tyranny, and they were convinced that if the aspirations of the European monarchies

Francisco de Miranda, a former general in the French Army, blazed the revolutionary trail in Latin America.

became so sour that they stifled democracy, then America should emphasize her withdrawal from the Old World by nurturing good feelings in the New.

Monroe's constituents were given ample opportunity to show

those feelings, for his presidency coincided not only with the Greek revolution but with the emancipation of Spanish America. If the United States could not influence events in the Balkans, she might at least extend a sympathetic hand to revolutionaries in the Andes.

Revolution in Latin America

Between 1810 and 1822 new republics sprang up from the Rio Grande to Tierra del Fuego with a rapidity unmatched until the ending of colonial rule in Africa in the 1960s. The desire for independence was originally stimulated by the example of the North American colonists in their struggle with Britain, but the timing of the individual revolts was determined by events in Europe and, in particular, by Napoleon's dominance of the Iberian Peninsula. The bonds linking Spain and her colonies had always been tenuous in time of war, and with Spanish administration breaking down, it appeared an easy task to cast them aside entirely.

The struggle was to prove a difficult one, however. The wars that ended Spain and Portugal's three-hundred-year domination of Latin America passed through two principal phases. During the first phase, from 1809 to 1816, the colonists were repressed everywhere except in the area around the Plate River. But during the second phase, between 1816 and 1825, the independence movement gained striking successes, and the colonists cast aside colonial exploitation in 4 million square miles of the South American subcontinent. The area liberated was five times as large as the English colonies that had successfully defied George III half a century earlier.

Basically, the Latin American revolt was a struggle for liberation from Spain rather than for individual liberty, and some of the new governments were as reactionary as any in Europe. Agustín de Iturbide, who proclaimed Mexico's independence from Spain in 1821, relied on support from the Church and the landowners to suppress a genuine republican movement and to ensure the survival of the constitutional monarchy over which he presided as Emperor. Brazil, which declared itself independent of Portugal in 1822, kept a monarchical structure of administration and accepted the rule of the Portuguese royal family until 1889.

Latin America's founding fathers

Despite these fundamentally conservative elements, the wars for independence produced three outstanding leaders who may be regarded as the founding fathers of Latin America: Francisco de Miranda, Simón Bolívar and José de San Martin. Miranda, a Creole from Caracas, Venezuela, was a failure in his own lifetime but blazed the revolutionary trail that

Simón Bolívar, who became master of Peru, Colombia and Bolivia.

Bolívar followed to free Colombia and Venezuela, and San Martín followed to liberate Chile and Peru. Miranda had witnessed the triumph of the American colonists in 1781, had enlisted in the army of the First French Republic and had risen to the rank of general. Long years of exile in London enabled him to interest William Pitt and the future Duke of Wellington in the liberation of South America. He received British money, and for a time he hoped for an army of British redcoats. But in 1811 he was left to command the Venezuelan insurgents without any foreign assistance. The Spanish loyalists outclassed Miranda militarily and he was captured and sent to Spain. He died in a dungeon in Cadiz in 1816, and his death marked the nadir of the rebels' cause. Bolívar, Miranda's principal lieutenant, was forced to flee from Venezuela and seek refuge in Jamaica, and it seemed as if the whole future of Latin America rested with the troops San Martín was laboriously collecting on the Andean slopes in western Argentina.

San Martín was a veteran officer who had fought for Spain in the homeland and in Africa. His Peninsular experiences served him well in 1817. Few battle feats in the nineteenth century surpass the achievement of San Martín's "Army of the Andes," an intrepid force of five thousand men who dragged wagons and guns over the hump of Mount Aconcagua and through the Uspallata Pass into Chile. It was a grim but effective march. The Spaniards, taken by surprise, were overwhelmed in the Battle of Chacabuco on February 12, 1818, and Santiago, the principal Spanish stronghold, was occupied. A revolutionary government was established under Bernardo O'Higgins (the son of an Irish soldier who had enlisted in the Spanish Army), and on the first anniversary of the Battle of Chacabuco, Chilean independence was formally proclaimed. In the north, Bolívar returned from his sanctuary in Jamaica, organized a base at Angostura, and proceeded westward across the Andes to destroy Spanish power in the northwest.

A great pincer movement then began to threaten the heart of

William Pitt the Younger, British Prime Minister who supported the South American revolutionary cause.

rows off the Spanish yoke

George Canning, British Foreign Secretary who accorded recognition to the South American rebels.

Spanish authority in Peru and in Quito, as Ecuador was then called. San Martín made use of a fleet improvised by Admiral Lord Cochrane, an independently minded British naval officer and former Member of Parliament. Cochrane's squadron had mastery of the Pacific coast and was able to transport San Martín's troops northward so that they could land where they chose and shape the military campaign by command of the sea. The Spanish Viceroy was forced to evacuate Lima, and the independence of Peru was proclaimed in July, 1821. Two years earlier Bolívar had defeated the Spanish armies in Venezuela and established Great Colombia, a region comprising the whole of the northwestern quarter of the subcontinent. The Latin American peoples seemed at last to be masters of their own fate.

At the end of July, 1822, one of the most surprising abnegations in history took place in Guayaquil, a small port almost equidistant from Lima and the Isthmus of Panama. In this steaming equatorial harbor San Martín met Bolívar and acknowledged the primacy of the man who had liberated the north. Believing that Bolívar's plans for a broad confederation were politically more ambitious than anything that he could offer, San Martín retired from political life. (He died a quarter of a century later in voluntary exile in France.) Bolívar assumed responsibility for

the armed forces of Peru and, after four long months of grueling marches, led them to a final victory at Ayacucho, nine thousand feet up in the Andes, in December, 1824. In the following year he established a new inland republic, named after its liberator.

In 1825 Bolívar's star still seemed ascendant. He regarded himself not so much as a soldier but as an intellectual and a lawgiver who, from his studies of Locke and the Enlightenment, had something new to offer in the theory and practice of politics. He was only forty-two—younger than George Washington at the time of Bunker Hill—when he became master of Peru, Colombia and Bolivia. His active mind was already planning "a league of good neighbors" designed to keep all the Spanish-speaking peoples at peace with one another.

It was too noble a concept for his compatriots, and Bolívar died a disillusioned man some five years later. Separatist movements and conspiracies among his most trusted subordinates had convinced him, even by 1826, "that our America can only be ruled by an able despotism." But autocracy, however enlightened, was ill-suited to the Latin temperament. Bolívar saw, or thought he saw, anarchy around him, and as his "Great Colombia" disintegrated, the vision of a United States of Latin America receded for all time.

Yet Bolívar's basic achievements were never in serious danger. A

return to colonial rule for any of the newly emancipated lands in South America was out of the question. The Russians at one time offered the King of Spain vessels to transport a punitive expedition to the Orinoco or the Plate rivers. But neither the British nor the Americans would have permitted it to cross the Atlantic. For, though no foreign power gave formal assistance to the Spanish colonists in their revolts, there was no doubt of the sympathies of the governments in London and Washington. George Canning, who became British Foreign Secretary in 1822, accorded conditional recognition to the rebel governments established by the colonists soon after he came to office. His act was not entirely a disinterested one, for it permitted British bankers and merchants to tighten their grip on South American trade and commerce. The United States followed Britain closely in giving diplomatic recognition, although the two English-speaking nations continued to eye each other with suspicion.

Toward the end of 1823, Canning proposed joint Anglo-American action to ensure the integrity and independence of the newly emancipated colonies. It was clearly to the interest of both governments to safeguard the right of trading freely with Spanish America and to exclude, so far as was possible, intervention by other European states. But Monroe and his Secretary of State, John Quincy Adams, distrusted Canning's pro-

posal. They had no wish, as Adams told his cabinet colleagues, "to be a cock-boat in the wake of the British man-of-war." Adams proposed a definition of American policy that he left to President Monroe to enunciate. Thus it was that in December, 1823, the President dispatched to Congress the famous Monroe Doctrine: no part of the Americas should be used for future colonization; any attempt by European powers to extend their influ-

John Quincy Adams: he first proposed the "Monroe Doctrine."

ence across the Atlantic would be interpreted by the United States as a danger to its own peace and security; the United States would not interfere in Europe's quarrels but expected Europe to accept that the political system of the Americas was essentially different and distinct. For more than a hundred years this doctrine was the lodestar of American foreign policy, though at the time Canning maintained that the young Republic could effect such proud isolation only by grace of the Royal Navy. It marked the final interment of the Spanish Empire on the mainland of South America (although Cuba was to remain a Spanish possession until the very end of the century).

The real importance of the Monroe Doctrine lay in the future—at a time when the United States fleet was sufficiently powerful to cast a shield of defense around the whole continent. But even in 1823, Monroe's bold words were significant. They reflected a new national self-confidence and an assumption that the armies of Europe would never be permitted to traverse the American lands. The fledgling Republic, ignored or at best disdainfully patronized by the European states, had come of age. This development would soon be reflected in her domestic politics as well as in her world standing.

Latin America gains Independence 1800-30

Dates show when independence gained

CUBA
1821 MEXICO
VENEZUELA
GUIANA
1830
COLOMBIA 1819
ECUADOR
1830
PERU
1821
BOLIVIA
1825
1818
1811
CHILE
1810
ARGENTINA
PATAGONIA Conquered by Argentina 1879

Independent Empire 1822
Republic 1889
BRAZIL

PARAGUAY
URUGUAY
1828

— Boundary of Greater Colombia 1819 In 1830 broke up into Venezuela, Colombia and Ecuador
◯ Former Portuguese territory
◯ Former Spanish territory

The People's President

The American electorate overwhelmingly rejected John Quincy Adams and his National Republican Party in the presidential election of 1828 and endorsed Andrew Jackson—the first populist candidate—for the nation's highest office. Adams called the defeat of his aristocratic, Eastern party "the ruin of our cause," but the populace did not agree. Like many of them, Jackson was a tenant farmer's son, a brawler and a self-made man. Soldiers and civilians alike referred to the Democratic candidate as "Old Hickory," and while few of them could remember his enlisting in Washington's Continental Army at the age of thirteen, fewer could forget his stunning victory over Major General Pakenham at New Orleans in the War of 1812. They swept Jackson into the White House, and he returned the favor by making the Democratic Party the champion of unlimited franchise, free education and equal opportunity.

For weeks before the raw inauguration morning of March 4, 1829, the roads to Washington were clogged with hard-featured homespun figures— farmers and mechanics, rivermen, artisans and backwoodsmen. All of them were converging on the still-unfinished capital to see "the man of the people," General Andrew Jackson, sworn in as the seventh President of the United States. The General's election in 1828 had been bitterly personal: President John Quincy Adams, the incarnation of Eastern aristocratic pretensions, had opposed Jackson, who emerged as hero-general of the West, the very symbol of what Adams had disdainfully called "the common man."

Scurrilities overshadowed issues in the 1828 campaign, a contest that witnessed the emergence of two fledgling parties—Adams' National Republicans and the Jacksonian Democrats—from the single chrysalis of Jefferson's Democratic Republicans. The ascetic Adams found himself labeled a Sybarite, a spendthrift, a monarchist—even a procurer. National Republicans in turn denounced Jackson as a gambler, a drunkard, a duelist, a slave dealer and a cockfighter. They even intimated that he was insane.

The Republicans' most successful propaganda effort was the Coffin Handbill, a lurid broadside edged with coffin silhouettes that accused Jackson of having had six militiamen arbitrarily shot as deserters in the War of 1812. Such accusations fell within the accepted limits of political abuse, but Adams' supporters went beyond those loose limits when they attacked the General's wife—the plump, good-hearted, pipe-smoking Rachel, whom Jackson had married after her first marriage had presumedly ended in divorce. Now, thirty-seven years later, Jackson found himself charged with having cohabited with Rachel before their marriage. "Ought a convicted adulteress and her paramour husband be placed in the highest office of this free and Christian land?" one Adams pamphlet asked.

Only Jackson's position as presidential candidate kept him from challenging the pamphlet's author. "How hard it is to keep the cowhide from these villains!" he lamented to a close friend.

For the friends of Jackson, the election's outcome had never been in doubt, but even they were astonished at its sweep. The General triumphed over his rival with 178 votes in the Electoral College to Adams' 83. In the popular voting, Adams trailed by 508,064 votes to Jackson's 647,276. "The ruin of our cause," the defeated President called the final tally —"the overwhelming ruin of our administration."

Jackson's triumph turned to ashes the following month when his beloved Rachel died. He was convinced that she had been hounded to her grave by the vituperative malevolence of Adams' pamphleteers. "In the presence of this dear saint I can and do forgive my enemies," he said as he stood at her graveside. "But those vile wretches who have slandered her must look to God for mercy."

Although it was sensed rather than seen at the time, Jackson's election marked the third American revolution. The first, which gave birth to the Declaration of Independence, was political rather than social, establishing an aristocratic republic. Washington was elected its first President by a propertied Federalist minority. In his aloof dignity —with his state receptions, his canary-yellow coach emblazoned with his family arms, and his wife's assumption of the honorific title of Lady Washington—Washington saw himself as above politics, a Republican regent for the whole people. Jefferson's hairbreadth election in 1800 marked the second American revolution, "as real a revolution in the principles of our government," Jefferson himself concluded, "as that of 1776 was in form." The persistent sweeping away of property qualifications for voting and the continued extension of the franchise to the mass of white American males made the triumph of Jefferson's Democratic Republicans over the Federalists inevitable.

Andrew Jackson, the first President to come from the New West and the first self-made man to live in the White House.

Opposite above The group of rustic log cabins which was Andrew Jackson's home from 1804–19, near Nashville, Tennessee; and (*below*) his home after 1819, again near Nashville, but now a luxurious mansion typical of the antebellum South.

A caricature of Jackson used against him in the 1832 election when he sought and secured re-election. His enemies accused him of monarchical ambitions.

Rachel Jackson, "Old Hickory's" wife. The fact that Jackson had married her before she was legally divorced was used as propaganda against him in the 1828 election campaign.

For Washington's courtliness Jefferson had substituted republican simplicity—even going so far as to walk to his own inauguration. Yet Jefferson was a doctrinaire democrat by nature and a patrician by inheritance. Except for the single-term interlude of John Adams, the Virginia-based political dynasty of which Jefferson was a member guided the destinies of the new nation for its first thirty-six years. As the master of the elegant Monticello, he remained a diffident theorist of democracy. Americans of limited means and learning—the bulk of the population—who were no longer content to be ruled by their self-appointed betters, rallied to him.

If Jefferson was the spokesman of common men, Jackson was their embodiment, and his election marked the end not only of Adams but of the Virginia dynasty as well. Though himself a wealthy frontier planter, Jackson personified the radical plebeian element in American politics. "Andy," as his supporters called him, was the first President to be called by his first name and the first self-made man to occupy the White House. The third American revolution, which was brought about by Jackson's election, was in essence a populist revolution. Before Jackson's inauguration, Daniel Webster remarked of the violent, self-willed President-elect that "when he comes he will bring a breeze with him. Which way it will blow I cannot tell."

The first six Presidents were men set apart by manners, breeding and education, but any ambitious man might measure himself against Andy Jackson, the tenant farmer's son. Jackson's father had come from the north of Ireland to settle in the Waxhaws, an upland frontier region of the Carolinas where he died in 1767, a month before his son Andrew was born. Andy grew up a thin, freckled boy with reddish hair and the proverbial short temper said to accompany such coloring. Considered the bright boy of the local church school (as quick with his fists as with his mind), he soon found his interests turning from books to horse racing, cockfighting and fisticuffs. Yet when the Philadelphia papers (which were brought to the Waxhaws each week by overland mail) began to carry news of the Revolution, young Jackson was often picked as the public reader, since he "could read a paper clean through without getting hoarse ... or stopping to spell out the words."

At the age of thirteen, Andy and his sixteen-year-old brother Robert joined Washington's Continental Army. Andy was promptly taken prisoner by the English. An arrogant British officer ordered the boy-soldier to clean his boots, and when he refused, the officer struck at him with his sword. As Andy raised his hand to ward off the blow, the blade cut to the bone and then glanced aside and laid open his scalp. Jackson would bear the white jagged scar—and a hatred of England—the rest of his life.

After the war, Andy stayed for a time with a family friend in Charleston, South Carolina, where for six months he was apprenticed to a saddler. Relieved from his semiservitude by an inheritance

BORN TO COMMAND.

OF VETO MEMORY.

HAD I BEEN CONSULTED.

KING ANDREW THE FIRST.

of several hundred pounds (left him by an Irish grandfather), Jackson lived the more expansive life of a gambler and horseman until his legacy ran out. From Charleston he moved on to Salisbury, North Carolina, where he was long remembered as a "most roaring, rollicking, game-cocking, horse-racing, card-playing mischievous fellow ... the head of rowdies hereabouts." His ambitions kept pace with his amusements as he studied law with his friend, John McNairy. Before he was old enough to vote, he had passed his bar examination and was admitted to practice.

North Carolina's Western District then extended to the Mississippi, and when McNairy was elected judge of that district's superior court, he appointed his friend and fellow student public prosecutor. With Bacon's *Abridgement of the Law* in his saddlebag and a black wench whom he had bought for two hundred dollars his only company, Andy set out across the Blue Ridge Mountains in 1788. He met McNairy along the way and joined the first caravan over the new Nashville Road. By October the two had reached the Cumberland River settlement of Nashville, which consisted of a pair of taverns, a distillery, two stores, a ramshackle courthouse and a fringe of cabins—all surrounded by a rail fence to keep out stray buffalo.

Jackson found Nashville a debtors' haven but within a month the young prosecutor had changed all that as he enforced writs of execution that had been neglected for years. Creditors and property owners soon acclaimed him, and clients flocked to his makeshift office. Money was scarce, but land was cheap, and most of his legal fees were paid in acres or slaves. Almost before he knew it, the zealous young prosecutor found himself a landowner.

The moral pattern completed

Andy first boarded at the widow Donelson's blockhouse, ten miles down the Kentucky Road from Nashville, and there he met his landlady's sloe-eyed married daughter, Rachel Donelson Robards. Rachel was then living apart from her husband, and when she returned to him in 1790 it was for a brief, unsuccessful attempt at reconciliation. Jackson was sent by the Donelson family to bring her home. The aggrieved Robards threatened to follow—until Jackson threatened to cut off his ears.

After Robards sued for divorce, Rachel fled to Natchez, the Spanish city on the Mississippi. Only thirty miles north of Natchez, at Bayou Pierre, Jackson had earlier set up a log house and trading post to sell slaves and supplies to the wealthier settlers flocking west. When he learned of the divorce action, he followed Rachel to Natchez. Unaware that the divorce would not be made final for another two years, he married her in August, 1791, in the mansion of one of his customers.

Jackson brought his bride back to Nashville, to a plantation he had bought from her brother. There, once settled, he not only traded in cotton, slaves, horses and land but also continued to practice law. When the Western District became a state, he is said to have proposed its name of Tennessee. The new governor, John Sevier, once the ruler of the outlaw state of Franklin, appointed Jackson Tennessee's first congressman. Albert Gallatin, Jefferson's urbane former Secretary of the Treasury, remembered the Tennessee congressman as a "tall, lanky, uncouth-looking personage . . . queue down his back tied with an eel-skin . . . dress singular . . . manners those of a rough backwoodsman." After Tennessee's first senator was expelled for "a high misdemeanor," Jackson was appointed to the United States Senate, but he soon resigned because of financial difficulties. In 1798 he became a justice of the state superior court.

On the bench Justice Jackson was fair and decisive, if impatient of legal subtleties. Nor did his judicial robes tame his violent spirit. When, after a falling-out, Sevier taunted him with "taking a trip with another man's wife," Jackson clubbed him down with his walking stick and then challenged him to a duel. (That duel never took place, but several years later Jackson did kill a man on the dueling field because he had maligned Rachel. In return he received a bullet near the heart that would cause him pain for the rest of his life.) While he was still a justice Jackson was involved in his most famous brawl, which took place in Nashville during the War of 1812. He spotted his enemies, Jesse and Thomas Hart Benton, on the street and went for them with a horsewhip. The Bentons replied with pistols, and in the free-for-all that followed, Jackson's shoulder was shattered by a bullet. He was carried, presumably dying, to the Nashville Inn where, in the course of the next few hours, two mattresses were soaked through with his blood. The wound was not a fatal one, however, and a few months later, with his arm in a sling, the indomitable

Jackson was able to conduct a militia expedition against the Creek Indians. And when the theater of war shifted to the South, Jackson rallied the defenses of New Orleans against an assault led by Wellington's brother-in-law, Major General Sir Edward Pakenham.

The Battle of New Orleans—fought a fortnight after the British and American commissioners had met at Ghent and signed a peace treaty—made "Old Hickory," as the soldiers called Jackson, the most popular military figure since Washington. Legend would celebrate the American victory as the triumph of Jackson's iron will and the skill of his freeborn Kentucky riflemen who coolly picked off the advancing redcoats until the British fled the field. The facts were more prosaic. In an example of military folly not to be equaled until Balaklava, Major General Pakenham sent his men in close formation across a long rice field to assault an earthwork at the opposite end. The sheltered Americans could direct almost pointblank cannon fire from their vantage, and the British were literally blown to pieces. Pakenham was shot dead, and over two thousand of his men fell with him. Jackson lost a mere eight militiamen, with thirteen more wounded. At the battle's end some five hundred redcoats—

John Quincy Adams, defeated by Jackson in the 1828 election. Adams was the incarnation of Eastern aristocratic pretensions.

An anti-Jackson election cartoon of 1832. The election was fought over the future of the Bank of the United States which Jackson was intent on destroying.

"The reign of King Mob"

who had prudently played dead—rose from the field like ghosts to surrender.

"I cannot believe," Henry Clay later testily observed of his rival for the presidency, "that the killing of 2,500 Englishmen at New Orleans qualifies a person for the various, difficult and complicated duties of the chief magistracy." Nevertheless the battle legend fixed Old Hickory as the nation's hero and the people's friend, and this single engagement almost elected him to the presidency in 1824 and carried him in triumph to the White House four years later. As he rode from his inauguration to his reception, frail-looking and still in mourning for Rachel, crowds followed him on foot and, heedless of invitation, surged through the White House rooms, overturning the refreshment tables, smashing glasses and clambering on damask chairs and sofas with their muddy boots. Women fainted, men fought, liquor was rushed out in buckets. Finally Jackson's friends had to link arms to protect him and lead him away from his exuberant supporters. "The reign of King Mob seemed triumphant," the patrician Supreme Court Justice Joseph Story observed.

Jackson had no definite plans on taking office. Sensing the bond between himself and ordinary people, he felt that he belonged to them and they to him, that where he led they would follow. His fundamental beliefs were few and simple. He believed that the American union of states was indissoluble; he distrusted banks and paper money; he accepted unreflectingly the premise that the interests of the majority were the measure of national interests. At his inauguration many of his supporters had carried hickory brooms as a token of the "clean sweep" of federal officeholders that they awaited from their leader—and they were not disappointed.

Jackson is commonly believed to have introduced the spoils system into American political life.

Actually the spoils system was a practice older than the Republic and one which Jackson never applied as ruthlessly as he has been accused of doing. In his first year in office, he removed approximately a tenth of the 11,000 federal officeholders, many of whom could justly be accused of indifference, inefficiency, corruption and superannuation. Public office, he felt, was not a private right, and he believed that appointments should be for four years only. His attack was directed at the entrenched and encrusted bureaucracy, but his political purge turned out to be worse than the bureaucratic disease itself: he dismissed many able men for partisan motives, and he established a national precedent of favoritism to the detriment of honest and efficient government.

Two issues dominated Jackson's two terms in office: the power of the Bank of the United States, and the threat of disunion, centered chiefly in South Carolina. The Bank of the United States was established after the financial chaos following the War of 1812. Its numerous branches served the country well, aiding commercial operations and providing the country with the soundest paper currency that it had ever known. In the opinion of a present-day economist, "the Bank often served the public and on a few occasions this was done at the expense of the stockholders." Issuing only a fifth of the nation's bank notes, and holding only a third of the total bank deposits, the Bank was never the monopoly claimed by its enemies. Nevertheless it was a private vested interest, not subject to regulation; it did control state bank currencies and dominated the domestic and foreign exchange markets; and it was not above making loans to

Political billiards, a cartoon showing the Tsar and the Turkish Sultan playing billiards for possession of Turkey, as Europe's sovereigns look on. Jackson, third from the left, watches in civilian clothes.

deserving politicians. For Jackson, the Bank was a "hydra of corruption," a truckler to "the rich and powerful" that stood for "the advancement of the few at the expense of the many." When Nicholas Biddle, the Bank's president, attempted to renew its charter in the 1832 presidential election year, the recharter bill sponsored by Henry Clay easily passed both houses of Congress. "The Bank is trying to kill me," Jackson told his Vice President, Martin Van Buren, when the measure passed, *"but I will kill it!"*

The 1832 election was fought on the issue of the Bank, with "Harry of the West" Clay, the candidate of the National Republicans, opposing Old Hickory. It resulted in an overwhelming victory for Jackson, who this time swept the Electoral College and carried the country by a two-to-one popular majority. Because the Bank's original charter did not expire until 1836, Jackson effectively undermined its power after his reelection by withdrawing government deposits and placing them in state banks. Jackson, who was intent on destroying the Bank as if it were an opponent on the field of honor, was too economically illiterate to grasp the implications of his actions. As a result, the United States, which had become one of the leaders in bank techniques, soon became one of the most backward. Inflation and depression followed.

Slave-holding Southern planter though he was, Jackson was first of all a Unionist. When, in resentment over the so-called Tariff of Abominations, South Carolina's John C. Calhoun claimed the rights of individual states to nullify "unconstitutional" acts of the national government, Jackson met the challenge at a Jefferson's birthday dinner. Staring grim-faced at Calhoun, the President proposed a standing toast: "Our Union: It must be preserved." Calhoun's fingers trembled so in drinking that the wine ran down the side of his glass.

Faced with a take-over of South Carolina's state government and gravely disturbed by the Nullifiers' threat to withdraw from the Union and set up a separate government, Jackson announced that if, in their defiance, they shed one drop of blood, he would hang the first Nullifier he could get his hands on from the first tree he could find. Neither office, age nor sorrow could dim his combative nature. The day after he left the presidency he remarked that he had only two regrets: he had not been able to shoot Clay and to hang Calhoun!

Jackson's predecessors had all been Neoclassicists who shared an enlightenment faith in reason and natural law. Jackson brought the Romantic Movement to political life, replacing reason and proportion with energy and feeling. More by instinct than intent, he changed the face of American politics and brought about the emergence of the mass man. He made the Democratic Party the party of those who believed in unlimited franchise, free education and equal opportunity. Through his violent and impulsive person he projected the age's leading ideas: that the unchecked development of the individual was paramount; that formal training and traditional learning were unnecessary; that thought should be subordinate to action. Yet Jackson, the people's friend, never saw fit to challenge the institution of slavery, and it was he who was largely responsible for the vindictive anti-intellectualism, the distrust of the educated man, that would subsequently run through American political life.

In his last months, Jackson's thoughts centered on Texas, where he feared that the independent settlers would become "hewers of wood and drawers of water for the ... [British] aristocracy." He lived just long enough to see the Lone Star State become part of the Union. Justice John Catron, whom Jackson had appointed to the Supreme Court, wrote of the fierce, dying old man:

If he had fallen from the clouds into a city on fire, he would have been at the head of the extinguishing hosts in an hour. He would have blown up a palace to stop the fire with as little misgiving as another would have torn down a board shed. In a moment he would have willed it proper and in ten minutes the thing would have been done. . . . He cared not a rush for anything behind: he looked ahead.

FRANCIS RUSSELL

An anti-Jackson cartoon of 1831 entitled *Rats leaving a Falling House.* Jackson was hated by the Eastern commercial classes.

659

The House of Rothschild

As the nineteenth century entered its fourth decade, life was changing in Europe no less than in the United States. Revolution, war and its aftermath had imposed a heavy financial burden on the Continental aristocracy, many of whom were already in debt to bankers or to less reputable financial adventurers. Extravagance and speculative attempts to improve old properties only further aggravated matters, and even Metternich (who received annual grants from the Tsar, the King of Naples and his own sovereign) needed personal financial backing from the House of Rothschild and other great Austrian and Swiss bankers. In some parts of Europe an almost morbid cupidity was elevated into a cult of money for its own sake, a philosophy which frequently went side by side with harebrained schemes of rash investment. The extremes that such cupidity reached in France were satirized in the novels of Balzac—who was a victim of that very vice

Tsar Nicholas I, who treated government as an endless military parade.

in his own private life.

These developments had effects far beyond the world of finance. In the late 1820s a bourgeois class of successful bankers, industrialists and traders began to set a tone of cultural taste distinct from the old values of aristocratic society. Indeed, between 1830 and 1848 the emergent bourgeoisie in France, Austria, Germany and Britain imposed their smug complacency and cozy respectability on the classes socially above them. That mood, which ultimately pervaded the courts of Europe, was in marked contrast to the Romanticism that still fired the passions of most students. Yet in a sense both views

were equally escapist.

Outwardly, however, the old European aristocracy was fighting an obstinate rearguard action to retain its political rights. In Vienna, Metternich continued to believe that the affairs of the whole Continent passed through his elegant hands. He sat at the great window in the Ballhausplatz each day studying reports from secret agents and ambassadors, ever alert against a revival of the Jacobin peril. Tsar Nicholas I—who, as a lad of eighteen, had ridden triumphantly into Paris in 1814 alongside his brother Alexander—ruled in St. Petersburg as though all government were an endless military parade. He could cow a mob by the strength of his personality; in the summer of 1831 he would have need of the talent.

By 1830 alarming dispatches were already reaching Nicholas from Warsaw, where the Poles were restive under Russian discipline. And they were not the only source of disaffection in the Europe of 1829-30. There was trouble among students in Italy and Germany, where nationalist sentiment catalyzed latent unrest, and there was trouble in Brussels, where citizens had already wearied of the union with Holland that had been imposed on Belgium in 1815. But it was toward France that Metternich and Nicholas looked most anxiously, for as Metternich, who was the Austrian Chancellor himself, declared, "When Paris sneezes, Europe catches cold."

Paris sneezes

The political health of France seemed no worse in the summer of 1830 than it had in the preceding six years. A punitive expedition was dispatched to Algiers to discipline its ruler, an Arab dignitary of piratical inclination who had slapped the face of the French Consul with his fan. The city was taken with ease, and Algieria remained a French possession until 1962. It was, however, the last foreign prize to be captured by the restored Bourbon monarchy. Louis XVIII had died in 1824 and had been succeeded by his brother, Charles X. Charles, who had fled precipitately from the kingdom upon the outbreak of the great French Revolution in 1789, was a religious bigot who relied for political advice on the Duc de Polignac, a devout obscurantist.

As long as France was materially

prosperous—a condition that lasted until the very end of Charles X's reign—his subjects treated the laws against sacrilege with tolerant disdain and even accepted measures that safeguarded aristocratic estates. There was much in the capital, however, to remind Parisians of the halcyon days of both the Revolution and the Empire. Lafayette, who had fought beside the Americans at Brandywine and Yorktown and who had commanded the French National Guard in 1789, was still a parliamentary deputy. Talleyrand, the old cynic who was consecrated Bishop of Autun four months before the Bastille fell and who had served the Directory, Napoleon and Louis XVIII as Foreign Minister, waited hopefully in the wings to make a farewell bow on the diplomatic stage. A fading galaxy of Napoleonic marshals—Jourdan, Macdonald, Marmont, Mortier, Oudinot, Soult, Victor—passed tactfully in their memories over days of humiliation and betrayal. Romanticism was turning the Bonapartist odyssey into legend, and it was becoming daringly fashionable to have served the Emperor. Lesser known veterans, gaunt figures with game legs or missing fingers, clustered around the cafés of the Palais-Royal seeking to rekindle the comradeship of the Grand Army. Frustrated by the tedium of the present, France was shadow-acting the recent past.

In July, 1830, the *dramatis personae* of the Revolution reemerged briefly to startle a Europe that had almost forgotten them. On July 26,

Charles X who succeeded Louis XVIII as King of France in 1824.

Charles X and Polignac attempted a minor coup by issuing ordinances aimed at ending representative government and abolishing liberty of the press. Their move enraged the people of Paris, and for three days barricades choked the narrow streets. Someone hoisted a tricolor flag over Notre-Dame and the King, who had already decided that he was safer amid the trees and water gardens of Rambouillet than in the capital, set out on a journey that took him to Cherbourg, and, ultimately, to exile in Edinburgh. A courier sped in the opposite direction bearing an Act of Abdication to Lafayette in the Hôtel de Ville; the revolutionary patriarch was once more master of Paris.

Louis-Philippe I

Although republicans had directed the new revolution, France remained a monarchy, for the radical party was not yet organized and the Bonapartists had no candidate

Marshal Soult, one of the greatest of Napoleon's generals.

at hand. Lafayette, always happier as a constitutional royalist than as a conservative republican, and Talleyrand, who sensed that Europe would not tolerate a French Republic, urged the Duke of Orleans to accept the vacant throne. They were supported by younger liberal intellectuals like Louis Thiers and François Guizot and by the banker Jacques Lafitte. The Duke of Orleans, a distant cousin of Charles X and a descendant of Louis XIII, had fought in the armies of the First Republic as a young man. Less than two decades later he was proclaimed "Louis-Philippe I, King of the French by the Grace of God and the Will of the People." It was, after all, an age of compromise.

As Metternich had feared, the fall of the Bourbon dynasty produced a liberal effervescence throughout the Continent. The rulers of the German states of Brunswick, Hesse-Cassel and Saxony were forced to abdicate, and their successors pledged themselves to introduce liberal constitutions. Early in 1831 trouble spread to Italy as revolts broke out in Modena and Parma and in the Papal States. Those risings were all aimed primarily against Austrian domination of the peninsula and they were all suppressed by Austrian troops. Tsar Nicholas I, who was to breathe fire and fury against "that infamous July Revolution" for the next eighteen years, urged his fellow autocrats in Berlin and Vienna to stand together in defense of the monarchical principle and to form a "rampart against revolutionary doctrines." It was an idea that Metternich found wholly acceptable, and it worked for more than a decade (largely because all of East-Central Europe was disturbed by an armed rebellion against Russian rule in Poland).

The July Revolution reaches Belgium

In Western Europe the July Revolution had its greatest effect in Belgium. Four weeks after the flight of Charles X, moderate liberals in Brussels began to demand an

Louis Thiers, a French intellectual who supported Louis Philippe's claim to the throne.

autonomous administration. The rebels insisted that "Belgium is no Dutch colony," but the Dutch ignored them. Tempers mounted, and in the last week of September, 1830, violent fighting broke out in the streets of Brussels. That series of clashes culminated in a withdrawal of troops and a proclamation of Belgian independence on October 4.

The birthplace of the radical William Cobbett at Farnham in Surrey.

The breach between the Dutch and the Belgians was broadened three weeks later when Dutch artillery bombarded Antwerp. During this period the Belgians were fortunate in two respects: the Polish revolt neutralized any repressive measures contemplated by the Eastern autocracies, and the British and French both supported the Belgian cause (despite their distrust of one another's motives). Before the end of the year an international conference in London had formally declared the union of Belgium with the Netherlands to be dissolved, but it was not until April of 1839 that the Treaty of London recognized Belgium as "an independent and perpetually neutral state."

Tory rule ends

Belgian independence was the first diplomatic success for Lord Palmerston, who became Foreign Secretary as a member of Earl Grey's cabinet in November, 1830. His appointment was a sign that political life was changing in Britain as well as on the Continent under the impact of the news from Paris that the Bourbons had fallen. For over twenty-three years the Tories had held a majority in the House of Commons, that gentlemanly but unrepresentative institution against whose composition the reformers had long railed in vain. A general election held within a few weeks of the July Revolution cost the Tories some thirty seats (although party distinctions were so blurred in those days that nobody could agree on the precise shift of allegiance). The Duke of Wellington, who had been Prime Minister since the first weeks of 1828, struggled to keep the Whigs out of office, but his government was defeated on a minor issue

and the King invited Earl Grey to form an administration pledged to parliamentary reform. There had been no Whig government since the days of Charles James Fox; a new era had dawned in British politics.

More than Tory rule was passing out of English life that summer, for 1828 was the year in which William Cobbett, the radical champion of an idealized free peasantry, completed his *Rural Rides*. Cobbett was deeply conscious both of the insidious spread of the towns and of the disappearance of the old interdependence between a yeoman farmer and his laborers. He found it ominous that starving field workers from the southern counties should have rioted to demand two shillings and sixpence a day and should have suffered savage punishment for their protestations. Classes were becoming more sharply segregated, even in the countryside. Farmers who sought "to ape their betters" were stock characters of gentle ridicule for the novelist— but they were unsympathetic

employers of labor as well.

The year 1830 also brought a change of monarch. George IV, King since 1820, and Regent for his deranged father for nine years before that, died in June. He was succeeded by his brother, William IV, who shared with Louis-Philippe of France an unregal quality of genial approachability. Few people mourned "Prinney's" passing; he had been a liar, a fop and a selfish hedonist whose monumental rudeness stuck in the mind more easily than his moments of charm. Yet he had shown taste in fashion and architecture and had recognized the genius of urban architect John Nash, who balanced crescents and terraces with a consciousness of open space. Under Nash's supervision Regency London and Regency Edinburgh became pioneering achievements in urban vistas, despite the fact that George's grandiose plans remained unfulfilled. Indeed, during the King's last years, the delicate combination of gaiety and classicism that was Regency at its best had disappeared, and vulgar adornment was becoming an end in itself.

The transition to bourgeois habits was as marked in London as in Paris or Vienna. In 1829 George Shillibeer introduced a horsedrawn omnibus—already a feature of French urban life—to the streets of the capital. For sixpence a Londoner could travel from the Bank of England to Regents Park in a coach whose side panels showed the eventual destination in elaborately ornamented classical seals. And up in Lancashire, the greatest social revolution in many decades had begun to change the face of the English countryside.

The Quadrant in Regent Street, part of Nash's plan for rebuilding London.

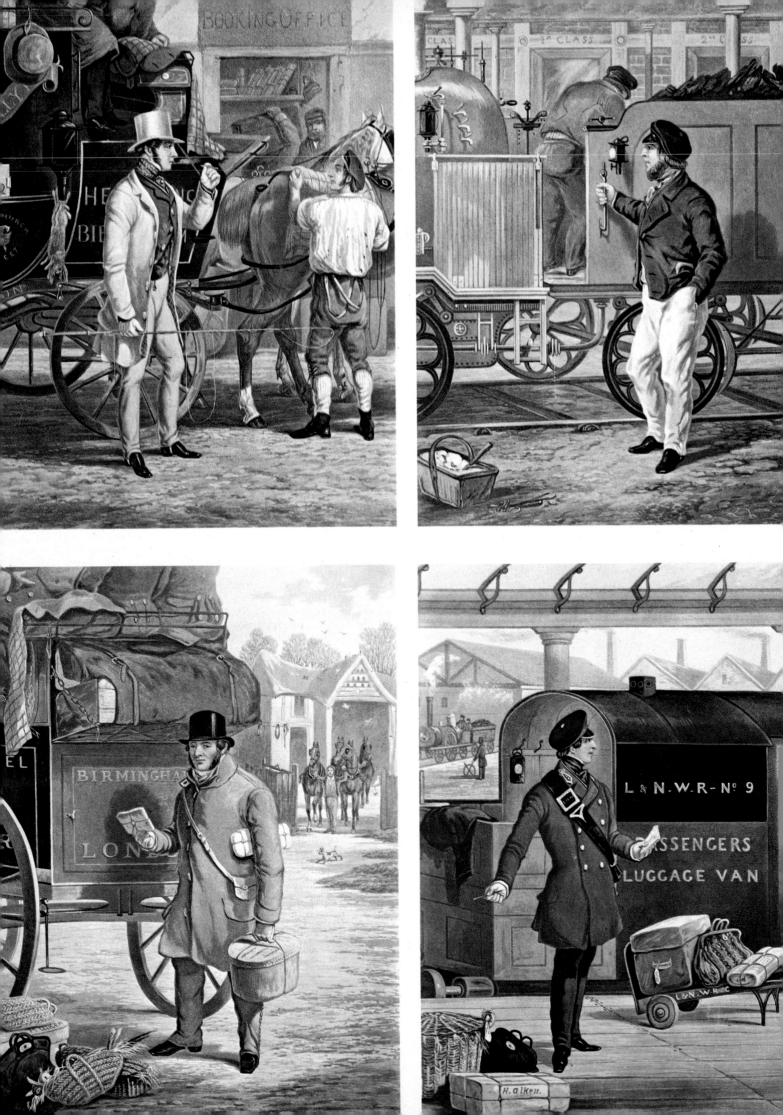

The Age of Steam

England in 1830 was rent by domestic unrest: persistent demands for parliamentary reform and frequent calls for repeal of the Corn Laws threatened to split the Duke of Wellington's cabinet and topple the Tory regime. In an effort to distract the disgruntled populace, the Duke's unpopular government pumped £100,000 in public funds into the construction of a rail link between Liverpool and Manchester. On September 15, 1830, the Duke and a galaxy of political and social luminaries boarded the eight special trains that were making their maiden run to Manchester. Nearly a million spectators—some jeering, most cheering—lined the roadbed to watch the lead locomotive, Northumbrian, sweep by at twenty-four miles per hour. The Age of Steam had begun.

The official opening of the Liverpool and Manchester railway on Wednesday, September 15, 1830—the climax of eight years of persistent scheming and hazardous construction—marked an achievement that was to have a profound effect on the development of national economies. The Duke of Wellington, Tory Prime Minister, had consented to preside over the ceremonies inaugurating what was appropriately referred to in the press as a "great national undertaking." For not only was the line the first British railway to link two populous towns; the railway company that built it had received a loan of £100,000 from public funds in 1828 to hasten its completion.

The weather on the morning of the fifteenth was fine. Thanks to skillful publicity—including the timely issue of an excellent illustrated history of the project by Henry Booth, treasurer of the Liverpool and Manchester Railway Company, and preliminary trips for directors, their families and friends on three previous Saturdays—large crowds (estimated at from 500,000 to about 1 million people) assembled at both terminals and along the track. The directors and their engineer, George Stephenson, had chosen eight locomotives for the occasion. The leading one, *Northumbrian*, was to be followed at intervals by seven other trains hauled by the locomotives *Phoenix, North Star, Rocket, Dart, Comet, Arrow* and *Meteor*.

At the Crown Street station in Liverpool, the air was festive as passengers boarded the carriages. The lead cars carried not only dignitaries, including the Duke, but musicians as well. At about 10:40 A.M. the carriages began rolling down by force of gravity through the tunnel that took the railway from Liverpool to Edgehill, where the locomotives were attached and the trains dispatched. The passengers were awed by the tunnels and excavations through rock and treacherous shale. The railway viaduct built over the Sankey Brook and the parallel Sankey Canal (where a grandstand had been built to accommodate a thousand spectators) "particularly

obtained the Duke's attention, and 'magnificent!' and 'stupendous!' were heard frequently to issue from his lips." The trains reached a speed of twenty-four miles an hour and the three leading locomotives soon arrived at Parkside, seventeen miles from Liverpool.

At this point a tragic accident occurred. The trains stopped, as arranged, to take on more water, and in spite of printed official placards requesting passengers not to dismount from their carriages, many did so. Among them was one of the two M.P.s for Liverpool, William Huskisson, a liberal Tory who had resigned from Wellington's cabinet soon after it had been formed in 1828 and had since been estranged from the Duke. Huskisson had recently undergone an operation, and he also suffered from the aftereffects of paralysis in one leg. The Duke, who wisely did not get down from the state carriage, shook hands with Huskisson in a gesture of reconciliation. Suddenly the *Rocket*, the fourth locomotive in the procession, was heard approaching Parkside on the parallel line of rails. The Duke ordered: "Huskisson, do get to your place! For God's sake get to your place!" But Huskisson held the handle of the wide door open for others hurrying to climb into the car, thus putting himself in the path of the oncoming *Rocket*. He failed to get inside in time. As far as can be ascertained, either the locomotive or the first car hit him. He stumbled and fell screaming onto the line, directly in the path of the second car.

The Earl of Wilton hurriedly improvised a tourniquet from a handkerchief, but Huskisson apparently knew that his wounds would prove fatal and cried out: "Where is Mrs. Huskisson? I have met my death. God forgive me." George Stephenson, who had designed the *Rocket*, now took charge. Two carriages were uncoupled from the *Northumbrian* and the remaining one became an improvised ambulance. The dying politician, together with two surgeons who happened to be in the party, sped forward to Eccles Bridge with George Stephenson at

George Stephenson, designer of *The Rocket* and initiator of many early British railways.

Opposite Uniforms showing the contrast between the coaching era and the age of steam; (*above*) drivers and (*below*) guards of 1832 and 1852.

The first railway accident

The Rocket, one of the eight locomotives chosen for the opening run of the Liverpool and Manchester Railway.

The opening of the Liverpool and Manchester Railway; this picture shows the scene at Edgehill, on the outskirts of Liverpool, where the locomotives were attached to carriages and dispatched to Manchester.

the controls of the locomotive. Huskisson was taken into the vicarage of his friend the Reverend Thomas Blackburne of Eccles, while George Stephenson set off toward Manchester "at a most terrific rate [after] travelling from the place where the accident happened to Eccles Bridge at the rate of thirty-five miles per hour." Stephenson collected four Manchester surgeons and returned to Eccles. Despite their efforts, Huskisson died the same evening at 9 o'clock.

The terrible accident had dissipated the good spirits of the morning, and the Duke wished to abandon the rest of the trip to Manchester. But the boroughreeves of Manchester and Salford pressed him to allow the full ceremonies to proceed. They gave as their reason the fear that the disappointment of the immense crowds gathered at the Manchester terminus in Ordsall Lane might break out into widespread rioting, particularly as the Duke's government was not outstandingly popular. The Duke agreed to continue, but the fears of the boroughreeves proved unjustified. Although there were occasional shouts in favor of parliamentary reform and against the Corn Laws, together with frequent hissing and hooting at the Liverpool Row Boats as the Duke's train steamed nearer to Manchester, the dissenters "appeared to be gathered from the lowest grades of the community." Another factor dampened any excessive ebullience: the fine morning weather at Liverpool had been replaced by cold winds, driving rain and thunder by the time the locomotives arrived at Manchester.

The Duke acknowledged both the cheers and the jeers in his usual restrained manner. On arrival at Manchester he and "the principal party" remained in their car while the rest of the expedition—almost eight hundred strong—partook of the customary "cold collation" in the upper floor of a railway warehouse. The Duke, however, did not isolate himself from the masses: "... he went through a most fatiguing office for more than an hour and a half, in shaking hands with thousands of people to whom he stooped over the handrail of the carriage . . . Many women brought their children to him, lifting them up that he might bless them, which he did, and during the whole time he had scarcely a minute's respite." About 4:30 P.M., after a warning by Joseph Lavender, deputy constable of Manchester, that the Manchester crowds were getting out of hand, the Duke's train began the journey back to Liverpool. The last locomotive reached Liverpool around 11 P.M., and its passengers soon discovered that the splendid entertainments planned for the evening and the following day had been either canceled or much reduced. Politically and socially it had been an unsatisfactory day; from a technological aspect, however, the day had been extremely successful.

Railways had appeared in Britain as early as the 1590s when short lines were laid in Nottinghamshire and in Shropshire. Primitive four-wheeled, horse-drawn trucks carried coal from the mines to rivers and main roads over these early lines. By the end of the seventeenth century the construction of these wagonways had become a task requiring considerable capital and engineering skill, particularly on the coalfields of Northumberland and Durham. The early rails were of hardwood, but by the eighteenth century cast iron was being used for the points and crossing rails, the areas of greatest

wear and tear. In 1767–68, during a period of low prices in the iron trade, the Coalbrookdale Iron Company of Shropshire laid down a wagonway using only cast-iron rails, and after that time wooden rails gradually went out of use.

In the 1780s the steam engine became sufficiently advanced in design to permit the construction of steam locomotives. Thomas Newcomen of Dartmouth had devised the first commercially profitable stationary steam engine between 1705 and 1712, and by the 1760s hundreds of Newcomen-type engines were at work pumping water out of coal mines. In 1769 James Watt secured his famous patent for the separate condenser, a device that cut fuel consumption in the Newcomen engine by two-thirds. With Watt's second patent (granted in 1781 for the "sun and planet" motion) it became possible to apply the improved steam pumping engine to give rotary motion to machinery. The Frenchman Nicolas J. Cugnot, independently of Watt, built a small steam carriage in Paris in 1769, but found that the carriage lacked sufficient power and was unstable.

As early as 1784 William Murdock, the gifted foreman of Matthew Boulton and James Watt's Soho Engineering Works, had constructed a small working model of a road locomotive, but Watt did not encourage Murdock to experiment further. It was left to Richard Trevithick to build both the first high-pressure road locomotive (1801) and the first locomotive to be used successfully on a railway (1804). The times were propitious for such an innovation. Two of the chief items in the expense of working a colliery were horses and their forage. During the Napoleonic Wars, and particularly after 1808, the demands of the British armies in the Iberian Peninsula forced up the price of horses considerably. It is not surprising therefore that colliery agents and engineers spent considerable time and energy during those years in trying to devise steam-driven "horses."

George Stephenson entered the contest later, and

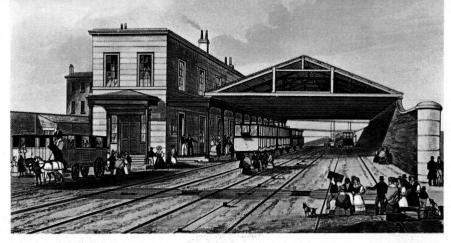

Liverpool railway station in the 1830s. The Liverpool and Manchester Railway was the first British railway to link two populous towns.

he did not produce his first engine until 1814. But his locomotive was noteworthy because it was the first to run on an edge rail rather than on a flanged plateway. (In the former the wheel has a projecting edge, or flange, to keep it on the track; in the latter the rail is flanged.) The old wagonways needed technical improvement once the "point of effort" on the railway had moved from the ground underneath the horses' hooves to the rails underneath the wheels of the new locomotives. Between 1815 and 1819 Stephenson concentrated on improving the fixing and jointing of the rails and the structure of the engine wheels. Birkinshaw's patent of 1820s, which enabled wrought-iron rails to be rolled cheaply enough to be a substitute for the brittler cast-iron rail, also proved to be an important factor in the early success of the locomotive railway.

Stephenson's first great success came with the construction of the famous Stockton and Darlington line. Opened in 1825, it was the first railway used for the public carriage of goods by locomotive (fare-paying passengers were not carried on the line until 1833). Although Stephenson also worked on the Bolton and Leigh line, which opened in 1829, and the Canterbury and Whitstable line, opened in 1830, he is chiefly remembered for his work on the Liverpool and Manchester Railway. That railway project had been discussed as early as 1822. The discussions demonstrated the power of Britain's

Trains on the Liverpool and Manchester Railway show the great difference between first-class (*top*) and second-class (*bottom*) travel.

The Iron Duke travels on the iron road

The Liverpool and Manchester Railway where it crosses the Bridgewater Canal. Railways soon took over the canal's role in transportation.

Below, from left to right
James Watt, inventor of the separate condenser; I. K. Brunel, who pioneered the building of suspension bridges; William Huskisson, one of the first railway accident victims; George Bradshaw, famous for compiling the first railway timetable.

newest and fastest growing industry: cotton.

The Industrial Revolution was in full swing, the national production of goods and services of nearly all kinds was expanding rapidly, and the existing network of rivers, canals and turnpike roads needed supplementing by some speedier and more economical method of transport. The traffic of goods between Liverpool and Manchester—largely raw cotton and cotton goods—was estimated to be about a thousand tons per week in the early 1820s. By the late 1820s that traffic had increased to an estimated thirteen hundred tons, and most of it had to be carried by water, either along the Mersey and Irwell rivers or along the canal system of the trustees of the Duke of Bridgewater. However, neither of the managements of these two systems gave much evidence of being able to speed the time for the passage of goods between Liverpool and Manchester or of being able to cope with the ever-increasing volume of such traffic, and a railroad was proposed to meet the growing demands.

Proponents of the railroad also argued that merchants and industrialists would be able to make the journey between the two cities, transact their business without undue haste, and return home in the early evening to their families—something that was not possible using the stagecoach. Passenger traffic was not stressed as much, however, as freight traffic in the debates on the proposed line.

Liverpool merchants, bankers and professional men promoted the measure in Parliament, and after four years of scheming, struggle and disappointment, the Liverpool and Manchester Railway Company finally was incorporated in 1826. By then the promoting group, popularly known as the Liverpool Party, contained a sizable minority from Manchester. The group had substantial links with the Quaker businessmen who had financed the Stockton and Darlington railway, the Peases and the Richardsons. There were still, however, great difficulties to be overcome. The line had to be run over the treacherous Chat Moss at the Manchester end at a cost of an extra £30,000; at the Liverpool end costly excavations and tunnels had to be made. George Stephenson made serious mistakes in some of his surveys, and as late as 1828–29 no final decision had been taken as to whether the line should be operated by locomotives or by a series of stationary steam engines hauling the trains and wagons over short distances by means of ropes. Stephenson held out strongly in favor of locomotives. To decide the issue, the directors of the company decided to hold the famous Rainhill Trials in October, 1829. The demonstration of the power and reliability of Stephenson's *Rocket* at these trials decided the question unequivocally. As Stephenson had predicted, the locomotive held out the greatest promise for increased power and speed. Railways could now be thought of not merely as feeder lines to rivers, canals and highways, but as potential vanquishers of the fastest form of transport then known—the stagecoach.

Official French, Prussian, Austrian and Russian observers, busy taking note for their governments on the tremendous upsurge of industrial and technological change taking place in post-Napoleonic

Britain, watched the growth of British railways with interest. The progress of railway construction in Britain also aroused lively interest in the United States, which was faced with the problems presented by vast distances. At least two British pamphlets on the Liverpool and Manchester railway had been issued in pirated editions in America by the end of 1830, and by 1840 the United States was not only constructing railways but was building some of its own locomotives. In Britain itself Birmingham was linked to the Liverpool and Manchester railway by 1837, and one year later the opening of the line from London to Birmingham created the first trunk system.

The 1840s saw a vast extension of the network as the result of the Railway Mania of 1844–47, and in the 1850s the drive to build national railways spread across Europe from Belgium, which had inaugurated a state-owned system in 1834. At the side of the railways ran the new electric telegraph, which linked capital cities with the provinces and further extended the power of governments that had already started to transport their armies by rail. During the Crimean War (1853–56) the first military railway made its appearance at Balaklava, and the construction of a strategic rail network was pressed forward in India after the mutiny of 1857. Railways proved decisive in the unification of Italy, for in 1859 Napoleon III's troops traveled by troop train from France into northern Italy to defeat the Austrians at Magenta and Solferino.

The Civil War in the United States provided the second example in history of the large-scale use of railways in military operations, and General Sherman's march through Georgia in 1864 effectively cut the Confederacy in two largely because of his systematic destruction of railway track and rolling stock. During the Civil War, construction began on the first through railway from the Atlantic to the Pacific. The Union Pacific Railroad Company extended its New York–Omaha line westward, while at the same time the Central Pacific Railroad Company pushed its track eastward from Sacramento. They met on May 10, 1869, at Promontory, Utah, and the first through train from Sacramento to New York reached its destination on July 29, 1869, after a journey of six and a half days. In the early 1870s railways were being laid down in the United States at the rate of ten thousand miles a year.

The opening up of Argentina and Uruguay by

667

Above *Rain, Steam and Speed— The Great Western Railway* by J. M. W. Turner. *Below* *The Railway Station*, a painting of Paddington Station by William Frith.

Extending the railway network

railways financed largely by British capital brought the wheat and meat of the pampas and prairies down to the ports for shipment to Britain. Similarly, in Australia, New Zealand and South Africa railway construction proved to be an indispensable preliminary to the first stages of economic development. Meanwhile the locomotive grew mightily in size and tractive power, and the substitution of steel rails for iron rails from the 1860s on made for smoother and safer running.

By the 1890s Europe was crisscrossed by a complex and efficient railway network. Over these lines, toward Hamburg, Bremen, Gothenburg, Rotterdam, Liverpool and Le Havre, came the surplus peasant population of Europe on its way to the New World, and Russian Jews fleeing before anti-Semitic pogroms. Even backward Russia, with its broad-gauge tracks, was reasonably well provided with railways by 1900, with nearly 48,000 miles open. The construction of the Trans-Siberian railroad from Vladivostok to Chelyabinsk, where it would join with the Russian European system, was begun in 1891 and completed in 1904, during the Russo–Japanese War.

The Edwardian era marked the apogee of the railway age in Britain, when railways reigned supreme as a means of land transport. Although the gasoline-driven internal combustion engine came rapidly into use after 1906, no long-distance transport worth mentioning, either of passengers or goods, was done by road before 1914. But World War I ultimately was responsible for the ascendancy of the car and truck; for the widespread use of gasoline-driven vehicles in military operations paved the

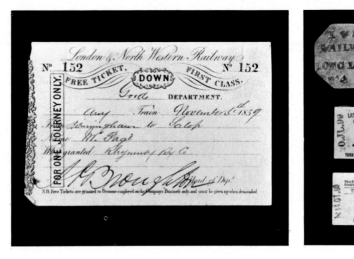

way for a rapid expansion of road transport at the expense of railway transport in the 1920s and 1930s. The railway age, which had lasted for less than a century, was clearly coming to an end. By then, however, patterns of trade, the development of markets for goods and services, and the movements of populations had been permanently altered.

W. H. CHALONER

Early train tickets. Railway tickets at first were varied in appearance.

Victorian travel was crowded and uncomfortable, as this painting by William Maw Egley shows.

"Dark, Satanic Mills"

The opening of the Liverpool-Manchester railway symbolized more than a revolution in transport and communications, for it coincided with the start of a reform era in government that was long overdue in Britain. In fact, passengers traveling on Stephenson's new railway were inevitably exposed to one of the political anachronisms of the age. Midway between Liverpool and Manchester the line passed the village of Newton. Though few in number, Newton's residents were doubly fortunate: they lived in an enclave of rural Lancashire as yet unsullied by the "dark, Satanic mills," and in each parliamentary election they enjoyed the privilege of returning two members to the House of Commons. The quarter of a million inhabitants of Manchester, on the other hand, remained politically unrepresented at Westminster. And so, for that matter, did the three great manufacturing

Earl Grey, who put through the First Reform Bill in 1832.

centers of Sheffield, Leeds and Birmingham. The removal of such anomalies was essential if the British people were to escape the violence that accompanied every major change on the Continent.

In 1831 and 1832 there seemed to be a very real prospect of popular insurrection in the English cities. Earl Grey's Whig government had indicated its desire to overhaul the electoral system, redistributing seats to ensure representation for the new industrial towns and to achieve the abolition of "rotten boroughs" and "pocket boroughs." But the radical "political unions" that had sprung up in Birmingham and other cities in the Midlands wanted more: they demanded a broad extension of the franchise. The Tory-dominated House of

Popular dissatisfaction caused riots in many towns, such as Bristol, where the Bishop's palace was burned.

Lords blocked all Grey's attempts at reform, however, and there were serious riots in Derby, Nottingham and Bristol.

In June of 1832, Grey and his colleagues finally managed to steer a Parliamentary Reform Bill through the House of Lords and into the statute book, but the measure itself fell far short of radical aspirations. The franchise was still limited to comparatively wealthy taxpayers, most of whom were property owners. (Thus the "reformed" House of Commons that met in 1833 had actually been elected by only one-sixth of the adult males in the country.) The radicals complained that the Reform Bill had merely transferred political power from the old landed aristocracy to the new oligarchs of industry and commerce, and working-class agitation continued. For the most part that dissent was conducted through the movements that had developed outside Parliament (and often in opposition to it); the rapidly expanding middle classes seemed content to seek redress of their grievances from the House of Commons.

The Grey and Melbourne ministries that managed British affairs for most of the 1830s were the last collective manifestation of the Whig ideal in politics, although the robustly amateur prejudices that formed the essence of Whig government survived until the mid-sixties. The Whig belief in ordered liberty prompted many reforms whose attainment was rooted deeply in the past. It made possible, for example, the triumph of the great anti-slavery campaign that William Wilberforce had resolutely championed since the days of Pitt and Fox. An act providing for the emancipation of all slaves in British possessions was passed in 1833, the year of Wilberforce's death.

The Utilitarians and the Chartists

Other influences at work at this time were gradually transforming the Whigs into the Liberals of Victorian England. Jeremy Bentham (who died in 1832 in his eighty-fifth year) was patriarch of the Philosophic Radicals, a group of political intellectuals who had been seeking to sweep away the centuries-old inefficiency of local and national administration for two generations. It was these Utilitarians who reformed the bumbling government in towns and cities through the Municipal Corporations Act of 1835, and it was they who launched sustained attacks on the entrenched privileges of the Church of England.

There was a less sympathetic side to the Utilitarians, however, for although they were prepared to give state protection to children employed in the factories, their coldly unemotional belief in the virtues of hard work made them unable to appreciate the rigors imposed on adults by an industrial society. Lord Shaftesbury—who was, at this time, beginning his twenty-year campaign for im-

Jeremy Bentham, patriarch of the Philosophic Radicals.

proved factory conditions—won far more support from Whigs like Melbourne and Palmerston (and even from that highly individualistic Tory, Disraeli) than from the archpriest of the Benthamites, Edwin Chadwick. The most characteristic piece of Benthamite legislation was the Poor Law Amendment Act of 1834 which made public relief of the destitute more systematic and uniform by establishing workhouses. Unhappily for both the Benthamites and the poor, these "uninviting places of wholesome restraint"—the phrase is Chadwick's—rapidly became a disgrace (as Dickens' powerful pen was to reveal before the end of this decade).

The Whigs, distrusting democrats no less than despots, frowned upon movements of popular agitation. For a brief ten months in 1834 a Grand National Consolidated Trades Union, with a membership of half a million, championed workers' rights, but in that same year six farmworkers at Tolpuddle in Dorset received savage sentences for union activity. The laboring classes soon sought other outlets for their accumulated indignation. From 1838 to 1842, for example, the popular radical movement known as Chartism pressed for annual parliaments, elected by universal male suffrage, as a panacea for Britain's ills. There were violent outbursts in 1839 at Birmingham and Newport, but Chartism was too weakly led and too confused in objectives ever to constitute a serious danger to entrenched interests. It declined in appeal during 1842 when splits developed between the North and Midland sections of the movement. In 1848 it stirred once more, but when its climactic spring demonstration ended in a rain-swept fiasco, Chartism was ridiculed into the

Republic!"

scrap heap of good intentions.

There was a more fundamental reason for the failure of Chartism than simply its surface imperfections. Throughout the nineteenth century the British people had responded far less easily to general ideas than the people of the Continental cities did. It was almost as if the collective mind of the English populace could comprehend only a particular problem for which there seemed a practical solution. At no time was this more clearly shown than in the "hungry forties." After the bad harvests of 1839, 1840 and 1841, the principal worry of the middle classes and the laborers was the price of food. They flocked to meetings of the Anti-Corn Law League, the movement founded in Manchester in 1839 by Richard Cobden and John Bright to advocate the abolition of all duties upon imported corn. The simple clarity of the League's purpose and the personal magnetism of its two leaders made it the most formidable pressure group a democratic society had ever known. The Tories, who

Sir Robert Peel, who founded the London police and repealed the Corn Laws.

had come into office in 1841 under Sir Robert Peel, soon found that the League's reiterated complaint (that they were keeping the price of bread high for the benefit of their landowning supporters) was hard to counter.

Famine in Ireland

The summer of 1845 was one of endless rain, and the English harvest was ruined. There was even worse tragedy in Ireland, where the potato crop was found to be diseased—a disaster that robbed more than half the Irish population of its staple diet. With famine stalking Ireland and threatening England, Peel insisted on repealing the Corn Laws in June of 1846. Prices were stabilized and corn imports rose so rapidly that within five years a quarter of England's bread supply depended on overseas grain. But starvation continued to take its toll in Ireland.

Cobden and Bright had won a victory for free trade. As the British found that they could sell more manufactured goods by admitting food and raw materials without import duties, all protectionist tariffs were swept away. The Tory Party was hopelessly split. The Peelites, of whom Gladstone was the most eminent, made common cause with the Liberals; the Tory rump, shocked and dismayed, sought a new philosophy of conservatism under Benjamin Disraeli. The year 1846 proved a truer watershed in British politics than 1832, the year in which the Reform Act was passed.

Reform reaches the Continent

Many of the problems that confounded the parliamentarians of Westminster also affected their counterparts across the Channel on the mainland of Europe. This was particularly true in France, where the reign of Louis-Philippe had fallen short of the revolutionary expectations of July, 1830. The new franchise instituted by the July Monarchy was little broader than the one it replaced. Parliament was narrowly bourgeois in composition, obstinately hostile toward workers' demands and closely attached to protectionist tariffs.

The French government appeared to be extremely unstable during this period (which saw thirteen ministries in eighteen years). In truth, power remained in the hands of a small circle of men who moved from one ministerial post to another, and there were only sixty different office-holders within those thirteen ministries. The strongest political figure was François Guizot, whose narrow conservatism kept the franchise firmly in the hands of the "men of property" (and thereby excluded 97 per cent of the French male population).

Radical insurrections in Lyons in 1831 and in Paris and Lyons in April, 1834, were repressed with more severity than the contemporaneous riots in England, and press laws imposed in 1835 made it impossible for a movement comparable to the Anti-Corn Law

John Bright; with Richard Cobden he founded the Anti-Corn Law League.

League to develop in France. Both countries suffered from the bad harvests of the 1840s and from mercantile panic over rash investment. The collapse of railway booms in northeastern England and central France ruined thousands of small speculators in 1847. Uncertainties over the future development of industry thus made life insecure for capitalists and for workers on both sides of the Channel

By the mid-forties Germany and Austria were also suffering from the growing pains of industrial capitalism (despite the fact that those countries were still dominated by an agrarian society that was almost feudal in its restraints on free labor). In Berlin, Frankfurt and Vienna, young agitators were demanding representative institutions; in Hungary the brilliant orator and journalist Lajos Kossuth was arousing the intense patriotism of his fellow countrymen and calling for a responsible government that was independent of Vienna; and in four of the Italian states, liberals were putting pressure on their rulers in the hope of obtaining constitutions. There was unrest throughout Europe—most of it aimed at the conservative sterility of the Metternich System.

Indeed, the Austrian Chancellor was still at the center of affairs in Vienna, just as he had been each year since 1809. "If they throw me out, the whole structure will collapse," he remarked early in 1848, sublimely indifferent to the signs of the approaching storm.

During the last week of February, 1848, the storm did break—not over Austria, but in Paris. A campaign for extension of the suffrage was to culminate with a reform banquet in the capital, but the meeting was proscribed by the authorities. Barricades went up in the labyrinthine alleys of the old city. There was shooting, and the mood of the Parisians turned ugly. Louis-Philippe, who, in his seventy-fifth year, could well recall losing his father to the guillotine, thought it wiser to abdicate and seek refuge in England. Few dynasties have toppled more gracefully, but few have had such slender foundations.

When news from Paris reached St. Petersburg, Tsar Nicholas I thundered at the officers of his guard: "Gentlemen, saddle your horses! France is a republic!" It was a premature alarm, for with the Romantic poet Lamartine incongruously seated at Talleyrand's old desk in the French Foreign Office, the mood of the country was neither Jacobin nor Bonapartist. There was a danger to the Tsar's autocratic principles, however, for the reports that had stirred him to choleric wrath also sent quivers across the Rhine and the Alps and down the Danube to Vienna and Budapest. Within three weeks of Louis-Philippe's abdication, rioting in the Austrian capital forced Metternich to resign, and Germany, Italy and Hungary resounded with nationalist sentiment. Before the end of the year barricades of revolution had gone up in twenty European cities—from Seville in southern Spain to Poznan in Prussian Poland.

Metternich's appraisal had been right: the structure had collapsed. But what would take its place? A confederation of European republics, as Mazzini hoped for in Italy? Independence for the historic master peoples of Europe, as Kossuth believed in Hungary? "Healthy national egoism," as a delegate of the German pre-Parliament in Frankfurt demanded? There were numberless solutions. And one at least had the merit of originality. The dream-child of a twenty-nine-year-old German refugee, it was to be found among a score of manifestoes circulating that year in Paris. Communism had arrived.

A Manifesto for the Masses

"The proletarians ... have a whole world to conquer" concluded the authors of the Communist
Manifesto, *a succinct twenty-three-page document issued in London in February of 1848.
The document's authors—Karl Marx and Friedrich Engels—were both exiles from their
native Germany. The bold conclusion that they reached in the closing paragraph of the
Manifesto was the result of months of collaboration and years of study. In the course of their
research, Marx and Engels had considered (and then either incorporated or rejected) the
overlapping tenets of Chartism, utopian socialism, and a dozen similar contemporary socialist
movements. Their synthesis concluded with a phrase that was to become international
communism's clarion call, one that would inspire riots and revolution around the world:
"Workers of the world, unite!"*

Title page of the first issue of
the *Neue Rheinische Zeitung*
to appear after the 1848
revolution, edited by Marx.

Opposite Karl Marx, the
father of Communism.

A specter haunts Europe—the specter of communism.
All the powers of old Europe have entered into a holy
alliance to hunt down and exorcise this specter: the Pope
and the Tsar, Metternich and Guizot, the French radicals
and the German police.

Thus begins the *Communist Manifesto*, a twenty-three-
page document that first appeared in London at the
end of February, 1848. Its German coauthors,
Karl Marx and Friedrich Engels, were both excellent theorists as well as fiery agitators. They had been
commissioned by the International Communist
Federation to outline the concepts, characteristics
and aims of the communist movement. At that time
the Federation was only one of the many socialist
groups in existence. Its members were refugees and
political outcasts of various nationalities, most of
them workers and craftsmen living in several European capitals under the leadership of the German
communist cell.

Socialism, together with its offshoot communism,
had begun to appear in both France and England in
the 1820s. It took the form of an intellectual and
emotional protest against the paradoxical situation
that the historian E. Halévy denounced as "pauper-
ism engendered by the invention of machinery."
Between 1820 and 1830, the progressive ideas of
Marx's three great forerunners began to circulate.
Those men—Robert Owen in England and the
Comte de Saint-Simon and Charles Fourier in
France—were what one might term utopian
socialists. They were indefatigable in their attempts
to bring about social reform, and they dreamed of a
perfect society in which the exploitation of man by
man would no longer exist. They made little or no
attempt, however, to deal with the vital problems of
state, government or political power, and they
reckoned on achieving their aims through persuasion rather than revolution.

The communist movement in France, on the other
hand, was fanatically republican, egalitarian and
revolutionary. It represented a trend toward violent
and direct action against the established order, and
in both its ideas and its membership it had far more
appeal for the working class. The leaders of this
"working-class socialism" deliberately challenged
utopian socialism, which had grown fashionable in
the *salons*. They suspected, not without reason, that
this form of socialism was more concerned with
reforming the old capitalist structure of society than
with replacing it with a brand new world.

The clandestine atmosphere of conspiracy and
revolutionary violence that characterized the republican secret societies—especially the society known
as the Seasons—during the reign of Louis-Philippe
was fertile ground for the growth of the spontaneous
type of communism that existed up to 1840. In
May, 1839, an uprising inspired by the Seasons was
crushed by the French Army and the National
Guard. A German secret society called the Federation of the Just, which had taken part in the insurrection, was virtually wiped out. The members of
this federation, whose motto was "all men are
brothers," were craftsmen, workmen and a few progressive intellectuals. They had been steeped in the
atmosphere of the Parisian communist movement,
but they still retained certain ideals and tendencies
that were alien to it. The theorist and leader of the
Federation of the Just was a tailor named Weitling,
the son of a French officer and a German maid-
servant. His steadfast belief in revolutionary action
was combined with a passionate longing for
evangelical fraternity.

The 1839 uprising was followed by a decade of
apparent calmness, but beneath the surface violent
upheavals were going on. Paris, the great center of
the European revolutionary movement, had become the cradle of social theories and ideals and the
meeting place for exiles, revolutionaries and agitators from every country and from all levels of
society. Theories varied widely: Etienne Cabet's
nonviolent, idealistic version of communism was
based on dreams of future utopias; Louis Blanc's

The Communist Manifesto in the *Red Republican*, a magazine that idolized the Republicans of the French Revolution. In the bleak years after 1848, when it was first published, republication of the Manifesto encouraged socialists not to abandon their ideals.

a life of exile—first in Paris, later in Brussels and finally in London, where he remained until his death in 1883.

In Paris, he became friendly with the Russian Mikhail Bakunin, a dedicated agitator and anarchist and a sworn enemy of the state who at a later date was to become Marx's archenemy. Marx, with his prodigious passion for reading, plunged into the study of the French Revolution. He became conscious for the first time of the problem of classes, and of the proletariat and the working-class movement. He showed a marked preference for communism over socialism, which was too middle class for his liking. Communism, he believed, was far more suited to the needs and hopes of the working-class proletariat, the class in bondage. Unfortunately, the communism of that time, as taught and disseminated by its supporters, was doctrinally far too simple for Marx. Nor had he reached the stage of realizing the vital importance of economics. That importance was to be revealed to him by his compatriot Friedrich Engels.

Engels was also a left-wing Hegelian philosopher, two years younger than Marx. He came from a family of rich textile manufacturers, and his father had sent him to England to learn the business. Engels was shocked at the sight of so much misery and poverty among the working classes. He was profoundly interested in Chartism, the movement of the British industrial working class for political reforms, notably universal male suffrage. He compared the movement to the utopian socialism of Owen, became engrossed in the study of the classical economists, and was haunted by the phenomenon of periodic crises of overproduction. It was just at the time that Engels was about to publish his remarkable work, *The Condition of the Working Classes in England* (1845), that he established the close intellectual and emotional relationship with Marx that was to last until Marx's death. The two men were convinced that with their combined knowledge and experience they held all the keys to social evolution, and they set themselves the task, between 1845 and 1847, of working out their doctrine. That doctrine was to be unmistakably proletarian in character as well as strictly scientific in concept and expression. The emancipation of the proletariats would be the work of the proletariats themselves—a radical new approach to communism.

Marx wanted to collaborate with Proudhon, for whom he had the greatest respect. They had long discussions on the subject of Hegel's philosophy during the winter of 1844–45, but Proudhon ultimately refused to work with him, having no wish for another new dogma or religious intolerance. Even worse, Proudhon would not accept the necessity for action, professing that he no longer believed in the virtue of revolution. In May, 1846, there was a complete break between them, and in June of the following year Marx published a pamphlet with the ironic title of *Misère de la Philosophie* (*Poverty of Philosophy*), reversing the title of Proudhon's *Philosophie de la Misère*.

socialism was based on the organization of work and called on the state to subsidize the "national workshops." Then, in 1840, Pierre Joseph Proudhon, a typographer and self-educated man, made his appearance on the scene, attracting the shocked attention of the public with his pamphlet "What is Property?" Proudhon condemned private ownership, arguing instead that property should be in the hands of those who actually do the work. According to his theory, voluntary associations formed by these workers eventually would replace tyrannical state governments.

It was in the Paris of the 1840s, the Paris of Proudhon, Louis Blanc, and Cabet, that foreigners burning with revolutionary ideals gathered together. And it was to Paris that Karl Marx, a native of the Rhineland, came toward the end of October, 1843. Marx was an extremely talented twenty-six-year-old Hegelian philosopher. Because his left-wing beliefs excluded him from an academic or journalistic career in Prussia, he was condemned to

674

The class struggle—premise of Marxism

A far more serious and definitive break, which affected the immediate plans of Marx and Engels, had already occurred with the blond tailor Weitling, the theorist of the Federation of the Just. Since the disastrous uprising of 1839 in Paris, the Federation of the Just had gone through a difficult time. In order to avoid punishment, they had broken up and scattered to Switzerland, Belgium and England. A group eventually re-formed in Paris, but by that time London had become the main center of the movement. Dutch, Hungarian, Slavic and Scandinavian exiles in the English capital grouped themselves together around a central German contingent. When the leaders of the London-based movement invited Marx and Engels to become active members of the Federation, they agreed—but only on the condition that Weitling's theory, tainted with utopianism, be replaced by their own political philosophy.

In March, 1846, a stormy meeting took place in Brussels between Weitling, who had come there to justify his opinions, and his two powerful adversaries. A Russian delegate's eyewitness account of this meeting describes Engels as tall, upright and distinguished, "like an Englishman"; Marx, looking like a lion under his mane of thick black hair, was revealed by the dictatorial, cutting tone in his voice. Marx accused Weitling of deceiving the people by inciting them to revolt without having any solid foundations on which to base his action. His reply to Weitling's moving defense was to strike the table with his fist, causing the lamp to shake, and comment: "Ignorance has never helped anyone yet!"

Marx and Engels emerged victorious from the confrontation in Brussels. During the summer of 1847 the Federation of the Just accepted their doctrine and changed its name to the International Communist Federation. Their slogan "all men are brothers" was replaced by "workers of the world, unite," and the task of drawing up a manifesto presenting the views and aims of these new-style communists was given to Marx in collaboration with Engels. The latter's first draft took the form of a catechism with twenty-five questions and answers, but that format was soon abandoned in favor of a straightforward narrative, presented almost as a historical drama. Because of the exceptional talent of the authors, there is an extraordinary mythical quality and feeling of enchantment about their analysis, even though it claims to be completely scientific in its approach.

Marx and Engel's fundamental premise in the *Manifesto* was that "the history of all human societies up to the present time has been the history of the class struggle." From this premise sprang the inescapable laws governing historical developments. The first prehistoric societies almost certainly had been classless, with goods belonging to all. But that communist condition had disappeared when certain men seized control of the land, forcing others to work for them. Thus society became divided into the exploiters and the exploited. This feudal agricultural system was itself replaced when an emerging commercial class, the capitalists, established a manufacturing economy through a series of revolutions in methods of production and means of communication. Later on, manufacture was in turn replaced by the infinitely superior methods of large-scale industry. As a result of the expansion of trade and the establishment of world markets, the industrial middle class, or capitalists, had to make way for industrial magnates, owners of huge industrial complexes—the modern bourgeoisie. In this way, the bourgeoisie itself played an extremely revolutionary role in the course of history.

Such praise, however, was more in the nature of an obituary, since Marx saw the destruction of the modern bourgeoisie as a necessary stage in the historical development of society. According to his theory, every economic system that is based on exploitation carries within it the seeds of its own destruction. In the capitalist system, the bourgeoisie had created "its own gravediggers"—the modern working class, the proletariat. Marx felt certain that at a given stage in history the proletarians, who were constantly growing in numbers, would become conscious of their growing strength. Forced to sell themselves day after day like bales of merchandise, and totally enslaved by capital, they would come to look upon law, ethics and religion as bourgeois prejudices concealing bourgeois interests. Moreover, while all earlier historical movements had been minority movements, or carried out on behalf of minorities, the working-class movement would be a spontaneous surging forward by the vast majority in the interests of that vast majority. The proletariat, the lowest stratum of contemporary

Left Friedrich Engels, who co-authored the Manifesto.

François Guizot, the French Prime Minister, whom the Manifesto accused of joining in an unholy alliance with Pope Pius IX, Tsar Nicholas I of Russia and the Austrian Prime Minister, Prince Metternich, to crush the specter of communism.

Dudley Street, Seven Dials, London, by Doré. Marx's concern with class may in part have sprung from his knowledge of London's slums. Dudley Street was very close to Dean Street where Marx lived for a time in London. Both Marx's sons and his daughter died of privation.

Right The British Museum, where Marx wrote *Das Kapital*, as it was in the 1850s.

Robert Owen's institution at New Lanark, Scotland. In his social ideas Owen was a precursor of Marx, but unlike Marx his social attitudes were translated into action.

society, could raise itself and stand erect on its own feet only by smashing to pieces the superstructure of that society.

This despotic domination by the proletariat, however, would bear no resemblance whatsoever to dominations in the past. It would serve merely as a period of transition, a stage in the process leading to the eventual dissolution of all classes and all states. It would represent a transitory historical necessity, for the exploited oppressed class would be able to free itself only "by, at the same time, freeing the whole of society from exploitation, oppression and class struggles, once and for all." The *Communist Manifesto* finished with a call to action:

The communists . . . openly proclaim that the only way they can achieve their aims is by the violent destruction of the old order of society. The ruling classes may well tremble at the thought of a communist revolution! The proletarians have nothing to lose in the struggle apart from their chains. They have a whole world to conquer—workers of the world, unite!

When the *Manifesto* was first published in London

at the end of February, 1848, Paris was in a state of revolution and that revolution spread like an epidemic all over Europe to Sicily, Tuscany, Lombardy, Venice, Naples, Rome, Vienna, and Prussia. It was only in France, however, that a socialist (or partially socialist) revolution took place, with socialist theorists such as Louis Blanc, Pierre Leroux, Philippe Buchez and Proudhon all trying to impose their particular policies. The situation ended tragically: the violent uprising of the Parisian working class during the historic June Days of 1848 was suppressed with considerable difficulty after a battle that raged for four long days in the barricaded streets of the capital.

When the forces of reaction gained total victory after 1850, it seemed as if the working class had been permanently driven back into its original hopeless situation. The socialist theorists returned to their utopian dreams of the years preceding 1848, and it was not until 1864 that the passionate call to action of the *Communist Manifesto* encouraged them to fresh efforts. The International Working Men's Association—which later on was to change its name

The revolution of 1848

The view from the Place de la Bastille during the Paris Commune of 1871, when workers erected barricades in the streets.

to the First International—was founded. Within the space of ten years, however, Marx himself had put an end to the First International, after clashing first with Proudhon's supporters and then, far more seriously, with Bakunin and his devotees. Bakunin was a volcanic giant of a Russian whose concept of anarchism rejected any form of temporary dictatorship by the proletariat, or any provisional administration by the state.

Meanwhile, the uprising of the Commune in Paris in 1871—a violent, bloody offshoot of the Franco–Prussian War—had served as a rousing inspiration to the working-class movements in every country. It lacked a realistic basis entirely, however, and achieved very little; moreover, French socialism suffered a severe setback as a result of it. On the other hand, the victory of the Prussians over France, which led to Germany unity, had a very beneficial effect on German socialism. Marx and Engels took advantage of the opportunity to impose Marxism on the German Social Democratic Party, which was to enjoy a remarkable success in the years to come. At the same time, the *Communist Manifesto* emerged from its state of semiretirement. Its circulation in German, the language in which it had originally been written, led to its being translated into English, French, Russian and many other languages as new socialist parties were created both within and outside Europe in the 1880s. This growth gave rise to the idea of a new International, more powerful and more permanent than the first—and the Second International was founded in Paris in 1889. On May 1, 1890, militant workers demonstrated in both America and Europe and demanded the establishment of an eight-hour working day.

After several years of internal struggle for power,

the Second International finally eliminated all the non-Marxist groups, especially the anarchists. Taking as its model the superbly organized German branch of the party—which some thought was too bureaucratic in its structure—the new International described itself as "social-democratic." The former qualification of "communist"—the word that had been deliberately chosen by the authors of the *Manifesto* to emphasize the proletarian violence and the defiance toward the bourgeois world adopted by "scientific socialism"—had apparently been dropped in the course of the organization's development. It was not until the first abortive Russian Revolution of 1905—which momentarily shook the Tsarist regime, encouraged the formation of *soviets*, or councils of worker delegates, brought Trotsky to the fore and provided Lenin, the Bolshevik leader, with valuable experience—that violence and defiance were reinstated.

The social-democratic International was swept out of existence by the catastrophic world war of 1914–18; it was totally unable to prevent the war's outbreak or the vast majority of the socialist leaders and members from supporting their own countries. But during the war, Lenin set about founding a new body that was genuinely dedicated to world revolution; in his eyes, the Russian revolution would be by no means the most important. He intended that this new International, which he would rebuild on the ruins of the second, should be efficient, highly disciplined and controlled by professional revolutionaries. He would call this Third International "Communist" in memory of the original *Communist Manifesto,* the historic document out of which the modern communist movement had developed.   JEAN JACQUES CHEVALLIER

КАПИТАЛЪ

КРИТИКА ПОЛИТИЧЕСКОЙ ЭКОНОМІИ.

The title page of the second volume of the Russian edition of *Das Kapital,* published in 1855. This translation has played an important role in subsequent European history as a result of the Communist revolution in Russia.

Public unrest

By the close of 1848 it was clear that the old order would withstand the impact of revolution. The Hohenzollern dynasty still reigned in Berlin, and the House of Hapsburg still ruled in Vienna (under the management of an eighteen-year-old emperor, Francis Joseph). No radical movement threatened the Romanov throne in Russia, and although the Pope had been forced to flee to Gaeta, the governments of Catholic Europe were all but competing with each other for the honor of restoring His Holiness to Rome. Even the French had eschewed socialism: they had elected Charles Louis Napoleon Bonaparte, the nephew of a legend and the only daringly safe candidate among the six contenders, as President of the Second Republic.

The radical tide was on the ebb throughout Europe by Christmas of 1848, but it had deposited clusters of determined rebels who were still gasping for survival among the flotsam of the barricades. The Roman Republic of Mazzini and Garibaldi successfully defied the forces of repression until it was crushed by an army of the French Republic in July. The Venetians, led by Daniele

Kossuth, leader of the Magyar rebels.

Manin, retained their independence until August, 1849, despite a cholera epidemic and a long siege by the Austrians.

Peace had returned to Germany by 1848, but the federal constitution that was written by the all-German assembly that met in Frankfurt that winter proved unacceptable to the German princes. And in the spring those deputies were sent about their business by

Prussian soldiers. In Hungary, by contrast, there was no peace that Christmas. A grim civil war dragged on in the featureless steppeland of the middle Danube as Kossuth's Magyars resisted attempts by Austrians and Croats to restore the unified Hapsburg Empire from which Hungary had sought its freedom. In August, 1849, the Hungarian will for national liberty finally broke, and the last Magyar militia surrendered to the Russian troops that Tsar Nicholas I, an ever-vigilant gendarme of autocracy, had put at the disposal of the young Francis Joseph. Counter-revolution was triumphant throughout Europe by the late summer of 1849.

Results of the revolutions

It would be a mistake to dismiss the 1848 revolutions as dramatic failures. The authority of absolute monarchy declined in each of the principal areas of insurrection. Louis Napoleon's France, for example, was in many ways a negation of the ideals of the barricades, but its plebiscites did pay lip service to the principle of universal male suffrage. Frederick William IV of Prussia restored the privileged position of the great landowners in local administration, but he retained a partially elected legislature in which, by 1859, liberals formed a majority. Karl Philipp Schwarzenberg and Alexander Bach, the mentors of Francis Joseph, ruled the Austrian Empire through a centralized bureaucracy,

Frederick William IV of Prussia.

but no one sought to reimpose feudal obligations on the emancipated peasantry.

Socialism was indeed discredited, and yet each of these countries tacitly accepted the notion that the state had obligations toward the teeming millions who were being drawn into the expanding factory system. Nationalism seemed a total casualty (partly as a result of its exclusive intolerance of the claims

Emperor Francis Joseph who conquered the Magyars with the help of Russian troops.

of other peoples), but the reputations of Garibaldi and Kossuth outside their own countries were so high that freedom for Italy and Hungary became a crusading cause of liberals everywhere, much as Greek freedom had been in the days of Byron. In England, enterprising manufacturers named a blouse and a biscuit after Garibaldi and brewers honored the Hungarian patriot on the signboards of public houses. Popular acclamation could hardly have gone further.

The 1848 revolutions had little direct effect on either Britain or the United States. The Chartist demonstration in South London on April 10 was such a failure that Thomas Carlyle, the chronicler of more shattering events in France, wrote complacently to his wife of "the No Revolution we have just sustained." In Tipperary a Young Ireland group attacked a police post without success, but elsewhere all was peaceful.

Across the Atlantic, men were busy with other matters: gold was discovered sixty miles east of Sutter's Fort in California in January, and in central New York State a mysterious series of table-tappings led to the creation of the cult of spiritualism. The Mormons, who had trekked to the Great Salt

Lake in the previous year, were building a temple and a tabernacle below the Wasatch Mountains, and General Zachary Taylor, who had recently precipitated (and won) a war with Mexico, was elected President by a nation that retained its liking for battle-scarred heroes.

Yet Europe's troubles were changing America almost imperceptibly. For one thing, the peak period of immigration coincided with the 1848 revolutions. Irish, fleeing from the famine, provided eastern cities with a ready labor force for industry and railway construction; and four thousand German-speaking political refugees—the vanguard of an invasion that made Milwaukee virtually a German city within ten years—settled in Wisconsin. The contribution of these ardent idealists to American life was considerable. Carl Schurz, the best known of the German-born Wisconsiners, supported the Republicans so effectively in the 1860 election that he virtually put Lincoln in the White House. The 1848 revolutions did indeed have far-reaching ramifications.

"Pam's" England

In England the man of the hour was Lord Palmerston, who had first held ministerial office in October of 1809 (two months before his eventual colleague, Gladstone, was born). At the age of sixty-one, "Pam" returned as Foreign Secretary in Lord John Russell's ministry

Lord John Russell, later Earl Russell.

(which was formed when Peel's government broke up in the summer of 1846). He was to dominate the Cabinet for all but twenty-eight months of the next nineteen years, in more than half of which he served as Prime Minister.

Palmerston's robust and cavalier temperament won him affection and acclaim from the British people who admired his jolly waistcoats and jauntily tilted hat, envied the excellence of his racing stables and delighted in the patriotic bluster of his diplomacy. He shared their liking for Garibaldi and Kossuth and their suspicion of all foreign sovereigns. In 1850 he sent a naval squadron to blockade Greece in order to obtain compensation for Don Pacifico, a moneylender born in Gibraltar—and therefore a British subject—whose house in Athens had been ransacked by an angry crowd. Such high-handed behavior led to protests from the French and Russians, and it shocked Queen Victoria. But it gratified her subjects!

Lord Palmerston who believed in treating foreigners arrogantly.

Lamentably, Palmerston's judgment on foreign affairs, astute in the 1830s, became increasingly wayward as he grew older. Yet his popularity never waned. "He is Mamma England's spoilt child," a Tory opponent acidly observed some two years after the Don Pacifico affair, but there were many at home and abroad who saw him as John Bull incarnate (an image that pleased his constituents in Tiverton but aroused disquiet among foreign statesmen).

An era under glass

Palmerston was by no means typical of early Victorian England. He lacked its earnest desire for self-

The Crystal Palace, built for the Great Exhibition of 1851.

improvement and its prim concern with the virtues of hard work. The principal festival of the age, the Great Exhibition of 1851, was essentially alien to all he represented. It was an attempt to show the world the material prosperity that industry had brought to Britain, and it harnessed science to national prestige for the first time. At least 6 million people visited the six-hundred-yard-long palace of glass that Joseph Paxton had erected amid the elm trees of Hyde Park. There they could admire the new precision tools from Whitworth and Armstrong, the self-acting cotton mules from Bradford, the steel knives of Sheffield, and the telegraph cable that was to be laid under the Channel that very year. Foreign products almost equaled those from Britain, and visitors could see power looms and labor-saving devices from America, women's fabrics from France, glassware from Bohemia, and—inconspicuous among the thousands of exhibits—some steel cannon manufactured by a Herr Krupp of Essen, Germany.

The Exhibition had been conceived in the ever-inquiring mind of Prince Albert, the Queen's consort. The weary visitor might be revived by tea and buns in one of the many refreshment rooms, but there were no bars and no alcohol. The motto of the Exhibition had been chosen by the Prince and was printed at the front of the four-volume official catalog: "The Earth is the Lord's and all that therein is." *The Times* of London caught the spirit of the opening when it reported that the occasion was like the Day of Judgment.

The mysterious Orient

Among the distinguished visitors shown in the specially commissioned painting of the Exhibition was a Chinaman in national costume, complete with fan. He was not, as was presumed at the time, the official representative of the Manchu Emperor but the master of a Chinese junk that was anchored in the Thames. Yet the publicity he attracted was evidence of the interest aroused by the Orient.

The Dutch and Portuguese had traded along the China coast since the sixteenth century. English ships had sailed up the Pearl River to Canton as early as 1637, and from the end of the seventeenth century until 1833 the East India Company retained a monopoly of Chinese seaborne trade, carrying silks and tea back to its docks along the Thames. The narratives written by eighteenth-century travelers of their journeys in the Orient made Chinese ornamental gardens and handpainted wallpaper fashionable in the 1760s, and the philosophers of the Enlightenment admired all that they heard of Chinese customs.

By the middle of the nineteenth century, these generous sentiments had given way to a conviction that the Chinaman was a quaint but distinctly inferior human animal. The reason for this change in attitude was the alleged susceptibility of the Chinese to opium, which had been smuggled from India into China by unscrupulous British merchants. In 1841 Chinese attempts to stamp out the opium trade led to a disgraceful war between Britain and China.

The 1842 Treaty of Nanking ceded the island of Hong Kong to Britain and stipulated that five Treaty Ports (Amoy, Canton, Foochow, Nangpo and Shanghai) should be opened to foreign trade at reasonable tariffs. The Chinese also agreed to compensate merchants for the loss of revenue from the opium trade. Collectively these measures gave the Europeans a stranglehold over the primitive Chinese economy. They were followed by concessions to the French and to the United States, which benefited particularly from the right to induce coolies to cross the Pacific and to labor in California under conditions that were hardly better than slavery.

As the American vessels sailed the Pacific, they passed close to the islands of Japan. For centuries the shoguns of Japan had rigorously preserved their country's isolation by stamping out all attempts of European nations to establish trading posts and by concentrating on building up a flourishing native economy. But with the Chinese coast wide open to foreign trade, it became increasingly difficult for the Japanese to maintain their policy of deliberate seclusion.

American warships entered Japanese waters in 1846 and again in 1849, and a forceful descent on the islands could not long be delayed. It remained to be seen if Japan would submit—as China had done

Street scene in Hong Kong, which has been a British colony since 1842.

—to foreign mastery or if she would use her tightly knit authoritarian system to bridge the gap between her culture and that of the industrialized West. Either solution was possible in July, 1853, when Commodore Perry's steam frigates anchored in the great bay below Mount Fuji.

Perry Opens Japan

1854

One of Millard Fillmore's last acts as President was to entrust Commodore Matthew C. Perry with the task of delivering a highly important official communiqué to the Emperor of Japan. In mid-July of 1853—four months after Fillmore was turned out of office—Perry delivered two letters to the Emperor. The first—Fillmore's—was diplomatic and conciliatory; the second, written by Perry himself, was somewhat more specific and far more threatening. It virtually commanded the Japanese to open their country to foreign trade. To underscore the gravity of his request, the Commodore announced that he would return the next year—with a larger fleet—to hear the Emperor's reply. Unhappily for the insular Japanese, Perry was as good as his word—and on March 31, 1854, the Japanese were induced to sign a treaty opening two harbors to foreign shipping. After centuries of self-imposed isolation, Japan had finally accepted membership in the family of nations.

On July 8, 1853, four ships of the United States Navy, two of them steamers, dropped anchor off the harbor of Uraga at the entrance of Edo (now Tokyo) Bay. In command of the squadron was Commodore Matthew C. Perry, a large and formidable martinet of fifty-nine who was popularly known as "Old Bruin" or "The Old Hoss."

Perry had with him a letter to the Emperor of Japan from President Millard Fillmore. That letter began by pointing out that Oregon and California lay directly opposite Japan and that steamships could cross the Pacific in eighteen days. The President declared that it would be profitable for Japan and the United States to engage in mutual trade, and he asked the Emperor to change the ancient laws that prohibited foreign trade except with the Chinese and the Dutch. Fillmore then proffered a half-promise that can only be described as insincere:

If your imperial majesty is not satisfied that it would be safe altogether to abrogate the ancient laws which forbid foreign trade, they might be suspended for five or ten years, so as to try the experiment. If it does not prove as beneficial as was hoped, the ancient laws can be restored. The United States often limit their treaties with foreign states to a few years, and then renew them or not, as they please.

The American President's letter went on to appeal for good treatment of American mariners shipwrecked on Japanese shores and concluded with a request that American vessels be allowed to stop in Japan for coal, provisions and water.

Fillmore's letter breathed conciliation from start to finish, and its courteous phraseology seemed to imply no hidden threat. Commodore Perry had composed his own letter to the Emperor, however, and his missive, while repeating the main points made by the President, contained certain passages that conveyed an unmistakable warning to the Japanese. Perry observed that no friendship between

his country and Japan could long exist "unless Japan ceases to act towards Americans as if they were her enemies." He expressed the hope that the Japanese government would "see the necessity of averting unfriendly collision between the two nations, by responding favorably to the propositions of amity, which are now made in all sincerity." Then he added:

Many of the large ships-of-war destined to visit Japan have not yet arrived in these seas, though they are hourly expected; and the undersigned, as an evidence of his friendly intentions, has brought but four of the smaller ones, designing, should it become necessary, to return to Edo in the ensuing spring with a much larger force.

Perry refused Japanese demands that he sail to Nagasaki, the only port where foreigners were officially received, and he adamantly declined to meet any but the highest officials. He was equally firm in resisting Japanese procrastination, asserting that the President's letter must be accepted with due formality within three days. And less than a week after his ships dropped anchor the redoubtable Commodore disembarked with a bodyguard of just under three hundred sailors and marines. After delivering his messages, Perry announced that he would be back the following year—with a larger squadron—to accept a reply to his President's requests. Before heading out to sea the Commodore sailed farther up the Bay of Edo to within sight of the shogun's capital. (The shoguns were hereditary military dictators who had been the real rulers of Japan since the twelfth century.)

When the "black ships," as the Japanese called them, returned in February, 1854, there were eight of them instead of four. The Americans and the Japanese began negotiations immediately, and it soon became clear that the latter, although bargaining all the way, were ready to bow step by step to superior force. The Japanese fought hard against proposals for a trade treaty, however, and in the end

A Japanese Prefect with his two attendants. This portrait was drawn in the year Perry arrived in Japan.

Opposite Perry's "Black Ships," which caused a sensation when they appeared in Tokyo Bay in 1853.

Right A contemporary Japanese painting of Commodore Perry.

Perry did not insist upon their signing one. But he did secure the opening of two harbors, Shimoda and Hakodate, as ports of refuge, and he did extract the reluctant promise that after eighteen months an American consul would be allowed to take up residence at Shimoda. Furthermore, Perry obtained for his country that invaluable concession known as "the most favored nation clause":

> If at any future day the government of Japan shall grant to any other nation . . . privileges and advantages which are not herein granted to the United States ... these same privileges and advantages shall be granted likewise to the United States and to the citizens thereof without any consultation or delay.

Perry's treaty, signed at the fishing hamlet of Yokohama on March 31, 1854, marked the end of Japan's long seclusion from the world. Perry had put his foot in the door; others were soon to open it further. Indeed, if Perry had not forced it open, a Russian or British naval commander certainly would have done so. Japan was not to be left alone— the very idea of doing so would have appeared

Commodore Perry meeting the Imperial Commissioners at Yokohama.

The lure of the Orient

whimsical to the confident American or European businessman of that day. Within five years the British, Russians, Dutch and French had persuaded the shogun's government to sign commercial treaties, and the first American consul, Townsend Harris, had obtained the same benefits for the United States. The treaties, which forced the Japanese to accept a low scale of import duties and to concede extraterritorial rights to the nationals of eighteen countries, were regarded by the Japanese as unequal. But foreign pressure seemed irresistible, and by 1860 a community of European and American merchants was well established along the waterfront at Yokohama.

For most Westerners all this represented the attainment of a dream. After gold was discovered in California in the 1840s the Orient developed a new lure for Americans. China and Japan seemed to be not only potential markets of great value, but also fruitful fields for the missionary, the engineer, the educator and the doctor. Moreover, Britain's victory in the Opium War and her subsequent annexation of Hong Kong had left Americans both fearful and jealous of British commercial competition in the Far East. (There was, in addition, the menace of Russian expansion which threatened to engulf the Japanese islands.) It is not surprising, therefore, that lobbies representing both businessmen and missionary boards pressed Congress to promote America's Manifest Destiny in the Orient. The outcome was presidential authorization of the Japan expedition under Commodore Perry.

For Americans the consequences of Perry's mission were almost wholly beneficial for many years. However, the Civil War, which broke out seven years after Perry's treaty, restricted American expansion during the 1860s. But in succeeding decades trade between the United States and Japan flourished, America becoming Japan's largest single market, especially for silk. Before World War II, America's commerce with Japan was worth a good deal more than its trade with China. Yet long before that war began, Japan had become America's Oriental bogey—a supposed threat to California,

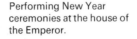
Performing New Year ceremonies at the house of the Emperor.

The "barbarians" from the west

Perry delivering his letter from President Fillmore to the Imperial Commissioners.

a shadow over the Philippines and a genuine menace to America's "sister republic," China.

For the Japanese the immediate consequences of Perry's visit and the subsequent treaties were generally unpleasant. The commercial benefits were small; the cultural shocks were intense. Whatever they thought of it in later years, the Japanese who greeted Perry in 1853 undoubtedly resented what amounted to an invasion of their territory. It is true that long before Perry's arrival, one or two scholars and officials had openly questioned the wisdom of the policy of strict seclusion that had been bequeathed to Japan in the seventeenth century by Iyemitsu, the third shogun of the Tokugawa line. They argued that there was much to be learned from Western nations and that only by intercourse with them could Japan make itself strong enough to

hold its own in the world. But those who advocated the opening of the country to foreign commerce did so precisely because they saw a potential menace to Japan's independence in the activities of the Western powers in the Far East. Closer contact with "barbarians" might be inevitable; it was nonetheless regrettable. Further, the instinctive sentiment of the samurai class—the warrior elite—was decidedly antiforeign, and for some years after Perry's arrival powerful elements in Japan remained basically unreconciled to the opening of the country.

At the time of Perry's first visit in 1853, the Japanese government took the unprecedented step of seeking the advice of provincial lords, leading scholars and certain important merchants as to the answer to be given to President Fillmore's letter. The replies received in Edo varied. Some wanted to fight Perry as soon as he reappeared. Some warned that granting Perry's concessions would only encourage the Westerners to demand further concessions later on, and they urged that the policy of national isolation be firmly maintained. Others advocated temporary concessions to the Americans to enable Japan to build up its defenses. One widely expressed view was that Japan should study and master the technical skills of the foreigners in order to turn the tables on them in future years.

In other words, in their reaction to foreign interference the Japanese were divided into two broad categories. Some were fanatical isolationists; others were pragmatic. But all were patriotic in the sense that they believed in the special virtue and destiny of their land, ruled "from ages eternal" by a line of monarchs descended from the Sun.

Politically the country was thrown into growing confusion. Perry's treaty indeed was a deadly blow to the prestige of the shogun's government in Edo. The very word *shogun* was a contraction of a longer title meaning "barbarian-suppressing generalissimo." If the shogun failed in this fundamental duty, the respect due to his office must necessarily diminish. And in fact the shogunate's reaction to Perry's visit—seeking outside advice—suggested a loss of nerve. The Emperor's court at Kyoto, long

An American sketch of a business session in progress between Perry and the Japanese.

684

Sumo wrestlers carrying bundles of rice ashore in the harbor of Yokohama.

powerless, began to assert itself, nagging at the shogun's government in Edo for its failure to stand up to the foreigners. Certain provincial lords attempted to expel the intruders by firing on their vessels, but such ventures proved ineffective and merely demonstrated the superior armaments possessed by the Western powers. Gradually, even the most die-hard patriots were forced to recognize that the foreigners had come to stay. Curiosity began to conquer prejudice; and among younger Japanese especially, admiration struggled with dislike. The loser in all the welter of emotional confusion was the Tokugawa shogunate, for here was a government that seemed both incompetent and out of date. And as the shogunate lost face, the prestige of the monarchy rose.

The collapse of the shogunate and, in 1868, its replacement by a new regime—the turn of events known as the Meiji restoration—was the prelude to a process of modernization that would astonish the world. The slogan of the Meiji oligarchy, accepted with enthusiasm as a national ideal, was "a rich country with strong armed forces." The second part of that phrase was the more important. In the development of industry and communications, the needs of the army and navy were given priority. In the new system of state education, obligations took precedence over rights. There was nothing novel in all this. A warrior society, homogeneous, ethnocentric and impregnated by Confucian concepts of duty, was adapting itself to the power politics of the contemporary world and was girding itself for two prime tasks: first, to remove the "unequal" treaties, and second, to join the great

A contemporary Japanese sketch of a group of minstrel performers.

The phoenix of Asia

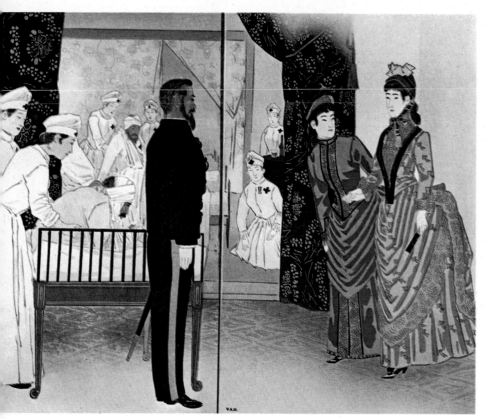

By the end of the century Japan had adopted Western customs in peace and war. This Japanese print shows Russian officers visiting wounded soldiers during the Russo-Japanese War of 1904–5.

Right Trade soon followed as a result of Perry's expedition. A Japanese illustration of 1861 showing a visiting American businessman.

imperial powers in the struggle for markets, spheres of influence and overseas colonies. Young samurai who had taken up arms when Perry landed at Uraga ("effeminate-looking Japanese," the expedition's historian called them) would see these goals achieved in their lifetime. By the twentieth century Japan had become a modern, militarily strong industrial state.

Thus, insult and humiliation—for that is what Western intrusion meant to the nineteenth-century Japanese—proved to be a challenge, a stimulus to effort. The twentieth century had scarcely begun before Japan was allied, on terms of formal equality, with Great Britain (an association that restored to the people of Japan the pride that had been lost half a century earlier). An apt pupil of the West, Japan then proceeded to demonstrate to the East that the West was not invincible. Victory over the Russians in 1905 made Japan, for a time at any rate, the hero of all Asia from the Yellow Sea to the Red Sea.

There are Japanese historians—controversial figures who presage an academic fashion of the 1970s—who claim that the era from the twilight years of the shogunate to the national surrender in 1945 should be seen as a kind of Hundred Years War against the West, in which Japan led Asia to eventual freedom and independence. According to this interpretation, the struggles for national freedom in India, Ceylon, Burma, Southeast Asia and, indeed, China itself were inspired by Japan's example.

The argument is that Japan demonstrated that an Asian country could modernize itself and become an industrial power with a minimum of foreign help.

Then, by defeating Russia in 1905, Japan demonstrated that white men could be beaten in war by Asians. Those historians see Japanese intervention in China as the stimulus that awakened the Chinese to the threat of imperial aggression. Thus, as the agent of fate or of historical necessity, Japan was the rough midwife of Mao's revolution and of the rise of China as a great power. That process of obtaining Asiatic independence, which began with victory in the Russo–Japanese War, was completed in World War II when Japan's conquests during the early engagements destroyed the remaining prestige of the white colonial powers and its grant of nominal independence to their colonial territories made the postwar independence of these territories inevitable.

Such a remarkable and, at first sight, bizarre theory cannot be dismissed out of hand. It deserves serious consideration, for there can be no doubt that Japan was a catalyst in the growth and eventual triumph of Asian nationalism. But for Japan to claim exclusive credit for that triumph—and to ignore the profound influence of forces such as Marxism and the Russian Revolution—is absurd. That Japanese aggression in China, particularly from 1937 on, brought chaos and, as a consequence of that chaos, Communism to that country can hardly be denied. In that negative and destructive sense Japan was perhaps the midwife of Mao's revolution—but that was never the role in which Japan saw itself. In any case, Mao's success is not something on which the Japanese can fairly congratulate themselves.

There is somewhat more substance to the claims

made for Japan's role in Asia during World War II. The first shattering blows (symbolized by the collapse of Singapore) meant a final loss of prestige for Westerners in Asia—a loss that later successes never completely effaced. There is no question that the false independence granted to European colonies occupied by the Japanese meant that real independence could not be denied these territories by their Western rulers in the postwar years. Here the Japanese played what could be described as a constructive role in Asian affairs, although the cost at the time to many of those concerned tended to be expensive in terms of human life and dignity.

The phoenix that has risen from the rubble of the ruined and prostrate Japan of 1945 has astonished the Western world. By the year 2000, Japan—which is already the third greatest economic power on earth—may conceivably have a standard of living that is higher than that of any other nation. Enormous industrial energy was released by the opening of Japan, but its potential dates from an earlier age. The closing of the country by the shogunate in the seventeenth century forced a stopper into a barrel that effervesced with vitality. Had seclusion not been imposed upon them, the Japanese—notable seafarers—would undoubtedly have discovered and probably have colonized areas of the globe such as Australia and New Zealand well ahead of any European power. Perry, and those who hastened to follow his lead, withdrew the stopper from the barrel and released a new and remarkable political force, one that was destined to be both the scourge and the liberator of Asia.

RICHARD STORRY

Within a few years of Perry's arrival Japan had brought her armies up to Western standards. They are here vanquishing Chinese troops.

Left By the end of the nineteenth century Japan had an advanced railway system. This picture is of Mihorabashi station.

687

Russian Expansion

The United States was not the only great power to show a new interest in the Far East in the 1850s. During that decade the massive and cumbersome empire of the tsars began to consolidate the gains of earlier centuries. Isolated Russian outposts had been established on the bleak coasts of the northern Pacific as early as 1650, but for two centuries the powerful Chinese Empire had restricted these settlements to icebound wastes that were frequented only by trappers and seal hunters. In 1847 the Russians inaugurated an eastward sweep. The Tsar appointed a young and enterprising colonialist, Count Nikolai Muravyov, as Governor General of Eastern Siberia, and for the next fourteen years every effort was made to secure Russian control of the mouth of the Amur River and to strengthen Russian influence over the Chinese government at the capital, Peking.

Muravyov's policy reached a climax in 1858 with the establishment of an imperial city at the head of a natural harbor on the Pacific. Significantly, Muravyov named this Russian counterpart to San Francisco Vladivostok, "Domination of the East." Its very name seemed a challenge to nations whose vessels had long traded in Far Eastern waters (although the next half-century was to reveal that Russia's greatest rival in the Far East was neither Britain nor the United States but Japan).

Russia's eastward expansion and America's westward expansion almost coincided in time, and yet there were few major nations in the world that were as dissimilar in character as the autocratic Tsarist Empire and the vigorous Republic. It is true that the economies of large areas in both countries depended on forced labor, and it is also true that the institution of slavery in the southern United States was no more morally defensible than the bonds of serfdom in Russia, but industrial capitalism was far more advanced in America than it was in the predominantly agrarian society of the Tsar's semi-feudal Empire.

Although the Russian flag flew over more than a sixth of the land surface of the globe in the mid-1850s, Russia had only fifteen towns with more than 50,000 inhabitants (their combined population was almost precisely the same as that of New York, Philadelphia, Baltimore and Boston). Russia also lagged behind the major European countries and the United States in communications and industry: it was only in 1851, after nine years of construction, that a railway linking the principal cities of Moscow and St. Petersburg was completed —and even this undertaking was financed by American capital and supervised by American engineers. By 1855 Russia had only one-fifth as many miles of railways as the United States.

Russian industry was still largely unmechanized at the turn of the century. Cotton spinning, for example, was largely carried out in domestic houses rather than factories—and in 1850 there were four times as many spindles in New England alone as in the whole of Russia. Where factories did exist, working conditions were grim: as late as 1860 serfs constituted more than four-fifths of the labor force in textile factories and about three-quarters of the labor force in steel and iron foundries.

Yet, for all its backwardness, Russia remained one of the great powers throughout the century. The Tsar's Empire seemed an almost limitless wasteland, capable of mobilizing hundreds of thousands of ruthless warriors and thrusting them deep into Europe— as the Hungarians had discovered in 1849. The Russian "bogey," with its Cossack raiders and its endless columns of infantry clad in long yellowish-gray greatcoats that almost swept the ground, was a very real apparition in the 1840s and 1850s. After the failure of the 1848 revolutions, Tsar Nicholas I acted so boldly in Europe that his power appeared to menace the security of the whole Continent. It was for this reason, more than any other, that the British and French governments drifted into the futile tragedy of the Crimean War.

War in the Crimea

The origins of the Crimean War lie far back, in old clashes of outlook and interest. To some extent, it can be argued that Louis Napoleon (who had proclaimed himself Emperor Napoleon III in 1852)

Emperor Napoleon III. France, like Britain, feared Russian domination in the East.

committed French troops to the conflict in the hopes of recovering the prestige that France had lost through his uncle's disastrous campaign in 1812. Anglo-Russian dissension, on the other hand, was caused by the "Eastern Question," the series of problems raised by the apparent inability of the Sultan's government in Constantinople to hold the Ottoman Empire together. The Russians, who had long been aware of the feebleness of their Turkish neighbor, had begun to move south around the Black Sea as early as 1790, and they had fought largely indecisive wars against Turkey from 1806 to 1812 and in 1828–29.

Each Russian move was regarded with suspicion by the British, who believed that the Tsar's army and navy were a danger to the stability of the Middle East and a threat to the overland route between Europe and India. The bolstering up of the Turkish Empire became an axiom of British foreign policy, for the British were anxious to prevent the Russian fleet's sailing through the narrow straits of the Bosporus and into the Mediterranean. The principal instrument in interpreting this policy was the British Ambassador in Constantinople, Viscount Stratford de Redcliffe, a diplomat who spent almost a quarter of a century in the Turkish capital. During those years, Stratford de Redcliffe's sympathy and patience stood in marked contrast to the bullying arrogance of a succession of Russian representatives in Constantinople.

The immediate cause of war between Russia and Turkey in 1853 was the Sultan's refusal of a Russian demand that the Tsar should be recognized as protector of all Christians living within the Ottoman Empire. The Turks would never have dared to declare war on Russia had they not felt assured of French and British support—and

British cavalry camp during the Crimean War.

Sick Man of Europe"

Hagia Sophia in Constantinople. Despite its ill-treatment of religious minorities, the Ottoman Empire was always able to count on Western support.

in 1853 they had reason to feel assured. Franco-Russian relations had been severely strained by a dispute over the custody of the holy places in Palestine, and the distrust in which the Tsar was held in Britain had been intensified by his proposals for the eventual partition of "the Sick Man of Europe," as he called Turkey.

When the Russian Navy caught and destroyed the Turkish fleet in the harbor at Sinope, the British and French became genuinely alarmed. There was no other force capable of protecting the approaches to the Bosporus and Constantinople, and the British and French squadrons were moved into the Black Sea. An ultimatum was sent to the Tsar from London and Paris in March of 1854, and war followed at the end of the month. That conflict had been caused not so much by deliberate aggression as by fear, misunderstanding and confusion. There are few conflicts that could have been so easily avoided.

Sebastopol under siege

The Crimean War was curiously limited in scope and objectives. The British and French armies served as ancillary forces to their navies, for there was never any serious attempt at invasion in depth of the Russian Empire. There were naval raids in the Baltic and against Muravyov's outposts on the peninsula of Kamchatka in the Far East, but by September, 1854, the war had settled down to a long siege of Sebastopol, the principal Russian naval base in the Crimea.

The siege itself lasted for a year

but the two most famous battles of the campaign, Balaklava and Inkerman, were both fought within two months of the initial landing. At Balaklava, British cavalry repulsed a Russian raid on the main British base. In the course of the engagement, confusion over orders led the Light Brigade to launch its famous, fatal frontal charge on the Russian gun positions.

Inkerman was one of the bloodiest encounters of the century in Europe. After six hours of hand-to-hand fighting, the combined casualty figures were over 16,000 killed and wounded—and yet, like so much else in the war, the outcome of the battle was largely inconclusive. The appallingly cold winter that followed decimated the besiegers and intensified administrative chaos, and the only real good that came from the war was an improvement in nursing services in both Britain and Russia. The work of Florence Nightingale and her thirty nurses at Skutari is well known; they revolutionized the character of military hospitals and won such renown and respect that they were able to continue to press for reforms in civil nursing when they returned to Britain. And at precisely the same time, the Grand Duchess Elena Pavlovna was organizing the first community of Russian nurses to care for the wounded in Sebastopol itself.

The fall of Sebastopol in September, 1855, virtually ended active operations, although the Russians gained a victory over the Turks when they captured the stronghold of Kars in the Caucasus in November. Fighting gradually died away in the main theaters of war. Napoleon III was anxious to reduce the

size of the French contingent (which outnumbered the British four to one), and none of the allied commanders seriously contemplated an advance into southern Russia.

Some of the dispute's original bitterness evaporated with the death of Tsar Nicholas I in March of 1855. His thirty-seven-year-old successor, Alexander II, was far less of a military martinet than his father. He was unwilling to see the War prolonged or extended, and when Austria threatened to enter the Crimean War as an ally of the French and British, the new Tsar

Florence Nightingale: who created modern nursing on the battlefields of the Crimea.

accepted proposals for peace. A conference was convened in Paris to draw up a peace treaty. It met from the end of February until mid-April of 1856, and the actual treaty was signed on March 30.

Treaty of Paris

The most important provision in the Treaty of Paris was a prohibition on all warships and fortifications in the Black Sea. At the same time the Russians renounced their claims to a religious protectorate over the Christian subjects of the Sultan. The Crimean War thus appeared to have achieved its two most immediate objectives. By taking the first steps toward recognizing Rumanian independence, the Treaty also sought to keep the Russians away from the Danube and to counter the aggressive intentions of the Tsar.

The Treaty was not a good settlement, however, for it merely postponed Russia's southward thrust.

The neutralization of the Black Sea remained valid only so long as the attention of Europe was not distracted elsewhere, and when, in 1870, the Russians announced that they no longer considered themselves bound by the demilitarization clauses, the European great powers were too preoccupied by the struggle between France and Prussia to take any action stronger than a written protest. So long as the Turkish government remained unreformed and unrepentant, the capricious cruelty of its officials in the Balkan lands kept the Eastern Question alive. Within twenty years of the Treaty of Paris it had become clear that the Crimean War had solved nothing.

Yet both the war and the Congress of Paris had long-term effects outside the strict limits of the Eastern Question. Alexander II felt that the war had exposed fundamental weaknesses in the structure of the Russian state. Although never sympathetic to radicalism, the Tsar was a human autocrat, and he was determined to modernize his Empire. Nine months after the signing of the Treaty of Paris, he personally presided at the first meeting of a commission to prepare for the emancipation of the Russian serfs. And in March of 1861 an edict was promulgated that liberated 20 million serfs and endowed them with plots of land (for which they were to pay "redemption debts," spread over fifty years, to the state). Other reforms swiftly followed: a legal code, representative local government, improvements in education, and the substitution of conscription for the inequitable forced levy that had long provided the army with its recruits. New railways improved communications and speeded the export of grain.

The Congress itself had one unexpected consequence. In January, 1855, the small north Italian kingdom of Piedmont —which was anxious to prove its status as an influential European power—had entered the Crimean War as an ally of France and Britain. Piedmontese troops participated in the battle of Chernaya in August of 1855 and acquitted themselves well. "Out of this mud, Italy will be made," a Piedmontese soldier is alleged to have declared during the battle—and in a sense he was right. At the Congress of Paris the Piedmontese Prime Minister, Count Cavour, placed the Italian Question on the agenda of Europe.

The Emergence of Italy 1856

The bitter struggle in the Crimea had reached a virtual stalemate by 1855, when Sardinia's shrewd Prime Minister, Count Camillo Benso di Cavour, dispatched a 15,000-man army to aid the French and British. Indeed, hostilities ceased little more than a year later—but by that time the Prime Minister's move had earned his tiny kingdom a hearing at the peace congress in Paris and had netted Sardinia a powerful ally in Napoleon III. Cavour's attempts to unify Italy under his sovereign, Victor Emmanuel II, received an invaluable assist from Napoleon some three years later, when 120,000 French troops landed at Genoa to aid Cavour in repulsing the Austrians from Piedmont. Within two months the neighboring province of Lombardy was Cavour's, and less than a year later Victor Emmanuel was proclaimed King of Italy.

The *Risorgimento*, the name given to the Italian unification movement, was largely the achievement of three men: Giuseppe Mazzini, Giuseppe Garibaldi and Count Camillo Benso di Cavour. Of the three, only Cavour, the head of the Sardinian government, had the means at his disposal to achieve the aims that had long been voiced so passionately by Italian patriots. Aspirations of independence had naturally found expression in the works of Machiavelli, Alfieri and Ugo Foscolo. But not until the 1830s were those aspirations consciously directed toward national unity.

Mazzini promoted a unification movement in the 1830s and encouraged insurrections against Austrian rule, but the republic of Rome that his movement established was suppressed by the French in 1849. In the previous year, King Charles Albert of Sardinia (Piedmont) granted his kingdom a constitution and declared war on Austria. He was defeated at the battles of Custoza and Novara and abdicated in 1849 in favor of his son, Victor Emmanuel II. The young King invited Cavour to join the government—first as Minister of Agriculture and Commerce, later as Minister of Finance, and finally in October, 1852, as Prime Minister—despite the fact that he strongly disliked him.

Cavour's political genius was soon revealed: he introduced social and economic reforms to Sardinia (in order to win French and British sympathy) and then—in his first daring act of diplomacy—he persuaded his King to send a small contingent of 15,000 men to the Crimea to fight with the allied armies against Tsarist Russia in 1855.

Cavour's bold move demonstrated Piedmont's solidarity with the Western powers, and when hostilities ended in the Crimea and a diplomatic congress was convened in Paris to draw up the terms of the peace treaty, Cavour took part in those peace talks. He was careful to adopt a reserved and modest attitude toward the great powers. Cavour's primary objective was to gain the sympathies, through informal private meetings, of ministers who

had already been shocked by the little they knew about the triumphant antiliberal forces in most of the Italian states, above all in Rome. The Emperor Napoleon III listened sympathetically; the British Minister, Lord Clarendon, and Count Walewski, the French president of the congress, condemned the reactionary policies of both the Papal States and the Kingdom of the Two Sicilies (as Naples and Sicily were called at the time). Cavour, for his part, pointed out that the revolutionary upheavals in the Italian peninsula, fostered by the stupidity and blind indifference of absolutist rulers, were a potential danger not only to the Kingdom of Sardinia but to the peace of Europe as a whole. The congress ended stormily with the majority of the delegates expressing themselves clearly in favor of Italian reforms in spite of Austria's determined opposition. From then on, Europe could no longer ignore the Italian problem.

Cavour returned home in triumph. He had already persuaded the French Emperor that war against Austria was the only way to achieve the aims voiced so persistently by the Italian people. He then informed the Sardinian Parliament that he and the Austrian delegates to the peace congress in Paris had parted company "with the firm conviction that they were further away than ever from finding some form of compromise between the policies of the two countries, and that the principles upheld by each country were irreconcilable."

In the eyes of Italian liberals, the leader of the Piedmontese government had now become the champion of what was to be, from that time on, a national cause. Cavour's future success depended on two conditions: first, that a military alliance be formed with France, and second, that Austria be provoked into declaring war on Piedmont (so that the latter would not appear to be the aggressor in the eyes of the world).

On July 21, 1858, Cavour and Napoleon III reached a secret verbal agreement that France would come to the aid of Sardinia if Austria attacked

Pope Piux IX, whose early liberalism was translated into bigoted reaction after the revolutions of 1848 had threatened the Papal States. His determined opposition to the movement for Italian unity was almost successful.

Opposite Garibaldi looking over the city of Capua.

The March of the Thousand

Count Cavour, Prime Minister of the Kingdom of Sardinia, and architect of the *Risorgimento*.

Cavour's homeland. War between the Franco–Sardinian alliance and Austria seemed inevitable. The latter no longer made any secret of its military buildup along the Piedmontese frontier, while on the other side, a marriage between Princess Clotilda, eldest daughter of the King of Sardinia, and Prince Jerome Napoleon, the Emperor's cousin, united the two dynasties. French clerics, who wielded great influence at the Court in the Tuileries, were strongly opposed to a conflict that might lead to the end of the temporal power of the papacy. But on April 23, 1859, Austria sent an ultimatum to Piedmont enjoining her to disarm within three days. As a result of that ultimatum, tantamount to a declaration of war, hostilities finally broke out.

Austrian troops crossed the Ticino, on the frontier of Austrian Lombardy, into Piedmont. The French immediately intervened: Napoleon III landed at Genoa on May 12, and his army of 120,000 joined forces with a Piedmontese army of some 60,000 men. The first attack—and the first victory of the Franco–Piedmontese forces—took place near the small village of Montebello. It was carried out with such spirit that the Austrian general mistakenly thought the enemy was making a frontal attack and hurriedly withdrew his soldiers to the south. A second confrontation took place at the village of Magenta, which the French soldiers occupied with difficulty, house by house, on June 4. Four days later, King Victor Emmanuel and Napoleon III made a triumphal entry into Milan.

The next great battle began on the morning of June 24, on the hills south of Lake Garda, where the Franco–Piedmontese forces were suddenly confronted by the massed Austrian army. The terrible battle that followed was waged violently and relentlessly throughout the day along a seven-mile front. Fighting was fiercest around the villages of Solferino—which was finally occupied by the French late in the evening—and San Martino, which a Piedmontese army led by King Victor Emmanuel gained and lost four times before re-occupying it for a fifth time at about six o'clock in the evening. The Austrian troops were forced to retreat during a terrific storm to the fortress of Peschiera. The losses suffered in the course of the day's fighting totaled 25,000 killed or wounded.

The whole of Italy waited breathlessly for the liberation of Venetia, for according to the agreement drafted at Plombières and ratified at Turin, that region, together with Lombardy and Piedmont, was to form part of the independent kingdom of northern Italy. To the Italians' considerable surprise, the news suddenly came through that the Austrian and French emperors had met at Villafranca di Verona on July 8—without the knowledge of Victor Emmanuel—and had signed an armistice. Lombardy was to be ceded to Napoleon III, who, in turn, would hand it over to Piedmont. The other Italian states were to form a federation presided over by the Pope, while Venetia, although belonging to the federation, would continue to be an Austrian possession.

The Italian people were profoundly disillusioned when they heard the news, and Napoleon's popularity on the peninsula evaporated overnight. Cavour tried desperately to enlist the help of the army, bitterly reproached his King for having accepted such terms and handed in his resignation. Victor Emmanuel had realized more clearly than Cavour, however, that it would be unwise to sever relations with an ally to whom he already owed so much.

Napoleon III's decision had been determined by a number of factors. The first was a simple question of humanity, for he had been profoundly moved by the horrifying sight of the battlefield at Solferino piled high with corpses, and he was afraid that the battles to follow might be even more bloody and violent. (The Prussian government had indicated that it might invade France if French victories against the Austrians continued.) Equally serious was the growing unrest among clerical circles in France itself. Finally, Napoleon III was reluctant to see Italy expand beyond the frontiers already defined by his uncle when he had created the Kingdom of Italy for his stepson, Eugène de Beauharnais.

The peace treaty that was concluded at Zurich on November 10, 1859, envisaged a confederation of Italian states under their former rulers. In actual fact, however, the dispossessed rulers had no chance whatsoever of recovering their states by force. The whole of central Italy longed to be united with Piedmont, and plebiscites held in 1860 in Parma, Modena, Tuscany and the Papal States of Bologna and Romagna approved such a union. Yet the uninspired, timid Sardinian government that had replaced Cavour lacked the necessary authority

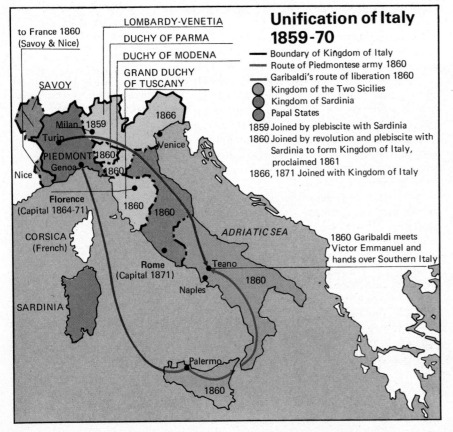

Unification of Italy 1859-70

to France 1860 (Savoy & Nice)

LOMBARDY-VENETIA
DUCHY OF PARMA
DUCHY OF MODENA
GRAND DUCHY OF TUSCANY
SAVOY

— Boundary of Kingdom of Italy
══ Route of Piedmontese army 1860
— Garibaldi's route of liberation 1860
⬤ Kingdom of the Two Sicilies
⬤ Kingdom of Sardinia
⬤ Papal States

1859 Joined by plebiscite with Sardinia
1860 Joined by revolution and plebiscite with Sardinia to form Kingdom of Italy, proclaimed 1861
1866, 1871 Joined with Kingdom of Italy

1860 Garibaldi meets Victor Emmanuel and hands over Southern Italy

Milan 1859
Turin
PIEDMONT 1860
Genoa 1860
Nice
Venice 1866
Florence (Capital 1864-71) 1860
CORSICA (French)
ADRIATIC SEA
Rome (Capital 1871) 1860
Teano
Naples 1860
SARDINIA
Palermo
1860

and initiative to take advantage of the situation and press for union. The King, realizing the dilemma, overcame his personal resentment toward Cavour and recalled him on January 20, 1860.

The movement for national unity had found a leader once again. Cavour had little difficulty in making Napoleon III realize that it was impossible for him to oppose the Italian people's desire for union with Piedmont, since Napoleon himself had been elected to power by popular vote. As a reward for recognizing the plebiscites in Italy, France was given Savoy on March 24, 1860, hs well as the county of Nice—which, as Cavour was quick to point out in the Sardinian Parliament, was really far more Provençal than Italian in character.

After northern Italy and Tuscany were united, few difficulties arose in integrating populations that differed widely in character and traditions. The Hapsburgs had been infinitely superior to the Popes and the Spanish Bourbon dynasty in the art of government, and since the eighteenth century they had carried out beneficial reforms in northern Italy, specifically in Milan and Florence. Enormous cultural, economic and even religious differences existed between northern and southern Italy.

Nonetheless, even though rebellion broke out in the spring of 1860 in the Kingdom of the Two Sicilies, it was morally out of the question for Piedmont to launch an attack on the Kingdom of Naples or on the Papal States (which were openly protected by France). Cavour could and did encourage Garibaldi to aid the rebels, however, and the National Society, a large patriotic association, supplied him with arms and money. Cavour secretly allowed volunteers to seize two ships in the port of Genoa, and those vessels were used to transport roughly one thousand volunteers (known as Red Shirts) to Sicily. They arrived off the port of Marsala on May 11, and four days later they came face to face with Bourbon troops at Calatafini. The

enemy was in an advantageous position on a steep, terraced hillside, but the Garibaldini, who were inferior in numbers and arms, attacked with such ferocity and bravery that they finally won. Garibaldi had already publicly proclaimed himself dictator of Sicily in the name of King Victor Emmanuel. The Bourbon government, for its part, inundated the chancelleries of Europe with protests against the perfidy of the Piedmontese government.

Within the space of a few days, Garibaldi's army was reinforced by local volunteers who had flocked to join it from all parts of the island. The army then set off to conquer Palermo. On May 27, after cunningly drawing the main force of the garrison out of Palermo and into the interior of the island, Garibaldi's finest men forced their way into the town after a bayonet attack. Even then they were not in complete control, since the Neapolitan fleet was anchored in the port of Palermo, and large contingents of the Neapolitan army still occupied the citadel. After ten days of fierce fighting, the Bourbons asked for an armistice, and on June 6 they evacuated Palermo.

From that moment on, the victory of Garibaldi's legendary Expedition of the Thousand was assured. Turin came out in open support of the force, ships from Genoa supplied reinforcements, and Francesco Crispi, Garibaldi's deputy, reorganized the civil administration of Sicily. A final battle took place at Milazzo on July 20, where government forces were still in control. The Bourbons were again defeated.

It remained to be seen whether the brave condottiere would carry on the revolutionary struggle in the south of the Italian mainland. At the request of Napoleon III, Victor Emmanuel wrote an official letter to Garibaldi ordering him not to cross the Straits of Messina to the mainland. Cavour, however, secretly countermanded these orders, and on the night of August 19, Garibaldi crossed the Straits and landed in Calabria. The Bourbon troops

The triumphal entry of Victor Emmanuel into Brescia, where generations of repression led to great rejoicing when Austrian rule was cast off.

Left The famous meeting between Garibaldi and Victor Emmanuel at Teano, outside Naples on October 26, 1860, at which Garibaldi handed over command of his soldiers to the King.

A photograph of Garibaldi in old age.

Pius IX : the prisoner in the Vatican

A dramatic painting of Garibaldi galloping into battle.

Right A meeting of conspirators. The unification of Italy was hindered by the ambitions and rivalries of European powers.

Marshal McMahon, leader of the French troops in Italy. France's support helped the Kingdom of Naples and the Papal States to withstand for a time the movement for unity.

On October 26, a meeting took place on the outskirts of Naples between King Victor Emmanuel and Garibaldi, who handed over the command of his troops to his monarch and went into voluntary retirement on the island of Caprera, which he had made his home. Now only the fortress of Gaeta remained to be taken. But because of French warships lying off the coast, it was impossible for Victor Emmanuel to blockade the fortress from the seaward side. Once again, the Italian monarch was forced to negotiate with Napoleon III, reproaching him for violating the very principle he himself had laid down at Villafranca—the principle of nonintervention in Italian affairs. The Emperor finally gave way and withdrew his fleet in January, 1861. The fortress finally surrendered, and on February 12, Francis II, the former King of the Two Sicilies, went aboard a ship that Napoleon had placed at his disposal and made his way to Rome. There he set up residence in the Farnese Palace.

During that same month, the first all-Italian Parliament sat in Turin. On the momentous day of March 14 it was unanimously agreed that Victor Emmanuel was to be proclaimed King of the newly created Kingdom of Italy. The new state was immediately recognized by England and, a few weeks later, in April, 1861, by the United States and Switzerland.

It now remained for Venice and Rome, together with the surrounding region of Latium, to be incorporated into the new Italy. For political reasons Rome was clearly going to be the most difficult to conquer, for France, anxious that it should remain the great center of Christendom, persisted in giving the city its protection. Even Mazzini, who had wanted Garibaldi to march on Rome, was persuaded of the impossibility of taking the city at that time and turned his attention to Venice. In 1861, however, the time was not yet ripe for either of them to be conquered, and the Italian nationalists were forced to wait for more favorable circumstances.

Unfortunately, Cavour died prematurely on June 6, scarcely three months after the achievement

stationed there completely lost heart and refused to fight. Garibaldi, most anxious not to lose any more time, hurried on to Naples, accompanied only by a few officers. All along the route he was acclaimed as the great liberator of Italy, and on September 7 he entered Naples in the midst of an enthusiastic reception. The Bourbon king, Francis II, had left the capital the previous day and had made his way to the naval fortress of Gaeta, where he and his remaining supporters took refuge.

Cavour, for his part, was determined that the initiative should remain firmly in the hands of the Piedmontese government. Consequently, he persuaded Victor Emmanuel to act on his own, and Piedmont invaded the Marches and Umbria. The inadequate forces defending these provinces (Catholic volunteers recruited in France, Belgium and Ireland) were no match for the regular Piedmontese troops. In spite of the valor of the "papal zouaves," they suffered a crushing defeat.

of the great task he had tirelessly pursued for twelve years. Before he died, however, he outlined the work that lay ahead for his successors: to make Rome the capital of the new Italy. After Cavour's death, the task was carried on by a group of politicians whose policies and attitudes had been molded by this great statesman. They were just as hard-working and unbiased as he had been, as moderate and realistic in their approach, as utterly devoted to their country. Yet they lacked one essential ingredient: his innate political genius.

Garibaldi, however, had still not relinquished the idea of conquering Rome in a surprise attack similar to that carried out by the Thousand, and from 1862 on, he grew increasingly restless. In August he landed near Catania at the head of twenty-five hundred volunteers recruited in Sicily; he immediately marched into Calabria. Rattazzi, the Italian Prime Minister, would have been quite ready to shut his eyes to what was going on, but Napoleon III made it clear that any attack launched by Garibaldi on papal territory would constitute a declaration of war. Rattazzi had no choice but to give way in the face of Napoleon's threat.

The next efforts to win Rome were diplomatic. The Turin government, led by Marco Minghetti, engaged in lengthy discussions with Paris about the departure of the French garrison from Rome. They finally agreed in 1864 that the French troops should leave within two years in return for a firm commitment on the part of the Italian government that Garibaldi would not embark on any new adventures. As a guarantee of good faith, the capital of Italy was transferred from Turin to Florence. The transfer provoked great disturbances in Turin, and the King himself was seriously displeased. Minghetti was forced to resign and was succeeded by General de la Marmora.

In September, 1867, Garibaldi again resumed his strong propaganda activities throughout the country in an effort to force the hand of the government and to conquer Rome. The Italian government was sent another warning by France, which must have been perfectly aware of the fact that Rattazzi was powerless to prevent the infiltration of revolutionary elements across the open frontiers of Latium or even stop the flight of Garibaldi from Caprera to take over the leadership of the revolutionaries. Finally, Napoleon III decided to take things into his own hands, and in October he ordered his fleet based at Antibes to set sail for Civitavecchia. On October 26 Garibaldi was victorious against the papal forces at the village of Monteretondo, but a few days later, on November 3, he clashed with French troops at Mentana and suffered a defeat.

Italian bitterness over that defeat contributed to the breaking down of the Franco–Italian alliance. In 1870, after war had broken out between France and Germany, King Victor Emmanuel was prepared to send his Italian troops to fight side by side with his French ally of 1859, but his parliament refused to permit him to do so. Instead, when the French garrison had been withdrawn from Rome after the first defeats of the French army, Italian regular troops entered the Holy City. Pius IX was anxious to avoid bloodshed; he rejected, however, the formal agreement between Italy and France, known as the Law of Guarantees, which recognized the complete spiritual autonomy of the Pope and also assured him the status of a reigning monarch over a certain number of buildings in the city of Rome. He considered himself to be a prisoner in the Vatican.

At the end of the nineteenth century, after the colonial setbacks suffered by Italy in East Africa, a new expansionist movement began to develop. After World War I that movement increased enormously under the Fascists. It brought about a reversal in alliances and led to Italy's defeat in 1945 and to the monarchy's fall.   MAURICE VAUSSARD

The Emigrants

The resurrection of Italy has a dramatic quality that contemporaries thought unique in nineteenth-century nationalism. It fired the imagination and sympathy of men and women who lived hundreds of miles from the peninsula and who were never likely to see for themselves the silvery green of the olive trees or the trim silhouettes of the cypresses that lined Tuscany's roads. The shopkeepers, clerks and laborers who brought their families to Piccadilly to cheer Garibaldi on his London visit in 1864 were thrilled to be in the presence of a figure who personified the Romantic image to which they clung as an antidote to the drudgery of a regimented life. The calculations of Cavour and the moral reasoning of Mazzini meant nothing to them, and the concept of the term "Italy" itself meant little more. The spectators were content that, in an age of conformist pruriency, there should still be a soldier-hero who combined cavalier dash with simplicity of purpose.

In the urban areas of Europe and along the eastern seaboard of the United States there were many thousands for whom such rapturous excursions were no substitute for adventure. And in the European countryside there were thousands more who instinctively felt that only in new lands could they achieve material betterment. The stream of emigration from Britain reached a higher level in the 1850s than it had during any previous decade, and it flowed strongly from other Western European countries as well. Most settlers went to North America—a continent whose

A southwestern view of the rapidly growing town of San Francisco in 1850.

people were also on the move westward. In the United States the movement was a far more rapid one than it was in Canada, where Winnipeg was an outpost with only two hundred inhabitants as late as 1870. During the 1850s great numbers of English-speaking immigrants settled in California and the Australian colonies. In each case the prime attraction to adventurers was the quest for gold.

Gold !

The Californian gold rush began in December of 1848 when President Polk confirmed earlier tales of dust and nuggets in a message to Congress. By that time rumors had already caused frenzied excitement in the new trading post of San Francisco, and within a month of Polk's message more than sixty vessels crammed with fortune-seekers were on their way around Cape Horn. As soon as the winter snow line receded, thousands of wagons set off westward along the California Trail and the Old Spanish Trail from Santa Fe. Many died along the route from cholera (which they picked up at contaminated waterholes in the Great Plains) or from a mysterious "mountain fever" in the Rockies. Some were attacked by Indians and some perished from starvation

in the awesome desolation of the Sierra Nevada. Yet more than 80,000 people arrived at the ramshackle mining camps before the end of the year, and San Francisco became a city of 25,000 inhabitants (larger than Boston had been at the start of the century). Vigilante committees and lynch law—both common forms of frontier justice—proved to be ineffective means of maintaining law and order, and even the admission of California as the thirty-first state in 1850 failed to assure ordered government.

During the next ten years countless fortunes were made and lost in the roaring shanty towns of the Mother Lode. The discovery of silver in Nevada eventually tempted prospectors eastward to Mount Davidson, and soon after that gold was found in Colorado. From 1859 on, wealth came not to those with "a washbowl on my knee" but to the engineers who could afford expensive machinery. The true "miners' frontier," a crudely vigorous society of retributive democracy, was a phenomenon of the 1850s.

Many aspects of the American experience were repeated in Australia in August of 1851 when gold was discovered in a colony that had been officially created only six weeks previously (and named after Queen Victoria). Men rushed out from Melbourne so precipitately that the newly designated colonial capital was left with only a handful of officials and no more than two policemen to control the hordes of fortune-hunters who were flocking ashore from vessels in Port Phillip Bay.

Seven times as many immigrants arrived in Victoria in 1852 as in 1850, and the total population of Australia almost trebled in the course of the decade. An average of three ships a day sailed up the Yarra River to Melbourne in 1853 and, for a few months, real estate in the city was five times as expensive as in London. At Ballarat, Bendigo, Eaglehawk and Castlemaine prospectors found nuggets only a few inches below the surface of the

sandy soil. Drunkenness, gambling, theft and murder became commonplace in the mining camps and in the streets of Melbourne itself. But, as in California, the boom years of lawlessness lasted only as long as did the alluvial deposits. Mining companies that sank deep shafts and employed laborers at a fixed wage replaced the pick-and-shovel prospectors, and rough discipline eventually tamed the threat of social anarchy (although not in time to prevent an armed rebellion of German and Irish immigrants in

A gold digger at work in Colorado.

the gold fields at the end of 1854). Many of the later settlers went not to the "diggings" that had lured them across the globe but to farms where wool and wheat assured a less capricious income.

Australia transformed

The Victoria gold rush completed a transformation of the Australian scene that had begun in New South Wales in 1815 with the foundation of Bathurst, the first town in the interior. The fact that New South Wales had been established as a penal settlement gave the Australian colonies a bad name for many years. Convicts were transported to New South Wales from 1788 to November, 1840 (and, on a more liberal basis, from 1848 to 1851). They were also settled in Tasmania from 1803 to 1853. Although the free population outnumbered the convicts and "emancipists" (ex-convicts) as early as 1834, the existence of a criminal element in the population delayed political development.

The administrative authorities' distrust of their constituents was well illustrated by the fate of the original discoverer of gold at Ballarat. Because he had a criminal

Broadway, New York in the 1850s.

America and Australia

A view of Sydney harbor in 1860. Australia rapidly developed from a penal colony into a great nation.

record, it was assumed that he had stolen the gold, melted it down and put forward his claim in order to speculate on land prices. He was duly whipped for having made known his discovery, and it was only when a clergyman arrived back at Melbourne with a nugget that the authorities were willing to acknowledge that there really was gold along the inland rivers. And even then the colonial governor tried to keep the news secret for fear of its effect on the criminal underworld.

The governor's attitude was not shared by the enthusiasts of the National Colonization Society in London. Gibbon Wakefield, the most persuasive propagandist of Australasian emigration in Britain, declared that with the increase of settlers after the gold rush "a colony was precipitated into a nation."

Wakefield was right. The Australian Colonies Government Act, which permitted the colonies to draft constitutions and form legislatures on whatever franchise they wished, preceded the gold rush by a year, but it was the sudden tide of immigrants in the fifties that gave the Australian state councils a new sense of independence and authority. New South Wales adopted a constitution in November, 1855, and Victoria, South Australia and Tasmania soon followed its example. Queensland was established as a separate self-governing colony in 1859. Western Australia, although recognized as a colony in 1829, was considered to be too thinly populated for self-government until 1890. (At the request of its own settlers, it had continued to receive transported convicts from 1850 to 1867.)

But even after the adoption of self-government, there remained limitations imposed from London: British troops were stationed in the colonies until 1870, and proposals for a federation were rejected because it was felt that Australia was too large and varied in character to possess common interests. Federation was only achieved by the Australian Commonwealth Act of 1900.

The cities of Melbourne and Sydney had characters of their own by 1860. Each had a university, libraries, theaters, broad gaslit streets and fashionable suburban villas by the waterside. Their citizens had already shown a passion for sporting contests, and when the first cricket match between Victoria and New South Wales was arranged at Melbourne in 1856, the state legislature, with a nice sense of priorities, suspended its sittings until after the close of play.

By 1856 settlement had still touched only the fringe of a continent almost as large as Europe or the United States. The Outback was a challenge like the American frontier. Robert Burke and William Wills crossed Australia from south to north in 1861 (only to perish on the return journey), and John Stuart trekked from Adelaide to Darwin in 1862. Explorers had led the way; it was hoped that pioneers would follow. The immigrant ships sailed southward from Europe for another thirty years, but the returns were small compared with the North American prairies, and the Australian colonies never again experienced as rapid a change as they had in the golden fifties.

Colonizing an empire

There were, of course, other colonies in which the British people could satisfy an urge for new adventure. Fear of French ambitions in the South Pacific induced the British government to annex the islands of New Zealand in 1840. The Treaty of Waitangi (which solemnized the annexation) solemnly guaranteed the lands of the Maori chieftains in return for a formal cession of sovereignty. Sheep raising brought wealth to South Island in the 1850s, and the colony was granted responsible government as early as 1856. But wars with the Maoris hampered the development of North Island and discouraged immigration. The discovery of gold at Otago in 1861 and at Westland in 1865 led to a small-scale rush of miners and helped to push the number of settlers up to the quarter-million mark by 1870, but New Zealand never captured the imagination of emigrants as Australia had done.

In the early part of the century more British emigrants had gone to Canada than to any other colony. Some 50,000 settlers—mostly from Scotland and Ireland—crossed the Atlantic in the course of 1832, but a conflict between nominated legislative councils and popularly elected assemblies led to an armed rebellion in 1837, and the number of settlers declined for several years. In 1839, however, Lord Durham (who had served as Governor for six months in the previous year) published his famous *Report on the Affairs of British North America*. In it he courageously proposed the granting of responsible government to the Canadian provinces.

Durham's concept of empire was a revolutionary one, but its implementation in 1840 enabled the Canadians to boost their seaborne trade and avoid dependence upon the far stronger American states to the south. Federation—an essential preliminary to the opening up of the interior by a transcontinental railway—followed in 1867.

Neither the West Indies nor South Africa attracted many settlers during these years. The abolition of all sugar duties (by Russell's Free Trade government of 1846–52) was a severe blow to the West Indian planters, and the islands, which had been such a source of fortune in the previous century, offered no reward for the surplus working population of the home country. Cape Colony was also unpopular, partly because government-sponsored emigrants in the 1820s had found farming conditions difficult. The proud independence of the Boers—which led them to set out on the Great Trek of 1836–37 in order to find regions for settlement free from the restraints of British authority—did not make for unity, and the fighting qualities of the native Kaffirs hampered expansion northward. During the economic depression of 1841 more than 38,000 emigrants left Britain for Canada or Australasia; only 150 departed for Cape Colony.

There remained the mysterious appeal of India. The shadow of political authority still rested with the East India Company, but a succession of governors general had modernized the Indian states and prepared the way for Indians to assist in administering their homeland. The British ruling classes were prouder of the guardianship that they believed they were exercising in India than they were of the new colonial settlements. The events of 1857 were to shatter all their assumptions.

A Maori war dance: the Maoris accepted British sovereignty in 1840.

Mutiny in India

During the first half of the nineteenth century, the enormous British mercantile combine known as the East India Company forced a program of sweeping reforms upon the inhabitants of the Indian subcontinent. British insistence upon legal and social equality gravely threatened India's centuries-old caste system and stirred deep resentment among upper-class Moslems and Hindus alike. In May of 1857, that welling unrest resulted in a series of Bengal Army mutinies. Those risings were led by native troops (known as sepoys), who were primarily upper-caste Hindus—members of the class that was most threatened by British reforms. The rebellions were ultimately suppressed, but not before the stunned British had been forced to acknowledge that a kingdom won by the sword could be lost by the sword. Englishmen in all parts of the world began to reconsider the relevance of their reforming zeal.

Lord Lawrence, ruler of the Punjab during the Indian Mutiny, later Viceroy of India.

Opposite British troops storming the batteries at Badle-Serai.

The year 1857 began badly for the Bengal Army of the East India Company. There was trouble with the native troops, or sepoys, in February and again at the beginning of May. These disturbances were summarily dealt with, but on May 10, the sepoys quartered at the great cantonment of Meerut revolted, murdered their officers and headed for Delhi, home of the titular Emperor, Bahadur Shah. An octogenarian pensioner of the East India Company, Bahadur Shah was a bad poet and a mystic who believed that he could change himself into a gnat in order to visit faraway places incognito. Moreover, he was a descendant of the Moguls, and for two hundred years—from the middle of the sixteenth century to the middle of the eighteenth—the Moguls had dominated the land as well as the imagination of India. (The East India Company itself had sheltered its power in Northern India under a Mogul grant.) On May 12 the mutineers proclaimed the terrified Bahadur Shah Emperor of India. The mutiny had become a rebellion.

Fortunately for the British, the mutiny spread slowly. There was no concerted uprising; instead, garrisons mutinied at different times, some not until the revolt had almost been crushed. The sporadic nature of the mutiny gave the East India Company two advantages. First, trouble never spread beyond the Bengal Army. The Bombay and Madras armies stayed substantially loyal, and so did the forces that had recently been recruited in the Punjab. Second, except for the Bengal Army's home country, the Hindi-speaking area of the United Provinces and Central India, the Company was able to suppress the mutinies as they arose. In such key cities as Lahore, Peshawar, Karachi and Barrackpore, the sepoys were successfully disarmed.

The mutineers, however, captured Delhi in May. By the end of June Cawnpore had fallen, and the city's capitulation was followed by the infamous massacre of the entire British garrison there, including women and children. The siege of Lucknow began at the end of June. By the beginning of October, 1857, Delhi had been recaptured from the mutineers and thoroughly sacked, but the rebels controlled the entire Ganges Valley except for Bengal and a large part of Central India. Roughly 130,000 mutineers had been joined by several princes and great landlords. The princes were mostly dispossessed; often, as in the case of the most famous of them all, the Rani of Jhansi, they revolted under pressure from the mutineers rather than of their own free will. The landlords were heavily concentrated in Oudh, the eastern half of the United Provinces, where the mutiny had wide popular support.

October marked the high point of the mutineers' success. During the next nine months the British recaptured the rebel-held area bit by bit. In December, at the second Battle of Cawnpore, the East India Company won back much of the central United Provinces. The relief of Saugor in February restored a large part of Central India, and the recapture of Lucknow in March and of Azimgarh in April returned the eastern United Provinces to the Company's domination. When Jhansi fell in April and Bareilly in May, the Company's authority was restored in the western United Provinces as well.

The mutiny was substantially over. There was a last flare-up at Gwalior in June, 1858; after that, only the mopping-up of guerrillas remained. That, too, was finished by the end of 1858, though the last embers did not flicker out until the rebels' great leader, Tantia Topi, was executed in April, 1859.

The roots of the Sepoy Rebellion lay in the changes that had taken place in India during the preceding thirty years. In 1818, with the final defeat of the Mahrattas—Hindu warriors who had replaced the Moguls as the great power in India—the British had become the unquestioned lords of India. From the 1820s onward they had felt free to reform Indian society according to their own ideals, and at an ever-increasing pace.

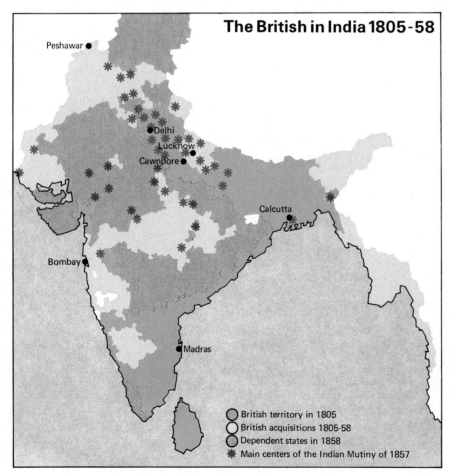

Indian cavalry attacking British infantry during the Mutiny.

The reforms were many. Perhaps the first that really alarmed the Indians who retained their original customs was the Charter of 1813, which allowed missionaries unrestricted entry. The missionaries lost no time in proselytizing, and their often unrestrained attacks on Hinduism and Islam caused widespread and increasing offense. They also established many schools and colleges, and they did much to introduce social reforms. Ram Mohan Roy indeed traveled all the way to Westminster to press for reforms, defying the old Hindu prohibition against crossing the black water.

Soon the far-reaching reforms began. Suttee (the burning alive of a widow with her husband's corpse), Thuggee (human sacrific to the Goddess Kali) and female infanticide were all banned. Hindu widows were allowed to remarry (child marriage and the high mortality rate produced many young widows condemned to a life of hardship). Hindu converts to Christianity were given the right to inherit family property.

The suspicion began to spread among Indians that the British intended to Christianize them. In the literal sense, this was untrue. Occasionally a government official or an army officer would prove to be a zealous evangelist; but for the most part the government was uninterested, even hostile toward such activities. From the early 1830s on, however, the British did begin the westernization of India. As Thomas Macaulay, the Whig historian who was for a time a member of the Indian Governor-General's Council, told the British House of Commons in 1833:

> We must do our best to form a class of persons Indian in Blood and colour, but English in taste, in opinions, in morals, and in intellect. . . . It may be that by good government we may educate our subjects into a capacity for better government . . . that they may, in some future age, demand European institutions. . . . Whenever it comes, it will be the proudest day in English history. To have found a great people sunk in the lowest depths of slavery and superstitions, to have so ruled them as to have made them desirous and capable of all the privileges of citizenship, would indeed be a title of glory all our own.

Macaulay's words were truly prophetic: those who rule India today are the heirs of his policy, but at the time his words were a threat to many educated Indians. The Persian and Sanskrit that had given them their position would no longer suffice for their sons. The power that they had been accustomed to would in future go to Englishmen and the *babus* (clerks) who knew English.

The British insistence on equality threatened the Indians even more severely. Individual British

The British in India 1805-58

Peshawar

Delhi
Lucknow
Cawnpore

Calcutta

Bombay

Madras

○ British territory in 1805
○ British acquisitions 1805-58
○ Dependent states in 1858
✳ Main centers of the Indian Mutiny of 1857

British justice—destroyer of traditional society

officials were frequently great respecters of rank and ancient lineage, but the British government did insist upon certain qualifications before a man could get a job. More significantly, British law made all men equal in the courts: a Brahmin could be hung as easily as an Untouchable, the testimony of an unbeliever was worth as much as that of a true believer (a Moslem), and the greatest feudal noble could be made a defendant—or even an accused—by the lowliest of his tenants. In the new railway trains an Untouchable could sit next to a Brahmin for the price of a ticket.

But it was Governor-General Dalhousie's policy of annexation, rather than the imposition of British law, that gave teeth to frustration. After Dalhousie arrived in 1848, he lost no time in extending the Company's empire. He annexed the Punjab beyond the Sutlej, took over the State of Oudh (whose kings had always been totally loyal to the Company), annexed princely states whose rulers died without natural heirs, and dispossessed thousands of semi-feudal landlords, especially in the Deccan and in Oudh, who could not show good title to their land. Dalhousie's motive was to protect the peasant. He saw the prince and the landlord as oppressors and the British official as a liberator—and he had plenty of evidence to support his view, especially in Oudh. In 1854 the British Governor in Lucknow, the capital of Oudh, reported on: "the vile life of the King, the misery of the unprotected cultivators, 78 of whose villages are plundered or burnt each year, the inhabitants tortured, slain or sold into slavery. In upholding the sovereign power of this effete, incapable dynasty, we do so at the cost of 5 million people."

Dalhousie vainly warned the King of Oudh. The King and his feudal nobles, the Talukdars, took no heed. In 1856, therefore, Dalhousie acted, informing the Court of Directors in London: "In humble reliance on the blessing of the Almighty (for millions of His creatures will draw happiness from the change), I approach the execution of this duty [the annexation of Oudh] gravely ... but calmly and altogether without doubt." Nor did Dalhousie act without realizing the possible consequences of his actions: "Insurrection may rise like an exhalation

from the earth, and cruel violence, worse than all the excesses of war, may be suddenly committed by men who to the very day on which they broke out in their frenzy of blood have been regarded as a harmless and timid race."

The British threat to the old society of India was particularly upsetting for the sepoys of the Bengal Army. They came, by and large, from Oudh, and they were frequently upper-caste Hindus or Moslems of good family. Dalhousie's reforms benefited their tenants and the poor and seemed to endanger the sepoys and their relatives. Further, a considerable number of them felt loyalty for the traditional royal house of Oudh, despite the weakness and debauchery of successive rulers. Many sepoys had

A rare contemporary photograph showing the damaged palace at Lucknow, where a small British garrison and some loyal sepoys held out until reinforcements arrived from Cawnpore.

An English family on the point of death. Many women and children were murdered during the Indian Mutiny.

Victoria—Empress of India

relatives among the courtiers—court retainers whom Dalhousie's annexation of Oudh had left jobless.

To those troubles were added more immediate problems in the Bengal Army itself. Pay was in arrears. Some British officers and noncommissioned officers (NCOs) displayed an intolerable racial arrogance toward their men. Many were ignorant of the feelings and even the religious beliefs of the sepoys—and it was that atmosphere that made the Affair of the Greased Cartridge so important.

In 1856 the Enfield rifle was introduced into India. It required a new cartridge that had to be bitten open before loading. Those cartridges were heavily greased. The rumor spread that the grease was made of pig and beef fat. But Moslems will not eat meat from pigs, and cows are sacred to Hindus. The rumor was therefore profoundly upsetting to the sepoys, whose position in their home villages would be destroyed if it were true. In truth, the grease was probably mutton fat, but the government was slow and hesitant about making the truth clear. The British Commander in Chief, for instance, took no action against an NCO of his own guard who taunted some junior NCOs with having lost caste from biting these cartridges. Once the mutiny had started, it was too late. As John Lawrence, himself later Viceroy, put it: "The misfortune of the present state of affairs is this—each step we take for our own security is a blow against the regular Sepoy. He feels this, and on his side takes a further step, and so we go on, until we disband or destroy them, or they mutiny and kill their officers."

Without the sepoys there would have been no mutiny. The motives of others outside the Bengal Army were mixed; they probably would not have taken the initiative to create a rebellion by themselves. The Nana Sahib himself, the villain of Cawnpore, the murderer of British women and children, was probably coerced by the mutineers into rebellion; he may not even have ordered the murders. The landlords of Oudh were moved by a mixture of patriotism, resentment over villages lost for lack of title, their loyalty to the deposed royal house and a general love of anarchy. The peasantry of Oudh followed their local nobles as they had always done. The Mogul princes snatched at a chance to restore the glory of their house.

It was all much too muddled and local. Above all,

it was too much an army mutiny to be called a war of independence. The men who took up arms against the British were not forerunners of Gandhi and Nehru who were striving for a free, united India. They were backward-looking members of a hierarchical society who were fighting for the privileges and the traditions that the reforms of the East India Company had begun to threaten. Yet so great was the gulf that the mutiny created between Indians and Britons in northern India that for two generations men like Nehru and Maulana Azad thought of it as a great national revolt against foreign rule.

The gulf between the races was caused by the very nature of the war. British officers had been murdered unawares; many thereafter found themselves totally unable to trust Indians. The artillery had been vital in intimidating and disarming mutinous regiments; the artillery thereafter was kept in British hands. The sepoys had been Brahmins and Moslems; for nearly fifty years the British in the north nurtured a suspicion of Brahmins and still more of Moslems. Indians had murdered British women and children; thereafter, in Northern India, the idea of Indian treachery lingered in many minds.

But the atrocities were not confined to one side. Colonel Neill and his men behaved little better than the Nana Sahib and his:

They [the British] were hunting down criminals of all kinds and hanging them up with as little compunction as though they had been pariah-dogs or jackals or vermin of a baser kind. . . . Volunteer hanging parties went out into the districts, and amateur executioners were not wanting to the occasion. One gentleman boasted of the number he had finished off quite "in an artistic manner," with mango-trees for gibbets and elephants for drops, the victims of this wild justice being strung up, as though for pastime, in the "form of a figure of eight."

And a British clergyman records having seen "a row of gallowses, on which the energetic colonel was hanging mutineer after mutineer. . . . On one occasion, some young boys, who perhaps in mere sport had flaunted the rebel colours and gone about beating tom-toms, were tried and sentenced to death."

Above all, the mutiny was a shocking reminder to the British that they had won India by the sword

The Marquess of Dalhousie, Governor-General of India during the Indian Mutiny.

Right A painting by an unknown Indian artist, thought to show Wajid Ali Shah embracing the Governor-General, Lord Hardinge, on his visit to Lucknow.

Illuminations at Peshawar celebrating the visit of Canning, the first Viceroy. As a result of the Mutiny India passed from the East India Company to the British Crown.

and could lose it by the sword. After the mutiny, even in the halcyon days of the 1880s and 1890s, British confidence in their own permanence was never complete. The suspicion always lingered that the great early administrators had been right, that British rule was only for a time, though perhaps for quite a long time.

The most disastrous result was social. Relationships between Indians and Englishmen had been intimate in the early days when Indians were potentates and Englishmen had Indian mistresses. They had weakened considerably in the generation before the mutiny. In Northern India they weakened further in the half century after. Clubs were often for white men only, and British social life went on largely within the British community. The Briton knew his soldiers or the peasants of his district or his policemen. He talked to his servants and his clerks, and he chatted with the great men of the district when they came to call or to ask a favor. But rarely again in Northern India did Britons relax in Indian company to the extent that they had at one time when the officers of Cawnpore had played billiards with the Nana Sahib.

The mutiny had more material consequences too. The first was the abolition of the East India Company in August, 1858, followed on November 1 by Queen Victoria's proclamation announcing the transfer of India's affairs to the Crown and offering a full amnesty to her Indian subjects. The Bengal Army was disbanded and the native contingent in the Indian Army was reduced. Moreover, the British contingent was raised in such a manner as to bring the premutiny ratio of one Briton to six Indians up to one Briton to two Indians. Indians were also debarred from the artillery.

There were rewards for those who had remained loyal and punishments for those who had revolted. The new regiments that had been raised in the Punjab were retained, and landlords who had helped refugees were given extra villages. The Sikhs, who had swarmed to the British colors, were favored; the Moslems of the United Provinces were suspect for a generation. Bengal, Bombay, Madras, the Punjab progressed socially and economically; the Hindi-speaking areas, the mainspring of the revolt, remained backward.

For the British, the mutiny was a lesson on the dangers of reforming zeal. The new government of the Queen showed none of the radicalism of Lord Dalhousie. Adopted heirs were recognized; annexation of princely states was terminated, and the British Viceroy was very slow to interfere even with the most grievous misgovernment. The Talukdars of Oudh were guaranteed their rights, and religion was left untouched. (Untouchability went on, and child marriage was not stopped until Indian opinion itself demanded legislation). The British government enforced law and order, built railways and public works and defended the frontiers. It no longer tried to change Indian society, except by the slow and indirect method of Western-style education, and there were some who criticized even that.

Such caution meant that when the demand for social reform did arise in India, the leaders of it more and more joined the parties that were asking for self-government. Yet they were all men whose minds had been formed by British-style education. The true victory of the British over the mutiny was that the leaders of the independence movement that followed were nearly all reformers. Not one was descended from a rebel of 1857.　TAYA ZINKIN

Mutineers suprised by the 9th Lancers. A drawing from the book *Campaign in India 1857–58* which was dedicated to Queen Victoria.

The Victorian Novel

The excesses of the Indian mutiny shocked English society. They disturbed the calm complacency of mid-Victorian London and temporarily discredited the patronizing assumption that British sovereignty universally bestowed beneficent rule. There was a startling contrast between the news from India and the sedate tone of government in Westminster. Only a few months earlier members of the House of Commons had fulminated against commanding officers who permitted regimental bands to give concerts in the Royal Parks on Sunday afternoon. Then, in November, 1857, those members read in their newspapers how the women and children in Lucknow had caught the distant sound of marching drums and had realized that relief was at hand; *that* regimental band had also been playing on a Sunday. The Queen herself wrote of "the horrors of shame and every outrage" of Cawnpore, although she felt that detailed accounts of the tragedy should have been suppressed to spare the victims' relatives the pain of knowledge.

There was indeed a difference between the reports from Delhi and the normal reading matter of the English middle classes. The year of the mutiny—1857—saw the publication of Trollope's *Barchester Towers*, Borrow's *Romany Rye*

and Dinah Mulock's *John Halifax, Gentleman*. The younger generation could be excited by Ballantyne's *Coral Island* or uplifted by the didactic morality of Hughes' *Tom Brown's Schooldays*. Readers who preferred their fiction in monthly installments (and there were, at this time, many thousands of serialized novels being published in Britain and the United States) had a chance to finish *Little Dorrit* by Dickens, to begin *The Virginians* by Thackeray, and to complete *Scenes of Clerical Life* by a highly praised new novelist who called herself George Eliot. Tennyson, Poet Laureate since 1850, was tuning his muse to Arthurian legend and was momentarily less in favor than Matthew Arnold, who had been elected Professor of Poetry at Oxford. John Ruskin, who had surprised his readers in 1856 by ending Volume III of *Modern Painters* with a digression on the Crimean War, was puzzling earnest listeners in Manchester with lectures on "The Political Economy of Art."

The cultural taste of the decade was certainly eclectic, although perhaps a little amateur in its enthusiasm and disapprobation. It was also strangely homemade. At both the beginning and end of the century, the English mind was open to easy dominance by Continental ideas, but in the second half of the fifties it was almost as insular as Lord Palmerston, the Prime Minister. Frith caught the glorious vulgarity of Derby Day on canvas, and Landseer, still the

favorite artist of the Queen and her subjects, brought his admirably Anglicized lions to the foot of Lord Nelson's column in Trafalgar Square. Even the medieval escapism of the pre-Raphaelite brother-

John Ruskin, most influential of Victorian art critics.

hood was essentially English in character and detail, for all its exploitation of early Indian art. Only architecture—from the mock-Renaissance edifices in Pall Mall to the Flemish Gothic façade of St. Pancras Station—continued year after year to be foreign in inspiration.

Enter the tourist

During the fifties and sixties the middle classes for the first time began to afford foreign travel. In 1855, Thomas Cook—who had been organizing railway excursions from Leicester for ten years—had the enterprise to arrange a special trip to Paris. Soon Cook's Tours were conveying English visitors to Switzerland and Italy as well as France. Leisure travel became an industry before 1870 and grew rapidly in the following two decades, especially after the introduction of sleeping cars—an American innovation—in 1873.

The English were the most numerous and determined of foreign tourists (although Germans, complete with the loftily patronizing guidebooks of Herr Baedeker, flocked to Venice, Florence and Paris). It is probable that travel of this nature merely confirmed established national prejudice, but it did at least represent a change in social habit.

In general, the French saw no need to leave their native land unless, like Victor Hugo, their political conscience forced them into exile. As in earlier centuries,

a small number of French critics did travel, and their astringent comments on neighboring countries have rare value. Hippolyte Taine, for example, was in England in 1861–62; and although his conclusion that Englishwomen had long teeth because they persisted in eating too much meat and long feet because they tramped for miles across rain-sodden fields may have lacked generosity, his observation of the social distinctions separating the propertied classes from the laborers helped to explain why Karl Marx found London such an ideal center for studying capitalism.

Taine's London

Taine noted the five miles of prosperous houses that covered the hills of south London; the iron resolution of the businessmen with perpendicular black hats and rolled umbrellas who arrived each morning at the railway termini; and the massive Italianate squares of London's West End. He contrasted this repository of wealth with squalid alleys "in the shade of the monumental streets," where "pale

The first advertisement for Cook's Tours —the beginning of organized tourism.

children nestled on mud-stained stairs." And he noted the mean rows of gray houses in the liquid fog of "dockland," an area as large as many Continental cities where the "submerged tenth" of the population hid their lives in despairing shame.

No doubt Taine exaggerated: working-class districts were as much a part of the Industrial Age as the steam engine, and brutality and degradation in the Parisian

Queen Victoria and the Prince Consort typified Victorian taste.

Hippolyte Taine, the first writer to examine the structure of London society.

slums were every bit as bad as that in London's (as Zola's sociological novels record). The mortality rate was actually higher in the poorer parts of Berlin than in similar areas of London, Birmingham or Liverpool. The extraordinary feature of mid-Victorian London was the size of each stratum of society. The commercial aristocracy could be numbered in thousands, rather than in hundreds (as it was in New York, Baltimore and Boston during America's Gilded Age), and by 1861 the chronically poor in London were reckoned at a quarter of a million.

Until the last quarter of the century, there was a lamentable failure to provide an adequate water supply for London or to institute proper drainage. Consequently, the stench from the Thames became so bad by the summer of 1858 that the House of Commons was almost uninhabitable. England, like most of Western Europe, had been ravaged by an epidemic of cholera in 1831–33,

but it was not until the disease returned on a large scale in 1865–1866 that a royal commission was established to discover "the requirements necessary for civilized social life." (Parliament accepted responsibility for educating the local authorities in public health during the next decade.) Yet, paradoxically, the Victorians always stressed the need for tidiness and cleanliness. In one of his lighter moments, the great Prussian historian, Heinrich von Treitschke, declared: "The English think Soap is Civilization." And there was justice in his dictum, for Victorian cleanliness—like the godliness that it proverbially stood next to—was a visible sign of an inner respectability.

Religion revived

Religious speculation was still the greatest intellectual exercise during the 1850s. This was true not only of Victorian England but also of Europe in general. Even Mazzini, who was regarded by the Catholic Church as a "red revolutionary," claimed to be acting in the name of "God and the People," and his personal manifesto, *The Duties of Man* (published in 1860), listed service to God alongside service to the family and the nation as obligations of the good citizen. Similarly, Auguste Comte, the Frenchman who founded Positivism, stated that it was impossible to transform philosophy into a worship of humanity without incorporating a mystical element and compiling a Positivist catechism to ensure an ordered scheme of life.

The Roman Catholic Church was less willing than its opponents to compromise, and from 1854 to 1870 Pope Pius IX endeavored to counter what he regarded as irreligious tendencies by resolute pronouncements of dogma. In 1854 the Pope proclaimed the dogma of the Immaculate Conception of the Virgin Mary, and ten years later his *Syllabus of Errors* condemned the fashionable ideas of science and the liberalism that the French priest, Lamennais, had urged the Church to accept as early as 1830. This new ultramontanism posed questions of conscience for sincere believers in many lands, and throughout the late fifties and sixties the air was heavy with ponderous theological debate.

In England the principal storm over religious matters and dogma

broke in the early forties (although it continued as a ground swell for almost half a century after that date). At the end of the Napoleonic Wars the Church of England accepted its privileged position as part of the established state without excessive exertion of the mind or undue concern for its pastoral obligations. The religious pacemakers in the new industrial towns were either Wesleyan dissenters or representatives of the evangelical minority within the Established Church, and it was from this group that such conscientious public servants as William Wilberforce and Lord Shaftesbury emerged.

In the 1830s a movement developed at the University of Oxford that sought to make the Church of England more self-consciously aware of its pre-Reformation heritage and less dependent on its explicitly Protestant tradition. The Oxford Movement was led by John Keble, John Henry Newman and Edward Pusey, all of whom

Sir Charles Lyell, the geologist who challenged the chronological assumptions of the Old Testament.

believed in reviving liturgical ceremonial (long ignored in the Church of England) and in establishing settlements in working-class districts (where the Church could bring both consolation and color into a drab existence).

The Oxford Movement aroused intense opposition from conservatively minded Protestants (who were ever-vigilant against popery), and it was this hostility which drove many Tractarians—as Newman's supporters were called—into the Roman Catholic Church. Newman himself was received into the Church of Rome in 1845 (and was created a Cardinal in 1879), but Keble and Pusey never seceded from the Church of England. Many

of the greatest minds in the country were focused on the Tractarian dispute: Gladstone, for example, wrote twice as many books and articles on religious topics between 1838 and 1858 as he did on political matters. In the early days of the Oxford Movement, Lord Melbourne complained: "Things have come to a pretty pass when religion is allowed to invade the sphere of private life." That point of view had become totally out of date by the late 1850s.

The machine age

Side by side with this revival of interest in religion there went a new spirit of scientific inquiry. Michael Faraday made possible the harnessing of electrical energy by his formulation of the principles of electromagnetic induction in 1831 and his discovery of diamagnetism in 1845. James Joule informed the British Association in 1843 that he had established the primary facts of the conservation of energy and had formulated the first law of thermodynamics. Eight years later William Thomson advanced the second law of thermodynamics (on which most developments in physical chemistry and engineering have subsequently been based).

Nor was such scientific progress limited to Britain. The work of a German, Hermann von Helmholtz, complemented the research of Joule and Thomson, and Volta, Ampère and Ohm were as much fathers of electricity as Faraday. Indeed, Italian, French and German scientists were no less interested in the spread of physical knowledge than the British.

Other disciplines were also coming under scrutiny. The geological studies of Sir Charles Lyell challenged the chronological assumptions of the Old Testament, and Mathias Schleiden's cell theory of living organisms, formulated in 1838, revolutionized the field of biology. As yet, however, the British public had taken little notice of these developments in science. Lyell, who was a polite pillar of society, advanced his theories with an air of apology, and Joule's address to the British Association was hardly reported. By the time the British Association met at Oxford in 1861, all that had changed, for in 1859 Darwin had published *The Origin of Species*. Science stood confidently arraigned at the bar of public opinion.

Ape or Angel?

The "most dangerous man in England"—at least in the year 1859—was a gentle and retiring invalid named Charles Darwin. The middle-aged naturalist earned that epithet with the publication of a single volume of scientific speculation, The Origin of Species. That work, which was based on data collected over a period of many years, suggested that "natural selection," rather than God's Will, dictated which species survived and flourished, and which became extinct. Most significantly of all, Darwin's treatise implied that man himself was subject to the same laws of necessary adaptation—what Darwin called "survival of the fittest"—which affected the finches that the biologist had observed in the Galapagos archipelago in the 1830s. In denying Genesis and advocating evolution, Darwin sparked a heated debate among world scholars. Many rejected Darwin's "monkey theory," but ultimately none could refute it.

Charles Darwin's diary for late July and early August, 1858, contains the laconic entry: "Began abstract of species book." Like everything about Darwin except the sweep of his scientific imagination, that casual note was unpretentious and matter-of-fact. One could scarcely have guessed—indeed, Darwin himself did not yet know—that after twenty years of patient preparation he had begun work on a book that was permanently to revolutionize men's attitude toward the natural world as perhaps no other work had ever done. For the book to which Darwin referred was *On the Origin of Species by Means of Natural Selection, or the Preservation of Favoured Races in the Struggle for Life,* a colossal milestone in the history of man's understanding of nature. Its publication was to earn Darwin both enduring fame and temporary vilification as "the most dangerous man in England."

There could hardly have been a less likely person for such denunciation than Darwin, who was a gentle invalid with the tastes of an English country gentleman and a devoted husband and father who impressed his acquaintances with his almost child-like simplicity and goodness. Certainly no such suspicion can have crossed the minds of the other middle-class guests at the King's Head Hotel on the Isle of Wight, where Darwin and his family were staying when he began the book that was ultimately to win its author a resting place alongside Sir Isaac Newton in Westminster Abbey. Yet "Darwinism" was subsequently to become virtually synonymous with militant atheism, callousness and aggression.

All but a very few of Darwin's scientific colleagues would have been astonished to discover that the modest, rather inarticulate, somewhat plodding naturalist was the greatest scientific genius of their century—and the greatest English scientist since Newton. Darwin was known as the author of an entertaining and informative scientific travel journal, *The Voyage of the Beagle,* as an able geologist with a touch of originality, and as an unrivaled authority on barnacles (which he had spent eight years studying). Only a chosen few knew that the patient, laborious, genuinely humble man of science was, in scientific terms, a revolutionary—and was so, moreover, in an area that touched the tenderest religious and moral feelings of the Victorian world, the question of the origin of species.

More accurately, only a few had known of Darwin's genius prior to July, 1858. And the rest might never have known, but for an event that occurred on June 18 of that year—an event that was to force Darwin out of his long secretiveness. On that date Darwin received a paper from a young naturalist in the East Indies, Alfred Russel Wallace, that showed that Wallace had hit independently on the key idea of Darwin's own work. Horrified at the prospect of a squalid controversy over precedence, Darwin called in leading men of science to arbitrate—and Wallace's paper was read (together with one Darwin had written in 1844) to a meeting of the Linnean Society in London on July 1. Darwin had declared himself at last.

Curiously, the papers written by Darwin and Wallace produced little stir in the sceptical atmosphere of a learned society. Speculation on the origin of species was not uncommon; the question was whether Darwin's theory would prove the key to the problem. Darwin's supporting evidence, accumulated during years of research, was the basis for the "species book" that he began to write in late July of 1858 while his family enjoyed their South Coast holiday.

On April 5, 1859, Darwin sent the first three chapters of that book to his publisher, John Murray. Murray was somewhat doubtful. What would "natural selection" mean to the public? Why was the book called an "abstract"? Would it sell? One of his advisers suggested that Darwin publish only the part of the work that dealt with pigeons and include a brief statement of his theory with it. Modest though he was, Darwin fortunately objected

ON

THE ORIGIN OF SPECIES

BY MEANS OF NATURAL SELECTION,

OR THE

PRESERVATION OF FAVOURED RACES IN THE STRUGGLE
FOR LIFE.

By CHARLES DARWIN, M.A.,
FELLOW OF THE ROYAL, GEOLOGICAL, LINNÆAN, ETC., SOCIETIES;
AUTHOR OF 'JOURNAL OF RESEARCHES DURING H. M. S. BEAGLE'S VOYAGE
ROUND THE WORLD.'

LONDON:
JOHN MURRAY, ALBEMARLE STREET.
1859.

The title page of the first edition of *On the Origin of Species*

Opposite Charles Darwin "the most dangerous man in England."

The voyage of the Beagle

Erasmus Darwin, grandfather of Charles Darwin, and precursor of much of his thinking.

Right Down House, Kent, where Darwin lived for many years.

Canon Charles Kingsley, Regius Professor of History at Cambridge. He was one of Darwin's earliest supporters.

to the proposal. Murray's doubts about whether the book would sell proved unfounded. He printed 1,250 copies, and published the book in November 1859. A second edition was called for immediately.

Years earlier, when he had first revealed his secret to his friend, the botanist Joseph Hooker, Darwin had written that his admitting to a belief in evolution, or "transmutation" as it was then called, was "like confessing a murder." The immediate reaction to *The Origin of Species* showed that Darwin's apprehensions were well founded. The book raised a storm of controversy from which Darwin held aloof as far as he could. He had tried, he said, to ensure that his book was "not more *un*-orthodox than the subject makes inevitable. I do not bring in any discussion about Genesis," he added, but his disclaimer was in vain. Darwin's theory was passionately denounced by orthodox believers. A distinguished scientist to whom Darwin had sent a copy of the book wrote back that he had found it "grievously mischievous" and that it had greatly shocked his moral sense. One journal observed that the book was "subversive of the foundation of both religion and morality."

The subversiveness of the book did not lie simply—or even mainly—in the fact that it contradicted the literal word of the book of Genesis, although there were some to whom that fact alone was affront enough. Orthodox, educated opinion had recently learned to interpret at least some of the Bible's statements about the creation in a figurative way. The science of geology, for example, had

revealed that the formation of the earth's crust was a matter of millions of years rather than six days. "Days" had subsequently been interpreted as symbolizing epochs of enormous duration. It is even possible that the idea of evolution as a scientific interpretation of God's command to "let the earth bring forth the living creature after his kind, cattle and creeping things and beasts of the earth," might have been accepted without too much anguish. The crucial row arose over a creature who was not discussed at all in *The Origin of Species*, (although Darwin was to do him full justice in later works): that creature was man.

The new geology had not yet ventured any observations about man. The earth itself might be unimaginably old, and the evidence locked in the earth might suggest that whole species had arisen and then become extinct. But man was still taken to be a creature whose story spanned only some six thousand years. Adam was a still plausible ancestor for such a species, and knowledge of man's early history was still based largely on the Old Testament. To see mankind as a product of evolution from lower animal and amphibian species—as cousin to the apes and descended from them—seemed a shocking debasement of human nature. *That* concept was what made "Darwinism" subversive. Critics called Darwinism "the monkey theory," a low, materialistic doctrine which asserted that "there is no God, and the ape is our Adam."

Darwin's theory soon won distinguished converts among leading scientists who were impressed by the ingenuity of his arguments and the sheer weight of the evidence that supported them. However, not even Darwin's closest friends were easily won over. The belief that each species was fixed for all time, exactly as it had issued from the hands of God (if not on the sixth day of the Creation, at least at some distinct point in time), was still the orthodox belief in 1859, not only among the laity but also in the scientific community. That belief had occasionally been challenged, it is true. In 1844, for example, a

John Murray, the publisher of the *Origin of Species*. He thought Darwin's theory was "as absurd as ... a fruitful union between a poker and a rabbit."

book called *The Vestiges of Creation* had caused a sensation when it was published anonymously by the Scottish publisher Robert Chambers. Like many such "challenges," *Vestiges* was scientifically disreputable, and it served to discredit rather than further the concept of evolution.

Darwin could sympathize with the attitude of those who doubted evolution on scientific grounds (he too regarded *Vestiges* as rubbish). He had come to the idea of evolution—against the weight of scientific opinion and against his own earlier acceptance of the "fixity" of species—with some difficulty, and his acceptance of that radical view had come only after a voyage around the world. Darwin's interest in evolution had first been aroused in the late 1830s while he was traveling around South America as ship's naturalist aboard the naval survey ship H.M.S. *Beagle*. He had been struck then by the close resemblances between species in the same area and by their similarity to extinct species of the area, which suggested that they had come from a common stock and had become distinct species only in the course of time and as they spread outward. Why should species be so distributed if each were the result of a unique, divine creation?

Darwin did not invent the doctrine of evolution. The idea had been considered by the ancient Greeks, and it had been toyed with by the thinkers of the eighteenth-century Enlightenment. It was only in the nineteenth century, however, that men's understanding of the fossil record of the successive forms of life became adequate to support a theory of evolution, just as it was only in the nineteenth century that the new, drastically revised estimates of the age of the earth allowed sufficient time for biological evolution. It would have been utterly incredible to suppose that life had developed its complex and varied forms in a mere six thousand

Darwin and his Precursors

1721
Charles de Montesquieu conceives of the possibility of change in species

1753
Denis Diderot sees possibility of common ancestor for all living bodies

1760
Carl Linnaeus doubts the unchangeability of organisms

1785
James Hutton attacks traditional Biblical chronology and the idea of a universal flood

1794
Erasmus Darwin propounds an early theory of evolution

1809
Jean Baptiste de Lamarck helps make evolutionary ideas respectable

1817
William Smith's *Stratigraphical System of Organized Fossils* throws doubts on the Biblical concept of creation

1830
Sir Charles Lyell's *Principles of Geology* opposes ideas of catastrophe in pre-history

1844
Robert Chambers in his anonymous *Vestiges of the Natural History of Creation* advocates a crude — and unpopular — theory of evolution

1858
Darwin and Wallace publish short articles on evolution and natural selection

1859
Publication of *The Origin of Species by means of Natural Selection*

Man, the heir of the apes

Thomas Malthus, whose theories on economics helped Darwin arrive at his theory of evolution.

years (the long-accepted estimate of the earth's duration). Moreover, the fact that much of that six-thousand-year period was recorded history and contained no historical record of dramatic biological transformations added to its implausibility.

More significantly, the idea of evolution was congenial to the belief in progress so characteristic of the period. It also appealed to many people because it seemed more truly scientific than the theory of special creations. Ever since the seventeenth century, physicists and chemists had refused to concede that God's intervention was a direct cause of physical occurrences, but biologists were still obliged, in explaining the origin of living species, to speak, as Darwin said, as though "elemental atoms have been commanded suddenly to flash into living tissues." If it could be established that the species had emerged gradually, in accordance with the operation of a natural law of organic development, then biology too could dispense with the need to invoke sudden and incalculable Divine Intervention to explain its subject matter.

But what law of development could explain evolution? The inadequacy of pre-Darwinian explanations was largely responsible for the scepticism about evolution that was felt by scientists, and that theoretic shortcoming was coupled with the fact that the fossil record of the earth's history was too fragmentary to prove whether life had developed from the simplest beginnings through successively more complex forms. Evolutionist doctrines had been reduced to the level of sheer guesswork. The noted nineteenth-century evolutionist and zoologist J.B. de Lamarck had held that creatures acquired new organs to satisfy new needs and then passed these modifications on to their offspring in the next generation. There was no evidence for Lamarck's speculation, and Darwin himself held that the Frenchman's theory was nonsense.

Like virtually all nineteenth-century biologists,

The *Beagle*, on which Darwin made an important voyage, to South America.

Darwin did believe that attributes acquired in an animal's lifetime could be passed on to the next generation—a belief no longer accepted by scientists. He did not subscribe to several of the less appealing contemporary explanations of evolution (among them Chambers' belief that a whole new species could arise from a single monstrous birth). After a superficial reading of Darwin's work his publisher, John Murray, seems to have thought that *The Origin of Species* was a reworking of Chambers' *Vestiges*, for he declared that Darwin's theory was "as absurd as though one should contemplate a fruitful union between a poker and a rabbit."

A plausible explanation of evolution was one of Darwin's two great achievements; the other was the almost infinite pains and the very remarkable success with which he anticipated objections to his theory and vindicated it through numerous references to a vast compendium of natural observations. He thus set evolutionary theory on a completely new path. From this point on, testable theory replaced wild guesswork in accounting for the variety of living things.

In his autobiography Darwin declared that he owed his discovery of the mechanism of evolution to the economist Thomas Malthus, whose work he read shortly after his return from the voyage of the *Beagle*. At the time his mind was full of the puzzling evidence for evolution he had encountered in South America. Malthus had pointed to the discrepancy between the capacity of populations to expand and their limited food supply; Darwin applied Malthus' theory to the problem of species that so preoccupied him. Populations were kept down by restrictions on their food supply. But which elements in the population survived and left offspring? In a natural state, those best adapted to their environment survived, Darwin answered. That was the law of "natural selection." It led to the formation of new species through the commonly

observed and apparently random variations that occurred in offspring. *Some* of these variations conferred an advantage on their possessors; those fortunate few had been "selected" by nature for survival and perpetuation just as a dog breeder selects the variations he wishes to encourage. Darwin wrote: "Owing to this struggle for life, any variation, however slight, if it be in any degree profitable to an individual of any species, in its infinitely complex relations to other organic beings and to external nature, will tend to the preservation of that individual, and will generally be inherited by its offspring."

The concept of natural selection was Darwin's greatest contribution to evolutionary theory, but it was also the point at which Darwin's theory most rudely shattered traditional notions of God and nature. Evolution would have been a less revolutionary doctrine had it merely asserted a development of living forms, in the general direction of greater complexity and specialization, while accounting for this development in terms of an overall

cosmic purpose. Darwin, however, would have none of such purposeful evolution. "Never use the words higher and lower," he wrote in the margin of his copy of *The Vestiges of Creation*. Nature was not purposeful. So far as science could tell, man was not the result of some long-prepared cosmic plan. Natural selection was simply the result of scarcity working upon blind chance—the occurrence of chance variations in offspring. It would select *anything* if it was better adapted to the environment than its competitors. Within the realm of Darwinian theory, science and emotion were obliged to part company; man's sense of purpose could not be projected into nature, and man himself appeared to be the random product of a blindly struggling nature.

Theologians quickly came to terms with the Darwinian world. Charles Kingsley, a novelist and theologian who was one of the earliest to accept Darwin's theory, wrote to him: "I have gradually learnt to see that it is just as noble a conception of the Deity to believe that He created primal forms capable of self-development as to believe that He required a fresh intervention to fill the [voids] which He himself had made." Humanists like Sir Julian Huxley, himself the grandson of Darwin's great champion T. H. Huxley, have found excitement in the idea that in man evolution has produced, albeit blindly, a creature capable of purposive control of his environment and of his destiny as a species. Nevertheless, it seems unlikely that anyone now can ever feel quite the same sense of community with the natural world as when nature's ends were thought of as divinely attuned to those of men, and Adam, quickened into life by the finger of God Himself, was little more than a great-grandfather. Twentieth-century thought, and doctrines like existentialism and logical positivism, presuppose the purposelessness of the physical world to an extent that would have been almost unthinkable in the early nineteenth century.

Some, it is true, have found positive inspiration in the idea of a struggle for existence. To some war became "a biological necessity"; the law of competition in business was "the survival of the fittest." Marx announced that *The Origin of Species* provided "a basis in natural science for the class-struggle in history," and Darwinian ideas formed an integral part of Hitler's doctrine of racial superiority. Such uses of Darwinism have diminished in recent years, for the problems of human society are too complex and their solution too much a matter of human preference to be resolved by a simple formula like the survival of the fittest. Societies themselves do whatever selecting is done on grounds quite different from nature's.

One subsequent development in which Darwin would undoubtedly have rejoiced has been the development of the science of genetics. To Darwin the causes of the mutations on which his theory rested remained a mystery. Genetics has now begun to penetrate the mystery, and modern biology rests equally on Mendelian genetics and Darwinian evolution by natural selection.   J. W. BURROW

Left above A. R. Wallace, whose ideas on evolution evolved along lines similar to Darwin's. In 1858 he and Darwin published joint articles on natural selection.

Left below A cartoon entitled *The Lion of the Season* published in *Punch* during the controversy that followed the publication of Darwin's book. The alarmed flunkey exclaims "Mr. G-g-g-o-o-o-rilla" as the guest enters.

Below Samuel Wilberforce, Bishop of Oxford, and T. H. Huxley (*bottom*), one of Darwin's most vociferous supporters. Wilberforce's attacks on Darwinism and his vicious controversy with Huxley at the British Association meeting in 1860 rallied many Church people against evolutionary ideas.

Apes or angels?

In November, 1864, Benjamin Disraeli, one of the most gifted British parliamentary debaters, summarized the Darwinian controversy in a speech at Oxford. "Is Man an ape or an angel?" he asked, adding, "I, my lord, am on the side of the angels." So, indeed, were most men and women in the Western world. Popular pride in progress and achievement rejected "new-fangled theories" that traced descent from the primitive anthropoids. Familiar concepts of Divine Revelation had a comforting reassurance that made belief in evolution appear not merely blasphemous but amoral. The possibility of reconciling Genesis and genetics overtaxed conventional minds.

But Darwinism could not be dismissed in a slick Disraelian phrase. It provided a powerful reinforcement for thinkers who were already seeking to explain

Herbert Spencer, the greatest exponent of Darwinism as a social philosophy.

natural phenomena in materialistic terms. Historical analysts and social theorists had sought tentative scientific rules of causation for many years, and they were delighted when Darwin was able to show that a synthesis of inquiry could produce an intellectually satisfactory means of speculation. It is hardly surprising that Karl Marx offered to dedicate *Das Kapital* to Darwin in admiration for his

researches on the morphology of science (an honor that Darwin hastily, but politely, declined), for Marx believed—with some justice—that he was doing for the new discipline of sociology what Darwin had done for biology.

The principle of evolution was gradually extended to other spheres. Darwin's cousin, Sir Francis Galton, applied it to psychological analysis of the relationship between heredity and ability in 1869; Sir Edward Tylor applied it to anthropology in 1871; and Walter Bagehot extended it to the growth of political institutions and customs in 1873. The greatest exponent of Darwinism as a social philosophy was Herbert Spencer, whose *Programme of a System of Synthetic Philosophy* was published in 1860 when its author was forty years old. In the United States, Spencer's impact on educational thought was more direct than Darwin's, whose theories continued to arouse virulent hostility in the Bible Belt areas until the twentieth century. Between them, Darwin and Spencer dominated late Victorian thought as completely as Bacon and Descartes had dominated that of the late sixteenth and seventeenth centuries.

Yet if the scientific age had found its prophet in Darwin, it was to gain its most revered figures from the field of medicine. Joseph Lister, Louis Pasteur and Robert Koch advanced the study of antiseptics and the isolation and identification of dangerous viruses in the last third of the century. During that same period the science of bacteriology and the introduction of preventive inoculation grew out of the work that Louis Pasteur was doing in Paris.

Public education comes of age

Herbert Spencer—who was considerably more optimistic than many of his contemporaries—believed in the ultimate inevitability of human perfection, and yet he saw the good life as attainable only through technological improvement. He therefore urged that science, rather than classical studies, form the basis of education. His theories were ahead of their time in England, where "public schools"—those exclusive institutions where "muscular Christians" imparted the grace of Homer and the wisdom of Cicero to the future rulers of the British Empire with

Louis Pasteur, who made great contributions to bacteriological science.

numerous strokes of the birch—were reaching their zenith in the 1860s.

Secondary education in Germany and France, on the other hand, was already coming to terms with the new applied sciences, and American academies had always offered a broader curriculum than the English public schools. There were some six thousand academies—almost all of them private institutions controlled by boards of trustees—in the United States on the eve of the Civil War, and the comprehensive educational tradition of Jefferson and Benjamin Franklin still survived in the more prosperous communities of the rapidly expanding American nation.

Steel and steam

Many of the inventions of the earlier part of the century had come not from the brains of distinguished scientists but from the practical application of natural ingenuity by mechanics and artisans. After 1850, however, technical progress was more complex and necessarily more interrelated. The spread of railways across continents required cooperation between men who could build tunnels and bridges, carry telegraphic signaling along the track and understand the stresses and strains of the new processes in making steel. Similarly, the application of the dynamo to generate electricity depended on adapting the researches of the physicist to the mass demands of the factory system.

The second stage of the Industrial Revolution was less dramatic in its immediate impact and more specialized than the first stage had been, but its effects were even more far-reaching. The globe itself was encompassed by science, and the successful laying of the cable for an electric telegraph under the Atlantic in 1866 marked the dawn of a new age in communications.

It would be a mistake to antedate the triumphs of steel and steam, however. British shipyards built more vessels in the 1860s and 1870s than ever before, outstripping all the other European powers combined. But although a few steel ships were launched in the sixties, most vessels were made of iron until the middle of the eighties because it was so much cheaper. Many ships of the period were composites of wood resting on an iron frame (the famous *Cutty Sark* was constructed in this way in 1869). The earliest British steamship lines (the Peninsular and Orient and the Cunard companies) had begun their services in 1839 and 1840 respectively. But it was not until 1883 that the tonnage of British steamships registered at Lloyds was greater than the tonnage of British sailing ships. Significantly, that change coincided with the Cunard Line's introduction of the first all-steel transatlantic liners (which were illuminated by incandescent electric light and were powered by triple expansion engines).

Before the revolution in shipping was complete, sail momentarily reached the acme of perfection. The loveliest and fastest ships in the world were the Yankee Clippers of the 1850s—long, narrow, tall-masted vessels with gracefully curved concave bows and an enormous spread of sail. In 1854 one of these vessels sailed 464 nautical miles in a day's run—an average speed of 20 knots—and another crossed from Boston to Liverpool in the record time of twelve days and six hours. The preeminence of the clipper ships was short-lived. Iron, screw-driven steamers forced them off the Atlantic run at the end of the fifties, and a decade later the oceanic sailing vessels of all countries suffered a fatal blow when the opening of the Suez Canal destroyed the need for crossings to the Orient and Australasia by way of the Cape. The future was with steam, but for some ten years the majesty of the clippers reigned supreme.

The Suez Canal, which provided a link between East and West.

Extremism in America

America in the clipper-ship era was a land still full of hope and promise, but its promise was tragically marred by contradictions in wealth and culture. Literary leadership was concentrated in a small area of Massachusetts where Henry W. Longfellow, Oliver Wen-

Henry Wadsworth Longfellow, author of *Hiawatha*.

dell Holmes, Henry Thoreau and Nathaniel Hawthorne lived almost under the shadow of Emerson's study (making the village of Concord—at that particular moment—an intellectual center as eminent as Paris or Oxford). But there was a world of difference between the broad visions of the New England intelligentsia and the narrow hatreds and suspicion of the rural masses. The 1854 elections in Massachusetts gave the Know-Nothing Party—a movement composed of bigots who opposed immigrants, Catholics and any liberals who championed what they considered un-American ideas—an overwhelming victory in the contests for the state senate, the lower house and the governorship.

The Know-Nothings went on to make substantial gains in Maryland, New York State and Louisiana. At the same time extremists ousted moderates from the humanitarian crusades for bettering conditions in the towns and from the crusade to rid the rural South of the scourge of slavery. And in the Southern states themselves, orators like William Yancey of Alabama and journalists like Robert Rhett of the *Charleston Mercury* began to beat the drums of secession.

At mid-century, the United States was divided into three vast regions: the South, which was still predominantly dependent upon a cotton crop; the North, in which factory towns had not as yet destroyed the rustic landscape; and a Middle Border region—Michigan, Ohio, Illinois, Iowa, Indiana, Wisconsin and Minnesota—that was almost as populous as the other two traditional areas and provided a vital link with the receding frontier.

California, which lay across the plains and mountains on the edge of that frontier, was admitted as the thirty-first state in 1850.

Although the issues splitting the nation emerged from the irreconcilable conflict of North and South, it was in the Middle Border region that the greatest changes in the character of the American way of life were taking place. These were the states that held the balance between the older sections. Had the northwestern markets tied themselves to the Mississippi and the South rather than to the railroads and the North, the great crisis in the American Union might

Ralph Waldo Emerson, one of the creators of American literature.

have been resolved in a different form. Chicago, incorporated as a city of four thousand people in 1837, held the key to America's future twenty years later, and there at least hope and promise seemed undimmed.

Hog butcherer to the nation

In the early 1850s the largest factory in Chicago was Cyrus Hall McCormick's plant, which manufactured mechanical reapers. McCormick was able to produce his machines at the unprecedented rate of ten a day and to sell them to the new farmers of the Great Plains by shrewd advertising and easy conditions of payment. In the ten years before the Civil War men such as McCormick—whose family was to become the best known industrial dynasty in Chicago—helped transform the city into the world's first farming metropolis. The lakeside community became a monster market town for livestock and the forwarding of grain, and railways converged on its stockyards from eight different directions.

Chicago was not alone in its prosperity. Fifty times as much wheat passed through Milwaukee in 1860 as in 1851, and trade down the Ohio and Mississippi valleys reached such a peak in 1860 that no less than 3,566 riverboat cargoes were unloaded at New Orleans in the last year of peace. The really significant development of those ten years was the growth of railway mileage in the state of Illinois: it leaped from a mere 110 miles of track in 1850 to 2,867 miles in 1860. Small wonder that in May, 1860, the six-year-old Republican Party held its national convention in Chicago and chose, on its third ballot, the only presidential candidate capable of carrying Illinois in the election—Abraham Lincoln of Springfield.

The Union imperiled

At the end of the antebellum period, agriculture, industry and business seemed to be flourishing everywhere except in the older slave states. But in 1857 a cyclical depression (resulting from land speculation and overdevelopment of railways) threw the economy into momentary confusion. The panic caused real distress in the industrial cities of the east and brought hardship to the sheep farmers of Ohio, but it made little difference to the growing productivity of the wheat lands.

Unfortunately, the depression also confirmed the political leaders of the South in the belief that their wealth, based upon cotton and spared by the depression, was "permanent," whereas that of the North was "fugitive and fictitious."

With every year that passed the divisions separating North from South grew deeper and deeper. Far more was at stake than even the gross human indignity of slavery: it was the failure of rival societies to understand each other. On a bright spring day in 1861, incomprehension exploded into the tragic futility of war as the commander of a low gray Federal fort in the waters of Charleston harbor defied South Carolina's demand for unconditional surrender. Two years and eighty days after the first shots were fired on Fort Sumter, the Confederate tide swept over the market town of Gettysburg, only to recede through wheat fields and peach orchards after the greatest battle of the American Civil War.

A Nation Divided

Spurred by his stunning victory at Chancellorsville, Confederate General Robert E. Lee began to plan an invasion of the populous and heavily industrialized North in early June of 1863. Lee's army of "starving ragamuffins" converged on the Pennsylvania farming community of Gettysburg, and on the last day of June his troops clashed with General George G. Meade's superior Union forces. The battle momentarily appeared to swing in Lee's favor on July 3, when General George Pickett's men broke through the Union lines shortly after two in the afternoon. Pickett's troops were unable to hold the vantage they had gained, however, and twenty minutes later they were forced to withdraw. On July 4, as Lee's bloodied army began its retreat to Virginia, word reached the General that the Southern stronghold of Vicksburg had fallen. In a single day, the Confederacy had been dealt two mortal blows.

It has been said that as Pickett's Virginian Division broke into the Union line on July 3, 1863, the Muse of History for a moment took up her pen to inscribe a new name in the list of nations. In Washington, sixty miles to the south, Abraham Lincoln prayed for victory: the nation, he felt, could not stand "another Fredericksburg or Chancellorsville." What was being decided in the hills above the little Pennsylvanian town of Gettysburg was whether the United States would go forward as a single and major nation. On July 1, 2 and 3, 1863, the scales trembled in an even balance.

The thirteen colonies which declared their independence of Britain in 1776 were scattered down a thousand miles of coast. Their origins and their interests were highly diverse. Only in 1781 was even a loose Confederation formed. It was with the greatest difficulty that the States were then persuaded into a closer unity. In 1787 delegates drafted the present Constitution. Over the following seventy years, it became a matter of dispute whether the Union was no more than a contract between states from which any given could, if it wished, withdraw. At first the state loyalties remained intense. It was a President of the United States, John Adams, who, speaking of "my country," meant Massachusetts.

But the North was receiving immigrants without the old local loyalties; and industry and communications developed rapidly. The South, a larger and more rural and scattered area to start with, missed much of this. Economically, too, iron and wheat, in the North, contrasted with cotton and tobacco in the South. It was seldom that a trading or banking policy was as beneficial to one as to the other. When in 1831 South Carolina came into collision for the first time with the Union authorities, the issue was not slavery but tariffs. The South Carolina legislature, standing on its overriding "sovereignty", passed a resolution "nullifying" a tariff law. The President, Andrew Jackson,

himself a Southerner, was clearly prepared to enforce the Federal law with troops if necessary, and South Carolina gave way.

But the most important of the issues dividing the country was Negro slavery. From the start the burgeoning new society had been disfigured by this huge and horrible excrescence. At first it seemed likely that it could gradually be restricted, then eliminated. In 1784 an Ordinance to forbid slavery in all the territory beyond the Appalachians was defeated in the Congress by only one vote—and this area would have included the future Kentucky, Tennessee, Alabama and Mississippi. The immediate abolition of the slave trade was voted for in 1787 by the moderate states of North and South, like Pennsylvania and Virginia, and opposed by South Carolina and Massachusetts. Under a compromise the trade was finally allowed to go on for twenty years, bringing a huge reinforcement to the slave population.

Meanwhile, just as southern expansion moved across the rich bottom lands of Alabama and Mississippi, perfect for cotton, Eli Whitney in 1794 invented the cotton gin, and within a decade the new fiber had swept the world. Its harvesting became the great citadel of Negro slavery.

In the first decades of the nineteenth century the movement against slavery still made headway in the non-cotton South. In 1831, a small slave rebellion (Nat Turner's) produced an intense reconsideration in the Virginia legislature. A motion to abolish slavery at that very session was only lost by 73 to 58, while a more moderate bill for gradual emancipation failed by only one vote. But this was almost the last sign of a serious movement against slavery in the South. The beginnings of a powerful Abolitionist movement in the North drew the lines. The Abolitionists must be distinguished from the many moderate northerners who opposed slavery. The former called for the dissolution of the Union as "an Agreement with Hell and a Covenant

Abraham Lincoln, who was responsible for the abolition of slavery in the United States.

Opposite The Battle of Gettysburg, 1863, where Robert E. Lee's Confederate army was defeated by General Meade's Union force.

John Brown: a martyr for the abolitionists

General Robert E. Lee and his officers who led the "starving ragamuffins" at the Battle of Gettysburg.

A contemporary drawing showing troops at the Rappahannock before the Battle of Fredericksburg.

with Death", and appealed for rivers of blood.

In the South, partly as a result of this agitation, a pro-slavery fanaticism emerged. It no longer became possible to discuss the subject rationally. Abraham Lincoln put it "that the institution of slavery is founded upon both injustice and bad policy, but that the promulgation of abolition doctrines tends rather to increase than abate its evils." As a young man he had seen slave auctions in New Orleans, and detested it. Yet he saw the difficulty of eradicating it at once rather than gradually without "producing a greater evil even to the cause of human liberty itself."

But the slavery question only gradually came to the fore as America's main political theme. In 1820 the Missouri Compromise (by which Missouri was admitted as a slave state, but slavery was otherwise excluded from all the new areas north of 36° 30',) took the issue out of the central area of politics for a generation. But the Mexican War of 1848 and the annexation of vast new territories in the

Southwest, once again raised the question of the political balance between the slave and the free states. By a new Compromise of 1850, designed once again to remove slavery as a major political issue, California was admitted as a free state while for the remainder of the area slavery was to be neither excluded nor imposed.

In 1854, however, the whole basis of previous agreements about the territories was destroyed by the Kansas–Nebraska Act: even in territories north of the Missouri Compromise line slavery was to become legal if approved by a majority of settlers—the so-called "Squatter Sovereignty." This was seen as a Southern political aggression, and it brought many Northerners of moderate views to the reluctant conclusion that they must oppose an insatiable South and support the new Republican Party which now arose with just such a program. It also led to a frightful guerrilla war in Kansas.

In 1857 came the "Dred Scott" decision of the Supreme Court, ruling that Congress had no power to prohibit slavery in the territories, and that, constitutionally, fugitive slaves must indeed be handed back to their Southern owners. This was increasingly abhorrent to Northerners, and several Northern states offered active resistance to the federal law. This in turn strengthened in the South the feeling that the Union was a fiction already, only obeyed by Northern states when it suited them.

One of the prominent Abolitionist terrorists of Kansas was John Brown. In 1859, with the support of the movement's leaders, he and a small band of followers seized the Arsenal at Harpers Ferry on the Maryland–Virginia border. As Lincoln, repudiating the raid, put it, "It was an attempt by white men to get up a revolt among slaves, in which the slaves refused to participate." Brown was captured and executed for treason—a martyr for the abolitionists, a portent of terror for the South.

For the election of 1860, Lincoln, by now the

"Slave Hound of Illinois" to the Abolitionists, won the Republican nomination over more extreme contenders. The Democrats were split in three factions by the slavery issue, and Lincoln won the Presidency on a minority vote. But even if the Democrats had combined, Lincoln would still have won with majorities, though not large ones, over almost all the North. Thus the election registered a country already divided along a geographical line.

But Lincoln regarded the preservation of the Union and enforcement of its laws as his overriding duty. When he came to power he offered every conceivable guarantee to the South that no Federal interference with slavery would take place. However, the extremists in South Carolina regarded the mere election of a Republican President as itself grounds for dissolving the Union. On December 20, 1860, they passed an ordinance of secession. Over the next six weeks, this was followed by Mississippi, Florida, Alabama, Georgia, Louisiana and Texas. At the beginning of February these came together to found the Confederate States of America.

The War did not start for some weeks. South Carolina claimed that Federal forces should move from the forts they held in its territory. The crux came when Lincoln, after dispute in the cabinet, decided to send in further supplies to Fort Sumter. On April 14, 1861, the Confederate General Beauregard ordered the bombardment of Fort Sumter, and the war began.

The secession of the other states had been rejected by Virginia, North Carolina, Tennessee and Arkansas, where big Union majorities carried the day. Only when Lincoln now called for troops to put down the Deep South did a revulsion of feeling take place, and the states of the Middle South themselves seceded in turn. Even now four slave states remained on the Union side. And many officers from the seceding states remained with the Union army—the Union division which repulsed

General Grant commanded the Union Army in its disastrous attack on Lee's Confederate troops.

Pickett's Charge was commanded by the North Carolinian Gibbon. All the same, Fort Sumter finally drew the lines. In North and South alike, fierce patriotisms—one for the Union and one for secession—swept the populations, only to wilt somewhat under the strains of war.

On the face of it, the South had no chance of victory. The North's population was 19 million and the white population of the South only $5\frac{1}{2}$ million. An advanced industrial country was fighting a backward agricultural one; and Southern agriculture was then concentrated on crops irrelevant to survival. In making the struggle after all into such a near thing, "the paramount factor," a Northern historian remarks, "was Robert E. Lee." Opposed to both secession and slavery, he had been approached to take command of the Union Army, but had felt that he could not take arms against Virginia and had "gone with his state". He was to be the only Great Captain who almost consistently extracted victory, until his resources were at an end, from situations in which he was always in inferior numbers and fighting an enemy equally well-trained and organized and officered, and far better equipped. Even the South's most determined ideological opponents could not forbear a cheer, as when Friedrich Engels wrote to Karl Marx, "they fight quite famously."

The first attempt to deal with the rebels was defeated at Bull Run in 1861. The following year saw Lee's defeat of McClellan in the Seven Days Battle, and of Pope at the Second Manassas, and Jackson's victories over the lesser Union armies in the Valley Campaign. Meanwhile in the West, New Orleans had been captured, and Eastern Tennessee conquered by the North. Powerful Southern counter blows at Shiloh and elsewhere never achieved more than partial and temporary success.

Lee's first invasion of the North was blocked at the Antietam in September. Lincoln took the opportunity to issue the Emancipation Proclamation. All slaves in territory under rebel control (though not in Union areas) were declared free, as from the end of the year, as a war measure.

717

Chancellorsville: victory of the "starving ragamuffins"

Above A contemporary print showing a typical Southern plantation scene.

Below A photograph showing Federal troops occupying General Robert E. Lee's mansion.

Lincoln had won the old Union men from the start by refusing to abolish slavery and setting the Union first. He now drew on the more radical anti-slavery forces. But above all, the Proclamation, bringing the issue openly to the front, made it extremely difficult for the Confederacy to appeal to the European powers whose support was in the long run as essential to them as it had been to George Washington in the Revolution.

The year ended on the Virginia front with another great victory for Lee at Fredericksburg. In May 1863, a further Union attempt to march on Richmond, with a greater superiority than ever, ended with Lee's masterpiece at Chancellorsville, where, as the New York papers complained, sixty thousand "starving ragamuffins" defeated 130,000 men of the "finest army on the planet."

On June 2, 1863, Lee set his Army in motion for an invasion of the North, with the aim of at best drawing the Union Army out from its impregnable position north of the Rappahannock, and conquering a peace in Washington. At worst, he wished to transfer the fighting from the wasted fields of Virginia. By the end of June he had crushed the Federal forces in the Shenandoah

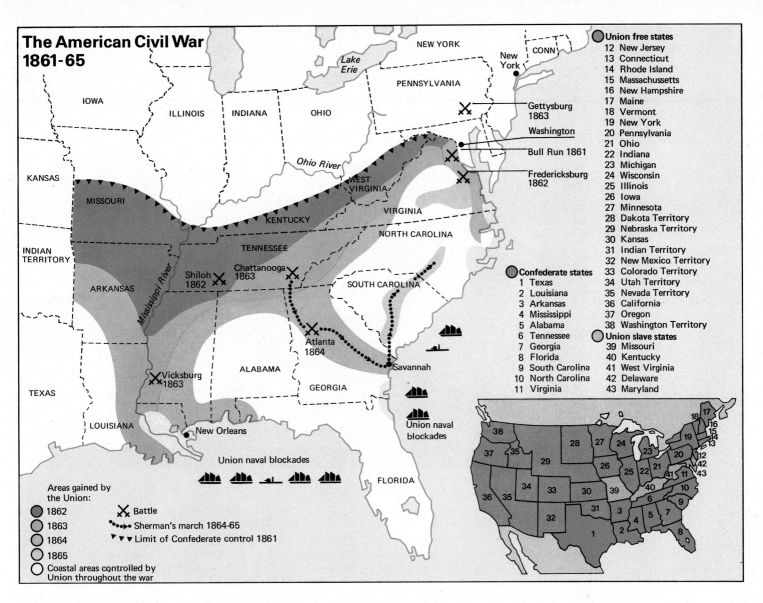

The American Civil War 1861-65

NEW YORK

Lake Erie

PENNSYLVANIA

New York

CONN

IOWA

ILLINOIS   INDIANA   OHIO

Ohio River

Gettysburg 1863

Washington

KANSAS

MISSOURI

WEST VIRGINIA

VIRGINIA

Bull Run 1861

Fredericksburg 1862

INDIAN TERRITORY

KENTUCKY

NORTH CAROLINA

ARKANSAS

TENNESSEE

Shiloh 1862   Chattanooga 1863

SOUTH CAROLINA

Mississippi River

Atlanta 1864

TEXAS

Vicksburg 1863

ALABAMA

Savannah

GEORGIA

LOUISIANA

New Orleans

Union naval blockades

Union naval blockades

FLORIDA

Union free states
12 New Jersey
13 Connecticut
14 Rhode Island
15 Massachussetts
16 New Hampshire
17 Maine
18 Vermont
19 New York
20 Pennsylvania
21 Ohio
22 Indiana
23 Michigan
24 Wisconsin
25 Illinois
26 Iowa
27 Minnesota
28 Dakota Territory
29 Nebraska Territory
30 Kansas
31 Indian Territory
32 New Mexico Territory
33 Colorado Territory
34 Utah Territory
35 Nevada Territory
36 California
37 Oregon
38 Washington Territory

Confederate states
1 Texas
2 Louisiana
3 Arkansas
4 Mississippi
5 Alabama
6 Tennessee
7 Georgia
8 Florida
9 South Carolina
10 North Carolina
11 Virginia

Union slave states
39 Missouri
40 Kentucky
41 West Virginia
42 Delaware
43 Maryland

Areas gained by the Union:
○ 1862
○ 1863
○ 1864
○ 1865
○ Coastal areas controlled by Union throughout the war

✕ Battle
•••• Sherman's march 1864-65
▼▼▼ Limit of Confederate control 1861

Valley at the second Battle of Winchester, and had marched through Maryland far into Pennsylvania. His leading corps, Ewell, was already on the Susquehanna. The Union Army of the Potomac had swung north to keep between him and Washington. The usually faultless Stuart, commanding the Southern cavalry, had been roughly handled at Brandy Station by the Union cavalry commander Pleasonton, and then, to reach his post on Lee's flank, he had ridden all the way round the Union Army, and was now out of touch. So in this alien territory Lee was without his eyes. On June 30 one of his brigades clashed in Gettysburg with the cavalry covering the Union left. Next day two Southern divisions were brought up to develop the situation, and the Northern First Corps arrived before the cavalry were driven in. The battle had begun. During the day the Northern Eleventh Corps came up on the right. But finally Ewell's Corps of Lee's Army, marching south from the Susquehanna drove them through Gettysburg on to the hills to the south.

Ewell, under orders to capture the hills if practicable, now failed to advance—the first tactical error of a series. Meade, the new Union Commander, came up in the night. Hearing that

the hills made a good defensive position, he had decided to fight there. The battle of the second and third day consisted of a series of Southern attacks from northeast, north and west on this position: it has been described as being like a fish-hook with its curve to the north at Cemetery Hill, its barb to the east at Culp's Hill, and its longer shank to the west as Cemetery Ridge, running from Cemetery Hill to the hills called the Round Tops at the southern end. The area round Little Round Top is a mass of rocks and gullies, culminating in a small hill a few hundred yards to the west—the Devil's Den. From there the ground dips westward then rises to the Peach Orchard. Lee (76,000 men) had about the same force as Napoleon at Waterloo, Meade (95,000) the equivalent of Wellington and Blucher combined. The Southern infantry had established a marked superiority, but the Northern artillery was greatly superior, in quality as well as quantity.

Lee's plan was to throw Longstreet's Corps, less Pickett's Division (not yet up) on the Union left. The other corps commanders had orders to demonstrate, converting this into attack as Longstreet's battle got going. Longstreet moved slowly. It was not until 4 P.M. that Hood's Division started

719

Lincoln: architect of victory and emancipation

A photograph of the dead on the battlefield of Gettysburg. This is one of the earliest war photographs; such views showed the grim reality of war.

to fight forward towards Little Round Top, then unoccupied. Warren, Chief Engineer of the Army of the Potomac, had climbed the hill to make a reconnaissance, when he saw the crisis—the key to the whole left flank was on the point of being lost, and with it the battle. He hastily detached nearby units on his own initiative and rushed them to the hill, which they were just able to save after bitter fighting. Meanwhile, Longstreet captured the Devil's Den and drove gradually forward in the Peach Orchard. Meade gradually brought up reinforcements until Longstreet was halted by more than half the Union army. But the other Southern corps failed to take advantage of the weakening of the troops facing them. It was not until 6 P.M. that Johnson's Division of Ewell's Corps captured part of the Union position on Culp's Hill and only at 8 P.M. did an attack by two brigades actually break the line on Cemetery Hill, having to retreat for lack of the expected support.

The odds against a Southern victory had steadily deteriorated. But it is the third day and the tremendous climax of Pickett's Charge which are taken as the High Tide of the Confederacy. Lee had again decided on a double blow. Johnson and Longstreet were ordered to strike early and simultaneously. Meade too pressed the fight on Culp's Hill, and by 11 o'clock Johnson had withdrawn to its base. Longstreet's column of nine brigades made its spirited and desperate assault at 2 o'clock. Inadequate support was given on the flanks, but in the teeth of a frightful Northern barrage the column broke into the Union lines on a hundred yard front. After twenty minutes close fighting the Virginians

withdrew, having lost all their regimental commanders. Meade had no reserves in hand to follow up the shattered units.

With this celebrated incident the battle was over apart from ineffective cavalry actions on either flank.

Gettysburg was no Waterloo. Lee remained on the field the following day, ready for another fight. But he had already decided to withdraw. On July 14, he crossed the Potomac and by August 4, the two armies again faced each other over the Rapidan, and the campaign was over.

As Lee fell back to Virginia the news arrived from the West that Grant had captured Vicksburg, the Southern stronghold on the Mississippi, which he had cut off in a brilliant campaign the previous May, after numerous repulses. The double blow to the Confederacy was, in the long run, deadly. But further efforts were possible. In September the South, for the first time, concentrated slightly superior forces at Chickamauga in northwest Georgia and won a great victory. Grant reversed the verdict at Chattanooga in November. He was then transferred to command against Lee.

1864 saw Sherman in northwest Georgia and Grant in Virginia facing the last great Southern armies, of Joseph Johnston and Lee respectively. Johnston conducted a fighting retreat back to Atlanta, while Lee, in his most remarkable campaign yet, won a series of defensive victories ending in the frightful slaughter of Cold Harbor, and Petersburg, which almost broke the North's will to fight. In August Lincoln considered that he could not win the 1864 election. But the deadlock was

broken by the fall of Atlanta, in September. Several victories in the Shenandoah Valley also heartened the North, as did the capture of Mobile.

In November there was one last scare. A Southern army, under Hood, re-entered Tennessee but was defeated there in December. Meanwhile Sherman "marched through Georgia," then the Carolinas. Lee's front remained in being before Richmond, but the whole hinterland was wasting away. In April the break finally came. Lee had to abandon his positions and after a week of desperate fighting, down to 7,000 infantry, he surrendered to Grant at Appomattox Court House. The other Southern armies followed suit in the next two months, and the war was over.

Lincoln, the supreme architect of victory and emancipation, stood for a reconciliation with the South "with malice towards none." His aim was the immediate readmission into the Union of all states accepting, as the South now did, the end of slavery and secession. His successor, Andrew Johnson, took a similar line but, lacking Lincoln's political skill, was soon in conflict with the radical Republicans. A great struggle (in which Johnson was nearly impeached by the Senate) took place over the whole future of the South. It left worse resentments than those of war and defeat.

By the beginning of 1866 all the Southern states had elected new governments, and all except Mississippi had abolished slavery, even before the Thirteenth Amendment became law. But most of them still retained various civic disqualifications for Negroes (as, indeed, did many of the Northern states). The Republican extremists objected to this on two grounds, one idealistic and one factious. They feared that the South would perpetuate a sort of covert slavery. And they feared that the re-entry of the Southern states under white control would mean the end of the Republican grip on Congress. Finally, and more reputably, a Fourteenth Amendment was passed in 1866 granting citizenship and civil rights to everyone. Most of the Southern states failed to carry this out effectively, and in March 1867 a Reconstruction Act imposed military government on all the ex-Confederate states except Tennessee. Many whites were disfranchised, and most of the South produced Republican governments based on the Negro vote. The Southern states were all readmitted to the Union under these Reconstruction governments by 1870. But it was only possible to maintain these administrations by Federal troops, and the North was not in the long run prepared to use force.

In 1876 the disputed presidential contest was settled on the tacit compromise that the Southern Democrats would acquiesce in the election of the Republican Hayes, while Hayes would withdraw troops from the South. Thereafter, till recent times, the "Solid South" remained Democratic, though it was not until the nineties that the Negroes were in effect exluded from voting.

Thus the results of the War, in the long run, were that slavery had been abolished, but that the racial problem had not been solved—as it has yet to be. But the Union had been saved, and the foundation, for good or ill, of the huge power of the modern United States had been laid.

ROBERT CONQUEST

The Battle of Hampton Roads in 1862, fought at the mouth of the River James. The Confederate ship *Virginia* sank the Union vessel *Cumberland* but was forced to withdraw, leaving the eastern seaboard in the hands of the Union.

Federal victory

The American Civil War was the most significant historical event between the collapse of the Napoleonic Empire in 1815 and the assassination of Archduke Francis Ferdinand at Sarajevo a century later. It was also one of the longest and bloodiest conflicts involving a major world power. On the afternoon of Palm Sunday, 1865, General Robert E. Lee rode into the village of Appomattox Court House and surrendered to General Ulysses S. Grant. As he did so, the Federal soldiers stationed around the surrender site noted that an all-but-forgotten stillness had fallen over the sloping fields and wooded hillocks of Virginia. After four tragic years and the loss of more than 600,000 American lives, the war of secession was finally over, and even General Grant (who was by no means a sensitive commander) seemed conscious of the scars of war. "Let all the men who claim to own a horse or mule take their animals home with them to work their farms," he declared that Sunday, modifying the original terms offered to Lee. The Union general ordered his troops not to cheer at the humiliation of their compatriots, and for a moment there seemed to be hope of reconciliation. That hope was illusory. Lincoln was shot at Ford's Theater in Washington on Good Friday,

and the sharp agony of battle was succeeded by the nagging sore of Reconstruction.

It would be misleading to place all the blame for the swift evaporation of the generous sentiment that attended Lee's surrender on the mood of the American people; harsh retribution was a characteristic of the 1860s. At no other time in the nineteenth century was man so alive to the hideous realities of war and so incapable of restraining his appetite for bloodshed. These were the years of the Geneva Convention on protection of the wounded and of the foundation of the Red Cross movement. They were also the years in which Tolstoi, working on his estate in rural Russia, destroyed the glamour of battle in the searing pages of *War and Peace*.

Yet in the whole decade there were only three months free from reports of military campaigns, and even this brief interlude witnessed a punitive expedition by British troops against the Maoris in New Zealand. In September of 1862 the newly appointed chief minister of Prussia, Otto von Bismarck, declared: "The great questions of the day will not be decided by speeches and majority votes—that was the great mistake of 1848-49—but by iron and blood." His words startled even his fellow Prussians, and yet they were not so much a threatening boast as a statement of fact, which was valid for Europe and beyond.

Leo Tolstoi, one of Russia's greatest novelists and moralists.

The Iron Chancellor

The shadow of Bismarck hangs heavily over the 1860s. In a rare moment of self-criticism in his later years Bismarck reproached himself: "Without me three great wars would not have happened and 80,000 men would not have perished." At the time, however, such considerations left him unmoved. Convinced of the inevitability of German unity—but determined that it should come about under the direction of Prussian landowners rather than middle-class liberals—Bismarck took advantage of each successive emergency to achieve his objective.

His supremely opportunistic instinct prompted Bismarck to lead Prussia (in alliance with Austria)

Von Moltke, who made the Prussian Army an almost invincible war machine.

into an 1864 war with Denmark that netted Prussia the partly German-speaking Danish province of Schleswig-Holstein. That war also enabled him to use the future disposal of these territories as an excuse for war against Austria and the other German states in the summer of 1866. The Danish campaign lasted ten weeks, the Austrian only seven.

The invincible Prussian Army was a new and unique military machine that had been perfected

by General Helmuth von Moltke (who had become chief of the Prussian general staff in 1857). Its success sprang from three main causes: the work of staff officers who had been trained to interpret war as an exact science; the use of railways for the rapid transportation of troops; and a revolution in firearms that enabled the Prussian breech-loading rifles to fire six times as rapidly as the older weapons of their opponents.

The victory of Prussia over Austria in the Battle of Sadowa—fought on the Bohemian Plain on July 3, 1866—stunned Europe. The balance of power swung decisively in Bismarck's favor; a North German Confederation came into being, uniting all the German states north of the Main River under Prussian hegemony; and the defeated Austrian Emperor Francis Joseph was induced to create the Dual Monarchy of Austria-Hungary and to cede "home rule" to his Magyar-speaking subjects. Nor were the ultimate effects of Bismarck's triumph limited to Central Europe. With ominous foresight one of Napoleon III's marshals declared: "It is France that has been defeated at Sadowa."

Slaughter in South America

While two powerful armies kept an uneasy watch on each other across the Rhine, the most protracted war of the era was being fought more than six thousand miles away in South America. Its casualties were to outnumber those of Moltke's campaigns and of the conflict between the Union and the Confederacy in the United States.

In March of 1865, General Francisco López, the dictator of Paraguay, carried his country into a struggle with Brazil, Argentina and Uruguay that lasted until López himself was killed five years later. This bitter war cost the Paraguayans three-quarters of a million lives in battle or its aftermath, and the Republic of Paraguay, which had been as efficient as any in Latin America in the 1850s, became impoverished and unstable. After 1870 it was permitted to exist only through the rivalry of its neighbors and the goodwill of arbitrators in distant Washington.

The Paraguayan tragedy passed almost unnoticed in the Western world. It was otherwise with

Mexico, where the folly of Napoleon III disastrously involved the French Army in an expedition originally intended to support the claims of European bondholders against Benito Juárez (whose government had announced the suspension of payments on all foreign debts). With the United States racked by civil war and unable to enforce the Monroe Doctrine, Napoleon III and his ministers gambled on building a Mexican empire, independent in status but closely linked to France for purposes of commerce and investment.

In June, 1864, Maximilian of Hapsburg, the brother of Francis Joseph, was crowned Emperor of Mexico and established an orderly and liberal administration. His power rested on the 25,000 French bayonets that kept the supporters of Juárez isolated in the mountains. There were occasional skirmishes, although more casualties resulted from disease and the climate than from guerrilla attacks. Once the Civil War ended north of the Rio Grande, the United States govern-

Benito Juarez, who suspended payment on foreign debts in Mexico.

ment adopted a menacing attitude, and Napoleon III ordered the withdrawal of French forces. The last units left on March 12, 1867, and Maximilian's charade of empire barely survived their departure. Within nine weeks he had been captured by Juárez, and within fourteen he was dead—shot by a firing squad on the hillside above Querétaro. Nothing remained of the Mexican Empire except clusters of graves among the cactus; a widowed, demented Empress living in exile in Belgium; and an oil painting by Manet—who had been so moved by the news of Maximilian's death that he had tried to capture the poignancy of the execution on canvas.

The execution of the Emperor Maximilian of Mexico, whose power rested solely on French arms.

Napoleon III

The whole Mexican episode was a crippling blow to the waning prestige of Napoleon III. In the ten years that followed the Crimean War, "the sphinx in the Tuileries" seemed the natural arbiter of the world's problems. A French garrison protected the Pope in Rome; a French force was sent to police Syria and Lebanon when disorder shook the Levant in 1860; and a French expedition marched beside the British to Peking, where Chinese discourtesy to foreign diplomats was punished by the burning of the Summer Palace.

Napoleon III's influence did not depend entirely upon military dispositions. The Rumanians, as a Latin people, could count on his support in their struggle for independence from the Sultan; the Tsar's Polish subjects had his sympathy and, occasionally, his encouragement; and Prince Nikita of Montenegro, whose reign was to last for more than half a century, owed his survival to French diplomatic intervention when Turkish troops marched on the mountain principality a few months after his accession. A portrait of Napoleon III was still hanging in an honored position in the royal palace at Cetinje when Austrian invaders finally chased Nikita into exile in 1916.

Elsewhere, however, gratitude had a less enduring quality. Sadowa and Querétaro dissolved the aura of French primacy, and Napoleon became conscious that he had over-

taxed his resources. In December of 1866 he withdrew the garrison from Rome (where French troops had been stationed for seventeen years). His cleric-advisers, terrified by the Garibaldian specter of Italian nationalism, forced Napoleon to send them back again ten months later. His grip on events seemed to slacken at home and abroad, and as pressure mounted from the radical opposition, autocracy gave way to representative government. In the first months of 1870 a liberal empire (headed by a prime minister who was responsible to a parliament) was proclaimed. Napoleon himself might declare that he had always believed in "liberty with order," but there were many in Paris who felt that it was a little late to be discovering first principles and that the donor of these concessions was both a tired and sick man.

Splendor of the Second Empire

Nevertheless, the last years of the Empire glittered with surface achievements. Baron Haussmann's boulevards—and the landscaping of the Bois de Boulogne—gave Paris a grace that other capitals sought to emulate. The Exhibition of 1867 surpassed both its predecessor and London's Crystal Palace in splendor. And while the Mexican adventure was reaching its tragic anticlimax, Napoleon was host to an unprecedented galaxy of foreign dignitaries: the Tsar of Russia; the Sultan of Turkey; the kings of Belgium, Denmark, Greece, Prussia, Sweden and Spain; the Prince

of Wales; and even Herr von Bismarck.

Earnest visitors to the gaslit capital found much that was frivolous and vulgar that summer. Entertainment included the Folies-Bergère, the masked balls, the jingles of Offenbach's music, and the scandal of the cancan. But the Exhibition caught the spirit of the Second Empire. It was an assertion of industrial progress, a parade of military panache, and proof that France remained a center of the arts. Its 15 million visitors seemed most interested in locomotives, interior furnishings and a lightweight metal called "aluminum"—and the greatest thrills were certainly the many captive balloons from which one could see all of Paris. But a Gallery of Art did exhibit works by Corot and Ingres, and the private pavilions of Manet and Courbet set up on the outer fringe of the grounds did display the new Impressionism to a public that declined to understand it. The Emperor, who had long been conscious of the social problems of industrialism, insisted that there should be sections of the Exhibition concerned with housing and conditions of factory life. He had lost none of his talent for window dressing.

Paris retained its gaiety through three seasons after the Exhibition closed. On May 25, 1870, an elegant audience enthusiastically applauded the first night of a new ballet at the Opera. The work was entitled *Coppelia*, and the triumph of the evening belonged to Guiseppina Bozzacchi, a young seventeen-year-old Italian who created the role of Swanhilda. She was hailed as a great ballerina in the making—but her career was doomed, for *Coppelia* was the last grand premiere of the Second Empire. Within two months the diplomats had blundered into war with Prussia; within four, France was a republic and Paris was encircled by the invading armies; within six, the Parisians were eating dogs, cats and rats and young Signorina Bozzacchi was dead, a victim of "siege-fever."

The decade was ending, as it had begun, in carnage and destruction. The devastation that had blighted the American South and turned Paraguay into a desert threatened Paris. The royal château of Saint-Cloud, like the Summer Palace at Peking, was left a charred ruin. And in the aftermath of war, flames consumed the Tuileries.

A Proclamation at Versailles 1871

In 1789, the year that the Bastille fell, Germany did not exist. Middle Europe was a patchwork of 350 sovereign states, dominated—but not controlled—by Prussia. Internecine squabbling was frequent at that time and national self-awareness was nonexistent. Ironically, it was Napoleon Bonaparte, Prussia's greatest foe, who first sparked a feeling of patriotism in the German people by annexing half of Prussia in 1807. Six years later—following Napoleon's humiliating and catastrophic Russian campaign—Prussia formed an alliance with the Tsar. By midcentury, it had become a power to reckon with—and by 1870, Prussia's Chancellor, Otto von Bismarck, felt sufficiently confident of his nation's military prowess to provoke France into a declaration of war. Prussia's victory was swift, and on January 18, 1871, William I of Prussia was proclaimed Emperor of Germany at Versailles. The German Empire had been born.

On January 18, 1871, Prussian troops in full-dress uniform formed ranks outside Louis XIV's palace at Versailles. At the time, the Franco–Prussian War was only some six months old, but Prussian forces had already routed the French troops at Sedan, captured the Emperor Napoleon III and 100,000 of his troops, besieged Paris and established their general headquarters at Versailles. And now the German states were to be formally unified; Germany was about to be proclaimed an empire under the Prussian King William I; and the Hohenzollerns, once petty local princes, were on the point of becoming the most powerful rulers in Europe.

January 18 had been chosen for the ceremony because it was the anniversary of the crowning of the first Prussian King, Frederick I, at Königsberg in 1701. The choice of setting was also symbolic: in the Hall of Mirrors at Versailles the brilliant court of Louis XIV had attended the Sun King's ceremonies. Now delegations from all the German regiments in the field were mustered in the enormous room, and they presented their battle-torn flags in a forest of color. In the middle of the gallery, between two tall center bays, an altar had been set up, and opposite it a raised dais had been built.

Precisely at midday a role of drums was heard from outside, an abrupt military command echoed down the gallery—which had suddenly fallen silent—and the King of Prussia made his entrance followed by other German rulers, princes and generals. He mounted the small dais and took his seat. On his right was the heir to the throne, the Crown Prince, and on his left was Chancellor Otto von Bismarck, wearing the uniform of Colonel of the Horse Guards. A detachment of infantry played a fanfare on muted trumpets, and the official court preacher delivered a long sermon. At the end of his harangue a choir of soldiers sang the Te Deum.

In a brief speech William I thanked the representatives of the German states who had offered him the title of Emperor and declared it his duty to accept it. Bismarck then read the Emperor's proclamation:

Accordingly, we and our successors will bear henceforth the title of Emperor in all affairs concerning the German Reich. We hope that with God's blessing we shall be able to lead our country, under the banner of its former splendor, toward a happier future. We shall assume the imperial dignity in a spirit of national fidelity, to preserve the rights of our Reich, to ensure peace, to defend our independence in prosperity, and to defend liberty.

At this point the Grand Duke of Baden, a man of enormous stature, cried loudly: "Long live His Majesty the German Emperor William I!" The whole assembly broke into frenzied cheers and some officers drew their swords and brandished them in the air. The German Empire had been born.

Strictly speaking, the ceremony had not been a coronation but simply a proclamation. But that was enough. "It was a historic day and a day of rejoicing," the Chancellor's secretary noted in his diary. "The ceremony was impressive, and was held amid a great military display. Everybody who was present said that it was an unforgettable sight." In point of fact, the event had transformed the fate of Germany, had changed the map of Europe, and it would ultimately affect the destinies of the world.

The achievement of German unity satisfied a relatively recent aspiration. The Holy Roman Germanic Empire, which had reached the apogee of its power in the Middle Ages, would later be referred to as a forerunner of the German Empire, but the two empires were actually vastly different. The First Reich, as the Holy Roman Empire came to be called, had been a loose, haphazard group of principalities that made no pretension to be the embodiment of any racial or national sentiment. It comprised such disparate territories as the Kingdom of Italy, the Kingdom of Arles, Holland and the Duchy of Burgundy. One Emperor, Frederick II

William I of Prussia, who was proclaimed Emperor of Germany at Versailles.

Opposite An English cartoon of Bismarck, who was regarded by many as Europe's most capable statesman. In the "Ems dispatch" he deliberately provided a *casus belli* for the French.

Berlin's will for leadership

A French newspaper attack on the unpreparedness of the French Army at Sedan, showing Napoleon III, more interested in his cigar than his ragged army. The Battle of Sedan allowed the German army to enter Paris almost unopposed.

The Emperor proclaimed in Versailles' Hall of Mirrors.

of Hohenstaufen, who was the grandson of Frederick Barbarossa, spoke Italian, French and Arabic—but no German.

In 1789, the year the Bastille fell, what is now called Germany was a patchwork of 350 sovereign states. Bismarck noted in his *Thoughts and Recollections*: "In Germany up to the outbreak of the French Revolution there was no sign of the emergence of a German nation." In fact, such signs were hardly discernible before 1807. But in that year Napoleon I reduced Prussia's territory by more than half by the Treaty of Tilsit. This brutal treatment embittered the Germans and brought about a national self-awareness; hatred for France became the banner of

German nationalism. A year later the first patriotic association, the Tugendbund, was founded. Its outspoken members urged all Germans to unite in resistance to foreign oppression, but in less than two years the Tugendbund was dissolved at the insistence of the French Emperor. German patriots were given another opportunity to vent their passions against the French in 1813, following Napoleon's disastrous and ill-advised Russian campaign. The whole of Germany rose against the French Emperor in the early months of 1813 and replaced the alliance with France by a treaty with the Tsar.

It was the German revolt that sealed Napoleon's fate. In October of 1813, the great conqueror suffered a decisive defeat at Leipzig—thanks in large part to the efforts of his former German allies. By April, 1815, a Frankfurt financier was able to write: "The memory of the humiliating domination that Germany suffered for ten years has developed a national spirit that has dispersed small local jealousies." The idea of a German nation had been launched; the man who was indirectly responsible was Napoleon.

In 1815 the government at Berlin initiated a German Confederation, a military alliance that included Austria as well as the German states. For the next several decades Austria and Prussia vied for a position of dominance in the Confederation. Not until one or the other established hegemony would unification move forward. The issue finally was decided in the Austro–Prussian War of 1866: Prussia triumphed at the Battle of Sadowa, and the war came to a swift and abrupt end.

Before the 1866 war, Prussia's growing ambitions had aroused lively reactions from the other German kingdoms, who feared that their independence was threatened. They could foresee the day when they might find themselves completely absorbed by their bigger neighbor. At the outbreak of war Bavaria had openly taken Austria's side. But Prussia's victory at

Sadowa not only eliminated the Austrian competition, it also unleashed enormous patriotic enthusiasm throughout Germany. From then on Prussia acted as a rallying point for the German territories.

On June 25, 1867, Prussia founded the North German Confederation. At the time, the Confederation comprised only Saxony and the small principalities that were too insignificant and weak to offer any obstacle to Prussian predominance. The other German states made a great point of holding themselves aloof. The southern states—Bavaria, Württemburg, Baden and Hesse-Darmstadt—showed themselves more and more reticent in the face of what they called the "will for leadership of Berlin." The most antagonistic without doubt was the King of Württemburg, Charles IV, brother-in-law of the Tsar of Russia. He made no secret of his feelings and of his will to resist anything that could be interpreted as disguised annexation. When he received Prince Frederick Charles of Prussia in 1868, he treated him with such coolness that it was tantamount to an insult. Charles even thought of linking the other southern kingdoms into an independent league that would be opposed to the northern confederation, although this meant that Germany would be cut in two.

This diplomatically perilous situation was to be temporarily resolved when Bavaria, Württemburg, Baden and Hesse all affirmed their resolution to preserve their freedom. At the same time, in separate treaties, each concluded a defensive military alliance with Berlin. It was agreed that if one of the signatories were to be attacked by a third power, the others would come to its assistance immediately. France almost immediately tested those new alliances—and in the process provoked the final achievement of German unity—by making the disputed succession to the Spanish throne an international issue. At the beginning of July, 1870,

the Spanish throne was vacant. Leopold of Hohenzollern-Sigmaringen, a petty German prince and a distant cousin of King William I, declared his willingness to accept the Spanish throne, and he did so with William's full permission. When the news became public, the French were furious. They asserted vigorously that the arrival of a Prussian on the throne of Spain constituted "an encircling movement against France." Buoyed by their recollection of Napoleon's exploits, they proclaimed their complete unwillingness to suffer "this intolerable provocation."

William I was astounded and extremely troubled by the violence of these reactions. At seventy-three,

Paris cooked in its own juice—by Germany and the Devil—a French cartoon of 1871.

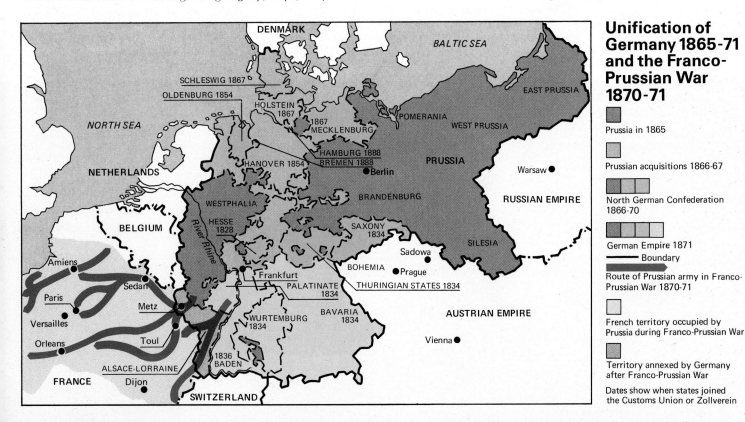

Unification of Germany 1865-71 and the Franco-Prussian War 1870-71

- ▨ Prussia in 1865
- ▢ Prussian acquisitions 1866-67
- ▨▨▨ North German Confederation 1866-70
- ▨▨▢▢ German Empire 1871
- ▬ Boundary
- ▬ Route of Prussian army in Franco-Prussian War 1870-71
- ▢ French territory occupied by Prussia during Franco-Prussian War
- ▨ Territory annexed by Germany after Franco-Prussian War
- Dates show when states joined the Customs Union or Zollverein

Unity achieved through a common cause for anger

A cartoonist's view of the aging Napoleon III. Like the Prussian King, he had no wish to fight, but popular feeling in France made war inevitable.

A railway bridge near Dijon being patrolled by German soldiers during the Franco-Prussian War.

he was anxious for peace, and he agreed to bring pressure on his cousin to persuade him to withdraw his candidacy, which the young prince promptly did. For France the diplomatic victory was a sizable one, and the incident was considered closed. Unfortunately, when news of the concession reached Paris it inflamed the high feelings that had been aroused. France's demands escalated, and it now insisted on what it called "guarantees for the future." The French ambassador presented these new demands to William at Ems, where the King was peacefully taking the waters. William answered that the renunciation of the throne was sufficient in itself. The meeting between the French Ambassador and the King took place in an atmosphere of extreme courtesy, but in Berlin Chancellor Bismarck, urged on by the military faction, deplored the evidence in his sovereign of what he considered "an excess of goodwill." He released the account that he had received of the meeting (now known as the "Ems dispatch"), but first he edited it in order to make it as offensive as possible to the French. The German text, already couched in unpleasant terms, was mistranslated by the French, and consequently the truth became doubly distorted.

No one in Paris was interested in checking the accuracy of the dispatch, which had no official sanction whatsoever. The people of Paris were enraged, and Emperor Napoleon III, aging and in failing health, was not sufficiently strong to resist such an outbreak of popular anger. In what was undeniably an unprovoked act of aggression, France declared war on Prussia on July 16, 1870.

France's move gave the other side of the Rhine the chance to implement the defensive alliances concluded in 1867. King Louis II of Bavaria, who was extremely anti-Prussian, hesitated for some hours, but under pressure from his compatriots he finally agreed to support the spirited resistance that had swept over the rest of the country. In fact the southern states were unanimous in declaring their "solidarity with Prussia, who was a victim of French megalomania." In two days the German bloc cohered. Bismarck was to admit later:

I considered a war with France entirely necessary for our national development. I never doubted that the establishment of the German Empire must be preceded by a victory over France. The nation could only achieve unity through a common cause for anger.

France's declaration of war was to prove cause enough. On September 3, 1870, the very day after the Prussian triumph at Sedan, Bismarck set about the task of giving his dream of a unified empire concrete form. He summoned Rudolph von Delbrück, who had been his closest collaborator in Berlin, to Versailles and charged him with drawing up a proposed constitution. The text was ready by the end of September. It predicted the formation of a German Empire, subject to the control of Prussia, into which the states would become integrated. The text was to be submitted to the interested parties.

At this point a rather strange thing happened: William I of Prussia, who was foremost among the "interested parties" and most likely to benefit from Delbrück's proposed constitution, proved extremely hesitant about the entire matter. The King was adverse to the title of Emperor, which he considered strongly reminiscent of the Holy Roman Empire, and it took considerable time to persuade him that the title was the only acceptable one. He finally resigned himself to it with what his son tells us was a "feeling that he was being given a cross to bear that would weigh heavily on his shoulders and on the Royal House of Prussia."

Although this first obstacle had been overcome, there still remained the difficulty of obtaining the agreement of the states who were being invited to surrender any real degree of sovereignty. The negotiations were delicate, but Bismarck was to display all the qualities of a great statesman. He directed his first efforts to winning over Bavaria, whose acceptance he thought would bring the others in its train. The negotiations were protracted. As Bismarck was later to explain:

The King of Bavaria, Louis II, expressed his agreement with the cause of German unity but nevertheless his primary concern was to maintain the federal principle which safeguarded the privileges of his country. I well

remember the idea that he put forward during the discussions at Versailles and that from a political point of view was quite unrealistic. He demanded that the Presidency of the Confederation should alternate between the Royal House of Prussia and that of Bavaria. I was perplexed as to how I could give so impractical a plan some reality.

Fortunately for Bismarck, Louis II, intelligent as he was, was an artist rather than a statesman, and his sensibilities were more highly developed than his resolution. Among other eccentricities, he was possessed with a mania for building palaces of all kinds. The Chancellor accordingly encouraged these expensive tastes by giving him, under the pretext that it was a "contribution to the arts," a personal subsidy of 100,000 thalers a year. Louis rapidly came to the conclusion that he could not long stand out against the movement that was infecting all the German peoples. What he now sought was the maximum personal advantage. Bismarck was prepared to make concessions as long as they did not compromise the essential matter. He agreed that Bavaria was to be accorded favorable treatment: it was to maintain its own diplomatic representation abroad and it was to continue to issue its own postage stamps. Furthermore, Bavaria's coinage would still bear the head of its ruling prince, and its army corps would maintain their separate designations. It was even stipulated that if the house of Hohenzollern became extinct, the royal crown would pass to the house of Wittelsbach at Munich. Satisfied with all these concessions, Louis II ratified the constitution.

On November 23, Bismarck entered the room where his secretaries were working. "Gentlemen," he said in a shaking voice, "the Bavarian treaty has been signed. German unity is a fait accompli and our King has become the German Emperor!" He ordered champagne to be brought and then, sitting down in the middle of his colleagues, he gave his version of events:

It is possible that I might have gained more from Munich. Our newspapers in Berlin will not be satisfied. Whoever later on writes a straightforward historical account will blame me for being too accommodating. He will say: "The fool could have demanded more and the

German guns bombard Paris.

other party would have had to concede it." But it is my contention that the other party should be satisfied. The agreement that we have signed is not perfect, but it is all the more firm for that. Treaties mean nothing when those who enter into them have only signed under duress.

In truth the minor rulers had no illusions about their ability to resist the Emperor; they knew what was in store for them. Bismarck himself, in safeguarding the individualities of old Germany, did not seem in fact to have wished to do more than to contrive the means for change. The ministries in Berlin quickly developed their overwhelming ascendancy, as the natural tendency toward centralization came irresistibly into play. The constant absorption of the smaller and weaker states by the more powerful and dynamic ones became ever more rapid; a system that had once been flexible became ever more rigid. Soon there was only one rule: "The state rather than the province." The law of the German Empire—rather than local law—predominated. In a short space of time the federal German Empire became a monolithic Empire. And this was not the only distortion. From its very beginning, the Empire carried the seeds of far more formidable things to come.

The Empire was conceived at a time of war and had its infancy in a time of victory. It began by inheriting the responsibility for Alsace and Lorraine, which had been annexed against the wishes of their inhabitants. As soon as elections were held in 1874, the populations of these provinces elected as their representatives to the Federal Parliament fifteen deputies devoted to protest. The two provinces whose destinies had been disposed of by force were never to accept the imposition; and the annexation was to engender a lasting hatred among the French, who were intent upon revenge. There followed an armaments race that lasted for half a century and bore heavily on the fate of Europe.

As far as Germany itself was concerned, the ceremony of January 18, 1871—in an invaded country and in a historical setting whose very choice was a mark of insolence, among all the trappings of war and the rattling of sabers—was to stamp upon the new German Empire a military character that was to permeate and dominate it. All this was to lead inevitably to the catastrophe of World War I and its natural consequence, World War II. German unity was a perfectly natural aspiration, but the manner in which it came about had deplorable consequences, and both Germany and France were responsible for the results.

GEORGES ROUX

Léon Gambetta, who led the resistance to the Germans after the defeat at Sedan.

Left The last German soldier in Paris.

729

German learning

The magnitude of the Prussian victory in 1871 ensured Bismarck's supremacy among the world's diplomats for the next two decades. All major international problems —apart from disputes between Britain and the United States—were referred to the German Chancellor for advice and guidance, if not for solution. And when the statesmen of Europe met in 1878 to settle the affairs of Turkey and her Balkan neighbors, it seemed natural that they should gather in the German capital for their formal deliberations. Similarly, it was in Berlin that a fourteen-nation conference met from November of 1884 to February of 1885 to determine boundaries for the newly acquired spheres of colonial settlement in Central Africa. Both France and Italy sought Bismarck's support when they vied over acquisition of Tunis in the early 1880s—and it is testimony to the Iron Chancellor's powers of dissimulation that each government subsequently

Gottlieb Daimler, who developed the first internal combustion engines using petrol.

believed that it alone had received his assurance of sympathetic patronage for its endeavors and ambitions.

Yet the Age of Bismarck witnessed more than a triumph of German statecraft. It also saw the influence of specifically Germanic learning and culture reach its zenith. During this period, Teutonic "higher criticism" subjected

Biblical passages to ponderous analysis; Ernst Haeckel asserted man's mastery of the universe; and Wilhelm Wundt anatomized man's physiological psychology. In an equally specialized but different field, Nikolaus Otto and Gottlieb Daimler perfected the first internal combustion engines—Otto, in 1876, using a "silent gas engine" and Daimler, a decade later, using petrol. In that same year—1886— Heinrich Hertz proved the existence of electromagnetic waves, a discovery that was used some nine years later by the Italian inventor Marconi for transmitting the first wireless messages.

Nor was the German achievement limited to the physical sciences. Those were the years in which the cult of Wagnerian opera —the very apotheosis of Romanticism—spread beyond the confines of the composer's fatherland. Historians throughout Europe followed Leopold von Ranke's search for a new objectivity, and Heinrich Schliemann promoted the science of archaeology with the thoroughness of a Prussian and the enthusiasm of a born Romantic. Even socialist thought, which had been predominantly French in inspiration earlier in the century, looked to the Germans Wilhelm Liebknecht and August Bebel for leadership. It was only in the field of fiction and in the visual arts that France retained her traditional supremacy; nothing in European painting matched the imaginative craftsmanship of Manet and the Impressionists, whose genius dominated the Parisian salons of the early 1870s.

Germany under Bismarck

Bismarck took little personal interest in the culture of his age. He remained loyal to the stolid Lutheranism of the Junkers, the class of Prussian landowners that he typified. During the nineteen years in which he was Germany's Chancellor he championed the established order, and during his tenure the political balance in Europe acquired a permanence not unlike the equilibrium that Metternich had sought to sustain half a century earlier.

The Chancellor believed that the wars of 1864, 1866 and 1870 had won Prussia all the territories that it could absorb without a fundamental change in its social structure. The Reich of 1871 was large

The Italian inventor Marconi, who transmitted the first wireless messages.

enough to satisfy the patriotic ardor of the German people and yet sufficiently limited in size to be administered by the Prussian civil service and the Junkers. Bismarck knew that the concept of a Greater Germany was an illusion of the middle classes—a dream whose realization would involve the political elimination of the Junkers. He therefore resisted all pan-Germanic movements, whether they had the backing of industrial magnates or of members of the General Staff. He would never have approved the foreign policy of Hitler's Third Reich.

Yet Bismarck could not entirely ignore new ideas. He bowed reluctantly to the general demand for colonies and authorized settlements in Tanganyika, the Cameroons and Southwest Africa in the 1880s. The Chancellor's gesture was a temporizing one, designed to mollify his critics; Bismarck realized that such undeveloped territories could be no more than expensive and politically dangerous toys for the German people for years to come. By the late 1880s he was prepared to experiment with social welfare schemes for industrial workers, although he remained narrowly conservative at heart. And while he was particularly opposed to all forms of "internationalism" (whether Roman Catholic or socialist in origin), he was equally suspicious of the bellicose nationalism of the younger generation. So long as William I remained Kaiser, Bismarck was secure in the knowledge that his

sovereign shared his viewpoint. The accession of the twenty-nine-year-old William II in 1888 changed that situation, and Bismarck's failure to understand the spirit of the new Germany he had created led to his dismissal by the young Kaiser two years later.

Bismarck's foreign policy

German foreign policy after 1871 reflected Bismarck's general desire for stability. He became a pillar of peace because he feared that any European war—even one that did not involve Germany—would enable the victor to impose a new settlement on the great powers (and thereby destroy his principal achievement). He knew that the greatest danger for Germany was a war of revenge initiated by France, but he assumed that the French would not risk a campaign without allies and he believed that he could counter any such threat by keeping the Third Republic diplomatically isolated.

The key to Bismarck's foreign policy lay not so much in his negative attitude toward France as in his dealings with his mighty neighbor to the east. Good relations with Russia were essential, for the Russians were natural geographic allies of the French in any struggle against Germany. Except for a brief period in 1879, therefore, there was a close understanding between the governments in Berlin and St. Petersburg throughout the Age of Bismarck.

The Chancellor also favored cooperation with Austria-Hungary, partly to forestall any Paris-Vienna combination and partly to hold in check the dangerous friction between the Austrians and Russians in southeastern Europe. The League of the Three Emperors, a loose understanding between Russia, Germany and Austria-Hungary, enabled the Eastern autocracies to work together from 1873 to 1875, but it could not survive the strain of the Eastern Crisis of 1875–78. The League was renewed more formally in 1881 and lasted until 1887 (when Balkan tensions once again aggravated relations between the Austrians and the Russians). Bismarck maintained close relations with the Russians during his last three years in office, however, and a secret Russo-German pact known as the Reinsurance Treaty was signed. This kept "the wires" to St. Petersburg open from 1887 to 1890.

Collaboration with Russia was only one aspect of Bismarck's diplomacy. He built up a system of secret defensive alliances at the same time to ensure military support from other European powers if Germany were attacked by France and/or Russia at some future date. An Austro-German alliance concluded in 1879 was transformed into a Triple Alliance of Germany, Austria-Hungary and Italy three years later, and that combination of European Central Powers lasted—at least theoretically—until the coming of World War I. (The Italians, who slipped out of the German orbit after Bismarck's fall, remained neutral in 1914). The weakness of Bismarck's system of alliances was that it required a Chancellor of his caliber to make it function, and none of his successors could reach such heights of statesmanship.

The Balkan question

"The whole of the Balkans are not worth the bones of a single Pomeranian Grenadier," Bismarck once remarked in disgust, and the sentiment was one with which most of his compatriots would have agreed. But Balkan questions plagued the European chancelleries in the 1870s and 1880s, just as they were to do—with tragic consequences

for Germany and the world— from 1911 to 1914. Misrule by the Sultan's officials in the Balkans provoked risings in the Turkish provinces of Bosnia-Herzegovina and Bulgaria in 1875–76. These revolts were suppressed by Turkish irregulars with a bestiality that was widely reported by American and British newspaper correspondents, and the Russians seized the reports as evidence that the Turks were unfit to administer those territories.

Public opinion in Britain was divided over the news of the Balkan atrocities. The Liberal opposition, led by Gladstone, campaigned vigorously for concerted action that would force the Turks to make concessions to the Balkan nationalities; the Conservative government of Disraeli, fearing that any limitation of the Sultan's sovereignty would only benefit Russia, disputed the reports as press exaggerations. There was, of course, some justification for the Conservative position. Like the Russians, most of the inhabitants of Bulgaria and Bosnia-Herzegovina were Slavs and members of the Orthodox Church, and public sentiment in the Tsar's Empire was strongly pan-Slav. It came as no surprise, therefore, when Alexander II declared war on Turkey in April of 1877 and sent a powerful army southwards through the Balkan Mountains to liberate Bulgaria and expel the Turks from Europe.

Although the Russians were held up for several months by Turkish resistance at Plevna, the first cavalry units reached the Sea of Marmora in February, 1878. The Sultan sued for peace, and a month later he signed the Treaty of San Stefano. That agreement startled the European powers, for besides giving the Russians considerable territory in the Caucasus it created a Bulgarian principality that included almost all of Macedonia and a long stretch of the Aegean coast. It was assumed that Greater Bulgaria would become a Russian satellite, and the Treaty was viewed by other nations as a means by which the Tsar could extend his power into the western Balkans and to the shores of the Mediterranean.

Opinion rapidly hardened against the Treaty of San Stefano, which was the supreme triumph of the pan-Slavs, both in Vienna, where the new Bulgaria had trespassed on Austria's Balkan interests, and in London, where there had long been an exaggerated fear of Russian influence in the eastern Mediterranean. The Tsar reluctantly accepted an offer from Bismarck to act as "honest broker" in settling the Eastern Question, and the Congress of Berlin was convened in July, 1878.

Treaty of Berlin

The resultant Treaty of Berlin destroyed the work of the pan-Slavs. The Russians kept their gains in the Caucasus but Greater Bulgaria became little more than an unrealized dream of the nationalists in Sofia. A small autonomous Bulgarian principality was set up, but the southern part of Bulgaria remained subject to Turkish rule under a Christian governor. Most of Macedonia was restored to Turkey. The Austrians were authorized to occupy Bosnia-Herzegovina and the British to occupy the island of Cyprus, but both of these territories remained within the Turkish Empire. Essentially, the Berlin settlement determined the fate of the Balkans for the next thirty years (even though the artificial division of Bulgaria was ended in 1885 by a further revolt).

The Treaty of Berlin provided neither a good settlement nor a just one, but it was remarkably effective. It was only in Russia that its terms aroused widespread resentment. Pan-Slavism had been

the first sentiment to stir the Russian masses since they had rallied in defense of their country against the Napoleonic invasion of 1812. The Russian press and the

William Gladstone, leader of the Liberal Party. He supported the cause of Balkan nationalism against the Turks.

Russian Church—a curious combination of the new and the old— had fanned public indignation until war with Turkey assumed the proportions of a crusade. Even before the 1877 invasion, Russian volunteers had set out from Moscow and St. Petersburg to aid their brother Slavs in the Balkan lands, and a Russian translation of Gladstone's pamphlet denouncing the Bulgarian horrors had sold ten thousand copies in a few weeks during the autumn of 1876. Small wonder then that the Treaty of Berlin seemed to be an anticlimax, and a deliberate denial of Russia's historic mission.

Inevitably, these events had repercussions on Russia's internal politics. While the pan-Slav agitation was at its height, most of the Russian intelligentsia resigned themselves to the absence of constitutional liberties. After the Treaty of Berlin, however, demands were made for representative institutions that would enable the voice of the Russian people to penetrate the citadels of Tsardom. But if genuine liberalism did exist among responsible Russians at this stage, Alexander II was not given an opportunity to respond to it, for in March of 1881 the politics of murder triumphed over reason.

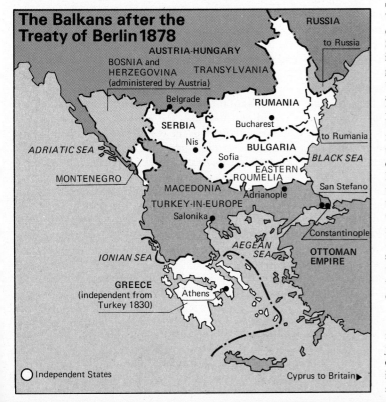

The Balkans after the Treaty of Berlin 1878

RUSSIA
to Russia
AUSTRIA-HUNGARY
BOSNIA and HERZEGOVINA (administered by Austria)
TRANSYLVANIA
Belgrade
RUMANIA
SERBIA
Bucharest
Nis
to Rumania
ADRIATIC SEA
BULGARIA
Sofia
BLACK SEA
MONTENEGRO
EASTERN ROUMELIA
MACEDONIA
Adrianople
San Stefano
TURKEY-IN-EUROPE
Salonika
Constantinople
AEGEAN SEA
OTTOMAN EMPIRE
IONIAN SEA
GREECE (independent from Turkey 1830)
Athens
○ Independent States
Cyprus to Britain ▶

Assassination of Alexander II

Even before the 1825 Decembrist Revolt—an abortive military coup that Nicholas I, Tsar of All the Russias, had ruthlessly suppressed—underground terrorist groups were plotting to overthrow the Romanov dynasty. By the middle years of the nineteenth century, plots to assassinate his son Alexander II were as frequent—and as notorious—as the blizzards that swept the Russian steppes. In an effort to placate his enemies, Alexander inaugurated a program of Great Reforms—culminating in the 1861 decree that emancipated Russia's serfs—but his foes could not be appeased. In 1879 a Nihilist organization known as People's Will secretly condemned the Tsar to death. Their initial attempts to execute that sentence were thwarted, but on March 13, 1881, the anarchists achieved their goal: Tsar Alexander was mortally wounded by a bomb blast that shook every European throne.

Nicholas Rysakov, Tsar Alexander's assassin, from a drawing made during his trial.

Opposite Tsar Alexander II who was assassinated by members of the terrorist organization, People's Will. By contemporary Russian standards Alexander was a liberal ruler.

In the early afternoon of Sunday, March 13, 1881, the Emperor Alexander II of Russia set off for his Winter Palace in St. Petersburg after a routine visit to the Mikhaylovsky Cavalry Parade Ground. He sat alone in his carriage. A liveried coachman rode on the box, mounted Cossacks wearing fur caps and scarlet coats escorted him, and sleighs conveying the St. Petersburg Chief of Police and other officers followed behind. It was a dull day and the gaudy imperial cortege contrasted sharply with the dirty snow underfoot.

As the Tsar himself had every reason to suspect, revolutionary conspirators had been keeping him under surveillance for several months in an effort to establish the pattern of his movements within the capital—a necessary preliminary to killing him with high explosives. These plotters, sometimes known as Nihilists, belonged to the underground terrorist political organization People's Will. They had secretly condemned Alexander to death in the late summer of 1879, and since that time they had made several determined attempts on his life: Nihilist saboteurs had blown up a train in which the Tsar was thought to be traveling north from the Crimea, and they had engineered a huge explosion inside the Winter Palace that killed many unintended victims but left the Tsar himself unscathed.

On March 13, 1881, those abortive attempts were finally crowned by success. As the Emperor's carriage swept westward down Engineer Street toward the Catherine Quay, Sophia Perovsky, the terrorist and qualified schoolmistress who directed the assault in the field, posted herself on the far side of the canal at a point where she could observe the Tsar's approach. When his carriage came into view she signaled with her handkerchief, alerting the four young men under her command who lurked on the Quay, each holding a cumbersome hand grenade disguised in an improvised wrapping.

After reaching the end of Engineer Street, the imperial carriage turned north along the Quay. It had covered about a hundred yards when the first Nihilist, Nicholas Rysakov, threw his bomb, which exploded with a great crash near the back axle. The vehicle held together, and Alexander would have been well advised to drive on at full speed without pausing to investigate, but he insisted on dismounting and walking back to where his assailant, already under arrest, stood amid a group of police and onlookers. Some words were exchanged and the Tsar turned back toward his carriage. At that moment a second member of the murder squad, Ignaty Grinevitsky, suddenly struck, throwing his grenade directly at the Emperor from close range.

Alexander was hurled back against the canal railing, mortally wounded. His blood gushing over the snow and his clothing in tatters, the monarch called weakly to be taken to his palace to die. He perished there soon afterwards, and at 3:55 P.M. the palace flag was lowered in mourning. The Tsar's assailant also died, a victim of his own bomb.

Within a few days the police had arrested many of those involved in the conspiracy, and on April 15, 1881, five condemned terrorists of People's Will (including Sophia Perovsky and Rysakov) were hanged on an enormous scaffold that was erected for the occasion on the Semyonovsky Parade Ground. The execution, which was performed most inexpertly by a drunken, red-shirted hangman to the sound of drum rolls, was attended by foreign diplomats, Russian military units and a huge crowd of sightseers.

The Tsar's assassination climaxed a decade of increasing revolutionary violence. At the beginning of the 1870s, the Russian revolutionary movement was expanding, but political conspirators still numbered in the hundreds, and they remained relatively peacefully inclined. Most of these dissidents hoped to effect a change of regime through the peasantry. That downtrodden and ill-used social

И БЛИСТАТЕЛЬНЫЕ ПОДВИГИ РУССКИХЪ ВОЙСКЪ ВЪ БОРЬБѢ ЗА СВОБОДУ СЛАВЯНЪ 1877 ГОДА.

Assassination of a reforming monarch

The Winter Palace,
St. Petersburg, to which
Alexander was returning when
he was assassinated.

Right Sophia Perovsky, the
schoolmistress and terrorist
who gave the signal when
the Tsar's carriage was
approaching.

A drawing from the *Illustrated
London News* showing
Rysakov's bomb exploding.

group seemed ripe for mutiny—and it was potentially well-poised to overturn the Tsar, if only because peasants comprised four-fifths of the Russian population. But how were these "dark people" to be shown the light and plunged into revolutionary action? Hundreds of young revolutionaries went out into the rural areas of Russia in the summers of 1873 and 1874 and attempted to teach the *muzhik* to revolt—but with poor results. Most Russian peasants were loyal to the throne.

Frustrated in their attempts to agitate rural Russia, the revolutionaries switched their attention to the towns during the late 1870s. They formed more tightly knit conspiratorial associations at the same time, but their frustrations continued to grow. Many of them were arrested and thrown into prison without a trial. Their periods of incarceration provided the rebels with plenty of opportunities to hatch revolutionary plots, and in 1879 a number of them banded together to form People's Will, a group specifically organized for the purpose of political terror by assassination. The slaughter of the Emperor in 1881 was only the climax to a series of assassinations that had taken the lives of several prominent victims.

Alexander's assassination echoed around the world, and the *New York Herald* was not the only periodical to regret the death of such a "far-seeing and beneficent prince." Although many deplored the tragedy, many others applauded the assassination as a severe blow to the monarchic principle. (The *New York Herald* also printed a paean in honor of Sophia Perovsky, for example.) Marx and Engels saw the event as one that would eventually lead to the establishment of a Russian commune.

Inside Russia the assassination did not provoke a general uprising, nor did it frighten the new Tsar into enacting far-reaching liberal reforms. After a brief spasm of excitement, the population at large relapsed into political indifference, and soon thereafter the new Tsar, Alexander III, revealed himself to be a far more reactionary ruler than his father had ever been. He rejected certain modest political concessions that had been accepted in principle by Alexander II just before his death, and he submitted to the influence of such diehard reactionaries as Constantine Pobedonostsev and Count D. A. Tolstoy. Alexander III's regime enacted a series of counterreforms that whittled away—but by no

means undid—the progressive measures that the assassinated Alexander II had introduced in the early, liberal years of his reign.

Meanwhile, a reorganized political police force was engaged in crushing the broken remnants of People's Will. Some of the conspirators were sent to Siberia and some were incarcerated in fortress dungeons, while others sought refuge in foreign exile. The few active revolutionaries who remained in the Russian Empire virtually abandoned tsaricide as a political tactic (although the year 1887 did bring the hatching of a plot to kill Alexander III—on the anniversary of his father's death and by a similar method). The conspiracy was foiled by the police and led to the execution of Alexander Ulyanov, Lenin's brother. Lenin himself was a mere schoolboy at the time, and the prospects for a Russian revolution seemed distant indeed in the middle of Alexander III's reign.

Although the assassination on the Catherine Quay proved disastrous to the assassins' immediate cause, it did shake the confidence of Russia's autocrats to a greater extent than any other event of the century, including a previous attempt to unseat a Tsar. That occurrence, known as the Decembrist Revolt of 1825, had instead led to a temporary strengthening of the monarchic principle. It was, nevertheless, the first revolutionary outbreak in Russian history.

For some years before 1825, political conspirators—most of whom were army officers—had been plotting to overthrow the Russian autocracy and to replace it with a constitutional monarchy or republic. After the death of Alexander I in November 1825, Nicholas I's claim to the throne was widely disputed, and in the ensuing confusion the disaffected officer-revolutionaries—the Decembrists—struck the blow that they had been secretly discussing for so long. They persuaded the rank and file of certain units to mutiny and then led the mutinous soldiers—several thousand strong—to the Senate Square in St. Petersburg, hoping that their presence would spark a general rising among the troops. Throughout most of the freezing day the soldiers paraded in the square. They undertook no military operations, but they also refused to heed numerous appeals to disperse. In the end, the new Tsar was forced to bring up artillery units and drive the rebels off with gunfire, causing many casualties.

The "first Russian revolution" was over. It was followed by a rigorous investigation and trial that appeared to have effectively destroyed the infant revolutionary movement and that provided the new Emperor—a notorious martinet—with an opportunity to assert his authority at the very outset of his reign. He then set up a special security organization, the Third Section and the Corps of Gendarmes, to combat subversion in his Empire. Strict censorship and control of education helped to hold the country in an iron grip during his regime (which is sometimes regarded as a prototype of the twentieth-century police state). Like Catherine the Great, Paul I and Alexander I before him, Nicholas I was

obsessed with the idea that an upheaval comparable to the French Revolution of 1789 might take place in Russia. A series of minor revolutions did indeed occur in Central and Western Europe during Nicholas' reign, and they prompted the Tsar to impose even stricter regimentation inside his Empire.

The death of Nicholas I in 1855, and the accession of his son Alexander II, brought about an immediate rise in morale in most sections of Russian society. Hopes of a change for the better were encouraged when, in the year following his accession, the new Tsar solemnly announced that he intended to emancipate the serfs of his Empire, claiming that it was better to accomplish that reform "from above" than to allow it to come "from below." Fear of peasant revolution may have inspired that great reform, but Alexander also sponsored important new legislation affecting many other branches of the administration. For a time the notoriously backward Russian Empire seemed likely to enter the second half of the nineteenth century as a nation aspiring to a degree of political, social and economic development comparable to that attained in the more advanced countries of the world.

At the very time that the Great Reforms were being enacted, however, general disillusionment was setting in. The year of emancipation—1861—was also a year of widespread peasant rioting. The first important student demonstrations broke out in St. Petersburg the same autumn. Nihilists distributed secretly printed pamphlets calling for the massacre of the Tsar, while terrible fires—of unknown origin but attributed by some to revolutionary arsonists—devastated parts of St. Petersburg. To cap these disasters a revolutionary ex-student, Dmitry Karakozov—who was, in effect, the first practicing Russian political terrorist—made an unsuccessful attempt to assassinate the Tsar by shooting at him in the Summer Garden in St. Petersburg on April 16, 1866. In the following year a Pole fired at Alexander during a visit to Paris.

Fearing unknown assassins, Alexander gave

The hanging of the terrorists convicted of the assassination of Alexander II.

V. K. Pleve, the Minister for the Interior, who tried to exterminate the terrorists. He himself was assassinated in 1904.

735

The coronation of Tsar Alexander II in 1856. The splendor of the Russian Court and high society contrasted with the miserable conditions of the populace.

The barricades of the unsuccessful 1905 Revolution. After Alexander's assassination the revolutionary movement grew gradually in size and reached its peak in 1917.

virtual control of the Empire's internal management to Peter Shuvalov, his chief of political police from 1866 to 1874. During the last decade and a half of his reign, the Emperor's reforming impetus was very much in abeyance and accordingly those were years of comparatively severe political reaction. Even so, Alexander II remains the most effective sponsor of humane reform among Russia's supreme rulers—Tsars and Soviet dictators alike—and it was a harsh dispensation of fate which decreed that he, rather than Nicholas I, should be struck down by revolutionary violence. (Some four years after Alexander's death a similar fate overtook Abraham Lincoln, who shares with the Russian

Emperor the achievement of having abolished slavery in an extensive section of the globe.)

After a long setback following the assassination of Alexander II, the Russian revolutionary movement gradually gathered new strength in secret. From the 1880s onward, Russian subversives living in temporary or permanent exile abroad played an especially important role in plotting the overthrow of the imperial system. But until the turn of the century, Russian revolutionary development, both at home and abroad, proceeded very largely on the plane of words. The age was one in which revolutionaries concentrated more on hammering out doctrine than on initiating action. Expatriate Russians published many pamphlets and periodicals on presses located outside Russia and smuggled such material into the Empire in quantity. During that period those same expatriates remained comparatively inactive in fomenting strikes and street demonstrations; no leading Russian statesmen were assassinated during the years 1881–1901.

If fringe groups such as the Anarchists are excluded, Russian revolutionaries can be said to have fallen into two opposed camps by the turn of the century. One of these groups was the Narodniks (Populists), so termed because they continued to champion the *narod*, or common people (in effect, the peasantry). That group ultimately took the name Socialist Revolutionaries and founded, at the beginning of the twentieth century, the Socialist

Revolutionary Party, a largely clandestine body. At the same time they secretly established a small and virtually independent fighting organization, which was to revive the tactic of political terror by assassination on a scale unprecedented in Russia.

That terror campaign began in a small way in 1901, when a former student murdered the Minister of Education. The next year saw the assassination of D. S. Sipyagin, who was Minister for the Interior and therefore included overall responsibility for the police among his many duties. His successor was V. K. Pleve, who tried to contain growing revolutionary violence by severe repressive measures. Despite such tactics—or because of them—Pleve himself fell victim to an assassin: on July 27, 1904, his carriage was blown to piece by a bomb.

The following year saw the outbreak of the unsuccessful Russian Revolution of 1905, sometimes termed the dress rehearsal for 1917. Widespread military and naval mutinies, manifold peasant riots, large-scale strikes and popular demonstrations—all lacking any effective central organization—were features of that disturbed year. Other significant episodes of 1905 were a sizable uprising in Moscow and a short-lived operation in St. Petersburg of a Soviet of Workers' Deputies which attempted to usurp some of the functions of government. Its members were arrested wholesale on December 15, 1905.

Meanwhile political assassination—chiefly of minor police officials, but including a Governor-General of Moscow, a Town Captain of St. Petersburg and several provincial governors—increased to the point where victims numbered in the hundreds. Reprisals by police and troops, combined with numerous summary death sentences awarded by military courts and field courts-martial, caused thousands of fatalities among the population. Those operations completely eclipsed the political terror and counterterror of Alexander II's last years. And though no successful attempt was made on the life of Nicholas II, who had succeeded to the Russian throne, several plots to kill him were devised. The police, using a network of informers

posing as revolutionaries, managed to thwart those plots, and by 1907 the imperial government had so effectively asserted its authority that revolution once more appeared to be on the retreat.

The other large semiclandestine revolutionary group of the late imperial period, the Russian Marxist movement, attracted less public attention than the more flamboyant Socialist Revolutionaries. That lack of notoriety was partly due to the Marxists' rejection of assassination as a means of accomplishing revolution—not as a matter of principle, but because they considered it ineffective. In 1898 the Marxists founded the Russian Social Democratic Workers' Party at Minsk; five years later, at the Second Congress in London, the Party split into two violently opposed factions—the Bolsheviks and the Mensheviks. Lenin, who was the leader of the Bolsheviks, did not seem particularly dangerous to the Russian political police of the period. On the contrary, his habit of quarreling viciously with rival Social Democrats (while recruiting a small and apparently harmless cadre of followers who were blindly loyal to him) seemed a positive advantage to the authorities for it split, and so weakened, an important section of the revolutionary movement.

Although Lenin would not have sponsored Alexander II's assassination (which he regarded as a mistaken political tactic), he was wholeheartedly committed to the use of violence wherever he saw a prospect of political gain. Indeed, the assassination of Tsar Alexander II gains new significance when examined in the context of Lenin's successful revolutionary coup of November, 1917. Unfortunately for Russia, political changes such as have often occurred in other countries through peaceful evolutionary means have frequently been brought about there by violence. The slaughter of the reforming Tsar was just such a tragic landmark in history—and it dealt a serious blow to the increasingly discredited monarchic principle throughout Europe. It shook every throne in Europe by removing an autocrat who, for all his reforms, had some claim to be regarded as the world's premier despot.

RONALD HINGLEY

Tsar Alexander III, whose reign was more repressive than that of his father, Alexander II.

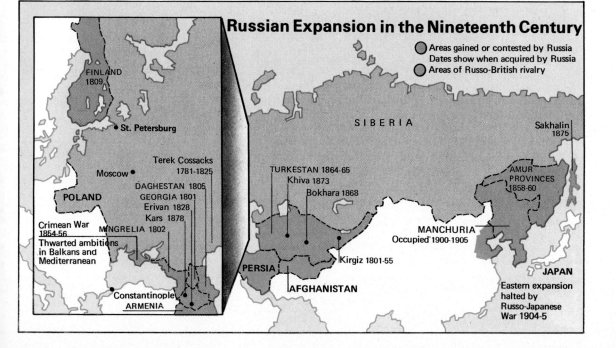

Russian Expansion in the Nineteenth Century

- ● Areas gained or contested by Russia Dates show when acquired by Russia
- ● Areas of Russo-British rivalry

FINLAND 1809

St. Petersburg

SIBERIA

Sakhalin 1875

Terek Cossacks 1781-1825

Moscow

DAGHESTAN 1805

POLAND

GEORGIA 1801

Erivan 1828

Kars 1878

MINGRELIA 1802

Crimean War 1854-56

Thwarted ambitions in Balkans and Mediterranean

Constantinople

ARMENIA

TURKESTAN 1864-65

Khiva 1873

Bokhara 1868

PERSIA

AFGHANISTAN

Kirgiz 1801-55

AMUR PROVINCES 1858-60

MANCHURIA
Occupied 1900-1905

JAPAN

Eastern expansion halted by Russo-Japanese War 1904-5

Parliamentary developments

"Parliaments are the great lie of our time." With that caustic generalization, Konstantin Pobedonostsev, the Chief Minister of Tsar Alexander III, inadvertently epitomized the contrast between Russia and the other nations of Europe in the late nineteenth century. While the Russian Empire tightened the bonds of autocracy through a series of repressive laws in the early 1880s, representative governments flourished in other parts of Europe on a far broader basis than had seemed possible thirty years before. Universal manhood suffrage was established in France and Germany in 1871; in Switzerland in 1874; in Spain in 1890; and in Belgium in 1893. It was introduced—with certain minor exemptions—in Britain in 1884 and in Holland in 1890. The franchise in Italy, although broadened in 1882, remained limited by property and educational qualifications until the eve of World War I. Lip service was paid to the

Emperor Mutsuhito of Japan who established the beginning of representative government in Japan.

concept of democratic control in the Balkan States, but political realities fell far short of constitutional provisions. There alone, perhaps, Pobedonostsev's remark had some justification.

In Britain, the last third of the century saw the classic parliamentary duel between the liberalism of Gladstone and the conservative philosophy of empire and social reform grafted to the old Tory Party by Disraeli. It was also an era of great parliamentarians on the Continent. The German Center Party, led by Ludwig Windthorst,

and the German National Liberals, led by Count Bennigsen, ensured that the Reichstag in Berlin was no mere echoing vault for Bismarck's thunder. The eloquence of such master craftsmen as Léon Gambetta, Jules Ferry and Georges Clemenceau made the Chamber of Deputies in Paris the real center of French political life and an effective bastion against the neo-Bonapartism of the right. And the parliament in Budapest—although by no means representative of all Hungary's nationalities—achieved under Kalman Tisza a dignity comparable to the institutions at Westminster.

Nor were these developments limited to Europe. The Congress of the United States was more powerful than the presidency in the last decades of the century, and in 1889 the Japanese Emperor Mutsuhito approved a constitution that established a Chamber of Peers and a Diet elected on a limited franchise. On the other hand, Sultan Abdul Hamid II rescinded political concessions forced on him by the Great Powers during the Eastern crises of 1875 and 1878 and continued to rule Turkey despotically until 1908. In Latin America power remained in the hands of self-perpetuating oligarchies that reduced parliamentary life to a completely empty formality.

On Liberty and liberal reform

The most venerated theorist of Western liberalism was John Stuart Mill (1806–73), whose great plea for minority rights, *On Liberty,* was published as early as 1859. Although Mill was primarily concerned with British institutions, he was much influenced by French traditions and spent several months each year in France. He enjoyed a respect on the Continent that was rare among English political writers, and his work was even translated into Serbo-Croat by the exiled Peter Karageorgevich (who was to ascend the Serbian throne in 1903).

In Britain itself Mill educated both the main parties: it was Disraeli, a Conservative, who pushed through the Second Parliamentary Reform Act of 1867 (which gave the vote to more than 1 million town laborers), but it was Gladstone, a Liberal, who passed the Third Reform Act of 1884 (which extended the franchise to 2 million farm workers). Yet there

was a significant limit to Mill's influence even in his native land. During the debates on the 1867 act, Mill proposed that any woman who paid taxes ought, by right, to enjoy the vote. His motion was overwhelmingly defeated in the House of Commons and his championship of female suffrage was scorned in *Punch* and satirized by

John Stuart Mill, the most venerated theorist of Western liberalism, and author of the classic plea for minority rights, *On Liberty.*

Gilbert and Sullivan, whose operas were then at the peak of their popularity. The first country to give women the right to vote was New Zealand, which did so in 1893.

The 1870s and 1880s were decades of domestic reform in Britain. Under Gladstone's leadership the Liberals laid the foundations of a national system of education, checked the scourge of alcoholism by controlling the sale of liquor, recognized the principle of privacy in casting votes in an election, established a more equitable system of entry into the higher ranks of the civil service and the army and centralized the judicature. Disraeli and the Conservatives were responsible for the earliest attempts to deal with slum clearance on a national scale and for giving governmental backing to local authorities' attempts to improve sanitation and

hygiene (and thereby stamp out cholera and limit the spread of other infectious diseases). The Disraeli government of 1874–80 was also the first administration to allow trade unionists to undertake peaceful picketing during a strike. And it was the Conservatives, under Lord Salisbury, who extended the principle of democratic control to smaller communities by the Local Government Act of 1888.

The Irish Question

Throughout this period British politics were dominated by the Irish Question and, in particular, by Parliament's failure to understand the Irish tenancy system or to perceive that the life of an Irish tenant farmer was more akin to that of an Eastern European peasant than that of an English farmer. Gladstone's Irish Land Act improved the status of the tenants, but it came too late to check violence and outrage. The brilliant political tactics of Charles Stewart Parnell and his Irish Party in the House of Commons kept the Irish Question in the forefront of people's minds for nearly ten years—until, in 1886, Gladstone himself became convinced that only Home Rule for Ireland would provide an answer. Nearly a hundred of Gladstone's own supporters at Westminster revolted at his proposal to set up an Irish parliament in Dublin, and the Liberal Party was sundered (just as

Charles Stewart Parnell, leader of the Irish Party, whose brilliant tactics forced Gladstone to support Home Rule for Ireland.

Peel's Tories had been over repeal of the Corn Laws forty years earlier). It was not until after World War I that a compromise solution gave self-government to southern Ireland, and even that settlement maintained close links between Ulster and Parliament at Westminster.

Religion on the Continent

Ireland was one of the few problems in British politics to involve religious issues, for the southern Irish were overwhelmingly Roman Catholic, and Ulster was staunchly Protestant. On the Continent, however, religion still dominated political life. This interest was maintained partly because governments distrusted the social implications of the doctrine of Papal Infallibility (which had been promulgated at the Vatican Council of 1870 and required the obedience of Roman Catholics to papal pronouncements on questions of faith and morals). Between 1873 and 1879 a fundamental conflict of beliefs arose in Germany. During that *Kulturkampf* the authorities sought—unsuccessfully—to subordinate the Roman Catholic Church to state regimentation by insisting upon inspection of Church schools and by an attempt to forbid priests to introduce controversial issues into their sermons.

Relations between Church and State were also strained at this time in Austria, Spain, Italy and Belgium. However, the most protracted disputes over Church rights in education arose in France in the 1880s—and apart from a brief interlude in the early 1890s they continued until the eve of World War I. The radical statesman, Jules Ferry, was responsible for the momentous law of March, 1882, that established free, nonclerical and compulsory primary education in France but which insisted on the teaching of essentially Christian ethics without the propagation of a specifically religious faith. Later, radical politicians attacked the alleged support given by the Catholic episcopate to anti-Republican movements of the right, and in 1905 the French government even went so far as to abrogate the Concordat, which had regulated Church-State relations since the time of Napoleon.

The Third Republic

These waves of anticlericalism in France were evidence of the growing self-confidence of the Republican leaders. In 1871 it had seemed as if the Third Republic would last no longer than its two predecessors. The bloody suppression of the Paris Commune in May

Georges Clemenceau, known as "The Tiger." His biting tongue destroyed many governments in France but kept him out of office for thirty years.

of 1871 had dealt a blow to French politics from which it had only just recovered at the turn of the century. Socialism was in eclipse after 1871, and the French provinces imposed a socially conservative government on the chastened capital. From 1871 to 1876 the monarchists were actually in a majority in both chambers of the National Assembly. They were, however, divided among supporters of the houses of Bourbon, Orleans and Bonaparte, and as Louis Thiers, the old Orleanist who served as the first President of the Republic, declared: "There is only one throne and three people cannot sit on it." The French electorate gradually resigned itself to a moderately conservative republicanism (whose representatives gained control of the lower house, or Chamber of Deputies, in 1876 and of the upper house, or Senate, in 1879).

Administrations under the Third Republic were notoriously short-lived. Between 1871 and 1914 there were fifty-eight governments under thirty-four different prime ministers (compared with twelve governments and seven premiers in Britain). A complicated and variable system of proportional representation led to a multiplicity of political parties. Each government was a coalition formed for one

political purpose, and once this purpose was achieved, the coalition tended to disintegrate. Moreover, if deputies voted against a ministry and forced it to resign, their action did not involve them in the risks and expense of a general election (as it would have done in Britain), and there was thus a greater willingness to overthrow governments in France than in countries with a more rigid constitutional structure. The system also had the effect of keeping strong personalities who were unwilling to compromise with other political factions out of the highest office. Thus Léon Gambetta, the archetypal Republican of the 1870s, was Prime Minister for only nine weeks, and Clemenceau, "the Tiger" whose biting tongue destroyed innumerable governments, did not become Prime Minister until 1906—after thirty years' experience in the Chamber and the Senate.

General Boulanger, leader of a proposed coup d'etat in Paris, whose nerve failed at the last minute.

Critics of the Republic exploited instances of corruption to demand constitutional reform from time to time. Their favorite panacea was a strong executive, modeled on the American presidency, and in 1889 it seemed as if they might have their way. There was danger of a military coup d'etat in Paris, for the political right had found a handsome and popular political champion in General Boulanger. But the General's nerve failed at the last moment and the Republican constitution remained fundamentally unchanged until the disasters of 1940. The Third Republic was a narrowly bourgeois regime, but it had qualities of durability unknown in France since the Revolution, and it ensured the French people a prosperity and world prestige that had seemed unattainable after the defeat of 1870.

The climax of the age of steam

All these developments went side by side with a growth of industrial production that was most marked in the United States but affected Britain, Germany, France, Austria-Hungary and northern Italy as well. The world output of steel multiplied sevenfold in the last twenty years of the century, and production of pig iron more than doubled. At the same time the climax of the Steam Age brought about a revolution in the supply of food. The first transcontinental railway in the United States had been opened in 1869—the same year in which the completion of the Suez Canal speeded up communications between Europe and the Far East. It was followed by the Canadian Pacific Railway in the mid-1880s and by three other routes that eventually linked the American prairies with the Atlantic and Pacific coasts. After 1876, refrigeration in ships and on freight cars enabled frozen meat from Australasia and the Americas to be conveyed to Europe.

The rapidly expanding urban population of Europe benefited from these fresh sources of food, but the farmers were alarmed. A flood of corn from the American Midwest, coupled with the likelihood that railways would soon open up the rich granary of southern Russia, posed new challenges. Of great concern was the fact that the price of home-produced wheat was in danger. Farmers in most Continental countries demanded governmental protection, and industrialists also seemed eager to counter foreign competition. Bismarck's Germany erected tariff walls in 1879. France and Austria-Hungary safeguarded manufactures in 1881 and agriculture in 1885. The Russians and the Spanish (who had never entirely accepted free trade) increased their tariffs in the late 1870s. Italy turned to protection in 1887, Sweden in 1888, and Switzerland in 1891. The United States responded with tariffs higher than any in Europe. Britain, still the largest exporter of industrial machinery in the world in 1880, stuck to her principles of free trade despite the protests of landlords and farmers.

Elsewhere, the liberal interlude of free trade and laissez-faire was receding rapidly; the advent of big business was soon to revolutionize the pattern of industrial society.

The Birth of Big Business

In August of 1859, a speculator named Edwin Drake struck "black gold" near Titusville, Pennsylvania—and the American oil rush was on. Four years later, John D. Rockefeller bought his first oil refinery in Cleveland, Ohio. By the end of the decade, Rockefeller and his partners had built their refinery into the largest oil-cracking operation in Cleveland—and they had begun to expand. By 1872, Rockefeller's company had taken over thirty-four rival firms and virtually dominated Cleveland's refining capacity; nine years later they controlled 90 per cent of the country's oil pipelines as well. In 1882, Rockefeller's holdings were merged into the Standard Oil Trust. That vast combine, which produced 80 per cent of the nation's refined oil, was notable for two reasons. First, it was probably the largest manufacturing firm on earth, and second, it was run by a centralized and efficient administration that was to characterize American Big Business.

John D. Rockefeller, who created the giant Standard Oil Trust.

Opposite 26 Broadway, headquarters of the Standard Oil Trust in the late nineteenth century.

The Standard Oil Trust was formed in January, 1882, when stockholders of forty companies (all of which were owned or controlled by the Standard Oil Company of Ohio) signed an agreement to place their stock in the hands of nine trustees. The trustees, chief executives of firms wholly or partially owned by Standard Oil, were given power "to exercise supervision over the affairs of several Standard Oil Companies, and, so far as practicable, over several other companies or partnerships, any portion of whose stock is held." In exchange the stockholders received dividend-bearing certificates from the Trust.

At the time that the agreements were signed, Standard Oil was already a huge enterprise operating in several states of the Union. Under existing United States law, however, corporations chartered in one state were not permitted to own or hold stock property in another. Thus the Standard Oil Trust formed in 1882 was part of a plan worked out by the company's recently acquired legal counselor, Samuel T. C. Todd, to circumvent these regulations and bring the sprawling combination under central control. Under the trusteeship device, Standard Oil ceded control of its wholly owned corporations to those corporations' trustees. That gesture was a mere technicality of course; the directors of Standard Oil remained in firm control of the huge combine.

The formation of the trust marked the culmination of a decade of effort by John D. Rockefeller and his associates to bring order and stability to one of the youngest and most chaotic of American industries. From the moment that Edwin Drake's celebrated drilling rig first gushed oil at Titusville, Pennsylvania, in August, 1859, the atmosphere in the producing region had been characterized by hectic exploration, optimistic speculation, soaring land prices, conspicuous waste and rapidly increasing output. Competition was hardly less keen in the refining of crude oil. In 1863, the year Rockefeller entered the industry, a small refinery could be built in Cleveland for as little as seven thousand dollars—and by the end of the decade Cleveland had at least twenty-six refining firms. Others were located in the oil-producing region around Titusville, in Pittsburgh, and in many of the large consuming centers of the nation. Refineries were also built in New York, Philadelphia and Baltimore to serve the rapidly growing export trade.

Technological developments in the manufacture of coal oil in both Europe and America during the 1850s had helped prepare world markets for petroleum, and the relatively cheap new fuel rapidly displaced coal oil, candles and whale oil as a source of light. Yet the output of crude oil rose even faster than the growing demand—from 2,000 barrels in 1859 to 4,800,000 barrels in 1869 and to nearly 10 million barrels in 1873. However, despite this phenomenal increase, by 1868 both prices and profits were falling.

By the end of the 1860s the firm of Rockefeller, Andrews and Flagler was refining three thousand barrels a day, about 10 per cent of Cleveland's output. It was already the largest refinery in the city. But up to that point the firm's growth had been largely internal, derived from ploughed-back profits, bank loans and the investments of a tightly knit, carefully selected group of partners. However, after incorporating the firm as the Standard Oil Company of Ohio in 1870 with a capital of a million dollars, Rockefeller and Flagler began implementing a strategy of growth through combination. As they purchased other refineries in Cleveland (beginning with the plant belonging to their largest competitor), they offered either shares in Standard Oil or cash, at a price based on an appraisal of "use value" rather than a cost of the investment to former owners. By the end of 1872 they had purchased thirty-four firms and had Cleveland's refining capacity firmly within the Standard Oil Company. From there they moved into the oil regions of

The growth of "the monster"

The Drake oil well at Titusville, Pennsylvania in 1861. Drake's operation typified the small-scale methods in use before Standard Oil developed more modern techniques.

Pittsburgh, New York and West Virginia, and by the late seventies they were an interstate group controlling a large share of the refining capacity of the nation. During the years between 1877 and 1881 Rockefeller and Flagler fought a great industrial war with opponents who were as ambitious and determined as themselves, among them the Empire Transportation Company and the Pennsylvania Railroad. Their victory gave Standard Oil control over most of the existing pipelines as well.

To Rockefeller and Flagler the aggressive purchasing of other refineries, undertaken at a time when other refiners were experiencing serious difficulties, was a constructive plan to bring order to a chaotic industry. But to many contemporaries, the plan represented an evil conspiracy. In fact, few can defend the methods by which the combine was created. Standard Oil bargained sharply for rebates and drawbacks from railways on its large oil shipments before pipelines became important. It spied on competitors in order to steal their customers; it cut prices to force competitors to sell out; and it used bribes freely.

To attribute the success of the Standard Oil group simply to a more unscrupulous use of business methods, however, is to miss those factors that explain Rockefeller and Flagler's achievement. First of all, they used bank loans freely to finance their operations. The purchases of the 1870s required considerable amounts of money (since most rivals unwisely took cash rather than shares in the new firm), and Rockefeller and Flagler's willingness to go into debt reflects Standard Oil's faith in the industry's future and contrasts sharply with the fears of many of its competitors. Rockefeller once said that he wore out the knees of his trousers asking for bank loans. The reputation for utter reliability that Rockefeller acquired in Cleveland (*before* he went into the oil industry) gave him

access to these loans and thus the means to act flexibly and boldly.

Another feature of Standard's growth was its persistent and discriminating search for men as well as material assets. The firm eventually absorbed such able and formidable rivals as Ambrose McGregor, H. H. Rogers, Oliver Payne, Charles Pratt and John D. Archbold. One aspect of Rockefeller's genius for organization was his ability to win over other brilliant men to work for him and his careful attention to the choice of both high and middle managers during the company's early years. Once a man was selected, Rockefeller gave him responsibility and trusted him to discharge it. He was always willing to listen to advice and arguments against his own views, and he preferred

Workmen laying a pipeline in the early 1890s.

decisions made on the basis of discussion. In one sense, Standard Oil destroyed individualism in the oil industry and laid the foundations of huge bureaucratic corporate giants. But in its early years it also set a remarkable example of cooperation among highly able and extremely aggressive men who were given full scope for their individual abilities.

A significant development in the 1880s (one which set a pattern for future rivals in the international oil industry) was the increasing tendency toward vertical integration—that is, toward the control of operations covering every phase of oil production. Standard had already purchased a few marketing outlets before the eighties and had built and acquired pipelines. The firm then moved into the marketing of its own products at home and began acquiring foreign outlets for its growing export trade. This movement into marketing was characteristic of many large firms in America during this decade, for unprecedented urban growth and railway expansion offered great inducements to manufacturers to bypass traditional middlemen.

In some respects Standard was never again to hold so dominant a position in the world's oil industry as it did in the mid-1880s. As new producing regions were opened in Texas, Oklahoma and California at the end of the century, Standard found itself unable to expand fast enough to maintain control, and new firms were created to fill the gap. Standard Oil's world-wide monopoly was further eroded by the discovery of oil in several other parts of the globe during the last two decades of the century. Indonesia, Russia and Burma were beginning production, and in none of these regions could Standard monopolize the new supplies of crude.

By this time Standard Oil had good reason for *not* wanting to appear to be without competitors. Almost from the very beginning of Rockefeller and Flagler's bold initiatives in the 1870s, the firm's activities had been under attack in legislatures and courts. Indeed, much of the popular view of "the monster" arose from publicity attached to legislative hearings in the states in which the company operated, and from civil and criminal proceedings taken against it in the courts by its rivals. As the most highly publicized trust, Standard's reputation suffered not only from the evasiveness of its officers as witnesses, but also from Rockefeller's refusal to undertake public relations activity to answer attacks. Meanwhile Henry Demarest Lloyd's book, *Wealth Against Commonwealth* was published in 1894. It anticipated the attacks of other muckrakers—notably Ida Tarbell's *History of the Standard Oil Company*—that became common in the next decade.

As trusts became more powerful, the public

Red Hot, Pennsylvania, characteristic of the boom towns that appeared for brief periods in the 1860s. Red Hot was built in 1869 and has produced no oil since 1871.

An early retailer of oil.

Dissolved by court order

outcry against them became more strident, for such concentrations of wealth conflicted with traditional mores and with the view Americans had of themselves. Further, as common-law prohibitions on restraint of trade proved inadequate to satisfy public opinion or cope with combinations across state boundaries, the clamor for effective legislative restraint grew. As a result, in 1890 the Sherman Anti-Trust Act was put on the federal statute books. This act made it illegal to combine or conspire to restrict interstate or foreign trade.

Few prosecutions were attempted under the Sherman Act until after a huge wave of mergers had been consummated between 1898 and 1904. Once trust-busting had begun, however, Standard Oil was too conspicuous to escape prosecution. The Supreme Court decision of 1911 in the case of Standard Oil constituted a landmark in the continuous search of the American courts for guidelines for dealing with large firms. The Court announced the famous "rule of reason," which stated that a combination was countervening the Sherman Act if it harassed competitors unreasonably. Deciding that Standard Oil had done so, the Court ordered its dissolution into a number of separate enterprises. This decree could not be made effective overnight, and for a time some community of interest still marked the relations between the constituent firms of the old trust. By 1920, however, Standard Oil of New Jersey, which was still the largest oil company in the world after dissolution, was competing with its former member companies.

Thus Standard Oil had been a factor both in the passing of the antitrust law and in its subsequent elaboration by the courts. This imposing body of complex law undoubtedly played a part in improving business practices, in markedly slowing down the merger movement in manufacturing, and in

making oligopoly rather than monopoly the characteristic of large firms in American manufacturing industry. From Thurman Arnold's appointment as Attorney General in the late 1930s to the present, antitrust law has continued to develop vigorously, and antitrust policy has remained a significant watchdog of the private sector. Antitrust law has been more significant than the regulatory commissions, such as the Federal Trade Commission, that were initially organized in response to unregulated bigness. Today neither the horizontal mergers of Standard Oil in the 1870s nor the vertical integration of the 1880s would be tolerated. Yet recent sharpening of swords against conglomerates (combines of firms engaged in unrelated activities) indicates that in the 1960s, as in the 1900s, the public's fear of bigness is greater than its appreciation of economic arguments for and against trusts. No firm can have any guarantee against prosecution. In the twentieth century the American public has become persuaded of the economic advantages of size, but it is not convinced that these advantages will necessarily be exploited in the public interest without competition.

As for Standard Oil, in spite of the re-creation of competition within the United States by the courts as well as competition from new oil-producing regions, the firm Rockefeller created prospered. Nevertheless, the dissolution of the combination in 1911 presented the largest remaining firm, Jersey Standard, with a number of problems. Standard of New York had been the marketing agent for exports in Europe and Asia and had owned most of the organization's tanker fleet. The dismembered company was strong in refining but weak in foreign marketing branches and in supplies of crude oil.

Fears that aggressive growth at home might bring antitrust prosecution led Standard Oil of New Jersey to look abroad for expansion. Here it met

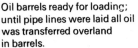

Samuel Dodd, an early associate of Rockefeller's.

Oil barrels ready for loading; until pipe lines were laid all oil was transferred overland in barrels.

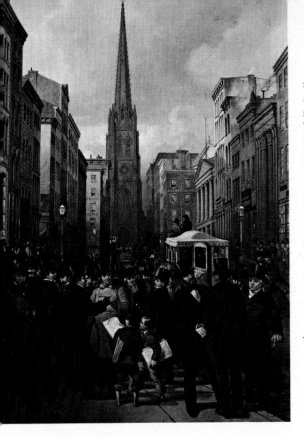

rivals worthy of it, notably the Shell Oil Company, which, as a merger of a marketing firm and a rich crude-oil producer, was fully integrated. Other large American firms, fearing a decline in the domestic oil supply, also joined in the scramble for concessions abroad. Over the next half century few parts of the world were untouched by the great international oil firms. Despite the competition, Standard Oil was operating in thirty-four countries by 1966, and four-fifths of its refining capacity was outside the United States. It was the largest of the seven great international oil companies.

The large international oil firms became examples par excellence of the separation of ownership and management. The leading executives of these firms, not the shareholders, made decisions as to how much of the profits were to be retained, how much released in dividends, and how to manage investment of those retained earnings. Decisions by these men affected living standards in the richer parts of the world both directly, through the degree of success in improving and cheapening oil, and indirectly, through the contributions to governments in taxes. Furthermore, as economic growth in developed nations came to depend increasingly upon technological change, the promotion of research to find new products and to improve the means of producing, transporting and marketing oil placed large firms in a key position to help sustain growth. During this process, the great oil firms diversified into new products, mostly related to their central activities. Jersey Standard, for example, has extensive worldwide interests in petrochemicals, synthetic chemicals and fibers, plastics, synthetic rubber, paint and petroleum resins as well as fertilizers, the manufacture of industrial gases and equipment, and chains of motels.

Although there may be little widespread popular suspicion of these large firms in the United States and Western Europe today, they have become a symbol of economic imperialism to much of the Third World. It is not difficult to see parallels with the hostility and suspicion encountered by Standard Oil in late nineteenth-century America. One basis for the suspicion is taxes: modern firms are taxed wherever they operate, but as integrated international firms, they have some control over where they pay taxes and thus over the amounts paid. Another is the relative stability of price and supply of oil over long periods of time, in spite of occasional price wars among the giants and apparently disruptive international incidents such as Iranian nationalization or the closing of the Suez Canal. The great companies have clearly cooperated for certain purposes—for example, in jointly exploiting oil concessions.

Yet in spite of all their evident power (demonstrated recently by a remarkable stability in spite of rapid growth since the late 1950s and the re-emergence of the Soviet Union as a major oil exporter), these huge international business institutions do experience some limitations on their freedom of action. As one example, governments have taken increasing shares of income in the form of taxes and higher royalties. For another, even without the threat of nationalization, these firms now operate within confines of diplomacy and public relations unknown to the founders of Standard Oil. In consequence, they have given subsidies to medical welfare, education and highways, and have invested in other types of development in regions where they operate. Further, the growth of oil industries in underdeveloped countries is slowed by a basic drawback: in relation to earnings, it employs so few people. Even a big refinery cannot provide the massive numbers of jobs for rapidly increasing agricultural populations that railway construction, the iron and steel industries and mining did in the nineteenth century. Finally, the American companies are still constrained by the antitrust laws. In 1962, for example, United States courts forced Jersey Standard and Sonoco to break up a combination of their Far Eastern interests (Stanvac), formed in 1933 to give them marketing outlets and sources of crude oil.

Industrial circumstances, of course, have not remained constant since the beginnings of the modern oil industry. The creation of the large firm was an achievement in ordering the environment and pooling resources for cooperative endeavor. But that environment keeps changing. The permanent achievement of Rockefeller and his associates was not the control of an industry but the creation of a massive organization and the means of making it work. To survive, bureaucratic firms have had to remain somewhat flexible and aggressive. Since the late 1950s the greater role of governments and the appearance of new supplies and new firms have reintroduced competition, reflected in falling prices. All firms have learned that they cannot afford to ossify.

CHARLOTTE ERICKSON

Education transforms society in Wester

Urban developments

Although industry changed the character of all of Western Europe and the eastern United States by the start of the 1880s, it was only in Britain that town dwellers outnumbered the rural population. Two-thirds of the French people and 72 per cent of the inhabitants of the United States still lived in communities of less than two thousand in 1880. Even by the end of the century the proportion in both countries was no more than 60 per cent in rural settlements to 40 per cent in the towns. Conditions were only slightly different in the German Empire, where the percentage of the urban population rose from 41.4 in 1880 to 54.4 in 1900. Elsewhere, despite heavy industrialization, most families continued to live in the country until after the turn of the century.

By 1880 factories and mass production had imposed a common pattern of social existence, predominantly urban in form, upon most of these countries. That pattern was reflected in the architecture of the period as the designing of public buildings and private houses sank to a nadir of unenterprising pretentiousness. The town halls of Victorian England were an acknowledged aesthetic joke, but such drab uniformity of ugliness was not limited to any one country. The new Hôtel de Ville in Paris, the Metropolitan Museum of Art in New York, the Law Courts in London and the civic buildings along the Ringstrasse in Vienna were all completed by the early 1880s, and each was a mere

William Morris, poet and painter, whose designs for furniture and books helped improve public taste.

pastiche of earlier styles, alien to its environment.

Private dwellings in most of the industrialized nations lost much of their character, largely through the cheapness of railway transport (which enabled heavy materials to be carried over long distances at a reasonable cost, thereby destroying local variations in construction that harmonized with the landscape). Brick walls and gray slate roofs invaded both the suburbs of the larger cities and the villages beyond them as speculative builders followed the railway lines deeper and deeper into the countryside. The threat of urban blight made necessary legislation to safeguard Epping Forest near London, the Forest of Fontainebleau and the Vienna Woods.

There were, of course, a number of artists and writers in various lands who reacted against the

encroachment of industry. In England, for example, the poet and painter William Morris sought to educate the taste of the public by producing furniture, tapestry and wallpaper of artistic quality and by founding (in 1877) a Society for the Protection of Ancient Buildings. There were few manufacturers who shared Morris' charmingly naïve aesthetic socialism, however, and the domestic arts suffered as much as architecture did from urban uniformity.

In general, furniture manufacturers sacrificed good design for cheapness of production and substituted vulgar decoration for craftsmanship. Among the proletariat, traditional clothing that was natural to particular occupations was giving way to cheap suits that were imitative of those worn by socially superior clerical workers. All over Western Europe national costumes rapidly became archaic curiosities. Like folk music, they were preserved only by enthusiasts who had a sense of their people's heritage. Technological invention confounded and confused all the arts as machines began to turn out more and more commodities of standard pattern. In the 1830s Ralph Waldo Emerson had complained: "Things are in the saddle and rule mankind." The pace of the next four decades served only to emphasize the frightening wisdom of his words.

At the time, however, men believed that they were more civilized than ever before, and perhaps they were right. Slavery, except in the darkest recesses of the hidden continents, had been abolished by the 1880s. There was no killing in the name of religious conformity

and, west of the Asian border, there were virtually no political prisoners. Almost every government had accepted an obligation to mitigate the worst rigors of poverty, and advocates of penal reform had secured the abolition of the more barbaric punishments, although it is sometimes forgotten that the last public hanging in Britain—one of the "advanced" countries—was held in the summer of 1868.

Evolution and education

The most encouraging improvement in both Europe and the United States at the end of the third quarter of the century was in education. In 1850, over a third of the adult population of Britain and

Student life in Germany. Great progress was made in education in Europe and America toward the end of the century.

the German states and fully half the adult population of France and Belgium were illiterate. Standards were far lower in Southern and Eastern Europe, and even in the United States a million adult whites could neither read nor write. Great advances were made in the next thirty years: the state assumed responsibility for primary education in Austria in 1868; in Britain in 1870; Germany in 1872; Switzerland in 1874; Italy in 1877; France and Holland in 1878; and Belgium in 1879. High schools grew rapidly in the United States in the decade following the Civil War, and the establishment of the U.S. Office of Education in 1867 tacitly recognized federal responsibility for the growth of teaching facilities, even if administration was left primarily to the individual state authorities.

By 1900, illiteracy had fallen to less than 5 per cent in Britain, France, Belgium, Germany and Scandinavia and to 10 per cent for

The Hôtel de Ville in Paris: the architecture of the late nineteenth century was often unimaginative and consisted chiefly of revivals of early styles.

urope and North America

Andrew Carnegie, who made a great fortune in steel and used much of it to endow libraries and universities.

the total population (white and black) of the United States. But in Russia, the eastern provinces of Austria-Hungary, and the Iberian, Italian and Balkan peninsulas, the proportion of illiterates remained high. At the turn of the century more than half the population of Europe was still unable to read or write. The figure was even higher in Latin America, Asia and Africa.

The spread of literacy in Europe and the United States had profound social consequences. A "popular press" was created in Britain, Germany, Italy and France. It owed much to the sensationalist journalism introduced into America by Joseph Pulitzer in the early 1880s (and which was later carried to extremes by William Randolph Hearst). More newspapers were sold than ever before, and twice as many books were printed in 1900 as in 1880. Free public libraries seemed a natural corollary to free primary education, and many were established by local authorities.

In the last decade of the century, industrial magnates came forward as patrons of the new mass culture. The Scottish-born American steel king, Andrew Carnegie, began to endow libraries on a large scale. Over 2,800 Carnegie libraries were set up in America alone between 1889 and 1919, and the British people also benefited from his philanthropy. Carnegie's example was followed by other millionaires on both sides of the Atlantic, although many preferred to limit their endowments to higher education—presumably in the belief that their nations needed trained engineers, administrators and technicians in order to maintain a high

level of prosperity in an increasingly competitive world.

The new luxury: leisure

Leisure habits were also changing by the middle of the nineteenth century. With the spread of organized work, sports became less casually haphazard, for both participants and spectators had begun to expect regulation and control in their recreation as well as in their daily lives. The establishment of the Football Association in London in 1863 was an event of some historic importance for Britain and for the world; within half a century the Association's code was to become England's first universally acceptable cultural export since William Shakespeare.

The game ceased to be a preserve of the English upper classes early in the 1870s when local churches began to organize football clubs as healthy alternatives to less morally defensible pastimes. Professional football players were authorized by the Association in 1885, and three years later twelve clubs in the English Midlands and in Lancashire formed the first football league. At the same time, the version of football originally played at Rugby School was growing in popularity (although the relative sophistication of its rules denied it the wide appeal of soccer). The English Rugby Union was established in 1871, and the first international match (between England and Scotland) was played in that same year —a full season before the earliest soccer international. Significantly, American football became an organized game in the same period.

W. G. Grace, whose skill made cricket a popular sport in the British Empire.

The first intercollegiate match was played between Rutgers and Princeton in 1869, and a code of rules was drawn up in 1873.

Summer sports were more highly organized in the United States than in Europe. The rules of baseball had been drawn up in New York in 1845, and even before the Civil War fifty clubs were playing a regular series of matches that were watched by admission-paying spectators. Professional teams sprang up after 1869, and in 1876 the National League was established. Lawn tennis was recognized as a sport in 1877 (the year in which the first Wimbledon Championship was held), and the U.S. Lawn Tennis Association was formed in 1881. Golf, which had made rapid progress in Britain in the 1880s, was introduced into Pennsylvania in 1887.

Cricket had long been the national sport of England, but it took the skill of Dr. W. G. Grace— in the years between 1870 and 1886 —to bring spectators into the cricket grounds in large numbers. The first team to leave England visited the United States and Canada in 1859, but the sport never took root in North America and it was the Australians who lifted it to international level. The first Test Matches between England and Australia were played at Melbourne in 1876–77, but a far greater stimulus to the game sprang from the Australian team's successful visit to England in 1878. There had been cricket clubs in Paris, Berlin, Frankfurt and other European cities from the early 1860s, and a successful "cricket week" was held at Hamburg in 1865. But from 1878 on cricket became almost a symbol of British sovereignty. Cricket fields, like the roads of classical Rome, were to survive the collapse of an Empire and provide a beneficent legacy for later generations.

The scramble for Africa

Throughout the 1870s and 1880s, the imagination of the newly educated millions was increasingly excited by a broader prospect of imperial power than had seemed possible a quarter of a century earlier. Improved methods of communication, better medical knowledge, the work of such intrepid explorers as David Livingstone and Henry M. Stanley, and a quest for new raw materials combined to make these decades an epoch of

Henry M. Stanley, intrepid explorer of darkest Africa.

imperialism. Sir Charles Dilke's *Greater Britain* (published in 1870) and Sir John Seeley's *The Expansion of England* (1883) gave the sentiment of colonization a powerful stimulus. The acquisition, administration and development of less materially advanced territories was seen as a divinely ordained mission, an obligation for the white man. Colonies were acquired—sometimes for purposes of trade, often for prestige, and occasionally as strategic bases to offset threats (frequently imaginary) from other powers. Older areas of settlement (such as southeast Asia and the Far East) were not neglected, but these years witnessed, above all, a "scramble for Africa."

The sentiment of imperialism was most marked in Britain, but it soon spread to Germany, France and Italy. Even Gladstone, who was condemned by his Tory opponents for being a "little Englander," could write of empire as "part of our patrimony."

By November of 1885 the railway was open as far as Kimberley, nearly five hundred miles northeast of Capetown. But within a few months it became clear that the line had not yet penetrated deep enough, for in 1886 rich reefs of gold were discovered in the Witwatersrand, another two hundred and fifty miles beyond Kimberley.

The Riches of the Rand   1886

In an attempt to preserve the isolated tranquility of their adopted homeland, the Boer farmers of the South African Transvaal shared a phenomenal secret for more than thirty years. From the 1850s until 1886, they alone knew that incalculably rich reefs of gold ore had been discovered on a plateau south of the capital city of Pretoria. Such momentous news could not be suppressed indefinitely, of course, and in the summer of 1886 gold was "rediscovered" in the Transvaal. On September 8, the gold fields of the Rand—as the main reef was called—were opened to public prospecting, and within a decade those fields were producing 2 million troy ounces of gold per year, or one quarter of the world's output. In that same decade the Transvaal experienced a wildly accelerated industrial revolution and a staggering population explosion that turned the once pastoral veld into a microcosm of modern capitalism.

Johannesburg owes its existence to an accident of geology, not to any conditions of geography, commerce, strategy or politics. The South African metropolis was, quite literally, founded on gold. In the 1880s, deposits of gold-bearing rock were discovered at various places in the pastoral republic of the Transvaal, an isolated territory that lacked both sea and rail connections with its neighbors. A well-established tradition holds that gold was first discovered in the Transvaal in the 1850s, but that the news was deliberately suppressed by the government in an effort to preserve the region's isolated tranquility. In 1877 the Transvaal Republic was annexed by the British, who returned it to the Boers (Afrikaner farmers) after the British defeat at Majuba in 1881.

Ironically, gold was "rediscovered" in the Transvaal less than two years after the Boers and the British negotiated the 1884 Convention of London, which granted the Afrikaners de facto independence in internal affairs. At that time, the white population of the Transvaal numbered perhaps 50,000, most of whom lived in Pretoria, the capital, or in one of two small towns, Potchefstroom and Rustenburg. There were, in addition, a dozen or so respectably sized villages, and a mining camp had recently sprung up in the east. The boundaries of this primitive republic were defined by the Vaal River in the south and the Limpopo in the north. Between these lines, and in the vaguely defined regions to the west and east, lived roughly three-quarters of a million African tribesmen. The revenue of the state, in the year preceding the founding of Johannesburg, amounted to £177,000.

By 1886, a number of prospectors claimed they had found gold deposits in payable quantities on the plateau south of Pretoria. In February of that year, an adventurer named George Walker came upon what was later identified as the Main Reef Leader, an outcrop of gold-bearing rock that stretched down thousands of feet below the surface.

If a date can be ascribed to the founding of Johannesburg, it is September 8, 1886, the day that the gold fields of the Main Reef were proclaimed public diggings. The isolation of the Transvaal had ended.

The center of the new deposits seemed to be under a ridge called the Witwatersrand ("the ridge of white waters") not because it was abundant in streams but because mica deposits in the rocks gave the illusion, from a distance, of cascades. The surroundings were bleak and arid, and the essential characteristic of the Rand, as the ridge came to be called, was that the gold was hard to reach. This was no Klondike or Yukon in which the lone prospector might make his fortune. Its development depended upon the application of the skills of the engineer, the geologist and the chemist, backed by a large labor force and sustained by immense capital investment. In the words of Professor S. E. Frankel:

> The geological character of the gold field is unique. It is marked by the exceptional continuity in length and breadth of its general low grade ore deposits. The history of the Rand is the history of the adaptation of modern industrial and financial methods to the exploitation of a mining field, continually dumbfounding the prophets both as to the area and the scale of operations economically most suited to it.

The discovery of the gold fields had far-reaching implications; the vibrations could be felt throughout the Western world. In 1888, the Rand produced 230,000 troy ounces of gold; in 1889 it produced 369,000 ounces; in 1892, 1,210,000; and in 1894, over 2 million—more than a quarter of the world's output. Within a few years, the Rand had become linked to the money markets of the world, and investors throughout Europe and the Americas felt that they had a stake in the Transvaal Republic. The nature of the industry led naturally to a high level of combinations, and great mining firms began to emerge. Many of the "Randlords," as the mining magnates came to be called, had already made

Cecil Rhodes, Prime Minister of Cape Colony. He aimed at uniting the races of South Africa under the British Crown.

Opposite Boers returning from hunting. The Boers were descended from Dutch farmers who settled in Cape Colony and the Transvaal.

From left to right Julius Wernher and Alfred Beit, mining magnates of Johannesburg; John X. Merriman, who described Johannesburg as "Monte Carlo superimposed upon Sodom and Gomorrah;" Johannes Rissik, the Transvaal gold surveyor after whom Johannesburg was named.

Diggers at work in the Transvaal gold fields.

their fortunes in the exploitation of the diamond fields of Kimberley in the 1870s. Their backgrounds were diverse. The great capitalists included such men as Julius Wernher and Alfred Beit, Cecil Rhodes and Barney Barnato, Adolf Goertz and George Albu, Sammy Marks and Abe Bailey. In the wake of the giants came the lesser men. The Johannesburg Stock Exchange became a lively, and sometimes a frenetic, center of speculation. John X. Merriman, a politician of Whiggish outlook, described Johannesburg as "Monte Carlo superimposed upon Sodom and Gomorrah"; J. A. Hobson referred to it as "the new Jerusalem."

The name of the town was intended as a compliment to two officials of the Transvaal Republic—Johannes Rissik, the surveyor, and Christian Johannes Joubert, the head of the Department of Mines.

The settlement's European population is said to have reached three thousand within a year, but the first census in the Transvaal was not taken until 1896. According to that survey, Johannesburg contained some 50,000 whites and roughly 50,000 Africans, Indians and "Coloureds" (persons of mixed race). Less than seven thousand of the whites were Transvaalers; the remainder came from Britain, the British colonies, Russia, France, the United States, Germany and Holland. Johannesburg was a polyglot metropolis, overshadowing the Transvaal and threatening to transform the nature of the entire region. For that reason the hospitality that the Transvaal government had originally showed toward the developers of Johannesburg swiftly turned to mistrust. At the same time, the new wealth that the gold fields brought to the Transvaal treasury

Monte Carlo superimposed upon Sodom and Gomorrah

gave the government command of resources that it had never previously possessed. Revenue increased from £177,000 in 1885 to £1,557,000 in 1889. By 1896 that figure had reached £3,912,000. President Kruger's Republic had become spectacularly solvent, but as Kruger viewed the situation, the new wealth flooding the Transvaal brought with it a serious threat to his nation's independence.

The history of the Boers was one of continuous struggle to escape from the jurisdiction of Britain. The Boers were descendants of the *Voortrekkers* who had emigrated from the Cape Colony in the 1830s, had moved north into the wilderness and had come at last to the Transvaal, their Promised Land. Britain had engulfed them in 1877, but they had won back their independence in 1881. Now it was threatened again, this time by "the money power." To assert his Republic's independence, President Kruger successfully revived the construction of a railway line to the port of Lourenço Marques, giving the Transvaal an outlet to the sea that was beyond British control. He regarded the inhabitants of Johannesburg as foreign fortune hunters—*Uitlanders*, or "men from outside"—who were not to be regarded as equal to the older inhabitants, the burghers of the Republic.

In the 1880s, the law governing the acquisition of Transvaal citizenship was reasonably hospitable to the newcomer—five years' residence and the payment of a fee of £25. Nonwhites were excluded from political rights and were not regarded as citizens. Male citizens elected the Volksraad, or legislative assembly, the President of the Republic and the Commandant General. In 1890, the voting law was changed to require a minimum of fourteen years' residence and the attainment of the age of forty. That move effectively disfranchised the majority of the Uitlanders. (Independence, Kruger knew, could be lost as easily through the ballot box as at the mouth of a gun.) Those who chose might acquire the right—after two years' residence—to vote in elections to fill the newly created "second Volksraad."

One of the characteristics of South Africa was that the region, from the beginning, was less a multiracial society than a geographical expression. As the suffrage dispute indicated, South Africa was a territory in which people of different origins, language, color and religion coexisted without forming a community. Uitlanders and Boers regarded each other with hostile incomprehension. James Bryce wrote:

Hearing nothing but English spoken, seeing nothing all round them that was not far more English than Dutch … it was natural that the bulk of the Uitlanders should deem themselves to be in a country which had become virtually English and should see something unreasonable and even grotesque in the control of a small body of persons whom they deemed in every way their inferiors.

Flora Shaw, a redoubtable woman journalist, wrote in 1892 that "Johannesburg at present has no politics. It is much too busy with material problems.

It is hideous and detestable, luxury without order; sensual enjoyment without art; riches without refinement; display without dignity."

The Johannesburgers might have had no politics, but they had, or thought they had, grievances about the way in which they were governed. Among other things, they considered themselves overtaxed, and the Randlords objected to the official policy of granting monopolies for the manufacture of dynamite, which was indispensable for mining operations. In retrospect, the grievances appear small, even illusory. It was W. E. H. Lecky who argued that if the Uitlanders suffered the disadvantages of aliens, it was because they had deliberately placed themselves under a "detestable government" for the sake of making money. The fact of the matter was that the Transvaal was experiencing, in accelerated form, the wrenching dislocations of

Old Park Station, Johannesburg. The city developed rapidly after the Main Reef rocks were declared public diggings.

Bottom Simmonds Street, Johannesburg. At first dealings on the stock exchange took place in Simmonds Street between chains that closed the street to traffic.

The Jameson Raid

Above President Kruger of the Transvaal. He tried hard to establish the Transvaal's independence from British jurisdiction.

Below left Joseph Chamberlain, British colonial secretary; he was strongly criticized for his handling of the Jameson Raid.

Below right Dr L. S. Jameson, leader of the abortive raid. The effect of the raid was to increase hatred between the British and Afrikaners, making the Boer War virtually inevitable.

sudden industrialization, coupled with an influx of immigrants that produced the effects of a population explosion. Furthermore, the capitalists were there to stay. It had seemed at one time that the gold fields might be exhausted so far as profitable extraction went.

Johannesburg and Pretoria were thirty miles apart. To travel that distance was to move from one world to another. Two nationalisms were in conflict—a cocky jingoism in Johannesburg, a farouche hatred of foreigners in Pretoria. The conflict became violent in 1895, when a plot was hatched in Johannesburg to support a rising led by a detachment of volunteers from Cecil Rhodes' chartered territory to the north. Certain aspects of that rising, known as the Jameson Raid, resemble a musical comedy staged in a casino, and English poet and traveler Wilfred Blunt called it a "gangrene of Colonial rowdyism." The consequences were tragic, however. Dr. Jameson's force was rounded up by a Boer commando unit fifteen miles from Johannesburg, and Jameson himself was handed over to the British government for trial.

Four members of the Johannesburg plotters were sentenced to death for their part in the abortive coup, but all four were allowed to ransom themselves. Cecil Rhodes, then Prime Minister of the Cape, was deeply implicated, and the finger of suspicion was also pointed at Joseph Chamberlain, the Colonial Secretary. There is no proof of Chamberlain's complicity, but the manner of the inquiry in London—"the lying-in-state at Westminster," as one sceptic described it—gave the strong impression that a great deal was being suppressed. The Kaiser, with characteristic impetuosity, sent a telegram of support to Kruger that momentarily lifted the episode to the level of an international incident. In South Africa, the raid sharpened the racial animosities between English and Afrikaner. It was, in fact, the preliminary skirmish that made the Boer War a virtual inevitability.

That war, when it came in 1899, was at bottom a conflict of nationalisms, fought to secure British paramountcy in South Africa. The conflict has frequently been portrayed as a consequence of capitalism—and in that sense, Johannesburg provided the impetus for a new development of Marxist theory. The progenitor of that theory was J. A. Hobson, who generalized what he understood to be the experience of South Africa into a theory of imperialism. (Lenin, building on Hobson's foundations, portrayed imperialism as the last stage of capitalism.) But to the men who made the decisions at the time, the issue was one of politics rather than economics. To Sir Alfred Milner, the High Commissioner at the Cape, the importance of the gold strike lay in the fact that power was being transferred from the Cape Colony to the Transvaal Republic. In that shift he saw a danger to British power. As far as the British High Commissioner was concerned, the war was fought to preserve the imperial position and to destroy Afrikaner nationalism by force. Britain ultimately achieved a military victory in South

Africa, but in so doing it endowed the Afrikaners with a permanent resentment of British rule.

The history of Johannesburg might be regarded as a textbook demonstration of the errors in the cruder forms of the Marxist thesis. The city's wealth has grown continuously throughout the twentieth century; at the same time, its political importance has declined. It is the metropolis of South Africa, and yet it has never been a dominating center of politics. In this weakness may be seen the failure of the South African English to develop skills in the theory or practice of government.

For a brief period after the Boer War, Milner conducted the government of the Transvaal from Johannesburg. If he had been allowed to do so, he would have made Johannesburg the capital city. "The more I see of Pretoria," he wrote, "the more I am impressed by its unfitness to be the capital of anything.... It will certainly never be the capital of British South Africa, if that country is going to remain a part of the Empire." The British government refused to agree. In the opinion of Joseph Chamberlain, Johannesburg was disqualified because of the preeminence of the mining industry. "I do not wish," he wrote, "to be understood as holding that the moral tone of Johannesburg society is lower than that of similar society elsewhere; my objection is that it necessarily lacks that diversity which in other great cities renders public opinion healthy and impartial." And so the curious duality has continued: wealth lies in Johannesburg, but political decisions are made in Pretoria.

G. H. LE MAY

Above A Boer farmhouse in the Transvaal showing the influence of Dutch domestic architecture; and (*below*) a Boer family at rest. The discovery of gold in the Transvaal brought to an end the peaceful and isolated existence of the Boers.

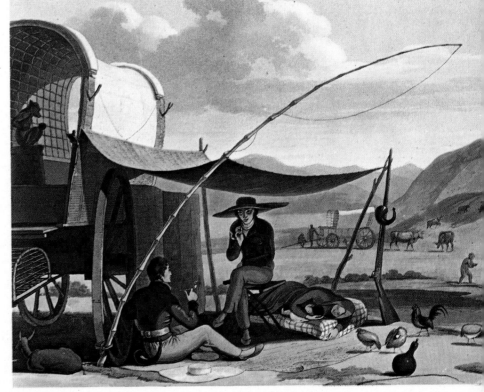

International relations

Throughout the last decade of the century international relations were in a state of flux, with new issues continually modifying traditional enmities. After Bismarck's resignation as German Chancellor in the year 1890, military power on the Continent was evenly balanced between the Triple Alliance (Germany, Austria-Hungary and Italy) and the Franco-Russian Alliance. Bismarck had always feared a French-Russian combination, and it took only four years for one to come into being after his fall from power. Each group viewed the other with suspicion and hostility. The French still hankered for the return to Alsace-Lorraine, lost to Germany in 1871 after the Franco-Prussian War; the Russians distrusted Austrian projects of railway construction in the Balkans; and the Italians resented French predominance around the shores of the Mediterranean. Old problems persisted: Turkey, "the sick man of Europe" for half a century, was by now a permanently incurable invalid, and so long as Strasbourg, the historic capital of Alsace, remained a German city, there was no possibility of reconciliation between the French Third Republic and Kaiser William II's Reich. But the existence of the two rival armed camps meant that, at least in Europe, there was deadlock over many questions. National prestige, as well as economic pressure, forced all of the great powers except Austria-Hungary to seek expansion in other parts of the globe. From the founding of Johannesburg until the defeat of the Tsar's armies in the Russo-Japanese War of 1904–5, imperial enterprise and rivalries in Africa and the Far East dominated world politics.

The sun never sets . . .

During these years Great Britain was in a unique position. Her widespread colonial possessions gave her an advantage over late starters in the scramble for empire and they enabled her to avoid attachment to either of the opposing camps. Successive British governments accepted freedom from long-term commitments as a principle of conduct as sacrosanct as America's Monroe Doctrine. Lord Salisbury, who was both Prime Minister and Foreign Secretary from 1886 to 1892 and again from 1895 to 1900, declared: "British policy is to drift lazily downstream, occasionally putting out a boat-hook to avoid a collision."

Salisbury did not believe, as is sometimes maintained, that "splendid isolation" was a virtue in itself, for he was prepared to

General Charles Gordon; after a distinguished career in China he was killed at the Siege of Khartoum.

cooperate with other nations to preserve peace in the Mediterranean and Far East. But he distrusted the apparent rigidity of the Bismarckian system of alliances. British independence relied instead upon the might of the Royal Navy and, in particular, on the standard —first declared publicly in 1889— that the British fleet would be "at least equal to the naval strength of any two other countries." That axiom of naval policy was not finally abandoned until 1912.

From 1890 until 1907 the supremacy of British battleships and cruisers was maintained by ensuring that their numbers were at least 10 per cent higher than those of any two other combined fleets. Only a Continental league (Germany, Russia and France, for example) could have limited the exercise of British power in this period. Although such a project was debated from time to time, especially by the Russians, old resentments within Europe rendered it impracticable.

Africa and Asia

The three main areas of imperial dispute were southern Africa, the Upper Nile Valley, and northern China. Sympathy shown by Germany for the Boer Republic of the Transvaal led, in 1896, to the first serious rift in Anglo-German relations—a coolness that continued until the end of the war waged by the British against the Boers from 1899 to 1902. In general, the British regarded the Franco-Russian combination, rather than the Triple Alliance, as particularly designed to limit their imperial expansion in Africa and Asia.

After 1882, British troops occupied Egypt, and British proconsuls administered the country in much the same way their counterparts did India. But in 1885 the revolt of a Moslem religious fanatic known as the Mahdi forced the British to withdraw garrisons from the Sudan, an area whose fate was inevitably linked to that of Egypt by the waters of the Nile. The rebuff that the British suffered at the hands of the Mahdi was intensified by the fact that his warriors had killed General Gordon, a great hero of late Victorian England, when they took Khartoum at the beginning of 1885.

In 1896, the knowledge that the French were sending an expedition eastward across Africa to claim the Sudan led Lord Salisbury to authorize a military campaign to avenge Gordon's death and to overthrow the tyrannical government of the Mahdi's successor, the Khalifa. General Kitchener defeated the Khalifa's dervishes at Omdurman in the first week of September, 1898, and proceeded up the Nile to the small town of Fashoda (which was already occupied by the French). For a few weeks it seemed that Britain and France would go to war over the future status of the Sudan, but the French ultimately gave way and agreed to withdraw. Kitchener was left as master of the Nile, but the humiliation imposed by the British at Fashoda rankled France for years to come.

At the same time, the British were close to war with France's ally, Russia. The Tsar's armies were the only troops in the world that could be transported across the

President McKinley. The war he declared on Spain led to the U.S. gaining the Philippines, and Puerto Rico.

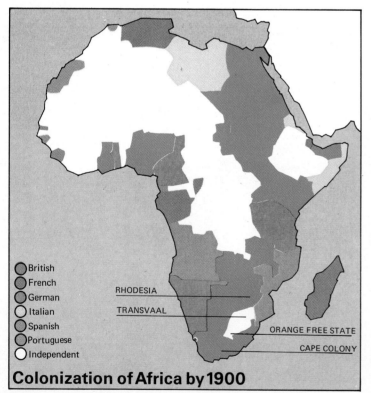

British
French
German
Italian
Spanish
Portuguese
Independent

RHODESIA

TRANSVAAL

ORANGE FREE STATE

CAPE COLONY

Colonization of Africa by 1900

globe without running the gauntlet of British sea power, for after 1891 the thin steel line of the Trans-Siberian Railway linked Europe and the farthest regions of Asia. Influential groups in St. Petersburg and Moscow wanted to carry the Russian frontier southward into Manchuria and Korea, and Lord Salisbury believed that Anglo-Russian friction in the Far East could be avoided only by a preliminary agreement defining their spheres of influence.

American imperialism

Public opinion in the United States was also influenced by imperialist sentiment in these years. The younger Republican Party politicians,

Friedrich Nietzsche, whose writings were later interpreted as supporting totalitarianism.

backed by the newly influential Hearst press, wanted to expand in the Pacific. (At the same time, the Republicans were protesting the brutally repressive colonial administration of Spanish Cuba, where an insurrection had broken out in 1895). In February, 1898, the American battleship *Maine* blew up mysteriously in Havana with 260 men on board. Without waiting for evidence of Spanish complicity and despite conciliatory proposals for colonial reform from Madrid, President McKinley yielded to the general clamor, and on April 20, 1898, Congress formally authorized a declaration of war against Spain.

In the course of that conflict, the Americans gained striking naval victories in the Philippines (which were also a Spanish colonial possession) as well as in Cuba, where an expeditionary force was landed.

After less than ten weeks of fighting, the Spaniards sued for peace. The United States gained the Philippines, Guam and Puerto Rico, and American troops occupied Cuba, which was formally proclaimed an independent republic in 1902. Although this "splendid little war" appealed to long-established beliefs in decolonization, it marked the emergence of the United States as a nation with interests outside the American continent. As such, it was more of a turning point than its champions in New York and Washington realized at the time.

Bloody Sunday

The general mood of Europe and the United States was more aggressive in the last years of the century than it had been in the several decades before. Social tension mounted between classes within the various countries and there were ugly incidents of racial conflict. Peasant risings in Sicily led to the arrest of socialist leaders there, and riots in Milan in 1897 caused the imposition of martial law in northern Italy. The 1894 Pullman strike in Illinois resulted in a major clash between the federal authorities and the American Railway Union, and units of the regular army were called in to quell the strikers. In November of 1887 the Life Guards were called to London to clear Trafalgar Square of radical demonstrators; there were a hundred casualties—including two men so seriously injured that they later died. The bitterness caused by this incident (Bloody Sunday) led to greater militancy in the incipient socialist movement throughout the next fifteen years. Anarchism and syndicalism (the accomplishment of workers' control of industry through strike action) hampered industrial development in France and Spain as well.

Unrelated but equally violent outbursts occurred in France in 1898. They were prompted by the anti-Semitism of the French General Staff, which had imprisoned Captain Alfred Dreyfus for espionage in 1894 and had continued to deny him justice even when it became clear that he was the innocent victim of the High Command's prejudice against Jewish officers. Racial envy also led to serious riots in a number of cities in the Hapsburg monarchy, notably Prague, and throughout Eastern Europe the Jews were rapidly becoming the

Bloody Sunday: the Life Guards arrive in Trafalgar Square to quell an early Socialist riot.

whipping boys of nationalistic demagogues.

Intellectuals, too, were influenced by the rejection of liberal humanitarian philosophy, and the ideas of Friedrich Nietzsche, first put forward in the 1880s, gained rapid popularity. Like Rousseau, Nietzsche was misunderstood and misrepresented. His followers read into his texts what they themselves wanted—a call for the exercise of authority in the state unrestrained by morality. It was a sorry prospect for the twentieth century.

The new internationalism

A number of writers and public figures were alive to the dangers of that warlike atmosphere, however, and they were anxious to counter the hostile fragmentation of the European community. There had been a growing movement for international arbitration ever since 1872, when Gladstone submitted an Anglo-American dispute to a five-nation tribunal. (The dispute involved compensation claimed by the United States for damages inflicted by the *Alabama* and other commerce raiders built in Britain for the Confederacy.) The foundation of an Interparliamentary Union in 1889—and the establishment of the Second Socialist International in the same year—pointed the way toward closer collaboration between peoples. So too did the decision taken in June, 1894, to revive the Olympic Games, after a lapse of fifteen hundred years (although only nine countries sent participants to the first modern Olympiad, held in Athens in 1896).

Alfred Nobel, the Swedish inventor of dynamite who died in December, 1896, left his fortune to a trust fund that was to award annual prizes not only for literature and the sciences, but for the encouragement of peace between nations. And in August, 1898, Tsar Nicholas II of Russia proposed an international conference to limit armaments and check the drift to war. The Tsar's motives were mixed (Russia was feeling the financial burden of maintaining a large army and a modern fleet), but a conference attended by representatives from twenty-six nations did gather at The Hague in May, 1899. Little was achieved on disarmament, but an International Court of Arbitration was established to resolve "disputes involving neither honor nor vital interests." Slowly and hesitantly the conscience of mankind was beginning to react against the shadow of war.

The Olympic Games and The Hague Peace Conference attracted wide attention in the press, but another momentous gathering passed almost unnoticed. The Jewish people of Europe had taken a greater part in the political life of the Continent during the nineteenth century than ever before, but Jews had attained cabinet rank only in France, Holland and Italy. Their share of political responsibilities, even in the countries where they were not actively oppressed, was out of all proportion to the contribution they made to economic life. By the 1890s a number of them sought to solve their dilemma by establishing a Jewish national state. And in August of 1897 the first Zionist Congress opened in Basel.

"Next year, in Jerusalem"

For nearly two thousand years, Jews in all corners of the globe have concluded the celebration of the Passover seder with the ritual line "Next year, in Jerusalem." That phrase expresses an ancient dream, one that centuries of pogroms and persecution failed to extinguish. The Zionist dream—of one day returning to the ancestral homeland in Palestine—became a tangible possibility on August 29, 1897, when the First Zionist Congress met in Basel, Switzerland. But for the singleminded dedication of Theodore Herzl, a Paris-based correspondent for a Viennese newspaper, that Congress might never have convened. Shocked out of his political complacency some five years earlier by the Dreyfus Affair, Herzl had begun to study, to discuss— and ultimately to promote—the idea of a separate Jewish state. The modern Zionist movement that Herzl founded was to survive his own untimely death, two world wars, and half a century of waiting before that dream was finally fulfilled.

Dr. Theodore Herzl, who first suggested the idea of a separate Jewish state and called the Zionist Congress to work for this aim.

Opposite The Rabbi by Marc Chagall, who was a Russian Jew.

On August 29, 1897, Dr. Isidore Schalit, a man with a wide forehead and a small goatee, hoisted a strange-looking blue and white flag with the Star of David emblazoned on it above the Petit Casino in Basel. He then entered the large concert hall, mounted the dais, struck the podium with his gavel and solemnly informed his tense, expectant audience: "The Zionist Congress is open."

Dr. Schalit's pronouncement opened the First Zionist Congress in Basel, and it marked the first international conference of delegates of the Jewish people, who had been living a life of exile for two thousand years. The Congress had been convened to determine the situation of Jews all over the world and to find a solution to what was popularly known as the "Jewish question." There were 202 delegates, hundreds of curious onlookers and dozens of journalists crowded together in the large hall when the Congress came to an end on August 31. By that time the delegates had formulated one of the most momentous resolutions in the history of the Jewish people: "Zionism seeks to secure for the Jewish people a legally guaranteed home in Palestine."

That official resolution was to be the cornerstone of Zionist policy in the years to come and was to lead ultimately to the creation of the State of Israel. The resolution itself was largely the result of the untiring efforts of a Viennese journalist, Dr. Theodore Herzl, who had been advocating such a declaration since 1895. But the idea was not a new one. Indeed, ever since the dispersal of the Jewish people following Emperor Titus' destruction of the Second Temple in Jerusalem in A.D. 70, the hope of a return to Zion had dominated the prayers and dreams of the Jewish people. From time to time, various groups and individuals had tried to return to the Promised Land, but those attempts were isolated and doomed to failure. It was not until the nineteenth century that the Jews' centuries-old longing was transformed into a political and social philosophy, one that gave birth to a movement of renaissance and national liberation.

To a certain extent that movement was the result of the disappointment experienced by Jews who had tried to become assimilated into non-Jewish society. Their failure to do so prompted Jewish intellectuals such as Moses Hess and Peretz Smolenskin to preach a nebulous form of nationalism that advocated a return to Palestine. The movement was given impetus by a wave of anti-Semitism in Eastern Europe. In 1881 a series of bloody pogroms spread through Tsarist Russia, beginning with a pogrom at Elisabethgard in April. A month later disturbances occurred in Kiev and Odessa, and by Christmastime more than 150 Jewish communities in Russia had been devastated by pogroms.

As a result of those pogroms, a Jewish doctor from Odessa named Leo Pinsker published a pamphlet entitled "Auto-Emancipation" in which he suggested that the Jews were deluding themselves about their future. According to Pinsker there was only one solution for them: the creation of a Jewish home in Palestine. Responding to the doctor's exhortations, a small group of students set out for Palestine, where they hoped to establish a settlement. With the generous help of Baron Edmund Rothschild, they created the first agricultural colonies in the land of Israel. Interest in Pinsker's proposal continued to grow, and in 1884 the inaugural congress of a new Jewish society was held at Katowice. That society was called *Hoveve Zion* ("Lovers of Zion"), and its primary aim was the return of the Jews to the Middle East and the acquisition of Palestine as a Jewish home.

The first man who dared to pronounce the words "Jewish state" was Dr. Theodore Herzl. Curiously, Herzl was the last Jew one would have expected to be nationalistic. He was thoroughly cosmopolitan and totally integrated into non-Jewish society, and

Dr. Herzl: "a royal scion of the House of David"

Dr. Isidore Schalit, who opened the First Zionist Congress at Basel in 1897.

The entrance to the ancient Jewish ghetto in Prague. For two thousand years the Jewish people had been living in exile.

he had even gone so far as to propose that all children, Christian and Jewish alike, should have a common baptism to erase all differences of race. Herzl, who was employed as Paris correspondent of the great Viennese newspaper *Neue Freie Presse*, was a brilliant journalist who mixed with French writers and artists and lived and worked in a world where Jewish problems were rarely discussed. His majestic figure, deep magnetic eyes and long black beard were familiar in the corridors of the Palais Bourbon and the Parisian literary salons.

In 1894, a scandal known as the Dreyfus Affair shook Paris. Dreyfus' trial, which began on December 19, radically altered Herzl's life. The agitated doctor later wrote:

I became a Zionist as a result of the Dreyfus trial. I can still see the accused entering the court, dressed in his artillery uniform, decorated with gold stripes; the shouts of the frenzied crowd jamming the street in front of the Ecole Militaire still resound in my ears: "Death to the Jews!" Death to all the Jews because one of them was a traitor? And was he really a traitor? The Dreyfus case represents more than an error in the law. It expresses the desire of the vast majority of people in France: to condemn a Jew and, through him, all Jews. Since that time "down with the Jews" has become a war-cry.

Herzl found the trial profoundly disturbing. For two months he shut himself away in his home, and during that time he produced a pamphlet entitled "The Jewish State." In it Herzl argued that Jews provoke anti-Semitism wherever they live and that their weakness makes them the scapegoats of every misfortune that occurs. Moreover, Herzl observed, the inner strength of Jews and their money make them the object of jealousy and hatred. Herzl's solution to the dilemma was a political one: the creation of a separate Jewish state, legally guaranteed by the civilized nations.

When Herzl showed his manuscript to a friend, the journalist Friedrich Schiff, the latter burst into tears. Herzl naturally assumed that his friend's tears were tears of emotion, but in reality Schiff was crying because he believed that the doctor had gone mad. Schiff advised Herzl to see a psychiatrist, and in following his friend's advice Herzl met Dr. Max Nordau, a man of great spiritual and moral authority in the Jewish world. After reading "The Jewish State," Nordau said to its author: "If you are mad, then that makes two of us. I am absolutely with you."

The idea of a separate Jewish state had been launched. Herzl, neglecting his other work, arranged to have his pamphlet printed and threw himself into the struggle. By then that struggle had become a political one, aimed at convincing heads of state that they should give the Jewish people a home in Palestine, then a part of the Ottoman Empire. At the same time Herzl sought to convince the Jews themselves that his solution was the right one. He was beset with difficulties and disappointments in his attempts to do so. Herzl did succeed in obtaining audiences with kings and princes, statesmen, ministers, royal councillors. He met Kaiser Wilhelm, the Turkish Sultan, the King of Italy, and the Pope as his fiery enthusiasm, his cultivation and his radiant belief opened all doors to him. Herzl's idea was that the Jewish people, if they made a tremendous financial effort, could succeed in finding the necessary money to restore the catastrophic finances of the Ottoman Empire. In return, the doctor asked for Turkish permission to create a Jewish national home in Palestine.

The kings of Europe received Herzl courteously, even warmly, and the Sultan himself appeared to be interested in the plan. It was only after several years of exhausting journeys and long negotiations that Herzl realized that all his efforts had been in vain. No one was going to let him have Palestine.

The Jewish reaction to his plan was an even greater disappointment for him. The Lovers of Zion had no faith in his solution; they were not interested in political action, and they were suspicious of this man who played the diplomat in royal courts. They continued to advocate their own solution: the colonization of Palestine, acre by acre, village after village. Moreover, the Lovers of Zion feared that Herzl's efforts would harm the Zionist movement by raising the issue in public. They were astounded and baffled by this proud, distinguished Jew who did not suffer from an inferiority complex and who dared to talk as an equal to kings. In their opinion, silence and discretion were the necessary conditions of success.

The Jews who favored integration also attacked Herzl, and he soon discovered that there were very few Jews in the world who were ready to demand their own state. The harried doctor did find one supporter, however: in an obscure synagogue in Plonsk, Poland, a ten-year-old boy declared that the true Messiah had just appeared on earth and that he would lead the children of Israel back to their country. The boy, who was to make the Zionist cause his personal religion, was named David Grin. He later changed his name to David Ben-Gurion.

In 1897, in spite of the persistent opposition to his

plans, Herzl decided to convene a Zionist Congress, one that would guarantee widespread Jewish support of Zionism. Difficulties arose almost immediately: the Congress, which had originally been scheduled to convene in Munich, had to be postponed because of the violent opposition of the Bavarian rabbis, who embarked on a furious propaganda campaign against Zionism. Basel was hurriedly selected as an alternate location, and Herzl then turned his attention to the problem of rounding up delegates.

Herzl's fund-raising campaign was a dismal failure: only several tens of thousands of the world's 10 to 12 million Jews voted—and a mere 202 delegates actually attended the Congress. Their ranks did include a number of distinguished personalities of the contemporary Jewish world, however—among them the writer Ahad Kaam; the Jewish leaders Ussischkin, Sokolov, Motzkin and Sirkin; and the future historian, Joseph Klausner. The Congress also included businessmen who happened to be on holiday in Switzerland, and some European university students who had been mandated by their countries to attend the Congress.

As the date set for the opening of the Congress approached, it appeared that the meeting hall would be half empty during the discussions. Such a brutal rebuff to the Zionists spelled disaster for the movement. And then a master stroke was devised by Herzl, an astute psychologist. He informed the delegates that they were to attend the inaugural meeting of the Congress wearing evening dress and white tie—thus creating a most solemn and dignified atmosphere at the opening session. It was an inspiring sight: the huge hall, sober and elegant in appearance, the flags of Israel bedecking the walls, the feeling of the audience that they were taking part in a historic event. Herzl himself dazzled the delegates, and one witness of the occasion wrote:

It was quite extraordinary; what had happened? This man was not the Dr. Herzl that I had seen before, and with whom I was in discussion as recently as the night before. Before us stood a marvellous superior being, kingly in bearing and stature, with profound eyes in which could

be seen a quiet majesty and an indescribable sadness. This was not the elegant Dr. Herzl of Vienna; this man was a royal scion of the House of David, risen from the dead, clothed in legend, fantasy and beauty. Everyone remained seated, holding their breath, as if in the presence of a miracle. . . . Then, a burst of applause filled the hall; for fifteen minutes, the delegates clapped, shouted and waved their handkerchiefs. The dream of two thousand years was just about to come true; it was as if Messiah, son of David, had appeared amongst us; and in the middle of this joyous tumult, I was filled with an overpowering desire to cry out at the top of my voice so that everyone would hear: *"Hehi hamelech!* Long live the King!"

Herzl, calm and solemn, walked up to the podium. As newly elected President of the Congress, he proceeded to make his inaugural address, elaborating on his main idea: the creation of a Jewish state in Palestine. Max Nordau, Herzl's faithful friend and colleague, spoke next. He described the situation of the Jews throughout the world, and that topic served as the theme of most of the speeches.

The last day of the meeting, August 31, was devoted to questions of finance. Before adjourning,

Early settlers in Ekron, Palestine. Small groups of Jews had gone to Palestine to set up agricultural colonies before the idea of a Jewish state was seriously considered.

The Second Zionist Congress in Basel in 1898. The Zionist Congress became an institution in Jewish life and took place annually.

The Balfour Declaration

Arthur Balfour. The Balfour Declaration of 1917 promised British support for the creation of a Jewish national home in Palestine.

the delegates decided on the creation of a Jewish Colonial Bank and a Jewish National Fund—the *Keren Kayemet Leisrael*—which was empowered to purchase plots of land in Palestine and hand them out to Jewish immigrants.

The Congress had tremendous repercussions throughout the Jewish world. Zionism had replaced the flabby hopes of a nostalgic return to Zion with a clearly defined program that crystalized all previous efforts and showed world Jewry the road to follow. The struggle was far from over, however. During the years that followed, Herzl traveled across Europe and the Middle East, attempting without success to arouse interest in the Zionist cause among Europe's political powers. Herzl—who had given up journalism to devote himself full-time to the political struggle and to the publication of the Zionist journal *Die Welt*, which he had launched—was frequently in financial difficulty during this period. The Zionist Congress had become an institution in Jewish life, however, and it took place regularly year after year.

The first great crisis of Zionism occurred in 1903. On the evening of Easter Sunday, an atrocious pogrom broke out in Kishinev, Russia. Before it ran its course, 45 men, women and children were massacred, 1,000 were wounded and more than 1,500 houses were destroyed. Horrified by the catastrophe, the leaders of the Zionist movement began to cast about for a speedy solution to the Jewish problem. Herzl allowed himself to be talked into accepting a proposition made by the British government for Jewish immigration to Kenya (a plan that the Zionists mistakenly called "The Uganda Plan").

Dr. Chaim Weizmann, who took over the leadership of the Zionist movement after World War I.

Herzl considered that plan little more than one that would deal only with the most urgent problems. He put this proposition before the Zionist Congress that was in session in Basel, and chaos erupted at the meeting. The principal leaders of the revolt were the Russian delegates, for whom it was a case of "Palestine or nothing." Herzl, red with anger, got up in the midst of the violent discussion and quoted a famous line from the Bible: "If I forget thee, O Jerusalem, may my right hand wither." He managed to convince the Russian delegation not to walk out of the Congress, but the Uganda Plan was doomed. A commission sent to Kenya by the Congress reached a negative conclusion, and the plan was finally dropped by the Zionist organization.

In 1904, Herzl, who had become sick and worn out by his strenuous efforts to promote a Jewish state, died at the age of forty-four. His death came as a tragic shock to the Zionist movement. At Plonsk, David Ben-Gurion wrote to his friend Fuchs: "The loss is as great and as cruel as the eternal suffering of a race as unfortunate as ours.... The sun has gone down, but its light shines as brightly as ever." A new crisis threatened the very existence of the Zionist movement. Groups and associations began to break away from the main body of the movement, which Herzl's untimely death had left leaderless. The English Zionist leader, Israel Zangwill, left the Zionist movement in order to found the Jewish Territorial Organization. Zangwill's organization, whose mission was to find land in Palestine or elsewhere suitable for the founding of a Jewish colony, did not return to the main Zionist movement until 1917.

That year—1917—was to be the great turning point in the history of Zionism. In 1917 a new man, one who had not previously played a leading role in the movement, appeared on the scene. That man was Chaim Weizmann, a Russian-born chemist who had settled in Manchester, England. Weizmann worked for the British government during World War I. At its height, he solved England's acute shortage of explosives by discovering synthetic acetone, a chemical that made the continuing manufacture of munitions possible. The president of the Committee for War Munitions, David Lloyd George, was profoundly grateful to Weizmann and wanted to reward him for his valuable work. Weizmann asked him "to do something for his people." It happened that Great Britain needed the support of the Jewish community at this time and Lloyd George, then Prime Minister, was only too happy to oblige. His government therefore proposed the formation of a Jewish national home in Palestine—in the hopes that such a move would prompt influential Zionists in the United States to urge the American government to declare war on the Central Powers. (The creation of a national home in Palestine—under British protection—would also enable His Majesty's government to control that country.) England's offer was made in the middle of the war, at a time when it was easy to promise land

and countries that had not even been conquered. Thus, on November 2, 1917, Arthur James Balfour, British Secretary of State for Foreign Affairs, wrote a letter to Lord Rothschild that read:

His Majesty's government views with favour the establishment in Palestine of a national home for the Jewish people, and will use their best endeavours to facilitate the achievement of his object, it being clearly understood that nothing shall be done which may prejudice the civil and religious right of existing non-Jewish communities in Palestine, or the rights and political status enjoyed by Jews in any other country.

I should be grateful if you would bring this declaration to the knowledge of the Zionist Federation.

The Balfour Declaration was received with both joy and surprise by the Jewish world. Surprise—since it far exceeded the wildest dreams of the Zionist leaders. For the first time, Zionist leaders really began to believe in their movement; they could suddenly entertain the hope that Herzl's dream would actually come true. The Zionist leaders' rejoicing over the Balfour Declaration was premature, however. Many believed that the Jewish state would be handed to them as soon as the war was over, and few saw clearly what lay ahead. Among those who did remain cool and calm was Ben-Gurion, who wrote:

England has not given us back Palestine. Even if the whole country were conquered by England, it would not be ours just because Great Britain agreed to it and because the other countries gave their assent. . . . Only the Hebrew people themselves can transform their right to the country into a tangible fact, and they must, with their bodies and with their souls, with their strength and with their capital, build a National Home for themselves, and achieve their national redemption.

At the end of World War I, Great Britain obtained a mandate over Palestine. The National Jewish Home became a reality. During the thirty years that followed, Weizmann and Ben-Gurion became the two great leaders of the Zionist world; yet their points of view on the best methods of creating a Jewish state were very different. Dr. Weizmann appeared as the natural successor to Herzl: he believed that the Jewish people would achieve their aims through diplomatic action vis-à-vis the Great Powers—in this instance, Great Britain. Ben-Gurion, on the other hand, was a realist. He advocated mass immigration to Palestine, reclamation of the land, the founding of new towns and colonies, and the creation of a Jewish economic, social and military force in Palestine itself. He realized that Great Britain's interests in the Arab world would eventually lead to a reevaluation of England's pro-Zionist policy—and might even cause the British government to change that policy radically. For this reason the Jews had to establish themselves firmly in the country and be prepared to fight not only the Arabs but also the British.

Tension between Jews and Arabs increased over the years, and bloody clashes broke out between the two communities in 1920–21, 1929–30 and 1936. In 1936 the British change of policy in favor of the Arabs that Ben-Gurion had long feared and long anticipated took place.

At the end of World War II the Jewish community in Palestine had increased to 600,000 people. It now found itself in conflict with both Great Britain and the Arabs, and this conflict increased in intensity. In addition to clashes between Jews and Arabs, anti-British terrorism began to develop. Finally, faced with a situation that had gotten entirely out of hand, Great Britain decided to evacuate Palestine and leave it to the people living there.

"At Basel I created the Jewish state," wrote Herzl in 1897. "If I stated that in public today, it would be received with laughter all over the world. Perhaps in five years time, however, and certainly within fifty, the whole world will understand."

On November 29, 1947—fifty years after the First Zionist Congress—the General Assembly of the United Nations voted in favor of the creation of a Jewish state in Palestine. MICHAEL BAR-ZOHAR

A view of Jerusalem painted by Edward Lear in the latter half of the nineteenth century.

1745	1755	1765	1775	1785	1795	1805

1803

Beethoven's Rededicated Masterpiece — A brilliant young German composes a vast new symphony that both fascinates and bewilders its first audiences

● **1791**
Declaration of the Rights of Man (preamble to First French Revolutionary constitution)

● **1792-1802**
French Revolutionary wars

● **1792**
Convention establishes First Republic in France

● **1793**
Execution of Louis XVI of France; Reign of Terror (until fall of Robespierre, 1794)

● **1795**
Third and final partition of Poland: gains by Russia, Prussia and Austria

● **1795**
Prussia and Spain make peace with France

● **1797**
Treaty of Campo Formio confirms French victory in Italian campaign

● **1798**
Bonaparte's Egyptian campaign ends when British destroy French fleet at Aboukir

● **1799**
Bonaparte assumes power as First Consul (till 1804)

● **1803**
Louisiana Purchase: United States acquires French North American territories

● **1803**
Resumption of war between Britain and France

● **1804**
French *Code Civile* instituted

● **1804**
Coronation of Napoleon as Emperor

● **1805**
British defeat French in naval battle of Trafalgar

● **1805**
Austerlitz: Napoleon defeats Russians and Austrians

● **1806**
Jena: Napoleon defeats Prussians

● **1806-12**
Russo-Turkish wars

● **1807**
Treaties of Tilsit: peace bet France and Russia; humiliat of Prussia

● **1808-14**
Peninsular War in Spain

● **1810-22**
Argentina, Chile, Mex Peru and Ecuador gai independence from S

1755	1765	1775	1785	1795	1805

...rd von Blücher ...1819 ...an general

Charles X 1757-1836 *King of France* · **Michel Ney** 1767-1815 *Marshal of France* · **William Wordsworth** 1770-1850 *English poet* · **Simon Bolivar** 1783-1830 *South American revolutionary* · **Nicholas I** 1796-1855 *Tsar of Russia* · **Louis Napoleon Bonaparte** 1803-73 *(Napoleon III)*

...aul Marat ...03 ...revolutionary

Maximilien Robespierre 1758-94 *French revolutionary* · **Joachim Murat** 1767-1815 *King of Naples, Marshal of France* · **Walter Scott** 1771-1832 *Scottish novelist and poet* · **Stendhal (Henri Beyle)** 1783-1842 *French novelist* · **Franz Schubert** 1797-1828 *Austrian composer* · **Ralph Waldo Emerson** 1803-82 *U.S. man of letters*

...l Kutuzov ...813 ...n field-marshal

Horatio Nelson 1758-1805 *British admiral* · **Andrew Jackson** 1767-1845 *U.S. general and President* · **James Mill** 1773-1836 *British philosopher* · **Lord Palmerston** 1784-1865 *British statesman* · **Adolphe Thiers** 1797-1877 *French statesman* · **Richard Cobden** 1804-65 *British statesman*

...cisco Goya ...-1828 ...ish painter

James Monroe 1758-1831 *U.S. President* · **John Quincy Adams** 1767-1848 *U.S. statesman, President* · **Louis Philippe** 1773-1850 *King of France* · **Alessandro Manzoni** 1785-1873 *Italian writer* · **William I** 1797-1888 *King of Prussia, Emperor of Germany* · **Benjamin Disraeli** 1804-81 *Earl of Beaconsfield*

...ny Bentham ...1832 ...h philosopher

Georges Danton 1759-94 *French revolutionary* · **Francis I** 1768-1835 *Emperor of Austria* · **Klemens von Metternich** 1773-1859 *Austrian statesman* · **François Guizot** 1787-1874 *French statesman, historian* · **Charles Albert** 1798-1849 *King of Sardinia* · **Giuseppe Mazzini** 1805-72 *Italian statesman*

...é de Mirabeau ...1 *French statesman, ...ate revolutionary*

William Wilberforce 1759-1833 *British statesman* · **Joseph Bonaparte** 1768-1844 *King of Naples, then of Spain* · **Jane Austen** 1775-1817 *English novelist* · **Lord Byron** 1788-1824 *English poet* · **Auguste Comte** 1798-1857 *French philosopher* · **Louis Auguste Blanqui** 1805-81 *French revolutionary*

...s James Fox ...806 ...Whig statesman

Claude Saint-Simon 1760-1825 *French social philosopher* · **Napoleon Bonaparte** 1769-1821 *French general, statesman and Emperor* · **J.M.W. Turner** 1775-1851 *English painter* · **Robert Peel** 1788-1850 *English statesman* · **Alexander Pushkin** 1799-1837 *Russian poet* · **Ferdinand de Lesseps** 1805-1904 *French engineer, diplomat*

...sco de Miranda ...816 ...uelan patriot

Mikhail Barclay de Tolly 1761-1818 *Russian field-marshal* · **Mohammed Ali** 1769-1849 *Pasha of Egypt* · **Bernardo O'Higgins** 1776-1842 *Chilean statesman* · **Louis Daguerre** 1789-1851 *French physicist, inventor* · **Honoré de Balzac** 1799-1850 *French novelist* · **Benito Juarez** 1806-72 *Mexican statesman*

...Alexandre Berthier ...815 *Marshal of ..., Prince of Neuchâtel*

George IV 1762-1830 *King of Great Britain (earlier Prince Regent)* · **Lord Castlereagh** 1769-1822 *British statesman* · **Alexander I** 1777-1825 *Tsar of Russia* · **Percy Bysshe Shelley** 1792-1822 *English poet* · **Felix Schwarzenberg** 1800-52 *Austrian statesman* · **John Stuart Mill** 1806-73 *English political philosopher*

...arles de Talleyrand ...54-1838 *French ...esman and bishop*

William Cobbett 1763-1835 *British reformer* · **Arthur Wellesley, Duke of Wellington** 1769-1852 *British soldier, statesman* · **Nathan Rothschild** 1777-1836 *London banker* · **Lord Durham** 1792-1840 *British Liberal statesman* · **Friedrich Wöhler** 1800-82 *German chemist* · **Robert E Lee** 1807-70 *U.S. Confederate general*

Marie Antoinette 1755-93 *Queen of France* · **Jean-Baptiste Bernadotte** 1763-1844 *French Marshal, King of Sweden as Charles XIV* · **Alexander von Humboldt** 1769-1859 *German explorer, scientist* · **José de San Martin** 1778-1850 *South American revolutionary* · **Lord John Russell** 1792-1878 *British Liberal statesman* · **Helmuth von Moltke** 1800-91 *Prussian field-marshal* · **Giuseppe Garibaldi** 1807-82 *Italian patriot*

Gerhard von Scharnhorst 1755-1813 *Prussian general* · **Robert Fulton** 1765-1815 *U.S. inventor, engineer* · **George Canning** 1770-1859 *British Tory statesman* · **Lord Melbourne** 1779-1848 *British Whig statesman* · **Matthew C. Perry** 1794-1858 *U.S. naval officer* · **Lord Shaftesbury** 1801-85 *British social reformer*

Louis XVIII 1755-1824 *King of France* · **Eli Whitney** 1765-1825 *U.S. inventor* · **Lord Liverpool** 1770-1828 *British Tory statesman* · **Karl von Clausewitz** 1780-1831 *Prussian military theorist and general* · **John Keats** 1795-1821 *English poet* · **John Henry Newman** 1801-90 *English religious thinker, cardinal*

Karl von Stein 1757-1831 *Prussian reformer, statesman* · **William IV** 1765-1837 *King of Great Britain* · **Georg Hegel** 1770-1831 *German philosopher* · **Jean Ingres** 1780-1867 *French painter* · **Frederick William IV** 1795-1861 *King of Prussia* · **Victor Hugo** 1802-85 *French writer*

Paul Lafayette 1757-1834 *French general, statesman* · **Thomas Malthus** 1766-1834 *English economist* · **Frederick William III** 1770-1840 *King of Prussia* · **George Stephenson** 1781-1848 *British engineer* · **Thomas Carlyle** 1795-1881 *Scottish man of letters* · **Lajos Kossuth** 1802-94 *Hungarian nationalist leader*

1805	1820	1835	1850	1865	1880	1895

Charles Darwin
1809-82
English naturalist

Karl Marx
1818-83 *German
political philosopher*

William Thomson (Lord
Kelvin) 1824-1907 *British
mathematician, physicist*

Andrew Carnegie
1835-1919 *U.S.
industrialist, philanthropist*

Louis II
1845-86
King of Bavaria

Alfred Tennyson
1809-92
English poet

Albert
1819-61 *Consort
to Queen Victoria*

Ferdinand Lassalle
1825-64 *German
socialist leader*

Joseph Chamberlain
1836-1914 *British
imperialist statesman*

Alexander III
1845-95
Tsar of Russia

William Ewart Gladstone
1809-98 *British
Liberal statesman*

Gustave Courbet
1819-77
French painter

Francisco Lopez
1826-70
President of Paraguay

Georges Boulanger
1837-91 *French
general, statesman*

Charles Stewart Parnell
1846-91
Irish statesman

Camillo Cavour
1810-61
Italian statesman

John Ruskin
1819-1900 *English
art critic and writer*

Joseph Lister
1827-1912
English surgeon

Leon Gambetta
1838-82
French statesman

Vyacheslav Pleve
1846-1904
Russian statesman

William Thackeray
1811-63
English novelist

Victoria
1819-1901
Queen of Great Britain

Henrik Ibsen
1828-1906
Norwegian dramatist

Paul Cézanne
1839-1906
French painter

Alexander Graham Bell
1847-1922
U.S. inventor

Charles Dickens
1812-70
English novelist

Victor Emmanuel II
1820-78 *King of
Sardinia, then Italy*

Leo Tolstoy
1828-1910
Russian writer

John D. Rockefeller
1839-1937 *U.S.
industrialist, philanthropist*

Thomas Edison
1847-1931
U.S. inventor

Alexander Herzen
1812-70 *Russian
revolutionary writer*

Friedrich Engels
1820-95 *German
political philosopher*

Robert Cecil, Marquis of
Salisbury 1830-1903
British statesman

Emile Zola
1840-1902
French novelist

Mohammed Ahmed (the
Mahdi) 1848-84
Sudanese rebel leader

Alfred Krupp
1812-87 *German
armaments manufacturer*

Florence Nightingale
1820-1910 *English
nursing reformer*

Porfirio Diaz
1830-1915
Mexican dictator

Alfred T. Mahan
1840-1914 *U.S.
naval strategist*

Mutsuhito
1852-1912
Meiji Emperor of Japan

Søren Kierkegaard
1813-55
Danish philosopher

Nana Sahib
c. 1821-59 *Leader
of Sepoy rebellion*

Francis Joseph
1830-1916
Emperor of Austria

Anton Dvořák
1841-1904
Czech composer

Cecil Rhodes
1853-1902 *British
statesman, colonialist*

David Livingstone
1813-73 *Scottish
missionary and explorer*

Charles Baudelaire
1821-67
French poet

Maximilian of Hapsburg
1832-67
Emperor of Mexico

Pierre Renoir
1841-1919
French painter

Alfred Dreyfus
1859-1935
French soldier

Richard Wagner
1813-83
German composer

Gustave Flaubert
1821-80
French novelist

Edouard Manet
1832-83
French painter

Nikolaus Otto
1832-91
German engineer

Oliver Wendell Holmes Jr.
1841-1935
U.S. jurist

William II
1859-1941
Emperor of Germany

Andrew Johnson
1808-75
U.S. President

Mikhail Bakunin
1814-76
Russian anarchist

Feodor Dostoyevsky
1821-81
Russian novelist

Alfred Nobel
1833-96 *Swedish
inventor, philanthropist*

Abdul Hamid II
1842-1918
Ottoman Sultan

Theodor Herzl
1860-1904 *Hungarian
journalist, Zionist leader*

Edgar Allan Poe
1809-49
U.S. writer

Otto von Bismarck
1815-98
German statesman

Heinrich Schliemann
1822-90
German archaeologist

Charles Gordon
1833-85 *British
general, administrator*

Robert Koch
1843-1910 *German
bacteriologist*

Anton Chekhov
1860-1904
Russian writer

Pierre-Joseph Proudhon
1809-65
French social theorist

Henry Thoreau
1817-62 *U.S. man
of letters, naturalist*

Louis Pasteur
1822-95
French chemist

Johannes Brahms
1833-97
German composer

Henry James
1843-1916
U.S. novelist

William Jennings Bryan
1860-1925
U.S. political leader

Abraham Lincoln
1809-65
U.S. President

Alexander II
1818-81
Tsar of Russia

Francis Galton
1822-1911
English scientist

William Morris
1834-96 *English
artist, poet*

Friedrich Nietzsche
1844-1900
German philosopher

Jean-Baptiste Marchant
1863-1934
French soldier, explorer

1811

"General" Lud's Army — Roving bands of jobless English textile workers vandalize the labor-saving machines that have robbed many of them of their livelihood

1812

Retreat from Russia — Cossack raiding parties and an awesome Russian winter combine to decimate Napoleon's Grand Army as it retreats from Moscow

1824

Death of a Poet — England's foremost Romantic poet dies in Greece attempting to aid insurgent natives in the struggle against their Ottoman oppressors

1829

The People's President — American voters overwhelmingly endorse Andrew Jackson, populist candidate and hero of the Battle of New Orleans, for the nation's highest office

1830

The Age of Steam — In an effort to restore domestic tranquility, an unpopular Tory Prime Minister inaugurates Britain's first railway amid considerable fanfare

1848

A Manifesto for the Masses — The last line of Marx and Engels' *Communist Manifesto* — "Workers of the world, unite!" — sparks riot and revolution around the world

1854

Perry Opens Japan — A bold U.S. naval commander all but single-handedly forces the isolationist Japanese to open their country to international trade

1856

The Emergence of Italy — Sardinia's astute Prime Minister capitalizes on European rivalries to piece together the first modern Italian state

1857

Mutiny in India — Upper-caste Hindus serving in the British-led Bengal Army rebel against the reforms instituted by their English overlords

1859

Ape or Angel? — British naturalist Charles Darwin's scandal-provoking "monkey theory" of natural Selection denies Genesis and advocates evolution

1863

A Nation Divided — The defeat of Robert E. Lee's valiant army of "starving ragamuffins" at Gettysburg deals the Confederacy a mortal blow

1871

A Proclamation at Versailles — Bismarck's dream of a united Germany is fulfilled when his sovereign, William I of Prussia, is proclaimed Emperor of Germany in Versailles' Hall of Mirrors

1881

Assassination of Alexander II — Political terrorists assassinate Russia's reforming Tsar, and their terrible deed is noted with alarm by every autocrat in Europe

1882

The Birth of Big Business — Industrialist John D. Rockefeller's immense holdings are merged into the Standard Oil Trust, the world's largest manufacturing firm

1886

The Riches of the Rand — The discovery of vast reefs of gold ore transform the peaceful farmlands of the Transvaal into a booming industrial center

1897

"Next year, in Jerusalem" — The dedication of a single man brings the centuries-old dream of a separate Jewish state a step closer to realization

---

● **1812-14** Anglo-American War

● **1813** of Leipzig: German unite to throw off eonic yoke

● **1814** e Colony ceded by Dutch Great Britain

● **1814** Napoleon is exiled to Elba; peace of Paris reinstates rench borders of 1792

● **1814-15** Congress of Vienna

● **1815** Napoleon escapes from Elba and is finally defeated at the Battle of Waterloo

● **1815** tablishment of the Quadruple liance, Holy Alliance and ngress System (till 1822)

● **1815** russia initiates a German onfederation, including ustro-Hungary

● **1818** British control all India after defeat of Mahratta

● **1820** Missouri Compromise: no new slave states in USA north of 36° 30' N.

● **1820** Britain formally annexes the whole of Australia

● **1822** Brazilian independence from Portugal

● **1823** Monroe Doctrine: no European interference in the Americas tolerated by USA

● **1825** Decembrist Revolt in Russia: a repressive regime follows its failure

● **1828-29** Russo-Turkish war: Russia obtains free navigation through Bosphorus

● **1830** July Revolution in France; uprisings in Germany, Italy, Belgium, Poland (till 1831)

● **1832** Reform Bill enfranchises middle-class men in Britain (1 in 6 of adult males)

● **1833** Abolition of slavery in British possessions

● **1834** Poor Law Amendment Act reforms British poor law

● **1836-37** Great Trek by Boers of Cape Colony

● **1838-48** Chartist movement in Britain

● **1839** Mohammed Ali's revolt in Asia Minor checked by European powers

● **1839-42** Sino-British Opium War: Hong Kong and trade concessions to Britain

● **1840** New Zealand becomes British colony

● **1845** Republic of Texas annexed to USA; leads to U.S.-Mexican War (1846-48)

● **1846** Corn Law Repeal in Britain: a victory for Free Trade

● **1848** California Gold Rush

● **1849** Hungarian, Roman and Venetian republics suppressed

● **1850** Missouri Compromise abandoned: struggle over slavery in Kansas

● **1850** Austro-Prussian Treaty of Olmütz transfers Geman leadership to Austria till 1866

● **1850-64** Taiping Rebellion in China: Ch'ing dynasty retains power with aid of British under Gordon

● **1852** Second French Empire

● **1853-56** Crimean War

● **1856** Treaty of Paris stipulates demilitarization of Black Sea (adhered to till 1870)

● **1859** War of Austria against France and Sardinia concluded at Solferino

● **1861** Liberation of 20 million serfs opens Alexander II's program of reform in Russia

● **1864** International Working Men's Association founded (later First International)

● **1865-70** War of the Triple Alliance between Paraguay and Argentine, Brazil and Uruguay

● **1866** Prussians defeat Austrians at Sadowa

● **1867** Canadian Federation

● **1867** Karl Marx's *Das Kapital*, Vol. I

● **1867** Disraeli's Reform Bill enfranchises British urban working men

● **1867** Alaska purchased by USA from Russia

● **1867-79** State primary education introduced in USA and Western Europe

● **1869** Suez Canal completed; Union Pacific and Central Pacific railroads join to span USA

● **1870** Unification of Italy completed

● **1873** League of the Three Emperors (Germany, Austria, Russia)

● **1875-78** Eastern Crisis: Treaty of Berlin (1878) destroys Pan-Slav Greater Bulgaria

● **1875** Suez Canal: Disraeli purchases half share of stock for Great Britain

● **1879-91** Tariff walls erected by USA and Europe except Britain

● **1881-82** Pogroms in Russia

● **1882** British occupation of Egypt and Sudan

● **1882** Triple Alliance between Germany, Austria-Hungary and Italy — "Central Powers"

● **1884** Gladstone's Reform Bill: universal manhood suffrage attained in Britain

● **1884-85** Congress of Berlin to decide spheres of colonial settlement in Central Africa

● **1886** Gladstone's Irish Home Rule Bill splits the British Liberal Party

● **1887** Secret Russo-German "Reinsurance Treaty"

● **1889** Second International founded in Paris, and foundation of Interparliamentary Union

● **1890** Radical workers' demonstrations in Europe and USA (May 1st)

● **1894** Franco-Russian alliance

● **1896-1906** Dreyfus Affair discredits French monarchists and clericalists

● **1898** Spanish-American War: U.S.A. acquires Philippines Guam and Puerto Rico

● **1899-1900** Boxer Rising in China provoked by European imperialist rivalry

● **1899-1902** Boer War: British commercial interests preserved, but political enmity of Boers intensified

● **1900** Australian Commonwealth Act creates federation

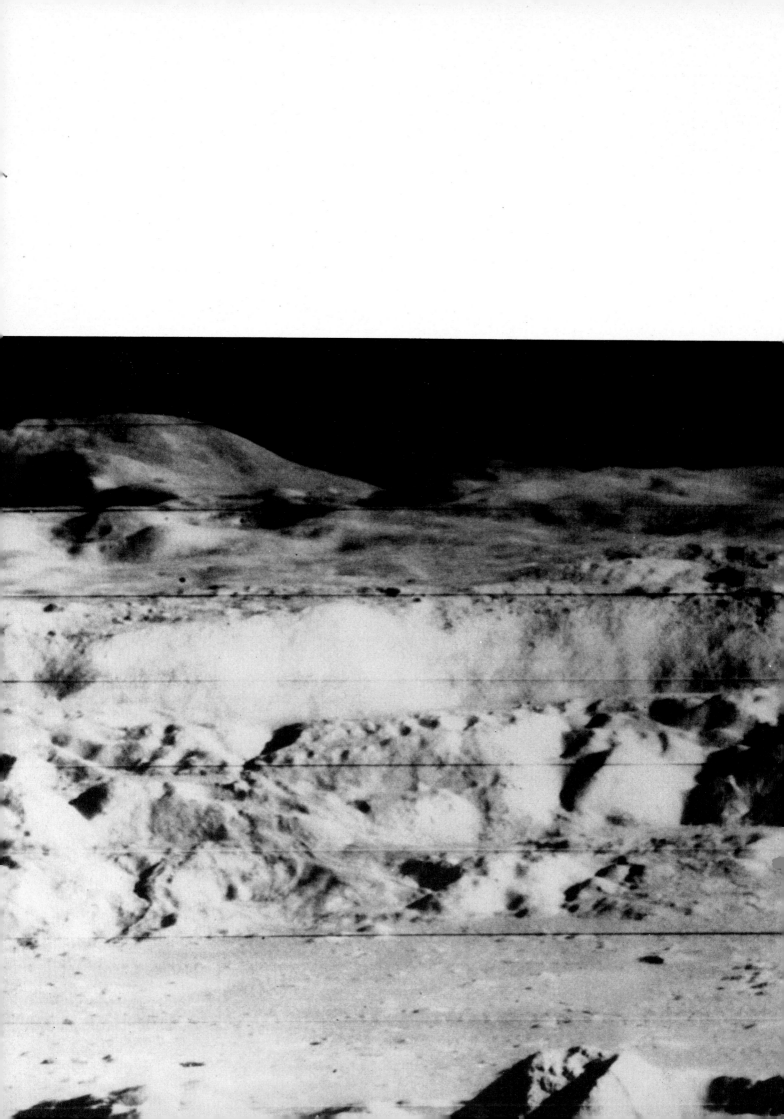

Our Twentieth-Century World

Introduction by **Hugh Thomas**

1903-1969

Introduction

The milestones of the twentieth century have been of two sorts: first, scientific or technological changes that have revolutionized the lives of ordinary people; second, moments when the leaders of the nation states of the world have attempted to grapple with the direct political consequences and the long-term effects of these innovations.

This epoch will doubtless be recalled as one during which the pace of scientific change outran the capacity of political society to organize these developments within viable, humane and predictable systems. In such a light, Henry Ford's decision in 1908 to produce cheap motor cars is symbolic of the new era. So too are the Wright brothers' flight in 1903; the invention of the first moving picture by Edison in 1905; the first commercial wireless broadcast by Westinghouse in 1920, and the first television transmission in 1927; or the discovery of vitamins by Sir Frederick Hopkins in 1906.

The ordinary man would undoubtedly have a list of similar turning points. The coming of the telephone, of contraception, refrigeration, electricity for lighting and cooking, penicillin, washing machines and central heating have transformed ordinary life for a majority of people in culturally advanced countries. Partly in consequence, there have been massive social changes, such as the virtual emancipation of women in the advanced countries, the disappearance of the autocratic family, much increased travel among all classes, and freer sex life (increasingly liberated from fear of venereal disease or unwanted babies).

These advances, however, have had their obverse sides. For example, radio and television, instruments of popular enlightenment, have also been used by artful governments to establish or preserve tyrannies. Wirelesses have frequently been used for spying and eavesdropping. For countless political prisoners, particularly in Russia, the electric light has become a symbol of a kind of torture unimaginable in the less-sophisticated past. The motor car has become an accessory to violent crime, and in advanced countries it causes as many deaths each year as serious diseases do. The airplane has transformed war as well as tourism. The disappearance of the old family life has not always been replaced by a richer social system, while the effect of refrigeration on food has not been an unmixed blessing.

In many ways, scientific advance has been directly harnessed to destruction and cruelty. The twentieth century—although generally one of social improvement and heightened governmental concern for the lives of the poor—has been dominated by the machine gun, the tank, the B-52, the nuclear bomb and, finally, the missile. It has been marked by wars more bloody and destructive than those of any other age, and it has been characterized by tyrants whose control over entire populations has permitted them to imprison hundreds of thousands of innocent people for years without the rest of the world's knowing what was happening. It is, therefore, a matter of opinion as to whether the era can really be characterized as progressive or not. There can be little question that the casualty of the century has been the sense of easy optimism that was a mark of nineteenth-century liberals. Thus the 1960s end with the two main powers of the world, the United States and the Soviet Union, depending for their defense upon an arsenal of nuclear weapons, which, if used, could perhaps end human life altogether.

The political milestones of this period are not always easy to relate to the scientific, medical or technological breakthroughs (even though some military innovations, such as the tank or the nuclear weapon, owe their genesis specifically to political decisions). In general, the history of the era consists of a struggle by governments, ruling classes, revolutionary sects and other institutions such as the Church to adapt themselves to, or take advantage of, those new scientific opportunities. On the whole, governments, classes and sects alike have failed before the human complexities of the task. The old world order, which was based on the economic and military power of Western Europe,

Introduction

was smashed in the course of World War I, and the three multinational empires of Eastern Europe (Austria, Turkey and Russia) were smashed along with it. And in World War II, the big global empires (Britain, France and the Netherlands) received fatal blows. The new world order that took their place, and that is based on American-Russian competition, is no more stable than that of the pre-1914 world.

The first critical political turning point was the failure of the great European powers to avert war in 1914 following the murder of the Austrian Archduke Franz Ferdinand. Even more important was the failure of the warring parties to reach an armistice when it became evident that the war could not be won swiftly by either side. The blame for this was plainly Germany's, since Germany, whatever its intentions before the conflict, clearly decided in the course of the war's first months to establish mastery over Europe by means of territorial acquisitions. The continuance of the war caused the mobilization of vast numbers of men, the gearing of civilian populations to the war effort through unprecedented propaganda campaigns, widespread famine in Central Europe and Russia, the Russian Revolution, the breakup of the Austro-Hungarian Empire into its constituent parts, and the United States' entry into the war on the side of France and Britain. That last event led to an armistice and to a revolution in Germany, in the course of which the German imperial monarchy was replaced by the Social Democratic Republicans.

The failure of the Allies to achieve a reasonable peace, their boycott of Germany at the peace conference, and the refusal of the U.S. Senate to ratify the peace treaty led to the creation of a new world power system based on the weakened Western democracies, Britain and France (which were sustained only by their empires and by their somewhat uncertain alliances with the new states of Eastern Europe). This system did not outlast the brief period of relief that followed the end of the war. The European continent was dominated by fear of Russian-style revolutions,

and this led first the Italian and then the German middle classes to follow Mussolini and Hitler and their new nationalist revolutionary movements of the right. With the coming of the depression, all of the new states of Eastern Europe except Czechoslovakia turned toward authoritarian governments of the right.

Nor did the economic crisis affect only Europe or only the industrial sectors of society: the collapse of business confidence began in the United States and, by causing a general collapse of world trade, affected all primary producing countries. (For instance, no country suffered more in the world depression than Cuba, the main sugar supplier of the world.) During that same period—the 1930s—the Russian Communist dictatorship entered its darkest phase, with the forced industrialization of the country under Stalin's five-year plans, the persecution and murder of several million small landholders, and the assassination of thousands of Communists whom Stalin believed to be possible opponents of his regime.

World War II was the consequence of revived German nationalism under Hitler's extremist leadership. While swiftly conquering the problem of unemployment at home by means of a lavish rearmament program and a public works scheme, Hitler also embarked upon a policy of expansion that he initially justified as a way of redressing the discrepancies in the Treaty of Versailles. A case could easily be made for the military reoccupation of the Rhineland, for the incorporation of Austria and the Sudeten Germans into the Reich, and for an end to the anomaly of the free city of Danzig. Hitler's methods were so hysterical, however, that it seemed certain that war would eventually come, and his invasion of the already mutilated state of Czechoslovakia caused a still pacifist Britain and its neighbor France to come to the tardy realization that there could be no effective appeasement of Hitler's demands. The British therefore gave a guarantee to Poland in March, 1939, and war followed the German invasion of that country in September. From a historical vantage point, it now seems that the best chance of stopping Hitler without reinvolving Europe in war would have been in 1936, at the time of the remilitarization of the Rhineland.

During the course of World War II, Germany and its Italian and Japanese allies overwhelmed the European continent, most of European Russia, the French Empire in North Africa, the British and French empires in the Far East, and large parts of China. The Japanese attack on Hawaii and the German attack on Russia, both of which came in 1941, persuaded the world's two non-European industrial giants to enter the war on Britain's side, and from then on the outcome of the war was really a foregone conclusion. Nevertheless, the expansionist powers held on until 1945, when the war in Europe was concluded by a massive Anglo-American invasion of northern France and a major Russian advance into Eastern Europe. In the Far East, the war was ended by the Allies' use of the first atomic bomb on Hiroshima. This weapon, which had been devised in America largely through the efforts of refugees from Europe, was used to avoid the immense loss of American lives that would have been caused by an invasion of Japan.

The United States' use of the atom bomb has long been considered one reason for the consequent cold war of the post-1945 era—and there can be little doubt that it did nothing to soothe the pathologically suspicious Russian mentality as to the intentions of the West. But the real cause of the cold war was the intractability of the Soviet system and the desires of Stalin to create a bulwark of pro-Russian states in Eastern Europe under the dictatorial auspices of the local Communist parties.

The collapse of the European empires led to the establishment of many new states which, while desiring aid from without, were uncertain of their social structures and political institutions. Thus the cold war, whose first and foremost theater was Europe (as expressed in the perpetual crises over Berlin, Hungary, and Czechoslovakia), has also been waged in all post-imperial societies, from Iran to Vietnam and from the Congo to Ghana. The Middle East, with its variety of pressures (in particular, the establishment of the new state of Israel), has in fact been a greater area of possible international strife than Europe—as the Suez Crisis of 1956 suggested. That event effectively marked the passing of Anglo-French imperial power in the Middle East, while the Six-Day War of June, 1967, showed how easy it still was for resolute small states, such as Israel and Egypt, to act quite independently of—and occasionally against—the desires of their main international protectors. In addition, the cold war also became extended—through the Guatemalan and Cuban revolutions of 1953 and 1959—to the post-imperial regions of Hispanic America.

Further anxieties derived from the arms race, which began as soon as it became clear that Russia as well as the United States possessed nuclear weapons. After 1949 both countries began manufacturing hydrogen bombs, weapons many times more powerful than the one that destroyed Hiroshima. Their example was followed by Britain, France and China. The arms race was extended to the question of the means of delivery of these weapons, and that, in turn, led to the missile race. In 1957, the Russian Sputnik added yet another dimension—the space race, an exercise in prestige politics whose benefits to the majority of the world have yet to be shown.

For twenty years after 1945, the bloodshed of World War II caused a general feeling that war and violence were at all costs to be avoided and that slow methods of arbitration were always to be preferred to swift but bloody battlefield decisions. This attitude led to many compromises and errors of judgment but, apart from the war in Korea, major conflict was avoided. In recent years, this view has seemed increasingly illusory. Indeed, the evidence suggests that the spread of knowledge and education has taught mankind little in the way of self-control and less in the art of living with other men. HUGH THOMAS

771

Wings over Kitty Hawk 1903

With four men, a boy, a dog and his brother Wilbur as his only audience, Orville Wright revved the engine of the frail-looking biplane that the brothers had constructed, slipped the restraining wire, and set off on man's first successful powered flight in a heavier-than-air craft. Orville's flight over the sand dunes of Kitty Hawk, North Carolina, on the morning of December 17, 1903, lasted only twelve seconds and covered less than 220 feet—but in those brief seconds history was made. The brothers made three additional flights that morning, one of which lasted for almost a minute and covered 852 feet—conclusive proof that their initial feat was no accident. The Wrights' technological triumph was complete; one of man's oldest dreams had been realized. Within a few decades the brothers' invention was to revolutionize both travel and warfare and "change the face of the world."

The air age took almost exactly a century to be ushered in after Sir George Cayley laid the foundations of aerodynamics and flight control in 1799. That century progressed through widespread theory and experimentation to the masterly gliding flights of the German engineer Otto Lilienthal, and finally, in 1903, to the world's first powered, sustained and controlled flights in an airplane by the brothers Wilbur and Orville Wright.

The Wright brothers' first flight—an event that was ultimately to revolutionize transportation and warfare and to "shrink" the world—must have seemed peculiarly matter-of-fact to the two chief actors: they were merely completing the first phase of the careful experiments that had started with their wing-warping kite of 1899 and had then passed through three seasons of increasingly successful gliding.

The scene was the sandy and windy coast of the Atlantic Ocean by the Kill Devil Sand Hills, some four miles south of the small fishing village of Kitty Hawk, North Carolina. The date was Thursday, December 17, 1903, and the time was about 10:35 A.M. Wilbur and Orville had risen early and had hoisted a signal to tell the crew of the Kill Devil Life Saving Station that an attempt was to be made to fly. Four men, a boy, and a dog came over to watch; one of the men was to stand by the camera set up to record the happenings.

At about 10:15 A.M., while a brisk wind blew from the north, the final preparations were made. The aircraft—called the *Flyer*—was a biplane with a forward elevator and a double rear rudder. There was a 12-horsepower gasoline engine, lying on the lower wing, that drove two pusher airscrews (behind the wings) via bicycle chains encased in tubes. The wings could be "warped"—that is, they could be given a helical twist so that the wings on one side presented a greater angle against the airflow than those on the other. This device, used in conjunction with the rear rudder, allowed the machine to be

rolled (banked) at will and was the main achievement of the Wrights' flight-control experiments.

The frail-looking but tough little machine could not take off from the sand on wheels and was therefore fitted with skids. The brothers devised a forty-foot wooden rail, laid down into the wind, on which a wheeled yoke ran freely; the skids of the airplane were laid across this yoke. The pilot lay prone on the lower wing, and the machine was restrained by a wire until the engine had been revved up to its maximum speed. Then the wire was slipped, and the *Flyer* sped down the rail. When the craft's speed was great enough for the wings to raise it into the air, it lifted off the wheeled yoke.

For the first trial, on December 14, 1903, the brothers had flipped a coin to see who would make the attempt, and Wilbur had won. He had been too brusque with the controls, however, and the machine had stalled and ploughed into the sand just beyond the end of the rail.

Then, on December 17, it was Orville's turn; and at approximately 10:30 all was ready for the second trial. Orville had the engine going full pelt. He slipped the restraining wire, and the *Flyer* ran along the rail and was off into the air. It remained airborne for about twelve seconds. Since it was flying into a brisk wind, this meant that it actually had flown considerably more than the distance covered over the ground, which was only some 220 feet. In those brief seconds history was made. As Orville said:

This flight lasted only twelve seconds, but it was nevertheless the first in the history of the world in which a machine carrying a man had raised itself by its own power into the air in full flight, had sailed forward without reduction of speed, and had finally landed at a point as high as that from which it started.

This flight was not the end of the trials, however. In all, four flights were made that morning between 10:30 and just after noon, with the brothers taking turns as pilots. The fourth flight—which Wilbur

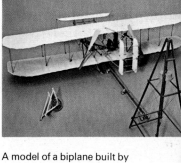

A model of a biplane built by the Wright brothers in 1908, five years after their first flight.

Opposite Wilbur (*top left*) and Orville Wright; and (*below*) a model of their craft with Wilbur lying down at the controls.

773

A photograph of Louis Blériot making the first powered flight across the English Channel in 1909.

Wilbur Wright came to Europe in 1908 to demonstrate the brothers' aircraft. He is shown here preparing for takeoff at Le Mans, France.

flying machine had come at last.

From the beginning we have employed entirely new principles of control; and as all the experiments have been conducted at our own expense without assistance from any individual or institution, we do not feel ready at present to give out any pictures or detailed description of the machine.

There are four vital points about the Wright brothers that are often overlooked and that have led to a great deal of misunderstanding of these great men. The first is that these initial powered flights were the culmination of three strenuous seasons of gliding (1900–1902), by the end of which the Wrights had mastered three-axis flight control, which was the true secret of their success in aviation. In other words, before they built their first powered *Flyer* in 1903, they had learned to control pitch, yaw and roll in a glider.

Second, the naïve idea, so often expressed, that the four flights on December 17, 1903, were looked upon by the Wrights as a "final" achievement is far from the truth. The flights were only tentative and were considered simply to have proved that Orville and Wilbur's research and development had proceeded along the right lines. If the brothers had made nothing more than those four brief flights, they would have been considered significant pioneers, but not much more. Their real achievement is that they progressed through their powered *Flyer* II of 1904, to their *Flyer* III of 1905, which could easily fly for half an hour and could bank, turn, circle and do figure eights. This *Flyer* III was the first practical airplane in history; its airborne duration was not to be exceeded by any other pioneer until September, 1908.

The third consideration is a peculiar one and touches upon problems of national psychology. Americans have perhaps overworked the notion illustrated by the saying "from log cabin to White House"—the belief that there is a chance for every-

piloted—lasted for fifty-nine seconds and covered 852 feet of ground and over half a mile in air distance. It is both interesting and amusing to note that nobody else in the world was to remain in the air in an airplane for twelve seconds until November, 1906; no one else was to remain aloft for fifty-nine seconds until November, 1907.

In a joint statement to the Associated Press on January 5, 1904, the Wrights said:

Only those who are acquainted with practical aeronautics can appreciate the difficulties of attempting the first trials of a flying machine in a twenty-five-mile gale. As winter was already well set in, we should have postponed our trials to a more favorable season, but for the fact that we were determined, before returning home, to know whether the machine possessed sufficient power to fly, sufficient strength to withstand the shocks of landings, and sufficient capacity of control to make flight safe in boisterous winds, as well as in calm air. When these points had been definitely established, we at once packed our goods and returned home, knowing that the age of the

Bachelor sons of a widower bishop

body, and that everybody has a chance of becoming President. Applied to the Wright brothers, this doctrine has emerged as the legend that they were humble lads—only one stage from being hicks. The myth pictures them as youngsters who "by guess and by golly" knocked up an odd contraption, tinkered about with it until it seemed to be promising, got in and—more by luck than good judgment—managed to take off the ground in their homemade creation. Nothing could be further from the truth.

The Wrights were bachelor sons of a widower bishop who was a member of a nonconformist sect called the United Brethren. The family also included a married son Lorin and the brothers' beloved sister Katharine, who ran the Wright household very efficiently. Their religious background produced two noticeable features in the Wright brothers. First was a strict ethic, which taught them honesty and integrity. The second was that, having been brought up with a Biblical background, they both wrote excellent English—simple, straightforward, and expressive. This was to stand them in excellent stead when it came to their aeronautical studies and their correspondence with the great American aviation pioneer Octave Chanute and a growing number of men who became involved with their activities over the years.

Building on these foundations, the brothers went through the customary education of the time and then struck out on their own. They became first-class mechanics and, after setting up a successful bicycle shop, progressed to designing and manufacturing an excellent bicycle of their own—the Van Cleeve. The mechanical know-how that Wilbur and Orville acquired in the bicycle business was of great service when they took to designing and building aircraft. But of equal importance—and one of the most remarkable features of their lives—was their almost innate gift for research in aerodynamics, the results of which surprised even modern masters such as Theodore von Karman. There are thousands of notes, diagrams and letters (many of them now published) to prove that gift. Almost as remarkable—some would perhaps say *more* remarkable—was their ability as airplane pilots, an ability that rapidly evolved in both brothers alike. They were not only the first men to fly, but the first true pilots; their friends have said that it was hard to choose between them when it came to piloting ability.

Perhaps most misunderstood of the four vital points concerning the brothers has been the Wrights' influence on the history of aviation. Unfortunately, certain prejudiced writers on both sides of the Atlantic have tried to show that the work of the Wrights was isolated and influenced no one. This is quite untrue. That misconception has developed because of the brothers' regrettable decision to stop flying at the end of 1905 and not to fly again until they had a guaranteed buyer for their machines. Such a buyer did not materialize until 1908. Their refusal to fly for this long period was to protect their invention.

Nevertheless, their vital influence on European

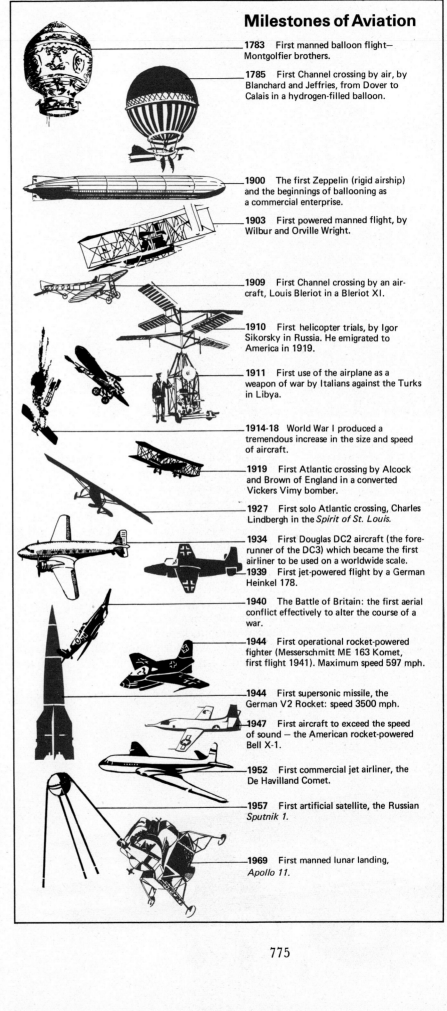

Milestones of Aviation

1783 First manned balloon flight—Montgolfier brothers.

1785 First Channel crossing by air, by Blanchard and Jeffries, from Dover to Calais in a hydrogen-filled balloon.

1900 The first Zeppelin (rigid airship) and the beginnings of ballooning as a commercial enterprise.

1903 First powered manned flight, by Wilbur and Orville Wright.

1909 First Channel crossing by an aircraft, Louis Bleriot in a Bleriot XI.

1910 First helicopter trials, by Igor Sikorsky in Russia. He emigrated to America in 1919.

1911 First use of the airplane as a weapon of war by Italians against the Turks in Libya.

1914-18 World War I produced a tremendous increase in the size and speed of aircraft.

1919 First Atlantic crossing by Alcock and Brown of England in a converted Vickers Vimy bomber.

1927 First solo Atlantic crossing, Charles Lindbergh in the *Spirit of St. Louis.*

1934 First Douglas DC2 aircraft (the forerunner of the DC3) which became the first airliner to be used on a worldwide scale.

1939 First jet-powered flight by a German Heinkel 178.

1940 The Battle of Britain: the first aerial conflict effectively to alter the course of a war.

1944 First operational rocket-powered fighter (Messerschmitt ME 163 Komet, first flight 1941). Maximum speed 597 mph.

1944 First supersonic missile, the German V2 Rocket: speed 3500 mph.

1947 First aircraft to exceed the speed of sound — the American rocket-powered Bell X-1.

1952 First commercial jet airliner, the De Havilland Comet.

1957 First artificial satellite, the Russian *Sputnik 1.*

1969 First manned lunar landing, *Apollo 11.*

An eminently respectable gathering in 1894 inspects Sir Hiram Maxim's flying machine. The Wrights were the first to succeed, but far from the first to attempt to fly.

A model of a Voisin biplane built in 1908. After the Americans, the French were the most advanced aeronauts.

experimentation had been at work ever since 1902 and 1903, when illustrations and descriptions of their gliding achievements became available in France. This material proved to be the direct inspiration for the revival of interest in aviation in Europe, especially when the grand old man of American aviation, Octave Chanute, lectured to the French pioneers in April of 1903. Chanute showed his audience excellent photographs and gave them accounts of the Wrights' masterly glider flying. The French, led by Ferdinand Ferber and Ernest Archdeacon, started to build Wright-type gliders, and with these machines the revival of European aviation was launched.

In 1908 it was decided that Orville should stay in the United States to fly the acceptance tests that had now been agreed to by the Army Signal Corps at Fort Myer, Virginia, while Wilbur was destined for Europe. Financial arrangements were completed by early 1908, and Wilbur went over to France. In August he made his first public flights, and in the words of the Count de La Vaulx—one of France's great aviation pioneers—Wilbur's wonderful new aircraft had, in a matter of weeks, "revolutionized the aviator's world." When Wilbur started to fly, no one in Europe really understood flight control—that is, the proper control of an airplane in the air, especially control in roll combined with control in yaw and pitch. The Wright airplane could be banked, turned, circled and generally maneuvered with the greatest of ease, whereas the primitive European machines had to be maneuvered with great care and could only be turned with difficulty.

European praise for the Wright machine knew no bounds, and as Wilbur piled triumph upon triumph, the Continental pioneers began to realize what essential lessons had to be learned from the Wrights. Wilbur's audience was by turns astounded, dismayed and, to give them credit, repentant—repentant of their six years of disbelief and dismayed at the memory of their six years of aeronautical fumbling. With no proper control in their hands, and no image of true flight in their minds, they were now experiencing a painful moment of truth.

The veteran pioneer Léon Delagrange spoke for all his honest countrymen when he exclaimed: "Well, we are beaten! We just don't exist." "No one can estimate," said one French spokesman, "the consequences that will result from this new

"A power which controls the fate of nations"

method of locomotion, the dazzling beginnings of which we salute today." "For us in France," exclaimed French aviator Louis Blériot, "and everywhere, a new era in mechanical flight has commenced ... It is marvelous." "It is a revelation in airplane work," said René Gasnier; "who can now doubt that the Wrights have done all they claimed? ... We are as children compared with the Wrights."

The French aviation press was equally repentant and enthusiastic, noting that Wilbur's demonstration was "one of the most exciting spectacles ever presented in the history of applied science." François Peyrey wrote:

I had the good fortune to find myself at Hunaudieres on August 8th, 1908, the date of the memorable demonstration. I shall try to give an idea of the incomparable mastery of the American aviators in the marvelous art of imitating the birds. For a long time—for too long a time—the Wright brothers have been accused in Europe of bluffing; perhaps even in their own land. Today they are hallowed by France, and I feel an intense pleasure in counting myself among the first to make amends for such flagrant injustice. ... It would also be just as puerile to challenge the first flight of December 17, 1903 in North Carolina as it would be to deny the experiences in La Sarthe. ... From the stands [on the race course] an immense acclamation goes up from the witnesses of this prowess. ...

The London *Times*, in its report of the flight demonstration in France, observed:

All accounts ... published in this morning's paper from the correspondents on the spot, attest the complete triumph of the American inventor ... the enthusiasm was indescribable ... all accounts agree that the most admirable characteristic of yesterday's flight was the steady mastery displayed by Mr. Wright over his machine.

The Europeans thus acquired a proper understanding of flight control for the first time, and it effected the revolution necessary to bring about the final conquest of the air. The world—not only of aviation but of politics and power—soon endorsed the now famous statement of Major B.F.S. Baden-Powell, the past president of the Royal Aeronautical Society: "That Wilbur Wright is in possession of a power which controls the fate of nations is beyond dispute."

Between August 8 and August 13, 1908, Wilbur made nine flights, the longest lasting just over eight minutes. He then received permission to use the great military ground, the Camp d'Auvours, seven miles east of Le Mans. Here, from August 21 to the last day of December, 1908, he made 104 flights and was airborne for about twenty-five and a half hours, thus making some twenty-six hours for the combined French locations that year. Wilbur's astonishing 1908 season at Auvours included: taking up passengers on some sixty occasions; fourteen flights of between one-quarter and one-half an hour's duration; six of between one-half and three-quarters of an hour; six of between one and two hours; a record flight (on December 31) of two hours, twenty minutes and twenty-three seconds; and one flight (on December 18) to gain the altitude record of 360 feet.

The influence exerted by the great inventors of

the world—especially those who are the true initiators—lays the foundations upon which their followers can build and sparks them into action. This vital role of first achiever, director and energizer was admirably fulfilled in the realm of aviation by the brothers Wilbur and Orville Wright. The final word belongs to the great French aeronaut and historian Charles Dollfus:

It is therefore incontestably the Wright brothers alone who resolved, in its entirety, the problem of human mechanical flight. ... This resulted from their tests from 1903 to 1905. Men of genius—erudite, exact in their reasoning, hard workers, outstanding experimenters, and unselfish—the brothers Wilbur and Orville Wright have, more than anyone else, deserved the success which they achieved. They changed the face of the globe.

CHARLES GIBBS-SMITH

Aviation rapidly captured the public's imagination and demonstrations were soon being held all over Europe. A poster announces an "Aviation Week" to be held at Reims.

Russian discontent

On July 30, 1903, the Second Congress of the All-Russian Social Democratic Party convened in a smelly, flea-infested warehouse in Brussels. After a few days, the smells, the fleas and the Belgian police caused the delegates to move to London. The Bolshevik Party, which would seize control of Russia in 1917, emerged out of the dissensions of that Congress.

In January, 1905, a series of Russian Army defeats in the war against Japan sparked a revolution against Tsar Nicholas' regime. In many ways that revolt was a dress rehearsal for 1917, for although the abortive coup of 1905 had no formal connection with the successful revolution of 1917, it was an indication of the acute revolutionary situation in tsarist Russia. The events of 1905 revealed the massive discontent of the Russian people. And the Second Congress guaranteed that there would ultimately be a party ruthless enough to exploit that discontent.

At the beginning of the twentieth century Russia possessed an autocratic monarchy, a parasitic nobility and a corrupt bureaucracy —all of which exploited a vast semifeudal peasantry. Stirrings of protest from intellectuals and students were met by police brutality, and peasant risings were put down by regiments of Cossacks; as discontent increased, so did oppression.

Peasants and factory workers alike were ready recruits for revolution. Much of the best pasture, woodland and water was in the hands of aristocrats who did not bother to farm it, and few peasants had the money to live above subsistence level, nor to pay for improvements. Famine was rampant. A repressed proletariat was emerging in the larger industrial areas where slum housing conditions, long working hours, child labor and low wages caused widespread discontent.

Despite the secret police and the constant threat of execution, exile or flogging, there was a flourishing revolutionary movement in existence. At first it had been an anarchist movement, primarily concerned with peasant problems. Then, in 1898, the Marxist Social Democratic Party was founded at Minsk, and a new sort of revolutionary appeared to challenge the old order. Even at the outset the new party was split. The older leaders believed the organization's main task was to make the workers aware they were being exploited. Vladimir Ilich Ulyanov thought differently. Such a process, he said, would only lead to reformism— that is, to a series of small improvements in contemporary economic conditions rather than a change of regime. In 1902, Ulyanov published *What Is To Be Done?* under his pen name, Lenin. In that work he claimed that the working class was incapable of creating its own revolutionary ideology, and that such a task would have to be undertaken by an elite of professional revolutionaries. The ideological conflict between Lenin and the older members of the party was raised at the Second Party Congress. Through skillful committee work and not a little underhandedness, Lenin and his followers emerged from the Congress as the *Bolshinstvo*, or majority, while those who preferred a more democratic notion of the party were left with the stigma of *Menshinstvo*, or minority. The result

The battleship *Potemkin* on which the crew mutinied during the 1905 revolution in Russia.

of this clash decided the course of revolution, for the Bolsheviks were committed to dictatorship. But the importance of this commitment lay in the future; for a time the revolution proceeded without Lenin.

In 1903, there were eighty-seven strikes in St. Petersburg, and elsewhere peasant bands burned down manor houses and murdered their landlords. The government, which hoped to divert attention from domestic troubles with a successful war, brought Russia into conflict with Japan. Instead of victories, there were only disastrous defeats, and on January 22, 1905, a huge crowd of pilgrims marched to the Winter Palace in St. Petersburg to petition Tsar Nicholas II for reform. The pilgrims, who were peacefully singing hymns and carrying pictures of the Tsar, were fired on by the palace guards. The 1905 Revolution had begun.

Further reports of catastrophic military defeats, such as the annihilation of the Baltic fleet at Tsushima, soon forced the Tsar to make concessions to his people. A constitution was promised, and a parliament, the Duma, was set up. But Nicholas' move came too late. Workers in St. Petersburg spontaneously created their own councils, called soviets, and under the leadership of a young Social Democrat, Leon Trotsky, the soviets became the real power in the land. Blind fear of the proletariat caused the middle classes to panic. They rallied to the government, and the Tsar was able to suppress the soviets. The powerless Duma remained in existence—a pathetic façade of democracy without a champion. Lenin said that supporting the Duma "was haggling with Tsarism over the dead bodies of the workers."

The revolution was dead, but its consequences were incalculable. The Bolsheviks learned from their mistakes, and in 1917 they did not hesitate to lead the people. "All power to the soviets!" they cried.

Reverberations from the experiences of the soviets were not confined to Russia alone. Throughout Asia and the Arab world— where the Russo-Japanese War symbolized the struggle between oppressed nations and European imperialists—the 1905 Revolution was seen as part of the struggle against tyranny. It unleashed a wave of unrest in Asia that spread from the Middle East to Vietnam.

The Far East

India suffered grave disturbances in 1905. There were agricultural riots in the Punjab and terrorist outbreaks in Bengal as popular opinion turned against British colonialism. To run their vast empire, the British had been forced to educate the Indians, and by 1900 there were five universities in India. An educated middle class arose that was aware of the French and American revolutions and of Western democratic ideals. They wanted to know why India could not be self-governing like Canada and Australia. The British tried to stem the tide by instituting the Morley-Minto reforms of 1909, which were aimed at creating "a class of persons, Indian in blood and colour, but English in taste, in opinion, in morals and in intellect." The creation of these Westernized Oriental Gentlemen, or "wogs" as they were derisively known, was a temporary measure. In the long run, British rule was doomed.

Meanwhile, in China, a third

Russian soldiers at Port Arthur during the Russo-Japanese War 1904-5.

revolution was brewing. However, like the Russian movement, it was directed less against Western imperialism than against despotism at home. Nevertheless, it was the impact of Western trade and ideas that triggered the disturbances. Like every Chinese dynasty since 200 B.C., the ruling Manchu dynasty rested on the three pillars of Confucianism, agriculture and the myth of universal empire. These pillars were badly shaken in the nineteenth century when the importation of manufactured goods was coupled with a vast population explosion to create intense peasant unrest. The resulting T'ai P'ing Rebellion (1850–64), took fourteen years to crush, and by that time knowledge that powerful nations existed beyond the seas had shattered the myth of universal empire.

Defeat in the war with Japan convinced many Chinese intellectuals that their country had to be Westernized, but the Dowager Empress Tzu Hsi refused to make concessions. Peasant discontent surfaced in 1900 in the form of the Boxer Rebellion, and the "Westernizers" were shunted aside. Encouraged from abroad by their exiled leader, Sun Yat-sen, they continued to plot.

Actual revolution began almost by accident. An explosion in Hankow in October, 1911, led police to the conspirators, and forced them into an immediate uprising. The civil war that followed soon reached an impasse, but the deadlock was broken when the cynical regent, Yüan Shih-k'ai, procured the abdication of the young Emperor in return for being made President of the new Republic. The Son of Heaven had abdicated, and 2,132 years of imperial rule had been brought to an end—

yet it was barely the beginning of the Chinese Revolution.

These developments in Russia, India and China were the first signs that the balance of world power was destined to shift dramatically in the twentieth century. The days of European domination were numbered, and Europe itself was moving inexorably toward the great holocaust of World War I. Outwardly, the situation on the Continent appeared calm enough: there had been no major European conflict since the Franco-Prussian War of 1870, and statesmen prided themselves on having entered the age of compromise and arbitration. To a large extent this was true, but behind every compromise lurked systems of attack and defense that had been erected in case those compromises ever failed.

An age of alliances

At the same time, European diplomacy was elaborating a system of increasingly rigid alliances. The first was formed in 1879, when Bismarck concluded the Dual Alliance with Austria-Hungary. This agreement enabled the German Chancellor to have a say in Austrian policy—and thereby prevent an Austro-Russian war over the Balkans. In later years, with less experienced statesmen at the helm of German policy, this agreement meant that Germany was committed to supporting Austrian adventures.

The Dual Alliance soon generated others. France, still smarting from the blows Germany had inflicted in 1870, concluded a formal alliance with Russia in 1894. Henceforth, German military thinking revolved around the problem of

how to defeat both France and Russia simultaneously. The solution hit upon by General Alfred von Schlieffen, the German Chief of Staff, was to knock out France in a lightning thrust and then to wage a longer campaign against Russia.

At this time, the Franco-Russian alliance might have been countered by an Anglo-German understanding, but several factors made such an arrangement impossible. Germany was seen as the cause of Britain's deteriorating position in world trade, and allegations were made that the Germans were selling shoddy goods by using the trademarks of respected British firms. The German monarch's Wagnerian conception of Germany's role in world politics did not help matters. Through such reckless gestures as sending a telegram of support to the Boer leader, Paul Kruger, the touchy and tactless Kaiser effectively eliminated all chances for amiable Anglo-German negotiations.

Britain's recognition that an alliance with Germany was impossible paved the way for a rapprochement with France. And such a détente was indeed necessary, for years of Anglo-French quarrelling over Egypt had come to a head in 1898 at Fashoda, when a small French expedition led by the explorer Jean Baptiste Marchand was confronted by General Horatio Kitchener's forces on the Upper Nile. The confrontation almost precipitated a war, but France recognized England's superior naval power and backed down. The incident served as a necessary purgative in Anglo-French relations; France finally recognized that she could do nothing about the British in Egypt. Edward VII's triumphant visit to Paris in 1903 soothed the memories of Fashoda, and in 1904 the prospect of the Russo-Japanese War expedited the conclusion of the Anglo-French détente.

Conflict in the Balkans

Meanwhile, the Russian defeat in 1905 had turned her away from the Far East and toward the Balkans. Russia's withdrawal from the Far East removed many points of dispute with Britain, but her renewed interest in the Balkans inevitably led to conflict with Austria. Anxious to remove dissension in Central Asia, the British agreed to a 1907 convention with Russia that dealt with Persia, Afghanistan and Tibet.

Germany, which had begun to feel intensely claustrophobic, tried to bully England out of its new alliances. The Kaiser's tactics only served to crystallize Europe into two armed camps—one, on the periphery, held together by German threats; the other, on the inside, desperate to break out.

Theodore Roosevelt, U.S. President 1901–9.

While Europe prepared for war, America slipped quietly into a period of prosperity. Under the presidency of Theodore Roosevelt, industry surged ahead and foreign negotiations brought significant financial gains. The key to Roosevelt's foreign policy was his determination to "speak softly and carry a big stick." The most significant application of his statement came in 1903, when he asked Colombia to lease the Isthmus of Panama, the narrowest point between the Atlantic and Pacific Oceans, so the United States might build an inter-ocean canal. Colombia refused, and the Panamanians rebelled against their colonial governors. The new independent Republic thereby created was immediately granted the beneficent protection of the United States—and the land needed for the canal was leased forthwith to the United States.

Roosevelt did not stand for re-election in 1908, and he was succeeded by William Howard Taft. Taft was a cautious man who used his powers sparingly, yet during his period of office momentous changes occurred in the American way of life. Scientific and technological advances began to make a real impact on the lives of the masses. Gramophones and refrigerators were becoming common, and Henry Ford's new automobile offered mobility to the average wage earner.

Chinese troops on their way to fight the Boxer rebels in 1900.

779

1908 | An Automobile for the Masses

"History is bunk," Henry Ford asserted—even as the company he founded made automotive history year after year. In 1908 the first Model T rolled out of Ford's Detroit plant; in the next two decades Ford would produce some 15 million nearly identical Model Ts by his refined assembly-line process. Those boxy, spartan, economical automobiles were to revolutionize American life, bringing low-cost locomotion to rural regions, mobility to the middle class, and privacy to courting couples. Equally important, Ford's landmark decision to institute voluntarily an eight-hour, five-dollar day for his employees inaugurated a new era of labor-management relations. By 1923, Ford's loyal employees were turning out more than 2 million Model Ts a year, and it could truly be said that Henry Ford had put America on wheels.

A 1915 Model T Ford.

Opposite The first mass-production line in America: the Ford plant at Highland Park, Michigan. (*Top*) Magneto assembly workers; (*bottom*) dropping the engine onto the chassis.

"I will build a motor car for the great multitude," Henry Ford once said. "It will be constructed of the best materials, by the best men to be hired, after the simplest designs that modern engineering can devise. But it will be so low in price that no man making a good salary will be unable to own one."

Such heady promises were foreign to the American Gothic temperament of the former Michigan farm boy whose fascination with engines had drawn him into the business of building automobiles. But Henry Ford kept his word, and in October, 1908, his first Model T—an oblong, boxlike machine that bespoke not beauty but stark utility—rolled out of the Piquette Avenue Ford plant in Detroit and, after vigorous hand cranking, sputtered to life.

"The way to make automobiles is to make one automobile like another automobile," Ford once said, "to make them all alike ... just as one pin is like another pin when it comes from a pin factory, or one match is like another match." His philosophy was soon put to the test, for with Model T production under way, the building of other Ford models was abruptly suspended. Model T and Ford became synonymous, and not only were all Ford cars alike in late 1908, but they changed very little over the next nineteen years. Except for technical modifications and an occasional face-lifting, the first car to be affectionately dubbed the Tin Lizzie was very much kin to the car being sold in 1927 (when, after exceeding 15 million in number, the Model T was finally retired).

What made the car so popular? For one thing, it was inexpensive. Automobiles were still considered rich men's toys in the first decade of the twentieth century. Most cars cost well over one thousand dollars and fully half were priced above two thousand. Stripped of accessories—which was how it left the factory—the first Model T Runabout, a two-passenger roadster, could be purchased for

eight hundred and fifty dollars. The Model T's high performance and appealing homeliness transcended the bounds of trade, profession or status. It was comparatively simple to operate, and for a man with a slight mechanical bent, easy to maintain. It had been the dream of an unprepossessing machinist, a man whose patchy education and apparent disregard for scholarship could prompt him to say, "History is bunk," even though the company he had founded made history year after year.

Henry Ford had been born in 1863 on a forty-acre farm in Dearborn township, two miles east of Michigan's Rouge River. Although an indifferent student, he was an impassioned tinkerer. He helped his father with the farm work—not by plowing or reaping, but by hammering out hinges on a forge and fixing wagons, farm implements and harnesses. "My toys were all tools," he wrote in *My Life and Work*, one of two autobiographical books that bear Ford's name.

At seventeen, Ford left the family farm and took the first of a series of factory jobs in Detroit. During his early years in that city he repaired and operated a number of steam engines and, according to his memoirs, even "built a steam engine that ran." Through the English and American mechanics' magazines that came into shops where he worked, Ford followed some of the progress being made toward development of the internal combustion engine. It was only a matter of time before he would abandon the idea of steam in favor of this more promising means of power.

Shortly after his marriage to twenty-one-year-old Clara Bryant in April, 1888, he began talking of the feasibility of building a "horseless carriage." He was not alone, of course. Almost three hundred American inventors were striving to put self-propelled, wheeled vehicles in operation in the waning years of the nineteenth century. Very few of these

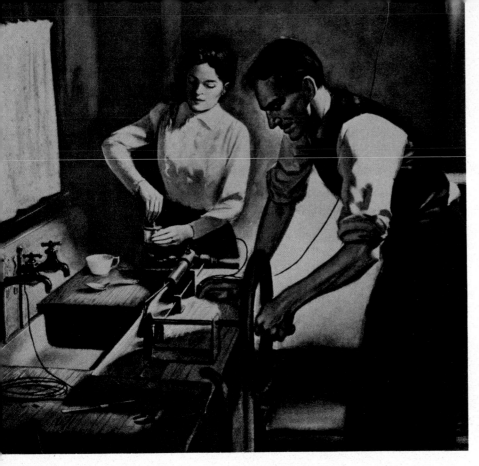

men were aware of the work being done in Europe—specifically by Gottlieb Daimler and Karl Benz, who both took out individual German patents on self-propelled vehicles within six months of one another in the mid-1880s.

Henry Ford began building a gasoline engine in his workshop behind the house on Bagley Street, Detroit, that he shared with his wife and infant son Edsel. His first engine was a simple one-cylinder contraption that he tried out in his wife's kitchen on Christmas Eve, 1893. Soon he was at work on a two-cylinder version, which he eventually mounted in a small carriage that rode on four bicycle wheels. This quadricycle was the first of a series of experimental vehicles conceived and built by Ford—cars whose performance on the road and in competition brought him the recognition, and much of the financial backing, that he needed to begin manufacturing automobiles. The Ford Motor Company, formed in 1903, produced eight different models before the Model T came along. There were two- and four-cylinder cars and a six-cylinder luxury vehicle that weighed one ton, cost twenty-five hundred dollars and could go fifty miles per hour. It was the last high-priced Ford to be built until 1922, when the company acquired Lincoln.

The Model T, introduced when the Ford Motor Company was only five years old, was no radical piece of auto engineering. Almost its only unique aspect was the way it seized and held a special place in American life. In 1908 Ford built 6,000 cars; in

Above A fanciful painting of the young Henry Ford building the engine for his quadricycle in the kitchen of his Detroit home.

Below The first gas station in Ohio—and possibly in America. Motorists drove their cars in the front door and out the back.

The first production line

1909, the first full year of Model T production, the output rose to 10,000. From then on, production figures showed a rarely interrupted rise each year (some years they actually doubled) until they reached their peak of 2 million in 1923.

Preceding the production boom—and possibly anticipating it—Ford had sought a place to build a new and bigger factory. In 1906 the company purchased sixty acres in an area called Highland Park at the north end of Detroit. Construction had progressed far enough for the company to begin moving in on New Year's Day, 1910. Over the next four years, as facilities were being completed, a staggering array of the latest precision machinery appeared in the plant: 3 million dollars' worth of lathes, planers, milling machines, drill presses, borers and grinding machines.

The presence of this equipment signaled the development of new methods for putting vehicles together. Previously, the men who built cars had been mechanical jacks-of-all-trades. They moved about the factory—to the parts bins or the tool cribs—and worked on a car from bare frame to finished product. As output increased, however, this leisurely and somewhat disorganized method of assembly proved inefficient. By 1908, line production, which already was in use in other industries, was being tried out by auto manufacturers, and most earnestly by Ford.

The idea was simply to save time and motion. Gravity slides and conveyor belts made it possible to move the work from man to man and machine to machine, keeping each man virtually in one spot. Various Model T components—engine, radiator, chassis, steering gear—were put together this way in individual subassemblies. But final assembly of all the components was accomplished pretty much as it had always been—by many hands doing many jobs to produce a finished car.

Line production was only partly successful because, like lanes of irregularly flowing traffic, some lines were fast and others slow. Cars were assembled in spurts, and much of the time that was gained along the line was lost in the chaos of final assembly. But during 1912 and 1913 the company thoroughly refined its assembly-line procedure, and Ford became the first auto manufacturer to turn entirely to mass production. In place of the various subassemblies, a continuously moving assembly line was installed. It started at one end of the factory and moved along at an even pace as one component after another was fed into the line and then added in sequence—until a completed car could be rolled away. A second assembly line was in operation by the end of 1913, and a few months later four lines were functioning.

The results were almost unbelievable. Whereas in August, 1913, it had taken twelve and a half hours to assemble a Model T chassis, the time span had shrunk to an hour and thirty-three minutes by the following January. And mass production techniques continued to improve.

Despite its efficiency, the Ford Motor Company was producing almost more cars than it could handle, and, as a result, labor was becoming demoralized. As pressure for greater output increased, working conditions grew steadily worse. Workers had to function in cramped spaces and remain in uncomfortable positions for long stretches of time. Machines were placed so close together that Ford himself later recalled that they appeared to have been "piled right on top of one another."

Worst of all was the dull and stultifying routine that factory work had assumed. Instead of helping to complete one car at a time, a skilled mechanic was now required to work on a great many cars doing only one job, the same job, with maddening repetition. The monotony of the work and the continual emphasis on speed sparked simmering resentment among Ford workers. Their bitterness reached a peak in the summer of 1913 when the company ended its policy of rewarding individual initiative with bonuses. Now the average worker knew that no matter how much he applied himself, he could earn no more than the standard wage: $2.34 a day. Disillusioned, a great many Ford workers began drifting to other jobs.

Clearly, a new labor policy was needed. Factory jobs could not be made more interesting. Moreover, because teamwork and precision had taken precedence over individual initiative, job satisfaction was no longer a factor in cementing company loyalty. Henry Ford, accustomed to pouring much of his profit back into the business, decided to invest some capital in a most important resource: manpower. On January 5, 1914, he announced that the Ford workday would shrink from nine to eight hours and the minimum wage would rise to five dollars a day.

The response to this surprise announcement was

The automobile rapidly gained acceptance throughout the world. King George V of England with his Daimler at military exercises in 1914.

A 1919 Model T Ford. The body style is somewhat different from that of the 1915 model, but the concept remains the same.

A 1913 British Daimler, which cost ten times as much as a Model T Ford.

immediate and galvanic. The next morning 10,000 job applicants appeared outside the factory and, in their passion, threatened to storm the gates. They came again, day after day, huddling together in the near-zero weather. They were a hungry, sorry lot, and most of them were doomed to disappointment, for only a handful could be hired. But their presence was viable proof that, in terms of the workingman, Ford's labor policy was a triumphant success.

The business community reacted adversely. Its mouthpiece, the *Wall Street Journal*, called the five-dollar day an "economic crime," and influential bankers denounced Henry Ford as a traitor to his class. They were wrong, of course, at least as far as his company's fortunes were concerned. Buoyed by higher wages, Ford employees were working faster, more efficiently and, considering the cost of assembling each car, for less money. The increased output more than offset the wage hike, and not only did the turnover of personnel diminish, but absenteeism was also markedly cut.

Despite grave predictions, the five-dollar day did not prove injurious to industry in general. Henry Ford recalled that it had had little effect at first, though he would have been delighted if other firms had been compelled to raise wages to the level he had set. Hadn't he promised to build a car for the "great multitude"? The more money workingmen earned, he reasoned, the more Model Ts he could expect to sell. To add impetus to mass sales, he periodically reduced prices. And he once promised that if he could sell 300,000 cars in a given twelve-month period, each purchaser would get fifty dollars back.

In the second decade of the century, the Model T's success seemed unassailable. The car had crotchets and failings, but once a part of the American scene it was as firmly entrenched as folklore. And the jokes and jests made at the car's expense worked like free advertising to further the legend.

The first attempt at streamlining the Model T took place in 1917 as graceful curves replaced some of the clumsy, squarish design that had been its hallmark. That year more than three-quarters of a million Model Ts were built. The next year production dipped somewhat when the company turned over some of its facilities to the manufacture of ambulances, trucks, aircraft engines, caissons and steel helmets during the period America participated in World War I. However, within three weeks of the armistice, civilian auto production had resumed, and by early December, 1918, the daily output of Model Ts had reached one thousand vehicles and was still climbing.

On January 2, 1919, Henry Ford announced another corporate milestone. Henceforth, he said, the Ford Motor Company would pay a daily wage of six dollars. This was not quite the windfall for workers it may have seemed, for the cost of living had more than doubled in five years. Still, the rise was significant. Other employers had matched Ford's wage scale, but none had exceeded it.

Ford's success spiral—higher and higher wages, lower and lower prices—was contingent on an always-expanding market. Thus when a depression hit the country in 1920 and caused a general drop in auto sales, the effect on the Ford Motor Company

Farewell to the Tin Lizzie

A 1921 bus based on the Model T Ford: the Model T was used as the basis for many types of vehicles.

was nearly devastating. Henry Ford had been borrowing huge sums of money to buy out his minority stockholders. And during the previous three years the company had spent nearly 100 million dollars on an expansion program that included construction of a new factory on the Rouge River near Springwells, Michigan.

When another price cut failed to produce enough of a sales spurt, Ford performed a financial coup that made him few friends but won him everlasting respect as a canny and crafty businessman. In mid-1921 he had 93,000 surplus cars assembled and shipped—cash on delivery—to dealers across the country. By this bold action he successfully divided his financial burden among a large group of men who dared not refuse to shoulder it, since a dealer's refusal would risk the possibility of having to forfeit his franchise.

Thus Henry Ford and the Model T survived. But many Ford executives and a number of farsighted dealers began to be aware of a shift in the public taste. They realized that with the growing prosperity of the 1920s, the spartan, inelegant Model T would soon cease to satisfy the great multitude for whom it had been created. Henry Ford at age sixty seemed more conciliatory than ever, yet in matters affecting the Model T, which had long since become his alter ego, he was more unyielding than ever. He dismissed requests for a wholesale redesigning of the car by insisting that "so far as I can see, the only trouble with the Ford car is that we can't make it fast enough."

In 1926 the Model T chassis was lowered, the radiator was raised, and for the first time since 1913 the car came in a choice of colors: fawn gray, gun-metal blue, phoenix brown or highland green. But only a modest increase in sales resulted. Another price cut was instituted, but this failed to alter the sales trend at all. In 1926 Ford's share of the market fell below 40 per cent for the first time since 1918; it threatened to drop to 25 per cent in 1927.

It was widely rumored that the long-lived Tin Lizzie would be discontinued, but Henry Ford kept insisting that "the Ford car will continue to be made in the same way." A few months later, however, the company announced that production of the car would cease. The last of 15,007,033 Model Ts came off the line on May 26, 1927. Nine months later the more contemporary, but otherwise conservative, Model A was introduced with enormous marketing fanfare.

"The Model T was a pioneer," Henry Ford said in retrospect. "There was no conscious public need of motor cars when we first made it. There were few good roads. This car blazed the way for the motor industry and started the movement for good roads everywhere."

In his history of the Ford Motor Company, Alan Nevins summed up the Model T's myriad virtues this way: "No other single machine, in all probability, did so much to induce people of provincial mind to begin thinking in regional and national terms; none did so much to knit together different parts of the county, the state and the country; none did more to create the sense of a freer and more spacious life." MERVYN KAUFMAN

Henry Ford, photographed in 1909—one year after the appearance of the first Model T.

Soldiers escorting a traction engine along the Strand during the railwaymen's strike in England in 1911.

Giddy visions of war dominated the imaginations of statesmen and citizens alike as Europe approached the brink of World War I. Excited throngs jammed the streets of every major European capital to cheer declarations of war; other world events shrank by comparison. Socialists parties in France and Germany ignored their commitment to the universal brotherhood of man and voted war credits with enthusiasm; large crowds sang "God Save the King" outside Buckingham Palace. For many, war promised relief from the dreary sameness of their everyday lives, for the war was viewed on a grand and heroic scale.

In a more tragic vein, the conflict also served as a safety valve for civil violence. Long before the war, most European countries had been torn by internal struggles, and these upheavals contributed as much to the crisis of 1914 as did the folly of diplomats.

The years preceding the outbreak of hostilities saw violence on a scale never previously witnessed in peacetime. Bomb throwing and assassinations were commonplace, and in 1908, Georges Sorel's handbook of political violence, *Réflexions sur la Violence*, appeared. Sorel's work, which was swiftly adopted by the working-class movement, asserted that violence had a valuable moral and political function. Throughout Europe, workers turned to the doctrine of revolution known as anarcho-syndicalism, which advocated the strike as labor's chief weapon. A series of strikes followed, which culminated in the general strike that sparked the Russian Revolution.

In the arts too the prevailing mood was violent. The futurists advocated movement and violence as ends in themselves, and their paintings were obsessively concerned with racing cars and speedboats. In music, awareness of the tenor of the times was less enthusiastic but nonetheless acute. The savage,

David Lloyd George, Liberal statesman and Prime Minister 1916–22.

tramping rhythms of Mahler's Sixth Symphony, published in 1904, were strangely prophetic of the horrors to come. Equally ominous themes were to be found in such musical landmarks of the prewar period as Igor Stravinsky's *Rite of Spring*, in which savage and primeval rhythms abound, and Jean Sibelius' Fourth Symphony,

in which the prevailing mood is one of desolation. But perhaps the most prophetic musical utterance of all, in the summer of 1914, was Gustav Holst's *Planet Suite*. A section called *Mars* seemed a bleak and relentless assertion of war's cruel brutalities.

Unrest in France

Most of Europe was affected by the growth of irrationalism and violence. In France, the main workers' union, the *Confederation Général du Travail*, wholeheartedly adopted anarcho-syndicalism in response to rising prices. A series of strikes, including one by civil servants, kept France in a state of almost perpetual industrial unrest. This social crisis was not confined to the working classes. An anti-Semitic, rabidly nationalist organization, *Action Française*, had grown out of the Dreyfus scandal, and its street gangs, the shock troops of the radical right, attacked Jews and workers. Perhaps the strongest indication of the state of tension came in 1914 when Madame Caillaux, the wife of the ex-Premier, murdered the editor of *Le Figaro* in retaliation for a press campaign against her husband.

Female suffrage

The problems faced by France, however, seemed mild in comparison with those of Britain. There, giant strikes and a British Army mutiny rocked the complacence of the Liberals. All over Europe,

governments faced the problems of mass politics. The tempers of the ill-educated masses could easily be aroused by the new pulp press, and appeals to this audience were increasingly made via the violent or the spectacular. Everywhere rabble-rousing replaced the select and dignified politics of the previous century. In England issues arose that were to involve the masses and bring the threat of civil war.

The existing social order came under attack from every direction. In a population of 34 million, only 5 million owned half of the nation's wealth. Upper-class opulence contrasted sharply with working-class slums. Liberal Prime Minister David Lloyd George tried to redress the balance in 1909 with his People's Budget, which was designed to tax unearned income; but the House of Lords, sensing a challenge to aristocratic privilege, rejected the budget. A struggle ensued, and victory finally went to the Liberals, but not before fistfighting erupted in Parliament. Die-hard Conservatives did not surrender. They had been forced to give way over the budget, but they were determined to fight again over the Irish demand for Home Rule. When non-Catholic Orangemen formed the Ulster Volunteer Force to resist Home Rule, they were egged on by the Conservatives. "We strongly challenge the government to interfere with us if they dare," said Sir Edward Carson, a Conservative leader. While the government stood helplessly by, private armies drilled in Ireland. The Ulster Volunteer Force squared off against the

Suffragettes guarding the coffin of Emily Davison, who died after throwing herself under the hooves of the King's horse at the Derby in an attempt to draw attention to the movement for female suffrage.

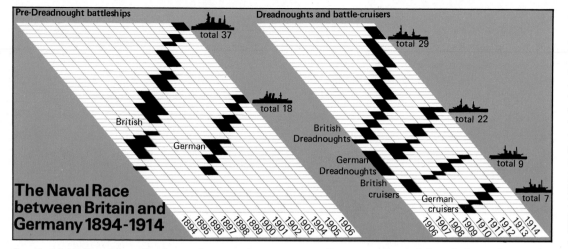

Pre-Dreadnought battleships — total 37 — British — German — total 18

Dreadnoughts and battle-cruisers — total 29 — British Dreadnoughts — German Dreadnoughts — British cruisers — total 22 — German cruisers — total 9 — total 7

1894 1895 1896 1897 1898 1899 1900 1901 1902 1903 1904 1905 1906 — 1906 1907 1908 1909 1910 1911 1912 1913 1914

The Naval Race between Britain and Germany 1894-1914

fanatical Irish Republican Brotherhood, and every time the government passed the Home Rule Bill in the House of Commons, it was stopped in the House of Lords.

The Liberals were faced with another threat to public order. Emmeline Pankhurst's suffragettes had begun to rebel against the smothering repressions of contemporary values. Revealing her sympathy with the trends of the times, Mrs. Pankhurst declared "the argument of the broken pane is the most valuable argument in modern politics." The government failed to respond to suffragette demands, and on November 18, 1910, a group of women marchers were assaulted by police and onlookers. The suffragettes replied with extreme militancy. Emily Davison threw herself under the King's horse at Epsom, and in March of 1912 every plate glass window in the West End was smashed. Imprisoned suffragette crusaders went on a hunger strike, only to be force-fed with great brutality.

The Liberal bureaucracy could not cope with the situation; violence was answered with violence. Some militant trade union leaders like Arthur J. Cook adopted anarcho-syndicalist tactics, and strikes became a regular event.

The threat of socialism

All over Europe the story was the same. In Spain, the central government in Madrid could think of no better way to deal with regionalism in Catalonia than to hire professional gunmen whose task was to stir up violence and provide the government with an excuse for suspending constitutional guarantees. Nor did Europe alone hold a monopoly on violence. In 1910 the Mexican Revolution broke out,

inaugurating ten years of savage and bloody civil war. Emiliano Zapata led the peasants against the military in a struggle that eventually cost the lives of over a quarter of a million people. The most dangerous outbursts of violence took place in the chaos of the Balkans, where a series of assassinations were attempted by a Serbian nationalist secret society known as the Black Hand.

During this same period, the decay of the Turkish Empire and the weaknesses of Austria-Hungary tempted various Balkan races to fight for national self-determination. Racial and political barriers rarely coincided in the Balkans, and consequently racial minorities frequently found themselves looking across their borders to compatriots who might liberate them. Serbs and Croats in Austria looked to Serbia, and Rumanians in Hungarian Transylvania looked to Rumania. Slavs throughout the Balkans were determined to break free of Hapsburg domination. "Better a terrible end than an endless terror," Slav leaders said.

These Slavic groups were tied by race and religion to Russia, which kept a perpetual eye on Slav affairs, and that special relationship posed a serious dilemma for Austria. To reunite the Slavic peoples, Austria would either have to conquer the Slavs who had gained independence as a result of the decline of Turkey —and in so doing risk war with Russia—or release those Slavs still under Austrian rule and thereby shatter the integrity of the Hapsburg Empire.

In Austria, as in other European countries, men of violence were coming to the fore. The military party under Count Conrad von Hötzendorf wanted to eliminate the problem by destroying Serbia. The Austrian Foreign Minister, Alois

Lexa Aehrenthal, sought to solve the problem with a dazzling display of diplomatic virtuosity. Anxious to seize Bosnia-Herzegovina and extend the Austrian threat to Serbia, Aehrenthal made a shady deal with the Russian Foreign Minister, Aleksandr Izvolsky, whereby Austria would annex Bosnia and Russia would seize the Dardanelles. Austria promptly moved into Bosnia, while Russia, which was unable to seize the Dardanelles without Austrian support—which was not forthcoming—was left high and dry. Following its diplomatic humiliation, Russia determined not to back down again. "Mark my words," said Izvolsky, "the Eastern Question is now insoluble without a conflict."

As Russia and Austria glared at each other across the Balkans, their allies, Britain and Germany, were drawing further apart. The British Foreign Office had come to the conclusion that the only interpretation of German policy which fitted the known facts was that Germany

wanted war. Germany, rapidly becoming more assertive in European politics, offended and disturbed the British with its well-publicized effort to outbuild the Royal Navy. As the world's major naval power, the British concluded that the German expansion was directed at them. Their reply was twofold: they began to concentrate their strength in the North Sea, leaving the Mediterranean more to the French (a division of labor that further committed the British to the French alliance); and, spurred by public opinion, they also began to increase the rate at which they were building Dreadnoughts.

Fanned by a sensational press, this arms race soon polarized existing antagonisms. Oppressed by the drabness of their everyday lives, the masses sought—and found— blood and thunder in the press. Diplomacy was followed as avidly as a national sport. In England the *Daily Express* and the *Daily Mail* became jingoistic guardians of national honor, and even *The Times* selected its information to stress the German menace. The German press was, if anything, more rabid. Both the *Neue Prussische Zeitung* and the *Deutsche Zeitung* demanded the creation of a navy able to wrest maritime supremacy from the British. Sensible diplomats were helpless. The masses demanded excitement, and they got it from international affairs. To them, national honor was everything. And when the band of Serbian nationalists known as the Black Hand claimed its most distinguished victim, the Austrian Archduke Franz Ferdinand, war became inevitable.

Launching a Dreadnought at Portsmouth.

787

Assassination Sparks the Great War

By the spring of 1914, imperial Germany was spoiling for war. Germany's leaders were determined to break up the Triple Entente of Britain, France and Russia that had isolated Germany in Europe and thwarted its territorial ambitions. And when a young Bosnian nationalist assassinated Archduke Franz Ferdinand, heir to the throne of Germany's lone ally, Austria-Hungary, the Kaiser had the "incident" he had been looking for. In the diplomatic controversy growing out of the assassination, the Kaiser threw his full support behind Austria-Hungary and against Russia. This set in motion a series of political and military maneuvers that made a full-scale Continental war virtually inevitable. The scope and inflexibility of Germany's master plan for mobilization—the infamous Schlieffen Plan—necessarily involved both England and France in any conflict between the Kaiser and the Tsar. And thus when Germany declared war on Russia on August 1, World War I was launched.

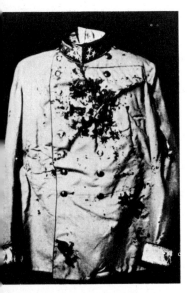

The blood-stained uniform of Archduke Franz Ferdinand, heir to the Austro-Hungarian Empire, after his assassination on June 28, 1914.

Opposite Kaiser Wilhelm II of Germany with his commander in chief, Helmuth von Moltke, on the Western Front at the beginning of World War I.

On June 28, 1914, in a narrow street in Sarajevo, the capital of Bosnia, two shots were fired setting off the train of events that culminated in the start of World War I six weeks later. Those two shots were fired by a Bosnian student, Gavrilo Princip, one of three young Bosnian nationalists who had traveled to Sarajevo on the instructions of a Serbian secret organization known as the Black Hand. The shots were fired at the Archduke Franz Ferdinand, the heir-presumptive to the throne of Austria-Hungary.

Why did this particular event lead to war? In 1912, all the Balkan states with the exception of Rumania had attacked Turkey—a crisis considerably more serious than a single assassination—yet there had been no wider repercussions. And since that time the ambassadors of the Great Powers had met regularly in London under the chairmanship of Sir Edward Grey, the British Foreign Secretary, to ensure that their countries were not dragged into war by the deeds of the belligerents.

Outwardly, the international situation in 1914 was much more settled than it had been in 1912. Indeed, one of the major antagonisms of international relations—the rivalry between Britain and Germany—seemed to be dying down. Britain had met some of Germany's colonial grievances; Britain's objections to German penetration of the Turkish Empire had finally been overcome in early 1914; and a contingent agreement for the division of the Portuguese colonies between Germany and England had also been concluded at that time. Moreover, each nation had seemed to accept the existence of the other's navy.

But this was only the surface reality. The division of the world into two power blocs was largely a result of German policy, a policy that concentrated

on raising Germany from a Continental to a world power. Its basis was Germany's economic expansion, which had succeeded in radically transforming its social, political and economic structure during the preceding generation. This rapid expansion in all spheres of economic life only heightened the Germans' awareness of the inadequacy of the country's sources of raw materials and created the general conviction, reinforced by nationwide propaganda, that Germany's frontiers had become too narrow. Germany's territorial ambitions ran counter to the designs of the other imperialist powers, and those powers were provoked into a policy of containment.

Germany's diplomacy never waivered in its ultimate objective—the expansion of Germany's power—although it vacillated in its methods. (At one time that policy emphasized rapprochement; at another, it aggressively insisted on Germany's claims.) Between 1912 and early 1914, Germany attempted to reach an understanding—which, it was hoped, would lead ultimately to an alliance—with Britain. But its efforts in this direction left it clearly subordinate to Britain and made it apparent that its objectives were not to be attained without a fundamental restructuring of the relations between Britain, France and Russia. This Germany had manifestly failed to do by peaceful means; the only alternative was preventive war against any nation that thwarted Germany's efforts to achieve its territorial objectives. But why did Sarajevo provide the opportunity for such a preventive war, and, more importantly, why did the assassination of Franz Ferdinand lead to the outbreak of a more horrific general war?

It is easy enough to see how the assassination at Sarajevo could lead to a localized conflict in the Balkans. After all, Franz Ferdinand had come to

The storm clouds gather

Franz Ferdinand. His death sparked the war that ended an epoch.

Right The arrest of Gavrilo Princip after the assassination at Sarajevo.

Bosnia to attend Austro-Hungarian army maneuvers that were nothing more than a gesture to remind the Balkan Slavs of Austria-Hungary's power. The Hapsburg monarchy had been rocked in the 1860s by the secession of its Italian and German members, and had only prevented the same thing from happening to its Hungarian domains by taking the Magyar aristocracy into partnership.

By 1914 the existence of the Austro-Hungarian Empire was being threatened by a movement of Slav nationalism. Partnership with the Slavs was out of the question because the Magyars would not tolerate a further dilution of their power, and consequently the only road open to the Hapsburgs was to bring the Slavs to heel. There were those in Vienna who felt that the crime committed against Austria at Sarajevo provided an excellent opportunity to teach the Slavs a lesson. Both Count Franz Conrad von Hötzendorf, the Chief of Staff, and Count Leopold von Berchtold, the Foreign Minister, felt that a demonstration against Serbia (which was suspected of being behind the assassination) would be a good way to reassert Austria's prestige.

At this point, the issue became considerably more complicated. An operation to humiliate the Slavs could well rouse Russia, the protector of the Slav nations, and the Austrians needed to be reassured that they had the support of their German allies before making their move against Serbia. Yet for seven days they did nothing. The immediate indignation arising from the assassination was allowed to evaporate, and Austria's subsequent action appeared to be concerned less with avenging an insult than with crushing the Serbs. On July 4, a full week after the assassination, the Austrians sent a letter to Kaiser Wilhelm II, asking for his support.

The Germans, who were so conscious of being isolated by the Triple Entente of Britain, France and Russia that they were prepared to do almost anything for their only certain ally, Austria-Hungary, readily pledged their support. The Kaiser, who was the decisive factor, became violently excited, gave the Austrians the go-ahead, and promised German support in case of Russian intervention. In doing so, the Kaiser sided with the generals who opined that, if preventive war against Russia was inevitable, it ought to come before Russian industrialization made it a more formidable enemy. In any case, the Kaiser was convinced that the Russians would back down, and he therefore made a chivalrous gesture that he felt was unlikely to be put to the test. This gesture strengthened the Austrians' resolve to be firm.

Nevertheless, the Austrians still hesitated. At the best of times Austrian policy was dilatory and hesitant; now it was held back by the knowledge that French President Raymond Poincaré was visiting St. Petersburg. Strong immediate action therefore could not be taken against Serbia—on the chance that the fire-eating Poincaré might encourage the Russians to take a pro-Slav stand.

Almost a month passed and nothing happened: Europe breathed a sigh of relief. Perhaps Sarajevo had just been one of those minor events in the Balkans.

But on July 23, Poincaré left St. Petersburg, and the diplomatic log jam began to break. At 6 P.M. on July 24, Austria-Hungary presented a provocative ultimatum to Serbia, one that was tantamount to an Austrian takeover of Serbia's internal policies. That ultimatum had a forty-eight-hour time limit. When it was presented, Serbia's Prime Minister Nikola Pašić was away, and he did not return until 5 A.M. on July 25. By that time eleven hours of the forty-eight had expired. That day, Sir Edward Grey suggested to Lichnowsky, the German ambassador in London, that Britain and Germany ask Austria to extend its time limit or accept mediations by France, Italy, Britain and Germany. Grey's move convinced the Germans that Britain was so anxious to avoid trouble that it would not intervene. Feeling free to encourage their Austrian allies, the Germans did not pass on Grey's message until after the ultimatum had expired. In fact, Theobald von Bethmann-Hollweg, the German Chancellor, seems to have had war with Russia and France as his main objective at this time. And he was apparently prepared to gamble on the possibility of Britain's entry into that war. If war had not ensued, Germany's diplomatic victory would have been sizable nonetheless. France's failure to support the Russians—and Russia's failure to support the Serbs—could quite easily have called the whole alliance system into question.

On July 24, the Germans notified the other powers that they felt that the Austrian ultimatum was reasonable and, attempting to create a peaceable impression, urged the powers to localize any conflict. The Russians stated that they could not acquiesce in the demise of Serbia, and the French announced that they would meet their obligations to Russia. This encouraged the Serbs to reject the Austrian ultimatum completely, although their reply was conciliatory. The Serbs refused to accept

unconditional surrender, and the Austrians immediately broke off diplomatic relations. Yet when the Kaiser saw the Serbian reply to the Austrian ultimatum, he said, "All reason for war has gone."

It was a reasonable conclusion, drawn by an intelligent and reasonable—if excitable—man. But the Kaiser had not reckoned with two forces, and these were the factors that transformed the small-scale local disagreement between Austria and Serbia into a Continental and then into a world war. One factor was the determination of Chancellor Bethmann-Hollweg and the German Chief of Staff, Helmuth von Moltke—and the interests they represented—to have their preventive war. The other was the rigidity of the Germans' military plans. By July 28, the Kaiser was genuinely afraid of the possibility of a European war, and he suggested that the Austrians save their honor by a token occupation of Belgrade, the Serbian capital. Bethmann-Hollweg held back the Kaiser's sane proposals until after Austria had declared war on Serbia. At this point the Russians decided to mobilize as a gesture of support for Serbia, to show that the Russian bear was not sleeping. This might have caused the Austrians to have second thoughts, but they were emboldened by messages telegrammed by Moltke.

Even at this point general war was not inevitable. Bethmann-Hollweg sued for British neutrality, in exchange for which he promised to forego annexation of French and Belgian territory. But the British stood firm, and Bethmann-Hollweg, who knew that the odds on a German victory had been dramatically diminished by Britain's move, lost some of his nerve. He pressed the Austrians to modify their plans in accordance with the earlier British proposals of a "halt in Belgrade." He did not want the Austrians to drop the matter entirely, however. Indeed, he was aware that the Russians would reject the British proposals. He was attempting a sleight of hand, one that was intended to lay the blame for any hostilities on Russia. (He hoped thereby to alter British

intentions.) The appearance of Russian aggression would greatly assist him in another objective—the winning over of the German public, especially the Social Democrats.

The Russians held the stage in the next act. A partial mobilization might have balked the Germans, but such a move was impossible. Russia's plans for mobilization were such that, if the country only partially mobilized against Austria, the chaos on the railway system would effectively preclude any wider mobilization. To prevent Russia from being left defenseless in case of German attack, any Russian mobilization had to be total. Yet that massive mobilization was meant only as a diplomatic maneuver, and not a decision for European war.

Russia's mobilization was precisely what Germany had been waiting for. Two ultimatums were immediately dispatched: one to Russia, demanding

A French infantry regiment leaving for the front in 1914. Five million Frenchmen were killed in Flanders during World War I.

German student-conscripts, with flowers in their helmets, at the beginning of the war.

"A stab from behind"

German and British biplanes
and triplanes fighting.

Opposite Two World War I
posters. Both sides felt that
they were fighting a crusade
against the forces of evil.

demobilization against Germany and Austria, and one to France, demanding that it make explicit its stand in the event of a German attack on Russia. War had become inevitable, primarily because of the nature of Germany's only military plan, the infamous Schlieffen Plan.

Of all the Great Powers, Germany alone had two potential enemies, France and Russia. It therefore faced the special problem of fighting two major wars simultaneously. Because of Russia's enormous size and huge manpower resources (which threatened a long, drawn-out war during which the French could break into Germany from the west), it was necessary to knock out France before Russia could mobilize. That was the battle plan devised by Alfred von Schlieffen, who had been German Chief of Staff before Moltke. Thinking that France's network of frontier fortresses was impregnable, Schlieffen proposed that the German armies outflank the French lines by means of a wheeling movement through Belgium. Such a move involved two problems, the consequences of which seem to have been ignored. First of all, the forcible violation of Belgian territory was likely to arouse the British, for whom the neutrality of the Low Countries was a fundamental policy. Secondly, in purely military terms, the Schlieffen Plan involved pouring four army groups through the railway junction at Aachen. One army would have to be through and on its way before the next one arrived, and that meant incredibly ingenious and intricate synchronization of railway timetables. It also meant that once German mobilization started, it could end only with troops leaving Aachen and violating Belgian neutrality. Thus for Germany mobilization meant war, and war on both France and Russia.

The part played by this plan in escalating the war and in ensuring that one particular interest prevailed in the German ruling class was enormous. Even as the Kaiser was ordering mobilization, news came of a British offer to guarantee French neutrality—provided Germany would refrain from attacking Russia. The Kaiser thought peace might

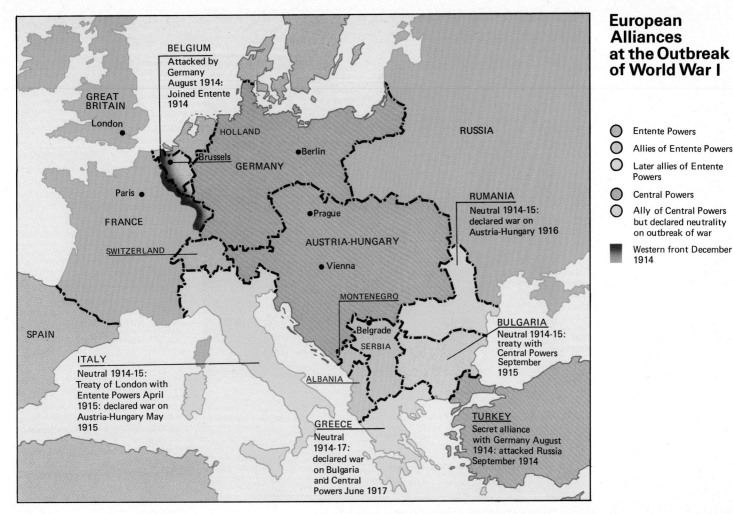

European Alliances at the Outbreak of World War I

BELGIUM
Attacked by Germany August 1914: Joined Entente 1914

RUMANIA
Neutral 1914-15: declared war on Austria-Hungary 1916

BULGARIA
Neutral 1914-15: treaty with Central Powers September 1915

TURKEY
Secret alliance with Germany August 1914: attacked Russia September 1914

GREECE
Neutral 1914-17: declared war on Bulgaria and Central Powers June 1917

ITALY
Neutral 1914-15: Treaty of London with Entente Powers April 1915: declared war on Austria-Hungary May 1915

- ◯ Entente Powers
- ◯ Allies of Entente Powers
- ◯ Later allies of Entente Powers
- ◯ Central Powers
- ◯ Ally of Central Powers but declared neutrality on outbreak of war
- ■ Western front December 1914

still be saved, but Moltke told him that it would not be possible to stop German mobilization (since doing so would involve the rerouting of 11,000 trains.) In any case, Russian mobilization was a threat to Germany's split-second timing. It had to press on —to force Russia to demobilize or to prevent Russia from getting a start and nullifying Germany's advantage of speed.

On August 1, Germany declared war on Russia. Two days later, it declared war on France. By August 3, the Balkan quarrel had been transformed, with the help of the Schlieffen Plan, into a European war involving France, Germany and Russia. So far, the British had managed to stay out, although there was a division of opinion inside the cabinet as to Britain's best course of action. This division of opinion may have been a factor encouraging belligerence on the Continent—encouraging the Germans to bank on British neutrality and the French to count on British support.

At this point, Schlieffen chalked up his greatest posthumous victory: in accordance with an 1839 treaty guaranteeing the independence and neutrality of Belgium, the British asked the Germans to respect that neutrality. The exigencies of the Schlieffen Plan ensured that the Germans could not comply with the British request (which Bethmann-Hollweg described as "stabbing a man from behind, while fighting for his life"). He could not believe that the British would go to war, "all for just a word, neutrality, just for a scrap of paper."

That Bethmann-Hollweg could use such an expression about an international treaty reflects the Germans' cavalier approach to international relations and their willingness to engage in a Continental war, even at the risk of making it a world war. The Schlieffen Plan was part and parcel of this approach. Once the tenuous truce had been broken, the scope and inflexibility of the Plan made world war a virtual inevitability.   BRIAN GROGAN

Over the Top. British troops advancing in Flanders.

In October, 1914, barely four months after Sarajevo, the United States ambassador in London, Walter Hines Page, wrote to President Wilson: "It is not the same world as it was last July." Page's observation was a profoundly accurate one, for the first clashes of World War I had ended an epoch that began in the Renaissance. When the war began, Europe dominated the world. The emperors of Germany, Austria, Turkey and Russia ruled the territory between the Rhine and Vladivostok, and Great Britain ruled the seas. When it ended, the four empires were in ruins, Europe was drained and exhausted, and the political structure of the world as we know it today had emerged.

General staffs, clinging to the tactics used in the Franco-Prussian War, became obsessed by dreams of vast frontal offensives against the enemy's strongest point. But advances in military technology—including the development of the machine rifle and the Maxim gun—and the use of railways for moving vast numbers of troops to the front turned such frontal assaults into suicide missions. These two factors interacted to create a horrific stalemate on the Western Front, where troops arriving at the battlefield by rail were soon mowed down by the concentrated rifle fire of the defensive forces. The limitations of rail transport were underscored by every breakthrough, for beyond the railhead an army could progress no faster than its slowest walker. Before enough troops could walk through the gap in the enemy defense, enemy reinforcements could be brought up by rail. As a result, Europe's manhood was inexorably decimated; thousands were killed or maimed in vast offensives that rarely gained more than a few hundred yards.

Trench warfare

The only way generals on both sides could see to break the deadlock was to mount giant offensives. The resulting slaughter was apalling, for while attacks proceeded on foot, defense was mechanized. The worst carnage occurred in 1916, the year the Germans decided to knock France out of the war by bleeding her to death. In February they attacked the fortress of Verdun, a symbol of French national pride that the French vowed to defend at any price. In the ensuing five-

French soldiers in a trench in 1916.

month struggle, the French and Germans lost 600,000 men. The Battle of the Somme in July had little more point.

The war at sea

The war at sea was no more decisive, although it was slightly less bloody than the land war. It was also something of an anticlimax after the fierce naval rivalry of the prewar years. The Royal Navy eagerly awaited a second Trafalgar, this time with the much-vaunted German High Seas Fleet as the victims. The Germans wisely stayed in port, at least until May, 1916, when they inaugurated a scheme to entrap isolated British ships. But the only major naval battle of the conflict took place off the west coast of Denmark. This naval clash, known as the Battle of Jutland, was indecisive, but it did keep the German fleet in port for the rest of the war. Aside from Jutland, the Royal Navy confined itself to two tasks. The first was participating in the disastrous Allied attacks on Gallipoli and Salonika in an effort to turn the German flank; the second was organizing an economic blockade that cut off Germany's food supply—a crippling blow.

The German reply to the Royal Navy's blockade led to the great turning point of the war. Unable to combat the British on the seas, the Germans decided to do so under the seas, and the first U-boats attacked in 1915. In May of that year the

British passenger liner *Lusitania* was sunk; among the victims were 128 U.S. citizens. There was a huge outcry in America, in part because the Germans had medals struck to commemorate the sinking. But the Germans, who did not have enough submarines to justify all-out submarine warfare, soon called a halt to the attacks.

At this stage, the United States was determined to stay out of the war. It was enjoying a most profitable neutrality, derived in part from the fact that Britain and France were compelled to sell their assets in America to obtain American loans to buy American goods. However, by early 1917 the British blockade of Germany was

beginning to take effect, and Admiral Alfred von Tirpitz was convinced that England must be starved by submarine attacks on every ship—belligerent or neutral —entering or leaving its ports. President Wilson protested, but the Germans, who hoped to destroy Britain before America could intervene, ignored his pleas. On February 3, the United States severed diplomatic relations with Germany. Later that month, the U.S. State Department released the Zimmermann note, in which the German foreign office had instructed its ambassador in Mexico to arrange a German-Mexican-Japanese alliance against America. On March 15, an American ship was sunk without warning and on April 2, 1917, President Wilson asked for a declaration of war on Germany. America, the sleeping giant, had awakened, and its entry into the war foreshadowed the end of Europe's hegemony over the civilized world.

Duplicity in the Middle East

One of the greatest changes brought about by the war was in the colonial sphere. Before the war the challenge to European imperialism was hardly noticed; by 1917, the end of colonialism was a clear possibility. Revolutionary movements in all corners of the globe benefited by the war. Germany supplied the Bolsheviks with cash and shipped Lenin to Russia in the hope that revolution would destroy the Russian war effort. And German rifles were shipped to Ireland, where war had not blunted the desire for

Admiral Alfred von Tirpitz, German Minister of Marine, during the war years.

he onslaught of new weapons

Home Rule. Britain was no less guilty. Anxious to protect their oil interests in Persia and to secure the Suez Canal from Turkey—which had entered the war on the side of Germany—the British encouraged Arab nationalism against the Turks. As early as 1915, they were negotiating with ibn-Ali Husein, the Sherif of Mecca, to stimulate an Arab revolt. In the course of negotiations, the British promised to help in the formation of independent Arab kingdoms in Arabia,

American forces landing in France in 1917.

Palestine, Iraq and Syria. Operating on that assurance, Husein's son, Faisal, joined with T. E. Lawrence in an Arab war against the German-Turkish lines. (Unbeknown to the Arabs, the British and French at this time had already arranged the Sykes-Picot Agreement—a plan for partitioning the Arab world between Britain and France.)

As if this display of bad faith were not enough, the British also promised Palestine to the Jews. Throughout the war, Zionism had grown in influence, largely through the efforts of the leader of British Zionism, Chaim Weizmann. Weizmann, a Russian-born chemist at the University of Manchester, managed to convert the British Cabinet to the idea of a Jewish national state. He accomplished this by emphasizing the usefulness of a Jewish state to the defense of Suez and by shrewdly suggesting that a pro-Jewish gesture was required to offset the unfavorable effect Russian

anti-Semitism was having on the Allied cause in America. In a letter from Foreign Secretary Arthur James Balfour to the Jewish financier Lord Rothschild (the letter was later known as the Balfour Declaration) Britain pledged itself to the idea of a Jewish Palestine.

Colonial unrest was not confined to the Near East during this period. Indeed British problems were brewing in India, where the Morley-Minto reforms had proven ineffective. The outbreak of war had provoked a display of enthusiastic Indian support for the British government. Hundreds of thousands of Indians had volunteered to serve in the British Army, and a million pounds had been contributed to the war effort. But the war had two corrosive effects on the British position. First, it gave Indians an intoxicating glimpse of independence, as the Indian Army took over imperial duties to release British units for Europe. In business and administration, Indians had a chance, small though it was, to see what they were capable of. Second, they began to realize how weak their British masters were.

Revolutionary chaos in Russia left the way open for a German and Turkish advance on India. The British were simply not strong enough to deal with such an attack —especially if they could not guarantee the absolute loyalty of

The Easter Week Rising in Dublin, 1916. Violence continued in Ireland in spite of the war.

their Indian subjects—and in August, 1917, the British were obliged to issue a declaration promising "increasing association of Indians in every branch of the administration and the gradual development of self-governing institutions." It was just as well they did, for nationalist extremists had gained control of the Congress movement. Moreover, India had at last found great leaders capable of mobilizing its vast population. Mohandas K. Gandhi was a lawyer

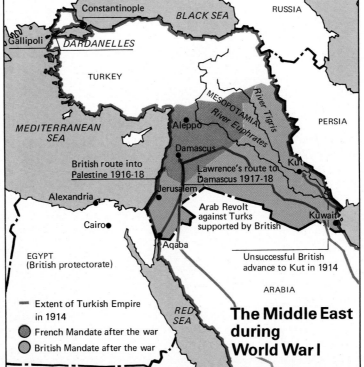

The Middle East during World War I

who had worked in South Africa, where he defended Indians against prejudicial laws. In the course of his work he had discovered the power of the device of civil disobedience. Jawaharlal Nehru was educated at Harrow and Cambridge, and in England he became aware of Western techniques of political organization. Together, Gandhi and Nehru turned Indian nationalism into a mass phenomenon. It would take years, but they had discovered the key to British withdrawal.

World War 1 was more of a European than a world war, for it represented the death throes of the old order rather than global conflict. The requirements of total war placed strains on the administrative and organizational skills of governments, and Europe's notions of the functions of government changed. Rationing and control of raw materials laid the basis for planned economics and welfare states. The growth of government propaganda machines—in liberal England as well as in militarist Germany—showed how far the war had forced acceptance of the needs of mass society on Europe. In February, 1917, that strain led to the final collapse of the Russian government. Agonies stifled since 1905 suddenly found their voice, and Russia began a descent into chaos. Governments succeeded one another with terrifying rapidity, and for a while it looked as if reactionary generals might succeed with a counter-revolutionary coup. Then Lenin intervened with a decision that would alter the course of world history.

1917 "Peace, Bread and Land"

St. Petersburg—Peter the Great's glittering capital, his "window on the West"—changed names twice during the first decades of the twentieth century. In 1914, as an expression of wartime patriotism, Peter's city was given the Russian name Petrograd. A decade later, that name was changed to Leningrad, to honor the man who meanwhile had toppled the Russian government. Ironically, it was to Petrograd—the city that would eventually bear his name—that Lenin traveled in 1917. And it was there, on October 23, that he met with the Central Committee of the Bolshevik Party to plot the overthrow of the moderate Provisional Government that had replaced the monarchy the preceding February. A fortnight later, Lenin's followers arrested the entire Provisional Government. A new government, a new state and a new society were proclaimed. Its rallying cry was "Peace, Bread and Land," and its ambition was to transform the world.

Lenin, architect of the revolution and ruler of Russia.

Opposite Petrograd, no surrender. A poster dating from the revolution.

On the evening of October 23, 1917, a number of nondescript, shabby men, some of them in disguise, slipped unobtrusively into a small, middle-class flat in the city of Petrograd (which had been known, until a few years before, as St. Petersburg, and which was soon to be renamed Leningrad). The surroundings were informal. For ten hours the talk concentrated on one topic only: should this group seize control of the government of Russia?

The get-together was, in fact, a full session of the Central Committee of the Bolshevik faction of the Russian Social Democratic Workers' Party. The leader of the group was Vladimir Ilich Ulyanov, better known as Lenin. He was forty-seven years old, tiny and bald, with small, deep-set eyes and high cheekbones. He generally wore a small Vandyke and moustache. For this occasion, however, he had taken the precaution of putting on a wig and shaving off his beard. Also present were Lev Davydovich Bronstein, better known as Leon Trotsky, and Iosif Vissarionovich Dzhugashvili, better known as Stalin. Trotsky was relatively tall, with a shock of bushy hair and a goatee. He had a powerful, musical voice and piercing blue eyes behind spectacles. Stalin was very small, with a slightly withered left arm, pockmarks, yellowish eyes and a heavy moustache.

Lenin had called the Committee together to make a proposal: he had decided it was time for an insurrection. During the ten hours of discussion he swung over to his own view all those who had not already been in agreement with him. Once made, the decision set in motion preparations that a fortnight later were to destroy the Russian government and institute a regime made up of Bolsheviks committed to the novel enterprise of transforming Russia, and indeed the whole world, into a socialist society. This was the first time in history that power was taken by a group of people in a conscious attempt to implement a preconceived theory not merely for personal reasons but to change society as a whole.

The tsarist government had been battered into helplessness by its long and exhausting involvement, during the preceding two and a half years, in World War I. Its resources were drained and its people exasperated by the strains of a war that, while seeming to lead nowhere, was at the same time exacting an immense toll of killed and wounded soldiers. But there was also a political element in the restiveness of the Russian people. The Russian intelligentsia—educated people of all classes who believed in changing things for the better—had given rise to a revolutionary movement in the last third of the nineteenth century. One branch of this movement believed in using the collective traditions of the peasantry to build a new society on the basis of some form of socialism; the other branch pinned its hopes for a socialist transformation of Russia on the industrial working class, or proletariat. This second branch had come to be dominated by the ideas of Karl Marx, whose major work, *Das Kapital*, had been translated from German into Russian before appearing in any other language.

Marx held that the middle classes, while perfecting capitalism, were simultaneously creating an indispensable working class. He thought that as capitalism evolved, it was bound to bring about the polarization of society into a smaller and smaller group getting richer and richer, and a larger and larger group getting poorer and poorer. He predicted that this larger group would ultimately be driven to despair by its misery; then, under the leadership of the proletariat, it would bring about the overthrow of the bourgeoisie through the extinction of capitalism and would install a new society based on socialism.

Russian Marxists thought that Russia would follow these general lines, and that as capitalism sank its roots (a little belatedly) in Russia, it would go through the process of creating the working class that would eventually bring about the destruction of capitalism. Russian Marxists accordingly accepted the development of capitalism as a way of bringing about the general rise in the economic level of the

The abortive revolution of 1905 ended when troops opened fire on the workers.

country that would ultimately ensure the triumph of the working class. Hence many Marxists worked together with other nonsocialist critics of the tsarist autocracy. In 1905, these critics had staged a dramatic though unsuccessful insurrection against the Tsar. Lenin had called the 1905 Revolution a "dress rehearsal" for the two revolutions of 1917—the February Revolution that undid tsarism and his own Bolshevik insurrection.

Yet when tsarism vanished so quickly, all political groups were unprepared. The concerted attack in 1905 had been beaten back, the revolutionary movement scattered in defeat. Before the outbreak of World War I in 1914, the prospects for a revolution in Russia had in fact been very somber. Still, when tsarism was shattered by the strain of the war, the revolutionary training and political experience of Petrograd intellectuals and workers very naturally produced the Soviet of Workers' Deputies (named after a similar institution that had sprung up and been dissolved in the 1905 Revolution and its aftermath) as one half of the new regime. Since the well-known leaders of the Russian revolutionary movement were all abroad or in exile in February, 1917, the Soviet was organized, more or less spontaneously, by secondary figures and by the rank and file of many parties and organizations. But as the more famous leaders began drifting back to Russia, the Soviet grew more and more powerful.

The link between the Provisional Government and the Soviet of Workers' Deputies was bizarre. The Provisional Government was theoretically sovereign, and acknowledged as such by the Soviet. Yet in practice it could do nothing without the specific permission or authorization of the Soviet. The power of the Soviet rested firmly with workingmen who were indispensable to the performance of the most vital functions—telegraph operators, railway men, printers, factory workers. Hence its agreement was needed before anything could be done. In addition, from the very beginning peasants as well as soldiers were represented in the Soviet; indeed the Soviet represented some 95 per cent of the population.

Meanwhile, World War I continued to place an agonizing strain on the country's resources. Russia faced a grave economic crisis. The morale of peasants and soldiers (who were, of course, mostly peasants themselves) continued to fall. More important, the revolution had raised hopes, and the clamor for instant reform grew. Peasants demanded land; workers, better wages and working conditions; the minorities, autonomy. The Provisional Government believed in the war, largely for patriotic reasons, and it tried to soothe all elements of the population with promises of reforms that would take place after the war had been won. Meanwhile, the people were kept locked to the treadmill of the war and its gargantuan demands.

Until Lenin returned to Russia in April, 1917, he had accepted the impossibility of a socialist party's taking power there. He was distinguished from the Mensheviks, a rival faction in the Social Democratic

Party, not so much by his interpretation of Marx as by his differing view of how the revolutionary party should be organized. Lenin believed in restricting the membership of the revolutionary party to full-time professionals; the Mensheviks thought it should be open to all "sympathizers." This difference of approach between Bolsheviks and Mensheviks was rooted in an ambiguity of Marxism itself.

Marx had predicted that the transition from capitalism to socialism was both inevitable and dependent upon the armed proletariat. Abstractly, there was no contradiction between the two points—the proletariat, made "self-conscious" by the increasing misery of its exploitation under capitalism, was to organize itself with the help of the revolutionary party; then it was to arm and to bring about the transition to socialism. In practice, however, the theory was open to two interpretations. One maintained that since the transition to socialism was inevitable, socialist parties needed to do nothing more than quietly educate the proletariat to its future responsibilities. On the other hand, since it was the armed proletariat that was to bring about the transition to socialism, a second view held that the organization of the proletariat—aimed, naturally, at an eventual coup d'etat through conspiracy—was the main task of the revolutionary party. Historically, the socialist parties on the Continent, including the Russian Mensheviks, clung to the first view; the Bolsheviks under Lenin took the second.

To be sure, Lenin's views on organization required a theoretical justification in Marxist terms. When he came back to Russia in April, 1917, he had contrived a variation of Marxism that enabled him to give his preoccupation with organization that theoretical justification. This variation was borrowed from Leon Trotsky, a younger Marxist who had been hovering for years outside all partisan affiliations. Trotsky, in collaboration with a cosmopolitan Marxist called Parvus (born Helphand), had worked out a Marxist twist of his own. His version maintained that since the Russian bourgeoisie was too weak to crush tsarism and carry out the requisite perfection of capitalism before the Russian proletariat grew strong enough to oust it, the proletariat would have to take power in order to accomplish a bourgeois revolution. Afterward, on the basis of the accomplishments of a bourgeois revolution, the proletariat would be able to construct socialism.

Lenin adopted this theory to support the streamlined party hierarchy he had created, and he made himself a contender for power. Trotsky, attracted by this combination, gave up his independence and joined the Bolshevik Party a couple of months before the insurrection. Lenin, by accepting Trotsky's theory, and Trotsky, by accepting Lenin's concept of the revolutionary party as a tightly knit caucus of dedicated professionals, made a fusion of theory and practice that enabled the Bolsheviks, by setting a course for the seizure of power, to elude the dilemma of their socialist rivals. In short, Lenin—unlike his rivals—had been flexible enough to change his mind.

Since that time, various Communist historians

Above The Red Guards attacking the Winter Palace during the last days of the Provisional Government.

Below Each factory raised a detachment of Red Guards in preparation for the revolution.

Stalin—Lenin's other face

Marc Chagall's picture entitled *Peace in a Hut, War in a Palace* epitomizes the period.

have attempted to smother Lenin's change of mind underneath a mountain of mythology. It has suited the Soviet regime to pretend that from the time that Lenin was born he had been proceeding stage by stage along the path laid down by the omniscience of Marx. Many enemies of the Soviet regime have, for their own reasons, concurred in this view. Yet it is plain that something special happened when Lenin arrived in Petrograd in April, 1917. His first speech flabbergasted not only his opponents and rivals but his own followers, who had also been clinging to "general Marxist" formulations. When he said that the proletariat—represented, of course, by the Bolsheviks—could and should take power, the Bolsheviks themselves were dumbfounded. His justifying this proposal by a theory borrowed from Trotsky, who was ten years younger and a non-Bolshevik to boot, made it no more palatable. Lenin needed all his personal authority and powers of persuasion to bring his followers around.

The decision made during that fateful ten-hour reunion of the Bolshevik Central Committee in that flat in Petrograd crystallized the program Lenin had announced in April. The decision was all the more momentous because Lenin played a role that in history has been rare: without him no Bolshevik insurrection was conceivable. In view of the consequences of the Bolshevik triumph, Lenin has surely been one of the greatest world-shakers in history.

Lenin's decision was a sine qua non for action. The Bolsheviks had been growing stronger in the Soviet between April and October, so that the relative weight of the Soviet vis-à-vis the Provisional Government had been increasing. After Lenin's arrival the Bolsheviks, no longer hampered by a doctrine that enforced subordination, had tended to be even more independent of the Provisional Government than the Soviet as a whole had been. Thus the rivalry between the Soviet and the Provisional Government was complicated by pressure within the Soviet to eliminate the Provisional Government. But sovereignty could not be sovereignty unless it was proclaimed to be such. The de facto power that had been exercised by the Soviet could not become state power until it was acknowledged—until the legal conception underlying the authority of the Provisional Government was replaced by another conception. Hence Lenin's decision to take power was an indispensable step.

Following the April announcement, Lenin had demonstrated his capacity not merely for theory but for effective politics—organization plus propaganda. He had skillfully harped on the afflictions besetting Russia, on the groaning of the workers, peasants and soldiers. He had also streamlined his own party and had given both its rank and file and its commanders a firm sense of purpose. He had provided the intellectual contingent of his party with "sound Marxist theory" for a daring enterprise, while at the same time carrying on a broad-gauge campaign aimed at the man in the street, a campaign in which the slogan that was to carry the day was the down-to-earth phrase, "Peace, Bread and Land!"—all

quite irrelevant to the ideas of classical Marxism.

During the night of November 6–7, a fortnight after the midnight reunion in the Petrograd flat, the Military Revolutionary Committee commanded by Trotsky arrested the entire Provisional Government. (Shortly before, a handful of party people and a small number of troops had seized the Winter Palace, the seat of the Provisional Government.) With scarcely any hubbub, the Bolshevik militia—the Red guards—occupied the Tauride Palace, the post offices and the railway stations, the national bank, the telephone exchanges, the power stations and other strategic points. It took only a few hours to obliterate the Provisional Government, and there were virtually no casualties. Though the Bolsheviks had been proclaiming their general intentions for weeks, the confusion and discouragement of their opponents, the support (or apathy) of the military, and the reluctance of the Bolsheviks' socialist rivals to move against their fellow socialists ensured an almost complete lack of resistance.

A new government, a new state and a new society were proclaimed. The overthrow had happened with dreamlike ease, against a background of turbulence, discontent, suffering and futility. The enthusiasm of the Bolsheviks was boundless; they had achieved a titanic victory so effortlessly that they had not even bothered to work out a program. They thought themselves on the verge of a vast ground swell that was about to transform the world; they expected to be caught up at any moment by similar eruptions and similar seizures of power throughout Europe and then the world at large. (It is true that in Russia a movement of resistance sprang up in the wake of the insurrection. A civil war raged for several years with much bloodshed and many atrocities on both sides. But the superior capacities of the Red Army, newly organized and commanded by Leon Trotsky, settled the issue decisively in favor of the Bolsheviks.)

Yet the victory of the Bolsheviks did not spread

A cartoon entitled *The First Coalition* which satirizes the doomed Provisional Government.

800

immediately, and for decades no revolution succeeded anywhere. The Bolsheviks, isolated in an exhausted country, found themselves obliged, in spite of the material difficulties and in the teeth of their traditional theories, to construct something that could be called socialism. They had thought that the élan of the suffering peoples, an élan generated by the tug of history, would be enough to bring about a transition to an ideal society; in fact, it was brute force—as well as a zeal for construction—that was needed for the realization of their large-scale innovations. Indeed, an apparatus of constraint was created that has survived to this day.

As the illusions about world revolution were swept away, the rigors of Soviet life emerged in stark relief. Lenin himself, who clung to his hopes for world revolution until a year before he died in 1924, was deeply disturbed by a feeling that the "machine had gotten out of control." The necessities of administering the vast country that the Bolsheviks had captured turned former writers, speakers and thinkers into a corps of bureaucrats. And as the bureaucracy expanded, the power it symbolized came to be concentrated in the hands of the man who controlled the allocation of personnel—Joseph Stalin, the General Secretary of the Central Committee.

Even before Lenin's death Stalin had become the most important man in the party apparatus; from 1928 to his death in 1953 he was the most important man in the country. He had emerged triumphant from the ferocious infighting that broke out in the Bolshevik Party as it found itself confronting the insoluble problem of creating socialism where none was possible (while at the same time pretending that all had been foreseen by Marxist analysis). Using his growing power within the administration, Stalin outmaneuvered, crushed, and finally exterminated all other party opposition. His virtual eradication of the Trotskyites during the 1930s was accompanied by a massive slaughter of the top strata of the party, the army, the state and all major institutions, as well as of vast sections of the population as a whole. Trotsky himself was assassinated in exile by Stalin's political police in 1940. From the time of Stalin's fiftieth birthday in 1929, he wielded well-nigh absolute power through his control of the political police, the Soviet Communist Party, the Soviet Union and the many Communist parties that belonged to the Third International founded by Lenin. In addition, he institutionalized the worship of his own person as a paramount—indeed, almost godlike—authority in all fields of activity.

Lenin's fateful decision affected not only Russia but the world. The chain of events it set in motion came to encompass vast numbers of people. Many countries on the western borders of the Soviet Union came under its power after Russia helped defeat Nazi Germany in World War II. China, in particular, was swept into the Communist orbit. In fact, Lenin's interpretation of Karl Marx molded the lives of more than a third of the human race and made Marxism one of the most potent forces in history.

JOEL CARMICHAEL

The Bolsheviks Fight for Survival

1918

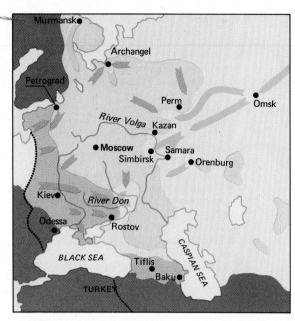

- ⬤ Controlled by Bolsheviks
- ⬤ Occupied by Germany or her allies
- ⋯⋯ Russian front in 1918
- ➤ Red Army advance
- ➤ White Army advance
- ➤ Allied intervention
- ➤ German advance
- ◯ Territory lost by Treaty of Brest-Litovsk

1919

- ◯ Controlled by Bolsheviks
- ➤ Red Army advance
- ➤ White Army advance
- ➤ Allied intervention
- ◯ Controlled by Allies

1920

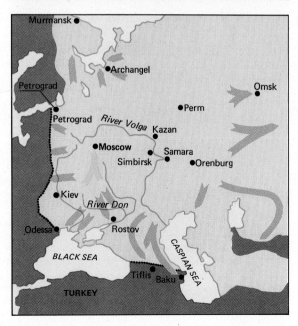

- ◯ Controlled by Bolsheviks
- ⋯⋯ Limits of Bolshevik power at the end of 1920
- ➤ Red Army advance
- ➤ White Army advance

Russia's Revolution

During the five years immediately following the end of World War I, Europe was preoccupied with three issues that convulsed the Continent until 1945. The rise of communism belongs symbolically to one end of this period; the rise of fascism to the other. The third issues derived from the Treaty of Versailles, for that treaty, which concluded the "war to end all wars," embodied blunders that allowed the new forces to engage in another horrific war within a generation. Versailles, a peace made by European powers to solve European problems in a way that ultimately led to the further devastation of Europe, masked the fact that Europe was no longer the focal point of the globe. It was only because Russia and the United States withdrew into shells of isolationism that the illusion of Europe's pre-eminence was temporarily preserved.

The erosion of Russia's old order by revolution began during the war. In 1918, the new Bolshevik government published and denounced the secret treaties made by the Tsar's government with its allies. They then exhorted the workers of the West to begin their own revolutions—a move that alarmed Western European governments and in a short time effectively isolated the Bolsheviks from gaining support.

The first hint of how extensive that isolation was to become came at Brest-Litovsk, where Germany and Russia met to make terms. Without troops in the trenches, the Bolsheviks were at a disadvantage at the treaty table. Realizing their weakness, they compensated by using the negotiations as a form for revolutionary propaganda. When the Germans ultimately advanced to within one hundred miles of Petrograd, the Bolsheviks were forced to sign away Poland, Lithuania, the Baltic provinces, Transcaucasia and the Ukraine.

The Germans' bold move at Brest-Litovsk seemed to prove the continuing strength of imperial Germany, but that might was illusory. In January of 1918, over 1 million German workers went on strike against the harshness of their government's conditions at Brest-Litovsk. In Austria-Hungary, disaffection was even more serious. Food supplies were low and in some places strikes were followed by the establishment of soviets. In February, there was a mutiny in the fleet. The trouble was suppressed, but there were other ominous signs. Matters were soon made worse by the arrival of prisoners of war freed by the Bolsheviks. These prisoners, who had been fed antiwar and revolutionary propaganda during their internment, had a corrosive effect on the rest of the Austrian Army. There was a rash of mutinies. Alarmed by this trend, the Germans got their Austrian allies to agree to joint military forces and a customs union—a virtual abdication by the Hapsburgs. The subject races of the Hapsburg Empire were not slow to take advantage; Czechs and other Slavs soon demanded a federation.

Europe after the Treaty of Versailles

- German losses
- formerly Austro-Hungarian
- formerly Russian
- newly independent states
- Austria and Hungary become two separate states

FINLAND
ESTONIA
LATVIA
LITHUANIA
DENMARK
Schleswig
HOLLAND
East Prussia
U.S.S.R.
GERMANY
POLAND
Rhineland Demilitarized 1919-36
BELGIUM
CZECHO SLOVAKIA
FRANCE
Alsace-Lorraine
AUSTRIA
HUNGARY
Tran-sylvania
SWITZERLAND
RUMANIA
YUGOSLAVIA
ITALY
BULGARIA

In January of 1918, the month of the general strike in Germany, President Wilson published his Fourteen Points. The document proclaimed that the Allies were fighting for democracy and national self-determination and gave an enormous boost to the various national groups of Central Europe. The Hapsburg Empire was beginning to break up as peasant revolts spread over Hungary and Yugoslavia, and things were hardly better for Germany. In March, the Germans launched a vast all-or-nothing offensive in the west. It carried them to within fifty miles of Paris, but the Allied lines held, and by August there were Allied counteroffensives. The German fleet mutinied and there was revolution in Munich. Neatly evading responsibility, the German High Command resigned in favor of a democratic government, which then had to take the odium of defeat.

The Treaty of Versailles

The war was over. But four years of slaughter, destruction and racial propaganda left open wounds. This was reflected in the Treaty of Versailles. It was a dictated settlement, imposed upon the defeated by the victors without negotiation or compromise. The framers of the treaty had two main objectives. The first—and more readily understandable—was to reorganize Europe in such a way that another war could not follow. The other objective, suggested by President Wilson, was "to liberate the captive nationalities, to re-unite those branches of the same family which have long been arbitrarily divided, and to draw frontiers in accordance with the ethnic masses." But the mentality of Europe in the wake of four years of total war made both aims impossible. The conflict between high-sounding principles and harsh practical realities was irreconcilable, and the settlement satisfied neither.

The conference met in an atmosphere of bitterness. Britain had suffered nearly 1 million dead and 1.5 million wounded. France had lost nearly 2 million dead and had been subjected to a crippling devastation. Lord Northcliffe's pulp press howled "HANG THE KAISER" and "MAKE THE GERMANS PAY," and in France public demands for vengeance were even stronger. The diplomats who gathered at Versailles were leaders of democratic countries, and as such they were subject to the wishes of their people.

The "Big Four," Lloyd George, Orlando, Clemenceau and Wilson at the Versailles Peace Conference in 1919.

Even those representatives who personally felt less vindictive than the baying hordes at home were anxious that someone else meet the staggering wartime bill. The French leader Georges Clemenceau was in complete agreement with his countrymen when he claimed "we do not have to beg pardon for our victory."

This general frame of mind made it highly unlikely that material aims would be sacrificed at the conference table for Wilson's idealistic theories. And indeed the resulting settlement struck its fiercest critic, the noted English economist John Maynard Keynes, as "a web of sophistry." Behind a smokescreen of Wilsonian platitudes, the peace basically reflected the material interest of the Allies: Germany was stripped of its industrial wealth by the French; *Anschluss* ("union") with Austria was forbidden; and the Rhineland was demilitarized. The principle of national self-determination was used as a convenient formula for dismembering Germany: Lithuania needed an outlet to the sea, and was given the Baltic seaport of Memel and its 100,000 Germans; Czechoslovakia needed a strong mountain frontier with Germany, and was given the Carpathians and 3.5 million Germans. The Germans were also presented with a gigantic reparations bill.

Vindictive peace terms

The uniform vindictiveness of the peace terms disguised Allied disunity, masking the falling-out that had taken place between the British and French. After the first surge of postwar belligerency, the British had shifted their stance, becoming more reasonable than the French. After all, British war aims were largely achieved. The German fleet had been scuttled, and Germany's colonies forfeited. France, on the other hand, felt only a bit more secure than it had been before the war. Vanquished Germany seemed much stronger in men and resources than victorious France, and hence the French were anxious to humble Germany so utterly that it might never rise again. Here again the treaty reflected neither viewpoint. Because the British would not agree to the total mutilation of Germany, the treaty was neither harsh enough to prevent German recovery nor lenient enough to encourage the Germans to accept it. It was not accepted as satis-

factory even at the time. A British diplomat, summing up the failure of Versailles, declared: "We came confident that the new order was about to be established, we left convinced that the new order had merely befouled the old."

The whole of the Versailles settlement was based on the premise of American support. It was a sign of the shifting balance of world forces that when this American support failed to materialize, the

A riot during the Spartacist revolt in Berlin in January, 1919. There was much civil unrest in Germany as a result of the Germans' defeat and disillusionment.

settlement slowly began to disintegrate. The end of European domination of world affairs had been evident before 1914, but the war made the process irrevocable. With Wilson's declaration of the principle of self-determination and Lenin's denunciation of imperialism, permanent cracks appeared in the structure of European imperialism.

Colonial troops returned home from the battlefields of Europe with new notions of democracy, self-government and national independence. Together with a new self-confidence, these notions formed the basis of a new resolve to obliterate the old concept of the inferior status of colonies. The revelation of the cynicism with which the Western powers bartered away colonial territories further discredited the imperialists and provoked violent reactions.

In the Arab world, the disclosure of the Sykes-Picot Agreement gave a sharp boost to Arab nationalism. In 1919, the Wafd Party was founded in Egypt, and it was followed in 1920 by the Destour Party in

Tunisia. The year 1919 also saw the convening of a Pan-African Congress in Paris. The Bolsheviks, quick to realize the revolutionary potential of oppressed colonial peoples, kept a steam of anti-imperialist propaganda flowing into Africa.

Colonial self-awareness

Throughout Asia these same factors contributed to an increased sense of self-awareness among colonial nations. This was particularly so in India. In accordance with the promises made in 1917, the British began implementing self-government for the Indians. The resulting Government of India Act of 1919 was a sham, however, for it retained complete British control of the central government. The legislature was to contain democratically elected Indians, but it had no control over ministers. Indian nationalists were bitterly disappointed. In view both of the 1917 promise and the great efforts made by Indians on Britain's behalf during the war, much more had been expected. Throughout 1918 there were riots and disturbances, and they grew worse as demobilization of European troops took place.

At this point, Mohandas K. Gandhi emerged as the leader of the Indian nationalists. Throughout 1919, he inspired outbreaks of civil disobedience. Initially, those outbreaks were confined to the educated classes, but with the help of Jawaharlal Nehru, Gandhi managed to extend the Congress movement to other social classes. The process of welding a political machine from village to village and province to province was barely in its infancy, but it did mark a great step forward for Indian nationalism. Disorders reached a climax in 1919 at Amritsar in the Punjab, when British troops fired on a mob of rioting Indians, killing 379 and wounding about 1,000. Amritsar became a symbol of British cruelty and did much to increase the trend to militancy.

The revolt against the West continued in China, where revolution was progressing with Mandarin slowness. During the war, the European powers had more or less abandoned China. Japan had been allowed to seize German territory and had taken the opportunity to overrun large areas. Chinese President Yüan Shih-k'ai hesitated to

resist, and a series of army mutinies destroyed his power. Army generals began to rule in their own interests, and during this period the Chinese countryside was pillaged and robbed. Robber bands and private armies roamed the land. In the long run this devastation turned the peasantry into a revolutionary force that longed for a strong, stable, reforming government of the sort that the communists were ultimately to offer. In the short run, the main result was a revulsion against the Western powers, who were held responsible for the chaos.

Bleak as prospects seemed for the West in Asia, things hardly appeared much better at home. In the aftermath of war, rising prices and inflation created discontent among the lower middle classes, especially in Germany and Italy. In Germany that discontent combined with resentment of the harshness of Versailles; in Italy, with disappointed

Victorious British troops marching through the Strand in 1919.

war aims. Patriotic disappointment was swelled by the existence of large numbers of ex-servicemen. All over Europe, demagogues emerged who were ready to exploit discontent, ready to throw the blame on socialism and democracy, and ready to launch aggressive programs of nationalist expansion. Before the war, violence had been advocated in many quarters as a mode of political action; five years after the war, those who had advocated violence as a political tool saw their advice put into practice in Italy.

The Blackshirts March on Rome   1922

"Either the government of Italy is given to us, or we shall seize it by marching on Rome!"
Benito Mussolini's bold declaration electrified the thousands of Fascists who had gathered in the
Piazza del Plebiscito in Naples on October 24, 1922, to hear their fiery young leader.
Responding to Mussolini's oratory, the crowd chanted "Roma! Roma! Roma!" Il Duce's words
had convinced the Blackshirts that a march on Rome would topple Luigi Facta's already troubled
government; those words had not convinced Mussolini himself. Indeed, his indecisiveness was so
acute that the leaders of the march gave serious thought to proceeding without him. By the time
Mussolini did reach Rome, Facta had resigned and King Victor Emmanuel had called upon the
Fascist leader to form a new government. The task of restoring order fell to Mussolini, who two
years later became the youngest prime minister in Italy's history.

During the afternoon of October 24, 1922, thousands upon thousands of black-shirted Fascists marched into the Piazza del Plebiscito in Naples. They stood at rigid attention in the square and listened to the words of their leader, Benito Mussolini. "I assure you in all solemnity that the hour has struck," Mussolini called out to them in his deep, emotive voice. "Either the government of Italy is given to us, or we shall seize it by marching on Rome. It is a matter of days, of hours. … I guarantee, I swear to you, that the orders will reach you." Responding to the power of Mussolini's oratory, the assembled Fascists took up his cry, shouting in unison, "*Roma! Roma! Roma!*"

Later that day Mussolini and other leading officers of the Fascist Party held a secret meeting in the Hotel Vesuvio. They discussed the arrangements for the march on Rome that Mussolini had proposed. It was decided that the Fascist militia should be mobilized as soon as the Blackshirts returned to their homes from the party congress in Naples. Four days later—following Fascist-provoked riots in which police and radio stations, post offices, prefectures, trade union premises and the offices of anti-Fascist newspapers would be occupied in all the principal towns—the Fascist militia would concentrate at various selected points and then converge upon the capital. The march was to be directed by four leading Fascists into whose hands all power was given.

Those *Quadrumviri*, as they were later to be known, were Michele Bianchi, a thirty-nine-year-old journalist who was Secretary-General of the Party and a dedicated, not to say fanatical, Fascist whose proud claim it was that he had been a member of the Party "from the first hour"; Italo Balbo, twenty-six years old, brave, good-looking, intelligent, the hero of the *squadristi* (the violent Fascist action groups); Cesare Maria de Vecchi, a landowner and lawyer, conservative and monarchist, who had distinguished himself as an army officer during World War I; and General Emilio de Bono, a small, frail, white-bearded officer of fifty-eight who had taken over the leadership of the Fascist militia while remaining in the regular army.

Mussolini himself remained outside the quadrumvirate. Indeed, in Balbo's opinion, his hesitant, capricious character entirely unsuited him for the organization and leadership of a determined coup d'etat. Balbo noted afterward that Mussolini was so vacillating that he had to be firmly told: "We are going to Rome, either with you or without you. It's up to you. Make up your mind."

Mussolini prudently returned to Milan as soon as the decision to march on Rome had been taken at Naples, and he determined to remain there until the crisis was resolved either by force or by compromise. He had not yet finally decided, despite his forthright address to the Blackshirts in the Piazza del Plebiscito, that a peaceful solution might not be reached even then.

There is little question that the Prime Minister, the good-natured and easygoing Luigi Facta, was prepared to make a deal with the Fascists if, by doing so, he could prolong his own government's life. So were the three other principal contenders for Facta's office, Antonio Salandra, Saverio Nitti and Giovanni Giolitti, all of whom had held the office in the past and with each one of whom Mussolini was in touch either directly or through an intermediary.

All over Italy the Fascists were preparing for action. Mobilization had started: public buildings had been occupied; prominent anti-Fascists had been detained; telephone wires had been cut, trains requisitioned, rifles and cars commandeered. And the militia had begun to concentrate for the coming march. Perugia, where the *Quadrumviri* had

A Fascist poster from the 1930s.

Opposite Benito Mussolini, Italy's "man of destiny," dominating the ancient city of Rome.

King Victor Emmanuel refuses to sign

Fascist leaders arrive in the capital after the march on Rome, October, 1922.

Mussolini taking the salute at a shipping review at Portofino, 1926.

established their headquarters in the Hotel Brufani, was one of several towns already firmly under Fascist control. In Rome, at eleven o'clock on the night of October 27, 1922, Luigi Facta handed his government's resignation to the King.

Remaining in office until a successor could be found, Facta called an emergency cabinet meeting for five o'clock the next morning. The cabinet members decided to proclaim a state of siege at noon. The proclamation, drafted on the spot, was to be fixed to the walls of Rome at 8:30 A.M.; the Italian Army was to be commanded to prevent the threatened march on the capital; all Fascist troublemakers were to be arrested to prevent outbreaks of violence.

Facta departed immediately for the Villa Savoia, Victor Emmanuel's official residence, where he planned to obtain the King's signature on the proclamation. But in the night Victor Emmanuel had been warned that the Army might well refuse to oppose the Fascists; he had also been advised that opposition might lead to civil war. Therefore, to Facta's consternation, he refused to sign.

When Mussolini heard that the King's refusal to sign the proclamation had forced the government to revoke the state of siege, he knew that he had won. Urged on all sides to leave immediately for the capital, he confidently replied that he would do so only when he received a written request from the King to form a government. When that request at last arrived, he left immediately for the railway station.

The march on Rome—so feared by the government, so revered in the party's later propaganda—was less than orderly. The headquarters of the *Quadrumviri*, isolated in Perugia, was able to exercise little control over the converging columns in a situation that changed confusingly from hour to hour. The various groups marched independently, without a coordinated plan. Four thousand men came down to Civitavecchia, two thousand to Monterotondo, and about eight thousand to Tivoli. (Some three thousand more remained in reserve at Foligno, near Perugia.) The men in each of the three marching columns were unaware of the progress of their comrades. No arrangements had been made for sleeping quarters on the way; most groups were short of food; some were unarmed. By the time they reached their concentration points north of Rome, a heavy rain had begun to fall, and some of them,

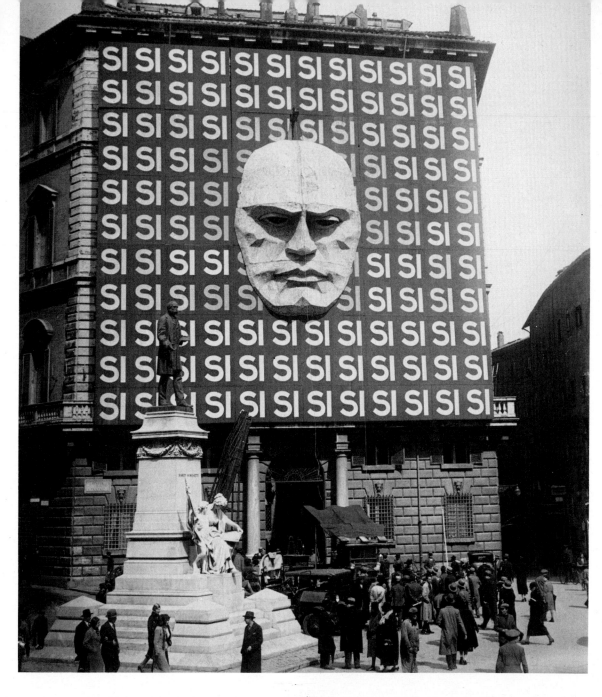

A 1934 Fascist poster.

Gabriele D'Annunzio, poet, and war hero.

wet and hungry, decided that they had had enough and went home.

Yet under the threat of less-organized opponents than these, stronger governments have fallen. And when, on the day after Mussolini's arrival in Rome, the thousands of *squadristi* still encamped outside the city were brought in by special trains to march in triumph past the Quirinal, the world could no longer doubt that a new age in the history of Italy was dawning.

To most Italians that dawn was both overdue and welcome. Italy had been on the victorious side during World War I, but she had failed to gain most of the territories that her allies had promised her. She obtained some islands in the Aegean and the Adriatic, parts of the Dalmatian coast, the Tyrol and Trieste. Yet she was denied the former German colonies, and she was also denied the Yugoslavian port of Fiume. Fiume had been seized by the nationalist poet and aviator Gabriele D'Annunzio in a characteristically theatrical gesture in 1919; however

D'Annunzio's eagle-plumed followers had been thrown out of Fiume with their cloaks and daggers after three months of rodomontade.

Reviled by disappointed nationalists, Italy's successive parliamentary governments, weak and irresolute, were equally reviled by the country's workers. Strikes and industrial revolts were as widespread in the north as was brigandage in the south. Workers' soviets were set up in the factories; Socialists and Communists marched through the streets shouting revolutionary slogans; rioters, protesting against the ever-rising cost of living, attacked public buildings, barracks, banks and trains. Inflation was aggravated by subsidies which did not relieve the distress of a painfully impoverished country that had been left billions of lire in debt by the sudden end of economic help from her allies. At the same time, the problems of unemployment were increased by the demobilization of thousands of soldiers, and the problems of crime were magnified by the army of no less than 150,000 deserters who

807

Above A rally in Rome's Piazza Venezia in 1939.

Below Victor Emmanuel III, King of Italy, meets Mussolini after the Fascist takeover.

Porto a Vostra Maestà l'Italia di Vittorio Veneto riconsacrata dalla Vittoria

had grown accustomed to living by their wits.

It was in those conditions of violence, distress and industrial unrest that Fascism had been born. In March, 1919, a group of men had met in a room at the Milan Association of Merchants and Shop-keepers in the Piazza San Sepolcro. The group in-cluded a disparate ragbag of discontented Socialists and syndicalists, republicans, anarchists, unclassifi-able revolutionaries and restless soldiers. Many of the latter had been *Arditi* (commandos in the Italian Army), and some of them were wanted by the police. Their self-appointed leader was Benito Mussolini, the son of a blacksmith from the Romagna. Musso-lini was an ex-soldier himself, formerly a school-teacher and now a journalist. As early as February, 1918, this dynamic young man with the pale face and staring dark eyes had been advocating the emergence of a dictator "ruthless and energetic enough to make a clean sweep." Three months later, in a widely reported speech at Bologna, he had hinted that he himself might prove such a man.

At the meeting in Milan, he advocated the for-mation of a *Fascio di Combattimento*, a group of fighters. Their insignia was to be the fasces, symbol of author-ity in ancient Rome—an axe surrounded by rods tightly bound together for strength and unity. The "Fascist" movement spread rapidly, gaining wider and wider support from the discontented young, from the frightened middle class, from industrialists and merchants who deeply resented the growing power and pretensions of the workers, from land-owners who feared for the loss of their rents, and from patriots who believed that the Fascists were members of the one movement that could bring Italy to a position of respect and power in Europe.

By the time of the elections of 1921, the movement had gained sufficient support for thirty-five of its candidates, including Mussolini himself, to be elected to Parliament. The following November the Fascist Party was founded—and thereafter Fascism grew more and more arrogant, meeting violence with greater violence. Squads of Fascists armed with knives and cudgels (or with revolvers brought back from the war) attacked their enemies with a ferocity and regularity that soon resulted in a situation almost comparable to civil war.

Yet although Mussolini had achieved power by force, he exercised it initially with restraint. He seemed anxious to demonstrate that he was not only the leader of Fascism but the head of the government of a united Italy. Less than a third of his cabinet were members of his party. He made it clear, however, that he intended to govern authoritatively and per-sonally. He appointed himself President of the Council, Minister of the Interior and Minister of Foreign Affairs. He demanded—and obtained by an overwhelming majority—full dictatorial powers for a year to carry out what he considered to be essential reforms. And that year proved long enough for him to push through a law guaranteeing the party that secured the largest number of votes in the elections the right to claim two-thirds of the seats in the Chamber. In the elections of 1924 the Fascists received over 65 per cent of the votes, and Mussolini, the youngest prime minister the Italians had ever had, was confirmed in an office that he was to retain for twenty years.

The first few years of those two decades were the halcyon days of Mussolini's party. The people were tired of strikes and riots; they were responsive to the flamboyant, choreographic techniques and the medieval trappings of Fascism; they were ready to accept a dictatorial regime—and the so-called corporative state—if the dignity of the country were to be restored and its national economy stabilized. And Fascism in those halcyon days—although never achieving the miracles claimed for it by its tireless propagandists—*did* seem a worthwhile adventure. Something *was* done to improve the conditions of the workers, to stabilize the economy, to inaugurate an ambitious program of public works (including the draining of the Pontine Marshes), to induce greater administrative efficiency, to promote national interests.

Thus it was that Mussolini's popularity was able to survive the violence and fraud of the 1924 elections and the murder of the brave and gifted Socialist leader Giacomo Matteotti by Fascist thugs. Skillfully presenting himself to the people as Italy's man of destiny, Mussolini was accepted as such—and it was not only Italians who fell under the sway of that proudly jutting jaw, those black wide-open eyes, those wonderfully expressive gestures. He was compared—without a hint of irony—to Napoleon and to Cromwell, and hailed as a genius and as a superman by public figures all over Europe and in America. Had he not reinvigorated his divided and demoralized country? Had he not succeeded—where even Cavour had failed—in reconciling the state with the papacy? Had he not carried out his social reforms and public works without jeopardizing the interests or losing the support of the industrialists and landowners? Who else could have achieved all this? No one but Mussolini, *Il Duce*, who—as slogans painted on walls all over Italy proclaimed—*ha sempre ragione*, "is always right."

Yet all the while an anti-Fascist resistance was at work, increasing in numbers as the dictatorship grew more oppressive and as it became increasingly evident that Mussolini was, behind the bluster of his brilliant propaganda, childish and coarse, unstable and irresolute, constitutionally deceitful and pathologically egotistic. As the years progressed, *Il Duce* revealed that he really had little conception of how to run a government, no patience with difficult work, a horror of decisions. He was capable of writing "approved" on two conflicting memoranda emanating from two different ministries—and then of going into another room where one of his mistresses lay waiting to satisfy the urgent demands of a sexual appetite that approached satyriasis. In his callous xenophobia, his wild arrogance, and his willful misapprehension of Italy's fundamental necessities (and with his health rapidly deteriorating and his gifts declining) he led Italy first into the invasion of Abyssinia and then into an alliance with Hitler and

Su loro ricade la colpa!

a world war that destroyed the power of Italian Fascism forever.

In April, 1945, as the World War II Allies drove the Germans into headlong retreat, Mussolini was shot by Communist partisans while attempting to flee into the mountains. His body was later strung up by the heels in front of a screaming mob in Milan, the city where Fascism had been born—the city where Mussolini first learned he had come to power through the Fascist march on Rome.

CHRISTOPHER HIBBERT

An Italian war poster: an attack on Churchill and Roosevelt as murderous gangsters.

Berlin—vice ridden symbol of Europe

According to popular myth, the decade of the 1920s was a rowdy, rollicking era between World War I and the depression years. The decade has consequently acquired a sort of happy-go-lucky glamour, symbolized by the flapper, the "good-time girl" of the speakeasy, whose search for pleasure was probably an expression of postwar anxiety. But the almost lengendarily vice-ridden Berlin of the Weimar Republic is a better symbol of the period.

Behind the sequined façade of the Jazz Age lay a world of violence and insecurity. Before it was over the decade was to witness the beginnings of political terror in Soviet Russia, the emergence of Nazi gangsterism in German politics, a great general strike in Britain, and revolutionary rumblings in China and India. The war left in its wake the economic uncertainties of dwindling credit and rising unemployment. And the aftermath of the Versailles Treaty saw the beginnings of a new quest for security by Western diplomats. Portents of a second war loomed.

Economic insecurity affected the greatest number of people. The war left a much-impoverished Europe, and Europe's poverty affected the rest of the world. The demographic cost, in terms of those killed and those not born because of the war, has been estimated at 20 million.

The "Black Bottom," a new dance of the 1920s. The gaiety of the Jazz Age was a reaction to the anxieties and hardships of the war years.

Even worse was the destruction of the prewar economic structure. The war had created a need for self-sufficiency, which led to a degree of industrial and agricultural overexpansion that could not be justified or maintained after the war. This alone was a cause of unemployment. Governments tried to

Some women were able to shake off the restrictions of the prewar years and enjoy the pleasures of the 1920s.

stave off disaster by resorting to protective tariffs that strangled international trade.

Inflation

In any case, the war had destroyed the necessary confidence for trade. Goods often had to be unloaded and reloaded at borders in Central Europe because rolling stock was likely to be confiscated in other countries. The almost inevitable slump that followed saw numerous currency disasters as governments used the printing press to hide the fall in real wealth. The German mark fell to one-billionth of its prewar value; the Russian ruble to one-four-hundred-millionth. Economic instability led to political chaos, and the existence of thousands of unemployed led to the creation of private armies by Fascist parties in Germany and Eastern Europe.

Unemployment was temporarily checked in the middle of the decade when Europe's industrial output reached the 1913 level. But relief was short-lived. Every European nation owed money to the United States, and since America was self-sufficient it had to be paid in gold. The flow of gold to the United States made European currencies even more unstable. Increasingly, American capital began to dominate the economy of Europe and other parts of the world.

Uncertainty in economic affairs was matched during the twenties by equal uncertainty in international relations. The two most dynamic forces during this period were the frantic desires of the French to be forever free of German attack and

the determination of the Germans to break free of the crippling provisions of the Treaty of Versailles. These opposing forces were allowed free play for three reasons. First, the United States had deserted its responsibilities as a world power and had left Europe to its own devices while enjoying a short-lived boom. Second, diplomats in Britain, which was France's ally, were not altogether certain that the Germans did not have a point about the vindictiveness of the treaty. Much influenced by *The Economic Consequences of the Peace*, John Maynard Keynes' savage criticism of Versailles, the makers of Britain's foreign policy were loath to support France in what they saw as the "crucifixion" of Germany. The lack of British and American support merely made the French quest for security all the more frantic and further encouraged German opposition to Versailles. The third and perhaps most disruptive factor in the diplomacy of the 1920s was the role of the Russians. Isolated themselves, the Bolsheviks tried to keep international relations in a state of chaos. Ruled out as a threat to their former enemy's eastern frontier, they joined Germany in the 1922 Treaty of Rapallo. That agreement, a considerable blow to the Versailles settlement, gave both Russia and Germany a new bargaining power with which to face the Western powers.

To a large extent, the French attitude was understandable. France had emerged from the war victorious, but it was psychologically a defeated nation. For four years France had suffered the indignities normally associated with defeat and occupation,

including the plunder of industrial machinery and the destruction of mines. It then saw Germany, untouched by the ravages of war, made stronger by the removal of the Russian threat from its eastern frontier. Thus for the French, the Treaty of Versailles became an attempt to right the seeming injustice of the war. Devoted therefore to crushing Germany at every possible opportunity, France was vicious in her exaction of reparations payments. When Germany failed to meet them in 1923, French troops occupied the Ruhr. At the same time, France attempted to encircle Germany through a network of alliances: with Belgium in 1920 and with Poland, Czechoslovakia, Rumania and Yugoslavia in 1921.

The Treaty of Locarno, showing the signatures and seals of Great Britain, Belgium, Germany, Italy, Czechoslovakia and Poland.

Locarno: a truce of exhaustion

France's attitude poisoned international relations by strengthening both Germany's distrust of the Western powers and its determination to break the 1919 settlement. Britain was just as determined to smooth things over, and moved to cancel all war debts—a major cause of bitterness between France and Germany. The British move was blocked by Washington, but this new spirit of appeasement did achieve a major success in France, where there was a dawning realization that the nation's vindictive postwar policy was merely playing into the hands of nationalist extremists in Germany. The efforts of British Prime Minister James Ramsay MacDonald created an atmosphere of mutual sympathy that was crowned in 1925 by the Treaty of Locarno. At that gathering

MacDonald convinced Edouard Herriot of France and Gustav Stresemann of Germany to agree to a treaty in which Britain guaranteed the frontiers of France and Germany against aggression by either side.

Locarno was perhaps as much a truce of exhaustion as a triumph of appeasement. There had been too much violence and hatred in the preceding decade for it all to be resolved overnight. Germany was still resentful of its defeat and anxious for a chance to recover. And France was still conscious of the German capacity for recovery. Moreover, the Germans never seriously believed that the British would support them in a crisis. Therefore, France went on seeking a net of encircling allies and Germany went on stealthily rearming—with Soviet help. In time Locarno might have worked, but before it had a chance to inspire the necessary confidence, the world economic crisis broke. Thereafter, extremists were able to distract attention from domestic social and unemployment problems by attacks on the Treaty of Versailles.

While Western Europe was blindly heading for catastrophe, events of enormous significance were taking place in Russia. During these years, Russia's bureaucracy began to develop into the monolith that it is today. The growth of a terrorist police force started at an early stage, for in a world of civil war, foreign intervention, economic chaos and counterrevolutionary enemies, the Bolsheviks soon became obsessed with the need to crush opposition before it crushed them. Absolute power was taken by the party on the theory that vast tracts of land stretching across two continents could only be ruled by a strong bureaucratic structure.

The Bolsheviks, who had taken up revolution in the first place to eradicate oppression, injustice and terror, and all the things associated with absolute power, were soon faced by a dilemma. White Russian terrorists, backed by British and American aid, had to be crushed in a savage civil war, and the Bolsheviks were forced to sacrifice their ideals to protect the essential framework of the revolution. Grain was forcibly requisitioned, and opposition was brutally wiped out. Conditions became so bad by 1921 that the sailors of the Kronshtadt naval base—the most revolutionary force in the country—mutinied against the government. A heartbroken Trotsky put down the revolt, and at the Tenth Party Congress, Lenin placed a ban on opposition within the party, thereby changing it from a free association of independent, critical-minded ideologists to a tightly disciplined bureaucratic machine. At the same time Lenin instituted the New Economic Policy, whereby the wrecked economy was to be revived by the temporary reintroduction of free enterprise. But all of these measures were temporary. By the end of 1923, Trotsky was advocating the waiving of the ban on opposition and the economy was visibly stronger.

The death of Lenin

At this point the greatest tragedy of the Bolshevik Revolution occurred. In January, 1924, Lenin died. His death resulted in a struggle for power the outcome of which molded contemporary Russia. The ultimate victor of this struggle was Joseph Stalin, a cold, brutal bureaucrat from the Caucasus. Unlike most of the Bolshevik leaders, who were cultured and cosmopolitan, the Asiatic Stalin was narrow and crude, and bitterly jealous of Trotsky's many-faceted genius. He had risen in the party through his ability and willingness to take over the administrative tedium that the other Bolsheviks shunned. Through his posts on various committees, Stalin had accumulated vast power and had filled the ranks of the party with his nominees.

Just before he died, Lenin began to sense that the bureaucratic

Leon Trotsky, premier of Russia 1917–25, exiled by Stalin in 1929 and murdered in Mexico in 1940.

machine was moving independently of him, and in his political testament he wrote: "I propose to the comrades to remove Stalin from that position [General Secretary of the Central Committee]." Lenin's proposal was buried with him a short time later, and Stalin used his accrued power to gain the leader-

Joseph Stalin, who, after Lenin's death in 1924, rose to become the dictatorial and ruthless head of the Russian government.

ship of the party.

The effects of Stalin's victory in the Soviet struggle for power are incalculable. The main tenet of Stalinism was "Socialism in One Country." Originally used to counter Trotsky's notion of "Permanent Revolution," Stalin's phrase struck a chord in the hearts of thousands of party workers who were tired after eight years of war and revolution. The concept involved the abandonment of the universality of Marxist thought and a concentration on Russia's well-being. Internally, this meant the beginning of the five-year plans for industrialization and the forced collectivization of agriculture. Abroad, it meant that the interests of world communism were sacrificed to the domestic needs of the Soviet Union. As Trotsky put it: the Comintern was transformed from the vanguard of the world revolution into the frontier guard of Russia.

Under Stalinism, foreign Communist parties were totally subjected to orders from Moscow. The result was that the German Communist Party embarked on the series of blunders that facilitated the rise of Hitler, and the Spanish Communist Party concentrated on persecuting anarchists and Trotskyites rather than fighting the Nationalists in the Civil War. The first country to suffer from Stalin's jaundiced interpretation of the prospects of world revolution was China. At the time, the Chinese

Communist Party was extremely small and the Russians tended to back Sun Yat-sen's Kuomintang. In 1925, Sun Yat-sen died and the leadership of the Kuomintang was taken over by the Russian-trained Chiang Kai-shek. In 1927, Chiang began to take advantage of a national movement of revulsion against the warlords. As his campaign progressed, the Communist Party made large numbers of conversions. The merchant and landlord classes that formed the basis of Chiang's backing grew fearful of social revolution, and to quiet their fears Chiang began to move against the Communists. Stalin, who believed that the first stage of the Chinese revolution could only be won through an alliance with the Kuomintang, ordered the Communists to surrender to Chiang. Instead, the Communists were massacred at Shanghai in 1927. Led by Mao Tse-tung, the shattered remnants began a guerrilla war against a program of "encirclements" by the Kuomintang.

While fascism took hold in Italy and the Nazi movement gained power in Germany, the United States seemed to be escaping the drama and misery of the postwar world. Economic chaos in European countries had left a corresponding political confusion in which millions of unemployed tried to salvage their self-respect in violent nationalist

Chiang Kai-shek, leader of the Chinese Communist Party in the 1920s and later leader of the Nationalist Party.

and fascist movements. But the United States was on a spending spree. Beginning with the Florida real estate boom of 1925, America was caught up in a bubble of stock market speculation that soon burst, bringing misery and ruin to millions of individuals throughout the world, increasing the already dangerous instability of Europe, and hastening the economic decline of the once-great imperialist powers.

Panic on Wall Street

Trading on the floor of the New York Stock Exchange began normally on Thursday, October 24, 1929. The market, which had faltered in early September, steadied, and then sagged heavily on October 21, was admittedly in serious trouble—and Wall Street investors had cause to be cheered by the opening hour of trading. What followed cheered none, and ruined many. As the volume of stocks being traded grew, prices began to drop. The ticker fell minutes, then hours behind as thousands of speculators rushed to sell. By the end of the day, 12,894,650 shares had been traded, the market was a shambles, and the speculative bubble that had involved untold thousands of small investors had burst. A committee of brokers issued a statement declaring that the market was "fundamentally sound," but their false optimism could do nothing to reverse the trend. The crash that followed triggered a decade of worldwide depression, mass unemployment, bitter class warfare and desperate nationalism.

Gold bullion bars. The collapse of the New York stock market and the subsequent depression forced many nations to abandon the Gold Standard.

Opposite Crowds in Wall Street during the Depression.

The New York Stock Exchange on Wall Street looks much the same outside today as it did in the 1920s, taking up three buildings on an oblong site in the heart of America's financial district, with its main trading room concealed behind an elaborate classical façade. On Thursday, October 24, 1929, trading at the Exchange began normally enough, at ten o'clock, with the buying and selling of the shares of America's largest companies. But the orderliness lasted only about an hour. Suddenly, no one was buying shares; everyone was selling, in growing haste and panic. As the prices offered for shares slithered and plunged, the ticker carrying the record to investors and directors in all parts of the United States failed to keep pace with the rush. More and more orders to sell poured in to the brokers. The mounting excitement and alarm inside the Stock Exchange spread to the noisy street outside, where a great crowd gathered, a quick prey to the rumors of suicide and ruin.

By midday the worst was over. The market had been soothed by the news that the country's leading bankers were pooling their resources to sustain the market prices of shares. But enough damage had been done to earn October 24 the name Black Thursday. "Measured by disorder, fright and confusion," comments the economist J. K. Galbraith, "it deserves to be so regarded. That day 12,894,650 shares changed hands, many of them at prices that shattered the dreams and the hopes of those who had owned them. Often there were no buyers, and only after wide vertical declines could anyone be induced to bid."

Many other days were equally "black" during the weeks of the Great Crash in the autumn of 1929. The warning signs that the Stock Exchange boom was faltering were clearly present during the early part of October: after years of almost uninterrupted rise, shares had started to drop in price. Most people, having lived through nearly a decade of glittering industrial and speculative boom, were incredulous.

As often happens in times of grave economic crisis, public leaders were afraid of hastening calamity by issuing the warnings they should have given, and instead the public was reassured that the economy was sound. Some shrewd men quietly sold while the going was good, however. (Millionaire Bernard Baruch recalled, years later, that after landing in New York after a grouse-shooting holiday in Scotland, he decided on the spot to sell everything he could—just before the Great Crash.)

The slide started in earnest on Monday, October 21; over 6 million shares were sold that day. A brief rally followed, and it held until October 23. But on that Wednesday several million shares were sold, the volume rapidly increased and prices tumbled as thousands of investors belatedly tried to cut their losses. On Black Thursday itself—thanks to the support from big bankers and financiers—the market actually recovered at the end of the day. But although prices were steadier, about another 8 million shares changed hands by the end of the week.

The bubble had burst. The following week the slide was more precipitous still, as those who had bought "cheap"—even on Black Thursday—were forced to sell again at derisory prices. The panic worsened among rich and not so rich, corporate and individual investors in all parts of the United States. The Stock Exchange closed for several days. During the week there were tremulous signs of a revival, but the fall in share prices—now dramatically undermining the financial stability of the whole economy —continued until the middle of November (and intermittently for several years thereafter). The index of industrial share prices in the United States fell from about 200–210 in 1929 to 30–40 in 1932. Thousands were ruined financially, while, paradoxically, a few made their fortunes. In the meantime, for the rest of the world as for America itself, the Great Crash was overshadowed by the Depression.

One simple explanation for the Great Crash of

Losing touch with industrial reality

Bernard Baruch, one of the few who saw the danger signals before the crash and sold out at the peak of the market.

Trading on the floor of the Stock Exchange.

1929 is that so many thousands of Americans had been seized during the previous years by the fever of speculation (which pushed them into investments well beyond their resources) that a disastrous finale was inevitable. Bernard Baruch referred to the "frenzy of stock market gambling that preceded the 1929 crash [as] a reflection of the curious psychology of crowds which has been demonstrated again and again in human history." Those who were in New York in 1929 recall how obsessed the whole city seemed, bankers and brokers, taxi drivers and shop assistants, with the possibility of growing rich overnight by dealing in shares. Speculation ran wild, indulged by the bland optimism of most of America's political and financial leaders.

The prices of shares had begun to climb in 1927, and in 1928 the boom moved into top gear and finally lost touch with industrial reality. More and more people began not only to invest in shares in the confident hope of rapid gain but to invest on borrowed money. The practice of margin trading—that is, buying additional stock with money borrowed against previously purchased shares—became commonplace. The interest paid by margin trading was so high that it in turn attracted a rising volume of finance into New York.

Meanwhile, the small investor's position was made more dangerous by the fact that the industrial boom

in America—soundly based a few years before on increasing productivity and the rising sales of such products as cars, houses and electrical equipment—was tailing off. A disastrous paradox was emerging: anyone with a rudimentary knowledge of economics knew that the value of shares ultimately depended upon the prosperity and earnings of the companies in which they were held—but as shares rose to new speculative heights in the United States in 1928 and 1929, industrial prosperity was faltering.

There seem to have been two main reasons for the Depression in the United States: the saturation of the market for industrial goods and the policy of the financial authorities (which aimed at keeping prices and wages steady and, as a result, directed the benefits of rising productivity into profits without stimulating fresh consumer demand). By mid-1929, there were fairly clear signs of overproduction. Moreover, there were serious weaknesses in the country's financial and economic structure, weaknesses that the Great Crash was sharply to expose. According to Professor Galbraith, those flaws were: the inequitable distribution of income, which gave too much economic influence to investment and luxury spending; a corrupt company structure, with too many grafters and swindlers; an archaic banking structure, overstretched and overfragmented; the persistent surplus in American trade, leading to an

influx of gold into the United States and an outflow of dubiously secured loans; and the poor economic thinking on the part of those in authority. These factors served to worsen and to prolong the Depression once it was truly launched by the Great Crash.

Like the toppling of great financial empires in the United States in the autumn of 1929, the exposure in England, a short while before, of the swindles of Clarence Hatry (who built up a great business empire that foundered on forgery) made industry more vulnerable to the onset of depression. But Europe's economic weaknesses, so glaringly revealed by the financial collapse of 1929, could be traced back to the end of World War I, eleven years earlier.

Economic historians point to a tangle of events and errors that made a slump of some kind almost inevitable. World War I had left a sorry legacy of dislocated world trade, along with vast problems of war debts and reparations. It also brought about a substantial increase in production of raw materials and foodstuffs, which led to surpluses and sagging commodity prices when the war was over, and in turn to less demand for industrial products. Agricultural gluts were further increased by improvements in farming techniques and science.

The financial systems of the major industrial countries grew more and more unstable. In particular, Germany was forced to borrow from the United States to pay for reparations; France suffered from the flight of capital abroad; and the United Kingdom struggled unsuccessfully to rebuild its position as the world's great source of capital. For a time, the system was held together largely by American willingness to send money abroad. But when the Stock Exchange boom tempted investors to keep their dollars at home, where they earned more, the pressure on debtor nations to cut back on their imports and increase their earnings at each other's expense became immense. The Great Crash was like a match applied to high explosives.

In 1934, a few years after the Crash, Professor Robbins of the London School of Economics reflected the shocked reaction to the Great Depression that is still discernible in the attitudes of millions of people today. The world depression that followed the stock market crash, he wrote:

… has dwarfed all preceding movements of a similar nature both in magnitude and in intensity. … Production in the chief manufacturing countries of the world shrank by anything from 30 to 50 per cent, and the volume of world trade in 1932 was only a third of what it was three years before. It has been calculated by the International Labor Office that in 1933, in the world at large, something like 30 million persons were out of work. There have been many depressions in modern economic history, but it is safe to say there has never been anything to compare with this.

In Europe, the financial crisis was triggered by the collapse of Austria's largest bank—the Credit-Anstalt—early in 1931. Banking assets held in Austria were immediately affected, notably those of the German banks that felt the first shock. Despite British and American efforts to help the Germans

Above The front page of the *Boston Daily Globe* on Friday, October 25, 1929. The crash did not immediately affect the attitudes of investment analysts, as the stockbroker's advertisement at the foot of the page shows.

Below Brokers relaxing on the floor of the Exchange in mid-October, 1929. The crash wiped the smiles from many faces.

Herbert Hoover, who was unable to prevent the disaster.

Right Crowds waiting to hear the latest news outside the Stock Exchange at the height of the crisis.

Selling a car to raise money. Many hard-pressed investors were forced to take even more drastic steps.

$100 WILL BUY THIS CAR MUST HAVE CASH LOST ALL ON THE STOCK MARKET

financially, the Reichsbank was forced to impose controls on foreign exchange, and this in turn prompted panic withdrawals of funds from London and other financial centers in Europe. As confidence in Britain's abilities to sustain its industry and maintain the Gold Standard was eroded, and as the country's financial reserves ebbed away, the only solution seemed to be the formation of a National Government. This was followed by the abandonment of the Gold Standard in September, 1931.

For Germany, the Depression meant the final loss of American finance and a swift rise in unemployment, the latter being one of the factors that helped the Nazi Party climb to power and led to Adolf Hitler's assumption of the Chancellorship in 1933. For the United States, the Crash brought about the New Deal policies of President Roosevelt. In Japan, the Depression caused a rise in unemployment, possibly to as high as 3 million. The Japanese economy was still heavily agricultural, while industry relied for its basic labor on thousands of small workshops. The shock of the Depression stimulated Japanese industry to achieve a vigorous expansion in the 1930s, chiefly through the development of heavy industry and exports, which were stimulated by government subsidies, protection and low wages.

In these ways, the Great Crash on Wall Street helped to shape the world economic and political structure in the 1930s. The years 1929–34 were a true watershed of history. The 1920s, for all the problems that existed—and despite a shaky world economy and the lingering shock caused by the slaughter of World War 1—were years tinged with optimism. Universal peace seemed within grasp. The problems of industry were grave but also, most people seemed to believe, soluble by free societies. The Soviet Union, the great dissenter, stood aside, revealing only its progressive aspects to the few admirers from the West.

In the economic field, the belief that the clock should and could be put back was nicely exemplified by Britain's return to the Gold Standard in 1925, a decision announced by its Chancellor of the Exchequer, Winston Churchill. But the return to the Gold Standard heralded increasing financial turbulence, not a return to the calm and prosperity of the days before World War 1. For the Gold Standard had been effect as much as cause: it had worked before 1914 because of comparative political stability, economic confidence, and the steady flow of gold discoveries. And it had worked because of the industrial lead established by Great Britain as center of the Empire and creator of the Industrial Revolution, a lead that enabled the City of London

The international consequences of the Depression

President Roosevelt, who faced the task of
reconstruction after the Depression.

to finance world trade with supreme confidence,
based on fairly small gold reserves.

The 1930s were the years of slump, mass unemployment, protection, increasingly bitter class warfare, and a desperate nationalism that fostered the
totalitarianisms of Germany, Italy and Japan. Those
movements won sympathizers for reasons that included the disillusionment of millions with the
capacity of liberal capitalism to withstand the challenge of communism. In the 1920s, men still tended
to look back to the partly imaginary halcyon days
of pre-World War I and to believe that these could
be restored. The Great Depression shattered those
imaginings: there was clearly no going back. The
choice in the 1930s seemed to be to go forward to the
controlled societies of either fascism or communism.
Only after World War II did the strength of modern
capitalism, reformed by welfare and by Keynsian
economic ideas that had been rejected in the late
1920s, emerge as a challenging and highly successful
contender for men's allegiances.

The kind of abuses that led to Black Thursday and
its aftermath would be impossible in the established
stock exchanges of the world today, since regulations
are stricter and perhaps economies more balanced,
even if people are no less greedy and gullible. But
for millions, those abuses are a symbol of the black
side of financial capitalism. For many others, by no
means hostile to free enterprise, they are a reminder
that the price of prosperity, like the price of freedom,
is constant vigilance.   GEORGE BULL

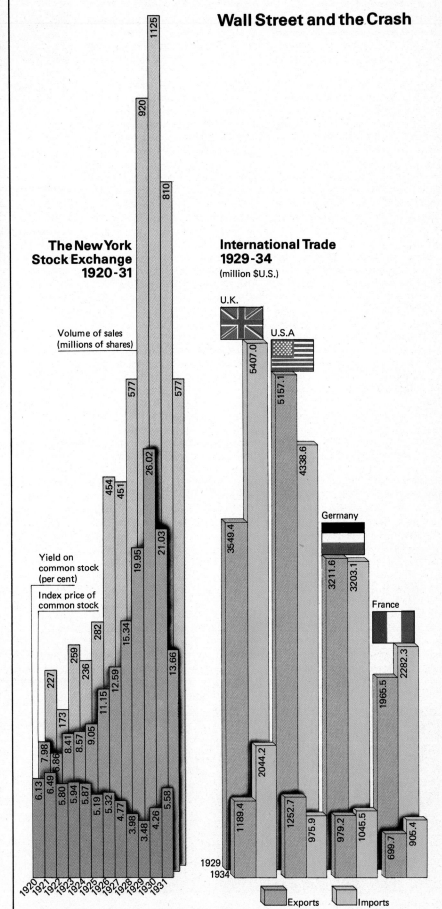

Wall Street and the Crash

**The New York
Stock Exchange
1920-31**

Volume of sales
(millions of shares)

Yield on
common stock
(per cent)

Index price of
common stock

**International Trade
1929-34**
(million $U.S.)

U.K.

U.S.A

Germany

France

1929
1934

Exports   Imports

Drabness, loss of freedom, cultural sterility-

In the wake of the great depression

Before the Great Depression, Europe was already experiencing major economic and political upheavals. Social and economic troubles had brought Mussolini to power in Italy, had fed Nazi propaganda in the Weimar Republic, and had produced a general strike in Britain. But it was the crash of the American stock market that really crippled the world's economies, for as a market and supplier of capital, the United States was foremost in the world. The crash hit America worst—national income fell 38 per cent between 1929 and 1932—but other nations suffered almost as badly from the collapse of world trade. As America withdrew capital from abroad, debtor nations cut their imports and prices plummeted. There was less demand for raw materials in developed countries and less demand for manufactured goods in underdeveloped countries. International trade ground to a halt.

It is in the light of this economic disaster that most of the significant events of the 1930s—from the rise of Hitler to the coming of World War II—must be viewed. Until late in the thirties, the world suffered from America's economic collapse. In the big money years of the Jazz Age, successive U.S. governments had declined to intervene and limit overspeculation. Under President Calvin Coolidge inflation had free rein, and industrial production rose so sharply that high pressure advertising had to be developed to market the surplus goods. But affluence hid poverty. While industry and commerce boomed, farming languished. Agriculture rapidly became a semidepressed sector of the economy, and even before the crash took its toll, the

conditions described in John Steinbeck's novel *The Grapes of Wrath* were destroying the small farmers of the Midwest. It was the same story after the depression, only in more extreme terms. For the majority, the crash brought hunger and poverty; for a lucky few, it brought enormous riches.

After America, Germany was hardest hit by the depression. Massive unemployment and other miseries following the crash created a recruiting paradise for extremist groups, and savage street fighting erupted between the Communists and the Nazis. German industrialists began subsidizing Hitler in the hope that they could use him to destroy socialism.

The instability of the postdepression years was spread far and wide. Germany owed America more than 1 billion dollars; Australia owed 181 million; Canada, 164 million. These were all short-term loans, and they were called in with catastrophic speed. Australia and Canada were forced to deflate their currencies and reduce wages, and both suffered a drop in living standards. France did not owe nearly as much, but in the collapse of world trade its economy was badly hit. Economic instability bred political unrest there as elsewhere. France had thirteen changes of government between 1929 and 1933.

The British also suffered badly in terms of unemployment, although many of their problems were caused by the obsolescence of basic industries. Asian competitors were ruining Britain's textile industry, and the coal and steel industries were hit when postwar reconstruction drew to a close and the European railway network was completed. Political instability of the sort that affected the rest of Europe never hit Britain, but economic problems did produce Sir Oswald Mosley's Blackshirts.

Riots in Paris in 1934. Economic depression caused political unrest in France and there were frequent changes of government

Economic nationalism in South America

Elsewhere, perhaps the most significantly affected area was South America. The crash underscored Latin America's highly precarious dependence on foreign capital and markets. Aware that their natural resources, properly developed, could provide decent living standards, many governments embarked on policies of economic nationalism, often based on the corporatism of Mussolini's Fascism. Authoritarian regimes proliferated: in Brazil, the "disciplined democracy" of Getulio Vargas; in the Dominican Republic, the dictatorship of Rafael Trujillo; in Argentina, Augustín Justo's state planning of a New Deal. In Mexico, by way of exception, Lázaro Cárdenas founded his socialist regime on labor support.

The depression brought massive unemployment to South America and shattered working-class living standards by reducing the prices of raw materials, especially coffee. The consequent discontent was often savagely repressed: in El Salvador, by the fascist dictatorship of Hernández Martínez; in Honduras, by the military dictator, Tiburcio Carías; and in Guatemala, by the regime of Jorge Ubico.

The Japanese in Asia

Western influence in Asia was largely economic, and the depression naturally cut back investments there as well. British economic influence declined sharply and the Japanese were able to advance into former British spheres of influence, largely at the expense of the Americans (for whom dominance of the Far East was a vital strategic interest). Japan, which had been a major power in Far Eastern affairs from the time of the Sino-Japanese War of 1894–95, suffered a great

population explosion in this period. That increase, coupled with an urgent need for resources, forced Japan to adopt an expansionist foreign policy to provide outlets for both emigration and raw materials.

The overpopulated island empire soon moved against both Manchuria and China—traditional targets of Japanese expansion—and by 1931, Japan had outstripped its Western rivals in China. (This was a relatively easy task because Chiang Kai-shek's weak Kuomintang government was preoccupied with subduing Mao Tse-tung's growing peasant army.) Ruthless Japanese competition had long kept Chinese industry in a subservient position, and while the financial crash reduced the influence of other powers, Japan had avoided most of the worst results of the depression by a program of large-scale rearmament. Thus, by the time Japan was ready to move into Manchuria in September of 1931, its forces were strong and China's economy, weak. Japan's aggression was the first serious blow to the system of international relations established at Versailles; the League of Nations was unable to effect Japanese withdrawal, and that demonstration of its weakness would encourage similar moves by Hitler and Mussolini.

Another area of Asian opposition to Western encroachment was India, where the increasingly militant Congress movement was gaining strength. British government readiness to meet the movement's demands proceeded less from Britain's economic weakness than from the recognition of a growing chorus of discontent. The work of Gandhi and Nehru in organizing the Congress Party into a mass body with support from the educated middle classes and peasants was beginning to bear fruit. This highly integrated party, which was rapidly mobilizing the masses, could not be ignored, and in 1928 the British set

Sir Oswald Mosley, founder of the British Union of Fascists, at a rally.

ussia's price for industrialization

up the Simon Commission to look into the question of India's readiness for self-government. Indians boycotted the Commission both because it contained no Indians and because it seemed insulting to have an inquiry into their fitness to govern themselves. Motilal Nehru, father of Jawaharlal, said the British were treating the Indians like schoolboys who could go up a class if they were good. The Commission ultimately recommended a measure of provincial self-government and a federal state structure, and in 1930 a round table conference met in London to discuss these points.

At the conference, Congress leaders demanded immediate self-government and dominion status. Gandhi began his second civil disobedience campaign by distilling salt from sea water, which symbolically challenged Britain's salt monopoly. Violent riots swept India, and Gandhi and other leaders were arrested. The Mahatma was released in 1931 after he had called off the campaign, and he was invited to London for the second round table conference. While there, he disconcerted George V by appearing at Buckingham Palace "with no proper clothes on and bare knees." The King's parting remark to this saintly leader of millions was: "Remember, Mr. Gandhi, I won't have any attacks on my empire." The conference ground to a halt over the issue of minority representation, but by that time nationalist enthusiasm had dwindled to the point where Gandhi was forced to abandon his policy of civil disobedience.

Russian collectives

Economically, Russia was even further removed from the Wall Street crash than India. Having won the struggle for power within the Bolshevik Party, Stalin ruthlessly began thrusting barbaric, semi-Asiatic Russia into the twentieth century. By the end of the twenties, the Bolsheviks realized that drastic action was necessary to solve Russia's economic problems. The New Economic Policy had brought production back to prewar levels, but they knew that capital was necessary if the economy were to expand further. The world's credit was closed to Russia, thus capital would have to be accumulated within Russia itself. Such a goal could only be achieved by drastic reductions in domestic consumption, and this in itself involved an enormous problem. The Bolshevik Revolution had originally been a proletarian revolution of urban industrial workers bent on the socialization of property, but because the industrial proletariat was small and weak, the Bolsheviks had increasingly identified themselves with the peasants. In fact, it was the sheer weight of peasant discontent that overthrew the Tsar. But the peasant was only an inadvertent revolutionary, one whose main aim was the personal ownership of land. Thus the Bolshevik Revolution was based on a contradiction between the socialist revolution of the towns and the bourgeois revolution of the countryside. Socialism could not be built

Indians in Madras protesting against the Simon Commission, set up in 1928 to investigate India's readiness for self-government.

until the peasantry ceased to be a conservative property-owning force. And as long as Russian agriculture was fragmented into millions of small holdings, the rate of production necessary for economic expansion could never be reached.

In 1929, Stalin embarked upon a program of forced collectivization of agriculture to solve the dual problems of increasing production and socializing the peasantry. Trotsky and Zinoviev had long advocated the need for a collectivized system of agriculture, one which they suggested could be built gradually by first setting up model collectives that would convince the peasants of the benefits of collectivization. Stalin brutally implemented this scheme. He ordered villages surrounded by companies of machine gunners who herded the villagers into collectives that often had no tractors or fertilizers. At the same time, the first Five-Year Plan in industry was begun. Peasants were uprooted

to work under harsh factory conditions and were forced to live in hovels in shanty towns. Ruthless drill and discipline forced them into the routine of modern industry. In the country peasant groups responded by slaughtering livestock and burning crops; in the towns, by smashing machinery. Stalin replied with a comprehensive system of terror that prevented rebellion by destroying all sense of security. Midnight arrests, torture and imprisonment became common.

The price paid by the Russian people for industrialization was large in terms of cultural sterility, loss of personal freedom and drab living conditions. But in the long run Russian industry was to reap the benefits of the regimen imposed by Stalin. Other aspects of Stalinism had more tragic results. In his passion to protect Russia from a hostile capitalist world, the Soviet leader subjugated foreign Communist parties to the needs of Russia's domestic policy.

In a world hit by the Great Depression, the opportunities offered the Communist movement were many. But Stalin, who feared that a global upheaval might damage Russia's plans for reconstruction, refused to sanction all-out revolutionism by the parties of the Comintern. He shattered working-class solidarity by authorizing attacks on non-communist workers' parties, and in all corners of Europe that directive fostered the growth of fascism. In Germany, for example, the Communist Party might have rallied the German working class by cooperation with Social Democrats. Instead, they helped the Nazis destroy the government's followers. And when the Reichstag, Germany's parliament building, suddenly and mysteriously burst into flame, Hitler found an excuse to turn against the Communists.

A demonstration in London against Japanese goods during the Sino–Japanese War of 1933.

The Burning of the Reichstag

The flames that consumed Germany's parliament building on the night of February 27, 1933, also destroyed the tattered remains of the Weimar Republic—and with it Germany's post-World War I democracy. A young Dutch Communist was arrested and charged with the crime, but by that time the opportune burning of the Reichstag had given Adolf Hitler and his Nazi Party an excuse to seize control of Paul von Hindenburg's tottering regime. On the day after the fire, Hitler—who had been Germany's Chancellor for less than a month—persuaded Hindenburg to sign a decree suspending those sections of the constitution dealing with civil liberties. Hitler moved swiftly in the resulting vacuum, purging Communists and Social Democrats from the government and then moving against trade unions, Jews, intellectuals, pacifists, liberals and dissidents of all kinds. The process of Nazification had begun; before it was ended, it would affect the entire world.

On the night of February 27, 1933, the German parliament building in Berlin, the Reichstag, was set on fire. The culprit apparently was a young Dutch Communist, Marianus van der Lubbe, who was found in the empty building even as the flames were consuming it. Symbolically and in harsh reality, the fire marked the death of German democracy. Called a Communist prelude to revolution, the fire was used as an excuse to destroy the left-wing and democratic forces that still stood in the way of the total Nazification of Germany.

On January 30, 1933, Adolf Hitler had been made German Chancellor as a result of a deal with anti-Republican conservatives who had hoped to use him to destroy the Weimar Republic. Hitler had accepted because his farcical attempt to seize power in 1923 had convinced him that his revolution could best be made with, rather than against, the power of the state. But although he had the Chancellorship, the Nazis were still in a minority. Even at the crest of their popular success in the elections of July, 1932, they had polled only 37 per cent of the vote. Hitler's immediate task was to overcome the opposition of the other 63 per cent of the German people. New elections were arranged for March 5, 1933. For the first time, the Nazis would have at their disposal state resources of press and radio, together with police rights to smash the meetings of their opponents.

The election campaign built up throughout February, with posters, bonfires, marches and film shows (backed by the naked terror of the brown-shirted thugs of the *Sturmabteilung*, the Nazi militia). Then, at a most opportune moment, came the Reichstag fire. So opportune was it, in fact, that it might almost have been planned by the Nazis themselves. Years of speculation on this point has made only one thing clear: it is highly unlikely the whole truth will ever be known.

Despite the great doubt there may be as to who was responsible, there is none regarding who reaped the benefit. The Nazis had been anxious for something sensational to terrify the public before the election and for an excuse to smash their left-wing rivals. On the day after the fire, Hitler got President Paul von Hindenburg to sign a decree "for the Protection of the People and State" that suspended those sections of the constitution dealing with individual and civil liberties. It was the beginning of the process of *Gleichschaltung*, or "coordination," whereby the whole of German life and culture was to be totally Nazified.

The Reichstag fire was merely an occasion and not a cause, however. Indeed, many historians have seen the events of 1933 as the inevitable outcome of German history. It can hardly be denied that Hitler found his greatest support among educated, respectable people, nor that most of the Nazis' ideas were widely current and eminently respectable before World War I. From the middle of the nineteenth century on, many of these ideas had become intellectual commonplaces in Germany. They sprang both from the hopes placed in German unification and from disappointment when these hopes were not fulfilled. Because Germany remained split into many small states for so long, many thinkers began to search for a cultural German unity. To find it, they returned to a romanticized medieval age.

When Otto von Bismarck achieved political unification in 1871, there was nonetheless bitter disappointment: the new empire failed to provide spiritual unity. The backward-looking search for a cultural unity became more intense. A reaction against the reality of modern Germany began, and a scapegoat was found in the Jews, who symbolized modernity.

Propaganda for the Hitler Youth.

Opposite The burning of the Reichstag on February 27, 1933. Symbolically, and in harsh reality, the fire marked the death of German democracy.

Hermann Göring addressing the Reichstag in September, 1932.

Georgi Dimitrov, an associate of van der Lubbe. After World War II Dimitrov became President of Bulgaria.

Here was a crisis in Germanic culture, and it was not just confined to a few intellectuals. Widespread spiritual despair produced its own prophets, and their books were read by millions. In the 1890s Julius Langbehn published *Rembrandt Als Erzeiher*, a confused essay on Germanism. It asserted the physical superiority of the Germans, argued the need to exterminate lesser races—especially the Jews— and called for a great Führer to lead Germany to greatness. Such ideas were very popular, and by the end of the century the conflict between everyday materialism and the potential spiritual vitality of the German race was a cliché of right-wing thought.

These ideas provided a sympathetic context for the Nazis later on, but the really influential set of ideas was the mixture of racism and social Darwinism propagated by Houston Stewart Chamberlain, an English friend of the Kaiser. In a series of books, notably his *Die Grundlagen des Neunzehnten Jahrhunderts* (*The Foundations of the Nineteenth Century*), he interpreted world history as a ruthless struggle for the survival of the fittest nation and depicted the German race as locked in a mortal struggle with the Jews.

Most of the men behind such ideas were eccentrics, yet they became completely respectable. *Volkish* ("folk," or "nationalist") ideologists, rabidly nationalistic Pan-Germans, and anti-Semites were prominent in the teaching profession. History textbooks under the Empire and the Weimar Republic were soaked in such notions. The *Wandervogel* movement, which gave rise to the world youth hostels, was permeated with anti-Semitism and the leadership cult. The Pan-German League, nationalistic, anti-Jewish and imperialistic, had a considerable influence among generals, admirals, industrialists, civil servants, agriculturalists and university pro-

fessors, who enthusiastically embraced Pan-German schemes for the Germanization of Eastern Europe and for the clearing away of the Slavs. It is not surprising, then, that Hitler was so readily accepted by upper and middle classes.

Between 1909 and 1913, in the doss houses and gutter politics of Vienna, Hitler formed the ruthless ideas that were to bring him to power in the 1930s. There he developed the notion that brutality is the essential life-force; acquired the ability to cheat, lie, deceive and flatter; and gained considerable skill in manipulating others' weaknesses. In Vienna, too, he learned his political stock in trade: his obscene anti-Semitism, his crude social Darwinism, his Pan-German clichés. Added to the unprecedented ruthlessness of his ideas was the manic power of his personality. Many witnesses say that when talking to Hitler, it was impossible to resist falling under the spell of his eyes.

The main factor in Hitler's favor in the twenties and thirties was the sheer weakness of the Weimar Republic. The currency of *Volkish* and anti-Semitic ideas was itself inimical to democracy. But more particularly, in the years of insecurity after 1918, Weimar was physically threatened by both the right and the left wings. The right associated the Republic with surrender and treachery. The aristocracy, the Junker landowners, industrialists, bankers and the officer corps opposed it from the first. Former servicemen, fueled by right-wing propaganda, identified their personal grievances with Germany's humiliation, a resentment that was channeled into violence against the regime. The Social Democrats, the presumed guardians of the Republic, had lost much support by their deal with the German Army at the beginning of the regime. Their failure to proceed to social reform left them open to attack by the Communists, who concentrated on creating disorder and confusion in the belief that a revolutionary situation would carry them automatically to power. All they achieved was to increase the unscrupulousness of German political life and to make the way easier for the real cutthroats.

Perhaps the greatest burden carried by the Weimar Republic was its reliance on the German Army, which placed it at the mercy of the hostile right and deprived it of support from the left. Throughout the twenties, the Army, by its enthusiastic opposition to the left and its ambiguous sympathy toward the right, dangerously hampered the Republic in its freedom of action.

An equally dangerous thorn in the side of the Republic was the judiciary. Political opposition by the left was ruthlessly crushed, thereby discrediting the Republic with its supporters. Attacks by the right, vicious slander and numerous political murders were condoned because the judiciary, permeated with *Volkish* and Pan-German ideas, felt that these attacks were more patriotic than was support for the democratic Republic.

In this environment, Hitler began building his movement. The support of veteran Ernst Röhm brought him former servicemen for his paramilitary

The weakness of the Weimar Republic

S.A., as well as the patronage of the Bavarian authorities. At the same time, Hitler was attaining a mastery of propaganda, of simple repetitions, of black-and-white statements. Believing that passion and aggression attract the masses, he developed a technique of verbal violence. Virulent posters, salutes, uniforms and a hierarchy of command gave his movement a veneer of power. Mass meetings created a sense of belonging. Gang fights and the smashing of opponents' meetings gave an impression of irresistible strength.

Hitler's debut on the national stage came in 1923. The French had occupied the Ruhr to speed up reparations payments, and the German government had replied by encouraging passive resistance. More paper money was printed to make good the wages of Ruhr workers, and an already inflationary situation spiraled absurdly. When Chancellor Gustav Stresemann made the sensible and courageous decision to recommence reparations, the right howled about betrayal.

In Bavaria several groups toyed with the idea of overthrowing the Republic. Hitler in particular worked his supporters into such a state that even when the Berlin government began to master its difficulties, he could not draw back. After trying to take over the government of Bavaria, Hitler marched his troops into Munich. But the police and the German Army for once held firm, and the Nazis lost their nerve. It was a total fiasco—yet Hitler managed to profit from it. Above all, he learned that power could not be taken without the support of the establishment and the Army. At the same time, he turned his trial into a political triumph before the press of Germany and the rest of the world. With the compliance of the judges, he put the prosecution witnesses in the dock, indicted the Republic, and gained much praise from the right wing for his forthright declaration of war on democracy.

Hitler received a five-year sentence, of which he served only nine months. During his imprisonment, he began the dictation of *Mein Kampf*. The royalties from that book were to be his main income for the next few years, for after the 1923 crisis, things improved for the Republic and simultaneously went badly for the Nazis. Membership in the party increased slowly, but Hitler kept it together until his big break came in 1929.

Stresemann was then negotiating to fix reparations for fifty-nine years in return for evacuation of the Rhineland. The parties of the right—Alfred Hugenberg's Nationalists, Class' Pan-Germans, Franz Seldte's *Stahlhelm* veterans party—were joining in a huge protest. Hitler was enlisted to drum up mass support. The campaign failed to stop implementation of the Young Plan—by which Germany was to pay reparations over a period of fifty-nine years on a graded scale—but the resources of Alfred Hugenberg's vast newspaper empire made Hitler a national figure and attracted for him the attention of industry and big business.

This attention put Hitler in a strong position when the Depression broke out at the end of 1929. Unem-

ployment rocketed to 3 million in September, 1930, and to 6 million the following year. Again the middle classes were hit. The loss of their respectability enabled Hitler to exploit their fears and resentments. For the elections in September, 1930, the Nazis launched a violent campaign. Slogans, posters, demonstrations, rallies, mob oratory gave the impression that the Nazis were the party of energy, determination and success—a party that could get Germany out of its economic chaos. Hitler offered the middle classes the nationalistic, virile solution that they had previously found only in their *Volkish*

Left Policemen looking at the gutted Reichstag.

Marianus van der Lubbe, the young Dutchman who was supposedly responsible for the Reichstag fire. Göring later said "The only one who knows about the Reichstag is I, because I set it on fire."

A room in the Reichstag. Within minutes of the start of the fire, the whole building was ablaze.

Middle-class and right-wing support

reading. He gave them objects for their resentments: the French, the corrupt politicians of the Weimar Republic, Jewish speculators. Nazi propaganda appealed to everyone, in particular the youth of Germany. In the elections, the Nazis received 107 seats, making them the second largest party in the Reichstag.

The increasing precariousness of the government encouraged the Nazis to attack it. At the same time, Hitler was consolidating support with the conservative right, whose members found his extremism distasteful but who were basically sympathetic to his ideas. In September, 1930, he made an open overture to the Army during a trial of officers accused of spreading Nazi propaganda. He spoke flatteringly of the great German Army and promised that a Nazi regime would build a huge one. Nazi strength was attractive to General Kurt von Schleicher, the power behind the German Army, who was trying to organize a government satisfactory to the armed forces. Schleicher had hopes of using the Nazis to build a strong government. Hitler, for his part, began to realize that for all his increased strength

he was no nearer power, and so he grew more sympathetic to a partnership with those who could get power for him.

As 1932 approached, the economic crisis worsened—and in state elections the Nazis polled 35 per cent of the votes. Hitler resisted overtures from Schleicher because he hoped to gain an absolute majority in the national elections in March. The campaign was fought with unprecedented bitterness. The Communists weakened the left by attacking the Social Democrats on orders from Moscow. A huge push with posters, films, records, marches and rallies brought the Nazi vote to 11.5 million, and in the April reelection the vote increased to 13.5 million. Yet Hitler was still faced with the problem of how to turn an electoral success that fell short of a majority to political advantage.

At this stage Schleicher adopted the tragic role of *deus ex machina*. He informed the Chancellor, Heinrich Brüning, that Brüning no longer enjoyed the support of the Army. Schleicher, who felt it his duty to the Reich to find a strong Chancellor, drafted Franz von Papen, a conservative dandy. But von Papen and his cabinet of barons were so unpopular that they had to rule by presidential decree. Meanwhile, the Nazis unleashed a wave of violence. On July 17, at Altona, 19 people were killed and 285 wounded. Schleicher and von Papen used the incident as an excuse to remove the Social Democratic government of Prussia, one of the last bastions of the Republic. In the July elections, the Nazis received 230 seats, making them the strongest single party. Yet they were as far away from power as ever. The S.A. was getting restless, but Hitler was determined to gain power legally. The Nazis demonstrated their indispensability to the government in September when they voted with a Communist motion of censure against von Papen. However, in the elections that followed von Papen's defeat, the Nazis, while they remained the largest party, lost 2 million votes. Their myth of inevitable success was broken, and von Papen was confident that another election would see their downfall. Unfortunately for von Papen, Schleicher decided to intervene at this stage. He was jealous of von Papen's growing independence and of his influence over President Hindenburg, and he was annoyed at the hostility between von Papen and the Nazis, since his object in giving von Papen power had been to get Nazi support for strong government. Schleicher therefore told Hindenburg that von Papen's policy of doing without the Nazis could not work. On December 2, 1932, Schleicher became Chancellor himself, confident that he could both get the support of the Nazis and keep them under control.

Schleicher was to be defeated by the same sort of intrigue as that which had brought him to power. Hitler was making a deal with von Papen, and between them they could muster the support for a government, which Schleicher could not. Hindenburg was impressed by the extent of the Nazis' electoral backing. By January 20, it was obvious that Schleicher's attempt to build a national front had

A military parade in the 1930s. Hitler bought the support of the army by promising to modernize and enlarge it.

failed. When he asked for emergency powers, Hindenburg refused. Hitler by this time had also secured the support of Hugenberg's Nationalists. On January 28, Schleicher resigned; on the thirtieth Hindenburg offered Hitler the Chancellorship.

Hitler had made it. Von Papen was as confident of controlling him as Schleicher had been. But with the power of the state behind Hitler, there would be no moving him. The aftermath of the Reichstag fire showed his determination to destroy his enemies and entrench his own power. Hitler had gained power by the skill and unscrupulousness with which he had exploited the selfishness of the right, the complaisance of the Army, the weakness of the left, and the general confusion of the period. Yet there was more to his victory than trickery. The fact remains that the Nazis received more votes than any other party. There was widespread sympathy for them throughout the right, and enthusiastic support among the middle classes.

Hitler might have been unique in his sheer unscrupulousness, but there were other parties of the right near enough to him to suggest that the Nazis were far from being a lone aberration of German politics. If they were unique, it was in the intensity of their urge for naked power. Indeed, the real significance of the Reichstag fire may be seen to be its illustration of this. In 1932, Hitler said to Hermann Rauschning: "We shall never capitulate. We may go under but we will take a whole world with us." On the day that he was made Chancellor, he said: "No power in the world will ever get me out of here alive." The Reichstag fire was the prelude to a series of events, from the liquidation of the Jews to World War II, which showed that Hitler meant exactly what he said.

PAUL PRESTON

M. Hitler déclare la paix au monde.

Above Hitler declares peace on the world, a French cartoon published in 1936.

Hitler ascending the steps at the beginning of the Nürnberg rally, 1933.

The emergency decree signed by President Hindenburg on the day after the Reichstag fire gave Hitler free rein to begin the Nazification of Germany. A series of political purges followed. The most significant of these was the Night of the Long Knives, June 30, 1934. On that night, Ernst Röhm and a number of other leaders of the leftist group known as the *Sturmabteilung* ("stormtroopers"), or simply the S.A., were hauled from their beds and shot. At the time the S.A. was locked in an intense rivalry with the German Army, and Röhm had aroused the jealousy of both Hermann Göring and Heinrich Himmler. The Army, overjoyed at the removal of the S.A., swore its undying loyalty to Hitler. (That loyalty would not be shaken until after Hitler had overrun most of Europe and his army faced defeat at Stalingrad.) The German Army was not the only group that supported Hitler with equanimity. When Hindenburg died in August 1934, a 90 per cent majority of the German people approved Hitler's assumption of the presidency.

Most Germans regarded the Nazi regime with hope and confidence. Only a minority of liberals, pacifists and Jews lived in terror of the Gestapo and concentration camps; the majority rejoiced over Hitler's intention to make Germany a great military power once again and to free it from the shackles of the Treaty of Versailles.

The last page has yet to be written explaining the history of Nazi Germany and the psychology behind such excesses as anti-Semitic legislation that deprived Jews of basic human rights, forbade their marrying gentiles, and barred them from making a career in all but the most menial occupations.

The cultural cost of Nazism was gigantic. In the process of creating a specifically Nazi culture, the liberal humanitarianism of Goethe and Beethoven and the sophisticated art of Heine, Mahler and Kafka were abandoned; in their place a mindless and barbaric cult was erected.

Rearmament was the key to Hitler's economic success. And while this was secretly taking place, Hitler pursued a foreign policy designed to throw other world powers into confusion about his ultimate aims. Still not absolutely sure of his position, Hitler played the respectable diplomat during this period. For the moment, the dreams of his book, *Mein Kampf*, of sweeping aside the Slavs in search of *Lebensraum* ("living space") for a greater Germany, were shelved. In 1934 Germany was still militarily weak, and its neighbors to the east and west—Poland and France, respectively—were hostile and suspicious. The long-term aim of Hitler's policy—world domination —was temporarily dropped in favor of the short-term aims of destroying the Treaty of Versailles and of rearming without provoking war.

The Nazi leader inaugurated his ambitious scheme on May 17, 1933, with a "peace" speech that completely disconcerted the Western powers. In that speech he renounced all offensive weapons—provided everyone else did the same. Hitler's declaration was only a means to an end, however, for as the Führer himself observed: "My party comrades will not fail to understand me when they hear me speak of universal peace, disarmament, and mutual security pacts." Less than six months later, Germany withdrew from the disarmament conference in Geneva on the grounds that the other participants had not renounced offensive weapons. Neither Britain nor France protested Hitler's move; he had successfully cashed in on the superficial reasonableness of his case and on the eagerness of Britain and France to appease him. The Nazi leader followed this first diplomatic triumph with an even greater one: in January, 1934, he signed a non-aggression pact with Poland and thereby created a huge breach in France's security network of Eastern alliances.

Hitler's policy was always double-edged. While he spoke publicly of peace, he secretly encouraged the subversive activities of Austrian Nazis. In July of 1934, this group organized a putsch in which the Chancellor, Engelbert Dollfuss, was shot. Nothing came of the attempted coup, but it did demonstrate Hitler's determination to effect a union with Austria. In March, 1935, Hitler announced Germany's rearmament, but the other major powers did nothing until April, when Britain, France

Dr. Engelbert Dollfuss, Austrian Chancellor, murdered by the Nazis.

and Italy issued a joint condemnatory declaration at Stresa. No effective action was taken, however, largely because Hitler softened the blow with verbiage about war never coming again. Each time he circumvented another provision of the Treaty of Versailles, his position at home strengthened. The German leader's most brilliant diplomatic stroke was yet to come, however. In the spring of 1935 Hitler offered Britain a limitation of German naval strength to 35 per cent of that of the Royal Navy, and Britain promptly took the bait. The Anglo-German Naval Agreement, signed in June of that year, convinced the British of Hitler's sincerity and, in the process, destroyed the four-month-old Stresa Agreement (which had established a common British, French and Italian front against Germany).

Hitler's bold foreign policy led to fresh triumphs in 1936. Complaining that the Franco-Russian alliance invalidated the Treaty of Locarno, he shattered that treaty by marching his troops into the Rhineland. On the same day, he proposed a nonaggression pact with France and Belgium. Behind a smokescreen of rationality, he had destroyed the Versailles system, and the meek reaction of the Western powers convinced Hitler that he could do with them as he wished.

The era of appeasement

Western policy of appeasement was shown at its most flaccid later in 1936, when Hitler joined Mussolini in openly aiding Franco in Spain. Appeasement, which culminated in the betrayal of the Czechs at Munich, proceeded from understandable, if not entirely creditable motives. In the twenties the policy in Britain sprang from a widely held belief that prolonged and strenuous efforts to secure peace were of greater value than the politically easy resort to war. It also derived from the belief there that the Germans had been harshly treated at Versailles because of French vindictiveness. In both Britain and France, there was a strong determination to avoid a repetition of the holocaust of World War I.

Appeasement was no answer to an Adolf Hitler bent on war, but few saw this at the time. An informed minority, Winston Churchill and Robert Vansittart among them, saw the danger, but their warnings fell on deaf ears. The British ambassador in Berlin, Sir Horace Rumbold, wrote home that "the German is an inexorable Oliver Twist. Give him something and it is a jumping-off ground for asking for something else."

Both the French and British governments were preoccupied with unemployment, however, and the enormous social problems left in the wake of the depression. There was no enthusiasm in either country for a resolute foreign policy. The people were war-weary, and the governments hoped to spend what little money they had on something more socially useful than armaments. France in particular was faced by violence from the extreme right and left. Accordingly, both of the Western democracies listened eagerly to Hitler's talk of peace, hoping against hope that war could be avoided. Even those who suspected that war could not be avoided hoped it might be put off for a time. The determination not

Persecution of the Jews in Germany in the 1930s; a Jewess sitting on a bench marked "Only for Jews," hides her face.

Sir Robert Vansittart, one of the few people in the mid-thirties to realize the danger of Hitler.

to antagonize Hitler was an indication of the enduring exhaustion of World War I.

The New Deal

In the United States, meanwhile, Roosevelt's New Deal was consolidating American capitalism and democracy. The horrors of Nazism were ignored in the United States as they were in England and France, for America had troubles of its own. Franklin D. Roosevelt became President in March, 1933, at a time when national income and productivity were only half what they had been in 1929. Bread lines, vagrancy and shanty towns bore witness to the crippling poverty that had left 12 million workers unemployed. America also faced a political problem, a threat to democracy that was perhaps best illustrated by Senator Huey Long's attempts to set up a quasi-fascist dictatorship in Louisiana.

To avoid social, economic and political catastrophe, Roosevelt pledged himself to "a new deal for the American people." He began by restoring confidence in the banking system. After temporarily closing all banks, Roosevelt reopened first the Federal Reserve Bank and then those private banks that were solvent. A huge program of public works raised wages, created more purchasing power, and rejuvenated the entire economy. Agricultural production was limited in order to raise prices. The popularity of the New Deal was such that in the 1936 elections, Roosevelt was reelected with a plurality of 9 million votes.

The New Deal was to bear its greatest fruit during the war. Measures first adopted to counter the depression were later to be the basis of America's huge wartime industrial, agricultural and armaments program.

Industrialization in Russia

In Stalin's Russia, industrialization and collectivization were proceeding at an enormous human cost. Thousands were shot or deported as full collectivization began, while in industry, gigantic strides forward were accompanied by huge sacrifices of human life. An American engineer who worked for five years on the Magnitogorsk project, reported: "I would wager that Russia's battle of ferrous metallurgy alone involved more casualties than the Battle of the Marne." The priority of heavy industry over consumer production, of *raison d'état* over popular interest, resulted in the terrible conditions described by Arthur Koestler: "I could not help noticing the Asiatic backwardness of life; the apathy of the crowds in the street, tramways and railway stations; the incredible housing conditions which make all industrial towns appear one vast slum (two or three couples sharing one room divided by sheets hanging from washing lines)."

The catastrophic reduction in living standards necessitated by Stalin's rapid industrialization resulted in a tremendous conflict between the people and the Communist Party. An increase in coercion and an intensification of police methods became essential, since

the Party was forced to carry out enormous social and economic transformations in a hostile environment. Toughness in carrying out unpopular orders became the highest qualification for Communist Party office, and men like Vyacheslav Molotov and Lazar Kaganovich came to the fore. Old Bolsheviks recoiled at the excesses of Stalinism—compulsory direction of labor, imprisonment in work camps, mass terror, the growth of crude Russian nationalism. Occasionally, when the old guard seemed to forget its responsibilities to the ideals of Bolshevism, Trotsky, a lone voice in exile, reminded them through the pages of his *Bulletin Oppozitsii* that the revolution was being betrayed. And when members of Stalin's own clique began expressing their fears that the revolution's ideals were being buried in a mound of tyranny, suffering and oppression, the Russian leader decided that the old guard had to be eliminated.

At the time, Politburo member Sergei Kirov was advocating a liberalizing of the regime, and when Kirov was mysteriously assassinated in Leningrad in December, 1934, it was a signal for the purges to begin. Absurd charges—of attempting mass poisoning of the workers, of being Nazi agents, of attempting to restore capitalism—were used to justify the liquidation of the great figures of the revolution. Lev Borisovich Kamenev, Grigori Zinoviev, Aleksei Rykov, Nikolai Bukharin, Mikhail Tukhachevski and a host of lesser figures were shot after humiliating confessions had been wrung out of them.

Stalin thus created the Russia of cold war legend, the police state, where free thought is ruthlessly stifled and insufferable living conditions prevail. The positive achievement of Stalinism was that it tore primitive, rural Russia out of its feudal backwardness, hurling it, almost fully industrialized, into the twentieth century. When Hitler

attacked Russia, it would be his undoing. This was so because Stalin had prepared Russia for modern warfare.

While Europe moved toward war, the two giants of the periphery, Russia and America, developed into the states that were to confront each other after the war. Several other postwar developments can also be traced to the thirties. In India, for example, the balance of power was shifting further away from the British. Increasing numbers of influential people were acknowledging that Britain must

Leo Kamenev, one of the great figures of the Russian Revolution, liquidated during the Stalinist purges of 1934.

either recognize the power of the Congress movement and transform India into a self-governing dominion and a loyal member of the Commonwealth or embark on a savage policy of repression that could benefit no one and would shatter India's economy.

Middle Eastern troubles

In the Middle East, British hegemony was further threatened by the Palestine problem, which was making enemies on both sides for the English. There had been sporadic violence between the local Arabs and the first Jewish settlers for years, but Hitler's rise to power brought a new urgency to the problem. Many previously assimilated Jews were forced to turn to Zionism in search of decent human rights, and as the Zionist movement grew, Arabs became alarmed at the prospect of increased Jewish immigration. To the consternation of the British, riots and assassinations increased. It was thus an unusually troubled world that received the news of the outbreak of the Spanish Civil War in July, 1936.

Working on a Tennessee Valley Authority dam project, one of the public works programs set up in 1933 as part of Roosevelt's New Deal.

The Spanish Civil War

The strongly worded pronunciamiento *broadcast by a Canary Islands radio station on July 18, 1936, was aimed—both literally and figuratively—at Madrid. The bold rhetoric of the manifesto was attributed to "the Commanding General of the Canaries"; its actual author was General Francisco Franco, who was soon to emerge as the leader of the military cabal that was bent on overthrowing the Second Spanish Republic. Assisted by the Axis Powers, which provided air transport for his troops, Franco landed some 15,000 members of his personally trained Army of Africa on Spanish soil in August of 1936. Romantics have tended to view the three-year civil war that followed as a contest between democracy and fascism; the truth is a little less clear-cut. The country that Franco invaded was rapidly sinking into anarchy. The authoritarian regime that Franco established at least gave Spain its first stable government in more than a century.*

The badge worn by members of the International Brigade, which fought against Franco in the Spanish Civil War.

Opposite A poster issued by the Republicans attacking Franco's supporters for their vested interests.

The military conspiracy against the Second Spanish Republic began in earnest in February, 1936, but General Francisco Franco did not commit himself to it until the end of June. On June 23, from his "exile" in the Canary Islands (where the newly elected Popular Front government had sent him as military governor), he made what he considered a final attempt to bring the government to its senses. In a long letter to the new Prime Minister, Casares Quiroga, he dwelt at length upon Army grievances and gave warning of "grave dangers" facing Spain. In Franco's mind, this curious letter hinted that he was available to restore order in an increasingly chaotic situation—if called upon to do so.

Casares Quiroga, who suffered from advanced consumption and had no desire to acknowledge that the Republic was in danger, ignored Franco's warning. His silence was the nonevent that ended Franco's prolonged season of doubt. Just in time—for the conspirators were about to act without him—he decided to join the military rebellion.

General Emilio Mola, known to the plotters as *el Director*, had planned to act on July 14, but he postponed his move until the seventeenth because of some last-minute quarrels on a common program acceptable to the disparate groups on the Nationalist side. The extra three days gave the Nationalists time to complete arrangements for conveying Franco from the Canaries to Morocco, where he was to take command of the insurgent forces in Africa. A British civil plane, chartered by the Nationalists, picked the General up at Las Palmas. News that the uprising had begun reached Franco before he left. He immediately telegraphed all divisional generals in Spanish Morocco and throughout Spain, appealing to them to rally to the Nationalist cause.

Franco also drafted an old-style *pronunciamiento*, known today as the Manifesto of Las Palmas, which was remarkable on several counts. For one thing the Manifesto, as broadcast by Radio Tenerife on July 18, 1936, was not attributed to Franco by name but to "the Commanding General of the Canaries." This reticence on Franco's part is explained by the fact that the General, a latecomer to the conspiracy, was not at that time the leader of the Nationalist movement. With Mola as the organizer, the conspirators had, in fact, designated General José Sanjurjo—a prestigious officer then in exile in Portugal—as Commander in Chief. Nevertheless, the tone and wording of the Manifesto made it quite clear that Franco considered himself the natural leader of the rebels now that he had decided to join them. That was the second remarkable aspect of the Manifesto.

A third point was that, in the face of the fact that the Republic's persecution of the Church was a major issue on the Nationalist side (and for all Franco's later reputation for piety), the Manifesto made no mention of religion. Instead, it promised "liberty and fraternity without libertinage and tyranny; work for all; social justice, accomplished without rancor or violence, and an equitable and progressive distribution of wealth without destroying or jeopardizing the Spanish economy."

Franco's immediate problem was how to convey the Army of Africa across the Straits of Gibraltar. This small but formidable force, whose professionalism owed much to Franco's efficient discipline, was potentially the key to a Nationalist victory. But it was almost useless where it was. The bulk of the Spanish fleet was in Republican hands, the crews having turned on their Nationalist officers and murdered them. The vessels, led by the battleship *Jaime* I, were steaming toward the international port of Tangier, where their presence would threaten any attempted crossing by sea.

In this situation, Franco made the fateful decision to seek the assistance of the Axis Powers. He first turned to Mussolini, who rebuffed his emissary. A second emissary, sent by Mola on July 25, persuaded *Il Duce* to change his mind. Five days later, twelve three-engined Italian Savoia-Marchetti 81s took off for Morocco; only nine actually arrived. Meanwhile,

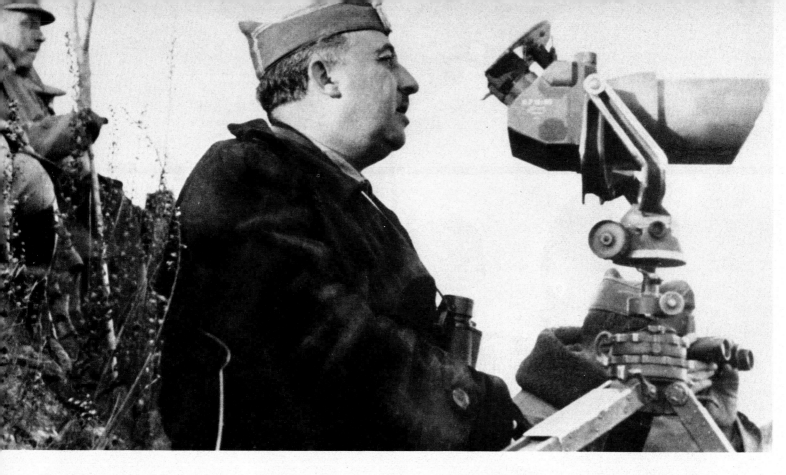

Franco put his case to two local Nazis, who took off
for Berlin on July 22. Hitler received them on July
26 at Bayreuth, where he was attending a Wagner
festival, and on the advice of Admiral Canaris,
the head of German military intelligence—who
thought highly of the Spanish general—he decided
to back Franco. Shortly after the two Nazi emissaries
returned to Morocco, Hitler's first planes started
arriving. The first group consisted of twenty JU 52
maximum-capacity transports and six Heinkel 51
fighters. They immediately started ferrying Nationalist troops across to the mainland. Together, the
German and Italian aircraft transported up to five
hundred men and fifteen tons of material a day
across the Straits. Within a few weeks, some 15,000
men were ready for action against the Republic.

Franco, meanwhile, was neutralizing the Republican fleet and preparing a naval convoy of his own.
Five warning telegrams were issued to the control
committee of the international zone at Tangier, and
on August 7, they were followed by an ultimatum
that gave the committee forty-eight hours to get rid
of the Republican fleet. In a crucial vote, the British
member of the control committee sided with the
Italian member in supporting a motion that Madrid
should be requested to remove its warships. On the
ninth, the last of them steamed out of Tangier.

Although this removed an immediate danger, the
Republican naval blockade was still in force. Over-
ruling objections from his naval staff, Franco had
already decided—before sending his ultimatum to
Tangier—to go ahead with his convoy plan. At 5 P.M.
on August 5, three thousand troops set off from
Ceuta, in the gunship *Dato*, the coastal patrol ship
Uad Kert, a tugboat and three merchantmen. Chal-

lenged by the *Alcala Galiano*, a Republican destroyer,
the *Dato* engaged her in an unequal artillery duel,
which ended in the *Dato's* favor when the Nationalist
Air Force put the *Alcala Galiano* to flight.

Franco had won the Battle of the Straits and had
gotten his troops to the mainland. Within two
months, his tough and professional Army of Africa
had a string of military successes to its credit, and
Franco had been proclaimed Chief of State and
Generalissimo of the armed forces of Nationalist
Spain. His one serious political rival, General Mola,
met his death in an air crash on June 3, 1937.
Less than two years later, the Republic was crushed.

A race to extremism

And thirty years after the Republic's defeat, Generalissimo Francisco Franco y Bahamonde was still Chief of State in the Nationalist Spain that was his by military victory.

The Spanish Second Republic was the direct outcome of the municipal elections of 1931, elections in which nearly all the cities and large towns voted overwhelmingly in favor of the Republican parties. King Alfonso XIII, fearing civil conflict, went into voluntary exile, though he did not abdicate—a fact that made it possible for the Monarchists to deny the legitimacy of the Republic. The Monarchists, and the King himself, had largely discredited themselves in public opinion by Alfonso's tolerance of the dictatorship of General Primo de Rivera (1923–30), which began well with modernizing achievements but ended in financial decline and general discontent. The first years of the Republic were dominated by Manuel Azaña, who began as War Minister and later became in turn Prime Minister and President. A gifted writer, Azaña was determined to curb the power of two of the three pillars of traditional Spain —the Church and the Army. (The third pillar, the monarchy, had already been broken.)

However defensible these objections may have been, Azaña aroused much antagonism by the arrogance and tactlessness with which he pushed through his anticlerical and antimilitary reforms. Conservative opinion had already been alarmed by Azaña's declared indifference in the face of a wave of church and convent burnings in the early days of the Republic. An ill-timed and ill-organized attempt to overthrow the Republic was made in August, 1932, by General Sanjurjo, who was first sentenced to death but was later reprieved and exiled. A fellow plotter, Colonel Varela, was won over to the ultraconservative Carlist cause during his imprisonment and later trained the "God, King and country" *Requetés*, or militias, of the Traditionalist Communion, as the Carlists should properly be called. (The Carlists were supporters of Don Carlos, pretender to the Spanish throne.) Although he had been approached by the plotters, Franco stayed aloof.

The Azaña phase of the Republic ended (as it had begun) in a wave of strikes and violence, in which the hand of the Anarchists and their trade union organization, the C.N.T., was visible. The next phase was dominated by the young right-wing Catholic leader Gil Robles, whose party, the C.E.D.A., topped the polls in the general elections of November, 1933, though it did not gain an absolute majority and was not included in the first post-election government. The two years of center-right government that followed are known to the Spanish left as the "two black years" (*bienio negro*). The trend toward extremism gathered speed and strength. Primo de Rivera's son, José Antonio, founded a Spanish fascist party, the Falange Española, with a radical social program and—in distinction to Nazism and Italian Fascism—support for religion. On the left, the Anarchists declared war on the new government, called strikes, burned churches and proclaimed "libertarian communism" in the villages. The small

Hitler and Franco inspecting a guard of honor before their meeting at Hendaye, France, in 1940.

Communist Party gained new members and fresh influence in alliance with the revolutionary left-wing Socialists, led by Largo Caballero. Political murders became commonplace.

The entry of Gil Robles' party into the government in October, 1934, sparked a left-wing revolution that took the form of a Socialist-led general strike, the proclamation of Catalonia's independence, and a miners' insurrection in Asturias jointly led by the Socialists, Communists and Anarchists. Called in by the War Ministry, General Franco restored order with brutal efficiency and considerable loss of life. The crushing of the Asturian revolt left the Army (except the officers promoted by Azaña) determined to combat revolutionary anarchy —which they called "communism"—and the left bent on revenge against the "fascists."

The general elections of February, 1936, confirmed the race to extremism. The Popular Front of Azaña's left-center, together with the Socialists and Communists—and supported by Anarchist and Trotskyite votes at polling time—dominated the Cortes, or Parliament. The Front won 258 seats, as opposed to 152 for the right and only 62 for the center. Street clashes became more and more frequent, not merely between the Falangists and Communists, but also between the relatively moderate Socialist followers of Indalecio Prieto and the Largo Caballero Socialists, who preached violent revolution. The climax was the abduction of the Monarchist politician Calvo Sotelo, who was murdered on July 13 by uniformed Republican police in retaliation for the murder of a policeman by Falangists the previous day.

By this time, the military plot against the Republic was far advanced. The Carlist *Requetés* were well

Don Manuel Azaña, who succeeded Zamora as President of the Republic.

Franco, the key to Nationalist victory

General Francisco Franco, as he appears today.

A painting showing soldiers being executed by a firing squad.

trained and organized, and the Falangist militias were training too. Within the Army, opposition to the Republic had crystallized around the semisecret *Unión Militar Española* (U.M.E.) formed in 1934. In terms of serious organization, Mola's conspiracy began at the time of the Popular Front's electoral victory. It was his achievement to unite the rival Monarchist groups (called Carlist and Alfonsist from their support of rival Bourbon contenders for the vacant throne) with the anti-Monarchist and anticapitalist Falange, and to win financial support from bankers and industrialists.

The polarization of Spanish politics coincided with the rise of the totalitarian dictatorships in Europe: those of Stalin in the Soviet Union, Hitler in Germany, and Mussolini in Italy. In the age of appeasement, the dominant concern of the Western democracies, especially Britain, was to keep out of the Spanish Civil War when it began. Hence their support for a nonintervention policy. Despite the Nonintervention Committee, however, the Spanish Civil War became an international free-for-all, with Russia, Mexico and France aiding the Republic, and Germany and Italy intervening with decisive effect on Franco's side. The popular concept of the war as a struggle between democracy and fascism is rooted in these circumstances. But this was essentially a true civil conflict, with indigenous Spanish origins.

Franco's decision to join the military rebellion against the Spanish Republic was one of the turning points of contemporary history. Under any of the General's contemporaries, Nationalist chances would have been considerably slimmer. If Franco had stayed out, the mantle of leadership would have presumably fallen upon the swashbuckling Queipo de Llano, the "radio general" who had bluffed his way into Seville at the outset of the Civil War. It is difficult to imagine the more conservative Nationalists taking orders from this flamboyant character with vaguely leftist views (who was the initiator of an abortive coup against Alfonso XIII).

Nor is it at all certain that Hitler would have provided transport for the Army of Africa had it not been under Franco's orders. And Mussolini, though he had promised planes, did not actually send them until he was sure that the Nazis were doing likewise. In all senses, then, Franco's belated decision to intervene was decisive.

The historical consequences of that decision, and of the victory guaranteed by his inflexible will as much as by Axis aid, were, however, ironical. Public opinion, identifying Franco with his Axis allies, wrongly saw the Nationalist conquest as the murder of Spanish democracy by international fascism. It would have been truer to see it as the victory of traditional Spain over the revolutionary left and international communism.

To present the outcome of the Civil War in this way is not to accept the Nationalist myth in preference to the Republican. What the Nationalists called "communism" embraced Azaña's anticlerical radicalism as well as revolutionary anarchism and the Spanish Communist Party, with its international allies. But Spanish democracy was already menaced when the Civil War began, and it died shortly after that. Law and order began to collapse in the political

violence that occurred from February to July, 1936. Thereafter two developments marked Republican Spain: first, a sweeping Anarchist revolution, with destruction of records, the emptying of prisons, the seizure of properties, the burning of Church property, and the torture and killing of clergy; and second, a carefully planned takeover of the Republican state by the Communists, carried out under the supervision of Comintern officers who, for Stalin's purposes, "used" such public figures as Largo Caballero and Dr. Negrín (who shipped the Republic's gold to Russia). The takeover would doubtless have been more complete had it not been for Stalin's reluctance —probably for general foreign-policy reasons—to let the Spanish Communist Party be shown to be in control of the Republican government. If the Republican forces had won, Spain would probably not have been a parliamentary democracy, but a Communist-controlled "people's democracy"—an outpost of the Soviet Union.

Paradoxically, the fact that Franco was in power in Madrid, helped to victory by Nazi aid, did not much help Hitler in World War II—for Franco, proclaiming Spain's neutrality or nonbelligerency (the formula varied to meet the fluctuations of fortune in World War II), resisted all Hitler's threats or blandishments. Losing patience, Hitler planned to invade the peninsula, but abandoned his plans when the bulk of his forces got bogged down on the Russian front. Gibraltar stayed British; the Allied campaign in North Africa was safeguarded; and Rommel was defeated. In the House of Commons on May 25, 1944, Winston Churchill praised Franco's Spain's contribution to the Allied successes in the Mediterranean. On the Axis side, General Jodl singled out "General Franco's repeated refusal to allow German armed forces to pass through Spain to take Gibraltar" as one of the major causes of Germany's defeat.

Franco's decision to seek Nazi and Italian Fascist help, however, was fateful in other ways. The "fascist" label stuck, and Spain was ostracized for many years after the defeat of the Axis Powers, deprived of Marshall Aid for postwar reconstruction and kept out of NATO. Some would see in this international odium a fitting punishment for Franco's original sin in seeking Axis aid. But his importance in European history cannot be denied. He gave Spain the longest period of peace it had known for a century and a half; his resistance to Hitler's demands contributed to the Allied victory; and he prevented the spread of Soviet Communism to southwestern Europe.

BRIAN CROZIER

Picasso's painting commemorating the bombing of Guernica.

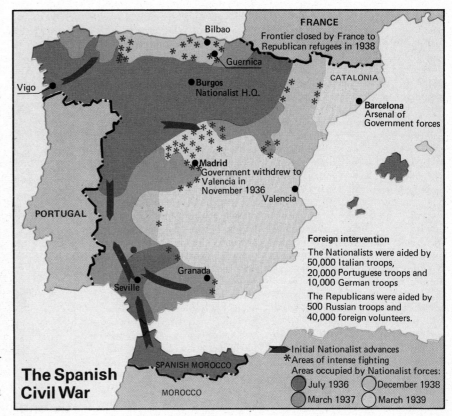

The Spanish Civil War

FRANCE
Frontier closed by France to Republican refugees in 1938

Bilbao
Guernica
CATALONIA
Vigo
Burgos
Nationalist H.Q.
Barcelona
Arsenal of Government forces

Madrid
Government withdrew to Valencia in November 1936
Valencia

PORTUGAL

Granada
Seville

SPANISH MOROCCO
MOROCCO

Foreign intervention

The Nationalists were aided by 50,000 Italian troops, 20,000 Portuguese troops and 10,000 German troops

The Republicans were aided by 500 Russian troops and 40,000 foreign volunteers.

Initial Nationalist advances
Areas of intense fighting
Areas occupied by Nationalist forces:
July 1936   December 1938
March 1937   March 1939

Tension in the Far East as Japanese landlus

Between 1936 and 1939, European political interest focused almost exclusively on the Spanish Civil War. The official postures European powers adopted toward the Spanish conflict symbolize attitudes that exploded into World War II: Britain and France banned supplies to the legally elected Second Republic and joined the Nonintervention Committee, while Hitler and Mussolini boldly intervened on the side of a fellow fascist, the insurgent Francisco Franco. Russia, the only major power to intervene officially on the side of the Spanish government, seemed more concerned with the destruction of anarchists and Trotskyites than winning the war.

This pattern of international relations after 1936 merely etched earlier patterns more clearly. In 1934, for example, Mussolini had attacked Ethiopia. The League of Nations was prevented from issuing effective sanctions against Italy by the French, who feared another major European catastrophe. These fears soon spread to the British and resulted in the Hoare-Laval Pact, which suggested the partition of Ethiopia. Neither Mussolini nor Hitler failed to identify safe targets of opportunity: when England and France abandoned Spain and Ethiopia, the fascists moved in.

Right-wing elements in both England and France regarded Franco as the savior of Christian society, while the left supported the Republic. This division in itself precluded a decisive policy, particularly when coupled with the fear of general war that infected both sides of the Channel. The two countries therefore set up a Nonintervention committee (which would prove ineffective in preventing fascist aid to Franco as well as Soviet aid to the Republic).

Ironically, Soviet policy toward the Spanish Civil War could not have been less revolutionary. Russia had already abandoned both the German and Chinese Communists in favor of Hitler and Chiang Kai-shek, thus demonstrating the basically conservative nature of Stalinist foreign policy. Stalin was interested only in Russia's security (a fact made abundantly clear when he signed a nonaggression pact with Hitler in 1939).

In 1936 Stalin was still trying to court the Western Allies, largely because Hitler was casting covetous eyes on the Ukraine. Thus Stalin could not permit the Spanish Republic to collapse—not out of revolutionary zeal, but because the

Italian troops during the invasion of Ethiopia in 1935.

alternative, a fascist regime in Spain, would increase France's growing timidity. But he did not want to risk fostering an all-out civil war to keep the republic alive, lest it alienate the conservative British and French. Consequently, Soviet policy in Spain seemed contradictory: on the one hand Russia supplied enough arms to keep the Republic alive; on the other it ruthlessly purged Republican revolutionary elements. By prolonging the conflict, Stalin hoped to trap Hitler in a war of attrition, one that would prevent a premature attack in the East. The Russians saw the Nonintervention Committee established in London as a hypocritical sham, and both Hitler and Mussolini cheerfully took advantage of its ineffectiveness. For Hitler, limited intervention meant keeping France preoccupied with the threat of a fascist state to the south, embarrassing the Russians, and keeping the international diplomatic situation unbalanced. There was also the possibility of solid economic advantage in the capture of Spain's mineral resources, and the valuable combat experience to be gained by the Condor Legion—Germany's "volunteers" who fought for Franco. Mussolini gained much less. The League of Nations' failure to cope with the Ethiopian crisis had encouraged Mussolini's tendency to use force and had made him eager to expose the decadence of the democracies. He saw Spain as a battleground in his much-vaunted crusade against Marxism, and, like Hitler, he saw the war as an opportunity for his army to gain practical experience. Italy's entry into the Spanish Civil War was designed to throw international affairs into a state of uncertainty, which the Italian leader could then exploit. It seemed an opportunity to assert ideological solidarity with a discipline of fascism, but it proved to be a huge miscalculation. Italy's large-scale intervention won little prestige, ruled out rapprochement with Britain and France, and threw Mussolini firmly into Hitler's camp.

The war itself was marked by atrocities on both sides. Anarchistic assassinations by the Republicans were matched by the insurgent Nationalists, whose Moorish troops spread terror wherever they went. The actual rising in July, 1936, soon crystallized into a physical division of Spain. The crucial issue was the siege of Madrid, which dragged on until 1939. A huge Nationalist assault was repelled by the courage and determination of Madrid's defenders (with the help of Russian arms), but Franco's better armed and better trained troops gradually conquered Republican territory. The Nationalists' greatest triumph came in February of 1939 when Catalonia fell. In that action the Nationalists were assisted by a Communist-inspired strategy to prevent arms from reaching the anarchists of the Catalan militias. In the last analysis, however, foreign arms and aid were probably the crucial factors in deciding the victory. The intensive bombing of civilians, which had already occurred in Ethiopia and would later take place in Poland, was practiced widely in Spain. The terrible climax came on April 26, 1937, when the Basque town of Guernica was

bombed by German aircraft. In the raid 1,600 unarmed, undefended civilians lost their lives.

Realizing "Mein Kampf"

The Spanish Civil War did not basically alter the major issues of European foreign policy. By 1937, Hitler was ready to switch from the restricted policy of removing the limitations of the Treaty of Versailles to the bolder course of implementing the aims outlined in his book *Mein Kampf*. The British and the French made a massive diplomatic effort to turn the tide of Hitler's ambition, but from 1936 to 1939 German aggression proceeded unchecked. During that period, Hitler kept to his shrewd policy of conquering his victims one at a time. In Austria and Czechoslovakia, for example, Nazi-inspired disruption of public life created fruitful problems for Hitler to "solve." *Anschluss* ("union") with Austria was achieved under the pretext of preventing the maltreatment of Austrian nationalists. (Hitler was able to point out that he was merely applying Wilsonian principles of national self-determination.) *Anschluss* completely changed the Central European balance of power and opened the way to further expansion, for Vienna was the traditional gateway to southeastern Europe. The German Army was at the edge of the Hungarian plain and at the threshold to the Balkans. In the north, Czechoslovakia's defenses were outflanked.

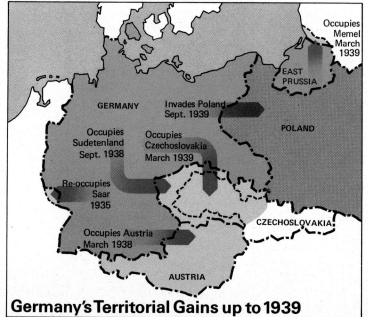

Germany's Territorial Gains up to 1939

nd warlust mount

Neville Chamberlain with Mussolini: Chamberlain thought he could influence the fascist dictators by meeting them frequently; instead he was duped by them.

The ease with which *Anschluss* was affected in Austria and the absence of protest by the democracies tempted Hitler to look next to Czechoslovakia. Created in 1919 as a democracy and an ally of France, Czechoslovakia was a hateful symbol of Versailles. Moreover, the crack Czech Army had to be eliminated before any move to the East could be made. The take-over of Czechoslovakia resembled that of Austria: the Sudetenlanders, residents of a heavily German section of eastern Czechoslovakia, began making unacceptable demands and creating unrest. Hitler was then able to intervene to "prevent civil war and the oppression of a minority."

The British Prime Minister, Neville Chamberlain, believed that conceding the Sudetenland might tempt Hitler into a negotiated settlement of other pressing issues. But Hitler played on Western fears by parading his own readiness for war, and was therefore able, in the ill-famed Munich Agreement, to persuade Chamberlain to concede German occupation of the Sudetenland. Then, believing the democracies would allow anything, Hitler took the rest of Czechoslovakia in March, 1939. It was his first miscalculation, for it forced the British to realize that Hitler could not be relied upon unless he was faced by serious threats of war.

Tension in the Orient

That realization brought war in Europe nearer—but war in the Far East was also brewing at this time, and for this Hitler was only indirectly responsible. German ambitions in Europe were matched by Japanese ambitions in the Pacific. The preoccupation of the Western powers with the threats posed by Hitler and Mussolini both encouraged and facilitated Japanese aggression, which was directed against all countries with interests in the Far East. This became clear with the Japanese invasion of Manchuria in 1931 and was further emphasized by the Amau Declaration of April, 1934, which made China a protectorate of Japan and proclaimed that Japan had the exclusive right to maintain peace and order in East Asia.

In July of 1934, Japan provoked China into open war. The Sino-Japanese conflict that followed is sometimes regarded as the first stage of World War II. Mao Tse-tung's Communists and Chiang Kai-shek's Kuomintang formed a shaky coalition to combat the Japanese onslaught. At Mao's insistence, the coalition inaugurated a policy of giving up land to gain time. The Chinese encouraged the Japanese to take more territory than they could handle, to overextend their lines of communication, and to penetrate so deeply into hostile territory that it was relatively easy for the Chinese to surround them. This design was in accord with the theory of guerrilla warfare that Mao had evolved, a theory that has been recognized as one of his most original concepts. The theory is summed up in one of Mao's famous quotations: "The enemy advances, we retreat; the enemy halts, we harass; the enemy retreats, we pursue." During the late 1930s, Mao perfected this policy and simultaneously strengthened the Communist Party by creating strong links between the Red Army and the peasants.

For a brief time, the Japanese benefited enormously from Mao's scheme. By the beginning of 1939, they had made huge advances inland and had secured most of the major coastal cities. The Japanese instituted harsh measures in an effort to break the Chinese people's will to fight, but these outrages merely served to further arouse the nation against them. (It also gained support for the Communists, who emerged as the only resolute fighters against Japan.)

Despite attacks on their Chinese holdings, the Western powers were as inept in the face of Japanese aggression as they were before Hitler. The British concession at Tientsin was blockaded; British and American shipping was attacked; and the American gunboat *Panay* was sunk. Yet all the American and British governments did was register protests. Meanwhile, the richest, most populous and most developed provinces in China fell to the Japanese, whose success served warning on the rest of the world of their determination to dominate the Pacific.

War in Europe

In Europe, Hitler was no less hesitant than the Japanese about taking what he wanted. The destruction of independent Czechoslovakia had been a great Nazi victory, for it meant that the one army in Eastern Europe that might have halted Germany's eastward advance had been eliminated. As Czechoslovakia was stripped of its fortifications, arms and munitions works, Hitler's dreams became even more ambitious.

The next step was the acquisition of the Polish Corridor. Hitler began making demands for Danzig. But the Poles, who refused, had learned the lesson of Czechoslovakia and began to prepare for war. When the Germans became more threatening, the British and the French—who had also learned a vital diplomatic lesson at Czechoslovakia's expense—pledged themselves to support the Poles. Undaunted by the Anglo-French pledge, convinced of Germany's invincibility, and enraged at the British, Hitler tore up the Anglo-German Naval Agreement

The evacuation of British troops from Dunkirk.

and the Polish Nonaggression Pact. In May of 1939, he signed the Pact of Steel with Mussolini, which emboldened him to risk war over Poland. At the same time Hitler temporarily shelved his crusade against what Nazis termed the "Jewish-Bolshevik world conspiracy" and signed a nonaggression pact with Stalin. This pact safeguarded Hitler's eastern flank.

When the Stalin-Hitler pact was announced, Britain reaffirmed her guarantees to Poland. Hitler reiterated his demands to the Poles, and when they were not met at 6:30 a.m. on September 1, 1939, Germany invaded Poland. Two days later Britain and France declared war on Germany. Poland quickly fell before Germany's Panzer divisions and the Stuka dive-bombers of the Luftwaffe, and Hitler then offered to make peace with the Western Allies. By this time, however, the Allies were demanding the restoration of Austria and Czechoslovakia as well as Poland. Hitler decided that another victory was necessary to bring the Allies to heel. Fearing an Allied move against Germany's Scandinavian ore supplies, he launched an attack on Norway and Denmark in April, 1940.

A British expedition to Norway failed disastrously and set off a parliamentary crisis that saw Chamberlain replaced by Winston Churchill. The new Prime Minister had barely taken office when the Germans swept through Holland and Belgium, and in May they expelled the British from France. The British evacuation from Dunkirk—aboard pleasure cruisers, fishing boats and anything else that floated—saved a large percentage of the expeditionary force. But the British now faced Hitler alone, for Germany controlled Europe from the Spanish border to the North Cape. The island kingdom's defiance—in the face of seemingly insurmountable odds—was summarized by Churchill: "You ask, What is our aim? I can answer in one word: Victory—Victory at all costs, victory in spite of all terror; victory, however long and hard the road may be." The cost was to be gigantic—the surrender of Britain's world preeminence, economic dependence upon the United States, and acquiescence to Russia's domination of Eastern Europe. All this was still in the future, when, in the late summer of 1940, the tide began to turn against the dictators on the Continent.

The Battle of Britain

Winston Churchill's stirring observation about the six-week air battle over Britain—"Never in the field of human conflict was so much owed by so many to so few"—was quite literally true. Great Britain, whose population numbered some 47 million in the late summer of 1940, was saved from imminent invasion by the skill and valor of slightly more than one thousand Royal Air Force pilots—one-third of whom were killed during the battle. Bucking odds that occasionally approached thirty to one, the battered RAF exacted a heavy—and increasingly telling—toll on Hitler's Luftwaffe. As the Germans' numerical superiority dwindled, so did their optimism. In early August, Air Marshal Göring had promised to smash the RAF within two weeks; by mid-September it was obvious that he had failed. England was saved.

Winston Churchill in a characteristic pose, from the portrait by Sickert.

Opposite A German pilot bales out of his Messerschmitt 109 fighter.

The Battle of Britain was fought over the English Channel and southeastern England during six weeks in August and September, 1940. The struggle waged by the British and German air forces was the most momentous air battle in world history. In previous wars, and in the Polish, Norwegian and French campaigns of World War II, military aircraft had been used like artillery—to provide close support for invading armies and to damage the enemy's communications. In the Battle of Britain, the fighting was solely in the air, and the armies and navies of both sides remained in reserve to await the outcome. The air battle was a preliminary to Hitler's planned invasion of Britain, but it was so essential that when Hitler lost it, he abandoned the invasion.

The Royal Air Force's victory did not win the war, nor was German power crippled by it. Hitler conquered the Balkans and embarked on his greatest campaign—the one against Russia—within a few months of his failure to smash England. In that sense the Battle of Britain was not decisive, like the battles of Salamis or Waterloo. But it saved Britain from defeat at the moment when defeat seemed probable. It gained time for the British to strengthen their home defenses against a renewal of the threat of invasion and to extend the war to the Atlantic and the Mediterranean, where their strategic advantages outmatched those of the Germans. It imposed a check upon unbroken German successes, and although it left Hitler still with many options, he chose the wrong one by invading Russia. Above all, the air battle preserved the British Isles as a base from which the Continent of Europe was eventually reconquered.

After the defeat of France in June, 1940, Hitler had only one enemy left: Great Britain and the Empire. He held the shores of the Atlantic and the North Sea from northern Norway to the Spanish frontier, and the Continent in depth from Brittany to central Poland. With Italy now his active ally, and with Russia, Japan, Spain and the United States in their very different ways at least neutralized,

the balance of power in his favor was overwhelming. On the European mainland only the fortress of Gibraltar remained in hostile hands. The German armed forces were elated and intact.

Although this situation had been foreseen and indeed planned, Hitler had given no thought to the strategy that should flow from it. He did not know what to do with his triumph. Nurtured on the mentality of World War I, he was nonplussed when his continental army reached the limits of the Continent. To defeat Britain by cutting its imperial communications and occupying the French provinces of North Africa was a concept alien to him. He hesitated, toying first with the idea of starving Britain into submission by unrestricted U-boat warfare and air attacks on its ports, and then, intermittently, with the idea of invading the country. He still hoped that political methods might render military methods unnecessary. Britain might be induced to make peace if its leaders were convinced of the impossibility of victory. Hitler could offer peace on terms so generous that even Churchill would find them preferable to annihilation.

The British position was not quite so hopeless as Hitler allowed himself to assume. The majority of Britain's best-trained troops had returned safely from Dunkirk and central France and were now being rapidly reequipped from reserve stores and new production. The fleet had scarcely been affected by the campaign in the West and only marginally by the Norwegian disaster, and it was still greatly superior to the German. The RAF, thanks to the difficult refusal to involve more than a small part of it in the later phases of the campaign in France, still had sixty fighter squadrons left intact. The spirits of the people, the armed forces, factory workers and the government were exhilarated by the prospect of single combat, and Churchill enhanced their optimism by expressing it so nobly. Several of the defeated allied governments had taken sanctuary in Britain and had added ships and men to British reserves. In default of a French government-in-exile, de Gaulle

The London Blitz: St. Paul's Cathedral surrounded by smoke and flame. Miraculously, the cathedral survived.

Lord Dowding, commander of Fighter Command during the Battle of Britain.

by German air superiority over it. The key to the Channel and its northern shoreline was the airspace above, and this could not be won as part of the invasion battle itself. It must be won beforehand in a preliminary contest between the air forces of each side in order to prevent British reconnaissance of German preparations, to protect the German ships and barges from air attack while still at sea and the troops when they landed, and to give German bombers every opportunity to harass British defenses and prevent the movement of British reserves.

This, in essence, was why the Battle of Britain was fought.

The Germans were convinced that they could smash the southern defenses of the RAF within one or two weeks. Air Marshal Göring had promised it. The Luftwaffe had 1,050 first-line fighters at the end of July, and some 500 in reserve; the RAF (having lost 430 aircraft during the fighting in France) had 625 in the first line and 230 in reserve. Because the Germans could bomb any part of Great Britain from their long continental coastline, Air Chief Marshal Sir Hugh Dowding, Commander in Chief of RAF Fighter Command, could not concentrate all his squadrons on the most vulnerable sector in the southeast; he was obliged to hold back half his force to defend the factories of the Midlands and the north against a threat that never materialized.

Thus the superior strength of the Luftwaffe was magnified by its possession of the initiative. The Germans could mass their squadrons against any point they chose, and London, the largest and most vulnerable target of all, lay within their fighter range. Against all this the British held certain advantages. They were fighting over their own country and nearby coastal waters, and their pilots would at least be safe from capture if shot down. They had, in the Spitfire and the Hurricane, two fighter planes that were superior in turning speed—but not in height ceiling—to the German Messerschmitt 109. They had a chain of radar stations that could give them adequate warning of the size, direction and height of approaching raids in time to send up home squadrons to meet the German planes on more level terms. Still, the RAF was outnumbered by two to one generally, and by as much as thirty to one in individual engagements, and their enemies had the advantages of concentration and surprise. The struggle could be won by the RAF only if British pilots could shoot down at least three German planes for every two they lost themselves; if the production of new aircraft could keep pace with British losses; if fresh pilots could be trained in time to take the place of the dead and wounded; and if the enemy made errors of strategy that would ease the strain.

All these things occurred. The greatest cause for anxiety on the British side was the problem of pilot replacement. Other commands were skimmed of young pilots to fill the gaps in Fighter Command. As the novices began to fill the cockpits of the veterans, the quality—although not the mettle—of the fighter pilots inevitably declined. The Germans had no equivalent worries, having started with

rallied to his illegal standard thousands of young Frenchmen. The untouched Empire and the Mediterranean bases still existed. Britain could survive on 60 per cent of its prewar imports, and Germany could neither stop them at their sources nor seriously interfere with their passage.

By such arguments the British reached the conclusion that surrender was not only unthinkable but unnecessary. They could survive. But how could they win? Their answer was a little more tentative: by the counterblockade of Germany; by air bombing; by the revolt of the European peoples under German occupation. Nobody spoke yet of the liberation of Europe by invasion. But in the closing words of Churchill's great speech of June 4, 1940, the significance of which was obscured by their splendor, he pointed to the ultimate, the only real solution: "... until in God's good time the new world with all its power and might steps forth to the rescue and liberation of the old."

The United States did what it could to help England "by all steps short of war," but Britain had to face the immediate dangers alone. Both Britain and Germany soon reached the same conclusion— the British in June, the Germans in July—that the war could be ended in 1940 only by a successful invasion of England; that invasion would have no chance of success unless Germany could put ashore some thirty well-equipped divisions; and that such an operation was impossible unless British naval superiority in the English Channel could be matched

Surrender: unthinkable and unnecessary

merchant shipping. The Germans had sunk 30,000 tons, but the proportion of their losses to British aircraft shot down foreshadowed later averages: at least 286 German aircraft were destroyed, while only 148 British planes were lost.

In mid-August the main attack began with an assault on the radar installations and southern airfields of Fighter Command. This was clearly the right tactic for the Luftwaffe. By sending over large bomber fleets escorted by clouds of fighters, Göring hoped to draw the defenders into the air and defeat them by attrition (while simultaneously making further resistance impossible by destroying RAF bases and the warning system). Two things went wrong with this plan. First, German losses of both fighters and bombers rapidly whittled down the numerical superiority with which they had started. Secondly, German pilots failed to press home their initial advantage and abandoned too soon the tactics by which they might have won. They attached so little importance to the radar system that although five stations were temporarily damaged and one (in the Isle of Wight) was destroyed, the system was allowed to continue to operate efficiently throughout the air battle. Similarly, in early September, at the critical moment when five forward airfields and six of the seven sector stations had suffered extensive damage, Göring switched his main effort further inland to attack factories and oil installations. "Had the enemy continued his heavy attacks on the airfields," wrote Air Vice-Marshal K. R. Park, who was in command of the southeastern group of Fighter Command, "the fighter defenses of London would have been put in a perilous state."

This was the turning point. Göring was persuaded to divert the Luftwaffe to the outskirts of London by the optimistic reports of his pilots that the RAF was on the verge of collapse. At the same time, Hitler was sufficiently stung by the British bombing of Berlin to insist that the Luftwaffe retaliate on London. On September 7, the day on which the British prematurely issued the codeword Cromwell to warn that invasion was imminent, three hundred German bombers escorted by six hundred fighters attacked the docks and oil depots on the lower Thames. On the fifteenth, the day still celebrated as Battle of Britain Day, German bombers attacked London itself, losing sixty aircraft to twenty-six British. As

A radar tower on the south coast of England. Stations like this one enabled RAF planes to get airborne in time to intercept the Luftwaffe.

Left German Dornier bombers over the East End of London at the height of the Blitz.

Spitfire pilots run to their planes—a common event during the Battle of Britain.

greater reserves and having recovered from captivity the four hundred pilots shot down during the battle for France. The loss rate of fighter aircraft was also of critical concern to the British. Their losses so greatly exceeded replacements during the crux of the air battle (from August 24 to September 6) that, in the words of the Air Ministry's report, "in three weeks more of activity on the same scale, the fighter reserves would have been completely exhausted." But from September 7 on, the losses fell below the output of new machines, and at the end of the air battle the reserves were in fact greater than at the beginning.

By German reckoning the air battle proper began on August 7. During the preceding month the Luftwaffe had carried out a series of test raids on Channel

Messerschmitt 109s flying up the English Channel past the White Cliffs of Dover.

A Supermarine Spitfire. These fighters were clearly superior to their Luftwaffe opponents.

soon as the Luftwaffe turned against London, RAF Fighter Command, which had been perceptibly weakening, began to recover strength. Pressure was taken off the vital sector stations. (Because the strength of the British defenses made daylight raids too costly, much of the German bombing was by night, when at that stage of the war the fighter aircraft had almost no role to play.)

In mid-September the Germans admitted to themselves that the attack had failed. The RAF was as active as ever. Civilian morale was unaffected by the bombing. The British still dominated the Channel by sea and continued to fight in the air. The weather was beginning to worsen. On September 14, Admiral Erich Raeder advised Hitler that "the present air situation does not provide conditions for carrying out the invasion, as the risk is still too great." Hitler agreed. On the nineteenth he postponed the invasion, and on the twenty-third he gave orders for the dispersal of the invasion fleet. The British and German armies were allowed to believe that the plan might be revived in the spring of 1941, but Hitler himself had very different ideas. He was already preparing to switch the weight of his attack against the Soviet Union.

In retrospect, the British air victory can be attributed to four factors. First, in the mid-1930s the British had had the foresight to design and construct a fleet of superb fighter aircraft and to exploit the discovery of radar. They had kept their fleet intact by denying the French the twenty fighter squadrons that could have made little difference to the battle in France after it had passed the point of no recovery, but that were enough to decide the issue in Britain two months later.

Second, Churchill knew that he could count on high civilian morale. He could take for granted his countrymen's support when he rejected Hitler's offer of peace. He was confident that they would endure air attack by day and night. He and Lord Beaverbrook, the Minister for Aircraft Production, could demand from the aircraft factories unparalleled efforts to replace the broken weapons of air defense.

Third, the Germans failed to appreciate the effort needed to knock out a well-trained and scientifically superior defense, or to allow for its recuperative powers.

Finally—and this will be remembered when the details of the air battle are forgotten—the spirit of dedication, adventurousness and rivalry among the fighter pilots of both sides stimulated them to deeds of unexampled valor. The difference was that Dowding's men were fighting for survival, while Göring's were fighting to finish a war that they considered already won. During the air struggle, 414 British and Allied pilots were killed. That seems a small number for so great a victory. But it was a high proportion—about one-third of those engaged. It was this very slenderness of the fighting force, added to the greatness of the issue, that has given the Battle of Britain the quality of a crusade. "Never in the field of human conflict was so much owed by so many to so few." Churchill's famous words were spoken on August 20, before the air battle had reached its climax. They were a prophesy, but they lived to become a verdict.

How much, in fact, was owed to these men? Perhaps it is best summed up by Churchill's remark to de Gaulle in August of that year: "Sooner or later the Americans will come in, but on condition that we here won't flinch. That's why I can't think of anything but the fighter air force." What was at stake was the only base from which a counterattack on Germany could one day be launched. No one will ever know whether the invasion of Britain would have succeeded, or would even have been attempted, if the RAF had been defeated. The British Navy and Army might have succeeded if the Air Force had failed. For the Germans it would still have been a very perilous operation. They would

A victory for civilian morale

have been obliged to organize and protect a sea crossing for an initial force of more than twenty divisions, and would afterwards have had to maintain them in face of an undefeated navy.

But while invasion would still have been a gamble, it is probable that Hitler would have risked it if the Luftwaffe had won the first round. In 1945 Field Marshal Karl Rudolf von Runstedt, who was to command the expedition, told his interrogators: "We looked on the invasion as a sort of game." At the time, however, it was not a game to the Luftwaffe, nor to Hitler. Otherwise he would never have retrained and deployed so great an army on the French coast, nor damaged the economy of Europe by withdrawing from its ports and canals so great an armada of shipping and barges, nor foregone adventures elsewhere when his fortunes were at their peak. From what historians have discovered about his secret intentions, he thought of the attack on Russia as an alternative, not a substitute, for the decisive struggle with Britain. Although victory in the air would certainly have led to the continuance of the war with Britain as a first priority, Hitler would first have considered the use of his bomber force alone. The bomber, not the fighter, was the true instrument of air power. The cities of England would have been defenseless if Fighter Command had failed; the ports would have been unusable, the factories wrecked. How long could the British people have withstood the barrage?

The air battle saved Britain from invasion or unendurable air attack. It probably saved the nation from defeat. It provided the British people with clear proof that defiance had not been foolhardy. It created in the free world—and above all in the United States—a wave of admiration and hope that resulted in immediate practical help (such as the arming of the Home Guard with American rifles and the exchange of fifty American destroyers for British bases in the Western Atlantic). The United States could not enter the war unless Germany or its allies challenged a vital American interest. But after the Battle of Britain, the British became for the United States what France had been to Britain, with the difference that Britain was undefeated. The longer the British kept their islands intact, the more honorable and viable seemed their cause, the more essential their survival. The United States did not enter the war to save Britain. But Britain was the United States' base in Europe and became its closest ally. The defeat of Germany assumed in President Franklin Roosevelt's mind equal importance with the defeat of Japan. None of this would have happened if Britain had been defeated in the summer of 1940. By far the greater part of the American war effort would have been deployed in the Far East, and Russia might have overrun the whole of Europe and much of the Middle East and North Africa. Speculation on what might have been is unprofitable beyond a certain point, but it is legitimate to call the Battle of Britain a milestone not only of World War II, but of the history of the entire century and the entire world.   NIGEL NICOLSON

A German ground crew rearms a Messerschmitt before sending it back into the battle.

A reconstructed Luftwaffe fighter base.

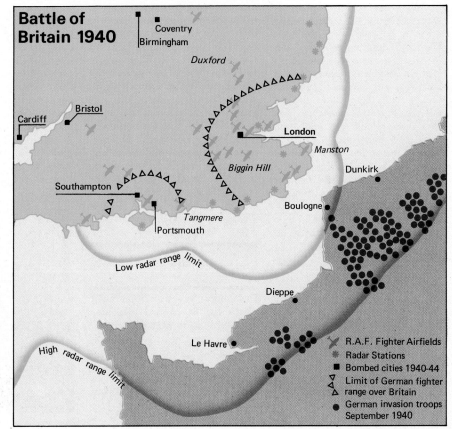

Battle of Britain 1940

Coventry
Birmingham
Duxford
Bristol
Cardiff
London
Manston
Biggin Hill
Dunkirk
Southampton
Boulogne
Tangmere
Portsmouth
Low radar range limit
Dieppe
High radar range limit
Le Havre

✕ R.A.F. Fighter Airfields
✳ Radar Stations
■ Bombed cities 1940-44
▽ Limit of German fighter
△ range over Britain
● German invasion troops
September 1940

The Battle of Britain ensured that military conquest of English soil would not be the means whereby the Germans ended the British challenge to their domination of Europe. But a war of vast proportions remained to be fought. For the moment, Britain and Germany were the only protagonists, and this was one of Germany's greatest assets. Germany, which had yet to reach its full economic potential, could draw on the resources of conquered Europe and of neutral states such as Sweden, Switzerland and Russia. Britain, on the other hand, had to rely upon the limited assistance of the governments-in-exile of the defeated European powers and the resources of its Empire. And at the time, that Empire was facing grave military and political problems: India was on the verge of open rebellion and, in the Middle East, Palestine was proving a liability. Britain's colonial forces were meager; the best was the Indian Army, but it was better equipped for police action against tribesmen than for modern warfare. Elsewhere the British Empire was undermanned and underequipped.

The British, however, chose to fight on. They could have accepted generous surrender terms from Hitler by acquiescing to German domination of Europe. But the British would not surrender, regardless of cost. The price would have to be paid after the war. Without consulting the Indians, the British colonial leadership brought India into the conflict merely by announcing that war had broken out. The leaders of the Congress Party described this action as a disgrace and a humiliation. They were prepared to fight Hitler but felt they should first be given power, so they might then fight as Britain's independent ally. In order to avoid opposition in India—opposition they could ill-afford—the British were obliged to promise self-government to India immediately after the war.

Another price paid was the handing of world economic domination to the United States in return for aid against the Germans. The British were able to buy goods from America, but it cost them their dollar reserves, salable stock and securities. Moreover, since American industry was not equipped for war, much of the first British money spent went into building and tooling factories. This facilitated American rearmament, but hardly helped Britain in the short term.

Stalemate in Europe

For a time Britain had to proceed alone. Because the British were in no position to invade the European mainland, and because the Germans had failed to invade Britain, both sides settled on a war of attrition that was carried out by mutual blockade and strategic bombing. The use of bombers was one of the characteristic features of the military history of the war, but

The bombed interior of the House of Commons.

its utility at the time seems to have been exaggerated. Both sides justified the use of saturation bombing by describing their raids as logical means of retaliating against the air strikes of the other. The effect of those raids was to devastate cities, but it did not significantly affect war production or civilian morale. Indeed, bombing merely cemented national unity. In 1940 Churchill said: "There is one thing that will bring Hitler down and that is an absolutely devastating, exterminating attack by very heavy bombers on the Nazi homeland." Certainly, civilians on both sides were made to feel the weight of the war, but one result of the bombing was to dissolve the hostility between civilians and fighting men that had been a feature of World War 1.

Success in Africa

In addition to safeguarding their island, the British had to deploy forces abroad to protect the Empire. By August of 1940, the Italians had captured British Somaliland and had swept sixty miles into Egypt to Sidi Barrâni, thus making the Mediterranean an important British war zone. Strategists were anxious to protect the route to India—a concern for empire

endorsed by Churchill, who declared: "I have not become the First Minister of the Crown in order to preside over the liquidation of the British Empire." While defending their West African possessions, the British were able to score an important victory: in November, 1940, a British air attack destroyed half of the Italian fleet in the harbor of Taranto. And in December, General Archibald Wavell began his desert offensive. He drove the Italians back to Tobruk by January, and to Benghazi by February. This British success, coupled with British resistance to Mussolini's attack on Greece, forced the Germans to come to the Italians' aid in the Mediterranean and the Balkans, and showed Hitler that his alliance with Italy was more of a liability than an asset.

In February, 1941, the brilliant German General Erwin Rommel arrived in Africa. At the time, British lines were overextended, and Rommel's crack Afrika Korps succeeded in driving Wavell's forces back into Egypt within a fortnight. In April, the Nazis began their Balkan blitzkrieg, racing through Yugoslavia and Greece. Things looked black for the British. U-boat attacks were taking a heavy toll on shipping, and financial reserves were running low. But the situation was not as bleak as it seemed, for Hitler's new commitments had overextended German lines and stretched German reserves. Moreover, America was beginning to realize that its own security depended upon British survival. This insight had been prompted by a pact signed by Germany, Italy and Japan in September, 1940. In this pact Japan recognized the new order in Europe, and the Axis Powers recognized the new order in Asia.

"Co-prosperity" in the Orient

Japan's projected "new order in Asia" ran contrary to the basic tenets of American foreign policy. The defeat of France and Holland in Europe had left French Indochina and the Dutch East Indies open to Japanese infiltration and eventual conquest. The Japanese hoped to create the Greater East Asia Co-prosperity Sphere, an empire comprising Indochina, Burma, Malaya, Borneo, Thailand and the Dutch East Indies—and, ultimately, Australia, New Zealand and India. Hitler and Mussolini thought that by supporting Japanese designs on Europe's Asiatic colonies, they could successfully deter the United States from giving further aid to Britain. Instead, Anglo-American cooperation increased during this period. In January of 1941, in response to a plea from Churchill, President Franklin D. Roosevelt asked Congress to allow him to send war materials and supplies to Great Britain. Payment for those supplies was to be made in goods and services after the war rather than in cash during the war. Roosevelt's program developed into the Lend-Lease scheme of March, 1941, when Britain began receiving overage U.S. destroyers in exchange for ninety-nine year leases on British bases in the Atlantic.

Barbarossa!

Unable to defeat Britain immediately, Hitler decided to fulfill his dream of crushing what he called the "Jewish-Bolshevik world conspiracy." *Lebensraum* ("living space") for the German master race, the destruction of the "inferior" Slavic race, and the wealth

A U.S. destroyer blows up during the Japanese attack on Pearl Harbor in 1941.

Japanese troops during the invasion of Malaya.

of the Ukraine had all tempted Hitler for some time. (His decision to move against the "conspiracy" had actually been made in 1940, but it had been delayed by the Balkan and Mediterranean campaigns.) In June of 1941, confident that Russia was militarily and politically weak and would quickly disintegrate, Hitler launched a new blitzkrieg: a force of over 3 million poured into Russia as part of Operation Barbarossa. Such an expedition had been a disaster for Napoleon; it was to prove the same for Hitler. Russia's great weapons—the fierce winter, the vast spaces and the huge resources of manpower—were soon to decimate Germany's military might. Meanwhile, the pressure was off Britain, which quickly extended its friendship to Russia. Churchill swallowed his hatred of Bolshevism and declared: "The Russian danger is our danger and that of the United States." As he put it: "If Hitler invaded Hell, I would make at least a favorable reference to the Devil in the House of Commons."

The German Army quickly penetrated deep into Russia, taking thousands of prisoners. The attack was divided into three parts: one thrust to Leningrad, one to Moscow and one to Kiev. The Russians were surprised along a 1,200-mile front, and their poorly trained, poorly equipped and poorly deployed forces were soon overwhelmed. But the technique of blitzkrieg was misplaced in Russia, a vast country that could not be knocked out by a single blow. Despite this, the Germans almost achieved their goal. In fact, a month after the attack Hitler was thinking of demobilizing his troops. But the Germans did not have the strength to take all three of their objectives and, although they did reach the suburbs of Moscow, they were then driven back by Marshal Georgi Zhukov's troops. Soon the

German Army of 3 million was tied down by bitter winter conditions and the Russians were preparing a massive counteroffensive.

Day of infamy

Hitler's attack on Russia had increased the strain on his own resources and had extended the scope of the conflict. A similar situation was about to develop in the Far East, where the Japanese were pursuing an increasingly aggressive foreign policy. In July of 1941, they had entered Indochina, thereby menacing Malaya, the Dutch East Indies and the Philippines. The Americans, British and Dutch retaliated by freezing Japanese assets, closing the Panama Canal to the Japanese, and placing an embargo on oil, rubber, tin and other strategic raw materials essential to Japan. To a certain extent, this forced Japan's hand, since without these materials the Japanese would either have to capitulate or seize the areas that could supply their needs. Japan decided to strike while it still had supplies of war materials. On the morning of December 7, 1941, Japanese carrier-based planes attacked Pearl Harbor, the huge American naval base in Hawaii, and destroyed half the American fleet. It was a heavy blow, both physically and psychologically, and it brought an outraged and united America into the war. Hitler, who

felt that U.S. aid to Britain already constituted war and was afraid lest Roosevelt beat him to the punch, tied the Atlantic and Pacific theaters together by declaring war against America first.

The situation for Britain became much more hopeful. Hitler's two mistakes—invading Russia and declaring war on America—had brought into being an Anglo-American-Soviet alliance of herculean strength. Victory was now inevitable, although disasters remained to be faced.

Surrender in Singapore

On the day after Pearl Harbor, the Japanese invaded Malaya, smashing the complacent British, who had placed their hopes on the inadequate defenses of Singapore. There had been no civil defense preparations in the event of an air strike, and Japanese bombers were able to attack a brightly lit harbor. Churchill sent two of the British Navy's most powerful ships, the battleship *Prince of Wales* and the battlecruiser *Repulse*, to aid the colony. Both were sunk by Japanese aircraft in the Strait of Malacca on December 10. This incident sealed the fate of Malaya and shattered the prestige of the Royal Navy. With the U.S. Navy also crippled, the Japanese were free to fall on the British, Dutch and American possessions in the area. Hong Kong fell on Christmas Day, 1941; Manila fell one week later; and on January 12, 1942, attacks were launched against the Dutch East Indies. The British attempted to hold Singapore as a foothold in the Far East, but the city, which was prepared only for a sea attack, quickly capitulated to the Japanese troops who had hacked their way through the jungle and attacked from the rear. The surrender of Singapore on February 15 was one of the biggest defeats ever suffered by the British Empire. In March, the Dutch East Indies were taken.

General Percival, the British commander at Singapore, on his way to surrender Singapore to the Japanese on February 15, 1942.

Defeating the Desert Fox

Depressed by Far Eastern defeats, the British could only view with alarm the situation in North Africa. There, in May of 1942, Rommel's desert offensive had carried the Germans perilously close to Cairo. The victory would prove a costly one for the "Desert Fox," because General Bernard Montgomery, the commander of the British Eighth Army, realized that Rommel's lines of communication were too long and that it would now be possible to defeat him. He waited until October, slowly building up his forces, and then attacked the German forces at El Alamein to win the first decisive British victory of the

General Erwin Rommel, commander of the German Army in Africa.

war. The week-long struggle at El Alamein eliminated the danger to the Suez Canal and enabled the British to launch a counterattack. By November, Rommel's Afrika Korps was in retreat.

Triumph in the Pacific

As Rommel was plotting his assault on Cairo and Suez, the Japanese High Command was planning a second Pearl Harbor in the Pacific. That air strike, against the U.S. fleet's only mid-Pacific base, was designed to eliminate the remnants of the U.S. Navy and remove the last obstacle to an invasion of Australia. To achieve its goal, the Imperial Japanese Navy assembled the largest armada the world had ever seen and sent it steaming toward Midway Island. The ensuing sea battle was the turning point in the Pacific war.

Midway to Victory 1942

On December 7, 1941, carrier-based Japanese airplanes attacked the U.S. naval base at Pearl Harbor and destroyed fully half the American fleet. President Roosevelt labeled December 7 "a date which will live in infamy" and called for a declaration of war against the Axis Powers, but even as he did so the Imperial Japanese Navy began to prepare a second massive strike against the Pacific Fleet. Unbeknown to the High Command, an extraordinary code-breaking coup had enabled American intelligence units to "read" the Japanese Navy's top-secret communiqués. As Admiral Yamamoto's Carrier Striking Force—the largest such armada the world had ever seen— steamed toward Midway Island, the Americans closed in. This time the element of surprise was on their side, and in the ensuing battle Yamamoto's fleet was decimated and Japan's supremacy in the Pacific was ended. As Chester A. Nimitz, commander of the Pacific Fleet, observed, the U.S. Navy was "midway" to victory in the Pacific.

The Japanese Imperial High Command was infected, during the first half of 1942, with what several of its members characterized in postwar interviews as "victory disease." None of history's major empires were acquired with such ease and speed. Between 1940 and 1942, the myriad peoples of most of the Far East and the Western Pacific became subjects of what Tokyo termed the Greater East Asia Co-Prosperity Sphere. The chief symptom of victory disease, according to its victims, was an arrogant assumption that whatever next step might be selected, victory was assured.

Early in 1942, some members of the Imperial High Command proposed an offensive against India and Ceylon. Others backed the strategy of isolating Australia—cutting its lifeline to the United States by seizing Fiji, New Caledonia, and Samoa. Admiral Isoroku Yamamoto, Commander in Chief of the Imperial Japanese Navy, was of a different mind.

Yamamoto, who had studied at Harvard and served as naval attaché in Washington, had an abiding respect for America's industrial might. He argued that Japan's chances of consolidating its newly won empire depended upon an immediate naval victory over the United States—a victory of Pearl Harbor proportions—followed by a negotiated peace with Washington.

Yamamoto's hand was strengthened by the surprise Doolittle-Halsey raid on April 18, 1942, which caused little damage to Tokyo and other Japanese cities but severely damaged Japanese pride. Three weeks later, the Battle of the Coral Sea—the first naval action fought entirely by carrier aircraft, with the combatant ships never once sighting each other —proved that the U.S. Pacific Fleet was a dangerous foe, and Yamamoto's plan for a decisive naval engagement proceeded without further debate.

His timetable called for the great battle to take place early in June, almost exactly six months after Pearl Harbor. Yamamoto's objective was to smoke

out the American fleet by threatening its one remaining important Pacific base, the Hawaiian Islands.

Operation MI, as it was designated, involved a primary objective, a diversionary thrust and four major striking forces. Yamamoto assembled the mightiest armada the world had ever seen: 162 major craft, including 8 aircraft carriers, 11 battleships, 22 cruisers, 67 destroyers, and 21 submarines. The diversion was aimed at the Aleutian Islands, which extend southwest from Alaska. The primary objective, involving the bulk of the Japanese Combined Fleet, was Midway Island, the westernmost outpost of the Hawaiian chain.

The core of the Midway Operation was Vice-Admiral Chuichi Nagumo's Carrier Striking Force —fleet carriers *Akagi*, *Kaga*, *Hiryu* and *Soryu*. All were veterans of Nagumo's Pearl Harbor attack. Backing up Nagumo was Yamamoto's Main Body, a powerful surface force that included seven battleships. Finally, there was the Occupation Force, a heavily escorted transport group that intended to seize Midway.

Yamamoto assumed that the Americans would be as surprised by Operation MI as they had been by the Pearl Harbor attack; that they would react instinctively and steam into one of the traps he was baiting at Midway and off the Aleutians; that whatever course the Americans chose, their movements would be shadowed and reported by a picket line of Japanese submarines stationed off Pearl Harbor. Every contingency was covered—as long as the Americans reacted as they were expected to react.

Quite unknown to Yamamoto, Admiral Chester W. Nimitz, commander of the U.S. Pacific Fleet at Pearl Harbor, was the beneficiary of a remarkable code-breaking achievement by the Navy's Combat Intelligence Unit. The "black chamber" cryptanalysis operations had established that Midway was the objective of the Japanese Combined Fleet, had

Admiral Isoroku Yamamoto, Commander in Chief of the Imperial Japanese Navy.

Opposite An American gun crew closing the breach of a 16-inch gun, from a painting by Lieutenant Commander Dwight C. Shepler.

Midway: a victory for cryptography

The Battle of Midway June 4-5, 1942

At 04:30 Japanese bombers and fighters launched from 1 Carrier Striking Force to attack Midway inflicting heavy damage. Return attack by Midway-based bombers on Japanese carriers proves costly and ineffective.

At 10:25 thirty-five dive-bombers from Task Forces 16 and 17 attack *Akagi, Soryu* and *Kaga*, and cripple them. A second strike, launched by Japanese dive-bombers at 14:35 on *Yorktown*, destroys her.

Shortly after 17:00, dive-bombers from Task Force 16 attack *Hiryu* and cripple the carrier. The shattered *Yorktown* is protected by a screening force.

Apart from *Mikuma* of the Cruiser Division which was attacked by Midway-based bombers, 1 Carrier Striking Force was the only part of the Japanese fleet which took part in the action. Yamamoto's Main Body cruised hundreds of miles away from the carriers, thus depriving them of any aid.

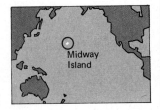

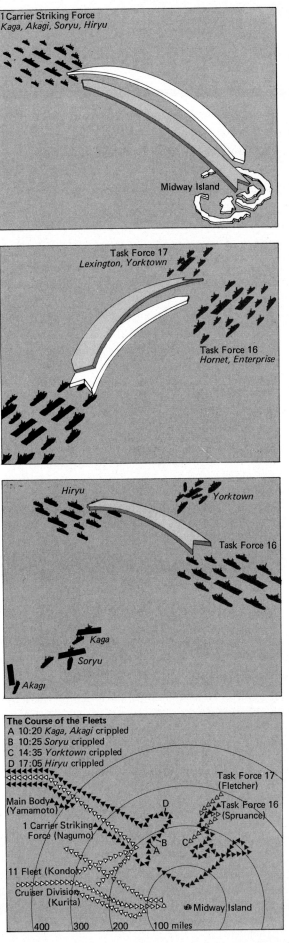

1 Carrier Striking Force
Kaga, Akagi, Soryu, Hiryu

Midway Island

Task Force 17
Lexington, Yorktown

Task Force 16
Hornet, Enterprise

Hiryu

Yorktown

Task Force 16

Kaga

Soryu

Akagi

The Course of the Fleets
A 10:20 *Kaga, Akagi* crippled
B 10:25 *Soryu* crippled
C 14:35 *Yorktown* crippled
D 17:05 *Hiryu* crippled

Main Body
(Yamamoto)

Task Force 17
(Fletcher)

D

Task Force 16
(Spruance)

1 Carrier Striking
Force (Nagumo)

B   C

A

11 Fleet (Kondo)

Cruiser Division
(Kurita)

Midway Island

400   300   200   100 miles

worked out in precise detail its composition, and had calculated its timetable with amazing accuracy.

Fleet carriers *Hornet* and *Enterprise* were recalled from the South Pacific, armed and fueled at Pearl Harbor, and dispatched toward Midway. The *Yorktown*, which had suffered severe internal damage from an aerial bomb in the Coral Sea action, was patched together by the prodigious efforts of Pearl Harbor's dockyard workers and sent off to join her two sister carriers.

By the afternoon of June 2, the U.S. battle fleet was on station well to the north of Midway. Task Force 17, composed of *Yorktown* and a cruiser-destroyer escort, was commanded by Rear Admiral Frank Jack Fletcher. Task Force 16, consisting of *Hornet* and *Enterprise* and their escorts, was under Rear Admiral Raymond A. Spruance. Fletcher, who had fought the Battle of the Coral Sea, was in tactical command. The combined strength of the two task forces was just 25 fighting vessels and 233 aircraft. Nimitz' strategy was to maintain the edge his intelligence officers had given him by secreting his forces until the last possible moment, relying on aircraft from Midway to locate the enemy. Nagumo's Carrier Striking Force was designated as the primary American target.

These rapid preliminary moves effectively canceled Yamamoto's contingency insurance. The picket line of Japanese submarines took position off the Hawaiian chain a full day too late to detect that Fletcher and Spruance had slipped out of Pearl Harbor. As the various elements of the Combined Fleet converged on Midway, the Japanese were blissfully unaware that the foe was reacting contrary to all their predictions.

Yamamoto's battle plan commenced precisely on schedule at dawn on June 3, 1942. The Aleutian strike force raided installations at Dutch Harbor and readied amphibious forces to seize the islands of Attu and Kiska at the tip of the Aleutian chain. Nimitz held Task Forces 16 and 17 on station, ignoring the gambit. The Occupation Force steamed along slowly, seven hundred miles west of Midway, marking time until the sea battle was decided. Angling in from the northwest was Nagumo's Carrier Striking Force, twenty-four hours' steaming time from the launching point for an air strike on the island. Some three hundred miles astern of Nagumo was Yamamoto's Main Body, waiting in the wings for the opportunity to draw the American fleet within range of its great naval rifles.

In midmorning on June 3, a Midway-based Catalina flying boat radioed that it had sighted Japanese ships due west of the island. Nimitz surmised that this was the Occupation Force: game far too small on which to waste his precious advantage of surprise.

The following morning, before dawn, eleven Catalinas lumbered off the Midway lagoon. *Yorktown* also launched a dawn search, but to the north, as a precaution. Everything pointed to the Carrier Striking Force's being to the northwest of Midway, and it was up to the Cats to locate it. At about the same time, Admiral Nagumo dispatched a 108-plane strike toward Midway. Almost as an afterthought, he ordered his cruisers to catapult seven float planes for a search to the north.

The early morning hours passed with agonizing slowness aboard the three American carriers. At 5:45 A.M. a message was intercepted from one of the Catalinas reporting "many enemy planes heading Midway." The tension increased. Then, eighteen minutes later, the key message came: the Carrier Striking Force had been sighted and tracked. The Cats had done their job. Spruance's Task Force 16 drove hard at twenty-five knots on a southwesterly course to bring its planes within range. After recovering *Yorktown*'s search planes, Fletcher followed.

At Midway, every plane that could fly was sent aloft, either to defend the island or to attack the enemy fleet. At 6:30 A.M. Midway came under heavy attack. Although the enemy bombers wrecked most of Midway's installations, they failed to crater the airfield enough to knock it out. The Japanese flight commander radioed Nagumo that a second strike would be required to neutralize Midway before any landing could be attempted.

At this point—it was now 7:15 A.M.—Nagumo made the first in a series of crucial decisions. He had prudently held back a one-hundred-plane reserve force in case any American ships were sighted. He now ordered those planes rearmed with fragmentation and incendiary bombs for a second strike.

Only a few minutes before, some 175 miles to the northeast, Raymond Spruance too had made a crucial decision. It was calculated that the Japanese carriers could be caught at an exceedingly vulnerable moment—rearming and refueling the returned Midway attack force—if Task Force 16 launched its planes immediately. Yet the range was still too great to assure the safe return of the relatively "short-legged" American fighters and bombers.

Spruance did not hesitate. He all but emptied *Enterprise* and *Hornet*, gambling everything on one single, massive surprise strike. Fletcher launched a partial strike force from *Yorktown*, keeping back a half deck-load of dive bombers and fighters for contingencies.

The Japanese Admiral, meanwhile, was undergoing increasing mental pressure. An uncoordinated but gallant series of attacks by Midway's airmen was forcing the Carrier Striking Force into radical defensive maneuvers, but only a handful survived the vicious Zeros and the antiaircraft fire.

In the midst of these attacks, one of the Japanese float planes launched earlier radioed a vague sighting: enemy ships to the northeast. Shortly after 8 A.M. the cruiser *Tone*'s search plane amplified the sighting by identifying one of the ships as a carrier. Nagumo hesitated. Contrary to all predictions, American ships had somehow slipped into the battle zone. Nagumo finally ordered the planes of his reserve force to be rearmed with torpedoes and armor-piercing bombs in anticipation of a naval action.

By this time, however, Nagumo's Midway strike force had returned, low on fuel and impatient to land. The Japanese Admiral was faced with yet another decision. He had thirty-odd dive bombers and torpedo planes on his decks, all properly armed for an immediate attack on the American ships. But his combat air patrol was too low on fuel to provide them with a fighter escort. With the harassing attacks

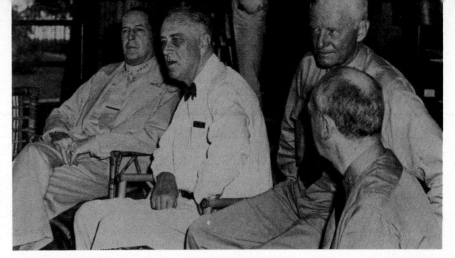

President Roosevelt (center), with General MacArthur (left), Admiral Chester Nimitz, and Admiral William Leahy (right) planning the final drive to liberate the Philippines.

Above The Mitsubishi Type O fighter—known as the Zero—used by the Japanese Navy in its attack on Midway.

Left A close-up of the Japanese cruiser *Mogame*, showing its superstructure wrecked and burning after an attack by U.S. planes during the Battle of Midway.

U.S. aircraft carrier *Yorktown* receiving a direct hit from a Japanese plane. While being towed to Pearl Harbor after the battle, the *Yorktown* was torpedoed and sunk by Japanese submarines.

An artist's impression of the Battle of Midway shows the Japanese carrier *Kaga* being attacked by U.S. Dauntlesses.

from Midway driven off at last, Nagumo made his decision: he ordered the reserve force transferred below decks in order to take aboard the Midway strike force. Once all his aircraft were rearmed and refueled, he would launch a balanced, fully equipped attack on the U.S. carrier that the *Tone*'s scout plane had sighted. As a precaution, he ordered a 90° course change, veering northeast—away from Midway and toward the American Task Force. Nagumo needed an hour's grace to prepare his new attack, and he anticipated that his course change would throw off any further enemy attacks.

Due to scattered clouds and haze—and the need to economize on fuel—the American squadrons had become badly scattered after taking off from their carriers. When they arrived over the expected intercept point one by one, they found nothing. The leader of *Hornet*'s dive bomber and fighter squadrons, assuming that the Japanese had held course but increased speed, turned toward Midway—and flew right out of the battle. The leaders of the other squadrons surmised that the Japanese had changed course and began to search to the northeast.

The first to sight the elusive Carrier Striking Force was the *Hornet*'s remaining squadron—Torpedo 8's fifteen Devastators. Even though he had no fighter escort, Lieutenant Commander John Waldron ordered an immediate attack. The lumbering, obsolete Devastators never had a chance. Patrolling Zeros shot down every one of Waldron's planes before they could get close enough for effective torpedo runs. One man survived.

Waldron's attack was made about 9:30 A.M. In the next forty-five minutes the torpedo squadrons from *Enterprise* and *Yorktown* tried their luck. None of their torpedoes found a target, and twenty more Devastators went cartwheeling into the sea. Free of attack once more, arming and refueling of their planes completed, *Akagi*, *Kaga*, *Hiryu* and *Soryu* turned into the wind to begin launching planes. By this time it was 10:20 A.M.

At that precise moment, Admiral Nagumo could not be blamed for feeling a surge of confidence. Despite more than three hours of intermittent attacks—eight of them in all—not one of his vessels had been even slightly damaged. Midway had been hit hard and nearly seventy U.S. planes had been shot down. He was about to hurl an overwhelming force against the American fleet—which was the objective of the whole massive operation.

But Nagumo's moment of confidence was brief. Some 14,000 feet above the Carrier Striking Force, the pilots and gunners of the dive-bomber squadrons from *Enterprise* and *Yorktown* were staring in frank amazement at the sight below. "This was the culmination of our hopes and dreams," recalled an *Enterprise* pilot.

As the Dauntless pilots carefully lined up their targets and rolled over into their dives, not a single Japanese fighter challenged them. Every Zero of the combat air patrol was far below, fresh from the slaughter of the U.S. torpedo bombers. Lacking radar, the first warning—the only warning—of impending doom for the men aboard the Japanese ships was the high-pitched shriek of diving planes.

The Douglas SBD Dauntless was a good scout plane and a superb dive-bomber, with remarkable stability in even the steepest dive. Now, within the space of just six minutes on that fateful fourth of June, the forty-seven Dauntlesses exacted a frightful toll of the Carrier Striking Force.

The *Enterprise* pilots took *Akagi* and *Kaga* as their targets and the *Yorktown* planes attacked *Soryu*; the fourth Japanese carrier, *Hiryu*, was too far away to be reached with any chance of success.

Three bombs struck *Akagi*, two of them in the

The Pacific initiative won

midst of the forty planes lined up for take-off. The fully armed and fueled planes exploded in a chain-reaction of destruction. In a matter of minutes Nagumo's flagship was aflame from stern to stern.

A similar grim fate overtook huge old *Kaga*. Rivers of blazing aviation gasoline spilled through the holed flight deck and ignited bomb and torpedo magazines. Nearly continuous explosions sent great gusts of flame and smoke in every direction. The *Yorktown* pilots were no less accurate. Three bombs tore *Soryu*'s flight deck apart, flinging planes overboard and spreading fires among the carelessly stowed bombs that the deck crews had failed to secure during the morning's frantic arming and re-arming. *Soryu*'s engines died and she wallowed to a stop.

As the Dauntlesses pulled out of their dives and raced for safety—pursued by the vengeful Zeros—they left behind a chaotic scene. Huge billows of black smoke from the three burning Japanese carriers stained the bright blue sky. Circled by anxious escorts, *Soryu* drifted aimlessly, her water mains ruptured and her fires beyond control. *Kaga* slowly lost headway and stopped, her hangar deck a white-hot inferno. *Akagi*, her rudder jammed, turned in slow circles like a wounded animal.

Despite the stunning turn of events, the battle was not yet over. Admiral Nagumo's surviving carrier, *Hiryu*, launched a strike force that tracked down Admiral Fletcher's *Yorktown*. Two waves of dive bombers and torpedo planes put three bombs and two torpedoes into the U.S. carrier. *Yorktown* lost power and took on a severe list; Fletcher, fearing she would capsize, ordered her abandoned.

Within two hours *Yorktown* was avenged. As soon as he had refueled and rearmed his planes, Spruance dispatched twenty-five Dauntlesses to attack *Hiryu* and once again the aim of the American pilots was deadly: four direct hits cut the carrier to pieces.

One by one, the once-proud carriers of Nagumo's command went to the bottom. Shortly after 7 P.M. *Soryu* slid stern-first under the calm sea; ten minutes later, *Kaga* followed. And at dawn on June 5 the still-burning hulks of *Akagi* and *Hiryu* were torpedoed by their own escorts.

A day later the battered *Yorktown* was discovered by a Japanese submarine as she was being towed toward Pearl Harbor. Two torpedoes sealed her fate; on June 7, sixteen hours later, she rolled over and sank.

Admiral Yamamoto had learned of the debacle shortly before 11 A.M. on June 4. Rallying quickly, he assembled a cruiser force to seek a night action with the American task forces—but to no avail. Finally, in the early hours of June 5, Yamamoto ordered a general retirement. The next day Spruance's airmen caught up with the lagging heavy cruiser *Mikuma* and sank her.

Nothing had prepared the Japanese for a defeat of such unimaginable proportions. Yamamoto was utterly disconsolate as the Combined Fleet steamed toward home waters. He had lost four fleet carriers, a heavy cruiser, over three hundred aircraft, and

thirty-five hundred men.

On the American side, many shared credit for the decisive victory. The Combat Intelligence Unit's coup had made it possible for the United States to enter the battle as an underdog with a chance of victory. Knowing Japanese intentions and dispositions, the battle became a duel not between two mismatched battle fleets, but between Task Forces 16 and 17 and Nagumo's Carrier Striking Force—three carriers against four. Yamamoto's massive battleships might as well have stayed in Tokyo Bay for all they accomplished. Nimitz used his advantage brilliantly and decisively, and his commanders—Fletcher, and especially Spruance—directed the battle with equal brilliance.

Midway must be ranked with El Alamein and Stalingrad as one of World War II's turning points. On that glorious fourth of June the whole complexion of the war in the Pacific changed. Midway won America the time to mobilize its enormous war potential. Never again would the Imperial Navy sail the Pacific with safety or security. Two months later, at Guadalcanal in the Solomons, the United States took the offensive against Japan; six months later the initiative was firmly in American hands, never to be relinquished.   STEPHEN W. SEARS

Top A memorial service for U.S. forces killed in the Battle of Midway. U.S. losses were light in comparison with the damage inflicted on the Japanese.

Above American troops landing on the island of Okinawa, 350 miles from Japan, in 1945.

849

Surrender at Stalingrad

"The Russians are done for," Adolf Hitler assured his Chief of Staff in June of 1942—and by all rights they should have been. Seventy per cent of Hitler's military might was committed to the 1,250-mile-long Eastern Front, and nothing seemed capable of stopping the German Army as it swept eastward toward the vital oil fields of the Caucasus. Indeed, the campaign in the southeast was meeting with so little opposition that the Führer decided to launch a simultaneous campaign against Stalingrad, a major industrial city on the Volga River. And there, for the first time, Hitler's armies ran into stiff resistance. The siege of Stalingrad lasted from August until February, 1943, and when it ended 85 per cent of the city lay in ruins, close to 150,000 German troops were dead, 60,000 Sixth Army vehicles had been captured or destroyed, and the Wehrmacht's eastward thrust had been halted.

Joseph Stalin, Russian dictator after whom Stalingrad was named.

Opposite Russian soldiers defending a ruined building in Stalingrad, November, 1942.

The Battle of Stalingrad was one of the most costly and catastrophic reverses ever suffered by German arms. It marked the limit of the Wehrmacht's advance into Russia and the eastward limit of the Red Army's long retreat. More significantly, the German Army's defeat at Stalingrad proved to be the turning point not only in the struggle between Hitler's Third Reich and the Soviet Union but also in World War II in Europe, for Germany had committed 70 per cent of its military strength to the disastrous campaign on the Eastern Front. After Stalingrad, the strategic initiative remained with the Russian commanders who steadily advanced to Berlin despite two major German counterblows.

By June of 1942, one year after Hitler's invasion of the U.S.S.R., over 3 million of his troops—Italian, Rumanian, Hungarian and Finnish as well as German—were deployed along a 1,250-mile front from Finland to the Sea of Azov. Hitler was convinced that the Russians had spent their main reserves in attempts to regain lost territory, notably around Kharkov, where three armies had been encircled and mauled in May. "The Russians are done for," the German leader assured his Chief of Staff.

There seemed to be little to halt Germany's eastward drive. But which objective should have priority? German troops could take Stalingrad, then wheel north and cut the communications of the Soviet forces defending Moscow, the very heart of Russia. That was one alternative. Another was to push south to the oil fields of the Caucasus. Germany needed oil to prosecute the war and had already drawn heavily on its reserves. Capture of those supplies would not only solve Hitler's oil shortage but would also cripple the Red Army's mobility.

Thus the oil fields of Maikop, Grozny and Baku beckoned as tempting—and plausible—German targets, provided that the northern flank of a thrust between the Black Sea and the Caspian Sea could be protected. To some extent the Don and Volga rivers did afford such protection, but the gap between the rivers would have to be held, and to achieve that goal the Wehrmacht must seize Stalingrad. That was the other alternative.

The German High Command should have chosen one or the other—the Caucasus or Stalingrad. Instead, they resolved to tackle both simultaneously, and in so doing they eventually stretched their resources to the limit and beyond. The ease of their advance had induced overconfidence, and the unexpectedly quick fall of Rostov on July 23, 1942, merely reinforced this optimism. Hitler had already decided it was no longer essential to take Stalingrad and cover the northern flank *before* Field Marshal Siegmund List's Army Group A headed south for the Caucasus. While List forged south, Field Marshal Maximilian von Weichs' Army Group B was to form a defensive front on the middle Don, cut off the narrow isthmus between the Don and Volga rivers, and advance on Stalingrad.

The Sixth Army, which was commanded by a fifty-two-year-old Hessian named Friedrich Paulus, was to lead the way. Originally, General Hermann Hoth's Fourth Panzer Army was to have had that honor, but at the last minute it was directed to help Army Group A across the lower Don east of Rostov. Only then did Hoth's troops turn northeast to Kotelnikovo, seventy miles from Stalingrad. As a result, the Sixth Army's progress was slower than desired, and the Russians were given more time to organize the defenses of what was to become the most famous city of the war.

Joseph Stalin had been sent to the city in 1918 (when it was still named Tsaritsyn after a local river) to serve as commissioner for food supplies in southern Russia. He soon organized the irregular Red units there, transformed them into the first regular regiments of the Red Army, and beat off three attacks by a White Russian force. From 1925 to 1962, when it was renamed Volgograd, the town was called Stalingrad, and by 1939 it had grown into the third largest industrial center in the U.S.S.R., with nearly half a

million inhabitants. Standing as it did at one end of the canal that linked the Volga and Don rivers, the city became a major river port for timber, oil, iron and steel. A vital center, to be sure—yet one wonders whether the Germans, and Hitler in particular, would have become so obsessed with the place had its name still been Tsaritsyn.

The main German summer offensive of 1942 opened on June 28, with two separate army groups being launched against widely divergent targets. In North Africa, General Erwin Rommel had just achieved a disrupting victory and was heading for the Nile. In southern Russia, the many Germans who despised the African campaign as a sideshow looked forward to an even more spectacular success.

The Sixth Army, moving across the open, almost treeless steppe between the Don and the Volga, met little resistance until Stalingrad came into view. Late on August 23, leading units broke through the northern suburbs and reached the Volga. That night the Luftwaffe systematically bombed the city. Tens of thousands of Russian civilians were left homeless, and thousands more were killed or injured in that

terror raid. The Germans then seeded the Volga with mines. They hoped to close the vital river and strangle the flow of supplies and reinforcements, but the Russians destroyed the mines.

The Russians formed a new "Stalingrad front" under General Andrei Yeremenko, whose three-man military council included, as Party representative, the energetic Nikita Khrushchev, afterward Prime Minister of the U.S.S.R. Yeremenko had three armies under his command. The most notable of them was the Sixty-Second, which was led by the future Marshal Vasily Chuikov, who was responsible for the defense of Stalingrad.

In the city itself a desperate struggle was fought for every street and house, for every square, cellar, factory and gutted building. The destruction was so great that when the battle was finally over, 85 per cent of Stalingrad lay in ruins, and it was called "the city without an address."

The Germans, who had failed to take the city by storm, believed that they were winning the war of attrition—when all the time they were wearing down their own strength and committing more troops to the battle than the Russians were. During September and October, reinforcement of Stalingrad's defending forces was kept to the necessary minimum, and it barely covered Russian losses. This was partly deliberate policy, for the defenders of Stalingrad were fighting to give the Russian High Command time in which to assemble a force large enough to inflict a decisive counterstroke.

Indeed, a million troops, 900 tanks, 1,100 aircraft and over 1,300 guns were assembled north of the Don under command of Marshal Georgi Zhukov, and the secret of their presence was maintained. In addition General Paulus failed to wipe out several Russian bridgeheads on the right bank of the Don during his advance on Stalingrad in

Stalingrad: "the city without an address"

August. Paulus' omission left his northern flank vulnerable to attack.

That attack came on November 19 when Konstantin Rokossovski's Sixty-Fifth Soviet Army stormed out of the Kletskaya bridgehead, eighty miles northwest of Stalingrad, and struck the weak Third Rumanian Army guarding Paulus' left flank. In four days the Rumanians lost 75,000 men, 34,000 horses and the heavy weapons of 5 divisions. At the same time the other prong of the mammoth Russian offensive, which aimed at encircling and then annihilating all the troops under Paulus' command, swept out of a bridgehead just south of Stalingrad and attacked the Fourth Rumanian Army. Here too the Russians broke through and captured the bridge on which the Sixth Army relied for all supplies.

As a result of the Soviet pincer movement, some 330,000 German and Rumanian troops were trapped between the Don and Volga rivers. When Hitler heard of the encirclement and of a proposal that Paulus be allowed to fight his way out to the west, he banged his fist on the table and twice shouted: *"Ich bleibe an der Wolga!"* ("I stay on the Volga!") On November 22 Hitler designated Stalingrad a fortress that must be held at all costs and canceled the orders from Army Group B for a breakout.

Hitler next summoned the brilliant General Erich von Manstein, whose army had captured Sevastopol in July, and ordered him to take command of the newly created Army Group Don, comprising the Sixth Army, the Fourth Panzer Army, and what remained of the two Rumanian armies. Eleven divisions were hurried in from France, Poland, Germany and other parts of Russia. Manstein, who believed that Paulus could no longer break out unaided, planned to cut a south-north corridor through which the Sixth Army could be replenished (and thus enabled to hold out longer). To this he obtained the Führer's agreement, but Manstein also planned to order Paulus to push south to aid the rescue operation, and then, having restored the Sixth Army's mobility with stocks of fuel from his column of vehicles laden with supplies, he would fetch the troops out of the Stalingrad "cauldron."

After several postponements, Hoth's Fourth Panzer Army struck northeast from Kotelnikovo on December 12 and at once encountered fierce opposition. With seventy-five miles to go, Hoth forced his way across the Aksay River, and on December 19 his battered force reached the Myshkova River. The German spearhead was barely thirty miles from the cauldron's southern edge, and the encircled German soldiers at Stalingrad grew more hopeful when they heard the distant gunfire. Hoth's troops had suffered immense losses, however, and his offensive strength dwindled rapidly—so much so that Manstein felt he could not get through by himself.

Manstein had come to believe that Paulus and the Sixth Army must concentrate against one short length of the perimeter and blast a way through to meet the rescuers. Accordingly, he ordered Paulus to break out. When Paulus collected his sixty remaining tanks and several hundred trucks, he found

A group of German generals captured during the battle.

German Field Marshal Paulus arriving at Red Army Headquarters for interrogation after the German surrender.

that the vehicles had fuel for twenty miles at most. The gap between the two armies was thirty miles. What if Hoth failed to advance any further? What if his own columns became stuck halfway through? The risks were great, of course, especially while he was keeping back the Russians. But not to use this slender chance meant abandoning all hope of saving the trapped Sixth Army.

Paulus felt that unless Manstein could extract from Hitler permission for a total breakout—and by December 22 he had not done so—he would not risk

Defeated German troops in the snow near Stalingrad.

Shattering the myth of German invincibility

The red flag of victory being raised over a shattered Stalingrad.

Right Drive the Nazi German villains from our land—an appeal to patriotism.

Forward to Victory, a Russian Army poster.

the venture. The last opportunity for retreat passed, and in mid-December a new and admirably timed Soviet offensive smashed through the Italian Eighth Army below Voronezh on the Middle Don and pushed south toward Millerovo and the Donets River. This advance promptly sealed the fate of Paulus' Sixth Army, because Manstein was compelled to detach part of his force to counter the new threat and also to build up a front to guard Rostov. As a result the depleted Fourth Panzer Army, which had failed to breach the Russians' Myshkova River-line defenses, was driven back over the Aksay to Kotelnikovo, its point of departure, on December 27. The rescue bid had failed, at a cost of 300 tanks and 16,000 troops.

The new Russian threat to Rostov also placed the whole operation of List's Army Group A in jeopardy. In August Group A had captured the oil fields at Maikop, but it had failed to reach the Black Sea at Tuapse or to secure Grozny, let alone to advance to Baku on the Caspian. Army Group A had been starved of equipment and reinforcements because of the Stalingrad battle, and the Wehrmacht's resources were simply not adequate to sustain the three-pronged advance against the Caucasian oil fields while the worsening situation on the Volga embroiled more and more troops. And so, two days after the Fourth Panzer Army had retreated over the Aksay to the Don, Hitler decided to order Army Group A to begin a withdrawal.

Inside the irrevocably isolated Fortress Stalingrad, which Hitler had taken under personal (albeit long-distance) command, most of the soldiers were without special winter clothing. Morale had deteriorated since the failure of Manstein's rescue attempt, and the men, cold outside, were also cold within for lack of food. During December, nearly 80,000 troops under Paulus' command were lost through death, disease, wounds or sheer hunger and cold, thereby reducing his force to 250,000. For the Germans the situation was already past redemption, but for Hitler, who had become obsessed by the struggle, Stalingrad's retention was a matter of political as well as military prestige. Although it could be argued that the Sixth Army tied down huge Russian forces, this was a diminishing return, and not nearly enough of the Red Army had been drawn in to prevent the whole of Germany's southern sector of the Eastern Front from collapsing.

The Russians, lucidly aware that matters lay to their advantage, addressed terms of surrender to General Paulus on January 8, 1943. The German commander rejected the terms, whereupon the Soviets launched an all-out concentric offensive. Since Zhukov had nearly half a million men along the Stalingrad perimeter, Paulus was outnumbered

ВПЕРЕД! ПОБЕДА БЛИЗКА!

ВОИНЫ КРАСНОЙ АРМИИ! КРЕПЧЕ УДАРЫ ПО ВРАГУ! ИЗГОНИМ НЕМЕЦКО-ФАШИСТСКИХ МЕРЗАВЦЕВ С НАШЕЙ РОДНОЙ ЗЕМЛИ!

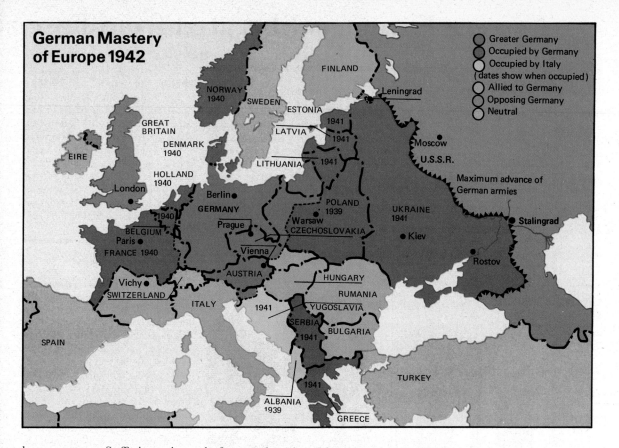

German Mastery of Europe 1942

Greater Germany
Occupied by Germany
Occupied by Italy
(dates show when occupied)
Allied to Germany
Opposing Germany
Neutral

FINLAND
NORWAY 1940
SWEDEN
ESTONIA
GREAT BRITAIN
EIRE
DENMARK 1940
LATVIA 1941
LITHUANIA 1941
HOLLAND 1940
London
Leningrad
Moscow
U.S.S.R.
Berlin
GERMANY
Prague
Warsaw
POLAND 1939
CZECHOSLOVAKIA
UKRAINE 1941
Maximum advance of German armies
Stalingrad
BELGIUM 1940
Paris
FRANCE 1940
Vienna
Kiev
Vichy
SWITZERLAND
AUSTRIA
HUNGARY
Rostov
ITALY
RUMANIA
SPAIN
1941
YUGOSLAVIA
SERBIA 1941
BULGARIA
TURKEY
1941
ALBANIA 1939
GREECE

by two to one. Suffering grievously from malnutrition and frostbite, Paulus' exhausted men could not hold off the Russian tanks.

On January 24, Paulus signaled to Hitler that effective command was no longer possible, further defense was senseless, and collapse inevitable. As expected, the Führer refused to countenance surrender, insisting still that the Sixth Army hold its positions to the last.

Four days later the Red Army broke through to the Volga from the west, and entire German battalions were wiped out or silenced. Declaring that there was no record of a German marshal's having been taken prisoner, Hitler promoted Paulus to the rank of field marshal—but his action could not prevent Paulus from surrendering on the last day of January. On February 2 the final pocket of resistance —six mangled divisions—yielded in the face of a massive assault. Some 90,000 prisoners fell into Russian hands, and 85,000 of them never returned to their homes. Close to 150,000 German and Rumanian troops perished within the cauldron as it dwindled in size and split apart.

When the radio announced the Sixth Army's surrender, a hush fell over the German people, who only days before had read posters that declared: *Stalingrad—unsterbliches Vorbild deutschen Kämpfertums* ("Stalingrad—immortal example of German fighting spirit"). Four days of national mourning were ordered, and places of entertainment closed for that period. The catastrophe undermined Germany's influence with neutral countries, heartened resistance movements in occupied territory, and encouraged anti-Nazi groups within Germany and the Wehrmacht. Many intelligent senior officers by then realized that ultimate defeat was inevitable, and they were converted to the belief that "some-

thing must be done"—by which they meant that Hitler must be removed from power.

On January 24, the Allies announced their policy of unconditional surrender at Casablanca, a move that complicated the work of conspirators. This new development was largely offset by the disasters at Stalingrad and by the defeats in North Africa. In the latter theater, the Eighth Army reached Tripoli by January 23. Tunis fell on May 7, and 250,000 Axis troops were obliged to lay down their arms.

Defeat at Stalingrad irrevocably shattered the myth of German invincibility that had already been severely shaken at the Battle of El Alamein three months earlier. It was now the Russians' turn to be overconfident when they regained Kursk and Kharkov. Barely three weeks after Stalingrad, the brilliant Manstein launched a counterblow that was so effective that the Red Army was compelled to relinquish Kharkov and 6,000 square miles of recently regained territory.

The German Army's resilience demonstrated what a close-run battle Stalingrad had been. Had the Germans taken the city and thwarted the great Russian counteroffensive, their attack on the oil fields could have been reinforced as well as protected. And Army Group A might well have captured not only Grozny and Baku but the Caucasus as well. Indeed, it might have fought its way into Persia and Iraq and headed for the rich oil fields around Mosul and Kirkuk. Had such a threat developed in November it is not impossible that General Bernard Montgomery's Eighth Army would have been obliged to call off its pursuit of Rommel's defeated troops and that the whole course of the war might have been altered. ANTONY BRETT-JAMES

The memorial to the dead of Stalingrad.

By February 3, 1943, when Germany conceded that it had lost the Battle of Stalingrad, all significant Axis advances had been checked. Thereafter, the problem was to recapture territory seized earlier by the Germans and Japanese. Throughout the rest of 1943, the Axis powers were rolled steadily back, and by 1944, they were being regularly defeated in every theater of the war. In the Far East the Japanese had tried to compensate for the defeat at Midway by an attack on the American force in the Solomon Islands at Guadalcanal. But in so doing they dangerously overextended their lines of communication, and in November of 1942 the Japanese suffered a sizable naval defeat off the Solomons.

German problems stemmed from Hitler's abandonment of his early policy of limited objectives achieved one at a time, in favor of an all-out attempt to execute the wild schemes outlined in *Mein Kampf*. The invasion of Russia was an immense military millstone, and by strictly adhering to the principles of Nazism, the Germans complicated the campaign even further. As they advanced eastward, the Germans were welcomed by populations that, out of expediency and a desire to free themselves from the rigors of Stalin's social policies, let them pass unhindered. But the Germans soon alienated these peoples. Rigidly following Hitler's plan for German expansion into eastern living space, Heinrich Himmler's dread secret police, the Gestapo and S.S. inaugurated a brutal policy of racial liquidation. Millions of Poles, Czechs and even Russians perished through starvation or forced labor. As a result, the conquered peoples resisted the Germans even more bitterly.

The most horrific task embarked upon by Himmler was the "final solution" of the Jewish "problem." This incomprehensibly monstrous scheme involved the arrest, deportation, internment and ultimate elimination, in the gas chambers and by other means, of roughly 6 million European Jews. For the most part, Himmler's program met little or no effective opposition. But in April, 1943, in a final, heroic—and doomed—gesture, the Jews who had been herded into the ghetto of Warsaw to starve rose against their tormentors. The ghetto was ultimately razed, and the survivors deported. Such brutality was not just the work of the secret police; atrocities against prisoners,

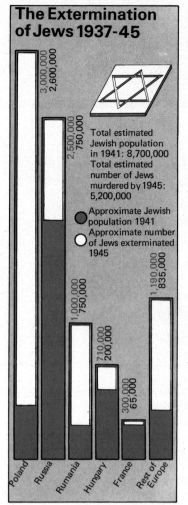

The Extermination of Jews 1937-45

3,000,000
2,600,000

2,500,000
750,000

Total estimated Jewish population in 1941: 8,700,000
Total estimated number of Jews murdered by 1945: 5,200,000

● Approximate Jewish population 1941
○ Approximate number of Jews exterminated 1945

1,000,000
750,000

710,000
200,000

300,000
65,000

1,190,000
835,000

Poland | Russia | Rumania | Hungary | France | Rest of Europe

particularly in Russia, were also committed by regular soldiers of the German Army. In occupied Europe, the Nazis themselves did more than anyone to keep alive the many resistance groups that had appeared to harass the German occupation forces.

Victories in the Pacific

As the war in the Pacific entered its final phase, a huge offensive was launched by General Douglas MacArthur. U.S. strategy consisted of knocking out major Japanese island bases and leaving the troops isolated and ineffective in between. The U.S. scheme was a brilliant and effective exploitation of Japan's overextension, and as early as February, 1944, Australian and U.S. troops had taken much of New Guinea. Their amphibious forces soon gained control of the Solomon and the Marshall islands. And in March, British and Indian forces repelled a Japanese attack on Imphal in Burma, signaling the end of the Japanese threat to the Indian subcontinent.

A setback in Italy

The Allies were no less successful in Europe. Sicily was occupied on July 9, 1943. The prospect of imminent invasion (linked to a widespread revulsion against fascism in general and the German occupation in particular) led to the downfall of Mussolini. And despite his fears of brutal German reprisals, Italy's new leader, Marshal Pietro Badoglio began making overtures for surrender. Under the impression

The corpses of Mussolini and his mistress, Clara Petacci, hanging in Milan's Piazzali Loreto, in April, 1945.

that Italy would fall without a struggle, Churchill pressed for an invasion of the mainland. The Americans, who preferred a landing in France, wavered. By the time agreement had been reached for a landing in September, the Germans had brought in fresh troops. The expeditionary force that reached the Italian mainland on September 2 met stiff German resistance, and the Allies could make only slow progress. After nine months of fierce fighting, they finally entered Rome in June, 1944, and that city became the first European capital to be freed from Nazi rule.

The whole question of an Italian theater of war posed serious political problems for the Allies. Although the battle for Italy involved German troops, it hardly accorded with Russia's urgent demands for the opening of a second front. Once the Germans realized there was not going to be an attack on northern France, they were able to release several divisions—twenty-seven according to Stalin—for the Russian Front. Moreover, the shipping required for the Italian operation cut down Allied supplies to Russia,

and embittered Soviet-Western relations.

The Allies' failure to open what Stalin considered a genuine second front in Europe (until late in the war when the Russians were driving into Eastern Europe) convinced the Russians that Germany had been defeated largely through their own efforts. Russia, Stalin concluded, would have to depend on its own unilateral action to ensure its future security.

Carving up Europe

It was for this reason that the Russians thought increasingly in terms of zones of influence, a topic discussed at the Allied foreign ministers' meeting that was held in Moscow in October, 1943. If nothing else, that meeting demonstrated that the Western Allies, as much as the Russians, thought in terms of spheres of influence. Earlier in the war, American leaders, fearful of upsetting millions of U.S. voters of Eastern European origin, had been reluctant to involve themselves in the carving up of Central and Eastern Europe. But as early as 1942, Secretary of War Henry L. Stimson had come to the conclusion that "there is no doubt that the Soviet government has tremendous ambitions with regard to Europe."

The Russian push west

The year 1944 brought the Russians huge military successes. In a series of sweeps they began to push the Germans back into Eastern and Central Europe. The Allies' actions in Italy had established that the country that liberated another country could then determine that nation's political, social and economic future, and the Russians were determined to capitalize on the precedent. In January they reached Poland; in March, Rumania. By the middle of the year, the Russians had pushed west as far as Warsaw and were about to take Yugoslavia and Bulgaria. By this time they had 225 infantry and 22 armored divisions in Central Europe—a military reality that inevitably affected the question of the political control of the liberated areas. The British, who recognized the Russian threat, favored a division of spheres of influence, which they said might save some of Eastern Europe from communism.

The Americans, on the other

hand, were reluctant to enter into any agreements that might prevent their challenging Soviet control of such areas after the war. However, with Roosevelt's acquiescence Churchill made a deal with Stalin.

Operation Overlord

In June, 1944, the Allies landed in northern France and began the push that would bring them face to face with the Russians in the middle of Germany. Operation Overlord, as the landing was called, was executed with extreme precision. On D-Day, June 6, a force of 1,200 fighting ships, 4,000 assault craft, 1,600 merchant vessels and 13,000 aircraft deposited some 156,000 Allied troops on the beaches of Normandy. The Germans, whose best divisions were in Russia, were slow to react. The troops stationed in Normandy were deceived by dummy attacks on another part of the coast, and they therefore missed an opportunity to launch a crippling counterattack while the Allies were still disembarking. Anticipating another attack, the Germans kept their forces dispersed, thereby allowing the Allies to build up great numerical superiority.

With the aid of the French resistance, a rapid push through France began. As the Western Front collapsed, several high-ranking German officers attempted to pave the way for surrender through an abortive attempt on Hitler's life. By July, a few courageous officers, including Rommel, had formulated a plot to assassinate the Führer. Colonel Klaus Schenk, Count von Stauffenberg, planted a bomb in Hitler's headquarters, but through a freakish mischance, the German leader escaped almost unhurt. Meanwhile, the German position in the West deteriorated rapidly, and on August 23-24, General Patton's armored column liberated Paris.

V-E Day

The war in Europe was almost over. By January of 1945, a giant Russian offensive had thrust deeply into Germany, and Hitler had incarcerated himself in the Reich Chancellery in Berlin. While the confused Führer ordered nonexistent armies about, Marshal Georgi Zhukov's forces pressed to within forty-five miles of Berlin itself. On the Western Front, a German counteroffensive through the Ardennes

collapsed, and the Allies advanced rapidly. By March, they had reached the Rhine and had swarmed across a bridge—left standing by a German oversight—at Remagen. On April 30, Hitler committed suicide in a bunker below the Reich Chancellery, and eight days later Germany surrendered.

Yalta

Two issues remained to be decided in 1945: the war in the Far East had yet to be won, and the terms of a postwar settlement had yet to be reached. Both of these issues were central to the conference held by Roosevelt, Churchill and Stalin at the Crimean coastal resort of Yalta in Feburary. Anxious to bring Russia into the war with Japan, the Americans made concessions to the Russians on several key issues. First was the division of Europe into spheres of influence. Second, a pro-Soviet government would be set up in Poland. Third, Germany would be disarmed, demilitarized, partitioned and made subject to reparations, the details of which were to be worked out by a commission that would meet in Moscow. Roosevelt agreed to the partitioning of the Third Reich despite the opposition of many of his advisers, who were against the granting of spheres of influence to the Russians. The American President had little choice but to acquiesce, for the Russians were in all-but-total military control of Eastern Europe, and Roosevelt was really only recognizing a fait accompli. Many State Department officials who were secretly anxious

Churchill, Roosevelt and Stalin at the Potsdam Conference.

to break this control hesitated to do so lest the Allies lose Russian support against the Japanese or provoke Stalin into signing a separate peace treaty with the Germans.

After the war, the Russians tended to stick to the letter of the Yalta agreements, while the Allies attempted to reverse them. In fact, Allied determination to negate the accords became apparent even before the war was over. The defeat of the Germans removed the fear of the Russians' making a separate peace, and the death of Roosevelt (on April 12, 1945) removed a major obstacle to denying the Russians their sphere, so the emboldened Allies began to move. The American ambassador in Moscow, Averell Harriman, convinced America's new President, Harry S Truman, that it was time to take a hard line with the Russians. His first step was to slash Lend-Lease aid to Russia. Next, he refused to withdraw behind the agreed upon demarcation line in Germany.

Potsdam

At this point, doubts about the course of the war in the Far East forced the Americans to ease their pressure on the Russians. At the Potsdam Conference, held in July and August of 1945, the Americans made a series of wide-ranging demands on the Russians that were not entirely in accord with the agreements reached at Yalta. They called for Russia to evacuate its sphere, for free elections to be held therein, and for an economically strong Germany to be rebuilt without reparations. The conference became deadlocked. Stalin felt the Americans were attempting to break the Yalta agreements. The Americans, on the other hand, were confident they could settle the outstanding issues to their satisfaction by a demonstration of power—and the war against Japan provided the opportunity for this.

Japan's collapse

In June, 1944, the Japanese had been pushed back to their own shores, but they had already shown signs of being willing to fight to the death. America felt that the use of a terrifying new weapon—the atom bomb—might frighten the Japanese into submission, thus preventing a long struggle and saving thousands of American lives. Oddly, it seems that such leaders as General Douglas MacArthur, commander in chief of the U.S. Pacific Command, and others intimately connected with the struggle against Japan, were not consulted about using the bomb until August 1: five days later an atomic bomb leveled Hiroshima.

Raising the Russian flag on the Reichstag in Berlin.

1945 Fireball over Hiroshima

At 2:45 a.m. on August 6, 1945, the American bomber Enola Gay *lifted off a runway in the Mariana Islands and swung north toward Japan. Some five and a half hours later, after a flight that was devoid of incident, the aircraft was over its target: Hiroshima, a major communications center for the Imperial Japanese Army. At seventeen seconds past 8:15, the* Enola Gay's *bomb doors opened and her cargo fell away. Forty-three seconds later, Hiroshima was obliterated by the first major atomic explosion in world history. Some 78,500 persons were killed in the holocaust that followed, and the practice of war changed convulsively and irrevocably. As a four-mile-high mushroom cloud formed over the leveled city, the world entered the Atomic Age.*

Harry S Truman, who gave the order for atom bombs to be used against Japan.

Opposite An atomic explosion similar to the ones that devastated Hiroshima and Nagasaki.

For the first five thousand years of the history of war, the development of weapons followed a simple pattern of changes discovered from individual experience and made practicable only when technology made one of its limited advances. The first of the climactic inventions—gunpowder—required two hundred years to become effective in war and another four centuries to reach its zenith. Then, abruptly, in the mid-twentieth century, the pattern changed: at fifteen minutes past eight on the morning of August 6, 1945, an American aircraft released one bomb over the Japanese city of Hiroshima. Forty-three seconds later Hiroshima had been obliterated. The nature and practice of major war had changed convulsively, and the history of man had entered a new era.

The moment of origin of the atomic bomb can be argued. Indeed, it may lie in the very beginnings of nuclear physics; it seems more probable, however, that historians will eventually place it at Ernest Rutherford's brilliant determination of the internal structure of the atom at Cambridge University, England, in 1911. The precision of his experiments led, by an inevitable and almost automatic process, to the final bombardment and splitting of the uranium atom by Otto Hahn and Fritz Strassmann in Berlin in late 1938.

The importance of the Germans' achievement was not immediately apparent either to politicians or to military leaders, although it was to scientists. Rutherford warned Sir Maurice Hankey, Secretary to the British cabinet, that Hahn and Strassmann's experiment was a highly significant one. In America, members of the considerable group of scientists who had left Fascist Italy and Nazi Germany in previous years were shocked. In March, 1939, Enrico Fermi, the Italian Nobel Prize winner, was put in touch with the U.S. Navy Department to discuss experiments he had made that confirmed the Germans' work, but the discussions were without significant result. In midsummer, with Germany's attack on Poland imminent, the Hungarian physicists Leo

Szilard and Eugene Wigner approached Albert Einstein and asked him to urge President Franklin D. Roosevelt and the U.S. government to take steps to develop an atomic weapon. Einstein was reluctant at first, but in August, with the assistance of Szilard and another scientist, Edward Teller, he wrote to Roosevelt asking that the project be started.

Roosevelt ordered action, but initial efforts met with delays, difficulties and lack of funds. Not until two years later, on December 6, 1941, was Vannevar Bush, head of the U.S. Office of Scientific Research and Development, able to announce governmental consent to an all-out drive to develop an atomic weapon. On December 7, in grim coincidence, the Japanese Navy launched its attack on Pearl Harbor.

By June, 1942, an almost inconceivably vast, top-secret program of atomic bomb development (called the Manhattan Project) had been initiated under the authoritarian command of Brigadier General Leslie Groves. By December Fermi had induced the first controlled nuclear chain reaction in an unused squash court at the University of Chicago, and J. Robert Oppenheimer had begun research on the explosive aspects of a bomb. In 1943 the giant experimental laboratories at Los Alamos were functioning, the Oak Ridge National Laboratory in Tennessee and other enormous components of production had been set up, and more than half a million were on the Manhattan Project's payroll.

A test device was in the final stages of completion on May 8, 1945—V-E Day—when Germany surrendered. On July 16, as Harry S Truman—who had become President after Roosevelt's death—was driving through the ruins of Berlin, an atomic bomb was triumphantly tested at Alamogordo in the desert of New Mexico. By that time, three billion dollars had been spent on the project. In the interim Italy had collapsed, Germany had gone down in absolute defeat, and Japan alone was left fighting.

Approximately a year previously, the Manhattan Project had organized its own separate "air force," with its own Boeing B-29 superfortresses, its own

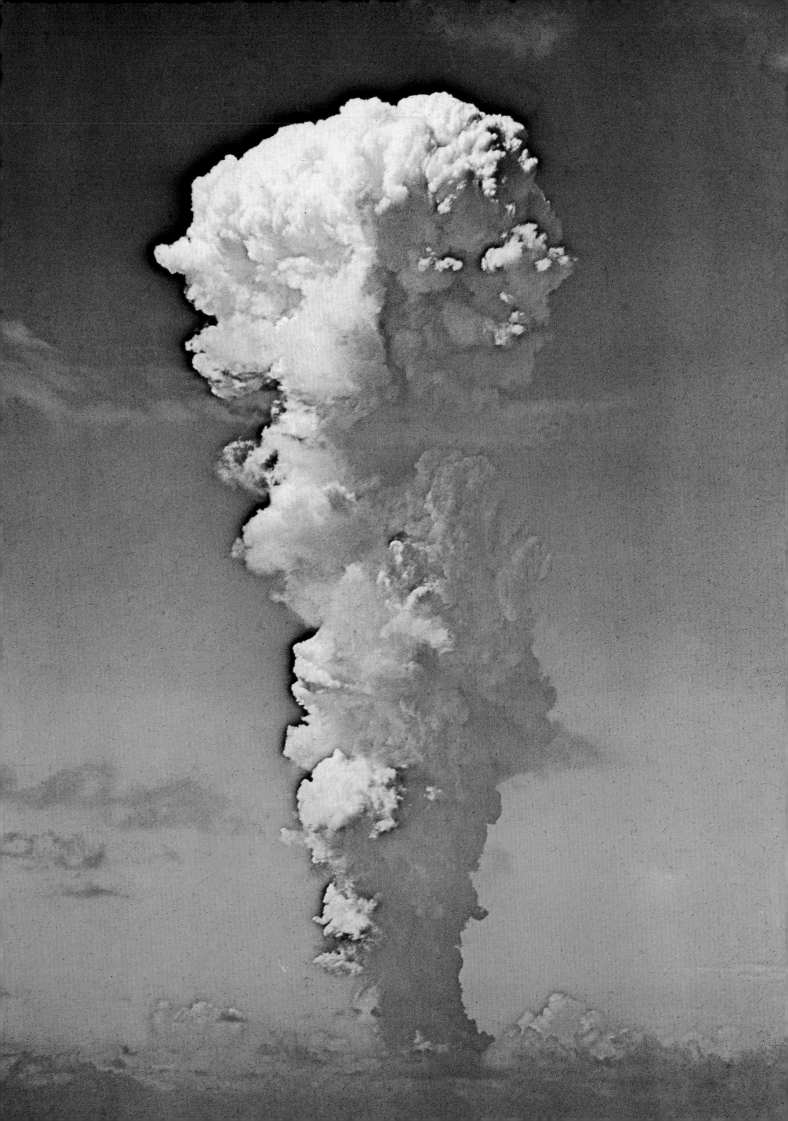

Choice of a target

Enola Gay, the B-29 Superfortress that dropped the bomb on Hiroshima.

Right Little Boy, the bomb detonated over Hiroshima. The ten-foot-long bomb weighed 9000 pounds.

An aerial view of Hiroshima showing the extensive damage done by the bomb.

transport aircraft and armament section, its own training program and rules, and a strength of seventeen hundred officers and men. Only Colonel Paul Tibbets, Jr., its commanding officer, was fully briefed on its purpose: to drop the first atomic bomb. In February, 1945, Admiral Chester Nimitz, commander in chief of the U.S. Pacific Fleet, was told the plan. General Douglas MacArthur, commander of U.S. forces in the Pacific, had not been informed. Tinian Island in the Marianas, a site that was secure, strategically located, and had a major air base, was chosen for the use of the 509th Composite Group, the Manhattan Project's private air force.

American forces were already dangerously close to the Japanese homeland. Iwo Jima had long been in their hands; Okinawa collapsed by June 22; B-29 fire raids and naval carrier attacks were sweeping across Honshu. As early as April, the Japanese sent out peace feelers through Allen Dulles' Office of Strategic Services in Switzerland; the effort failed, however, for lack of support in Tokyo.

Two months later Koichi Kido, a member of Japan's government, approached Emperor Hirohito

himself and secured approval for a peace plan, to which the Japanese Supreme Council agreed on June 18. By coincidence, on that same day President Truman confirmed the plan for Olympic, the name for the opening assault on Japan due in November and the invasion of Honshu, the main island, in March, 1946.

As Okinawa fell, the Japanese made fresh approaches to the Russian ambassador to Tokyo; when the Japanese Army objected, it was rebuked by the Emperor, in an exceptional intervention. The Russians were, in any event, uncooperative. On July 7, Hirohito ordered a fresh approach through Russia that dealt in part with the question of unconditional surrender, but this failed also.

Just two days before, the cruiser *Indianapolis* had left the San Francisco Navy Yard, carrying on board the charge for the first nuclear weapon. Ten days later the Allied Powers meeting at Potsdam presented this ultimatum to Japan:

We call upon the government of Japan to proclaim now the unconditional surrender of all Japanese armed forces. ... The alternative for Japan is prompt and utter destruction.

This was the atom warning, but no indication of the nature or the power of the weapon was given. Japan failed to respond. Procrastination in the Japanese government, furious opposition by Army officers, and political refusals to acknowledge reality inhibited action.

The weapon had now acquired a dynamic of its own. Inexorably, the steps that led to its use were taken. The target had to be a substantial city, untouched by previous bombings but large enough to provide a convincing demonstration. Kyoto, the ancient capital of Japan, headed the first list of choices, which included Hiroshima and Kokura. Kyoto was spared, for although General Curtis LeMay believed the destruction of its temples and its palaces would be a compelling shock to Japan, Henry L. Stimson, the U.S. Secretary of War,

considered that its destruction would be impermissible vandalism. Hiroshima became the primary target, Kokura the second and Nagasaki was added.

The city was a major communications base. From it, Japanese armies had sailed for the China War, for the Russian War and for the invasion of Malaya. In 1945 it had been designated Japan's Southern Command Headquarters in preparation for the anticipated American invasion, and the Emperor was to move to it if Tokyo was threatened. Hiroshima's population was 340,000, but evacuation had reduced it to 245,000 at the time of the atomic attack.

While President Truman was at sea returning from the Potsdam Conference, the final moves were made. At 1:37 A.M. on August 6, three reconnaissance aircraft were dispatched—to Hiroshima, Nagasaki and Kokura—to ascertain cloud cover

861

Making the unthinkable possible

Emperor Hirohito inspects bomb damage in Tokyo.

over the targets. At 2:45, *Enola Gay*, the aircraft carrying the bomb, took off, with Colonel Tibbets using every desperate inch of Tinian's runway. At two-minute intervals the instrument and photographic planes followed. After them came a standby plane. Two hours later, two more photographic planes followed.

The flight was uneventful. At dawn Iwo Jima was distantly visible to the northeast, and at 4:55 the accompanying planes assumed a broad arrow formation. There was no sign of Japanese air activity. All three reconnaissance planes reached their target cities. Kokura was clear; Nagasaki and Hiroshima had some cloud cover. At 7:45 the pilot of the *Straight Flush*, the plane over Hiroshima, signaled: "Advice: bomb primary." Then he turned for home.

The *Enola Gay* was already at bombing altitude, six miles above the Pacific. At ten minutes to eight she crossed the coastline of Shikoku. As inexorably as the takeoff and the flight, the testing of the bomb's electrical circuits proceeded. There was no Japanese jamming on the frequency of the proximity fuse, no hang-up in the aircraft's electronics.

At nine minutes past eight, Tibbets said casually, "We are about to start the bomb run. Put on your goggles. When you hear the tone signal, pull the goggles over your eyes ..." Two minutes later *Enola Gay* reached the starting point of the bomb run, only seventeen seconds late after traveling fifteen hundred miles. At exactly 8:15 and seventeen seconds the bomb doors opened, the bomb dropped, righted itself and fell away. As the nose of *Enola Gay* flung up, Tibbets jerked the plane around in a violent evasive maneuver and swung away. On his left the instrument plane dropped its three parachute loads of recording and transmitting gear and swung

urgently clear. There were just forty-three seconds in which to reach a safe distance.

The flash from the explosion all but blinded those who looked directly at it through special polarized glasses. The fireball was 1,800 feet across. The shock wave hit the *Enola Gay* a minute later. Afterward, as they turned to fly past the southern outskirts of Hiroshima, the co-pilot, staring at the boiling dust and flame that roared up into the four-mile cloud, said quietly: "My God, what have we done?"

There had been no second air alert in Hiroshima. The first had been canceled after the *Straight Flush* left the area and the *Enola Gay*'s run was assumed to be just another reconnaissance. It would have made small difference. A few people saw parachutes in the sky—the instrument parachutes. No one saw the bomb, only the blinding, inconceivable flash that seared consciousness.

It is not possible to say how many died in the first instant of the flame that engulfed the central area of Hiroshima. The fire that followed was fed by thousands of little charcoal cooking fires burning in the flimsy houses that collapsed in flames in a circle three miles across. Those trapped in the wreckage died as the fire storm grew. Those wandering—blinded, scorched, with the skin peeling off them and their faces in shreds from the first horror of that flame— died in the fire storm also. But most of those in the center were killed by the blast itself.

It is believed that 78,500 people perished on the first morning. How many died later is unclear; people are still dying from causes attributable to the blast. Medical attention was all but impossible. Half the city's doctors were dead and most of the rest were wounded: 1,650 of the city's nurses were dead or injured. Ten thousand people crawled or

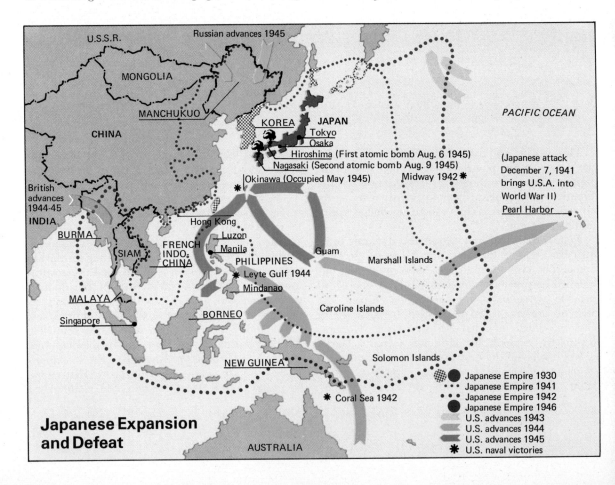

Japanese Expansion and Defeat

were carried to the one surviving hospital. Medicine, drugs and bandages were destroyed, food was burned or inedible, water over large areas was undrinkable. Aid from outside was slow in coming, relief incompetent (Japan, it is necessary to remember, was a shattered country even before Hiroshima).

It is at this point that the moral questions begin. Was the bomb inhuman? In Tokyo on the night of March 9–10, 1945, at least 83,800 had died in uncontrollable fires. In February the RAF had killed 25,000 in Dresden (35,000 more were missing). The bomb dropped on Hiroshima was inhuman, but it was neither less nor more inhuman as an instrument of slaughter than the conventional systems it superseded.

Was the bomb necessary? The situation that existed in Japan for three days after the bomb had fallen was incomprehensible to Western minds. Despite the shattering proof of the weapon's potential, the absolute deadlock between the two sides in control of Tokyo continued. In the end the crisis required the personal intervention of the Emperor to resolve it, and even his decision was unacceptable to sections of the Army, the Navy and the Air Force. Indeed, elements of the Army committed the sacrilege of seizing the Imperial Palace in an attempt to prevent the Emperor from invoking the ancient precedent of The Voice of the Crane—the act of speaking directly to the nation—through the modern device of broadcasting.

Had the Army imposed its will on the Emperor or had the Emperor decided to fight on, the consequences would have been immeasurable. Japan was already defeated, but substantial forces still existed in the homeland, adequate quantities

The Industrial Promotion Center in Hiroshima has been left in its damaged state as a memorial to the victims of the first atomic bomb.

of ammunition and equipment were available and preparation for fanatical resistance had been made. No one who had watched the Japanese garrison on Iwo Jima accept annihilation or had seen the bitter desolation of Okinawa could believe that a Japan under the control of Korechika Anami, the War Minister, and the Navy and Army chiefs of staff, Admiral Toyoda and General Umezu—and backed (genuinely or under duress) by the Emperor—would not have fought the most terrible defensive battle of history. To break such resistance would have required fire storms in every remaining city and town in Japan and the annihilation of whole populations, as well as the destruction of the armed forces by conventional means.

The horror of the first atomic bomb lies not in the death and desolation of Hiroshima, nor even in the subsequent destruction of Nagasaki by the second bomb, but in the scientific and the technological potential that it unleashed. It made possible the unthinkable. Even before Hiroshima, men at the Los Alamos atomic center were talking of the "super" bomb. At Hiroshima the explosion yielded a power equivalent to 13,000 tons of TNT (the early figure of 20,000 was inaccurate).

But even that was not enough. Spurred by the genius of Edward Teller, scientific research was even then moving irresistibly toward a hydrogen bomb. To measure the explosive power of this superbomb it was necessary that scientists coin a new unit—megaton—to enable military men to calculate its effect in terms of a million tons of TNT. To carry such a bomb, new delivery systems were necessary, for aircraft delivery was becoming obsolete. To satisfy these new needs, the 1944 development of the German V-2 rocket—deemed to have failed then because of the inadequacy of its explosives—became a dominant element of future war.

The involvement of the twentieth-century world in the consequences of nuclear physics, the extravagances of missile technologies, the incredibilities of lunar and planetary exploration, and the possibility of total destruction are the ultimate moralities rising from Hiroshima. DAVID DIVINE

On September 2, 1945, Japanese delegates sign an unconditional surrender on board the U.S.S. *Missouri* in Tokyo Bay. General Douglas MacArthur is standing at the microphones.

In the wake of Japan's surrender, Russia and the United States moved rapidly to consolidate their power and the ideological clash resulting from that confrontation rapidly became the dominant feature of the postwar world. This tense international situation was soon complicated by the Chinese Communists' victory in the civil war against Chiang Kai-shek, and by the emergence of what has come to be known as the Third World— the vast underdeveloped areas of the globe that owe political allegiance to neither power bloc. The Third World eventually became a battleground for the "superpowers," but in the immediate postwar period the conflict was confined largely to Europe.

The United States assumed leadership of the Western bloc during the first months of the postwar period, largely due to the decline of the United Kingdom, which was nominally victorious but economically shattered in 1945. The trading mechanisms by which Britain earned its livelihood had been destroyed, and the Empire on which it depended for much of its wealth had become a burden (particularly because wartime propaganda had given colonial peoples a taste for freedom). Overseas investments had been sold to finance the war, gigantic debts had been contracted, and through wartime neglect, capital assets—from industrial machinery to housing—had become run down. The British no longer had the power or the spirit to be an active imperialist power. In the face of this abdication from world power, America, which emerged from the war unscathed by Axis bombing and at the height of its industrial power, did not hesitate to take up the crown.

Reconstruction in Russia

Some 20 million able-bodied Russian men had lost their lives during the war, and many of the survivors were maimed or crippled. During 1945 and 1946, those who survived returned home from the Eastern Front. The scene that greeted them was one of awesome destruction: the coal mines, steel mills and factories built during the five-year plans had been flooded, dismantled or razed, and countless homes had been destroyed. For years after the war, 25 million people had to live in mud huts and dugouts, and to compound their

misery further, Russia was hit by a calamitous drought in 1946. Food rations were a quarter of what they had been in 1939, and industrial production was only 50 per cent of the prewar figure. Between the end of the war and the declaration of the Truman Doctrine in 1947, the Russian leaders attempted to resolve the acute shortage of manpower by rapidly demobilizing

Marshal Tito, the Communist President of Yugoslavia. He pursued an independent policy and refused to allow his country to become a Russian pawn.

their armies. That demobilization was undertaken with such alacrity that the number of men in uniform dropped from 11.5 million in 1945 to under 3 million in 1947. Allied fears notwithstanding, Russia was not in any position to launch a serious attack on Western Europe in the late 1940s.

By the terms of the agreements signed at the Yalta and Potsdam

conferences, Stalin had committed himself to respect the predominance of capitalism in postwar Western Europe. And, at least initially, he seemed inclined to do just that. The Russian dictator prevailed upon the Communist parties in Italy and France to collaborate with right-wing governments, and when a Greek revolt was crushed by British tanks, neither *Pravda* nor *Izvestia* made unfavorable comment. The Yugoslav revolution was carried out by Tito against the instructions of Stalin (and while Stalin was advising Mao Tse-tung to yield to Chiang Kai-shek's Kuomintang). Even within the Russian sphere of influence in Eastern Europe, the process of Stalinization was quite slow. Fearful of antagonizing the West, Stalin allowed anti-Communist parties some representation in coalition governments in Poland and Hungary.

Between 1945 and 1950, Russia achieved a near-miraculous economic recovery by subordinating the economy of Eastern Europe to Russian needs. The recuperative process was slow in the immediate postwar years, and the financial brunt was borne by East Germany, from which war reparations were extracted. In addition, industrial plants in the Eastern Zone of occupied Germany were dismantled and confiscated to replace machines damaged in Russia during the war.

The cost of reconstructing Russia was staggering. State planning concentrated on heavy industry—coal, steel, machine tools, oil wells, railway lines and power stations— and the needs of the consumer were temporarily ignored.

Postwar America

Faced with the problem of converting from a wartime to a peacetime economy, America desperately needed to reopen its old trade outlets and to find new ones. The war had brought an industrial boom that had virtually eliminated unemployment, and if wartime increases in industrial capacity were not to produce another crisis of overproduction, overseas markets would have to be maintained and extended. This necessity brought conflict with Russia, as W. C. Bullitt, U.S. Ambassador to Russia, observed in 1946: "Every time the Soviet Union extends its power over another area or state, the United States and Great Britain lose another normal market." The Allies' pursuit of outlets for the goods produced by their overheated postwar economies was both intense and risky. It led, almost

Eduard Beneš, the Czech Social Democrat whose government was swept aside by the communists.

immediately, to a confrontation with Russia in Eastern Europe, and the desire to roll back Soviet domination in that region owed more than a little to Allied economic interests.

"Stalinization"

In response to this threat, the Russians sought security in "Stalinization," the total subjection of Eastern Europe to Russia's political and economic needs. The Kremlin realized that a communized Eastern Europe was necessary if the Russians were to block the penetration of U.S. capital and trade. In addition, it was a useful physical barrier against a revived Germany.

Stalin's brusque and sometimes brutal program of "consolidation"

Andrei Gromyko signing the United Nations charter, June, 1945. Stalin feared the antagonism of the West.

Greek troops keeping watch on a mountain pass during the civil war.

allies staged a phenomenal postwar recovery, and by 1952 their overall production was double that of 1938.

NATO

In March of 1948, Britain, France and the Low Countries signed the Brussels Treaty, which provided for joint military and economic cooperation in the event of an armed attack on Western Europe. A provision of this treaty created a permanent military committee staffed by representatives of the signatory powers. A year later, the North Atlantic Treaty grew from this provision. It was signed in Washington, D.C. on April 4, 1949, and led to the now-familiar European defense organization, NATO. In ratifying the treaty, the United States committed itself to its first peacetime alliance and, rather more fundamentally, to defending the territorial integrity of the non-Communist world.

United Nations

To assist the North Atlantic Treaty Organization in its peace-keeping operations, the Allies sought to strengthen the fledgling United Nations. The U.N. was an offshoot of the Yalta Conference and had functioned as a relief and rehabilitation bureau during the final years of the war and the immediate postwar period. On October 9, 1944, a group of delegates representing the Big Three powers and China had met at Dumbarton Oaks, an estate in Washington, D.C., to propose that the United Nations be established on a permanent basis. And in the spring of 1945, representatives of fifty nations convened in San Francisco to draw up a charter.

Less than six months later, the new organization found itself embroiled in a violence-ridden crisis over the partitioning of India. In the next month, the rioting subsided, and some progress was made toward reconciling Hindu and Pakistani differences. Two years later, an integration of the two factions seemed possible. Then, without warning, an assassin's bullet cut down the father of Indian independence.

Trygve Lie, first Secretary General of the United Nations.

in Eastern Europe met its first significant resistance in Czechoslovakia, where President Eduard Benes' Social Democratic Party categorically refused to merge with the Communists. In July of 1947, the Benes government momentarily accepted, and then, under intense pressure from Moscow, rejected an offer of Western aid. The Czech move so disconcerted the Russians that they engineered a coup d'etat the following February. A Communist-dominated government replaced the Benes coalition, and a sweeping purge eliminated all liberal opposition to the new regime.

In Yugoslavia, where local Communists—rather than Soviet troops—had been instrumental in expelling the Nazis, "consolidation" proved impossible. The leader of the Yugoslav partisans, Josip Broz (known as Tito), indicated a willingness to cooperate closely with Stalin, but he refused to permit his country to become a Soviet pawn. Relations between the two Communist leaders became increasingly tense during 1947–48, and in the spring of 1948 they broke down entirely. Russia withdrew its technical advisers from Yugoslavia, and Tito applied for—and received—Western aid.

Truman Doctrine

To counter Stalin's westward thrust, the U.S. State Department inaugurated a policy of "containment" on a worldwide scale. That program, first articulated by the noted Kremlinologist George F. Kennan in the winter of 1946, became official U.S. policy on March 12, 1947. On that date, President Truman called upon Congress to appropriate several hundred million dollars to be used to combat Communist incursions in Greece and Turkey.

The American President's request, which was triggered by news of civil warfare between antimonarchist forces and government troops in Greece, served as the basis for a broad statement of America's global aims. The policy, which became known as the Truman Doctrine, asserted that the United States was committed to helping free peoples "maintain their institutions and their national integrity against aggressive movements that seek to impose on them totalitarian regimes."

Marshall Plan

In practice, the Truman Doctrine took the form of massive economic aid and joint military alliances. The first aspect of the doctrine, which was officially known as the European Recovery Program and popularly known as the Marshall Plan (after U.S. Secretary of State George C. Marshall), was born some two weeks after Truman's 1947 speech. During the next four years, the U.S. government poured 12 billion dollars into Western Europe—half of which went to Great Britain, France and Germany. The results were more than gratifying. Spurred by Marshall Plan grants and loans, America's

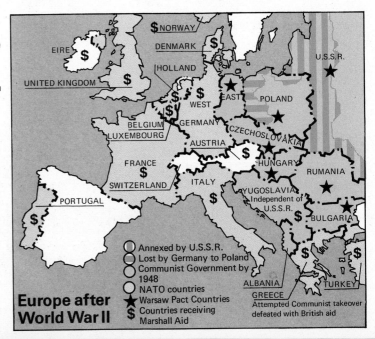

Europe after World War II

- Annexed by U.S.S.R.
- Lost by Germany to Poland
- Communist Government by 1948
- NATO countries
- ★ Warsaw Pact Countries
- $ Countries receiving Marshall Aid

NORWAY · DENMARK · EIRE · HOLLAND · UNITED KINGDOM · U.S.S.R. · WEST GERMANY · EAST · POLAND · BELGIUM · LUXEMBOURG · CZECHOSLOVAKIA · AUSTRIA · HUNGARY · FRANCE · SWITZERLAND · ITALY · RUMANIA · YUGOSLAVIA Independent of U.S.S.R. · PORTUGAL · BULGARIA · ALBANIA · GREECE Attempted Communist takeover defeated with British aid · TURKEY

Murder of the Mahatma 1948

On January 30, 1948, a fanatic Hindu nationalist fired three shots at pointblank range into the frail body of Mohandas Karamchand Gandhi, the father of Indian independence. A day later some 2 million Indians gathered outside New Delhi to witness the ritual cremation of the man who had won the sovereignty of the subcontinent of India through nonviolent means. The terrible irony of Gandhi's violent death was not lost on his disciples and admirers around the world. The British Attorney General called the Mahatma "the most remarkable man of the century," and George Marshall, the U.S. Secretary of State, eulogized: "Gandhi was the spokesman for the conscience of all mankind." In thirty-four years of public life, Mahatma Gandhi had never held public office—and yet by the sheer force of his personal example he had liberated colonial India, quelled civil strife, and given the world a hopeful alternative to violence.

Jawaharlal Nehru, who had become India's Prime Minister on August 15, 1947, when India won its independence, did not see eye to eye on many issues with Vallabhbhai Patel, Deputy Prime Minister. Their dispute, like many others, had been dropped into the lap of Mohandas Karamchand Gandhi, the "super prime minister." On the afternoon of January 30, 1948, Patel conferred intensely with Gandhi at Birla House in New Delhi. Finally Gandhi tore himself away. He was scrupulously punctual, and the interview had made him late for his daily five o'clock prayer meeting. He walked with big strides toward the grounds of Birla House, where some five hundred persons had been waiting. As he approached, most of the worshipers rose. Some edged forward. Those nearest bent to kiss his feet. Gandhi pressed his palms together in the traditional Hindu greeting.

At that moment a young man stepped into Gandhi's path and fired three shots from a small automatic pistol. After the second bullet hit him, blood began to stain the Mahatma's white shoulder-wrap and shawl. He murmured, "*Hey, Rama*" ("Oh, God"). As the third shot struck, Gandhi collapsed on the ground, dead.

The body was brought back into the house and washed and anointed according to Hindu rites. Suggestions were heard that the Mahatma be embalmed. His son Devadas and his closest disciples objected. They wanted no worship. It was decided to cremate Gandhi the next day.

A million people lined the route from Birla House to the banks of the sacred Jumna River, where a funeral pyre had been prepared. Another million assembled around the pyre. The Pope, the Dalai Lama, the Archbishop of Canterbury, the Chief Rabbi of England, the King of England, President Harry S Truman, the President of France and the governments of all major and minor countries telegraphed condolences. The United Nations lowered its flag to half-mast.

Gandhi's life was remarkable in that he had been an indifferent pupil, a mediocre law student in London, and a failure as an attorney in Bombay. He was made great by struggle. Made aware of the indignities suffered by Indians in South Africa, he launched a twenty-one-year campaign against inequality and prejudice. His weapons were truth, reason and peaceful determination. Together these merged into an arsenal of combat that he called "civil disobedience."

Gandhi was not, at the inception of his public career, a complete pacifist or an anti-imperialist. He enlisted in the British forces in South Africa to succor the wounded on Boer War battlefields, and he recruited Indians for the British Army in World War I. But after his return to India in 1915 he gradually became the foremost fomenter of Indian nationalism.

As India neared independence, Gandhi's life became a tragedy. The Government of India Act of 1935 gave the eleven provinces of British India a degree of self-government subject to the veto of the British governors, extended the franchise to approximately 30 million persons and introduced separate electorates for religious communities. The Act thus created a large battlefield where Hindus and Moslems could compete for political power. This opportunity tempted Mohammed Ali Jinnah, who had established a lucrative law practice in England and who had earlier cooperated with the Indian Congress Party of Gandhi, Nehru, Patel and Maulana Abul Kalam Azad, to return to India. In the 1937 elections, the first held under the Act, the Indian Congress Party won overwhelmingly—even in the totally Moslem Northwest Frontier Province. The Congress Party used these victories to enhance its power at the expense of Jinnah's Moslem League. Relations between the two large religious communities were further exacerbated by social developments. In 1940 Pakistan—a separate Moslem state in the Indian subcontinent—became accepted

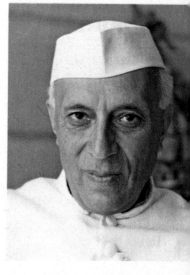

Jawaharlal Nehru, first Prime Minister of independent India.

Opposite Mohandas Gandhi, the Mahatma: "Spokesman for the conscience of all mankind."

867

One India or two?

Gandhi as a young barrister in Johannesburg. The plight of South Africa's colored community sparked Gandhi's interest in social reform.

Right Mohammed Ali Jinnah with Lord Mountbatten. Jinnah led the campaign for a separate Moslem state of Pakistan, and he became Pakistan's first Governor-General.

Gandhi with the last Viceroy of India, Earl Mountbatten of Burma, and Lady Mountbatten, two months before independence.

Moslem League doctrine. Henceforth, riots between Hindus and Moslems grew in number and ferocity.

Mahatma Gandhi was a doer. His keen political sense told him that World War II was the appropriate time for Britain to liberate India. He therefore planned a "Quit India" civil disobedience movement. Challenged by those who felt that Britain could not leave the country just when the Japanese were knocking at India's eastern door and Field Marshal Rommel was moving on Suez, Gandhi, to the astonishment of some of his closest disciples, said the British armed services could stay and also run the railways and manage the ports. Either by clear thinking or by intuition, he felt that, given the rising tide of violence and Hindu-Moslem tension, it would be best to grant India self-government while British forces remained in the land to guarantee order. And indeed it would seem, in the light of what happened during the three years after the war, that independence during wartime could have prevented the partition of India and saved the lives of hundreds of thousands of persons. In June, 1942, Gandhi launched his "Quit India" movement; it quickly turned to violence and also turned into a fiasco. Gandhi and hundreds of Congress Party leaders were imprisoned.

After his release in 1944, Gandhi knew that only the constitutional, legal way to independence lay open to him; for with violence filling the Indian air, he could no longer resort to the method by which he had achieved most of his victories and acquired most of his influence.

Gandhi accordingly welcomed the announcement by Labour Prime Minister Clement R. Attlee in the House of Commons on February 20, 1947, that Britain would quit India "by a date not later than June, 1948." The fear that England, in her enfeebled postwar state, might face a rebellious India that had wrenched itself loose from Gandhi's control gave wings to the Labour government's desire to implement its ideological commitment to Indian independence. In pursuance of Attlee's statement, an impressive British Cabinet Mission arrived in New Delhi on March 24, 1946, to negotiate with all parties and outstanding personalities in India. On May 16 the Mission published its plan for the independence of India.

The Mission stated that it had examined "closely and impartially the possibility of a partition of India" and found that in the proposed West Pakistan 37.93 per cent of the population would be non-Moslem (Hindus and Sikhs), and in the proposed East Pakistan the percentage of non-Moslems would be as high as 48.31, while 20 million Moslems would remain outside Pakistan in the Indian Union. "These figures show," the Mission declared, "that the setting up of a separate state of Pakistan on the lines claimed by the Moslem League would not solve the communal minority problem." Therefore the Mission was "unable to advise the British government that the power which at present resides in British hands should be handed over to two entirely separate sovereign states."

Instead, the Mission Plan provided for a federal system of government well suited to India's provincial fissures. The central authorities in New Delhi would deal with defense, foreign relations and communications, and presumably with currency and finance. India would be divided into three subfederations, one in the west, largely Moslem, a second in the east with a bare Moslem majority, and the core in the center, overwhelmingly Hindu.

Firmly denied Pakistan by the Mission Plan, the Moslem League, under Jinnah's presidency, unanimously accepted the three-subfederation scheme as the next best. The Congress Party hesitated. The socialists, then still members of the Congress Party, disliked the religious basis of the plan. Others were apprehensive that Hindu and Sikh regions might become encased in the western and eastern Moslem

federations. Nehru suspected that the British again proposed to divide in order to rule. But Gandhi trusted the British government. The All-India Congress Committee approved the Mission Plan on July 7 by a vote of 200 to 51.

"Now happened one of those unfortunate events which changed the course of history," wrote Maulana Abul Kalam Azad in *India Wins Freedom*:

On July 10, Jawaharlal [Nehru] held a press conference in Bombay in which he made a statement that Congress would enter the Constituent Assembly "completely unfettered by agreements and free to meet all situations as they arise…. Congress had agreed only to participate in the Constituent Assembly and regarded itself free to … modify the Cabinet Mission Plan as it thought best."

The consequences of Nehru's intervention are history. Because Nehru, the Congress Party President, had rejected the Mission Plan, Jinnah jumped to the fresh opportunity, rescinded the Moslem League's approval of the Cabinet scheme and again proposed Pakistan on July 27. He then proclaimed August 16 Direct Action Day. Calcutta, India's most populous city, became the first victim. Moslems killed Hindus, Hindus retaliated, rioting continued for four days and nights and at least 5,000 persons were killed and 15,000 wounded.

Gandhi went to Calcutta to bid the waves of hate to recede. "I am not going to leave Bengal," he pledged, "until the last embers of trouble are stamped out. I may stay on here for a whole year or more. If necessary I will die here." From Calcutta he traveled to Noakhali in the water-logged delta of the Ganges and Brahmaputra rivers. Jinnah's Direct Action Day had rent the district with civil strife. Many villages were in ashes.

He remained in Noakhali from November 7, 1946, to March 2, 1947. During that period he lived in forty-nine villages. By the time the seventy-seven-year-old leader left Noakhali, he was satisfied with the signs of intercommunity peace.

The Mahatma would have remained in Bengal but for reports reaching him from Bihar, the province that borders Bengal, of Hindu retaliatory violence against Moslems. He moved on to Bihar, where he again proved to have a magic touch.

Admiral Lord Louis Mountbatten arrived in New Delhi on March 22, 1947, to become the twentieth and last British Viceroy of India. The next day Jinnah stated that unless Moslems received Pakistan, India faced "terrific disasters." He had it in his power to unloose them. Mountbatten summoned Gandhi from Bihar. The Mahatma and the Viceroy conferred for two and a quarter hours on March 31.

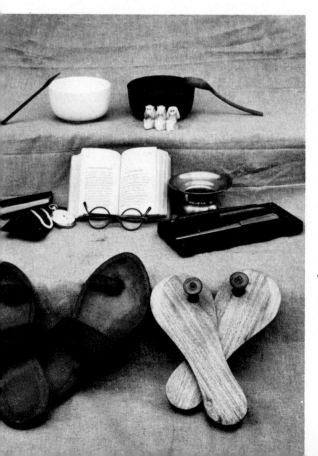

869

Five additional talks followed in the next twelve days. Jinnah was received in audience an equal number of times.

His talks with Mountbatten concluded, Gandhi returned to Bihar. Unless he could prove that the two religious communities were living in amity, Jinnah was right and Pakistan inevitable. Gandhi foresaw that partition would not solve the problems of the Indian subcontinent or reduce the level of violence. Segregation, he knew from experience, intensified hostility. Hence his total commitment to building a Hindu-Moslem bridge rather than widening the chasm.

General Lord Wavell, the preceding Viceroy, had chosen a provisional, all-Indian government with Nehru as Prime Minister and with Moslem League participation. In view of the widespread disorders, the Congress Party blundered into giving Patel the Home Ministry to cope with and letting the finance portfolio go to Liaqat Ali Khan, Jinnah's first lieutenant. By every stratagem possible the Moslem Leaguers in the provisional cabinet made it their business to prove that the Congress Party and the Moslem League, in harness together, pulled in opposite directions and could not run India.

The person most responsible for the partition of

India was Jinnah. Lord Mountbatten, addressing the Royal Empire Society in London on October 6, 1948 (after his withdrawal from office in New Delhi), told how it happened. "Mr. Jinnah made it abundantly clear from the first moment that so long as he lived he would never accept a United India. He demanded partition; he insisted on Pakistan." The Congress leaders, on the contrary, favored an undivided India, but they agreed they would accept partition to prevent civil war. Mountbatten was "convinced that the Moslem League would have fought." The question before them, Mountbatten declared, was how to partition. The Congress Party refused to let non-Moslem areas go to Pakistan. "That automatically meant a partition of the great provinces of the Punjab and Bengal," Mountbatten said. The Punjab was almost half Hindu and Sikh; Bengal almost half Hindu. Mountbatten continued:

When I told Mr. Jinnah that I had their provisional agreement [the agreement of Congress] to partition he was overjoyed. When I said that it logically followed that this would involve partition of the Punjab and Bengal he was horrified. He produced the strongest arguments why these provinces should not be partitioned. He said they had national characteristics and that partition would be disastrous. I agreed, but I said how much more must I now feel that the same considerations applied to the partitioning of the whole of India. He did not like that, and started explaining why India had to be partitioned, and so we went round and round the mulberry bush until finally he realized that either he could have a United India with an unpartitioned Punjab and Bengal or a divided India with a partitioned Punjab and Bengal, and he finally accepted the latter situation.

Jinnah was unable to crack Mountbatten's logic, but Gandhi had an answer. He, the champion of Indian independence, favored delayed independence. The British, he knew, could not surrender power to the Moslem minority. Therefore if they wanted to leave—and they so obviously did—they would have to hand over power to the Congress Party to rule an undivided India. Nehru and Krishna Menon did not share this faith. On the principle that half an India is better than none, they felt they must seize what the British offered.

So it happened that on August 15, 1947, India became free and divided: Pakistan, two lobes a thousand miles apart, hung like elephant's ears from the body of India. The day that should have marked his crowning achievement was to Gandhi a day of mourning.

The trisection of India had provoked an immediate catastrophe: a great migration commenced. Fifteen million people, crazed by fear and horrified by mass atrocities, rushed from their ancestral homes —Moslems out of India into Pakistan, Hindus and Sikhs out of Pakistan into India. The fertile Punjab, rent in two by partition, poured forth a column of half-starved humanity fifty-seven miles long, crawling in the direction of Delhi to escape death. Vultures hovered overhead, waiting for the many who would collapse by the wayside. The Nehru government set up camps to catch the Punjabis before they reached the capital, but endless thou-

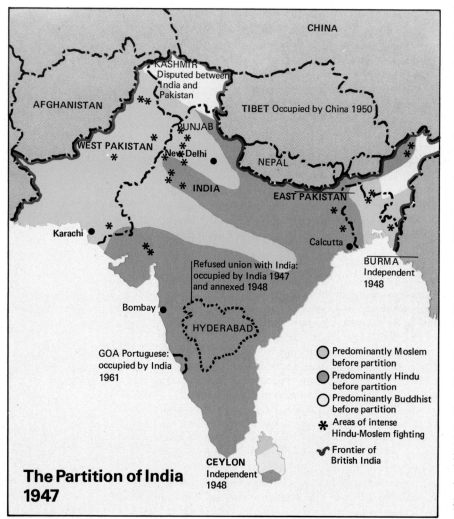

The Partition of India 1947

CHINA

KASHMIR Disputed between India and Pakistan

AFGHANISTAN

TIBET Occupied by China 1950

PUNJAB

WEST PAKISTAN

New Delhi

NEPAL

INDIA

EAST PAKISTAN

Karachi

Calcutta

Refused union with India: occupied by India 1947 and annexed 1948

BURMA Independent 1948

Bombay

HYDERABAD

GOA Portuguese: occupied by India 1961

○ Predominantly Moslem before partition
◑ Predominantly Hindu before partition
○ Predominantly Buddhist before partition
✳ Areas of intense Hindu-Moslem fighting
ᴠ Frontier of British India

CEYLON Independent 1948

sands eluded the thin cordons. In Delhi they slept on pavements, in doorways, in deserted homes. Anything belonging to a departed or lingering Moslem was fair loot.

Gandhi plunged into the eye of this tornado of madness determined to still the storm with counsels of love and peace. Slowly, in part through exhaustion, in part as a result of Gandhi's untiring talking, Delhi seemed to become an oasis of peace. Yet Gandhi was not satisfied; moslems still were afraid to walk through the capital city of free India. On January 13, 1948, he decided to fast. On the third day of the fast Gandhi dictated a statement asking the government of India to pay Pakistan 550 million rupees (approximately $180 million), a huge sum for the nearly empty treasury of New Delhi, as Pakistan's share of the assets of prepartitioned India. The Nehru Cabinet had previously refused to pay. On Gandhi's demand, it did.

The day after his fast the Mahatma was carried in a chair to the prayer meeting on the grounds of Birla House, where he had been staying. The next day he was again carried to prayers. During prayers a handmade bomb was hurled at him, but Gandhi was not injured. The young man who had thrown the bomb, Madan Lal, was a Hindu refugee from the Punjab who had found shelter in a Delhi mosque only to be evicted when, in deference to Gandhi's wishes, the police began returning mosques to Moslem worshipers. He had seen Hindus shot down in Punjab towns.

After Madan Lal's failure, Nathuram Godse came up from Bombay. He was a thirty-five-year-old editor and publisher of a Hindu Mahasabha weekly and a high-degree Brahman. He began loitering about Birla House. In the pocket of his khaki jacket he carried a small automatic pistol. Godse said at his trial that he was exasperated by India's payment of half a billion rupees to Pakistan. "I sat brooding intensely," he told the court, "on the atrocities perpetuated on Hinduism and on its dark and deadly future if left to face Islam outside and Gandhi inside." On the afternoon of January 30, he killed Mohandas K. Gandhi.

Godse and eight others found guilty of conspiracy were hanged. Gandhi, who opposed every manner of killing, would not have approved. Nonviolence had been his banner and civil disobedience his ultimate weapon. The latter helped him achieve the liberation of India, and for him the freedom of India was the prelude to the rise of free Indians, countrymen free of corruption in politics and devoted to Gandhian ideals. In this goal he failed. India remains a democracy thanks to the legacy of the British, the heritage of Gandhi and the turbulent personality of Nehru, the Westernized infidel. But although all official Indians and many unofficial Indians pay lip service to Gandhi, he is dead in India except in the hearts of the very few. "Generations to come will scarce believe," Albert Einstein once said of Gandhi, "that such a one as this ever in flesh and blood walked upon this earth."

LOUIS FISCHER

Above Gandhi's memorial at Cape Comorin in southern India; and (*below*) the centerpiece of the Gandhi memorial, which contains the Mahatma's ashes.

HAGANAH Ship
EXODUS1947

Israeli Independence

Six months before the State of Israel officially came into being, it was already fighting for its life against terrorist attacks by Arab commandos. At the time, Palestine was still under British mandate and the Palestinian Jews had no legal army. The task of defending the substantial Jewish population of the region was therefore entrusted to an irregular army known as the Haganah. Then, on November 29, 1947, the United Nations General Assembly voted 33 to 12 to partition Palestine in such a way as to create a separate Jewish state. The Arabs' reaction was immediate and violent, and during the first phase of the war that followed, the Arabs gained several substantial victories. The united Arab offensive was finally brought to a halt in the spring of 1949, and later that year Israel concluded armistice terms with its neighbors. Israel joined the family of nations—and intermittent guerrilla warfare became a fact of life in the Middle East.

At dawn on May 14, 1948, dozens of workmen were swarming over the modest building that housed the Tel Aviv Museum on the Boulevard Rothschild. They hurriedly converted the main hall of the Museum, set up a platform with tables and chairs in the middle, hung two enormous flags on the wall, and placed between them a large portrait of Theodore Herzl. Rows of seats were hastily installed on the balcony to accommodate the Philharmonic Orchestra.

At four o'clock in the afternoon, the car carrying David Ben-Gurion, the President of the National Directory, stopped in front of the Museum. The diminutive figure with the legendary mane of white hair saluted the guard of honor and ran up the steps of the building. He entered the main hall, where the other members of the Directory, those of the National Council, more than a hundred guests, notables, journalists and photographers were waiting. Ben-Gurion rose and read out Israel's declaration of independence to a visibly moved audience:

... On November 29, 1947, the General Assembly of the United Nations adopted a resolution providing for an independent Jewish state in Palestine, and invited the inhabitants of the country to take the necessary steps to put this plan into effect.

As a result, we, the members of the National Council, representing the Jewish people in Palestine and the world Zionist movement, are united today at a solemn assembly. In the light of natural law and the history of the Jewish people, as well as in accordance with the resolution of the United Nations, we proclaim the foundation of the Jewish state in the Holy Land which will bear henceforth the name of the State of Israel.

... The State of Israel will be open for the immigration of Jews from every country in which they have been dispersed. It will develop the country for the benefit of all its inhabitants. It will be founded on the principles of liberty, justice and peace, just as they were conceived by the prophets of Israel. It will respect the complete social and political equality of all its citizens, without distinction of religion, race or sex. It will guarantee freedom of religion,

conscience, education and culture. It will protect the holy places of all religious faiths, and it will sincerely apply the principles of the Charter of the United Nations.

... We wish for peace and good neighborliness, and we offer our hand to all those states which surround us. We invite them to cooperate with the independent Jewish nation for the common benefit of all.

At the end of the reading, the document was signed by the thirty-seven members of the National Council, and Ben-Gurion became Prime Minister of the State of Israel. Notably absent from the ceremony was the aged and ailing Dr. Chaim Weizmann, the future President of the State of Israel. At the time of the signing, Weizmann was visiting the United States, where he was directing all his efforts toward persuading President Truman to give the new state official recognition.

The efforts of this celebrated scholar and Zionist leader were not in vain. At two o'clock in the morning of May 15, Ben-Gurion was suddenly awakened by his aide-de-camp, who brought him a telegram. The United States had just recognized Israel. Some hours later a second telegram brought the news that Israel had also been recognized by the Soviet Union.

The Jewish State might well have been created ten years earlier, even before World War II. At that time there were some 450,000 Jews in Palestine, and they had the support of Great Britain, the mandatory power in Palestine. Successive British governments had been generally faithful to the Balfour Declaration of November 2, 1917, which advocated the establishment of a Jewish "national home" in the Holy Land.

The honeymoon between Zionism and His Majesty's government came to an end in February, 1939, during a conference at St. James's Palace in London. That conference, which brought together both Jewish and Arab delegates, was presided over by Neville Chamberlain. Great Britain, which was

The Israeli Declaration of Independence, signed by the thirty-seven members of the National Council in the Tel Aviv Museum on May 14, 1948.

Opposite Jewish immigrants arriving illegally at Haifa in 1947. After World War II, Jewish immigration to Palestine increased rapidly despite British attempts to limit the influx.

873

A modern village in Israel. Since Israel's independence the landscape of Palestine has been transformed with the aid of American grants and German war reparations.

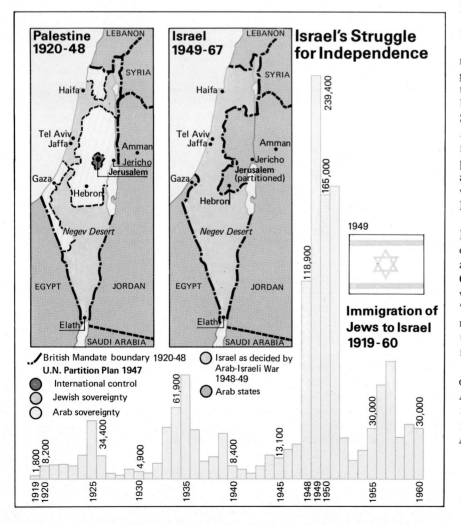

Israel's Struggle for Independence

Palestine 1920-48
LEBANON
SYRIA
Haifa
Tel Aviv
Jaffa
Amman
Gaza
Jericho
Jerusalem
Hebron
Negev Desert
EGYPT
JORDAN
Elath
SAUDI ARABIA

Israel 1949-67
LEBANON
SYRIA
Haifa
Tel Aviv
Jaffa
Amman
Gaza
Jericho
Jerusalem (partitioned)
Hebron
Negev Desert
EGYPT
JORDAN
Elath
SAUDI ARABIA

British Mandate boundary 1920-48

U.N. Partition Plan 1947
- International control
- Jewish sovereignty
- Arab sovereignty

- Israel as decided by Arab-Israeli War 1948-49
- Arab states

1949

Immigration of Jews to Israel 1919-60

1919: 1,800
1920: 8,200
1925: 34,400
1930: 4,900
1935: 61,900
1940: 8,400
1945: 13,100
1948: 118,900
1949: 239,400
1950: 165,000
1955: 30,000
1960: 30,000

preoccupied with the deteriorating international situation, decided to initiate a rapprochement with the Arab peoples of the Middle East at the expense of the Jews in Palestine. A white paper was published that announced a series of severe new measures, all disadvantageous to the Jews. They included the lowering of the immigration figures, a ban on the Jews' acquiring further territory, and the confirmation of the minority status of Jews in Palestine. From this time on, the Jewish leaders in Palestine were to engage more and more in a policy of resistance to England, whom they accused of duplicity.

More than 30,000 Palestinian Jewish men and women enlisted in the British Army in the war against Hitler, but they were also actively engaged in fighting the white paper. An extraordinary congress, organized by the American Committee for Zionist Affairs, took place in the Biltmore Hotel in New York on May 12, 1942. With one abstention, the six hundred delegates voted for the proposal that Ben-Gurion had brought from Palestine, a proposal that after the war Palestine be transformed into a "Jewish Commonwealth integrated into the new structure of world affairs." Zionism had made a further step forward. Until now it had been content with a national home in Palestine. It was now demanding an independent state.

The real fight for the creation of that state began at the end of World War II. In the new state of world affairs, the Palestinian Jews had the advantage of some firm alliances: the new President of the United States, Harry S Truman, was a confirmed friend of the Zionist cause; the Soviet Union was coming to the realization that by assisting in the creation of a Jewish state in Palestine it would be able to supplant British influence in this area of the world; and world opinion had turned a favorable eye upon the national aspirations of the Jews after the terrible slaughter that had cost 6 million of them their lives.

On the other hand, the attitude of the new Labour government in Great Britain hardened, and it refused to budge. Had England shown a little flexibility, history might well have been different, but in the face of British intransigence the Jews were forced toward more and more extreme behavior.

On February 14, 1947, Great Britain referred the matter to the United Nations. The international organization sent a commission of inquiry to Palestine that was composed of representatives from Canada, Uruguay, Guatemala, Peru, India, Iran, Holland, Sweden, Yugoslavia, Czechoslovakia and Australia. And in September the commission published its recommendations. By eight votes to three, it proposed the partition of Palestine into a Jewish state and an Arab state. On November 29, by thirty-three votes to twelve, the General Assembly of the United Nations adopted the plan of partition.

The territory allotted to the Jews by the United Nations comprised three narrow strips of land: part of Galilee, a narrow strip extending along the coast, and the Negev desert (which stretched south to the Gulf of Aqaba). These three separate territories were linked together by tiny points of contact called "kissing points." Similar points united the remaining parts of Palestine, which had been allocated to the Arabs. Jerusalem was to become an international city.

The Arabs refused to accept the plan, and on the day following the voting they went into action. Apparently unconcerned about the presence of 100,000 British soldiers in Palestine, Arab commandos killed seven Jewish travelers on the roads. And thus the war of independence in Israel broke

The birth of the Arab refugee problem

out, six months before the Jewish State came into being.

In 1949 the war came to an end, and the State of Israel had to be accepted as a fact. Through the mediation of Dr. Ralph Bunche, Israel concluded armistice terms with its neighbors. There were those in Israel who were sufficiently unsophisticated to believe that the armistice was the prelude to a final peace between the Jewish State and its Arab neighbors, but they were soon disillusioned. The Arabs, smarting under their defeat, refused to conclude peace with Israel.

There were two principal stumbling blocks to improvement in the atmosphere between Israel and its neighbors: the question of the frontiers and the tragic question of the refugees. Hundreds of thousands of Arab refugees who had left their homes during the fighting were anxious to return. Israel refused, for fear that its people would be submerged by the Arab influx.

The Arab states also refused to integrate the refugees into their population and their economy. They preferred to keep them clustered in wretched camps along the frontiers of the Jewish State and to use them as a political weapon.

As time passed, the situation along the demarcation lines of the armistice agreement became more and more precarious, and military incidents between Israelis and Arabs established themselves as a normal occurrence in Middle East affairs. In spite of the insecurity that prevailed along its frontiers, and in spite of its difficult economic situation, Israel

embarked upon a historic enterprise—the reuniting of the exiles. The young state opened its doors wide to immigration. In accordance with the Law of Return voted by the Israeli parliament, every Jew in the world had the right to become an immigrant and to settle in Israel.

Experts predicted that Israel's wide-open immigration policy would result in an economic catastrophe. They maintained that the State of Israel was incapable of absorbing so many people, to whom it could offer neither homes nor jobs. Their fears were in part borne out, for during the first years of the "return" the new arrivals did live in appalling conditions. Camps of tents and huts covered the countryside, an austere economic regime was put into operation, and the budget was balanced only by donations and loans from abroad. In spite of all those difficulties, Israel succeeded in integrating the returnees. Between 1948 and 1969, some 1,280,000 immigrants arrived in Israel, whose Jewish population now totals almost 2.5 million.

Israel's basic problem was that of defense. From 1948 on, military experts thought little of the chances of 1 or 2 million Jews holding their own against tens of millions of Arabs. But as the years passed, Israel not only succeeded in defending itself against its enemies but even asserted an undeniable military ascendancy. The Israeli Army, which had been forged in the course of the war of independence, was organized and consolidated under the aegis of David Ben-Gurion, President of the Council and Minister of Defense from 1948 to 1953.

Israel's Territorial Gains in the Six Day War 1967

- Gained from Syria
- Gained from Jordan
- Gained from Egypt

ISRAEL
Jerusalem
Suez Canal
Negev Desert
Sinai Desert
JORDAN
SAUDI ARABIA
EGYPT

Israeli troops crossing the Sinai Desert during the Six-Day War of 1967, while a truckload of Egyptian prisoners is driven towards Israel.

Shattering the delicate balance of the Middle East

Jaffa during the 1948 war.

Planting the Israeli flag at Elath during the 1948 war. Elath is Israel's only port on the Gulf of Aqaba and is the terminus of a new oil pipeline.

In 1953 Ben-Gurion resigned from office and settled in the kibbutz of Sde Boker in the Negev. His intention was to set an example for the nation's youth and attract those youths to the pioneer work of reclaiming the desert, but his example was not followed. Ben-Gurion was replaced as President of the Council by Moshe Sharett, who also held the office of Foreign Secretary. Sharett, who was a far more moderate man than Ben-Gurion, was to be bitterly disappointed in his efforts to find a basis for agreement with the Arabs. In February, 1955, Sharett's Minister of Defense resigned, and Ben-Gurion was asked to fill the vacant post. Following the general election of August, 1955, he once more became President of the Council.

At that time, an explosive situation was building up on the country's frontiers. Infiltrators, commandos who called themselves Volunteers for Death, and even regular units of the Egyptian Army were broadcasting terror in Israel, and the situation was the same on the Jordanian and Syrian frontiers. The Arab states were acting in concert against Israel. Ben-Gurion strongly advocated a firm line, and the Israeli Army, led by its commander in chief, General Moshe Dayan, reacted to every case of provocation with harsh reprisals against the neighboring states. Those provocations and reprisals soon became a vicious circle, one in which cause and effect were indistinguishable.

On September 17, 1955, the President of Egypt, Gamal Abdel Nasser, announced the signature of a commercial agreement with Czechoslovakia by the terms of which Egypt would receive several hundred tanks as well as large numbers of fighter and bomber aircraft. The delicately balanced equilibrium of the Middle East was shattered. In October, 1955, Nasser declared the Gulf of Aqaba completely closed to Israel's ships and planes, and a joint military command was established for the Egyptian, Syrian and Jordanian armies. Using the Gaza Strip, which was

The Arabs vigorously resisted the establishment of a Jewish state in Palestine. Here Arab rioters are burning goods in Jaffa harbor.

administered by Egypt, as a base, Arab terrorists penetrated deep into Israeli territory.

Israel, threatened with encirclement, decided to counter the Arab nations' move with a war of deterrence. In this Israel was encouraged by France and Great Britain, who had been preparing for military intervention in Egypt since July, 1956, when Nasser nationalized the Suez Canal. On October 22, 1956, a top-secret conference of Israeli, French and British leaders met at Sèvres, near Paris. Israel was represented by Ben-Gurion, France by several government ministers, and Great Britain by her Minister of Foreign Affairs, Selwyn Lloyd. A protocol was signed that constituted collusion between the three countries, and Israel attacked Egypt on October 29. That attack served as a pretext for the intervention of the Franco-British forces in Egypt. The war that Israeli troops waged in the Sinai Desert was a success, but the Franco-British landing was a disaster.

Israel emerged from the Sinai war as a state to be reckoned with. She had wiped out the strongest Arab army in the Middle East with no great difficulty,

and her prime military objects had been achieved. The Gulf of Aqaba was reopened to Israeli shipping, and peace was assured for several years.

In May of 1967, without any warning, Egypt dispatched troops to the Israeli frontier, drove the Bluecaps of the United Nations from the border region, and once more imposed the blockade on the Gulf of Aqaba. After an initial period of irresolution, the Israeli government decided to take action: Moshe Dayan, the conqueror of Sinai, was called upon to take over the Ministry of Defense, and General Itzhak Rabin was made commander in chief of the Israeli Army.

On June 5, the Israeli forces attacked Egypt. In a lightning action they occupied the whole of Sinai, wiped out the Egyptian Army and Air Force and reached the banks of the Suez Canal. Jordan and Syria intervened, only to suffer bitter defeats and to lose part of their territories to Israel. (The Jordanian part of Jerusalem, for example, fell into the hands of the Israelis, who annexed and reunited the city.)

In spite of their defeat the Arabs refused to negotiate peace terms with Israel, and the Jewish State continued to occupy the conquered territories. Israel had learned the lessons of war: it had found that even after many years, peace with the Arabs was a vain hope. It had also learned that the Israeli Army was far stronger than the united armies of its neighbors, and that the danger of the complete destruction of the Jewish State by the Arab states could definitely be discounted.

By creating a completely new nation, the beleaguered and, when necessary, bellicose State of Israel has brought about a profound change in the lives of millions of Jews scattered around the world. At the same time, its emergence has profoundly upset the established order and social structure of the surrounding states and has created a hotbed of unresolved tension in the Middle East.

MICHEL BAR-ZOHAR

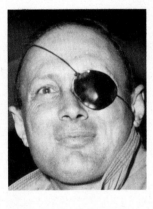

Moshe Dayan, Defense Minister of Israel and a former member of the Stern Gang, one of the terrorist organizations set up by the Jews in Palestine before 1948.

Left David Ben-Gurion, Israel's first Prime Minister.

877

Red Victory in China 1949

The city of Nanking, longtime capital of Generalissimo Chiang Kai-shek's Nationalist regime, was all but abandoned by the time Mao Tse-tung's troops reached the city's bridges on April 23, 1949. Chiang, his vice president Li Tsung-jên and the Kuomintang government had fled, leaving Nanking's terrified populace to face the advancing Communists. The Reds' bloodless "capture" and pacific occupation of the city marked the beginning of the end of the protracted and bitter civil war that had been raging in China for more than two decades. Moreover, it signaled the imminent collapse of the Kuomintang (which had failed to incorporate the Communists in 1923 or 1936—or to eradicate them in 1934). Refusing to capitulate, Chiang and his fugitive government withdrew to Formosa, where they continue to pose an ideological—if not a military— threat to the Communists. From 1949 on, mainland China has belonged to Mao.

The Communists entered Nanking, the Nationalist capital, on April 23, 1949—and to some, Communist hegemony in mainland China begins on that date, although the National Day is celebrated by virtue of an arbitrary decision on October 1, 1949. Canton was not occupied until mid-October of 1949, however, and the large South China Sea island of Hainan was taken still later. On October 1, the Nationalists still had a foothold in Fukien, facing the Formosa Straits. Yunnan, bordering on French Indochina, did not fall until mid-December, and Chengtu, the capital of Szechwan, held out until the twenty-seventh. Actually, in April, 1949, Nanking was a capital in name only. The head of state, Generalissimo Chiang Kai-shek, had resigned on January 21 and both he and the government had departed.

The undefended city did not fall in a military sense; it was merely taken over as a result of a bid that had been made elsewhere and some time before. There had been no fighting, although a few days earlier the Communists, poised on the north bank of the Yangtse River, had indulged in some rather symbolic shelling. Tens of thousands of civilians (who were fleeing an expected massacre that never took place) had been streaming eastward in the direction of Shanghai, only to find themselves already cut off. The armies of Mao Tse-tung were quietly, almost unobtrusively, marching into what had been— except during the Japanese occupation and during the puppet Wang Ching-wei regime—the capital of Kuomintang China for twenty-two years.

No great crowds were about in the streets of Nanking either to curse or to cheer the newcomers. Curiously enough, the Communists were wearing the same uniforms as the Kuomintang troops, although theirs were woven of coarser cotton and were a little greener in shade. The shops had put up their shutters, as had always been the rule in China wherever and whenever the military moved in. Everyone was expecting the worst from the soldiery,

and when the soldiers failed to conform to tradition, the very first reaction of the people was one of puzzlement rather than gratitude. The Communist troops did not loot, rob, ransack, or rape—yet even their decorous behavior, breaking with tradition, was disquieting to the populace. The psychological effect was tremendous. It was, in the fullest sense of the word, revolutionary.

The propaganda machine was immediately set in motion as the Communist Army's team of artists, who had arrived with the vanguard, began chalking multicolored pictures on walls. The almost invariable subject was a soldier with a red star on his cap who was freeing the oppressed Chinese people from the imperialists and the "Kuomintang bandits." The drawing was often excellent and the style always typically Russian. The local press resumed publication with new staffs. Less than two hours after the first Communist soldiers had entered Nanking, the radio station was broadcasting again—and even giving the details of programs for the whole week to come. The police, who had for the most part remained at their posts, appeared to have undergone lightning brainwashing. Overnight their surliness and arrogance became smiling politeness to all.

The Chinese Communist Party had come into being on July 1, 1921. It was organized by a Russian Comintern delegate named Gregori Voitinsky, and its early members had all had their political training in Europe: Chou En-lai and Li Li-san in France, Chu Teh in Germany, Ch'ü Ch'iu-pai in Russia. At the time it was essentially a party of intellectuals, one that held little appeal for the proletarian masses. When, for survival's sake, it joined hands with the Kuomintang in 1923, its officially recorded membership did not exceed three hundred.

The Kuomintang, under Sun Yat-sen, the "Father of the Chinese Revolution," was the only organized revolutionary force in the country at the time. No actual merger ever took place, but the Communist Party, Russian-dominated and officially playing

Chiang Kai-shek as a young revolutionary in the Kuomintang.

Opposite A poster commemorating the Communist victory over Chiang Kai-shek in 1949.

The funeral of Dr. Sun Yat-sen, who founded the Kuomintang and pushed China into the twentieth century.

1925 did not palpably affect the situation. What was later to be known as the Northern Expedition—the campaign to capture North China from its ruling warlords—was being feverishly prepared for in South China in that year, and Soviet advice was more than ever required, even though the leaders of the right wing of the Kuomintang, Hu Han-min and Chiang Kai-shek himself, already had their misgivings as to the future of Kuomintang-Communist cooperation. The Chinese Communists were by then efficiently using the Kuomintang machinery to their own ends, and they were successful to such an extent that by 1926 their party membership had risen to some 45,000.

In July of the same year, the Northern Expedition got under way and made rapid progress under the military leadership of Chiang Kai-shek. The Yangtse River—halfway to Peking—was reached the following spring. Almost at once the breach between the Communists and the Kuomintang became an accomplished fact, with the former establishing themselves at Hankow and Chiang setting up his capital at Nanking and dominating the Lower Yangtse Valley.

From then on, the Northern Drive was forgotten. The warlords, far more frightened by the growing influence of the Communists than by Chiang Kai-shek's nationalism, gradually came to terms with him. At the same time, a new civil war broke out. The tide ran against the Communists, who were forced to retreat southward. The first Chinese Soviet

second fiddle to the Kuomintang, did its best to infiltrate and subvert Sun's party. Sun Yat-sen was willing to welcome Soviet assistance, especially in the fields of party organization and propaganda technique, and the Communists were in a position to provide it. Moreover, the Western democracies, by consistently ignoring Dr. Sun, actually forced him to throw himself into the arms of the Russians.

Indeed, it was with the Russians, not the Chinese Communists, that Sun Yat-sen entered into virtual political partnership early in 1923. His death in

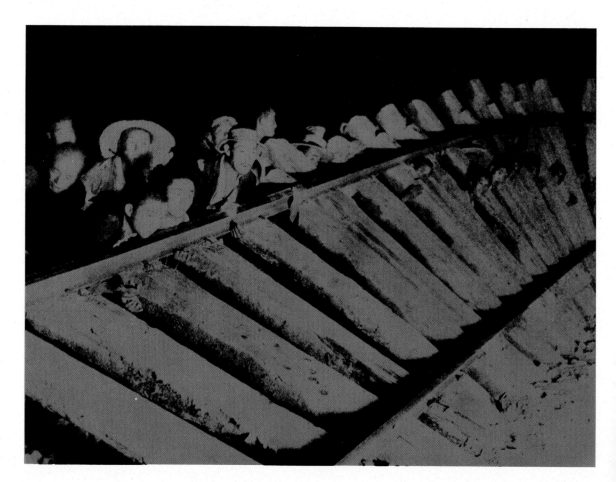

Communist guerrillas overturning a railway line in order to cut enemy supply lines.

880

Sun Yat-sen: partner of the Russians

Republic was founded in the southeastern province of Kiangsi in 1931. It took the Nationalists no less than five military campaigns to drive out the Communists, and it was not until the fall of 1934 that the Communists' exodus north—known as the Long March—began. By a very roundabout way it brought them to the northwestern province of Shensi, where Yenan became their new capital in December, 1936. For a whole year they had fought their way, not through China, but rather around China, and during that time Mao Tse-tung's political leadership asserted itself.

In these years, other things had been happening in China. There had been the 1931 Japanese aggression, which resulted in the virtual annexation of Manchuria and further encroachments in North China. Another Japanese invasion was imminent in 1936, and everyone in China knew it. It had been widely stated that the Nationalists were then prepared to come to terms with imperialist Japan, but nothing could have been further from the truth. In 1936, Chiang Kai-shek was as acutely aware of the new Japanese threat as everyone else and, it would seem, ready to face it. Still, he made it very plain that he wanted to liquidate the Communists first. A sixth campaign had already been planned against them. The man in charge was the "Young Marshal," Chang Hsueh-liang. His headquarters were at Sian, close to Communist territory. He had all the troops and equipment he needed. Yet he wavered—and so, in December, 1936, Chiang himself flew to Sian,

where Chang Hsueh-liang at once arrested him.

The Communist forces had numbered 130,000 when they left their Kiangsi capital late in 1934. A bare 30,000 had reached Yenan after the Long March. The exhausted, if heroic, body of men, hard put to find its feet on new ground, lacking arms and generally unfit, was in no position to resist Chang Hsueh-liang, had he obeyed his orders. But Chang hesitated, the Communists captured Yenan, and a few days later the Sian "incident" occurred. It was Communist General Chou En-lai who went to Sian

Students organized by Mao Tse-tung singing anti-Japanese songs. During the Japanese occupation the Red Army became the focus for patriotic resistance.

The Red Army marching into Nanking on April 23, 1949.

A recent picture of Mao Tse-tung.

attack on Britain's Far Eastern possessions brought the whole Anglo-Saxon world into the war on the side of China. The events also brought a host of American military and diplomatic personnel to Chungking, China's wartime capital.

The Japanese North China forces had been progressing rapidly southward along the main roads and railways, but they had not advanced along a continuous front, steamroller fashion, and so had left in their rear a vast military, political and administrative vacuum. The Communists began to fill this vacuum, and by the end of World War II in 1945, they had secured for themselves considerable popular support in many provinces.

At Chungking, Chou En-lai, shrewd and brilliant as ever, was concentrating on the Americans, mostly the diplomats, and in so convincing a manner that, years before a pro-Nationalist China lobby had come into being in the U.S. Congress, there existed a pro-Mao faction within the Department of State, where the view prevailed that the Chinese Communists were democratically minded and that their general purpose was to bring about liberal reforms.

Thus when the Japanese capitulated, the position of the Chinese Communists became extremely strong, both nationally and internationally. They were ready for a resumption of the civil war (actually there had been many military clashes between the Communists and the Nationalists during the official truce), but appearances had to be considered and foreign sympathies retained. The Nationalists, on the other hand, were in a difficult situation: they had no illusions about the Reds' plans for total national domination, but they had lost much ground since 1936 when the Communists, although practically at bay, had made their bid to take over China.

In fact, hostilities were resumed immediately after the Japanese capitulation (August 15, 1945) when the Communist commander in chief, ordered his troops in North China to disarm the Japanese. Thanks to a prompt American airlift, the Nationalists beat them to it. Nevertheless, the truce had come to a spectacular end, even though both sides continued to proclaim their desire for peace.

By the end of the year, the situation had deteriorated to such an extent that President Truman sent General George C. Marshall to China as a mediator. His efforts resulted in yet another truce agreement, signed on January 10, 1946, and the setting up in Peking of a tripartite commission—Kuomintang, Communist and American—to see that it was properly abided by. It never was. A year later, first the Americans, then the Communists left the commission.

The stage was set for a last act, during which the fortunes of civil war at first seemed to favor the Nationalists, who beat back three Communist offensives led by Lin Piao, and even succeeded in occupying Yenan. The unaccountable capitulation of General Fu Tso-yi, in whom Chiang Kai-shek placed great trust, and whose forces in North China greatly outnumbered the Communists, soon turned the tide. All Nationalist resistance then collapsed,

to negotiate with Chiang, and, indeed, to rescue him. A Kuomintang-Communist truce ensued, and a united anti-Japanese front (later made official and formal) was agreed upon.

The probable truth of the matter is that in 1936, as in 1923, the Communist Party in China could not have survived without entering into some sort of partnership with the Kuomintang.

During the war with Japan, an uneasy truce was maintained, both sides being aware that the struggle for power had merely been postponed. In December, 1941, Pearl Harbor and the simultaneous Japanese

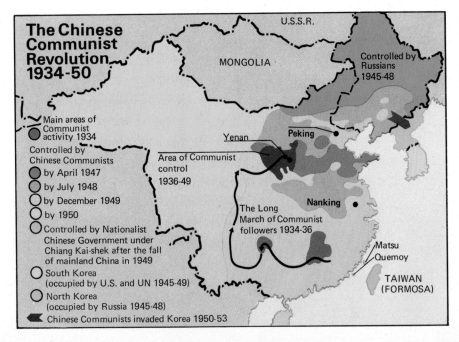

The Chinese Communist Revolution 1934-50

- Main areas of Communist activity 1934
- Controlled by Chinese Communists
  - by April 1947
  - by July 1948
  - by December 1949
  - by 1950
- Controlled by Nationalist Chinese Government under Chiang Kai-shek after the fall of mainland China in 1949
- South Korea (occupied by U.S. and UN 1945-49)
- North Korea (occupied by Russia 1945-48)
- Chinese Communists invaded Korea 1950-53

U.S.S.R.

MONGOLIA

Controlled by Russians 1945-48

Yenan   Peking

Area of Communist control 1936-49

The Long March of Communist followers 1934-36

Nanking

Matsu
Quemoy

TAIWAN (FORMOSA)

Nationalist collapse in the North

The victorious Red Army entering Peking on January 31, 1949.

and Nanking fell a short time after Peking.

Relations between Washington and the Nationalist government had been uneasy for a long time. Ever since the war years when General Stilwell, Chiang Kai-shek's American Chief of Staff, was wont to call Chiang "the peanut" in the rather public privacy of his own circle of friends (and even before the press), and when the U.S. Embassy was engaged in rather active flirtation with Yenan, there had been considerable mutual distrust. Even before the Japanese collapse of 1945, America and China had been on rather strained terms.

After V-J Day and the almost immediate resumption of civil war in China, the Americans engaged in various efforts at mediation, trying to bring about at least a modus vivendi. But both the Kuomintang and the Communists were playing the game only as far as it suited them and wondering at Yankee political blindness. Washington's diplomacy had come to favor the Reds more and more and continued to do so even after the Marshall truce was broken in 1946, and the Communists, seeing no further reason to placate the Americans, abruptly attacked them in their propaganda. What happened then is reported in a recent edition of Taipei's official *China Year Book* in the following words: "At this juncture, when the Chinese Communists openly launched their anti-American movement, the American Government stopped its supply of arms to the Chinese Government without taking any

action against the Chinese Communists despite the latter's violations of the American-mediated truce agreement."

By 1949, after the Communist takeover of the mainland, the Americans were ready to write Nationalist China off. In order to prepare public opinion at home and abroad for such a change in foreign policy, the State Department published a white paper that amounted to a denunciation of the Kuomintang regime and a discreet assurance of American goodwill toward the Communists. This document, the first official hint of an American desire for disengagement in East Asia, was received in Taiwan with much anger. Taiwan would obviously soon stand alone.

On March 1, 1950, Chiang Kai-shek, who had tendered his resignation as President of the Chinese Republic, withdrew it and resumed office. It was at that point an act of courage, for the position of Taiwan looked almost desperate and Chiang could well have taken refuge on the other side of the Pacific Ocean, as many of his friends had done.

On June 25, Communist North Korea invaded the Republic of South Korea. The United States, which promptly came to the embattled South Koreans' aid, eventually extended its military protection to include Chiang's endangered government-in-exile. With the U.S. Seventh Fleet patrolling the Straits of Formosa, the survival of Chiang Kai-shek's regime was no longer in doubt. JACQUES MARCUSE

Lin Piao, Mao's heir apparent, holding a copy of the *Sayings of Chairman Mao.*

By the end of the 1940s, China was bursting its seams, for despite the country's immense size, less than 15 per cent of the mainland was arable, and the country's burgeoning population desperately needed new sources of food and raw materials. Excluded from international trade by the Western powers' "containment" policy, Mao's regime turned on its southern, northern, and western neighbors.

One of the first countries to be directly affected by the ominous external manifestations of Red China's internal chaos was India. In that country, Chinese harassment took the form of intermittent border disputes, the most serious of which occurred in October of 1959. India's own internal problems had begun in earnest more than a decade earlier, when attempts to partition the subcontinent between Hindu and Moslem factions had resulted in bloody riots.

Mahatma Gandhi's colleague, Jawaharlal Nehru, had inherited a bitterly divided nation, and his first years in office were devoted almost exclusively to restoring civil concord. On January 1, 1949, a Hindu-Pakistani cease-fire agreement ended the clash over the northeastern province of Kashmir, and an uneasy truce followed. Nehru, a gentle and pacific leader, presided over the internally uneasy, externally threatened and eternally bankrupt subcontinent for fifteen years. During that time he established himself as one of the world's leading "neutralists" and a formidable international mediator. (Nehru won such wide international respect and such deep domestic loyalty that within a few years of his death in 1964, his daughter, Indira Gandhi, was selected as Premier.)

Berlin blockade

Mahatma Gandhi had been dead less than three months when events in occupied Germany shifted the world's attention away from India. On April 2, 1948, Soviet authorities halted all barge traffic in the Russian-occupied Eastern Zone. The Russians' provocative move—part of a general policy of harassment designed to thwart the Allies' attempts to establish effective joint control over the divided country—was rescinded three days later, but the matter was far from closed. On June 18, the Russians terminated

United Nations troops in South Korea.

interzonal passenger traffic in both directions, and six days after that they cut all land communications between the Western Zone and Berlin, which lay entirely within the Eastern Zone and was administered jointly by the Big Four. On June 28, the United States and Great Britain inaugurated a massive airlift of fuel and foodstuffs to the isolated city, and by the time the blockade was finally lifted Allied transport planes had delivered 2.3 million tons of supplies to the beleaguered German metropolis. Three hundred and twenty-two days and 277,264 mercy flights later, the blockade was officially lifted. By that time two municipal assemblies—one Communist, the other pro-West—had been elected, and the city had been divided into armed Eastern and Western zones.

Conflict in Korea

Germany's fate was to be Korea's as well, for there too Allied occupation forces had found themselves unable to agree on a means of propelling the Koreans toward independence. The ensuing stalemate played havoc with the country's economy, for the north-south division agreed upon at Potsdam effectively isolated the agricultural south (the U.S. zone) from the industrialized north (the Russian zone). In August of 1948, the South Koreans abandoned hope of uniting the country, declared all lands south of the 38th parallel part of the Republic of South Korea, and elected Syngman

Rhee their President. The North Koreans promptly retaliated by proclaiming the lands above the parallel the Peoples' Democratic Republic.

On June 25, 1950, North Korean troops burst across the 38th parallel at eleven separate points and invaded South Korea in force. Rhee's government called upon the United Nations for assistance, and the United States independently and immediately came to the South Koreans' aid. At the time, Russia's delegates to the United Nations were boycotting all committees that included representatives of the Nationalist Chinese government-in-exile—and their boycott included the Security Council. For this reason, the Council was able to pass a resolution calling for the United Nations' armed intervention in the Korean conflict without fear of a Russian veto.

In September a counteroffensive launched against the invading North Korean armies pushed them back to the 38th parallel, and in October General Douglas MacArthur, commander in chief of the combined U.N.-U.S. forces, crossed the parallel and pressed his attack north to the borders of Manchuria. At this point, the war took a dramatic, significant and costly turn: on November 26, the Communist Chinese Army intervened on the North Koreans' side. On January 1, 1951, this rejuvenated force broke through U.N. lines, and on January 4 they took Seoul, South Korea's capital. Unable to achieve a clear-cut military victory,

the U.N. forces were obliged to negotiate. Cease-fire talks, initiated in July, were soon broken off, but on October 25, 1951, formal negotiations were resumed.

Armistice talks dragged on for months, as efforts to negotiate a settlement were repeatedly scuttled by the Communists. (In July of 1952, for example, the Russians' exercised their veto power in the Security Council for the forty-ninth time in the Council's seven-year history, that time to prevent a Red Cross investigation of unsubstantiated Chinese allegations of germ warfare, charges that were then stalling the talks.) On July 26, 1953, an armistice was finally signed, and fighting officially halted the next day. The 50,000 American combat troops still stationed in South Korea, and subsequent international crises such as the 1968 *Pueblo* incident, attest to the uncertainty of that settlement.

Hungary's "Freedom Fighters"

The weaknesses of the United Nations revealed by the Korean crisis were underscored by the catastrophe that befell Hungary in 1956. In October of that year, seething discontent among the subjugated masses erupted in the form of anti-Soviet rioting in Budapest. At the end of the month, seemingly

Russian tanks arriving in Budapest during the 1956 revolution.

responsive Soviet occupational troops withdrew from the Hungarian capital on the condition that riots cease. At that, Premier Imre Nagy promised the rebellious citizenry free elections—and the Soviets promptly reoccupied the city. János Kádár's puppet government was installed, tanks suppressed

Departing British troops waving to Danish United Nations soldiers taking over after the Suez invasion, 1956.

the hopelessly outclassed rebels, and Nagy was eventually executed. The United Nations twice condemned the Soviet action but was powerless to intervene.

Suez and the Six-Day War

The United Nations' most effective police action occurred at precisely the time that Nagy's regime was toppling. On June 13, 1956, Britain had relinquished its seventy-four-year occupation of the Suez Canal, a vital shipping link in its oil lifeline. Six weeks later, Egypt's mercurial President Gamal Abdel Nasser nationalized the Canal. Subsequently, Nasser successfully resisted the Western powers' concerted efforts—in the form of both diplomatic and economic pressure —to force him to back down.

On October 29, Israeli troops invaded the Sinai—and French and English forces promptly intervened by parachuting troops along the Suez Canal. In a rare show of unanimity, the U.N. Security Council dispatched a peace-keeping force to the Middle East, and by November 15, that unit had arrived to enforce a shaky cease-fire arranged a week earlier.

The Middle East remained a crisis-ridden region, however, and the already tense situation there was further exacerbated by the rapid arms buildup that occurred in the mid-1950s. Later events included a 1957 dispute between Syria and the United States; a dramatic East-West confrontation growing out of a border dispute between Turkey and Syria; intermittent border warfare between

Israel and her Arab neighbors; and the 1958 landing of U.S. troops in Lebanon. All presaged the swift, militarily shrewd and stunningly successful attack that Israel launched against the Arab nations in 1967. This air and ground strike, which began June 5, was directed primarily against missile sites and air bases in Egypt. Within a matter of hours, the Egyptian Air Force had been decimated (most of the planes

Gamal Abdul Nasser, President of Egypt.

were destroyed on the ground and a number of Russian-built missile sites were captured intact). Israel's other Arab neighbors promptly joined the fight, but the Israelis quickly occupied the strategically vital Gaza Strip and the Golan

Heights region of Syria and swept south and east to the banks of the Suez Canal. Jordanian territory on the west bank of the Jordan River also fell to Israeli commandos, as did the Old City of Jerusalem. On June 10, the "Six-Day War" was over. The Arabs had lost more than 2 billion dollars in equipment and armaments, and despite immense territorial gains, the Israelis had actually shortened and consolidated their borders.

"Perónitis" in South America

America's attention focused almost exclusively on Western Europe during the immediate postwar period, and relations with Latin America were largely neglected. For a time, at least, there seemed little cause for concern: the threat of Communist take-over, ubiquitous in Eastern Europe, had not yet spread to the Americas, and United States' dealings with its Central and South American neighbors were amiable and progressive. In 1947, for example, every Latin American state joined the United States in signing the Rio Treaty, thereby pledging reciprocal assistance in case of armed attack. A year later, the Pan-American Conference at Bogotá drew up plans for the Organization of American States, a pact that extended hemispheric cooperation into economic areas.

The amiability of the late 1940s was deceptive, however, for beneath the tranquil façade, two radically different forces were locked in bitter struggle. This clash— between rebel forces, who were attempting to establish genuine democracy in Latin America, and existing military dictatorships— served to entrench the juntas that were to dominate Latin American politics for the next two decades.

Foremost among South American dictators was Juan Perón, the high-handed, high-living ruler of the continent's richest country, Argentina. Perón, whose *descamisados* ("shirtless ones") had swept him into office in February of 1946, had subsequently embarked on a program of ruthless press censorship and rapid nationalization. In June of 1955, resentment against the Argentinian president's tyrannical tactics reached its peak, and mutinous military officers engineered a coup that resulted in Perón's ouster. The full significance of Perón's fall was first felt some eighteen months later in Cuba,

where a series of events suggested that the days of all Latin American dictators were numbered.

The bearded one

In November of 1956, while Perón fumed and plotted in exile, revolutionary forces in Cuba launched the first of a series of attacks on the oppressive dictatorship of Fulgencio Batista. Led by a young lawyer named Fidel Castro, the rebel forces camped in the Sierra Maestra region of eastern Cuba. They survived repeated government efforts to eradicate them (including a campaign of terror that resulted in some 20,000 executions over a two-year

Joseph McCarthy, who built America's suspicion of communism into a fear of everything that was liberal and intellectual.

period), and in November of 1958 —precisely two years after their initial uprising—Fidel's forces initiated a final offensive.

Within a month the government was tottering, and when Castro's three hundred-man force routed a government garrison ten times its size at Santa Clara, Batista fled. In the months that followed, Cuba rapidly entered the Soviet sphere, and in May of 1961 Castro's island was officially declared a socialist state.

In Cuba, the old order had proved incapable of coping with postwar demands for agrarian reform and truly representative government; in Algeria, the story was very much the same.

De Gaulle Returns to Power

By the spring of 1958, General Charles de Gaulle had spent nearly twelve years in self-imposed retirement. Following his resignation in 1946 as provisional president of France's shaky Fourth Republic, the General had watched twenty-one unstable coalition governments attempt to cope with the problems of postwar France. By 1958, the situation had grown grave indeed: the disaster at Dien Bien Phu had cost France its empire in Indochina; Tunisia and Morocco had also broken away; and Algeria was in open rebellion. On May 15, General Raoul Salan, commander in chief of French troops in Algeria, stepped onto the balcony of the Gouvernement Général in Algiers and declared: "Long live de Gaulle!" Deserted by the military and rent by political infighting, the troubled Fourth Republic was dying. Its final act was to call upon "the greatest of all Frenchmen" to form a new government.

Raoul Salan, commander in chief of the French forces in Algeria and one of the rebel leaders. He was sentenced to death *in absentia* in 1961.

Opposite Charles de Gaulle.

At 6 P.M. on May 13, 1958, a European mob swept through the seat of Algeria's Gouvernement Général crying "Long live French Algeria!" For several years a bitter civil war had raged between Algerian Moslems, who were demanding self-rule, and Algeria's European settlers, who were implacably opposed to independence. Through demonstrations, strikes, and incidents, the Europeans hoped to prevent the government in Paris from negotiating with the insurgents of the National Liberation Front (FLN), the leading nationalist group, for a political solution to the Algerian problem. By storming the Gouvernement Général, the Europeans, for the first time in the long history of Algerian colonization, were openly rejecting the authority of the French Republic.

The police showed few signs of serious resistance to the actions of the mob on May 13. By and large the police did not conceal their sympathies for the cause of French Algeria. At first the French Army held back, but then, in the face of mounting tension, it showed its hand. One of the Army's outstanding commanders was General Jacques Massu, who had made his reputation by cleaning out pockets of FLN resistance at the earlier Battle of Algiers. Massu made a dramatic public appearance before the crowds of demonstrators and proclaimed: "The Army is on your side!"

Shortly before 9 P.M. on May 13, Massu made a second appearance and read from the telegram that he had just addressed to the President of the Republic, René Coty:

I, General Massu, hereby inform you of the creation, under my presidency, of a civil and military Committee for Public Safety. This has been made necessary by the gravity of the situation and the vital need to maintain order and avoid bloodshed. We demand the setting up in Paris of a government capable of keeping Algeria as an integral part of Metropolitan France.

The Army had crossed the Rubicon and the death throes of the Fourth Republic had begun. For several months, in fact, the Fourth Republic had survived only by a series of makeshift measures. Behind its façade, the structure was tottering. Ever since Charles de Gaulle had resigned as provisional president in 1946, the Republic had failed to achieve stability. Between December, 1946, and May, 1958, no less than twenty-one governments had come to power—having an average life of six months.

"The system," as de Gaulle nicknamed the Fourth Republic, had become the pawn of political parties. Since the liberation of France in 1944, the Communist Party had monopolized nearly a quarter of the votes at each election and had become the only substantial force in a rapidly declining democracy. By opposing all governments in power, the Communists had, in effect, joined forces with the Gaullist opposition.

France had emerged from war and occupation destroyed, pillaged and demoralized. The reconstruction had allowed all sorts of feudal systems to develop, and among these, political syndicates were not the least self-interested. The country was deeply divided. The German occupation had brought about a direct confrontation between the Resistance forces and the Vichyists. Since the war, international developments had brought the defenders of national independence and the partisans of European integration face to face. A permanent state of conflict existed between those who claimed they wanted to preserve the French Empire and those who, through idealism or self-interest, wanted a return to the limits of Metropolitan France.

Prime Minister Winston Churchill and General de Gaulle walk down Paris' Champs Élysées after honoring the war dead at the Arc de Triomphe in November, 1944. De Gaulle's wartime experiences as leader of the Free French led to a distrust of Britain and the United States that became apparent in French foreign policy after 1958.

French parachutists landing at Dien Bien Phu in 1954. On May 7 the Communists captured this key stronghold, and shortly afterwards they overran Hanoi, the capital of French Indochina. French power collapsed in Vietnam, Africa, Syria and Lebanon during the postwar period.

Since November, 1956, war had been dragging on in Algeria. One million privileged citizens of European origin were living on an average yearly income of 450,000 francs and were paying only indirect taxes. On the other hand, there were 8.5 million Moslems living on an average yearly income of 16,000 francs. Although they represented 90 per cent of the population, they provided very few of the elite and the intellectuals. Only one Moslem child in seventy-five went to school. These desperate masses were increasingly turning their eyes toward the Third World, where colonization was giving way to independence everywhere.

In 1958 the whole of political life in France was carried on atop the Algerian volcano. In Paris, the word "government" had become a joke. On March 13 the Paris police, who were dissatisfied with their lot, had besieged the Chamber of Deputies and threatened the people's representatives. Then, on May 13, the Army uprising in Algeria broke out.

The regime, which had lost control of its own police force, now saw its own Army turning upon it.

The news of the uprising threw political circles into complete chaos. The government of Félix Gaillard had been overthrown on April 15. Pierre Pflimlin was invested as the new Premier on the night of May 13, thanks to the support of the Communist Party. Indecisive, ill-informed and torn between the various political groups, Pflimlin struggled to maintain his position. One moment he would send a telegram expressing confidence to the Army leaders, and the next he would cast about for the means of crushing their insubordination. Parliament became a humming beehive of rumors.

But throughout the whole country, an increasingly powerful trend was becoming apparent. The French people realized that "the system" was dead. From now on, people would listen to those who advocated changing the regime (either from the conviction that it was now essential to build a stable state, or from the desire to hang on to Algeria). Among all the solutions proposed, one stood out more and more clearly: appeal to General de Gaulle, the man who had symbolized resistance in 1940, the man who had liberated the country and restored its national sovereignty. He alone could stand up to the storm that had been let loose. On May 14, Hubert Beuve-Méry, the editor of Le Monde, made a resounding editorial appeal: "Speak to us, General!" L'Aurore, renowned for its stubborn anti-Gaullism, made the same plea. On the eve of the May 13 uprising, Alain de Serigny, editor of Echo d'Alger and a notorious opponent of Gaullism, caused some surprise. Despite his Pétainist convictions, he wrote: "I beseech you, General, speak, speak to us quickly—your words will be deeds."

The most decisive event of all took place on May 15, when General Raoul Salan, commander in chief of the French troops in Algeria, cried out from the

The Algerian volcano

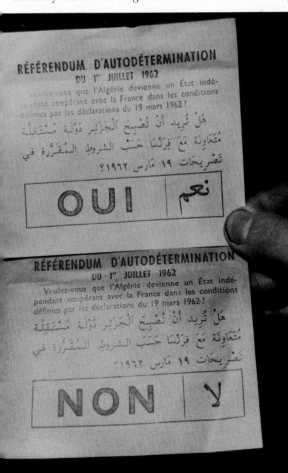

balcony of the Gouvernement Général: "Long live de Gaulle!" After two days of confusion and uncertainty, the leaders of the Algerian secession—a secession that the official government in Paris was contesting—had made it known that they were ready to return to allegiance if de Gaulle were recalled to power.

The man to whom all these appeals were made was living in retirement in the village of Colombey-les-deux-Eglises in northeastern France. In 1946 he had voluntarily renounced power to avoid being involved in party intrigues. "We are near the end of the illusion," the General had written. "We must prepare the remedy."

In the face of the rapidly deteriorating situation, de Gaulle remained silent. His supporters were striving to influence all malcontents in his favor: Algerians, soldiers and citizens alike. Every Frenchman was waiting for a sign. It was only when the military leaders in Algeria made it clear that they

desired continued allegiance to France that de Gaulle broke the silence. On May 15, at 6 P.M., the General's secretary in Paris broadcast de Gaulle's statement: "In view of the country's increasing tribulations, I declare to the people that I am ready to assume the powers of the Republic."

De Gaulle's message caused delirium among his supporters. In government circles there was complete panic. The hard-line ministers were pressing for a tough handling of the "sedition," and the government was vainly attempting to stifle the news by introducing censorship. Equally vain were the politicians' tortuous antifascist orders and the unions' attempts to call a general strike: at the Renault factories, scarcely three hundred workers out of 80,000 obeyed a union strike order.

In the French Parliament there was panic and acute demoralization. Its corridors were the scene of maneuvers to rally or renounce support. Everyone was caught in the dilemma: on the one hand, there was the fear of de Gaulle (with his demonstrated hostility toward party intrigue), and on the other there was fear of an invasion by the French troops of Algiers. But little by little, the deputies came to accept the first of the two less-than-desirable options. Socialist leaders who had been corresponding with or making secret visits to de Gaulle were gradually tempted to finish the business by joining the appeal to the General, and the combined pressure of these new supporters forced Pflimlin to hold a secret meeting with the General.

The interview took place on the night of May 26 at St. Cloud. Even before Pierre Pflimlin could reach a decision about the issues raised in these discussions, a new communiqué burst like a bombshell: "I have taken the first step," said General de Gaulle, "in the regular procedure necessary to set up a republican government." It was generally thought that de Gaulle had accelerated developments to prevent an invasion by the mutineers; the process from this point was irreversible. The President of the Republic, René Coty, made an official appeal to General de Gaulle, "the greatest of all Frenchmen." On June 2, Parliament elected him Premier by 329 votes to 224, adopted a constitutional law, and entrusted the General with full powers of government for six months. The Fourth Republic was dead.

On March 25, 1957, France and five other nations had signed the Treaty of Rome, establishing the Common Market. But there had been no positive step taken toward executing these plans. Bogged down in the Algerian war and paralyzed by internal contradictions, the Fourth Republic could hardly devote itself to the reconstruction of Europe. Its economy was stagnant, its finances in ruins; France was definitely "the sick man of Europe." The return of de Gaulle—well known for his attacks on the Eurocrats, a resolute opponent of any submission to supernationality, and a stubborn defender of national independence—seemed to other Europeans a formidable threat to the plans that they had momentarily cherished. All de Gaulle's skill was needed to dispel this prejudice. And, although he

General Jacques Massu, hero of the 1958 revolt.

Above left President René Coty and Prime Minister Felix Gaillard (left). Gaillard's government, the twentieth in twelve years, fell one month before the Algerian revolt erupted.

Voting cards used in the 1962 referendum that gave Algeria its independence.

Rebel French troops in Algeria during the 1958 troubles. Their faces have been blacked out by Algerian censors.

was to give life to the Common Market, he could not totally eclipse a certain mistrust.

On June 2, 1958, when Maurice Couve de Murville took up his duties as Foreign Minister—a position that he was to hold for ten years—France occupied an insignificant place in the concert of nations. All its resources were incapable of bringing the war in Algeria to a satisfactory end, and the instability of its government had made France's pretention to the role of Great Power seem ridiculous. The return of de Gaulle was to dispel these uneasy specters. The world rediscovered the man who, almost alone, had embodied France during the war

years. From the moment he returned to power de Gaulle occupied himself with the regeneration of his country. "France," he said, "must embrace her century." Within France itself, the foundations of a stable state were laid with the constitution of September 4, 1958. By the referendum of 1962, the President of the Republic was to be elected by universal suffrage, a move that indisputably gave increased power and prestige to the President. Finances were put to rights, the foreign debt was paid back before it was due, and the Bank of France accumulated reserves of dollars and gold. France reestablished a strong currency, which it was

A cartoon of De Gaulle published in 1958, and (far right) a recent photograph. His Fifth Republic sought to restore France to greatness without the ties of a colonial empire.

Establishing the principle of independence

The changes that de Gaulle brought about within his country and the consequences of his acts on universal developments make the General one of the few men who has shaped the history of the twentieth century. Powerless, he watched the fall of the Third Republic, which he had foretold in his wartime writings. The Free French, which he assembled, took part in the victory of liberal Europe against Hitler's Europe. He founded two republics. One, the Fourth—paralyzed by the impotence of the state and subject to political intrigue—lasted only twelve years. The other—the Fifth—also reached its twelfth year, but without its founder. Whatever its fate, it remains de Gaulle's Republic.

EDOUARD SABLIER

De Gaulle on a visit to North Africa.

to maintain until the crisis of May, 1968.

Throughout the ten years of de Gaulle's rule, on-lookers asked themselves two questions: how far-reaching were the changes that de Gaulle had imposed on France, and what would happen when he had gone? The terrible crisis that France experienced in May, 1968—and that led ultimately to the departure of de Gaulle in April, 1969—revealed how solid the Fifth Republic truly was. The crisis and its consequences also revealed the tenacity of those who clung to the past. Wealthy landowners, small industrialists, businessmen, farmers and local leaders all reacted violently against any reform that would erode their privileges or their way of life.

But the stability restored by the Fifth Republic also created new difficulties. Serving a strong state, the administration gave birth to a new race of young technocrats whose omnipotence could not be threatened by any ministerial crisis. At the same time, ministers who knew that their positions were safe only as long as the head of state approved them were generally less preoccupied with making progress in their departments than with satisfying de Gaulle. It is undeniable, however, that French life underwent more transformations in ten years of Gaullism that it had in the preceding half-century.

As for the second question, "post-Gaullism" seemed to have found a temporary solution in the relative continuity that prevailed after the departure of the General. De Gaulle led France in an irreversible direction, but the principle of national independence, which had been severely shaken in the debacle of 1940, was no longer questioned.

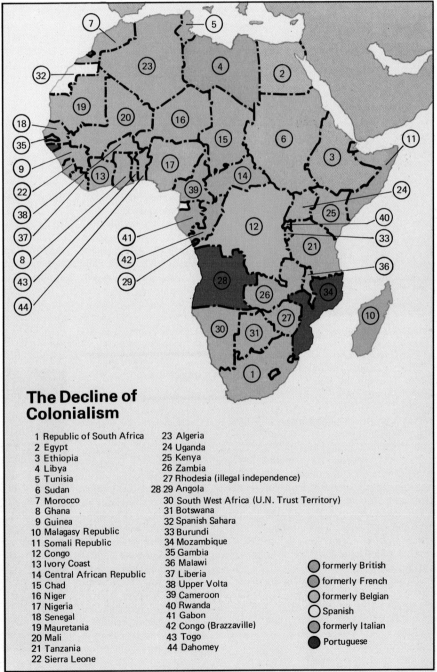

The Decline of Colonialism

1 Republic of South Africa
2 Egypt
3 Ethiopia
4 Libya
5 Tunisia
6 Sudan
7 Morocco
8 Ghana
9 Guinea
10 Malagasy Republic
11 Somali Republic
12 Congo
13 Ivory Coast
14 Central African Republic
15 Chad
16 Niger
17 Nigeria
18 Senegal
19 Mauretania
20 Mali
21 Tanzania
22 Sierra Leone

23 Algeria
24 Uganda
25 Kenya
26 Zambia
27 Rhodesia (illegal independence)
28 29 Angola
30 South West Africa (U.N. Trust Territory)
31 Botswana
32 Spanish Sahara
33 Burundi
34 Mozambique
35 Gambia
36 Malawi
37 Liberia
38 Upper Volta
39 Cameroon
40 Rwanda
41 Gabon
42 Congo (Brazzaville)
43 Togo
44 Dahomey

- formerly British
- formerly French
- formerly Belgian
- Spanish
- formerly Italian
- Portuguese

On October 5, 1957, Tass, the official Soviet news agency, announced to a stunned and unprepared world that a team of Russian scientists and technicians had successfully placed a man-made satellite in orbit around the earth. This event, which instantly captured the imaginations of scientists and laymen around the world, ushered in a new age of exploration—and gave the world a new vocabulary. Sputnik 1, as the Russian's spherical aluminium satellite was called, lived only twenty-two days before its simple transmitter went dead. But in those three weeks tracking stations around the globe were able to pick up and record Sputnik's familiar "beep." The "space race" was on.

Russia's first earth satellite (Sputnik).

The Russians followed their initial triumph in space with a second coup: one month after Sputnik, they orbited a satellite carrying an eleven-pound mongrel dog. The double Soviet triumph gave Russia a commanding lead in space and yielded incalculable benefits in terms of international prestige. Shocked and dismayed, U.S. government officials called for a reassessment and restructuring of America's laggard space program, and educators across the country reevaluated their scientific curricula.

During 1958, the United States launched five small data-gathering satellites, all of which were considerably more sophisticated than Sputnik 1, but eight other attempts failed. As the two countries' technological know-how grew, both attempted increasingly bold

experiments. In 1959, for example, the Russians launched a series of lunar probes designed to photograph the dark side of the moon, while the United States orbited the world's first weather satellite.

Man in space

U.S. space race morale suffered a dramatic setback in April of 1961 when the Russians used one of their huge booster rockets (which were much more powerful than those developed by U.S. scientists) to place a Soviet cosmonaut, Yuri Gagarin, in orbit. The first man ever successfully to orbit the earth, Gagarin remained aloft for 108 minutes at a maximum altitude of 203 miles. Gagarin's single orbit of the earth was followed four months later by Gherman Titov's seventeen-orbit space ride—yet another indication of Soviet technological supremacy. Chagrined and challenged, President John F. Kennedy announced a 20 billion dollar, nine-year program to place an American astronaut on the moon by 1970.

A year after Kennedy's announcement, the U.S. was finally ready to put its first astronauts into orbit, and before the year was out, the burgeoning U.S. space program had three technically flawless manned space flights to its credit. The first of these was John H. Glenn's three-orbit flight on February 20, 1962. Unlike Soviet flights, the first U.S. effort was conducted—from countdown to splashdown—before a worldwide television audience.

Africa's new look

As the world's two richest nations allocated increasingly larger portions of their national budgets to the space race, the world's poorest nations moved toward independence. In March of 1957, Ghana became a member of the United Nations General Assembly, and in the next six years, twenty-three former African colonies followed suit. Fourteen of these newly independent nations joined the United Nations in 1960 alone, and by 1963 the map of Africa was almost completely redrawn. The process of decolonialization was a dislocating and frequently violent one, and nowhere was this more true than in the Congo, where anticolonial rioting erupted during the first weeks of January, 1959.

Contention in the Congo

Distressed by the persistent pattern of civil disorder in its only colony, the Belgian government called for round-table discussions regarding the Congo Question in January of 1960. In April of that year, free elections were held in the Congo, and Patrice Lumumba's Nationalist Party won a clear-cut majority. Lumumba became Prime Minister of the new Republic, and his closest political rival, Joseph Kasavubu, was appointed President.

After a single week of peaceful independence, the Congolese Army mutinied and Lumumba was obliged to call upon the United Nations to quell the insurrection. The U.N. Emergency Force responded promptly but refused to place itself at Lumumba's command. The Congolese Prime Minister then requested—and received—Soviet aid, a move that prompted the rebellious President of Katanga, Moise Tshombe, to declare his province independent of the central government. As matters worsened, President Kasavubu dismissed Lumumba—only to be turned out of office himself by Colonel Joseph Mobutu. Mobutu promptly expelled the Russians and incarcerated Lumumba (who died—or was assassinated—while in police custody in February, 1961).

One tragic consequence of the unresolved Congolese power struggle was the death of U.N. Secretary-General Dag Hammarskjöld, who was killed in an airplane crash while en route to a meeting

with Tshombe in September of 1961. Four months later, Tshombe and the central government settled their differences, and in June of 1964 the United Nations pulled its troops out of the Congo.

The Congo Question was far from settled, however. Two months before the U.N. troops departed, secessionist forces in Kivu Province —followers of the slain Lumumba —staged a series of disruptive raids and skirmishes around Stanleyville, and it was not until 1966 that the central government was finally successful in suppressing rebellion.

Biafra

The familiar pattern of coup and countercoup, secession and coalition was repeated in Nigeria beginning in 1967. Over a two and a half year period that ended in January, 1970, the rebellious leaders of Biafra, as the secessionist region of southeastern Nigeria was known, resisted government efforts to reunite the divided country.

By December of 1969, the rebels were isolated and dependent upon an emergency airlift for food and medical supplies. This airlift was largely financed by a loosely knit, worldwide organization of private citizens who had been galvanized into action by news reports that some 1 million Biafrans—mostly women and children—were dying of kwashiorkor, a wasting disease caused by protein deficiency. By the first weeks of 1970, the insurrectionists had been starved into submission. The rebel leader, General Odumegwu Ojukwu,

Patrice Lumumba, Prime Minister of the Congo, being carried shoulder-high by an enthusiastic crowd.

escaped into exile, and his chief of staff, Philip Effiong, formally capitulated to Yakubu Gowon's federal government troops.

Insurrection in Indochina

Africa was not the only continent to suffer the agonies of decolonialization during the late 1950s. France's reluctant decision to

Moise Tshombe, Prime Minister of breakaway Katanga. He later died in an Algerian prison.

abandon Indochina ultimately proved more costly and crisis-fraught than its efforts to disengage itself in Africa. Spurred by news that the French Army fortress at Dien Bien Phu (in what is now North Vietnam) had fallen to Ho Chi Minh's rebel troops in early May of 1954, the foreign ministers meeting in Geneva agreed to armistice terms to end the dispute. One of these terms called for dividing Vietnam into a pro-West southern sector and a Communist northern region.

Ten months after the armistice was signed, civil war flared in Saigon, and Premier Ngo Dinh Diem ordered government troops to launch a full-scale campaign against the insurgents. Six months later, on October 26, 1955, Diem felt sufficiently confident of victory to proclaim the establishment of the Republic of South Vietnam. His regime was anything but stable, however, as the temporarily successful military coup of November

11, 1960, demonstrated. The South Vietnamese Army restored Diem to power the next day, but both he and his supporters in Washington were severely shaken by the plot.

To consolidate Diem's power and ensure his future, a three-day conference between delegates from South Vietnam and the United States was called in 1961. Diem's representatives emerged from that meeting with a number of firm commitments from the United States. Among them were a promise of some 40 million dollars' worth of American arms and a commitment to pay and equip 20,000 South Vietnamese troops to augment Diem's 150,000-man standing army. The United States also agreed to increase the size of its 685-man advisory force by assigning trained specialists and field observers to work with Diem's troops.

In March of 1962, Diem's rejuvenated South Vietnamese Army, bolstered by American aid and advisers, launched Operation Sunrise, a vast government campaign to eliminate the Vietcong rebels once and for all.

"De-Stalinization"

Soviet space triumphs during the late 1950s tended to eclipse a significant political development, one that would shape the coming decade as much as the space race. It began in 1956 as a program of gradual "de-Stalinization" and it eventually caused a major rift between Russia and Red China. But its beginnings were so low-key that they passed almost unnoticed

by the Western press. Khrushchev's program of de-Stalinization, introduced at the Twentieth Soviet Party Congress in Moscow in 1956, called for an end to the "cult of personality" that had grown up around Russia's wartime leader. The Chinese Communist leadership,

Ho Chi Minh, leader of the Vietnamese resistance to France, and then President of North Vietnam.

staunchly Stalinist, flatly denounced the change, which caused a serious breach between Moscow and Peking. This falling-out was accentuated by the Soviet reaction to China's sweeping program of communization in the mid-1950s. Khrushchev greeted the plan coolly, and when a subsequent economic crisis forced Mao Tse-tung's regime to abandon the program in 1959, Khrushchev's misgivings appeared confirmed.

As the rift widened, diplomatic

exchanges between the two Communist monoliths became increasingly strained and in 1959 the Russians withdrew their promise to help the Chinese develop an atomic capacity. The Chinese retaliated in April of 1960 by publishing *Long Live Leninism*, an anti-Soviet broadside that so enraged Khrushchev that he summarily withdrew from China all Soviet technicians and Soviet aid.

In the fall of that year, an extraordinary gathering of international Communist leaders was arranged, and representatives of eighty-one Communist parties met in Moscow in November to iron out the Sino-Soviet split. The delegates emerged from the meeting exuding amiability and spouting words of reconciliation, but in reality the dispute was unresolved. In fact, the rift had worsened, as the events of October, 1961, were to prove. In that month, Russia publicly denounced the Albanian Communist Party for siding with the Chinese, then abruptly broke diplomatic relations wih the tiny Balkan nation.

Open antagonism became open warfare in 1962, when Turkic nomads in Sinkiang Province in western China rose against their government, dealt the Red Army a severe blow, and fled across the border into Soviet Central Asia. Two subsequent incidents were to drive the wedge still deeper. The first was China's attack on India's nothern border in October of 1962 —an act the Russians said was a grave threat to world peace. The second occurred in Cuba, where Russia's tactical retreat outraged the Chinese.

The evacuation of wounded soldiers after the fall of Dien Bien Phu.

Pope John's Vatican Council

The College of Cardinals that convened in 1958 following the death of Pius XII found itself unable to settle on a successor to the austere and authoritarian Pope. To resolve the deadlock, the College settled on a compromise candidate, Angelo Cardinal Roncalli. Two and a half months after his election as Pope John XXIII, the supposedly uncontroversial Roncalli announced to an astonished world that he intended to call an Ecumenical Council. The Council—the first since 1870—was convened at the Vatican on October 11, 1962, and was charged with the task of adapting the Church to meet the challenges of the modern world. Weeks before the opening of the second session of the Council, John XXIII died and his work passed into the hands of his more conservative successor, Paul VI. The reforms that followed were small, but the spirit of reform that survived was substantial.

John XXIII, elected by a compromise.

Opposite The opening of the Vatican Council on October 11, 1962, in St. Peter's.

An Ecumenical Council of the Catholic Church is a curiosity in the modern world. Nowadays, grand ritual occasions are few and far between. A Pontifical High Mass in the basilica of St. Peter's before some twenty-three hundred bishops in resplendent dress is an extraordinary, impressive and photogenic event, and the Pontifical Mass that was celebrated in St. Peter's on October 11, 1962, naturally enchanted its worldwide audience. On that day a rather fat and undistinguished looking, but peaceful, cheerful and kindly old man was carried aloft into the basilica where his elderly congregation awaited him. Papa Roncalli—Pope John XXIII—had come to open his Council. Many of the watchers were unsure what the Council could achieve, and many of the bishops were unsure what they would be allowed to achieve. But all agreed that the Second Vatican Council must take its course and its hope from John. He had called it into being; it was a child that he must educate and set on its way.

Four years earlier, the cardinals had been strongly divided on the choice of a successor to the austere and authoritarian Pius XII. They could not agree, and so decided on a stopgap measure. Cardinal Roncalli seemed to meet their requirements excellently. At seventy-seven he could not be expected to last too long. He had risen in the diplomatic service of the Church and was well regarded from Istanbul to Paris. As Archbishop of Venice he had performed his pastoral work with humble devotion and charm. Most important for a compromise choice, he was neither a theoretician nor a theologian, and he had little experience in the central Roman administration of the Church. It was therefore felt that the Curia—the civil service of the Church—would have no trouble keeping him in hand. When Roncalli became John XXIII, however, he quickly gave evidence of the strong and simple virtues of his peasant ancestry. His natural sympathy for all peoples had been happily fostered by diplomatic experience. His long absence from Rome left him uncontaminated by the narrow and exclusive Roman outlook. Even his simplicity and lack of intellectual brilliance was turned to good advantage: theory never got in the way of human relations. "Are you a theologian?" he once asked an Anglican priest. "No? So much the better—neither am I!" He would talk to anyone, from Khrushchev to members of the Orthodox Church. He tried to serve where he could help most. He did not have a great mind, but doctrinal matters are only part of a pope's preoccupation; as Bishop of Rome he had a duty to comfort the sick, the poor and the unfortunate. He visited hospitals, slums and prisons as no other pope has done in recent times. The people listened to him because he could draw up from his own experience the right words for their condition. (He even told prisoners that his uncle had gone to jail for poaching.)

Pope John had his ear closely tuned to the stirring ground swell of twentieth-century humanity. He was far more able than the busy, efficient men in the Roman Curia to detect the widening separation between the secular world and the Roman Catholic Church. In January, 1959, two and a half months after his election, John XXIII announced to a surprised world that he intended to call an Ecumenical Council to be held at the Vatican.

"An Ecumenical Council," an unconventional churchman once said, "is a football match in which all the players are bishops." According to Abbot Butler's more prosaic definition, an Ecumenical Council is a meeting of the bishops in communion with the Holy See. "Together with the Pope, these bishops constitute the *magisterium*, or teaching body, of the Church and are also its supreme executive and governing body." An Ecumenical Council can define doctrine and make practical laws. In the past, Councils had been summoned to respond to special occasions—to fight particular heresies, or to formulate important doctrine. The first, at Nicaea in A.D. 325, was called by the Emperor Constantine to denounce the Arian heresy. The last before the

The escaped prisoner of the Curia

Three progressive cardinals. (*Left*) Cardinal Bea, a Jesuit reformer in the Vatican. (*Center*) Cardinal Suenens, Archbishop of Malines. He pointed out the dangers in the Church's traditional approach to contraception. (*Right*) Cardinal Frings, another leading liberal at the Council.

The Uniate Patriarch Maximos IV Saigh of Antioch, whose presence reminded the Council that the Roman Catholic Church has many varieties of religious rites and practices.

Second Vatican Council had been held in 1869–70. That nineteenth-century Council, also held at the Vatican, had promulgated the doctrine of papal infallibility.

What was the extraordinary occasion for the Second Vatican Council? The answer is: nothing in particular. What new dogma did John propose to define? The answer again is none. "I am not infallible," he once told some startled Greek visitors: "The Pope is only infallible when he speaks *ex cathedra*. But I will never speak *ex cathedra*." And he never did. The aim that John had in mind for his Council was both very simple and rather vague, quite unlike the obvious problems that had faced earlier Councils. The key to John's intentions was given by the word *aggiornamento*, by which he meant that the Catholic Church should be brought up to date and should adapt to the state of the world. On October 11, in his opening address to the Council, he suggested to the assembled fathers what their tasks would be: first to renew life within the Church—a revision of old thinking, old laws, old liturgy and old doctrine; then to attempt to promote Christian unity; and lastly to come together with the contemporary world and work toward a real understanding of modern conditions and problems.

Pope John put forward this revolutionary plan with his usual optimism. Others in the Church thought that his program would lead to either unresolvable problems or appalling results. The Pope was proposing that the Church give up many of the habits that it had cultivated in the four hundred years since the Reformation. To many Catholics, particularly those in the Roman Curia, this was a very fearful idea. All commentators on the Second Vatican Council agree that the villain of the piece was the Curia, and it is understandable why this should be so.

For centuries the real power in the Curia had been held by a small group of elderly Italians who were convinced that Catholicism was an Italian, perhaps even a Roman, affair. Though in theory the pope was above the Curia and the source of its power, in practice he was very often a prisoner to his curial

civil service. Ever since the Reformation, the centralizing and authoritarian traditions in the Church had encouraged the Curia to make the important decisions in Church government. The members now claimed this work as a right. They therefore viewed Pope John's Council plans with much apprehension. All three points in the Pope's program worried them. If John merely intended a renewal of the Church, then they claimed that a Council was not necessary: the Curia alone had the information and power to initiate reforms within the Church. But if the Pope really intended to push forward his other two points —Christian unity and adaptation to the secular world—then he was threatening the Roman Curia itself, which for hundreds of years had proclaimed Catholic exclusiveness and incompatibility with the temporal world.

On that Thursday in October when Pope John faced the bishops for the first time, the chances for the Council's success were finely balanced. In the last hundred years the Catholic Church had taken many steps toward reform and a revaluation of older attitudes. The encyclical *Rerum Novarum* (1891) of Leo XIII had shown that Rome was aware of modern economic and social problems. This promising direction was followed by Pius XI and by John himself in his encyclical *Mater et Magistra* (1961). Pius XII had been greatly interested in modern sciences, and his encyclical *Divino afflante Spiritu* had caused a great revival in Catholic Biblical studies. For some time Rome had even edged demurely toward Christian unity. Here, too, John had made the decisive move: in June, 1960, he formed a Secretariat for Unity under Cardinal Bea, a Jesuit of liberal bent, and this body had a powerful effect on the Council. On the other hand, much about Rome was extremely backward-looking. The attitudes of curial cardinals such as Ottaviani and Ruffini were very still. Some hopeful progressive movements, such as the worker-priest movement in France and Belgium, had been frowned on and finally suppressed by Rome. And no one was certain whether or not a Council composed largely of bishops would be able to stand against the disapproval of the cardinals of the Curia.

The events of the Second Vatican Council have usually been presented as a struggle between the progressives and the conservatives—the progressives led by the cardinals of the northern European hierachies, in particular France and Germany, and the conservatives ranging behind certain members of the Curia, supported by many Italian and Spanish bishops. Generally, this division was no doubt true enough. But the bishops were by no means consistent or united.

Pope John, in his innocent way, had hoped that the entire Council would be over by Christmas, 1962. But the devious politics and the necessity to make speeches in rusty Latin ensured a slow start. By the end of the first session, on December 8, only the liturgy had received a full discussion. But although the progress was slow, it was promising. Non-Catholic observers may have thought that the purpose of the Council was to conduct a flirtation with the outside world, but to Catholics the first aim of the Council was to encourage a renewal of life within the Church. The liturgy, dealing with the forms of Catholic worship, received the first attention. And from this, other benefits were reaped. The attempt to go back behind patristic sources and the accretions of tradition, back to the first Biblical sources, was obviously pleasing to Protestants, and so a step toward Christian unity. Also, the translation of parts of the Mass into local languages helped to involve the laity in the service and fostered a kind of decentralization away from Rome. By the end of the first session, the reformers were reasonably pleased with the Council's efforts.

Then, in the months of preparation for the second session, a tragedy occurred. On June 3, 1963, John XXIII, the greatly loved and greatly admired Pope, died. The Council, into which he had breathed his own spirit of kindliness and tolerance, passed into the hands of his successor, Papa Montini—Pope Paul VI. Montini had been a member of the Curia for many years, yet on some matters he was known to have progressive opinions. However, no one was sure whether he could avoid the blandishments of his old companions in the Curia and continue the direction given by Pope John.

At the opening of the second session, on September 29, 1963, the signs were hopeful. In a fine and moving speech, Pope Paul outlined the work still to be done. He stressed the idea of service. He, the Pope, was "the servant of the servants of God"; and the Church was to serve the world, "not to despise it, but to appreciate it; not to condemn it, but to strengthen and save it." Within the Church, he looked on the bishops as a college that, together with the pope, would play a large part in the doctrinal and practical government of the Church. The bishops, not the members of the Curia, were "the

Pope John XXIII giving his blessing at a Vatican ceremony.

heirs of the Apostles." He recognized the common religious patrimony that Catholics share with other Christian denominations, and he asked forgiveness for any damage that Catholics might have inflicted on the Christian community in the past.

The course of the second, third and fourth sessions did not run easily. Progressives and conservatives were as embattled as ever. The Curia still attempted to stifle promising movements. And Pope Paul, after his generous beginning, played a curiously ambiguous part—delaying, indecisive and often an apparent hostage to the Curia. In both the second session, in 1963, and the third session, in 1964, there were dangerous crises. None of the liberalizing measures had an easy passage. The question of the collegiate responsibility of the bishops was violently attacked by the Curia, which quite rightly saw here a threat to its own power. The Curia also went some way to persuade Paul that a synod of bishops would undermine his own primacy. The revival of the diaconate (an order of laymen with powers of assisting the priests), although begged for by the South American bishops, was strongly resisted by those reluctant to see laymen get a foot in the Church. The measure on religious liberty needed all the force and political ability of the North American cardinals and bishops to push it through. The Declaration on the Jews—although promoted with ardor by Cardinal Bea's Secretariat for Unity, and despite the German Cardinal's humble acknowledgment of the Nazi crimes against the Jews—still had to struggle for votes.

All these measures were to some extent theological matters. When the Council attempted to face the modern world, progress was even harder. In

November, 1964, the Council very cautiously approached the question of sexual morality. The Pope had already reserved to himself the decision on the contraceptive pill, but Cardinals Leger and Suenens and Patriarch Maximos IV Saigh discreetly tried to pour some light on the Church's traditionally dark view of sex, pointing out the human consequences of overpopulation. At least the Church was ready to discuss this fearful topic. The final document passed by the Council was the Pastoral Constitution on the Church in the Modern World. Tardily, but hopefully, the Church began to point the way forward.

The constitutions, decrees and declarations passed by the Second Vatican Council mark a definite shift in the attitudes of the Roman Catholic Church, the largest Christian community in the world. From the time of the Reformation until 1962, the Catholic Church was afflicted with Counter-Reformation mentality, a mentality mainly concerned with the preservation of the Church's rights, authority, privileges and exclusiveness. As a result, the Church naturally drifted apart from other religions, both Christian and non-Christian, and from the secular world. Whatever the value of its doctrinal truths, in human affairs the Church was becoming inflexible and out of touch with reality. Consequently, the Catholic religion had begun to lose its hold on contemporary man and no longer greatly influenced the course of modern life.

Taking its inspiration from Pope John, the most human of pontiffs, the Second Vatican Council gave the Church a chance to change its ways. If the suggestions of the Council are put into effect, the Church will become less centralized, closer to the people and to other religions, more able to answer the moral perplexities and practical dilemmas of modern life. Whether or not the leads will be taken up is the problem that is as yet unresolved. The habits of more than four hundred years are not easily set aside. The results of progressive action are not always what one would expect; sometimes they intensify the evils they hope to stamp out. Events in Rome since the close of the Council in 1965 have shown that the advance of reform is always slow, and frequently painful.

MICHAEL FOSS

Pope Paul, surrounded by bishops, attending mass in St. Peter's.

Left Bishops leaving St. Peter's after attending a session of the Council.

Pope Paul entering Jordan on a visit to the Holy Land. Paul, a former Vatican diplomat and Archbishop of Milan, has traveled more widely than any previous pope.

The Cuban Missile Crisis 1962

President John F. Kennedy was still glancing over the morning papers when National Security Adviser McGeorge Bundy burst into his bedroom on the morning of October 16, 1962. Bundy confronted the President with "hard photographic evidence" that Russian technicians were constructing a series of offensive missile sites on the island of Cuba. During the next few days, Kennedy, Bundy and some fifteen other high officials and trusted advisers met regularly to ponder a response to the Soviet government's provocative move. In a dramatic televised speech to the nation on October 22, the President announced the Russians' action and called for a naval blockade to prevent further shipments from reaching Castro's island. The crisis was far from resolved, however; the missile sites remained, and it would take some highly unorthodox diplomacy to secure their removal.

In the nuclear age the greatest threats to international peace burst upon the world unannounced. The Cuban missile crisis of October, 1962, certainly happened that way. The first intimation that the whole of mankind was standing on the brink of a nuclear holocaust came on the evening of Monday, October 22, when President John F. Kennedy, in a broadcast to the American people, somberly warned them of the existence of "a deliberately provocative and unjustified change in the status quo which cannot be accepted by this country."

That "change in the status quo" was, of course, the construction in Cuba of a series of Russian-built missile sites—each with the power to point a nuclear dagger at the heart of any city in the southeastern United States. The construction of these missile sites had been a remarkably well-kept secret on the part of the Russians and the Cubans. Although work on them had almost certainly been going on throughout the previous two months, the President himself had heard of this clandestine development only six days earlier.

The U.S. government as a whole had been aware that from July on an unprecedented stream of Soviet ships had been moving toward Cuba. There were even reports from Cuban refugees of truck convoys on the island that were hauling long, tubular objects shrouded in tarpaulins. The U.S. intelligence community's view, however, was that all this activity betrayed only defensive precautions. It was, not surprisingly, a view that the Russians themselves did everything to encourage. On two separate occasions in September, messages were indirectly passed from the Kremlin to President Kennedy reassuring him that there was nothing alarming in this activity and that the Soviet Union had absolutely no desire to embarrass him in any way while the mid-term elections were still unresolved.

The only American government official who appears to have been suspicious of these assurances—and to have convinced himself that all the goings-on

in Cuba could bear a very sinister interpretation indeed—was John McCone, the Director of the Central Intelligence Agency. However, throughout this period McCone was not at his post in Washington: during September he was on his honeymoon in the south of France, and his warnings—sent in four separate telegrams from his holiday hideout at Cap Ferrat—seem to have been disregarded by his colleagues. Certainly they were not passed on to the President.

Four weeks later—on the morning of Tuesday, October 16—the President had to listen to a very different report. While he was still in his pajamas reading the morning papers, his National Security Adviser, McGeorge Bundy, burst into his bedroom to give him the grim news that "hard photographic evidence" now existed which disclosed that the Russians had imported offensive nuclear missiles into Cuba after all. The hard photographic evidence was the result of a stepped-up series of U-2 flights over Cuba that John McCone had personally ordered upon his return to Washington. The photographs left no room for doubt that the same telltale ground pattern of offensive missile sites previously seen only in the Soviet Union was now imprinted on the soil of Cuba, only ninety miles from the American coast.

President Kennedy had spent the previous day in a strenuous orgy of domestic political campaigning in New York State. But he lost no time in adjusting himself to the crisis. His first order was for the establishment of a task force to meet together in the greatest secrecy to consider the various options that the new situation left open to the United States. The first meeting of this informal group of presidential advisers (later to be called the Executive Committee of the National Security Council) took place in the White House that very morning. In attendance were some fifteen people. Only four of them (the Vice-President, Lyndon Johnson; the Secretary of State, Dean Rusk; the Secretary of Defense, Robert McNamara; the Chairman of the Joint Chiefs of

Ernesto "Che" Guevara, Castro's lieutenant and confidant whose life work was fomenting revolution in Latin America.

Opposite Soviet Premier Khrushchev and Cuban Premier Castro embrace at the United Nations in 1960.

Playing "chicken"—the nuclear game

in the Executive Committee of the National Security Council who wanted invasion to be the first move—and it was only at the Saturday afternoon meeting that they were finally overruled by the President.

On October 21—after the decision in favor of the naval blockade had been taken but before the President had announced it to the world—Dean Acheson (who, a decade earlier, had been President Truman's Secretary of State) slipped out of Washington with the delicate mission of warning the governments in London, Paris and Bonn about what was to come; a similar arrangement was simultaneously made for the Canadian Premier, John Diefenbaker, to be forewarned.

Among the ships steaming toward Cuba—ships that the United States was now publicly pledged to intercept and, if necessary, forcibly board in a search for arms—were no less than twenty-five Soviet vessels. With his Monday evening broadcast announcing the naval blockade President Kennedy had, in effect, launched the first game of "chicken" of the nuclear era. If the approaching ships stayed on course, and if the U.S. Navy stood firm at the five-hundred-mile interception barrier it had thrown around Cuba, then sooner or later the two greatest powers in the world would necessarily be gazing at each other not across a conference table but at opposite ends of a gun barrel.

At the highest level of government in Washington the greatest anxieties were naturally enough fixed on what would happen on the high seas. After the signing of a presidential proclamation, the Cuban block-

Havana, no longer the cosmopolitan city it was before Castro's revolution.

Right Fidel Castro haranguing a crowd.

Andrei Gromyko, Russian Foreign Minister. It was his task to justify the erection of the missile bases to the United Nations.

Staff, General Maxwell Taylor) had been summoned chiefly because of the nature of the offices they held. The rest—the President's brother, Robert Kennedy; three of his most intimate White House aides; and private citizens like Dean Acheson—were made part of the group simply because they were types of people whom the President wanted at his elbow.

Most accounts of the Cuban missile crisis go out of their way to emphasize the smooth and well-ordered manner in which the American decision-making process worked. But the truth seems to have been rather different. At least in its early stages, the special ad hoc group charged with the responsibility of advising the President had difficulty in reaching any united conclusion at all. Certainly it was not in any position to put a collective proposal forward until the afternoon of Saturday, October 20, when, at the second of its meetings attended by the President, the decision in favor of a naval blockade of Cuba was made.

Even the decision to blockade was regarded by most of those present at that meeting as, at best, an interim measure. The general consensus was that if it was not enough by itself to convince the Kremlin that the missiles would have to be removed, then the United States would still have to be prepared to resort to an air strike, to be followed if necessary by a land invasion of Cuba. There were those, of course,

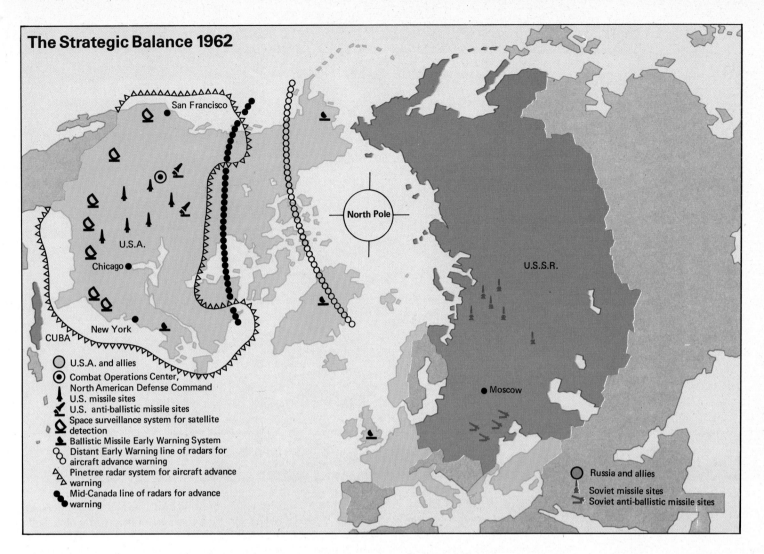

The Strategic Balance 1962

Legend:
- U.S.A. and allies
- Combat Operations Center, North American Defense Command
- U.S. missile sites
- U.S. anti-ballistic missile sites
- Space surveillance system for satellite detection
- Ballistic Missile Early Warning System
- Distant Early Warning line of radars for aircraft advance warning
- Pinetree radar system for aircraft advance warning
- Mid-Canada line of radars for advance warning

- Russia and allies
- Soviet missile sites
- Soviet anti-ballistic missile sites

Map labels: San Francisco, U.S.A., Chicago, New York, CUBA, North Pole, U.S.S.R., Moscow

ade was formally imposed at 10 A.M. on Wednesday, October 24. At that time two Soviet ships—the *Gagarin* and the *Komiles*—were within a few miles of the quarantine barrier; between them a Russian submarine had been detected moving into position. For the President's group of advisers, who were meeting in the White House at that moment, it was perhaps the tensest period of the whole crisis. What if the ships failed to stop or, worse, what if the Soviet submarine started to fire torpedoes at the shadowing American ships? So seriously was the danger taken that orders had already been given for depth charges to be dropped on the submarine if at a given sonic order it failed to surface. Dramatically, just before the moment of actual confrontation came, an unconfirmed report was received that the approaching Russian ships had stopped dead in the water. Within the hour the U.S. Office of Naval Intelligence confirmed that all twenty Russian vessels nearest to the barrier had either stopped or turned around.

For President Kennedy, this was merely a temporary reprieve, not a solution to the crisis. The principal objection to the naval blockade tactic all along had been that it amounted in practice to no more than locking the stable door after the horse had been stolen. Intelligence reports reaching Washington confirmed that work was still going on furiously within Cuba on the rocket sites. The naval blockade might prevent the importation of further armaments into Cuba; it could not stop the Russians and the Cubans from making the most effective use possible of the nuclear arsenal they already had on the island.

President Kennedy had been only too conscious of this difficulty from the beginning; indeed it had provided the main argument for those (including all the Joint Chiefs of Staff) who advocated a "surgical" air strike as the only answer to the Russian challenge. The President, however, preferred to try the path of persuasion first. With that aim in view he had been in private correspondence with Premier Khrushchev from the time of the delivery of his broadcast. Initially, Khrushchev's reactions were not encouraging: his first letter simply accused the United States of "outright banditry" and his second gloatingly pointed out that, as all the arms shipments needed were already in Cuba, there was no point in the maintenance of the United States' blockade.

But this second letter—which has never been published in its entirety—also gave the first signs that the Russian leader might be prepared for a negotiated settlement after all. In the course of what one who read it later described as "a confused, almost maudlin message," Mr. Khrushchev apparently suggested that he would be prepared to send no further weapons to Cuba and to withdraw or dismantle those already there if the United States, for its part, would call off its naval blockade and give a solemn pledge never to invade Cuba.

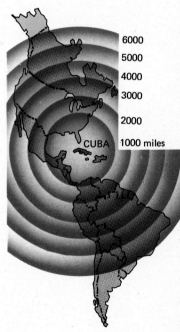

6000
5000
4000
3000
2000
1000 miles

CUBA

CHERRY PICKER

LAUNCH PAD WITH ERECTOR

MISSILE READY BLDGS

LAUNCH PAD WITH ERECTOR

OXIDIZER VEHICLES

FUELING VEHICLES

An aerial view of a Russian missile base in Cuba. It was on such evidence that President Kennedy ordered the blockade.

The relief in Washington was short-lived, however, for the very next day—Saturday, October 27—the Executive Committee of the National Security Council found itself confronted with a much more formal letter from the Kremlin raising the "price" on any deal. This time the Soviet leaders were insisting that in return for their taking their missiles out of Cuba, the United States must remove its nuclear bases from Turkey. Nor was this the only bad news received in the White House that morning. On his way into the meeting, the Attorney General, Robert Kennedy, received word from the FBI that Soviet diplomats in New York were preparing to destroy all confidential documents—an invariable embassy precaution on the eve of war. As if that were not doom-laden enough, the news also came that

morning that an American U-2 had been shot down by a Russian surface-to-air missile while on a flight mission above the Cuban mainland. The understanding from the beginning of the crisis had been that once this happened, the United States would have no choice but to order a retaliatory air strike against the Soviet missile bases. Against the advice of many of his advisers, the President decided to stay his hand: there would, he directed, be no immediate act of retaliation while one final effort was made to reach a settlement.

The shape that effort took was certainly unorthodox. On the advice of his brother, the Attorney General, President Kennedy simply decided to ignore the formal letter that had been received that morning, which stiffened the Soviet terms. Instead a reply

A Russian ship carrying aircraft as deck cargo, photographed by an American reconnaissance aircraft.

A great might-have-been

President Kennedy and the Joint Chiefs of Staff meet in the oval office of the White House.

was drafted and sent to Mr. Khrushchev solely on the basis of his earlier, much more personal letter. In this reply the President made it clear to Khrushchev that the proposals he had made contained within them the ingredients of a settlement—though at the same time he sternly insisted that the first move would have to come from the Russians.

That Saturday night in Washington very few of those who had lived with the crisis during the past twelve days had any confidence that this final gambit—desperate, almost despairing—could possibly work. Indeed, arrangements went ahead for an air attack on Cuba early the following week, with the President even issuing a proclamation for the activation of twenty-four squadrons of the Air Force Reserve. But miraculously, the next morning, October 28, there arrived a dramatic message from Khrushchev agreeing to the President's terms. The Soviet government, the communication announced, had given "a new order to dismantle the arms, which you described as offensive, and to crate and return them to the Soviet Union." The Cuban missile crisis was over.

The American government's suspicion at the time was that the Soviet Union was trying for a trade or a deal, and there is some evidence to support that theory in the penultimate Soviet letter demanding the withdrawal of American missiles from Turkey in return for an agreement by the Russians to dismantle the nuclear installations they had built in Cuba. The rapidity with which the Soviet Union retreated from this position hardly suggests that it can have been a central part of the Kremlin's plan.

But a more plausible explanation remains: that the Soviet government was simply conducting a probe to see what it could get away with. Its miscalculation—if there was one—arose from its assumption that the U.S. Administration would respond to the crisis according to the normal formulas of time-honored diplomacy. When the Russians discovered that the new and youthful American President—perhaps still smarting from his humiliation over the abortive Bay of Pigs invasion of Cuba in the spring of 1961—was determined instead to convert the crisis into a full-scale public nuclear confrontation, they had no choice but to back down. Certainly there is nothing in the Soviet government's behavior or reactions during those thirteen days to suggest that it had ever contemplated, let alone accepted, that a piece of classic, if reckless, *realpolitik* adventurism could lead to nuclear war.

In the end, of course, the Cuban missile crisis changed nothing in terms of the international power balance. Paradoxically, what it did do was to improve, if only fleetingly, the whole climate of Soviet-American relations.

What other fruits it might have had no one will ever know. By one of those ironic twists of fate the two men who, perhaps more than any others, had been brought to understand just how tenuous the thread of human survival is lingered only briefly thereafter on the world stage. Within thirteen months of those thirteen days that remain his principal claim to fame, President Kennedy was assassinated. Less than a year after that, Chairman Khrushchev fell from power in the Soviet Union. In much more than the obvious and direct sense, the Cuban missile crisis remains one of the great might-have-beens of history. ANTHONY HOWARD

A monument commemorating the Cuban Revolution; in the foreground is a statue of Jose Marti, a Cuban revolutionary leader of the nineteenth century.

Left The General Assembly of the United Nations. The Cuban crisis was discussed at length by the United Nations.

905

The United States Lockheed U–2 spyplane in which Gary Powers was shot down.

A spirit of Détente

For a time at least, the peaceful spirit of Vatican II seemed infectious. During the first years of the new decade, cold war tensions abated, and the United States and Russia moved toward a genuine détente. Between 1959 and 1963, Russian Premier Nikita Khrushchev purposefully pursued a policy of "peaceful coexistence" that he had first articulated in 1956 and reiterated in 1959 at the Twenty-first Party Congress in Moscow. According to Khrushchev, peaceful coexistence with the West was no longer a practical, temporary compromise—as in Stalin's day—but an enduring policy of Russia's new, consumer-oriented Communist state.

Détente seemed better suited to Soviet economic and military policy in the early 1960s than hostile confrontation, and Khrushchev actively and vocally sought improved East-West relations. In September of 1959 he paid a state visit to the United States (President Eisenhower's plans to reciprocate were scrubbed in the wake of the U-2 disaster). And in June of 1961 the Soviet leader met with President Kennedy in Vienna. One of the topics they discussed was the stalled nuclear treaty. On July 15, 1963, these talks were revived, and on August 5 Great Britain, the United States and the Soviet Union signed a limited nuclear test-ban treaty.

The new spirit of détente, which was embodied in the 1963 papal encyclical *Pacem in Terris*, was further evidenced by the meeting between German Chancellor Konrad Adenauer and French President Charles de Gaulle in Paris. As a result of this series of conferences, strained relations between the two were eased and a program of mutual economic and military cooperation was agreed upon. In the same year, President Kennedy proposed a joint U.S.-U.S.S.R. space program, and Premier Khrushchev called for a NATO-Warsaw Treaty Organization nonaggression pact.

March on Washington

As international tensions eased, domestic tensions grew in the United States. In the late summer of 1963, only days after the test-ban treaty was signed, more than 200,000 Americans—white as well as black—converged on the Washington Monument in what was described as "the greatest assembly for the redress of grievances" that the American capital had ever seen. A century after the signing of the Emancipation Proclamation, outraged blacks and sympathetic whites joined together in protest against what they saw as the nation's failure to ensure the privileges granted to blacks in Lincoln's Emancipation Proclamation and guaranteed by the Constitution.

The demonstration in Washington was entirely peaceful, but it was both preceded and followed by less peaceful "sit-ins" and "lie-ins" across the South and eventually across the nation. Increasingly militant black organizations demanded an end to segregation in public transportation, public schools, and housing; equal job opportunities; and the dropping of the so-called color bar in legislatures, the military high command, and the civil service.

The fire this time

Ultimately, the civil rights movement would bear fruit in the form of the Civil Rights Bill of 1965, which eliminated literacy tests and other prejudicial voting procedures, and in the Supreme Court's 1969 call for "immediate" integration of public schools. Before that time, however, the country was obliged to endure what many called America's "second civil war." The first major clash of this war occurred in the late summer of 1965 in Watts, Los Angeles' Negro ghetto. A five-day riot erupted that devastated

Martin Luther King, leader of the non-violent wing of the civil rights movement. He was later assassinated.

a 150-block area of the city. By the time the disorder was quelled, 34 persons (including 28 Negroes) had died, another 1,032 had been injured, and 3,952 had been arrested.

By 1967 racial unrest had become the dominant domestic issue in the United States as fresh rioting broke out in Newark, New Jersey, and Detroit, Michigan. The Newark riots, which began July 12, lasted six days and eventually enveloped nearly half the city, were followed five days later by a monumental civil insurrection in Detroit. These riots, which reached proportions unprecedented in American history, had to be forcibly put down by local law-enforcement agencies and armed federal troops.

Rebellion in Russia

The Soviet Union was not immune from internal dissension during this period, and as Premier Khrushchev's overtures to the West became more frequent and more cordial, opposition to his policy of peaceful coexistence grew. In mid-October of 1964, rebellious Politburo members ousted the seventy-year-old Premier and stripped him of his party rank. Khrushchev's successors, Aleksei N. Kosygin and Leonid I. Brezhnev, announced that they planned "no change in basic foreign policy," but in ensuing months Western Kremlinologists grew increasingly pessimistic about the prospects of a continuing détente.

Khrushchev's ouster was only one of a number of events occurring during 1963 and 1964 that severely jeopardized the world's hopes for peace. On November 2, 1963, for example, a military clique in South Vietnam deposed—and later executed—President Ngo Dinh Diem. Twenty days later American President John F. Kennedy was assassinated while his motorcade was making its way through the streets of downtown Dallas, Texas.

Kennedy's successor, Lyndon B. Johnson, had been in office less than a year when an incident occurred in the South China Sea that was radically to alter U.S. foreign policy in the Far East and eventually plunge the United States into a second ground war in Asia. On August 2 and again on August 4, 1964, North Vietnamese PT boats reportedly fired upon two U.S. destroyers cruising in the Gulf of Tonkin—off North Vietnam's

Nikita Khrushchev with Chinese leader Mao Tse-tung.

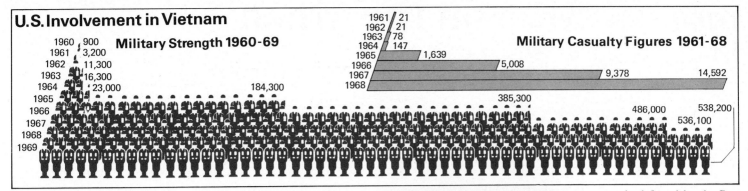

U.S. Involvement in Vietnam

Military Strength 1960-69

Year	Strength
1960	900
1961	3,200
1962	11,300
1963	16,300
1964	23,000
1965	184,300
1966	385,300
1967	486,000
1968	536,100
1969	538,200

Military Casualty Figures 1961-68

Year	Casualties
1961	21
1962	21
1963	78
1964	147
1965	1,639
1966	5,008
1967	9,378
1968	14,592

castern coast. Although neither American vessel was damaged, President Johnson ordered a retaliatory air strike against North Vietnamese coastal bases and an oil depot.

In ensuing months, U.S. troop strength in South Vietnam escalated rapidly in response to stepped-up infiltration from North Vietnam. Before the Gulf of Tonkin incident, the number of American troops in South Vietnam had risen slowly to almost 16,000; in the next four years it would swell to more than half a million.

Dominican crisis

President Johnson's willingness to use U.S. troops was underscored by his decision to land Marine assault troops at Santo Domingo in April of 1965. These forces—eventually numbering 19,000—promptly quelled antigovernment rioting in the Dominican Republic's capital, thereby preventing an imminent leftist coup. By May 5, a truce had been negotiated, and U.S. forces began to withdraw from the island.

The same pattern was soon to be repeated in South Vietnam, where intransigent rebel troops with widespread popular support continued to resist combined U.S. and South

Vietnamese efforts to expel or eliminate them. Repeated heavy bombing raids directed against supply depots and infiltration routes in North and South Vietnam and neighboring Laos hindered but failed to halt insurgent activity in the south, and in March of 1968, President Johnson announced his intention to severely restrict American bombing in the north in an effort to break the stalemate. Johnson also called for peace talks to settle the conflict. Hanoi responded promptly and affirmatively, and formal discussions began in Paris in May.

Cease-fire talks soon deadlocked over North Vietnamese demands for an unconditional bombing halt and U.S. demands for prompt withdrawal of North Vietnamese troops. As both the talks in Paris and the fighting in Southeast Asia dragged on, antiwar demonstrations and antiadministration broadsides grew more frequent and more vehement. With college students and the radical press—and later, college faculties and the established press—reiterating their demands for a solution to the Vietnam War, Johnson kept his pledge of the preceding March that he would not seek reelection in November of 1968, but would confine himself instead to seeking "an honorable settlement" to the war during the

Alexander Dubcek, leader of the short-lived Czech reform government.

remaining months of his term.

Johnson's startling announcement was only the first of a series of events that would stun, discourage and confuse U.S. voters in the spring and summer of 1968. In June, New York Senator Robert F. Kennedy, brother of the assassinated President and a contender for the Democratic presidential nomination, was mortally wounded on the eve of his primary campaign victory in California. Kennedy's death came only weeks after the assassination of the Reverend Martin Luther King, Jr., organizer of the 1963 March on Washington, D.C., Nobel Peace laureate, and a longtime leader of the American civil rights movement. The double tragedy of their deaths deprived dissident American minorities of both political and spiritual leadership and opened the way for a chaotic presidential race in which the Democratic candidate, Vice-President Hubert H. Humphrey,

was narrowly defeated by the Republican contender, Richard M. Nixon.

The Prague spring

A few days before the riot-marred Democratic convention in Chicago nominated Hubert Humphrey as its standard-bearer, word reached the West that Russian tanks had rolled into Prague, Czechoslovakia's capital, to suppress the liberal regime of Alexander Dubcek. The decade, which had begun with such promise, seemed likely to end in

A battle between Parisian students and police in 1968. A year later President de Gaulle resigned after failure of an election reform.

chaos and confusion. Traditional party bonds had been sundered, Korean tensions had been renewed, and the specter of Soviet repression loomed over Eastern Europe. China was reeling under the impact of Mao Tse-tung's abortive 1966 Cultural Revolution, England was enduring a period of economic austerity, and France was casting about for a successor to Charles de Gaulle.

With so little to be optimistic about at the end of the 1960s, the world anticipated the United States' attempt to land two men on the moon with special fervor.

Averell Harriman, leader of the American delegation at the Paris peace talks, with South Vietnamese General Ky, December, 1968.

Man on the Moon

Some 350 years after Galileo Galilei first trained his improved refracting telescope on the moon and studied its craters, two American astronauts landed in one of those flat, dry, dusty basins. By that time, the Apollo Space Program inaugurated by President Kennedy was eight years old, and the Apollo 11 mission was four days old. Six additional hours were to elapse before Neil A. Armstrong, civilian commander of the moon flight, was ready to announce to an impatient worldwide audience of more than 350 million people that he was about to descend the lunar module's ladder and step out onto the moon's surface. At 10:45 p.m. on Sunday, July 20, 1969, Armstrong took his first tentative step—and the world exulted. Few could deny that on purely technological terms the U.S. Space Program's remarkable achievement was indeed a "giant leap for mankind."

A Saturn rocket blasting off from Cape Kennedy.

Opposite The moon, photographed by the Apollo astronauts from their capsule.

A sharp command cut through the relaxed atmosphere in the Mission Control Center in Houston. It was the voice of Eugene Kranz, the Apollo 11 flight director. "Everyone at his desk, please," he called out curtly. "I want absolute silence." He then ordered the doors to be locked and guarded. There must be no risk of anyone's bursting in and distracting attention—even for a second—while his engineers were helping Neil A. Armstrong and Col. Edwin E. ("Buzz") Aldrin, Jr. to land on the moon.

A poll was taken to ascertain, in these last seconds, whether the landing attempt should proceed. "Communications?" Kranz called out. "Go," replied the communications engineer. "Medical?" The answer again was "Go." Some twelve times Kranz asked the question, and the verdict was unanimous. If there had been a single "No go," the landing mission might have been aborted. But all answered in the affirmative, some quietly and others with an emphatic shout.

Now Mission Control was resolved. The capsule communicator spoke swiftly to the two astronauts who were circling the moon, 239,000 miles away. "Eagle, you're to go for PDI." The initials "PDI" meant "power descent initiation," prelude to the trickiest part of the mission. Few people at Mission Control had any fears that the astronauts would be marooned on the moon after a safe landing. The take-off had been rehearsed dozens of times with mock-up lunar modules. But landing was very different. The lunar module was so delicate, and the moon's gravity so much less than the earth's, that the only place a moon landing could be practiced was on the moon itself.

After clearance for the landing had been given, Buzz Aldrin replied, "Roger, understand." Aldrin was the co-pilot of Eagle, code name for the lunar module. Neil Armstrong, the commander, pressed a button on his instrument panel to initiate Eagle's computer landing program, and Eagle's descent engine flamed immediately. The lunar module

paused in its 50,000-foot lunar orbit. Lower and lower it approached the moon's surface, ever more slowly.

At an altitude of 39,000 feet there came a second of terror. Eagle's landing computer was flashing its alarm panel. For a split second nobody knew whether or not something had gone dangerously wrong, and back at Houston, General Samuel L. Phillips, head of the Apollo Space Program, bit clean through his cigar. (Christopher Kraft, the director of flight operations, later called this computer malfunction "a matter of grave concern.") The computer had become saturated with the demands placed upon it. If Eagle had been unmanned, there is no doubt that it would have crashed. The astronauts were compelled to take partial manual control. Armstrong directed the craft while Aldrin called out speed and altitude.

No sooner had this danger passed than a fresh one appeared. The gravitational pull of mysterious "mascons," great lumps of solid matter beneath the moon's surface, were throwing Eagle off course. Armstrong stared through one of Eagle's triangular windows and saw to his horror that she was about to land in a jagged crater "big enough to house the Houston Astrodome." He took over full manual control. Finding a smoother place, he began his final descent. Mission Control's nervousness was intense; if the descent engines faltered now, the two men would perish. The engine held. The landing probes on Eagle's legs signaled "lunar contact," and Armstrong cut the engine. Eagle settled into the Sea of Tranquillity. "Houston," radioed Armstrong, "Tranquillity Base here. The Eagle has landed."

The Apollo 11 mission had begun four days earlier, on Wednesday, July 16, 1969, at the Cape Kennedy Space Center in Florida, and the occasion provoked the most passionate excitement. Five hours before liftoff, which was due to occur at Launch Pad 39A at exactly 9:32 A.M. local time, thousands of carloads of people converged on the Space Center,

The answer to crime?

The Flight of Apollo 11

1. Lift-off from Cape Kennedy.
2. The burned-up first stage of the *Saturn V* launching vehicle falls away.
3. *Saturn* second stage falls away and *Saturn* third stage puts the craft into earth orbit.
4. *Saturn* third stage is fired to put the craft out of orbit and into moon trajectory.
5. The command-service module (C-SM) detaches from *Saturn* third-stage.
6. C-SM turns to join up with the lunar module (LM).
7. LM and C-SM dock.
8. LM and C-SM jettison *Saturn* third stage.
9. The spacecraft nears the moon.
10. The spacecraft fires rockets to put it into low orbit. As it orbits the moon two astronauts enter LM.
11. LM separates from C-SM.
12. LM descends to moon firing retro-rockets.
13. LM lifts off from moon leaving its descent stage behind and goes into orbit.
14. LM and C-SM dock. Astronauts return to C-SM.
15. LM is jettisoned.
16. Rockets fire C-SM out of orbit and into earth trajectory.
17. Before entering earth's atmosphere, the command module with the astronauts inside detaches from the service module.
18. Command module enters earth's atmosphere.
19. Parachutes break the module's descent to earth to 25 mph.

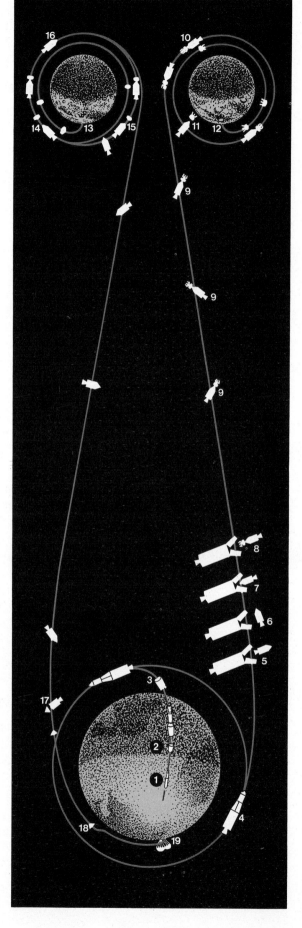

causing solid lines of traffic for nearly twenty miles. At 5 A.M., the entire eastern night sky blazed with one great light—the white glare from a floodlit Saturn v rocket. The Saturn, which was 364 feet in height and capable of putting a weight of 150 tons into orbit, was, at the time, the most powerful rocket ever made. The dazzling beacon was visible for thirty miles, and it sent a glare out over the horizon that seemed to call men's spirits to it like a modern Star of Bethlehem.

By 8 A.M., astronauts Armstrong, Aldrin and Col. Michael Collins, pilot of the command ship Columbia, were inside their spacecraft on top of the rocket. Everyone listened to the crisp voice of Jack King, the official launch commentator. "We are still go for Apollo 11." The minutes passed. "Astronauts report it feels good. T-minus 25 seconds. Twenty seconds and counting. T-minus 15 seconds; guidance is internal. Twelve, eleven, ten, nine—*ignition sequence starts*. Six, five, four, three two, one, zero—*all engines running, liftoff! We have liftoff on Apollo 11!*"

The blinding explosion of light was like a signal to the crowd. Hundreds of thousands of people rose from their seats yelling: "Go! Go! Go!" The rocket appeared to hear them and obey. With the equivalent combined horsepower of 543 jet fighters, the roar of five giant engines struck the spectators with a force that made every wooden and metal structure tremble. When three-quarters of its 7 million pounds of thrust had built up, the rocket began to rise, making the earth shake almost visibly. Great clouds of ice, which the supercooled propellant had deposited on the hull, were shaken loose by the monstrous vibration and they showered down on the launch site.

The journey from the earth to the moon, a voyage that had caused considerable wonder in the previous missions of Apollo 8 and Apollo 10, had by now become almost routine. After the first two stages of the rocket had burned out and been jettisoned, and after the spacecraft had made several orbits of the earth, Mission Control in Houston advised the astronauts that they were "Go for TLI" (the abbreviation stands for "translunar injection"). The third stage was then fired to accelerate the spacecraft to 25,000 m.p.h., the velocity needed to break away from earth orbit and fly to the moon.

An ingenious maneuver then took place. The three astronauts in the command ship Columbia separated their craft from the third rocket stage, and moved on ahead until they were some one hundred feet away. They slowly turned the module around and retraced their path until their front "docking probe" faced the front end of the third stage. The third stage then unfolded its flowerlike "petals," revealing Eagle packed up inside. Columbia's docking probe locked on to Eagle, and the two craft were fixed together. A short burn of her side engines was sufficient to push Columbia away from the third stage. The journey to the moon was now well under way, with the two craft tumbling continuously over each other so that the fierce heat of the sun would not burn too long on any part.

At 1:26 P.M. (Eastern Daylight Time) on Saturday, July 19, the three-day coast to the moon was complete, and the trajectory of the two linked spaceships carried them behind the moon. During the thirty-four minutes that the craft were out of touch with Houston, Columbia's powerful rocket engines slowed the ships' speed and thrust the two into a low lunar orbit.

On Sunday morning, Armstrong and Aldrin crawled through a hatch and into Eagle's tiny cabin. When they were certain that the lunar module's instrumentation was in working order, they initiated Eagle's separation from Columbia. Leaving Collins orbiting some seventy miles above the moon's surface, Armstrong and Aldrin began their hazardous descent to the moon. At 4:17 P.M. on Sunday, July

20, the lunar module touched down at Tranquillity Base. The Eagle had landed.

More than 350 million people sat before their television sets that night, impatiently awaiting the first steps on the moon. At last, at 10:45 P.M., they heard Armstrong's voice: "The hatch is coming open." A few minutes later, he was on the porch at the top of Eagle's ladder.

Armstrong had begun to operate the television camera, and Houston interrupted: "Man, we're getting a picture on the TV. Okay, now we can see you coming down the ladder." As he reached the foot of the ladder and took his step on the lunar soil, Armstrong uttered the sentence that will surely be remembered a thousand years from now: "That's one small step for a man; one giant leap for mankind."

Aldrin soon followed him down the frail ladder, confidently jumping the last two rungs. They then set in motion three scientific experiments: a laser reflector to detect minute movements in the earth's crust—and thereby warn of impending earthquakes; an experiment to measure the gases of the solar wind; and a seismic device to detect rumblings beneath the moon's surface. In addition, they collected several bags of rocks that were carried home for analysis. Their "walk"—in gravity one-sixth that of the earth's—consisted of swift hops and jumps. It was interrupted by a radio telephone call from President Nixon, who told them: "Because of what you have done, the heavens have become a part of man's world."

These events produced popular excitement on an extraordinary scale. In New York, crime dropped to a fraction of its normal rate, and one police chief wished it were possible to have a moonwalk every

Yuri Gagarin, the first man to orbit the earth, seen in the cabin of his spaceship *Vostok* before his flight.

A photograph of the large crater of Goclenius, taken as the space capsule orbited the moon.

"A galactic telephone directory"

The Apollo astronauts leaving their quarters for the ride out to the launch pad at Cape Kennedy.

The Earth as seen from space. South America is visible on the left and the African coast on the right.

night. In London, hundreds of thousands of people stayed up all night to watch the moon landing on a giant television screen in Trafalgar Square. In Rome, Pope Paul VI solemnly performed a blessing as he watched his screen. In North Vietnam, the Communist leaders were so concerned over the moon landing's effect on the morale of their fighting men that they told them that the Russians, not the Americans, had walked on the moon. In Russia itself, parts of the moonwalk were shown on television with the grudging official comment that it was "a great scientific achievement." In America, Monday, July 21, 1969, was declared an official holiday.

As the weeks passed and calmer minds began to appraise the importance of Apollo 11, it became apparent even to the least imaginative men that a milestone in history had been reached. The changes it produced would be subtle and gradual, and its impact might not be felt on a substantial proportion of mankind for several generations. But in the future, when the colonization of the solar system should begin in earnest, with whole planets climatically altered to support large populations in a healthy atmosphere, and when the first manned expeditions to the stars should depart (perhaps to settle in some remote world and never to return), Apollo 11 would be recalled as the decisive act that opened the way. Significantly, only churchmen, not historians or sociologists, challenged President Nixon's remark that the week of the Apollo mission was "the greatest week in history since the Creation." Evolutionists might argue that the Creation lasted somewhat longer than a week, and clergymen lamented that the President had omitted the life of Christ from his catalog—but it is difficult to see the decisive moment that liberated man from his own planet in any other context than one of gigantic consequence.

Just as modern astronomers have abandoned all concepts of the universe that gave a special or central position to earth or the solar system, so an increasing number of scientists had abandoned the thesis that man may have evolved on our planet through a vast series of accidents. It is asserted that evolution might have taken one of millions of other possible routes, and those scientists agree that it could well have done so. But if that had happened, they say, the result would have been essentially the same as if it had not: one species would have acquired intelligence and grown to dominate the others. All that was needed was eyesight that distinguished perspective and color, a well-coordinated brain, the ability to stand several feet off the ground, and members resembling fingers. Armed with these tools, there would be nothing to prevent such creatures from establishing a machine technology and traveling through space.

Such thinking leads at once to two fantastic implications. Apollo 11, or something like it, may have happened millions of times before, and will probably happen millions of times again. Even if only ten million stars, from the hundred thousand million suns in our galaxy, bear technologically intelligent life, then countless alien civilizations must have passed the critical moment of a first landing on another celestial body. The second implication is that Apollo 11 was inevitable from the moment when life first appeared on earth. The human species, which finally prevailed over all other life-forms, was impelled into technological progress by those inventive powers and exploratory urges that it had acquired during millions of years of struggle for survival. To believe that this tough creature could refrain from expensive and dangerous exploration is to ignore man's biological nature. Forty centuries of urban civilization is too short a time in which to cast off the aggressive habits of 3 million years.

Access to the far side of the moon will enable an

An astronaut with his cumbersome life support pack. The moon's thin atmosphere enabled the astronauts to move freely despite their bulky equipment.

Below A footprint left by the Apollo 11 astronauts in the dust on the moon's surface.

Bottom One of the first tasks the astronauts performed was to plant the American flag on the moon's surface.

experiment to be performed that may confirm the truth of all these suspicions. A search will be made for intelligent radio or optical messages from civilizations on planets in orbit around other suns. To await this shattering communication, an automatic radio-receiving device will be installed among the remote craters. It will switch itself on during the fourteen-day-long lunar nights, when there will be no radio interference from the sun or from the busy people of earth. The moment it detects an artificial pattern in signals from any of the neighboring stars, it will trigger an alarm, and a cautious reply will be sent into space.

Earth at that point will have become listed in what Arthur Clarke has called the "galactic telephone directory." Because of the vast distances, resulting interstellar conversations will take many years to complete. Even the nearest star, Proxima Centauri, is four and a third light years away (a light year is the distance light travels in a year, moving at 670 million miles per hour.) A radio message would take just under nine years to make the trip there and back. But to some scientists, the prospect of such a long drawn-out conversation is undaunting. "Imagine that a reply to one of your messages was scheduled to be received forty years from now," writes Professor Edward Purcell of Harvard University. "What a legacy for your grandchildren!"
ADRIAN BERRY

1900 | **1910** | **1920** | **1930**

● 1903
Wings Over Kitty Hawk
Orville Wright's brief flight over North Carolina sand dunes realizes one of man's oldest dreams and revolutionizes transportation

● 1922
The Blackshirts March on Rome
An ill-organized but highly effective march on Italy's capital brings Benito Mussolini and his Blackshirts to power

● 1908
An Automobile for the Masses
An innovative mechanic from Detroit perfects an unlovely, inexpensive motor car — the Model T — and puts America on wheels

● 1929
Panic on Wall Street
Amid wild trading and wilder rumors, the speculative bubble of the late 1920s finally bursts, and America is plunged into a decade of depression

● 1914
Assassination Sparks the Great War
In the diplomatic confusion following the assassination of Austria-Hungary's heir-presumptive, Europe moves irrevocably toward war

● 1933
The Burning of the Reichstag
Germany's ambitious Chancellor, Adolf Hitler, seizes upon a highly suspicious incident to consolidate his control of the country

● 1917
"Peace, Bread and Land!"
Lenin returns from exile to lead a Bolshevik coup that topples Russia's provisional government and establishes a new, Communist state

● 1936
The Spanish Civil War
Assisted by the Axis Powers, General Francisco Franco lands an invasion army in his native Spain and overthrows the Second Republic

● 1900
Planck's quantum theory

● 1917
U.S.A. enters World War I

● 1924
Zinoviev letter forgery leads to fall of first British Labour government

● 1933
New Deal reform legislation begun in U.S.A.; U.S.A. and Canada abandon Gold Standard

● 1901
U.S.A.: assassination of President McKinley; Roosevelt President

● 1918
Wilson's Fourteen Points: principle of national self-determination

● 1925
Locarno Pact guarantees Germany's western borders and allows her entry to League of Nations

● 1934
Nazi *putsch* in Austria: assassination of Dollfuss

● 1903-21
Second wave of pogroms in Russia

● 1918
Votes for women in Britain

● 1934
China: "Long March" north of Communist guerrillas under Mao Tse-tung

● 1904
Building of Panama Canal under U.S. protection

● 1919
Treaty of Versailles

● 1925
Trotsky asserts opposition to Stalin's "Communism in One Country": exiled 1929

● 1904-5
Russo-Japanese War establishes Japan as world power

● 1919
League of Nations, World Court, International Labor Organization established

● 1935-36
Italy conquers Ethiopia: League of Nations powerless

● 1926
General Strike in Britain

● 1905
First Russian Revolution: foundation of "Soviets"

● 1919
Gandhi's civil disobedience campaign in India: troops fire on Indians at Amritsar

● 1936
Coup by military in Japan

● 1926
First television transmission

● 1905
First moving picture devised by Edison

● 1936
Rome-Berlin Axis: military pact

● 1920
Votes for women in U.S.A.; prohibition of alcohol (until 1933)

● 1927
China: massacre of Communists by Nationalists in Shanghai begins civil war

● 1907
Anglo-Russian Convention on Persia, Afghanistan and Tibet; 1904 Anglo-French Entente expanded to Triple Entente (Britain, Russia, France)

● 1937
Sino-Japanese War: fall of Peking, Shanghai and Nanking

● 1921
Russia: Kronstadt mutiny; ban on opposition in Party; New Economic Policy

● 1928-29
First Five Year Plan in USSR; forced collectivization; virtual dictatorship of Stalin

● 1910
Mexican Revolution

● 1923
Turkey declared a republic under reform regime of Ataturk

● 1931
Financial crisis reaches climax in Europe: National Government and abandonment of Gold Standard in Britain

● 1910
Union of South Africa created

● 1911
Revolution in China: imperial rule overthrown

● 1923
French troops occupy the Ruhr (until 1925) because Germany does not pay war reparations

● 1931
Sino-Japanese War: Japan withdraws from League of Nations

● 1915
First U-boat (submarine) attacks: sinking of the *Lusitania*

● 1923
Acute inflation in Germany: Hitler's unsuccessful "beer-hall *putsch*" in Munich

● 1933
Hitler Chancellor of Germany; Germany leaves Geneva Disarmament Conference and League of Nations

● 1916
Einstein completes his general theory of relativity

● 1924
Death of Lenin

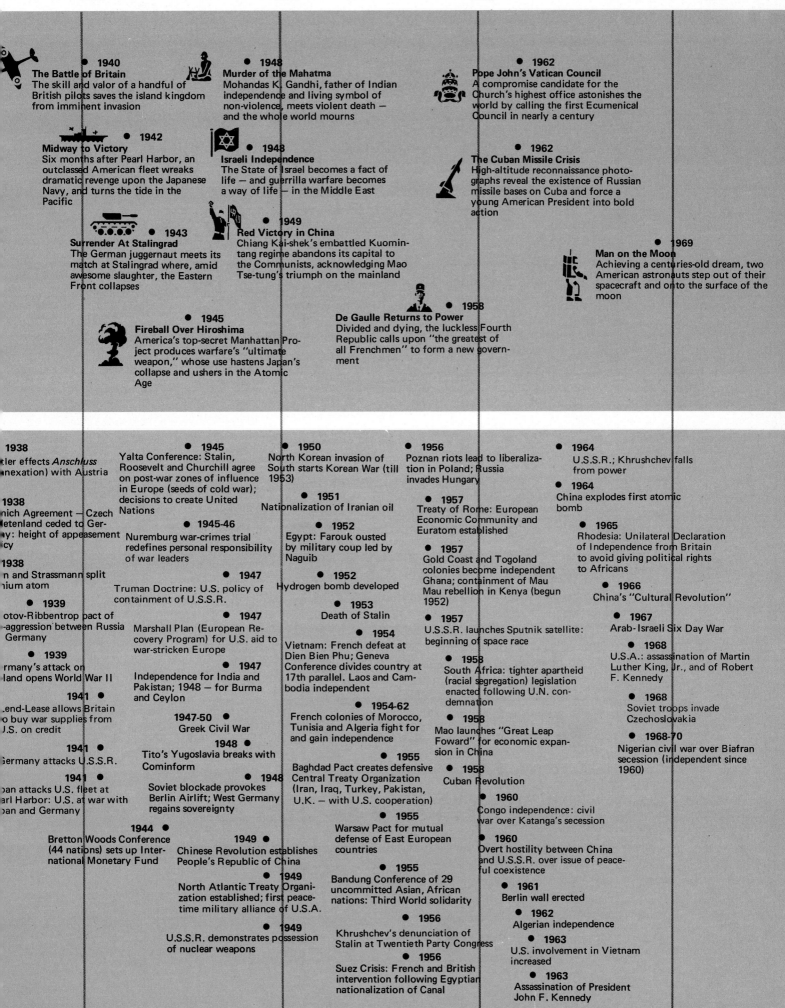

1940   **1950**   **1960**   **1970**

● **1940**
The Battle of Britain
The skill and valor of a handful of British pilots saves the island kingdom from imminent invasion

● **1942**
Midway to Victory
Six months after Pearl Harbor, an outclassed American fleet wreaks dramatic revenge upon the Japanese Navy, and turns the tide in the Pacific

● **1943**
Surrender At Stalingrad
The German juggernaut meets its match at Stalingrad where, amid awesome slaughter, the Eastern Front collapses

● **1945**
Fireball Over Hiroshima
America's top-secret Manhattan Project produces warfare's "ultimate weapon," whose use hastens Japan's collapse and ushers in the Atomic Age

● **1948**
Murder of the Mahatma
Mohandas K. Gandhi, father of Indian independence and living symbol of non-violence, meets violent death — and the whole world mourns

● **1948**
Israeli Independence
The State of Israel becomes a fact of life — and guerrilla warfare becomes a way of life — in the Middle East

● **1949**
Red Victory in China
Chiang Kai-shek's embattled Kuomintang regime abandons its capital to the Communists, acknowledging Mao Tse-tung's triumph on the mainland

● **1958**
De Gaulle Returns to Power
Divided and dying, the luckless Fourth Republic calls upon "the greatest of all Frenchmen" to form a new government

● **1962**
Pope John's Vatican Council
A compromise candidate for the Church's highest office astonishes the world by calling the first Ecumenical Council in nearly a century

● **1962**
The Cuban Missile Crisis
High-altitude reconnaissance photographs reveal the existence of Russian missile bases on Cuba and force a young American President into bold action

● **1969**
Man on the Moon
Achieving a centuries-old dream, two American astronauts step out of their spacecraft and onto the surface of the moon

● **1938**
tler effects *Anschluss* (annexation) with Austria

● **1938**
nich Agreement — Czech detenland ceded to Germany: height of appeasement cy

● **1938**
n and Strassmann split nium atom

● **1939**
otov-Ribbentrop pact of -aggression between Russia Germany

● **1939**
rmany's attack on land opens World War II

1941 ●
end-Lease allows Britain o buy war supplies from U.S. on credit

1941 ●
Germany attacks U.S.S.R.

1941 ●
pan attacks U.S. fleet at arl Harbor: U.S. at war with pan and Germany

1944 ●
Bretton Woods Conference (44 nations) sets up International Monetary Fund

● **1945**
Yalta Conference: Stalin, Roosevelt and Churchill agree on post-war zones of influence in Europe (seeds of cold war); decisions to create United Nations

● **1945-46**
Nuremburg war-crimes trial redefines personal responsibility of war leaders

● **1947**
Truman Doctrine: U.S. policy of containment of U.S.S.R.

● **1947**
Marshall Plan (European Recovery Program) for U.S. aid to war-stricken Europe

● **1947**
Independence for India and Pakistan; 1948 — for Burma and Ceylon

1947-50 ●
Greek Civil War

1948 ●
Tito's Yugoslavia breaks with Cominform

1948 ●
Soviet blockade provokes Berlin Airlift; West Germany regains sovereignty

1949 ●
Chinese Revolution establishes People's Republic of China

● **1949**
North Atlantic Treaty Organization established; first peacetime military alliance of U.S.A.

● **1949**
U.S.S.R. demonstrates possession of nuclear weapons

● **1950**
North Korean invasion of South starts Korean War (till 1953)

● **1951**
Nationalization of Iranian oil

● **1952**
Egypt: Farouk ousted by military coup led by Naguib

● **1952**
Hydrogen bomb developed

● **1953**
Death of Stalin

● **1954**
Vietnam: French defeat at Dien Bien Phu; Geneva Conference divides country at 17th parallel. Laos and Cambodia independent

● **1954-62**
French colonies of Morocco, Tunisia and Algeria fight for and gain independence

● **1955**
Baghdad Pact creates defensive Central Treaty Organization (Iran, Iraq, Turkey, Pakistan, U.K. — with U.S. cooperation)

● **1955**
Warsaw Pact for mutual defense of East European countries

● **1955**
Bandung Conference of 29 uncommitted Asian, African nations: Third World solidarity

● **1956**
Khrushchev's denunciation of Stalin at Twentieth Party Congress

● **1956**
Suez Crisis: French and British intervention following Egyptian nationalization of Canal

● **1956**
Poznan riots lead to liberalization in Poland; Russia invades Hungary

● **1957**
Treaty of Rome: European Economic Community and Euratom established

● **1957**
Gold Coast and Togoland colonies become independent Ghana; containment of Mau Mau rebellion in Kenya (begun 1952)

● **1957**
U.S.S.R. launches Sputnik satellite: beginning of space race

● **1958**
South Africa: tighter apartheid (racial segregation) legislation enacted following U.N. condemnation

● **1958**
Mao launches "Great Leap Foward" for economic expansion in China

● **1958**
Cuban Revolution

● **1960**
Congo independence: civil war over Katanga's secession

● **1960**
Overt hostility between China and U.S.S.R. over issue of peaceful coexistence

● **1961**
Berlin wall erected

● **1962**
Algerian independence

● **1963**
U.S. involvement in Vietnam increased

● **1963**
Assassination of President John F. Kennedy

● **1964**
U.S.S.R.; Khrushchev falls from power

● **1964**
China explodes first atomic bomb

● **1965**
Rhodesia: Unilateral Declaration of Independence from Britain to avoid giving political rights to Africans

● **1966**
China's "Cultural Revolution"

● **1967**
Arab-Israeli Six Day War

● **1968**
U.S.A.: assassination of Martin Luther King, Jr., and of Robert F. Kennedy

● **1968**
Soviet troops invade Czechoslovakia

● **1968-70**
Nigerian civil war over Biafran secession (independent since 1960)

Paul von Hindenburg
1847-1934 *German field marshal, statesman*

Wilhelm II
1859-1941 *German Kaiser*

Neville Chamberlain
1869-1940 *British statesman*

Albert Schweitzer
1875-1965 *Alsatian philosopher, missionary*

Franklin D. Roosevelt
1882-1945 *U.S. President*

Boris Pasternak
1890-1960 *Russian poet, novelist*

Nikita Khrushch
1894- *Russian statesm*

Ivan Pavlov
1849-1936 *Russian physiologist*

Raymond Poincaré
1860-1934 *French statesman*

Mohandas Gandhi
1869-1948 *Indian leader*

Pius XII
1876-1958 *Pope*

Igor Stravinsky
1882- *Russian composer*

Dwight D. Eisenhower
1890-1969 *U.S. general, President*

Juan Perón
1895- *Argentinian statesm*

Henry Cabot Lodge
1850-1924 *U.S. statesman*

David Lloyd-George
1863-1945 *British statesman*

Henri Matisse
1869-1954 *French painter*

Konrad Adenauer
1876-1967 *German statesman*

Franz Kafka
1883-1924 *Czech novelist*

Ho Chi Minh
1890-1969 *Vietnamese Communist leader*

Trygve Lie
1896-1968 *Norwegian statesman, U.N. Sec. G*

Ferdinand Foch
1851-1929 *French general*

Henry Ford
1863-1947 *U.S. industrialist*

Frank Lloyd Wright
1869-1959 *U.S. architect*

Leon Trotsky (L.D. Bronstein)
1879-1940 *Russian revolutionary leader*

Pierre Laval
1883-1945 *French politician*

Charles de Gaulle
1890- *French general, statesman*

Georgi Zhuk
1896-1969 *Russian gene*

Joseph Joffre
1852-1931 *Marshal of France*

George V
1865-1936 *King of England*

Lenin Vladimir I. (Ulyanov)
1870-1924 *Russian revolutionary leader*

Joseph Stalin (Dzhugashvili)
1879-1953 *Russian statesman*

Benito Mussolini
1883-1945 *Italian dictator*

Erwin Rommel
1891-1944 *German field marshal*

Bertold Brecht
1898-1956 *German playwri*

James Keir Hardie
1856-1915 *British socialist statesman*

Erich Ludendorff
1865-1937 *German general*

Marcel Proust
1871-1922 *French novelist*

Albert Einstein
1879-1955 *German-American physicist*

John Maynard Keynes
1883-1946 *British economist*

Averell Harriman
1891- *U.S. statesman*

Trofim Lysenk
1898- *Russian genetic*

Theobald von Bethmann-Hollweg
1856-1921 *German statesman*

Sun Yat-sen
1866-1925 *Chinese revolutionary*

Ernest Rutherford
1871-1937 *British physicist*

Kemal Ataturk
1880-1938 *Turkish leader*

Walther Gropius
1883-1969 *German architect*

Haile Selassie
1891- *Emperor of Ethiopia*

Henry Moor
1898- *British sculpt*

Woodrow Wilson
1856-1924 *U.S. President*

J. Ramsay MacDonald
1866-1937 *British statesman*

Orville Wright
1871-1948 *U.S. aircraft inventor*

Béla Bartók
1881-1945 *Hungarian composer*

Harry S Truman
1884- *U.S. President*

Francisco Franco
1892- *Spanish general, dictator*

Hussein ibn Ali
1856-1931 *Sherif of Mecca*

Wilbur Wright
1867-1912 *U.S. aircraft inventor*

Grigori Rasputin
1872-1916 *Russian monk*

John XXIII
1881-1963 *Pope*

Chiang Kai-shek
1886- *Chinese general, statesman*

Tito (Josip Broz)
1892- *Yugoslav statesman*

Sigmund Freud
1856-1939 *Austrian psychiatrist*

Marie Curie
1867-1934 *French chemist, physicist*

Arnold Schoenberg
1874-1951 *Austrian composer*

Georges Braque
1881-1963 *French painter*

David Ben-Gurion
1886- *Israeli statesman*

Hermann Göring
1893-1946 *German Nazi leader*

George Bernard Shaw
1856-1950 *British dramatist*

Stanley Baldwin
1867-1947 *British statesman*

Chaim Weizmann
1874-1952 *Russian-British Zionist leader*

Kliment Voroshilov
1881-1969 *Russian field marshal*

John Foster Dulles
1888-1959 *U.S. statesman*

Mao Tse-tung
1893- *Chinese statesman*

Theodore Roosevelt
1858-1919 *U.S. President*

Nicholas II
1868-1918 *Tsar of Russia*

Winston Churchill
1874-1965 *British statesman*

Pablo Picasso
1881- *Franco-Spanish painter*

Adolf Hitler
1889-1945 *German Nazi leader*

Jomo Kenyatta
1893- *Kenyan statesman*

Max Planck
1858-1947 *German physicist*

Maxim Gorki
1868-1936 *Russian author*

Carl Jung
1875-1961 *Swiss psychiatrist*

Alexander Kerensky
1881-1970 *Russian statesman*

Jawaharlal Nehru
1889-1964 *Indian statesman*

Aldous Huxley
1894-1964 *British writer*

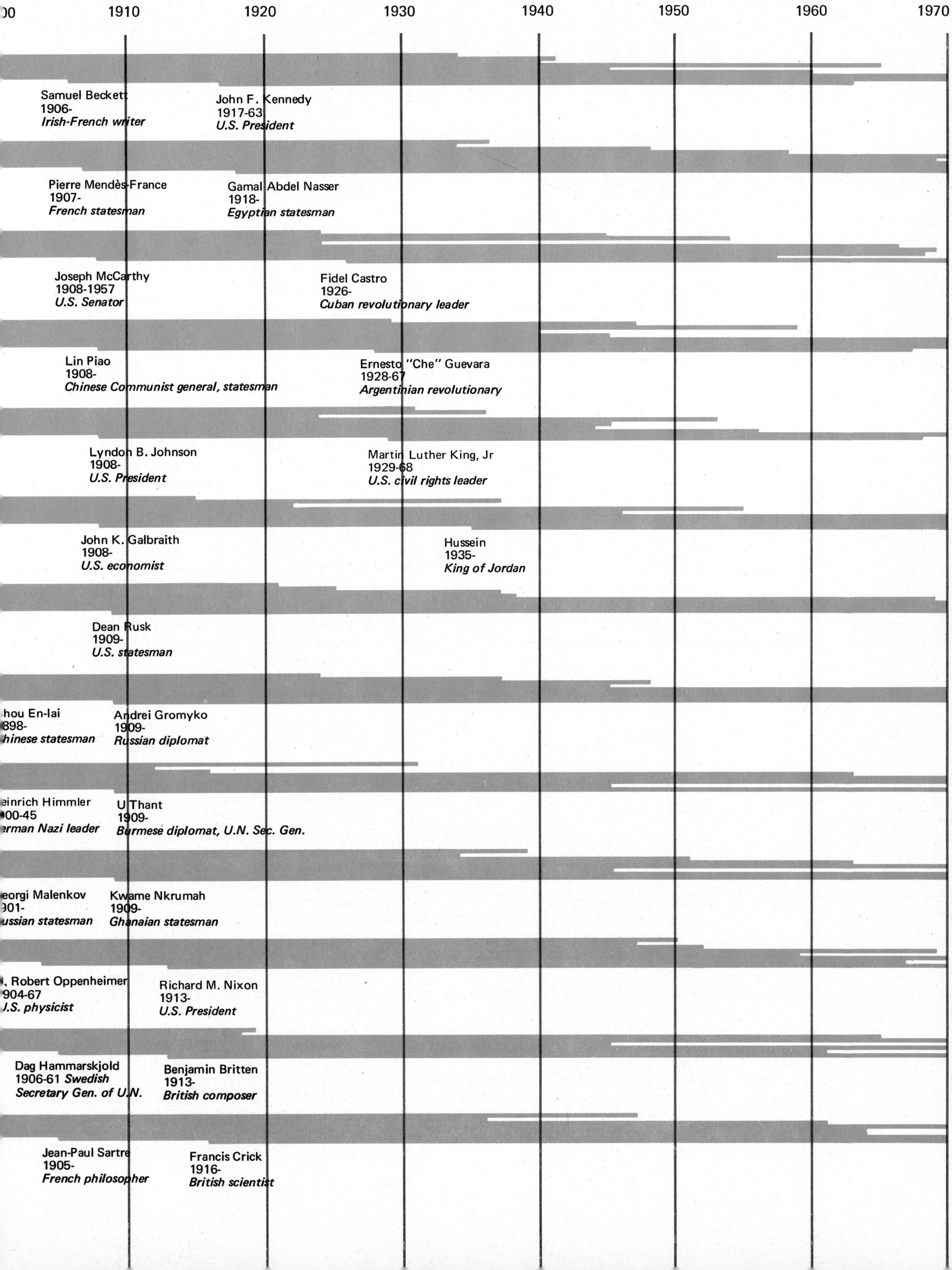

00
1910
1920
1930
1940
1950
1960
1970
Samuel Beckett
1906-
Irish-French writer
John F. Kennedy
1917-63
U.S. President
Pierre Mendès-France
1907-
French statesman
Gamal Abdel Nasser
1918-
Egyptian statesman
Joseph McCarthy
1908-1957
U.S. Senator
Fidel Castro
1926-
Cuban revolutionary leader
Lin Piao
1908-
Chinese Communist general, statesman
Ernesto "Che" Guevara
1928-67
Argentinian revolutionary
Lyndon B. Johnson
1908-
U.S. President
Martin Luther King, Jr
1929-68
U.S. civil rights leader
John K. Galbraith
1908-
U.S. economist
Hussein
1935-
King of Jordan
Dean Rusk
1909-
U.S. statesman
hou En-lai
898-
hinese statesman
Andrei Gromyko
1909-
Russian diplomat
einrich Himmler
00-45
erman Nazi leader
U Thant
1909-
Burmese diplomat, U.N. Sec. Gen.
eorgi Malenkov
901-
ussian statesman
Kwame Nkrumah
1909-
Ghanaian statesman
. Robert Oppenheimer
904-67
.S. physicist
Richard M. Nixon
1913-
U.S. President
Dag Hammarskjold
1906-61 Swedish
Secretary Gen. of U.N.
Benjamin Britten
1913-
British composer
Jean-Paul Sartre
1905-
French philosopher
Francis Crick
1916-
British scientist

Acknowledgments

The editors, authors and publishers wish to thank the authorities of the following museums, collections and art galleries by whose kind permission the illustrations are reproduced:

ALEPPO: National Museum, 31/1
AMSTERDAM: Rijksmuseum, 480/*1*, 547/*2*, 550/*2*
ANKARA: Archaeological Museum, 31/*1*, 48/5, 66/1
ASSISI: S. Francesco, 343/2
ATHENS: Acropolis Museum, 74/1, 85/2
    Deutsches Archäologisches Institute, 74/5
    National Museum, 38/1, 38/2, 39, 81
BAGDAD: Iraq Museum, 20/2, 20/4, 21/1
BAMBERG: Staatliche Bibliothek, 243/4
BAYEUX: Musée, 261/4, 263/1, 263/2, 264, 265/1
BEAULIEU, England: The Montagu Motor
    Museum, 780, 784, 785
BEIRUT: National Museum, 53/1
BERLIN (EAST): Staatliche Museen, 14/1, 14/2
    21/2, 48/1, 48/6, 55/1, 67/1, 85/5, 88/5, 137/1
BERLIN (WEST): Deutsche Staatsbibliothek,
    31/2, 110/1, 110/2, 277/1
    Staatlichen Museen—Münzkabinett, 220/1,
    243/3
    Germanisches National Museum, 497/2
    Provincial Museum, 418/2
BERN: Bürgerbibliothek, 220/2, 296
BORDEAUX: Musée des Beaux Arts, 651/1
BOSTON: Museum of Fine Arts, 122, 136/2
BOWDOIN COLLEGE: Museum of Art, Brunswick,
    Maine, 593/1
BRESCIA: Musei Civici, 14/1, 184/3, 189/1
BRUSSELS: Bibliotheque Royale, 354/*2*, 353/*3*
    Musee Royale de Beaux Arts, 435/*2*
CAIRO: Egyptian Museum, 12, 15/1, 15/2, 17/1,
    18, 40/2, 41/2, 58
    National Museum, 56/2
CAMBRAI: Bibliothèque Municipale, 304/2
CAMBRIDGE: Corpus Christi College, 319, 359/*3*
    Clare College, 280
    Gonville and Caius College, 285/1
CAMBRIDGE: Trinity College, 651/*3*
CAMBRIDGE (Massachusetts): Fogg Art Museum,
    Harvard University, 287/3
CHANTILLY: Musée Condé, 285/*3*
CHICAGO: Oriental Institute, 20/2, 21/2, 21/5
COMO: Museo Civico, 387
COPENHAGEN: Ny Carlsberg Glyptotek, 85/6,
    112, 115/1
    Nationalmuseum, 257/2
CRACOW: Wawel, Bibliotoka Kapitularna, 273
DAMASCUS: National Museum, 93/2
DELFT: Stedelijk Museum "Het Prinsenhof",
    149/1
DELPHI: Archaeological Museum, 80/4
DIJON: Bibliothèque Municipale, 279/1
DUBLIN: Chester Beatty Library, 446/*1*
    National Museum of Ireland, 177/2, 179/1
    Trinity College, 179/2
DURHAM: Gulbenkian Museum, 206/4, 250/3
EDINBURGH: National Museum of Antiquities
    of Scotland, 504
    Scottish National Gallery, on loan from Lord
    Rosenberry, 511/1

University Library, 201/*1*, 201/*2*, 335/*1*, 335/*3*
EPERNAY: Bibliothèque Municipale, 223/1
FLORENCE: Bargello, 187/3, 299, 341
    Biblioteca Laurenziana, 194, 353/2, 408/1,
    410/1, 411
    Biblioteca Nazionale, 86
    Cathedral, 344/1
    Horne Collection, 419/2
    Museo Archaeologico, 75/1
    Museo dell'Opera del Duomo, 340
    Museo St. Marco, 394/2
    Orfanotrionfo Bigallo, 347/*2*
    Palazzo Medici-Riccardi, 78
    Palazzo, Vecchio, 404/*3*
    Pitti, 402/*1*, 404/*1*, 438/*1*
    Raccolta, 384/*1*
    St. Apollonia, 351, 358/*2*
    St. Maria Novella, 342, 345/*3*
    Uffizi, 111/2, 396, 401/*1*, 402/*2*, 404/*2*, 405
ESCORIAL: 432
GETTYSBURG: National Military Park, 714
GENEVA: Bibliotheque Nationale (Publique?)
    et Universitaire, 411/2
GLOUCESTER: City Museum, 180/2
GRANADA: Capilla Real, 391/2
HALLE: Landemuseum für Vorgeschichte, 188
HERACLION (Crete): Archaeological Museum,
    33, 34/*1*, 34–5, 35
HERMITAGE, Tennessee: Ladies Hermitage
    Association, 654, 655
ISTANBUL: Archaeological Museum, 88, 89/2
JENA: Universitäts Bibliothek, 275/2
JERUSALEM: Central Zionist Archives, 758/1,
    760/2, 872
    Israel Defence Department, 876/2
    Israel Museum, 147/2, 149/1, 144/1, 144/3,
    144/4, 145/1, 145/2, 145/6, 757
JOHANNESBURG: Africana Museum, 750, 752/3
KARACHI: National Museum of Pakistan, 21/3,
    72/2, 93/1
KREMSMÜNSTER: Abbey, 224/1
KIBBUTZ SEDOT YAM: Caesarea Museum, 139/1
LE MANS: Musée, 271/1
LENINGRAD: Hermitage, 590/*1*, 544/*2*
LIEGE: Musée des Beaux Arts, 636
LILLE: Bibliotheque Municipale, 372/*2*
LISBON: Archivio de Indias, 422/*1*
    Museo de Arte Antigua, 73/*1*
LIVERPOOL: Walker Art Gallery, 650/2
LONDON: Admiralty, 588/2
    British Museum, 16/1, 16/3, 19/1, 19/2, 20/1,
    21/1, 21/2, 24/1, 27/4, 29, 30/1, 30/2, 30/3,
    30/4, 31, 41/1, 44/1, 48/1, 48/3, 48/5, 49/3,
    53/1, 55/2, 63/2, 65/1, 66/2, 66/3, 66/4,
    67/2, 67/4, 70/1, 70/2, 71/1, 71/2, 74/3,
    77/1, 78, 80/2, 82/2, 83, 84/3, 85/4, 87, 92,
    96, 100/2, 110/5, 111/5, 114/2, 117/2, 119/4,
    120, 121, 123/1, 123/2, 125/2, 126/1, 127/1,
    128/1, 129/2, 129/3, 130, 132/2, 133/1, 133/2,
    134/2, 137/2, 137/3, 137/4, 138, 142, 145/1,
    145/4, 145/7, 149/2, 173/3, 174, 180/1, 185,
    212/1, (property of R. Pinder-Wilson), 206/1,
    225/1, 227/1, 227/2, 231/2, 232/2, 260/2,
    261/2, 261/3, 269/2, 301/2, 308/1, 320/2,
    321/1, 321/2, 322/2, 331/2, 338/2, 348/1,

Acknowledgements

Museo Ostia, 76
Museo Villa Giulia, 79/2, 102/4, 103/2, 106/2
Palazzo del Conservatori, 164, 166/2
Palazzo Doria, 394/3, 434/1
Palazzo Medici-Riccardi, 382
Pecci Blunt Collection, 531
S. Giovanni in Laterano, 471/3
S. Maria dell'Anima, 414/1
S. Pietro in Vaticana, 341/2, 400/2
Sistine Chapel, 397, 398, 402, 403
Vatican Library, 194/1, 272, 300/2, 338/1
ROUEN: Bibliotheque Nationale, 371
ST. GALLEN: Stiftsbibliothek, 190, 242
SEVILLE: Alcazar, 359/1
SIENNA: Cattedrale, 377/2
Palazzo Publico, 346/1
Pinacoteca, 352, 375/2
SPARTA: Archaeological Museum, 84/1
STOCKHOLM: Antikvarsk-Topografiska Arkivet,
255/2
Kungliga Biblioteket, 223/4
National Museum, 475/2
SUBIACO: Sacro Spaco, 317
TEHERAN: Archaeological Museum, 67/4, 80/1
TOKYO: National Museum, 211/1, 213/2, 214/1
University, 682/1
TORTOSA-TARRAGONA: Coll. Joan Lamotte,
188/2
TOLEDO: Cathedral, 392
TRIER: Rheinishes Landesmuseum, 84/4, 136/2,
136/3
TROYES: Museum, 184/1
TUNIS: Bardo Museum, 116
UTRECHT: University Library, 221/2, 224/3, 246
VENICE: Accademia, 401/2
Museo di Palazzo, 400/1
VERSAILLES: Musée de, 448/2, 449/1, 514/1,
599, 603
VIENNA: Bildarchiv der Osterreichischen
Nationalbibliothek, 788
Gessellschaft des Musikfreunde, 620
Kunstgeschichtliche Sammlungen, 181/2
Kunsthistorisches Museum, 128/2, 131/1,
246, 367/2
Nationalbibliothek, 224/1, 240/2, 278/3,
535/2
Niederosterreichisches Landesmuseum, 136/5
Österreiches Nationale Bibliotheque, 331/1
VITTO, BARON: 385/2
WASHINGTON: Freer Gallery of Art, 172/3
Combat Art Section, U.S. Navy, 848/2
(Official U.S. Navy photo)
Department of Defense, 905/1
Department of Navy, 844, 847/2
National Gallery of Art, 598
Smithsonian Institution, 656/1, 657/2, 684/2
685
U.S. Signal Corps (Brady Collection) 716/1,
717/1, 717/2
U.S. War Department, 718/2
WINDSOR: Royal Library, 395/2
PRIVATE COLLECTIONS: 98/1, 98/2, 99, 207/1
582/1, 587/1, 588/1
Anglesey, Marquess of, 549
Koningsegg, Count of, 366/2

Mountbatten, Lord, 869/2
Portland, Duke of, 471/2
Radnor, Earl of, 505
Walston, Oliver, 695/3
Winsten, Clare, 866

Photographs were kindly supplied by the following:

Aerofilms, 376/1
Aldus Books, 565/2, 601/1
Alinari; 75/1, 79, 85/1, 85/2, 102/1, 102/3,
102/4, 103/1, 103/2, 103/3, 103/5, 106/1, 106/2,
111/1, 113, 114, 115/2, 118/2, 119/2, 118/3,
126/1, 128/4, 129/4, 129/5, 126/1, 132/1,
134/1, 144/2, 145/3, 153/1, 153/2, 165, 168/1,
168/2, 169, 173/4, 189, 192/1, 199, 215, 247,
271/2, 297/1, 337, 338/2, 340, 339/2, 340,
342, 343/1, 345/2, 345/3, 351, 352, 355/2,
356/2, 358/2, 384/1, 394/2, 394/3
American Stock Exchange, 814
Anderson, 56/2, 78, 103/7, 170/2, 196/1, 475/2,
343/2, 343/3, 367/3, 375/2, 377/2, 395/1, 398/2,
399, 402/2, 404/1, 404/3, 412/2, 435/1
Anderson-Giraudon, 692
Archives Photographiques, 282, 301/1
Arland, Jean, 413/2, 422/2
Arthaud, Michele, 21/1, 31/1, 54/2, 57/3, 173/2
Aufsberg, Lala, 274/3
Austin, James, 76, 109/1, 111/4, 113/1, 190/2
Bandy, I., 283/1, 283/2, 283/3, 285/2
Barnaby's Picture Library, 811/3, 874, 876/1,
877/1
Benrido Co. Ltd., 207/2, 208
Bertarelli, 808/2
Bildarchiv Foto Marburg, 725
Blainel, 497/1, 500/3
Boudot-Lamotte, 207/3, 265/2, 270/2, 271/1
Bredol-Lepper, 275
British Printing Corporation, 804, 805, 806,
807/2, 808/2, 815/2, 816/3, 821, 825/3, 831/1,
890/2
British Travel Association, 262, 268/1, 269/1,
305, 316, 330/2
Brogi, 197/1
Brown Brothers, 740, 860/3
Bulloz, Photo, 330/1, 369, 372/2, 373, 385/2,
338/3, 348/2, 513/2, 516/2, 609/2
Burn, Richard, 363/3
Burchall, Elea, 348, 380
Byzantine Institute, Dumbarton Oaks Field
Committee, 219/1
Camera Press, 672, 673, 885/2, 886, 827, 828/2,
829/3, 893/1, 901
Abe Capek, 94/1, 94/2, 94/3, 95/1, 95/2, 95/3,
172, 250
Cash, J. Allan, 109, 381/1
Centre Cultural Portugaise, 574/1
Chuzeville, Maurice, 49/1
Cianetti, F., 32, 37/2
Collection Viollet, 483/1, 500/1
Commune di Rome, 166/2
Conant, Kenneth John, (courtesy of the
Mediaeval Academy of America), 243/1
Connaissance de Arts, (R. Bonnefoy), 428/1

Acknowledgements

Ministry of Public Buildings and Works, 339/1
Morison History Project, 845
Moro, Milan, 806/2, 808/1
Moro, Rome, 889
Münchow, Ann, 217, 218/1, 218/3, 220/1, 221/1, 223/2, 223/3
Musées Nationaux: Photo de, 518/1
ND-Viollet, 295/2
Newsweek, 912/1
Niepce, Janine, 286/1
Novosti, 324–26, 328, 329, 541/1, 542/2, 544/2, 660/1, 677/2, 733, 735/2, 736/2, 737, 778, 797, 798, 799/2, 800, 811/2, 850, 852, 853/1, 853/3, 854, 855, 892/1, 902/2, 906/1, 906/3, 911/1
Northern Ireland Tourist Board, 177/1
Pepper, Curtis B., 164
Percheron, Réne, 49/5, 51, 53/3, 63/1, 77/1, 80/1, 89/1, 89/2, 90, 91/1, 135/1, 146, 147
Photo Picard, 104, 105, 107, 108
Picturepoint, 402, 403/1
Pont. Comm. di Arch. Sacra, 167/2
Paul Popper Ltd., 26, 107/3, 645/3, 730/1, 738/1, 747/2, 758/2, 779/1, 790, 818/2, 826/2, 834, 838/1, 842/2, 843, 864/1, 865/2, 877/3, 885/1, 889/2, 892/2, 896/2, 907/2
Powell, Josephine, 31/3, 34/1, 34/2, 35, 38/1, 42, 43, 56/6, 57/4, 57/5, 66/1, 67/4, 196/3, 203/2, 531/1
Prestel, Verlag, 284/1
Pritchard, 56/5
Public Building and Works, Ministry of, Edinburgh, Crown ©, 181/1
Public Works for Ireland, Commissioners of, 176/3
Putnam and Co. Ltd., 847/3 (from Japanese Aircraft of the Pacific War by R. J. Francillon)
Radio Times Hulton Picture Library, 327/2, 331, 354/1, 426, 428/2, 438/2, 472/3, 477/1, 486/2, 490/2, 490/3, 491/3, 503/2, 523/1, 530, 531/1, 538/1, 539/2, 556/1, 557/2, 564/3, 569/2, 573/2, 573/3, 591/1, 591/2, 593/1, 596/2, 596/2, 597/2, 600/1, 652/1, 652/2, 656/2, 734, 786/1, 786/2, 787, 794, 795, 802, 803, 810, 819/2, 827/1, 827/3, 864/3, 865/1, 877/2
Raeburn, C., 30/1, 53/1, 53/2
Rapho, Agence, 52, 72
Réalités, 318/2, (J. Guillot) 16/2, (J. L. Swiners) 50
Reece, Winstone, 230
Rizzoli-Editore, 397
Roberts, Rex, 446/1
Roger-Viollet, 278/2
Ronan, Colin, Picture Library, 427/2, 428/3, 528/2, 529/3
Roubier, Jean, 243/2, 279/2
St. John Nixon, 783
Scala, 86, 117/1, 166/1, 167/1, 170/1, 171/1, 185, 187/1, 187/2, 187/3, 191, 194/2, 195, 218/2, 241/1, 245, 276/2, 291, 294/2, 295/2, 295/3, 299, 303/1, 303/3, 341, 344/1, 346/1, 347, 350/1, 353/2, 382, 387, 390, 396, 400/2, 406, 407, 622/2, 636, 690, 694/1, 695/1
Search, 840/1, 841/1
Sewell, William, 878
Sheridan, Ronald, 206/3
Schmidt-Glassner, Helga, (C. J. G. Cotta'sche Verlag), 136/1, 321/3

Schwitter, Norma, 47/1, 47/2, 72/2, 73/2, 92/2, 93/1, 116
SECAS-B, Vilerbue, 97, 101/2
Smith, Edwin, 266/1, 230/1
Snark International, 642, 880/1
Sohio News Service, 743/2, 782/2
Society for Cultural Relations with the U.S.S.R., 327/1
Standard Oil of New Jersey, 741, 742/1, 742/2, 744/1, 745/2
Swedish Institute for Cultural Relations, 495
Swaan, Wim, 234, 235, 236/2, 237/1, 238, 302
The Times, 203
Thomas Photos, 423/3
Transworld Feature Syndicate, 902/3
Turkish Embassy, 56/4
Turkish Tourism Information Office, London, 437
Tweedie, Penny, 284/3
Ullstein, Bilderdienst, 415, 418, 419/1
Unione, Foto, 129/1
United Arab Republic Ministry of Information, 17/2
United Press International, 859, 875, 882, 883/2, 890/1, 890/3, 902/1, 905/3, 912/2
United States Air Force, 860/2
United States Information Service, 816/1, 827/2, 847/1, 849/2, 857/2, 858, 863/1, 864/2, 884, 885/3, 900, 904, 908, 909, 911/2, 913
Victoria & Albert Museum, 264
Warburg Institute, 136/4
Wellcome Foundation, 241/2, 241/4
Wheeler, Sir Mortimer, 20/3, 44/2, 45/1, 45/2, 46/1, 46/2
Wierzda, A., 273
Witty, Derrick, 442, 443/1
Zauho Press-Ziolo, 212/2
Zentrale Farbbild Agentur, 171/2

Picture research by Enid Moore, Patricia Quick, Michele Rimbeaud, Rowena Ross and Jane Caplan.

Maps and diagrams designed by DIAGRAM.

Index

Index

Canute, King, 259
Capet, Hugh, 260
Caphtor, 53
Capitol, the, 635, *635*
Caprara, Herbert, 532
Capua, 107, 108, 112, 116
Capuchins, The, 430
Cárdenas, Lázaro, 818
Cardinals, College, of, 276
Carias, Tiburcio, 818
Carlists, 831
Carnegie, Andrew, 747, *747*
Carolingians, The, 161, 162, 224
Carthage, 103, 105, 106, 107, 109, 110
Cartier, Jacques, 422
Cartwright, William, 630
Casablanca Conference (1943), 855
Casimir, John, 438, 448
Casimir the Great, 349
Cassites, 31
Cassius, Dio, historian, 132
Castlereagh, Viscount, 644
Castro, Fidel, 885, *900, 902*
Catal Hüyük, 11
Cateau-Cambresis (peace treaty), 431, 439
Cathari, 278, 286, 287
Cathay, 333, 386
Catherine of Aragon, 412, *413*
Catherine of Braganza, 523
Catherine of France (wife of Henry v), 370
Catherine the Great, 570, 590, *590*
Catinat, Marshal, 538
Cato, 111
Cauchon, Pierre, 374
Cavour, Count Camillo Benso di, 691–6, *692*
Cawnpore, 698
Caxton, William, 385, *385*
Cayley, Sir George, 773
Celestine v, Pope, 338
Celsius, Anders, 591
Celtic Church, 173
Celts, The, 180, 181
Central Pacific Railroad Company, 667
Cervantes, Miguel de, 474, *474*
Chacabuco, Battle of (1818), 652
Chadwick, Edwin, 670
Chaeronea, 85
Chamberlain, Houston, 822
Chamberlain, Joseph, 752, *752, 753*
Chamberlain, Neville, 835, *835, 873*
Chambers, Ephraim, 568
Chambers, William, 601

Champeau, Guillaume de, 280–2
Chancellorsville, Battle of (1863), 725, 728
Chandragupta, 93
Chandragupta ii, 172
Chao Kuang-yin, 250
Chardin, Jean Baptiste, 601
Charlemagne, Emperor, 161, 162, 215, *216*, 217–21, *218*, 220
Charles iv, Holy Roman Emperor, 349, 358, *358*
Charles v, Holy Roman Emperor, 390, *391*, 404, 405, 412, 416, 422, 431
Charles v, Holy Roman Emperor, 474, 477
Charles vi, Holy Roman Emperor, 548, 572
Charles Martel (the Hammer), 215
Charles i of England, 475, 482, *482*, 502–9, *504, 507, 511*, 519, 522, 523, 538, 556
Charles ii of England, *506*, 509, 511, 523
Charles v of France, 349, 359, 606
Charles vi of France, 366, 367, 369, 370
Charles vii of France, 369, 370, *370*, 372–4, 376
Charles viii of France, 394
Charles ix of France, 438
Charles x of France, 660, *660*
Charles of Lorraine, 534–7, *535*
Charles i of Spain, 404
Charles ii of Spain, 547, 548
Charles ix of Sweden, 482
Charles x of Sweden, 546
Charles xi of Sweden, 546
Charles xii of Sweden, 544, 546, 547, *547, 550*, 551, 552
Charles iv of Würtemburg, 727
Charles Albert of Sardinia (Piedmont), 691
Charles the Bold, 385
Charles the Simple, 258
Chartists, The, 670, 671, 673, 678
Chartres Cathedral, *284*, 287, *288–93*, 289–95
Chaucer, Geoffrey, 359, *359*
Cheops (Khufu), Pharoah, 17
Cherusci, 132
Chesapeake (frigate), 634
Chiang Kai-shek, 811, *811*, 818, 834, 835, 864, 879–83, *879*
China, 207, 250–1, 367, 392,

679, 778, 779, 803, 811, 835, 864, 879–84, 893, 907
Russian influence in, 688
Chippendale, Thomas, 601
Chitor, the Rana of, 442–3
Choiseul, Duc de, 579
Chosroes i, King, 197
Chosroes ii, King, 197
Chou En-lai, 879–81
Chou K'ou Tien, 10, 94
Christian ii of Denmark, 413
Christian iv of Denmark, 494, 500
Christian Civic League, 413
Christianity, 161–5, 167–72, 173, 175, 180, 181, 186, 187, 206, 224, 248, 274, 275
Christina of Sweden, 546, *546*
Chrysopolis, 170
Chuikov, Marshal V., 852
Church of England, 705
Churchill, Winston, 816, 826, 833, 836, *836*, 840, 842, 843, 856, *856, 888*
CIA, 901
Cimbri, 130
Cimmerians, 66, 67
Cisneros, Cardinal, 240
Civil Code, 641
Civil Rights Movement, 906
Clarendon, Lord, 691
Claudius, Emperor, *145*, 145
Clausewitz, Karl von, 638
Clay, Henry, 658, 659
Cleisthenes, 75
Cleitus, 90
Clemenceau, Georges, 739, *739*, 802, 803
Clement, v, Pope, 338, 346
Clement vi, Pope, 351, 352
Clement vii, Pope, 412, *412*, 422
Clement xiv, Pope, 590
Cleomenes, 87
Cleon, 115
Cleopatra, Queen of Egypt, 93, *121*, 121, 122, 123, 124, 125
Clermont, Council of, 279
Clermont (steamboat), 634
Cleveland, Ohio, 740
Clive, Robert, 580, 581, *581*
Clodianus, Gn. Lentulus, 112
Clovis, King, 186, 187, 214
Cluny, monks of, 243, 274
Cobbett, William, 627, 631
Cobden, Richard, 671
Cochrane, Admiral Lord, 652
Cogelin, Joseph Cuers de, 580
Cognac, League of, 412
Coke, Sir Edward, 321
Colbert, Jean Baptiste, 517, *517*, 518, 538
Cold Harbor, Battle of, 720

Coligny, Admiral Gaspard de, 438, *438*
Collins, Colonel Michael, 910, 911, *912*
Colman, Bishop of Lindisfarne, 179
Columba of Iona, St., 177, 178
Columbanus, St., 178
Colombia, 652, 653, 879
Colonna, Marco Antonio, 434, 435
Colonna, Prospero, 412
Colorado, 696
Columbus, Christopher, 333, *386*, 388, 389, 391, 392, 394
Comintern, 911
Common Market, 889
Commonwealth, 473, 509–11
Communist Manifesto, The, 672, *674*, 675, 676, 677
Condé (Huguenot commander), 438
Condé, Prince de, 513, *513*, 538
Condell, Henry, 472
Condor Legion, 834
Confederation with the Ecclesiastical Princes, 319
Confessio, see Patrick, St.,
Confucian code, 207
Confucius (K'ung Fu-Tsu), 95, *95*, 207
Congo, 892
Congress Party (Indian), 818, 819, 827, 842, 867–70
Congreve, William, *557*
Conrad iii, Emperor, 304
Conrad iv of Germany, 331
Conrad, Duke of Franconia, 224
Constance, Council of, 358, 366–7
Constance, 'Queen of Sicily', 339
Constans, Emperor, 171
Constantine, Emperor, 129, 162, *162*, 165, 171, *171*, 172, 173, 380, 382
Constantinople (Byzantium), 111, 129, 162, 165–71, *171*, 196, 197, 205, 214, 296, *302*, 379–82, *380*
Fall of, 298–305
Constantius Chlorus, 165
Constantius, son of Emperor Constantine, 171
Conti, Prince de, 513
Continental System, 630, 634, 637, 642, 645
Cook, Captain Thomas, 582, 583–9, *589*, 704
Coolidge, President Calvin, 818

925

Index

Index

Index

Index

Index

Index

936

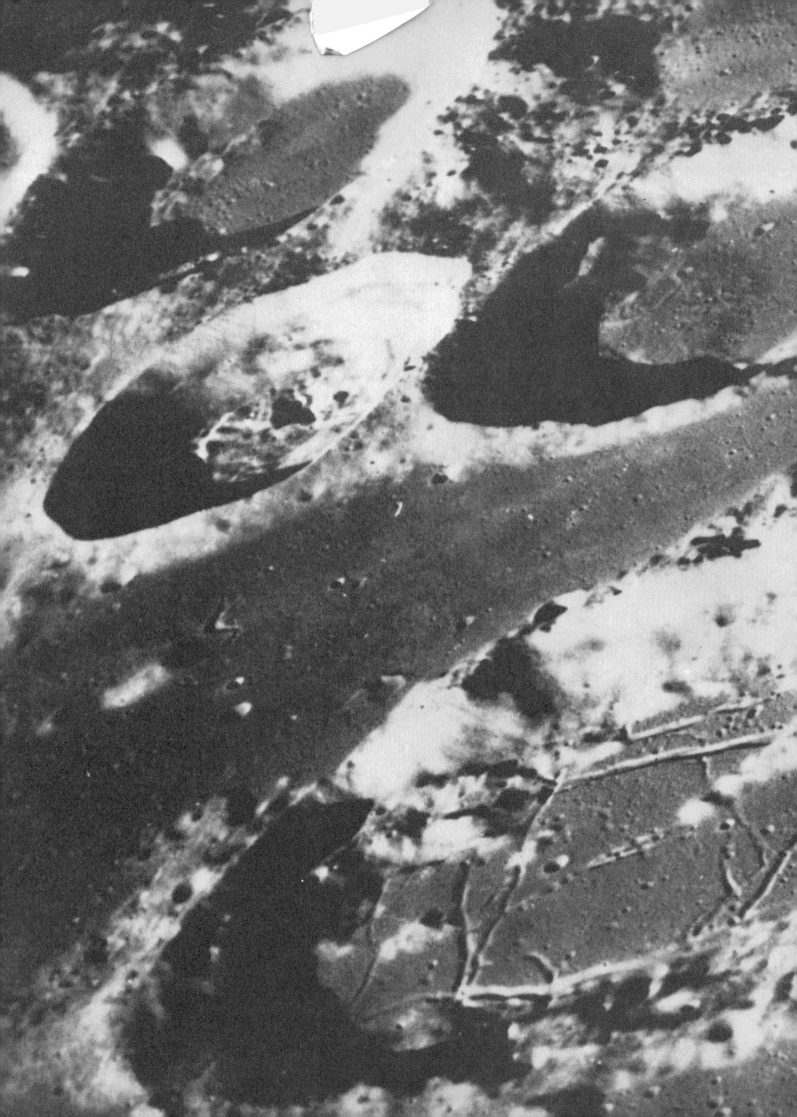